Lecture Notes in Computer Science 13092

More information about this subseries at https://link.springer.com/bookseries/7410

Mehdi Tibouchi · Huaxiong Wang (Eds.)

Advances in Cryptology – ASIACRYPT 2021

27th International Conference on the Theory
and Application of Cryptology and Information Security
Singapore, December 6–10, 2021
Proceedings, Part III

Springer

Editors
Mehdi Tibouchi
NTT Corporation
Tokyo, Japan

Huaxiong Wang
Nanyang Technological University
Singapore, Singapore

ISSN 0302-9743 ISSN 1611-3349 (electronic)
Lecture Notes in Computer Science
ISBN 978-3-030-92077-7 ISBN 978-3-030-92078-4 (eBook)
https://doi.org/10.1007/978-3-030-92078-4

LNCS Sublibrary: SL4 – Security and Cryptology

This Springer imprint is published by the registered company Springer Nature Switzerland AG
The registered company address is: Gewerbestrasse 11, 6330 Cham, Switzerland

Preface

Asiacrypt 2021, the 27th Annual International Conference on Theory and Application of Cryptology and Information Security, was originally planned to be held in Singapore during December 6–10, 2021. Due to the COVID-19 pandemic, it was shifted to an online-only virtual conference.

The conference covered all technical aspects of cryptology, and was sponsored by the International Association for Cryptologic Research (IACR).

We received a total of 341 submissions from all over the world, and the Program Committee (PC) selected 95 papers for publication in the proceedings of the conference. The two program chairs were supported by a PC consisting of 74 leading experts in aspects of cryptology. Each submission was reviewed by at least three PC members (or their sub-reviewers) and five PC members were assigned to submissions co-authored by PC members. The strong conflict of interest rules imposed by IACR ensure that papers are not handled by PC members with a close working relationship with the authors. The two program chairs were not allowed to submit a paper, and PC members were limited to two submissions each. There were approximately 363 external reviewers, whose input was critical to the selection of papers.

The review process was conducted using double-blind peer review. The conference operated a two-round review system with a rebuttal phase. After the reviews and first-round discussions the PC selected 233 submissions to proceed to the second round and the authors were then invited to provide a short rebuttal in response to the referee reports. The second round involved extensive discussions by the PC members.

Alongside the presentations of the accepted papers, the program of Asiacrypt 2021 featured an IACR distinguished lecture by Andrew Chi-Chih Yao and two invited talks by Kazue Sako and Yu Yu. The conference also featured a rump session which contained short presentations on the latest research results of the field.

The four volumes of the conference proceedings contain the revised versions of the 95 papers that were selected, together with the abstracts of the IACR distinguished lecture and the two invited talks. The final revised versions of papers were not reviewed again and the authors are responsible for their contents.

Via a voting-based process that took into account conflicts of interest, the PC selected the three top papers of the conference: "On the Hardness of the NTRU problem" by Alice Pellet-Mary and Damien Stehlé (which received the best paper award); "A Geometric Approach to Linear Cryptanalysis" by Tim Beyne (which received the best student paper award); and "Lattice Enumeration for Tower NFS: a 521-bit Discrete Logarithm Computation" by Gabrielle De Micheli, Pierrick Gaudry, and Cécile Pierrot. The authors of all three papers were invited to submit extended versions of their manuscripts to the Journal of Cryptology.

Many people have contributed to the success of Asiacrypt 2021. We would like to thank the authors for submitting their research results to the conference. We are very grateful to the PC members and external reviewers for contributing their knowledge and expertise, and for the tremendous amount of work that was done with reading papers and contributing to the discussions. We are greatly indebted to Jian Guo, the General Chair, for his efforts and overall organization. We thank San Ling and Josef Pieprzyk, the advisors of Asiacrypt 2021, for their valuable suggestions. We thank Michel Abdalla, Kevin McCurley, Kay McKelly, and members of IACR's emergency pandemic team for their work in designing and running the virtual format. We thank Chitchanok Chuengsatiansup and Khoa Nguyen for expertly organizing and chairing the rump session. We are extremely grateful to Zhenzhen Bao for checking all the LaTeX files and for assembling the files for submission to Springer. We also thank Alfred Hofmann, Anna Kramer, and their colleagues at Springer for handling the publication of these conference proceedings.

December 2021

Mehdi Tibouchi
Huaxiong Wang

Organization

General Chair

Jian Guo	Nanyang Technological University, Singapore

Program Committee Co-chairs

Mehdi Tibouchi	NTT Corporation, Japan
Huaxiong Wang	Nanyang Technological University, Singapore

Steering Committee

Masayuki Abe
Lynn Batten
Jung Hee Cheon
Steven Galbraith
D. J. Guan
Jian Guo
Khalid Habib
Lucas Hui
Nassar Ikram
Kwangjo Kim
Xuejia Lai
Dong Hoon Lee
Satya Lokam
Mitsuru Matsui (Chair)
Tsutomu Matsumoto
Phong Nguyen
Dingyi Pei
Duong Hieu Phan
Raphael Phan
Josef Pieprzyk (Vice Chair)
C. Pandu Rangan
Bimal Roy
Leonie Simpson
Huaxiong Wang
Henry B. Wolfe
Duncan Wong
Tzong-Chen Wu
Bo-Yin Yang
Siu-Ming Yiu
Yu Yu
Jianying Zhou

Program Committee

Shweta Agrawal	IIT Madras, India
Martin R. Albrecht	Royal Holloway, University of London, UK
Zhenzhen Bao	Nanyang Technological University, Singapore
Manuel Barbosa	University of Porto (FCUP) and INESC TEC, Portugal
Lejla Batina	Radboud University, The Netherlands
Sonia Belaïd	CryptoExperts, France
Fabrice Benhamouda	Algorand Foundation, USA
Begül Bilgin	Rambus - Cryptography Research, The Netherlands
Xavier Bonnetain	University of Waterloo, Canada
Joppe W. Bos	NXP Semiconductors, Belgium

Wouter Castryck	KU Leuven, Belgium
Rongmao Chen	National University of Defense Technology, China
Jung Hee Cheon	Seoul National University, South Korea
Chitchanok Chuengsatiansup	The University of Adelaide, Australia
Kai-Min Chung	Academia Sinica, Taiwan
Dana Dachman-Soled	University of Maryland, USA
Bernardo David	IT University of Copenhagen, Denmark
Benjamin Fuller	University of Connecticut, USA
Steven Galbraith	The University of Auckland, New Zealand
María Isabel González Vasco	Universidad Rey Juan Carlos, Spain
Robert Granger	University of Surrey, UK
Alex B. Grilo	CNRS, LIP6, Sorbonne Université, France
Aurore Guillevic	Inria, France
Swee-Huay Heng	Multimedia University, Malaysia
Akinori Hosoyamada	NTT Corporation and Nagoya University, Japan
Xinyi Huang	Fujian Normal University, China
Andreas Hülsing	Eindhoven University of Technology, The Netherlands
Tetsu Iwata	Nagoya University, Japan
David Jao	University of Waterloo and evolutionQ, Inc., Canada
Jérémy Jean	ANSSI, France
Shuichi Katsumata	AIST, Japan
Elena Kirshanova	I. Kant Baltic Federal University, Russia
Hyung Tae Lee	Chung-Ang University, South Korea
Dongdai Lin	Institute of Information Engineering, Chinese Academy of Sciences, China
Rongxing Lu	University of New Brunswick, Canada
Xianhui Lu	Institute of Information Engineering, Chinese Academy of Sciences, China
Mary Maller	Ethereum Foundation, UK
Giorgia Azzurra Marson	NEC Labs Europe, Germany
Keith M. Martin	Royal Holloway, University of London, UK
Daniel Masny	Visa Research, USA
Takahiro Matsuda	AIST, Japan
Krystian Matusiewicz	Intel Corporation, Poland
Florian Mendel	Infineon Technologies, Germany
Nele Mentens	Leiden University, The Netherlands, and KU Leuven, Belgium
Atsuko Miyaji	Osaka University, Japan
Michael Naehrig	Microsoft Research, USA
Khoa Nguyen	Nanyang Technological University, Singapore
Miyako Ohkubo	NICT, Japan
Emmanuela Orsini	KU Leuven, Belgium
Jiaxin Pan	NTNU, Norway
Panos Papadimitratos	KTH Royal Institute of Technology, Sweden

Alice Pellet–Mary	CNRS and University of Bordeaux, France
Duong Hieu Phan	Télécom Paris, Institut Polytechnique de Paris, France
Francisco Rodríguez-Henríquez	CINVESTAV, Mexico
Olivier Sanders	Orange Labs, France
Jae Hong Seo	Hanyang University, South Korea
Haya Shulman	Fraunhofer SIT, Germany
Daniel Slamanig	AIT Austrian Institute of Technology, Austria
Ron Steinfeld	Monash University, Australia
Willy Susilo	University of Wollongong, Australia
Katsuyuki Takashima	Waseda University, Japan
Qiang Tang	The University of Sydney, Australia
Serge Vaudenay	EPFL, Switzerland
Damien Vergnaud	Sorbonne Université and Institut Universitaire de France, France
Meiqin Wang	Shandong University, China
Xiaoyun Wang	Tsinghua University, China
Yongge Wang	UNC Charlotte, USA
Wenling Wu	Institute of Software, Chinese Academy of Sciences, China
Chaoping Xing	Shanghai Jiao Tong University, China
Sophia Yakoubov	Aarhus University, Denmark
Takashi Yamakawa	NTT Corporation, Japan
Bo-Yin Yang	Academia Sinica, Taiwan
Yu Yu	Shanghai Jiao Tong University, China
Hong-Sheng Zhou	Virginia Commonwealth University, USA

Additional Reviewers

Behzad Abdolmaleki
Gorjan Alagic
Orestis Alpos
Miguel Ambrona
Diego Aranha
Victor Arribas
Nuttapong Attrapadung
Benedikt Auerbach
Zeta Avarikioti
Melissa Azouaoui
Saikrishna Badrinarayanan
Joonsang Baek
Karim Baghery
Shi Bai
Gustavo Banegas
Subhadeep Banik
James Bartusek
Balthazar Bauer
Rouzbeh Behnia
Yanis Belkheyar
Josh Benaloh
Ward Beullens
Tim Beyne
Sarani Bhattacharya
Rishiraj Bhattacharyya
Nina Bindel
Adam Blatchley Hansen
Olivier Blazy
Charlotte Bonte
Katharina Boudgoust
Ioana Boureanu
Markus Brandt

Anne Broadbent
Ileana Buhan
Andrea Caforio
Eleonora Cagli
Sébastien Canard
Ignacio Cascudo
Gaëtan Cassiers
André Chailloux
Tzu-Hsien Chang
Yilei Chen
Jie Chen
Yanlin Chen
Albert Cheu
Jesús-Javier Chi-Domíguez
Nai-Hui Chia
Ilaria Chillotti
Ji-Jian Chin
Jérémy Chotard
Sherman S. M. Chow
Heewon Chung
Jorge Chávez-Saab
Michele Ciampi
Carlos Cid
Valerio Cini
Tristan Claverie
Benoît Cogliati
Alexandru Cojocaru
Daniel Collins
Kelong Cong
Craig Costello
Geoffroy Couteau
Daniele Cozzo
Jan Czajkowski
Tianxiang Dai
Wei Dai
Sourav Das
Pratish Datta
Alex Davidson
Lauren De Meyer
Elke De Mulder
Claire Delaplace
Cyprien Delpech de Saint Guilhem
Patrick Derbez
Siemen Dhooghe
Daniel Dinu
Christoph Dobraunig
Samuel Dobson
Luis J. Dominguez Perez
Jelle Don
Benjamin Dowling
Maria Eichlseder
Jesse Elliott
Keita Emura
Muhammed F. Esgin
Hulya Evkan
Lei Fan
Antonio Faonio
Hanwen Feng
Dario Fiore
Antonio Florez-Gutierrez
Georg Fuchsbauer
Chaya Ganesh
Daniel Gardham
Rachit Garg
Pierrick Gaudry
Romain Gay
Nicholas Genise
Adela Georgescu
David Gerault
Satrajit Ghosh
Valerie Gilchrist
Aron Gohr
Junqing Gong
Marc Gourjon
Lorenzo Grassi
Milos Grujic
Aldo Gunsing
Kaiwen Guo
Chun Guo
Qian Guo
Mike Hamburg
Ben Hamlin
Shuai Han
Yonglin Hao
Keisuke Hara
Patrick Harasser
Jingnan He
David Heath
Chloé Hébant
Julia Hesse
Ryo Hiromasa
Shiqi Hou

Lin Hou
Yao-Ching Hsieh
Kexin Hu
Jingwei Hu
Zhenyu Huang
Loïs Huguenin-Dumittan
Arnie Hung
Shih-Han Hung
Kathrin Hövelmanns
Ilia Iliashenko
Aayush Jain
Yanxue Jia
Dingding Jia
Yao Jiang
Floyd Johnson
Luke Johnson
Chanyang Ju
Charanjit S. Jutla
John Kelsey
Taechan Kim
Myungsun Kim
Jinsu Kim
Minkyu Kim
Young-Sik Kim
Sungwook Kim
Jiseung Kim
Kwangjo Kim
Seungki Kim
Sunpill Kim
Fuyuki Kitagawa
Susumu Kiyoshima
Michael Klooß
Dimitris Kolonelos
Venkata Koppula
Liliya Kraleva
Mukul Kulkarni
Po-Chun Kuo
Hilder Vitor Lima Pereira
Russell W. F. Lai
Jianchang Lai
Yi-Fu Lai
Virginie Lallemand
Jason LeGrow
Joohee Lee
Jooyoung Lee
Changmin Lee
Hyeonbum Lee
Moon Sung Lee
Keewoo Lee
Dominik Leichtle
Alexander Lemmens
Gaëtan Leurent
Yannan Li
Shuaishuai Li
Baiyu Li
Zhe Li
Shun Li
Liang Li
Jianwei Li
Trey Li
Xiao Liang
Chi-Chang Lin
Chengjun Lin
Chao Lin
Yao-Ting Lin
Eik List
Feng-Hao Liu
Qipeng Liu
Guozhen Liu
Yunwen Liu
Patrick Longa
Sebastien Lord
George Lu
Yuan Lu
Yibiao Lu
Xiaojuan Lu
Ji Luo
Yiyuan Luo
Mohammad Mahzoun
Monosij Maitra
Christian Majenz
Ekaterina Malygina
Mark Manulis
Varun Maram
Luca Mariot
Loïc Masure
Bart Mennink
Simon-Philipp Merz
Peihan Miao
Kazuhiko Minematsu
Donika Mirdita
Pratyush Mishra

Tomoyuki Morimae
Pratyay Mukherjee
Alex Munch-Hansen
Yusuke Naito
Ngoc Khanh Nguyen
Jianting Ning
Ryo Nishimaki
Anca Nitulescu
Kazuma Ohara
Cristina Onete
Jean-Baptiste Orfila
Michele Orrù
Jong Hwan Park
Jeongeun Park
Robi Pedersen
Angel L. Perez del Pozo
Léo Perrin
Thomas Peters
Albrecht Petzoldt
Stjepan Picek
Rafael del Pino
Geong Sen Poh
David Pointcheval
Bernardo Portela
Raluca Posteuca
Thomas Prest
Robert Primas
Chen Qian
Willy Quach
Md Masoom Rabbani
Rahul Rachuri
Srinivasan Raghuraman
Sebastian Ramacher
Matthieu Rambaud
Shahram Rasoolzadeh
Krijn Reijnders
Joost Renes
Elena Reshetova
Mélissa Rossi
Mike Rosulek
Yann Rotella
Joe Rowell
Arnab Roy
Partha Sarathi Roy
Alexander Russell
Carla Ráfols
Paul Rösler
Yusuke Sakai
Amin Sakzad
Yu Sasaki
Or Sattath
John M. Schanck
Lars Schlieper
Martin Schläfer
Carsten Schmidt
André Schrottenloher
Jacob Schuldt
Jean-Pierre Seifert
Yannick Seurin
Yaobin Shen
Yixin Shen
Yu-Ching Shen
Danping Shi
Omri Shmueli
Kris Shrishak
Hervais Simo Fhom
Luisa Siniscalchi
Daniel Smith-Tone
Fang Song
Pratik Soni
Claudio Soriente
Akshayaram Srinivasan
Douglas Stebila
Damien Stehlé
Bruno Sterner
Christoph Striecks
Patrick Struck
Adriana Suarez Corona
Ling Sun
Shi-Feng Sun
Koutarou Suzuki
Aishwarya T
Erkan Tairi
Akira Takahashi
Atsushi Takayasu
Abdul Rahman Taleb
Younes Talibi Alaoui
Benjamin Hong Meng Tan
Syh-Yuan Tan
Titouan Tanguy
Alexander Tereshchenko
Adrian Thillard

Emmanuel Thomé
Tyge Tiessen
Radu Titiu
Ivan Tjuawinata
Yosuke Todo
Junichi Tomida
Bénédikt Tran
Jacques Traoré
Ni Trieu
Ida Tucker
Michael Tunstall
Dominique Unruh
Thomas Unterluggauer
Thomas van Himbeeck
Daniele Venturi
Jorge Villar
Mikhail Volkhov
Christine van Vredendaal
Benedikt Wagner
Riad Wahby
Hendrik Waldner
Alexandre Wallet
Junwei Wang
Qingju Wang
Yuyu Wang
Lei Wang
Senpeng Wang
Peng Wang
Weijia Wang
Yi Wang
Han Wang
Xuzi Wang
Yohei Watanabe
Florian Weber
Weiqiang Wen
Nils Wisiol
Mathias Wolf
Harry H. W. Wong
Keita Xagawa
Zejun Xiang
Jiayu Xu
Luyao Xu
Yaqi Xu
Shota Yamada
Hailun Yan
Wenjie Yang
Shaojun Yang
Masaya Yasuda
Wei Chuen Yau
Kazuki Yoneyama
Weijing You
Chen Yuan
Tsz Hon Yuen
Runzhi Zeng
Cong Zhang
Zhifang Zhang
Bingsheng Zhang
Zhelei Zhou
Paul Zimmermann
Lukas Zobernig

Contents – Part III

Symmetric-Key Constructions

Homomorphic Encryption and Encrypted Search

NIZK and SNARKs

Lunar: A Toolbox for More Efficient Universal and Updatable zkSNARKs and Commit-and-Prove Extensions

Matteo Campanelli[1(✉)], Antonio Faonio[2], Dario Fiore[3], Anaïs Querol[3,4(✉)], and Hadrián Rodríguez[3]

[1] Aarhus University, Aarhus, Denmark
matteo@cs.au.dk
[2] EURECOM, Sophia Antipolis, France
antonio.faonio@eurecom.fr
[3] IMDEA Software Institute, Madrid, Spain
{dario.fiore,anais.querol,hadrian.rodriguez}@imdea.org
[4] Universidad Politécnica de Madrid, Madrid, Spain

Abstract. We study how to construct zkSNARKs whose SRS is *universal* and *updatable*, i.e., valid for all relations within a size-bound and to which a dynamic set of participants can indefinitely add secret randomness. Our focus is: efficient universal updatable zkSNARKs with linear size SRS and their commit-and-prove variants. We both introduce new formal frameworks and techniques, as well as systematize existing ones.

We achieve a collection of zkSNARKs with different tradeoffs. One of our schemes achieves the smallest proof size and proving time compared to the state of art for proofs for arithmetic circuits. The language supported by this scheme is a variant of R1CS that we introduce, called R1CS-lite. Another of our constructions directly supports standard R1CS and achieves the fastest proving time for this type of constraints.

These results stem from different contributions: (1) a new algebraically-flavored variant of IOPs that we call *Polynomial Holographic IOPs* (PHPs); (2) a new compiler that combines our PHPs with *commit-and-prove zkSNARKs* (CP-SNARKs) for committed polynomials; (3) pairing-based realizations of these CP-SNARKs for polynomials; (4) constructions of PHPs for R1CS and R1CS-lite. Finally, we extend the compiler in item (2) to yield commit-and-prove universal zkSNARKs.

Keywords: zkSNARK · Universal SRS · Polynomial commitments · IOP

1 Introduction

A zero-knowledge proof system [31] allows a prover to convince a verifier that a non-deterministic computation accepts without revealing more information than its input. In the last decade, there has been growing interest in zero-knowledge proof systems that additionally are *succinct* and *non interactive* [12,29,40,46], dubbed zkSNARKs. These are computationally-sound proof

M. Tibouchi and H. Wang (Eds.): ASIACRYPT 2021, LNCS 13092, pp. 3–33, 2021.
https://doi.org/10.1007/978-3-030-92078-4_1

systems (*arguments*) that are *succinct*, in that their proofs are short and efficient to verify: the proof size and verification time should be constant or polylogarithmic in the length of the non-deterministic witness. In circuit-based arguments for general computations the verifier must at least read the statement to be proven which includes both the description of the computation (i.e., the circuit) and its input (i.e., public input). But this is not succinct; by reading the whole circuit, the verifier runs linearly in the size of the computation. *Preprocessing zkSNARKs* try and work around this problem [13,28,32,44]. Here the verifier generates a *structured reference string* (SRS) that depends on a certain circuit C; it does this *once and for all*. This SRS can be used later to verify an unbounded number of proofs for the computation of C. This is a succinct system: while the cost of SRS generation does depend on $|C|$, proof verification does not have to.

Works on subversion-resistance show that CRS can be generated by a verifier with no impact on security [1,3,24]. But contexts with many verifiers, e.g. blockchains, require a trusted party. Solutions that mitigate this problem (e.g. MPC secure against dishonest majority [7]) are still expensive and often impractical as they should be carried out for each single C. To address this problem, Groth et al. [34] introduced the model of *universal and updatable SRS*. An SRS is *universal* if it can be used to generate and verify proofs for all circuits of some bounded size; it is *updatable* if any user can add randomness to it and a sequence of updates makes it secure if at least one user acted honestly. They proposed the first such zkSNARK, but their scheme requires an SRS of size *quadratic* in the number of multiplication gates of the supported arithmetic circuits (and similar quadratic update/verification time).

Recent works [18,19,21,27,45,53] have improved on this result obtaining universal and updatable SRS whose size is *linear* in the largest supported circuit. In particular, the current Marlin [19] and PLONK [27] proof systems achieve a proving time concretely faster than that of Sonic [45] while retaining constant-size proofs ([18,21,53] have instead polylogarithmic-size proofs). We also mention the very recent works of Bünz, Fisch and Szepieniec [17], and Chiesa, Ojha and Spooner [20] that proposed zkSNARKs in the uniform random string (URS) model, that is implicitly universal and updatable; their constructions have a short URS and poly-logarithmic-size proofs. Yet another universal zkSNARK construction is that in [41] which, despite its proofs of 4 group elements and comparable proving time, has an SRS which is not updatable.

Many of these efficient constructions (and the ones in this work) follow a similar blueprint to build zkSNARKs, which we now overview.

The Current Landscape of zkSNARKs with Universal SRS. A known modular paradigm to build efficient cryptographic arguments [36,37] works in two distinct steps. First construct an information-theoretic protocol in an abstract model, e.g., interactive proofs [31], standard or linear PCPs [13], IOPs [9,48]. Then apply a compiler that, taking an abstract protocol as input, transforms it into an efficient computationally sound argument via a cryptographic primitive. This approach has been successfully adopted to construct zkSNARKs with universal SRS in the recent works [17,19,27], in which the information theoretic object is an algebraically-flavored variant of Interactive Oracle Proofs (IOPs), while the cryptographic primitive are *polynomial commitments* [39]. Through polynomial commitments, a prover can compress a polynomial p (as a message much shorter than all its concatenated coefficients) and can later open the commitment at evaluations of p, namely to convince a verifier that $y = p(x)$ for public points x and y. In these IOP abstractions—called *algebraic holographic proofs* (AHP) in [19] and *polynomial IOPs*[1] in [17]—a prover and a verifier interact, one providing oracle access to a set of polynomials and the other sending random challenges (if public-coin). At the end of the protocol the verifier asks for evaluations of these polynomials and decides to accept or reject based on the responses. The *idealized low-degree protocols* (ILDPs) abstraction of [27] proceeds similarly except that in the end the verifier asks to verify a set of polynomial identities over the oracles sent by the prover (which can be tested via evaluation on random points). To build a zkSNARK with universal SRS starting from AHPs/ILDPs we let the prover commit to the polynomials obtained from the AHP/ILDP prover, and then use the opening feature of polynomial commitments to respond to the evaluation queries in a sound way. As we detail later, our contribution revisits the aforementioned blueprint to construct universal zkSNARKs.

1.1 Our Contribution

In this work we propose Lunar, a *family* of new preprocessing zkSNARKs in the universal and updatable SRS model that have constant-size proofs and that improve on previous work [19,27,45] as to proof size and prover running time.

In Table 1, we present a detailed efficiency comparison between prior work and the best representatives of our schemes, when using arithmetic circuit satisfiability as common benchmark. LunarLite has the smallest proof size (384 bytes over curve BN128; 544 bytes over BLS12-381)[2] and the lowest proving time compared to the state of art of universal zkSNARKs with constant-size proofs for arithmetic circuits. As we explain later, LunarLite uses a new arithmetization of arithmetic circuit satisfiability that we call R1CS-lite, quite similar to rank-1 constraint systems (R1CS). A precise comparison to PLONK depends on the circuit structure and how the number m of nonzero entries of R1CS-lite matrices depends on the number a of addition gates[3]; for instance, PLONK is faster for circuits with only multiplication gates, but LunarLite is faster when $m \leq 3a$.

If we focus the comparison on solutions that directly support R1CS (of which Marlin [19] is the most performant among prior work), our scheme Lunar1cs (fast & short) offers the smallest SRS, the smallest proof and the fastest prover. This comes at the price of higher constants for the size of the (specialized) verification key and verification time[4]. Lunar1cs (short vk) offers a tradeoff: it has smaller verification key and faster verification time, but slightly larger proofs, $3\times$ larger SRS, and $5m$ more $\mathbb{G}_1$-exponentiations at proving time than Lunar1cs (fast & short). Even with this tradeoff, Lunar1cs (short vk) outperforms Marlin

[1] Hereinafter we use AHP/PIOPs interchangeably as they are almost the same notion.
[2] BN128 is 100-bits-secure while BLS12-381 has 128-bits-security.
[3] Applying [14] PLONK's proving time drops to $8n + 8a$, but our analysis still holds.
[4] In practice this overhead is negligible. Lunar1cs (fast & short) takes 7 pairings to verify ($\approx$35 ms); faster schemes, including some from this work, take 2 ($\approx$10 ms).

in all these measures. We implemented Lunar's building blocks and we confirm our observations experimentally (check full version).

Table 1. Efficiency of universal and updatable *practical* zkSNARKs for arithmetic circuit satisfiability with $O(1)$ proofs. n: number of multiplication gates; a: number of addition gates; $m \geq n$: number of nonzero entries in R1CS(-lite) matrices encoding the circuit; N, N^*, A and M: largest supported values for $n, a+m, a$ and m respectively.

zkSNARK		size				time			
		$\lvert\mathsf{srs}\rvert$	$\lvert\mathsf{ek_R}\rvert$	$\lvert\mathsf{vk_R}\rvert$	$\lvert\pi\rvert$	KeyGen	Derive	Prove	Verify
Sonic	$\mathbb{G}_1$	$4N$	$36n$	—	20	$4N$	$36n$	$273n$	7 pairings
[45]	$\mathbb{G}_2$	$4N$	—	3	—	$4N$	—	—	
	$\mathbb{F}$	—	—	—	16	—	$O(m \log m)$	$O(m \log m)$	$O(\ell + \log m)$
MARLIN	$\mathbb{G}_1$	$3M$	$3m$	12	13	$3M$	$12m$	$14n+8m$	2 pairings
[19]	$\mathbb{G}_2$	2	—	2	—	—	—	—	
	$\mathbb{F}$	—	—	—	8	—	$O(m \log m)$	$O(m \log m)$	$O(\ell + \log m)$
(small proof)	$\mathbb{G}_1$	$3N^*$	$3n+3a$	8	7	$3N^*$	$8n+8a$	$11n+11a$	
(fast prover)	$\mathbb{G}_1$	N^*	$n+a$	8	9	N^*	$8n+8a$	$9n+9a$	
PLONK	$\mathbb{G}_2$	1	—	1	—	1	—	—	2 pairings
[27]	$\mathbb{F}$	—	—	—	7	—	$O((n+a)\log(n+a))$	$O((n+a)\log(n+a))$	$O(\ell+\log(n+a))$
	$\mathbb{G}_1$	M	m	—	10	M	—	$8n+3m$	7 pairings
LunarLite	$\mathbb{G}_2$	M	—	27	—	M	$24m$	—	
[this work]	$\mathbb{F}$	—	—	—	2	—	$O(m \log m)$	$O(m \log m)$	$O(\ell + \log m)$
	$\mathbb{G}_1$	M	m	—	11	M	—	$9n+3m$	7 pairings
Lunar1cs	$\mathbb{G}_2$	M	—	60	—	M	$57m$	—	
(fast & short)	$\mathbb{F}$	—	—	—	2	—	$O(m \log m)$	$O(m \log m)$	$O(\ell + \log m)$
	$\mathbb{G}_1$	$3M$	$3m$	12	12	$3M$	$12m$	$9n+8m$	2 pairings
Lunar1cs	$\mathbb{G}_2$	1	—	1	—	1	—	—	
(short vk)	$\mathbb{F}$	—	—	—	5	—	$O(m \log m)$	$O(m \log m)$	$O(\ell + \log m)$

Our main contribution to achieve this result is *to revisit the aforementioned blueprint to construct universal zkSNARKs* by proposing: (1) a new algebraically-flavored variant of IOPs, *Polynomial Holographic IOPs* (PHPs), and (2) a new compiler that builds universal zkSNARKs by using our PHPs together with *commit-and-prove zkSNARKs (CP-SNARKs)* [18] *for committed polynomials.* Additional contributions include: (3) pairing-based realizations of these CP-SNARKs for polynomials, (4) constructions of PHPs for both R1CS and a novel simplified variant of it, (5) a variant of the compiler (2) that yields a commit-and-prove universal zkSNARK. The latter is the first general compiler from (algebraic) IOPs to commit-and-prove zkSNARKs. A CP-SNARK permits to verify a proof through a commitment to an input (rather than an input in the clear) that, crucially, we can reuse among proofs[5]. Below we detail our contributions.

Polynomial Holographic IOPs (PHPs). Our PHPs generalize AHPs[6] as well as ILDPs. A PHP consists of an interaction between a verifier and a prover sending oracle polynomials, followed by a decision phase in which the verifier

[5] We compose CP-SNARKs as gadgets to modularly build complex schemes; as studied recently [18,54], they are useful to prove properties of committed values [11,35].

[6] PHPs generalize AHPs where the verifier is "algebraic", including all schemes in [19].

outputs a set of polynomial identities to be checked on the prover's polynomials (such as $a(X)b(X) - z \cdot c(X) \stackrel{?}{=} 0$, for oracle polynomials a, b, c and some scalar z), as well as a set of degree tests (e.g. $\mathsf{deg}(a(X)) < D$). The PHP model is close to ILDPs, but the two differ with respect to zero-knowledge formalizations: while ILDPs lack one altogether, we introduce and formalize a fine-grained notion of zero-knowledge—called $(\mathsf{b}_1, \ldots, \mathsf{b}_n)$-bounded zero-knowledge—where the verifier may learn up to b_i evaluations of the i-th oracle polynomial. When compared to AHPs, PHP has, again, a more granular notion of zero-knowledge, as well as verification queries that are more expressive than mere polynomial evaluations.

As we shall discuss next, these two properties of PHPs—expressive verifier's queries and a highly flexible zero-knowledge notion—naturally capture more (and more efficient) strategies when compiling into a cryptographic argument (e.g., we can weaken the required hiding property of the polynomial commitments and the zero-knowledge of the CP-SNARKs used in our compiler).

From PHPs to zkSNARKs Through Another Model of Polynomial Commitments. We describe how to compile a (public-coin) PHP into a zkSNARK. For AHPs and ILDPs [19,27], compilation works by letting the prover use polynomial commitments on the oracles and then open them to the evaluations asked by the verifier. Our approach, though similar, has a key distinction: *a different formalization of polynomial commitments with a modular design.*

Our notion of polynomial commitments is *modular*: rather than seeing them as a monolithic primitive—a tuple of algorithms for both commitment and proofs—we split them into two parts, i.e., a regular commitment scheme with polynomials as message space, and a collection of commit-and-prove SNARKs (CP-SNARKs) for proving relations over committed polynomials. We find several advantages in this approach.

As already argued in prior work on modular zkSNARKs through the commit-and-prove strategy [11,18], one benefit of this approach is *separation of concerns*: commitments are required to do one thing independently of the context (committing), whereas what we need to prove about them may depend on *where* we are applying them. For example, we often want to prove evaluation of committed polynomials: given a commitment c and points x, y, prove that $y = p(x)$ and c opens to p. But to compile a PHP (or AHP/ILDP) we also need to be able to prove other properties about them, such as checking degree bounds or testing equations over committed polynomials. Because these properties—and the techniques to prove them—are somehow independent from each other, we argue they should not be bundled under a bloated notion of polynomial commitment. Going one step further in this direction, we formalize commitment extractability as a proof of knowledge of opening of a polynomial commitment. This modular design allows us to describe an abstract compiler that assumes generic CP-SNARKs for the three aforementioned relations—proof of knowledge of opening, degree bounds and polynomial equations—and can yield zkSNARKs with different tradeoffs depending on how we instantiate them.

We also find additional benefits of the modular abstraction. First, a CP-SNARK for testing equations over committed polynomials more faithfully captures the goal of the PHP verifier (as well as the AHP verifier in virtually all known constructions). Second, we can allow for realizations of CP-SNARKs for equations over polynomials other than the standard one, which reduces the problem of (batched) polynomial evaluations via random point evaluation. As an application, we show a simple scheme for quadratic equations that can even have an empty proof (see below); our most efficient realizations exploit this fact.

From PHPs to zkSNARKs: Fine-Grained Leakage Requirements. Our second contribution on the compiler is to *minimize the requirements needed to achieve zero-knowledge.* As we shall discuss later, this allows us to obtain more efficient zkSNARKs. A straightforward compiler from PHPs to zkSNARKs would require *hiding* polynomial commitments and *zero-knowledge* CP-SNARKs; we weaken both requirements. Instead of "fully" hiding commitments, our compiler requires only *somewhat hiding* commitments. This new property guarantees, for each committed polynomial, leakage of at most one evaluation on a random point. Instead of compiling through "full" zero-knowledge CP-SNARKs, our compiler requires only $(\mathsf{b}_1, \ldots, \mathsf{b}_n)$-leaky zero-knowledge CP-SNARKs. This new notion is weaker than zero-knowledge and states that the verifier may learn up to b_i evaluations of the i-th committed polynomial.

We show that by using a somewhat-hiding commitment scheme and a $(\mathsf{b}_1, \ldots, \mathsf{b}_n)$-leaky zero-knowledge CP-SNARK that can prove the checks of the PHP verifier, one can compile a PHP that is $(\mathsf{b}_1 + 1, \ldots, \mathsf{b}_n + 1)$-bounded ZK into a fully-zero-knowledge succinct argument.

Although related ideas were used in constructions in previous works [27], our contribution is to systematically formalize (as well as expand) the properties needed on different fronts: the PHP, the commitment scheme, the CP-SNARKs used as building blocks and the interaction among all these in the compiler.

Pairing-Based CP-SNARKs for Committed Polynomials. We consider the basic commitment scheme for polynomials consisting of giving a "secret-point evaluation in the exponent" [32,39] and then show CP-SNARKs for various relations over that same commitment scheme. In particular, by using techniques from previous works [19,27,39] we show CP-SNARKs for: proof of knowledge of an opening in the algebraic group model [25] (which actually comes for free), polynomial evaluation, degree bounds, and polynomial equations. In addition to these, we propose a new CP-SNARK for proving opening of several commitments with a proof consisting of one single group element; the latter relies on the PKE assumption [32] in the random oracle model. Also, we show that for a class of quadratic equations over committed polynomials (notably capturing some of the checks of our PHPs), we can obtain an optimized CP-SNARK in which the proof is empty as the verifier can test the relation using a pairing with the inputs (the inputs are commitments, i.e., group elements). This technique is reminiscent of the compiler from [13] that relies on linear encodings with quadratic tests.

PHPs for Constraint Systems. We propose a variety of PHPs for the R1CS constraint system and for a simplified variant of it that we call R1CS-lite. In brief, R1CS-lite is defined by two matrices $\boldsymbol{L}, \boldsymbol{R}$ and accepts a vector $\boldsymbol{x}$ if there is a $\boldsymbol{w}$ such that, for $\boldsymbol{c} = (1, \boldsymbol{x}, \boldsymbol{w})$, $\boldsymbol{L} \cdot \boldsymbol{c} \circ \boldsymbol{R} \cdot \boldsymbol{c} = \boldsymbol{c}$. We show that R1CS-lite can express arithmetic circuit satisfiability with essentially the same complexity of R1CS, and its simpler form allows us to design slightly simpler PHPs. We believe this characterization of NP problems to be of independent interest.

Part of our techniques stem from those in Marlin [19]: we adopt their encoding of sparse matrices; also one of our main building blocks is the sumcheck protocol from Aurora of Ben-Sasson *et al.* [8]. But in our PHPs we explore a different protocol that proves properties of sparse matrices and we introduce a refined efficient technique for zero-knowledge in a univariate sumcheck. In a nutshell, compared to [8] we show how to choose the masking polynomial with a specific sparse distribution that has only a constant-time impact on the prover. This idea and analysis of this technique is possible thanks to our fine-grained ZK formalism for PHPs. By combining this basic skeleton with different techniques we can obtain PHPs with different tradeoffs (see Table 2).

Commit-and-Prove zkSNARKs from PHPs. We propose the first general compiler from an information-theoretic object such as (algebraic) IOPs—and more in general PHPs—to Commit-and-Prove zkSNARKs[7]. Recall that the latter is a SNARK where the verifier's input includes one (or several) *reusable* hiding commitment(s), i.e., to check that $\mathsf{R}(\mathsf{u}_1, \ldots, \mathsf{u}_\ell)$ holds for a tuple of commitments $(\hat{c}_j)_{j\in[\ell]}$ such that c_i opens to u_i. By reusable we mean that these commitments could be used in multiple proofs and with different proof systems since their commitment key is generated before the setup of the proof system. To obtain a CP-SNARK we cannot apply the committing methods for polynomials used in [19,27]: these require a known bound on how many times we will evaluate the polynomials. This is analogous to knowing a bound on the number of proofs over those same committed polynomials, which may be unknown at commitment time. Therefore we apply more stringent requirements and assume these commitments to be full-fledged hiding rather than just somewhat-hiding.

To obtain our commit-and-prove compiler we adapt our compiler to zkSNARKs to include the following key idea: we prove a "link" between the committed witnesses $(\mathsf{u}_j)_{j\in[\ell]}$—which open *hiding* commitments $(\hat{c}_j)_{j\in[\ell]}$—and the PHP polynomials $(p_j)_{j\in[n]}$—which open *somewhat-hiding* commitments $(c_j)_{j\in[n]}$. We design a specific CP-SNARK for this task, $\mathsf{CP}_{\mathsf{link}}$. Our construction works for pairing-based commitments and supports a wide class of linking relations which include those in our PHP constructions.

Simplifying a little bit, our techniques involve proving equality of images of distinct (committed) polynomials on distinct domains and they are of independent interest. In particular they can plausibly be adapted to compile other zkSNARKs with similar properties—e.g., Marlin or PLONK [19,27]—into CP-SNARKs *with commitments that can be reused among different proofs.*

Efficient CP-SNARKs with a universal setup are strongly motivated by practical applications. One of them is *committing-ahead-of-time* [10,18] in which we commit to a value possibly *before* we can predict what we are going to prove about it. A CP-SNARK with a universal SRS, like those in this work, can be a

[7] Here we do not consider the alternative approach of explicitly proving in the PHP a relation augmented with commitment opening; this is often too expensive [18].

requirement in the context of committing-ahead-of-time: if the setting requires committing to data *before* knowing what properties to prove about them (which can happen on-demand), the same setting can benefit from an (unspecialized) SRS string available *before* knowing what to prove about the committed data.

Our work improves on the efficiency of LegoUAC in [18], a modular CP-SNARK construction with universal setup for universal relations (and the only one in literature to the best of our knowledge). Our results are also complementary to those of [18] (in particular their *specialized* CP-SNARKs with universal setup) and to those of works on efficient composable CP-SNARKs on commitments in prime order groups, such as [11]: our universal CP-SNARK can be composed with the schemes in these works *as they can all be derived from the same SRS*, or with some of the transparent instantiations in [11].

1.2 Other Related Work

In this work we focus on practical zkSNARKs with a universal and updatable setup and constant-size proofs. Recent work builds on our formalizations to expand this area designing a fully algebraic framework for modular arguments [47]. Here we briefly survey other works that obtain universality through other approaches at the cost of a larger proof size.

Concurrent work in [42] proposes a new scheme with universal—but not updatable—SRS and an asymptotically linear prover (our prover is quasi-linear due to the use of FFT). By recursive composition they achieve an asymptotically $O_\lambda(1)$-size proof. In practice this is about 9× larger than some of our proofs.

Spartan [49] obtains preprocessing arguments with a URS; it trades a transparent setup for larger arguments and less efficient verification, ranging from $O(\log^2(n)$ to $O(\sqrt{n})$, depending on the instantiation.

Concurrent work in [43] extends Spartan techniques obtaining a linear-time prover. They obtain asymptotically constant-sized proofs through one step of recursive composition with Groth16 [33]; they do not discuss concrete proof sizes. This, however, yields a scheme with universal but not updatable setup. It would require an existing scheme with universal and updatable setup to achieve the latter; their work can thus be seen as complementary to ours.

Other works obtain universal SNARGS through a transparent setup and by exploiting the structure of the computation for succinctness. They mainly use two classes of techniques: hash-based vector commitments applied to oracle interactive proofs [4–6] or multivariate polynomial commitments and doubly-efficient interactive proofs [51,53,55–58].

Fractal [20] achieves transparent zkSNARKs with recursive composition—the ability of a SNARG to prove computations involving prior SNARGs. Their work also uses an algebraically-flavored variant of interactive oracle proofs that they call *Reed–Solomon encoded holographic IOPs.*

Another line of work, e.g., [2,8,15,16,26], obtains a restricted notion of succinctness with no preprocessing, a linear verifier and sublinear proof size.

1.3 Outline

See Sect. 2 for preliminaries. In Sect. 3 we define PHPs; we describe PHP constructions in Sect. 4. Section 5 describes how to compile PHPs to universal zkSNARKs. Concrete compilations for the Lunar zkSNARKs are in Sect. 6.

2 Preliminaries and Notation

Universal Relations. A *universal relation* $\mathcal{R}$ is a set of triples $(\mathsf{R}, \mathsf{x}, \mathsf{w})$ where R is a relation, $\mathsf{x} \in \mathcal{D}_\mathsf{x}$ is called the *instance* (or input), $\mathsf{w} \in \mathcal{D}_w$ the *witness*, and $\mathcal{D}_\mathsf{x}, \mathcal{D}_\mathsf{w}$ are domains that may depend on R. Given $\mathcal{R}$, the corresponding *universal language* $\mathcal{L}(\mathcal{R})$ is the set $\{(\mathsf{R}, \mathsf{x}) : \exists \mathsf{w} : (\mathsf{R}, \mathsf{x}, \mathsf{w}) \in \mathcal{R}\}$. For a size bound $\mathsf{N} \in \mathbb{N}$, $\mathcal{R}_\mathsf{N}$ denotes the subset of triples $(\mathsf{R}, \mathsf{x}, \mathsf{w})$ in $\mathcal{R}$ such that R has size at most N, i.e. $|\mathsf{R}| \leq \mathsf{N}$. In our work, we also write $\mathcal{R}(\mathsf{R}, \mathsf{x}, \mathsf{w}) = 1$ (resp. $\mathsf{R}(\mathsf{x}, \mathsf{w}) = 1$) to denote $(\mathsf{R}, \mathsf{x}, \mathsf{w}) \in \mathcal{R}$ (resp. $(\mathsf{x}, \mathsf{w}) \in \mathsf{R}$).

When discussing schemes that prove statements on committed values we assume that $\mathcal{D}_\mathsf{w}$ can be split in two subdomains $\mathcal{D}_\mathsf{u} \times \mathcal{D}_\omega$, and sometimes we use an even more fine-grained splitting of $\mathcal{D}_\mathsf{u} := (\mathcal{D}_1 \times \cdots \times \mathcal{D}_\ell)$ for some arity ℓ.

2.1 Algebraic Preliminaries

We denote by $\mathbb{F}$ a finite field, by $\mathbb{F}[X]$ the ring of univariate polynomials, and by $\mathbb{F}_{<d}[X]$ (resp. $\mathbb{F}_{\leq d}[X]$) the set of polynomials in $\mathbb{F}[X]$ of degree $< d$ (resp. $\leq d$).

We briefly describe some algebraic preliminaries (see full version for details):

Vanishing and Lagrange Basis Polynomials. For any subset $S \subseteq \mathbb{F}$ we denote by $\mathcal{Z}_S(X) := \prod_{s \in S}(X - s)$ the *vanishing polynomial* of S, and by $\mathcal{L}_s^S(X)$ the *s-th Lagrange basis polynomial*, which is the unique polynomial of degree at most $|S| - 1$ such that for any $s' \in S$ it evaluates to 1 if $s = s'$ and to 0 otherwise.

Multiplicative Subgroups. If $\mathbb{H} \subseteq \mathbb{F}$ is a multiplicative subgroup of order n, then its vanishing polynomial has a compact representation $\mathcal{Z}_\mathbb{H}(X) = (X^{|\mathbb{H}|} - 1)$. Similarly, for such $\mathbb{H}$ it holds $\mathcal{L}_\eta^\mathbb{H}(X) = \frac{\eta}{|\mathbb{H}|} \cdot \frac{X^{|\mathbb{H}|}-1}{X-\eta}$ [38,50,52]. Both $\mathcal{Z}_\mathbb{H}(X)$ and $\mathcal{L}_\eta^\mathbb{H}(X)$ can be evaluated in $O(\log n)$ field operations. We assume that $\mathbb{H}$ comes with a bijection $\phi_\mathbb{H} : \mathbb{H} \to [n]$, and we use elements of $\mathbb{H}$ to index the entries of a matrix $\boldsymbol{M} \in \mathbb{F}^{n \times n}$, i.e., $\boldsymbol{M}_{\eta,\eta'}$ denotes $\boldsymbol{M}_{\phi_\mathbb{H}(\eta),\phi_\mathbb{H}(\eta')}$, and similarly for vectors. For any vector $\boldsymbol{v} \in \mathbb{F}^n$, we denote by $v(X)$ its *interpolating polynomial* in $\mathbb{H}$, i.e., the unique degree-$(|\mathbb{H}| - 1)$ polynomial such that, for all $\eta \in \mathbb{H}$, $v(\eta) = \boldsymbol{v}_\eta$.

Univariate Sumcheck. We use the lemma from [8,19], which shows that for any $p \in \mathbb{F}_d[X]$ and multiplicative subgroup $\mathbb{H} \subset \mathbb{F}$, $\sigma = \sum_{\eta \in \mathbb{H}} p(\eta)$ iff there exists $q(X), r(X)$ such that $p(X) = q(X)\mathcal{Z}_\mathbb{H}(X) + Xr(X) + \sigma/|\mathbb{H}|$ with $\mathsf{deg}(r) < n - 1$.

Polynomial Masking. Given a subgroup $\mathbb{H} \subset \mathbb{F}$ and an integer $\mathsf{b} \geq 1$, $\mathsf{Mask}_\mathsf{b}^\mathbb{H}(p(X))$ is a shorthand for $p(X) + \mathcal{Z}_\mathbb{H}(X)\rho(X)$ for a randomly sampled $\rho(X) \leftarrow_\$ \mathbb{F}_{<\mathsf{b}}[X]$.

Definition 1 (Bivariate Lagrange polynomial). *The* bivariate Lagrange polynomial *for a multiplicative subgroup* $\mathbb{H} \subseteq \mathbb{F}$ *is* $\Lambda_\mathbb{H}(X, Y) := \frac{\mathcal{Z}_\mathbb{H}(X) \cdot Y - X \cdot \mathcal{Z}_\mathbb{H}(Y)}{n \cdot (X - Y)}$.

This polynomial has two properties useful for our work: for all $\eta \in \mathbb{H}$, $\Lambda_{\mathbb{H}}(X, \eta) = \mathcal{L}_\eta^{\mathbb{H}}(X)$, and it can be evaluated in $O(\log n)$ time (see full version).

Sparse Matrix Encodings. For a matrix $\boldsymbol{M}$, $||\boldsymbol{M}||$ denotes the number of its nonzero entries, which we call its *density.* We occasionally use encodings for sparse matrices inspired to [19]. Let $\mathbb{K}$ be another multiplicative subgroup of $\mathbb{F}$ such that $|\mathbb{K}| \geq ||\boldsymbol{M}||$. In brief, a sparse encoding of a matrix $\boldsymbol{M}$ is a triple of polynomials $(\mathsf{val_M}, \mathsf{row_M}, \mathsf{col_M})$ in $\mathbb{F}_{<|\mathbb{K}|}[X]$, where $\mathsf{row_M} : \mathbb{K} \rightarrow \mathbb{H}$ (resp. $\mathsf{col_M} : \mathbb{K} \rightarrow \mathbb{H}$) is the function such that $\mathsf{row_M}(\kappa)$ (resp. $\mathsf{col_M}(\kappa)$) is the row (resp. column) index of the κ-th nonzero entry of $\boldsymbol{M}$, and $\mathsf{val}_M : \mathbb{K} \rightarrow \mathbb{F}$ is the function that encodes the values of $\boldsymbol{M}$ in some arbitrary ordering. Hence it holds that for all $\kappa \in \mathbb{K}$, $\mathsf{val_M}(\kappa) = \boldsymbol{M}_{\mathsf{row_M}(\kappa), \mathsf{col_M}(\kappa)}$. We define the *matrix-encoding polynomial* of $\boldsymbol{M}$ as the bivariate polynomial $V_M(X, Y) := \sum_{\kappa \in \mathbb{K}} \mathsf{val_M}(\kappa) \cdot \mathcal{L}^{\mathbb{H}}_{\mathsf{row_M}(\kappa)}(X) \cdot \mathcal{L}^{\mathbb{H}}_{\mathsf{col_M}(\kappa)}(Y)$, and note that for all $\eta, \eta' \in \mathbb{H}$, $V_M(\eta, \eta') = \boldsymbol{M}_{\eta, \eta'}$.

The following lemma shows that a sparse encoding polynomial of a matrix $\boldsymbol{M}$ can be used to express linear transformations by $\boldsymbol{M}$. Proof in the full version.

Lemma 1 (Sparse Linear Encoding). *Let $\boldsymbol{M} \in \mathbb{F}^{n \times n}$ and let $V_M(X, Y)$ be its matrix-encoding polynomial. Let $\boldsymbol{v}, \boldsymbol{y} \in \mathbb{F}^n$ be two vectors and $v(X), y(X)$ be their interpolating polynomials over $\mathbb{H}$. Then $\boldsymbol{y} = \boldsymbol{M} \cdot \boldsymbol{v}$ if and only if $y(X) = \sum_{\eta \in \mathbb{H}} v(\eta) \cdot V_M(X, \eta)$.*

Joint Sparse Encodings for Multiple Matrices. When working with multiple matrices, it is sometimes convenient to use a sparse encoding that keeps track of entries that are nonzero in either of the matrices. This has the advantage of having a pair of $\mathsf{col}, \mathsf{row}$ polynomials common to all matrices. For example, for two matrices $\boldsymbol{L}, \boldsymbol{R}$, this encoding includes polynomials $\{\mathsf{val}_L, \mathsf{val}_R\}$ encoding their values, and polynomials $\{\mathsf{col}, \mathsf{row}\}$ that maintain the indices in which either of the matrix is nonzero. Namely, for any $\kappa \in \mathbb{K}$, we have $\mathsf{val}_L(\kappa) = \boldsymbol{L}_{\mathsf{row}(\kappa), \mathsf{col}(\kappa)}$ and $\mathsf{val}_R(\kappa) = \boldsymbol{R}_{\mathsf{row}(\kappa), \mathsf{col}(\kappa)}$. In this case though $|\mathbb{K}|$ is in the worst case $\geq ||\boldsymbol{L}|| + ||\boldsymbol{R}||$.

3 Polynomial Holographic IOPs

In this section we define our notion of Polynomial Holographic IOPs (PHP), that generalizes *algebraic holographic proofs* (AHPs) [19]. We show how to compile them into one another in the full version. In a nutshell, a PHP is an interactive oracle proof (IOP) system that works for a family of universal relations $\mathcal{R}$ that is specialized in two main ways. First, it is holographic, i.e., the verifier has oracle access to the relation encoding, a set of oracle polynomials created by a trusted party, the *holographic relation encoder* (or simply, *encoder*) $\mathcal{RE}$. Second, it is algebraic in the sense that the system works over a finite field $\mathbb{F}$: at each round the prover can send field elements or oracle polynomials to the verifier, while the latter can perform algebraic checks as queries over the prover's messages.

More formally, a Polynomial Holographic IOP is defined as follows.

Definition 2 (Polynomial Holographic IOP (PHP)). *Let $\mathcal{F}$ be a family of finite fields and let $\mathcal{R}$ be a universal relation. A Polynomial Holographic IOP over $\mathcal{F}$ for $\mathcal{R}$ is a tuple* $\mathsf{PHP} = (\mathsf{r}, \mathsf{n}, \mathsf{m}, \mathsf{d}, \mathsf{n_e}, \mathcal{RE}, \mathcal{P}, \mathcal{V})$ *where* $\mathsf{r}, \mathsf{n}, \mathsf{m}, \mathsf{d}, \mathsf{n_e} : \{0,1\}^* \rightarrow \mathbb{N}$ *are polynomial-time computable functions, and* $\mathcal{RE}, \mathcal{P}, \mathcal{V}$ *are three algorithms for the encoder, prover and verifier respectively, that work as follows.*

- **Offline phase:** *The encoder* $\mathcal{RE}(\mathbb{F}, \mathsf{R})$ *takes as input a field* $\mathbb{F} \in \mathcal{F}$ *and a relation description* R, *and returns* $\mathsf{n}(0)$ *polynomials* $\{p_{0,j}\}_{j\in[\mathsf{n}(0)]}$ *encoding* R.
- **Online phase:** *The prover* $\mathcal{P}$ *and verifier* $\mathcal{V}$ *run for* $\mathsf{r}(|\mathsf{R}|)$ *rounds and take respectively as input a tuple* $(\mathsf{R}, \mathsf{x}, \mathsf{w}) \in \mathcal{R}$ *and an instance* x*; the verifier has also oracle access to the polynomials encoding* R.
  In the i-th round, $\mathcal{V}$ *sends a message* $\rho_i \in \mathbb{F}$ *to the prover, and* $\mathcal{P}$ *replies with* $\mathsf{m}(i)$ *messages* $\{\pi_{i,j} \in \mathbb{F}\}_{j\in[\mathsf{m}(i)]}$, *and* $\mathsf{n}(i)$ *oracle polynomials* $\{p_{i,j} \in \mathbb{F}[X]\}_{j\in[\mathsf{n}(i)]}$, *such that* $\deg(p_{i,j}) < \mathsf{d}(|\mathsf{R}|, i, j)$.
- **Decision phase:** *After the* $\mathsf{r}(|\mathsf{R}|)$*-th round, the verifier outputs two sets of algebraic checks of the following type.*
  - *Degree checks: to check a bound on the degree of the polynomials sent by the prover. More in detail, let* $\mathsf{n_p} = \sum_{k=1}^{\mathsf{r}(|\mathsf{R}|)} \mathsf{n}(k)$ *and let* $(p_1, \ldots, p_{\mathsf{n_p}})$ *be the polynomials sent by* $\mathcal{P}$. *The verifier specifies a vector of integers* $\boldsymbol{d} \in \mathbb{N}^{\mathsf{n_p}}$, *which is satisfied if and only if* $\forall k \in [\mathsf{n_p}] : \deg(p_k) \leq d_k$.
  - *Polynomial checks: to check that certain polynomial identities hold for the oracle polynomials and the prover messages. Formally, let* $\mathsf{n}^* = \sum_{k=0}^{\mathsf{r}(|\mathsf{R}|)} \mathsf{n}(k)$ *and* $\mathsf{m}^* = \sum_{k=1}^{\mathsf{r}(|\mathsf{R}|)} \mathsf{m}(k)$, *and denote by* $(p_1, \ldots, p_{\mathsf{n}^*})$ *and* $(\pi_1, \ldots, \pi_{\mathsf{m}^*})$ *all the oracle polynomials (including the encoder's) and all the messages sent by the prover. The verifier can specify a list of* $\mathsf{n_e}$ *tuples, each of the form* $(G, v_1, \ldots, v_{\mathsf{n}^*})$, *where* $G \in \mathbb{F}[X, X_1, \ldots, X_{\mathsf{n}^*}, Y_1, \ldots, Y_{\mathsf{m}^*}]$ *and every* $v_k \in \mathbb{F}[X]$. *Then a tuple* $(G, \boldsymbol{v})$ *is satisfied if and only if* $F(X) \equiv 0$ *where*

$$F(X) := G(X, \{p_k(v_k(X))\}_{k\in[\mathsf{n}^*]}, \{\pi_k\}_{k\in[\mathsf{m}^*]})$$

  The verifier accepts if and only if all the checks are satisfied.

Efficiency Measures. *Given the functions* $\mathsf{r}, \mathsf{d}, \mathsf{n}, \mathsf{m}$ *in the tuple* PHP, *one can derive some efficiency measures of the protocol* PHP *such as the total number of oracles sent by the encoder,* $\mathsf{n}(0)$, *by the prover* $\mathsf{n_p}$, *by both in total,* n^**; or the number of prover messages* m^*. *In addition to these, we define the following shorthands for two more measures of* PHP*; degree* D, *and proof length* $\mathsf{L}(|\mathsf{R}|)$*:*

$$\mathsf{D} := \max_{\substack{\mathsf{R}\in\mathcal{R}\\ i\in[0,\mathsf{r}(|\mathsf{R}|)]\\ j\in[\mathsf{n}(i)]}} (\mathsf{d}(|\mathsf{R}|, i, j)), \qquad \mathsf{L}(|\mathsf{R}|) := \sum_{\substack{i\in[\mathsf{r}(|\mathsf{R}|)]\\ j\in[\mathsf{n}(i)]}} \mathsf{m}(i) + \mathsf{d}(|\mathsf{R}|, i, j).$$

PHP *should satisfy completeness, (knowledge) soundness and zero-knowledge:*

Completeness. *If for all* $\mathbb{F} \in \mathcal{F}$ *and any* $(\mathsf{R}, \mathsf{x}, \mathsf{w}) \in \mathcal{R}$, *the checks returned by* $\mathcal{V}^{\mathcal{RE}(\mathbb{F},\mathsf{R})}(\mathbb{F}, \mathsf{x})$ *after interacting with (honest)* $\mathcal{P}(\mathbb{F}, \mathsf{R}, \mathsf{x}, \mathsf{w})$ *are always satisfied.*

Soundness. *A PHP is* ϵ*-sound if for every field* $\mathbb{F} \in \mathcal{F}$*, relation-instance tuple* $(\mathsf{R}, \mathsf{x}) \notin \mathcal{L}(\mathcal{R})$ *and prover* $\mathcal{P}^*$ *we have* $\Pr[\langle \mathcal{P}^*, \mathcal{V}^{\mathcal{RE}(\mathbb{F},\mathsf{R})}(\mathbb{F}, \mathsf{x})\rangle = 1] \le \epsilon$.

Knowledge Soundness. *A PHP is* ϵ*-knowledge-sound if there exists a polynomial-time knowledge extractor* $\mathcal{E}$ *such that for any prover* $\mathcal{P}^*$*, field* $\mathbb{F} \in \mathcal{F}$*, relation* R*, instance* x *and auxiliary input* z*:*

$$\Pr\left[(\mathsf{R}, \mathsf{x}, \mathsf{w}) \in \mathsf{R} : \mathsf{w} \leftarrow \mathcal{E}^{\mathcal{P}^*}(\mathbb{F}, \mathsf{R}, \mathsf{x}, z)\right] \ge \Pr[\langle \mathcal{P}^*(\mathbb{F}, \mathsf{R}, \mathsf{x}, z), \mathcal{V}^{\mathcal{RE}(\mathbb{F},\mathsf{R})}(\mathbb{F}, \mathsf{x})\rangle = 1] - \epsilon$$

where $\mathcal{E}$ *has oracle access to* $\mathcal{P}^*$*, i.e., it can query the next message function of* $\mathcal{P}^*$ *(and rewind it) and obtain all the messages and polynomials returned by it.*

Zero-Knowledge. *A PHP is* ϵ-zero-knowledge *if there exists a PPT simulator* $\mathcal{S}$ *such that for every field* $\mathbb{F} \in \mathcal{F}$*, every triple* $(\mathsf{R}, \mathsf{x}, \mathsf{w}) \in \mathcal{R}$*, and every algorithm* $\mathcal{V}^*$ *the following random variables are within* ϵ *statistical distance:*

$$\mathsf{View}\big(\mathcal{P}(\mathbb{F}, \mathsf{R}, \mathsf{x}, \mathsf{w})\ , \mathcal{V}^*\big) \approx_\epsilon \mathsf{View}\big(\mathcal{S}^{\mathcal{V}^*}(\mathbb{F}, \mathsf{R}, \mathsf{x})\big)$$

where $\mathsf{View}\big(\mathcal{P}(\mathbb{F}, \mathsf{R}, \mathsf{x}, \mathsf{w}), \mathcal{V}^*\big)$ *consists of* $\mathcal{V}^*$*'s randomness,* $\mathcal{P}$*'s messages* $\pi_1, \ldots, \pi_{\mathsf{m}^*}$ *(which do not include the oracles), and* $\mathcal{V}^*$*'s list of checks, while* $\mathsf{View}\big(\mathcal{S}^{\mathcal{V}^*}(\mathbb{F}, \mathsf{R}, \mathsf{x})\big)$ *consists of* $\mathcal{V}^*$*'s randomness followed by* $\mathcal{S}$*'s output, obtained after having straightline access to* $\mathcal{V}^*$*, and* $\mathcal{V}^*$*'s list of checks.*

Remark 1 (About messages and constant polynomials). We explicitly model the prover's messages π_i, although they could be replaced by (degree-0) polynomial oracles evaluated on 0 during the checks. This is useful for zero-knowledge: while messages are supposed not to leak information on the witness (i.e., they must be simulated), this does not hold for the oracles. Thus, in our compiler, we will not need to hide messages π_i from the verifier, only the oracles.

On the Class of Polynomial Checks. Above we describe the class of polynomial checks of the verifier in full generality; nonetheless, when possible, we use more convenient notations. We note that this class includes low-degree polynomials like $G(\{p_i(X)\}_i)$ (e.g., $p_1(X)p_2(X)p_3(X) + p_4(X)$), in which case each $v_i(X) = X$, polynomial evaluations $p_i(x)$, in which case $v_i(X) = x$, tests over $\mathcal{P}$ messages, e.g., $p_i(x) - \pi_j$, and combinations of all these.

Public Coin and Non-adaptive Queries. In the rest of this work, we only consider PHPs that are public coin and non-adaptive: the messages of the verifier are random elements and its checks are independent of the prover's messages.

Below we define two additional properties that can be satisfied by a PHP:

Bounded Zero-Knowledge. This property will be useful for our compiler of Sect. 5. We require that zero-knowledge holds even if the view includes a bounded number of evaluations of oracle polynomials at given points.

However, we cannot allow evaluations on any possible point: specific points could leak bits of information of the witness. Thus we define a notion of "admissible" evaluations. Below we say that a list $\mathcal{L} = \{(i_1, y_1), \ldots\}$ is (b, C)-bounded where $\mathsf{b} \in \mathbb{N}^{\mathsf{n_p}}$ and C is a PT algorithm if $\forall i \in [\mathsf{n_p}] : |\{(i, y) : (i, y) \in \mathcal{L}\}| \le \mathsf{b}_i$ and $\forall (i, y) \in \mathcal{L} : \mathsf{C}(i, y) = 1$.

Definition 3 ((b, C)-Zero-Knowledge). *We say that* PHP *is* (b, C)*-Zero-Knowledge if for every triple* $(\mathsf{R}, \mathsf{x}, \mathsf{w}) \in \mathcal{R}$, *and every* (b, C)*-bounded list* $\mathcal{L}$, *the following random variables are within* ϵ *statistical distance:*

$$\left(\mathsf{View}(\mathcal{P}(\mathbb{F}, \mathsf{R}, \mathsf{x}, \mathsf{w}), \mathcal{V}), (p_i(y))_{(i,y)\in\mathcal{L}}\right) \approx_\epsilon \mathcal{S}(\mathbb{F}, \mathsf{R}, \mathsf{x}, \mathcal{V}(\mathbb{F}, \mathsf{x}), \mathcal{L}).$$

where $p_1, \ldots, p_{\mathsf{n_p}}$ *are the polynomials returned by the prover* $\mathcal{P}$.

Moreover, we say that PHP *is* honest-verifier zero-knowledge with query bound b (b*-HVZK for short) if there exists a PT algorithm* C *such that* PHP *is* (b, C)*-ZK and for all* $i \in \mathbb{N}$ *we have* $\Pr_{y \leftarrow\$ \mathbb{F}}[\mathsf{C}(i, y) = 0] \in \mathsf{negl}(\lambda)$.

3.1 PHP Verifier Relation

We formalize the definition of an NP relation that models the PHP verifier's decision phase. We shall use it in our compiler in Sect. 5.

Let $\mathsf{PHP} = (\mathsf{r}, \mathsf{n}, \mathsf{m}, \mathsf{d}, \mathsf{n_e}, \mathcal{RE}, \mathcal{P}, \mathcal{V})$ be a PHP protocol over a finite field family $\mathcal{F}$ for a universal relation $\mathcal{R}$, with D as its maximum degree. We define $\mathcal{R}_{\mathsf{php}}$ as a family of relations that express the checks of $\mathcal{V}$ over the oracle polynomials, which can be formally defined as follows.

Let $\mathsf{n_p}, \mathsf{n}^* \in \mathbb{N}$ be two positive integers, and consider the following relations:

$$\mathsf{R_{deg}}\left((d_j)_{j\in[\mathsf{n_p}]}, (p_j)_{j\in[\mathsf{n_p}]}\right) := \bigwedge\nolimits_{j\in[\mathsf{n_p}]} \deg(p_j) \stackrel{?}{\leq} d_j$$

$$\mathsf{R_{eq}}\left((G', \boldsymbol{v}), (p_j)_{j\in[\mathsf{n}^*]}\right) := G'\left(X, (p_j(v_j(X)))_{j\in[\mathsf{n}^*]}\right) \stackrel{?}{\equiv} 0$$

where $G \in \mathbb{F}[X, X_1, \ldots, X_{\mathsf{n}^*}]$ and $\boldsymbol{v} = (v_1, \ldots, v_{\mathsf{n}^*}) \in \mathbb{F}[X]^{\mathsf{n}^*}$. For a PHP verifier that returns a polynomial check $(G', \boldsymbol{v})$, $\mathsf{R_{eq}}$ expresses such check if one considers G' as the partial evaluation of G at $(Y_1 = \pi_1, \ldots, Y_{\mathsf{m}^*} = \pi_{\mathsf{m}^*})$. $\mathsf{R_{deg}}$ instead expresses the degree checks of a PHP verifier.

Given relations $\mathsf{R}_A \subset \mathcal{D}_\mathsf{x} \times \mathcal{D}_\mathsf{w}$ and $\mathsf{R}_B \subset \mathcal{D}'_\mathsf{x} \times \mathcal{D}_\mathsf{w}$ with a common domain $\mathcal{D}_\mathsf{w}$ for the witness, consider the product $\mathsf{R}_A \times \mathsf{R}_B \subset \mathcal{D}_\mathsf{x} \times \mathcal{D}'_\mathsf{x} \times \mathcal{D}_\mathsf{w}$ containing all the tuples $(\mathsf{x}_A, \mathsf{x}_B, \mathsf{w})$ where $(\mathsf{x}_A, \mathsf{w}) \in \mathsf{R}_A$ and $(\mathsf{x}_B, \mathsf{w}) \in \mathsf{R}_B$. For $\mathsf{n_e} \in \mathbb{N}$, let

$$\mathsf{R}_{\mathsf{n}^*,\mathsf{n_p},\mathsf{n_e}} := \mathsf{R_{deg}} \times \overbrace{\mathsf{R_{eq}} \times \cdots \times \mathsf{R_{eq}}}^{\mathsf{n_e}\text{ times}} \quad \text{and} \quad \mathcal{R}_{\mathsf{php}} := \left\{\mathsf{R}_{\mathsf{n}^*(|\mathsf{R}|),\mathsf{n_p}(|\mathsf{R}|),\mathsf{n_e}(|\mathsf{R}|)} : \mathsf{R} \in \mathcal{R}\right\}$$

where $\mathsf{n}^*(|\mathsf{R}|) = \sum_{i=0}^{\mathsf{r}(|\mathsf{R}|)} \mathsf{n}(i)$ and $\mathsf{n_p}(|\mathsf{R}|) = \sum_{i=1}^{\mathsf{r}(|\mathsf{R}|)} \mathsf{n}(i)$ are the number of total and prover oracle polynomials respectively, when running PHP with relation R.

4 Our PHP Constructions

We propose a collection of PHP constructions for two types of constraint systems: the by now standard rank-1 constraint systems [28] and an equally expressive variant we introduce in Sect. 4.1 called R1CS-lite.

R1CS-lite can be seen as a simplified version of R1CS with only two matrices. In brief, an R1CS-lite relation is defined by two matrices $\boldsymbol{L}, \boldsymbol{R}$ and is satisfied if

Table 2. Comparison of our PHP constructions, all with complexities: $O(m \log m)$ for $\mathcal{RE}$, $O(m \log m + n \log n)$ for $\mathcal{P}$ and $O(\ell + \log m + \log n)$ for $\mathcal{V}$. To have a simpler table, we assume $|\mathbb{K}| = m > 2n$, which is often the case. We call $|\pi| = 5n + 2m - 2\ell + 2\mathsf{b}_a + 2\mathsf{b}_b + 2\mathsf{b}_s + 6\mathsf{b}_q - 4$, and $|\pi'| = |\pi| + n - \ell + \mathsf{b}_w + 7\mathsf{b}_q$. For verifier checks, we denote by "deg" the number of degree checks that require a tight bound; the last two columns show the degree of the two polynomial checks: in the first one we have all $v_j(X) = y$ and in the second one all $v_j(X) = X$. "Rk" ("full") denote remark (resp. full version).

PHP		Degree	Oracles		Msgs	Proof length	$\mathcal{V}$ checks		
Name	Ref.		$\mathcal{RE}$	$\mathcal{P}$			deg	$\mathsf{deg}_{X,\{X_i\}}(G_1)$	$\mathsf{deg}_{X,\{X_i\}}(G_2)$
$\mathsf{PHP}_{\mathsf{lite1}}$	4.1	$2m$	8	7	1	$\|\pi\| + 2m$	2	2	2
$\mathsf{PHP}_{\mathsf{lite1x}}$	Remark 2	$2m$	5	7	1	$\|\pi\| + 2m$	2	2	3
$\mathsf{PHP}_{\mathsf{lite2}}$	full	m	24	7	1	$\|\pi\|$	2	2	2
$\mathsf{PHP}_{\mathsf{lite2x}}$	full	m	16	7	1	$\|\pi\|$	2	2	3
$\mathsf{PHP}_{\mathsf{r1cs1}}$	full	$3m$	9	8	1	$\|\pi'\| + 4m$	2	2	2
$\mathsf{PHP}_{\mathsf{r1cs1x}}$	full	$3m$	6	8	1	$\|\pi'\| + 4m$	2	2	3
$\mathsf{PHP}_{\mathsf{r1cs2}}$	full	m	57	8	1	$\|\pi'\|$	2	2	2
$\mathsf{PHP}_{\mathsf{r1cs2x}}$	full	m	42	8	1	$\|\pi'\|$	2	2	3
$\mathsf{PHP}_{\mathsf{r1cs3}}$	full	$3m$	12	8	1	$\|\pi'\|$	2	2	5

there exists a vector $\boldsymbol{c}$ such that $(\boldsymbol{L} \cdot \boldsymbol{c}) \circ (\boldsymbol{R} \cdot \boldsymbol{c}) = \boldsymbol{c}$. We show that R1CS-lite is as expressive as R1CS since it can represent arithmetic circuit satisfiability with essentially the same complexity as R1CS (see full version)[8]. It allows us to obtain PHP constructions (and resulting zkSNARKs) that are simpler and more efficient. More formally, R1CS-lite is defined as follows.

Definition 4 (R1CS-lite). *Let $\mathbb{F}$ be a finite field and $n, m \in \mathbb{N}$ be positive integers. The universal relation $\mathcal{R}_{R1CS\text{-}lite}$ is the set of triples*

$$(\mathsf{R}, \mathsf{x}, \mathsf{w}) := ((\mathbb{F}, n, m, \ell, \{\boldsymbol{L}, \boldsymbol{R}\}), \boldsymbol{x}, \boldsymbol{w})$$

where $\boldsymbol{L}, \boldsymbol{R} \in \mathbb{F}^{n \times n}$, $\max\{||\boldsymbol{L}||, ||\boldsymbol{R}||\} \leq m$, the first ℓ rows of $\boldsymbol{R}$ are $(-1, 0, \ldots, 0) \in \mathbb{F}^{1 \times n}$, $\boldsymbol{x} \in \mathbb{F}^{\ell - 1}$, $\boldsymbol{w} \in \mathbb{F}^{n - \ell}$, and for $\boldsymbol{c} := (1, \boldsymbol{x}, \boldsymbol{w})$, it holds $(\boldsymbol{L}\boldsymbol{c}) \circ (\boldsymbol{R}\boldsymbol{c}) = \boldsymbol{c}$.

In this section, we present one PHP for R1CS-lite relations and give the intuition to obtain other PHP variants. The PHPs for the R1CS language follow the same bare-bone protocol, differing mainly in the number of matrices and an additional witness vector. In Table 2 we give a summary of all our PHPs and their measures.

4.1 Our PHPs for R1CS-Lite

In all our constructions we use a variant of R1CS-lite in which we slightly expand the witness, and we express the witnesses and the check in polynomial form.

[8] Comparing to R1CS, the number of columns in R1CS-lite matrices do not change and the number of rows increase by the amount of public inputs, for the same circuit. The count of nonzero entries in R1CS-lite is smaller for virtually every circuit.

Definition 5 (Polynomial R1CS-lite). *Let $\mathbb{F}$ be a finite field, and $n, m \in \mathbb{N}$ be positive integers. The universal relation $\mathcal{R}_{polyR1CS\text{-}lite}$ is the set of triples*

$$((\mathbb{F}, n, m, \{\boldsymbol{L}, \boldsymbol{R}\}, \ell), \boldsymbol{x}, (a'(X), b'(X)))$$

where $\boldsymbol{L}, \boldsymbol{R} \in \mathbb{F}^{n\times n}$, $\max\{||\boldsymbol{L}||, ||\boldsymbol{R}||\} \leq m$, $\boldsymbol{x} \in \mathbb{F}^{\ell-1}$, $a'(X), b'(X) \in \mathbb{F}_{\leq n-\ell-1}[X]$, and such that, for $\mathbb{L} := \{\phi_{\mathbb{H}}^{-1}(i)\}_{i\in[\ell]}$, $\boldsymbol{x}' = (1, \boldsymbol{x})$, $a(X) := \sum_{\eta\in\mathbb{L}} \boldsymbol{x}'_{\phi_{\mathbb{H}}(\eta)} \cdot \mathcal{L}_{\eta}^{\mathbb{H}}(X) + a'(X) \cdot z_{\mathbb{L}}(X)$ and $b(X) := 1 + b'(X) \cdot z_{\mathbb{L}}(X)$, it holds, over $\mathbb{F}[X, Z]$,

$$a(X) + Z \cdot b(X) + \sum_{\eta,\eta'\in\mathbb{H}} (\boldsymbol{L}_{\eta,\eta'} + Z \cdot \boldsymbol{R}_{\eta,\eta'}) \cdot a(\eta') \cdot b(\eta') \cdot \mathcal{L}_{\eta}^{\mathbb{H}}(X) = 0 \quad (1)$$

In the full version we prove that $\mathcal{L}(\mathcal{R}_{R1CS-lite}) \equiv \mathcal{L}(\mathcal{R}_{polyR1CS\text{-}lite})$.

Our PHP $\mathsf{PHP}_{\mathsf{lite1}}$. We describe the main ideas of our protocol $\mathsf{PHP}_{\mathsf{lite1}}$. The prover's goal is to convince the verifier that the polynomials $a(X), b(X)$ satisfy Eq. (1). To this end, the relation encoder $\mathcal{RE}$ encodes the matrices $\boldsymbol{L}, \boldsymbol{R}$ by using a joint sparse encoding (see Sect. 2.1), which consists of four polynomials $(\mathsf{val}_L, \mathsf{val}_R, \mathsf{col}, \mathsf{row})$ in $\mathbb{F}_{<|\mathbb{K}|}[X]$. In this case we use a multiplicative subgroup $\mathbb{K} \subset \mathbb{F}$ of minimal cardinality such that $|\mathbb{K}| \geq 2m \geq ||\boldsymbol{L}|| + ||\boldsymbol{R}||$.

By applying the sparse linear encoding of Lemma 1 to the matrices $\boldsymbol{L}$ and $\boldsymbol{R}$ and using the property of the bivariate Lagrange polynomial that $\Lambda_{\mathbb{H}}(X, \eta) = \mathcal{L}_{\eta}^{\mathbb{H}}(X)$, Eq. (1) can be expressed as

$$\begin{aligned} 0 &= a(X) + Z \cdot b(X) + \sum_{\eta\in\mathbb{H}} a(\eta) \cdot b(\eta) \cdot (V_L(X, \eta) + Z \cdot V_R(X, \eta)) \\ &= \sum_{\eta\in\mathbb{H}} (a(\eta) + Z \cdot b(\eta)) \cdot \Lambda_{\mathbb{H}}(X, \eta) + a(\eta) \cdot b(\eta) \cdot V_{LR}(X, \eta, Z) \end{aligned} \quad (2)$$

where, exploiting the use of $\mathsf{col}, \mathsf{row}$ common to $\boldsymbol{L}, \boldsymbol{R}$, $V_{LR}(X, Y, Z)$ equals:

$$V_L(X, Y) + Z \cdot V_R(X, Y) = \sum_{\kappa\in\mathbb{K}} (\mathsf{val}_L(\kappa) + Z \cdot \mathsf{val}_R(\kappa)) \cdot \mathcal{L}_{\mathsf{row}(\kappa)}^{\mathbb{H}}(X) \cdot \mathcal{L}_{\mathsf{col}(\kappa)}^{\mathbb{H}}(Y)$$

In order to show that $a(X), b(X)$ satisfy Eq. (2), the verifier draws random points $x, \alpha \leftarrow_{\$} \mathbb{F}$ that are used to "compress" the equation from $\mathbb{F}[X, Z]$ to $\mathbb{F}$. Then, the prover's task becomes to show that

$$\sum_{\eta\in\mathbb{H}} (a(\eta) + \alpha \cdot b(\eta)) \cdot \Lambda_{\mathbb{H}}(x, \eta) + a(\eta) \cdot b(\eta) \cdot V_{LR}(x, \eta, \alpha) = 0$$

This is done via a univariate sumcheck over $p(X) := (a(X) + \alpha \cdot b(X)) \cdot \Lambda_{\mathbb{H}}(x, X) + a(X) \cdot b(X) \cdot V_{LR}(x, X, \alpha)$. However, since $p(X)$ depends on the witness, we make the sumcheck zero-knowledge by doing it over $p(X) + s(X)$ for a random polynomial $s(X)$ sent by the prover in the first round. Although this resembles the zero-knowledge sumcheck technique of [8], we propose an optimized way to randomly sample a sparse $s(X)$, which is sufficient for the bounded zero-knowlegde of our PHP. So, for the sumcheck the prover sends two polynomials $q(X), r(X)$ such that $s(X) + p(X) = q(X) \cdot z_{\mathbb{H}}(X) + X \cdot r(X)$. The verifier checks this equation by evaluating all the polynomials on a random point $y \leftarrow_{\$} \mathbb{F} \setminus \mathbb{H}$. To do this, the verifier can compute on its own (in $O(\log n)$ time) the polynomials $\Lambda_{\mathbb{H}}(x, y)$, $\mathcal{Z}_{\mathbb{H}}(y)$, and query all the others, except for $V_{LR}(x, y, \alpha)$. For the latter the prover sends a candidate value σ and runs a univariate sumcheck to convince the verifier that $\sigma = \sum_{\kappa \in \mathbb{K}} (\mathsf{val}_L(\kappa) + \alpha \cdot \mathsf{val}_R(\kappa)) \cdot \mathcal{L}^{\mathbb{H}}_{\mathsf{row}(\kappa)}(x) \cdot \mathcal{L}^{\mathbb{H}}_{\mathsf{col}(\kappa)}(y)$.

In what follows we give a detailed description of the PHP protocol $\mathsf{PHP}_{\mathsf{lite1}}$.

Offline Phase $\mathcal{RE}(\mathbb{F}, n, m, \{\boldsymbol{L}, \boldsymbol{R}\}, \ell)$. The holographic relation encoder takes as input a description of the specific relation and outputs eight polynomials

$$\{\mathsf{col}(X), \mathsf{row}(X), \mathsf{cr}(X), \mathsf{col}'(X), \mathsf{row}'(X), \mathsf{cr}'(X), \mathsf{vcr}_L(X), \mathsf{vcr}_R(X)\} \in \mathbb{F}_{\leq |\mathbb{K}|}[X].$$

The polynomials $\{\mathsf{col}, \mathsf{row}, \mathsf{val}_L, \mathsf{val}_R\}$ are the joint sparse encoding of $\{\boldsymbol{L}, \boldsymbol{R}\}$. The holographic relation encoder computes:

$$\mathsf{cr}(X) := \sum_{\kappa \in \mathbb{K}} \mathsf{col}(\kappa) \cdot \mathsf{row}(\kappa) \cdot \mathcal{L}^{\mathbb{K}}_{\kappa}(X)$$
$$\{\mathsf{vcr}_M(X) := \sum_{\kappa \in \mathbb{K}} \mathsf{val}_M(\kappa) \cdot \mathsf{cr}(\kappa) \cdot \mathcal{L}^{\mathbb{K}}_{\kappa}(X)\}_{M \in \{L, R\}}$$
$$\mathsf{col}'(X) := X \cdot \mathsf{col}(X), \quad \mathsf{row}'(X) := X \cdot \mathsf{row}(X), \quad \mathsf{cr}'(X) := X \cdot \mathsf{cr}(X)$$

Essentially, the polynomials $\mathsf{cr}(X), \mathsf{vcr}_L(X)$ and $\mathsf{vcr}_R(X)$ are low-degree extensions of the evaluations in $\mathbb{K}$ of $(\mathsf{col}(X) \cdot \mathsf{row}(X))$, $(\mathsf{val}_L(X) \cdot \mathsf{col}(X) \cdot \mathsf{row}(X))$ and $(\mathsf{val}_R(X) \cdot \mathsf{col}(X) \cdot \mathsf{row}(X))$ respectively, while $\mathsf{col}', \mathsf{row}'$ and cr' are a shifted version of col, row and cr each. The intuition behind expanding the sparse encoding of $\boldsymbol{L}$, $\boldsymbol{R}$ in this way is to keep the polynomial checks of the verifier of the lowest possible degree. In particular we are interested in obtaining a PHP where $\mathsf{deg}_{X, \{X_i\}}(G) \leq 2$ as it enables interesting instantiations of our compiler. As an example, by adding $\mathsf{cr}(X)$ we can replace terms involving $\mathsf{col}(X) \cdot \mathsf{row}(X)$ with $\mathsf{cr}(X)$. This shall become more clear when looking at the decision phase.

Online Phase $\langle \mathcal{P}((\mathbb{F}, n, m, \{\boldsymbol{L}, \boldsymbol{R}\}, \ell), \boldsymbol{x}, (a'(X), b'(X))), \mathcal{V}(\mathbb{F}, n, m, \boldsymbol{x}) \rangle$.

Round 1: $\mathcal{P} \xrightarrow{\{\hat{a}'(X), \hat{b}'(X), s(X)\}} \mathcal{V}$

The prover samples polynomials $q_s(X) \leftarrow\!\!\$\, \mathbb{F}_{\mathsf{b}_s + \mathsf{b}_q - 1}[X]$ and $r_s(X) \leftarrow\!\!\$\, \mathbb{F}_{\mathsf{b}_r + \mathsf{b}_q - 1}[X]$, and sets $s(X) := q_s(X) \cdot \mathcal{Z}_{\mathbb{H}}(X) + X \cdot r_s(X)$. Note that, whenever $\mathsf{b}_r + \mathsf{b}_q \leq n$, the pair $q_s(X), r_s(X)$ is a unique decomposition of $s(X)$, and also $s(X) \in \mathbb{F}_{\leq n + \mathsf{b}_s + \mathsf{b}_q - 1}[X]$. $\mathcal{P}$ sends $s(X)$ to $\mathcal{V}$ together with randomized versions of the witness polynomials $\hat{a}'(X) \leftarrow\!\!\$\, \mathsf{Mask}^{\mathbb{H} \setminus \mathbb{L}}_{\mathsf{b}_a + \mathsf{b}_q}(a'(X)) \in \mathbb{F}_{\leq n - \ell + \mathsf{b}_a + \mathsf{b}_q - 1}[X]$ and $\hat{b}'(X) \leftarrow\!\!\$\, \mathsf{Mask}^{\mathbb{H} \setminus \mathbb{L}}_{\mathsf{b}_b + \mathsf{b}_q}(b'(X)) \in \mathbb{F}_{\leq n - \ell + \mathsf{b}_b + \mathsf{b}_q - 1}[X]$.

Round 2: $\mathcal{V} \xrightarrow{x, \alpha} \mathcal{P} \xrightarrow{\{q(X), r(X)\}} \mathcal{V}$

The verifier sends two random points $x, \alpha \leftarrow\!\!\$\, \mathbb{F}$. The prover uses the pair x, α to "compress" the check of Eq. (1) over $\mathbb{F}[X, Z]$ into the sumcheck statement

$\sum_{\eta \in \mathbb{H}} p(\eta) = 0$ over $\mathbb{F}$ for the polynomial $p(X) := (\hat{a}(X) + \alpha \cdot \hat{b}(X)) \cdot \Lambda_{\mathbb{H}}(x, X) + \hat{a}(X) \cdot \hat{b}(X) \cdot V_{LR}(x, X, \alpha)$ where, for $\boldsymbol{x}' = (1, \boldsymbol{x})$, we have

$$\hat{a}(X) := \hat{a}'(X) \cdot z_{\mathbb{L}}(X) + \sum_{\eta \in \mathbb{L}} \boldsymbol{x}'_{\phi_{\mathbb{H}}(\eta)} \cdot \mathcal{L}_{\eta}^{\mathbb{H}}(X) \in \mathbb{F}_{\leq n + \mathsf{b}_a + \mathsf{b}_q - 1}[X],$$
$$\hat{b}(X) := \hat{b}'(X) \cdot z_{\mathbb{L}}(X) + 1 \in \mathbb{F}_{\leq n + \mathsf{b}_b + \mathsf{b}_q - 1}[X],$$

Next, $\mathcal{P}$ computes and sends polynomials $q(X) \in \mathbb{F}_{\leq 2n + \mathsf{b}_a + \mathsf{b}_b + 2\mathsf{b}_q - 3}[X]$ and $r(X) \in \mathbb{F}_{\leq n-2}[X]$—such that $s(X) + p(X) = q(X) \cdot z_{\mathbb{H}}(X) + X \cdot r(X)$—to prove the univariate sumcheck $\sum_{\eta \in \mathbb{H}} s(\eta) + p(\eta) = 0$. Note that by construction $\sum_{\eta \in \mathbb{H}} s(\eta) = 0$; its role here is to (sufficiently) randomize $q(X), r(X)$ in a way that their evaluations do not leak information about the witness (Theorem 2).

Round 3: $\mathcal{V} \xrightarrow{\quad y \quad} \mathcal{P} \xrightarrow{\quad \sigma,\ \{\, q'(X), r'(X) \,\} \quad} \mathcal{V}$

The verifier sends a random point $y \leftarrow_{\$} \mathbb{F} \setminus \mathbb{H}$. The prover uses y to compute $\sigma \leftarrow V_{LR}(x, y, \alpha)$ and then defines the degree-($|\mathbb{K}| - 1$) polynomial

$$p'(X) := \sum_{\kappa \in \mathbb{K}} (\mathsf{val}_L(\kappa) + \alpha \cdot \mathsf{val}_R(\kappa)) \cdot \mathcal{L}_{\mathsf{row}(\kappa)}^{\mathbb{H}}(x) \cdot \mathcal{L}_{\mathsf{col}(\kappa)}^{\mathbb{H}}(y) \cdot \mathcal{L}_{\kappa}^{\mathbb{K}}(X)$$

The goal of the prover is to convince the verifier that $\sum_{\kappa \in \mathbb{K}} p'(\kappa) = \sigma$ and

$$\forall \kappa \in \mathbb{K} : p'(\kappa) = (\mathsf{val}_L(\kappa) + \alpha \cdot \mathsf{val}_R(\kappa)) \cdot \mathcal{L}_{\mathsf{row}(\kappa)}^{\mathbb{H}}(x) \cdot \mathcal{L}_{\mathsf{col}(\kappa)}^{\mathbb{H}}(y)$$

These two statements can be combined in such a way that $\mathcal{P}$ does not need to send $p'(X)$, which is implicitly known by $\mathcal{V}$ as it depends on $\mathcal{RE}$ polynomials.

The first claim, since $\mathsf{deg}(p') < |\mathbb{K}|$, reduces to proving that its constant term is $\frac{\sigma}{|\mathbb{K}|}$, for which $\mathcal{P}$ sends $r'(X) \in \mathbb{F}_{\leq |\mathbb{K}| - 2}[X]$ such that $p'(X) = X \cdot r'(X) + \frac{\sigma}{|\mathbb{K}|}$.

The second claim, by definition of $\mathcal{L}^{\mathbb{H}}(\cdot)$, means proving that $\forall\ \kappa \in \mathbb{K}$:

$$n^2 p'(\kappa)(x - \mathsf{row}(\kappa))(y - \mathsf{col}(\kappa)) = \big(\mathsf{val}_L(\kappa) + \alpha \mathsf{val}_R(\kappa)\big) \mathsf{row}(\kappa) \mathsf{col}(\kappa) z_{\mathbb{H}}(x) z_{\mathbb{H}}(y).$$

By definition of $p'(X)$ and of the relation polynomials, $\mathcal{P}$ can define

$$t(X) := \frac{\sigma}{|\mathbb{K}|} \cdot n^2 \cdot (xy + \mathsf{cr}(X) - x \cdot \mathsf{col}(X) - y \cdot \mathsf{row}(X)) + r'(X) \cdot n^2 \cdot (xy \cdot X + \mathsf{cr}'(X) -$$
$$x \cdot \mathsf{col}'(X) - y \cdot \mathsf{row}'(X)) - (\mathsf{vcr}_L(X) + \alpha \cdot \mathsf{vcr}_R(X)) \cdot z_{\mathbb{H}}(x) \cdot z_{\mathbb{H}}(y) \in \mathbb{F}_{\leq 2|\mathbb{K}| - 2}[X]$$

that equals 0 on any $\kappa \in \mathbb{K}$. This way, $\mathcal{P}$ computes $q'(X) := \frac{t(X)}{z_{\mathbb{K}}(X)} \in \mathbb{F}_{\leq |\mathbb{K}| - 2}[X]$ and sends σ and $\{q'(X), r'(X)\}$ to $\mathcal{V}$.

Decision Phase. The verifier outputs the following degree checks

$$\mathsf{deg}(\hat{a}'), \mathsf{deg}(\hat{b}'), \mathsf{deg}(s), \mathsf{deg}(q), \mathsf{deg}(q') \overset{?}{\leq} \mathsf{D}_{\mathsf{snd}} \tag{3}$$
$$\mathsf{deg}(r) \overset{?}{\leq} n - 2 \tag{4}$$
$$\mathsf{deg}(r') \overset{?}{\leq} |\mathbb{K}| - 2 \tag{5}$$

and the following two polynomial checks:

$$s(y) + \Big(\hat{a}'(y) \cdot z_{\mathbb{L}}(y) + \sum_{\eta \in \mathbb{L}} x'_{\phi_{\mathbb{H}}(\eta)} \cdot \mathcal{L}^{\mathbb{H}}_{\eta}(y) \Big) \Big(\Lambda_{\mathbb{H}}(x,y) + \sigma(\hat{b}'(y) \cdot z_{\mathbb{L}}(y) + 1) \Big)$$
$$+ (\hat{b}'(y) \cdot z_{\mathbb{L}}(y) + 1) \cdot \alpha \cdot \Lambda_{\mathbb{H}}(x,y) - q(y)\, z_{\mathbb{H}}(y) - y\, r(y) \stackrel{?}{=} 0 \tag{6}$$

$$\frac{\sigma}{|\mathbb{K}|} \cdot n^2 \cdot (xy + \mathsf{cr}(X) - x \cdot \mathsf{col}(X) - y \cdot \mathsf{row}(X))$$
$$+ r'(X) \cdot n^2 \cdot (xy \cdot X + \mathsf{cr}'(X) - x \cdot \mathsf{col}'(X) - y \cdot \mathsf{row}'(X))$$
$$- (\mathsf{vcr}_L(X) + \alpha \cdot \mathsf{vcr}_R(X)) \cdot z_{\mathbb{H}}(x) \cdot z_{\mathbb{H}}(y) - q'(X) \cdot z_{\mathbb{K}}(X) \stackrel{?}{=} 0 \tag{7}$$

Above, we highlight the oracle polynomials in *gray*, the prover messages in blue, and the coefficients of the verifier's polynomial checks in red. This is to help seeing how the above checks fit the form described in Definition 2.

In the first degree check, $\mathsf{D}_{\mathsf{snd}}$ is an integer that can be chosen by the verifier and governs the soundness error as shown in Theorem 1. While for correctness we need $\mathsf{D}_{\mathsf{snd}} \geq \mathsf{D} - 1$, where D is the degree of the PHP (shown below), this bound does not need to be tight (i.e., $\mathsf{D}_{\mathsf{snd}} = \mathsf{D} - 1$) as is the case for the degree checks on r and r'. This observation has an impact on our compiler where, by choosing $\mathsf{D}_{\mathsf{snd}}$ to be the maximal degree supported by the commitment scheme, one does not need to create a proof for degree checks of the form "$\leq \mathsf{D}_{\mathsf{snd}}$".

Security Analysis. We state knowledge soundness and zero-knowledge of $\mathsf{PHP}_{\mathsf{lite1}}$; full proofs are in the full version.

Theorem 1 (Knowledge Soundness). *Our protocol* $\mathsf{PHP}_{\mathsf{lite1}}$ *is* ϵ*-knowledge-sound with* $\epsilon = \frac{|\mathbb{H}|}{|\mathbb{F}|} + \frac{2\mathsf{D}_{\mathsf{snd}} + |\mathbb{H}|}{|\mathbb{F} \setminus \mathbb{H}|}$.

Theorem 2 (Zero-Knowledge). *Our PHP protocol* $\mathsf{PHP}_{\mathsf{lite1}}$ *is perfect zero-knowledge. Furthermore, it is perfect* b*-HVZK with* $\mathsf{b} = (\mathsf{b}_a, \mathsf{b}_b, \mathsf{b}_s, \mathsf{b}_q, \mathsf{b}_r, \infty, \infty)$.

For an intuition about soundness we refer to the intuitive description of the construction. For b-HVZK, we present the main ideas. Following a rather standard argument, we have that up to b_a (resp. b_b) evaluations of $\hat{a}'$ (resp. $\hat{b}'$) are randomly distributed due to their construction through Mask. Instead, up to b_q (resp. b_r) evaluations of q (resp. r) can be argued random thanks to the randomness of the polynomials q_s and r_s defining $s(X) = q_s(X) \cdot z_{\mathbb{H}}(X) + X \cdot r_s(X)$. In particular, this uses that for $\gamma \in \mathbb{F} \setminus \mathbb{H}$, $s(X)$ is $(\mathsf{b}_s + \mathsf{b}_q)$-wise independent even conditioned on $r_s(X)$, and that the honest $q(X)$ is determined by $(p(X) + s(X) - Xr(X))/z_{\mathbb{H}}(X)$, where $p(X)$ is that defined in round 2.

Remark 2 ($\mathsf{PHP}_{\mathsf{lite1x}}$*: a variant with fewer relation polynomials).* We present a variant of $\mathsf{PHP}_{\mathsf{lite1}}$, that we call $\mathsf{PHP}_{\mathsf{lite1x}}$, which has fewer relation polynomials.

In particular, the $\mathcal{RE}$ of $\mathsf{PHP}_{\mathsf{lite1x}}$ does not output $\mathsf{col}'(X), \mathsf{row}'(X)$ and $\mathsf{cr}'(X)$, and the second polynomial check, of degree 3 with a public term X, becomes:

$$n^2 \cdot \left(X \cdot r'(X) + \frac{\sigma}{|\mathbb{K}|} \right) \cdot \left(xy + \mathsf{cr}(X) - x \cdot \mathsf{col}(X) - y \cdot \mathsf{row}(X) \right) \\ - \left(\mathsf{vcr}_L(X) + \alpha \cdot \mathsf{vcr}_R(X) \right) \cdot z_{\mathbb{H}}(x) \cdot z_{\mathbb{H}}(y) - q'(X) \cdot z_{\mathbb{K}}(X) \stackrel{?}{=} 0 \quad (8)$$

$\mathsf{PHP}_{\mathsf{lite2}}$**: Separate Sparse Matrix Encodings.** We propose another PHP for R1CS-lite called $\mathsf{PHP}_{\mathsf{lite2}}$. $\mathsf{PHP}_{\mathsf{lite2}}$ is very similar to $\mathsf{PHP}_{\mathsf{lite1}}$, indeed its first two rounds of the online phase are identical. The main difference is that in $\mathsf{PHP}_{\mathsf{lite2}}$ the matrices $\{\boldsymbol{L}, \boldsymbol{R}\}$ are encoded in sparse form separately. Namely, $\boldsymbol{L}, \boldsymbol{R}$ are represented with the functions $\{\mathsf{val}_M, \mathsf{row}_M, \mathsf{col}_M\}_{M \in \{L,R\}}$ so that, for any $\kappa \in \mathbb{K}$, $\mathsf{val}_M(\kappa) = \boldsymbol{M}_{\mathsf{row}_M(\kappa), \mathsf{col}_M(\kappa)}$. The main benefit of this choice is that we can work with a subgroup $\mathbb{K} \subset \mathbb{F}$ such that $|\mathbb{K}| \geq m \geq \max\{||\boldsymbol{L}||, ||\boldsymbol{R}||\}$, which is half the size of the one needed in $\mathsf{PHP}_{\mathsf{lite1}}$. Using this encoding, the $V_{LR}(X, Y, Z)$ polynomial in Eq. (2) here becomes

$$\sum_{\kappa \in \mathbb{K}} \left(\mathsf{val}_L(\kappa) \cdot \mathcal{L}^{\mathbb{H}}_{\mathsf{row}_L(\kappa)}(X) \cdot \mathcal{L}^{\mathbb{H}}_{\mathsf{col}_L(\kappa)}(Y) + Z \cdot \mathsf{val}_R(\kappa) \cdot \mathcal{L}^{\mathbb{H}}_{\mathsf{row}_R(\kappa)}(X) \cdot \mathcal{L}^{\mathbb{H}}_{\mathsf{col}_R(\kappa)}(Y) \right)$$

So, in round 3 of $\mathsf{PHP}_{\mathsf{lite2}}$ the prover's goal is to show that $\sigma = V_{LR}(x, y, \alpha)$ for the equation above. This is done analogously to $\mathsf{PHP}_{\mathsf{lite1}}$ except that here $\{\mathsf{val}_M, \mathsf{row}_M, \mathsf{col}_M\}_{M \in \{L,R\}}$ are expanded in a total of 24 relation polynomials for the goal of keeping 2 the degree of the second polynomial check. See Table 2 for a summary of $\mathsf{PHP}_{\mathsf{lite2}}$ measures and its variant $\mathsf{PHP}_{\mathsf{lite2x}}$, and the full version for a detailed description.

5 Compiler from PHPs to Universal zkSNARKs

We start with the definitions for our compiler. Some of the following notions are standard or were introduced in previous works, while some others are new. For space reasons, we defer to the full version for formal definitions.

Commitment Schemes. In our work we use the notion of *type-based commitments*, introduced by Escala and Groth [22]: these are a generalization of regular commitments that unify several committing methods into the same scheme. As done in [11], in this work we exploit the formalism of type-based commitments to describe commit-and-prove zero-knowledge proofs that work with commitments of different types, tailoring different properties for the same message space.

More in detail, a type-based commitment scheme is a tuple of algorithms $\mathsf{CS} = (\mathsf{Setup}, \mathsf{Commit}, \mathsf{VerCom})$ that works as a commitment scheme with the difference that the Commit and VerCom algorithms take an extra input type that represents the type of c. All the possible types are included in the type space $\mathcal{T}$. Having different types helps for a more granular description of the security properties of the commitment scheme. For example, a commitment scheme for a set of types $\{\mathsf{type}_1, \mathsf{type}_2\}$ could be trapdoor hiding for commitments of type type_1 and could be computationally hiding for commitments of type type_2. In this case, we say that the commitment scheme is type_1-trapdoor hiding and type_2-computationally hiding. We assume succinct commitments.

zkSNARKs with Universal and Specializable SRS. A zkSNARK with specializable universal SRS for a family of relations $\{\mathcal{R}_{\mathsf{N}}\}_{\mathsf{N}\in\mathbb{N}}$, introduced by Groth et al. [34], is a tuple of algorithms $\Pi = (\mathsf{KeyGen}, \mathsf{Derive}, \mathsf{Prove}, \mathsf{Verify})$ where KeyGen is probabilistic and upon input public parameters and size bound N produces the srs and a trapdoor td_{k}, Derive is deterministic and upon input srs and $\mathsf{R} \in \mathcal{R}_{\mathsf{N}}$ produces $\mathsf{ek}_{\mathsf{R}}, \mathsf{vk}_{\mathsf{R}}$, and the prover Prove and verifier Verify act as usual. We require the standard notions of completeness, succinctness, knowledge-soundness and zero-knowledge.

Universal CP-SNARKs. We adapt the notion of commit-and-prove SNARKs of [18] to universal relations. Very roughly speaking, a universal CP-SNARK for a family of relationships $\mathcal{R}$ and a commitment scheme CS is a universal SNARK for a family of relations $\mathcal{R}^{\mathsf{Com}}$ which includes all the relations $\mathsf{R}^{\mathsf{Com}}$ such that $\mathsf{R}^{\mathsf{Com}}(\mathsf{x}, c, \mathsf{w}) = 1$ if and only if $\mathsf{R}(\mathsf{x}, \mathsf{w}) = 1$ and c *is a commitment that opens to* w and $\mathsf{R} \in \mathcal{R}$. As in [18], in the definition we add syntactic sugar to this idea to handle relations where the domain of the witness is more fine grained and split over $\ell + 1$ subdomains for a fixed $\ell \in \mathbb{N}$.

More in detail, we denote a universal CP-SNARK as a tuple of algorithms $\mathsf{CP} = (\mathsf{KeyGen}, \mathsf{Derive}, \mathsf{Prove}, \mathsf{Verify})$ where: (i) $\mathsf{KeyGen}(\mathsf{ck}, \mathsf{N}) \rightarrow \mathsf{srs} := (\mathsf{ek}, \mathsf{vk})$ generates the structured reference string. (ii) $\mathsf{Derive}(\mathsf{srs}, \mathsf{R}) \rightarrow (\mathsf{ek}_{\mathsf{R}}, \mathsf{vk}_{\mathsf{R}})$ is a deterministic algorithm that takes as input an srs produced by $\mathsf{KeyGen}(\mathsf{ck}, \mathsf{N})$, and a relation $\mathsf{R} \in \mathcal{R}_{\mathsf{N}}$. (iii) $\mathsf{Prove}(\mathsf{ek}, \mathsf{x}, (c_j)_{j\in[\ell]}, (\mathsf{u}_j)_{j\in[\ell]}, (o_j)_{j\in[\ell]}, \omega) \rightarrow \pi$ outputs the proof for $(\mathsf{x}, \mathsf{w}) \in \mathsf{R}$ and $\mathsf{w} = (\mathsf{u}_1, \ldots, \mathsf{u}_\ell, \omega)$. (iv) $\mathsf{Verify}(\mathsf{vk}_{\mathsf{R}}, \mathsf{x}, (c_j)_{j\in[\ell]}, \pi) \rightarrow \{0, 1\}$ rejects or accepts the proof. Sometimes we use a more general notion of knowledge soundness for CP-SNARKs introduced by Benarroch *et al.* [11] named *knowledge soundness with partial opening.* The intuition is to consider adversaries that explicitly return valid openings for a subset of the commitments that they return, thus enabling to formally define knowledge soundness in the context where not all the commitments need to be extracted.

In the basic completeness notion of Universal CP-SNARKs, the CP-SNARK is required to work with commitments of any type. We also define a weaker notion of completeness in which the CP-SNARK works only when certain witnesses are committed with a specific type. We call this notion *T-restricted completeness.* This is useful if we want to use a CP-SNARK that supports only a subset T of the types of the commitment scheme. We give a few examples. Suppose the commitment scheme has two different types, $\mathsf{type}_1, \mathsf{type}_2$, and there exists a CP-SNARK that only works with commitments of type_1. Alternatively, a CP-SNARK for a relation with $\ell_1 + \ell_2$ committed witnesses could work only when the first ℓ_1 commitments are of type type_1 and the subsequent ℓ_2 commitments are of type type_2. And clearly, more fine-grained combinations are possible.

Commitment-Only SRS. We say that a universal CP-SNARK has a *commitment-only* SRS if the key generation algorithm is deterministic. Notice that for Universal CP-SNARK with commitment-only SRS the notion of zero-knowledge in the SRS model is not achievable. In fact, formally speaking, the commitment key ck is part of the description of a relation; thus, the actual SRS of the CP-SNARK would be the empty string. However, the classical result of [30] shows that NIZK in the plain model exists only for trivial languages. Therefore we consider a weaker notion of zero-knowledge for these CP-SNARKs, that we call trapdoor-commitment zero-knowledge in the SRS model, where the trapdoor necessary for simulation comes from the commitment key of CS.

5.1 Compiler's Building Blocks

Commitments to Polynomials. Recall that a PHP verifier has access to two sets of oracle polynomials: those from the relation encoder (which describe the relation) and those from the prover (which should supposedly convince the verifier to accept a public input x). The compiler commits to polynomials in both sets; it requires all these commitments to be binding, but not to fully hide any of these polynomials.

The commitments for the relation encoding polynomials—whose type we denote by `rel`—do not need to hide anything: they open to polynomials representing the relation, which is public information. The polynomial commitments of type `rel` have weaker requirements for one more reason. Besides not requiring them to be hiding, we will not require them to be extractable (i.e., we do not assume a CP-SNARK that has knowledge soundness for them, here is the reason to use the notion of knowledge soundness with partial opening).

Above, we ignored leakage when committing to relation encoding polynomials; we cannot do the same when committing to the polynomials from the PHP prover as they contain information about the witness. If we do not prevent *some* leakage we will lose zero-knowledge. At the same time we will show that we do not need full hiding for these polynomials either, just a relaxed property that may hold even for a deterministic commitment algorithm. We call this property *somewhat-hiding*—defined below—and denote its type by `swh`.

In the remainder of this section we will assume CS to be a polynomial commitment scheme; i.e., a commitment scheme in which the message space $\mathcal{M}$ is $\mathbb{F}_{\leq d}[X]$ for a finite field $\mathbb{F} \in \mathcal{F}$ and an integer $d \in \mathbb{N}$. Without loss of generality we assume d to be an input parameter of Setup.

Definition 6 (Somewhat-Hiding Polynomial Commitments). *Let* $\mathsf{CS} = (\mathsf{Setup}, \mathsf{Commit}, \mathsf{VerCom})$ *be a type-based commitment scheme for a class of polynomials* $\mathbb{F}_{\leq d}[X]$ *and a class of types* $\mathcal{T}$*, and that works as in Type-Based Commitment Schemes, but where we allow* Commit *to be deterministic. Then* CS *is said to be* type-typed somewhat-hiding *if there exist three algorithms* $(\mathsf{ck}, \mathsf{td} = (\mathsf{td}', s)) \leftarrow \mathcal{S}_{\mathsf{ck}}(s)$ *where* $s \in \mathbb{F}$*,* $(c, st) \leftarrow \mathsf{TdCom}(\mathsf{td}, \gamma)$ *and* $o \leftarrow \mathsf{TdOpen}(\mathsf{td}, st, c, f)$ *such that: (1) the distribution of the commitment key returned by* $\mathcal{S}_{\mathsf{ck}}$ *with a uniformly random* $s \leftarrow_{\$} \mathbb{F}$ *as input is identical to the one of the key returned by* Setup*;*

(2) for any $f \in \mathbb{F}_{<d}[X]$*,* $(c, o) \approx (c', o')$ *where* $(c, o) \leftarrow \mathsf{Commit}(\mathsf{ck}, \mathsf{type}, f)$*,* $(c', st) \leftarrow \mathsf{TdCom}(\mathsf{td}, f(s))$ *and* $o' \leftarrow \mathsf{TdOpen}(\mathsf{td}, st, c', f)$*.*

CP-SNARKs for the Commitment Scheme. We assume that the commitment scheme CS is equipped with a CP-SNARK $\mathsf{CP}_{\mathsf{php}} = (\mathsf{KeyGen}_{\mathsf{php}}, \mathsf{Prove}_{\mathsf{php}}, \mathsf{Verify}_{\mathsf{php}})$ for a relation family $\mathcal{R}' \supseteq \mathcal{R}_{\mathsf{php}}$ (we defined $\mathcal{R}_{\mathsf{php}}$ in Sect. 3.1), and with a CP-SNARK $\mathsf{CP}_{\mathsf{opn}} = (\mathsf{KeyGen}_{\mathsf{opn}}, \mathsf{Prove}_{\mathsf{opn}}, \mathsf{Verify}_{\mathsf{opn}})$ for the (trivial) relation family $\mathcal{R}_{\mathsf{opn}} = \{\psi, (p_j)_{j \in [\ell]} : \ell \in \mathbb{N}\}$ whose instance is the empty string ψ and witnesses are tuples of polynomials. A CP-SNARK for $\mathcal{R}_{\mathsf{opn}}$ is essentially a *proof of knowledge* of the openings of ℓ commitments.

Leaky Zero-Knowledge. We define a weaker zero-knowledge notion that is sufficient to be satisfied by the $\mathsf{CP}_{\mathsf{php}}$ CP-SNARK in our compiler. This new property allows better efficiency and flexibility of the compiled protocols. Intuitively, a CP-SNARK for relations over committed polynomials is *leaky zero-knowledge* if its proofs may leak information about a bounded number of evaluations of these polynomials. More in detail, a CP-SNARK is (b, C)-leaky zero-knowledge if there exists a ZK simulator that has access to a list of leaked values $\{\mathsf{u}_{i_j}(y_j)\}_{(i,j)}$ where the list $\{(i_j, y_j)\}_{j \in \mathbb{N}}$ is (b, C)-bounded (see Sect. 3).

5.2 The Compiler

At a high level, we follow the known paradigm stemming from [40,46] in which the prover commits to the oracles, answers the verifier's queries generated using a random oracle and proves correctness of these answers. A high-level description of the compiled SNARK $\Pi = (\mathsf{KeyGen}, \mathsf{Derive}, \mathsf{Prove}, \mathsf{Verify})$ follows:

- The KeyGen algorithm runs the setup of the commitment scheme CS and generates keys for the auxiliary CP-SNARKs.
- The Derive algorithm, when deriving a specialized SRS for a specific relation R, commits to all the polynomials returned by the relation encoder $\mathcal{RE}(\mathsf{R})$ using `rel`-typed commitments.
- The prover Prove algorithm executes internally the PHP prover $\mathcal{P}$, at each round of $\mathcal{P}$ it commits the polynomials from $\mathcal{P}$ using `swh`-typed commitments; it proves it knows their opening using $\mathsf{CP}_{\mathsf{opn}}$; concatenate the commitments, the proofs and the rest of the messages from $\mathcal{P}$. It computes a hash of the partial transcript, which it then uses as the next message to feed to the $\mathcal{P}$. At the last round it uses $\mathsf{CP}_{\mathsf{php}}$ to prove that the *PHP* verifier $\mathcal{V}$ would accept.
- The verifier checks all the CP-SNARK proofs of opening for the commitments and executes the decision stage of $\mathcal{V}$ with input the instance and the random oracle hash values computed over the partial transcripts. It thus generates an instance for $\mathsf{CP}_{\mathsf{php}}$ and checks the related CP-SNARK proof.

For compactness in the exposition, we state the main result of the section in one theorem, however in the full version we restate the theorem in two steps: first we compile to universal *interactive* argument systems, and secondly we compile the latter argument systems to SNARKs using the Fiat-Shamir transform—thus the following theorem holds in the random oracle model.

Theorem 3. *Let* $\mathsf{PHP} = (\mathsf{r}, \mathsf{n}, \mathsf{m}, \mathsf{d}, \mathsf{n_e}, \mathcal{RE}, \mathcal{P}, \mathcal{V})$ *be a non-adaptive public-coin PHP over a finite field family* $\mathcal{F}$ *and for a universal relation* $\mathcal{R}$. *Let* CS *be a type-based commitment scheme for a class of polynomials* $\mathbb{F}_{<d}[X]$ *and a class of types* $\mathcal{T} = \{\mathtt{rel}, \mathtt{swh}\}$ *that is* $\mathcal{T}$*-binding and* $\mathtt{swh}$*-somewhat-hiding and equipped with CP-SNARKs* $\mathsf{CP_{opn}}$ *for* $\mathcal{R}_{\mathsf{opn}}$ *and* $\mathsf{CP_{php}}$ *for* $\mathcal{R}_{\mathsf{php}}$.

- *The scheme* $\Pi = (\mathsf{KeyGen}, \mathsf{Derive}, \mathsf{Prove}, \mathsf{Verify})$ *is a zkSNARK with specializable universal SRS for the family of relations* $\mathcal{R}$.
- *If* $\mathsf{CP_{opn}}$ *is TP-ZK, and, for a checker* C, PHP *(resp.* $\mathsf{CP_{php}}$*) is* $(\mathsf{b}+1, \mathsf{C})$*-bounded honest-verifier zero-knowledge (resp.* (b, C)*-leaky zero-knowledge) then* Π *is zero-knowledge in the SRS model.*

Remark 3 (On completeness). It is sufficient for $\mathsf{CP_{php}}$ to be T-restricted complete, with $T = \left((\mathtt{rel})^{\mathsf{n}(0)} \| (\mathtt{swh})^{\mathsf{n_p}}\right) \in \mathcal{T}^{\mathsf{n}^*}$, to obtain the completeness of Π.

Remark 4 (On updatable SRS). If the commitment key generated by Setup is updatable [21,34], and $\mathsf{CP_{opn}}$ and $\mathsf{CP_{php}}$ have commitment-only SRS then the SRS of Π is updatable.

Intuition on Security Proof. The proof of knowledge soundness follows the standard argument of simulating a prover for the PHP extracting the polynomials from the commitments sent by the adversary and use the binding property of the commitments together with the knowledge soundness of $\mathsf{CP_{php}}$ to prove that the verifier of the PHP protocol would indeed accept.

We now provide an intuition about zero-knowledge; for simplicity we describe it as if the protocol involved a single committed polynomial. First, observe that we assume a PHP with $b+1$-bounded ZK—i.e., we can simulate interaction with an honest prover even after we have leaked $b+1$ evaluations of the polynomial. Since we assume a commitment scheme that is only somewhat-hiding (Definition 6), we are actually leaking one evaluation of the committed polynomial (in particular on a random point). We now combine this fact with the ZK property we are assuming on the CP-SNARKs in the compiler—b-leaky ZK—and this allows us to still simulate an interaction with an honest prover that is indistinguishable after further b leaked evaluations.

Compiler to Universal CP-SNARK. We briefly explain how to adapt our compiler to turn PHPs into CP-SNARKs. More details appear in the full version.

We consider a natural sub-class of PHP where the extractor for the knowledge soundness satisfies a stronger property usually denoted as *straight-line extractability* in the literature. In particular, we assume there exists an extractor $\mathsf{WitExtract}$ that on input the polynomials sent by a malicious prover interacting with the verifier can extract the valid witness.

Recall that the instances for CP-SNARKs are tuples of the form $(\mathsf{x}, \hat{c}_1, \ldots, \hat{c}_\ell)$ for a value $\ell \in \mathbb{N}$, where x is an instance for the relation and $\hat{c}_1, \ldots, \hat{c}_\ell$ commits to chunks of the witness. The commitments $\hat{c}_1, \ldots, \hat{c}_\ell$ are just classical commitments (in the sense that they are hiding and binding, but there are no restrictions on other properties they might have). Therefore we consider CP-SNARKs for typed-commitment schemes with class of types $\mathcal{T} = \{\mathtt{rel}, \mathtt{swh}, \mathtt{lnk}\}$, where the latter type is reserved for the input commitments (and thus the commitment scheme is lnk-typed hiding and lnk-typed binding).

The compiler to a CP-SNARK is exactly the same as the compiler presented before but where the prover, after having computed all the commitments $c_1, \ldots, c_{n_p}$ (and the proofs for $\mathsf{CP_{opn}}$ and $\mathsf{CP_{php}}$), additionally computes a CP-SNARK proof for the relation $\mathcal{R}_{\mathsf{link}}$ that says that the commitments $\hat{c}_1, \ldots, \hat{c}_\ell$ open to values $\mathsf{u}_1, \ldots, \mathsf{u}_\ell$ and the commitments $c_1, \ldots, c_{n_p}$ open to polynomials $p_1, \ldots, p_{n_p}$ such that $\mathsf{WitExtract}(p_1, \ldots, p_{n_p}) = (\mathsf{u}_1, \ldots, \mathsf{u}_\ell, \omega)$, therefore creating a link between the computed proof and the input commitments $\hat{c}_1, \ldots, \hat{c}_\ell$.

6 Instantiating Our Compiler: Our Universal zkSNARKs

We propose different instantiations of the building blocks needed by our compiler of Sect. 5: *(i)* (type-based) pairing-based commitment schemes for polynomials; *(ii)* a collection of CP-SNARKs for various relations over such committed polynomials. Next, we describe different options to combine them together in our compiler, when applied to our PHP constructions (see Table 2). The resulting zkSNARKs offer different tradeoffs in terms of SRS size, proof size, and verification time. Table 1 summarizes the most interesting among these schemes.

We denote a bilinear group setting by a tuple $(q, \mathbb{G}_1, \mathbb{G}_2, \mathbb{G}_T, e)$, where $\mathbb{G}_1$, $\mathbb{G}_2$, $\mathbb{G}_T$ are additive groups of prime order q, and $e : \mathbb{G}_1 \times \mathbb{G}_2 \rightarrow \mathbb{G}_T$ is an efficiently computable, non-degenerate, bilinear map. We focus on Type-3 groups and use the bracket notation of [23], i.e., for $g \in \{1, 2, T\}$ and $a \in \mathbb{Z}_q$, we write $[a]_g$ to denote $a \cdot P_g \in \mathbb{G}_g$, where P_g is a fixed generator of $\mathbb{G}_g$.

6.1 Pairing-Based Commitment Schemes for Polynomials

We show two type-based commitment schemes, denoted CS_1 and CS_2 respectively, with type set $\{\mathtt{rel}, \mathtt{swh}\}$ and for degree-d polynomials. The commitment of a polynomial p is essentially the *evaluation in the exponent* of p in a secret point s, following the scheme of Groth [32] and Kate et al. [39]. Slightly more in detail, in both schemes, the commitment key ck contains encodings of powers of a secret point s, and a commitment of type swh to a polynomial $p(X)$ is a group element $[p(s)]_1$. The only difference between the two schemes are the commitments of type rel, which in CS_1 are $[p(s)]_1$ whereas in CS_2 are $[p(s)]_2$. As discussed in the next section, the advantage of having some polynomials committed in $\mathbb{G}_2$ is that one immediately gets a way to test quadratic equations over committed polynomials where each quadratic term involves exactly one polynomial of type rel. Both types of commitments are computationally binding under the power-discrete logarithm assumption [44]; we prove commitments of type swh to also be somewhat hiding.

Remark 5 (On updatability of our SNARKs*).* Since the commitment schemes CS_1 and CS_2 that we work upon generate keys that only contain monomials in the exponent, our constructions are updatable in the sense that participants can easily re-randomize them at will. Pointing to previous works on updatable SNARKs, *"a CRS that consists solely of monomials (...) is updatable"* [34].

6.2 Pairing-Based CP-SNARKs for CS_1 and CS_2

We show CP-SNARKs for various relations over polynomials committed using CS_1 or CS_2. Our CP-SNARKs work over both commitment schemes unless explicitly stated otherwise. A full description of these schemes is in the full version.

Proof of Knowledge: "I know p and c opens to p". We show two schemes. (i) $\mathsf{CP}_{\mathsf{opn}}^{\mathsf{AGM}}$ is a trivial scheme in which the proof is the empty string and is knowledge-sound in the algebraic group model [25]; this is an observation already done in previous work, e.g., [19,27]. (ii) $\mathsf{CP}_{\mathsf{opn}}^{\mathsf{PKE}}$, is *novel* and provides extractability based on the mPKE assumption and, when used on more than one commitment, on the random oracle heuristic. In a nutshell, this scheme uses the classical technique of giving as a proof a group element $\pi_{\mathsf{opn}} = \gamma \cdot c$, where $\gamma \in \mathbb{F}$ is a secret but such that π_{opn} can be publicly computed if one knows the opening of c. What is new in our scheme is a way to batch this proof for ℓ commitments in such a way that we have only one extra group element as a proof, instead of ℓ elements.

Polynomials Evaluation: "$\left(p_i(x_i) = y_i\right)_{i\in[\ell]}$". We first give a CP-SNARK for single polynomial evaluation—"$p(x) = y$"—$\mathsf{CP}_{\mathsf{eval},1}$, secure under the d-SDH assumption and the extractability of $\mathsf{CP}_{\mathsf{opn}}$, and then we extend it into a CP-SNARK $\mathsf{CP}_{\mathsf{eval}}$ to support batching. Both schemes stem from techniques in [39].

Polynomial Equations: A CP-SNARK $\mathsf{CP}_{\mathsf{eq}}$ for general polynomial equations, e.g., $a(X)b(X) - 2c(X)d(X)e(X) = 0$), relying mainly on $\mathsf{CP}_{\mathsf{opn}}$ and $\mathsf{CP}_{\mathsf{eval}}$. It is based on the idea of doing evaluations on a random point, with optimizations from [27], based on the linearity of the commitment, to minimize proof size.

Quadratic Polynomial Equations: A novel CP-SNARK for quadratic polynomial equations[9] specific to commitment scheme CS_2; although less general than $\mathsf{CP}_{\mathsf{eq}}$, $\mathsf{CP}_{\mathsf{qeq}}$ is more efficient since its proof may simply be empty, while verification consists of some pairing checks over the commitments. The basic intuition is simple: to check that $G(p_1(X), \ldots, p_\ell(X)) = 0$ for a quadratic polynomial G it is possible to homomorphically compute G over the values $(p_1(s), \ldots, p_\ell(s))$ in the target group using pairings and the linear property of the commitments. For this to be possible, for each quadratic monomial $p_i(X)p_j(X)$, we need at least one of $[p_i(s)]_2$ or $[p_j(s)]_2$ in $\mathbb{G}_2$. This holds if they are committed through different types, i.e., one as `rel` and the other as `swh`. Otherwise, if they are both in the same group, we let the prover create one of the two polynomials committed in the "symmetric" group. Interestingly, for carefully designed equations, the $\mathsf{CP}_{\mathsf{qeq}}$ proof can be empty and all the verifier needs to do is verifying a pairing product.

Degree Bound: "$(\mathsf{deg}(p_i) \leq d_i)_{i\in[\ell]}$". Two CP-SNARKs—$\mathsf{CP}_{\mathsf{deg}}^{(\star)}$ and $\mathsf{CP}_{\mathsf{deg}}^{(2)}$—such that $\mathsf{CP}_{\mathsf{deg}}^{(\star)}$ works over both commitment schemes while $\mathsf{CP}_{\mathsf{deg}}^{(2)}$ works only over CS_2. The basic idea is to commit to the shifted polynomial $p^*(X) = X^{D-d}p(X)$

[9] Here "quadratic" means it supports products of at most two polynomials.

and then prove that the polynomial equation $X^{D-d} \cdot p(X) - p^*(X) = 0$ using a CP-SNARK for polynomial equations, either $\mathsf{CP}_{\mathsf{eq}}$ or $\mathsf{CP}_{\mathsf{qeq}}$. This idea is extended in order to batch together these proofs for several polynomials.

6.3 Available Options to Compile Our PHPs

We discuss how to combine the aforementioned CP-SNARKs for committed polynomials to obtain CP-SNARKs for the $\mathcal{R}_{\mathsf{php}}$ relations corresponding to our PHPs. All our PHPs have a similar structure in which the verifier checks consist of one vector $\boldsymbol{d}$ of degree checks, and two polynomial checks $((G'_1, \boldsymbol{v}_1), (G'_2, \boldsymbol{v}_2))$. Hence, for each PHP the corresponding relation $\mathcal{R}_{\mathsf{php}}$ can be expressed as:

$$\mathsf{R}_{\mathsf{deg}}((d_j)_{j\in[\mathsf{n_p}]}, (p_j)_{j\in[\mathsf{n}(0)+1,\mathsf{n}^*]}) \wedge \left\{\mathsf{R}_{\mathsf{eq}}((G'_i, \boldsymbol{v}_i), (p_j)_{j\in[\mathsf{n}^*]})\right\}_{i\in\{1,2\}}$$

where G'_i is the partial evaluation of G_i on the prover message σ.

In all the PHPs, in the first polynomial check the $\boldsymbol{v}_{1,j}(X)$ are constant polynomials (in particular, they all encode the same point, i.e., $\forall j : \boldsymbol{v}_{1,j}(X) = y$), while in the second check they are the identity, i.e., $\forall j : \boldsymbol{v}_{2,j}(X) = X$. Furthermore, in those PHPs where $\mathsf{deg}_{X,\{X_i\}}(G_2) = 2$, the second R_{eq} relation can be replaced by its specialization for quadratic equations.

We use two main compilation options for our PHPs (outlined in Fig. 1):

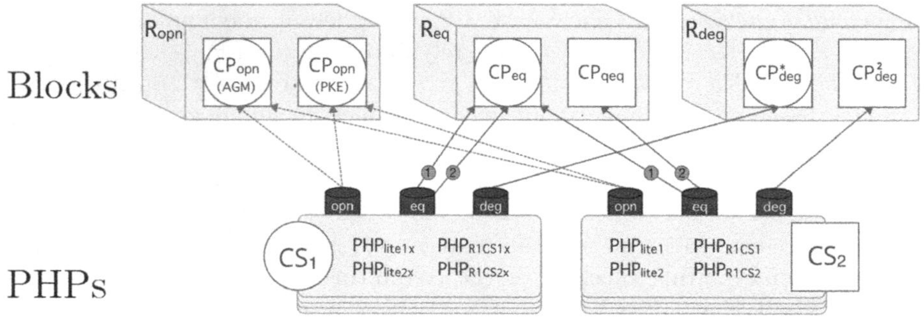

Fig. 1. Different options to compile our PHPs. We mark compatibility with commitment schemes CS_1 and CS_2 respectively by a circle and a square (both shapes mean full compatibility). Dotted lines mean either option is possible. An index 1 or 2 for an arrow to R_{eq} denotes whether it refers to the first or second polynomial check.

6.4 Zero-Knowledge Bounds When Instantiating PHPs

Our compiler assumes a CP-SNARK $\mathsf{CP}_{\mathsf{php}}$ that can be (b, C)-leaky-ZK to compile a PHP protocol that is $(\mathbf{1} + \mathsf{b})$-bounded ZK (see Theorem 3), as the commitments reveals one evaluation per oracle polynomial. Among the CP-SNARKs we propose to realize $\mathsf{CP}_{\mathsf{php}}$, the only one that is leaky-ZK is the $\mathsf{CP}_{\mathsf{eq}}$ scheme.

Its leakage is due to the fact that the proof includes evaluations of those polynomials that end up in the set S used to optimize the proof size. Note that this concern arises only when using it to prove the first polynomial check. Indeed, in all of our schemes *the second polynomial check involves only oracle polynomials that are not related to the witness*, and thus for those polynomials the amount of leakage does not matter. We discuss how to choose b for the b-leaky-ZK of $\mathsf{CP_{eq}}$ when proving the first polynomial check in all of our PHPs.

PHPs for R1CS-lite. The first polynomial check is the same in both constructions. Through the syntax for relation $\mathsf{R_{eq}}$ we write the polynomial G'_1 as

$$G'_1(X_a, X_b, X_s, X_q, X_r) := X_a \cdot X_b \cdot g_{a,b} + X_a \cdot g_a + X_b \cdot g_b + X_q \cdot g_q + X_r \cdot g_r + X_s + g_0$$

where the goal is to prove that on a given y, $G'_1((p_j(y))_{j \in [5]}) = 0$, that is:

$$\hat{a}'(y)\hat{b}'(y) \cdot g_{a,b} + \hat{a}'(y) \cdot g_a + \hat{b}'(y) \cdot g_b + s(y) + q(y) \cdot g_q + r(y) \cdot g_r + g_0 \stackrel{?}{=} 0$$

To this end, $\mathsf{CP_{eq}}$ chooses a set S of size 1; for instance it reveals $\hat{b}'(y)$ and nothing more. Thus, $\mathsf{CP_{eq}}$ for this polynomial check is b-leaky-ZK with $\mathsf{b} = (\mathsf{b}_a, \mathsf{b}_b, \mathsf{b}_s, \mathsf{b}_q, \mathsf{b}_r) = (0, 1, 0, 0, 0)$. From Theorem 3, $\mathsf{PHP_{lite1}}$ and $\mathsf{PHP_{lite2}}$ need to be $(1, 2, 1, 1, 1)$-bounded ZK, and we can optimize the degrees and instantiate $\mathsf{PHP_{lite*}}$ with $\hat{a}' \in \mathbb{F}_{\leq n+1}[X]$, $\hat{b}' \in \mathbb{F}_{\leq n+2}[X]$, $q_s \in \mathbb{F}_{\leq 1}[X]$, $r_s \in \mathbb{F}_{\leq 1}[X]$.

PHPs for R1CS. All these constructions need to be $(1, 2, 1, 1, 1, 1)$-bounded ZK. The analysis is the same as for R1CS-lite; we omit details for lack of space.

6.5 Our Resulting zkSNARKs and CP-SNARKs

In the full version we provide a table with the efficiency of all the zkSNARKs obtained through the different options to instantiate the compiler on all of our PHPs. We also discuss how those measures are obtained and give the costs for the CP-SNARKs resulting from the commit-and-prove compiler. We recall that the most representative zkSNARKs (in the algebraic group model) are shown in Table 1 together with a comparison with the state of the art. We recall that all our constructions are universal and updatable.

We note that instantiating our proofs under the mPKE assumption (instead of the AGM) is significantly more efficient than for those in [19]. The overhead of instantiating our proofs under mPKE is: for us, have 4 more $\mathbb{G}_1$ elements and the prover needs up to $3n + 6m$ more $\mathbb{G}_1$ exponentiations: in [19], 11 more $\mathbb{G}_1$ elements in the proof and $11n + 5m$ more exponentiations to the prover.

Acknowledgments. This work has received funding in part from the European Research Council (ERC) under the European Union's Horizon 2020 research and innovation program under project PICOCRYPT (grant agreement No. 101001283), by the Spanish Government under projects SCUM (ref. RTI2018-102043-B-I00), CRYPTOEPIC (ref. EUR2019-103816), and SECURITAS (ref. RED2018-102321-T), by the

Madrid Regional Government under project BLOQUES (ref. S2018/TCS-4339), and by research grants from Protocol Labs, and by Nomadic Labs and the Tezos Foundation. The first and second authors were at the IMDEA Software Institute while developing part of this work. Additionally, the project that gave rise to these results received the support of a fellowship from "la Caixa" Foundation (ID 100010434). The fellowship code is LCF/BQ/ES18/11670018.

References

1. Abdolmaleki, B., Baghery, K., Lipmaa, H., Zajkac, M.: A subversion-resistant SNARK. In: Takagi, T., Peyrin, T. (eds.) ASIACRYPT 2017, Part III. LNCS, vol. 10626, pp. 3–33. Springer, Cham (2017). https://doi.org/10.1007/978-3-319-70700-6_1
2. Ames, S., Hazay, C., Ishai, Y., Venkitasubramaniam, M.: Ligero: lightweight sublinear arguments without a trusted setup. In: ACM CCS 2017, pp. 2087–2104 (2017). https://doi.org/10.1145/3133956.3134104
3. Baghery, K.: Subversion-resistant simulation (knowledge) sound NIZKs. In: Albrecht, M. (ed.) IMACC 2019. LNCS, vol. 11929, pp. 42–63. Springer, Cham (2019). https://doi.org/10.1007/978-3-030-35199-1_3
4. Ben-Sasson, E., et al.: Computational integrity with a public random string from quasi-linear PCPs. In: Coron, J.-S., Nielsen, J.B. (eds.) EUROCRYPT 2017, Part III. LNCS, vol. 10212, pp. 551–579. Springer, Cham (2017). https://doi.org/10.1007/978-3-319-56617-7_19
5. Ben-Sasson, E., Bentov, I., Horesh, Y., Riabzev, M.: Scalable zero knowledge with no trusted setup. In: Boldyreva, A., Micciancio, D. (eds.) CRYPTO 2019, Part III. LNCS, vol. 11694, pp. 701–732. Springer, Cham (2019). https://doi.org/10.1007/978-3-030-26954-8_23
6. Ben-Sasson, E., Chiesa, A., Goldberg, L., Gur, T., Riabzev, M., Spooner, N.: Linear-size constant-query IOPs for delegating computation. In: Hofheinz, D., Rosen, A. (eds.) TCC 2019, Part II. LNCS, vol. 11892, pp. 494–521. Springer, Cham (2019). https://doi.org/10.1007/978-3-030-36033-7_19
7. Ben-Sasson, E., Chiesa, A., Green, M., Tromer, E., Virza, M.: Secure sampling of public parameters for succinct zero knowledge proofs. In: 2015 IEEE Symposium on Security and Privacy, pp. 287–304 (2015). https://doi.org/10.1109/SP.2015.25
8. Ben-Sasson, E., Chiesa, A., Riabzev, M., Spooner, N., Virza, M., Ward, N.P.: Aurora: transparent succinct arguments for R1CS. In: Ishai, Y., Rijmen, V. (eds.) EUROCRYPT 2019, Part I. LNCS, vol. 11476, pp. 103–128. Springer, Cham (2019). https://doi.org/10.1007/978-3-030-17653-2_4
9. Ben-Sasson, E., Chiesa, A., Spooner, N.: Interactive oracle proofs. In: Hirt, M., Smith, A. (eds.) TCC 2016. LNCS, vol. 9986, pp. 31–60. Springer, Heidelberg (2016). https://doi.org/10.1007/978-3-662-53644-5_2
10. Benarroch, D., Campanelli, M., Fiore, D.: Commit-and-Prove Zero-Knowledge Proof Systems. ZKProof.org (2020)
11. Benarroch, D., Campanelli, M., Fiore, D., Gurkan, K., Kolonelos, D.: Zero-knowledge proofs for set membership: efficient, succinct, modular. In: Financial Cryptography and Data Security (2021). https://doi.org/10.1007/978-3-662-64322-8_19
12. Bitansky, N., Canetti, R., Chiesa, A., Tromer, E.: From extractable collision resistance to succinct non-interactive arguments of knowledge, and back again. In: ITCS 2012, pp. 326–349 (2012)

13. Bitansky, N., Chiesa, A., Ishai, Y., Paneth, O., Ostrovsky, R.: Succinct non-interactive arguments via linear interactive proofs. In: Sahai, A. (ed.) TCC 2013. LNCS, vol. 7785, pp. 315–333. Springer, Heidelberg (2013). https://doi.org/10.1007/978-3-642-36594-2_18
14. Boneh, D., Drake, J., Fisch, B., Gabizon, A.: Efficient polynomial commitment schemes for multiple points and polynomials. Cryptology ePrint Archive, Report 2020/081 (2020)
15. Bootle, J., Cerulli, A., Chaidos, P., Groth, J., Petit, C.: Efficient zero-knowledge arguments for arithmetic circuits in the discrete log setting. In: Fischlin, M., Coron, J.-S. (eds.) EUROCRYPT 2016, Part II. LNCS, vol. 9666, pp. 327–357. Springer, Heidelberg (2016). https://doi.org/10.1007/978-3-662-49896-5_12
16. Bünz, B., Bootle, J., Boneh, D., Poelstra, A., Wuille, P., Maxwell, G.: Bulletproofs: short proofs for confidential transactions and more. In: 2018 IEEE Symposium on Security and Privacy, pp. 315–334 (2018). https://doi.org/10.1109/SP.2018.00020
17. Bünz, B., Fisch, B., Szepieniec, A.: Transparent SNARKs from DARK compilers. In: Canteaut, A., Ishai, Y. (eds.) EUROCRYPT 2020, Part I. LNCS, vol. 12105, pp. 677–706. Springer, Cham (2020). https://doi.org/10.1007/978-3-030-45721-1_24
18. Campanelli, M., Fiore, D., Querol, A.: LegoSNARK: modular design and composition of succinct zero-knowledge proofs. In: ACM CCS 2019, pp. 2075–2092 (2019). https://doi.org/10.1145/3319535.3339820
19. Chiesa, A., Hu, Y., Maller, M., Mishra, P., Vesely, N., Ward, N.: Marlin: preprocessing zkSNARKs with universal and updatable SRS. In: Canteaut, A., Ishai, Y. (eds.) EUROCRYPT 2020, Part I. LNCS, vol. 12105, pp. 738–768. Springer, Cham (2020). https://doi.org/10.1007/978-3-030-45721-1_26
20. Chiesa, A., Ojha, D., Spooner, N.: Fractal: post-quantum and transparent recursive proofs from holography. In: Canteaut, A., Ishai, Y. (eds.) EUROCRYPT 2020, Part I. LNCS, vol. 12105, pp. 769–793. Springer, Cham (2020). https://doi.org/10.1007/978-3-030-45721-1_27
21. Daza, V., Ràfols, C., Zacharakis, A.: Updateable inner product argument with logarithmic verifier and applications. In: Kiayias, A., Kohlweiss, M., Wallden, P., Zikas, V. (eds.) PKC 2020, Part I. LNCS, vol. 12110, pp. 527–557. Springer, Cham (2020). https://doi.org/10.1007/978-3-030-45374-9_18
22. Escala, A., Groth, J.: Fine-tuning Groth-Sahai proofs. In: Krawczyk, H. (ed.) PKC 2014. LNCS, vol. 8383, pp. 630–649. Springer, Heidelberg (2014). https://doi.org/10.1007/978-3-642-54631-0_36
23. Escala, A., Herold, G., Kiltz, E., Ràfols, C., Villar, J.: An algebraic framework for Diffie-Hellman assumptions. In: Canetti, R., Garay, J.A. (eds.) CRYPTO 2013, Part II. LNCS, vol. 8043, pp. 129–147. Springer, Heidelberg (2013). https://doi.org/10.1007/978-3-642-40084-1_8
24. Fuchsbauer, G.: Subversion-zero-knowledge SNARKs. In: Abdalla, M., Dahab, R. (eds.) PKC 2018, Part I. LNCS, vol. 10769, pp. 315–347. Springer, Cham (2018). https://doi.org/10.1007/978-3-319-76578-5_11
25. Fuchsbauer, G., Kiltz, E., Loss, J.: The algebraic group model and its applications. In: Shacham, H., Boldyreva, A. (eds.) CRYPTO 2018, Part II. LNCS, vol. 10992, pp. 33–62. Springer, Cham (2018). https://doi.org/10.1007/978-3-319-96881-0_2
26. Gabizon, A.: AuroraLight: improved prover efficiency and SRS size in a Sonic-like system. Cryptology ePrint Archive, Report 2019/601 (2019)
27. Gabizon, A., Williamson, Z.J., Ciobotaru, O.: PLONK: permutations over Lagrange-bases for oecumenical noninteractive arguments of knowledge. Cryptology ePrint Archive, Report 2019/953 (2019)

28. Gennaro, R., Gentry, C., Parno, B., Raykova, M.: Quadratic span programs and succinct NIZKs without PCPs. In: Johansson, T., Nguyen, P.Q. (eds.) EUROCRYPT 2013. LNCS, vol. 7881, pp. 626–645. Springer, Heidelberg (2013). https://doi.org/10.1007/978-3-642-38348-9_37
29. Gentry, C., Wichs, D.: Separating succinct non-interactive arguments from all falsifiable assumptions. In: 43rd ACM STOC, pp. 99–108 (2011). https://doi.org/10.1145/1993636.1993651
30. Goldreich, O., Oren, Y.: Definitions and properties of zero-knowledge proof systems. J. Cryptol. **1**, 1–32 (1994)
31. Goldwasser, S., Micali, S., Rackoff, C.: The knowledge complexity of interactive proof systems. SIAM J. Comput. **1**, 186–208 (1989)
32. Groth, J.: Short pairing-based non-interactive zero-knowledge arguments. In: Abe, M. (ed.) ASIACRYPT 2010. LNCS, vol. 6477, pp. 321–340. Springer, Heidelberg (2010). https://doi.org/10.1007/978-3-642-17373-8_19
33. Groth, J.: On the size of pairing-based non-interactive arguments. In: Fischlin, M., Coron, J.-S. (eds.) EUROCRYPT 2016, Part II. LNCS, vol. 9666, pp. 305–326. Springer, Heidelberg (2016). https://doi.org/10.1007/978-3-662-49896-5_11
34. Groth, J., Kohlweiss, M., Maller, M., Meiklejohn, S., Miers, I.: Updatable and universal common reference strings with applications to zk-SNARKs. In: Shacham, H., Boldyreva, A. (eds.) CRYPTO 2018, Part III. LNCS, vol. 10993, pp. 698–728. Springer, Cham (2018). https://doi.org/10.1007/978-3-319-96878-0_24
35. Hopwood, D., Bowe, S., Hornby, T., Wilcox, N.: Zcash protocol specification. Technical report, 2016–1.10. Zerocoin Electric Coin Company (2016)
36. Ishai, Y.: Efficient Zero-Knowledge Proofs: A Modular Approach. Simons Institute. Lecture (2019)
37. Ishai, Y.: Zero-Knowledge Proofs from Information-Theoretic Proof Systems - Part I. ZKProof.org, Blog entry (2020)
38. Ivanov, K.G., Saff, E.B.: Behavior of the Lagrange interpolants in the roots of unity. In: Ruscheweyh, S., Saff, E.B., Salinas, L.C., Varga, R.S. (eds.) Computational Methods and Function Theory. LNM, vol. 1435, pp. 81–87. Springer, Heidelberg (1990). https://doi.org/10.1007/BFb0087899
39. Kate, A., Zaverucha, G.M., Goldberg, I.: Constant-size commitments to polynomials and their applications. In: Abe, M. (ed.) ASIACRYPT 2010. LNCS, vol. 6477, pp. 177–194. Springer, Heidelberg (2010). https://doi.org/10.1007/978-3-642-17373-8_11
40. Kilian, J.: A note on efficient zero-knowledge proofs and arguments (extended abstract). In: 24th ACM STOC, pp. 723–732 (1992)
41. Kosba, A.E., Papadopoulos, D., Papamanthou, C., Song, D.: MIRAGE: succinct arguments for randomized algorithms with applications to universal zk-SNARKs. In: USENIX Security 2020, pp. 2129–2146 (2020)
42. Kothapalli, A., Masserova, E., Parno, B.: Poppins: a direct construction for asymptotically optimal zkSNARKs. Cryptology ePrint Archive, Report 2020/1318 (2020)
43. Lee, J., Setty, S., Thaler, J., Wahby, R.: Linear-time zero-knowledge SNARKs for R1CS. Cryptology ePrint Archive, Report 2021/030 (2021)
44. Lipmaa, H.: Progression-free sets and sublinear pairing-based non-interactive zero-knowledge arguments. In: Cramer, R. (ed.) TCC 2012. LNCS, vol. 7194, pp. 169–189. Springer, Heidelberg (2012). https://doi.org/10.1007/978-3-642-28914-9_10
45. Maller, M., Bowe, S., Kohlweiss, M., Meiklejohn, S.: Sonic: zero-knowledge SNARKs from linear-size universal and updatable structured reference strings. In: ACM CCS 2019, pp. 2111–2128 (2019). https://doi.org/10.1145/3319535.3339817

46. Micali, S.: Computationally sound proofs. SIAM J. Comput. **30**(4), 1253–1298 (2000)
47. Ràfols, C., Zapico, A.: An algebraic framework for universal and updatable SNARKs. In: Malkin, T., Peikert, C. (eds.) CRYPTO 2021, Part I. LNCS, vol. 12825, pp. 774–804. Springer, Cham (2021). https://doi.org/10.1007/978-3-030-84242-0_27
48. Reingold, O., Rothblum, G.N., Rothblum, R.D.: Constant-round interactive proofs for delegating computation. In: 48th ACM STOC, pp. 49–62 (2016). https://doi.org/10.1145/2897518.2897652
49. Setty, S.: Spartan: efficient and general-purpose zkSNARKs without trusted setup. In: Micciancio, D., Ristenpart, T. (eds.) CRYPTO 2020, Part III. LNCS, vol. 12172, pp. 704–737. Springer, Cham (2020). https://doi.org/10.1007/978-3-030-56877-1_25
50. Trefethen, L., Berrut, J.P.: Barycentric Lagrange interpolation. SIAM Rev. **46**(3), 501–517 (2004)
51. Wahby, R.S., Tzialla, I., shelat, A., Thaler, J., Walfish, M.: Doubly-efficient zkSNARKs without trusted setup. In: 2018 IEEE Symposium on Security and Privacy, pp. 926–943 (2018). https://doi.org/10.1109/SP.2018.00060
52. Wu, H., Zheng, W., Chiesa, A., Popa, R.A., Stoica, I.: DIZK: a distributed zero knowledge proof system. In: USENIX Security 2018, pp. 675–692 (2018)
53. Xie, T., Zhang, J., Zhang, Y., Papamanthou, C., Song, D.: Libra: succinct zero-knowledge proofs with optimal prover computation. In: Boldyreva, A., Micciancio, D. (eds.) CRYPTO 2019, Part III. LNCS, vol. 11694, pp. 733–764. Springer, Cham (2019). https://doi.org/10.1007/978-3-030-26954-8_24
54. Yamashita, K., Tibouchi, M., Abe, M.: On the impossibility of NIZKs for disjunctive languages from commit-and-prove NIZKs. IEEE Access (2021). https://doi.org/10.1109/ACCESS.2021.3056078
55. Zhang, J., Xie, T., Zhang, Y., Song, D.: Transparent polynomial delegation and its applications to zero knowledge proof. In: 2020 IEEE Symposium on Security and Privacy, pp. 859–876 (2020). https://doi.org/10.1109/SP40000.2020.00052
56. Zhang, Y., Genkin, D., Katz, J., Papadopoulos, D., Papamanthou, C.: vSQL: verifying arbitrary SQL queries over dynamic outsourced databases. In: 2017 IEEE Symposium on Security and Privacy, pp. 863–880 (2017). https://doi.org/10.1109/SP.2017.43
57. Zhang, Y., Genkin, D., Katz, J., Papadopoulos, D., Papamanthou, C.: A zero-knowledge version of vSQL. Cryptology ePrint Archive, Report 2017/1146 (2017)
58. Zhang, Y., Genkin, D., Katz, J., Papadopoulos, D., Papamanthou, C.: vRAM: faster verifiable RAM with program-independent preprocessing. In: 2018 IEEE Symposium on Security and Privacy, pp. 908–925 (2018). https://doi.org/10.1109/SP.2018.00013

Gentry-Wichs is Tight: a Falsifiable Non-adaptively Sound SNARG

Helger Lipmaa(✉) and Kateryna Pavlyk

Simula UiB, Bergen, Norway

Abstract. By the impossibility result of Gentry and Wichs, non-falsifiable assumptions are needed to construct (even non-zero-knowledge) adaptively sound succinct non-interactive arguments (SNARGs) for hard languages. It is important to understand whether this impossibility result is tight. While it is known how to construct adaptively sound non-succinct non-interactive arguments for NP from falsifiable assumptions, adaptively sound SNARGs for NP from non-falsifiable assumptions, and adaptively sound SNARGs for P from falsifiable assumptions, there are no known non-adaptively sound SNARGs for NP from falsifiable assumptions. We show that Gentry-Wichs is tight by constructing the latter. In addition, we prove it is non-adaptively knowledge-sound in the algebraic group model and Sub-ZK (i.e., zero-knowledge even if the CRS is subverted) under a non-falsifiable assumption.

Keywords: Falsifiable assumptions · Gentry-Wichs · Non-adaptive soundness · SNARG · SNARK · Sub-ZK

1 Introduction

Due to excellent efficiency properties, zk-SNARKs (zero-knowledge succinct non-interactive arguments of knowledge, [22]) are currently the most popular argument systems for NP. Zk-SNARKs are usually defined in the CRS model, where a universally trusted third party generates a CRS used by both the prover and the verifier. A more realistic model is subversion zero-knowledge (Sub-ZK, [1,3,5,14]); a Sub-ZK SNARK is zero-knowledge even if the CRS was subverted. Zk-SNARGs are zero-knowledge succinct non-interactive argument systems that are not necessarily knowledge-sound. NIZKs are non-interactive zero-knowledge argument systems that are not necessarily succinct.

Unfortunately, known SNARKs for NP are based on non-falsifiable assumptions. Gentry and Wichs [17] showed that this is (in a quite precise sense) unavoidable. Their impossibility result balances four aspects of efficient NIZKs: succinctness, adaptive soundness, reliance on falsifiable assumptions, and hardness of the languages. All four aspects are highly desirable:

(1) Succinctness plays a crucial role in the practical adaptation since non-succinct NIZKs are not efficient enough for applications like cryptocurrencies.

M. Tibouchi and H. Wang (Eds.): ASIACRYPT 2021, LNCS 13092, pp. 34–64, 2021.
https://doi.org/10.1007/978-3-030-92078-4_2

Table 1. Some known (im)possibility results. Impossibility results mean that one cannot achieve all ∘'s at the same time. Possibility results achieve ✓'s but do not achieve ✗'s. AS = adaptive soundness, s = succinctness, HL = hard languages, FA = falsifiable assumptions, PZK = perfect zero-knowledge, BBR = black-box reduction.

AS	s	HL	FA	PZK	Some papers
					Impossibility results
∘	∘	∘	∘		Gentry-Wichs [17] (BBRs), [7] (nonuniform BBRs)
∘		∘	∘	∘	[4] (direct BBRs), [38] (BBRs), [7] (non-uniform BBRs)
					Possibility results: the tightness of Gentry-Wichs
✓	✗	✓	✓	✗	Feige-Lapidot-Shamir [13]
✓	✓	✓	✗	✓	SNARKs [22]
✓	✓	✗	✓		Delegation schemes [29,21] (ZK is irrelevant)
✗	✓	✓	✓	✓	The current paper
					Additional possibility result: tightness of [38]
✗	✗	✓	✓	✓	Groth-Ostrovsky-Sahai [25]

(2) A falsifiable assumption is an assumption where a challenger can efficiently decide whether the adversary broke it. Non-falsifiable assumptions are controversial in general [36].
(3) Adaptive soundness guarantees that the SNARK stays sound even if the malicious prover can choose the input $\mathbb{x}$ after seeing the CRS. Non-adaptive soundness guarantees soundness only if $\mathbb{x}$ is chosen before the CRS is fixed.
(4) Most of the applications need SNARKs for hard languages (i.e., languages with hard subset membership problem) like circuit satisfiability; SNARKs for easy languages have their uses, but they are limited.

Gentry and Wichs [17] proved that non-falsifiable assumptions are needed to construct (even non-zero-knowledge) adaptively sound succinct non-interactive arguments (SNARGs) for hard languages under black-box reductions. Assuming black-box reductions (or stronger non-uniform black-box-reductions, [7]), Gentry-Wichs is known to be tight in three aspects, see Table 1. First, non-succinct adaptively sound falsifiable NIZKs are known for NP [13]. Second, adaptively sound falsifiable SNARGs are known for P [21,29] (note that in this case, zero-knowledge is not important). Third, adaptively sound non-falsifiable SNARGs are known for NP [16,22,23,31,32,37]. However, it is a major open problem *whether Gentry-Wichs is tight in the fourth aspect; i.e., whether non-adaptively sound falsifiable SNARGs for hard languages are possible.*[1]

Our Contributions. We construct the first **fa**lsifiable **n**on-**a**daptively sound SNARG FANA for NP. Thus, Gentry-Wichs is tight. We also prove that FANA is both non-adaptively knowledge-sound and Sub-ZK (zero-knowledge, even if the CRS is maliciously generated, [1,3,5,14]). While the last two properties are not related to Gentry-Wichs, they are important in applications.

[1] Note that even non-succinct falsifiable adaptively sound NIZKs for NP do not exist when one aims to obtain perfect zero-knowledge, [38]. The impossibility result of [38] is known to be tight, see Table 1. Thus, we will focus on [17].

FANA is inspired by [10,12] who proposed two NIZKs (DGPRS and FLPS) for well-known constraint systems SSP [9] and SAP [23], correspondingly. We emphasize that DGPRS and FLPS do not seem to be good starting points for our goal:

(a) They are quasi-adaptive SNARGs (QA-SNARGs [27]). (We use the term QA-SNARG instead of the common QA-NIZK to emphasize the succinctness property.) In QA-SNARGs, the NP language is parameterized by a language parameter lpar. Both the quasi-adaptive soundness and zero-knowledge properties hold only if lpar is honestly generated. Since the latter is an undesirable trust assumption, we aim to avoid it by constructing a SNARG and not a QA-SNARG.
(b) They are quasi-adaptively sound [27] (which means the argument system is sound against an adversary who chooses the input $\mathbb{x}$ after seeing lpar and crs), and thus they do not seem to be candidates for *non-adaptive* NIZKs.
(c) They are commit-and-prove argument systems, having a non-succinct perfectly-binding commitment and are thus not succinct.
(d) They are for the SSP [9] and the SAP [23], which are less standard and less powerful constraint systems compared to the QAP [16].
(e) They are not known to be knowledge-sound.
(f) They are not known to be Sub-ZK.

We solve Items a to c by carefully modifying the construction and the soundness proof of [10,12]. In DGPRS and FLPS, the prover commits to the input $\mathbb{x}$ and the witness $\mathbb{w}$ by using a perfectly-binding and several succinct commitment schemes, including a *functional SSB commitment scheme* [12]. Functional SSB commitment schemes satisfy the following helpful property: for a small locality parameter q ($q < 10$ in DGPRS and FLPS), one can reprogram its commitment key ck during the security proof so that the reduction will obtain q linear combinations of the input and witness coordinates; moreover, in existing schemes, the commitment length is $q + 1$ group elements.

The quasi-adaptive soundness proof of [10,12] consists of several games. Assume that $\mathcal{A}$ is a successful soundness adversary. The first game is the classic (quasi-adaptive) soundness game. In the second game, one picks a random J, which is a guess for the SSP/SAP/QAP constraint that is not satisfied. One aborts if the guess was wrong. (This results in n-time security loss where n is the number of constraints.) Crucially, one uses the perfectly binding commitment scheme to extract values required to do this check. In the third game, one additionally modifies the commitment key of the functional SSB scheme to be a function of J. One can do so due to the "function-set hiding" property [12] of the functional SSB scheme. One then shows that the last game is secure by constructing two different reductions to two different security assumptions.

In comparison, we check whether the reduction guessed a non-satisfied constraint correctly by using the succinct functional SSB commitment. Thus, we do not need the perfectly binding commitment at all, solving Item c. Hence, we have a succinct NIZK, i.e., a SNARG. Moreover, since the language parameter

lpar in DGPRS and FLPS is the commitment key of the perfectly-binding commitment scheme and we will not use the latter at all, FANA will not have lpar. Importantly, it means that FANA is not a QA-NIZK but a usual NIZK. This solves Item a. Moreover, since FANA is secure under a variant of the security assumptions of [10,12], we have a falsifiable SNARG.

At this moment, it might seem that we have breached the Gentry-Wichs impossibility result since DGPRS and FLPS are quasi-adaptively sound. However, this is not the case. Namely, since we use the functional SSB commitment to check whether the Jth constraint is satisfied, we cannot do a check (and a conditional abort) before changing the commitment key. In the case of (quasi-)adaptive soundness, $\mathbb{x}$ (and thus also the unsatisfied constraint's number) can depend on ck, where the latter depends on J. A malicious prover can thus, after seeing ck, choose $\mathbb{x}$ so that the Jth constraint is satisfied.

We solve this seeming contradiction by resorting to non-adaptive soundness, i.e., we ask $\mathcal{A}$ to output $\mathbb{x}$ before seeing ck so that it cannot depend on J that is embedded in ck. In this case, the security proof follows. This solves Item b. Since we now have a non-adaptively sound SNARG for NP under falsifiable assumptions, we have also shown that Gentry-Wichs is tight. We emphasize that while this change to [10,12] may sound simple, it is pretty surprising: as we already argued, DGPRS and FLPS do not seem to be suitable starting points for our endeavor. It also results in a multiple changes to the construction of the SNARG, including the omission of perfectly-binding commitment and lpar.

Additional Features. While we have already solved our main open problem, to make FANA more attractive in practice, we will also tackle Items d to f. In addition, we will base FANA on an—arguably—better falsifiable assumption, which also results in slight efficiency gain. Due to this, FANA's argument length and verifier's complexity are almost the same as in FLPS.

Finally, FANA relies on the González-Hevia-Ràfols bilateral subspace QA-NIZK BLS from [19]. For FANA to be non-adaptively sound, non-adaptively knowledge-sound, and Sub-ZK, BLS has to satisfy quasi-adaptive σ-strong soundness, adaptive knowledge-soundness, and Sub-ZK. Here, quasi-adaptive σ-strong soundness is a new security property of QA-SNARGs that lies between quasi-adaptive soundness and quasi-adaptive strong soundness [28]. We prove that BLS satisfies all three properties. Since bilateral subspace QA-NIZKs have many independent applications, this constitutes a contribution of independent interest.

QAP (Item d*).* DGPRS is for SSP (Square Span Program, [9]), a constraint system that has an efficient reduction to Boolean circuit satisfiability. In many applications, it is desirable to construct a (QA-)SNARG for arithmetic circuits. FLPS is for SAP (Square Arithmetic Program, [23,24]), a constraint system that has an efficient reduction to arithmetic circuit satisfiability for circuits that consist of addition and square gates. The use of square gates instead of general multiplication gates results in a factor of two overhead.

The constraint system QAP (Quadratic Arithmetic Program, [16]) models efficiently arithmetic circuits with general multiplication gates. FANA is directly for QAP. In the pairing-based setting, SNARKs for QAP have one complication compared to SNARKs for SSP and SAP: namely, in the former, the prover outputs an element in both source groups. Hence, differently from DGPRS and FLPS, we use functional SSB commitments in both source groups $\mathbb{G}_1$ and $\mathbb{G}_2$. In the soundness proof, this means adding one more game to change the functional SSB ck in both groups. Adding another commitment means that, at least when using the same approach as DGPRS and FLPS, SNARKs for QAP are necessarily less efficient. We mitigate it by using a different assumption.

Better Assumption. The q-type assumptions S-TSDH (Square Target Strong Diffie-Hellman) and SA-TSDH (Square Arithmetic Target Strong Diffie-Hellman) used in [10] and [12] respectively, look quite complicated.[2] To argue that such assumptions are sensible, one can prove that they hold in the *generic group model* (GGM). In a GGM proof, one considers a generic adversary that is only allowed to (i) execute group operations in the source and target groups, (ii) perform the pairing operation, and (iii) check for equality of two group elements. GGM is a very restrictive model. One of the many criticisms against GGM is that the target group $\mathbb{G}_T$ is a subgroup of the finite field, and thus it is questionable whether it can be modeled as a generic group, [26]. Indeed, one can use the finite field structure to operate on the elements of the $\mathbb{G}_T$. To address this issue, [26] defined the *semi-GGM*, where one assumes that only the source groups are generic. A significant drawback of S-TSDH and SA-TSDH is that, in their definition, the adversary can output a value in the target group. Thus, they are not (known to be) secure in the semi-GGM.

Moreover, the adversary of the $\{*\}$TSDH assumptions is required to output some elements together with their "knowledge components" [8]. To prove soundness under $\{*\}$TSDH assumptions, the prover of the SNARG must also output the knowledge components. Due to this, $\{*\}$TSDH assumptions "force" one to design SNARGs that might not be optimal.

Instead of $\{*\}$TSDH assumptions, we introduce a very different-looking assumption QA-LINRES. QA-LINRES (see Definition 2) holds in the algebraic group model (AGM, [15]).[3] Since the QA-LINRES adversary does not have to output "knowledge components", QA-LINRES allows to design more efficient SNARGs. Even without counting the cost of perfectly-binding commitment in DGPRS and FLPS, FANA is efficiency-wise competitive with DGPRS and FLPS despite being for QAP and thus involving one more functional SSB commitment.

Knowledge-Soundness (Item e). In many applications, knowledge-soundness is desirable. It is especially important in the case of succinct NIZKs, where the verifier only has access to a succinct commitment to the witness. Such commitments can be information-theoretically opened to an exponential number of witnesses, and it is important to know which witness was used by the adversary. Unfortunately, neither DGPRS nor FLPS is known to be knowledge-sound.

[2] DGPRS, FLPS, and FANA also rely on two standard assumptions SKerMDH [19] and DDH. We focus on the least standard assumptions, S-TSDH and SA-TSDH.

[3] We recall that the AGM is a modern, somewhat more realistic alternative to the GGM. In particular, like the semi-GGM, the AGM of [15] considers only the source groups to be "algebraic". Thus, QA-LINRES also holds in the semi-GGM.

Sub-ZK (Item f). DGPRS and FLPS are proven to be sound and zero-knowledge, assuming that both lpar and crs are *trusted.* Since in many applications, it is crucial to avoid trust assumptions (like crs's correctness), this situation is not satisfactory. Instead, one should aim to prove Sub-ZK [5]. It is known that the most efficient zk-SNARK [23] is also Sub-ZK [1,3,14] under non-falsifiable assumptions. As noted in [2], non-falsifiable assumptions are also needed due to the well-known impossibility result of [18]. In Theorem 2, we prove that FANA is Sub-ZK assuming that BLS is Sub-ZK.

Efficiency. The FANA argument π is succinct, consisting of 9 elements of $\mathbb{G}_1$ and 5 elements of $\mathbb{G}_2$.

The Bilateral Subspace Argument. FANA uses a bilinear subspace argument system that, in particular, allows one to prove that different commitments in both $\mathbb{G}_1$ and $\mathbb{G}_2$ commit to the same message. As a contribution of independent interest, we study the quasi-adaptively strongly sound and perfectly zero-knowledge González-Hevia-Ràfols bilateral subspace argument system BLS [19].

Let σ be an efficiently computable function. We define a new soundness notion for QA-SNARGs, σ-strong soundness, that lies between soundness and strong soundness [28]. Since BLS is quasi-adaptively strongly sound, it is also quasi-adaptively σ-strongly sound for any efficiently computable σ. While quasi-adaptive strong soundness of BLS is known to be sufficient for the non-adaptive (knowledge-) soundness of FANA, we show that it suffices that BLS is σ_x-strongly sound for a particular function σ_x. There are two primary motivations for introducing the new security notion. First, it allows one to capture the exact security property of BLS needed by FANA. Second, it may be possible (though we leave it for future work) to construct more efficient bilinear subspace argument systems that are σ_x-strongly sound but not strongly sound.

In Theorem 1, we prove BLS is adaptively sound under the non-falsifiable assumption $\mathrm{SKerMDH}^{\mathrm{dl}}$ from [2]. We prove that BLS is adaptively knowledge-sound in the AGM under the $\mathrm{SDL}^{\mathrm{dl}}$ assumption from [2]. (See Theorem 1.) Both $\mathrm{SKerMDH}^{\mathrm{dl}}$ and $\mathrm{SDL}^{\mathrm{dl}}$ belong to the family of non-adaptive oracle assumptions, where the adversary is initially given access to the oracle who solves the discrete logarithm assumption. After that, the adversary has to break either the SKerMDH or the SDL [6] assumption on a fresh instance. We believe such assumptions are significantly more realistic than knowledge assumptions underlying efficient zk-SNARKs.

As shown in [2], to prove that a QA-SNARG is Sub-ZK, one must prove that the QA-SNARG is both black-box zero-knowledge (that is, zero-knowledge, if lpar and crs are trusted) and non-black-box persistent zero-knowledge (that is, zero-knowledge, if lpar and crs are not trusted; this notion was defined in [2]). In the latter case, one assumes that one can extract the simulation trapdoor from a malicious crs. Zero-knowledge does not follow from persistent zero-knowledge since the former is black-box and the latter is non-black-box, [2]. In Theorem 1, we prove that (1) BLS is perfectly zero-knowledge, and (2) BLS is persistent zero-knowledge under a novel knowledge-assumption GHR-KE, similar to the KW-KE assumption [2].

Since bilateral subspace argument systems have many more applications, the BLS section constitutes a significant independent contribution.

Summary of Security Results. To not overwhelm the reader, we did not describe all security results in the introduction. As a corollary of various theorems of the current paper, we can informally state the following result.

Corollary 1 (Informal). FANA *is a SNARG that is non-adaptively sound under the falsifiable* SKerMDH, DDH, *and* QA-LINRES *assumptions (where the latter is a new falsifiable assumption that holds under the PDL assumption in the AGM). It is non-adaptively knowledge-sound in the AGM if additionally the non-falsifiable assumptions* $\mathrm{SKerMDH}^{\mathrm{dl}}$ *and* $\mathrm{SDL}^{\mathrm{dl}}$ [2] *hold. It is Sub-ZK under the* DDH *and the non-falsifiable* GHR-KE *assumption (where the latter is a new knowledge assumption that holds in the AGM).*

Full Version. Due to the lack of space, we postpone most of the security proofs and several additional results to the full version, [35].

Open Problems. To be precise, we showed that [17] is tight with respect to black-box reductions [17] and non-uniform black-box reductions [7]. We leave the study of general non-black-box reductions as an interesting open problem.

2 Preliminaries

For a matrix $\boldsymbol{A} = (A_{ij})$, $\boldsymbol{A}_i$ denotes its ith row and $\boldsymbol{A}^{(j)}$ denotes its jth column. The cokernel of $\boldsymbol{A}$ is defined as $\mathrm{coker}(\boldsymbol{A}) = \{\boldsymbol{a} : \boldsymbol{a}^\top \boldsymbol{A} = \boldsymbol{0}\}$. Let $\mathrm{colspace}(\boldsymbol{A})$ be the column space of $\boldsymbol{A}$. For matrices $\boldsymbol{A}$ and $\boldsymbol{B}$, denote $\boldsymbol{A}//\boldsymbol{B} := \left(\begin{smallmatrix}\boldsymbol{A}\\ \boldsymbol{B}\end{smallmatrix}\right)$.

Assume n is a power of two. Let ω be the nth primitive root of unity modulo p (ω exists, given that $n \mid (p-1)$.) Then,

- $Z(X) := \prod_{i=1}^{n}(X - \omega^{i-1}) = X^n - 1$ is the unique degree n monic polynomial, such that $Z(\omega^{i-1}) = 0$ for all $i \in [1, n]$.
- For $i \in [1, n]$, let $\ell_i(X)$ be the *ith Lagrange polynomial*, i.e., the unique degree $n-1$ polynomial, such that $\ell_i(\omega^{i-1}) = 1$ and $\ell_i(\omega^{j-1}) = 0$ for $i \neq j$. Let $Z'(X) = dZ(X)/dX = nX^{n-1}$. It is well known that

$$\ell_i(X) := \frac{Z(X)}{Z'(\omega^{i-1})(X - \omega^{i-1})} = \frac{(X^n - 1)\omega^{i-1}}{n(X - \omega^{i-1})} \quad \text{for } X \neq \omega^{i-1}.$$

Given $X \in \mathbb{Z}_p$, one can efficiently compute $\{\ell_i(X)\}_{i=1}^{n}$. $L_{\mathbb{z}}(X) := \sum_{i=1}^{n} \mathbb{z}_i \ell_i(X)$ is the interpolating polynomial of the vector $\mathbb{z} \in \mathbb{Z}_p^n$ at points ω^{i-1}.

We denote assignment by $\leftarrow$ and (uniformly random) sampling by $\leftarrow_{\$}$. PPT denotes probabilistic polynomial-time; $\lambda \in \mathbb{N}$ is the security parameter. We assume all adversaries are stateful, i.e., keep up a state between different executions. For an algorithm $\mathcal{A}$, $\mathrm{range}(\mathcal{A})$ is the range of $\mathcal{A}$, i.e., the set of valid outputs of $\mathcal{A}$, $\mathsf{RND}_\lambda(\mathcal{A})$ denotes the random tape of $\mathcal{A}$ (for given λ), and $r \leftarrow_{\$} \mathsf{RND}_\lambda(\mathcal{A})$ denotes the uniformly random choice of the randomizer r from $\mathsf{RND}_\lambda(\mathcal{A})$. By $y \leftarrow \mathcal{A}(x; r)$ we denote the fact that $\mathcal{A}$, given an input x and a randomizer r, outputs y. Let $\mathsf{negl}(\lambda)$ be an arbitrary negligible function, and $\mathsf{poly}(\lambda)$ be an arbitrary polynomial function. We write $a \approx_\lambda b$ if $|a - b| \le \mathsf{negl}(\lambda)$.

Bilinear Groups. A bilinear group generator $\mathsf{Pgen}(1^\lambda)$ returns $(p, \mathbb{G}_1, \mathbb{G}_2, \mathbb{G}_T, \hat{e}, [1]_1, [1]_2)$, where $\mathbb{G}_1$, $\mathbb{G}_2$, and $\mathbb{G}_T$ are three additive cyclic groups of prime order p, $\hat{e} : \mathbb{G}_1 \times \mathbb{G}_2 \to \mathbb{G}_T$ is an efficiently computable non-degenerate bilinear pairing, and $[1]_\iota$ is a fixed generator of $\mathbb{G}_\iota$. While $[1]_\iota$ is a part of p, for the sake of clarity, we often give it as an explicit input to different algorithms. We assume $n \mid (p-1)$, where n is a large deterministically fixed upper bound on the size of the statements that one handles in this bilinear group. As in [5], we assume that Pgen is deterministic and cannot be subverted. The bilinear pairing is of Type-3, i.e., there is no efficient isomorphism between $\mathbb{G}_1$ and $\mathbb{G}_2$. We use the by-now standard bracket notation, i.e., for $\iota \in \{1, 2, T\}$, we write $[a]_\iota$ to denote $a[1]_\iota$. We denote $\hat{e}([a]_1, [b]_2)$ by $[a]_1 \bullet [b]_2$. We use freely the bracket notation together with matrix notation, e.g., $\boldsymbol{AB} = \boldsymbol{C}$ iff $[\boldsymbol{A}]_1 \bullet [\boldsymbol{B}]_2 = [\boldsymbol{C}]_T$. For an integer (vector) a, we denote $[a]_* := ([a_1]_1, [a_2]_2)$.

Assumptions. Let $\kappa^*, \kappa \in \mathbb{N}$, with $\kappa^* \ge \kappa$, be small constants. Let p be a large prime. A PPT-sampleable distribution $\mathcal{D}_{\kappa^*,\kappa}$ is a *matrix distribution* [11] if it samples matrices $\boldsymbol{A} \in \mathbb{Z}_p^{\kappa^* \times \kappa}$ of full rank κ. $\mathcal{D}_{\kappa^*,\kappa}$ is *robust* [27] if it samples matrices $\boldsymbol{A}$ whose upper $\kappa \times \kappa$ submatrix $\bar{\boldsymbol{A}}$ is invertible. Denote the lower $(\kappa^* - \kappa) \times \kappa$ submatrix of $\boldsymbol{A}$ by $\underline{\boldsymbol{A}}$. Denote $\mathcal{D}_\kappa = \mathcal{D}_{\kappa+1,\kappa}$. We denote $\mathcal{D}_{\kappa+1,\kappa}$ by $\mathcal{D}_\kappa$. In the full version [35], we define five common distributions [11]: $\mathcal{U}_\kappa$ (uniform), $\mathcal{L}_\kappa$ (linear), $\mathcal{IL}_\kappa$ (incremental linear), $\mathcal{C}_\kappa$ (cascade), $\mathcal{SC}_\kappa$ (symmetric cascade). All mentioned distributions can be made robust with minimal changes.

Let $d_1(n), d_2(n) \in \mathsf{poly}(\lambda)$. $(d_1(n), d_2(n))$-*PDL (Power Discrete Logarithm,* [31,39]*)* holds relative to Pgen, if $\forall$ PPT $\mathcal{A}$,

$$\mathsf{Adv}^{\mathrm{pdl}}_{\mathsf{Pgen},d_1,d_2,\mathcal{A}}(\lambda) := \Pr\left[\begin{array}{l}\mathsf{p} \leftarrow \mathsf{Pgen}(1^\lambda), x \leftarrow_{\$} \mathbb{Z}_p^* : \\ \mathcal{A}(\mathsf{p}, [(x^i)_{i=0}^{d_1(n)}]_1, [(x^i)_{i=0}^{d_2(n)}]_2) = x\end{array}\right] \approx_\lambda 0.$$

The q-PDL assumption in $\mathbb{G}_1$ (resp., $\mathbb{G}_2$) is equal to the $(q,0)$-PDL (resp., $(0,q)$-PDL) assumption. The *symmetric discrete logarithm* (SDL [6]) assumption is equal to the $(1,1)$-PDL assumption.

Let $\iota \in \{1, 2\}$. *DDH*$_{\mathbb{G}_\iota}$ *(Decisional Diffie-Hellman)* holds relative to Pgen, if $\forall$ PPT $\mathcal{A}$, $\mathsf{Adv}^{\mathrm{ddh}}_{\mathsf{Pgen},\mathbb{G}_\iota,\mathcal{A}}(\lambda) := |\varepsilon^0_{\mathcal{A}}(\lambda) - \varepsilon^1_{\mathcal{A}}(\lambda)| \approx_\lambda 0$, where

$$\varepsilon^\beta_{\mathcal{A}}(\lambda) := \Pr[\mathsf{p} \leftarrow \mathsf{Pgen}(1^\lambda); x, y, z \leftarrow_{\$} \mathbb{Z}_p : \mathcal{A}(\mathsf{p}, [x, y, xy + \beta z]_\iota) = 1].$$

Let $\iota \in \{1, 2\}$. $\mathcal{D}_{\kappa^*,\kappa}$-*KerMDH*$_{\mathbb{G}_\iota}$ (Kernel Diffie-Hellman) holds relative to Pgen, if $\forall$ PPT $\mathcal{A}$, $\mathsf{Adv}^{\mathrm{kermdh}}_{\mathsf{Pgen},\mathbb{G}_\iota,\mathcal{D}_{\kappa^*,\kappa},\mathcal{A}}(\lambda) :=$

$$\Pr[\mathsf{p} \leftarrow \mathsf{Pgen}(1^\lambda); \boldsymbol{A} \leftarrow_{\$} \mathcal{D}_{\kappa^*,\kappa}; [\boldsymbol{c}]_{3-\iota} \leftarrow \mathcal{A}(\mathsf{p}, [\boldsymbol{A}]_\iota) : \boldsymbol{A}^\top \boldsymbol{c} = \boldsymbol{0}_\kappa \wedge \boldsymbol{c} \neq \boldsymbol{0}_\ell] \approx_\lambda 0.$$

$\mathcal{D}_{\kappa^*,\kappa}$-*SKerMDH* (Split Kernel Diffie-Hellman, [19]) holds relative to Pgen, if $\forall$ PPT $\mathcal{A}$, $\mathsf{Adv}^{\mathrm{skermdh}}_{\mathsf{Pgen},\mathbb{G}_\iota,\mathcal{D}_{\kappa^*,\kappa},\mathcal{A}}(\lambda) :=$

$$\Pr\left[\begin{array}{l}\mathsf{p} \leftarrow \mathsf{Pgen}(1^\lambda); \boldsymbol{A} \leftarrow_{\$} \mathcal{D}_{\kappa^*,\kappa}; ([\boldsymbol{c}_1]_1, [\boldsymbol{c}_2]_2) \leftarrow \mathcal{A}(\mathsf{p}, [\boldsymbol{A}]_1, [\boldsymbol{A}]_2) : \\ \boldsymbol{A}^\top(\boldsymbol{c}_1 - \boldsymbol{c}_2) = \boldsymbol{0}_\kappa \wedge \boldsymbol{c}_1 - \boldsymbol{c}_2 \neq \boldsymbol{0}_{\kappa^*}\end{array}\right] \approx_\lambda 0.$$

According to Lemma 1 of [19], if $\mathcal{D}_{\kappa^*,\kappa}$-KerMDH holds in generic symmetric bilinear groups, then $\mathcal{D}_{\kappa^*,\kappa}$-SKerMDH holds in generic asymmetric bilinear groups. The KerMDH assumption holds also for Type-1 pairings, where $\mathbb{G}_1 = \mathbb{G}_2$, but then one needs $\kappa \geq 2$, which affects efficiency.

Algebraic Group Model (AGM). The AGM is a new model [15] used to prove the security of a cryptographic assumption, protocol, or a primitive. Essentially, in the AGM, one assumes that each PPT algorithm $\mathcal{A}$ is algebraic in the following sense. Assume $\mathcal{A}$'s input includes $[\boldsymbol{x}_\iota]_\iota$ and no other elements from the group $\mathbb{G}_\iota$. We consider a less restrictive version of the AGM that gives the adversary additional access to random oracles. More precisely, assume $\mathcal{A}$ has an access to oracles $\mathcal{O}_1$ and $\mathcal{O}_2$. For $\iota \in \{1, 2\}$, $\mathcal{O}_\iota$ samples and outputs a random element $[q_{\iota k}]_\iota$ from $\mathbb{G}_\iota$. The oracle access models the ability of $\mathcal{A}$ to create random group elements without knowing their discrete logarithms.

We assume that if $\mathcal{A}$ outputs group elements $[\boldsymbol{y}_\iota]_\iota$, then $\mathcal{A}$ knows matrices $\boldsymbol{N}_\iota$, such that $\boldsymbol{y}_\iota = \boldsymbol{N}_\iota \binom{\boldsymbol{x}_\iota}{\boldsymbol{q}_\iota}$. Formally, a PPT algorithm $\mathcal{A}$ is *(*Pgen*-)algebraic* if there exists an efficient extractor $\mathsf{Ext}_\mathcal{A}$, such that for any PPT-sampleable distribution $\mathcal{D}$, $\mathsf{Adv}^{\mathrm{agm}}_{\mathsf{Pgen},\mathcal{D},\mathcal{A},\mathsf{Ext}_\mathcal{A}}(\lambda) :=$

$$\Pr\left[\begin{array}{l}\mathsf{p} \leftarrow_\$ \mathsf{Pgen}(1^\lambda); \mathbb{x} = ([\boldsymbol{x}_1]_1, [\boldsymbol{x}_2]_2) \leftarrow_\$ \mathcal{D}; r \leftarrow_\$ \mathsf{RND}_\lambda(\mathcal{A}); \\ ([\boldsymbol{y}_1]_1, [\boldsymbol{y}_2]_2) \leftarrow_\$ \mathcal{A}^{\mathcal{O}_1,\mathcal{O}_2}(\mathbb{x}; r); (\boldsymbol{N}_1, \boldsymbol{N}_2) \leftarrow \mathsf{Ext}_\mathcal{A}(\mathbb{x}; r) : \\ \boldsymbol{y}_1 \neq \boldsymbol{N}_1 \binom{\boldsymbol{x}_1}{\boldsymbol{q}_1} \vee \boldsymbol{y}_2 \neq \boldsymbol{N}_2 \binom{\boldsymbol{x}_2}{\boldsymbol{q}_2}\end{array}\right] = \mathsf{negl}(\lambda).$$

For $\iota \in \{1, 2\}$, $\mathcal{O}_\iota$ is an oracle that samples and returns a random element from $\mathbb{G}_\iota$. $[\boldsymbol{q}_\iota]_\iota$ is the list of all elements output by $\mathcal{O}_\iota$. The AGM states that for any PPT-sampleable $\mathcal{D}$ and PPT $\mathcal{A}$, there exists a PPT $\mathsf{Ext}_\mathcal{A}$, such that $\mathsf{Adv}^{\mathrm{agm}}_{\mathsf{Pgen},\mathcal{D},\mathcal{A},\mathsf{Ext}_\mathcal{A}}(\lambda) = \mathsf{negl}(\lambda)$.

Quadratic Arithmetic Program (QAP). QAP was introduced in [16] as a relation $\mathbf{R}$ where for an input $\mathbb{x}$ and a witness $\mathbb{w}$, $(\mathbb{x}, \mathbb{w}) \in \mathbf{R}$ can be verified by using a parallel quadratic check. QAP has an efficient reduction from the (either Boolean or Arithmetic) Circuit-SAT. Thus, an efficient zk-SNARK for QAP results in an efficient zk-SNARK for Circuit-SAT.

In QAP, one considers arithmetic circuits that consist only of fan-in-2 multiplication gates, but either input of each multiplication gate can be any weighted sum of wire values [16]. In arithmetic circuits, n is the number of multiplication gates, m is the number of wires, and $m_0 < m$ is the number of public inputs.

For the sake of efficiency, we require the existence of the n-th primitive root of unity modulo p, denoted by ω. (However, this is not needed for the new protocols to work.) Let $\boldsymbol{U}, \boldsymbol{V}, \boldsymbol{W} \in \mathbb{Z}_p^{n \times m}$ be instance-dependent matrices and let $\mathbb{z} \in \mathbb{Z}_p^m$ be a witness. A QAP is characterized by the constraint $\boldsymbol{U}\mathbb{z} \circ \boldsymbol{V}\mathbb{z} = \boldsymbol{W}\mathbb{z}$, where $\circ$ denotes the entrywise product of two vectors and $\mathbb{z} = \binom{\mathbb{x}}{\mathbb{w}}$. For $j \in [1, m]$, define $u_j(X) := L_{\boldsymbol{U}^{(j)}}(X)$, $v_j(X) := L_{\boldsymbol{V}^{(j)}}(X)$, and $w_j(X) := L_{\boldsymbol{W}^{(j)}}(X)$ to be interpolating polynomials of the jth columns of the corresponding matrices. Thus, $u_j, v_j, w_j \in \mathbb{Z}_p^{(\leq n-1)}[X]$. Let $u(X) = \sum_{j=1}^m \mathbb{z}_j u_j(X)$, $v(X) = \sum_{j=1}^m \mathbb{z}_j v_j(X)$, and $w(X) = \sum_{j=1}^m \mathbb{z}_j w_j(X)$. Then $\boldsymbol{U}\mathbb{z} \circ \boldsymbol{V}\mathbb{z} = \boldsymbol{W}\mathbb{z}$ iff $Z(X) \mid (u(X)v(X) - w(X))$

iff $u(X)v(X) \equiv w(X) \pmod{Z(X)}$ iff there exists a polynomial $h(X)$ such that $u(X)v(X) - w(X) = h(X)Z(X)$.

An QAP instance $\mathcal{I}_{\mathsf{qap}}$ is equal to $(\mathbb{Z}_p, m_0, \{u_j, v_j, w_j\}_{j=1}^{m})$. $\mathcal{I}_{\mathsf{qap}}$ defines the following relation:

$$\mathbf{R}_{\mathcal{I}_{\mathsf{qap}}} = \left\{ \begin{array}{l} (\mathbb{x}, \mathbb{w}) \colon \mathbb{x} = (\mathbb{z}_1, \dots, \mathbb{z}_{m_0})^\top \wedge \mathbb{w} = (\mathbb{z}_{m_0+1}, \dots, \mathbb{z}_m)^\top \wedge \\ u(X)v(X) \equiv w(X) \pmod{Z(X)} \end{array} \right\} \quad (1)$$

where $u(X)$, $v(X)$, and $w(X)$ are defined as above. Alternatively, $(\mathbb{x}, \mathbb{w}) \in \mathbf{R} = \mathbf{R}_{\mathcal{I}_{\mathsf{qap}}}$ if there exists a (degree $\leq n-2$) polynomial $h(X)$, such that the following key equation holds:

$$\chi(X) := u(X)v(X) - w(X) - h(X)Z(X) = 0, \quad (2)$$

On top of checking Eq. (2), the verifier also needs to check that $u(X)$, $v(X)$, and $w(X)$ are correctly computed: that is, (i) the first m_0 coefficients $\mathbb{z}_j$ in $u(X)$ are equal to the public inputs, and (ii) $u(X)$, $v(X)$, and $w(X)$ are all computed by using the same coefficients $\mathbb{z}_j$ for $j \in [1, m]$.

SAP and SSP. Square arithmetic programs (SAPs, [23]) are QAPs with the extra condition $\boldsymbol{U} = \boldsymbol{V}$; thus, all multiplication gates in the arithmetic circuit have equal inputs, i.e., they are square gates. Square span program (SSP, [9]) are QAPs with the restriction that $\boldsymbol{U} = \boldsymbol{V} = \boldsymbol{W}$; see [34]. There is an efficient relation between the arithmetic circuit evaluation problem and QAP/SAP and another one between the Boolean circuit evaluation problem and SSP. SSP is useful when the concrete zero-knowledge language is related to Boolean circuits.

2.1 Underlying Commitment Schemes

We will use several different commitment schemes that are all specific cases of the Multi-Pedersen commitment scheme.

EMP Commitment. Let $\iota \in \{1, 2\}$. Let q (the locality parameter) and n (the plaintext length) be two integers. Let $\mathcal{D}$ be a (matrix) distribution on $q \times (m+1)$ matrices. In the $(q, \mathcal{D})$-*Extended Multi-Pedersen commitment scheme* EMP [12,20], the commitment key is $\mathsf{ck} = [\boldsymbol{G}]_\iota$, where $\boldsymbol{G} \leftarrow_\$ \mathcal{D}$. The commitment $\mathsf{EMP.Com}(\mathsf{ck}; \boldsymbol{a}; r)$, where $\boldsymbol{a} \in \mathbb{Z}_p^m$ and $r \leftarrow_\$ \mathbb{Z}_p$, is defined as $[\boldsymbol{G}]_\iota \binom{\boldsymbol{a}}{r}$. The *interpolation commitment scheme* [33] is a perfectly-hiding EMP commitment scheme, with $\mathsf{ck} := [\ell_1(x), \dots, \ell_m(x), Z(x)]_\iota \in \mathbb{G}_\iota^{1 \times (m+1)}$ for a random trapdoor $x \leftarrow_\$ \mathbb{Z}_p$.

Functional SSB Commitment [12]**.** Let F be a fixed function. In general, F may depend on p, but we will not emphasize it for notational simplicity. In our applications, $F : a \mapsto [a]_\iota$ for $\iota \in \{1, 2\}$. Let $\mathcal{F}$ be a function family, where $f \in \mathcal{F}$ inputs a vector $\boldsymbol{x}$ and outputs an element from the domain of F. An F-*extractable functional somewhere statistically-binding (SSB) commitment scheme* [12] $\Gamma = (\mathsf{Pgen}, \mathsf{KC}, \mathsf{Com}, \mathsf{LExt}_F)$ for a function family $\mathcal{F}$ makes it possible to commit to a vector $\boldsymbol{x}$, such that the following properties hold. (1) The commitment key ck is chosen depending on the description of a function tuple $f_1, \dots, f_q \in \mathcal{F}$, (2) commitment keys corresponding to different function tuples are computationally indistinguishable, and (3) given the extraction key, one can extract from the commitment the vector $(F(f_1(\boldsymbol{x})), \ldots, F(f_q(\boldsymbol{x})))$.

More precisely, an *F-extractable functional SSB commitment scheme* $\Gamma = (\mathsf{Pgen}, \mathsf{KC}, \mathsf{Com}, \mathsf{LExt}_F)$ for a function family $\mathcal{F}$ consists of the following polynomial-time algorithms. We will omit algorithms (like trapdoor opening) and properties not needed in the current paper.

Parameter generation: $\mathsf{Pgen}(1^\lambda)$ returns parameters p (for example, group description). Recall that F depends on p.

Commitment key generation: for parameters p, a positive integer $n \in \mathsf{poly}(\lambda)$, a locality parameter $q \in [1, n]$, and a tuple $\mathcal{S} = (f_1, \ldots, f_{|\mathcal{S}|}) \subseteq \mathcal{F}$ with $|\mathcal{S}| \leq q$, $\mathsf{KC}(\mathsf{p}, n, q, \mathcal{S})$ outputs a commitment key ck and a trapdoor $\mathsf{td} = (\mathsf{ek}, \mathsf{tk})$. Here, ek is the *extraction key*, and tk is the *trapdoor key*. ck, ek, and tk implicitly specify p, the message space $\mathcal{M}$, the randomizer space $\mathcal{R}$, and the commitment space $\mathcal{C}$, s.t. $F(\mathcal{M}) \subseteq \mathcal{C}$. For any other input, KC outputs $(\mathsf{ck}, \mathsf{td}) = (\perp, \perp)$.

Commitment: for a commitment key $\mathsf{ck} \neq \perp$, a message $\boldsymbol{x} \in \mathcal{M}^n$, and a randomizer $r \in \mathcal{R}$, $\mathsf{Com}(\mathsf{ck}; \boldsymbol{x}; r)$ outputs a commitment $c \in \mathcal{C}$.

Local extraction: for $\mathsf{p} \in \mathsf{Pgen}(1^\lambda)$, a positive integer $n \in \mathsf{poly}(\lambda)$, a locality parameter $q \in [1, n]$, a tuple $\mathcal{S} = (f_1, \ldots, f_{|\mathcal{S}|}) \subseteq \mathcal{F}$ with $1 \leq |\mathcal{S}| \leq q$, $(\mathsf{ck}, (\mathsf{ek}, \mathsf{tk})) \in \mathsf{KC}(\mathsf{p}, n, q, \mathcal{S})$, and $c \in \mathcal{C}$, $\mathsf{LExt}_F(\mathsf{ek}; c)$ returns a tuple $(F(f_1(x)), \ldots, F(f_{|\mathcal{S}|}(x))) \in \mathcal{M}^{|\mathcal{S}|}$;

For $\{f_i\}_{i=1}^q \subseteq \mathcal{F}$ and vector $\boldsymbol{x}$ let us denote $\boldsymbol{x}_\mathcal{S} = (f_1(\boldsymbol{x}), \ldots, f_q(\boldsymbol{x}))$.

An *F-extractable functional SSB commitment scheme* Γ for function family $\mathcal{F}$ can satisfy the following security requirements.

Function-Set Hiding: $\forall \lambda$, PPT $\mathcal{A}$, $n \in \mathsf{poly}(\lambda)$, $q \in [1, n]$, $\mathsf{Adv}^{\mathsf{fsh}}_{\Gamma,n,q,\mathcal{A}}(\lambda) := 2 \cdot |\varepsilon^{\mathsf{fsh}}_{\Gamma,n,q,\mathcal{A}}(\lambda) - 1/2| \approx_\lambda 0$, where $\varepsilon^{\mathsf{fsh}}_{\Gamma,n,q,\mathcal{A}}(\lambda) :=$

$$\Pr\left[\begin{matrix}\mathsf{p} \leftarrow \mathsf{Pgen}(1^\lambda); (\mathcal{S}_0, \mathcal{S}_1) \leftarrow \mathcal{A}(\mathsf{p}, n, q) \text{ s.t. } \forall i \in \{0,1\}. \mathcal{S}_i \subseteq \mathcal{F} \wedge |\mathcal{S}_i| \leq q; \\ \beta \leftarrow_\$ \{0,1\}; (\mathsf{ck}_\beta, \mathsf{td}_\beta) \leftarrow \mathsf{KC}(\mathsf{p}, n, q, \mathcal{S}_\beta) : \mathcal{A}(\mathsf{ck}_\beta) = \beta\end{matrix}\right].$$

Intuitively, ck reveals computationally no information about $\mathcal{S}$.

Almost Everywhere Perfectly Hiding: $\forall \lambda$, unbounded $\mathcal{A}$, $n \in \mathsf{poly}(\lambda)$, $q \in [1, n]$, $\mathsf{Adv}^{\mathsf{aeph}}_{\Gamma,n,q,\mathcal{A}}(\lambda) := 2 \cdot |\varepsilon^{\mathsf{aeph}}_{\Gamma,n,q,\mathcal{A}}(\lambda) - 1/2| = 0$, where $\varepsilon^{\mathsf{aeph}}_{\Gamma,n,q,\mathcal{A}}(\lambda) :=$

$$\Pr\left[\begin{matrix}\mathsf{p} \leftarrow \mathsf{Pgen}(1^\lambda); \mathcal{S} \leftarrow \mathcal{A}(\mathsf{p}, n, q) \text{ s.t. } \mathcal{S} \subseteq \mathcal{F} \wedge |\mathcal{S}| \leq q; (\mathsf{ck}, \mathsf{td}) \leftarrow \mathsf{KC}(\mathsf{p}, n, q, \mathcal{S}); \\ (\boldsymbol{x}_0, \boldsymbol{x}_1) \leftarrow \mathcal{A}(\mathsf{ck}) \text{ s.t. } \boldsymbol{x}_{0\mathcal{S}} = \boldsymbol{x}_{1\mathcal{S}}; \beta \leftarrow_\$ \{0,1\}; r \leftarrow_\$ \mathcal{R} : \mathcal{A}(\mathsf{Com}(\mathsf{ck}; \boldsymbol{x}_\beta; r)) = \beta\end{matrix}\right].$$

Intuitively, given ck, that depends on $\mathcal{S}$, the commitment hides perfectly the values of x_i for $i \notin \mathcal{S}$.

Local F-Extractability: $\forall \lambda$, $\mathsf{p} \in \mathsf{Pgen}(1^\lambda)$, $n \in \mathsf{poly}(\lambda)$, $q \in [1, n]$, $\mathcal{S} = (f_1, \ldots, f_{|\mathcal{S}|}) \subseteq \mathcal{F}$ with $|\mathcal{S}| \leq q$, $(\mathsf{ck}, (\mathsf{ek}, \mathsf{tk})) \leftarrow \mathsf{KC}(\mathsf{p}, n, q, \mathcal{S})$, and PPT $\mathcal{A}$, $\mathsf{Adv}^{\mathsf{lext}}_{F,\Gamma,n,q,\mathcal{A}}(\lambda) :=$

$$\Pr[\boldsymbol{x}, r \leftarrow \mathcal{A}(\mathsf{ck}) : \mathsf{LExt}_F(\mathsf{ek}; \mathsf{Com}(\mathsf{ck}; \boldsymbol{x}; r)) \neq (F(f_1(\boldsymbol{x})), \ldots, F(f_{|\mathcal{S}|}(\boldsymbol{x})))] = 0.$$

$\mathsf{KC}(\mathsf{p}, n, q, [\boldsymbol{M}]_\iota \in \mathbb{G}_\iota^{q\times n})$:

Set implicitly $\mathcal{M} = \mathcal{R} = \mathbb{Z}_p^n$ and $\mathcal{C} = \mathbb{G}_\iota^{q+1}$;
Sample $\boldsymbol{R} \leftarrow_\$ \mathbb{Z}_p^{(q+1)\times(q+1)}$ so that it has full rank; Sample $\boldsymbol{\varrho} \leftarrow_\$ \mathbb{Z}_p^n$;
Set $[\boldsymbol{M}']_\iota \leftarrow \left[\begin{smallmatrix} \boldsymbol{M} & \boldsymbol{0} \\ \boldsymbol{\varrho}^\top & 1 \end{smallmatrix} \right]_\iota \in \mathbb{Z}_p^{(q+1)\times(n+1)}$;
Set $\mathsf{ck} \leftarrow \boldsymbol{R}[\boldsymbol{M}']_\iota \in \mathbb{G}_\iota^{(q+1)\times(n+1)}$, $\mathsf{td} \leftarrow (\mathsf{ek} \leftarrow \boldsymbol{R}^{-1}, \mathsf{tk} \leftarrow \boldsymbol{\varrho})$;
return $(\mathsf{ck}, \mathsf{td})$;

$\mathsf{Com}(\mathsf{ck}; \boldsymbol{x} \in \mathbb{Z}_p^n; r \in \mathbb{Z}_p)$	$\mathsf{LExt}(\mathsf{ek}; [\mathbf{c}]_\iota)$
return $\mathsf{ck}\left(\begin{smallmatrix} \boldsymbol{x} \\ r \end{smallmatrix}\right)$;	**return** $\mathsf{ek}[\mathbf{c}]_\iota$ without the last element;

Fig. 1. Functional SSB commitment scheme FSSB_ι for linear functions in $\mathbb{G}_\iota$.

Intuitively, given ck, that depends on $\mathcal{S}$, and an extraction key, one can extract $F(\boldsymbol{x}_\mathcal{S})$. (This property was called somewhere perfect F-extractability in [12].)

Computational Hiding: $\forall$ PPT $\mathcal{A}$, $n \in \mathsf{poly}(\lambda)$, $q \in [1, n]$, $\mathsf{Adv}^{\mathsf{ch}}_{\Gamma,n,q,\mathcal{A}}(\lambda) := 2 \cdot |\varepsilon^{\mathsf{ch}}_{\Gamma,n,q,\mathcal{A}}(\lambda) - 1/2| = \mathsf{negl}(\lambda)$, where $\varepsilon^{\mathsf{ch}}_{\Gamma,n,q,\mathcal{A}}(\lambda) :=$

$$\Pr\left[\begin{array}{l} \mathsf{p} \leftarrow \mathsf{Pgen}(1^\lambda); \mathcal{S} \leftarrow \mathcal{A}(\mathsf{p}, n, q) \text{ s.t. } \mathcal{S} \subseteq \mathcal{F} \wedge |\mathcal{S}| \le q; \\ (\mathsf{ck}, \mathsf{td}) \leftarrow \mathsf{KC}(\mathsf{p}, n, q, \mathcal{S}); (\boldsymbol{x}_0, \boldsymbol{x}_1) \leftarrow \mathcal{A}(\mathsf{ck}); \beta \leftarrow_\$ \{0,1\}; r \leftarrow_\$ \mathcal{R} : \\ \mathcal{A}(\mathsf{Com}(\mathsf{ck}; \boldsymbol{x}_\beta; r)) = \beta \end{array}\right].$$

Intuitively, given ck, that can depend on any $\mathcal{S}$, the commitment hides computationally the vector $\boldsymbol{x}$.

Construction. [12] constructed a functional SSB scheme for the family of all linear functions, see Fig. 1. It represents q linear functions by a matrix $[\boldsymbol{M}]_\iota \in \mathbb{G}_\iota^{q\times n}$, where each row contains coefficients of one function. Clearly, the commitment computes $[\mathbf{c}]_\iota \leftarrow \mathsf{Com}(\mathsf{ck}; \boldsymbol{x}; r) = \mathsf{ck}\left(\begin{smallmatrix} \boldsymbol{x} \\ r \end{smallmatrix}\right) = \boldsymbol{R}[\boldsymbol{M}']_\iota\left(\begin{smallmatrix} \boldsymbol{x} \\ r \end{smallmatrix}\right) = \left[\begin{smallmatrix} \boldsymbol{R}\boldsymbol{M}\boldsymbol{x}\boldsymbol{R}(\boldsymbol{\varrho}^\top \boldsymbol{x}+r) \end{smallmatrix}\right]_\iota$, while $\mathsf{LExt}(\mathsf{ek}; [\mathbf{c}]_\iota)$ computes $\mathsf{ek} \cdot [\mathbf{c}]_\iota = \boldsymbol{R}^{-1}[\boldsymbol{R}\boldsymbol{M}'\left(\begin{smallmatrix} \boldsymbol{x} \\ r \end{smallmatrix}\right)]_\iota = [\boldsymbol{M}'\left(\begin{smallmatrix} \boldsymbol{x} \\ r \end{smallmatrix}\right)]_\iota = \left[\begin{smallmatrix} \boldsymbol{M}\boldsymbol{x}\boldsymbol{\varrho}^\top \boldsymbol{x}+r \end{smallmatrix}\right]_\iota$, and returns $[\boldsymbol{M}\boldsymbol{x}]_\iota$.

Proposition 1 (**[12]**)**.** *Let* Pgen *be a bilinear group generator. Fix data size* n *and locality parameter* q*. The commitment scheme in Fig. 1 is (i) function-set hiding relative to* Pgen *under the* $DDH_{\mathbb{G}_\iota}$ *assumption: for each PPT* $\mathcal{A}$*, there exists a PPT* $\mathcal{B}$*, such that* $\mathsf{Adv}^{\mathsf{fsh}}_{\Gamma,n,q,\mathcal{A}}(\lambda) \le \lceil \log_2(q+1) \rceil \cdot \mathsf{Adv}^{\mathsf{ddh}}_{\mathbb{G}_\iota,\mathsf{Pgen},\mathcal{B}}(\lambda)$*. (ii) locally* F*-extractable for* $F = [\cdot]_\iota$ *(thus,* F *depends on* p*), (iii) almost everywhere perfectly-hiding, (iv) computationally-hiding. More precisely, for all PPT* $\mathcal{A}$*, there exist PPT* $\mathcal{B}_1$ *and unbounded* $\mathcal{B}_2$*, such that* $\mathsf{Adv}^{\mathsf{ch}}_{\Gamma,n,q,\mathcal{A}}(\lambda) \le \mathsf{Adv}^{\mathsf{fsh}}_{\Gamma,n,q,\mathcal{B}_1}(\lambda) + \mathsf{Adv}^{\mathsf{aeph}}_{\Gamma,n,q,\mathcal{B}_2}(\lambda)$*.*

Due to (iv), computational hiding does not have to be proven separately since it always follows from function-set hiding and almost everywhere perfect hiding.

2.2 Sub-ZK NIZK and QA-NIZK

In the current paper, we use both NIZKs and quasi-adaptive NIZKs [27]. To save space, we first give a complete description of QA-NIZKs (both since QA-NIZKs are less known and their security definitions subsume those of NIZKs) and then point out the differences in the case of NIZKs. We postpone the formal definitions of non-QA NIZKs to the full version [35].

A QA-NIZK argument system in the CRS model proves membership in the language $\mathbf{L}_{\mathsf{lpar}}$ defined by a relation $\mathbf{R}_{\mathsf{lpar}} = \{(\mathbb{x}, \mathbb{w})\}$, where both are determined by a language parameter lpar. In the honest case, lpar is sampled from a distribution $\mathcal{D}_{\mathsf{p}}$; let $\mathsf{setup.lpar}$ be the PPT algorithm that does this sampling. We assume that lpar contains p, and thus, we do not include p as an argument to algorithms that also input lpar; recall that we assumed that p cannot be subverted. A distribution $\mathcal{D}_{\mathsf{p}}$ is *witness-sampleable* if there exists a PPT algorithm $\mathsf{setup.ltrap}$ that samples $(\mathsf{lpar}, \mathsf{ltrap})$ such that lpar is distributed according to $\mathcal{D}_{\mathsf{p}}$, and the membership of lpar in $\mathbf{L}_{\mathsf{p}}$ can be efficiently verified given ltrap. The CRS crs can depend on lpar, but the simulator has to be a single algorithm that works for the whole collection of relations $\mathbf{R}_{\mathsf{p}} = \{\mathbf{R}_{\mathsf{lpar}}\}_{\mathsf{lpar} \in \text{image}(\mathcal{D}_{\mathsf{p}})}$. We will assume that crs contains lpar implicitly.

The zero-knowledge simulator is usually required to be a single (non-black-box) PPT algorithm that works for the whole collection of relations $\mathbf{R}_{\mathsf{p}} = \{\mathbf{R}_{\mathsf{lpar}}\}_{\mathsf{lpar} \in \text{image}(\mathcal{D}_{\mathsf{p}})}$; that is, one requires *uniform simulation* (see [27]). Following [1,3,14], we accompany the universal simulator Sim with an adversary-dependent extractor. We assume Sim also works when one cannot efficiently establish whether $\mathsf{lpar} \in \text{image}(\mathcal{D}_{\mathsf{p}})$. The simulator is not allowed to create new lpar or crs but has to operate with one given to it as an input.

A *Sub-ZK QA-NIZK argument system in the CRS model* for a set of witness-relations $\mathbf{R}_{\mathsf{p}} = \{\mathbf{R}_{\mathsf{lpar}}\}_{\mathsf{lpar} \in \text{image}(\mathcal{D}_{\mathsf{p}})}$ is a tuple of PPT algorithms $\Pi = (\mathsf{Pgen}, \mathsf{setup.lpar}, \mathsf{K}_{\mathsf{crs}}, \mathsf{PARV}, \mathsf{CV}, \mathsf{P}, \mathsf{V}, \mathsf{Sim})$. In the case of witness-sampleable languages, $\mathsf{setup.lpar}$ is replaced by $\mathsf{setup.ltrap}$. Here, Pgen is the parameter generation algorithm, $\mathsf{setup.lpar}$ is the language parameter generation algorithm, $\mathsf{setup.ltrap}$ is the corresponding $\mathsf{lpar}/\mathsf{ltrap}$ generation algorithm in the witness-sampleable case, $\mathsf{K}_{\mathsf{crs}}$ is the CRS generation algorithm, PARV is the lpar-verification algorithm, CV is the CRS verification algorithm, P is the prover, V is the verifier, and Sim is the simulator.

Π can satisfy the following security notions. Intuitively, quasi-adaptive soundness is soundness in the case when lpar is honestly generated. Quasi-adaptive strong soundness is soundness when lpar is honestly generated from a witness-sampleable distribution, and the adversary additionally gets access to ltrap. Adaptive soundness is soundness in the case of maliciously generated lpar. In all previous cases, the adversary sees crs before creating the input $\mathbb{x}$. Non-adaptive soundness is soundness in the case of maliciously generated lpar when the adversary has to fix $\mathbb{x}$ before seeing crs. Similar intuition holds in the case of various knowledge-soundness notions. Quasi-adaptive (knowledge)-soundness follows from adaptive (knowledge-)soundness. (Quasi-)adaptive soundness follows from (quasi-)adaptive knowledge-soundness.

Perfect Completeness: $\forall$ λ, PPT $\mathcal{A}$,

$$\Pr\left[\begin{array}{l}\mathsf{p} \leftarrow \mathsf{Pgen}(1^\lambda); \mathsf{lpar} \leftarrow \mathsf{setup.lpar}(\mathsf{p}); (\mathsf{crs}, \mathsf{td}) \leftarrow \mathsf{K_{crs}}(\mathsf{lpar});\\ (\mathbb{x}, \mathbb{w}) \leftarrow \mathcal{A}(\mathsf{crs}); \pi \leftarrow \mathsf{P}(\mathsf{lpar}, \mathsf{crs}, \mathbb{x}, \mathbb{w}) : \mathsf{PARV}(\mathsf{lpar}) = 1 \wedge\\ \mathsf{CV}(\mathsf{lpar}, \mathsf{crs}) = 1 \wedge ((\mathbb{x}, \mathbb{w}) \notin \mathbf{R}_{\mathsf{lpar}} \vee \mathsf{V}(\mathsf{lpar}, \mathsf{crs}, \mathbb{x}, \pi) = 1)\end{array}\right] = 1.$$

Computational Quasi-Adaptive Strong Soundness: defined if lpar is witness-sampleable. For any stateful PPT $\mathcal{A}$, $\mathsf{Adv}^{\mathrm{strsound}}_{\mathsf{Pgen},\Pi,\mathcal{A}}(\lambda) :=$

$$\Pr\left[\begin{array}{l}\mathsf{p} \leftarrow \mathsf{Pgen}(1^\lambda); (\mathsf{lpar}, \mathsf{ltrap}) \leftarrow \mathsf{setup.ltrap}(\mathsf{p}); (\mathsf{crs}, \mathsf{td}) \leftarrow \mathsf{K_{crs}}(\mathsf{lpar});\\ (\mathbb{x}, \pi) \leftarrow \mathcal{A}(\mathsf{lpar}, \mathsf{ltrap}, \mathsf{crs}) : \mathsf{V}(\mathsf{lpar}, \mathsf{crs}, \mathbb{x}, \pi) = 1 \wedge \neg(\exists \mathbb{w}. \mathbf{R}_{\mathsf{lpar}}(\mathbb{x}, \mathbb{w}) = 1)\end{array}\right] \approx_\lambda 0.$$

In the definition of computational quasi-adaptive soundness (also defined in the non-witness-sampleable case), the only difference is that one samples $\mathsf{lpar} \leftarrow \mathsf{setup.lpar}(\mathsf{p})$, and the adversary does not get ltrap as an input.

Computational Non-adaptive Soundness: $\forall$ stateful PPT $\mathcal{A}$, $\mathsf{Adv}^{\mathrm{nas}}_{\mathsf{Pgen},\Pi,\mathcal{A}}(\lambda) :=$

$$\Pr\left[\begin{array}{l}\mathsf{p} \leftarrow \mathsf{Pgen}(1^\lambda); (\mathsf{lpar}, \mathbb{x}) \leftarrow \mathcal{A}(\mathsf{p}); (\mathsf{crs}, \mathsf{td}) \leftarrow \mathsf{K_{crs}}(\mathsf{lpar}); \pi \leftarrow \mathcal{A}(\mathsf{crs}) :\\ \mathsf{PARV}(\mathsf{lpar}) = 1 \wedge \mathsf{V}(\mathsf{lpar}, \mathsf{crs}, \mathbb{x}, \pi) = 1 \wedge \neg(\exists \mathbb{w}. \mathbf{R}_{\mathsf{lpar}}(\mathbb{x}, \mathbb{w}) = 1)\end{array}\right] \approx_\lambda 0.$$

Computational Adaptive Soundness: $\forall$ stateful PPT $\mathcal{A}$, $\mathsf{Adv}^{\mathrm{as}}_{\mathsf{Pgen},\Pi,\mathcal{A}}(\lambda) :=$

$$\Pr\left[\begin{array}{l}\mathsf{p} \leftarrow \mathsf{Pgen}(1^\lambda); \mathsf{lpar} \leftarrow \mathcal{A}(\mathsf{p}); (\mathsf{crs}, \mathsf{td}) \leftarrow \mathsf{K_{crs}}(\mathsf{lpar}); (\mathbb{x}, \pi) \leftarrow \mathcal{A}(\mathsf{crs}) :\\ \mathsf{PARV}(\mathsf{lpar}) = 1 \wedge \mathsf{V}(\mathsf{lpar}, \mathsf{crs}, \mathbb{x}, \pi) = 1 \wedge \neg(\exists \mathbb{w}. \mathbf{R}_{\mathsf{lpar}}(\mathbb{x}, \mathbb{w}) = 1)\end{array}\right] \approx_\lambda 0.$$

Computational Adaptive Knowledge-Soundness: $\forall$ PPT stateful adversary $\mathcal{A}$, there exist a PPT extractor $\mathsf{Ext}_{\mathcal{A}}$, s.t. $\mathsf{Adv}^{\mathrm{aks}}_{\mathsf{Pgen},\Pi,\mathcal{A}}(\lambda) :=$

$$\Pr\left[\begin{array}{l}\mathsf{p} \leftarrow \mathsf{Pgen}(1^\lambda); r \leftarrow_{\$} \mathsf{RND}_\lambda(\mathcal{A}); \mathsf{lpar} \leftarrow \mathcal{A}(\mathsf{p}, r);\\ (\mathsf{crs}, \mathsf{td}) \leftarrow \mathsf{K_{crs}}(\mathsf{lpar}); (\mathbb{x}, \pi) \leftarrow \mathcal{A}(\mathsf{crs}; r); \mathbb{w} \leftarrow \mathsf{Ext}_{\mathcal{A}}(\mathsf{p}, \mathsf{crs}; r) :\\ \mathsf{PARV}(\mathsf{lpar}) = 1 \wedge \mathsf{V}(\mathsf{lpar}, \mathsf{crs}, \mathbb{x}, \pi) = 1 \wedge \mathbf{R}_{\mathsf{lpar}}(\mathbb{x}, \mathbb{w}) = 0\end{array}\right] \approx_\lambda 0.$$

A knowledge-sound argument system is called an *argument of knowledge.*

Computational (resp., Perfect) Zero Knowledge: $\forall$ PPT (resp., unbounded) adversary $\mathcal{A}$, $|\varepsilon_0^{zk} - \varepsilon_1^{zk}| \approx_\lambda 0$ (resp., $|\varepsilon_0^{zk} - \varepsilon_1^{zk}| = 0$), where $\varepsilon_b^{zk} :=$

$$\Pr[\mathsf{p} \leftarrow \mathsf{Pgen}(1^\lambda); \mathsf{lpar} \leftarrow \mathcal{D}_{\mathsf{p}}; (\mathsf{crs}, \mathsf{td}) \leftarrow \mathsf{K_{crs}}(\mathsf{lpar}) : \mathcal{A}^{\mathcal{O}_b(\cdot,\cdot)}(\mathsf{lpar}, \mathsf{crs}) = 1].$$

That is, $\mathcal{A}$ is given an oracle access to $\mathcal{O}_b(\cdot,\cdot)$, where $\mathcal{O}_0(\mathbb{x}, \mathbb{w})$ returns $\perp$ (reject) if $(\mathbb{x}, \mathbb{w}) \notin \mathbf{R}_{\mathsf{lpar}}$, and otherwise it returns $\mathsf{P}(\mathsf{lpar}, \mathsf{crs}, \mathbb{x}, \mathbb{w})$. Similarly, $\mathcal{O}_1(\mathbb{x}, \mathbb{w})$ returns $\perp$ (reject) if $(\mathbb{x}, \mathbb{w}) \notin \mathbf{R}_{\mathsf{lpar}}$, and otherwise it returns $\mathsf{Sim}(\mathsf{lpar}, \mathsf{crs}, \mathsf{td}, \mathbb{x})$.

Intuitively, zero knowledge in this sense corresponds to black-box zero-knowledge in the case when lpar and crs are trusted.

Computational (resp., Perfect) Persistent Zero Knowledge: $\forall$ PPT subverter $\mathcal{Z}$, there exists a PPT extractor $\mathsf{Ext}_{\mathcal{Z}}$, s.t. $\forall$ PPT (resp., unbounded) adversary $\mathcal{A}$, $|\varepsilon_0^{zk} - \varepsilon_1^{zk}| \approx_\lambda 0$ (resp., $|\varepsilon_0^{zk} - \varepsilon_1^{zk}| = 0$), where $\varepsilon_b^{zk} :=$

$$\Pr\left[\begin{array}{l}\mathsf{p} \leftarrow \mathsf{Pgen}(1^\lambda); r \leftarrow_\$ \mathsf{RND}_\lambda(\mathcal{Z}); (\mathsf{lpar}, \mathsf{crs}, \mathsf{aux}) \leftarrow \mathcal{Z}(\mathsf{p}, r); \mathsf{td} \leftarrow \mathsf{Ext}_{\mathcal{Z}}(\mathsf{p}, r) : \\ \mathsf{PARV}(\mathsf{lpar}) = 1 \wedge \mathsf{CV}(\mathsf{lpar}, \mathsf{crs}) = 1 \wedge \mathcal{A}^{\mathcal{O}_b(\cdot,\cdot)}(\mathsf{lpar}, \mathsf{crs}, \mathsf{aux}) = 1\end{array}\right].$$

The oracles are as above. Persistent zero-knowledge corresponds to non-black-box zero-knowledge in the case when lpar and crs are not trusted.

Π is *Sub-ZK* if it is both perfectly ZK and perfectly persistent zero-knowledge. ZK does not follow from persistent zero-knowledge in the case of QA-NIZKs [2] and thus, one has to prove both properties separately.

NIZKs. In the case of a (non-QA) NIZK, there is no language parameter and thus, no algorithms $\mathsf{setup.lpar}$ and PARV; other algorithms (including the adversary) do not take lpar as an argument or output it. Thus, $\Pi = (\mathsf{Pgen}, \mathsf{K_{crs}}, \mathsf{CV}, \mathsf{P}, \mathsf{V}, \mathsf{Sim})$. Moreover, one deals with a single non-parametrized language $\mathbf{L}$. Otherwise, all properties of QA-NIZKs carry over but in a simplified form. Note that (1) one is not interested in quasi-adaptive (strong) soundness and (2) Sub-ZK and persistent zero-knowledge coincide. We postpone the formal definitions of non-QA NIZKs to the full version [35].

SNARKs. A (QA-)NIZK is *succinct* ((QA-)SNARG) if the argument π has a sublinear (desirably, logarithmic) length in $\mathsf{poly}(\lambda)\,(|\mathbb{x}| + |\mathbb{w}|)$. A *(QA-)SNARK* is a (QA-)SNARG that is additionally knowledge-sound.

Gentry-Wichs Impossibility Result. Gentry and Wichs [17] proved that if an NP language $\mathbf{L}$ has a sub-exponentially (resp., exponentially) hard subset-membership proof and Π is a complete SNARG in the CRS model with $|\pi| = \mathsf{poly}(\lambda)\,(|\mathbb{x}| + |\mathbb{w}|)^{o(1)}$ (resp., $|\pi| = \mathsf{poly}(\lambda)\,(|\mathbb{x}| + |\mathbb{w}|)^c + o(|\mathbb{x}| + |\mathbb{w}|)$ for some constant $c < 1$) for $\mathbf{L}$, then there is a black-box reduction from the adaptive soundness of Π to a falsifiable assumption X only when X is false.

3 Sub-ZK Bilateral Subspace QA-SNARK

A bilateral subspace argument system, with $\mathsf{lpar} = [M]_*$, allows to prove that $[\mathbf{c}_1]_1 \in \mathbb{G}_1^{n_1}$ and $[\mathbf{c}_2]_2 \in \mathbb{G}_2^{n_2}$ satisfy $\binom{\mathbf{c}_1}{\mathbf{c}_2} \in \mathrm{colspace}\binom{M_1}{M_2}$. Following [10,12], we will use it to construct QA-SNARGs. Next, we prove that BLS, a variant of the González-Hevia-Ráfols bilateral subspace QA-SNARG, satisfies stronger properties, needed for FANA to be non-adaptively knowledge-sound and Sub-ZK.

First, let σ be any efficiently computable function. A distribution $\mathcal{D}_\mathsf{p}$ is σ-*witness-sampleable* if (1) there exists a PPT algorithm $\mathsf{setup.ltrap}_\sigma$ that samples $(\mathsf{lpar}, \sigma(\mathsf{ltrap}))$ such that lpar is distributed according to $\mathcal{D}_\mathsf{p}$, and (2) for any language trapdoor ltrap', such that the membership of lpar in the parameter language $\mathbf{L}_\mathsf{p}$ can be efficiently verified given ltrap', it holds that $\sigma(\mathsf{ltrap}) = \sigma(\mathsf{ltrap}')$. (In the context of the current paper, think of ltrap as the discrete logarithm of lpar, and $\sigma(\mathsf{ltrap})$ as an efficient—fixed—leakage function of ltrap.) We will prove that BLS satisfies the following new security property that follows from the quasi-adaptive strong soundness (see page 14):

Computational Quasi-Adaptive σ-Strong Soundness: defined if lpar is σ-witness-sampleable. For any stateful PPT $\mathcal{A}$, $\mathsf{Adv}^{\sigma-\mathrm{strsound}}_{\mathsf{Pgen},\Pi,\mathcal{A}}(\lambda) :=$

$$\Pr\left[\begin{array}{l}\mathsf{p} \leftarrow \mathsf{Pgen}(1^\lambda); (\mathsf{lpar}, \sigma(\mathsf{ltrap})) \leftarrow \mathsf{setup.ltrap}_\sigma(\mathsf{p}); (\mathsf{crs}, \mathsf{td}) \leftarrow \mathsf{K_{crs}}(\mathsf{lpar}); \\ (\mathbb{x}, \pi) \leftarrow \mathcal{A}(\mathsf{lpar}, \sigma(\mathsf{ltrap}), \mathsf{crs}) : \mathsf{V}(\mathsf{lpar}, \mathsf{crs}, \mathbb{x}, \pi) = 1 \wedge \\ \neg(\exists \mathbb{w}. \mathbf{R}_{\mathsf{lpar}}(\mathbb{x}, \mathbb{w}) = 1)\end{array}\right] \approx_\lambda 0.$$

This notion agrees with the quasi-adaptive strong soundness when $\sigma = id$ is the identity function and with the quasi-adaptive soundness if σ is a constant function. While BLS is quasi-adaptively strongly sound and thus also quasi-adaptively σ-strongly sound for any efficient σ, we find it instructive to define σ-strong soundness. In particular, for the non-adaptive soundness of FANA, we will need BLS to be σ_x-strongly sound for a well-defined function σ_x. It is possible that one can find a more efficient version of BLS that is quasi-adaptively σ_x-strongly sound but not quasi-adaptively strong sound.

Assume that the matrix security parameter is $\kappa = 2$ (if $\kappa = 1$ then SKerMDH does not hold, [19]). Assume $\tau := \text{corank}(\boldsymbol{M}) = n_1 + n_2 - \text{rank}(\boldsymbol{M}) \geq 1$; here, n_1, n_2 can be smaller or larger (only the latter case was studied in [19]) than m. For $\mathsf{lpar} \in \mathbb{G}_1^{n_1 \times m} \times \mathbb{G}_2^{n_2 \times m}$, where $\mathsf{lpar} = [\boldsymbol{M}]_*$, define the bilateral subspace language (also known as the subspace concatenation language, [19])

$$\mathbf{L}_{\mathsf{lpar}} := \left\{([\mathbf{c}_1]_1, [\mathbf{c}_2]_2) \in \mathbb{G}_1^{n_1} \times \mathbb{G}_2^{n_2} : \exists \mathbb{w} \in \mathbb{Z}_p^m . \left(\begin{smallmatrix}\mathbf{c}_1 \\ \mathbf{c}_2\end{smallmatrix}\right) = \left(\begin{smallmatrix}\boldsymbol{M}_1 \\ \boldsymbol{M}_2\end{smallmatrix}\right)\mathbb{w}\right\}.$$

That is, $\mathbf{c}_1 = \boldsymbol{M}_1\mathbb{w}$ and $\mathbf{c}_2 = \boldsymbol{M}_2\mathbb{w}$.

A distribution $\mathcal{D}_\kappa$ is *efficiently verifiable* [2], if there exists a PPT algorithm $\mathsf{MATV}([\bar{\boldsymbol{A}}]_2)$ that outputs 1 if $\bar{\boldsymbol{A}}$ is invertible (recall that we assume that the matrix distribution is robust) and well-formed with respect to $\mathcal{D}_\kappa$, and otherwise outputs 0. Clearly, the standard distributions (see the full version [35]) $\mathcal{U}_1$, $\mathcal{L}_\kappa$, $\mathcal{IL}_\kappa$, $\mathcal{C}_\kappa$, and $\mathcal{SC}_\kappa$ (for any κ) are verifiable [2], while the verification whether $[\bar{\boldsymbol{A}}]_2$ is invertible is intractable for $\mathcal{U}_\kappa$ if $\kappa > 1$. To be able to handle $\mathcal{U}_\kappa$, [2] added parts of $[\bar{\boldsymbol{A}}]_1$ to crs. However, in the $\mathcal{U}_\kappa$ case, they proved adaptive soundness under the SKerMDH^{dl} (that we will define in Sect. 3.1) assumption instead of the KerMDH^{dl} assumption (see [2] for more discussion), which resulted in the choice $\kappa = 2$. $[\bar{\boldsymbol{A}}]_1$ is always in crs of a bilateral subspace argument system and thus the adaptive soundness relies on (a variant of) the SKerMDH^{dl} assumption.

As before, assume that the distribution $\mathcal{D}_\kappa$ is robust. Extending the definition of [2], we say that $\mathcal{D}_\kappa$ is *efficiently verifiable*, if there exists an algorithm $\mathsf{MATV}([\bar{\boldsymbol{A}}]_1, [\bar{\boldsymbol{A}}]_2)$ that outputs 1 if $\bar{\boldsymbol{A}}$ is invertible and well-formed with respect to $\mathcal{D}_\kappa$ and otherwise outputs 0. Here, MATV gets two inputs, $[\bar{\boldsymbol{A}}]_1$ and $[\bar{\boldsymbol{A}}]_2$; there are cases when an efficient MATV does not exist when only $[\bar{\boldsymbol{A}}]_1$ is given as the input. In particular, under this definition, also $\mathcal{U}_2$ is efficiently verifiable.

We depict a slight variant of the González-Hevia-Ràfols bilateral subspace QA-SNARG argument system BLS for $\mathbf{L}_{[\boldsymbol{M}_1]_1, [\boldsymbol{M}_2]_2}$ in Fig. 2. Compared to [19], we add the CRS verification algorithm CV and assume the existence of $\mathsf{setup.ltrap}_\sigma$ for some efficiently computable function σ. As in [19], the prover's work is dominated by $2m\kappa$ exponentiations, the verifier's work is dominated by $(n_1 + n_2 + 2\kappa)\kappa$ pairings, and the argument consists of 2κ group elements. Theorem 1 generalizes a theorem from [19] to any $n_\iota \times m$ matrices $\boldsymbol{M}_\iota$ (even if $m > n_\iota$), given that $\tau := n_1 + n_2 - \text{rank}(\boldsymbol{M}) \geq 1$. This generalization is important since in FANA (see Eq. (4)), $m > n_2$. On top of the known results that BLS

$\mathbf{L}_{\mathsf{p}} = \{[\boldsymbol{M}]_* \in \mathbb{G}_1^{n_1 \times m} \times \mathbb{G}_2^{n_2 \times m} : \tau := n_1 - \text{rank}(\boldsymbol{M}_1) = n_2 - \text{rank}(\boldsymbol{M}_2) \geq 1\}$

$\mathsf{setup.lpar}(\mathsf{p})$

$([\boldsymbol{M}]_*, \sigma(\boldsymbol{M}_1, \boldsymbol{M}_2)) \leftarrow_\$ \mathsf{setup.ltrap}_\sigma(\mathsf{p});$
return $\mathsf{lpar} \leftarrow [\boldsymbol{M}]_*;$

$\mathsf{BLS.K_{crs}}(\mathsf{p}, \mathsf{lpar} = ([\boldsymbol{M}_1]_1, [\boldsymbol{M}_2]_2))$

$\boldsymbol{A} \leftarrow_\$ \mathcal{D}_\kappa;$ // $\boldsymbol{A} \in \mathbb{Z}_p^{(\kappa+1)\times\kappa}$, $\bar{\boldsymbol{A}}$ is invertible
$\boldsymbol{K}_1 \leftarrow_\$ \mathbb{Z}_p^{n_1 \times \kappa}; \boldsymbol{K}_2 \leftarrow_\$ \mathbb{Z}_p^{n_2 \times \kappa}; \boldsymbol{\Delta} \leftarrow_\$ \mathbb{Z}_p^{\kappa \times m};$
$\boldsymbol{C}_1 \leftarrow \boldsymbol{K}_1 \bar{\boldsymbol{A}}; \boldsymbol{C}_2 \leftarrow \boldsymbol{K}_2 \bar{\boldsymbol{A}};$ // $\boldsymbol{C}_\iota \in \mathbb{Z}_p^{n_\iota \times \kappa}$
$[\boldsymbol{P}_1]_1 \leftarrow \boldsymbol{K}_1^\top [\boldsymbol{M}_1]_1 + [\boldsymbol{\Delta}]_1;$
$[\boldsymbol{P}_2]_2 \leftarrow \boldsymbol{K}_2^\top [\boldsymbol{M}_2]_2 - [\boldsymbol{\Delta}]_2;$ // $[\boldsymbol{P}_\iota]_\iota \in \mathbb{G}_\iota^{\kappa \times m}$
$\mathsf{crs} \leftarrow ([\bar{\boldsymbol{A}}, \boldsymbol{C}_2, \boldsymbol{P}_1]_1, [\bar{\boldsymbol{A}}, \boldsymbol{C}_1, \boldsymbol{P}_2]_2);$
$\mathsf{td} \leftarrow (\boldsymbol{K}_1, \boldsymbol{K}_2);$
return $(\mathsf{crs}, \mathsf{td});$

$\mathsf{BLS.P}(\mathsf{p}, \mathsf{crs}; ([\mathbf{c}_1]_1, [\mathbf{c}_2]_2), \mathbf{w})$

$\boldsymbol{\zeta} \leftarrow_\$ \mathbb{Z}_p^\kappa;$
$[\boldsymbol{\psi}_1]_1 \leftarrow [\boldsymbol{P}_1]_1 \mathbf{w} + [\boldsymbol{\zeta}]_1;$
$[\boldsymbol{\psi}_2]_2 \leftarrow [\boldsymbol{P}_2]_2 \mathbf{w} - [\boldsymbol{\zeta}]_2;$ // $[\boldsymbol{\psi}_\iota]_\iota \in \mathbb{G}_\iota^\kappa$
return $\psi \leftarrow ([\boldsymbol{\psi}_1]_1, [\boldsymbol{\psi}_2]_2);$

$\mathsf{BLS.Sim}(\mathsf{p}, \mathsf{crs}; ([\mathbf{c}_1]_1, [\mathbf{c}_2]_2), \mathsf{td})$

$\boldsymbol{\zeta}' \leftarrow_\$ \mathbb{Z}_p^\kappa;$
$[\boldsymbol{\psi}'_1]_1 \leftarrow \boldsymbol{K}_1^\top [\mathbf{c}_1]_1 + [\boldsymbol{\zeta}']_1;$ // $[\mathbf{c}_\iota]_\iota \in \mathbb{G}_\iota^{n_\iota}$
$[\boldsymbol{\psi}'_2]_2 \leftarrow \boldsymbol{K}_2^\top [\mathbf{c}_2]_2 - [\boldsymbol{\zeta}']_2;$ // $[\boldsymbol{\psi}'_\iota]_\iota \in \mathbb{G}_\iota^\kappa$
return $\psi' \leftarrow ([\boldsymbol{\psi}'_1]_1, [\boldsymbol{\psi}'_2]_2);$

$\mathsf{BLS.V}(\mathsf{p}, \mathsf{crs}; ([\mathbf{c}_1]_1, [\mathbf{c}_2]_2), \psi)$

return $[\mathbf{c}_1]_1^\top \bullet [\boldsymbol{C}_1]_2 + ([\boldsymbol{C}_2]_1^\top \bullet [\mathbf{c}_2]_2)^\top \stackrel{?}{=} [\boldsymbol{\psi}_1]_1^\top \bullet [\bar{\boldsymbol{A}}]_2 + ([\bar{\boldsymbol{A}}]_1^\top \bullet [\boldsymbol{\psi}_2]_2)^\top;$ // in $\mathbb{G}_T^{1\times\kappa}$

$\mathsf{BLS.CV}([\boldsymbol{M}]_*, \mathsf{crs})$:

return 1 **if** the following checks all succeed

$\mathsf{crs} = ([\bar{\boldsymbol{A}}, \boldsymbol{C}_2, \boldsymbol{P}_1]_1, [\bar{\boldsymbol{A}}, \boldsymbol{C}_1, \boldsymbol{P}_2]_2);$
$[\boldsymbol{P}_1]_1 \in \mathbb{G}_1^{\kappa \times m} \wedge [\bar{\boldsymbol{A}}]_2 \in \mathbb{G}_2^{\kappa\times\kappa} \wedge [\boldsymbol{C}_1]_2 \in \mathbb{G}_2^{n_1 \times \kappa};$
$[\boldsymbol{P}_2]_2 \in \mathbb{G}_2^{\kappa \times m} \wedge [\bar{\boldsymbol{A}}]_1 \in \mathbb{G}_2^{\kappa\times\kappa} \wedge [\boldsymbol{C}_2]_1 \in \mathbb{G}_1^{n_2 \times \kappa};$
(♯) $[\bar{\boldsymbol{A}}]_1 \bullet [1]_2 = [1]_1 \bullet [\bar{\boldsymbol{A}}]_2;$
(∗) $[\boldsymbol{M}_1]_1^\top \bullet [\boldsymbol{C}_1]_2 + [\boldsymbol{M}_2]_2^\top \bullet [\boldsymbol{C}_2]_1 = [\boldsymbol{P}_1]_1^\top \bullet [\bar{\boldsymbol{A}}]_2 + [\boldsymbol{P}]_2^\top \bullet [\bar{\boldsymbol{A}}]_1;$
$\mathsf{MATV}([\boldsymbol{A}]_2) = 1;$

Fig. 2. The Sub-ZK bilateral subspace QA-SNARG BLS, for efficiently verifiable $\mathcal{D}_\kappa$.

is quasi-adaptively (strongly) sound and zero-knowledge, we prove that BLS is quasi-adaptively σ-strongly sound (for any efficient σ), adaptively sound, adaptively knowledge-sound, persistent zero-knowledge, and thus Sub-ZK. To state Theorem 1, we will first need to define several security assumptions.

3.1 New Security Assumptions

To state Theorem 1, we will first need to define two (non-falsifiable) non-adaptive security assumptions, $\text{SKerMDH}^{\text{dl}}$ and SDL^{dl}, that state that the SKerMDH and SDL [6] assumptions stay secure even if one is given a non-adaptive access to a discrete logarithm oracle in both $\mathbb{G}_1$ and $\mathbb{G}_2$. [30] used KerMDH to prove the quasi-adaptive soundness of their QA-SNARG Π_{kw} (assuming that lpar is honestly generated and witness-sampleable), and [2] used (non-falsifiable) non-adaptive interactive assumptions $\text{KerMDH}^{\text{dl}}$ and SDL^{dl} to prove the adaptive soundness and knowledge-soundness of Π_{kw}. Witness-sampleability makes it possible for the reduction to generate lpar together with ltrap, and then use the knowledge of ltrap. The use of a non-falsifiable but reasonable looking non-adaptive interactive assumption allows the reduction to obtain ltrap by using the (non-polynomial-time) discrete logarithm oracles. Thus, one does not have to assume anymore that lpar is honestly generated. See [2] for discussion.

The intuition behind using different assumptions, compared to [2], is similar to the reason why BLS is sound under the SKerMDH and not under the KerMDH assumption. See [19] for discussion.

For $\iota \in \{1,2\}$, the oracle $\mathrm{dl}_\iota([y]_\iota)$ returns the discrete logarithm y of $[y]_\iota$. *The* $\mathcal{D}_{\kappa^*,\kappa}$-SKerMDH^{dl} *assumption* [2] holds relative to Pgen, if $\forall$ PPT $\mathcal{A}$,

$$\mathsf{Adv}^{\mathrm{skermdhdl}}_{\mathcal{D}_{\kappa^*,\kappa},\mathsf{Pgen},\mathcal{A}}(\lambda) := \Pr\left[\begin{array}{l}\mathsf{p} \leftarrow \mathsf{Pgen}(1^\lambda); \mathsf{st} \leftarrow \mathcal{A}^{\mathrm{dl}_1(\cdot),\mathrm{dl}_2(\cdot)}(\mathsf{p});\\ \boldsymbol{A} \leftarrow_{\$} \mathcal{D}_{\kappa^*,\kappa}; ([\boldsymbol{c}_1]_1, [\boldsymbol{c}_2]_2) \leftarrow \mathcal{A}(\mathsf{p}, \mathsf{st}, [\boldsymbol{A}]_1, [\boldsymbol{A}]_2) :\\ \boldsymbol{A}^\top(\boldsymbol{c}_1 - \boldsymbol{c}_2) = \boldsymbol{0}_\kappa \wedge \boldsymbol{c}_1 - \boldsymbol{c}_2 \neq \boldsymbol{0}_{\kappa^*}\end{array}\right] \approx_\lambda 0.$$

The SDL^{dl} *assumption* [2] holds relative to Pgen, if for any PPT $\mathcal{A}$,

$$\mathsf{Adv}^{\mathrm{sdldl}}_{\mathsf{Pgen},\mathcal{A}}(\lambda) := \Pr\left[\begin{array}{l}\mathsf{p} \leftarrow \mathsf{Pgen}(1^\lambda); \mathsf{st} \leftarrow \mathcal{A}^{\mathrm{dl}_1(\cdot),\mathrm{dl}_2(\cdot)}(\mathsf{p}); x \leftarrow_{\$} \mathbb{Z}_p :\\ \mathcal{A}(\mathsf{p}, \mathsf{st}, [x]_1, [x]_2) = x\end{array}\right] \approx_\lambda 0.$$

In the version of SKerMDH^{dl} and SDL^{dl} from [2], $\mathcal{A}$ was only given access to the oracle dl_1. We decided to not change the name of the assumption.

[2] proved the persistent zero-knowledge of the Kiltz-Wee QA-SNARG argument system [30] under a new knowledge assumption KW-KE and then proved KW-KE's security in the algebraic group model, [15]. Since BLS is sufficiently different from [30], we need to define another knowledge assumption, GHR-KE (the *González-Hevia-Ràfols knowledge-of-exponent*). Intuitively, GHR-KE states that if one outputs an lpar and a crs, such that PARV and CV accept $(\mathsf{lpar}, \mathsf{crs})$ correspondingly, then one must know $\mathsf{td} = (\boldsymbol{K}_1, \boldsymbol{K}_2)$. This also gives an intuition of the role that is filled by PARV and CV. In the full version [35], we prove the security of GHR-KE in the AGM.

Definition 1. *Fix* $\kappa \geq 1$, $n > m \geq 1$, *and a distribution* $\mathcal{D}_\kappa$. *Let* $\mathsf{BLS.PARV}$ *and* $\mathsf{BLS.CV}$ *be as in Fig. 2.* $(\mathcal{D}_\mathsf{p}, \kappa, \mathcal{D}_\kappa)$-GHR-KE *holds relative to* Pgen *if for any PPT* $\mathcal{A}$, *there exists a PPT extractor* $\mathsf{Ext}_\mathcal{A}$, *s.t.* $\mathsf{Adv}^{\mathrm{ghrke}}_{\mathcal{D}_\mathsf{p},\kappa,\mathcal{D}_\kappa,\mathsf{Pgen},\mathcal{A},\mathsf{Ext}_\mathcal{A}}(\lambda) :=$

$$\Pr\left[\begin{array}{l}\mathsf{p} \leftarrow \mathsf{Pgen}(1^\lambda); r \leftarrow_{\$} \mathsf{RND}_\lambda(\mathcal{A}); (\mathsf{lpar} := [\boldsymbol{M}]_*, \mathsf{crs}) \leftarrow \mathcal{A}(\mathsf{p}, r);\\ (\boldsymbol{K}_1, \boldsymbol{K}_2) \leftarrow \mathsf{Ext}_\mathcal{A}(\mathsf{p}, r) : \mathsf{crs} = ([\bar{\boldsymbol{A}}, \boldsymbol{C}_1, \boldsymbol{P}_2]_1, [\bar{\boldsymbol{A}}, \boldsymbol{C}_2, \boldsymbol{P}_1]_2) \wedge\\ \mathsf{BLS.PARV}(\mathsf{lpar}) = 1 \wedge \mathsf{BLS.CV}(\mathsf{lpar}, \mathsf{crs}) = 1 \wedge\\ (\boldsymbol{P}_1 + \boldsymbol{P}_2 \neq \boldsymbol{K}_1^\top \boldsymbol{M}_1 + \boldsymbol{K}_2^\top \boldsymbol{M}_2)\end{array}\right] \approx_\lambda 0.$$

3.2 Security Proof of BLS

Theorem 1. *Fix* λ, n_1, n_2, m, *let* $\tilde{n} = n_1 + n_2$. *Let* $\kappa = 2$. *Let* σ *be any efficient function. Let* $\mathcal{D}_\mathsf{p}$ *be a matrix distribution on* $[\boldsymbol{M}]_* \in \mathbb{G}_1^{n_1 \times m} \times \mathbb{G}_2^{n_2 \times m}$, *such that* $\tilde{n} - \operatorname{rank}(\boldsymbol{M}) \geq 1$, *where* $\boldsymbol{M} := \binom{\boldsymbol{M}_1}{\boldsymbol{M}_2}$. *Then (1)* BLS *is perfectly complete and perfectly zero-knowledge. (2) If* $(\mathcal{D}_\mathsf{p}, \kappa, \mathcal{D}_\kappa)$-GHR-KE *holds relative to* Pgen, *then* BLS *is perfectly persistent zero-knowledge. (3) Assume* $\mathcal{D}_\kappa$ *is efficiently verifiable. If* $\mathcal{D}_\kappa$-SKerMDH^{dl} *holds relative to* Pgen, *then* BLS *is computationally adaptively sound. (4) Assume* $\mathcal{D}_\mathsf{p}$ *is* σ-*witness-sampleable and* $\mathcal{D}_\kappa$

is efficiently verifiable. If $\mathcal{D}_\kappa$-SKerMDH *holds relative to* Pgen *then* BLS *is computationally quasi-adaptively* σ*-strongly sound. (5) Assume that* $\mathcal{D}_\kappa$ *is robust. If* BLS *is computationally adaptively sound and* $\mathrm{SDL}^{\mathrm{dl}}$ *holds relative to* Pgen, *then* BLS *is computationally adaptively knowledge-sound in the AGM.*

4 A Non-adaptive SNARK FANA for QAP

Next, we propose a non-adaptively sound Sub-ZK SNARK FANA for QAP by following the ideas from [10,12] who proposed (quasi-adaptively sound) QA-SNARGs for SSP and SAP. A significant difference between QAP and SSP/SAP is that in QAP, one has to deal with different polynomials $u_j(X)$ and $v_j(X)$ in groups $\mathbb{G}_1$ and $\mathbb{G}_2$; this complicates the argument system since one has to include a functional SSB commitment in both groups. (In both [10,12], a functional SSB commitment is only given in $\mathbb{G}_1$.) On top of doing a version of the usual zk-SNARK with perfectly-hiding commitments to the evaluations $\mathsf{a} = A(x)$, $\mathsf{b} = B(x)$, and $\mathsf{c} = C(x)$ of three polynomials $A(X), B(X), C(X)$ (see Eq. (3); here, x is a trapdoor), we add (in both groups) a functional SSB commitment to specific values, explained later. We then use a bilateral subspace argument system [19] to show that all commitments are consistent.

More precisely, let $u(X)$, $v(X)$, and $w(X)$ be defined as in Sect. 2. In the new zk-SNARG, we define the following polynomials with randomizers r_a, r_b, r_c:

$$\begin{aligned} A(X) &= u(X) + r_a Z(X),\\ B(X) &= v(X) + r_b Z(X),\\ C(X) &= w(X) + r_c Z(X),\\ h(X) &= (A(X)B(X) - C(X))/Z(X)\\ &= (u(X)v(X) - w(X))/Z(X) + (r_a v(X) + r_b u(X) - r_c) + r_a r_b Z(X). \end{aligned} \tag{3}$$

V checks $[\mathsf{a}]_1 \bullet [\mathsf{b}]_2 - [\mathsf{c}]_1 \bullet [1]_2 = [h(x)]_1 [Z(x)]_2$, where $[\mathsf{a} = A(x), \mathsf{c} = C(x)]_1$, $[\mathsf{b} = B(x)]_2$ are circuit-dependent perfectly-hiding commitments. Intuitively, V checks $[V(x)]_2 = [0]_2$, where $V(X) := A(X)B(X) - C(X) - h(X)Z(X)$.

Let $[\boldsymbol{g}_u]_1 \leftarrow \mathsf{FSSB}_1.\mathsf{KC}(\mathsf{p}, m+2, N_1, [\mathbf{N}_u]_1)$ and $[\boldsymbol{g}_v]_2 \leftarrow \mathsf{FSSB}_2.\mathsf{KC}(\mathsf{p}, m+1, N_2, [\mathbf{N}_v]_2)$ be commitment keys of the functional SSB commitment scheme, with $\boldsymbol{g}_u \in \mathbb{Z}_p^{(N_1+1)\times(m+3)}$ and $\boldsymbol{g}_v \in \mathbb{Z}_p^{(N_2+1)\times(m+2)}$. Here, N_1 and N_2 are locality parameters set to $N_1 := 4$ and $N_2 := 2$. (We define $[\mathbf{N}_u]_1$ and $[\mathbf{N}_v]_2$ in Lemma 3; the choice of N_1 and N_2 will become later.)

In addition, we commit to the bases $\boldsymbol{u}(X) = (u_i(X))_{i=1}^m$, $\boldsymbol{v}(X) = (v_i(X))_{i=1}^m$, and $\boldsymbol{w}(X) = (w_i(X))_{i=1}^m$. For example, $[\mathsf{c}]_1 = \sum_{j=1}^m \mathbb{z}_j [w_j(x)]_1 + r_c [Z(x)]_1$. Since $w_j(X) = \sum_{i=1}^n W_{ij} \ell_i(X)$, then $[\mathsf{c}]_1 = \sum_{i=1}^n \sum_{j=1}^m W_{ij} \mathbb{z}_j [\ell_i(X)]_1 + r_c [Z(x)]_1 = \sum_{i=1}^n \sum_{j=1}^m (\boldsymbol{W}\mathbb{z})_i [\ell_i(X)]_1 + r_c [Z(x)]_1 = [\boldsymbol{g}_\ell]_1 \binom{\boldsymbol{W}\mathbb{z}}{r_c}$, where $[\boldsymbol{g}_\ell]_\iota := [\ell_1(x), \dots, \ell_n(x), Z(x)]_\iota$. Thus, $[\mathsf{c}]_1$ is an interpolation commitment [33] to the vector $\boldsymbol{W}\mathbb{z}$ (i.e., the vector of all output wires of all multiplication gates) with the randomness r_c. Similar formulas hold for $[\mathsf{a}]_1$ and $[\mathsf{b}]_2$.

Let $\hat{\boldsymbol{G}} = (\boldsymbol{I}_{m_0} \| \boldsymbol{0}_{m_0 \times (m-m_0)}) \in \mathbb{Z}_p^{m_0 \times m}$. Let $\hat{u}_i(X) = 0$ for $i \le m_0$ and $\hat{u}_i(X) = u_i(X)$ for $i > m_0$. Using $\hat{u}_i(X)$ instead of $u_i(X)$ helps us to prove efficiently that the prover used the correct public input $(\mathbb{z}_1, \ldots, \mathbb{z}_{m_0})^\top = \mathbb{x}$. We use BLS to prove that several commitments commit to the same message while using different commitment keys, with

$$\boldsymbol{H}_1 = \left(\begin{array}{ccc|ccc|cc} \hat{\boldsymbol{G}}^{(1)} & \ldots & \hat{\boldsymbol{G}}^{(m)} & \boldsymbol{0}_{m_0} & \boldsymbol{0}_{m_0} & \boldsymbol{0}_{m_0} & \boldsymbol{0}_{m_0} & \boldsymbol{0}_{m_0} \\ \hat{u}_1(x) & \ldots & \hat{u}_m(x) & Z(x) & 0 & 0 & 0 & 0 \\ w_1(x) & \ldots & w_m(x) & 0 & 0 & Z(x) & 0 & 0 \\ \boldsymbol{g}_u^{(1)} & \ldots & \boldsymbol{g}_u^{(m)} & \boldsymbol{g}_u^{(m+1)} & \boldsymbol{0}_{N_1+1} & \boldsymbol{g}_u^{(m+2)} & \boldsymbol{g}_u^{(m+3)} & \boldsymbol{0}_{N_1+1} \end{array}\right).$$

$$\boldsymbol{H}_2 = \left(\begin{array}{ccc|ccc|cc} v_1(x) & \ldots & v_m(x) & 0 & Z(x) & 0 & 0 & 0 \\ \boldsymbol{g}_v^{(1)} & \ldots & \boldsymbol{g}_v^{(m)} & \boldsymbol{0}_{N_2+1} & \boldsymbol{g}_v^{(m+1)} & \boldsymbol{0}_{N_2+1} & \boldsymbol{0}_{N_2+1} & \boldsymbol{g}_v^{(m+2)} \end{array}\right). \quad (4)$$

Here, $\boldsymbol{H}_1 \in \mathbb{Z}_p^{(m_0+N_1+3)\times(m+5)}$ and $\boldsymbol{H}_2 \in \mathbb{Z}_p^{(N_2+2)\times(m+5)}$. The witness is $(\mathbb{z}, r_a, r_b, r_c, r_u, r_v)$, where r_u and r_v are randomizers needed to randomize additional commitments.[4]

We use the bilateral subspace argument system to guarantee that

$$(\mathbb{x}//\mathsf{a}//\mathsf{c}//\tilde{\mathsf{c}}_u//\mathsf{b}//\tilde{\mathsf{c}}_v) \in \text{colspace}\left(\begin{smallmatrix} \boldsymbol{H}_1 \\ \boldsymbol{H}_2 \end{smallmatrix}\right). \quad (5)$$

That is, there exists $\mathsf{BLS}.\mathbb{w} = (\mathbb{z} = \left(\begin{smallmatrix} \mathbb{x} \\ \mathbb{w} \end{smallmatrix}\right), r_a, r_b, r_c, r_u, r_v)$, such that

- $[\mathsf{a}]_1 = \sum_{j=1}^m \mathbb{z}_j [\hat{u}_j(x)]_1 + r_a [Z(x)]_1 = \sum_{j=m_0+1}^m \mathbb{z}_j [u_j(x)]_1 + r_a [Z(x)]_1$,
- $[\mathsf{c}]_1 = \sum_{j=1}^m \mathbb{z}_j [w_j(x)]_1 + r_c [Z(x)]_1$,
- $[\tilde{\mathsf{c}}_u]_1 = \mathsf{FSSB}_1.\mathsf{Com}([\boldsymbol{g}_u]_1; \mathbb{z}//r_a//r_c; r_u)$,
- $[\mathsf{b}]_2 = \sum_{j=1}^m \mathbb{z}_j [v_j(x)]_2 + r_b [Z(x)]_2$, and
- $[\tilde{\mathsf{c}}_v]_2 = \mathsf{FSSB}_1.\mathsf{Com}([\boldsymbol{g}_v]_2; \left(\begin{smallmatrix} \mathbb{z} \\ r_b \end{smallmatrix}\right); r_v)$.

4.1 Description of FANA

We depict FANA in Fig. 3. The CRS of FANA consists of the public elements needed to compute all the commitments, $[h(x)]_1$, and the bilateral subspace argument system. The input of P and V is $\mathbb{x}$. The argument π includes $[\mathsf{a}, \mathsf{c}]_1$ and $[\mathsf{b}]_2$ (perfectly-hiding commitments to $\boldsymbol{U}\mathbb{z}$, $\boldsymbol{W}\mathbb{z}$, and $\boldsymbol{V}\mathbb{z}$, with randomizers r_a, r_c, and r_b) and $[\tilde{\mathsf{c}}_u]_1$ and $[\tilde{\mathsf{c}}_v]_2$ (functional SSB commitments to $\mathbb{z}//r_a//r_c$ and $\left(\begin{smallmatrix} \mathbb{z} \\ r_b \end{smallmatrix}\right)$). On top of that, the argument also contains $[h(x)]_1$ and a bilateral subspace argument $\mathsf{BLS}.\pi$. Here, $h(X)$ is as in the description of the QAP.

5 FANA: Assumptions and Soundness Proofs

5.1 The QA-LINRES Assumption

In the full version [35], we reproduce the known assumptions n-TSDH [37] (a well-known, relatively standard pairing-based assumption), n-S-TSDH (Assumption 7 and Assumption 8 in [10]; used to prove the soundness of the SNARG

[4] In [12], the structure of corresponding matrices was different, and thus one ended up with dimensions $[\boldsymbol{H}_1]_1 \in \mathbb{G}_1^{(2m+2)\times(2m+3)}$, $[\boldsymbol{H}_2]_2 \in \mathbb{G}_2^{5\times(2m+3)}$.In particular, they used Elgamal encryption as a perfectly-binding commitment in $\mathbb{G}_1$ (resulting in the addend $2m$ in the number of rows of $\mathbb{G}_1$).

$\mathsf{K_{crs}}(\mathsf{p}, \mathbf{R}_{\mathcal{I}_{\mathsf{qap}}})$: // n is implicit in $\mathsf{p}, \mathbf{R}$, matrices are as in Eq. (4)

$\mathbf{N}_u \leftarrow_\$ \mathbb{Z}_p^{N_1 \times (m+1)}$; $([\boldsymbol{g}_u]_1, \mathsf{td}_u) \leftarrow \mathsf{FSSB}_1.\mathsf{KC}(\mathsf{p}, m+2, N_1, [\mathbf{N}_u]_1)$;

$\mathbf{N}_v \leftarrow_\$ \mathbb{Z}_p^{N_2 \times (m+1)}$; $([\boldsymbol{g}_v]_2, \mathsf{td}_v) \leftarrow \mathsf{FSSB}_2.\mathsf{KC}(\mathsf{p}, m+1, N_2, [\mathbf{N}_v]_2)$;

$x \leftarrow_\$ \mathbb{Z}_p^*$; Create $\mathsf{BLS.lpar} \leftarrow [\boldsymbol{H}]_*$ as in Eq. (4);

$(\mathsf{BLS.crs}, \mathsf{BLS.td}) \leftarrow \mathsf{BLS.K_{crs}}(\mathsf{p}, \mathsf{BLS.lpar})$;

$\mathsf{crs} \leftarrow ([\boldsymbol{g}_u, (x^i)_{i=0}^n]_1, [\boldsymbol{g}_v, (x^i)_{i=0}^n]_2, \mathsf{BLS.lpar}, \mathsf{BLS.crs})$; $\mathsf{td} \leftarrow \mathsf{BLS.td}$;

return $(\mathsf{crs}, \mathsf{td})$;

$\mathsf{CV}(\mathsf{crs})$: Create $\mathsf{BLS.lpar} \leftarrow [\boldsymbol{H}]_*$ as in Eq. (4); Check $\mathsf{BLS.CV}(\mathsf{BLS.lpar}, \mathsf{BLS.crs}) = 1$;

$\mathsf{P}(\mathsf{crs}, \mathbb{x} = (\mathbb{z}_1, \dots, \mathbb{z}_{m_0}); \mathbb{w} = (\mathbb{z}_j)_{j=m_0+1}^m)$:

1. $r_a, r_b, r_c, r_u, r_v \leftarrow_\$ \mathbb{Z}_p$;
2. $A(X) \leftarrow \sum_{j=1}^m \mathbb{z}_j u_j(X) + r_a Z(X)$; $B(X) \leftarrow \sum_{j=1}^m \mathbb{z}_j v_j(X) + r_b Z(X)$;
3. $C(X) \leftarrow \sum_{j=1}^m \mathbb{z}_j w_j(X) + r_c Z(X)$;
4. $h(X) \leftarrow (A(X)B(X) - C(X))/Z(X)$;
5. $[\mathsf{a}]_1 \leftarrow \sum_{j=m_0+1}^m \mathbb{z}_j [u_j(x)]_1 + r_a [Z(x)]_1$; $[\mathsf{c}]_1 \leftarrow \sum_{j=1}^m \mathbb{z}_j [w_j(x)]_1 + r_c [Z(x)]_1$; $[\mathsf{b}]_2 \leftarrow \sum_{j=1}^m \mathbb{z}_j [v_j(x)]_2 + r_b [Z(x)]_2$;
6. $[\tilde{\mathsf{c}}_u]_1 \leftarrow \mathsf{FSSB}_1.\mathsf{Com}([\boldsymbol{g}_u]_1; \mathbb{z}//r_a//r_c; r_u)$;
7. $[\tilde{\mathsf{c}}_v]_2 \leftarrow \mathsf{FSSB}_2.\mathsf{Com}([\boldsymbol{g}_v]_2; \binom{\mathbb{z}}{r_b}; r_v)$;
8. $[h(x)]_1 \leftarrow \sum_{i=0}^{n-2} h_i [x^i]_1$;
9. $\mathsf{BLS}.\mathbb{x} \leftarrow [\mathbb{x}//\mathsf{a}//\mathsf{c}//\tilde{\mathsf{c}}_u]_1 // [\mathsf{b}//\tilde{\mathsf{c}}_v]_2$;
10. $\mathsf{BLS}.\pi \leftarrow \mathsf{BLS.P}(\mathsf{BLS.lpar}, \mathsf{BLS.crs}; \mathsf{BLS}.\mathbb{x}; (\mathbb{z}, r_a, r_b, r_c, r_u, r_v))$;
11. $\pi \leftarrow ([\mathsf{a}, \mathsf{c}, \tilde{\mathsf{c}}_u, h(x)]_1, [\mathsf{b}, \tilde{\mathsf{c}}_v]_2, \mathsf{BLS}.\pi)$.

$\mathsf{V}(\mathsf{crs}, \mathbb{x} = (\mathbb{z}_1, \dots, \mathbb{z}_{m_0}); \pi)$:

$\mathsf{BLS}.\mathbb{x} \leftarrow [\mathbb{x}//\mathsf{a}//\mathsf{c}//\tilde{\mathsf{c}}_u]_1 // [\mathsf{b}//\tilde{\mathsf{c}}_v]_2$;

check $\mathsf{BLS.V}(\mathsf{BLS.lpar}, \mathsf{BLS.crs}, \mathsf{BLS}.\mathbb{x}, \mathsf{BLS}.\pi)$ accepts and $([\mathsf{a}]_1 + \sum_{j=1}^{m_0} \mathbb{z}_j [u_j(x)]_1) \bullet [\mathsf{b}]_2 - [\mathsf{c}]_1 \bullet [1]_2 = [h(x)]_1 \bullet [Z(x)]_2$.

$\mathsf{Sim}(\mathsf{crs}, \mathsf{td} = \mathsf{BLS.td}, \mathbb{x} = (\mathbb{z}_1, \dots, \mathbb{z}_{m_0}))$:

1. $r_u, r_v, \mu_1, \mu_2, \mu_3 \leftarrow_\$ \mathbb{Z}_p$;
2. $[\mathsf{a}]_1 \leftarrow \mu_1 [Z(x)]_1 - \sum_{j=1}^{m_0} \mathbb{z}_j [u_j(x)]_1$; $[\mathsf{b}]_2 \leftarrow \mu_2 [Z(x)]_2$;
3. $[\mathsf{c}]_1 \leftarrow \mu_3 [Z(x)]_1$;
4. $[\tilde{\mathsf{c}}_u]_1 \leftarrow \mathsf{FSSB}_1.\mathsf{Com}([\boldsymbol{g}_u]_1; \mathbf{0}_{m+2}; r_u)$;
5. $[\tilde{\mathsf{c}}_v]_2 \leftarrow \mathsf{FSSB}_2.\mathsf{Com}([\boldsymbol{g}_v]_2; \mathbf{0}_{m+1}; r_v)$;
6. $[h(x)]_1 \leftarrow \mu_1 \mu_2 [Z(x)]_1 - \mu_3 [1]_1$;
7. $\mathsf{BLS}.\mathbb{x} \leftarrow [\mathbb{x}//\mathsf{a}//\mathsf{c}//\tilde{\mathsf{c}}_u]_1 // [\mathsf{b}//\tilde{\mathsf{c}}_v]_2$;
8. $\mathsf{BLS}.\pi \leftarrow \mathsf{BLS.Sim}(\mathsf{BLS.lpar} = [\boldsymbol{H}]_*, \mathsf{BLS.crs}, \mathsf{BLS.td}; \mathsf{BLS}.\mathbb{x})$.
9. $\pi \leftarrow ([\mathsf{a}, \mathsf{c}, \tilde{\mathsf{c}}_u, h(x)]_1, [\mathsf{b}, \tilde{\mathsf{c}}_v]_2, \mathsf{BLS}.\pi)$.

Fig. 3. New zk-SNARK FANA for QAP.

DGPRS for SSP), n-Q-TSDH (Assumption 8 in [10]; used to prove the soundness of range proofs and some other argument systems), and n-SA-TSDH [12] (used to prove the soundness of a SNARG for SAP). The last three assumptions are known to hold under if n-TSDH and a suitable knowledge assumption hold. One can similarly define a new TSDH-related assumption QA-TSDH (see the full version [35]) to prove the non-adaptive soundness of FANA.

While $\{\mathsf{S}, \mathsf{Q}, \mathsf{SA}, \mathsf{QA}\}$TSDH naturally extend the well-known assumption TSDH, they look complicated. Each of them is intrinsically related to the underlying language: S-TSDH is related to the SSP language, SA-TSDH is related to the SAP language, and QA-TSDH is related to the QAP language. Since SAP is a more involved language than SSP, SA-TSDH is more involved than S-TSDH.

Most importantly, in $\{\mathsf{S}, \mathsf{Q}, \mathsf{SA}, \mathsf{QA}\}$TSDH, $\mathcal{A}$ returns an element $[\nu]_T$ of the target group $\mathbb{G}_T$. The widely-accepted way to motivate the security of an assumption like $\{\mathsf{S}, \mathsf{Q}, \mathsf{SA}, \mathsf{QA}\}$TSDH is to analyze its security in the generic group model GGM, or in some of its weakenings like the algebraic group mode, AGM [15]. As explained in [26], in pairing-based settings, $\mathbb{G}_T$, being a subgroup of the multiplicative group of a finite field, should not be thought of as a generic group. Instead, [26] proposed the *semi-GGM*, where only $\mathbb{G}_1$ and $\mathbb{G}_2$ are considered to be generic groups. Since an $\{\mathsf{S}, \mathsf{Q}, \mathsf{SA}, \mathsf{QA}\}$TSDH adversary returns $[\nu]_T$ in the target group, $\{\mathsf{S}, \mathsf{Q}, \mathsf{SA}, \mathsf{QA}\}$TSDH is not secure in the semi-GGM.

Fortunately, this is a problem of the concrete assumptions, not intrinsic to the QA-SNARGs. We prove that FANA is sound under a different assumption, QA-LINRES, where the adversary *only returns elements in* $\mathbb{G}_1$ and $\mathbb{G}_2$.

Definition 2 (QA-LINRES). *n-Quadratic Arithmetic Linear Residuosity (n-QA-LINRES) holds relative to* Pgen, *if* $\forall$ *PPT* $\mathcal{A}$, $\mathsf{Adv}^{\text{qa-linres}}_{\mathsf{Pgen},n,\mathcal{A}}(\lambda) = \mathsf{negl}(\lambda)$, *where* $\mathsf{Adv}^{\text{qa-linres}}_{\mathsf{Pgen},n,\mathcal{A}}(\lambda) :=$

$$\Pr\left[\begin{array}{l} \mathsf{p} \leftarrow \mathsf{Pgen}(1^\lambda); x, y \leftarrow_{\$} \mathbb{Z}_p^*; \mathsf{ck} \leftarrow (([x^i]_1, [x^i]_2)_{i=0}^n, [y]_1, [y]_2); \pi \leftarrow \mathcal{A}(\mathsf{p}, \mathsf{ck}) : \\ \pi = \left(\mathsf{J}, [A(x), \alpha_u(x), \hat{\beta}_u, C(x), \alpha_w(x), \hat{\beta}_w, h(x)]_1, [B(x), \alpha_v(x), \hat{\beta}_v]_2\right) \wedge \\ A(x) = \alpha_u(x)(x - \omega^{\mathsf{J}-1}) + \hat{\beta}_u/y \wedge B(x) = \alpha_v(x)(x - \omega^{\mathsf{J}-1}) + \hat{\beta}_v/y \wedge \\ C(x) = \alpha_w(x)(x - \omega^{\mathsf{J}-1}) + \hat{\beta}_w/y \wedge A(x)B(x) - C(x) = h(x)Z(x) \wedge \\ \hat{\beta}_u\hat{\beta}_v \neq \hat{\beta}_w y \end{array}\right].$$

QA-LINRES is falsifiable since the challenger who created x and y can efficiently verify that the conditions hold. Like $\{*\}$TSDH, QA-LINRES is parameterized by n (the size of the instance) but does not depend on the instance otherwise.

Next, we will motivate the choice of the assumption. The penultimate equality above, $A(x)B(x) - C(x) = h(x)Z(x)$, is the key equation of the QAP. The first three equalities are explicitly motivated by the soundness proof of FANA; they intuitively guarantee that (say) when one divides the polynomial $A(X)$ with $X - \omega^{\mathsf{J}-1}$, then the remainder is (integer) β_u and the quotient is the polynomial $\alpha_u(X)$. To guarantee that (say) β_u is an integer (and thus does not depend on x), the $\{\mathsf{S}, \mathsf{Q}, \mathsf{SA}, \mathsf{QA}\}$TSDH assumptions introduce a new indeterminate y and require that the adversary also outputs $[\beta_u y]_1$. Since ck only contains $[y]_1$ (and no $[x^i y]_1$), it means that an algebraic adversary must know the integer β_u.

This trick means that in the case of the say SA-TSDH assumption (see the full version, [35]), the adversary has to return $[\beta_u, \beta_w]_1$ together with knowledge-components $[\hat{\beta}_w, \hat{\beta}_w]_1$; this makes the assumption more complicated. Moreover, in the soundness proof, the reduction has to extract all four elements. While

$[\beta_u, \beta_w]_1$ can be extracted from the perfectly-binding commitment scheme, the other two are extracted from the functional SSB commitment scheme, making the output of the functional SSB commitment longer. Following this blueprint, in the case of the QA-SNARG for QAP, there are three elements $[\beta_u, \beta_w]_1, [\beta_v]_2$ and thus there would be also three extra knowledge components $[\hat{\beta}_u, \hat{\beta}_w]_1, [\hat{\beta}_v]_2$.

In QA-LINRES, the adversary only has to return the knowledge-components $[\hat{\beta}_u, \hat{\beta}_w]_1, [\hat{\beta}_v]_2$ but not $[\beta_u, \beta_w]_1, [\beta_v]_2$. This results in a cleaner assumption (the adversary has to return fewer elements) and a more efficient QA-SNARG (the length of the functional SSB commitment is reduced by one group element).

Since the adversary of QA-LINRES does not output elements like $[\beta_u]_1$ together with their knowledge components anymore, the security of QA-LINRES cannot be directly ascertained under Damgård's knowledge-of-exponent assumptions. Hence, in the full version [35], we will prove that QA-LINRES holds in the AGM under the standard PDL assumption.

Theorem 2. *(1)* FANA *is perfectly complete. (2) If* BLS *is perfectly zero-knowledge and* FSSB_1 *and* FSSB_2 *are almost everywhere perfectly-hiding then* FANA *is perfectly zero-knowledge. (3) If* BLS *is perfectly persistent zero-knowledge,* FANA *is perfectly zero-knowledge, and* FSSB_1 *and* FSSB_2 *are computationally-hiding then* FANA *is Sub-ZK.*

Recall that if FSSB_ι is function-set hiding and almost everywhere perfectly-hiding, then it is also computationally-hiding; thus, for (3) it suffices if we assume function-set hiding and almost everywhere perfectly-hiding properties.

5.2 Non-adaptive Soundness of FANA

Our non-adaptive soundness proof proceeds in four games. In the last game, Game_4, we construct two reductions. The first reduction is to the quasi-adaptive σ-strong soundness (for a fixed σ_x) of BLS that guarantees that no PPT non-adaptive soundness adversary $\mathcal{A}$ is successful if there exists no witness $\mathsf{BLS}.\mathbb{w}$, s.t. Eq. (5) holds; this includes the case $\mathcal{A}$ used a wrong public input.

Assume now that there exists at least one witness $\mathsf{BLS}.\mathbb{w}$, such that Eq. (5) holds. Then, a successful $\mathcal{A}$ left at least one constraint unsatisfied. The adversary $\mathcal{B}_3$ (constructed in the second, QA-LINRES, reduction) samples $\mathsf{J} \leftarrow_\$ [1, n]$ and guesses that the Jth QAP constraint $(\boldsymbol{U}_\mathsf{J}\mathbb{z})(\boldsymbol{V}_\mathsf{J}\mathbb{z}) = \boldsymbol{W}_\mathsf{J}\mathbb{z}$ is unsatisfied. $\mathcal{B}_3$ aborts in Game_4 if the guess was correct. In Game_3 and Game_4, we modify the functional SSB scheme's commitment key to be able to extract six elements (namely, $([\hat{\alpha}_u(x), \hat{\beta}_u, \hat{\alpha}_w(x), \hat{\beta}_w]_1, [\hat{\alpha}_v(x), \hat{\beta}_v]_2$; other elements can be computed in a straightforward way) needed to break QA-LINRES. $\mathcal{B}_3$ works with the modified commitment keys; inside the QA-LINRES experiment, $\mathcal{B}_3$ aborts if $\mathcal{A}$ satisfied the Jth constraint. This incurs an n-times security loss.

Crucially, $\mathcal{B}_3$ makes the decision to abort based on the information in modified functional SSB commitment keys. Thus, we can only abort in the last game Game_4. This is the main reason why we have both a succinct argument (abortion is not based on information, extracted from the perfectly-binding commitment as in [10,12]) and non-adaptive soundness (in the adaptive case, $\mathcal{A}$ sees the modified commitment key before creating the input, and then it can covertly choose the unsatisfied constraint based on it).

With the modified commitment keys, $\hat{\beta}_u = \boldsymbol{U}_\mathsf{J}\mathbb{z}$, $\hat{\beta}_v = \boldsymbol{V}_\mathsf{J}\mathbb{z}$, and $\hat{\beta}_w = \boldsymbol{W}_\mathsf{J}\mathbb{z}$ for some $\mathbb{z}$. If $\mathcal{B}_3$ aborts, then $\hat{\beta}_u\hat{\beta}_v \neq \hat{\beta}_w$. (The quasi-adaptive σ_x-strong soundness of BLS guarantees that such a $\mathbb{z}$ exists.) Since $A(X) = \sum_{i=1}^{n} \boldsymbol{U}_i\mathbb{z}\ell_i(X) + r_a Z(X)$, we get $A(X) \equiv \boldsymbol{U}_\mathsf{J}\mathbb{z} \pmod{Z(X)}$ and thus $A(X) \equiv \boldsymbol{U}_\mathsf{J}\mathbb{z} \pmod{X - \omega^{\mathsf{J}-1}}$. Similarly, $B(X) \equiv \boldsymbol{V}_\mathsf{J}\mathbb{z} \pmod{X - \omega^{\mathsf{J}-1}}$ and $C(X) \equiv \boldsymbol{W}_\mathsf{J}\mathbb{z} \pmod{X - \omega^{\mathsf{J}-1}}$. Thus, for some polynomials $\alpha_u(X)$, $\alpha_v(X)$, and $\alpha_w(X)$,

$$A(X) = \alpha_u(X)(X - \omega^{\mathsf{J}-1}) + \hat{\beta}_u, \quad B(X) = \alpha_v(X)(X - \omega^{\mathsf{J}-1}) + \hat{\beta}_v,$$
$$C(X) = \alpha_w(X)(X - \omega^{\mathsf{J}-1}) + \hat{\beta}_w.$$

In the malicious case, $[\hat{\beta}_u]_1$, $[\hat{\beta}_v]_2$, and $[\hat{\beta}_w]_1$ can depend on x; e.g., $[\hat{\beta}_u]_1 = [\hat{\beta}_u(x)]_1$. Consider first the case $y = 1$. Then, the verification equation $A(X)B(X) - C(X) = h(X)Z(X)$ guarantees that $\hat{\beta}_u(X)\hat{\beta}_v(X) - \hat{\beta}_w(X) \equiv 0 \pmod{X - \omega^{\mathsf{J}-1}}$ as a polynomial while the QA-LINRES assumption states $\hat{\beta}_u\hat{\beta}_v \neq \hat{\beta}_w$. To obtain a contradiction, we need to guarantee that $\mathcal{B}_3$ returned $([\hat{\beta}_u, \hat{\beta}_w]_1, [\hat{\beta}_v]_2)$, such that $\hat{\beta}_u$, $\hat{\beta}_v$, and $\hat{\beta}_w$ do not depend on x. We achieve this by sampling a random y and adding $([y]_1, [y]_2)$ to crs; then an algebraic adversary can create (say) $[\hat{\beta}_u]_1 = [\boldsymbol{U}_\mathsf{J}\mathbb{z}y]_1$, such that $\hat{\beta}_u/y$ is in a non-trivial relation only if $\hat{\beta}_u$ does not depend on the trapdoor x.

Importantly, the non-adaptive soundness of FANA follows from falsifiable assumptions. Knowing which constraint J was unsatisfied, we use the local extractability of the functional SSB scheme to recover a succinct local witness that allows one to reduce the non-adaptive soundness to QA-LINRES. Thus, we do not need to have a perfectly-binding commitment. In comparison, [10,12] used witness-sampleability to extract some elements of that local witness from the perfectly-binding commitment scheme.

Let $\sigma_x : \mathsf{ltrap} \mapsto x$. Clearly, σ_x can be computed efficiently: given $(\boldsymbol{H}_1, \boldsymbol{H}_2)$, σ_x uses one of the entries of $\boldsymbol{H}_1$ that contains $Z(x)$ to compute the value of x. For $\iota \in \{1,2\}$, let FSSB_ι be the Fauzi-Lipmaa-Pindado-Siim functional SSB commitment scheme in $\mathbb{G}_\iota$. Let BLS be the González-Hevia-Ràfols bilateral subspace argument system. Let $N_1 = 4$ and $N_2 = 2$.

Theorem 3. *Assume that* FSSB_ι *is locally* $[\cdot]_\iota$*-extractable and function-set hiding for* $\iota \in \{1,2\}$, BLS *is quasi-adaptively* σ_x*-strongly sound, and* n-QA-LINRES *holds relative to* Pgen. *Then the QA-SNARK* FANA *from Fig. 3 is non-adaptively sound. More precisely, there exist PPT adversaries* $\mathcal{B}_1, \mathcal{B}'_1, \mathcal{B}_2, \mathcal{B}_3$ *against the function-set hiding property of* FSSB_1*, the function-set hiding property of* FSSB_2*, the quasi-adaptive* σ_x*-strong soundness of* BLS*, and the* n-QA-LINRES *assumption, respectively, such that*

$$\mathsf{Adv}^{\mathrm{nas}}_{\mathsf{Pgen},\mathsf{FANA},\mathcal{A}}(\lambda) \leq \mathsf{Adv}^{\mathrm{fsh}}_{\mathsf{FSSB}_1,m+2,N_1,\mathcal{B}_1}(\lambda) + \mathsf{Adv}^{\mathrm{fsh}}_{\mathsf{FSSB}_2,m+1,N_2,\mathcal{B}'_1}(\lambda) + \mathsf{Adv}^{\sigma_x-\mathrm{strsound}}_{\mathsf{Pgen},\mathsf{BLS},\mathcal{B}_2}(\lambda) + n \cdot \mathsf{Adv}^{\mathrm{qa\text{-}linres}}_{\mathsf{Pgen},n,\mathcal{B}_3}(\lambda).$$

For the quasi-adaptive σ_x-strong soundness of BLS, the language parameter distribution of BLS must be σ_x-witness-sampleable. On the other hand, [10,12] assumed that BLS.lpar is witness-sampleable and thus also lpar for their QA-SNARG (for SSP/SAP) is witness-sampleable; by this reason alone, their SNARGs are only quasi-adaptively sound (i.e., sound, assuming lpar is honestly generated). FANA is not a QA-SNARG and thus has no language parameter.

Proof. (of Theorem 3). The non-adaptive soundness proof consists of the following games. Let $\mathcal{A}$ be an adversary against the non-adaptive soundness. We recall that in the terminology of arithmetic circuits, $\mathcal{A}$ has two avenues of cheating: either by using a wrong public input or by leaving some constraints unsatisfied.

Game_1: this is the non-adaptive soundness game for non-QA NIZKs (see page 14 but remember that in the case of NIZKs, there is no lpar). The output is 1 if $\mathcal{A}$ produces a false accepting proof, i.e., either (1) there exists at least one constraint i, such that $(\boldsymbol{U}\mathbb{z})_i(\boldsymbol{V}\mathbb{z})_i \neq (\boldsymbol{W}\mathbb{z})_i$, or (2) the various committed values are either different or do not start with $\mathbb{x}$.

Game_2: This game also samples $\mathsf{J} \leftarrow_\$ [1, n]$ as a guess for the unsatisfied equation i in the case (1).

Game_3: Let $\delta_{uj}(X)$ (resp., $\delta_{wj}(X)$ / $\delta_Z(X)$) be the quotient of the division of $u_j(X)$ (resp., $w_j(X)$ / $Z(X)$) with $X - \omega^{\mathsf{J}-1}$. We will show later that the remainder is $U_{\mathsf{J}j}$ (resp., $W_{\mathsf{J}j}$ / 0). We redefine the commitment key of the FSSB_1 scheme as $([\boldsymbol{g}_u]_1, \mathsf{td}_u) \leftarrow \mathsf{FSSB}_1.\mathsf{KC}(\mathsf{p}, m+2, N_1, [\mathbf{N}_u]_1)$ for

$$[\mathbf{N}_u]_1 \leftarrow \begin{bmatrix} \delta_{u1}(x) & \dots & \delta_{um}(x) & \delta_Z(x) & 0 \\ U_{\mathsf{J}1}y & \dots & U_{\mathsf{J}m}y & 0 & 0 \\ \delta_{w1}(x) & \dots & \delta_{wm}(x) & 0 & \delta_Z(x) \\ W_{\mathsf{J}1}y & \dots & W_{\mathsf{J}m}y & 0 & 0 \end{bmatrix}_1 \in \mathbb{G}_1^{N_1 \times (m+2)}. \quad (6)$$

In Lemma 3, this change allows us to use the local extractability of FSSB_1 to extract $[\hat{\alpha}_u, \hat{\beta}_u, \hat{\alpha}_w, \hat{\beta}_w]_1 (= [\alpha_u(x), \hat{\beta}_u, \alpha_w(x), \hat{\beta}_w]_1)$ related to the QA-LINRES assumption (see Definition 2).

Game_4: Let $\delta_{vj}(X)$ be the quotient of the division of $v_j(X)$ with $X - \omega^{\mathsf{J}-1}$. We will show later that the remainder is $V_{\mathsf{J}j}$. We redefine the commitment key of the FSSB_2 scheme as $([\boldsymbol{g}_v]_2, \mathsf{td}_v) \leftarrow \mathsf{FSSB}_2.\mathsf{KC}(\mathsf{p}, m+1, N_2, [\mathbf{N}_v]_2)$ for

$$[\mathbf{N}_v]_2 \leftarrow \begin{bmatrix} \delta_{v1}(x) & \dots & \delta_{vm}(x) & \delta_Z(x) \\ V_{\mathsf{J}1}y & \dots & V_{\mathsf{J}m}y & 0 \end{bmatrix}_2 \in \mathbb{G}_2^{N_2 \times (m+1)}. \quad (7)$$

In Lemma 3, this change allows us to use the local extractability of FSSB_2 to extract $[\hat{\alpha}_v, \hat{\beta}_v]_2 (= [\alpha_v(x), \hat{\beta}_v]_2)$ related to the QA-LINRES assumption.

We show that in Game_4, either one can (1) break the quasi-adaptive σ_x-strong soundness of BLS or (2) with probability $1/n$, compute $[\hat{\beta}_u, \hat{\beta}_w]_1$ and $[\hat{\beta}_v]_2$, where $\hat{\beta}_u/y = \boldsymbol{U}_{\mathsf{J}}\mathbb{z}$, $\hat{\beta}_v/y = \boldsymbol{V}_{\mathsf{J}}\mathbb{z}$, and $\hat{\beta}_w/y = \boldsymbol{W}_{\mathsf{J}}\mathbb{z}$, and thus break QA-LINRES. (Here, we need FSSB_ι to be locally $[\cdot]_\iota$-extractable.)

See Fig. 4 for the formal description of all games.

Game_1 and Game_2 are clearly indistinguishable.

Lemma 1. *There exist a PPT adversary $\mathcal{B}_1$, such that* $|\Pr[\mathsf{Game}_3(\mathcal{A}) = 1] - \Pr[\mathsf{Game}_2(\mathcal{A}) = 1]| \leq \mathsf{Adv}^{\mathsf{fsh}}_{\mathsf{FSSB}_1, m+2, N_1, \mathcal{B}_1}(\lambda)$.

Game$_1$ / Game$_2$ / Game$_3$ / Game$_4$
$\mathsf{p} \leftarrow \mathsf{Pgen}(1^\lambda); \mathbb{x} \leftarrow \mathcal{A}(\mathsf{p});$ // Non-adaptive NIZK soundness adversary $\mathcal{A}$ (no lpar)
$\mathsf{J} \leftarrow_\$ [1, n];$ $(\mathsf{crs}, \mathsf{td}) \leftarrow \mathsf{K_{crs}}(\mathsf{p}); \pi \leftarrow \mathcal{A}(\mathsf{crs});$
if $\mathsf{V}(\mathsf{crs}, \mathbb{x}, \pi) = 1 \wedge \neg(\exists \mathbb{w}.\mathbf{R}(\mathbb{x}, \mathbb{w}) = 1)$ **then return** 1; **else return** 0; **fi** ;
$\mathsf{K_{crs}}(\mathsf{p})$
$\mathcal{N}_u \leftarrow_\$ \mathbb{Z}_p^{N_1 \times (m+1)}; ([\boldsymbol{g}_u]_1, \mathsf{td}_u) \leftarrow \mathsf{FSSB_1.KC}(\mathsf{p}, m+2, N_1, [\mathcal{N}_u]_1);$
Choose $[\mathcal{N}_u]_1$ as in Eq. (6); $([\boldsymbol{g}_u]_1, \mathsf{td}_u) \leftarrow \mathsf{FSSB_1.KC}(\mathsf{p}, m+2, N_1, [\mathcal{N}_u]_1);$
$\mathcal{N}_v \leftarrow_\$ \mathbb{Z}_p^{N_2 \times (m+1)}; ([\boldsymbol{g}_v]_2, \mathsf{td}_v) \leftarrow \mathsf{FSSB_2.KC}(\mathsf{p}, m+1, N_2, [\mathcal{N}_v]_2);$
Choose $[\mathcal{N}_v]_2$ as in Eq. (7); $([\boldsymbol{g}_v]_2, \mathsf{td}_v) \leftarrow \mathsf{FSSB_2.KC}(\mathsf{p}, m+1, N_2, [\mathcal{N}_v]_2);$
$x \leftarrow_\$ \mathbb{Z}_p^*$; Create $\mathsf{BLS.lpar} \leftarrow [\boldsymbol{H}]_*$ as in Eq. (4);
$(\mathsf{BLS.crs}, \mathsf{BLS.td}) \leftarrow \mathsf{BLS.K_{crs}}(\mathsf{p}, \mathsf{BLS.lpar});$
$\mathsf{crs} \leftarrow ([\boldsymbol{g}_u, (x^i)_{i=0}^n]_1, [\boldsymbol{g}_v, (x^i)_{i=0}^n]_2, \mathsf{BLS.lpar}, \mathsf{BLS.crs}); \mathsf{td} \leftarrow \mathsf{BLS.td};$
return $(\mathsf{crs}, \mathsf{td})$;

Fig. 4. Games in the proof of Theorem 3. Dotted boxed part is only in Game$_2$, dashed boxed part is only in Game$_3$, and boxed part is only in Game$_4$. The parts with several boxes are present in all corresponding games.

Proof. If $\mathcal{A}$'s success in the two games differs then one can distinguish between two different $[\boldsymbol{g}_u]_1$'s: the distinguisher $\mathcal{B}_1$ obtains $\mathbb{x}$ from $\mathcal{A}(\mathsf{p})$, creates crs from the correct Game$_2$ or Game$_3$ distribution but embedding $[\boldsymbol{g}_u]_1$ to it, and then obtains π from $\mathcal{A}$. If $\mathcal{A}$ succeeds, then $\mathcal{B}_1$ guesses that $[\boldsymbol{g}_u]_1$ was modified. Clearly, $\mathcal{B}_1$ has at least the same advantage as $\mathcal{A}$. □

The analysis of Lemma 2 is similar.

Lemma 2. *There exist a PPT adversary $\mathcal{B}_1'$, such that* $|\Pr[\mathsf{Game}_4(\mathcal{A}) = 1] - \Pr[\mathsf{Game}_3(\mathcal{A}) = 1]| \leq \mathsf{Adv}^{\mathsf{fsh}}_{\mathsf{FSSB}_2, m+1, N_2, \mathcal{B}_1'}(\lambda)$.

Finally, we bound the advantage of $\mathcal{A}$ in Game$_4$.

Lemma 3. *Assume* FSSB_1 *is locally* $[\cdot]_1$*-extractable and* FSSB_2 *is locally* $[\cdot]_2$*-extractable. There exist PPT adversaries* $\mathcal{B}_2$ *and* $\mathcal{B}_3$*, such that*

$$|\Pr[\mathsf{Game}_4(\mathcal{A}) = 1] \leq \mathsf{Adv}^{\sigma_{\mathsf{x}}-\mathsf{strsound}}_{\mathsf{Pgen},\mathsf{BLS},\mathcal{B}_2}(\lambda) + n \cdot \mathsf{Adv}^{\mathsf{qa\text{-}linres}}_{\mathsf{Pgen},n,\mathcal{B}_3}(\lambda).$$

Proof. Let $\mathcal{A}$ be a non-adaptive soundness adversary in Game$_4$. Let ev be the event that Eq. (5) does not hold, that is, there does not exist $\mathsf{BLS}.\mathbb{w} = (\mathbb{z}, r_a, r_b, r_c, r_{\mathsf{sph}}, r_u, r_v)$, such that Eq. (5) (and the paragraph after it) holds. Clearly,

$$\Pr[\mathsf{Game}_4(\mathcal{A}) = 1] \leq \Pr[\mathsf{Game}_4(\mathcal{A}) = 1|\mathsf{ev}] + \Pr[\mathsf{Game}_4(\mathcal{A}) = 1|\overline{\mathsf{ev}}].$$

First Reduction. We bound the first addend $\Pr[\mathsf{Game}_4(\mathcal{A}) = 1|\mathsf{ev}]$ by the advantage of an adversary $\mathcal{B}_2$ against the quasi-adaptive σ_x-strong soundness (see

$\mathcal{B}_2(\mathsf{p}, \mathsf{BLS.lpar} = [\boldsymbol{H}]_*, \sigma_x(\mathsf{BLS.ltrap}) = x, \mathsf{BLS.crs})$ // QA σ_x-strong soundness

$\mathbb{x} \leftarrow \mathcal{A}(\mathsf{p})$; // $\mathbb{x} = (\mathbb{z}_1, \ldots, \mathbb{z}_{m_0})$
$\mathbf{N}_u \leftarrow_\$ \mathbb{Z}_p^{N_1 \times (m+1)}$; $\mathbf{N}_v \leftarrow_\$ \mathbb{Z}_p^{N_2 \times (m+1)}$; // Generate crs
$([\boldsymbol{g}_u]_1, \mathsf{td}_u = (\mathsf{ek}_u, \mathsf{tk}_u)) \leftarrow \mathsf{FSSB}_1.\mathsf{KC}(\mathsf{p}, m+2, N_1, [\mathbf{N}_u]_1)$;
$([\boldsymbol{g}_v]_2, \mathsf{td}_v = (\mathsf{ek}_v, \mathsf{tk}_v)) \leftarrow \mathsf{FSSB}_2.\mathsf{KC}(\mathsf{p}, m+1, N_2, [\mathbf{N}_v]_2)$;
Create $\mathsf{BLS.lpar} \leftarrow [\boldsymbol{H}]_*$ as in Eq. (4);
$\mathsf{FANA.crs} \leftarrow ([\boldsymbol{g}_u, (x^i)_{i=0}^n]_1, [\boldsymbol{g}_v, (x^i)_{i=0}^n]_2, \mathsf{BLS.lpar}, \mathsf{BLS.crs})$;
$\pi \leftarrow \mathcal{A}(\mathsf{FANA.crs})$; // $\pi = ([\mathsf{a}, \mathsf{c}, \tilde{\mathsf{c}}_u, h(x)]_1, [\mathsf{b}, \tilde{\mathsf{c}}_v]_2, \mathsf{BLS}.\pi)$
$\mathsf{BLS}.\mathbb{x} \leftarrow ([\mathbb{x} // \mathsf{a} // \mathsf{c} // \tilde{\mathsf{c}}_u]_1 // [\mathsf{b} // \tilde{\mathsf{c}}_v]_2)$;
return $(\mathsf{BLS}.\mathbb{x}, \mathsf{BLS}.\pi)$;

$\mathcal{B}_3(\mathsf{p}, ([x^i]_1, [x^i]_2)_{i=0}^n, [y]_1, [y]_2)$ // QA-LINRES

$\mathbb{x} \leftarrow \mathcal{A}(\mathsf{p})$; // $\mathbb{x} = (\mathbb{z}_1, \ldots, \mathbb{z}_{m_0})$
$\mathbf{N}_u \leftarrow_\$ \mathbb{Z}_p^{N_1 \times (m+1)}$; $\mathbf{N}_v \leftarrow_\$ \mathbb{Z}_p^{N_2 \times (m+1)}$; // Generate crs
$([\boldsymbol{g}_u]_1, \mathsf{td}_u = (\mathsf{ek}_u, \mathsf{tk}_u)) \leftarrow \mathsf{FSSB}_1.\mathsf{KC}(\mathsf{p}, m+2, N_1, [\mathbf{N}_u]_1)$;
$([\boldsymbol{g}_v]_2, \mathsf{td}_v = (\mathsf{ek}_v, \mathsf{tk}_v)) \leftarrow \mathsf{FSSB}_2.\mathsf{KC}(\mathsf{p}, m+1, N_2, [\mathbf{N}_v]_2)$;
Create $\mathsf{BLS.lpar} = [\boldsymbol{H}]_*$ as in Eq. (4);
$\mathsf{BLS.crs} \leftarrow \mathsf{BLS.K_{crs}}(\mathsf{p}, \mathsf{BLS.lpar})$;
$\mathsf{FANA.crs} \leftarrow ([\boldsymbol{g}_u, (x^i)_{i=0}^n]_1, [\boldsymbol{g}_v, (x^i)_{i=0}^n]_2, \mathsf{BLS.lpar}, \mathsf{BLS.crs})$;
$\pi \leftarrow \mathcal{A}(\mathsf{FANA.crs})$; // $\pi = ([\mathsf{a}, \mathsf{c}, \tilde{\mathsf{c}}_u, h(x)]_1, [\mathsf{b}, \tilde{\mathsf{c}}_v]_2, \mathsf{BLS}.\pi)$
$[\hat{\alpha}_u, \hat{\beta}_u, \hat{\alpha}_w, \hat{\beta}_w]_1^\top \leftarrow \mathsf{FSSB}_1.\mathsf{LExt}(\mathsf{ek}_u; [\tilde{\mathsf{c}}_u]_1)$;
$[\hat{\alpha}_v, \hat{\beta}_v]_2^\top \leftarrow \mathsf{FSSB}_2.\mathsf{LExt}(\mathsf{ek}_v; [\tilde{\mathsf{c}}_v]_2)$;
$[\mathsf{a}']_1 \leftarrow [\mathsf{a}]_1 + \sum_{j=1}^{m_0} \mathbb{z}_j [u_j(x)]_1$;
if $[\hat{\beta}_u]_1 \bullet [\hat{\beta}_v]_2 = [\hat{\beta}_w]_1 \bullet [y]_2$ **then return** $\perp$;
else return $(\mathsf{J}, [\mathsf{a}', \hat{\alpha}_u, \hat{\beta}_u, \mathsf{c}, \hat{\alpha}_w, \hat{\beta}_w, h(x)]_1, [\mathsf{b}, \hat{\alpha}_v, \hat{\beta}_v]_2)$; **fi** ;

Fig. 5. The quasi-adaptive σ_x-strong soundness adversary $\mathcal{B}_2$ and the n-QA-LINRES adversary $\mathcal{B}_3$ in Lemma 3. $\mathcal{A}$ is a non-adaptive soundness adversary in Game_4.

page 15 for the definition) of BLS. In Fig. 5, we depict $\mathcal{B}_2$. $\mathcal{B}_2$ receives its input, sampled according to the distribution specified by Game_4. (The necessity to have $\sigma_x(\mathsf{ltrap}) = x$ as part of the input is precisely why BLS needs to be quasi-adaptively σ_x-*strongly* sound.) Given $\sigma_x(\mathsf{ltrap}) = x$, $\mathcal{B}_2$ constructs the rest of FANA.crs. Finally, $\mathcal{B}_2$ uses the output of $\mathcal{A}$ to break the quasi-adaptively σ_x-strong soundness of BLS. Thus, $\Pr[\mathsf{Game}_4(\mathcal{A}) = 1 | \mathsf{ev}] \le \mathsf{Adv}^{\sigma_x-\mathrm{strsound}}_{\mathsf{Pgen},\mathsf{BLS},\mathcal{B}_2}(\lambda)$.

Notably, quasi-adaptive σ_x-strong soundness of BLS suffices since BLS.lpar is a part of FANA.crs and thus honestly generated; moreover, σ_x is efficient.

Second Reduction. Assume $\mathsf{ev} = \mathsf{false}$. To bound the second addend $\Pr[\mathsf{Game}_4(\mathcal{A}) = 1 | \overline{\mathsf{ev}}]$, we construct an adversary $\mathcal{B}_3$ (see Fig. 5) against the n-QA-LINRES assumption. $\mathcal{B}_3$ queries $\mathcal{A}$ to obtain $\mathbb{x}$. After that, $\mathcal{B}_3$ uses its input to create FANA.crs according to the CRS distribution specified by the game (Game_3 or Game_4). $\mathcal{B}_3$ sends FANA.crs to $\mathcal{A}$, who outputs π. $\mathcal{B}_3$ uses the local extractability of FSSB_1 and FSSB_2 to extract certain values and then finishes as in Fig. 5, aborting when $\hat{\beta}_u \hat{\beta}_v \ne \hat{\beta}_w y$.

Let us explain why $\mathcal{B}_3$ succeeds with probability at least $1/n$. First, since FSSB_1 is locally $[\cdot]_1$-extractable and FSSB_2 is locally $[\cdot]_2$-extractable, $\mathcal{B}_3$ can extract $[\hat{\alpha}_u, \hat{\beta}_u, \hat{\alpha}_w, \hat{\beta}_w]_1 := [\mathbf{N}_u(\mathbb{z}//r_a//r_c)]_1 \leftarrow \mathsf{FSSB}_1.\mathsf{LExt}(\mathsf{ek}_u; [\tilde{\boldsymbol{c}}_u]_1)$ and $[\hat{\alpha}_v, \hat{\beta}_v]_2 := [\mathbf{N}_v(\binom{\mathbb{z}}{r_b})]_2 \leftarrow \mathsf{FSSB}_2.\mathsf{LExt}(\mathsf{ek}_v; [\tilde{\boldsymbol{c}}_v]_2)$. ($\mathsf{LExt}$ is defined as in Fig. 1).

We will next show that if that $\mathcal{B}_3$ does not abort, then it succeeds in breaking QA-LINRES. That is, the following conditions lifted from Definition 2 hold in relation to the values output by $\mathcal{B}_3$:

(a) $\hat{\beta}_u\hat{\beta}_v \neq \hat{\beta}_w y$,
(b) $\mathsf{a}' = \hat{\alpha}_u \cdot (x - \omega^{\mathsf{J}-1}) + \hat{\beta}_u/y$, where a' is as in Fig. 5 description of $\mathcal{B}_3$),
(c) $\mathsf{b} = \hat{\alpha}_v \cdot (x - \omega^{\mathsf{J}-1}) + \hat{\beta}_v/y$,
(d) $\mathsf{c} = \hat{\alpha}_w \cdot (x - \omega^{\mathsf{J}-1}) + \hat{\beta}_w/y$,
(e) $\mathsf{a}'\mathsf{b} - \mathsf{c} = h(x)Z(x)$.

Trivially, if $\mathcal{B}_3$ does not abort, then Item a holds. Since the FANA verifier accepts, $[\mathsf{a}']_1 \bullet [\mathsf{b}]_2 - [\mathsf{c}]_1 \bullet [1]_2 = [h(x)]_1 \bullet [Z(x)]_2$. Thus, Item e holds.

Next, since $\mathsf{ev} = \mathsf{false}$, there exists at least one $\mathsf{BLS}.\mathbb{w} = (\mathbb{z} = \binom{\mathbb{x}}{\mathbb{w}}, r_a, r_b, r_c, r_{\mathsf{sph}}, r_u, r_v)$, such that Eq. (5) holds. Fix *any* such $\mathsf{BLS}.\mathbb{w}$ (it does not have to be known to the reduction or even the one used by the adversary). Due to Eqs. (6) and (7), $\hat{\alpha}_u = \sum_{j=1}^{m} \mathbb{z}_j\delta_{uj}(x) + r_a\delta_Z(x)$ and $\hat{\beta}_u = (\sum_{j=1}^{m} \mathbb{z}_j U_{\mathsf{J}j})y = \boldsymbol{U}_{\mathsf{J}}\mathbb{z}y$. The quotient of $u_j(X)/(X-\omega^{\mathsf{J}-1})$ is $\delta_{uj}(X)$. Since $u_j(X) = \sum_{i=1}^{n} U_{ij}\ell_i(X)$, the remainder of $u_j(X)/(X - \omega^{\mathsf{J}-1})$ is $U_{\mathsf{J}j}$. Clearly, $Z(X) = \delta_Z(X)(X - \omega^{\mathsf{J}-1})$. Since Eq. (5) holds, $\mathsf{a}' = \sum_{j=1}^{m} \mathbb{z}_j u_j(x) + r_a Z(x) = \sum_{j=1}^{m} \mathbb{z}_j(\delta_{uj}(x)(x - \omega^{\mathsf{J}-1}) + U_{\mathsf{J}j}) + r_a\delta_Z(x)(x - \omega^{\mathsf{J}-1}) = \hat{\alpha}_u \cdot (x - \omega^{\mathsf{J}-1}) + \hat{\beta}_u/y$. Thus, Item b holds. Similarly, Item c and d hold. Hence, if $\mathcal{B}_3$ does not abort, then all five conditions hold.

Finally, we need to argue that $\mathcal{B}_3$ does not abort with a probability of at least $1/n$. Since $\mathsf{ev} = \mathsf{false}$, we have that $\mathsf{BLS}.\mathbb{w}$ starts with $\mathbb{w}$. Thus, according to Eq. (1), for $\mathcal{A}$ to be successful, there must exist an i such that $(\boldsymbol{U}\mathbb{z})_i(\boldsymbol{V}\mathbb{z})_i \neq (\boldsymbol{W}\mathbb{z})_i$. Since J is chosen uniformly at random and the non-adaptive soundness adversary $\mathcal{A}$ chooses the input before seeing crs, with probability $\geq 1/n$, the Jth constraint is not satisfied. Thus, with probability $\geq 1/n$, $A(X)B(X)-C(X)$ does not divide by $X-\omega^{\mathsf{J}-1}$, where A, B, C are defined as always. Then, $\beta := A(X)B(X)-C(X) \bmod (X-\omega^{\mathsf{J}-1})$ is non-zero. However, $\beta = (\boldsymbol{U}_{\mathsf{J}}\mathbb{z})(\boldsymbol{V}_{\mathsf{J}}\mathbb{z})-\boldsymbol{W}_{\mathsf{J}}\mathbb{z} = \hat{\beta}_u\hat{\beta}_v/y^2-\hat{\beta}_w/y$ and thus $\mathcal{B}_3$ does not abort with probability $\geq 1/n$. Thus, Item a holds with probability $\geq 1/n$.

Since (1) if $\mathcal{B}_3$ does not abort, then all five conditions hold, and (2) $\mathcal{B}_3$ does not abort with probability $\geq 1/n$, $\Pr[\mathsf{Game}_4(\mathcal{A}) = 1|\mathsf{ev}] \leq n \cdot \mathsf{Adv}^{\text{qa-linres}}_{\mathsf{Pgen},n,\mathcal{B}_3}(\lambda)$. □

Combining the lemmas proves the theorem. □

5.3 Adaptive Knowledge-Soundness of FANA

Theorem 4. *Assume the setting of Theorem 3. If* FANA *is non-adaptively sound and* BLS *is adaptively knowledge-sound, then* FANA *is non-adaptively knowledge-sound.*

Acknowledgment. We thank Prastudy Fauzi, Zaira Pindado, Carla Ràfols, Janno Siim, and anonymous reviewers for helpful comments.

References

1. Abdolmaleki, B., Baghery, K., Lipmaa, H., Zając, M.: A subversion-resistant SNARK. In: Takagi, T., Peyrin, T. (eds.) ASIACRYPT 2017, Part III. LNCS, vol. 10626, pp. 3–33. Springer, Cham (2017). https://doi.org/10.1007/978-3-319-70700-6_1
2. Abdolmaleki, B., Lipmaa, H., Siim, J., Zając, M.: On QA-NIZK in the BPK model. In: Kiayias, A., Kohlweiss, M., Wallden, P., Zikas, V. (eds.) PKC 2020, Part I. LNCS, vol. 12110, pp. 590–620. Springer, Cham (2020). https://doi.org/10.1007/978-3-030-45374-9_20
3. Abdolmaleki, B., Lipmaa, H., Siim, J., Zajac, M.: On subversion-resistant SNARKs. J. Cryptol. **34**(3), 1–42 (2021)
4. Abe, M., Fehr, S.: Perfect NIZK with adaptive soundness. In: Vadhan, S.P. (ed.) TCC 2007. LNCS, vol. 4392, pp. 118–136. Springer, Heidelberg (2007). https://doi.org/10.1007/978-3-540-70936-7_7
5. Bellare, M., Fuchsbauer, G., Scafuro, A.: NIZKs with an untrusted CRS: security in the face of parameter subversion. In: Cheon, J.H., Takagi, T. (eds.) ASIACRYPT 2016, Part II. LNCS, vol. 10032, pp. 777–804. Springer, Heidelberg (2016). https://doi.org/10.1007/978-3-662-53890-6_26
6. Bichsel, P., Camenisch, J., Neven, G., Smart, N.P., Warinschi, B.: Get shorty via group signatures without encryption. In: Garay, J.A., De Prisco, R. (eds.) SCN 2010. LNCS, vol. 6280, pp. 381–398. Springer, Heidelberg (2010). https://doi.org/10.1007/978-3-642-15317-4_24
7. Chung, K.M., Lin, H., Mahmoody, M., Pass, R.: On the power of nonuniformity in proofs of security. In: ITCS 2013, pp. 389–400 (2013)
8. Damgård, I.: Towards practical public key systems secure against chosen ciphertext attacks. In: Feigenbaum, J. (ed.) CRYPTO 1991. LNCS, vol. 576, pp. 445–456. Springer, Heidelberg (1992). https://doi.org/10.1007/3-540-46766-1_36
9. Danezis, G., Fournet, C., Groth, J., Kohlweiss, M.: Square span programs with applications to succinct NIZK arguments. In: Sarkar, P., Iwata, T. (eds.) ASIACRYPT 2014, Part I. LNCS, vol. 8873, pp. 532–550. Springer, Heidelberg (2014). https://doi.org/10.1007/978-3-662-45611-8_28
10. Daza, V., González, A., Pindado, Z., Ràfols, C., Silva, J.: Shorter quadratic QA-NIZK proofs. In: Lin, D., Sako, K. (eds.) PKC 2019, Part I. LNCS, vol. 11442, pp. 314–343. Springer, Cham (2019). https://doi.org/10.1007/978-3-030-17253-4_11
11. Escala, A., Herold, G., Kiltz, E., Ràfols, C., Villar, J.: An algebraic framework for Diffie-Hellman assumptions. In: Canetti, R., Garay, J.A. (eds.) CRYPTO 2013, Part II. LNCS, vol. 8043, pp. 129–147. Springer, Heidelberg (2013). https://doi.org/10.1007/978-3-642-40084-1_8
12. Fauzi, P., Lipmaa, H., Pindado, Z., Siim, J.: Somewhere statistically binding commitment schemes with applications. In: Borisov, N., Diaz, C. (eds.) FC 2021. LNCS, vol. 12674, pp. 436–456. Springer, Heidelberg (2021). https://doi.org/10.1007/978-3-662-64322-8_21
13. Feige, U., Lapidot, D., Shamir, A.: Multiple non-interactive zero knowledge proofs based on a single random string (extended abstract). In: 31st FOCS, pp. 308–317 (1990)

14. Fuchsbauer, G.: Subversion-zero-knowledge SNARKs. In: Abdalla, M., Dahab, R. (eds.) PKC 2018, Part I. LNCS, vol. 10769, pp. 315–347. Springer, Cham (2018). https://doi.org/10.1007/978-3-319-76578-5_11
15. Fuchsbauer, G., Kiltz, E., Loss, J.: The algebraic group model and its applications. In: Shacham, H., Boldyreva, A. (eds.) CRYPTO 2018, Part II. LNCS, vol. 10992, pp. 33–62. Springer, Cham (2018). https://doi.org/10.1007/978-3-319-96881-0_2
16. Gennaro, R., Gentry, C., Parno, B., Raykova, M.: Quadratic span programs and succinct NIZKs without PCPs. In: Johansson, T., Nguyen, P.Q. (eds.) EUROCRYPT 2013. LNCS, vol. 7881, pp. 626–645. Springer, Heidelberg (2013). https://doi.org/10.1007/978-3-642-38348-9_37
17. Gentry, C., Wichs, D.: Separating succinct non-interactive arguments from all falsifiable assumptions. In: 43rd ACM STOC, pp. 99–108 (2011)
18. Goldreich, O., Oren, Y.: Definitions and properties of zero-knowledge proof systems. J. Cryptol. **7**(1), 1–32 (1994)
19. González, A., Hevia, A., Ràfols, C.: QA-NIZK arguments in asymmetric groups: new tools and new constructions. In: Iwata, T., Cheon, J.H. (eds.) ASIACRYPT 2015, Part I. LNCS, vol. 9452, pp. 605–629. Springer, Heidelberg (2015). https://doi.org/10.1007/978-3-662-48797-6_25
20. González, A., Ráfols, C.: New techniques for non-interactive shuffle and range arguments. In: Manulis, M., Sadeghi, A.-R., Schneider, S. (eds.) ACNS 2016. LNCS, vol. 9696, pp. 427–444. Springer, Cham (2016). https://doi.org/10.1007/978-3-319-39555-5_23
21. González, A., Ràfols, C.: Shorter pairing based arguments under standard assumptions. In: Galbraith, S.D., Moriai, S. (eds.) ASIACRYPT 2019, Part III. LNCS, vol. 11923, pp. 728–757. Springer, Cham (2019). https://doi.org/10.1007/978-3-030-34618-8_25
22. Groth, J.: Short pairing-based non-interactive zero-knowledge arguments. In: Abe, M. (ed.) ASIACRYPT 2010. LNCS, vol. 6477, pp. 321–340. Springer, Heidelberg (2010). https://doi.org/10.1007/978-3-642-17373-8_19
23. Groth, J.: On the size of pairing-based non-interactive arguments. In: Fischlin, M., Coron, J.-S. (eds.) EUROCRYPT 2016, Part II. LNCS, vol. 9666, pp. 305–326. Springer, Heidelberg (2016). https://doi.org/10.1007/978-3-662-49896-5_11
24. Groth, J., Maller, M.: Snarky signatures: minimal signatures of knowledge from simulation-extractable SNARKs. In: Katz, J., Shacham, H. (eds.) CRYPTO 2017, Part II. LNCS, vol. 10402, pp. 581–612. Springer, Cham (2017). https://doi.org/10.1007/978-3-319-63715-0_20
25. Groth, J., Ostrovsky, R., Sahai, A.: Non-interactive zaps and new techniques for NIZK. In: Dwork, C. (ed.) CRYPTO 2006. LNCS, vol. 4117, pp. 97–111. Springer, Heidelberg (2006). https://doi.org/10.1007/11818175_6
26. Jager, T., Rupp, A.: The semi-generic group model and applications to pairing-based cryptography. In: Abe, M. (ed.) ASIACRYPT 2010. LNCS, vol. 6477, pp. 539–556. Springer, Heidelberg (2010). https://doi.org/10.1007/978-3-642-17373-8_31
27. Jutla, C.S., Roy, A.: Shorter quasi-adaptive NIZK proofs for linear subspaces. In: Sako, K., Sarkar, P. (eds.) ASIACRYPT 2013, Part I. LNCS, vol. 8269, pp. 1–20. Springer, Heidelberg (2013). https://doi.org/10.1007/978-3-642-42033-7_1
28. Jutla, C.S., Roy, A.: Shorter quasi-adaptive NIZK proofs for linear subspaces. Cryptology ePrint Archive, Report 2013/109 (2013). https://eprint.iacr.org/2013/109
29. Kalai, Y.T., Paneth, O., Yang, L.: How to delegate computations publicly. In: 51st ACM STOC, pp. 1115–1124 (2019)

30. Kiltz, E., Wee, H.: Quasi-adaptive NIZK for linear subspaces revisited. In: Oswald, E., Fischlin, M. (eds.) EUROCRYPT 2015, Part II. LNCS, vol. 9057, pp. 101–128. Springer, Heidelberg (2015). https://doi.org/10.1007/978-3-662-46803-6_4
31. Lipmaa, H.: Progression-free sets and sublinear pairing-based non-interactive zero-knowledge arguments. In: Cramer, R. (ed.) TCC 2012. LNCS, vol. 7194, pp. 169–189. Springer, Heidelberg (2012). https://doi.org/10.1007/978-3-642-28914-9_10
32. Lipmaa, H.: Succinct non-interactive zero knowledge arguments from span programs and linear error-correcting codes. In: Sako, K., Sarkar, P. (eds.) ASIACRYPT 2013, Part I. LNCS, vol. 8269, pp. 41–60. Springer, Heidelberg (2013). https://doi.org/10.1007/978-3-642-42033-7_3
33. Lipmaa, H.: Prover-efficient commit-and-prove zero-knowledge SNARKs. In: Pointcheval, D., Nitaj, A., Rachidi, T. (eds.) AFRICACRYPT 2016. LNCS, vol. 9646, pp. 185–206. Springer, Cham (2016). https://doi.org/10.1007/978-3-319-31517-1_10
34. Lipmaa, H.: Simulation-Extractable ZK-SNARKs Revisited. Technical Report 2019/612, IACR (2019). https://ia.cr/2019/612. Accessed 8 Feb 2020
35. Lipmaa, H., Pavlyk, K.: Gentry-Wichs Is Tight: A Falsifiable Non-Adaptively Sound SNARG. Technical report, IACR (2021)
36. Naor, M.: On cryptographic assumptions and challenges (invited talk). In: Boneh, D. (ed.) CRYPTO 2003. LNCS, vol. 2729, pp. 96–109. Springer, Heidelberg (2003). https://doi.org/10.1007/978-3-540-45146-4_6
37. Parno, B., Howell, J., Gentry, C., Raykova, M.: Pinocchio: nearly practical verifiable computation. In: 2013 IEEE Symposium on Security and Privacy, pp. 238–252 (2013)
38. Pass, R.: Unprovable security of perfect NIZK and non-interactive non-malleable commitments. In: Sahai, A. (ed.) TCC 2013. LNCS, vol. 7785, pp. 334–354. Springer, Heidelberg (2013). https://doi.org/10.1007/978-3-642-36594-2_19
39. Stachowiak, G.: Proofs of knowledge with several challenge values. Cryptology ePrint Archive, Report 2008/181 (2008). https://eprint.iacr.org/2008/181

Proofs for Inner Pairing Products and Applications

Benedikt Bünz[1(✉)], Mary Maller[2], Pratyush Mishra[3], Nirvan Tyagi[4], and Psi Vesely[5]

[1] Stanford University, Stanford, USA
buenz@stanford.edu
[2] Ethereum Foundation, Bern, Switzerland
[3] UC Berkeley, Berkeley, USA
[4] Cornell University, Ithaca, USA
[5] UC San Diego, San Diego, USA

Abstract. We present a generalized inner product argument and demonstrate its applications to pairing-based languages. We apply our generalized argument to prove that an inner pairing product is correctly evaluated with respect to committed vectors of n source group elements. With a structured reference string (SRS), we achieve a logarithmic-time verifier whose work is dominated by $6 \log n$ target group exponentiations. Proofs are of size $6 \log n$ target group elements, computed using $6n$ pairings and $4n$ exponentiations in each source group.

We apply our inner product arguments to build the first polynomial commitment scheme with succinct (logarithmic) verification, $O(\sqrt{d})$ prover complexity for degree d polynomials (not including the cost to evaluate the polynomial), and a SRS of size $O(\sqrt{d})$. Concretely, this means that for $d = 2^{28}$, producing an evaluation proof in our protocol is $76\times$ faster than doing so in the KZG commitment scheme, and the CRS in our protocol is $1000\times$ smaller: 13 MB vs 13 GB for KZG.

As a second application, we introduce an argument for aggregating n Groth16 zkSNARKs into an $O(\log n)$ sized proof. Our protocol is significantly faster ($>1000\times$) than aggregating SNARKs via recursive composition: we aggregate $\sim 130,000$ proofs in 25 min, versus 90 proofs via recursive composition. Finally, we further apply our aggregation protocol to construct a low-memory SNARK for machine computations that does not rely on recursive composition. For a computation that requires time T and space S, our SNARK produces proofs in space $\tilde{O}(S + T)$, which is significantly more space efficient than a monolithic SNARK, which requires space $\tilde{O}(S \cdot T)$.

1 Introduction

An inner product argument proves that an inner product relation holds between committed vectors. In this work, we present a new construction of inner product arguments for pairing-based languages that yields a logarithmic time verifier—a significant improvement over the linear time verifier of previous work. We use our new inner product argument to build (1) a new polynomial commitment

M. Tibouchi and H. Wang (Eds.): ASIACRYPT 2021, LNCS 13092, pp. 65–97, 2021.
https://doi.org/10.1007/978-3-030-92078-4_3

scheme that achieves novel asymptotic characteristics of succinct verification and opening proofs that can be computed in time square root of the polynomial degree as well as a square root sized SRS; and (2) a new approach for aggregation of Groth16 general-purpose SNARKs [Gro16] useful for verifiable computation, avoiding the expensive costs of recursive proving circuits. We provide an open-source Rust implementation of all our protocols and applications and benchmark them against the state of the art. Our benchmarks show that the asymptotic improvements translate to significant practical gains.

Inner Product Arguments. Inner product arguments (IPA) are core components of many primitives, including zero-knowledge proofs and polynomial and vector commitment schemes [Boo+16, Bün+18, Wah+18, LMR19, BGH19, Bün+20]. Despite the fact that the inner product arguments constructed in these works largely share the same core strategy as the original protocol in [Boo+16], they all spend significant effort in reproving security to accommodate for minor changes (introduced for efficiency and/or application-specific purposes). This repeated effort adds significant overhead in the process of auditing the security of inner product arguments, and enables errors to slip through unnoticed. Our first contribution is an abstraction of previous work into a generalized inner product argument (GIPA). While the techniques in GIPA are not novel, they do provide a unified view of all prior work, enabling simpler exposition and simpler security proofs. In particular, this means that our single security proof suffices to prove the security of all prior GIPA instantiations [Boo+16, Bün+18, LMR19], as well as the protocols introduced in this paper.

We additionally prove security for the non-interactive variant of GIPA in a generalization of the algebraic group model [FKL18], which we dub the *algebraic commitment model*. Because GIPA is a public-coin protocol, it can be transformed to a non-interactive argument using the Fiat–Shamir heuristic, and it is this variant that is used in applications—non-interactive Bulletproofs secures almost 2 billion USD of Monero [O'L18]. However, due to a technicality about modeling random oracles in recursive arguments (the generic transformation leads to a super-polynomial extractor), prior works provided no satisfactory security proof for these non-interactive variants. Our security proof remedies this oversight, and we envisage that our techniques may be useful in proving the security of other non-interactive and recursive protocols [BFS20].

Reducing Verification Cost. Making use of the high level GIPA blueprint, our second contribution is a protocol for reducing the verifier cost for specific inner product arguments over pairing-based languages. For a committed vector length of n, we reduce the verifier cost from $\mathcal{O}(n)$ for existing protocols [LMR19], to $\mathcal{O}(\log n)$, which is an exponential improvement. To do this, we introduce a new pairing-based commitment scheme with structured keys and prove its security. We then exploit a special structure of the "homomorphic collapsing" execution of GIPA (first observed in [BGH19]) with our commitment scheme. In particular, the outsourced computation is reduced to opening a KZG polynomial commitment scheme. We rely on a trusted setup that is updatable [Gro+18] and can be used for languages of different sizes (up to some maximum bound specified by the SRS).

Equipped with our new logarithmic-time verifier for inner products over pairing-based languages, we next turn to apply our techniques to two applications: (1) polynomial commitments, and (2) SNARK aggregation.

Polynomial Commitments. Polynomial commitment (PC) schemes [KZG10] are commitment schemes specialized to work with polynomials. A committer outputs a short commitment to a polynomial, and then later may convince a verifier of correctness of an evaluation of that committed polynomial at any point via a short evaluation proof, or "opening". PC schemes have been used to reduce communication and computation costs in a vast breadth of applications including proofs of storage and replication [Xu+16, Fis18], anonymous credentials [Cam+15, FHS19], verifiable secret sharing [KZG10, BDK13], and zero-knowledge arguments [Wah+18, Mal+19, Set20, GWC19, Xie+19, Chi+20].

In this work, we use a combination of inner product arguments in order to build a pairing-based polynomial commitment scheme that requires a universal structured reference string of size only $\sqrt{d}$ when committing to degree d polynomials, and where proving an evaluation claim only requires $\mathcal{O}(\sqrt{d})$ cryptographic operations (i.e., group/pairing operations not including scalar computation). We achieve this while maintaining constant-sized commitments, $\mathcal{O}(\log d)$-sized evaluation proofs, and $\mathcal{O}(\log d)$ verifier time.

This compares to a linear sized CRS for the widely used KZG [KZG10] commitment scheme. Concretely, this means that for polynomial of degree 2^{22}, KZG requires a large SRS of size ~400 MB. This can cause deployment hurdles in applications in decentralized systems, as this SRS needs to be stored by every prover. For example, in SNARKs relying on polynomial commitments [GWC19, Chi+20], the degree of the polynomial is roughly the size of the circuit, which can be large [Ben+14c, Wu+18]. A large SRS also has a non-trivial impact on security [GGW18]. In contrast, the SRS of our protocol has size 3MB, which is over 130× smaller, making deployment much easier.

Furthermore, as noted above, computing an evaluation proof requires only $\mathcal{O}(\sqrt{d})$ cryptographic operations, which is much better than KZG, which requires $\mathcal{O}(d)$ cryptographic operations. This is important for applications such as vector commitments [LY10] and proofs of space [Fis19], where a polynomial is committed to just once, but the commitment is opened at many different evaluation points.

SNARK Aggregation. A SNARK aggregation protocol takes as input many SNARK proofs and outputs a single aggregated proof that can be verified more quickly than individually verifying each SNARK. This is useful for applications where the batch of proofs will be verified many times by different clients. For example, this is the case in applications that aim to improve the scalability of decentralized blockchains by using SNARKs to prove the correctness of state transitions [Whi, Bon+20].

We use our inner product arguments to design an aggregation protocol for Groth16 [Gro16] SNARKs that enjoys the following efficiency properties when aggregating n proofs: (a) aggregation requires $\mathcal{O}(n)$ cryptographic operations, (b) the aggregated proof has size $\mathcal{O}(\log n)$, and (c) verification requires $\mathcal{O}(\log n)$ cryptographic operations, and $\mathcal{O}(n)$ field operations.

Our protocol offers asymptotic and concrete improvements over prior approaches that aggregate proofs via *recursive composition*. In more detail, these approaches create (another) SNARK for the circuit that contains n copies of the Groth16 verifier circuit [Ben+14a, Bow+20]. This entails constructing arithmetic circuits for computing pairings, which is expensive (for example, computing a pairing on the BLS12-377 curve requires ~15,000 constraints [Bow+20]). In contrast, our protocol "natively" works with pairing-based languages. This results in the following efficiency savings: (a) our protocol does not have to reason about arithmetic circuits for computing pairings, (b) our protocol does not have to compute FFTs, which require time $\mathcal{O}(n \log n)$, and (c) our protocol does not require special cycles or chains of curves [Ben+14a, Bow+20].

Put together, these savings allow us to aggregate proofs over $\sim 1400\times$ faster than the recursive approach. Furthermore, our protocol requires the verifier to only perform $\mathcal{O}(n)$ field operations, as opposed to $\mathcal{O}(n)$ cryptographic operations for the recursive approach.

Low-Memory SNARKs for Machine Computations. We leverage our aggregation protocol to construct a *low-memory SNARK* for (non-deterministic) machine computations. In more detail, if for a machine M, checking an execution transcript requires space S and time T, then our SNARK prover takes space $\tilde{\mathcal{O}}(S + T)$ to produce a proof for that execution. In comparison, constructing a monolithic proof for the entire computation at once requires space $\tilde{\mathcal{O}}(S \cdot T)$, whereas the only other solution for constructing low-memory SNARKs for machine computations requires recursive composition of proofs [Bit+13], which is concretely expensive.

Summary of Contributions

- We provide a unifying generalization of inner product arguments, identifying and formalizing the appropriate *doubly-homomorphic* commitment property.
- We prove security of the non-interactive Fiat-Shamir transform of this protocol, implying security for the entire family of protocols.
- We provide a new set of inner product arguments for pairing-based languages that improve verifier efficiency from linear to logarithmic by introducing a trusted structured setup.
- We construct a new polynomial commitment scheme with constant-sized commitments, opening time square root in the degree and square root sized CRS. The opening verifier runs in logarithmic time and opening proofs are logarithmic in size.
- We design an aggregator for Groth16 [Gro16] pairing-based SNARKs that produces an aggregated proof of logarithmic size. We apply our aggregator to construct a low-memory SNARK for machine computations *without relying on recursive composition.*
- We implement a set of Rust libraries that realize our inner product argument protocols and applications from modular and generic components. We evaluate our implementation, and find that our PC scheme is over $14\times$ faster to open than a KZG commitment [KZG10] for polynomials of degree 10^6, and

Table 1. Efficiency comparisons for polynomial commitment schemes. All numbers are given asymptotically. We use $\mathbb{G}_1, \mathbb{G}_2, \mathbb{G}_T$ to represent groups in a bilinear map, P to represent pairings, $\mathbb{G}_U$ to represent groups of unknown order, and $\mathbb{H}$ to represent hash functions. For simplicity we only specify the dominant costs e.g., if there are d $\mathbb{G}_1$ and d $\mathbb{G}_2$ group exponentiations we simple write d $\mathbb{G}_2$. Column 5 is the expected size of one commitment plus one opening proof at $d = 2^{20}$ over a BN256 curve.

Polynomial commitment	Communication complexity				Transparent setup	Time complexity		
	CRS	Commitments	Openings	$d = 2^{20}$		Commit	Open	Verify
Kate et al. [KZG10]	$d\ \mathbb{G}_1$	$1\ \mathbb{G}_1$	$1\ \mathbb{G}_1$	96b	no	$d\ \mathbb{G}_1$	$d\ \mathbb{G}_1$	$1\ P, \mathbb{G}_1$
Bulletproofs [Bün+18]	$d\ \mathbb{G}_1$	$1\ \mathbb{G}_1$	$\log(d)\ \mathbb{G}_1$	1.3 KB	yes	$d\ \mathbb{G}_1$	$d\ \mathbb{G}_1$	$d\ \mathbb{G}_1$
Hyrax [Wah+18]	$\sqrt{d}\ \mathbb{G}_1$	$\sqrt{d}\ \mathbb{G}_1$	$\log(d)\ \mathbb{G}_1$	33 KB	yes	$d\ \mathbb{G}_1$	$\sqrt{d}\ \mathbb{G}_1$	$\sqrt{d}\ \mathbb{G}_1$
DARKs [BFS20]	$d\ \mathbb{G}_U$	$1\ \mathbb{G}_U$	$\log(d)\ \mathbb{G}_U$	8.6 KB	yes	$d\ \mathbb{G}_U$	$d \log(d)\ \mathbb{G}_U$	$\log(d)\ \mathbb{G}_U$
Virgo [Zha+20]	1	$1\ \mathbb{H}$	$\log(d)^2\ \mathbb{H}$	183 KB	yes	$d \log(d)\ \mathbb{H}$	$d \log(d)\ \mathbb{H}$	$\log(d)^2\ \mathbb{H}$
Groth [Gro11]	$\sqrt[3]{d}\ \mathbb{G}_2$	$\sqrt[3]{d}\ \mathbb{G}_T$	$\sqrt[3]{d}\ \mathbb{G}_1$	25 KB	yes	$d\ \mathbb{G}_1$	$\sqrt[3]{d^2}\ \mathbb{G}_1$	$\sqrt[3]{d}\ P$
This work	$\sqrt{d}\ \mathbb{G}_2$	$1\ \mathbb{G}_T$	$\log(d)\ \mathbb{G}_T$	2.5 KB	no	$d\ \mathbb{G}_1$	$\sqrt{d}\ P$	$\log(d)\mathbb{G}_T$

that our aggregation scheme aggregates over 1400× faster than the alternative 2-chain approach.

Related Work. Lai, Malavolta, and Ronge [LMR19] introduced an inner product argument for pairing based languages. Their scheme runs over a transparent setup and is secure under the SXDH assumption. Their work improves on Groth and Sahai Proofs [GS08] which are a method to prove pairing-based languages under zero-knowledge without reducing to NP. Their proving costs are dominated by a linear number of pairings, their proof sizes are logarithmic and their verifier running costs are dominated by a linear number of group exponentiations. Our pairing based IPA's have much lower verification costs but we use a trusted setup. Our generalized IPA argument can be used to greatly simplify the security proofs for their Theorems 3.2, 4.1, 4.2 and 4.3, and we prove security of a non-interactive variant in the algebraic commitment model.

In Table 1, we compare the efficiency of various polynomial commitment schemes. [KZG10] introduced a pairing based polynomial commitment scheme with constant sized proofs. Their scheme is secure under an updatable setup in the algebraic group model. Groth [Gro11] designed a pairing based "batch product argument" secure under SXDH. This argument that can be seen as a form of polynomial commitment scheme and our two-tiered polynomial commitment techniques were inspired by this work. Under discrete-logarithm assumptions, Bayer and Groth designed a zero-knowledge proving system to show that a committed value is the correct evaluation of a known polynomial [BG13]. Both the prover and verifier need only compute a logarithmic number of group exponentiations, however verifier costs are linear in the degree of the polynomial. Wahby et al. proved that it is possible to use the inner product argument of Bulletproofs [Bün+18] to build a polynomial commitment scheme [Wah+18]. Bowe et al. [BGH19] argued that the inner product argument of Bulletproofs is also highly aggregatable, to the point where aggregated proofs can be verified using a one off linear cost and an additional logarithmic factor per proof. Attema and Cramer [AC20] recently provided an orthogonal generalization of the inner product argument. They show that the inner product argument can be seen as a black box compression mechanism for sigma protocols and show that it can be used as a proof system for secret shared data.

Polynomial commitment schemes have also been constructed using Reed-Solomon codes [Zha+20]. These commitments use highly efficient symmetric key primitives, however the protocols that use them require soundness boosting techniques that result in large constant overheads. Bünz et al. [BFS20] designed a polynomial commitment scheme in groups of unknown order such as RSA groups or class groups with efficient verifier time and small proof sizes. However, it requires super-linear commitment and prover time. Asymptotically, our scheme positions itself competitively among state-of-the-art PCs (see Table 1). In terms of concrete efficiency, the trusted setup scheme of Kate et al. [KZG10] allows for constant proof sizes and verifier time (versus our logarithmic results), whereas our protocol offers quadratic improvements to opening efficiency and the maximum degree polynomial supported by a SRS of a given size.

Prior aggregatable SNARKs have relied on efficiently expressing SNARK verifiers as as arithmetic circuits [Ben+14b, Ben+13b]. For pairing based SNARKs this was achieved through the use of pairing-friendly cycles [Ben+14a] or two-chains [Bow+20]. Known cycles and two-chains for the 128-bit security level require roughly 768-bit curves, which are ~10× more expensive than the roughly 384-bit curves used when recursion is not necessary. Bowe et al. introduce a novel approach to recursive SNARKs that works with cycles of standard (non-pairing) curves [BGH19]. Bünz et al. [Bün+20] generalize and formalize this approach. Chiesa et al. build a post-quantum recursive SNARK [COS20]. For all of these approaches we expect to significantly improve on prover time because we do not rely on expensive NP reductions.

Subsequent Work. Prior (full) versions of this work included an additional polynomial commitment construction based on GIPA that only requires an unstructured reference string. In this construction, the prover computes $\mathcal{O}(\sqrt{d})$ pairings and exponentiations, the opening proof consists of $\mathcal{O}(\log(d))$ group elements, and the verifier performs $\mathcal{O}(\sqrt{d})$ exponentiations for degree d univariate polynomials. Recent subsequent work [Lee20] introduced a new PC scheme (called Dory) that builds on, and improves upon, our unstructured-setup construction. The key improvement is that the verifier time of this scheme is $\mathcal{O}(\log d)$, which is achieved by cleverly switching the commitment key in every round of the GIPA protocol and folding the old commitment key into the committed vector. This is possible when GIPA is instantiated with a bilinear group as the key space of the commitment to one vector is the message space of the commitment to the other vector, and vice versa. It is therefore possible to combine keys and messages homomorphically. However, log-verification costs of Dory are concretely more costly than our log-verification structured-setup PC scheme ($\approx 6\times$): at $d = 2^{20}$, Dory's opening proofs are 18KB and computed in 6 s, while our scheme has proofs of size 2.5 KB computed in 1 s.

Further subsequent works have applied our inner product arguments to aggregate vector commitment opening proofs [Sri+21], construct incrementally-verifiable computation without recursion [Tya+21], and aggregate SNARKs in blockchain settings using existing trusted setups [GMN21].

2 Technical Overview

2.1 Generalized Inner Product Argument

The first contribution of our paper is a *generalized inner product argument* we denote GIPA. At a high level, our protocol generalizes the protocols of [Boo+16, Bün+18] as follows. The protocols of [Boo+16, Bün+18] enable proving the correctness of inner products of scalar vectors committed via the Pedersen commitment scheme [Ped92]. Our protocol generalizes their techniques to enable proving the correct computation of a large class of inner products between vectors of group and/or field elements committed to using (possibly distinct) *doubly homomorphic commitments.* We explain in more detail below.

Starting Point: Inner Product Arguments. The inner product argument (IPA) by [Boo+16] enables a prover to convince a verifier that two committed vectors (using Pedersen vector commitments) have a publicly known inner product. It does this by elegantly rescaling the committed vectors to half their size in each round. In each round the verifier sends a random challenge, which the prover uses to take a linear combination of the right and left half of the committed vectors, and they both rescale the commitment keys accordingly.

After $\log_2 m$ such reduction step the prover simply opens the commitment and the verifier checks that the product relation holds. In Bulletproofs [Bün+18] the authors improve on the IPA by committing to the two vectors and the scalar in a single commitment, while maintaining the halving structure of the argument. This enables sending just two commitments per round.

We observe that the same argument structure works for a much wider class of commitment schemes. In particular we require only that the commitment scheme is binding and has the homomorphic properties that enable the rescaling step. This property is that the commitment scheme is doubly homomorphic, i.e., homomorphic over the messages and the commitment keys.

Doubly Homomorphic Commitments. At a high level, a doubly homomorphic commitment scheme is a binding commitment scheme $(\mathsf{Setup}, \mathsf{CM})$ where the key space $\mathcal{K}$, message space $\mathcal{M}$, and commitment space $\mathcal{C}$ form abelian groups of the same size such that $\mathsf{CM}((\mathsf{ck}_1 + \mathsf{ck}_2); (M_1 + M_2)) = \mathsf{CM}(\mathsf{ck}_1, M_1) + \mathsf{CM}(\mathsf{ck}_1; M_2) + \mathsf{CM}(\mathsf{ck}_2, M_1) + \mathsf{CM}(\mathsf{ck}_2, M_2)$.

The Pedersen commitment $\mathsf{CM}(\boldsymbol{g}, \boldsymbol{a}) \to \prod_i g_i^{a_i}$ is the doubly homomorphic commitment used in Bulletproofs. Lai, Malavolta, and Ronge [LMR19] used a doubly homomorphic commitment for bilinear groups where the committed vectors consist of group elements in a bilinear group: $\mathsf{CM}(\boldsymbol{v}, \boldsymbol{v}', \boldsymbol{w}, \boldsymbol{w}'; \boldsymbol{A}, \boldsymbol{B}) \to \prod_i e(v_i, A_i)e(B_i, w_i), \prod_i e(v_i', A_i)e(B_i, w_i')$.

In some of our protocols the verifier already has access to one of the committed vectors. For instance, in the polynomial commitment scheme the verifier can simply compute the vector consisting of the monomials of the evaluation point. Such protocols are also captured by our abstraction since the identity commitment is doubly homomorphic. In the actual protocols, the prover doesn't send any scalings of these vectors, and the verifier simply computes them directly.

Inner Products. Building on our generalization of commitment schemes that work for inner product arguments, GIPA also generalizes the types of inner products that can be proven between committed vectors. It can be used not only to show inner products between field elements, but for arbitrary inner product maps $\langle \cdot, \cdot \rangle$ that are bilinear, i.e., for which $\langle \boldsymbol{a}+\boldsymbol{b}, \boldsymbol{c}+\boldsymbol{d} \rangle = \langle \boldsymbol{a}, \boldsymbol{c} \rangle + \langle \boldsymbol{a}, \boldsymbol{d} \rangle + \langle \boldsymbol{b}, \boldsymbol{c} \rangle + \langle \boldsymbol{b}, \boldsymbol{d} \rangle$. It immediately follows our generalized argument works for bilinear pairings. We apply GIPA to three different inner products:

$$\begin{array}{ll} \langle \cdot, \cdot \rangle : \mathbb{G}_1^m \times \mathbb{G}_2^m \mapsto \mathbb{G}_T, & \langle \boldsymbol{A}, \boldsymbol{B} \rangle = \prod_{i=0}^{m-1} e(A_i, B_i) \\ \langle \cdot, \cdot \rangle : \mathbb{G}_1^m \times \mathbb{F}^m \mapsto \mathbb{G}_1, & \langle \boldsymbol{A}, \boldsymbol{b} \rangle = \prod_{i=0}^{m-1} A_i^{b_i} \\ \langle \cdot, \cdot \rangle : \mathbb{F}^m \times \mathbb{F}^m \mapsto \mathbb{F}, & \langle \boldsymbol{a}, \boldsymbol{b} \rangle = \sum_{i=0}^{m-1} a_i b_i \end{array}$$

We refer to the first inner product as the inner pairing product.

Security Proof. We prove both the interactive and the non-interactive variant of GIPA to be knowledge-sound. The interactive security proof shows the $(k_1, \ldots, k_r)$-special soundness of GIPA protocols, which implies knowledge-soundness via a recent result of Attema and Cramer [AC20] (previous interactive security proofs showed only witness-extended emulation). In particular, we reduce the security of any GIPA instantiation to the binding of its commitment scheme.

We also prove knowledge-soundness of the non-interactive version of GIPA given by the Fiat-Shamir transform. It is known from folklore that applying the Fiat-Shamir transformation to a r-round interactive argument of knowledge with negligible soundness error yields a non-interactive argument of knowledge in the random oracle model where the extractor $\mathcal{E}$ runs in time $O(t^r)$ for an adversary that performs at most $t = \text{poly}(\lambda)$ random oracle queries. GIPA has $\log m$ rounds for $m = \text{poly}(\lambda)$ so this transformation yields a super-polynomial extractor. Given this, we directly prove the security of the non-interactive argument in the algebraic commitment model, a generalization of the algebraic group model [FKL18] for doubly-homomorphic commitments. In essence, whenever the prover outputs a commitment he must also give an opening to it with respect to some linear combination of commitment keys; the commitment schemes we consider can be shown to achieve this model in their own respective algebraic group models. Our security proof yields an efficient linear-time extractor and negligible knowledge-soundness. Given the generality of GIPA this also yields the first tight security analysis of non-interactive Bulletproofs [Boo+16, Bün+18] and the many related protocols [LMR19, BGH19, Bün+20].

TIPP and MIPP. Generically GIPA protocols have logarithmic communication but linear verifier time as computing the final commitment key takes a linear number of operations. We introduce TIPP, a logarithmic verifier variant for the inner pairing product and MIPP for the multi-exponentiation inner product.[1] These schemes use universal and updatable structured references string as commitment keys. Their commitments are based on that of Abe et al. [Abe+16], where given a commitment key $(v_0, v_1) \in \mathbb{G}_2$ the commitment to $(A_0, A_1) \in \mathbb{G}_1^2$ is given by $e(A_0, v_0)e(A_1, v_1)$, and the KZG polynomial commitment [KZG10].

Instead of the verifier having to compute the verification key itself, we leverage a recent insight by Bowe, Grigg, and Hopwood [BGH19]. The final commitment key in GIPA can be viewed as a polynomial commitment to a degree m polynomial that can be verified in $\log m$ time. Using the structured setup we can outsource computing the commitment key to the prover. The verifier simply verifies that the commitment key was computed correctly. This amounts to evaluating the polynomial at a random point and checking a KZG [KZG10] polynomial commitment proof.

2.2 Applications

We show how to use instantiations of our generalized inner product argument to obtain interesting applications: a polynomial commitment scheme where computing evaluation proofs for polynomials of degree d requires only $O(\sqrt{d})$ cryptographic operations, and a protocol for aggregating n Groth16 SNARKs [Gro16] to produce an aggregate proof of size $O(\log n)$ and verifiable in time $O(\log n)$.

Polynomial Commitment Following Groth [Gro11] we use two-tiered homomorphic commitments: i.e. commitments to commitments. Suppose we wish to commit to a polynomial

$$f(X,Y) = f_0(Y) + f_1(Y)X + \ldots + f_{m-1}(Y)X^{m-1} = \sum_{i=0}^{m-1} f_i(Y)X^i.$$

We can view this polynomial in matrix form

$$f(X,Y) = (1, X, X^2, \ldots, X^{m-1}) \begin{pmatrix} a_{0,0} & a_{0,1} & a_{0,2} & \cdots & a_{0,\ell-1} \\ a_{1,0} & a_{1,1} & a_{1,2} & \cdots & a_{1,\ell-1} \\ a_{2,0} & a_{2,1} & a_{2,2} & \cdots & a_{2,\ell-1} \\ \vdots & & & \ddots & \vdots \\ a_{m-1,0} & a_{m-1,1} & a_{m-1,2} & \cdots & a_{m-1,\ell-1} \end{pmatrix} \begin{pmatrix} 1 \\ Y \\ Y^2 \\ \cdots \\ Y^{\ell-1} \end{pmatrix}$$

One first computes commitments $A_0, \ldots, A_{m-1}$ to $f_0(Y), \ldots, f_{m-1}(Y)$. Next one commits to the commitments $A_0, \ldots, A_{m-1}$.

On receiving an opening challenge (x, y) the prover evaluates the first tier at x to obtain a commitment A to $f(x, Y)$. This is done using MIPP. The prover then opens the second tier commitment A at y in order to obtain $\nu = f(x, y)$. This is

[1] We actually introduce two variants of MIPP: MIPP_u, where both the vectors are committed, and MIPP_k where the verifier already knows the exponent, but it's of a structured form.

done using a KZG univariate polynomial commitment scheme [KZG10]. To apply our prover efficient polynomial commitment scheme to univariate polynomials, commit to $f(X, X^n)$ and open at (x, x^n).

Note that for $m \approx \ell \approx \sqrt{d}$ both the MIPP and the KZG commitment are only of square root size. This results in a square root reference string. In order to achieve square root prover time (in addition to evaluating the polynomial) the prover needs to store the $A_0, \ldots, A_{m-1}$ when committing to the polynomial. Using these values the resulting MIPP can be opened in $O(m) = O(\sqrt{d})$ time.

SNARK Aggregation and Proofs of Machine Computation Pairing-based SNARKs such as Groth16 can be proven and verified using only algebraic operations (e.g., field operations, group operations and pairings). This means we can aggregate by applying TIPP to the Groth16 verifier equations, such that whenever TIPP verifies the aggregator must have seen some verifying proof. In particular, to aggregate n Groth 16 proofs $\{(A_i, B_i, C_i)\}_{i=1}^n \in \mathbb{G}_1 \times \mathbb{G}_2 \times \mathbb{G}_1$, one first computes commitments to the A_i, B_i, C_i values. Then the aggregator computes $\prod_{i=1}^n e(A_i, B_i)^{r^{2i}}$ and $\prod_{i=1}^n C_i^{r^{2i}}$ for some random value r and proves these are correct using our pairing based arguments. Finally the verifier checks that these values satisfy a randomized version of the Groth16 verifier equations. Overall the verifier only performs one field multiplication per instance and $O(\log(n))$ cryptographic operations for the TIPP protocol.

Low-memory SNARKs for Machine Computation. We make use of the SNARK aggregation protocol to build a low-memory SNARK that does not rely on recursive computation. Our approach proceeds by producing an individual Groth16 proof for each machine step and aggregating these individual proofs. The key observation is that due to the structure of the intermediate computation state, i.e., the output of one computation step becomes the input to the next, we can speed up the verifier's work from linear in the number of computation steps to logarithmic with an additional inner product commitment to the intermediate states. See Sect. 8 for details.

2.3 Implementation

We implement a set of Rust libraries that realize our inner product argument protocols and applications. Our libraries consists of a number of modular and generic components: (a) a generic interface for inner products, and instantiations for scalar products, multi-scalar multiplication, and pairing products; (b) a generic interface for doubly-homomorphic commitments, with instantiations for Pedersen commitments, the commitments of [Abe+16], and trivial identity commitments; (c) a generic implementation of GIPA that relies on the above interfaces, and instantiations for the various concrete inner products and corresponding commitments; and (d) implementations of our polynomial commitment scheme and our aggregation scheme for Groth16 proofs. See Sects. 6 and 7 for evaluation details.

3 Notation

We denote by $[n]$ the set $\{1, \ldots, n\} \subseteq \mathbb{N}$. We use $\boldsymbol{a} = [a_i]_{i=1}^n$ as a short-hand for the vector $(a_1, \ldots, a_n)$, and $[\boldsymbol{a}_i]_{i=1}^n = [[a_{i,j}]_{j=1}^m]_{i=1}^n$ as a short-hand for the vector $(a_{1,1}, \ldots, a_{1,m}, \ldots, a_{n,1}, \ldots, a_{n,m})$; $|\boldsymbol{a}|$ denotes the number of entries in $\boldsymbol{a}$. We analogously define $\{a_i\}_{i=1}^n$ with respect to sets instead of vectors. If x is a binary string then $|x|$ denotes its bit length. For a finite set S, let $x \xleftarrow{\$} S$ denote that x is an element sampled uniformly at random from S. We also write $x \xleftarrow{\$} \mathsf{A}()$ to denote when an algorithm A samples and uses randomness in the computation of x.

Inner Pairing Product Notation. We introduce some special notation related to our inner pairing product argument, some of which is borrowed from the Pedersen inner product introduced in [Bün+18]. We write group operations as multiplication. For a scalar $x \in \mathbb{F}$ and vector $\boldsymbol{A} \in \mathbb{G}^n$, we let $\boldsymbol{A}^x = (A_1^x, \ldots, A_n^x) \in \mathbb{G}^n$, and for a vector $\boldsymbol{x} = (x_0, \ldots, x_{m-1}) \in \mathbb{F}^n$ we let $\boldsymbol{A}^{\boldsymbol{x}} = (A_0^{x_0}, \ldots, A_{m-1}^{x_{m-1}})$. For a bilinear group $(\mathbb{G}_1, \mathbb{G}_2, \mathbb{G}_T, q, g, h, e)$ and pair of source group vectors $\boldsymbol{A} \in \mathbb{G}_1^n$, $\boldsymbol{B} \in \mathbb{G}_2^n$ we define $\boldsymbol{A} * \boldsymbol{B} = \prod_{i=1}^n e(A_i, B_i)$. For two vectors $\boldsymbol{A}, \boldsymbol{A}' \in \mathbb{G}^n$ we let $\boldsymbol{A} \circ \boldsymbol{A}' = (A_0 A_0', \ldots, A_{m-1} A_{m-1}')$.

Let $\boldsymbol{A} \| \boldsymbol{A}' = (A_0, \ldots, A_{n-1}, A_0', \ldots, A_{m-1}')$ be the concatenation of two vectors $\boldsymbol{A} \in \mathbb{G}^n$ and $\boldsymbol{A}' \in \mathbb{G}^m$. To denote slices of vectors given $\boldsymbol{A} \in \mathbb{G}_?^n$ and $0 \leq \ell < n-1$ we write $\boldsymbol{A}_{[:\ell]} = (A_0, \ldots, A_{\ell-1}) \in \mathbb{G}^\ell$ and $\boldsymbol{A}_{[\ell:]} = (A_\ell, \ldots, A_{n-1}) \in \mathbb{G}^{n-\ell}$.

Languages and Relations. We write $\{(\mathbb{x}) : p(\mathbb{x})\}$ to describe a polynomial-time language $\mathcal{L} \subseteq \{0,1\}^*$ decided by the polynomial-time predicate $p(\cdot)$. We write $\{(\mathbb{x}; \mathbb{w}) : p(\mathbb{x}, \mathbb{w})\}$ to describe a NP relation $\mathcal{R} \subseteq \{0,1\}^* \times \{0,1\}^*$ between instances $\mathbb{x}$ and witnesses $\mathbb{w}$ decided by the polynomial-time predicate $p(\cdot, \cdot)$.

Security Notions. We denote by $\lambda \in \mathbb{N}$ a security parameter. When we state that $n \in \mathbb{N}$ for some variable n, we implicitly assume that $n = \text{poly}(\lambda)$. We denote by $\text{negl}(\lambda)$ an unspecified function that is *negligible* in λ (namely, a function that vanishes faster than the inverse of any polynomial in λ). When a function can be expressed in the form $1 - \text{negl}(\lambda)$, we say that it is *overwhelming* in λ. When we say that algorithm $\mathcal{A}$ is an *efficient* we mean that $\mathcal{A}$ is a family $\{\mathcal{A}_\lambda\}_{\lambda \in \mathbb{N}}$ of non-uniform polynomial-size circuits. If the algorithm consists of multiple circuit families $\mathcal{A}_1, \ldots, \mathcal{A}_n$, then we write $\mathcal{A} = (\mathcal{A}_1, \ldots, \mathcal{A}_n)$.

Arguments of Knowledge and Commitments. We use several standard notions in this paper such as interactive arguments of knowledge and commitments. For completeness, we include their definitions in the full version [Bün+19].

4 Generalized Inner Product Argument (GIPA)

We now generalize the inner product argument (IPA) from [Boo+16,Bün+18] to work for all "doubly homomorphic" inner product commitments. The generalized inner product argument (GIPA) protocol is described with respect to a doubly homomorphic inner product commitment and an inner product map defined over

$\mathsf{Prove}(\langle \mathsf{group} \rangle, \mathsf{ck} = (\mathsf{ck}_1, \mathsf{ck}_2, \mathsf{ck}_3);\ (\boldsymbol{a}, \boldsymbol{b}))$		$\mathsf{Verify}(\langle \mathsf{group} \rangle, \mathsf{ck}, C)$
	If $m = 1$	
	$a \in \mathcal{M}_1, b \in \mathcal{M}_2$ $\longrightarrow$	**Return** $\mathsf{CM}(\mathsf{ck};\ (a, b, a \circledast b)) == C$
	Else $m \geq 2$	
$m' = m/2$		$m' = m/2$
$z_L = \langle \boldsymbol{a}_{[m':]}, \boldsymbol{b}_{[:m']} \rangle$		
$z_R = \langle \boldsymbol{a}_{[:m']}, \boldsymbol{b}_{[m':]} \rangle$		
$C_L = \mathsf{CM}(\mathsf{ck}_1, \mathsf{ck}_2, \mathsf{ck}_3;\ \boldsymbol{a}_{[m':]} \Vert \boldsymbol{0}, \boldsymbol{0} \Vert \boldsymbol{b}_{[:m']}, z_L)$		
$C_R = \mathsf{CM}(\mathsf{ck}_1, \mathsf{ck}_2, \mathsf{ck}_3;\ \boldsymbol{0} \Vert \boldsymbol{a}_{[:m']}, \boldsymbol{b}_{[m':]} \Vert \boldsymbol{0}, z_R)$		
	$C_L, C_R \in \mathsf{Image}(\mathsf{CM})$ $\longrightarrow$	
	$x \in \mathbb{F}_p$ $\longleftarrow$	$x \xleftarrow{\$} \mathbb{F}_p$
$\boldsymbol{a}' = \boldsymbol{a}_{[:m']} + x \cdot \boldsymbol{a}_{[m':]}$		
$\boldsymbol{b}' = \boldsymbol{b}_{[:m']} + x^{-1} \cdot \boldsymbol{b}_{[m':]}$		
$\mathsf{ck}_1' = \mathsf{ck}_{1,[:m']} + x^{-1} \cdot \mathsf{ck}_{1,[m':]}$		$\mathsf{ck}_1' = \mathsf{ck}_{1,[:m']} + x^{-1} \cdot \mathsf{ck}_{1,[m':]}$
$\mathsf{ck}_2' = \mathsf{ck}_{2,[:m']} + x \cdot \mathsf{ck}_{2,[m':]}$		$\mathsf{ck}_2' = \mathsf{ck}_{2,[:m']} + x \cdot \mathsf{ck}_{2,[m':]}$
		$C' = \mathsf{Collapse}(x \cdot C_L + C + x^{-1} \cdot C_R)$
Recurse on $(\langle \mathsf{group} \rangle, (\mathsf{ck}_1', \mathsf{ck}_2', \mathsf{ck}_3), (\boldsymbol{a}', \boldsymbol{b}'))$		**Recurse** on $(\langle \mathsf{group} \rangle, (\mathsf{ck}_1', \mathsf{ck}_2', \mathsf{ck}_3), C')$

Fig. 1. Generalized inner product argument. Cases are based on the length m of the message (and correspondingly commitment key) vectors. Here, $\boldsymbol{0}$ is the vector containing m' sequential group identity elements for the appropriate group.

its message space. All of the inner pairing product arguments in this paper as well as the discrete-log inner product argument from [Boo+16, Bün+18] can be described as instantiations of GIPA, sometimes with non-black-box optimizations that do not work generally. The generalized version enables us to simplify the proof of security of the specific instantiations presented in the rest of the paper and provides a "compiler" that lets the reader plug in their own computationally binding "inner product commitment" to obtain a new inner product argument (of knowledge).

Protocol Intuition. The protocol works by reducing the instance from size m to $m/2$ each round. As an intuition, we will show how to reduce an instance with 2 expensive mappings $\circledast$ to an instance with just a single $\circledast$. Given a_1, a_2, b_1, b_2 a prover wants to convince a verifier that $(a_1 \circledast b_1) + (a_2 \circledast b_2) = c$ for an expensive map $\circledast$. To do this the prover sends cross terms $l = a_1 \circledast b_2$ and $r = a_2 \circledast b_1$. The verifier then sends a challenge x. Note that for $a' = x \cdot a_1 + a_2$ and $b' = x^{-1} \cdot b_1 + b_2$ we have that $a' \circledast b' = x \cdot l + c + x^{-1} \cdot r$. Since the prover has to commit to the cross terms l and r before knowing x, if x is uniformly sampled from a sufficiently large space then checking this latter equation implies that $c = (a_1 \circledast b_1) + (a_2 \circledast b_2)$ with overwhelming probability.

GIPA extends this idea to work for committed vectors $\boldsymbol{a}_1, \boldsymbol{a}_2, \boldsymbol{b}_1, \boldsymbol{b}_2$. It relies on *doubly* homomorphic commitments with a commitment key ck where $\mathsf{CM}(\mathsf{ck}, \boldsymbol{a}) = \mathsf{CM}(x^{-1} \cdot \mathsf{ck}, x \cdot \boldsymbol{a})$.

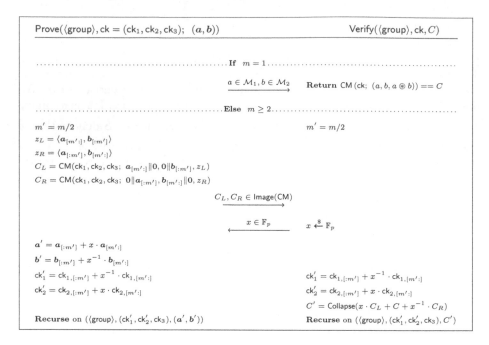

4.1 Doubly Homomorphic Commitments

We can apply GIPA over any commitment scheme which is "doubly-homomorphic." For example, consider the Pedersen commitment scheme:

$\underline{\mathsf{Setup}(1^\lambda) \to \mathsf{ck}}$	$\underline{\mathsf{CM}(\mathsf{ck}, \boldsymbol{a}) \to c}$
Return $(g_1, \ldots, g_m) \xleftarrow{\$} \mathbb{G}$	Return $g_1^{a_1} \cdots g_m^{a_m}$

This scheme allows us to commit to elements in the message space $\mathcal{M} = \mathbb{F}_p^m$ under commitment keys in the key space $\mathcal{K} = \mathbb{G}^m$ for a group $\mathbb{G}$ of prime order p. We denote the key space (i.e., the image of the setup algorithm) by $\mathcal{K}$. The commitment space is additively homomorphic because for all $\boldsymbol{a}, \boldsymbol{b} \in \mathcal{M}$ and $\boldsymbol{g} \in \mathcal{K}$ we have that $\boldsymbol{g}^{\boldsymbol{a}} \cdot \boldsymbol{g}^{\boldsymbol{b}} = \boldsymbol{g}^{\boldsymbol{a}+\boldsymbol{b}}$. The key space is also homomorphic because for all $\boldsymbol{g}, \boldsymbol{w} \in \mathcal{K}$ and $\boldsymbol{a} \in \mathcal{M}$ we have that $\boldsymbol{g}^{\boldsymbol{a}} \cdot \boldsymbol{w}^{\boldsymbol{a}} = (\boldsymbol{g} \circ \boldsymbol{w})^{\boldsymbol{a}}$. Thus, we consider the Pedersen commitment scheme to be *doubly-homomorphic* (i.e., homomorphic in both the commitment space and the key space).

Definition 1 (Doubly homomorphic commitment scheme). *A commitment scheme* (Setup, CM) *is* doubly homomorphic *if* $(\mathcal{K}, +)$, $(\mathcal{M}, +)$ *and* (Image(CM), +) *define abelian groups such that for all* $\mathsf{ck}, \mathsf{ck}' \in \mathcal{K}$ *and* $M, M' \in \mathcal{M}$ *it holds that*

1. $\mathsf{CM}(\mathsf{ck}; M) + \mathsf{CM}(\mathsf{ck}; M') = \mathsf{CM}(\mathsf{ck}; M_1 + M')$
2. $\mathsf{CM}(\mathsf{ck}; M) + \mathsf{CM}(\mathsf{ck}'; M) = \mathsf{CM}(\mathsf{ck} + \mathsf{ck}'; M)$

Observe that if CM is doubly homomorphic then for all $x \in \mathbb{Z}_p$ it holds that $\mathsf{CM}(x \cdot \mathsf{ck}; M) = \mathsf{CM}(\mathsf{ck}; x \cdot M)$.

4.2 Inner Product

We consider inner products as bilinear maps from two equal-dimension vector spaces over two groups to a third group.

Definition 2 (Inner product map). *A map* $\circledast : \mathcal{M}_1 \times \mathcal{M}_2 \to \mathcal{M}_3$ *from two groups of prime order* p *to a third group of order* p *is an* inner product map *if for all* $a, b \in \mathcal{M}_1$ *and* $c, d \in \mathcal{M}_2$ *we have that*

$$(a + b) \circledast (c + d) = a \circledast c + a \circledast d + b \circledast c + b \circledast d$$

Given an inner product $\circledast$ *between groups we define the inner product between vector spaces* $\langle , \rangle : \mathcal{M}_1^m \times \mathcal{M}_2^m \to \mathcal{M}_3$ *to be* $\langle \boldsymbol{a}, \boldsymbol{b} \rangle := \sum_{i=1}^{m} a_i \circledast b_i$

We use three different inner products in this paper. For the Pedersen commitment described above we have that $\circledast$ is multiplication between elements in $\mathbb{F}_p$ and $\langle , \rangle$ is the dot product. In TIPP we have that $\circledast : \mathbb{G}_1 \times \mathbb{G}_2 \to \mathbb{G}_T$ and $A \circledast B = e(A, B)$. In this case we refer to the resulting protocols as *inner pairing product* arguments. In MIPP we use the inner product $\circledast : \mathbb{G} \times \mathbb{F} \to \mathbb{G}$ and $A \circledast b = A^b$, a multiexponentiation inner product.

Inner Product Commitment. We further define an inner product commitment which consists of a doubly homomorphic commitment with a message space that is the Cartesian product of three message subspaces and an inner product that maps the first two message subspaces to the third. For GIPA the committed vectors and commitment keys halve in every round. If the commitments are constant sized, we can add commitments of different length. If not, we need to assume that the commitment key has a collapsing property such that additions of commitments are still well defined: Concretely we require that there exists a collapsing function $\mathsf{Collapse}$ to reduce the size of commitments with repeated entries. For example consider a commitment scheme with commitment key $[g_1, g_2, g_3, g_4] \in \mathbb{G}^4$ that commits a message vector with repeated entries, $[a_1, a_2, a_1, a_2] \in \mathbb{F}^4$ as $[g_1^{a_1}, g_2^{a_2}, g_3^{a_1}, g_4^{a_2}]$. Then, we can define a collapsing function that outputs the shorter commitment $[(g_1 g_3)^{a_1}, (g_2 g_4)^{a_2}]$ under a compressed commitment key $[g_1 g_3, g_2 g_4] \in \mathbb{G}^2$.

Definition 3 (Inner product commitment). *Let* $(\mathsf{Setup}, \mathsf{CM})$ *be a doubly homomorphic commitment with message space* $\mathcal{M} = \mathcal{M}_1^m \times \mathcal{M}_2^m \times \mathcal{M}_3$ *and key space* $\mathcal{K} = \mathcal{K}_1^m \times \mathcal{K}_2^m \times \mathcal{K}_3$ *defined for all* $m \in [2^j]_{j \in \mathbb{N}}$*, where* $|\mathcal{M}_i| = |\mathcal{K}_i| = p$ *is prime for* $i \in [3]$*. Let* $\circledast : \mathcal{M}_1 \times \mathcal{M}_2 \to \mathcal{M}_3$*. We call* $((\mathsf{Setup}, \mathsf{CM}), \circledast)$ *an* ***inner product commitment*** *if there exists an efficient deterministic function* $\mathsf{Collapse}$ *such that for all* $m \in [2^j]_{j \in \mathbb{N}}$*,* $M \in \mathcal{M}$*, and* $\mathsf{ck}, \mathsf{ck}' \in \mathcal{K}$ *such that* $\mathsf{ck}_3 = \mathsf{ck}'_3$ *it holds as*

$$\mathsf{Collapse}\left(\mathsf{CM}\left(\begin{array}{c|c} \mathsf{ck}_1 \| \mathsf{ck}'_1 & M_1 \| M_1 \\ \mathsf{ck}_2 \| \mathsf{ck}'_2 & M_2 \| M_2 \\ \mathsf{ck}_3 & M_3 \end{array}\right)\right) = \mathsf{CM}\left(\begin{array}{c|c} \mathsf{ck}_1 + \mathsf{ck}'_1 & M_1 \\ \mathsf{ck}_2 + \mathsf{ck}'_2 & M_2 \\ \mathsf{ck}_3 & M_3 \end{array}\right) .$$

We refer to the requirement above as the ***collapsing property****.*

Let $((\mathsf{Setup}, \mathsf{CM}), \circledast)$ be a binding inner product commitment as defined above. In Fig. 1 we present a generalized inner product argument defined for all $m \in [2^j]_{j \in \mathbb{N}}$. We prove that this protocol is an argument (resp., proof) of knowledge when instantiated with a computationally (resp., statistically) binding inner product commitment. The proof of the following theorem is presented in the full version [Bün+19].

Theorem 1 (GIPA **knowledge-soundness).** *If* $((\mathsf{Setup}, \mathsf{CM}), \circledast)$ *is a computationally (resp., perfectly) binding inner product commitment, then* $(\mathsf{Setup}, \mathsf{Prove}, \mathsf{Verify})$*, where* CM *and* $\circledast$ *instantiate the* Prove *and* Verify *algorithms presented in Fig. 1, has perfect completeness and computational (resp., statistical) knowledge-soundness for the relation*

$$\mathcal{R}_{\mathsf{IPA}} = \left\{ \begin{array}{r} (\mathsf{ck} \in \mathcal{K}_1^m \times \mathcal{K}_2^m \times \mathcal{K}_3 \; C \in \mathsf{Image}(\mathsf{CM}); \boldsymbol{a} \in \mathcal{M}_1^m, \boldsymbol{b} \in \mathcal{M}_2^m) : \\ C = \mathsf{CM}(\mathsf{ck};\; (\boldsymbol{a}, \boldsymbol{b}, \langle \boldsymbol{a}, \boldsymbol{b} \rangle)) \end{array} \right\} .$$

Non-interactive Argument. In order to turn the public-coin interactive argument into a non-interactive proof we rely on the Fiat–Shamir heuristic. This results in all challenges being generated from a cryptographic hash function instead of by a verifier. The proof for the following theorem is presented in the full version [Bün+19].

Theorem 2. *If* $((\mathsf{Setup}, \mathsf{CM}), \circledast)$ *is a computationally (resp., perfectly) binding inner product commitment then in the algebraic group model and modeling* Hash *as a random oracle* $\mathsf{FS}(\mathsf{GIPA})$ *is a non-interactive argument of knowledge against an efficient t-query adversary in the random oracle model.*

Efficiency. Let m be a power of 2 and $\ell = \log_2 m$, the number of rounds in the GIPA protocol. The prover communication consists of 2ℓ commitments, 1 $\mathcal{M}_1$ element, and 1 $\mathcal{M}_2$ element. When the commitment scheme used is constant-sized, an instantiation of GIPA produces log-size proof. The prover makes 2 commitments to $(m+1)$-element messages in the first round, 2 commitments to $(m/2+1)$-element messages in the second, and 2 commitments to $(m/2^{i-1}+1)$-element messages in the i-th. It holds that $2 \cdot \sum_{i=1}^{\ell} \left(\frac{m}{2^{i-1}} + 1\right) = 4m + 2\ell - 4 \approx 4m$. So we say the prover commits to a total of $4m$ elements. Before computing these commitments, however, the prover first must compute the z_L and z_R inner products, similarly requiring $2m$ invocations of $\circledast$ on $4m$ elements. Upon receiving the 2 commitments sent each round, the verifier uses them along with the challenge x_i it sampled that round to compute C', requiring 2ℓ multiplications in $\mathsf{Image}(\mathsf{CM})$.

The prover and verifier each compute ck' in each round, requiring $2m$ multiplications in $\mathcal{K}$. Some extensions of the GIPA protocol we'll introduce later use trusted setups to produced structured commitment keys. In these protocols, the verifier doesn't compute ck' themself in each round, but instead is sent the final rescaling $\mathsf{ck} \in \mathcal{K}_1 \times \mathcal{K}_2 \times \mathcal{K}_3$ that can be seen as a polynomial commitment in the verifiers challenges because of how the commitment key was structured. The verifier asks for an opening at a random point, which they can check with a small constant number of multiplications and pairings, and $O(\ell)$ field operations. This technique achieves a log-time verifier.

The prover alone computes $\boldsymbol{a}'$ and $\boldsymbol{b}'$, requiring m multiplications in each of $\mathcal{M}_1$ and $\mathcal{M}_2$. In some instantiations of GIPA, one or both of the vectors in $\mathcal{M}_1$ and $\mathcal{M}_2$ are included in full in the public input (i.e., the commitment performs the identity map on these inputs). In this case the verifier computes $\boldsymbol{a}'$ and/or $\boldsymbol{b}'$ themself.

4.3 Instantiation

GIPA can be instantiated with different commitments and inner product maps. In Bulletproofs [Bün+18] it is instantiated with the generalized Pedersen commitment defined above, where $\mathcal{K} = \mathbb{G}^m \times \mathbb{G}^m \times \mathbb{G}^m$, $\mathcal{M} = \mathbb{F}_p^m \times \mathbb{F}_p^m \times \mathbb{F}_p$, and $\circledast$ is the field addition operation. The reader can verify the commitment is a binding, doubly-homomorphic commitment scheme if the DL assumption holds for $\mathbb{G}$.

As a second example, in [LMR19] GIPA is instantiated for the inner pairing product $a \circledast b \equiv e(a, b)$ using the public-coin setup commitment scheme

$$\mathsf{CM}((\boldsymbol{v}, \boldsymbol{w}, 1);\ (\boldsymbol{A}, \boldsymbol{B}, \boldsymbol{A} * \boldsymbol{B})) = (\boldsymbol{A} * \boldsymbol{v}, \boldsymbol{w} * \boldsymbol{B}, \boldsymbol{A} * \boldsymbol{B}) \ .$$

Parts of the commitment may be computable directly from inputs to the verifier. For efficiency reasons the prover would not have to transmit that part of the commitment. We can formulate instantiations of GIPA for the inner pairing product map and the identity commitment scheme, which is perfectly (and thus statistically) binding.

An Improvement on [LMR19]**.** GIPA also directly yields an improvement to the protocol presented in [LMR19] for proving knowledge of committed vectors of source group elements such that their inner pairing product is a public target group element. Replacing Lai et al.'s commitment scheme with [Abe+16] results in a 2 times faster prover and verifier for the relation while retaining the same proof size and assumptions.

5 Log-Time Verifier Inner Pairing Product Arguments

We present three inner product protocols that build on GIPA with the use of a trusted setup. Informally, these protocols prove the following relations:

(1) TIPP: An inner pairing product argument that proves $Z \in \mathbb{G}_T$ is the inner pairing product between committed vectors $\boldsymbol{A} \in \mathbb{G}_1^m$ and $\boldsymbol{B} \in \mathbb{G}_2^m$.
(2) MIPP_u: An unknown-exponent multiexponentiation inner product argument that proves $U \in \mathbb{G}_1$ is the multiexponentiation product between committed vectors $\boldsymbol{A} \in \mathbb{G}_1^m$ and $\boldsymbol{b} \in \mathbb{F}^m$.
(3) MIPP_k: A known-exponent multiexponentiation inner product argument that proves $U \in \mathbb{G}_1$ is the multiexponentiation inner product between a committed vector $\boldsymbol{A} \in \mathbb{G}_1^m$ and an uncommitted vector $\boldsymbol{b} = [b^i]_{i=0}^{m-1}$ for $b \in \mathbb{F}$.

Our arguments achieve log-time verification by building on a recent observation about inner product arguments by Bowe, Grigg, and Hopwood [BGH19]. A specially structured commitment scheme allows the prover to send the final commitment key and a succinct proof (as a KZG polynomial opening) of its correctness, which is verified via a log-time evaluation of the polynomial and two pairings.

5.1 Inner Product Commitments with Structured Setup

We construct inner product commitments for our arguments that are structured-key variants of the pairing-based commitment for group elements introduced by Abe et al. in [Abe+16] and of the Pedersen commitment for field elements [Ped92]. The setup algorithms for the inner product arguments are input a security parameter λ and a max instance size $m \in \{2^n\}_{n \in \mathbb{Z}^+}$. A type 3 bilinear group description $\langle \mathsf{group} \rangle \leftarrow \mathsf{SampleGrp_3}(1^\lambda)$ is sampled. The structured setup proceeds by sampling random trapdoor elements $\alpha, \beta \xleftarrow{\$} \mathbb{F}$, and constructing the prover and verifier keys (SRS) as follows for generators $g \in \mathbb{G}_1$ and $h \in \mathbb{G}_2$:

$$(\langle \mathsf{group} \rangle, \mathsf{pk} = (\left[g^{\alpha^i}\right]_{i=0}^{2m-2}, \left[h^{\beta^i}\right]_{i=0}^{2m-2}), \mathsf{vk} = (g^\beta, h^\alpha)) \xleftarrow{\$} \mathsf{Setup}(1^\lambda, m)$$

The inner product commitment keys are derived by taking the even powers from the prover SRS as $\boldsymbol{w} = \left[g^{\alpha^{2i}}\right]_{i=0}^{m-1}$ and $\boldsymbol{v} = \left[h^{\beta^{2i}}\right]_{i=0}^{m-1}$. They are used as keys for the following inner product commitments. Observe that the vector commitment components of these inner product commitments are simply the structured-key variants of [Abe+16] and [Ped92]. The inner product values U, Z and the known vector $\boldsymbol{b}$ are committed to as the identity with keys initialized to 1.

(1) TIPP: $\mathsf{CM_{TIPP}}((\boldsymbol{v}, \boldsymbol{w}, 1_{\mathbb{G}_T});\ \boldsymbol{A}, \boldsymbol{B}, Z) := (\boldsymbol{A} * \boldsymbol{v}, \boldsymbol{w} * \boldsymbol{B}, Z)$
(2) MIPP_u: $\mathsf{CM_{MIPP\text{-}u}}((\boldsymbol{v}, \boldsymbol{w}, 1_{\mathbb{G}_T});\ \boldsymbol{A}, \boldsymbol{b}, U) := (\boldsymbol{A} * \boldsymbol{v}, \boldsymbol{w}^{\boldsymbol{b}}, U)$
(3) MIPP_k: $\mathsf{CM_{MIPP\text{-}k}}((\boldsymbol{v}, \boldsymbol{1}_{\mathbb{F}}, 1_{\mathbb{G}_T});\ \boldsymbol{A}, \boldsymbol{b}, U) := (\boldsymbol{A} * \boldsymbol{v}, \boldsymbol{b}, U)$

It follows directly from the q-ASDBP assumption (see full version [Bün+19]) that these commitments are binding with respect to both the commitment key and the proving SRS. Note that the commitment keys only use even powers of trapdoor elements. This is to prevent an adversary from using (g^β, h^α) to find collisions in the commitment scheme—observe that $e(g, h^\alpha) \cdot e(g^\alpha, h^{-1}) = 1_{\mathbb{G}_T}$. The proving SRS requires all powers in order to compute the succinct KZG polynomial opening proofs for the final commitment keys. This is the reason for our introduction of a new security assumption.

KZG Polynomial Commitments. As mentioned, we make use of the KZG polynomial commitment scheme [KZG10] which commits to polynomials of some max degree n. For polynomial $f(X) = \sum_{i=0}^{n-1} a_i X^i$ where $\boldsymbol{a} = [a_i]_{i=0}^{n-1}$, the commitment is computed with an analogously-structured trapdoor commitment key $\boldsymbol{ck} = \left[g^{\alpha^i}\right]_{i=0}^{n-1}$ as $\mathsf{KZG.CM}(\langle \mathsf{group} \rangle, \boldsymbol{ck}, \boldsymbol{a}) = \boldsymbol{ck}^{\boldsymbol{a}}$.

To open a point (x, y) where $y = f(x)$, KZG uses the polynomial remainder theorem which says $f(x) = y \Leftrightarrow \exists q(X) : f(X) - y = q(X)(X - x)$. The proof is just a KZG commitment to the quotient polynomial $q(X)$ where if $q(X)$ has coefficients $\boldsymbol{b}$, then $\mathsf{KZG.Open}(\langle \mathsf{group} \rangle, \boldsymbol{ck}, \boldsymbol{a}, x) = \boldsymbol{ck}^{\boldsymbol{b}}$. The verifier key consists of h^α, and the verifier runs $\mathsf{KZG.Verify}(\langle \mathsf{group} \rangle, h^\alpha, C, W, x, y)$ for commitment C and opening W and checks that $e(Cg^{-y}W^x, h) = e(W, h^\alpha)$.

5.2 Final Commitment Keys

Recall in GIPA, the verifier is required to perform a logarithmic amount of work to verify the final commitments C_L and C_R, using the challenges of each round of recursion to transform the commitments homomorphically. Assuming the commitments are of constant size this means that the verifier can efficiently check that these values are correct. However, the verifier must also perform a linear

$\mathsf{Prove}(\langle\mathsf{group}\rangle, f(X), \boldsymbol{g} = [g^{\alpha^i}]_{i=0}^{2m-2})$		$\mathsf{Verify}(\langle\mathsf{group}\rangle,\ (f(X), h^{\alpha}))$
$w = \mathsf{KZG.CM}(\langle\mathsf{group}\rangle, \boldsymbol{g}, f(X))$	$\xrightarrow{w \in \mathbb{G}_1}$	
	$\xleftarrow{z \in \mathbb{F}_p}$	$z \xleftarrow{\$} \mathbb{F}_p$
$\pi = \mathsf{KZG.Open}(\langle\mathsf{group}\rangle, \boldsymbol{g}, f(X), z)$	$\xrightarrow{\pi \in \mathbb{G}_1}$	**Return** $\mathsf{KZG.Verify}(\langle\mathsf{group}\rangle, h^{\alpha}, w, \pi, f(z))$

Fig. 2. The argument (of $\mathcal{R}_{ck}$) used to allow a prover to prove well-formedness of the final structured commitment key. The final commitment key w is interpreted as a KZG polynomial commitment that the prover must open at a random point. Shown for $w \in \mathbb{G}_1$, but holds analogously for $v \in \mathbb{G}_2$.

amount of work in rescaling the commitment key ck. Thus to achieve logarithmic verification time, when instantiating GIPA we need to avoid having the verifier rescale the commitment keys. We do this by outsourcing the work of rescaling the commitment keys to the prover.

The prover will compute the final commitment keys and then prove that they are well-formed, i.e., that they are exactly what the verifier would have computed in an unmodified instantiation of GIPA. Recall, we have structured our commitment keys as $\boldsymbol{w} = \left[g^{\alpha^{2i}}\right]_{i=0}^{m-1}$ and $\boldsymbol{v} = \left[h^{\beta^{2i}}\right]_{i=0}^{m-1}$. Without loss of generality, we will present the approach inspired by techniques from [BGH19] with respect to proving well-formedness of the final commitment key for $\boldsymbol{w} \in \mathbb{G}_1$; the techniques will apply analogously to $\boldsymbol{v} \in \mathbb{G}_2$.

In each round of GIPA, the commitment key is homomorphically rescaled by the round challenge x as:

$$\boldsymbol{w}' = \boldsymbol{w}_{[:m/2]} \circ \boldsymbol{w}_{[m/2:]}^{x} = \left[g^{\alpha^{2i}(1+x\alpha^{m+2i})}\right]_{i=0}^{m/2-1}.$$

Repeating this rescaling over $\ell = \log m$ recursive rounds with challenges $\boldsymbol{x} = [x_j]_{j=0}^{\ell}$, we claim (and show using an inductive argument in the full version [Bün+19]) that the final commitment key w takes the form:

$$w = g^{\prod_{j=0}^{\ell}\left(1+x_{\ell-j}\alpha^{2^{j+1}}\right)}.$$

We can then view this final commitment key w as a KZG polynomial commitment to the polynomial $f_w(X)$ defined below (and analogously v as the commitment to $f_v(X)$):

$$f_w(X) = \prod_{j=0}^{\ell}\left(1 + x_{\ell-j}X^{2^{j+1}}\right) \qquad f_v(X) = \prod_{j=0}^{\ell}\left(1 + x_{\ell-j}^{-1}X^{2^{j+1}}\right)$$

Thus, to prove the well-formedness of the final commitment keys, the prover will prove the following relation $\mathcal{R}_{\mathsf{ck}}$ making direct use of the KZG polynomial opening proof. Again, without loss of generality, the relation is presented with respect to the final commitment key $w \in \mathbb{G}_1$.

$$\mathcal{R}_{\mathsf{ck}} = \left\{ \left(\langle \mathsf{group} \rangle, w \in \mathbb{G}_2, f(X), h^{\alpha} \; ; \boldsymbol{g} = [g^{\alpha^i}]_{i=0}^{2m-2} \right) : w = g^{f(\alpha)} \right\}$$

Our protocol for proving $\mathcal{R}_{\mathsf{ck}}$ is given in Fig. 2. At a high level, the verifier produces a challenge point $z \in \mathbb{F}$. If the prover can provide a valid KZG opening proof of $f_w(z)$ for commitment w, then the verifier accepts. We formally prove the security of this argument system in the full version [Bün+19] in the algebraic group model.

5.3 TIPP: Inner Pairing Product

The TIPP protocol allows a prover to show that for $T, U, Z \in \mathbb{G}_T$, they know $\boldsymbol{A} \in \mathbb{G}_1$ and $\boldsymbol{B} \in \mathbb{G}_2$ such that T and U are pairing commitments to $\boldsymbol{A}$ and $\boldsymbol{B}$, and Z is the inner pairing product $Z = \boldsymbol{A} * \boldsymbol{B}$.

This description is not quite general enough to cover the needs of our applications, such as batch verification. For example, to check that m pairing equations are simultaneously satisfied (i.e., that $[Z_i = e(A_i, B_i)]_{i=0}^{m-1}$), it is not sufficient to prove that $\Pi_{i=0}^{m-1} e(A_i, B_i) = \Pi_{i=0}^{m-1} Z_i$. Rather, instead you must prove the inner pairing product of a random linear combination defined by verifier challenge $r \in \mathbb{F}$: $\Pi_{i=0}^{m-1} e(A_i, B_i)^{r^i} = \Pi_{i=0}^{m-1} Z_i^{r^i}$.

We support this by modifying the TIPP relation to include the linear combination challenge r. For notational simplicity, we will use powers of two (matching that of our commitment keys) and define a public vector of field elements $\boldsymbol{r} = [r^{2i}]_{i=0}^{2m-2}$. The prover first commits to T and U, and then the verifier send a random field element r. Thus, the TIPP relation is captured formally as follows:

$$\mathcal{R}_{\mathsf{TIPP}} = \left\{ \begin{pmatrix} \langle \mathsf{group} \rangle, \; g^{\beta} \in \mathbb{G}_1, \; h^{\alpha} \in \mathbb{G}_2, \; T, U, Z \in \mathbb{G}_T, \; r \in \mathbb{F} \; ; \\ \boldsymbol{w} = [g^{\alpha^{2i}}]_{i=0}^{m-1}, \boldsymbol{A} \in \mathbb{G}_1^m, \; \boldsymbol{v} = [h^{\beta^{2i}}]_{i=0}^{m-1}, \boldsymbol{B} \in \mathbb{G}_2^m, \\ \boldsymbol{r} = [r^{2i}]_{i=0}^{m-1} \in \mathbb{F}^m \end{pmatrix} : \begin{matrix} \\ T = \boldsymbol{A} * \boldsymbol{v} \; \wedge \; U = \boldsymbol{w} * \boldsymbol{B} \; \wedge \; Z = \boldsymbol{A}^{\boldsymbol{r}} * \boldsymbol{B} \end{matrix} \right\}.$$

Observe that if $T = \boldsymbol{A} * \boldsymbol{v}$ is a commitment to $\boldsymbol{A}$, then $T = \boldsymbol{A}^{\boldsymbol{r}} * \boldsymbol{v}^{\boldsymbol{r}^{-1}}$ is a commitment to $\boldsymbol{A}^{\boldsymbol{r}}$ under the commitment key $\boldsymbol{v}^{\boldsymbol{r}^{-1}}$. Intuitively, the argument proceeds by having the prover act as if it is working with a rescaled commitment key $\boldsymbol{v}' = \boldsymbol{v}^{\boldsymbol{r}^{-1}}$. TIPP runs the GIPA protocol with $\mathsf{CM}_{\mathsf{TIPP}}$ where the collapsing function is defined as the identity, $\mathsf{Collapse}_{\mathsf{id}}(C) = C$, over message $(\boldsymbol{A}^{\boldsymbol{r}}, \boldsymbol{B}, Z = \boldsymbol{A}^{\boldsymbol{r}} * \boldsymbol{B})$ and commitment key $(\boldsymbol{v}' = \boldsymbol{v}^{\boldsymbol{r}^{-1}}, \boldsymbol{w}, 1_{\mathbb{G}_T})$. Since all components of the commitment are compact, the identity collapsing function is sufficient.

Lastly, since the protocol is run over a rescaled commitment key $\boldsymbol{v}'$, the polynomial with which the prover proves the well-formedness of the final commitment key is also rescaled. It is as follows (derived in the full version [Bün+19]):

$$f'_v(X) = \prod_{j=0}^{\ell} \left(1 + x_{\ell-j}^{-1} (rX)^{2^{j+1}} \right)$$

$\mathsf{TIPP.Prove}(\langle\mathsf{group}\rangle, \mathsf{pk} = (\left[g^{\alpha^i}\right]_{i=0}^{2m-2}, \left[h^{\beta^i}\right]_{i=0}^{2m-2}), (T, U, Z, r), (\boldsymbol{A}, \boldsymbol{B}, \boldsymbol{w}, \boldsymbol{v}, \boldsymbol{r}))$
$\leftrightarrow \mathsf{TIPP.Verify}(\langle\mathsf{group}\rangle, \mathsf{vk} = (g^\beta, h^\alpha), (T, U, Z, r)):$

1. Prover rescales $\boldsymbol{A}$ and $\boldsymbol{v}$ with respect to linear combination challenge r:

$$\boldsymbol{A}' = \boldsymbol{A}^{\boldsymbol{r}} \qquad \boldsymbol{v}' = \boldsymbol{v}^{\boldsymbol{r}^{-1}}.$$

Run GIPA:

2. Prover and verifier run GIPA with $\mathsf{CM}_{\mathsf{TIPP}}$ and $\mathsf{Collapse}_{\mathsf{id}}$ with some minor changes:

$$\mathsf{GIPA}_{\mathsf{CM\text{-}TIPP}}.\mathsf{Prove}(\langle\mathsf{group}\rangle, (\boldsymbol{v}', \boldsymbol{w}, 1_{\mathbb{G}_T}), (\boldsymbol{A}', \boldsymbol{B})) \leftrightarrow \mathsf{GIPA}_{\mathsf{CM\text{-}TIPP}}.\mathsf{Verify}(\langle\mathsf{group}\rangle, \cdot, (T, U, Z))$$

   (a) The verifier does not take as input a commitment key, and does not perform commitment key rescalings during GIPA execution. The verifier takes as output the final commitment C, the final message values (A, B), and the recursive round challenges $\boldsymbol{x} = [x_j]_{j=0}^{\log m}$.
   (b) The prover stores the recursive round challenges $\boldsymbol{x}$ and the final commitment keys $(v, w) = (\mathsf{ck}_1, \mathsf{ck}_2)$.
   (c) The prover sends the final commitment keys (v, w) to the verifier.

Prove well-formedness of final commitment keys:

3. Define the following polynomials for $\ell = \log m$:

$$f_w(X) = \prod_{j=0}^{\ell} \left(1 + x_{\ell-j} X^{2^{j+1}}\right) \qquad f_v'(X) = \prod_{j=0}^{\ell} \left(1 + x_{\ell-j}^{-1} (rX)^{2^{j+1}}\right)$$

4. Prover and verifier run the argument from Figure 2 for each final commitment key v and w:

$$\mathsf{CK.Prove}(\langle\mathsf{group}\rangle, f_w(X), \left[g^{\alpha^i}\right]_{i=0}^{2m-2}) \leftrightarrow \mathsf{CK.Verify}(\langle\mathsf{group}\rangle, (w, f_w(X), h^\alpha))$$

$$\mathsf{CK.Prove}(\langle\mathsf{group}\rangle, f_v'(X), \left[h^{\beta^i}\right]_{i=0}^{2m-2}) \leftrightarrow \mathsf{CK.Verify}(\langle\mathsf{group}\rangle, (v, f_v'(X), g^\beta))$$

5. Verifier returns 1 if the above arguments accept and if $\mathsf{CM}_{\mathsf{TIPP}}((v, w, 1_{\mathbb{G}_T}); (A, B, e(A, B))) == C$.

Fig. 3. TIPP argument of knowledge for inner pairing product between committed vectors.

A full description of the protocol is given in Fig. 3. Because the protocol is public-coin, we can transform the interactive argument into a non-interactive proof using the Fiat-Shamir heuristic. In later sections, we may overload TIPP.Prove and TIPP.Verify as their non-interactive counterparts in which the prover will output a proof π that will be taken as an additional input by the verifier. This will be the case for MIPP_u and MIPP_k as well.

Communication and Time Complexity. Table 2 gives an overview of the communication and time complexity of our inner product protocols. Here we provide accounting for TIPP. The prover SRS consists of $2m$ elements in $\mathbb{G}_1$ and $2m$ elements in $\mathbb{G}_2$. The SRS consists only of monomials and therefore is updatable. The verifier's SRS consists of the group description, 1 elements in $\mathbb{G}_1$ and 1 elements in $\mathbb{G}_2$.

We calculate the prover computation. Our recursive argument requires $\log(m)$ rounds. The left and right commitments at each recursive round of GIPA require a total of $6m$ pairings to compute: $3m$ in the first round, $\frac{3m}{2}$ in the second round, and $\frac{3m}{2^{j-1}}$ in the j-th round. Homomorphically rescaling the commitment keys $(\boldsymbol{v}, \boldsymbol{w})$ and the messages $(\boldsymbol{A}, \boldsymbol{B})$ require a total of $2m$ exponentiations in each source group. The prover for the final commitment key costs $2m$ group

Table 2. Efficiency table for TIPP, MIPP_k, and MIPP_u. The verifier keys are succinct.

	Communication complexity		Time complexity	
	$\|SRS\|$	$\|\pi\|$	Prove	Verify
TIPP	$2m\ \mathbb{G}_1 + 2m\ \mathbb{G}_2$	$6\log m\ \mathbb{G}_T + 3\ \mathbb{G}_1 + 3\ \mathbb{G}_2$	$4m\ \mathbb{G}_1 + 4m\ \mathbb{G}_2 + 6m\ P$	$7\ P + 6\log m\ \mathbb{G}_T$
MIPP_u	$m\ \mathbb{G}_1 + 2m\ \mathbb{G}_2$	$2\log m\ \mathbb{G}_T + 3\ \mathbb{G}_1 + 2\ \mathbb{G}_2 + 1\ \mathbb{F}$	$3m\ \mathbb{G}_1 + 3m\ \mathbb{G}_2 + 2m\ P$	$6\ P + 2\log m\ \mathbb{G}_T$
MIPP_k	$2m\ \mathbb{G}_2$	$2\log m\ \mathbb{G}_T + 1\ \mathbb{G}_1 + 2\ \mathbb{G}_2$	$m\ \mathbb{G}_1 + 3m\ \mathbb{G}_2 + 2m\ P$	$4\ P + 2\log m\ \mathbb{G}_T + \log m\ \mathbb{F}$

exponentiations in each source group (for each commitment key). In total this sums to $6m$ pairings, $4m$ $\mathbb{G}_1$ exponentiations and $4m$ $\mathbb{G}_2$ exponentiations.

Regarding proof size, we have $6\log(m)$ $\mathbb{G}_T$ elements from the recursive argument, 1 $\mathbb{G}_1$ element and 1 $\mathbb{G}_2$ element from the final openings, and 2 $\mathbb{G}_1$ elements and 2 $\mathbb{G}_2$ elements from the final commitment key argument (i.e., w, v, and their proofs of correctness).

The verifier computes 7 pairings: 3 from the recursive argument and 4 from the final commitment key argument. Homomorphically rescaling the commitments in the recursive argument requires $6\log(m)$ exponentiations in $\mathbb{G}_T$. The verifier also computes $f(z)$ in the final commitment key argument which costs $2\ell = 2\log_2(m)$ field multiplications and additions.

Security. Here we prove soundness for TIPP in the algebraic group model.

Theorem 3 (Computational knowledge-soundness TIPP). *The protocol defined in Sect. 5.3 for the NP relation $\mathcal{R}_{\mathsf{TIPP}}$ has computational knowledge-soundness against algebraic adversaries under the q-ASDBP and $2q$-SDH assumptions.*

Proof. The commitment scheme $\mathsf{CM}((\boldsymbol{v}', \boldsymbol{w}, 1), (\boldsymbol{A}', \boldsymbol{B}, Z)) = (\boldsymbol{A}' * \boldsymbol{v}',\ \boldsymbol{w} * \boldsymbol{B}, Z) = (T, U, Z)$ is doubly homomorphic: the key space $\mathbb{G}_2^m \times \mathbb{G}_1^m \times \mathbb{F}$ is homomorphic under $\mathbb{G}_2$ multiplication, $\mathbb{G}_1$ multiplication, and $\mathbb{F}$ addition. The message space $\mathbb{G}_1^m \times \mathbb{G}_2^m \times \mathbb{G}_T$ is homomorphic under the respective group multiplications. The commitment space $\mathbb{G}_T \times \mathbb{G}_T \times \mathbb{G}_T$ is homomorphic under $\mathbb{G}_T$ multiplication. All groups have prime order p for $p > 2^\lambda$. The commitment scheme is also binding by the q-ASDBP assumption. This means that the commitment scheme is an inner product commitment. Thus either the adversary convinces the verifier of incorrect w, v, or by Theorem 1 an adversary that breaks knowledge-soundness can extract a valid m-ASDBP instance. An algebraic adversary that convinces a verifier of incorrect w, v can extract a valid $2m$-SDH instance by the security of $\mathcal{R}_{\mathsf{ck}}$ (Eq. 5.2).

5.4 MIPP_u: Multiexponentiation with Unknown Field Vector

In the MIPP_u protocol, a prover demonstrates knowledge for pairing commitment $T \in \mathbb{G}_T$ and KZG commitment $B \in \mathbb{G}_2$ of $\boldsymbol{A} \in \mathbb{G}_1^m$ as the opening of T and $\boldsymbol{b} \in \mathbb{F}^m$ as the opening of B where $U = \prod_{i=0}^{m-1} A_i^{r^{2i} b_i}$ for a public field element r. The public field element r, as in Sect. 5.3, allows the argument to be used for random linear combinations. The MIPP_u relation is captured formally as follows:

$$\mathcal{R}_{\mathsf{MIPP}\text{-}u} = \left\{ \left(\begin{array}{c} \langle \mathsf{group} \rangle,\ g^{\beta} \in \mathbb{G}_1,\ h^{\alpha} \in \mathbb{G}_2,\ T \in \mathbb{G}_T,\ B, U \in \mathbb{G}_1,\ r \in \mathbb{F}\ ; \\ \boldsymbol{w} = [g^{\alpha^{2i}}]_{i=0}^{m-1}, \boldsymbol{A} \in \mathbb{G}_1^m, \boldsymbol{v} = [h^{\beta^{2i}}]_{i=0}^{m-1}, \boldsymbol{b} \in \mathbb{F}^m, \\ \boldsymbol{r} = [r^{2i}]_{i=0}^{m-1} \in \mathbb{F}^m \end{array} \right) : \begin{array}{c} \\ T = \boldsymbol{A} * \boldsymbol{v}\ \wedge\ B = \boldsymbol{w}^{\boldsymbol{b}}\ \wedge\ U = \boldsymbol{A}^{\boldsymbol{r} \circ \boldsymbol{b}} \end{array} \right\}.$$

The MIPP_u argument proceeds analogously to TIPP if using the inner product commitment $\mathsf{CM}_{\mathsf{MIPP}\text{-}u}$ where k_U is initialized to $1_{\mathbb{G}_T}$:

$$\mathsf{CM}_{\mathsf{MIPP}\text{-}u}((\boldsymbol{v}, \boldsymbol{w}, k_U);\ \boldsymbol{A}, \boldsymbol{b}, U) := (\boldsymbol{A} * \boldsymbol{v}, \boldsymbol{w}^{\boldsymbol{b}}, k_U U)$$

However, we make a small optimization by replacing the above commitment scheme with a modified scheme $\mathsf{CM}'_{\mathsf{MIPP}\text{-}u}$ with a commitment size consisting only of one element in $\mathbb{G}_T$ (concretely ~25% reduction in size). Recall, the proof includes a logarithmic number of commitments, so cutting the commitment size by 25% more or less cuts the proof size by the same proportion.

Using $\mathsf{CM}'_{\mathsf{MIPP}\text{-}u}$ adds two additional random group elements $\hat{h}_1, \hat{h}_2 \xleftarrow{\$} \mathbb{G}_2$ to the prover key and verifier key $(\mathsf{pk}, \mathsf{vk})$ during setup. After setting (T, B, U, r), the verifier samples values $(c_1, c_2) \xleftarrow{\$} \mathbb{F}$ and sends them to the prover. The prover and verifier then each set $\hat{h}'_1 = \hat{h}_1^{c_1}$ and $\hat{h}'_2 = \hat{h}_2^{c_2}$. The values $\hat{h}'_1$ and $\hat{h}'_2$ become part of the commitment key for the following inner product commitment:

$$\mathsf{CM}'_{\mathsf{MIPP}\text{-}u}((\boldsymbol{v}, \boldsymbol{w}, (\hat{h}'_1, \hat{h}'_2));\ \boldsymbol{A}, \boldsymbol{b}, U) := (\boldsymbol{A} || \boldsymbol{w}^{\boldsymbol{b}} || U) * (\boldsymbol{v} || \hat{h}'_1 || \hat{h}'_2)$$

The prover then proceeds analogously to TIPP. First, running GIPA with $\mathsf{CM}'_{\mathsf{MIPP}\text{-}u}$ with the identity collapsing function over message $(\boldsymbol{A}^{\boldsymbol{r}}, \boldsymbol{b}, U = \boldsymbol{A}^{\boldsymbol{r} \circ \boldsymbol{b}})$ and commitment key $(\boldsymbol{v}' = \boldsymbol{v}^{\boldsymbol{r}^{-1}}, \boldsymbol{w}, (\hat{h}'_1, \hat{h}'_2))$. The verifier runs with commitment $C = T \cdot e(B, \hat{h}'_1) \cdot e(U, \hat{h}'_2$. The final commitment keys w and v are proved with respect to the same polynomials $f_w(X)$ and $f'_v(X)$.

A full description of the protocol is given in the full version [Bün+19]. Soundness follows for algebraic adversaries from the q-ASDBP and the q-SDH assumptions and the algorithm is proven secure in the full version [Bün+19].

5.5 MIPP_k: Multiexponentiation with Known Field Vector

In the MIPP_k protocol a prover demonstrates knowledge of $\boldsymbol{A} \in \mathbb{G}_1^m$ such that $\boldsymbol{A}$ commits to pairing commitment T under $\boldsymbol{v}$ and $U = \boldsymbol{A}^{\boldsymbol{b}}$ for a public vector $\boldsymbol{b} = [b^i]_{i=0}^{m-1}$ for $b \in \mathbb{F}$. The MIPP_k relation is captured formally as follows:

$$\mathcal{R}_{\mathsf{MIPP}\text{-}k} = \left\{ \left(\begin{array}{c} \langle \mathsf{group} \rangle,\ g^{\beta} \in \mathbb{G}_1,\ T \in \mathbb{G}_T,\ U \in \mathbb{G}_1,\ b \in \mathbb{F}\ ; \\ \boldsymbol{A} \in \mathbb{G}_1^m, \boldsymbol{v} = [h^{\beta^{2i}}]_{i=0}^{m-1}, \boldsymbol{b} \end{array} \right) : \begin{array}{c} \\ T = \boldsymbol{A} * \boldsymbol{v}\ \wedge\ U = \boldsymbol{A}^{\boldsymbol{b}}\ \wedge \boldsymbol{b} = [b^i]_{i=0}^{m-1} \end{array} \right\}.$$

For the known vector multiexponentiation inner product, we use an inner product commitment that commits to the vector $\boldsymbol{b}$ as itself using a key $\boldsymbol{k_b}$ initialized to $\boldsymbol{1}_{\mathbb{F}}$. Since the commitment is no longer compact, we use a collapsing function that collapses the vector by adding the first and second halves. This provides the required homomorphic properties of Definition 3.

$$\mathsf{CM}_{\mathsf{MIPP}\text{-}k}((\boldsymbol{v}, \boldsymbol{k_b}, 1_{\mathbb{G}_T});\ \boldsymbol{A}, \boldsymbol{b}, U) := (\boldsymbol{A} * \boldsymbol{v}, [k_{b,i} b_i]_{i=0}^{m-1}, U)$$

$$\mathsf{Collapse}_{\mathsf{MIPP}\text{-}k}(C = (C_A, \boldsymbol{C_b}, C_U)) = (C_A, [C_{b,i} + C_{b,(i+\frac{m}{2})}]_{i=0}^{\frac{m}{2}-1}, C_U)$$

If we were to run GIPA naively with this commitment, the proof size would be linear in the length of $\boldsymbol{b}$. However, we can use a similar to trick to how we calculate the final commitment keys (Sect. 5.2). Instead of sending the commitment to the rescaled message $\boldsymbol{b}$ at each recursive round, we observe that rescaling the structured vector $\boldsymbol{b}$ leads to a closed-form expression of the final b' message using recursive challenges $\boldsymbol{x} = [x_j]_{j=0}^{\log m} : b' = \prod_{j=0}^{\ell} \left(1 + x_{\ell-j}^{-1} b^{2^j}\right)$. This value b' can be computed in $\log m$ time by the verifier and allows for the prover to omit the commitment to $\boldsymbol{b}$, bringing the proof size back to logarithmic in m.

In addition, as in Sect. 5.4 for MIPP_u, we provide an optimized inner product commitment scheme $\mathsf{CM}'_{\mathsf{MIPP}\text{-}k}$ with commitment size equal to one element of $\mathbb{G}_T$ (when using the above trick to omit $\boldsymbol{b}$). The commitment $\mathsf{CM}'_{\mathsf{MIPP}\text{-}u}$ adds one additional random group element $\hat{h} \xleftarrow{\$} \mathbb{G}_2$ to the prover key and verifier key $(\mathsf{pk}, \mathsf{vk})$ during setup. After setting (T, U, b), the verifier samples value $c \xleftarrow{\$} \mathbb{F}$ and sends it to the prover. The prover and verifier then each set $\hat{h}' = \hat{h}^c$. The value $\hat{h}'$ becomes part of the commitment key for the following inner product commitment:

$$\mathsf{CM}'_{\mathsf{MIPP}\text{-}k}((\boldsymbol{v}, \boldsymbol{k_b}, \hat{h}');\ \boldsymbol{A}, \boldsymbol{b}, U) := ((\boldsymbol{A}||U) * (\boldsymbol{v}||\hat{h}'), [k_{b,i} b_i]_{i=0}^{m-1})$$

$$\mathsf{Collapse}'_{\mathsf{MIPP}\text{-}k}(C = (C_{A||U}, \boldsymbol{b} = [b^i]_{i=0}^{m-1})) = (C_{A||U}, [C_{b,i} + C_{b,(i+\frac{m}{2})}]_{i=0}^{\frac{m}{2}-1})$$

A full description of the protocol is given in the full version [Bün+19]. Soundness follows for algebraic adversaries from the q-ASDBP and the q-SDH assumptions and the algorithm is proven secure in the full version [Bün+19].

6 Log-Time Verifier Polynomial Commitments with Square Root SRS

In this section we introduce a polynomial commitment (PC) scheme with a square root sized SRS and opening time, and logarithmic proof sizes and verifier time. We use a two-tiered homomorphic commitment algorithm similar to the one from [Gro11] but with structured keys. We first describe how our PC can be used for bivariate polynomials, and then present a simple way to use it for univariate polynomials as well. In the full version [Bün+19], we show how these polynomial commitments can be made hiding for zero-knowledge applications.

Two-Tiered Inner Product Commitment. We describe a two-tiered inner product commitment for bivariate polynomials. It is based on the [Gro11] two tiered commitment. We use the structured-key variant of the [Abe+16] commitment introduced in Sect. 5.1 to commit to the KZG commitments [KZG10]. A brief description of KZG commitments was also given in Sect. 5.1. We describe our polynomial commitment in Fig. 4.

To commit to a polynomial $f(X,Y) = \sum_{j=0}^{m-1} f_j(Y)X^j$ given commitment key $ck = (\boldsymbol{g}, \boldsymbol{v}, \hat{h})$, the committer computes m KZG polynomial commitments $\boldsymbol{A} = [A_j]_{j=0}^{m-1}$ to y-polynomials $\boldsymbol{f} = [f_j(Y)]_{j=0}^{m-1}$ where say $f_j(Y)$ has coefficients $\boldsymbol{a}_j = [a_{i,j}]_{i=0}^{\ell-1}$: $A_j = \mathsf{KZG.CM}(\boldsymbol{g}, \boldsymbol{a}_j) = \boldsymbol{g}^{\boldsymbol{a}_j} = g^{\sum_{i=0}^{\ell-1} a_{i,j}\alpha^i}$. The committer then computes the pairing commitment [Abe+16] to the KZG commitments

$$T = \boldsymbol{A} * \boldsymbol{v} = \prod_{j=0}^{m-1} e(A_j, v_i) = \prod_{j=0}^{m-1} e(A_j, h^{\beta^{2j}}) \ .$$

Thus, $T = e(g,h)^{\sum_{i,j=0}^{\ell-1,m-1} a_{i,j}\alpha^i\beta^{2j}}$, and this commitment is binding under the q-ASDBP assumption and the q-SDH assumption.

Two-Tiered Opening. Our opening algorithm proves a commitment T to a polynomial $f(X,Y)$ evaluates to ν at a point $(x,y) \in \mathbb{F}^2$. We proceed in three steps. First the prover produces an opening for an outer tier partial evaluation $U = f(x,Y) = \prod_{i=0}^{m-1} A_i^{x^i}$ for a point $x \in \mathbb{F}$. Observe that U is a KZG commitment to the univariate polynomial $f(x,Y) = \sum_{j=0}^{\ell-1}(\sum_{i=0}^{m-1} a_{i,j}x^i)Y^j$. Second the prover produces a MIPP_k proof (see Sect. 5.5) that U is the inner product of the opening to T and the vector $\boldsymbol{x} = (1, x, \ldots, x^{m-1})$. Third the prover produce a KZG proof that ν is the evaluation of U at y. The prover returns U and the two proofs. The verifier simply checks the two proofs.

Theorem 4. *If there exists a bilinear group sampler* $\mathsf{SampleGrp}_3$ *that satisfies the* q-ASDBP *assumption in* $\mathbb{G}_2$ *and the* q-SDH *assumption, then the protocol in Fig. 4 is a polynomial commitment scheme with computational extractability against algebraic adversaries.*

Note that computing the partial opening U takes $m\ell$ $\mathbb{G}_1$ exponentiations if computing from scratch. Instead, if the KZG commitments to the y-polynomials $\boldsymbol{A}$ are given as input, U can be computed with only m $\mathbb{G}_1$ exponentiations. Thus, we pass $\boldsymbol{A}$, which was already computed during commitment, as auxiliary data to the opening algorithm to facilitate our square root degree opening time.

Supporting Univariate Polynomials. If we have a univariate polynomial, then we set $\ell m = d$ for d the degree of $f(X)$ and $f_i(Y) = a_{i\ell} + a_{i\ell+1}Y + \ldots + a_{(i+1)\ell-1}Y^{\ell-1} = \sum_{j=0}^{\ell-1} a_{i\ell+j}Y^j$. Observe now that $p(X,Y) = \sum_{i=0}^{m-1} f_i(Y)X^i$ is such that $p(X^\ell, X) = f(X)$ Thus we commit to $f(X)$ by committing to $p(X,Y)$. To evaluate $f(X)$ at x the prover evaluates the first tier at x^ℓ and the second at x. If $\ell \approx m$ then we have square root values $f_i(X)$ which each have degree square root in d. Hence our IPP arguments are ran over a square root number of commitments, which is what makes our verifier complexity and SRS size square root.

$\underline{\mathsf{Setup}(1^\lambda, \ell, m):}$
$\langle \mathsf{group} \rangle \leftarrow \mathsf{SampleGrp}_3(1^\lambda)$
$\hat{h} \xleftarrow{\$} \mathbb{G}_2;\ \ \alpha, \beta \xleftarrow{\$} \mathbb{F}$
$\boldsymbol{g} \leftarrow [g^{\alpha^i}]_{i=0}^{\ell-1}$
$\boldsymbol{v} \leftarrow [h^{\beta^{2i}}]_{i=0}^{m-1}$
$\mathsf{ck} \leftarrow (\langle \mathsf{group} \rangle, \boldsymbol{g}, \boldsymbol{v}, \hat{h})$
$\mathsf{ek} \leftarrow (\langle \mathsf{group} \rangle, \boldsymbol{g}, [h^{\beta^i}]_{i=0}^{2m-2}, \hat{h})$
$\mathsf{vk} \leftarrow (\langle \mathsf{group} \rangle, g^\beta, h^\alpha, \hat{h})$
Return $(\mathsf{ck}, \mathsf{vk})$

$\underline{\mathsf{Open}(\mathsf{ek}, T, (x, y), \nu, f(X, Y), [A_j]_{j=0}^{m-1})}$
$((\langle \mathsf{group} \rangle, \boldsymbol{g}, \mathsf{pk}, \hat{h}) \leftarrow \mathsf{ek}$
$U \leftarrow \prod_{j=0}^{m-1} A_j^{x^i}$
$\pi_1 \leftarrow \mathsf{MIPP}_k.\mathsf{Prove}(\langle \mathsf{group} \rangle, (\mathsf{pk}, \hat{h}), (T, U, x), (\boldsymbol{A}, \boldsymbol{v}, \boldsymbol{x}))$
$\pi_2 \leftarrow \mathsf{KZG.Open}(\langle \mathsf{group} \rangle, \boldsymbol{g}, f(x, Y), \nu)$
Return (U, π_1, π_2)

$\underline{\mathsf{CM}(\mathsf{ck}, f(X, Y)):}$
$[A_j]_{j=0}^{m-1} \leftarrow \prod_{i=0}^{\ell-1} g_i^{a_{i,j}}$
$T \leftarrow \prod_{j=0}^{m-1} e(A_j, v_j)$
Return T

$\underline{\mathsf{Check}(\mathsf{vk}, (T, (x, y), \nu), (U, \pi_1, \pi_2))}$
$b_1 \leftarrow \mathsf{MIPP}_k.\mathsf{Verify}(\langle \mathsf{group} \rangle, (g^\beta, \hat{h}), (T, U, x), \pi_1))$
$b_2 \leftarrow \mathsf{KZG.Verify}(\langle \mathsf{group} \rangle, h^\alpha, U, \pi_2, y)$
Return $b_1 \wedge b_2$

Fig. 4. A two-tiered inner product commitment.

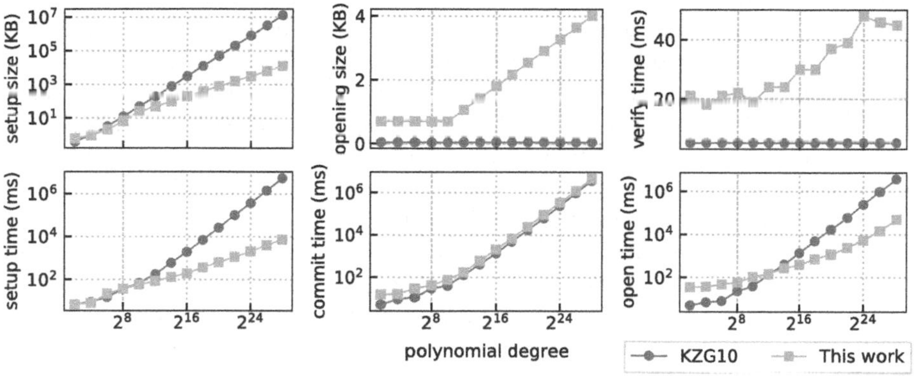

Fig. 5. Measured performance of the IPA polynomial commitment.

Evaluation. In Fig. 5, we compare the performance of our polynomial commitment scheme against the state-of-the-art KZG commitment scheme. In optimizing the IPA commitment scheme, we found that the MIPP_k proof was more expensive than the KZG proof. Therefore, it makes sense to skew the split of the polynomial so the MIPP_k proof is over a smaller vector than the KZG proof. We found a skew of $\kappa = 16$ to be optimal, leading to a split of $m = \frac{\sqrt{d}}{\kappa}$ and $\ell = \kappa\sqrt{d}$; this explains the hitch in the plots until the optimal tradeoff is able to be made at $d = 2^{10}$.

Both KZG and our IPA produce commitments of constant size (a single $\mathbb{G}_1$ element for KZG and a single $\mathbb{G}_T$ element for IPA). The differences are that KZG allows for constant opening proof sizes and constant verifier time (versus our logarithmic opening sizes and verifier time), whereas IPA allows for square root opening time and SRS size (compared to the linear complexity of KZG).

These asymptotic differences result in significant concrete tradeoffs between the two schemes. As expected, the IPA commitment, while expensive for low degree polynomials due to overhead of the inner product argument, quickly becomes much faster to compute opening proofs with breakeven degree being $d \approx 2000$; at $d = 10^6$, IPA is 14× faster, and at $d = 250 \times 10^6$ is 80× faster. Similar savings are made with respect to prover SRS size. For degree 10^6, IPA requires an SRS of size 800 KB, 60× smaller than the 50 MB SRS required by KZG. In contrast, the IPA verifier time and opening size grow logarithmically and thus do not get too large; verifier time remains below 50 ms even for polynomials of degree $d = 250 \times 10^6$, and opening proof size remains below 4 KB.

7 Aggregating SNARK Proofs

We now discuss how the inner pairing product can be used to verify that n independently generated SNARK proofs on independent instances can be aggregated to a $O(\log(n))$ sized proof. While zk-SNARKs have constant-sized proofs and verifiers, in many settings, such as blockchains, a verifier needs to read and verify many proofs created by independent provers. We show how an untrusted aggregator can use inner product arguments to aggregate these proofs into a small logarithmic sized proof. The verifiers only need to check the aggregated proof to be convinced of the existence of the underlying pairing-based SNARKs. We show our approach is concretely much faster than existing approaches relying on recursive composition and expensive pairing-friendly cycles of elliptic curves.

To date the most efficient zkSNARK is due to Groth [Gro16]; it consists of 3 group elements and requires checking a single pairing product equation to verify. We thus choose to describe our methods with respect to [Gro16], but note that they apply more generally to pairing-based SNARKs that do not use random oracles [GM17, Par+13]. We first provide some background on the [Gro16] SNARK, focusing on the verifier and not the prover, for it is the verification equations that we aim to prove are satisfied.

[Gro16] **Background.** We recall the following facts about the [Gro16] SNARK: The verification key is of the form:

$$\mathsf{vk} := (p = g^{\rho}, q = h^{\tau}, [s_j = g^{(\beta u_j(x) + \alpha v_j(x) - w_j(x))}]_{j=1}^{\ell}, d = h^{\delta}) \ .$$

Here $\rho, \tau, \delta, x \in \mathbb{F}$ are secrets generated (and discarded) during the generation of the proving and verification keys, ℓ is the statement size, and $u_j(X), v_j(X), w_j(X)$ are public polynomials that together with δ define a circuit representation of the computation being checked. The proof is of the form $\pi := (A, B, C) \in \mathbb{G}_1 \times \mathbb{G}_2 \times \mathbb{G}_1$. On input a verification key vk, an NP instance $\mathbb{x} := (a_1, \ldots, a_\ell) \in \mathbb{F}^\ell$, and a proof $\pi = (A, B, C)$, the verifier checks that $e(A, B) = e(p, q) \cdot e(\prod_{j=1}^{\ell} s_j^{a_j}, h) \cdot e(C, d)$.

A part of the [Gro16] trusted setup is *circuit-specific*, i.e., the s_j values constructed from $u_j(X), v_j(X), w_j(X)$ polynomials and d. Our protocol supports aggregating proofs over different circuits that share the non-circuit-specific part of their trusted setup, i.e., the p, q elements in the verification key.

Setup($\langle$group$\rangle$, $[\mathsf{vk}_i]_{i=0}^{n-1}$):
1. Construct commitment keys and prover and verifier keys. Note commitment keys $\boldsymbol{w} = \left[g^{\alpha^{2i}}\right]_{i=0}^{m-1}$ and $\boldsymbol{v} = \left[h^{\beta^{2i}}\right]_{i=0}^{m-1}$ are included in $\mathsf{pk}_{\mathsf{IPP}}$. Sample $\alpha, \beta \xleftarrow{\$} \mathbb{F}$:
$$(\mathsf{pk}_{\mathsf{IPP}} = (\left[g^{\alpha^i}\right]_{i=0}^{2m-2}, \left[h^{\beta^i}\right]_{i=0}^{2m-2}), \mathsf{vk}_{\mathsf{IPP}} = (g^\beta, h^\alpha)) \xleftarrow{\$} \mathsf{IPP.Setup}(m; \alpha, \beta)$$
2. Commit to circuit-specific elements of verification keys, $\mathsf{vk}_i = (p, q, [s_{i,j}]_{j=1}^{\ell}, d_i)$:
   (a) Commit to $\boldsymbol{d} = [d_i]_{i=0}^{n-1}$: $C_d \leftarrow \mathsf{CM}(\boldsymbol{w}, \boldsymbol{d}) = \boldsymbol{w} * \boldsymbol{d}$.
   (b) For each $j \in [\ell]$, commit to $\boldsymbol{s}_j$: $C_{s,j} \leftarrow \mathsf{CM}(\boldsymbol{v}, \boldsymbol{s}_j = [s_{i,j}]_{i=0}^{n-1}) = \boldsymbol{s}_j * \boldsymbol{v}$.
3. Return $(\mathsf{pk}_{\mathsf{agg}} = (\mathsf{pk}_{\mathsf{IPP}}, [\mathsf{vk}_i]_{i=0}^{n-1}, [C_{s,j}]_{j=1}^{\ell}, C_d, \boldsymbol{d}), \mathsf{vk}_{\mathsf{agg}} = (\mathsf{vk}_{\mathsf{IPP}}, p, q, [C_{s,j}]_{j=1}^{\ell}, C_d))$.

Agg($\mathsf{pk}_{\mathsf{agg}}, [(\mathbb{x}_i = [a_{i,j}]_j^{\ell}, \pi_i)]_{i=0}^{n-1}$):
$(\pi, r) \leftarrow \mathsf{AggHelper}(\mathsf{pk}_{\mathsf{agg}}, [(\mathbb{x}_i, \pi_i)]_{i=0}^{n-1}, \bot)$
Return π

Verify($\mathsf{vk}_{\mathsf{agg}}, [\mathbb{x}_i = [a_{i,j}]_j^{\ell}]_{i=0}^{n-1}, \pi_{\mathsf{agg}}$):
$[Z_{s,j}]_{j=1}^{\ell} \leftarrow [\prod_{i=0}^{n-1} s_{i,j}^{a_{i,j} r^{2i}}]_j^{\ell}$
$(b, r) \leftarrow \mathsf{VerHelper}(\mathsf{vk}_{\mathsf{agg}}, [Z_{s,j}]_j^{\ell}, \pi_{\mathsf{agg}}, \bot)$
Return b

Fig. 6. Aggregation of Groth16 SNARKs. The helper subprotocols for aggregation and verification are given in the full version [Bün+19].

Our Aggregation Protocol. Our aggregation protocol is described in Fig. 6. Given n instances $[[a_{i,j}]_{i=0}^{n-1}]_{j=1}^{\ell}$, proofs $[\pi_i = (A_i, B_i, C_i)]_{i=0}^{n-1}$, and circuit-specific verification keys $[[s_{i,j}]_j^{\ell}, d_i]_{i=0}^{n-1}$, verifying the pairing product equation for each proof π_i individually requires performing $3n$ pairings and $n\ell$ exponentiations. To reduce this computation to a single pairing product equation, the verifier can take a random linear combination between all equations. That is, the verifier samples $r \xleftarrow{\$} \mathbb{F}$, sets $\boldsymbol{r} = (1, r^2, \ldots, r^{2n-2})$ and then checks whether

$$\prod_{i=0}^{n-1} e((A_i)^{r^{2i}}, B_i) = e(p,q)^{\sum_i^{n-1} r^{2i}} \cdot e(\prod_{j=1}^{\ell} \prod_{i=0}^{n-1} s_{i,j}^{a_{i,j} r^{2i}}, h) \cdot e(\prod_{i=0}^{n-1} C_i^{r^{2i}}, d_i) \ .$$

If this equation holds, then with overwhelming probability each individual verification holds. It therefore suffices to check this one pairing product instead of checking all SNARKs individually.

We make use of two inner products arguments to prove that the above check succeeds. At a high level, the prover commits to $\boldsymbol{A}$, $\boldsymbol{B}$ and $\boldsymbol{C}$. First, the TIPP protocol is used to prove the evaluation of $\boldsymbol{A}^{\boldsymbol{r}} * \boldsymbol{B} = Z_{AB}$. The verifier must check Z_{AB} against the expected evaluation of the right-hand side of the above pairing product equation. To further help the verifier, a second evaluation of TIPP is used to prove the evaluation of $\boldsymbol{C}^{\boldsymbol{r}} * \boldsymbol{d} = Z_{Cd}$, where $\boldsymbol{d}$ is derived from the circuit-specific verification keys. The verifier then completes by evaluating and checking:

$$Z_{AB} = e(p,q)^{\frac{r^{2n}-1}{r^2-1}} \cdot e(\prod_{j=1}^{\ell} \prod_{i=0}^{n-1} s_{i,j}^{a_{i,j} r^{2i}}, h) \cdot Z_{Cd} \ ,$$

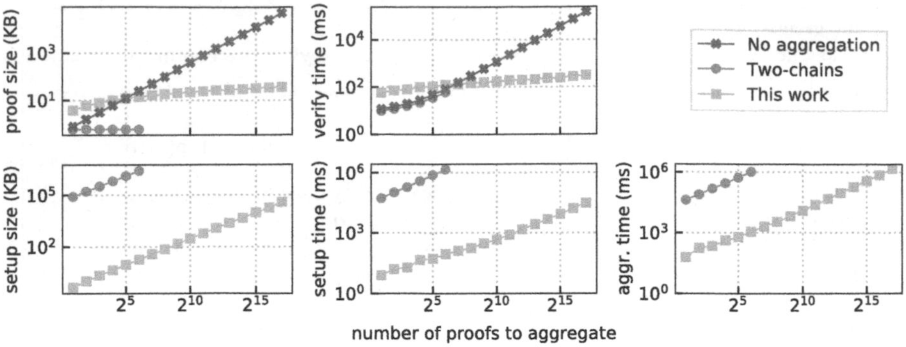

Fig. 7. Measured performance of TIPP aggregation of SNARK proofs compared to the cost of proving a one layer of recursion inside a SNARK.

which requires only two pairings, $\ell + 2$ exponentiations, and $O(\ell \cdot n)$ field operations. If aggregating over the same circuit, the circuit-specific setup of $\boldsymbol{d}$ is not needed and the protocol can be simplified to use MIPP_k instead of TIPP to derive Z_{Cd}.

Evaluation. In Fig. 7, we compare the performance for aggregating SNARK proofs using (a) our aggregation protocol, (b) using recursive SNARKs over a 2-chain [Bow+20], and (c) not aggregating at all (i.e., sending all proofs individually). The 2-chain approach proves inside another SNARK that each of the aggregated SNARKs is valid. The verification time for no aggregation consists of a single batched pairing check.

While our protocol does not produce constant-sized proofs, it does reduce setup size and aggregation time greatly. For example, when aggregating 64 proofs, our protocol is 900× faster than the 2-chain approach. Furthermore, the 2-chain approach is unable to scale further as it consumed too much memory. In fact, in the time it takes 2-chain approach to aggregate 64 proofs, our protocol can aggregate 65,000 proofs into a 35 kB proof that takes 300 ms to verify.

8 Low-Memory SNARKs for Machine Computations

We now show how to leverage our aggregation protocol in Sect. 7 to construct a *low-memory SNARK* for (non-deterministic) machine computations. A machine computation M consists of applying a sequence of operations $M = (\mathsf{op}_0, \ldots, \mathsf{op}_T)$ (from some operation set OpSet) over a fixed number of registers. We model that M can read and write to an external memory (of size S) using techniques for online memory checking [Bit+13, Ben+13a, Blu+91] in which the memory is represented as a Merkle tree. In this case, an arithmetic circuit P_i for each operation op_i can be built such that $|P_i| = \text{polylog}(S)$, given that op_i itself has complexity $\text{polylog}(S)$ and makes at most $\text{polylog}(S)$ reads or writes to memory. Taking this approach, we provide Theorem 5, which states that if a machine computation M executes using memory S over T operation steps, then our SNARK prover takes time $\tilde{\mathcal{O}}(\max_i(|P_i|)\cdot T)$ and space $\tilde{\mathcal{O}}(\max_i(|P_i|)+T+S)$ to produce a proof for that execution.

In comparison, constructing a monolithic proof for the entire computation at once requires the same time, but incurs a space usage of $\tilde{\mathcal{O}}(\sum_i(|P_i|)\cdot T+S)$. The only other solution for constructing low-memory SNARKs for machine computations requires recursive composition of proofs [Bit+13]. Recursive composition achieves a further improved space usage of $\tilde{\mathcal{O}}(\max_i(|P_i|) + S)$, but the time to prove, while asymptotically equivalent to the previous solutions, is concretely very expensive.

Definition 4 (Machine relation). *For a machine M with step operations $[\mathsf{op}_i]_{i=0}^{T-1}$, the NP relation $\mathcal{R}_M$ is the set of instance-witness pairs $(x, [\omega]_i^{T-1})$, such that M accepts $(x, [\omega]_i^{T-1})$ after the T step operations are applied.*

Theorem 5. *Let $\mathcal{R}_M$ be a machine relation for some machine M with step operations $[\mathsf{op}_i]_{i=0}^{T-1}$ that can be represented with arithmetic circuits $[P_i]_i^{T-1}$, and $\mathsf{op}_i \in \mathsf{OpSet}$ for all i. Then there exists a SNARK for $\mathcal{R}_M$ where*

(1) Setup takes time $\mathcal{O}(T + \sum_{\mathsf{op} \in \mathsf{OpSet}}(|P_{\mathsf{op}}|))$.
(2) Proving takes time $\tilde{\mathcal{O}}(\max_i(|P_i|)\cdot T)$ and uses space $\tilde{\mathcal{O}}(\max_i(|P_i|)+T+S)$, where S is the space required to compute M.
(3) Proof size is $\mathcal{O}(\log(T))$ and verification takes time $\mathcal{O}(\log(T))$.

Overview of Solution. We first introduce some notation. The full details of our protocol are given in the full version [Bün+19]. Machine M operates over a fixed set of ℓ registers. The statement for each operation circuit P_i consists of 2ℓ elements: ℓ input registers $[a_{i,j}]_{j=1}^{\ell}$ and ℓ output registers $[b_{i,j}]_{j=1}^{\ell}$. The circuit verifies that the output registers are valid with respect to applying the operation on the input registers. Importantly, the output registers of an operation are passed as the input registers to the next operation in sequence:

$$[b_{i,j}]_{j=1}^{\ell} = [a_{i+1,j}]_{j=1}^{\ell}\,.$$

The verifier does not need to be aware of all of the values the registers take on during intermediate steps of execution. Instead, it need only verify that the above "sequential" pattern of registers is present in the proofs for each operation step. This is the key observation we take advantage of to produce a log-time verifier.

As a strawman, consider the solution of proving an individual Groth16 SNARK for each operation step and aggregating using the protocol of Sect. 7. To verify, the verifier must receive and perform scalar computations over all of the intermediate statements, incurring linear proof size and verification time.

Instead, in our solution, the prover commits to all of the intermediate statements and proves to the verifier that they follow the sequential structure, i.e., the second half of the statement for proof i is the first half of the statement for proof $i+1$. The verifier can verify this in time ℓ with knowledge of only the initial register state $[a_{0,j}]_j^\ell$ and the final register state $[b_{T-1,j}]_j^\ell$. The prover commits to the inputs and outputs of all statements, $\boldsymbol{a}_j$, $\boldsymbol{b}_j$, to $C_{a,j}, C_{b,j}$. The prover then proves the sequential pattern between $\boldsymbol{a}_j$ and $\boldsymbol{b}_j$ holds, namely that the vectors are offset by one:

$$\begin{array}{llll} a_{0,j} & a_{1,j} & \dots & a_{T-1,j} & \\ & b_{0,j} & \dots & b_{T-2,j} & b_{T-1,j} \end{array}$$

The prover does this by homomorphically shifting the commitment to $\boldsymbol{b}_j$ using challenge r and taking the difference between the two vector commitments $C_{a,j}C_{b,j}^{-1/r^2}$, then providing a KZG opening proof that it opens to $a_{0,j} - b_{n-1,j}r^{2T-2}$ when evaluated on r. Lastly, the prover uses the commitments to precompute a part of the final pairing product verification check to help the verifier avoid the linear scalar computations. The prover computes and proves using MIPP_u the multiexponentiation inner products, $Z_{s,j} = \boldsymbol{s}_j^{\boldsymbol{a}_j \circ \boldsymbol{r}}$ and $Z_{s,\ell+j} = \boldsymbol{s}_{\ell+j}^{\boldsymbol{b}_j \circ \boldsymbol{r}}$ for $\boldsymbol{s}_j$ derived from circuit-specific verification keys. The verifier then completes the verification by checking the following pairing product equation:

$$Z_{AB} = e(p,q)^{\frac{r^{2n}-1}{r^2-1}} \cdot e(\prod_{j=1}^{2\ell} Z_{s,j}, h) \cdot Z_{Cd} \enspace ,$$

which requires only two pairings and $O(\ell)$ group operations. Our solution may be adapted to provide greater efficiency in the case of repeated application of a single step operation.

References

[Abe+16] Abe, M., Fuchsbauer, G., Groth, J., Haralambiev, K., Ohkubo, M.: Structure-preserving signatures and commitments to group elements. J. Cryptol. **29**(2), 363–421 (2015). https://doi.org/10.1007/s00145-014-9196-7

[AC20] Attema, T., Cramer, R.: Compressed Σ-protocol theory and practical application to plug & play secure algorithmics. In: Micciancio, D., Ristenpart, T. (eds.) CRYPTO 2020. LNCS, vol. 12172, pp. 513–543. Springer, Cham (2020). https://doi.org/10.1007/978-3-030-56877-1_18

[BDK13] Backes, M., Datta, A., Kate, A.: Asynchronous computational VSS with reduced communication complexity. In: Dawson, E. (ed.) CT-RSA 2013. LNCS, vol. 7779, pp. 259–276. Springer, Heidelberg (2013). https://doi.org/10.1007/978-3-642-36095-4_17

[BFS20] Bünz, B., Fisch, B., Szepieniec, A.: Transparent SNARKs from DARK compilers. In: Canteaut, A., Ishai, Y. (eds.) EUROCRYPT 2020. LNCS, vol. 12105, pp. 677–706. Springer, Cham (2020). https://doi.org/10.1007/978-3-030-45721-1_24

[BG13] Bayer, S., Groth, J.: Zero-knowledge argument for polynomial evaluation with application to blacklists. In: Johansson, T., Nguyen, P.Q. (eds.) EUROCRYPT 2013. LNCS, vol. 7881, pp. 646–663. Springer, Heidelberg (2013). https://doi.org/10.1007/978-3-642-38348-9_38

[BGH19] Bowe, S., Grigg, J., Hopwood, D.: Halo: recursive proof composition without a trusted setup. eprint 2019/1021

[Bit+13] Bitansky, N., Canetti, R., Chiesa, A., Tromer, E.: Recursive composition and bootstrapping for SNARKs and proof-carrying data. In: STOC 2013 (2013)

[Blu+91] Blum, M., Evans, W., Gemmell, P., Kannan, S., Naor, M.: Checking the correctness of memories. In: FOCS 1991 (1991)

[Bon+20] Bonneau, J., Meckler, I., Rao, V., Shapiro, E.: Coda: decentralized cryptocurrency at scale. eprint 2020/352

[Boo+16] Bootle, J., Cerulli, A., Chaidos, P., Groth, J., Petit, C.: Efficient zero-knowledge arguments for arithmetic circuits in the discrete log setting. In: Fischlin, M., Coron, J.-S. (eds.) EUROCRYPT 2016. LNCS, vol. 9666, pp. 327–357. Springer, Heidelberg (2016). https://doi.org/10.1007/978-3-662-49896-5_12

[Bow+20] Bowe, S., Chiesa, A., Green, M., Miers, I., Mishra, P., Wu, H.: ZEXE: enabling decentralized private computation. In: S&P 2020 (2020)

[Bün+18] Bünz, B., Bootle, J., Boneh, D., Poelstra, A., Wuille, P., Maxwell, G.: Bulletproofs: short proofs for confidential transactions and more. In: S&P 2018 (2018)

[Bün+19] Bünz, B., Maller, M., Mishra, P., Tyagi, N., Vesely, P.: Proofs for inner pairing products and applications. eprint 2019/1177

[Bün+20] Bünz, B., Chiesa, A., Mishra, P., Spooner, N.: Proof-carrying data from accumulation schemes. In: TCC 2020 (2020)

[Cam+15] Camenisch, J., Dubovitskaya, M., Haralambiev, K., Kohlweiss, M.: Composable and modular anonymous credentials: definitions and practical constructions. In: Iwata, T., Cheon, J.H. (eds.) ASIACRYPT 2015. LNCS, vol. 9453, pp. 262–288. Springer, Heidelberg (2015). https://doi.org/10.1007/978-3-662-48800-3_11

[Chi+20] Chiesa, A., Hu, Y., Maller, M., Mishra, P., Vesely, N., Ward, N.: Marlin: preprocessing zkSNARKs with universal and updatable SRS. In: Canteaut, A., Ishai, Y. (eds.) EUROCRYPT 2020. LNCS, vol. 12105, pp. 738–768. Springer, Cham (2020). https://doi.org/10.1007/978-3-030-45721-1_26

[COS20] Chiesa, A., Ojha, D., Spooner, N.: Fractal: post-quantum and transparent recursive proofs from holography. In: Canteaut, A., Ishai, Y. (eds.) EUROCRYPT 2020. LNCS, vol. 12105, pp. 769–793. Springer, Cham (2020). https://doi.org/10.1007/978-3-030-45721-1_27

[FHS19] Fuchsbauer, G., Hanser, C., Slamanig, D.: Structure-preserving signatures on equivalence classes and constant-size anonymous credentials. J. Cryptol. **32**(2), 498–546 (2018). https://doi.org/10.1007/s00145-018-9281-4

[Fis18] Fisch, B.: Poreps: proofs of space on useful data. eprint 2018/678

[Fis19] Fisch, B.: Tight proofs of space and replication. In: Ishai, Y., Rijmen, V. (eds.) EUROCRYPT 2019. LNCS, vol. 11477, pp. 324–348. Springer, Cham (2019). https://doi.org/10.1007/978-3-030-17656-3_12

[FKL18] Fuchsbauer, G., Kiltz, E., Loss, J.: The algebraic group model and its applications. In: Shacham, H., Boldyreva, A. (eds.) CRYPTO 2018. LNCS, vol. 10992, pp. 33–62. Springer, Cham (2018). https://doi.org/10.1007/978-3-319-96881-0_2

[GGW18] Gurkan, K., Gabizon, A., Williamson, Z.: Cheon's attack and its effect on the security of big trusted setups. https://ethresear.ch/t/cheons-attack-and-its-effect-on-the-security-of-big-trusted-setups/6692

[GM17] Groth, J., Maller, M.: Snarky signatures: minimal signatures of knowledge from simulation-extractable SNARKs. In: Katz, J., Shacham, H. (eds.) CRYPTO 2017. LNCS, vol. 10402, pp. 581–612. Springer, Cham (2017). https://doi.org/10.1007/978-3-319-63715-0_20

[GMN21] Gailly, N., Maller, M., Nitulescu, A.: SnarkPack: practical SNARK aggregation. eprint 2021/529

[Gro+18] Groth, J., Kohlweiss, M., Maller, M., Meiklejohn, S., Miers, I.: Updatable and universal common reference strings with applications to zk-SNARKs. In: Shacham, H., Boldyreva, A. (eds.) CRYPTO 2018. LNCS, vol. 10993, pp. 698–728. Springer, Cham (2018). https://doi.org/10.1007/978-3-319-96878-0_24

[Gro11] Groth, J.: Efficient zero-knowledge arguments from two-tiered homomorphic commitments. In: Lee, D.H., Wang, X. (eds.) ASIACRYPT 2011. LNCS, vol. 7073, pp. 431–448. Springer, Heidelberg (2011). https://doi.org/10.1007/978-3-642-25385-0_23

[Gro16] Groth, J.: On the size of pairing-based non-interactive arguments. In: Fischlin, M., Coron, J.-S. (eds.) EUROCRYPT 2016. LNCS, vol. 9666, pp. 305–326. Springer, Heidelberg (2016). https://doi.org/10.1007/978-3-662-49896-5_11

[GS08] Groth, J., Sahai, A.: Efficient non-interactive proof systems for bilinear groups. In: Smart, N. (ed.) EUROCRYPT 2008. LNCS, vol. 4965, pp. 415–432. Springer, Heidelberg (2008). https://doi.org/10.1007/978-3-540-78967-3_24

[GWC19] Gabizon, A., Williamson, Z.J., Ciobotaru, O.: PLONK: permutations over lagrange-bases for oecumenical noninteractive arguments of knowledge. eprint 2019/953

[KZG10] Kate, A., Zaverucha, G.M., Goldberg, I.: Constant-size commitments to polynomials and their applications. In: Abe, M. (ed.) ASIACRYPT 2010. LNCS, vol. 6477, pp. 177–194. Springer, Heidelberg (2010). https://doi.org/10.1007/978-3-642-17373-8_11

[Lee20] Lee, J.: Dory: efficient, transparent arguments for generalised inner products and polynomial commitments. eprint 2020/1274

[LMR19] Lai, R.W.F., Malavolta, G., Ronge, V.: Succinct arguments for bilinear group arithmetic: practical structure-preserving cryptography. In: CCS 2019 (2019)

[LY10] Libert, B., Yung, M.: Concise mercurial vector commitments and independent zero-knowledge sets with short proofs. In: Micciancio, D. (ed.) TCC 2010. LNCS, vol. 5978, pp. 499–517. Springer, Heidelberg (2010). https://doi.org/10.1007/978-3-642-11799-2_30

[Mal+19] Maller, M., Bowe, S., Kohlweiss, M., Meiklejohn, S.: Sonic: zero-knowledge snarks from linear-size universal and updatable structured reference strings. In: CCS 2019 (2019)

[O'L18] O'Leary, R.: Monero to become first billion-dollar crypto to implement 'bulletproofs' tech. https://www.coindesk.com/monero-to-become-first-billion-dollar-crypto-to-implement-bulletproofs-tech

[Par+13] Parno, B., Gentry, C., Howell, J., Raykova, M.: Pinocchio: nearly practical verifiable computation. In: S&P 2013 (2013)

[Ped92] Pedersen, T.P.: Non-interactive and information-theoretic secure verifiable secret sharing. In: Feigenbaum, J. (ed.) CRYPTO 1991. LNCS, vol. 576, pp. 129–140. Springer, Heidelberg (1992). https://doi.org/10.1007/3-540-46766-1_9

[Set20] Setty, S.: Spartan: efficient and general-purpose zkSNARKs without trusted setup. In: Micciancio, D., Ristenpart, T. (eds.) CRYPTO 2020. LNCS, vol. 12172, pp. 704–737. Springer, Cham (2020). https://doi.org/10.1007/978-3-030-56877-1_25

[Sri+21] Srinivasan, S., Chepurnoy, A., Papamanthou, C., Tomescu, A., Zhang, Y.: Hyperproofs: Aggregating and maintaining proofs in vector commitments. eprint 2021/599

[Tya+21] Tyagi, N., Fisch, B., Bonneau, J., Tessaro, S.: Client-auditable verifiable registries. eprint 2021/627

[Wah+18] Wahby, R.S., Tzialla, I., Shelat, A., Thaler, J., Walfish, M.: Doubly-efficient zkSNARKs without trusted setup. In: S&P 2018 (2018)

[Whi] Whitehat, B.: Roll up: scale Ethereum with SNARKs. https://github.com/barryWhiteHat/roll_up

[Wu+18] Wu, H., Zheng, W., Chiesa, A., Popa, R.A., Stoica, I.: DIZK: a distributed zero knowledge proof system. In: USENIX Security 2018 (2018)

[Xie+19] Xie, T., Zhang, J., Zhang, Y., Papamanthou, C., Song, D.: Libra: succinct zero-knowledge proofs with optimal prover computation. In: Boldyreva, A., Micciancio, D. (eds.) CRYPTO 2019. LNCS, vol. 11694, pp. 733–764. Springer, Cham (2019). https://doi.org/10.1007/978-3-030-26954-8_24

[Xu+16] Xu, J., Yang, A., Zhou, J., Wong, D.S.: Lightweight delegatable proofs of storage. In: Askoxylakis, I., Ioannidis, S., Katsikas, S., Meadows, C. (eds.) ESORICS 2016. LNCS, vol. 9878, pp. 324–343. Springer, Cham (2016). https://doi.org/10.1007/978-3-319-45744-4_16

[Zha+20] Zhang, J., Xie, T., Zhang, Y., Song, D.: Transparent polynomial delegation and its applications to zero knowledge proof. In: S&P 2020 (2020)

[Ben+13a] Ben-Sasson, E., Chiesa, A., Genkin, D., Tromer, E.: Fast reductions from RAMs to delegatable succinct constraint satisfaction problems. In: ITCS 2013 (2013)

[Ben+13b] Ben-Sasson, E., Chiesa, A., Genkin, D., Tromer, E., Virza, M.: SNARKs for C: verifying program executions succinctly and in zero knowledge. In: Canetti, R., Garay, J.A. (eds.) CRYPTO 2013. LNCS, vol. 8043, pp. 90–108. Springer, Heidelberg (2013). https://doi.org/10.1007/978-3-642-40084-1_6

[Ben+14a] Ben-Sasson, E., Chiesa, A., Tromer, E., Virza, M.: Scalable zero knowledge via cycles of elliptic curves. In: Garay, J.A., Gennaro, R. (eds.) CRYPTO 2014. LNCS, vol. 8617, pp. 276–294. Springer, Heidelberg (2014). https://doi.org/10.1007/978-3-662-44381-1_16

[Ben+14b] Ben-Sasson, E., Chiesa, A., Tromer, E., Virza, M.: Succinct non-interactive zero knowledge for a von Neumann architecture. In: USENIX Security 2014 (2014)

[Ben+14c] Ben-Sasson, E., et al.: Zerocash: decentralized anonymous payments from Bitcoin. In: SP 2014 (2014)

Snarky Ceremonies

Markulf Kohlweiss[1,2(✉)], Mary Maller[3], Janno Siim[4], and Mikhail Volkhov[2]

[1] IOHK, Edinburgh, UK
[2] The University of Edinburgh, Edinburgh, UK
{mkohlwei,mikhail.volkhov}@ed.ac.uk
[3] Ethereum Foundation, London, UK
mary.maller@ethereum.org
[4] University of Tartu, Tartu, Estonia
janno.siim@ut.ee

Abstract. Succinct non-interactive arguments of knowledge (SNARKs) have found numerous applications in the blockchain setting and elsewhere. The most efficient SNARKs require a distributed ceremony protocol to generate public parameters, also known as a structured reference string (SRS). Our contributions are two-fold:

- We give a security framework for non-interactive zero-knowledge arguments with a ceremony protocol.
- We revisit the ceremony protocol of Groth's SNARK [Bowe et al., 2017]. We show that the original construction can be simplified and optimized, and then prove its security in our new framework. Importantly, our construction avoids the random beacon model used in the original work.

1 Introduction

Zero-knowledge proofs of knowledge [23] allow to prove knowledge of a witness for some NP statement while not revealing any information besides the truth of the statement. The recent progress in zero-knowledge (ZK) Succinct Non-interactive Arguments of Knowledge (SNARKs) [16,24,25,34,37] has enabled the use of zero-knowledge proofs in practical systems, especially in the context of blockchains [6,10,31].

Groth16 [25] is the SNARK with the smallest proof size and fastest verifier in the literature, and it is also competitive in terms of prover time. Beyond efficiency, it has several other useful properties. Groth16 is rerandomizable [33], which is a desirable property for achieving receipt-free voting [33]. Simultaneously, it also has a weak form of simulation extractability [3] which guarantees that even if the adversary has seen some proofs before, it cannot prove a new statement without knowing the witness. The prover and verifier use only algebraic operations and thus proofs can be aggregated [13]. Furthermore, Groth16 is attractive to practitioners due to the vast quantity of implementation and code auditing it has already received.

M. Tibouchi and H. Wang (Eds.): ASIACRYPT 2021, LNCS 13092, pp. 98–127, 2021.
https://doi.org/10.1007/978-3-030-92078-4_4

Every application using Groth16 must run a separate trusted setup ceremony in order to ensure security, and even small errors in the setup could result a complete break of the system. Indeed, the paper of the original Zcash SNARK [8] contained a small typo which resulted in a bug that would allow an attacker to print unlimited funds in an undetectable manner [20]. Some would use this example as a reason to avoid any SNARK with a trusted setup ceremony at all costs. And yet Groth16 is not only still being used, but many protocols are being actively designed on top of it, potentially for the reasons listed above. Thus we believe that if this SNARK ceremony is going to be used anyway, it is important to put significant effort on simplifying its description and verifying its security.

The primary purpose of this work is to take a formal approach to proving the security of the Groth16 setup ceremony of Bowe, Gabizon, and Miers [12] that is currently commonly used in practice. The first prominent application of the protocol was the Zcash Sapling ceremony, but it was also run by many other projects, for example Aztec protocol, Filecoin, Semaphore, Loopring, Tornado Cash, Plumo Ceremony, and Hermez. Some of these ceremonies are based on the project called Perpetual Powers of Tau (PPoT), which implements the first phase of [12], that is not specialized to any circuit—this implies that the project planning to run a ceremony can fork off the PPoT, reducing its own setup cost. In other words, [12] is by far the most popular ceremony protocol used in practice; but it is also modified, specialized, and re-implemented by many independent projects. We simplify the original protocol, specifically we remove the need for a random beacon. Our security proofs equally apply to the version of the protocol with a beacon already used in practice.

A number of different works have analysed the setup security of zk-SNARKs. The works of [1,7,11] propose specialized multi-party computation protocols for SRS generation ceremonies. A common feature of these protocols is that they are secure if at least one of the parties is honest. However, these schemes are not robust in the sense that all parties must be fixed before the beginning of the protocol and be active throughout the whole execution. In other words if a single party goes offline between rounds then the protocol will not terminate. Bowe, Gabizon, and Miers [12] showed that the latter problem could be solved if there is access to a random beacon—an oracle that periodically produces bit-strings of high entropy—which can be used to rerandomize the SRS after each protocol phase. Unfortunately, obtaining a secure random beacon is, by itself, an extremely challenging problem [9,27,30]. Secure solutions include unique threshold signatures [28], which themselves require complex setup ceremonies as well as verifiable delay functions [9,38,39] that require the design and use of specialized hardware. Practical realizations have instead opted for using a hash function applied to a recent blockchain block as a random beacon. This is not an ideal approach since the blockchain miners can bias the outcome.[1]

The work of Groth, Kohlweiss, Maller, Meiklejohn, and Miers [26] takes a different approach and directly constructs a SNARK where the SRS is updat-

[1] It is desirable for a setup ceremony to avoid dependence on setups as much as possible—we spurn random beacons but embrace random oracles.

able, that is, anyone can update the SRS and knowledge soundness and zero-knowledge are preserved if at least one of the updaters was honest.[2] Subsequent updatable SNARKS like Sonic [36], Marlin [15], and PLONK [21] have improved the efficiency of updatable SNARKs, but they are still less efficient than for example [25]. Mirage [32] modifies the original Groth16 by making the SRS universal, that is the SRS works for all relations up to some size bound. The latter work can be seen as complementary to the results of this paper as it amplifies the benefits of a successfully conducted ceremony.

1.1 Our Contributions

Our key contributions are as follows:

Designing a security framework. We formalize the notion of non-interactive zero-knowledge (NIZK) argument with a multi-round SRS ceremony protocol, which extends the framework of updatable NIZKs in [36]. Our definitions fix a syntax for ceremonies with Update and VerifySRS algorithms and take a game-based approach. This is less rigid than a multi-party computation definition (see for example [1] for a UC-functionality). Our security notion says that an adversary cannot forge a SNARK proofs even if they can participate in the setup ceremony. We call such a SNARK ceremonial. This notion is more permissible for the setup ceremony than requiring simulatability and is therefore easier to achieve. In particular, using our definitions we do not require the use of a random beacon (as is needed in [12]) or additional setup assumptions ([7] assumes a common random string and [1] assumes a trusted commitment key), whereas it is not clear that those could be avoided in the MPC setting. Our definitions are applicable to SNARKs with a multiple round setup ceremony as long as they are ceremonial.

Proving security without a random beacon. We prove the security of the Groth16 SNARK with a setup ceremony of [12] in our new security framework. We intentionally try not change the original ceremony protocol too much so that our security proof would apply to protocols already used in practice. Security is proven with respect to algebraic adversaries [18] in the random oracle model. We require a single party to be honest in each phase of the protocol in order to guarantee that knowledge soundness and subversion zero-knowledge hold. Unlike [12], our security proof does not rely on the use of a random beacon. However, our security proof does apply to protocols that have been implemented using a (potentially insecure) random beacon because the beacon can just be treated as an additional malicious party. We see this as an important security validation of real-life protocols that cryptocurrencies depend on.

Revisiting the discrete logarithm argument. The original paper of [12] used a novel discrete logarithm argument Π_{dl} to prove knowledge of update contributions. They showed that the argument has knowledge soundness

[2] Note that one can independently prove subversion ZK [2,17].

under the knowledge of exponent assumption in the random oracle model. While proving the security of the ceremony protocol, we observe that even stronger security properties are necessary. The discrete logarithm argument must be zero-knowledge and straight-line simulation extractable, i.e., knowledge sound in the presence of simulated proofs. Furthermore, simulation-extractability has to hold even if the adversary obtains group elements as an auxiliary input for which he does not know the discrete logarithm. We slightly modify the original argument to show that those stronger properties are satisfied if we use the algebraic group model with random oracles.

Thus, this work simplifies the widely used protocol of [12] and puts it onto firmer security foundations.

1.2 Our Techniques

Security Framework. Our security framework assumes that the SRS is split into φ_{max} distinct components $\mathsf{srs} = (\mathsf{srs}_1, \ldots, \mathsf{srs}_{\varphi_{max}})$ and in each phase of the ceremony protocol one of the components gets finalized. We formalize this by enhancing the standard definition of NIZK with an Update and VerifySRS algorithms. Given srs and the phase number φ, the Update algorithm updates srs_φ and produces a proof ρ that the update was correct. The verification algorithm VerifySRS is used to check that srs and update proofs $\{\rho_i\}_i$ are valid.

We obtain the standard updatability model of [36] if $\varphi_{max} = 1$. When modelling the Groth16 SNARK we set $\varphi_{max} = 2$. In that scenario, we split the SRS into a *universal* component $\mathsf{srs}_1 = \mathsf{srs}_u$ that is independent of the specific relation that we want to prove[3] and to a specialized component $\mathsf{srs}_2 = \mathsf{srs}_s$, which depends on a concrete relation $\mathcal{R}$. Both srs_u and srs_s are updatable; however, the initial srs_s has to be derived from srs_u and the relation $\mathcal{R}$. Thus, parties need first to update srs_u, and only after a sufficient number of updates can they start to update srs_s. The universal srs_u can potentially be reused for other relations.

In our definition of update knowledge soundness, we require that no adversary can convince an honest verifier of a statement unless either (1) they know a valid witness; (2) the SRS does not pass the setup ceremony verification VerifySRS; or (3) one of the phases did not include *any* honest updates. Completeness and zero-knowledge hold for any SRS that passes the setup ceremony verification, even if there were no honest updates at all. The latter notions are known as subversion completeness and subversion zero-knowledge [5].

Security Proof of Setup Ceremony. We must prove subversion zero-knowledge and update knowledge-soundness. Subversion zero-knowledge follows from the previous work in [2,17], which already proved it for Groth16 under

[3] Similarly to the universal updatability notions that share the same "independence", e.g. [36], srs_u still formally depends on the maximum size of the circuit, which can nevertheless be made large enough to be practically universal.

knowledge assumptions. The only key difference is that we can extract the simulation trapdoor with a discrete logarithm proof of knowledge argument Π_{dl} used in the ceremony protocol.

Our security proof of update knowledge-soundness uses a combination of the algebraic group model and the random oracle (RO) model. As was recently shown by Fuchsbauer, Plouviez, and Seurin [19] the mixture of those two models can be used to prove powerful results (tight reductions of Schnorr-based schemes in their case) but it also introduces new technical challenges. Recall that the algebraic group model (AGM) is a relaxation of the generic group model proposed by Fuchsbauer, Kiltz, and Loss [18]. They consider algebraic adversaries $\mathcal{A}_{alg}$ that obtain some group elements $G_1, \ldots, G_n$ during the execution of the protocol and whenever $\mathcal{A}_{alg}$ outputs a new group element E, it also has to output a linear representation $\vec{C} = (c_1, \ldots, c_n)$ such that $E = G_1^{c_1} G_2^{c_2} \ldots G_n^{c_n}$. Essentially, $\mathcal{A}_{alg}$ can only produce new group elements by applying group operations to previously known group elements. In contrast to the generic group model, the representation of group elements is visible to $\mathcal{A}_{alg}$, and thus security proofs in AGM are typically reductions to some group-assumptions (e.g. the discrete logarithm assumption).

Already the original AGM paper [18] proved knowledge soundness of the Groth16 SNARK in the AGM model (assuming trusted SRS). They proved it under the q-discrete logarithm assumption, i.e., a discrete logarithm assumption where the challenge is $(G^z, G^{z^2}, \ldots, G^{z^q})$. The main idea for the reduction is that we can embed G^z in the SRS of the SNARK. Then when the algebraic adversary $\mathcal{A}_{alg}$ outputs a group-based proof π, all the proof elements are in the span of the SRS elements, and $\mathcal{A}_{alg}$ also outputs the respective algebraic representation. We can view the verification equation as a polynomial Q that depends on the SRS and π such that $Q(SRS, \pi) = 0$ when the verifier accepts. Moreover, since π and SRS depend on z, we can write $Q(SRS, \pi) = Q'(z)$. Roughly, the proof continues by looking at the formal polynomial $Q'(Z)$, where Z is a variable corresponding to z, and distinguishing two cases: (i) if $Q'(Z) = 0$, it is possible to argue based on the coefficient of Q' that the statement is valid and some of the coefficients are the witness, i.e., $\mathcal{A}_{alg}$ knows the witness, or (ii) if $Q'(Z) \neq 0$, then it is possible to efficiently find the root z of Q' and solve the discrete logarithm problem.

Our proof of update knowledge soundness follows a similar strategy, but it is much more challenging since the SRS can be biased, and the $\mathcal{A}_{alg}$ has access to all the intermediate values related to the updates. Furthermore, $\mathcal{A}_{alg}$ also has access to the random oracle, which is used by the discrete logarithm proof of knowledge Π_{dl}. Firstly, since the SRS of the Groth16 SNARK contains one trapdoor that is inverted (that is δ), we need to use a novel extended discrete logarithm assumption where the challenge value is $(\{G^{z^i}\}_{i=0}^{q_1}, \{H^{z^i}\}_{i=0}^{q_2}, r, s, G^{\frac{1}{rz+s}}, H^{\frac{1}{rz+s}})$ where G and H are generators of pairing groups and r, s, z are random integers. We prove that this new assumption is very closely related (equivalent under small change of parameters) to the q-discrete logarithm assumption. In the case with an honest SRS [18] it was possible to argue that by multiplying all SRS elements by δ we get an equivalent argument which does not contain division, but it is harder to use the same reasoning when the adversary biases δ. The reduction still follows a similar high-level idea, but we need to introduce intermediate games that create a simplified environment before we can use the polynomial Q. For these games we rely on the zero-knowledge property and simulation extractability of Π_{dl}. Moreover, we have to consider that $\mathcal{A}_{alg}$ sees and adaptively affects intermediate states of the SRS on which the proof by π can depend on. Therefore the polynomial Q' takes a significantly more complicated form, but the simplified environment will reduce this complexity.

Revisiting the Discrete Logarithm Argument. One of the key ingredients in the [12] ceremony is the discrete logarithm proof of knowledge Π_{dl}. Each updater uses this to prove that it knows its contribution to the SRS. The original [12] proved only knowledge soundness of Π_{dl}. While proving the security of the setup ceremony in our framework, we observe that much stronger properties are needed. Firstly, Π_{dl} needs to be zero-knowledge since it should not reveal the trapdoor contribution. Secondly, Π_{dl} should be knowledge sound, but in an environment where the adversary also sees simulated proofs and obtains group elements (SRS elements) for which it does not know the discrete logarithm. For this, we define a stronger notion simulation-extractability where the adversary can query oracle $\mathcal{O}_{\mathsf{se}}$ for simulated proofs and oracle $\mathcal{O}_{\mathsf{poly}}$ on polynomials $f(X_1, \ldots, X_n)$ that get evaluated at some random points $x_1, \ldots, x_n$ such that the adversary learns $G^{f(x_1,\ldots,x_n)}$ or $H^{f(x_1,\ldots,x_n)}$.

We show that proofs can be trivially simulated when the simulator has access to the internals of the random oracle and thus Π_{dl} is zero-knowledge. We once again use AGM, this time to prove simulation-extractability. Since in this proof we can embed the discrete logarithm challenge in the random oracle responses, we do not need different powers of the challenge and can instead rely on the standard discrete logarithm assumption. We also slightly simplify the original Π_{dl} and remove the dependence on the public transcript T_{Π} of the ceremony protocol, that is, the sequence of messages broadcasted by the parties so far. Namely, the original protocol hashes T_{Π} and the statement to obtain a challenge value. This turns out to be a redundant feature, and removing it makes Π_{dl} more modular.

Implementation and Optimization. Partners in a joint research project have developed a Rust implementation[4] of our Update and VerifySRS algorithms for Groth16 building on the arkworks library with various optimizations such as batching and parallelization. This validates the correctness of our algorithms and intends to serve as an independent implementation to measure other solutions. We describe batched SRS update verification in the full version of this paper.

[4] https://github.com/grnet/snarky.

2 Preliminaries

PPT denotes probabilistic polynomial time, and DPT denotes deterministic polynomial time. The security parameter is denoted by λ. We write $y \xleftarrow{r} \mathcal{A}(x)$ when a PPT algorithm $\mathcal{A}$ outputs y on input x and uses random coins r. Often we neglect r for simplicity. If $\mathcal{A}$ runs with specific random coins r, we write $y \leftarrow \mathcal{A}(x; r)$. Uniformly sampling x from a set A is denoted by $x \leftarrow_{\$} A$. A view of an algorithm $\mathcal{A}$ is a list denoted by $\mathsf{view}_{\mathcal{A}}$ which contains the data that fixes $\mathcal{A}$'s execution trace: random coins, its inputs (including ones from the oracles), and outputs[5]. We sometimes refer to the "transcript" implying only the public part of the view: that is interactions of $\mathcal{A}$ with oracles and the challenger.

Let $\vec{a}$ and $\vec{b}$ be vectors of length n. We say that the vector $\vec{c}$ of length $2n-1$ is a convolution of $\vec{a}$ and $\vec{b}$ if $c_k = \sum_{(i,j)=(1,1);i+j=k+1}^{(n,n)} a_i b_j$ for $k \in \{1, \dots, 2n-1\}$. In particular, multiplying the polynomial $\sum_{i=1}^{n} a_i X^{i-1}$ with $\sum_{i=1}^{n} b_i X^{i-1}$ produces $\sum_{i=1}^{2n-1} c_i X^{i-1}$. When indexing families of values, we sometimes use semicolon to separate indices, e.g. $\{G_{\beta x:i}\}_{i=0}^{n}$ is a vector $G_{\beta x}$ indexed by i.

Bilinear Pairings. Let BGen be a bilinear group generator that takes in a security parameter 1^λ and outputs a pairing description $\mathsf{bp} = (p, \mathbb{G}_1, \mathbb{G}_2, \mathbb{G}_T, \hat{e}, G, H)$ where $\mathbb{G}_1, \mathbb{G}_2, \mathbb{G}_T$ are groups of prime order p, G is a generator of $\mathbb{G}_1$, H is a generator of $\mathbb{G}_2$, and $\hat{e} : \mathbb{G}_1 \times \mathbb{G}_2 \to \mathbb{G}_T$ is a non-degenerate and efficient bilinear map. That is, $\hat{e}(G, H)$ is a generator of $\mathbb{G}_T$ and for any $a, b \in \mathbb{Z}_p$, $\hat{e}(G^a, H^b) = \hat{e}(G, H)^{ab}$. We consider Type III asymmetric pairings, with $\mathbb{G}_1 \neq \mathbb{G}_2$ and without any efficiently computable homomorphism between $\mathbb{G}_1$ and $\mathbb{G}_2$.

2.1 Algebraic Group Model with RO and Discrete Logarithm Assumptions

We will use the algebraic group model (AGM) [18] to prove the security of Groth's SNARK. In AGM, we consider only algebraic algorithms that provide a linear explanation for each group element that they output. More precisely, if $\mathcal{A}_{alg}$ has so far received group elements $G_1, \dots, G_n \in \mathbb{G}$ and outputs a group element $G_{n+1} \in \mathbb{G}$, then it has to also provide a vector of integer coefficients $\vec{C} = (c_1, \dots, c_n)$ such that $G_{n+1} = \prod_{i=1}^{n} G_i^{c_i}$. We will use AGM in a pairing-based setting where we distinguish between group elements of $\mathbb{G}_1$ and $\mathbb{G}_2$. Formally, the set of algebraic coefficients $\vec{C}$ is obtained by calling the algebraic extractor $\vec{C} \leftarrow \mathcal{E}_{\mathcal{A}}^{\mathsf{agm}}(\mathsf{view}_{\mathcal{A}})$ that is guaranteed to exist for any algebraic adversary $\mathcal{A}$. This extractor is white-box and requires $\mathcal{A}$'s view to run.

[5] The latter can be derived from the former elements of the list, and is added to $\mathsf{view}_{\mathcal{A}}$ for convenience.

$\mathsf{RO}_t(\phi)$ `// Initially` $Q_{\mathsf{RO}} = \emptyset$

if $Q_{\mathsf{RO}}[\phi] \neq \bot$ **then** $r \leftarrow Q_{\mathsf{RO}}[\phi]$;
else $r \leftarrow\$ \mathbb{Z}_p$; $Q_{\mathsf{RO}}[\phi] \leftarrow r$
if $t = 1$ **then return** r **else return** G^r

Fig. 1. The transparent random oracle $\mathsf{RO}_0(\cdot) : \{0,1\}^* \rightarrow \mathbb{G}_1$, $\mathsf{RO}_1(\cdot) : \{0,1\}^* \rightarrow \mathbb{Z}_p$. We write $\mathsf{RO}(\phi)$ for the interface $\mathsf{RO}_0(\phi)$ provided to protocols.

Random Oracle. Fuchsbauer et al. [18] also show how to integrate the AGM with the random oracle (RO) model. In particular, we are interested in RO that outputs group elements. Group elements returned by $\mathsf{RO}(\phi)$ are added to the set of received group elements. To simulate update proofs we make use of a weakening of the programmable RO model that we refer to as a transparent RO, presented on Fig. 1. For convenience we will denote $RO(\cdot) := RO_0(\cdot)$. The simulator has access to $\mathsf{RO}_1(\cdot)$ and can learn the discrete logarithm r by querying $\mathsf{RO}_1(x)$. It could query $\mathsf{RO}_0(x)$ for G^r but can also compute this value itself. Constructions and the $\mathcal{A}$ in all security definitions only have access to the restricted oracle $\mathsf{RO}_0(\cdot)$.

One remarkable detail in using white-box access to the adversary $\mathcal{A}$ in the RO model is that $\mathsf{view}_{\mathcal{A}}$ includes the RO transcript (but not RO randomness), since it contains all requests and replies $\mathcal{A}$ exchanges with the oracles it has access to, including RO. Thus access to $\mathsf{view}_{\mathcal{A}}$ is sufficient for our proofs, even though we do not give any explicit access to the RO history besides the view of the adversary to the extractor.

Assumptions. We recall the (q_1, q_2)-discrete logarithm assumption [18].

Definition 1 (**(q_1, q_2)-dlog**). *The (q_1, q_2)-discrete logarithm assumption holds for* BGen *if for any PPT $\mathcal{A}$, the following probability is negligible in λ,*

$$\Pr\left[\mathsf{bp} \leftarrow \mathsf{BGen}(1^\lambda); z \leftarrow\$ \mathbb{Z}_p; z' \leftarrow \mathcal{A}(\mathsf{bp}, \{G^{z^i}\}_{i=1}^{q_1}, \{H^{z^i}\}_{i=1}^{q_2}) : z = z'\right].$$

In our main theorem it is more convenient to use a slight variation of the above.

Definition 2 (**(q_1, q_2)-edlog**). *The (q_1, q_2)*-extended *discrete logarithm assumption holds for* BGen *if for any PPT $\mathcal{A}$, the following probability is negligible in λ,*

$$\Pr\left[\begin{array}{l}\mathsf{bp} \leftarrow \mathsf{BGen}(1^\lambda); z, r, s \leftarrow\$ \mathbb{Z}_p \ s.t.\ rz + s \neq 0; \\ z' \leftarrow \mathcal{A}(\mathsf{bp}, \{G^{z^i}\}_{i=1}^{q_1}, \{H^{z^i}\}_{i=1}^{q_2}, r, s, G^{\frac{1}{rz+s}}, H^{\frac{1}{rz+s}}) : z = z'\end{array}\right].$$

The assumption is an extension of (q_1, q_2)-**dlog**, where we additionally give $\mathcal{A}$ the challenge z in denominator (in both groups), blinded by s, r, which $\mathcal{A}$ is allowed to see. Later this helps to model fractional elements in Groth16's SRS.

Notice that (q_1, q_2)-**edlog** trivially implies (q_1, q_2)-**dlog**, since $\mathcal{A}$ for the latter does not need to use the extra elements of the former. The opposite implication is also true (except for a slight difference in parameters) as we state in the following theorem. The proof is postponed to full version of this paper.

Theorem 1. *If* $(q_1 + 1, q_2 + 1)$-***dlog*** *assumption holds, then* (q_1, q_2)-***edlog*** *assumption holds.*

We also state two lemmas that are often useful in conjunction with AGM proofs.

Lemma 1 ([4]). *Let* Q *be a non-zero polynomial in* $\mathbb{Z}_p[X_1, \ldots, X_n]$ *of total degree* d. *Define* $Q'(Z) := Q(R_1 Z + S_1, \ldots, R_n Z + S_n)$ *in the ring* $(\mathbb{Z}_p[R_1, \ldots, R_n, S_1, \ldots, S_n])[Z]$. *Then the coefficient of the highest degree monomial in* $Q'(Z)$ *is a degree* d *polynomial in* $\mathbb{Z}_p[R_1, \ldots, R_n]$.

Lemma 2 (Schwartz-Zippel). *Let* P *be a non-zero polynomial in* $\mathbb{Z}_p[X_1, \ldots, X_n]$ *of total degree* d. *Then,* $\Pr[x_1, \ldots, x_n \leftarrow_{\$} \mathbb{Z}_p : P(x_1, \ldots, x_n) = 0] \leq d/p$.

3 Ceremonial SNARKs

We present our definitions for NIZKs that are secure with respect to a setup ceremony. We discuss the new notions of update completeness and update soundness that apply to ceremonies that take place over many rounds. We also define subversion zero-knowledge which is adjusted to our ceremonial setting.

Compared to standard MPC definitions, our definition of (update) knowledge soundness is not simulation-based and the final SRS may not be uniformly random. We believe that the attempt to realise standard MPC definitions is what led prior works to make significant practical sacrifices e.g. random beacons or players that cannot go offline. This is because a rushing adversary that plays last can manipulate the bit-decomposition, for example to enforce that the first bit of the SRS is always 0. We here choose to offer an alternative protection: we allow that the final SRS is not distributed uniformly at random provided that the adversary does not gain any meaningful advantage when attacking the soundness of the SNARK. This is in essence an extension of updatability definitions [26] to ceremonies that require more than one round.

We consider NP-languages $\mathcal{L}$ and their corresponding relations $\mathcal{R} = \{(\phi, w)\}$ where w is an NP-witness for the statement $\phi \in \mathcal{L}$. An argument system Ψ (with a ceremony protocol) for a relation $\mathcal{R}$ contains the following algorithms:

(i) A PPT parameter generator Pgen that takes the security parameter 1^λ as input and outputs a parameter p (e.g., a pairing description)[6]. We assume that $\mathsf{p} \leftarrow \mathsf{Pgen}(1^\lambda)$ and the security parameter is given as input to all algorithms without explicitly writing it.

[6] We disallow subversion of p in this paper but in real life systems also this part of the setup needs scrutiny. This is arguable easier since usually p is trapdoor free.

(ii) A PPT SRS update algorithm Update that takes as input a phase number $\varphi \in \{1, \ldots, \varphi_{max}\}$, the current SRS srs, and proofs of previous updates $\{\rho_i\}_i$, and outputs a new SRS srs′ and an update proof ρ'. It is expected that Update itself forces a certain phase order, e.g. the sequential one.
(iii) A DPT SRS verification algorithm VerifySRS that takes as an input a SRS srs and update proofs $\{\rho_i\}_i$, and outputs 0 or 1.
(iv) A PPT prover algorithm Prove that takes as an input a SRS srs, a statement ϕ, and a witness w, and outputs a proof π.
(v) A DPT verification algorithm Verify that takes as an input a SRS srs, a statement ϕ, and a proof π, and outputs 0 or 1.
(vi) A PPT simulator algorithm Sim that takes as an input a SRS srs, a trapdoor τ, and a statement ϕ, and outputs a simulated proof π.

The description of Ψ also fixes a default $\mathsf{srs}^{\mathsf{d}} = (\mathsf{srs}^{\mathsf{d}}_1, \ldots, \mathsf{srs}^{\mathsf{d}}_{\varphi_{max}})$. We require that a secure Ψ satisfies the following flavours of completeness, zero-knowledge, and knowledge soundness. All our definitions are in the (implicit) random oracle model, since our final SRS update protocol will be using RO-dependent proof of knowledge. Therefore, all the algorithms in this section have access to RO, if some sub-components of Ψ require it.

Completeness of Ψ requires that Update and Prove always satisfy verification.

Definition 3 (Perfect Completeness). *An argument Ψ for $\mathcal{R}$ is* perfectly complete *if for any adversary $\mathcal{A}$, it has the following properties:*

1. Update completeness:

$$\Pr\left[\begin{array}{l}(\varphi, \mathsf{srs}, \{\rho_i\}_i) \leftarrow \mathcal{A}(1^\lambda), (\mathsf{srs}', \rho') \leftarrow \mathsf{Update}(\varphi, \mathsf{srs}, \{\rho_i\}_i) : \\ \mathsf{VerifySRS}(\mathsf{srs}, \{\rho_i\}_i) = 1 \wedge \mathsf{VerifySRS}(\mathsf{srs}', \{\rho_i\}_i \cup \{\rho'\}) = 0\end{array}\right] = 0.$$

2. Prover completeness:

$$\Pr\left[\begin{array}{l}(\mathsf{srs}, \{\rho_i\}_i, \phi, w) \leftarrow \mathcal{A}(1^\lambda), \pi \leftarrow \mathsf{Prove}(\mathsf{srs}, \phi, w) : \\ \mathsf{VerifySRS}(\mathsf{srs}, \{\rho_i\}_i) = 1 \wedge (\phi, w) \in \mathcal{R} \wedge \mathsf{Verify}(\mathsf{srs}, \phi, \pi) \neq 1\end{array}\right] = 0.$$

Our definition of subversion zero-knowledge follows [2]. Intuitively it says that an adversary that outputs a well-formed SRS knows the simulation trapdoor τ and thus could simulate a proof himself even without the witness. Therefore, proofs do not reveal any additional information. On a more technical side, we divide the adversary into an efficient SRS subverter $\mathcal{Z}$ that generates the SRS (showing knowledge of τ makes sense only for an efficient adversary) and into an unbounded distinguisher $\mathcal{A}$. We let $\mathcal{Z}$ send st to communicate with $\mathcal{A}$.

Definition 4 (Subversion Zero-Knowledge (sub-ZK)). *An argument Ψ for $\mathcal{R}$ is* subversion zero-knowledge *if for all PPT subverters $\mathcal{Z}$, there exists a PPT extractor $\mathcal{E}_{\mathcal{Z}}$, such that for all (unbounded) $\mathcal{A}$, $|\varepsilon_0 - \varepsilon_1|$ is negligible in λ, where*

$$\varepsilon_b := \Pr\left[\begin{array}{l}(\mathsf{srs}, \{\rho_i\}_i, st) \leftarrow \mathcal{Z}(1^\lambda), \tau \leftarrow \mathcal{E}_{\mathcal{Z}}(\mathsf{view}_{\mathcal{Z}}) : \\ \mathsf{VerifySRS}(\mathsf{srs}, \{\rho_i\}_i) = 1 \wedge \mathcal{A}^{\mathcal{O}_b(\mathsf{srs}, \tau, \cdot)}(st) = 1\end{array}\right].$$

$\mathcal{O}_b$ is a proof oracle that takes as input $(\mathsf{srs}, \tau, (\phi, w))$ *and only proceeds if* $(\phi, w) \in \mathcal{R}$. *If* $b = 0$, *$\mathcal{O}_b$ returns an honest proof* $\mathsf{Prove}(\mathsf{srs}, \phi, w)$ *and when* $b = 1$, *it returns a simulated proof* $\mathsf{Sim}(\mathsf{srs}, \tau, \phi)$.

Bellare et al. [5] showed that it is possible to achieve soundness and subversion zero-knowledge at the same time, but also that subversion soundness is incompatible with (even non-subversion) zero-knowledge. Updatable knowledge soundness from [26] can be seen as a relaxation of subversion soundness to overcome the impossibility result.

We generalize the notion of update knowledge soundness to multiple SRS generation phases. SRS is initially empty (or can be thought to be set to a default value $\mathsf{srs}^{\mathsf{d}}$). In each phase φ, the adversary has to fix a part of the SRS, denoted by srs_φ, in such a way building the final srs. The adversary can ask honest updates for his own proposal of srs^*_φ, however, it has to pass the verification $\mathsf{VerifySRS}$. The adversary can query honest updates using UPDATE query through a special oracle $\mathcal{O}_{\mathsf{srs}}$, described in Fig. 2. Eventually, adversary can propose some srs^*_φ with update proofs Q^* to be finalized through FINALIZE query. The oracle does it if Q^* contains at least one honest update proof obtained from the oracle for the current phase. If that is the case, then srs_φ cannot be changed anymore and the phase $\varphi+1$ starts. Once the whole SRS has been fixed, $\mathcal{A}$ outputs a statements ϕ and a proof π. The adversary wins if $(\mathsf{srs}, \phi, \pi)$ passes verification, but there is no PPT extractor $\mathcal{E}_\mathcal{A}$ that can extract a witness even when given the view of $\mathcal{A}$.

Definition 5 (Update Knowledge Soundness). *An argument Ψ for $\mathcal{R}$ is update knowledge-sound if for all PPT adversaries $\mathcal{A}$, there exists a PPT extractor $\mathcal{E}_\mathcal{A}$ such that* $\Pr[\mathsf{Game}_{\mathsf{uks}}^{\mathcal{A},\mathcal{E}_\mathcal{A}}(1^\lambda) = 1]$ *is negligible in λ, where*

$$\mathsf{Game}_{\mathsf{uks}}^{\mathcal{A},\mathcal{E}_\mathcal{A}}(1^\lambda) := \begin{bmatrix} (\phi, \pi) \leftarrow \mathcal{A}^{\mathcal{O}_{\mathsf{srs}}(\cdot)}(1^\lambda); \textit{get } (\mathsf{srs}, \varphi) \textit{ from } \mathcal{O}_{\mathsf{srs}}; w \leftarrow \mathcal{E}_\mathcal{A}(\mathsf{view}_\mathcal{A}); \\ \textbf{\textit{return}} \ \mathsf{Verify}(\mathsf{srs}, \phi, \pi) = 1 \wedge (\phi, w) \notin \mathcal{R} \wedge \varphi > \varphi_{max} \end{bmatrix},$$

SRS update oracle $\mathcal{O}_{\mathsf{srs}}$ is described in Fig. 2.

If $\varphi_{max} = 1$, we obtain the standard notion of update knowledge soundness. In the rest of the paper, we only consider the case where $\varphi_{max} = 2$. In particular, in the first phase we will generate a universal SRS $\mathsf{srs}_u = \mathsf{srs}_1$ that is independent of the relation and in the second phase we generate a specialized SRS $\mathsf{srs}_s = \mathsf{srs}_2$ that depends on the concrete relation. We leave it as an open question whether ceremony protocols with $\varphi_{max} > 2$ can provide any additional benefits. We also note that we do not model the possibility of the protocol running for several relations honestly simultaneously, although $\mathcal{A}$ can construct such SRS variants on its own.

It is important to explain the role of the default SRS in the definition. Our definition allows $\mathcal{A}$ to start its chain of SRS updates from any SRS, not just from the default one; the only condition is the presence of a single honest update in the chain. The default $\mathsf{srs}^{\mathsf{d}}$ is only used as a reference, for honest users. This has positive real-world consequences: since the chain is not required to be connected

$\mathcal{O}_{\mathsf{srs}}(\mathsf{intent}, \mathsf{srs}^*, Q^*)$ `// Initially` $Q_1 = \cdots = Q_{\varphi_{max}} = \emptyset; \varphi = 1$

---

if $\varphi > \varphi_{max}$: **return** $\perp$; `// SRS already finalized for all phases`
$\mathsf{srs}_{\mathsf{new}} \leftarrow (\mathsf{srs}_1, \ldots, \mathsf{srs}_{\varphi-1}, \mathsf{srs}^*_{\varphi}, \ldots, \mathsf{srs}^*_{\varphi_{max}})$;
if $\mathsf{VerifySRS}(\mathsf{srs}_{\mathsf{new}}, Q^*) = 0$: **return** $\perp$; `// Invalid SRS`
if $\mathsf{intent} = \text{UPDATE}$:
  $(\mathsf{srs}', \rho') \leftarrow \mathsf{Update}(\varphi, \mathsf{srs}_{\mathsf{new}}, Q^*); Q_\varphi \leftarrow Q_\varphi \cup \{\rho'\}$;
  return (srs', ρ');
if $\mathsf{intent} = \text{FINALIZE} \wedge Q_\varphi \cap Q^* \neq \emptyset$:
    Assign $\mathsf{srs}_\varphi \leftarrow \mathsf{srs}^*_\varphi; \varphi \leftarrow \varphi + 1$;

Fig. 2. SRS update oracle $\mathcal{O}_{\mathsf{srs}}$ given to the adversary in Definition 5. UPDATE returns $\mathcal{A}$ an honest update for φ, and FINALIZE finalizes the current phase. Current phase φ and current SRS srs are shared with the KS challenger. $\{Q_{\varphi_i}\}_i$ is a local set of proofs for honest updates, one for each phase.

to any "starting point", clients only need to verify the suffix of Q^*, if they are confident it contains an honest update. In particular, clients that contribute to the SRS update can start from the corresponding proof of update.

We again note that when using the random oracle model in a sub-protocol, we assume that all of the above algorithms in our security model have access to RO.

4 Update Proofs of Knowledge

One of the primary ingredients in the setup ceremony is a proof of update knowledge whose purpose is to ensure that adversary knows which values they used for updating the SRS. In this section, we discuss the proof of knowledge given by Bowe et al. [12]. Bowe et al. only proved this proof of knowledge secure under the presence of an adversary that can make random oracle queries. This definition is not sufficient to guarantee security (at least in our framework), because the adversary might be able to manipulate other users proofs or update elements in order to cheat. We therefore define a significantly stronger property that suffices for proving security of our update ceremony.

4.1 White-Box Simulation-Extraction with Oracles

In this section, we provide definitions for the central ingredient of the ceremony protocol—the *update proof of knowledge* that ensures validity of each sequential SRS update. The proof of knowledge (PoK) protocol does not rely on reference string but employs a random oracle as a setup. Hence we will extend the standard NIZK definitions with $\mathsf{RO}_t(\cdot)$, defined in Fig. 1.

Since NIZK proof of knowledge is used in our ceremony protocol, we require it to satisfy a stronger security property than knowledge soundness or even simulation extraction. Instead of the standard white-box simulation-extractability

(SE), we need a property that allows to compose the proof system more freely with other protocols while still allowing the adversary to extract. This is somewhat similar to idea of universal composability (UC, [14]), but contrary to the standard UC, our extractor is still white-box. Another way would be to use an augmented UC model which allows white-box assumptions (see [29]). In this work we follow the more minimal and commonly used game-based approach.

We model influence of other protocols by considering a polynomial oracle $\mathcal{O}_{\mathsf{poly}}$ in the SE game of the update PoK.

The adversary can query the oracle $\mathcal{O}_{\mathsf{poly}}$ on Laurent polynomials $f_i(Z_1, \dots, Z_n)$ and it will output $G^{f_i(z_1,\dots,z_n)}$ for $z_1, \dots, z_n$ pre-sampled from a uniform distribution, and unknown to $\mathcal{A}$. We use Laurent polynomials since SRS elements, the access to which the oracle models, may have negative trapdoor powers.[7] By $\mathsf{deg}(f)$ we will denote the maximum absolute degree of its monomials, where by absolute degree of the monomial we mean the sum of all its degrees taken as absolute values. Formally, $\mathsf{deg}(c \cdot \prod_i Z_i^{a_i}) := \sum_i |a_i|$, and $\mathsf{deg}(f(Z_1, \dots, Z_n)) = \mathsf{deg}(\sum_i M_i) := \max\{\mathsf{deg}(M_i)\}$, where M_i are monomials of f. For example, $\mathsf{deg}(3x^2\alpha\delta^{-2} + y) = 5$. This notion is used to limit the degree of input to $\mathcal{O}_{\mathsf{poly}}$—we denote the corresponding degree $d(\lambda)$ (or d, interchangeably).

This empowered adversary still should not be able to output a proof of knowledge unless it knows a witness. Note that $\mathcal{O}_{\mathsf{poly}}$ is independent from the random oracle RO_t and cannot provide the adversary any information about the random oracle's responses. In general, $\mathcal{O}_{\mathsf{poly}}$ adds strictly more power to $\mathcal{A}$. The intention of introducing $\mathcal{O}_{\mathsf{poly}}$ is to account for the SRS of the Groth's SNARK later on.

In addition, our ceremony protocol for Groth's SNARK requires NIZK to be straight-line simulation extractable, i.e., that extraction works without rewinding and is possible even when the adversary sees simulated proofs. Below, we define such a NIZK in the random oracle model.

$\mathcal{O}_{se}(\phi)$	$\mathcal{O}^{\mathbb{G}_1}_{\mathsf{poly}}(f(Z_1, \dots, Z_{d(\lambda)}))$	$\mathcal{O}^{\mathbb{G}_2}_{\mathsf{poly}}(g(Z_1, \dots, Z_{d(\lambda)}))$
`// Initially` $Q = \emptyset$	**if** $\mathsf{deg}(f) > d(\lambda)$	**if** $\mathsf{deg}(g) > d(\lambda)$
$\pi \leftarrow \mathsf{Sim}^{\mathsf{RO}_1(\cdot)}(\phi)$	**return** $\perp$	**return** $\perp$
$Q \leftarrow Q \cup \{(\phi, \pi)\}$	**else return** $G^{f(z_1,\dots,z_{d}(\lambda))}$	**else return** $H^{g(z_1,\dots,z_{d}(\lambda))}$
return π		

Fig. 3. Simulation-extraction oracle and two d–Poly oracles—for $\mathbb{G}_1$ and $\mathbb{G}_2$. All used in $\mathsf{Game}_{\mathsf{sSE}}$.

Let L be a language and $\mathcal{R}$ the corresponding relation. The argument Ψ for $\mathcal{R}$ in the random oracle model consists of the following PPT algorithms: the parameter generator Pgen, the prover $\mathsf{Prove}^{\mathsf{RO}(\cdot)}$, the verifier $\mathsf{Verify}^{\mathsf{RO}(\cdot)}$, and

[7] See the description of Groth16 SRS, which has $1/\delta$ in some SRS elements.

the simulator $\mathsf{Sim}^{\mathsf{RO}_1(\cdot)}$. We make an assumption that all algorithms get $\mathsf{p} \leftarrow \mathsf{Pgen}(1^\lambda)$ as an input without explicitly writing it.

We assume that Ψ in the random oracle model satisfies the following definitions.

Definition 6. *An argument Ψ for $\mathcal{R}$ is* perfectly complete *in the random oracle model, if for any adversary $\mathcal{A}$,*

$$\Pr\left[(\phi, w) \leftarrow \mathcal{A}^{\mathsf{RO}(\cdot)}, \pi \leftarrow \mathsf{Prove}^{\mathsf{RO}(\cdot)}(\phi, w) : (\phi, w) \in \mathcal{R} \wedge \mathsf{Verify}^{\mathsf{RO}(\cdot)}(\phi, \pi) \neq 1\right] = 0.$$

Definition 7. *An argument Ψ for $\mathcal{R}$ is* straight-line simulation extractable *in the (RO, d−Poly)-model, if for all PPT $\mathcal{A}$, there exists a PPT extractor $\mathcal{E}_\mathcal{A}$ such that $Pr[\mathsf{Game}^{\mathcal{A}}_{\mathsf{sSE}}(1^\lambda) = 1] = \mathsf{negl}(\lambda)$, where $\mathsf{Game}^{\mathcal{A}}_{\mathsf{sSE}}(1^\lambda) =$*

$$\left[\begin{matrix} Q \leftarrow \emptyset; z_1, \ldots, z_{d(\lambda)} \leftarrow \mathbb{Z}_p; \\ (\phi, \pi) \leftarrow \mathcal{A}^{\mathcal{O}_{\mathsf{se}}, \mathsf{RO}, \mathcal{O}^{\mathbb{G}_1}_{\mathsf{poly}}, \mathcal{O}^{\mathbb{G}_2}_{\mathsf{poly}}}(1^\lambda); \\ w \leftarrow \mathcal{E}_\mathcal{A}(\mathsf{view}_\mathcal{A}); \end{matrix} : \begin{matrix} \mathsf{Verify}^{\mathsf{RO}(\cdot)}(\phi, \pi) = 1 \wedge \\ (\phi, w) \notin \mathcal{R} \wedge (\phi, \pi) \notin Q \end{matrix}\right]$$

The oracles $\mathcal{O}_{\mathsf{se}}, \mathcal{O}^{\mathbb{G}_1}_{\mathsf{poly}}, \mathcal{O}^{\mathbb{G}_2}_{\mathsf{poly}}$ are defined on Fig. 3.

Roughly speaking, the adversary wins if it can output a verifying statement and proof for which it does not know a witness, such that this proof has not been obtained from a simulation oracle. There are also up to $d(\lambda)$ random variables chosen at the start such that the adversary can query an oracle for arbitrary polynomial evaluations with maximum degree $d(\lambda)$ of these values in the group. With respect to the relation of this definition to more standard one we note two things. First, our definition is white-box (since $\mathcal{E}_\mathcal{A}$ requires $\mathsf{view}_\mathcal{A}$), and strong (in the sense that proofs are not randomizable). Second, our notion implies strong-SE in the presence of RO, which is the special case of $\mathsf{Game}_{\mathsf{sSE}}$ with $\mathcal{O}_{\mathsf{poly}}$ removed, and thus is very close to the standard non-RO strong-SE variant.

Definition 8. *An argument Ψ for the relation $\mathcal{R}$ is* perfectly zero-knowledge *in the random oracle model if for all PPT adversaries $\mathcal{A}$, $\varepsilon_0 = \varepsilon_1$, where $\varepsilon_b :=$ $\Pr\left[\mathcal{A}^{\mathcal{O}_b(\cdot), \mathsf{RO}(\cdot)}(1^\lambda) = 1\right]$. $\mathcal{O}_b$ is a proof oracle that takes as an input (ϕ, w) and only proceeds if $(\phi, w) \in \mathcal{R}$. If $b = 0$, $\mathcal{O}_b$ returns an honest proof $\mathsf{Prove}^{\mathsf{RO}(\cdot)}(\phi, w)$ and when $b = 1$, it returns a simulated proof $\mathsf{Sim}^{\mathsf{RO}_1(\cdot)}(\phi)$.*

Note that Sim is allowed to have access to RO discrete logarithms.

4.2 On the Security of BGM Update Proofs

We now prove that the proof system of [12] satisfies this stronger property.

Bowe et al. [12] proved that the proof system is secure under a Knowledge-of-Exponent assumption. Their analysis does not capture the possibility that an attacker might use additional knowledge obtained from the ceremony to attack the update proof. Our analysis is more thorough and assumes this additional knowledge. This means that we cannot use a simple Knowledge-of-Exponent assumption. Instead we rely on the algebraic group model; the AGM is to date the weakest idealized model in which Groth16 has provable security and thus we do not see this as being a theoretical drawback. The proof of knowledge is for the discrete logarithm relation

$$\mathcal{R}_{dl} = \{(\phi = (m, G^{y_1}, H^{y_2}), w) \mid y_1 = y_2 = w\},$$

where m is an auxiliary input that was used in the original [12] proof of knowledge. The auxiliary input is redundant as we will see, but we still model it to have consistency with the original protocol. We recall that one of our goals is also to confirm the security of ceremony protocols already used in practice.

The protocol is given formally in Fig. 4. First the prover queries the random oracle on the instance ϕ. The oracle returns a fresh random group element H^r. The prover returns $\pi = H^{rw}$. The verifier checks that the instance is well-formed ($y_1 = y_2$), and then checks that $\hat{e}(\pi, H) = \hat{e}(\mathsf{RO}(\phi), H^{y_2})$ which ensures knowledge of y_2. Intuition for the last equation is that $\mathsf{RO}(\phi)$ acts as a fresh random challenge for ϕ and the only way to compute $\pi = \mathsf{RO}(\phi)^{y_2}$ and H^{y_2} is by knowing y_2. The fact that in $\mathcal{R}_{dl}$ every ϕ with $y_1 = y_2$ belongs to $\mathcal{L}_{dl}$ (the exponent w always exists) justifies that we will call the correspondent equation "well-formedness check"; subsequently, we will refer to the other check as "the main verification equation".

$\mathsf{Prove}_{dl}^{\mathsf{RO}(\cdot)}(\phi, w)$	$\mathsf{Verify}_{dl}^{\mathsf{RO}(\cdot)}(\phi = (\cdot, G^{y_1}, H^{y_2}), \pi)$	$\mathsf{Sim}_{dl}^{\mathsf{RO}_1(\cdot)}(\phi = (\cdot, G^{y_1}, H^{y_2}))$
$G^r \leftarrow \mathsf{RO}(\phi)$; **return** G^{rw};	$G^r \leftarrow \mathsf{RO}(\phi)$; Verify that $\hat{e}(G^{y_1}, H) = (G, H^{y_2}) \wedge$ $\hat{e}(\pi, H) = \hat{e}(G^r, H^{y_2})$;	Assert $\hat{e}(G^{y_1}, H) = (G, H^{y_2})$; $r_\phi \leftarrow \mathsf{RO}_1(\phi)$; **return** $\pi \leftarrow (G^{y_1})^{r_\phi}$;

Fig. 4. A discrete logarithm proof of knowledge Π_{dl}.

Here we have moderately simplified the description from [12]:

- We allow the message m to be unconstrained. Thus if one were to hash the public protocol view, as current implementations do, our security proof demonstrates that this approach is valid. However, we can also allow m to be anything, including the empty string.
- The original protocol has the proof element in $\mathbb{G}_2$. We switched it to $\mathbb{G}_1$ to have shorter proofs.
- Our protocol includes the pairing based equality check for y in G^y and H^y in the verifier rather than relying on this being externally done in the ceremony protocol. The value G^y is needed by the simulator.

We are now ready to state the security theorem for Π_{dl}.

Theorem 2. *The argument* $\Pi_{dl} = (\mathsf{Prove}_{dl}^{\mathsf{RO}(\cdot)}, \mathsf{Verify}_{dl}^{\mathsf{RO}(\cdot)}, \mathsf{Sim}_{dl}^{\mathsf{RO}_1(\cdot)})$ *is (i) complete, (ii) perfect zero-knowledge in the random oracle model, and (iii) straight-line SE in the (RO,d−Poly)-model against algebraic adversaries under the* $(1,0)$-**dlog** *assumption in* $\mathbb{G}_1$.

Proof (sketch). Completeness and perfect zero-knowledge follow directly from the construction of the prover, verifier, and simulator algorithms. The proof of straight-line simulation extractability is considerably more challenging and we provide the proof in the full version of this paper. We only mention the high level idea here.

We consider security against algebraic adversaries $\mathcal{A}$. Both statement ϕ elements (G^y, H^y) and proof $\pi \in \mathbb{G}_1$ that $\mathcal{A}$ outputs are going to be in the span of elements that $\mathcal{A}$ queried from oracles. Coefficients of those spans are available in $\mathcal{A}$'s view $\mathsf{view}_{\mathcal{A}}$ due to $\mathcal{A}$ being algebraic. We construct an extractor $\mathcal{E}_{\mathcal{A}}$ that gets $\mathsf{view}_{\mathcal{A}}$ as an input and returns the coefficient k corresponding to the element $\mathsf{RO}(\phi) = G^r$. Rest of the proof focuses on proving that k is the witness y. Roughly speaking, the idea is to construct a discrete logarithm adversary $\mathcal{C}$ that embeds (a randomized) discrete logarithm challenge G^c into each of the random oracle queries that $\mathcal{A}$ makes. We show that unless $k = y$, $\mathcal{C}$ is able to compute the discrete logarithm c from $\mathsf{view}_{\mathcal{A}}$ with an overwhelming probablity. □

5 Groth16 is Ceremonial

We show that Groth16 is ceremonial for a setup ceremony similar to the one proposed in [12]. In this section, we start by giving an intuitive overview of the [12] ceremony protocol. After that, we recall the Groth16 argument and carefully model the ceremony protocol in our security framework.

5.1 Ceremony Overview

We briefly remind the main idea of the [12] ceremony protocol.

- The SRS contains elements of the form e.g. $(A_1, \ldots, A_n, T) = (G^x, G^{x^2}, \ldots, G^{x^n}, G^{\delta p(x)})$ where $p(X)$ is a public polynomial known to all parties, and x and δ are secret trapdoors.[8]
- Parties initialize the SRS to $(A_1, \ldots, A_n, T) = (G, \ldots, G, G)$.
- In the first phase any party can update $(A_1, \ldots, A_n)$ by picking a random $x' \in \mathbb{Z}_p$ and computing $(A_1^{x'}, \ldots, A_n^{(x')^n})$. They must provide a proof of knowledge of x'.
- The value T is publicly updated to $G^{p(x)}$ given $A_1, \ldots, A_n$.
- In the second phase any party can update T by picking a random $\delta' \in \mathbb{Z}_p$ and computing $T^{\delta'}$. They must provide a proof of knowledge of δ'.

[8] The polynomial $p(X)$ is introduced only in the scope of this example, and is not related to QAP.

In order to prove knowledge of x' they assume access to a random oracle $\mathsf{RO} : \{0,1\}^* \to \mathbb{G}_2$ and proceed as follows:

- The prover computes $R \leftarrow \mathsf{RO}(\mathsf{T}_\Pi \| G^x)$ as a challenge where T_Π is the public transcript of the protocol.
- Then prover outputs $\pi \leftarrow R^x$ as a proof which can be verified by recomputing R and checking that $\hat{e}(G, \pi) = \hat{e}(G^x, R)$. The original protocol is knowledge sound under (a variation of) the knowledge of exponent assumption, which states that if given a challenge R, the adversary outputs (G^x, R^x), then the adversary knows x.

Our protocol differs from the [12] in a few aspects related to both performance and security. Additionally to the RO switch to $\mathbb{G}_1$ and optionality of including T_Π in evaluation of RO, which we described in Sect. 4, we remove the update with the random beacon in the end of each phase. That means that SRS can be slightly biased, but we prove that it is not sufficient to break the argument's security. We consider this to be the biggest contribution of this work since obtaining random beacons is a significant challenge both in theory and practice. Our approach completely side-steps this issue by directly proving the protocol without relying on the random beacon model.

5.2 Formal Description

We present the version of Groth's SNARK [25] from [12] and adjust the ceremony protocol to our security framework by defining Update and $\mathsf{VerifySRS}$ algorithms which follow the intuition of the previous section.

Firstly, let us recall the language of Groth's SNARK. A Quadratic Arithmetic Program (QAP) is described by a tuple

$$\mathsf{QAP} = \left(\mathbb{Z}_p, \{u_i(X), v_i(X), w_i(X)\}_{i=0}^m, t(X)\right)$$

where $u_i(X), v_i(X), w_i(X)$ are degree $n-1$ polynomials over $\mathbb{Z}_p$, and $t(X)$ is a degree n polynomial over $\mathbb{Z}_p$. Let the coefficients of the polynomials be respectively u_{ij}, v_{ij}, w_{ij}, and t_j. We can define the following relation for QAP,

$$\mathcal{R}_{\mathsf{QAP}} = \left\{ (\phi, w) \;\middle|\; \begin{array}{l} \phi = (a_0 = 1, a_1, \ldots, a_\ell) \in \mathbb{Z}_p^{1+\ell}, \\ w = (a_{\ell+1}, \ldots, a_m) \in \mathbb{Z}_p^{m-\ell}, \\ \exists h(X) \in \mathbb{Z}_p[X] \text{ of degree } \leq n-2 \text{ such that} \\ \left(\sum_{i=0}^m a_i u_i(X)\right)\left(\sum_{i=0}^m a_i v_i(X)\right) = \sum_{i=0}^m a_i w_i(X) + h(X)t(X) \end{array} \right\}.$$

In particular, the satisfiability of any arithmetic circuit, with a mixture of public and private inputs, can be encoded as a QAP relation (see [22] for details).

Groth [25] proposed an efficient SNARK for the QAP relation, which is now widely used in practice. Bowe et al. [12] modified original argument's SRS to make it consistent with their distributed SRS generation protocol. The full description of the latter argument is in Fig. 5. For the intuition of the construction, we refer the reader to the original paper by Groth.

We adjust the SRS in Fig. 5 to our model with a ceremony protocols: the default SRS, update algorithm, and a SRS specialization algorithm are described

$\underline{\mathsf{Setup}(\mathcal{R}_{\mathsf{QAP}})}$: Sample $\tau = (\alpha, \beta, \delta, x) \leftarrow\$ (\mathbb{Z}_p^*)^4$ and return $(\mathsf{srs} = (\mathsf{srs}_u, \mathsf{srs}_s), \tau)$ s.t.

$$\mathsf{srs}_u \leftarrow \left(\{G^{x^i}, H^{x^i}\}_{i=0}^{2n-2}, \{G^{\alpha x^i}, G^{\beta x^i}, H^{\alpha x^i}, H^{\beta x^i}\}_{i=0}^{n-1}\right),$$

$$\mathsf{srs}_s \leftarrow \left(G^\delta, H^\delta, \{G^{\frac{\beta u_i(x)+\alpha v_i(x)+w_i(x)}{\delta}}\}_{i=\ell+1}^m, \{G^{\frac{x^i t(x)}{\delta}}\}_{i=0}^{n-2}\right).$$

$\underline{\mathsf{Prove}(\mathcal{R}_{\mathsf{QAP}}, \mathsf{srs}, \{a_i\}_{i=0}^m)}$: Sample $r, s \leftarrow\$ \mathbb{Z}_p$ and return $\pi = (G^A, H^B, G^C)$, where

$$A = \alpha + \sum_{i=0}^m a_i u_i(x) + r\delta, \qquad B = \beta + \sum_{i=0}^m a_i v_i(x) + s\delta,$$

$$C = \frac{\sum_{i=\ell+1}^m a_i(\beta u_i(x)+\alpha v_i(x)+w_i(x))+h(x)t(x)}{\delta} + As + Br - rs\delta.$$

$\underline{\mathsf{Verify}(\mathcal{R}_{\mathsf{QAP}}, \mathsf{srs}, \{a_i\}_{i=1}^\ell, \pi)}$: Parse π as (G^A, H^B, G^C) and verify that

$$\hat{e}(G^A, H^B) = \hat{e}(G^\alpha, H^\beta) \cdot \hat{e}(\prod_{i=0}^{\ell} G^{a_i(\beta u_i(x)+\alpha v_i(x)+w_i(x))}, H) \cdot \hat{e}(G^C, H^\delta).$$

$\underline{\mathsf{Sim}(\mathcal{R}_{\mathsf{QAP}}, \mathsf{srs}, \tau, \{a_i\}_{i=1}^\ell)}$: Return (G^A, H^B, G^C), where

$$A, B \leftarrow\$ \mathbb{Z}_p,\ C = \frac{AB - \alpha\beta - \left(\sum_{i=0}^\ell a_i(\beta u_i(x)+\alpha v_i(x)+w_i(x))\right)}{\delta}$$

Fig. 5. Groth's zk-SNARK description.

in Fig. 6.[9] We obtain the default SRS from the trapdoor $\tau = (1, 1, 1, 1)$. The algorithm Update samples new trapdoors and includes them in the previous SRS by exponentiation as was described in Sect. 5.1. For example, to update G^ι, where ι is some trapdoor, the updater will sample ι' and computes $(G^\iota)^{\iota'}$. Depending on the phase number $\varphi \in \{1, 2\}$, the algorithm will either update srs_u or srs_s. When updating srs_u, we also derive a consistent srs_s using the Specialize algorithm[10] which essentially computes srs_s with $\delta = 1$. This fixes a sequential phase update scenario, since updating srs_u after srs_s overwrites the latter.

Each update is additionally accompanied with an update proof ρ, which allows us to verify update correctness. For each trapdoor update ι', ρ contains $G^{\iota\iota'}$ (the element of the new SRS), $G^{\iota'}$, $H^{\iota'}$, and a NIZK proof of knowledge $\pi_{\iota'}$ for ι'. Since G^ι is part of the previous update proof, we can use pairings to assert well-formedness of $G^{\iota\iota'}$, $G^{\iota'}$, and $H^{\iota'}$. The first element of the update proof duplicates the element of the new SRS, but since we do not store every updated SRS but only update proofs, we must keep these elements.

Finally, we have a SRS verification algorithm VerifySRS in Fig. 7, that takes as an input srs and a set of update proofs Q, and then (i) uses pairing-equations to verify that srs is well-formed respect to some trapdoors, (ii) checks that each update proof $\rho \in Q$ contains a valid NIZK proof of discrete logarithm, and (iii) uses pairing-equations to verify that update proofs in Q are consistent with srs.

[9] Our Groth16 SRS follows [12] and not the original [25]. It additionally contains $\{H^{x^i}\}_{i=n-2}^{2n-2}$, $\{H^{\alpha x^i}\}_{i=1}^{n-1}$, and $\{H^{\beta x^i}\}_{i=1}^{n-1}$.

[10] This generality simplifies our model. In practice srs_s can be derived using Specialize only once just before starting phase 2.

Default SRS: Run Setup in Fig. 5 with $\tau = (1,1,1,1)$ to obtain $\mathsf{srs}^{\mathsf{d}}$.

$\underline{\mathsf{Update}(\mathcal{R}_{\mathsf{QAP}}, \varphi \in \{1,2\}, (\mathsf{srs} = (\mathsf{srs}_u, \mathsf{srs}_s), Q)):}$

If $\varphi = 1$:

1. Parse $\mathsf{srs}_u = (\{G_{x:i}, H_{x:i}\}_{i=0}^{2n-2}, \{G_{\alpha x:i}, G_{\beta x:i}, H_{\alpha x:i}, H_{\beta x:i}\}_{i=0}^{n-1})$;
2. Sample $\alpha', \beta', x' \leftarrow\$ \mathbb{Z}_p^*$;
3. For $\iota \in \{\alpha, \beta, x\}$: $\pi_{\iota'} \leftarrow \mathsf{Prove}_{dl}^{\mathsf{RO}(\cdot)}(G^{\iota'}, H^{\iota'}, \iota')$;
4. $\rho_{\alpha'} \leftarrow (G_{\alpha x:0}^{\alpha'}, G^{\alpha'}, H^{\alpha'}, \pi_{\alpha'})$;
5. $\rho_{\beta'} \leftarrow (G_{\beta x:0}^{\beta'}, G^{\beta'}, H^{\beta'}, \pi_{\beta'})$;
6. $\rho_{x'} \leftarrow (G_{x:1}^{x'}, G^{x'}, H^{x'}, \pi_{x'})$;
7. $\rho \leftarrow (\rho_{\alpha'}, \rho_{\beta'}, \rho_{x'})$;
8. $\mathsf{srs}'_u \leftarrow \left(\{G_{x:i}^{(x')^i}, H_{x:i}^{(x')^i}\}_{i=0}^{2n-2}, \{G_{\alpha x:i}^{\alpha'(x')^i}, G_{\beta x:i}^{\beta'(x')^i}, H_{\alpha x:i}^{\alpha'(x')^i}, H_{\beta x:i}^{\beta'(x')^i}\}_{i=0}^{n-1}\right)$
9. $\mathsf{srs}'_s \leftarrow \mathsf{Specialize}(\mathsf{QAP}, \mathsf{srs}'_u)$;
10. **return** $((\mathsf{srs}'_u, \mathsf{srs}'_s), \rho)$;

If $\varphi = 2$:

11. Parse $\mathsf{srs}_s = (G_\delta, H_\delta, \{G_{sum:i}\}_{i=\ell+1}^{m}, \{G_{t(x):i}\}_{i=0}^{n-2})$;
12. Sample $\delta' \leftarrow\$ \mathbb{Z}_p^*$;
13. $\pi_{\delta'} \leftarrow \mathsf{Prove}_{dl}^{\mathsf{RO}(\cdot)}(G^{\delta'}, H^{\delta'}, \delta')$;
14. $\rho \leftarrow (G_\delta^{\delta'}, G^{\delta'}, H^{\delta'}, \pi_{\delta'})$;
15. $\mathsf{srs}'_s \leftarrow \left(G_\delta^{\delta'}, H_\delta^{\delta'}, \{G_{sum:i}^{1/\delta'}\}_{i=\ell+1}^{m}, \{G_{t(x):i}^{1/\delta'}\}_{i=0}^{n-2}\right)$;
16. **return** $((\mathsf{srs}_u, \mathsf{srs}'_s), \rho)$;

$\underline{\mathsf{Specialize}(\mathcal{R}_{\mathsf{QAP}}, \mathsf{srs}_u):}$ `// Computes` srs_s `with` $\delta = 1$

17. Parse $\mathsf{srs}_u = (\{G_{x:i}, H_{x:i}\}_{i=0}^{2n-2}, \{G_{\alpha x:i}, G_{\beta x:i}, H_{\alpha x:i}, H_{\beta x:i}\}_{i=0}^{n-1})$;
18. $\mathsf{srs}_s \leftarrow \left(G, H, \{\prod_{j=0}^{n-1} G_{\beta x:j}^{u_{ij}} \cdot G_{\alpha x:j}^{v_{ij}} \cdot G_{x:j}^{w_{ij}}\}_{i=\ell+1}^{m}, \{\prod_{j=0}^{n} G_{x:(i+j)}^{t_j}\}_{i=0}^{n-2}\right)$;
19. **return** srs_s;

Fig. 6. Default SRS and update algorithm for Groth's SNARK

In the full version , we show how to make VerifySRS more efficient by using batching techniques. This will allow to substitute most of pairings in VerifySRS with significantly cheaper small-exponent multi-exponentiations.

6 Security

We prove the security of Groth's SNARK from Sect. 5 in our NIZK with a ceremony framework of Sect. 3.

Theorem 3 (Completeness). *Groth's SNARK has perfect completeness, i.e., it has update completeness and prover completeness.*

Proof. Let us first make a general observation that if some bitstring $s = (\mathsf{srs}, \{\rho_i\}_i)$ satisfies $\mathsf{VerifySRS}(s) = 1$, then there exists a unique $\alpha, \beta, x, \delta \in \mathbb{Z}_p^*$ that define a well-formed srs.

<u>$\mathsf{VerifySRS}^{\mathsf{RO}(\cdot)}(\mathsf{QAP}, \mathsf{srs}, Q)$:</u>

1. Parse $\mathsf{srs} = (\mathsf{srs}_u, \mathsf{srs}_s)$ and $Q = (Q_u, Q_s) = \{\rho_{u,i}\}_{i=1}^{k_u} \cup \{\rho_{s,i}\}_{i=1}^{k_s}$;
2. Parse $\mathsf{srs}_u = \left(\{G_{x:i}, H_{x:i}\}_{i=0}^{2n-2}, \{G_{\alpha x:i}, G_{\beta x:i}, H_{\alpha x:i}, H_{\beta x:i}\}_{i=0}^{n-1}\right)$ and assert that elements belong to correct groups;
3. For $i = 1, \ldots, k_u$:
   (a) Parse $\rho_{u,i} = (\rho_{\alpha'}^{(i)}, \rho_{\beta'}^{(i)}, \rho_{x'}^{(i)})$;
   (b) For $\iota \in \{\alpha, \beta, x\}$:
      i. Parse $\rho_{\iota'}^{(i)} = (G_{\iota}^{(i)}, G_{\iota'}^{(i)}, H_{\iota'}^{(i)}, \pi_{\iota'}^{(i)})$;
      ii. Assert $\mathsf{Verify}_{dl}^{\mathsf{RO}(\cdot)}(G_{\iota'}^{(i)}, H_{\iota'}^{(i)}, \pi_{\iota'}^{(i)}) = 1$;
      iii. If $i \neq 1$: Assert $\hat{e}(G_{\iota}^{(i)}, H) = \hat{e}(G_{\iota}^{(i-1)}, H_{\iota'}^{(i)})$;
4. Assert $G_{x:1} = G_x^{(k_u)} \neq 1$; $G_{\alpha x:0} = G_{\alpha}^{(k_u)} \neq 1$; $G_{\beta x:0} = G_{\beta}^{(k_u)} \neq 1$;
5. For $i = 1, \ldots, 2n-2$: Assert $\hat{e}(G_{x:i}, H) = \hat{e}(G, H_{x:i})$ and $\hat{e}(G_{x:i}, H) = \hat{e}(G_{x:(i-1)}, H_{x:1})$;
6. For $i = 0, \ldots, n-1$ and $\iota \in \{\alpha, \beta\}$: Assert $\hat{e}(G_{\iota x:i}, H) = \hat{e}(G, H_{\iota x:i})$ and $\hat{e}(G_{\iota x:i}, H) = \hat{e}(G_{x:i}, H_{\iota x:0})$;
7. Parse $\mathsf{srs}_s \leftarrow \left(G_\delta, H_\delta, \{G_{sum:i}\}_{i=\ell+1}^{m}, \{G_{t(x):i}\}_{i=0}^{n-2},\right)$ and assert that elements belong to correct groups;
8. For $i = 1, \ldots, k_s$:
   (a) Parse $\rho_{s,i} = (G_{\delta}^{(i)}, G_{\delta'}^{(i)}, H_{\delta'}^{(i)}, \pi_{\delta'})$;
   (b) Assert $\mathsf{Verify}_{dl}^{\mathsf{RO}(\cdot)}(G_{\delta'}^{(i)}, H_{\delta'}^{(i)}, \pi_{\delta'}) = 1$;
   (c) if $i \neq 1$ assert $\hat{e}(G_{\delta}^{(i)}, H) = \hat{e}(G_{\delta}^{(i-1)}, H_{\delta'}^{(i)})$;
9. Assert $\hat{e}(G_\delta, H) = \hat{e}(G, H_\delta)$ and $G_\delta = G_{\delta}^{(k_s)} \neq 1$;
10. For $i = \ell + 1, \ldots, m$: Assert $\hat{e}(G_{sum:i}, H_\delta) = \hat{e}(\prod_{j=0}^{n-1} G_{\beta x:j}^{u_{ij}} \cdot G_{\alpha x:j}^{v_{ij}} \cdot G_{x:j}^{w_{ij}}, H)$;
11. For $i = 0, \ldots, n-2$: Assert $\hat{e}(G_{t(x):i}, H_\delta) = \hat{e}(G_{t(x)}, H_{x:i})$, where $G_{t(x)} = \prod_{j=0}^{n} G_{x:j}^{t_j}$;

Fig. 7. SRS verification algorithm for Groth's SNARK

Update Completeness: Let $\mathcal{A}$ be an adversary that outputs $s = (\varphi, \mathsf{srs}, \{\rho_i\}_i)$ such that $\mathsf{VerifySRS}(s) = 1$. By the observation above, there exists some $\alpha, \beta, x, \delta \in \mathbb{Z}_p^*$ that map to a well-formed srs. It is easy to observe that by construction $\mathsf{Update}(\mathsf{QAP}, \varphi, (\mathsf{srs}, \{\rho_i\}_i))$ picks a new $\alpha', \beta', x' \in \mathbb{Z}_p^*$ (or δ' if $\varphi = 2$) and rerandomizes srs such that the new srs' has a trapdoor $\alpha\alpha', \beta\beta', xx' \in \mathbb{Z}_p^*$ (or $\delta\delta' \in \mathbb{Z}_p^*$). Since the srs' is still well-formed and ρ is computed independently, $\mathsf{VerifySRS}(\mathsf{srs}', \{\rho_i\}_i \cup \{\rho'\}) = 1$.

Prover Completeness: Suppose that $\mathcal{A}$ output $(\mathsf{srs}, \{\rho_i\}_i, \phi, w)$ such that $(\phi, w) \in \mathcal{R}_{\mathsf{QAP}}$, and $\mathsf{VerifySRS}(\mathsf{srs}, \{\rho_i\}_i) = 1$. It follows that srs is a well-formed SRS for Groth's SNARK. From here, the prover completeness follows from the completeness proof in [25]. □

Subversion zero-knowledge of Groth's SNARK was independently proven in [2] and [17] under slightly different knowledge assumptions. Our approach here differs only in that we extract the trapdoor from Π_{dl} proofs. For sake of completeness, we sketch the main idea below.

Theorem 4 (sub-ZK). *If Π_{dl} is a non-interactive proof of knowledge, then Groth's SNARK is subversion zero-knowledge.*

Proof (sketch). Let $\mathcal{Z}$ be a PPT subverter and $\mathcal{A}$ an unbounded adversary in the subversion zero-knowledge definition. We suppose that $\mathcal{Z}(1^\lambda)$ outputs $(\mathsf{srs}, \{\rho_i\}_i, st)$ such that $\mathsf{VerifySRS}(\mathsf{srs}, \{\rho_i\}_i) = 1$. The latter guarantees that srs is well-formed and that update proofs verify. To prove subversion zero-knowledge, we need to construct an extractor $\mathcal{E}_\mathcal{Z}$ that give $\mathsf{view}_\mathcal{Z}$ extracts the simulation trapdoor for srs. Idea behind $\mathcal{E}_\mathcal{A}$ is that we use straight-line extractability of Π_{dl} to extract $\iota_1, ..., \iota_m$ for $\iota \in \{x, \alpha, \beta, \delta\}$ from the proofs $\{\rho_i\}_i$ and then compute $\iota = \prod_i \iota_i$ to obtain the trapdoor $\tau = (x, \alpha, \beta, \delta)$. Given that $\mathcal{E}_\mathcal{A}$ outputs the correct trapdoor τ, proofs can be perfectly simulated as is proven in [25]. □

6.1 Update Knowledge Soundness

Theorem 5. *Let us assume the $(2n-1, 2n-2)$-**edlog** assumption holds. Then Groth's SNARK has update knowledge soundness with respect to all PPT algebraic adversaries in the random oracle model.*

Proof. Let $\mathcal{A}$ be an algebraic adversary against update knowledge soundness and let us denote the update knowledge soundness game $\mathsf{Game}_{\mathsf{uks}}$ by Game_0. We construct an explicit white-box extractor $\mathcal{E}_\mathcal{A}$ and prove it to succeed with an overwhelming probability. The theorem statement is thus $\mathsf{Adv}^{\mathsf{Game}_0}_{\mathcal{A},\mathcal{E}_\mathcal{A}}(\lambda) = \mathsf{negl}(\lambda)$. We assume that $\mathcal{A}$ makes at most q_1 update queries in phase 1 and at most q_2 in phase 2. Often we will use ι to denote any of the elements x, α, β or δ.

$\mathcal{E}_\mathcal{A}(\mathsf{view}_\mathcal{A})$

1. Extract the set of algebraic coefficients $T_\pi \leftarrow \mathcal{E}^{\mathsf{agm}}_\mathcal{A}(\mathsf{view}_\mathcal{A})$ and obtain $\{C_{i:x:j}\}^{m_1,m}_{i,j=(1,l+1)}$ from it, corresponding to the elements $\{(\beta u_i(x) + \alpha v_i(x) + w_i(x))/\delta\}$ in the second phase, where m_1 is the number of update queries made in the first phase, and m is the QAP parameter.
2. From $\mathsf{view}_\mathcal{A}$ deduce i_{crit_2} — $\mathcal{O}_{\mathsf{srs}}$ query index that corresponds to the last honest update in the final SRS.
3. Return coefficients $w = \{C_{i_{\mathsf{crit}_2}:x:j}\}^m_{j=l+1}$.

Fig. 8. The extractor $\mathcal{E}_\mathcal{A}$ for update knowledge soundness

Description of the extractor $\mathcal{E}_\mathcal{A}$. We present the extractor $\mathcal{E}_\mathcal{A}$ on Fig. 8. The extractor takes the adversarial view $\mathsf{view}_\mathcal{A}$ as an input and extracts AGM coefficients from $\mathsf{view}_\mathcal{A}$ when $\mathcal{A}$ produces a verifying proof. The goal of the extractor is to reconstruct the witness from this information.

The intuition behind its strategy is that, in Prove on Fig. 5, C is constructed as $\sum_i a_i(\alpha u_i(x) + \beta v_i(x) + w_i(x))/\delta$, and we would like to obtain precisely these

a_i as AGM coefficients corresponding to the $(\alpha u_i(x) + \ldots)/\delta$ elements of the *final* SRS. When $\mathcal{A}$ submits the final response $(\phi, \pi = (A, B, C))$, the proof element $C \in \mathbb{G}_1$ has the algebraic representation, corresponding to following $\mathbb{G}_1$ elements: (1) SRS elements that the update oracle outputs, (2) corresponding update proofs, and (3) direct RO replies. These sets include *all* the SRS elements that were produced during the update KS game, not only those that were included in the final SRS. The coefficient of elements $(\alpha u_i(x) + \ldots)/\delta$ that the extractor needs belong to the first category and in particular correspond to the second phase updates, since δ is updated there.

Let m_φ be the number of update queries that $\mathcal{A}$ makes in phase $\varphi \in \{1, 2\}$. We introduce the notion of the *critical* query—$i_{\mathsf{crit}_\varphi} \in \{1, \ldots, m_\varphi\}$ corresponds to the last honest update that $\mathcal{A}$ includes into the finalized SRS in phase φ. Technically, we define it in the following way. For every phase φ, the final SRS is associated with update proofs $\{\rho_{\varphi,i}\}_{i=1}^{k_\varphi}$ (contained in Q^* in Fig. 2) and at least one of them must be produced by honest update query for finalization to succeed. Suppose that $\rho_{\varphi,i_{max}}$ is the last honest update in that set, that is, the one with the largest index i. If $\rho_{\varphi,i_{max}}$ was obtained as the j-th update query, then we define $i_{\mathsf{crit}_\varphi} := j$.

The extractor $\mathcal{E}_\mathcal{A}$ can deduce $i_{\mathsf{crit}_\varphi}$, since $\mathsf{view}_\mathcal{A}$ includes $\mathcal{O}_{\mathsf{srs}}$ responses and Q^*. When $\mathcal{E}_\mathcal{A}$ obtains i_{crit_2}, it merely returns the AGM coefficients (which it can obtain from $\mathsf{view}_\mathcal{A}$ since $\mathcal{A}$ is algebraic) corresponding to the $(\alpha u_i(x) + \ldots)/\delta$ elements of update oracle response number i_{crit_2}. For now, there is no guarantee that these elements are in any way connected to the final SRS, but later we show that $\mathcal{E}_\mathcal{A}$ indeed succeeds.

Description of Game_1**.** We describe Game_1, that differs from Game_0 in that one of the honest updates in each phase is a freshly generated SRS instead of being an update of the input SRS. This simplifies further reasoning (Lemma 4), and also at a later step we build a reduction $\mathcal{B}$ that embeds the edlog challenge z into the trapdoors of the fresh SRS. For convenience, we describe Game_1 in terms of communication between the challenger $\mathcal{C}$ (top-level execution code of Game_1) and $\mathcal{A}$.

$\mathcal{C}$ of Game_1 maintains an update (current call) counter i_{call}, which is reset to zero in the beginning of each phase. Before the game starts, $\mathcal{C}$ uniformly samples two values i_{guess_1} and i_{guess_2}, ranging from $1, \ldots, q_1$ and $1, \ldots, q_2$ (upperbounds on the number of queries) correspondingly, in such a way attempting to guess critical queries $\{i_{\mathsf{crit}_\varphi}\}_\varphi$. In case the actual number of queries m_φ in a particular execution of $\mathcal{A}$ is less than $i_{\mathsf{guess}_\varphi}$, $\mathcal{C}$ will just execute as in Game_0 for phase φ. $\mathcal{C}$ will generate fresh SRS for at most two (randomly picked) update queries through $\mathcal{O}_{\mathsf{srs}}$, and it will respond to all the other update requests from $\mathcal{A}$ honestly. The successful guess formally corresponds to the event **lucky**, set during SRS finalization in Game_1.

It is not possible for $\mathcal{C}$ to generate an update proof for a fresh SRS as in Game_0 because it does not know the update trapdoors $\hat{\iota}'$ for critical queries—these values do not exist explicitly, since instead of updating an SRS, $\mathcal{C}$ generated a new one. Therefore, it uses a specific technique to simulate update proofs using the procedure $\mathsf{SimUpdProof}$. The task of $\mathsf{SimUpdProof}$ is to create $\rho_{\hat{\iota}'} = (G^{\hat{\iota}'}_{\hat{\iota}}, G^{\hat{\iota}'}, H^{\hat{\iota}'}, \pi_{\hat{\iota}'})$, which is a valid update proof from srs^* to a freshly generated srs'. Since $\mathcal{C}$ does not actually update srs^*, but creates a completely new one with z_ι trapdoors, we have $G^{z_\iota} = G^{\hat{\iota}\hat{\iota}'}$ where $\hat{\iota}$ is the trapdoor value of srs^* and $\hat{\iota}'$ is the new update trapdoor. Given the value $\hat{\iota}$ in clear, we can reconstruct $G^{\hat{\iota}'}$ by computing $(G^{\hat{\iota}\hat{\iota}'})^{\hat{\iota}^{-1}} = (G^{z_\iota})^{\hat{\iota}^{-1}}$.

This is the strategy of $\mathcal{C}$: it uses $\mathsf{view}_\mathcal{A}$ to extract the trapdoors ι_j for all the k_u updates that led to srs^*_φ, and thus obtains $\hat{\iota}$. Notice that these updates can be both honest and adversarial, but importantly, none of them are simulated (because we perform this procedure only once per phase), which guarantees that extraction succeeds. Next, $\mathsf{SimUpdProof}$ computes a product $\hat{\iota}$ of these extracted values, and using its inverse produces $(G^{\hat{\iota}'}, H^{\hat{\iota}'})$, which are the second and third elements of the update proof. The first element of $\rho_{\hat{\iota}'}$ is just an element of the new SRS (e.g. for $\iota = x$, it is $G^{\iota'}_{x:1}$, and for $\iota \in \{\alpha, \beta\}$ it is $G^{\iota'}_{\iota x:0}$), so we set the value to G^{z_ι}. The last element, the proof-of-knowledge of $\hat{\iota}'$, we create by black-box simulation, since Π_{dl} is perfectly ZK. Namely, since the challenger already has $\phi_{dl} = (\bot, G^{\hat{\iota}'}, H^{\hat{\iota}'})$, it passes it into Sim_{dl}, and attaches the resulting $\pi_{\iota'}$ to the update proof. Since we know z_ι in Game_1 (and therefore know ϕ_{dl} exponent $\hat{\iota}'$), it is not necessary to simulate the proof in Game_1—technically, the procedure only requires G^{z_ι}. However, simulation will be critical in the final part of our theorem, reduction to edlog, since in that case z_ι contains embedded edlog challenge for which the challenger does not know the exponent. This is why we introduce it here in Game_1.

We prove in the full version of this paper that the game Game_1 that we introduced is indistinguishable from Game_0 for $\mathcal{A}$ by relying on the zero-knowledge and simulation-extractability properties of Π_{dl}. We recall that $(1,0)$-**dlog** assumption is implied by $(2n-1, 2n-2)$-**edlog** assumption.

Lemma 3. *Assuming* $(1,0)$-***dlog****, the difference between advantage of* $\mathcal{A}$ *in winning* Game_0 *and* Game_1 *is negligible:* $\mathsf{Adv}^{\mathsf{Game}_0}_{\mathcal{A},\mathcal{E}_\mathcal{A}}(\lambda) \leq \mathsf{Adv}^{\mathsf{Game}_1}_{\mathcal{A},\mathcal{E}_\mathcal{A}}(\lambda) + \mathsf{negl}(\lambda)$.

Reconstructing the Proof Algebraically. For the next steps of our proof we will need to be able to reconstruct the proof elements, and the verification equation generically from the AGM coefficients we extract from $\mathcal{A}$. Almost all the elements that $\mathcal{A}$ sees depend on certain variables $\vec{\Psi}$ that are considered secret for the adversary (update trapdoors, RO exponents, critical query honest trapdoors). Since $\mathcal{A}$ can describe proof elements A, B, C as linear combinations of elements it sees, that depend on $\vec{\Psi}$, we are able to reconstruct the proof elements as functions $A(\vec{\Psi}), B(\vec{\Psi}), C(\vec{\Psi})$ (Laurent polynomials, as we will show later). That is, for the particular values $\vec{\psi}$ that we chose in some execution in Game_1, $A(\vec{\psi}) = A$ (but we can also evaluate $A(\vec{\Psi})$ on a different set of trapdoors). From these functions $A(\vec{\Psi}), B(\vec{\Psi}), C(\vec{\Psi})$ one can reconstruct a SNARK verification equation $Q(\vec{\Psi})$, such that $\mathsf{Verify}(\psi, \pi) = 1 \iff Q(\vec{\psi}) = 0$.

We note that it is not trivial to obtain the (general) form of these functions, because it depends on $\mathsf{view}_\mathcal{A}$—different traces produce different elements that $\mathcal{A}$

sees, which affects with which functions these elements are modelled. Therefore, we start by defining which *variables* are used to model elements that $\mathcal{A}$ sees.

We denote by $\vec{\Psi}$ this set of variables which are unknown to $\mathcal{A}$. This includes, first and foremost, the set of trapdoors that are used for the (critical) simulation update queries: $Z_x, Z_\alpha, Z_\beta, Z_\delta$ (these abstract the corresponding trapdoors $\{z_\iota\}$). To denote the expression that includes final adversarial trapdoors $\iota_j^{\mathcal{A}}$, we will use $\hat{Z}_\iota$ that is equal to the previously defined Z_ι, but now as a function of Z_ι: $\hat{Z}_\iota(Z_\iota) = Z_\iota \prod \iota_j^{\mathcal{A}}$ for $\iota \in \{x, \alpha, \beta\}$, and $\hat{Z}_\delta(Z_\delta) = Z_\delta / \prod \delta_j^{\mathcal{A}}$.[11]

The full list of variables that constitute $\vec{\Psi}$ is the following:

1. Critical honest trapdoor variables: $Z_\alpha, Z_\beta, Z_x, Z_\delta$.
2. Honest (non-critical) update trapdoors $\vec{T} = \{T_{i,\iota}\}$.
3. RO replies, which we, for convenience of indexing, split into three disjoint sets:
   - RO values for the critical queries $\vec{K} = \{K_\iota\}_{x,\alpha,\beta,\delta}$: these RO replies are used in PoK simulation by Game_1.
   - RO values for honest update proofs $\vec{R}_T = \{R_{T:i:\iota}\}_{i,\iota}$. First phase update query number $i \in \{1, \dots, m_1\}$ corresponds to three values $R_{T:i:x}$, $R_{T:i:\alpha}$, $R_{T:i:\beta}$, and second phase update query number $j \in \{1, \dots, m_2\}$ corresponds to $R_{T:j:\delta}$.
   - RO responses $\vec{R}_{\mathcal{A}}$ that $\mathcal{A}$ directly requests from RO. These are used by $\mathcal{A}$, in particular, but not only, to create PoKs for adversarial SRS updates.

We denote by $\vec{R} = \vec{R}_{\mathcal{A}} \cup \vec{R}_T$. Therefore, $\vec{\Psi} = (\{Z_\iota\}_\iota, \vec{K}, \vec{T}, \vec{R})$. Since we will be often working only with the first set of variables $\{Z_\iota\}$, we will denote it as $\vec{\Psi}_2$, and all other variables from $\vec{\Psi}$ as $\vec{\Psi}_1$.

Success in Lucky Executions. In general, the set structure of $Q(\vec{\Psi})$ can vary enormously, and it depends on many things, including the way $\mathcal{A}$ interacts with the challenger. Each interaction can present a different set of coefficients in $\mathcal{A}$ that will be modelled by different functions. Therefore, we would like to take advantage of the **lucky** event to simplify our reasoning and reduce the space of possible interactions.

We claim that **lucky** is independent from $\mathcal{A}$'s success in Game_1. In other words, in order to win Game_1 it suffices to only show the existence of a witness extractor in the case where the lucky indices correspond to $\mathcal{A}$'s critical queries.

$$\mathsf{Adv}_{\mathcal{A},\mathcal{E}_{\mathcal{A}}}^{\mathsf{Game}_1}(\lambda) = \Pr[\mathsf{Game}_1^{\mathcal{A},\mathcal{E}_{\mathcal{A}}}(1^\lambda) = 1] = \Pr[\mathsf{Game}_1^{\mathcal{A},\mathcal{E}_{\mathcal{A}}}(1^\lambda) = 1 \mid \mathbf{lucky}]$$

where q_1 and q_2 are polynomially bounded. Indeed, $\mathcal{A}$ is blind to whether we simulate or not, and so we can assume independence of events: $\Pr[\mathsf{Game}_1^{\mathcal{A},\mathcal{E}_{\mathcal{A}}}(1^\lambda) = 1 \mid \mathbf{sim}_i]$ is the same for all simulation strategies $\mathbf{sim}_i$, including the lucky one.

[11] If $\hat{Z}_\iota$ is not equal $Z_\iota \prod \iota_j^{\mathcal{A}}$ as a function we have $\hat{Z}_\iota(\Psi) - Z_\iota \prod \iota_j^{\mathcal{A}} \neq 0$ but $\hat{Z}_\iota(\psi) - z_\iota \prod \iota_j^{\mathcal{A}} \equiv 0$ for $\iota \in \{x, \alpha, \beta, \delta\}$, and we break the $(2n-1, 2n-2)$-**edlog** problem as in Lemma 6.

$$\mathsf{Adv}^{\mathsf{Game}_1}_{\mathcal{A},\mathcal{E}_\mathcal{A}}(\lambda) = \sum_{i=0}^{q_1 q_2} \Pr[\mathsf{Game}_1^{\mathcal{A},\mathcal{E}_\mathcal{A}}(1^\lambda) = 1 \mid \mathbf{sim}_i] \frac{1}{q_1 q_2}$$
$$= \frac{1}{q_1 q_2} \sum_i \Pr[\mathsf{Game}_1^{\mathcal{A},\mathcal{E}_\mathcal{A}}(1^\lambda) = 1 \mid \mathbf{lucky}] = \Pr[\mathsf{Game}_1^{\mathcal{A},\mathcal{E}_\mathcal{A}}(1^\lambda) = 1 \mid \mathbf{lucky}]$$

Our choice of $\{i_{\mathsf{guess}_\varphi}\}_\varphi$, and thus the chosen simulation strategy $\mathbf{sim}_i$ is independent from the success of $\mathcal{A}$. This does not imply that we ignore some traces of $\mathcal{A}$, which would break the reduction. Instead, for each possible trace of $\mathcal{A}$, and thus each possible way it communicates with the challenger and the oracles, we only consider those executions in which we guess the indices correctly.

Defining the Function $Q(\vec{\Psi})$ for Game_1. Therefore, when in Game_1 the challenger guesses critical queries correctly (**lucky**), and $\mathcal{A}$ returns a verifying proof, the complexity is greatly simplified, and we can now define at least the high-level form of the function Q:

$$Q(\vec{\Psi}) := \left(A(\vec{\Psi})B(\vec{\Psi}) - \hat{Z}_\alpha \hat{Z}_\beta - \sum_{i=0}^{\ell} a_i(\hat{Z}_\beta u_i(\hat{Z}_x) + \hat{Z}_\alpha v_i(\hat{Z}_x) + w_i(\hat{Z}_x)) - C(\vec{\Psi})\hat{Z}_\delta \right) \tag{1}$$

such that $G^{A(\vec{\psi})} = A$ and similarly for B and C, where $\vec{\psi}$ is the concrete set of secret values used for a particular execution.[12] The function $Q(\vec{\Psi})$ reconstructs verification equation of the proof in this particular game execution: in particular, $Q(\vec{\psi}) = 0 \iff \mathsf{Verify}(\mathsf{srs}, \phi, \pi) = 1$.

Note that the form of functions $A(\vec{\Psi})$, $B(\vec{\Psi})$, and $C(\vec{\Psi})$ depends on the interaction with $\mathcal{A}$, and thus on the particular execution trace. But the general form of Q we have just specified is enough to argue the critical lemmas. The proof of the following Lemma, which shows exactly that, is deferred to the full version.

Lemma 4. *In* Game_1, *conditioned on event* **lucky**, *the general form of the function* $Q(\vec{\Psi})$ *reconstructing the main verification equation is as presented in Eq. 1, under* $(2n-1, 2n-2)$-***edlog***. *Moreover,* A, B, C *are Laurent polynomials in* $\vec{\Psi}_2$ *when viewed over* $\mathbb{Z}_p[\vec{C}, \vec{\Psi}_1]$, *where* $\vec{C}$ *are AGM coefficients, abstracted as variables. In other words,* $A, B, C \in (\mathbb{Z}_p[\vec{C}, \vec{\Psi}_1])[\vec{\Psi}_2]$ *are Laurent. Therefore,* Q *also is Laurent when viewed as* $(\mathbb{Z}_p[\vec{C}, \vec{\Psi}_1])[\vec{\Psi}_2]$ *element.*

Description of Game_2. The following game, presented on Fig. 9 extends Game_1 with two additions. Firstly, it introduces the event **bad**. The condition that we are trying to capture is whether $\mathcal{A}$ uses the elements that depend on trapdoors

[12] The form of the proof-independent parts of the verification equation is due to our critical-step-simulation strategy that we introduce in Game_1. That is, these values they only depend on the challenge variables Z_ι plus last adversarial trapdoors (e.g. $\prod \alpha_i^{\mathcal{A}}$ etc.). This is where guessing the *last* query really helps: otherwise these terms would also depend on Ψ_1, e.g. on $\vec{T}$.

$\mathsf{Game}_2^{\mathcal{A},\mathcal{E}_\mathcal{A}}(1^\lambda)$

$\mathsf{srs} \leftarrow \mathsf{srs}^\mathsf{d}, \varphi = 1,$
$Q_1, Q_2 \leftarrow \emptyset; i_\mathsf{call} \leftarrow 0; i_{\mathsf{guess}_1} \leftarrow\$ [0, q_1]; i_{\mathsf{guess}_2} \leftarrow\$ [0, q_2]; \{z_\iota\}_{\iota \in \{x,\alpha,\beta,\delta\}} \leftarrow\$ \mathbb{Z}_p;$
RO_t, $\mathcal{O}_\mathsf{srs}$ and $\mathsf{SimUpdProof}$ are constructed as in Game_1;
$(\phi, \pi) \leftarrow \mathcal{A}^{\mathcal{O}_\mathsf{srs},\mathsf{RO}}$;
$w \leftarrow \mathcal{E}_\mathcal{A}(\mathsf{view}_\mathcal{A})$;
$\mathbf{bad} := \left(\mathbf{lucky} \wedge Q(\psi_1, \{z_\iota\}) = 0 \wedge Q(\psi_1, \{Z_\iota\}) \not\equiv 0\right)$
return $\mathsf{Verify}(\mathsf{srs}, \phi, \pi) = 1 \wedge (\phi, w) \notin \mathcal{R} \wedge \varphi > \varphi_{max} \wedge \mathbf{lucky}$;

Fig. 9. Description of Game_2, an extension of Game_1 with **bad** event. $Q(\vec{\Psi}_1, \vec{\Psi}_2)$ is the function (Laurent polynomial in $\vec{\Psi}_2$) that corresponds to the way to reconstruct π and verification equation, where Ψ_2 corresponds to the trapdoor variables $\{Z_\iota\}$.

z_ι blindly or not. When **bad** does not happen, the adversary is constructing π in such a way that it works for any value of z'_ι ($Q(\psi_1, \{Z_\iota\})$ is a zero as a polynomial). Otherwise, we can argue that $\mathcal{A}$'s cheating strategy depends on the specific value of z_ι, even though it is hidden in the exponent ($Q(\psi_1, \{z_\iota\}) = 0$, but $Q(\psi_1, \{Z_\iota\})$ is a non-zero polynomial).

Secondly, we require that adversary wins only if the event **lucky** happens. Since lucky is an independent event, then $\Pr[\mathsf{Game}_2^{\mathcal{A},\mathcal{E}_\mathcal{A}}(1^\lambda) = 1] = \Pr[\mathsf{Game}_1^{\mathcal{A},\mathcal{E}_\mathcal{A}}(1^\lambda) = 1 \wedge \mathbf{lucky}] = \Pr[\mathsf{Game}_1^{\mathcal{A},\mathcal{E}_\mathcal{A}}(1^\lambda) = 1]/(q_1 q_2)$. The last transition is due to independence of winning Game_1 and **lucky** explained earlier ($\Pr[\mathsf{Game}_1^{\mathcal{A},\mathcal{E}_\mathcal{A}}(1^\lambda) = 1] = \Pr[\mathsf{Game}_1^{\mathcal{A},\mathcal{E}_\mathcal{A}}(1^\lambda) = 1 \mid \mathbf{lucky}]$). We can use the total probability formula to condition winning in Game_2 on the event bad.

$$\begin{aligned}\Pr[\mathsf{Game}_2^{\mathcal{A},\mathcal{E}_\mathcal{A}}(1^\lambda) = 1] &= \Pr[\mathsf{Game}_2^{\mathcal{A},\mathcal{E}_\mathcal{A}}(1^\lambda) = 1 \mid \neg\mathbf{bad}] \cdot \Pr[\neg\mathbf{bad}] \\ &+ \Pr[\mathsf{Game}_2^{\mathcal{A},\mathcal{E}_\mathcal{A}}(1^\lambda) = 1 \mid \mathbf{bad}] \cdot \Pr[\mathbf{bad}] \\ &\leq \Pr[\mathsf{Game}_2^{\mathcal{A},\mathcal{E}_\mathcal{A}}(1^\lambda) = 1 \mid \neg\mathbf{bad}] + \Pr[\mathbf{bad}].\end{aligned}$$

The next two lemmas will upperbound this probability. The Lemma 5 will bound the first term of the sum and the Lemma 6 bounds the second term.

Extractor Succeeds in Good Executions. In this subsection we present a lemma, that states that whenever $\mathcal{C}$ guesses the critical indices correctly, and event **bad** does not happen, the output of the extractor $\mathcal{E}_\mathcal{A}$ is a QAP witness. The proof of Lemma 5 is presented in the full version of this paper.

Lemma 5. *In* Game_2, *when* $\neg$**bad** *happens and* $\mathcal{A}$ *produces a verifying proof, then* $\mathcal{E}_\mathcal{A}$ *succeeds:* $\Pr[\mathsf{Game}_2^{\mathcal{A},\mathcal{E}_\mathcal{A}}(1^\lambda) = 1 \mid \neg\mathbf{bad}] = \mathsf{negl}(\lambda)$.

Description of the EDLOG Reduction. We show that the event **bad** can only happen with a negligible probability by making a reduction to the edlog assumption. If $\mathcal{A}$ triggers **bad**, then it could construct a proof in a manner that is specific to the SRS $\vec{\psi}_2$ and does not generalize to any other $\vec{\psi}'_2$. This means that $\mathcal{A}$ has knowledge of the exponent element, which is impossible assuming edlog. The proof of the following lemma is delayed to the full version.

Lemma 6. *The probability of* **bad** *in* Game_2 *is negligible under the* $(2n-1, 2n-2)$*-**edlog** assumption.*

Now, combining the results of Lemma 5 and Lemma 6 with previous game transitions:

$$\begin{aligned}
\Pr[\mathsf{Game}_0^{\mathcal{A},\mathcal{E}_\mathcal{A}}(1^\lambda) = 1] &\leq \Pr[\mathsf{Game}_1^{\mathcal{A},\mathcal{E}_\mathcal{A}}(1^\lambda) = 1] + \mathsf{negl}(\lambda) \\
&= (q_1 q_2) \Pr[\mathsf{Game}_2^{\mathcal{A},\mathcal{E}_\mathcal{A}}(1^\lambda) = 1] + \mathsf{negl}(\lambda) \\
&\leq (q_1 q_2)\big(\Pr[\mathsf{Game}_2^{\mathcal{A},\mathcal{E}_\mathcal{A}}(1^\lambda) = 1 \mid \neg\mathbf{bad}] + \Pr[\mathbf{bad}]\big) + \mathsf{negl}(\lambda) \\
&= (q_1 q_2)(\mathsf{negl}(\lambda) + \mathsf{negl}(\lambda)) + \mathsf{negl}(\lambda) = \mathsf{negl}(\lambda)
\end{aligned}$$

This concludes the proof of the update knowledge soundness theorem. □

Acknowledgements. This work has been supported in part by the European Union's Horizon 2020 research and innovation programme under grant agreement No. 780477 (project PRIViLEDGE). Janno Siim was additionally supported by the Estonian Research Council grant PRG49. An early version of this work [35] included a Sapling security proof that was funded by the Electric Coin Company.

References

1. Abdolmaleki, B., Baghery, K., Lipmaa, H., Siim, J., Zając, M.: UC-secure CRS generation for SNARKs. In: Buchmann, J., Nitaj, A., Rachidi, T. (eds.) AFRICACRYPT 2019. LNCS, vol. 11627, pp. 99–117. Springer, Cham (2019). https://doi.org/10.1007/978-3-030-23696-0_6
2. Abdolmaleki, B., Baghery, K., Lipmaa, H., Zając, M.: A subversion-resistant SNARK. In: Takagi, T., Peyrin, T. (eds.) ASIACRYPT 2017, Part III. LNCS, vol. 10626, pp. 3–33. Springer, Cham (2017). https://doi.org/10.1007/978-3-319-70700-6_1
3. Baghery, K., Kohlweiss, M., Siim, J., Volkhov, M.: Another look at extraction and randomization of Groth's zk-SNARK. Cryptology ePrint Archive, Report 2020/811 (2020). https://eprint.iacr.org/2020/811
4. Bauer, B., Fuchsbauer, G., Loss, J.: A classification of computational assumptions in the algebraic group model. In: Micciancio, D., Ristenpart, T. (eds.) CRYPTO 2020, Part II. LNCS, vol. 12171, pp. 121–151. Springer, Cham (2020). https://doi.org/10.1007/978-3-030-56880-1_5
5. Bellare, M., Fuchsbauer, G., Scafuro, A.: NIZKs with an untrusted CRS: security in the face of parameter subversion. In: Cheon, J.H., Takagi, T. (eds.) ASIACRYPT 2016, Part II. LNCS, vol. 10032, pp. 777–804. Springer, Heidelberg (2016). https://doi.org/10.1007/978-3-662-53890-6_26
6. Ben-Sasson, E., et al.: Zerocash: decentralized anonymous payments from bitcoin. In: 2014 IEEE Symposium on Security and Privacy, pp. 459–474. IEEE Computer Society Press, May 2014

7. Ben-Sasson, E., Chiesa, A., Green, M., Tromer, E., Virza, M.: Secure sampling of public parameters for succinct zero knowledge proofs. In: 2015 IEEE Symposium on Security and Privacy, pp. 287–304. IEEE Computer Society Press, May 2015
8. Ben-Sasson, E., Chiesa, A., Tromer, E., Virza, M.: Succinct non-interactive zero knowledge for a von neumann architecture. In: Fu, K., Jung, J. (eds.) USENIX Security 2014, pp. 781–796. USENIX Association, August 2014
9. Boneh, D., Bonneau, J., Bünz, B., Fisch, B.: Verifiable delay functions. In: Shacham, H., Boldyreva, A. (eds.) CRYPTO 2018, , Part I. LNCS, vol. 10991, pp. 757–788. Springer, Cham (2018). https://doi.org/10.1007/978-3-319-96884-1_25
10. Bowe, S., Chiesa, A., Green, M., Miers, I., Mishra, P., Wu, H.: ZEXE: Enabling decentralized private computation. In: 2020 IEEE Symposium on Security and Privacy, pp. 947–964. IEEE Computer Society Press, May 2020
11. Bowe, S., Gabizon, A., Green, M.D.: A multi-party protocol for constructing the public parameters of the Pinocchio zk-SNARK. Cryptology ePrint Archive, Report 2017/602 (2017). http://eprint.iacr.org/2017/602
12. Bowe, S., Gabizon, A., Miers, I.: Scalable multi-party computation for zk-SNARK parameters in the random beacon model. Cryptology ePrint Archive, Report 2017/1050 (2017). http://eprint.iacr.org/2017/1050
13. Bünz, B., Maller, M., Mishra, P., Vesely, N.: Proofs for inner pairing products and applications. Cryptology ePrint Archive, Report 2019/1177 (2019). https://eprint.iacr.org/2019/1177
14. Canetti, R.: Universally composable security: a new paradigm for cryptographic protocols. In: 42nd FOCS, pp. 136–145. IEEE Computer Society Press, October 2001
15. Chiesa, A., Hu, Y., Maller, M., Mishra, P., Vesely, N., Ward, N.: Marlin: preprocessing zkSNARKs with universal and updatable SRS. In: Canteaut, A., Ishai, Y. (eds.) EUROCRYPT 2020, Part I. LNCS, vol. 12105, pp. 738–768. Springer, Cham (2020). https://doi.org/10.1007/978-3-030-45721-1_26
16. Danezis, G., Fournet, C., Groth, J., Kohlweiss, M.: Square span programs with applications to succinct NIZK arguments. In: Sarkar, P., Iwata, T. (eds.) ASIACRYPT 2014, Part I. LNCS, vol. 8873, pp. 532–550. Springer, Heidelberg (2014). https://doi.org/10.1007/978-3-662-45611-8_28
17. Fuchsbauer, G.: Subversion-zero-knowledge SNARKs. In: Abdalla, M., Dahab, R. (eds.) PKC 2018, Part I. LNCS, vol. 10769, pp. 315–347. Springer, Cham (2018). https://doi.org/10.1007/978-3-319-76578-5_11
18. Fuchsbauer, G., Kiltz, E., Loss, J.: The algebraic group model and its applications. In: Shacham, H., Boldyreva, A. (eds.) CRYPTO 2018, Part II. LNCS, vol. 10992, pp. 33–62. Springer, Cham (2018). https://doi.org/10.1007/978-3-319-96881-0_2
19. Fuchsbauer, G., Plouviez, A., Seurin, Y.: Blind Schnorr signatures and signed ElGamal encryption in the algebraic group model. In: Canteaut, A., Ishai, Y. (eds.) EUROCRYPT 2020, Part II. LNCS, vol. 12106, pp. 63–95. Springer, Cham (2020). https://doi.org/10.1007/978-3-030-45724-2_3
20. Gabizon, A.: On the security of the BCTV pinocchio zk-SNARK variant. Cryptology ePrint Archive, Report 2019/119 (2019). https://eprint.iacr.org/2019/119
21. Gabizon, A., Williamson, Z.J., Ciobotaru, O.: PLONK: permutations over lagrange-bases for oecumenical noninteractive arguments of knowledge. Cryptology ePrint Archive, Report 2019/953 (2019). https://eprint.iacr.org/2019/953
22. Gennaro, R., Gentry, C., Parno, B., Raykova, M.: Quadratic span programs and succinct NIZKs without PCPs. In: Johansson, T., Nguyen, P.Q. (eds.) EUROCRYPT 2013. LNCS, vol. 7881, pp. 626–645. Springer, Heidelberg (2013). https://doi.org/10.1007/978-3-642-38348-9_37

23. Goldwasser, S., Micali, S., Rackoff, C.: The knowledge complexity of interactive proof-systems (extended abstract). In: 17th ACM STOC, pp. 291–304. ACM Press, May 1985
24. Groth, J.: Short pairing-based non-interactive zero-knowledge arguments. In: Abe, M. (ed.) ASIACRYPT 2010. LNCS, vol. 6477, pp. 321–340. Springer, Heidelberg (2010). https://doi.org/10.1007/978-3-642-17373-8_19
25. Groth, J.: On the size of pairing-based non-interactive arguments. In: Fischlin, M., Coron, J.-S. (eds.) EUROCRYPT 2016, Part II. LNCS, vol. 9666, pp. 305–326. Springer, Heidelberg (2016). https://doi.org/10.1007/978-3-662-49896-5_11
26. Groth, J., Kohlweiss, M., Maller, M., Meiklejohn, S., Miers, I.: Updatable and universal common reference strings with applications to zk-SNARKs. In: Shacham, H., Boldyreva, A. (eds.) CRYPTO 2018, Part III. LNCS, vol. 10993, pp. 698–728. Springer, Cham (2018). https://doi.org/10.1007/978-3-319-96878-0_24
27. Han, R., Yu, J., Lin, H.: RandChain: decentralised randomness beacon from sequential proof-of-work. Cryptology ePrint Archive, Report 2020/1033 (2020). https://eprint.iacr.org/2020/1033
28. Hanke, T., Movahedi, M., Williams, D.: Dfinity technology overview series, consensus system. arXiv preprint arXiv:1805.04548 (2018). https://arxiv.org/abs/1805.04548
29. Kerber, T., Kiayas, A., Kohlweiss, M.: Composition with knowledge assumptions. Cryptology ePrint Archive, Report 2021/165 (2021). https://eprint.iacr.org/2021/165
30. Kiayias, A., Russell, A., David, B., Oliynykov, R.: Ouroboros: a provably secure proof-of-stake blockchain protocol. In: Katz, J., Shacham, H. (eds.) CRYPTO 2017, Part I. LNCS, vol. 10401, pp. 357–388. Springer, Cham (2017). https://doi.org/10.1007/978-3-319-63688-7_12
31. Kosba, A.E., Miller, A., Shi, E., Wen, Z., Papamanthou, C.: Hawk: the blockchain model of cryptography and privacy-preserving smart contracts. In: 2016 IEEE Symposium on Security and Privacy, pp. 839–858. IEEE Computer Society Press, May 2016
32. Kosba, A.E., Papadopoulos, D., Papamanthou, C., Song, D.: MIRAGE: succinct arguments for randomized algorithms with applications to universal zk-SNARKs. In: Capkun, S., Roesner, F. (eds.) USENIX Security 2020, pp. 2129–2146. USENIX Association, August 2020
33. Lee, J., Choi, J., Kim, J., Oh, H.: SAVER: snark-friendly, additively-homomorphic, and verifiable encryption and decryption with rerandomization. Cryptology ePrint Archive, Report 2019/1270 (2019). https://eprint.iacr.org/2019/1270
34. Lipmaa, H.: Progression-free sets and sublinear pairing-based non-interactive zero-knowledge arguments. In: Cramer, R. (ed.) TCC 2012. LNCS, vol. 7194, pp. 169–189. Springer, Heidelberg (2012). https://doi.org/10.1007/978-3-642-28914-9_10
35. Maller, M.: A proof of security for the sapling generation of zk-SNARK parameters in the generic group model (2018). https://github.com/zcash/sapling-security-analysis/blob/master/MaryMallerUpdated.pdf. Accessed 26 Feb 2020
36. Maller, M., Bowe, S., Kohlweiss, M., Meiklejohn, S.: Sonic: zero-knowledge SNARKs from linear-size universal and updatable structured reference strings. In: Cavallaro, L., Kinder, J., Wang, X., Katz, J. (eds.) ACM CCS 2019, pp. 2111–2128. ACM Press, November 2019
37. Parno, B., Howell, J., Gentry, C., Raykova, M.: Pinocchio: nearly practical verifiable computation. In: 2013 IEEE Symposium on Security and Privacy, pp. 238–252. IEEE Computer Society Press, May 2013

38. Pietrzak, K.: Simple verifiable delay functions. In: Blum, A. (ed.) ITCS 2019, vol. 124, pp. 60:1–60:15. LIPIcs, January 2019
39. Wesolowski, B.: Efficient verifiable delay functions. In: Ishai, Y., Rijmen, V. (eds.) EUROCRYPT 2019, Part III. LNCS, vol. 11478, pp. 379–407. Springer, Cham (2019). https://doi.org/10.1007/978-3-030-17659-4_13

Efficient NIZKs for Algebraic Sets

Geoffroy Couteau[1(✉)], Helger Lipmaa[2(✉)], Roberto Parisella[2], and Arne Tobias Ødegaard[2]

[1] CNRS, IRIF, Université de Paris, Paris, France
couteau@irif.fr
[2] Simula UiB, Bergen, Norway
helger.lipmaa@gmail.com

Abstract. Significantly extending the framework of (Couteau and Hartmann, Crypto 2020), we propose a general methodology to construct NIZKs for showing that an encrypted vector χ belongs to an algebraic set, i.e., is in the zero locus of an ideal $\mathfrak{I}$ of a polynomial ring. In the case where $\mathfrak{I}$ is principal, i.e., generated by a single polynomial F, we first construct a matrix that is a "quasideterminantal representation" of F and then a NIZK argument to show that $F(\chi) = 0$. This leads to compact NIZKs for general computational structures, such as polynomial-size algebraic branching programs. We extend the framework to the case where $\mathfrak{I}$ is non-principal, obtaining efficient NIZKs for R1CS, arithmetic constraint satisfaction systems, and thus for NP. As an independent result, we explicitly describe the corresponding language of ciphertexts as an algebraic language, with smaller parameters than in previous constructions that were based on the disjunction of algebraic languages. This results in an efficient GL-SPHF for algebraic branching programs.

Keywords: Algebraic branching programs · Algebraic languages · Algebraic sets · NIZK · Pairing-based cryptography · SPHF · Zero knowledge

1 Introduction

Zero-knowledge arguments are fundamental cryptographic primitives allowing one to convince a verifier of the truth of a statement while concealing all further information. A particularly appealing type of zero-knowledge arguments, with a wide variety of applications in cryptography, are *non-interactive zero-knowledge arguments* (NIZKs) with a single flow from the prover to the verifier.

Early feasibility results from the 90's established the existence of NIZKs for all NP languages (in the common reference string model) under standard cryptographic assumptions. However, these early constructions were inefficient. In the past decades, a major effort of the cryptographic community has been directed towards obtaining *efficient* and *conceptually simple* NIZK argument systems for many languages of interest. Among the celebrated successes of this line of work are the Fiat-Shamir (FS) transform, which provides simple and efficient NIZKs but only offers heuristic security guarantees, and pairing-based NIZKs such as the Groth-Sahai proof system [21] (and its follow-ups).

M. Tibouchi and H. Wang (Eds.): ASIACRYPT 2021, LNCS 13092, pp. 128–158, 2021.
https://doi.org/10.1007/978-3-030-92078-4_5

The Quest for Efficient and Conceptually Simple NIZKs. The Groth-Sahai NIZK proof system was a major breakthrough in this line of work, providing the first provably secure (under standard pairing assumptions) and reasonably efficient NIZK for a large class of languages, capturing many concrete languages of interest. This proof system initiated a wide variety of cryptographic applications, and its efficiency was refined in a sequence of works. Unfortunately, the efficiency of Groth-Sahai proofs often remains unsatisfying (typically much worse than NIZKs obtained with Fiat-Shamir), and building an optimized Groth-Sahai proof for a specific problem is an often tedious process that requires considerable expertise. This lack of conceptual simplicity inhibits the potential for large-scale deployment of this proof system. Therefore, we view it as one of the major open problems in this line of work to obtain an efficient proof system where constructing an optimized proof for a given statement does not require dedicated expertise. The Fiat-Shamir transform offers such a candidate – and as a consequence, it has seen widescale adoption in real-world protocols – but lacks a formal proof of security. The recent line of work on quasi-adaptive NIZKs offers simultaneously simple, efficient, and provably secure proof systems, but these are restricted to a small class of languages – namely, linear languages. Some recent SNARK proof systems also offer generic and efficient methods to handle a large class of languages given by their high-level description; however, they all rely on very strong knowledge-of-exponent style assumptions.

The Couteau-Hartmann Argument System. Very recently, Couteau and Hartmann put forth a new framework for constructing pairing based NIZKs [9]. At a high level, their approach compiles a specific interactive zero-knowledge proof into a NIZK (as does Fiat-Shamir), by embedding the challenge in the exponent of a group equipped with an asymmetric pairing. The CH argument system enjoys several interesting features:

- It generates compact proofs, with efficiency comparable to Fiat-Shamir arguments, with ultra-short common reference strings (a single group element);
- It has a conceptually simple structure, since it compiles a well-known and simple interactive proof;
- It handles a relatively large class of *algebraic languages* [5,8], which are parameterized languages of the shape $\mathcal{L}_{\boldsymbol{\Gamma},\boldsymbol{\theta}} = \{\mathtt{x} : \exists \mathtt{w}, \boldsymbol{\Gamma}(\mathtt{x}) \cdot \mathtt{w} = \boldsymbol{\theta}(\mathtt{x})\}$, where $\mathtt{x}$ is the input, $\mathtt{w}$ is the witness, $\boldsymbol{\Gamma}$ and $\boldsymbol{\theta}$ are affine maps, such that $\mathtt{x}$ and $\boldsymbol{\theta}(\mathtt{x})$ are vectors and $\boldsymbol{\Gamma}(\mathtt{x})$ is a matrix. We call $(\boldsymbol{\theta}, \boldsymbol{\Gamma})$ the *matrix description* of the language $\mathcal{L}$. Since any NP language can be embedded into an algebraic language[1], this gives a proof system for all of NP.

These features make the CH argument system a competitive alternative to Fiat-Shamir and Groth-Sahai in settings where efficiency and conceptual simplicity are desirable while maintaining provable security under a plausible, albeit new, assumption over pairing groups. In a sense, Couteau-Hartmann achieves a sweet spot between efficiency, generality, and underlying assumption.

---

[1] The classical approach to do so for circuit satisfiability uses algebraic commitments to all values on the wire of the circuit; then the statement "all committed values are consistent and the output is 1" is an algebraic language.

Limitations of the CH Argument System. The CH transformation offers attractive efficiency features, but its core advantage is (arguably) its conceptual simplicity. As many previous works pointed out (see e.g. [25]), what "real-world" protocol designers need is a method that can easily take a high-level description of a language, and "automatically" generate a NIZK for this language without going through a tedious and complex process requiring dedicated expertise. Ideally, both the process of generating the NIZK description from the high-level language and the NIZK itself should be efficient.

With this in mind, CH provides an important step in the right direction, where producing the NIZK for any algebraic language is a straightforward generic transformation applied to its matrix description. However, it falls short of fully achieving the desired goal for two reasons.

First, it does not entirely remove the need for dedicated expertise from the NIZK construction; rather, it pushes the complexity of *building the NIZK* to that of *finding its matrix description* given a higher-level description of an algebraic language. However, it does not provide a characterization of which languages, given via a common higher-level description, are algebraic, neither does it give a method to construct their matrix description[2].

Second, the CH-compilation produces NIZKs whose soundness reduces to an instance of the novel ExtKerMDH family of assumptions. However, the particular assumption will only be falsifiable in the much more restricted setting of *witness-samplable* algebraic languages, which essentially seem to capture disjunctions of linear languages. Couteau and Hartmann focused on NIZKs based on the falsifiable variant, which severely limits the class of languages captured by the framework. It is much more desirable to base the security of all NIZKs produced by this framework on a single, plausible, well-supported assumption: this would avoid protocol designers the hurdle of precisely assessing the security of the specific flavor of the ExtKerMDH assumption their particular instance requires.

1.1 Our Contribution

We overcome the main limitations of the CH argument system. Our new approach, which significantly departs from the CH methodology, allows us to produce compact NIZKs for a variety of languages, with several appealing features.

A General Framework. We provide a generic method to compute, for several important families of languages, a different matrix description of the languages. We then construct a NIZK. We implicitly use the CH-compiler but in a way, different from [9]. We focus on the important setting of commit-and-prove NIZK argument systems, i.e. languages of the form $\{\mathsf{Com}(x_1), \ldots, \mathsf{Com}(x_n) \mid R(x_1, \ldots, x_n)\}$, where R is some efficiently computable relation. Our method allows us to automatically obtain a compact matrix description for many types of high-level relations.

[2] While we can always embed any language in an algebraic language, this can be inefficient; the CH proof system is efficient when the language is "natively" algebraic.

New NIZKs: Improved Efficiency or Generality. As a first byproduct, we obtain improved NIZKs for some important statements, such as set membership (see Table 1) or the language of commitments to points on an elliptic curve[3], as well as new NIZKs for very general classes of statements, such as R1CS, arithmetic constraint satisfaction systems (and thus for NP).

A Weaker Unified Assumption. As the second byproduct of our formal approach, we manage to base all NIZKs in our framework on a slightly weaker form of the extended Kernel Diffie-Hellman assumption, which we call the CED (family of) assumption(s) (for *Computational Extended Determinant* assumption). This turns out to have an important consequence: we show that all instances of our assumption can be based on a single plausible *gap assumption*, which states that solving the kernel Diffie-Hellman assumption in a group $\mathbb{G}_2$ (a well-known search assumption implied in particular by DDH) remains hard, even given a CDH oracle in a *different* group $\mathbb{G}_1$. On top of it, several of our NIZKs (like the one for Boolean Circuit-SAT) are based on a falsifiable CED assumption, while we also show that a slight modification of the NIZK for arithmetic circuits can be also based on a falsifiable variant of CED.

New SPHFs. Eventually, as another byproduct of our methodology, we obtain constructions of Smooth Projective Hash Functions (SPHFs) [17] for new languages (SPHFs were the original motivation for introducing the notion of algebraic language, and [5] gives a generic construction of SPHFs given the matrix description of an algebraic language), including languages describable by efficient algebraic branching programs.

1.2 Efficiency, Generality, and Security of Our NIZKs

The argument of Couteau and Hartmann [9] improves over (even optimized variants of) the standard Groth-Sahai approach on essentially all known algebraic languages. Couteau and Hartmann illustrated this by providing shorter proofs for linear languages (Diffie-Hellman tuples, membership in a linear subspace) and OR proofs (and more generally, membership in t out of n possibly different linear languages), two settings with numerous important applications (to structure-preserving signatures, tightly-secure simulation-sound NIZKs, tightly-mCCA-secure cryptosystems, ring signatures...). Our framework builds upon the Couteau-Hartmann framework, provides a clean mathematical approach to overcoming its main downside (which is that the matrix description of "algebraic languages" must be manually found), and significantly generalizes it. Our framework enjoys most of the benefits of the Couteau-Hartmann framework, such as its ultra-short common random string (a single random group element).

Efficiency. Our framework shines especially as soon as the target language becomes slightly too complex to directly "see" from its description an appropriate and compatible matrix description $\boldsymbol{C}$ of the language; then, we get significant

[3] NIZKs for this type of languages have recently found important applications in blockchain applications, such as the zcash cryptocurrency, see [25] and https://z.cash/technology/jubjub/.

Table 1. Comparison of set-membership proofs, i..e., NIZKs for $\mathcal{L}_{\mathsf{pk},F}$, where $F(X)$ is univariate, as in Lemma 7and 8and an additional lemma in the full version [10]. The verifier's computation is given in pairings. The Groth-Sahai computation figures are not published and based on our own estimation; hence, we have omitted the computation cost. Note that $|\mathbb{G}_2| = 2|\mathbb{G}_1|$ in common settings. In CHM and new NIZK, $|\mathbf{crs}| = |\mathbb{G}_2|$.

Argument	$\|\pi\|$	P comp.	V comp.
	Previous works		
Optimized GS [33]	$d\|\mathbb{G}_1\| + (3d+2)\|\mathbb{G}_2\|$	-	-
CHM NIZK + [9] $(\boldsymbol{\Gamma}, \boldsymbol{\theta})$, full version [10]	$(3d-1)\|\mathbb{G}_1\| + (3d-2)\|\mathbb{G}_2\|$	$(7d-4)\mathfrak{e}_1 + (3d-1)\mathfrak{e}_2$	$9d-2$
	New solutions		
CHM NIZK + new $\boldsymbol{\Gamma}, \boldsymbol{\theta}$, Lemma 8	$2d\|\mathbb{G}_1\| + (2d-1)\|\mathbb{G}_2\|$	$(5d-3)\mathfrak{e}_1 + 4d\mathfrak{e}_2$	$7d-1$
New NIZK, Lemma 7	$2d\|\mathbb{G}_1\| + (2d-1)\|\mathbb{G}_2\|$	$\leq 3d\mathfrak{e}_1 + (4d-2)\mathfrak{e}_2$	$7d-1$

efficiency improvements. We illustrate this on a natural and useful example: set membership proofs for ElGamal ciphertext over $\mathbb{G}_1$ (i.e., the language of ElGamal encryptions of $m \in S$ for some public set S of size d), see Table 1. It depicts the complexity of optimized Groth-Sahai proofs, the generic Couteau-Hartmann compilation of Maurer's protocol (denoted CHM) by using the language parameters $(\boldsymbol{\Gamma}, \boldsymbol{\theta})$ provided in [9], CHM NIZK for $(\boldsymbol{\Gamma}, \boldsymbol{\theta})$ automatically derived in the current paper from the matrix description $\boldsymbol{C}$, and our new NIZK. On the other hand, our modular approach provides significantly shorter proofs. Taking e.g. $d = 5$, we get a proof about 25% shorter compared to Groth-Sahai. Our approach also significantly improves in terms of computational efficiency. Moreover, since in our approach, we need to only encrypt the data in a single group, as opposed in two groups in the case of (asymmetric-pairing-based) Groth-Sahai, we have three times shorter commitments. In Sect. 8.2, we also discuss the case of multi-dimensional set membership proofs (where, depending on the structure of the set, our framework can lead to even more significant improvements).

Generality. Our framework also goes way beyond the class of languages naturally handled by Couteau-Hartmann. In particular, we show that our framework directly encompasses *arithmetic constraint satisfaction systems* (aCSPs), i.e., collections of functions $F_1, \ldots, F_\tau$ (called *constraints*) such that each function F_i depends on at most q of its input locations.[4] In particular, this efficiently captures arithmetic circuits, hence all NP languages.[5]

Rank-1 constraints systems (R1CS) are well-known to be powerful, since they capture *compactly* many languages of interest [16]. They have been widely used in the construction of SNARKs. aCSPs directly extend these simple constraints to arbitrary low-degree polynomial relations. Moving away from R1CS to more expressive constraint systems can potentially be very useful: in many

[4] That is, for every $j \in [1, \tau]$ there exist $i_1, \ldots, i_q \in [1, n]$ and $f : \mathbb{F}^q \to \mathbb{F}$ such that $\forall \chi \in \mathbb{F}^n, F_j(\chi) = f(\chi_{i_1}, \ldots, \chi_{i_q})$. Then F is satisfiable if $\forall j, F_j(\chi) = 0$.

[5] Technically, one could always take aCSPs, write them as a circuit satisfiability problem, and embed that into an agebraic language to capture it with the Couteau-Hartmann framework; the point of our framework is that, by capturing this powerful model directly, we can obtain much better efficiency on aCSPs.

applications of NIZKs with complex languages, an important work is dedicated to finding the "best" R1CS to represent the language. The increased flexibility of being allowed to handle more general constraints can typically allow to achieve a significantly more efficient solution. While systematically revisiting existing works and demonstrating that their R1CS system could be improved using aCSPs would be out of the scope of this paper, we point out that this generalization approach was successfully applied in the past: the work of [22] described a method to go beyond R1CS in "Bulletproof style" random-oracle-based NIZKs (this setting is incomparable to ours, as we focus on NIZKs in the standard model). They show how to handle general quadratic constraints, and demonstrate that this leads to efficiency improvements over Bulletproof on aggregate range proofs. Since aCSPs are even more general, handling any low-degree polynomials, we expect that this representation could lead to significant optimizations for many applications of NIZKs that rely on R1CS representations. However, we are aware of no previous random-oracle-less NIZKs that can handle aCSPs natively.

Furthermore, even in scenarios where R1CS does indeed provide the best possible representation, our framework leads to proofs more compact than Groth-Sahai. We illustrate this on Table 2 for the case of general boolean circuits. Here, the standard GOS approach [20] reduces checking each gate of the circuit to checking R1CS equations. When comparing the cost obtained with our framework to the cost achieved by a Groth-Sahai proof (using the optimized variant of [18]), we find that our framework leads to three times smaller commitments, 20% shorter argument, and almost a factor two reduction in computation.

On the Non-falsifiability of Our Assumption. When the algebraic branching program representation of the relation is multivariate, the corresponding matrix description may lead to a NIZK under a non-falsifiable assumption. This might appear at first sight to significantly restrict the interest of our framework: while our NIZKs are typically more efficient than Groth-Sahai, they are usually larger than SNARKs since they grow linearly with (the algebraic branching program representation of) the relation, while SNARKs have size independent of both the relation and the witness. Hence, if we allow non-falsifiable assumptions, wouldn't SNARKs provide a better solution?

We discuss this apparent issue in Sect. 10. First, we identify a large class of important cases where the underlying assumption becomes falsifiable; this includes Boolean circuits (and thus NP). Second, we provide a general approach to transform *any* NIZK from our framework into NIZKs under a falsifiable assumption, by replacing the underlying commitment scheme by a DLIN-based encryption scheme and double-encrypting certain values. This comes at the cost of increasing the commitment and argument size. Third, we argue that the gap assumption [30] underlying our framework is, despite its non-falsifiability, a very natural and plausible assumption; see Sect. 10 for more details. In particular, gap assumptions are generally recognized as much more desirable than knowledge of exponent assumptions. In essence, our assumption says that uncovering structural weaknesses in a group $\mathbb{G}_1$ does not necessarily imply the existence of structural weaknesses in another group $\mathbb{G}_2$; in particular, this assumption trivially holds in the generic bilinear group model (where a CDH oracle in $\mathbb{G}_1$ provides no useful information for breaking any assumption in $\mathbb{G}_2$).

Overall, we view our framework as providing a desirable middle ground between Groth-Sahai (which leads to less efficient NIZKs, but under the standard SXDH assumption) and SNARKs (which lead to more efficient NIZKs in general but require highly non-standard knowledge of exponent assumptions).

1.3 Technical Overview

Intuitive Overview. At a high level, the Couteau-Hartmann methodology compiles a Σ-protocol for languages of the form $\{\boldsymbol{x} : \exists \boldsymbol{w}, \boldsymbol{\Gamma}(\boldsymbol{x}) \cdot \boldsymbol{w} = \boldsymbol{\theta}(\boldsymbol{x})\}$, where $(\boldsymbol{\Gamma}, \boldsymbol{\theta})$ are linear maps, into a NIZK. This leaves open, however, the tasks of characterizing which languages admit such a representation, *finding* such a representation, and when multiple representations are possible optimizing the choice of the representation. We provide a blueprint for these tasks.

We focus on commit-and-prove languages, a large and useful class of languages. At the heart of our techniques is a general method to convert a set of low-degree polynomial equations $F_i(\boldsymbol{X})$ into a set of "optimized" matrices $\boldsymbol{C}_i(\boldsymbol{X})$ such that $\det(\boldsymbol{C}_i(\boldsymbol{X})) = F_i(\boldsymbol{X})$ with a specific additional structure. We call this matrix a *quasideterminental (QDR) representation* of the polynomial. Then, we directly construct a compact NIZK proof system for a QDR, using a variant of the Couteau-Hartmann methodology. We prove that the resulting proof system is sound under a CED assumption. Whenever F_i has a polynomial number of roots (e.g., univariate), the corresponding CED assumption is always falsifiable.

Constructing a QDR from a polynomial is a non-trivial task that highly depends on the representation of F_i. We provide a general framework to construct such QDRs from the *algebraic branching program* (ABP [29]) representation of F_i; hence, our framework is especially suited whenever the polynomials have a compact ABP representation. ABP is a powerful model of computation, capturing in particular all log-depth circuits, boolean branching programs, boolean formulas, logspace circuits, and many more.

Background. The rest of the technical overview requires understanding of some minimal background from algebraic geometry, see [11] for more. Let $\mathbb{F} = \mathbb{Z}_p$ and $\boldsymbol{X} = (X_1, \ldots, X_\nu)$. For a set $\mathcal{F}$ of polynomials in $\mathbb{F}[\boldsymbol{X}]$, let $\mathcal{A}(\mathcal{F}) := \{\chi \in \mathbb{F}^\nu : f(\chi) = 0 forall f \in \mathcal{F}\}$ be the *algebraic set defined by* $\mathcal{F}$. A subset $\mathcal{A} \subseteq \mathbb{F}^\nu$ is an *algebraic set* if $\mathcal{A} = \mathcal{A}(\mathcal{F})$ for some $\mathcal{F}$. Given a subset $\mathcal{A}$ of $\mathbb{F}^\nu$, let $\mathcal{I}(\mathcal{A})$ be the ideal of all polynomial functions vanishing on $\mathcal{A}$, $\mathcal{I}(\mathcal{A}) := \{f \in \mathbb{F}[\boldsymbol{X}] : f(\chi)$ for all $\chi \in \mathcal{A}\}$. Since each ideal of $\mathcal{F}[\boldsymbol{X}]$ is finitely generated [11], then so is $\mathcal{I}(\mathcal{A})$, and thus $\mathcal{I}(\mathcal{A}) = \langle F_1, \ldots, F_\tau \rangle$ for some F_i. $\mathcal{I}$ is principal if it is generated by a single polynomial. All univariate ideals are principal. For an ideal $\mathcal{I}$ with generating set $\{F_i\}$, $\mathcal{A}(\mathcal{I}) := \mathcal{A}(\{F_i\})$. We also define $\mathcal{Z}(F) := \mathcal{A}(\{F\})$.

Commit-and-Prove NIZKs for Algebraic Sets. For the sake of concreteness, we focus on commit-and-prove languages where the underlying commitment scheme is the ElGamal encryption scheme; it is easy to extend this approach to any additively homomorphic and perfectly binding algebraic commitment scheme. Let pk be an Elgamal public key and let $\mathcal{A}$ be an algebraic set. We provide a general methodology of constructing a NIZK argument for the language $\mathcal{L}_{\mathsf{pk},\mathcal{A}} = \{[\mathbf{ct}]_1 : \exists \chi \text{ such that } \mathsf{Dec}([\mathbf{ct}]_1) = [\chi]_1 \wedge \chi \in \mathcal{A}\}$ of Elgamal-encryptions of elements of $\mathcal{A}$. We define $\mathcal{L}_{\mathsf{pk},F} := \mathcal{L}_{\mathsf{pk},\mathcal{Z}(F)}$ when we are working with a single polynomial. Assuming $\mathfrak{I}(\mathcal{A}) = \langle F_1, \dots, F_\tau \rangle$, we prove that $\chi \in \mathcal{A}$ by proving that $F_i(\chi) = 0$ for each F_i. The resulting argument system is efficient (probabilistic polynomial-time), assuming that there is

(i) an efficient algorithm (to be run only once) that finds a small generating set $(F_1, \dots, F_\tau)$ for $\mathfrak{I}(\mathcal{A})$ where $\tau = \mathsf{poly}(\lambda)$, and
(ii) an efficient NIZK argument system to show that $F_i(\chi) = 0$ for each F_i.

Note that the NIZK for showing that $F_i(\chi) = 0$ for each i is a simple conjunction of NIZKs for showing for each i that $F_i(\chi) = 0$.

Now, i is a non-cryptographic problem from computational commutative algebra. The classical Buchberger-Möller algorithm [27] can find efficiently a finite Gröbner basis $\{F_i\}$ for all algebraic sets $\mathcal{A}$ that have a finite Gröbner basis. Other methods exist, and we will only mention a few. Most importantly, one can relate i to finding efficient arithmetic circuits and arithmetic constraint satisfaction systems (aCSPs), see Sect. 8.1. The main technical contribution of our work (on top of the general framework) is to propose an efficient solution to ii.

Constructing a Compact Proof System for $F(\chi) = 0$. Here, we follow the next blueprint: we construct

(iii) a small matrix $\boldsymbol{C}(\boldsymbol{X})$ (that satisfies some additional properties) of affine maps, such that $\det(\boldsymbol{C}(\boldsymbol{X})) = F(\boldsymbol{X})$, and
(iv) an efficient NIZK argument system for showing that $\det(\boldsymbol{C}(\chi)) = 0$ for committed χ.

To solve iv, we build upon the new computational extended determinant assumption (CED). The CED assumption is a relaxation of the ExtKerMDH assumption from [9], which itself is a natural generalization of the Kernel Diffie-Hellman assumption. At a high level, CED says that given a matrix in a group $\mathbb{G}_2$, it is hard to find an *extension* of this matrix over $\mathbb{G}_2$, together with a large enough set of linearly independent vectors in $\mathbb{G}_1$ in the kernel of the extended matrix (where $(\mathbb{G}_1, \mathbb{G}_2)$ are groups equipped with an asymmetric pairing). While CED is not falsifiable in general, it can be reduced to a natural gap assumption. The latter reduction does not work with the ExtKerMDH assumption.

Our reduction to the CED assumption proceeds by identifying the matrix $\boldsymbol{C}$, returned by the CED adversary, with the matrix $\boldsymbol{C}(\boldsymbol{X})$ from iii. Intuitively, we construct a reduction that, knowing the Elgamal secret key sk, extracts $[(\gamma \| \boldsymbol{C})(\chi)]_1$, where $[\chi]_1 = \mathsf{Dec}_{\mathsf{sk}}([\mathbf{ct}]_1)$, such that $\boldsymbol{C}(\chi)$ has full rank iff the soundness adversary cheated, i.e., $F(\chi) \neq 0$. In that case, the reduction can obviously break the CED assumption.

To ensure that the NIZK argument can be constructed, we require that $\boldsymbol{C}$ satisfies two additional properties. Briefly,(1) $\boldsymbol{C}(\boldsymbol{X})$ is a matrix of affine maps, (to ensure that the matrix is computable from the statement) and (2) the first column of $\boldsymbol{C}(\chi)$ is in the linear span of the remaining columns of the matrix for any $\chi \in \mathcal{Z}(F)$ (a technical condition which ensures that an honest prover can compute the argument). We say that then $\boldsymbol{C}(\boldsymbol{X})$ is a *quasideterminantal representation (QDR)* of F. We also give some conditions which make it easier to check whether a given matrix is a QDR of F.

Building NIZKs from QDRs. Assuming $\boldsymbol{C}(\boldsymbol{X})$ is a QDR of F, we propose a linear-algebraic NIZK argument $\boldsymbol{\Pi}_{\mathsf{nizk}}$ for showing that $\mathtt{x} \in \mathcal{L}_{\mathsf{pk},F}$. We prove that $\boldsymbol{\Pi}_{\mathsf{nizk}}$ is sound under a CED assumption. Importantly, CED is falsifiable if $\mathcal{A} = \mathcal{A}(F)$ has a polynomial number of elements. Otherwise, CED is in general non-falsifiable (except in some relevant cases, see Sect. 10), but belongs to the class of "inefficient-challenger" assumptions (usually considered more realistic than knowledge assumptions, see [31]). Furthermore, CED can be reduced to a single, natural *gap assumption*: the hardness of breaking DDH in a group $\mathbb{G}_2$ given a CDH oracle in a different group $\mathbb{G}_1$. We refer to Sect. 10.2 for more details.

Constructing QDRs. The remaining, *highly non-trivial*, problem is to construct a QDR of F, such that the constructed NIZK argument is efficient. In the rest of the paper, we study this problem.

First, we propose a general framework to construct NIZK arguments for $\mathcal{L}_{\mathsf{pk},F}$ where $F(\chi)$ can be computed by an efficient *algebraic branching program*. Let Π be an ABP that computes F, with the node set V and the edge set E, and let $\ell = |V| - 1$. Given the methodology of [23,24], one can represent Π as an $\ell \times \ell$ matrix $\mathsf{IK}(\boldsymbol{X})$, such that $\det(\mathsf{IK}(\boldsymbol{X}))$ is equal to the output of the ABP. We show that such $\mathsf{IK}(\boldsymbol{X})$ is a QDR. Thus, we obtain an efficient computationally-sound NIZK for $\mathcal{L}_{\mathsf{pk},F}$ under a CED assumption.

Applications. We consider several natural applications of our framework.

Univariate Polynomials. Given a univariate polynomial $F(X) = \prod(X - \xi_i)$ of degree-d, for different roots ξ_i, we construct a simple matrix $\boldsymbol{C}(X)$. The resulting NIZK argument is about 30% shorter and 20% more computationally efficient than the set membership proof that stems from [9, Section C]; see the comparison in Table 1.

Commitments to Points on an Elliptic Curve. We construct a NIZK argument to prove that the committed point (X, Y) belongs to the given elliptic curve $Y^2 = X^3 + aX + b$. Such NIZK proofs are popular in cryptocurrency applications, [4]. The construction of $\boldsymbol{C}(X, Y)$ is motivated by a classical algebraic-geometric (possibility) result that for any homogeneous cubic surface $F(X, Y, Z)$, there exists a 3×3 matrix of affine maps that has $F(X, Y, Z)$ as its determinant [14].

OR Proofs. In Sect. 6.2, we look at the special case of OR proofs and study three instantiations of our general protocol to OR arguments. We discuss the advantages and downsides of each.

Non-principal Ideals. Importantly, in Sect. 8, we capture the very general scenario where $\mathcal{I}(\mathcal{A})$ has a "nice-looking" generating set $(F_1, \dots, F_\tau)$ (i.e. τ is small and each polynomial has a small degree). Some cryptographically important examples include arithmetic circuits, R1CS, Boolean circuits, and arithmetic constraint satisfaction systems. Thus, we obtain efficient NIZKs for NP.

Full Version. Due to the lack of space, a significant amount of additional material (including all proofs) can be found in the full version of this paper, [10].

2 Preliminaries

For a matrix $\boldsymbol{A} \in \mathbb{Z}_p^{n \times n}$ and $i \in [1, n]$, let $\boldsymbol{C}_{(i,1)}$ be the submatrix obtained from $\boldsymbol{C}$ by removing the ith row and the first column.

Cryptography. A bilinear group generator $\mathsf{Pgen}(1^\lambda)$ returns $\mathsf{p} = (p, \mathbb{G}_1, \mathbb{G}_2, \mathbb{G}_T, \hat{e}, [1]_1, [1]_2)$, where $\mathbb{G}_1$, $\mathbb{G}_2$, and $\mathbb{G}_T$ are three additive cyclic groups of prime order p, $[1]_\iota$ is a generator of $\mathbb{G}_\iota$ for $\iota \in \{1, 2, T\}$ with $[1]_T = \hat{e}([1]_1, [1]_2)$, and $\hat{e} : \mathbb{G}_1 \times \mathbb{G}_2 \to \mathbb{G}_T$ is a non-degenerate efficiently computable bilinear pairing. We require the bilinear pairing to be Type-3, that is, we assume that there is no efficient isomorphism between $\mathbb{G}_1$ and $\mathbb{G}_2$. We use the additive implicit notation of [15], that is, we write $[a]_\iota$ to denote $a[1]_\iota$ for $\iota \in \{1, 2, T\}$. We denote $\hat{e}([a]_1, [b]_2)$ by $[a]_1 \bullet [b]_2$. Thus, $[a]_1 \bullet [b]_2 = [ab]_T$. We freely use the bracket notation together with matrix notation; for example, if $\boldsymbol{AB} = \boldsymbol{C}$ then $[\boldsymbol{A}]_1 \bullet [\boldsymbol{B}]_2 = [\boldsymbol{C}]_T$. We also assume that $[\boldsymbol{A}]_2 \bullet [\boldsymbol{B}]_1 := ([\boldsymbol{B}]_1^\top \bullet [\boldsymbol{A}]_2^\top)^\top = [\boldsymbol{AB}]_T$.

Let $\mathcal{P}_\nu := \{[a_0]_1 + \sum_{i=0}^{\nu} [a_i]_1 X_i : a_i \in \mathbb{Z}_p fori \in [0, \nu]\} \subset \mathbb{G}_1[\boldsymbol{X}]$ be the set of linear multivariate polynomials over $\mathbb{G}_1$ in ν variables.

Algebraic languages [8,9] are parameterized languages of the shape $\mathcal{L}_{\boldsymbol{\Gamma},\boldsymbol{\theta}} = \{\mathtt{x} : \exists \mathtt{w}, \boldsymbol{\Gamma}(\mathtt{x}) \cdot \mathtt{w} = \boldsymbol{\theta}(\mathtt{x})\}$, where $\mathtt{x}$ is the input, $\mathtt{w}$ is the witness, $\boldsymbol{\Gamma}$ and $\boldsymbol{\theta}$ are affine maps, such that $\mathtt{x}$ and $\boldsymbol{\theta}(\mathtt{x})$ are vectors, and $\boldsymbol{\Gamma}(\mathtt{x})$ is a matrix. One can construct Gennaro-Lindell smooth projective hash functions (GL-SPHFs [3,5,17]) for all algebraic languages.

Let $\mathsf{k} \in \{1, 2, \dots\}$ be a small parameter related to the matrix distribution. In the case of asymmetric pairings, usually $\mathsf{k} = 1$. Let $\mathcal{D}_{\ell\mathsf{k}}$ be a probability distribution over $\mathbb{Z}_p^{\ell \times \mathsf{k}}$, where $\ell > \mathsf{k}$. We denote $\mathcal{D}_{\mathsf{k}+1,\mathsf{k}}$ by $\mathcal{D}_\mathsf{k}$. We use the matrix distribution, $\mathcal{L}_1$, defined as the distribution over matrices $\left(\begin{smallmatrix} 1 \\ a \end{smallmatrix}\right)$, where $a \leftarrow_\$ \mathbb{Z}_p$.

In the Elgamal encryption scheme, the public key is $\mathsf{pk} = [1, \mathsf{sk}]_1$, and $\mathsf{Enc}_\mathsf{pk}(m; r) = (r[1]_1 \| m[1]_1 + r[\mathsf{sk}]_1)$. To decrypt, one computes $[m]_1 = \mathsf{Dec}_\mathsf{sk}([\mathsf{c}]_1) \leftarrow -\mathsf{sk}[c_1]_1 + [c_2]_1$. In what follows, we denote $[\mathsf{c}]_1 = \mathsf{Enc}(m; r)$ for a fixed public key $\mathsf{pk} = \left[\begin{smallmatrix} 1 \\ \mathsf{sk} \end{smallmatrix}\right]_1$. Elgamal's IND-CPA security is based on $\mathcal{L}_1$-KerMDH, that is, DDH.

The following Extended Kernel Diffie-Hellman assumption $\mathsf{ExtKerMDH}$ [9] generalizes the well-known KerMDH assumption [28]. We also define in parallel a new, slightly weaker version of this assumption, CED (*computational extended determinant*).

Definition 1. **($\mathcal{D}_\mathsf{k}$-$(\ell - 1)$-$\mathsf{ExtKerMDH}$).** *Let $\ell, \mathsf{k} \in \mathbb{N}$, and $\mathcal{D}_\mathsf{k}$ be a matrix distribution. The $\mathcal{D}_\mathsf{k}$-$(\ell - 1)$-$\mathsf{ExtKerMDH}$ assumption holds in $\mathbb{G}_\iota$ relative to* Pgen, *if for all PPT adversaries $\mathcal{A}$, the following probability is negligible:*

$$\Pr\left[\begin{array}{l} \mathsf{p} \leftarrow \mathsf{Pgen}(1^\lambda), [\boldsymbol{D}]_\iota \leftarrow_\$ \mathcal{D}_\mathsf{k}, ([\boldsymbol{\gamma} \| \boldsymbol{C}]_{3-\iota}, [\boldsymbol{\delta}]_\iota) \leftarrow \mathcal{A}(\mathsf{p}, [\boldsymbol{D}]_\iota) : \boldsymbol{\delta} \in \mathbb{Z}_p^{(\ell-1) \times \mathsf{k}} \wedge \\ \boldsymbol{\gamma} \in \mathbb{Z}_p^{\ell \times \mathsf{k}} \wedge \boldsymbol{C} \in \mathbb{Z}_p^{\ell \times \ell} \wedge (\boldsymbol{\gamma} \| \boldsymbol{C}) \left(\begin{smallmatrix} \boldsymbol{D} \\ \boldsymbol{\delta} \end{smallmatrix}\right) = \boldsymbol{0} \wedge \operatorname{rk}(\boldsymbol{\gamma} \| \boldsymbol{C}) \geq \ell \end{array}\right].$$

We define $\mathcal{D}_\mathsf{k}$-$(\ell - 1)$-CED analogously, except that we change the condition $\operatorname{rk}(\boldsymbol{\gamma} \| \boldsymbol{C}) \geq \ell$ to $\operatorname{rk}(\boldsymbol{C}) \geq \ell$.

CED is *weaker* than ExtKerMDH since a successful adversary has to satisfy a stronger condition ($\text{rk}(\boldsymbol{C}) \geq \ell$ instead of $\text{rk}(\gamma \| \boldsymbol{C}) \geq \ell$). (See the full version [10] for a reduction.) CED suffices for the security of all NIZK arguments of the current paper. Moreover, in Sect. 10.2, we reduce CED to a gap assumption. It seems that ExtKerMDH cannot be reduced to the same assumption. Finally, CED is a natural assumption since we always care about $\text{rk}(\boldsymbol{C})$ and not $\text{rk}(\gamma \| \boldsymbol{C}) \geq \ell$.

Despite the general definition, in the rest of the paper (following [9]), we will be only concerned with the case $\mathsf{k} = 1$ and $\mathcal{D}_\mathsf{k} = \mathcal{L}_1$.

NIZK Arguments. An adaptive NIZK Π for a family of language distribution $\{\mathcal{D}_\mathsf{p}\}_\mathsf{p}$ consists of five probabilistic algorithms: (1) $\mathsf{Pgen}(1^\lambda)$: generates public parameters p that fix a distribution $\mathcal{D}_\mathsf{p}$. (2) $\mathsf{kgen}(\mathsf{p})$: generates a CRS $\mathtt{crs}$ and a trapdoor $\mathtt{td}$. For simplicity of notation, we assume that any group parameters are implicitly included in the CRS. We often denote the sequence "$\mathsf{p} \leftarrow \mathsf{Pgen}(1^\lambda)$; $(\mathtt{crs}, \mathtt{td}) \leftarrow \mathsf{kgen}(\mathsf{p})$" by $(\mathsf{p}, \mathtt{crs}, \mathtt{td}) \leftarrow \mathsf{kgen}(1^\lambda)$. (3) $\mathsf{P}(\mathtt{crs}, \mathtt{lpar}, \mathtt{x}, \mathtt{w})$: given a language description $\mathtt{lpar} \in \mathcal{D}_\mathsf{p}$ and a statement $\mathtt{x}$ with witness $\mathtt{w}$, outputs a proof π for $\mathtt{x} \in \mathcal{L}_{\mathtt{lpar}}$. (4) $\mathsf{V}(\mathtt{crs}, \mathtt{lpar}, \mathtt{x}, \pi)$. On input of a CRS, a language description $\mathtt{lpar} \in \mathcal{D}_\mathsf{p}$, a statement and a proof, accepts or rejects the proof. (5) $\mathsf{Sim}(\mathtt{crs}, \mathtt{td}, \mathtt{lpar}, \mathtt{x})$. Given a CRS, the trapdoor $\mathtt{td}$, $\mathtt{lpar} \in \mathcal{D}_\mathsf{p}$, and a statement $\mathtt{x}$, outputs a simulated proof for the statement $\mathtt{x} \in \mathcal{L}_{\mathtt{lpar}}$.

Note that the CRS does not depend on the language distribution or language parameters, i.e. we define fully adaptive NIZKs for language distributions. The following properties need to hold for a NIZK argument.

A proof system Π for $\{\mathcal{D}_\mathsf{p}\}_\mathsf{p}$ is *perfectly complete*, if

$$\Pr\left[\mathsf{V}(\mathtt{crs}, \mathtt{lpar}, \mathtt{x}, \pi) = 1 \mid \begin{array}{c}(\mathsf{p}, \mathtt{crs}, \mathtt{td}) \leftarrow_{\$} \mathsf{K}_{\mathtt{crs}}(1^\lambda); \mathtt{lpar} \in \text{Supp}(\mathcal{D}_\mathsf{p});\\ (\mathtt{x}, \mathtt{w}) \in \mathcal{R}_{\mathtt{lpar}}; \pi \leftarrow_{\$} \mathsf{P}(\mathtt{crs}, \mathtt{lpar}, \mathtt{x}, \mathtt{w})\end{array}\right] = 1$$

A proof system Π for $\{\mathcal{D}_\mathsf{p}\}_\mathsf{p}$ is *computationally sound*, if for every efficient $\mathcal{A}$,

$$\Pr\left[\begin{array}{c}\mathsf{V}(\mathtt{crs}, \mathtt{lpar}, \mathtt{x}, \pi) = 1\\ \wedge \mathtt{x} \notin \mathcal{L}_{\mathtt{lpar}}\end{array}\middle| \begin{array}{c}(\mathsf{p}, \mathtt{crs}, \mathtt{td}) \leftarrow_{\$} \mathsf{K}_{\mathtt{crs}}(1^\lambda);\\ \mathtt{lpar} \in \text{Supp}(\mathcal{D}_\mathsf{p}); (\mathtt{x}, \pi) \leftarrow \mathcal{A}(\mathtt{crs}, \mathtt{lpar})\end{array}\right] \approx 0$$

with the probability taken over $\mathsf{K}_{\mathtt{crs}}$.

Π for $\{\mathcal{D}_\mathsf{p}\}_\mathsf{p}$ is *perfectly zero-knowledge*, if for all λ, all $(\mathsf{p}, \mathtt{crs}, \mathtt{td}) \in \text{Supp}(\mathsf{K}_{\mathtt{crs}}(1^\lambda))$, all $\mathtt{lpar} \in \text{Supp}(\mathcal{D}_\mathsf{p})$ and all $(\mathtt{x}, \mathtt{w}) \in \mathcal{R}_{\mathtt{lpar}}$, the distributions $\mathsf{P}(\mathtt{crs}, \mathtt{lpar}, \mathtt{x}, \mathtt{w})$ and $\mathsf{Sim}(\mathtt{crs}, \mathtt{td}, \mathtt{lpar}, \mathtt{x})$ are identical.

Σ-Protocols. A Σ-protocol [12] is a public-coin, three-move interactive proof between a prover P and a verifier V for a relation $\mathcal{R}$, where the prover sends an initial message a, the verifier responds with a random $e \leftarrow_{\$} \mathbb{Z}_p$ and the prover concludes with a message z. Lastly, the verifier outputs 1, if it accepts and 0 otherwise. In this work we are concerned with three properties of a Σ-protocol: completeness, optimal soundness and honest-verifier zero-knowledge.

CH Compilation. Couteau and Hartmann [9] compile Σ-protocols to NIZKs in the CRS model for algebraic languages by letting $[e]_2$ be the CRS. The basic Couteau and Hartmann compilation is for a Σ-protocol, inspired by [26], for algebraic languages. We will describe it in Sect. 9.

3 Quasideterminantal Representations

Next, we define quasideterminantal representations (QDRs) $\boldsymbol{C}(\boldsymbol{X})$ of a polynomial $F(\boldsymbol{X})$. We prove a technical lemma in Sect. 3.1 which shows how one can check whether a concrete matrix $\boldsymbol{C}(\boldsymbol{X})$ is a QDR of F. We use this definition in Sect. 4, where, given a QDR $\boldsymbol{C}(\boldsymbol{X})$, we define the NIZK argument for the associated language $\mathcal{L}_{\mathsf{pk},F}$ (defined in Eq. (1)), and prove its security.

We first define the class of languages we are interested in. Initially, we are interested in the case where $\mathcal{A} = \mathcal{A}(\{F\})$ for a single polynomial F. Fix $\mathsf{p} \leftarrow \mathsf{Pgen}(1^\lambda)$. For a fixed Elgamal public key pk, let $\mathtt{lpar} := (\mathsf{pk}, F)$. (Implicitly, $\mathtt{lpar}$ also contains p.) Let $[\mathbf{ct}]_1 = \mathsf{Enc}([\boldsymbol{\chi}]_1; \boldsymbol{r}) = (\mathsf{Enc}([\chi_i]_1; r_i))_i$. We use freely the notation $F(\mathsf{Dec}([\mathbf{ct}]_1)) = F([\boldsymbol{\chi}]_1) = [F(\boldsymbol{\chi})]_1$. In Sect. 4, we describe a general technique that results both in efficient NIZK arguments for languages

$$\mathcal{L}_{\mathsf{pk},F} = \{[\mathbf{ct}]_1 : \exists \boldsymbol{\chi} \text{ such that } \mathsf{Dec}([\mathbf{ct}]_1) = [\boldsymbol{\chi}]_1 \wedge \boldsymbol{\chi} \in \mathcal{Z}(F)\} \ . \tag{1}$$

For example, if $F(X) = X^2 - X$, then $\mathcal{L}_{\mathsf{pk},F}$ corresponds to the language of all Elgamal encryptions of Boolean values under the fixed public key pk.

Intuition. To motivate the definition of QDRs, we first explain the intuition behind the new NIZK argument. Recall from Definition 1 that an adversary breaks the $\mathcal{L}_1$-$(\ell-1)$-CED assumption if, given $[\boldsymbol{D}]_2 = [\binom{1}{e}]_2 \leftarrow_s \mathcal{L}_1$ (i.e., $e \leftarrow_s \mathbb{Z}_p$), he returns $([\boldsymbol{\gamma}\|\boldsymbol{C}]_1 \in \mathbb{G}_1^{\ell\times(\ell+1)}, [\boldsymbol{\delta}]_2 \in \mathbb{G}_2^{(\ell-1)\times 1})$, such that $\mathrm{rk}(\boldsymbol{C}) \geq \ell$ and

$$\boldsymbol{\gamma} + \boldsymbol{C}\binom{e}{\boldsymbol{\delta}} = \mathbf{0}. \tag{2}$$

Following [9], in our arguments $[e]_2$ (i.e., $[\boldsymbol{D}]_2$) is given in the CRS and $[\boldsymbol{\delta}]_2$ is chosen by the prover. More precisely, the prover sends $\mathsf{Enc}([\boldsymbol{\gamma}\|\boldsymbol{C}]_1)$ and $[\boldsymbol{\delta}]_2$ (together with some elements that make it possible to verify that Eq. (2) holds using encrypted values) to the verifier.

The matrix $\boldsymbol{C}$ must have full rank whenever the prover cheats, i.e. $F(\boldsymbol{\chi}) \neq 0$. We achieve this by requiring that $\det(\boldsymbol{C}(\boldsymbol{X})) = F(\boldsymbol{X})$. Then, $\mathrm{rk}(\boldsymbol{C}) = d$.

We guarantee that $\boldsymbol{C}$ is efficiently computable by requiring that $\boldsymbol{C}(\boldsymbol{X})$ is a matrix of affine maps, and $[\boldsymbol{C}]_1 = [\boldsymbol{C}(\boldsymbol{\chi})]_1$ for $[\boldsymbol{\chi}]_1 = \mathsf{Dec}([\mathsf{ct}]_1)$. This also minimizes communication since each element of $\mathsf{Enc}([\boldsymbol{C}(\boldsymbol{\chi})]_1)$ can be recomputed from $\mathsf{Enc}([\boldsymbol{\chi}]_1)$ by using the homomorphic properties of Elgamal.

On the other hand, assume that the prover is not honest (i.e., $\det(\boldsymbol{C}(\boldsymbol{\chi})) = F(\boldsymbol{\chi}) \neq 0$) but managed to compute $\mathsf{Enc}([\boldsymbol{\gamma}]_1)$ and $[\boldsymbol{\delta}]_2$ accepted by the verifier. Assume that the reduction knows sk (the language trapdoor). Then, the reduction obtains $[\boldsymbol{\chi}]_1$ by decryption and recomputes $[\boldsymbol{C}(\boldsymbol{\chi})]_1$. Since $\det(\boldsymbol{C}(\boldsymbol{\chi})) \neq 0$ but the verifier accepts (i.e., Eq. (2)), then one can break the CED assumption by returning $[(\boldsymbol{\gamma}\|\boldsymbol{C})(\boldsymbol{\chi})]_1$ and $[\boldsymbol{\delta}]_2$.

3.1 Definition

We now define quasideterminantal representations (QDRs) $\boldsymbol{C}(\boldsymbol{X})$ of polynomial F. QDRs are related to the well-known notion of determinantal representation from algebraic geometry, see the full version [10] for a discussion.

Definition 2 (Quasideterminantal Representation (QDR)). *Let* $F(\boldsymbol{X}) \in \mathbb{Z}_p[\boldsymbol{X}]$ *be a* ν*-variate polynomial. Let* $\ell \geq 1$ *be an integer. A matrix* $\boldsymbol{C}(\boldsymbol{X}) = (C_{ij}(\boldsymbol{X})) \in \mathbb{Z}_p[\boldsymbol{X}]^{\ell \times \ell}$ *is a* QDR *of* F*, if the following requirements hold. Here,* $\boldsymbol{C}(\boldsymbol{X}) = (\boldsymbol{h} \| \boldsymbol{T})(\boldsymbol{X})$*, where* $\boldsymbol{h}(\boldsymbol{X})$ *is a column vector.*

Affine map: *For each* i *and* j*,* $C_{ij}(\boldsymbol{X}) = \sum_{k=1}^{\nu} P_{kij} X_k + Q_{ij}$*, for public* $P_{kij}, Q_{ij} \in \mathbb{Z}_p$*, is an affine map.*
F-rank: $\det(\boldsymbol{C}(\boldsymbol{X})) = F(\boldsymbol{X})$.
First column dependence: *For any* $\boldsymbol{\chi} \in \mathcal{Z}(F)$*,* $\boldsymbol{h}(\boldsymbol{\chi}) \in \text{colspace}(\boldsymbol{T}(\boldsymbol{\chi}))$.

The quasideterminantal complexity $\mathsf{qdc}(F)$ *of* F *is the smallest QDR size of* F*. (Clearly,* $\mathsf{qdc}(F) \geq \deg(F)$*.)*

For example, $\boldsymbol{C}(X) = \begin{pmatrix} 0 & X \\ X-1 & 1-X \end{pmatrix}$ is a QDR of $F(X) = X(X-1)$. The first column dependence property follows since $\begin{pmatrix} 0 \\ \chi-1 \end{pmatrix} = \begin{pmatrix} \chi \\ 1-\chi \end{pmatrix} w$ iff $(\chi, w) = (0, -1)$ or $(\chi, w) = (1, 0)$, i.e., $\chi \in \mathcal{Z}(F)$. On the other hand, $\boldsymbol{C}(X) = \begin{pmatrix} X & 0 \\ 0 & X-1 \end{pmatrix}$ is not a QDR (of the same F) since $\begin{pmatrix} \chi \\ 0 \end{pmatrix} = \begin{pmatrix} 0 \\ \chi-1 \end{pmatrix} w$ iff $(\chi, w) = (0, 0)$.

The first column dependence property is nicely connected to a computational requirement we need for our NIZK. However, it can be difficult to check whether a given matrix satisfies this condition. We now give two alternative conditions that imply the first column dependence property, and which are easier to check.

Lemma 1. *Suppose a matrix* $\boldsymbol{C}$ *satisfies the affine map and* F*-rank properties. If it in addition satisfies one of the following properties, it also satisfies the first column dependence property.*

(1) High right rank: For any $\boldsymbol{\chi} \in \mathbb{Z}_p^{\nu}$*,* $\text{rk}(\boldsymbol{T}(\boldsymbol{\chi})) = \ell - 1$.
(2) Invertible right-submatrix: there exists i*, s.t.* $\det(\boldsymbol{C}_{(i,1)}(\boldsymbol{\chi})) \neq 0$ *for any* $\boldsymbol{\chi}$.

E.g., any matrix $\boldsymbol{C}(\boldsymbol{X})$ that contains non-zero elements on its upper 1-diagonal and only 0's above the upper 1-diagonal is automatically a QDR of $F(\boldsymbol{X}) := \det(\boldsymbol{C}(\boldsymbol{X}))$. See Sects. 5 and 6 for more.

3.2 Corollaries

The affine map property is needed since we use a homomorphic cryptosystem which makes it possible to compute $\mathsf{Enc}([C_{ij}(\boldsymbol{\chi})]_1) = \sum_{k=1}^{\nu} P_{kij} \mathsf{Enc}([\chi_k]_1) + Q_{ij} \mathsf{Enc}([1]_1)$ given only $\mathsf{Enc}([\boldsymbol{\chi}]_1)$. The F-rank property follows directly from the definition of CED. The first column dependence property, guarantees that the QDR $\boldsymbol{C}(\boldsymbol{X})$ satisfies the following two properties, required later:

Efficient prover: There exist two PPT algorithms that we later explicitly use in the new NIZK argument (see Fig. 2) for $\mathcal{L}_{\mathsf{pk},F}$. First, $\mathsf{comp}_1(\mathsf{p}, \boldsymbol{\chi}, \boldsymbol{C}(\boldsymbol{X}))$, that computes $[\boldsymbol{\gamma}]_1$ and a state st. Second, $\mathsf{comp}_2(st, [e]_2)$, that computes $[\boldsymbol{\delta}]_2$. We require that if $F(\boldsymbol{\chi}) = 0$, then $([\boldsymbol{\gamma}]_1, [\boldsymbol{\delta}]_2)$ satisfy Eq. (2). We denote the sequential process $([\boldsymbol{\gamma}]_1, st) \leftarrow \mathsf{comp}_1(\mathsf{p}, \boldsymbol{\chi}, \boldsymbol{C}(\boldsymbol{X}))$, $[\boldsymbol{\delta}]_2 \leftarrow \mathsf{comp}_2(st, [e]_2)$ by $([\boldsymbol{\gamma}]_1, [\boldsymbol{\delta}]_2) \leftarrow \mathsf{comp}(\mathsf{p}, [e]_2, \boldsymbol{\chi}, \boldsymbol{C}(\boldsymbol{X}))$.

$\mathsf{comp}_1(\mathsf{p}, \chi, \boldsymbol{C}(\boldsymbol{X}))$:	$\mathsf{comp}_2(st, \psi(e))$:
Write $\boldsymbol{C}(\chi) = (\boldsymbol{h} \\| \boldsymbol{T})(\chi)$; $\boldsymbol{y} \leftarrow_\$ \mathbb{Z}_p^{\ell-1}$;	Write $\boldsymbol{C}(\chi) = (\boldsymbol{h} \\| \boldsymbol{T})(\chi)$;
$\gamma \leftarrow \boldsymbol{T}(\chi)\boldsymbol{y}$; $st \leftarrow (\mathsf{p}, \chi, \boldsymbol{C}(\boldsymbol{X}); \boldsymbol{y})$;	Compute $\boldsymbol{w}$ such that $\boldsymbol{T}(\chi)\boldsymbol{w} = \boldsymbol{h}(\chi)$;
return $([\gamma]_1, st)$;	$\psi(\boldsymbol{\delta}) \leftarrow -(\boldsymbol{w}\psi(e) + \psi(\boldsymbol{y}))$; **return** $\psi(\boldsymbol{\delta})$;

Fig. 1. comp_i algorithms assuming $\boldsymbol{h}(\chi) \in \text{colspace}(\boldsymbol{T}(\chi))$. Here, $\psi = id$ in the case of the Σ-protocol, and $\psi = [\cdot]_2$ in the case of the NIZK argument.

Zero-knowledge: For $([\gamma]_1, [\boldsymbol{\delta}]_2) \leftarrow \mathsf{comp}(\mathsf{p}, [e]_2, \chi, \boldsymbol{C}(\boldsymbol{X}))$, $\boldsymbol{\delta}$ is uniformly random. This requirement is needed for the zero-knowledge property of the resulting NIZK argument.

To be able to construct an efficient Σ-protocol for $\mathcal{L}_{\mathsf{pk},F}$, we need to replace the efficient prover assumption with the following assumption.

Efficient prover over integers: as the "efficient prover" requirement, but one uses e everywhere instead of $[e]_2$, and $\boldsymbol{\delta}$ instead of $[\boldsymbol{\delta}]_2$.

In all our instantiations, the two variations of comp are related as follows: $\mathsf{comp}(\mathsf{p}, [e]_2, \chi, \boldsymbol{C}(\boldsymbol{X}))$ is the same as $\mathsf{comp}(\mathsf{p}, e, \chi, \boldsymbol{C}(\boldsymbol{X}))$ but applies an additional $[\cdot]_2$ to some of the variables.

Remark 1. We will explicitly need the independence of $[\gamma]_1$ from $[e]_2$ for Σ-protocols and thus for CH-compilation. It is not a priori clear if it is needed for NIZK arguments in general. However, if $\gamma = f(e)$ for some non-constant affine map f, then one cannot efficiently compute $[\gamma]_1$ given only $[e]_2$, since we rely on type-III pairings and those two values belong to different source groups. Thus, independence of $[\gamma]_1$ from $[e]_2$ seems inherent in the case of type-III pairings.

Lemma 2. *Assume F is as in Definition 2 and that $\boldsymbol{C}(\boldsymbol{X})$ is a QDR of F. Then (1) $\boldsymbol{C}$ has the efficient-prover property. (2) $\boldsymbol{C}$ has the zero-knowledge property.*

Finally, we show that any matrix which satisfies the efficient prover property as well as the affine map and F-rank properties must satisfy the first column dependence property. Thus, the latter property is actually needed.

Lemma 3. *Let $\boldsymbol{C}(\boldsymbol{X})$ be a matrix that satisfies the affine map, F-rank and efficient prover properties. Then $\boldsymbol{C}$ satisfies the first column dependence property.*

4 Argument for Algebraic Set of Principal Ideal

Fix $\mathsf{p} \leftarrow \mathsf{Pgen}(1^\lambda)$ and define $\mathcal{D}_\mathsf{p} := \{\mathtt{lpar} = (\mathsf{pk}, F)\}$, where (1) pk is an Elgamal public key for encrypting in $\mathbb{G}_1$, and (2) F is a polynomial with $\mathsf{qdc}(F) = \mathsf{poly}(\lambda)$, i.e., there exists a $\mathsf{poly}(\lambda)$-size QDR $\boldsymbol{C}(\boldsymbol{X})$ of F. (In Sects. 5 and 6, we will show that such QDRs exist for many F-s.)

Before going on, recall that $C_{ij}(\boldsymbol{X}) = \sum_{k=1}^{\nu} P_{kij} X_k + Q_{ij}$ for public P_{kij} and Q_{ij}. To simplify notation, we will use vector/matrix format, by writing $\boldsymbol{C}(\boldsymbol{X}) = \sum_{k=1}^{\nu} \boldsymbol{P}_k X_k + \boldsymbol{Q}$. As always, we denote $\mathsf{Enc}([\boldsymbol{a}]_1; \boldsymbol{r}) := (\mathsf{Enc}([a_i]_1; r_i))_i$. We often omit χ in notation like $[\boldsymbol{C}(\chi)]_1$, and just write $[\boldsymbol{C}]_1$.

$\mathsf{kgen}(\mathsf{p}, \mathtt{lpar})$: $e \leftarrow_{\$} \mathbb{Z}_p$; return $(\mathtt{crs}, \mathtt{td}) \leftarrow ([e]_2, e)$;

$\mathsf{P}(\mathtt{crs}, \mathtt{lpar}, \mathtt{x} = [\mathbf{ct}]_1, \mathtt{w} = (\boldsymbol{\chi}, \boldsymbol{r}))$: $([\boldsymbol{\gamma}]_1, [\boldsymbol{\delta}]_2) \leftarrow \mathsf{comp}(\mathsf{p}, [e]_2, \boldsymbol{\chi}, \boldsymbol{C}(\boldsymbol{X}))$;
$\boldsymbol{\varrho} \leftarrow_{\$} \mathbb{Z}_p^{\ell}$; $[\mathbf{ct}^{\gamma}]_1 \leftarrow \mathsf{Enc}([\boldsymbol{\gamma}]_1; \boldsymbol{\varrho}) \in \mathbb{G}_1^{\ell \times 2}$;
$[\boldsymbol{z}]_2 \leftarrow \boldsymbol{\varrho}[1]_2 + (\sum_{k=1}^{\nu} r_k \boldsymbol{P}_k) \left[\begin{smallmatrix} e \\ \boldsymbol{\delta} \end{smallmatrix} \right]_2 \in \mathbb{G}_2^{\ell}$.
Return $\pi \leftarrow ([\mathbf{ct}^{\gamma}]_1, [\boldsymbol{\delta}, \boldsymbol{z}]_2) \in \mathbb{G}_1^{2\ell} \times \mathbb{G}_2^{2\ell-1}$.

$\mathsf{V}(\mathtt{crs}, \mathtt{lpar}, \mathtt{x} = [\mathbf{ct}]_1, \pi)$: check $[\mathbf{ct}^{\gamma}]_1 \bullet [1]_2 + \sum_{k=1}^{\nu} ([\mathbf{ct}_k]_1 \bullet \boldsymbol{P}_k \left[\begin{smallmatrix} e \\ \boldsymbol{\delta} \end{smallmatrix} \right]_2) =^?$
$[0, 1]_1 \bullet (-\boldsymbol{Q} \left[\begin{smallmatrix} e \\ \boldsymbol{\delta} \end{smallmatrix} \right]_2) + \mathsf{pk} \bullet [\boldsymbol{z}]_2$.

$\mathsf{Sim}(\mathtt{crs}, \mathtt{td}, \mathtt{lpar}, \mathtt{x} = [\mathbf{ct}]_1)$: $\boldsymbol{\delta} \leftarrow_{\$} \mathbb{Z}_p^{\ell-1}$;
$\boldsymbol{z} \leftarrow_{\$} \mathbb{Z}_p^{\ell}$; $[\mathbf{ct}^{\gamma}]_1 \leftarrow \mathsf{Enc}(-\boldsymbol{Q}(\begin{smallmatrix} e \\ \boldsymbol{\delta} \end{smallmatrix})[1]_1; \boldsymbol{z}) - \sum_{k=1}^{\nu} [\mathbf{ct}_k]_1 \cdot \boldsymbol{P}_k(\begin{smallmatrix} e \\ \boldsymbol{\delta} \end{smallmatrix})$;
Return $\pi \leftarrow ([\mathbf{ct}^{\gamma}]_1, [\boldsymbol{\delta}, \boldsymbol{z}]_2) \in \mathbb{G}_1^{2\ell} \times \mathbb{G}_2^{2\ell-1}$.

Fig. 2. The new NIZK argument $\boldsymbol{\Pi}_{\mathsf{nizk}}$ for $\mathcal{L}_{\mathsf{pk},F}$.

4.1 Protocol Description

Let $\mathcal{L}_{\mathsf{pk},F}$ be defined as in Eq. (1). The new Σ-protocol and NIZK argument for $\mathcal{L}_{\mathsf{pk},F}$ are based on the same underlying idea. Since the new NIZK is a CH-compilation of the Σ-protocol, it suffices to describe intuition behind the NIZK.

In the new NIZK argument (see Fig. 2), P uses comp_1 to compute $[\boldsymbol{\gamma}]_1$ (together with state *st*), encrypts $[\boldsymbol{\gamma}]_1$ by using fresh randomness $\boldsymbol{\varrho}$, and then uses comp_2 (given $\mathtt{crs} = [e]_2$) to compute $[\boldsymbol{\delta}]_2$. If P is honest, then by the definition of QDRs of F, Eq. (2) holds, i.e., $\boldsymbol{\gamma} + \boldsymbol{C}(\boldsymbol{\chi})(\begin{smallmatrix} e \\ \boldsymbol{\delta} \end{smallmatrix}) = \mathbf{0}$. The latter is equivalent to $\boldsymbol{\gamma} + (\sum_k \boldsymbol{P}_k \chi_k)(\begin{smallmatrix} e \\ \boldsymbol{\delta} \end{smallmatrix}) = -\boldsymbol{Q}(\begin{smallmatrix} e \\ \boldsymbol{\delta} \end{smallmatrix})$. V needs to be able to check that the last equation holds, while given only an encryption of $[\boldsymbol{\gamma}]_1$. To help V to do that, P sends a vector of randomizers $[\boldsymbol{z}]_2$ to V as helper elements that help to "cancel out" the randomizers used by the prover to encrypt $[\boldsymbol{\gamma}]_1$ and $[\boldsymbol{\chi}]_1$.

The new NIZK argument is given in Fig. 2.

4.2 Efficiency

Next, we estimate of the efficiency of the NIZK argument. Note that if we use the comp algorithm given in Fig. 1, we see that the algorithm computes $\boldsymbol{w}$ and $\boldsymbol{y}$ such that $[\boldsymbol{\delta}]_2 = -(\boldsymbol{w}[e]_2 + \boldsymbol{y}[1]_2)$. This lets us write $\left[\begin{smallmatrix} e \\ \boldsymbol{\delta} \end{smallmatrix} \right]_2 = \left(\begin{smallmatrix} 1 \\ -\boldsymbol{w} \end{smallmatrix} \right)[e]_2 + \left(\begin{smallmatrix} 0 \\ -\boldsymbol{y} \end{smallmatrix} \right)[1]_2$. This allows us to compute $[\boldsymbol{z}]_2$ as $(\sum_{k=1}^{\nu} r_k \boldsymbol{P}_k) \left(\begin{smallmatrix} 1 \\ -\boldsymbol{w} \end{smallmatrix} \right)[e]_2 + (\boldsymbol{\varrho} + \sum_{k=1}^{\nu} r_k \boldsymbol{P}_k) \left(\begin{smallmatrix} 0 \\ -\boldsymbol{y} \end{smallmatrix} \right)[1]_2$, which can be done with 2ℓ exponentiations in $\mathbb{G}_2$. This leads to the following lemma. Its proof follows by direct observation.

Lemma 4. *Consider* $\boldsymbol{\Pi}_{\mathsf{nizk}}$ *with QDR* $\boldsymbol{C}$. *Define* $T_P(\boldsymbol{C}) := |\{(i,j) : \exists k, P_{kij} \neq 0\}|$, *and* $T_Q(\boldsymbol{C}) := |\{(i,j) : Q_{ij} \neq 0\}|$. *Let* $\mathfrak{c}$ *be the time needed to run* comp, $\mathfrak{e}_{\iota}$ *is the time of an exponentiation in* $\mathbb{G}_{\iota}$, *and* $\mathfrak{p}$ *is the time of a pairing. Then (1) the prover's computation is dominated by* $\mathfrak{c} + 2\ell \cdot \mathfrak{e}_1 + 2\ell \cdot \mathfrak{e}_2$, *(2) the verifier's computation is dominated by* $(T_P(\boldsymbol{C}) + T_Q(\boldsymbol{C})) \cdot \mathfrak{e}_2 + 2(2+\nu)\ell \cdot \mathfrak{p}$, *(3) the communication is* 2ℓ *elements of* $\mathbb{G}_1$ *and* $2\ell - 1$ *elements of* $\mathbb{G}_2$.

For the argument to be efficient, we need comp to be as efficient (according to Sect. 3.1, it must be efficient to solve the system $\boldsymbol{T}(\chi)\boldsymbol{w} = \boldsymbol{h}(\chi)$ for $\boldsymbol{w}$, where $\boldsymbol{C}(\boldsymbol{X}) = (\boldsymbol{h}\|\boldsymbol{T})(\boldsymbol{X})$), and the matrices $\boldsymbol{P}_k$ and $\boldsymbol{Q}$ to be sparse.

In Sect. 5, we propose a way to construct $\boldsymbol{C}(\boldsymbol{X})$ that satisfies these restrictions for any $F(\boldsymbol{X})$ that can be computed by a polynomial-size ABP. In Sect. 6, we study other interesting cases.

The estimate in Lemma 4 is often over-conservative. For example, let $\boldsymbol{\delta}' = \binom{e}{\boldsymbol{\delta}}$. If $P_{kij_1} = P_{kij_2} =: P'$ for $j_1 \neq j_2$, then the verifier has to perform one exponentiation $P'([\delta'_{j_1}]_2 + [\delta'_{j_2}]_2)$ instead of two. The same holds when $Q_{ij_1} = Q_{ij_2}$ for some $j_1 \neq j_2$. Moreover, when the exponent is a small constant (in the extreme case, 1 or -1), then one does not have to perform a full-exponentiation.

4.3 Security of the NIZK Argument

Theorem 1. *Let $\{\mathcal{D}_\mathsf{p}\}_\mathsf{p}$ be the family of language distributions, where $\mathcal{D}_\mathsf{p} = \{\mathtt{lpar} = (\mathsf{pk}, F)\}$ as before. Here, $F(\boldsymbol{X})$ is a ν-variate polynomial of degree d, where $\nu, d \in \mathsf{poly}(\lambda)$. Let $\boldsymbol{C}(\boldsymbol{X}) \in \mathbb{Z}_p[\boldsymbol{X}]^{\ell \times \ell}$ be a QDR of F. The NIZK argument $\boldsymbol{\Pi}_\mathsf{nizk}$ for $\{\mathcal{D}_\mathsf{p}\}_\mathsf{p}$ from Fig. 2 is perfectly complete and perfectly zero-knowledge. It is computationally (adaptive) sound under the $\mathcal{L}_1$-$(\ell-1)$-CED assumption in $\mathbb{G}_2$ relative to Pgen.*

5 Efficient Instantiation Based on ABP

In this section we construct QDRs, that we denote by $\mathsf{IK}(\boldsymbol{X})$, for any polynomial F that can be efficiently computed by algebraic branching programs (ABPs). This results in NIZKs for the class of languages $\mathcal{L}_{\mathsf{pk},F}$, where F is only restricted to have a small ABP. However, in many cases, the resulting matrix $\mathsf{IK}(\boldsymbol{X})$ is not optimal, and this will be seen in Sect. 7.1. Thus, following sections consider alternative construction techniques of such matrices.

5.1 Preliminaries: Algebraic Branching Programs

A branching program is defined by a directed acyclic graph (V, E), two special vertices $s, t \in V$, and a labeling function ϕ. An algebraic branching program (ABP, [29]) over a finite field $\mathbb{F}_p$ computes a function $F : \mathbb{F}_p^n \to \mathbb{F}_p$. Here, ϕ assigns to each edge in E a fixed affine (possibly, constant) function in input variables, and $F(\boldsymbol{X})$ is the sum over all $s-t$ paths (i.e., paths from s to t) of the product of all the values along the path.

Algebraic branching programs capture a large class of functions, including in particular all log-depth circuits, boolean branching programs, boolean formulas, logspace circuits, and many more. For some type of computations, they are known to provide a relatively compact representation, which makes them especially useful. See [23,24] and the references therein.

Ishai and Kushilevitz [23,24] related ABPs to matrix determinants as follows.

Proposition 1. *[24, Lemma 1] Given an ABP* $\mathsf{abp} = (V, E, s, t, \phi)$ *computing* $F : \mathbb{F}_p^\nu \to \mathbb{F}_p$*, we can efficiently (and deterministically) compute a function* $\mathsf{IK}(\chi)$ *mapping an input* $\chi \in \mathbb{F}_p^\nu$ *to a matrix from* $\mathbb{F}_p^{\ell\times\ell}$*, where* $\ell = |V| - 1$*, such that:*

1. $\det(\mathsf{IK}(\chi)) = F(\chi)$*,*
2. *each entry of* $\mathsf{IK}(\chi)$ *is an affine map in a single variable* χ_i*,*
3. $\mathsf{IK}(\chi)$ *contains only* -1*'s in the upper* 1*-diagonal (the diagonal above the main diagonal) and* 0*'s above the upper* 1*-diagonal.*

Specifically, IK *is obtained by transposing the matrix you get by removing the column corresponding to* s *and the row corresponding to* t *in the matrix* $\mathsf{adj}(\boldsymbol{X}) - \boldsymbol{I}$*, where* $\mathsf{adj}(\boldsymbol{X})$ *is the adjacency matrix for* abp*.*

Note that the matrix IK is transposed compared to what is found in [24, Lemma 1], to ensure consistency with the notation from the CED assumption.

5.2 NIZK for Algebraic Branching Programs

Lemma 5. *Let* $\mathsf{abp} = (V, E, s, t, \phi)$ *be an ABP that computes a* ν*-variate polynomial* $F(\boldsymbol{X})$*. Then* $\mathsf{IK}(\boldsymbol{X})$ *is a QDR of* F *with* $\ell = |V| - 1$*.*

In particular, $\mathsf{qdc}(F) \le |V| - 1$.

Efficiency of comp**.** We next specialize the general comp_i algorithms given in Fig. 1 to ABP. For this, we just have to write down how to efficiently do the next two steps: (1) Compute $\boldsymbol{\gamma} = \boldsymbol{T}(\chi)\boldsymbol{y}$. Due to the shape of $\mathsf{IK}(\chi)$ and thus of $\boldsymbol{T}(\chi)$, one can clearly compute $\boldsymbol{\gamma}$ as $\gamma_i \leftarrow \sum_{j=1}^{i-1} T_{ij}(\chi) y_{j-1} - y_i$ for each $i \in [1, \ell]$. (2) Solve $\boldsymbol{T}(\chi)\boldsymbol{w} = \boldsymbol{h}(\chi)$ for $\boldsymbol{w}$. Let $\boldsymbol{T}^*$ be the matrix obtained from $\boldsymbol{T}(\chi)$ by omitting its last row, and similarly let $\boldsymbol{h}^*$ be the vector obtained from $\boldsymbol{h}(\chi)$ by omitting its last element. One finds $\boldsymbol{w}$ by solving $\boldsymbol{T}^*\boldsymbol{w} = \boldsymbol{h}^*$ by forward substitution, as follows: $w_i \leftarrow \sum_{j=1}^{i-1} T_{ij}(\chi) w_j - h_i(\chi)$ for each $i \in [1, \ell - 1]$.

Lemma 6. *Let* $N(v)$ *be the neighbourhood of a node* v *in the underlying ABP. Assuming* $\boldsymbol{C}(\boldsymbol{X}) = \mathsf{IK}(\boldsymbol{X})$*, the computational complexity of* comp *is dominated by* $2(|E| - |N(s)|) - |N(t)|$ *field multiplications,* ℓ *exponentiations in* $\mathbb{G}_1$*, and* $2(\ell - 1)$ *exponentiations in* $\mathbb{G}_2$*.*

6 Applications

6.1 Univariate F (Set-Membership Proof)

Consider an algebraic set $\mathcal{A} \in \mathbb{Z}_p$ of size $\mathsf{poly}(\lambda)$, generated by τ univariate polynomials $F_1, \dots, F_\tau \in \mathbb{Z}_p[X]$. As before, we aim to prove that an Elgamal-encrypted χ satisfies $\chi \in \mathcal{A}$, i.e., $F_i(\chi) = 0$ for all i. In the univariate case, all ideals are principal [11, Section 1.5], and thus any ideal can be written as $\mathcal{I} = \langle F \rangle$ for some F. Thus, $\mathcal{A} = \mathcal{A}(F)$ for $F \leftarrow \gcd(F_1, \dots, F_\tau)$ [11, Section 1.5].

Moreover, $\mathcal{I}(\mathcal{A}(F)) = \mathcal{I}(F_{red})$ [11, Section 1.5], where F_{red} has the same roots as F but all with multiplicity one. That is, if $F(X) = \prod(X - \xi_i)^{b_i}$, for $b_i \ge 1$

$$s \xrightarrow{X-\xi_1} a_1 \xrightarrow{X-\xi_2} \cdots \xrightarrow{X-\xi_{d-1}} a_{d-1} \xrightarrow{X-\xi_d} t \qquad \mathsf{IK}_{path}(X) = \begin{pmatrix} X-\xi_1 & -1 & 0 & \dots & 0 \\ 0 & X-\xi_2 & -1 & \dots & 0 \\ \vdots & \vdots & \vdots & \vdots & \vdots \\ 0 & 0 & 0 & \dots & -1 \\ 0 & 0 & 0 & \dots & X-\xi_d \end{pmatrix}$$

Fig. 3. The ABP $\mathsf{abp}^d_{\mathsf{path}}(X, \boldsymbol{\xi})$ for $F(X) = \prod_{i=1}^d (X - \xi_i)$ and $\mathsf{IK}_{path}(X)$

and mutually different ξ_i, then $F_{red} = \prod(X - \xi_i)$. This *reduced polynomial* F_{red} can be efficiently computed as $F_{red} = F/\gcd(F, F')$, [11, Section 1.5]. Since we are constructiong NIZKs for algebraic sets, in this section, we will assume that $F(X) = F_{red}(X) = \prod(X - \xi_i)$ for mutually different roots ξ_i. (This will be the case if we assume $\mathcal{A} = \{\xi_i\}$ for polynomially many ξ_i.) Thus, it suffices to prove that $F(\chi) = 0$, where F is a reduced polynomial. As before, for efficiency reasons, we assume that F has degree $\mathsf{poly}(\lambda)$.

We now apply the ABP-based protocol to a univariate reduced polynomial F. We depict the ABP $\mathsf{abp}^d_{\mathsf{path}}(X, \boldsymbol{\xi})$ in Fig. 3. The ABP consists of a single path of length d with edges labelled by values $X - \xi_i$. Clearly, $\mathsf{abp}^d_{\mathsf{path}}(X, \boldsymbol{\xi})$ computes $F(X)$. The corresponding matrix $\mathsf{IK}_{path}(X)$ is also given in Fig. 3.

Lemma 7. *Let $F(X)$ be a univariate reduced polynomial. The ABP-based NIZK argument for $\mathcal{L}_{\mathsf{pk},F}$ has prover's computation of at most $3d$ exponentiations in $\mathbb{G}_1$ and $4d - 2$ exponentiations in $\mathbb{G}_2$, verifier's computation of $7d - 1$ pairings and at most d exponentiations in $\mathbb{G}_2$, and communication of $2d$ elements of $\mathbb{G}_1$ and $2d - 1$ elements of $\mathbb{G}_2$.*

6.2 Special Case: OR Arguments

In an OR argument, the language is $\mathcal{L}_{\mathsf{pk},X(X-1)}$, that we will just denote by $\mathcal{L}_{\{0,1\}}$, assuming that pk is understood from the context. The case of OR arguments is of particular interest because of its wide applications in many different scenarios. Indeed, one of the most direct applications of [9] is a new OR proof with the argument consisting of 7 group elements. Due to the importance of $\mathcal{L}_{\{0,1\}}$, in the full version [10], we will detail three example NIZK arguments that are all based on CED-matrices. The first argument is based on $\mathsf{abp}^2_{\mathsf{path}}$, and the other two arguments are based on known Σ-protocols from the literature. Interestingly, the third example is not based on ABPs; the added discussion clarifies some benefits of using the ABP-based approach.

6.3 Elliptic Curve Points

In Fig. 4, we depict an ABP and $\mathsf{IK}(X, Y)$ for the bivariate function $F(X, Y) = X^3 + aX + b - Y^2$ (i.e., one checks if (X, Y) belongs to the elliptic curve $Y^2 = X^3 + aX + b$). In Sect. 7.1, we will propose a non-ABP-based QDR for the same task. ABPs for hyperelliptic curves $Y^2 + H(X)Y = f(X)$ (where $\deg(H) \leq g$ and $\deg f = 2g + 1$) of genus g can be constructed analogously.

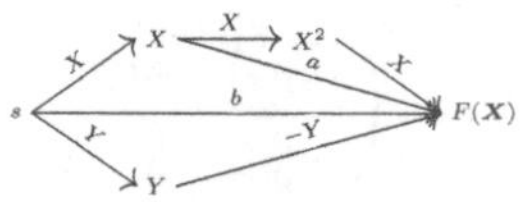

$$\mathsf{IK}(X,Y) = \begin{pmatrix} X & -1 & 0 & 0 \\ 0 & X & -1 & 0 \\ Y & 0 & 0 & -1 \\ b & a & X & -Y \end{pmatrix}$$

Fig. 4. ABP example for $F(X,Y) = X^3 + aX + b - Y^2$.

NIZK arguments that committed (X, Y) belongs to the curve are interesting in practice since one often needs to prove in zero-knowledge that a verifier of some pairing-based protocol accepts. Such a situation was studied in [4], who proposed to use cycles of elliptic curves, such that the number of points on one curve is equal to the size of the field of definition of the next, in a cyclic way. Using the NIZK, resulting from the example of the current subsection, one can use a bilinear group with group order p to prove that the encrypted coordinates belong to an elliptic curve where the finite field has size p.

Different Normal Form. Motivated by [32], we also consider the following less common normal form for an elliptic curve, $F(X,Y) = (X + aY)(X + bY)(X + cY) - X$, for mutually different a, b, c. Then, one can construct the following ABP-based 3×3 QDR: $\begin{pmatrix} X+aY & -1 & 0 \\ 0 & X+bY & -1 \\ -X & 0 & X+cY \end{pmatrix}$.

7 On Bivariate Case

Dickson [14] proved that for any degree-d bivariate polynomial $F(\boldsymbol{X})$, there exists a $d \times d$ matrix $\boldsymbol{C}(\boldsymbol{X})$ of affine maps that has $F(\boldsymbol{X})$ as its determinant. Plaumann *et al.* [32] described efficient algorithms for finding $\boldsymbol{C}(\boldsymbol{X})$ for some families of polynomials F; in their case, $\boldsymbol{C}(\boldsymbol{X})$ is usually symmetric and can satisfy some other additional requirement like semidefiniteness. Since the ABP-based approach often blow ups the dimension of the matrix, we will next use the results of [14,32] to construct a $d \times d$ matrix $\boldsymbol{C}(\boldsymbol{X})$. However, the resulting matrix is usually not a QDR, which results in additional complications. We provide several concrete examples in the case $F(X,Y)$ describes an elliptic curve. Plaumann *et al.* [32] provided also examples for the case $d \in \{4, 5\}$, noting however that finding a determinantal representation of F becomes very time-consuming for $d \geq 5$. In the full version [10], we will provide an example for $d = 5$. We refer to [32] for algorithms and general discussion.

7.1 Optimized Solutions for Elliptic Curves

Let $F(X,Y) = X^3 + aX + b - Y^2$ be a polynomial that describes an elliptic curve. In Sect. 6.3, we described a small ABP for checking that $(X,Y) \in E(\mathbb{Z}_p)$, where $E(\mathbb{Z}_p) : F(X,Y) = 0$. However, this resulted in a 4×4 matrix $\mathsf{IK}(X,Y)$. Next, we construct 3×3 matrices, of correct determinant, for two different choices of F. In general, there are several inequivalent linear symmetric determinantal representations of F, [32]. In both cases, we chose the matrix by inspection.

Case $F(X,Y) = X^3 + aX + b - Y^2$ for $a \neq 0$. In the full version [10], we show that in case there exists a 3×3 determinantal representation that is not a QDR, and discuss the possible issues that arise when one tries to use our NIZK argument in such a case.

Case $F(X,Y) = X^3 + b - Y^2$. We will tackle this case in the full version [10].

8 Handling Non-principal Ideals

Next, we extend the new framework to constructing a NIZK argument that an Elgamal-encrypted χ satisfies $\chi \in \mathcal{A}$ for any algebraic set $\mathcal{A} = \mathcal{A}(\mathfrak{I})$. Namely, assume that $\mathfrak{I}(\mathcal{A})$ has a known generating set $(F_1, \ldots, F_\tau)$ for some τ. We prove that $\chi \in \mathcal{A}$ by proving that $F_i(\chi) = 0$ for each F_i. Thus, $\mathcal{D}_\mathsf{p} = \{(\mathsf{pk}, \mathcal{A})\}$, where $\mathfrak{I}(\mathcal{A}) = \langle F_1, \ldots, F_\tau \rangle$ and each F_i has $\mathsf{qdc}(F_i) = \mathsf{poly}(\lambda)$.

The argument system can be implemented in polynomial time and space, assuming that (1) we know a generating set with small $\tau = \mathsf{poly}(\lambda)$ and with small-degree polynomials, (2) for each F_i, we know a small QDR $\boldsymbol{C}_i(\boldsymbol{X})$ of F_i, and (3) we can construct an efficient NIZK argument system for showing that $\det(\boldsymbol{C}_i(\boldsymbol{X})) = 0$. The previous sections already tackled the last two issues. In this section, we study issue (1). However, the issues are related. In particular, steps (2) and (3) are most efficient for specific type of polynomials F_i, and when solving (1), we have to take this into account.

8.1 NIZK for NP

Next, we use the described methodology to implement arithmetic circuits, and then extend it to R1CS (a linear-algebraic version of QAP [16]) and aCSPs (*arithmetic constraint satisfaction systems*), i.e., constraint systems where each constraint is a small-degree constant that depends on some small number of inputs. We also show how to directly use our techniques to implement the Groth-Sahai-Ostrovsky constraint system [20] that have efficient reductions to corresponding circuits. Interestingly, this seems to result in the first known pairing-based (random-oracle-less) NIZK for general aCSPs.

Arithmetic Circuits. Let $\mathfrak{C}$ be an arithmetic circuit over $\mathbb{Z}_p$, with n gates (including input gates) and m wires. We construct an algebraic set $\mathcal{A}_\mathfrak{C} = (\chi_1, \ldots, \chi_n) \in \mathbb{Z}_p^n$, such that $\chi \in \mathcal{A}_\mathfrak{C}$ iff $\mathfrak{C}(\chi) = 0$, as follows. First, χ corresponds to the vector of wire values. As in the case of QAP [16], we assume that each gate is a weighted multiplication gate that computes $F_i : (\sum_j u_{ij}\chi_{i_j})(\sum_j v_{ij}\chi_{i_j}) \mapsto \chi_i$ for public u_{ij}, v_{ij}, and i_j, where for the sake of efficiency, the sum is taken over a constant number of values.

1. First, each χ_i corresponds to the value of the output wire of ith gate, with χ_j, $j \leq \mathsf{m}_0$ corresponding to the inputs of the circuit. We also assume that the last few wire values correspond to the output values of the circuit.
2. Second, for each gate $i > \mathsf{m}_0$, we introduce the polynomial $F_i(\chi) = \chi_i - (\sum u_{ij}\chi_{i_j})(\sum v_{ij}\chi_{i_j})$.

Then $\mathcal{A}_{\mathfrak{C}} = \{(\chi_1, \ldots, \chi_m) : F_i(\chi) = 0 \text{ for all } i > \mathsf{m}_0\}$. To construct a NIZK for showing $\chi \in \mathcal{A}_{\mathfrak{C}}$, we do as before: (1) We let the prover Elgamal-encrypt χ. (2) We show that $F_i(\chi) = 0$ for all i by using the NIZK argument from Sect. 4. Note that each polynomial in this case is quadratic, and thus one can construct a 2×2 QDR $\boldsymbol{C}(\chi) = \begin{pmatrix} \sum u_{ij}\chi_{i_j} & -1 \\ -\chi_i & \sum v_{ij}\chi_{i_j} \end{pmatrix}$.

According to [21], the Groth-Sahai proof for this task has commitment length $(2m+1)(|\mathbb{G}_1| + |\mathbb{G}_2|)$ and argument length $(2m+2n+2)(|\mathbb{G}_1| + |\mathbb{G}_2|)$. The new NIZK has commitment length $2m|\mathbb{G}_1|$ and argument length $n(4|\mathbb{G}_1| + 3|\mathbb{G}_2|)$. Assuming $m \approx n$ and $|\mathbb{G}_2| = 2|\mathbb{G}_1|$, the new NIZK has 3 times shorter commitments/encrypts and 20% shorter proofs. The new NIZK has approximately 1.5–2 times smaller prover's and verifier's computation. Since the computation in [21] can probably be optimized, we have not included complete comparison.

Extension: R1CS. In R1CS (*rank-1 constraint system* [16]), one has n constraints $(\sum u_{ij}\chi_i)(\sum v_{ij}\chi_i) = \sum w_{ij}\chi_i$ in m variables χ_i, for arbitrary public matrices $U = (u_{ij})$, $V = (v_{ij})$, and $W = (w_{ij})$. There is clearly a simple reduction from arithmetic circuits to R1CS. The described solution for arithmetic circuits can be used to construct a NIZK argument system for R1CS, by defining $F_i(\chi) = (\sum u_{ij}\chi_i)(\sum v_{ij}\chi_i) - \sum w_{ij}\chi_i$ and $\boldsymbol{C}(\chi) = \begin{pmatrix} \sum u_{ij}\chi_{i_j} & -1 \\ -\sum w_{ij}\chi_{i_j} & \sum v_{ij}\chi_{i_j} \end{pmatrix}$.

Extension: Arithmetic Constraint Satisfaction Problems (aCSPs). Fix $\mathbb{F} = \mathbb{Z}_q$. Recall that for a $q \geq 1$, a q-aCSP instance F over $\mathbb{F}$ is a collection of functions $F_1, \ldots, F_\tau$ (called *constraints*) such that each function F_i depends on at most q of its input locations. That is, for every $j \in [1, \tau]$ there exist $i_1, \ldots, i_q \in [1, n]$ and $f : \mathbb{F}^q \rightarrow \mathbb{F}$ such that $F_j(\chi) = f(\chi_{i_1}, \ldots, \chi_{i_q})$ for every $\chi \in \mathbb{F}^n$. Then F is satisfiable if $F_j(\chi) = 0$ for each j.

One can extend R1CS to q-aCSP for small constant q, assuming that F_j are (small-degree) polynomials for which one can construct poly-size QDRs. Intuitively, F is the generating set for some polynomial ideal $\mathfrak{I} = \mathfrak{I}(\mathcal{A})$, and thus the examples of this subsection fall under our general methodology. One can possibly use some general techniques (see Sect. 8.2 for some examples) to minimize the generating sets so as to obtain more efficient NIZKs.

Specialization: Boolean Circuits. By using techniques from [20], one can construct a NIZK for any Boolean circuit that, w.l.o.g., consists of only NAND gates. Intuitively, one does this by showing that each wire value is Boolean, and then showing that each NAND gate is followed correctly. The latter can be shown by showing that a certain linear combination of the input and output wires of the NAND gate is Boolean. Thus, here one only uses polynomials of type $f_i(\chi) = A(\chi)^2 - A(\chi)$, where $A(\chi) = \sum a_{ij}\chi_j$ for some coefficients a_{ij}.

In Table 2, we compare the resulting NIZK with the optimized Groth-Sahai proof for Boolean circuits by Ghadafi *et al.* [18]. Here, m is the number of wires and n is the number of gates. In the case of the AES circuit described in [18], $m = 33880$ and $n = 34136$. Assuming $|\mathbb{G}_2| = 2|\mathbb{G}_1|$ and $\mathfrak{e}_2 = 2\mathfrak{e}_1$, we get that the NIZK of [18] has commitment length $203283|\mathbb{G}_1|$, argument length $814662|\mathbb{G}_1|$, prover's computation $1629324\mathfrak{e}_1$, and verifier's computation $1630336\mathfrak{p}$. The new NIZK has commitment length $67760|\mathbb{G}_1|$, argument length $680160|\mathbb{G}_1|$, and

Table 2. Comparison of falsifiable NIZKs for Boolean circuit satisfiability: the Groth-Sahai proof, as optimized by Ghadafi *et al.* [18], and the new NIZK from Sect. 8.1.Here, $|\mathbb{G}_\iota|$ is the length of one element from $\mathbb{G}_\iota$

Protocol	$\lvert\mathsf{crs}\rvert$	$\lvert\mathsf{com}\rvert$	$\lvert\pi\rvert$	P comp.	V comp.
Groth-Sahai [18]	$4(\lvert\mathbb{G}_1\rvert + \lvert\mathbb{G}_2\rvert)$	$2(m+1)(\lvert\mathbb{G}_1\rvert + \lvert\mathbb{G}_2\rvert)$	$(6m+2n+2)(\lvert\mathbb{G}_1\rvert + \lvert\mathbb{G}_2\rvert)$	$(12m+4n+4)(\mathfrak{e}_1+\mathfrak{e}_2)$	$16(2m+n)\mathfrak{p}$
New, Sect. 8.1	$\lvert\mathbb{G}_2\rvert$	$2m \cdot \lvert\mathbb{G}_1\rvert$	$(m+n)(4\lvert\mathbb{G}_1\rvert + 3\lvert\mathbb{G}_2\rvert)$	$(m+n)(5\mathfrak{e}_1+4\mathfrak{e}_2)$	$13(m+n)\mathfrak{p}$

prover's computation $884208\mathfrak{e}_1$, and verifier's computation $884208\mathfrak{p}$. Hence, the new NIZK has 3 times shorter commitments, 20% shorter arguments, and 1.84 times smaller prover's and verifier's computation.

8.2 Various Examples

Next, we give very generic background on generating sets and after that, we give some examples of the cases when it pays off directly to work with aCSPs (and not just arithmetic circuits) and then use the described methodology to construct the NIZK. We emphasize that one does not need a Gröbner basis and thus sometimes there exist smaller generating sets. In fact, there exist many alternative methods for constructing efficient aCSPs not directly related to generating sets at all; and the Gröbner basis technique is just one of them—albeit one that is strongly related to our general emphasis on polynomial ideals. As we see from the examples, the efficiency of NIZK depends on a delicate balance between the size of the generating set and the degree of the polynomials in that set. Really, it follows from Lemma 4 that if the generating set contains polynomials F_i for which QDRs have sizes ℓ_i, then the resulting NIZK has communication complexity $(2\sum \ell_i)(|\mathbb{G}_1| + |\mathbb{G}_2|) - \tau|\mathbb{G}_2|$.

Basic Background on Generating Sets. Generating sets of an ideal can have vastly different cardinality. For example, $\mathbb{Z}$ is generated by either $\{1\}$ or by the set of all primes. Since a Gröbner basis [7] is, in particular, a generating set, one convenient way of finding a generating set is by using a Gröbner basis algorithm; however, such algorithms assume that one already knows a generating set. Fortunately, the Buchberger-Möller algorithm [27] (as say implemented by CoCoA[6]) can compute a Gröbner basis for $\mathcal{I}(\mathcal{A})$, given any finite set $\mathcal{A}$.

Worst-Case Multi-dimensional Set-Membership Proof. We performed an exhaustive computer search to come up with an example of a 3-dimensional set of five points that has the least efficient NIZK argument in our framework. One of the examples we found[7] is $\mathcal{A} = \{(2,5,1),(2,4,2),(2,5,3),(1,2,4),(3,1,5)\}$. In this case, we found a reduced degree-lexicographic Gröbner basis

$$\left\{ \begin{array}{l} (y-z-2)(y+z-6), \frac{1}{18}(6x(3y-5)-37y+(z-4)z+68), \\ \frac{1}{9}\left(9x^2-33x+y-(z-4)z+22\right), \frac{1}{3}(-12x+5y+z(z(3z-23)+53)-34) \end{array} \right\}$$

[6] http://cocoa.dima.unige.it/.

[7] In the case of many other sets, the NIZK will be much more efficient. We will provide one concrete example in the full version [10].

that consists of three quadratic and one cubic polynomials. Clearly, here, each degree-d polynomial has an optimal-size $d \times d$ QDR. In the only non-trivial case (the cubic polynomial), one can use the matrix

$$\boldsymbol{C}_4(x, y, z) = \begin{pmatrix} z & 1 & 0 \\ 53/3 & 23/3 - z & -4 \\ x - 5y/12 + 17/6 & 0 & -z \end{pmatrix} .$$

Thus, one can construct a NIZK argument with communication of $2(2+2+2+3) = 18$ elements of $\mathbb{G}_1$ and $18 - 4 = 14$ elements of $\mathbb{G}_2$. Since, usually, elements of $\mathbb{G}_2$ are twice as long as elements of $\mathbb{G}_1$, it means that, in the worst case, such a NIZK argument will only be 4.6 times longer than a single OR proof. This is also the upper bound on the NIZK communication according to our exhaustive search, further discussion would be outside the scope of the current paper.

The most efficient known alternative seems to add (structure-preserving) signatures (SPSs) of 5 points to the CRS, letting the prover encrypt a signature of the chosen point, and then proving that the encrypted value is a valid signature of some point. This alternative has both a much larger CRS and worse concrete complexity compared to our NIZK argument. Moreover, it assumes that the underlying signature scheme is unforgeable.

Range Proofs. In the full version [10], we will show how to use our techniques to construct range proofs, i.e., proofs that the committed value χ belongs to some interval $[0, N]$. Couteau and Hartmann's approach can be used to propose range proofs of efficiency $\Theta(\log N)$ by using the binary decomposition of χ. In the full version [10], we note that the use of the NIZK from Sect. 6.1 helps us to obtain a NIZK with better verifier's computation.

9 Back to Algebraic Languages

The well-known methodology of diverse vector spaces (DVSs, [3,5]) has been used to successfully create efficient smooth projective hash functions (SPHFs) for algebraic languages. Moreover, by now several constructions of NIZKs based on such SPHFs are known, [1,9]. For all such constructions, the first step is to construct language parameters $\boldsymbol{\Gamma}$ and $\boldsymbol{\theta}$ (see Sect. 2). Unfortunately, existing constructions of the language parameters are all somewhat ad hoc.

Next, we improve on the situation by proposing a methodology to construct $(\boldsymbol{\Gamma}, \boldsymbol{\theta})$ for any $\mathcal{L}_{\mathsf{pk},\mathcal{A}}$, where $\mathcal{A}$ is any algebraic set for which Sect. 8 results in an efficient NIZK. We start the process from a QDR $\boldsymbol{C}_i$ of F_i, where $\langle F_1, \dots, F_\tau \rangle$ is some generating set of $\mathfrak{I}(\mathcal{A})$, and output concrete parameters $(\boldsymbol{\Gamma}, \boldsymbol{\theta})$. The problem of constructing such $\boldsymbol{C}_i$ was already tackled in the current paper, with many examples (including the case when $\boldsymbol{C}_i$ is based on an ABP). As the end result, we construct explicit language parameters $(\boldsymbol{\Gamma}, \boldsymbol{\theta})$ for a variety of languages where no such small parameters were known before. Moreover, even in the simple case of univariate polynomials, where previous solutions were known [5,9], the new parameters are smaller than before.

We consider various NIZKs that one can construct for given $(\boldsymbol{\Gamma}, \boldsymbol{\theta})$. For every fixed $(\boldsymbol{\Gamma}, \boldsymbol{\theta})$, the NIZK from Sect. 4 is more efficient than the QA-NIZK of [1] and usually more efficient than the CHM NIZK of [9]. Finally, we briefly discuss resulting GL-SPHFs [17] based on the new language parameters.

Preliminaries. We describe the CHM (Couteau-Hartmann-Maurer) Σ-protocol and the resulting NIZK in the full version [10]. There, we will also state the efficiency of their construction as a function of $(\boldsymbol{\Gamma}, \boldsymbol{\theta})$. We also restate Theorem 18 from [9] about the security of the CHM NIZK.

9.1 On Algebraic Languages for Elgamal Ciphertexts

Next, we derive language parameters $\boldsymbol{\Gamma}$ and $\boldsymbol{\theta}$ for an arbitrary $\mathcal{L}_{\mathsf{pk},F}$, such that $\boldsymbol{\theta}(\mathrm{x}) \in \operatorname{colspace} \boldsymbol{\Gamma}(\mathrm{x})$ iff $\mathrm{x} \in \mathcal{L}_{\mathsf{pk},F}$. In the case where $\mathfrak{I}(\mathcal{A}) = \langle F_1, \dots, F_\tau \rangle$ is not a principal ideal, one can then "concatenate" all τ parameters $\boldsymbol{\Gamma}(\mathrm{x})$ and $\boldsymbol{\theta}(\mathrm{x})$.

We start the derivation from the equation $\boldsymbol{T}(\boldsymbol{\chi})\boldsymbol{w} = \boldsymbol{h}(\boldsymbol{\chi})$ in Fig. 1. To simplify notation, let $\mathcal{E}(\chi; r) := \mathsf{Enc}([\chi]_1; r)^\top \in \mathbb{G}_1^2$ be a transposed ciphertext. Let $\mathcal{E}(\boldsymbol{T}(\boldsymbol{\chi}))$ (resp., $\mathcal{E}(\boldsymbol{h}(\boldsymbol{\chi}))$) denote an element-wise (transposed) encryption of $\boldsymbol{T}(\boldsymbol{\chi})$ (resp., $\boldsymbol{h}(\boldsymbol{\chi})$), where χ_i is encrypted by using randomizer r_i (that is, χ_i is "replaced" by $[\mathbf{ct}_i]_1^\top$) and constants are encrypted by using the randomizer 0. We define $[\boldsymbol{\Gamma}(\mathrm{x})]_1$ and $[\boldsymbol{\theta}(\mathrm{x})]_1$ as follows:

$$[\boldsymbol{\Gamma}(\mathrm{x})]_1 = (\mathcal{E}(\boldsymbol{T}(\boldsymbol{\chi})) \| \mathcal{E}(\mathbf{0}_{d\times d}, \boldsymbol{I}_d)) \in \mathbb{G}_2^{2d\times(2d-1)} , \quad [\boldsymbol{\theta}(\mathrm{x})]_1 = \mathcal{E}(\boldsymbol{h}(\boldsymbol{\chi})) \in \mathbb{G}_1^{2d} . \tag{3}$$

Thus, $[\boldsymbol{\Gamma}]_1 \boldsymbol{w}^* = [\boldsymbol{\theta}]_1$ is an "encrypted" version of $\boldsymbol{T}(\boldsymbol{\chi})\boldsymbol{w} = \boldsymbol{h}(\boldsymbol{\chi})$, where $[\boldsymbol{\Gamma}]_1$ contains additional columns and $\boldsymbol{w}^*$ contains additional rows (compared to $\boldsymbol{w}$) to take into account the randomizers used to encrypt χ_i. Note that $\mathcal{E}(\boldsymbol{C}(\boldsymbol{\chi})) = \mathcal{E}(\sum \boldsymbol{P}_k \chi_k + \boldsymbol{Q}; \sum \boldsymbol{P}_k r_k)$.

Example 1. Let $F(X) = (X-0)(X-1)$, and thus $d = 2$. Recall that then $\boldsymbol{C}(\chi) = \begin{pmatrix} \chi & -1 \\ 0 & \chi-1 \end{pmatrix}$ and thus $\boldsymbol{T}(\chi) = \begin{pmatrix} -1 \\ \chi-1 \end{pmatrix}$ and $\boldsymbol{h}(\chi) = \begin{pmatrix} \chi \\ 0 \end{pmatrix}$. Since $\mathsf{Enc}([0]_1; 1) = [1, \mathsf{sk}]_1$ and $\mathsf{Enc}([0]_1; 0) = [0, 0]_1$, Eq. (3) results in

$$[\boldsymbol{\Gamma}]_1 = \begin{pmatrix} \mathcal{E}(-1;0) & \| & \mathcal{E}(0;1)\ \mathcal{E}(0;0) \\ \mathcal{E}(\chi-1;r) & \| & \mathcal{E}(0;0)\ \mathcal{E}(0;1) \end{pmatrix} = \begin{bmatrix} 0 & \| & 1 & 0 \\ -1 & \| & \mathsf{sk} & 0 \\ \mathsf{ct}_1 & \| & 0 & 1 \\ \mathsf{ct}_2 - 1 & \| & 0 & \mathsf{sk} \end{bmatrix}_1 \in \mathbb{G}_1^{4\times 3} , \quad [\boldsymbol{\theta}]_1 = \begin{bmatrix} \mathsf{ct}_1 \\ \mathsf{ct}_2 \\ 0 \\ 0 \end{bmatrix}_1 .$$

A variation of this $[\boldsymbol{\Gamma}, \boldsymbol{\theta}]_1$ was given in [5,9]. To motivate Theorem 2, note that $w_1^* = w = -\chi$ is a solution of $\boldsymbol{T}(\chi) w_1^* = \boldsymbol{h}(\chi)$. Setting $\hat{\boldsymbol{w}} := (w_2^* \| w_3^*)^\top = r\begin{pmatrix} 1 \\ -w_1^* \end{pmatrix} = r\begin{pmatrix} 1 \\ \chi \end{pmatrix}$ results in $\boldsymbol{\Gamma}\boldsymbol{w}^* - \boldsymbol{\theta} = (0 \| 0 \| 0 \| -\chi(\chi-1))^\top$, which is equal to $\mathbf{0}_4$ iff $\chi \in \{0, 1\}$.

Theorem 2. $\mathcal{L}_{\mathsf{pk},F} = \mathcal{L}_{\boldsymbol{\Gamma},\boldsymbol{\theta}}$.

In the full version [10], we will give two more (lengthy) examples to illustrate how $\boldsymbol{w}^*$ is chosen.

Handling Non-principal Ideals. Assume $\mathfrak{I}(\mathcal{A})$ has a generating set $(F_1, \dots, F_\tau)$ for $\tau > 1$, and that for each F_i, we have constructed the language parameter $\boldsymbol{\Gamma}_i, \boldsymbol{\theta}_i$. We can then construct the language parameter for $\mathcal{L}_{\mathsf{pk},\mathcal{A}}$ by using the well-known concatenation operation, setting $\boldsymbol{\Gamma} = \begin{pmatrix} \boldsymbol{\Gamma}_1 & \dots & 0 \\ \dots & \dots & \dots \\ 0 & \dots & \boldsymbol{\Gamma}_\tau \end{pmatrix}$ and $\boldsymbol{\theta} = \begin{pmatrix} \boldsymbol{\theta}_1 \\ \dots \\ \boldsymbol{\theta}_\tau \end{pmatrix}$.

On the Couteau-Hartmann Disjunction. In the full version [10], we describe the Couteau-Hartmann disjunction that results in $\boldsymbol{\Gamma}$ of size $(3d-1)\times(3d-2)$ and compare it to Eq. (3). For the sake of completeness, we also reprove the efficiency of the CHM NIZK from [9].

9.2 Efficiency of Set-Membership NIZKs: Comparisons

In Table 1 we give a concrete efficiency comparison in the case of set-membership. This is motivated by the fact that this is probably the most complex language for which [9] provides a concrete NIZK with which we can compare our results. Because of the still large dimensions of $\boldsymbol{\Gamma}$, using the CHM Σ-protocol as in [9] for $\mathcal{L}_{\boldsymbol{\Gamma},\boldsymbol{\theta}} = \mathcal{L}_{\mathsf{pk},F}$ has quite a big overhead. Thus, the NIZK in Lemma 7 is quite a bit more efficient. However, it compares favorably to [9]. In the following lemma, we state its efficiency.

Lemma 8. *Let F be a univariate degree-d polynomial and let $\boldsymbol{C}(\boldsymbol{X})$ be the $\mathsf{abp}_{\mathsf{path}}$-based QDR of F from Sect. 6.1. Let $[\boldsymbol{\Gamma}]_1$ be constructed as in Eq. (3). Then, the CHM NIZK argument requires $(5d-3)\mathfrak{e}_1 + 4d\mathfrak{e}_2$ from the prover, $7d-1$ pairings from the verifier, and $4d-1$ group elements.*

Note that the computation of the language parameters $\boldsymbol{\Gamma}, \boldsymbol{\theta}$ induces some cost. However, this computation is usually done once in advance. It is also not expensive, both in the case of the new NIZK and the CHM NIZK [9] requiring one to compute $[\xi_i]_1$ for each root ξ_i.

9.3 GL-SPHFs for Algebraic Sets

We give an example of GL-SPHFs (Gennaro-Lindell smooth projective hash functions, [17]) based on the new $\mathtt{lpar} = (\boldsymbol{\Gamma}, \boldsymbol{\theta})$. We refer the reader to [3,5,13] for a formal definition of GL-SPHFs. Briefly, recall that an SPHF is defined for a language parameter $\mathtt{lpar}$ and associated language $\mathcal{L}_{\mathtt{lpar}}$. A SPHF consists of an algorithm $\mathsf{hashkg}(\mathtt{lpar})$ to generate the private hashing key hk, an algorithm $\mathsf{projkg}(\mathtt{lpar}, \mathsf{hk})$ to generate a public projection key hp from hk, and two different hashing algorithms: $\mathsf{hash}(\mathtt{lpar}, \mathsf{hk}, \mathtt{x})$ that constructs an hash H, given the input $\mathtt{x}$ and hk, and $\mathsf{projhash}(\mathtt{lpar}, \mathsf{hp}, \mathtt{x}, \mathtt{w})$ that constructs a projection hash pH, given the input $\mathtt{x}$ and its witness $\mathtt{w}$. It is required that (1) $\mathsf{H} = \mathsf{pH}$ when $\mathtt{x} \in \mathcal{L}_{\mathtt{lpar}}$, and that (2) H looks random when $\mathtt{x} \notin \mathcal{L}_{\mathtt{lpar}}$, given $(\mathtt{lpar}, \mathsf{hp}, \mathtt{x})$.

In the GL-SPHFs [17], $\mathtt{lpar}$ and the projection key hp can depend on $\mathtt{x}$, while in other types of SPHFs, $\mathtt{x}$ is only chosen after $\mathtt{lpar}$ and hp are fixed. In the "DVS-based" constructions of SPHFs of [5], one starts with $[\boldsymbol{\Gamma}]_1 \in \mathbb{G}_1^{n \times t}$ and $[\boldsymbol{\theta}]_1 \in \mathbb{G}_1^n$ that may or may not depend on $\mathtt{x} = [\boldsymbol{\Gamma}]_1 \mathtt{w}$. One samples a random $\mathsf{hk} = \boldsymbol{\alpha} \leftarrow_{\$} \mathbb{Z}_p^n$, and sets $\mathsf{hp} \leftarrow \boldsymbol{\alpha}^\top [\boldsymbol{\Gamma}]_1$. For $\mathtt{x} = [\boldsymbol{\Gamma}]_1 \mathtt{w}$, one computes $\mathsf{pH} = \mathsf{projhash}(\mathtt{lpar}, \mathsf{hp}, \mathtt{x}, \mathtt{w}) \leftarrow \mathsf{hp} \cdot \mathtt{w}$ and $\mathsf{H} = \mathsf{hash}(\mathtt{lpar}, \mathsf{hk}, \mathtt{x}) \leftarrow \mathsf{hk} \cdot \mathtt{x}$.

For any $\mathcal{A}(\mathcal{J})$ for which the NIZK of Sect. 4 is efficient, one can also construct an efficient SPHF by constructing $\boldsymbol{\Gamma}$ and $\boldsymbol{\theta}$ as in Eq. (3). In the full version [10], we will describe a GL-SPHF for the language of elliptic curve points.

10 On Falsifiability of CED

In the current paper, we significantly expand the class of languages for which the Couteau-Hartmann framework allows for the construction of efficient NIZKs. However, for many of these languages, the underlying variant of the CED assumption is not falsifiable. At first sight, even though the Couteau-Hartmann framework leads to particularly compact NIZKs, relying on a non-falsifiable assumption seems to limit the interest of the result severely: if one is willing to rely on non-falsifiable in the first place, then there are countless pairing-based SNARGs and SNARKs which will achieve much more compact proofs (albeit the prover cost will be much higher in general).

Next, we discuss the falsifiability of the CED assumption. In Sect. 10.1, we study the falsifiable CED case, by clarifying for which languages there exist (algebraic) polynomial-time algorithms to check $F(\chi) = 0$. In particular, we point out that for many examples of the current paper, the CED assumption is already falsifiable. After that, we concentrate on the cases when this is not so.

In Sect. 10.2, we show that despite their unfalsifiability, CED assumptions are fundamentally different in nature from knowledge-of-exponent assumptions (which underlie the security of existing SNARK candidates). We will prove that CED assumptions are implied by a new but natural *gap assumption* [30] that KerMDH stays secure in $\mathbb{G}_2$ even given a CDH oracle in $\mathbb{G}_1$.

In Sect. 10.3, we modify our NIZKs to make the CED assumption falsifiable by letting the prover additionally encrypt input elements in $\mathbb{G}_2$. If the polynomial F is quadratic, then the soundness reduction can use them to check whether the prover's inputs belong to the language or not, thus making CED falsifiable. Since each gate of an arithmetic circuit is a quadratic polynomial, one can construct a NIZK for arithmetic circuits under a falsifiable assumption. The reason why we do not start with this solution is the added cost. First, the additional elements make the argument longer. Second, as probably expected, one cannot use Elgamal but has to use the less efficient DLIN cryptosystem [6].

Thus, if CED is falsifiable, then one can use an Elgamal-based solution. Otherwise, one has a security-efficiency tradeoff: one can either rely on a non-falsifiable gap-assumption or use a slightly less efficient DLIN-based falsifiable NIZK.

10.1 On Languages for Which CED is Falsifiable

The CED assumption is falsifiable if there exists an efficient verification algorithm $\mathsf{V_f}$, such that given an arbitrary ciphertext tuple $\mathbf{x} = [\mathbf{ct}_1, \ldots, \mathbf{ct}_\nu]_1$ and an sk-dependent trapdoor $\mathbf{T}$, $\mathsf{V_f}(\mathsf{p}, \mathsf{pk}, \mathsf{x}, \mathbf{T})$ can efficiently check whether $\mathsf{Dec_{sk}}([\mathbf{ct}_1, \ldots, \mathbf{ct}_\nu]_1) \in \mathcal{L}_{\mathsf{pk},F}$. As in the rest of the paper, we take $\mathbf{T} = \mathsf{sk}$. Thus, given a ciphertext tuple $[\mathbf{ct}]_1$, $\mathsf{V_f}$ can use sk to decrypt it and obtain the plaintext $[\chi]_1$. $\mathsf{V_f}$ then forms the QDR $[\boldsymbol{C}(\chi)]_1$ from $[\chi]_1$. If $F(\chi) \neq 0$ (that is, $\mathsf{x} \notin \mathcal{L}_{\mathsf{pk},F}$), then $[\boldsymbol{C}(\chi)]_1$ has full rank. Otherwise, it has rank $< \ell$. Thus, if $F(\boldsymbol{X})$ is such that it is possible to check efficiently whether $F(\chi) = 0$, given $[\chi]_1$, we can construct an efficient falsifiability check $\mathsf{V_f}$. (Note that this approach is different from Couteau-Hartmann, who required $\mathbf{T}$ to be a matrix.)

First, if $|\mathcal{A}| = \mathsf{poly}(\lambda)$, then $\mathsf{V_f}$ just checks if $[\chi]_1$ is equal to $[\boldsymbol{a}]_1$ for any $\boldsymbol{a} \in \mathcal{A}$. Thus, the NIZK for the univariate case in Sect. 6.1 and the NIZK for boolean circuits in Sect. 8.1 rely on a falsifiable CED assumption. (This assumes that all polynomials have degree $\mathsf{poly}(\lambda)$, and the circuits are polynomial-size.) In general, the NIZK in the case of non-principal ideal, Sect. 8, is based on falsifiable CED iff $\mathcal{A}(\mathfrak{I})$ has polynomial size.

The outliers are the cases of principal ideals of multivariate polynomials (since then $|\mathcal{A}(\mathfrak{I})|$ can be exponential as in the set of points (X, Y) on an elliptic curve) and some instances of non-principal ideals where $|\mathcal{A}(\mathfrak{I})|$ is super-polynomial. In the latter case, we can clarify the situation further. Namely, given a generating set $\langle F_1, \ldots, F_\tau \rangle$, by Bézout's theorem, $\mathcal{A}(\mathfrak{I})$ has at most size $\prod \deg F_i$. Assuming each $\deg F_i$ is $\mathsf{poly}(\lambda)$, $\prod \deg F_i$ is super-polynomial if $\tau = \omega(1)$. Thus, constant-size set-membership arguments in Sect. 8.2 or aCSPs for constant-size arithmetic circuits in Sect. 8.1 are based on falsifiable CED. However, range proofs and superconstant-size arithmetic circuits are based on non-falsifiable CED.

The super-polynomial size of $\mathcal{A}(\mathfrak{I})$ does not mean that efficient $\mathsf{V_f}$ does not exist. E.g., assume $F_j(\boldsymbol{X}) = \prod_i (X_i - s_j)$ for each j. The ideal $\langle F_j \rangle$, for a single j, has exponential size. However, given $[\chi]_1$, one can check if $F_j(\chi) = 0$ by checking if $\chi_i = s_j$ for some j. This can be generalized to the case F_j is a product of affine multivariate polynomials $\sum a_{ik} X_k + b_{ik}$. Clearly, $F(\chi) = 0$ iff one of its affine factors is equal to 0. So, $\mathsf{V_f}$ can check if there exists an i such that $\sum a_{ik} [\chi_k]_1 + b_{ik} [1]_1 = [0]_1$. Generalizing this, one can efficiently establish whether $[\boldsymbol{C}]_1$ is full-rank if the Leibniz formula for the determinant, $\det(\boldsymbol{C}) = \sum_{\sigma \in S_n} (\mathrm{sgn}(\sigma) \prod_{i=1}^n C_{i,\sigma_i})$, contains only one non-zero addend.

On the other hand, since $\mathsf{V_f}$ has only access to $[\chi]_1$, there is not much hope that the CED assumption is falsifiable if F is a product of irreducible polynomials, such that at least one of them has a total degree greater than one, unless we add some additional, carefully chosen, elements to the proof for this purpose. In the general case, this is not efficient, but the number of additional needed elements might not be prohibitive for some applications.

Finally, the falsifiability of CED depends only on the polynomial F and not on the specific $\boldsymbol{C}$. One could find two different CED-matrices $\boldsymbol{C}_i$ for F, such that the first one results in a more efficient NIZK argument, but the second one has a specific structure enabling one to construct efficient $\mathsf{V_f}$.

10.2 CED as a Gap Assumption

We show that CED follows from a new gap assumption, which states that given $\mathsf{p} \leftarrow \mathsf{Pgen}(1^\lambda)$, even if one finds some structural properties in $\mathbb{G}_1$ that allows breaking CDH over this group, this does in general not guarantee an efficient algorithm for solving KerMDH [28] over the other group $\mathbb{G}_2$. More formally:

Definition 3. *Assume that the (exponential-time) oracle* $\mathcal{O}([x,y]_1)$ *outputs* $[xy]_1$. $\mathcal{D}_{\ell-1,\mathsf{k}}$-$\mathsf{CDH}_{\mathbb{G}_1}$$\not\Rightarrow$$\mathsf{KerMDH}_{\mathbb{G}_2}$ *holds relative to* Pgen, *if* $\forall$ *PPT* $\mathcal{A}$,

$$\Pr\left[\mathsf{p} \leftarrow \mathsf{Pgen}(1^\lambda); \boldsymbol{D} \leftarrow_{\$} \mathcal{D}_{\ell-1,\mathsf{k}}; [\boldsymbol{c}]_{3-\iota} \leftarrow \mathcal{A}^{\mathcal{O}}(\mathsf{p}, [\boldsymbol{D}]_\iota) : \boldsymbol{D}^\top \boldsymbol{c} = \boldsymbol{0}_\mathsf{k} \wedge \boldsymbol{c} \neq \boldsymbol{0}_{\ell-1}\right] \approx_\lambda 0 \ .$$

Theorem 3. *Let $\ell - 1, \mathsf{k} \in \mathbb{N}$. If the $\mathcal{D}_\mathsf{k}$-$\mathsf{CDH}_{\mathbb{G}_1} \not\Rightarrow \mathsf{KerMDH}_{\mathbb{G}_2}$ assumption holds relative to* Pgen, *then $\mathcal{D}_\mathsf{k}$-$(\ell - 1)$-CED holds in $\mathbb{G}_1$ relative to* Pgen.

Note that in particular, this re-proves the result of [9] that CED is secure in the generic bilinear group model (since a CDH oracle in $\mathbb{G}_1$ does not help to break any assumption in $\mathbb{G}_2$ in the generic bilinear group model).

10.3 DLIN-Based NIZK Based on Falsifiable CED

While constructing a Sub-ZK QA-NIZK, [2] had to check efficiently if $\boldsymbol{C}$ is invertible, given only $[\boldsymbol{C}]_1$. We will next study whether we can apply their technique. It is not straightforward to apply it since their case is somewhat different: there, $\boldsymbol{C}$ is a $\mathsf{k} \times \mathsf{k}$ (in particular, $\mathsf{k} \in \{1, 2\}$) public matrix sampled from $\mathcal{D}_\mathsf{k}$ and then given as a part of the CRS. In our case, $\boldsymbol{C}$ can have an arbitrary $\mathsf{poly}(\lambda)$ dimension, and it is reconstructed from the input to the NIZK argument.

To explain the technique of [2], consider the case $[\boldsymbol{C}]_1 \in \mathbb{G}_1^{2\times 2}$. [2] added to the CRS certain additional elements in $\mathbb{G}_2$ (namely, $[C_{11}, C_{12}]_2$), such that it became possible to check publicly (by using pairings) whether $\det \boldsymbol{C} = 0$ by checking whether $[C_{11}]_1 \bullet [1]_2 = [1]_1 \bullet [C_{11}]_2$, $[C_{12}]_1 \bullet [1]_2 = [1]_1 \bullet [C_{12}]_2$, and $[C_{22}]_1 \bullet [C_{11}]_2 = [C_{21}]_1 \bullet [C_{12}]_2$. One cost of publishing the additional elements in [2] was that it changed the assumption they used from KerMDH to the less standard SKerMDH assumption [19]. As we see next, we have to use the DLIN cryptosystem [6] instead of the Elgamal cryptosystem. However, as a result, we will obtain a NIZK for any F, computable by a poly-size arithmetic circuit, sound under a falsifiable CED assumption. Another benefit of it is to demonstrate that our framework is not restricted to Elgamal encryptions.

Next, we show how to construct a NIZK, based on a falsifiable CED assumption, for the polynomial $F(X, Y) = X^2 - Y$. We ask the prover to also encrypt X in $\mathbb{G}_2$. In the soundness reduction, a CED-adversary uses the latter, after decryption, to check whether $[X]_1 \bullet [X]_2 = [Y]_1 \bullet [1]_2$. We must ensure that the verifier only accepts the proof if $[X]_2$ is correct, i.e., $[X]_1 \bullet [1]_2 = [1]_1 \bullet [X]_2$. Since Elgamal is not secure given symmetric pairings, we cannot use the secret key or the same randomness in both groups. Hence, we use the DLIN encryption scheme (see the full version [10] for its definition). Given $\mathsf{sk} = (\mathsf{sk}_1, \mathsf{sk}_2)$ and $\mathsf{pk}_\iota = [1, \mathsf{sk}_1, \mathsf{sk}_2]_\iota$, we define $\mathtt{lpar} := (\mathsf{pk}_1, \mathsf{pk}_2, F)$. Then, $\mathcal{L}_{\mathtt{lpar}} := \{([\mathbf{ct}_1, \mathbf{ct}_2]_1, [\mathbf{ct}_1]_2)\}$, where $[\mathbf{ct}_1]_\iota = \mathsf{Enc}_\iota(X; r_1, r_2) = [r_1 \mathsf{sk}_1, r_2 \mathsf{sk}_2, X + r_1 + r_2]_\iota$ and $[\mathbf{ct}_2]_1 = \mathsf{Enc}_1(Y; r_3, r_4) = [r_3 \mathsf{sk}_1, r_4 \mathsf{sk}_2, Y + r_3 + r_4]_1$. We prove that $[\mathbf{ct}_1, \mathbf{ct}_2]_1$ are encryptions of X and Y such that $X^2 = Y$, by using the QDR $\boldsymbol{C}(X, Y) = \left(\begin{smallmatrix} X & -1 \\ -Y & X \end{smallmatrix}\right)$. The use of the DLIN encryption scheme just affects the efficiency and the communication size of the protocol. In addition, one can check that $[\mathbf{ct}_1]_1$ and $[\mathbf{ct}_1]_2$ encrypt the same X in two different groups by checking that $[\mathbf{ct}_1]_1 \bullet [1]_2 = [1]_1 \bullet [\mathbf{ct}_1]_2$.

Since the DLIN encryption is doubly-homomorphic like Elgamal, then the argument of Sect. 4.1 stays essentially the same, with Elgamal encryptions replaced by DLIN encryptions, and the dimensions of randomizers and ciphertexts increasing slightly. In the soundness proof, given that the prover also outputs $\mathsf{Enc}_2(X; r_1, r_2)$, the constructed CED adversary obtains plaintexts $[X, Y]_1, [Z]_2$ and, then can efficiently verify if the statement $X^2 = Y$ holds.

Combining this idea with the rest of our framework, we can construct a NIZK for any language of DLIN-encryptions for any F, based on a falsifiable CED assumption. This is since one can check that $F = 0$ by checking that an arithmetic circuit evaluates to 0, and each gate of an arithmetic circuit evaluates a quadratic function. For example, to prove that $Y^2 = X^3 + aX + b$, one can encrypt Y, Y', X, X', and X'', and then prove that $Y' = Y^2$, $X' = X^2$, $X'' = XX'$, and $Y' = X'' + aX + b$.

Acknowledgment. Geoffroy Couteau was partially supported by the ANR SCENE.

References

1. Abdalla, M., Benhamouda, F., Pointcheval, D.: Disjunctions for hash proof systems: new constructions and applications. In: Oswald, E., Fischlin, M. (eds.) EUROCRYPT 2015, Part II. LNCS, vol. 9057, pp. 69–100. Springer, Heidelberg (2015). https://doi.org/10.1007/978-3-662-46803-6_3
2. Abdolmaleki, B., Lipmaa, H., Siim, J., Zając, M.: On QA-NIZK in the BPK model. In: Kiayias, A., Kohlweiss, M., Wallden, P., Zikas, V. (eds.) PKC 2020, Part I. LNCS, vol. 12110, pp. 590–620. Springer, Cham (2020). https://doi.org/10.1007/978-3-030-45374-9_20
3. Ben Hamouda-Guichoux, F.: Diverse modules and zero-knowledge. Ph.D. thesis, PSL Research University (2016)
4. Ben-Sasson, E., Chiesa, A., Tromer, E., Virza, M.: Scalable zero knowledge via cycles of elliptic curves. In: Garay, J.A., Gennaro, R. (eds.) CRYPTO 2014, Part II. LNCS, vol. 8617, pp. 276–294. Springer, Heidelberg (2014). https://doi.org/10.1007/978-3-662-44381-1_16
5. Benhamouda, F., Blazy, O., Chevalier, C., Pointcheval, D., Vergnaud, D.: New techniques for SPHFs and efficient one-round PAKE protocols. In: Canetti, R., Garay, J.A. (eds.) CRYPTO 2013, Part I. LNCS, vol. 8042, pp. 449–475. Springer, Heidelberg (2013). https://doi.org/10.1007/978-3-642-40041-4_25
6. Boneh, D., Boyen, X., Shacham, H.: Short group signatures. In: Franklin, M. (ed.) CRYPTO 2004. LNCS, vol. 3152, pp. 41–55. Springer, Heidelberg (2004). https://doi.org/10.1007/978-3-540-28628-8_3
7. Buchberger, B.: An algorithm for finding the basis elements of the residue class ring of a zero dimensional polynomial ideal. Ph.D. thesis, University of Innsbruck (1965)
8. Chaidos, P., Couteau, G.: Efficient designated-verifier non-interactive zero-knowledge proofs of knowledge. In: Nielsen, J.B., Rijmen, V. (eds.) EUROCRYPT 2018, Part III. LNCS, vol. 10822, pp. 193–221. Springer, Cham (2018). https://doi.org/10.1007/978-3-319-78372-7_7
9. Couteau, G., Hartmann, D.: Shorter non-interactive zero-knowledge arguments and ZAPs for algebraic languages. In: Micciancio, D., Ristenpart, T. (eds.) CRYPTO 2020, Part III. LNCS, vol. 12172, pp. 768–798. Springer, Cham (2020). https://doi.org/10.1007/978-3-030-56877-1_27
10. Couteau, G., Lipmaa, H., Parisella, R., Ødegaard, A.T.: Efficient NIZKs for Algebraic Sets. Technical report, IACR (2021)

11. Cox, D.A., Little, J., O'Shea, D.: Ideals, Varieties, and Algorithms: An Introduction to Computational Algebraic Geometry and Commutative Algebra. Undergraduate Texts in Mathematics, 4th edn. Springer, Heidelberg (2015)
12. Cramer, R., Damgård, I., Schoenmakers, B.: Proofs of partial knowledge and simplified design of witness hiding protocols. In: Desmedt, Y.G. (ed.) CRYPTO 1994. LNCS, vol. 839, pp. 174–187. Springer, Heidelberg (1994). https://doi.org/10.1007/3-540-48658-5_19
13. Cramer, R., Shoup, V.: Universal hash proofs and a paradigm for adaptive chosen ciphertext secure public-key encryption. In: Knudsen, L.R. (ed.) EUROCRYPT 2002. LNCS, vol. 2332, pp. 45–64. Springer, Heidelberg (2002). https://doi.org/10.1007/3-540-46035-7_4
14. Dickson, L.E.: Determination of all general homogeneous polynomials expressible as determinants with linear elements. Trans. Am. Math. Soc. **22**(2), 167–179 (1921)
15. Escala, A., Herold, G., Kiltz, E., Ràfols, C., Villar, J.: An algebraic framework for Diffie-Hellman assumptions. In: Canetti, R., Garay, J.A. (eds.) CRYPTO 2013, Part II. LNCS, vol. 8043, pp. 129–147. Springer, Heidelberg (2013). https://doi.org/10.1007/978-3-642-40084-1_8
16. Gennaro, R., Gentry, C., Parno, B., Raykova, M.: Quadratic span programs and succinct NIZKs without PCPs. In: Johansson, T., Nguyen, P.Q. (eds.) EUROCRYPT 2013. LNCS, vol. 7881, pp. 626–645. Springer, Heidelberg (2013). https://doi.org/10.1007/978-3-642-38348-9_37
17. Gennaro, R., Lindell, Y.: A framework for password-based authenticated key exchange. In: Biham, E. (ed.) EUROCRYPT 2003. LNCS, vol. 2656, pp. 524–543. Springer, Heidelberg (2003). https://doi.org/10.1007/3-540-39200-9_33. https://eprint.iacr.org/2003/032.ps.gz
18. Ghadafi, E., Smart, N.P., Warinschi, B.: Practical zero-knowledge proofs for circuit evaluation. In: Parker, M.G. (ed.) IMACC 2009. LNCS, vol. 5921, pp. 469–494. Springer, Heidelberg (2009). https://doi.org/10.1007/978-3-642-10868-6_28
19. González, A., Hevia, A., Ràfols, C.: QA-NIZK arguments in asymmetric groups: new tools and new constructions. In: Iwata, T., Cheon, J.H. (eds.) ASIACRYPT 2015, Part I. LNCS, vol. 9452, pp. 605–629. Springer, Heidelberg (2015). https://doi.org/10.1007/978-3-662-48797-6_25
20. Groth, J., Ostrovsky, R., Sahai, A.: Non-interactive zaps and new techniques for NIZK. In: Dwork, C. (ed.) CRYPTO 2006. LNCS, vol. 4117, pp. 97–111. Springer, Heidelberg (2006). https://doi.org/10.1007/11818175_6
21. Groth, J., Sahai, A.: Efficient non-interactive proof systems for bilinear groups. In: Smart, N. (ed.) EUROCRYPT 2008. LNCS, vol. 4965, pp. 415–432. Springer, Heidelberg (2008). https://doi.org/10.1007/978-3-540-78967-3_24
22. Hoffmann, M., Klooß, M., Rupp, A.: Efficient zero-knowledge arguments in the discrete log setting, revisited. In: ACM CCS 2019, pp. 2093–2110 (2019)
23. Ishai, Y., Kushilevitz, E.: Randomizing polynomials: a new representation with applications to round-efficient secure computation. In: 41st FOCS, pp. 294–304 (2000)
24. Ishai, Y., Kushilevitz, E.: Perfect constant-round secure computation via perfect randomizing polynomials. In: Widmayer, P., Eidenbenz, S., Triguero, F., Morales, R., Conejo, R., Hennessy, M. (eds.) ICALP 2002. LNCS, vol. 2380, pp. 244–256. Springer, Heidelberg (2002). https://doi.org/10.1007/3-540-45465-9_22
25. Kosba, A.E., et al.: CØCØ: A Framework for Building Composable Zero-Knowledge Proofs. Technical Report 2015/1093, International Association for Cryptologic Research (2015). https://ia.cr/2015/1093. Accessed 9 Apr 2017

26. Maurer, U.: Unifying zero-knowledge proofs of knowledge. In: Preneel, B. (ed.) AFRICACRYPT 2009. LNCS, vol. 5580, pp. 272–286. Springer, Heidelberg (2009). https://doi.org/10.1007/978-3-642-02384-2_17
27. Möller, H.M., Buchberger, B.: The construction of multivariate polynomials with preassigned zeros. In: Calmet, J. (ed.) EUROCAM 1982. LNCS, vol. 144, pp. 24–31. Springer, Heidelberg (1982). https://doi.org/10.1007/3-540-11607-9_3
28. Morillo, P., Ràfols, C., Villar, J.L.: The kernel matrix Diffie-Hellman assumption. In: Cheon, J.H., Takagi, T. (eds.) ASIACRYPT 2016, Part I. LNCS, vol. 10031, pp. 729–758. Springer, Heidelberg (2016). https://doi.org/10.1007/978-3-662-53887-6_27
29. Nisan, N.: Lower bounds for non-commutative computation (extended abstract). In: 23rd ACM STOC, pp. 410–418 (1991)
30. Okamoto, T., Pointcheval, D.: The gap-problems: a new class of problems for the security of cryptographic schemes. In: Kim, K. (ed.) PKC 2001. LNCS, vol. 1992, pp. 104–118. Springer, Heidelberg (2001). https://doi.org/10.1007/3-540-44586-2_8
31. Pass, R.: Unprovable security of perfect NIZK and non-interactive non-malleable commitments. In: Sahai, A. (ed.) TCC 2013. LNCS, vol. 7785, pp. 334–354. Springer, Heidelberg (2013). https://doi.org/10.1007/978-3-642-36594-2_19
32. Plaumann, D., Sturmfels, B., Vinzant, C.: Computing linear matrix representations of Helton-Vinnikov curves. Math. Methods Syst. Optim. Control Oper. Theory **222**, 259–277 (2012)
33. Ràfols, C.: Stretching Groth-Sahai: NIZK proofs of partial satisfiability. In: Dodis, Y., Nielsen, J.B. (eds.) TCC 2015. LNCS, vol. 9015, pp. 247–276. Springer, Heidelberg (2015). https://doi.org/10.1007/978-3-662-46497-7_10

Theory

Bit Security as Computational Cost for Winning Games with High Probability

Shun Watanabe[1] and Kenji Yasunaga[2](✉)

[1] Tokyo University of Agriculture and Technology, Tokyo, Japan
shunwata@cc.tuat.ac.jp
[2] Tokyo Institute of Technology, Tokyo, Japan
yasunaga@c.titech.ac.jp

Abstract. We introduce a novel framework for quantifying the bit security of security games. Our notion is defined with an operational meaning that a λ-bit secure game requires a total computational cost of 2^λ for winning the game with high probability, e.g., 0.99. We define the bit security both for search-type and decision-type games. Since we identify that these two types of games should be structurally different, we treat them differently but define the bit security using the unified framework to guarantee the same operational interpretation. The key novelty of our notion of bit security is to employ two types of adversaries: inner adversary and outer adversary. While the inner adversary plays a "usual" security game, the outer adversary invokes the inner adversary many times to amplify the winning probability for the security game. We find from our framework that the bit security for decision games can be characterized by the information measure called the *Rényi divergence* of order 1/2 of the inner adversary. The conventional "advantage," defined as the probability of winning the game, characterizes our bit security for search-type games. We present several security reductions in our framework for justifying our notion of bit security. Many of our results quantitatively match the results for the bit security notion proposed by Micciancio and Walter in 2018. In this sense, our bit security strengthens the previous notion of bit security by adding an operational meaning. A difference from their work is that, in our framework, the Goldreich-Levin theorem gives an optimal reduction only for "balanced" adversaries who output binary values in a balanced manner.

Keywords: Bit security · Rényi divergence · Goldreich-Levin theorem

1 Introduction

The security levels of cryptographic primitives are usually measured by the attacker's cost for breaking them. We say a primitive P has λ-bit security if the attacker needs to perform 2^λ operations to break it. The idea behind the notion is that an ideal scheme should be secure as if the only effective attack is the brute-force search of the λ-bit secret key. The attacker can find the key by checking each candidate roughly 2^λ times or randomly guessing a key, which is

M. Tibouchi and H. Wang (Eds.): ASIACRYPT 2021, LNCS 13092, pp. 161–188, 2021.
https://doi.org/10.1007/978-3-030-92078-4_6

correct with probability $2^{-\lambda}$. In either way, the attacker needs a computational cost of roughly 2^λ operations to find the correct key. There is a trade-off between the computational cost T and the success probability ϵ for finding the key. Thus, a λ-bit secure primitive should satisfy the relation $T/\epsilon \geq 2^\lambda$ for any attacks. The quantity $\log_2(T/\epsilon)$ has been used to give an upper bound on bit security.

The above notion of bit security only captures *search* primitives such as one-way functions and signature schemes, where the attacker tries to find the correct answer from a wide range of the solution space. We also have another type of primitives, called *decision* primitives, such as pseudorandom generators and encryption schemes, where the attacker tries to distinguish two possible cases. Since the quantity of $\log_2(T/\epsilon)$ has an operational meaning only for search-type games, the corresponding notion for decision primitives has not been established.

Micciancio and Walter [19] introduced a unified framework for measuring bit security that captures both search and decision primitives. They discussed the validity of their definition by giving several results, including the tightness of the Goldreich-Levin hard-core predicate and a simple reduction of one-wayness of pseudorandom generators. Results obtained under their framework are compatible with what has been believed in the cryptography community. Notably, their bit security definition reflects the folklore (cf. [16]), claiming that the bit security of decision games is reciprocal of the "square" of the advantage. In the framework of [19], they consider a security game in which an attacker is allowed to output a failure symbol $\perp$; the advantage of the attacker is defined as the ratio between the mutual information and the Shannon entropy of random variables induced by the security game. However, these concepts seem to be introduced without satisfactory explanation. The security of cryptographic primitives cannot be verified by experiments, unlike physics. Thus, the compatibility of the results is not sufficient enough to justify the notion. It is desirable to build a security definition that has a firm operational meaning.

In this work, we revisit a theoretical treatment of bit security and introduce a new notion of bit security with an operational meaning. Specifically, we define *bit security* as the computational cost for winning the security game with high probability. We apply the same interpretation to both search and decision primitives but distinguish them since they should be structurally different. Below we explain the underlying idea of our framework of bit security.

In cryptography, the security of a primitive is usually defined through the security game. The game is played by an attacker and defines the success probability ϵ of the attacker. For example, in the security of one-way function f, an attacker is given $f(x)$ for random x and tries to output x' satisfying $f(x) = f(x')$. When the success probability is at most ϵ for any attackers with computational cost at most T, we say that f is (T, ϵ)-secure one-way function. Assume there is an attacker A that, given $f(x)$, can output x' with $f(x) = f(x')$ with computational cost T and success probability ϵ. What can we say about the cost of breaking the one-wayness? Suppose we run A in total N times, where A receives an independently generated challenge $f(x_i)$ for the ith time. The total cost is NT, and the success probability for finding a pair $(f(x_i), x'_i)$ satisfying $f(x'_i) = f(x_i)$ can be increased to roughly $N\epsilon$. Thus, it suffices to run A about

$1/\epsilon$ times to break one-wayness with high probability. The total cost of T/ϵ corresponds with the quantity described above. Hence, if f is a λ-bit secure one-way function, it must satisfy $T/\epsilon \geq 2^\lambda$ for any attackers.

The above formulation of bit security can be adopted for other search primitives. The success probability for those primitives is designed to be sufficiently small, and it may be increased by running the base attacker repeatedly. For *decision* primitives, the success probability of an attacker is designed to be close to 1/2. In a security game of a pseudorandom generator $g : \{0,1\}^\ell \to \{0,1\}^m$, an attacker tries to distinguish whether a given bit string y is from an output $g(x)$ for random $x \in \{0,1\}^\ell$ or a random sampling from $\{0,1\}^m$. A game is such that, after choosing a bit $u \in \{0,1\}$ randomly, the attacker obtains $y = g(x)$ if $u = 0$, and random $y \in \{0,1\}^m$ if $u = 1$, and finally outputs $u' \in \{0,1\}$ as a guess. The attack succeeds if $u' = u$. We usually require that, for any attacker with cost T, the success probability ϵ is bounded by $\epsilon \leq 1/2 + \delta$ for small $\delta \geq 0$.

Although the success probability for decision primitives should be close to 1/2, it can be amplified by running the base attacker repeatedly and making the final decision from the output sequence. Thus, bit security can be defined similarly as the computational cost for winning the security game with high probability. Note that there is a structural difference between games for search and decision primitives. For search primitives, an attacker receives independently generated challenges in repeated games and wins the game if it finds any successful solution. For decision primitives, an attacker needs to determine the secret bit u, which is consistent in every repeated game.

1.1 Our Contribution

We define a notion of bit security based on the above idea. Specifically, we define a game in which two types of adversaries exist. The first adversary A, called an *inner* adversary, is an attacker for the "usual" security game. The second adversary B, called an *outer* adversary, invokes A certain times to amplify the final success probability $\epsilon_{A,B}$. The bit security is defined as (the logarithm base 2 of) the computational cost of (A, B) necessary for achieving $\epsilon_{A,B} \geq 0.99$.

The condition for success differs depending on the types of games. For decision games, the inner adversary A tries to distinguish two cases whether the secret bit u equals 0 or 1. The outer adversary also tries to distinguish the two cases by observing answers from A sufficiently many times. The success condition of (A, B) is that B outputs b with $b = u$. For search games, where a secret u is chosen from $\{0,1\}^n$ for $n > 1$, at the ith invocation of A by B, the challenge x_i is generated independently and sent to A. The pair (A, B) succeeds if at least one invocation of A could find the correct answer of the underlying security game. Thus, as long as A chooses a value from a finite solution space, the bit security takes a finite value in search games.

Suppose an adversary A runs in time T_A and achieves the success probability ϵ_A for some security game. For the search game, the advantage of A is usually defined to be $\mathsf{adv}^{\mathsf{srch}} = \epsilon_A$. Our bit security is roughly given by $\log_2 T_A + \log_2(1/\mathsf{adv}^{\mathsf{srch}}) + O(1)$. This is compatible with the well-accepted quantification of bit security in the literature.

On the other hand, for the decision game, the advantage of A is usually defined to be $\mathsf{adv}^{\mathrm{decn}} = 2\epsilon_A - 1$. Our main message of this paper is that the usual notion of advantage $\mathsf{adv}^{\mathrm{decn}}$ is useful only for a certain class of adversaries. More specifically, we introduce a class of adversaries that output in a "balanced" manner, referred to as β-balanced adversaries. For instance, the linear test of pseudorandom generators is β-balanced for $\beta = 1/2$ since it outputs 0 and 1 with equal probability when the instance is from a true random generator. For that class of adversary, we show that our bit security is roughly given by $\log_2 T_A + 2\log_2(1/\mathsf{adv}^{\mathrm{decn}}) + O(1)$. Thus, it is compatible with the folklore (cf. [16]) that the bit security of decision games is reciprocal of the square of the advantage. However, for general adversaries, we demonstrate that the bit security is characterized by the *Rényi advantage* $\mathsf{adv}_A^{\mathrm{Renyi}} = D_{1/2}(A_0 \| A_1)$, where $D_{1/2}$ is the Rényi divergence of order $1/2$ and A_u is the random variable of the output of A under the condition that u is the secret bit. This new notion of advantage is closely tied to the optimal exponential convergence of the error probability in the Bayesian hypothesis testing [5, Section 11.9]. Using the Rényi advantage, we show that our bit security is roughly given by $\log_2 T_A + \log_2(1/\mathsf{adv}_A^{\mathrm{Renyi}}) + O(1)$.

When we consider a security reduction of a decision game to the corresponding search game, it turns out that the use of the Rényi advantage instead of the advantage $\mathsf{adv}^{\mathrm{decn}}$ is crucial. As a concrete example, let us consider the case of proving that a λ-bit secure pseudorandom generator (PRG) implies a λ-bit secure one-way function (OWF). Suppose that there is an inner adversary A for the OWF with success probability ϵ_A. Then, using this adversary A, we can build an inner adversary A' for the PRG; this adversary A' outputs 0 only when A succeeds in inverting the OWF and thus is extremely biased. For such a biased adversary, it turns out that the Rényi advantage $\mathsf{adv}_A^{\mathrm{Renyi}}$ and the advantage $\mathsf{adv}^{\mathrm{decn}}$ are both $\Omega(\epsilon_A)$. Then, our estimate of the bit security using the Rényi advantage provides that the bit security of the PRG is upper bounded by $\log_2 T_A + \log_2(1/\epsilon_A) + O(1)$, which proves the desired contradiction. However, using the advantage $\mathsf{adv}^{\mathrm{decn}}$, the bit security of the PRG is only upper bounded by $\log_2 T_A + 2\log_2(1/\epsilon_A) + O(1)$, which does not prove the desired contradiction.

Using our framework, in addition to the above example of the PRG to the OWF, we present several other security reductions. For the distribution approximation problem (a.k.a. approximate samplers), we show that the approximation precision for preserving the bit security is essentially the same for search and decision primitives as long as the distributions are close enough in the *Hellinger distance*. It solves another peculiar problem raised in [19] that decision primitives may require more precise approximation than search primitives. Regarding the Goldreich-Levin hard-core predicate [9,10], we observe that their reduction is tight as long as we consider β-balanced attackers for the hard-core predicate. Concretely, if a one-way function $f : \{0,1\}^n \to \{0,1\}^m$ is λ-bit secure, then the inner product function $\sum_i x_i \cdot r_i \bmod 2$ is a $(\lambda - O(\log_2 n))$-bit secure hard-core predicate for function $g(x,r) = (f(x), r)$ against adversaries A satisfying $\min_x \Pr[A = x] = \Omega(1)$. We observe that the well-known reduction from the Computational Diffie-Hellman (CDH) problem to the Decisional Diffie-Hellman

(DDH) problem shows that if the DDH problem has λ-bit security, then the corresponding CDH problem has $(\lambda - O(1))$-bit security. Although the DDH assumption is stronger than the CDH assumption, our result implies that the DDH problem may not necessarily have quantitatively higher bit security. In addition, we give a quantitative relationship between the IND-CPA security and the one-wayness of encryption schemes. We show that if an encryption scheme is λ-bit secure IND-CPA and the message space is of size 2^λ, it has $(\lambda - O(1))$-bit secure one-wayness. Finally, we show that a hybrid argument for distinguishing distributions can be generally applied in our framework.

1.2 Related Work

Our study is inspired by the bit security framework introduced by Micciancio and Walter [19]. They first defined the advantage of adversary A using the mutual information and the Shannon entropy. Then, they observed that their advantage could be approximated by $\mathsf{adv}^{\mathrm{srch}}_{\mathrm{MW}} = \alpha\beta$ for search games and $\mathsf{adv}^{\mathrm{decn}}_{\mathrm{MW}} = \alpha(2\beta - 1)^2$ for decision games, where α is the probability that A outputs values other than $\perp$ and β is the conditional probability that A succeeds in the game under the condition that A outputs values other than $\perp$. Their bit security is defined as $\min_A \log_2(T_A/\mathsf{adv}_{\mathrm{MW}})$, where T_A is the measure of resources of A. Their notion could solve peculiar problems in PRG and approximate samplers. However, it is not easy to understand the quantitative meaning of their bit security. Since the notion of bit security was introduced to offer an easy-to-understand simple metric, our new notion of bit security would be more appealing. In our framework, if a security game has λ-bit security, the game requires a total computational cost of 2^λ to win the game with high probability.

In [26], the closeness in Hellinger distance was used for the distribution approximation problem in the bit security framework of [19]. Although we have not found concrete relations between the frameworks of [19] and ours, the Hellinger distance plays a key role in both frameworks for the distribution approximation problem.

The Rényi divergence has been used in various problems in the information theory; see [23,25] and references therein. Since the Rényi divergence can be regarded as a proxy of distance, it has been used as a security metric on encryption [12], an approximation metric in lattice cryptography [2,4,15,22,24], differential privacy [20], and security analysis [14,17]. Our usage of the Rényi divergence is different from these cryptographic applications in the sense that the Rényi divergence naturally arises as a characterization of the operationally defined bit-security via the Bayesian hypothesis testing.

2 Preliminaries

We present several basic notions and their properties about probability distributions. Let P and Q be probability distributions over a finite set Ω. For a distribution P over Ω and $A \subseteq \Omega$, we denote by $P(A)$ the probability of event A, which is equal to $\sum_{x \in A} P(x)$.

The *total variation distance* between P and Q is

$$d_{\mathsf{TV}}(P,Q) = \max_{A \subseteq \Omega} |P(A) - Q(A)| = \frac{1}{2} \sum_{x \in \Omega} |P(x) - Q(x)|.$$

The *Hellinger distance* between P and Q is

$$d_{\mathsf{HD}}(P,Q) = \sqrt{\frac{1}{2} \sum_{x \in \Omega} \left(\sqrt{P(x)} - \sqrt{Q(x)}\right)^2} = \sqrt{1 - \sum_{x \in \Omega} \sqrt{P(x) \cdot Q(x)}},$$

which takes values in $[0,1]$. It holds that

$$d_{\mathsf{HD}}(P,Q)^2 \le d_{\mathsf{TV}}(P,Q) \le \sqrt{2} \cdot d_{\mathsf{HD}}(P,Q). \tag{1}$$

The Rényi divergence of order $1/2$ is

$$D_{1/2}(P \| Q) = -2 \ln \sum_{x \in \Omega} \sqrt{P(x)Q(x)}.$$

It holds that $1 - 1/t \le \ln t \le t - 1$ for $t > 0$. By using this inequality, we have that

$$d_{\mathsf{HD}}(P,Q)^2 \le \frac{1}{2} \cdot D_{1/2}(P \| Q) \le \frac{d_{\mathsf{HD}}(P,Q)^2}{1 - d_{\mathsf{HD}}(P,Q)^2} \le 2 \cdot d_{\mathsf{HD}}(P,Q)^2, \tag{2}$$

where the last inequality holds if $d_{\mathsf{HD}}(P,Q)^2 \le 1/2$. Thus, if $D_{1/2}(P \| Q) \ge x$, we have

$$d_{\mathsf{HD}}(P,Q)^2 \ge \min\left\{\frac{1}{2}, \frac{x}{2}\right\}. \tag{3}$$

3 Bit Security

Based on the idea described in Sect. 1, we introduce our framework of bit security. Section 3.1 provides a formal definition. Section 3.2 presents upper and lower bounds on the bit security, which will be used for security reductions.

3.1 Definition

We define an n-bit security game $G_{A,B} = (X, R, \{O_\theta\}_\theta)$ consisting of an algorithm X, a Boolean function R, and oracles $\{O_\theta\}_\theta$, played by an *inner* adversary A and an *outer* adversary B. The inner adversary A plays a usual security game. First, a secret $u \in \{0,1\}^n$ is chosen uniformly at random, and the challenge x is computed as $X(u)$. Given x, A tries to output a such that $R(u,x,a) = 1$ using oracle access to $\{O_\theta\}_\theta$. See Fig. 1. The success probability of A is

$$\epsilon_A = \Pr\left[u \xleftarrow{R} \{0,1\}^n; x \leftarrow X(u); a \leftarrow A^{\{O_\theta(\cdot)\}_\theta}(x) : R(u,x,a) = 1\right].$$

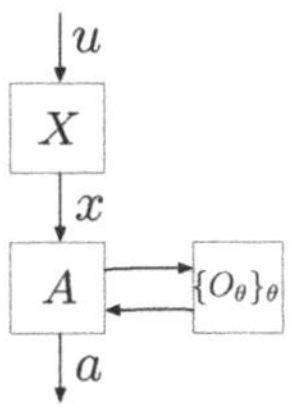

Fig. 1. A description of the inner adversary.

The outer adversary B can invoke the inner adversary A multiple times. We denote by A_i the ith invocation of A, which is the identical copy of A. The outer adversary B finally outputs b. The success condition of B depends on the type of games.

Decision Type ($n = 1$)**:** When $n = 1$, A tries to distinguish two cases whether $u = 0$ or $u = 1$. The outer adversary B also tries to tell apart from the two cases based on the answers $a_1, a_2, \cdots$ from $A_1, A_2, \cdots$, where $a_i \in \{0, 1\}$. Thus, the success probability of B is defined as

$$\epsilon^{\text{decn}}_{A,B} = \Pr\left[u \xleftarrow{R} \{0,1\}; b \leftarrow B^{O^{\text{decn}}_A} : b = u\right],$$

where O^{decn}_A is the oracle that, given the ith query, computes $x_i \leftarrow X(u)$ and replies with $a_i \leftarrow A_i^{\{O_\theta(\cdot)\}_\theta}(x_i)$. See Fig. 2.

A typical example of the decision-type primitive is the pseudorandom generator. In that case, the secret describes whether the algorithm X is the pseudorandom generator ($u = 0$) or the true random generator ($u = 1$). Then, upon observing the output x from $X(u)$, the goal of the inner adversary is to estimate the value of u. Usually, the success probability is given by $\frac{1}{2}(1 + \delta)$ for some small advantage δ. The purpose of the outer adversary is to boost the success probability of estimating u by aggregating the outputs of N independent invocations of the inner adversary.

Search Type ($n > 1$)**:** When $n > 1$, A tries to find any "correct" answer a satisfying $R(u, x, a) = 1$. Thus, B also tries to find any correct answer by invoking A_i's. At the ith invocation, a secret u_i is chosen independently and uniformly at random. Given $X(u_i)$, A_i replies with a_i. The final output of B is the list $\{(j, a_j)\}_j$ of all oracle replies. The success probability of B is defined as

$$\epsilon^{\text{srch}}_{A,B} = \Pr\left[b = \{(j, a_j)\}_j \leftarrow B^{O^{\text{srch}}_A} : \exists i, (i, a_i) \in b \land R(u_i, x_i, a_i) = 1\right],$$

where O^{srch}_A is the oracle that, given the ith query, chooses $u_i \in \{0, 1\}^n$ uniformly at random, computes $x_i \leftarrow X(u_i)$, and replies with $a_i \leftarrow A_i^{\{O_\theta(\cdot)\}_\theta}(x_i)$. See Fig. 3.

A typical example of the search-type primitive is the one-way function. In that case, the secret describes the input of the one-way function X. Then,

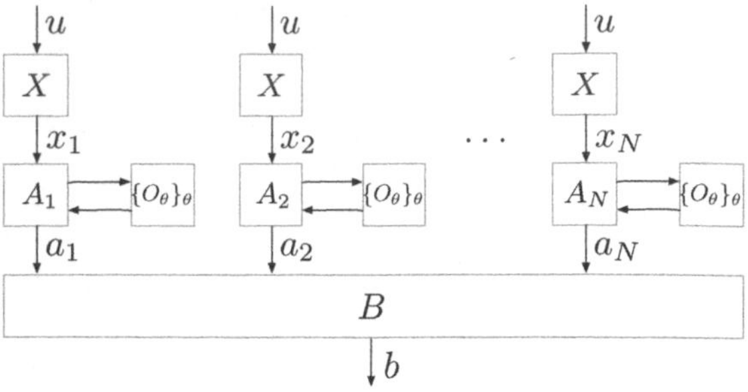

Fig. 2. A description of the outer adversary for $n = 1$.

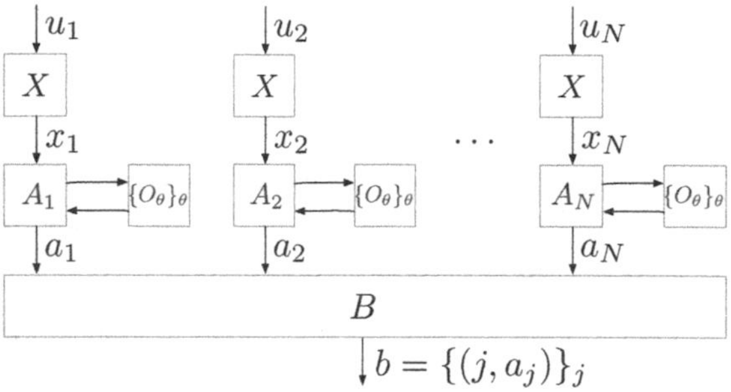

Fig. 3. A description of the outer adversary for $n > 1$.

upon observing the output of the one-way function, the goal of the inner adversary is to find an element in the inverse image of the given output. Usually, the success probability of the search-type game is tiny. Unlike the decision-type primitive, the outer adversary does not process the outputs obtained from the inner adversary; the role of the outer adversary is to invoke the inner adversary a sufficient number of times so that at least one correct estimate of the secret is included in the list.

The objective of the outer adversary B is to achieve the success probability of $1 - \mu$ for some small constant $\mu > 0$ with the least number $N = N_{A,B}$ of invocations of A. We assume that N outputs $a_1, \ldots, a_N$ are independently identically distributed according to a distribution determined by the behavior of the inner adversary A. This assumption implies that our definition captures the situation in which the outer adversary tries to amplify the success probability by observing multiple invocations of the inner adversary.

Let T_A denote the computational complexity for playing the inner game by A. Namely, it is the (worst-case) computational cost for running the experiment $\left[u \xleftarrow{R} \{0,1\}^n; x \leftarrow X(u); a \leftarrow A^{\{O_\theta(\cdot)\}_\theta}(x)\right]$. The bit security is defined as the computational cost of (A, B) necessary for achieving the success probability $\epsilon_{A,B} \geq 1 - \mu$.

Definition 1 (Bit Security). *The bit security of an n-bit game $G = (X, R, \{O_\theta\}_\theta)$ for error probability μ is defined to be*

$$\mathrm{BS}_G^\mu \triangleq \min_{A,B} \{\log_2(N_{A,B} \cdot T_A) : \epsilon_{A,B} \geq 1 - \mu\}$$
$$= \min_A \left\{\log_2 T_A + \log_2 \min_B\{N_{A,B} : \epsilon_{A,B} \geq 1 - \mu\}\right\},$$

where $N_{A,B}$ is the number of queries to A made by the outer adversary B.

The computational complexity of B is not considered in the definition. It is for simplicity. Most of the time is consumed by the $N_{A,B}$ times running of A. Compared to it, the computational cost of B is negligibly small. Indeed, in Sect. 3.2, we show that simple computations of B can achieve tight upper bounds on the bit security. We note that when $n = 1$, the restriction of the output range of A to $\{0, 1\}$ is necessary to ignore the computational cost of B. If A can output any values and we do not consider B's cost, B may trivially predict the value u by observing each A_i's view and performing a high-cost computation that is not counted.

By definition, the bit security of search primitives has a finite value if the output space of inner adversaries is finite. If an inner adversary A for a search-type game outputs $u \in \{0,1\}^\ell$, since a random guessing adversary has a success probability of at least $1/2^\ell$, the bit security is bounded above by $\ell + O(1)$. In contrast to this fact, decision games can have infinite bit security. For example, since the one-time pad has perfect secrecy, the bit security should be unbounded.

Measures of Computational Costs

We can adopt various measures of resources as computational complexity. The only restriction is that repeating the task with complexity T in total ℓ times takes the complexity of ℓT. This property is implicitly assumed in Definition 1.

We can assume that time complexity is employed to measure computational cost in this paper. Following the literature, one may also employ the circuit size as the computational cost. Note that there have been discussions about measuring the cost of attacks [3,6,13], especially in the non-uniform model.

Instantiations

Some instantiations of decision and search games in our framework are described in Table 1.

3.2 Upper and Lower Bounds

Since most cryptographic primitives are built upon unproven hardness assumptions, it is difficult to provide absolute bounds on the bit security of given

Table 1. Some instantiations of security games.

Game	Type*	X	R	$\{O_\theta(\cdot)\}_\theta$
OWF f	S	$f(u)$	$f(u) = f(a)$	—
PRG g	D	$\begin{cases} g(U_\ell) & u=0 \\ U_m & u=1 \end{cases}$	$u = a$	—
IND of (D_0, D_1)	D	D_u	$u = a$	—
IND security of (Enc, Dec)	D	$(m_0, m_1, \mathsf{Enc}(m_u))$	$u = a$	—
IND-CPA of (Enc, Dec)	D	pp	$u = a$	$O_e(q) = \mathsf{Enc}_{ek}(q)$ $O_c(q_0, q_1) = \mathsf{Enc}_{ek}(q_u)$
Unforgeability of (Sign, Vrfy)	S	vk	$a \notin \{O_s(q_i)\}_i$ $\wedge\ \mathsf{Vrfy}_{vk}(a) = 1$	$O_s(q) = (q, \mathsf{Sign}_{sk}(q))$
2nd-preimage resistance of h	S	(u, r)	$r \neq a\ \wedge$ $h_u(r) = h_u(a)$	—
Collision resistance of h	S	u	$a_1 \neq a_2 \wedge$ $h_u(a_1) = h_u(a_2)$	—
DDH	D	$\begin{cases} (g, g^c, g^d, g^{cd}) & u=0 \\ (g, g^c, g^d, g^e) & u=1 \end{cases}$	$u = a$	—
CDH	S	(g, g^c, g^d)	$a = g^{cd}$	—

*S = Search, D = Decision

primitives. In this section, we present an upper bound (Theorem 1) and a lower bound (Theorem 2) on the bit security in terms of the success probability of an inner adversary. In Sect. 4, those upper bound and lower bound are used to discuss the relative loss of the bit security during reductions of cryptographic primitives.

First, we derive an upper bound. To that end, for a given inner adversary A with success probability ϵ_A, we shall derive an upper bound on the number $N_{A,B}$ of invocations necessary to attain the outer adversary's success probability $1-\mu$. For the search-type game, the number $N_{A,B}$ can be upper bounded by a simple bound on the geometric distribution.

Lemma 1 (Upper bound for $n > 1$). *Let G be a search-type security game, and A be its inner adversary with success probability $\epsilon_A \in (0,1]$. Then, there exists an outer adversary B such that $\epsilon_{A,B} \geq 1-\mu$ and*

$$N_{A,B} = \left\lceil \frac{1}{\epsilon_A} \ln(1/\mu) \right\rceil.$$

Proof. We consider an adversary B that simply invokes A_i in total $N = N_{A,B}$ times. The success probability of B is $\epsilon_B = 1-(1-\epsilon_A)^N$. We need to guarantee that $\epsilon_B \geq 1-\mu$, i.e., $(1-\epsilon_A)^N \leq \mu$. Since

$$(1-\epsilon_A)^N \leq \exp(-N\epsilon_A),$$

it suffices to choose $N = \lceil (1/\epsilon_A)\ln(1/\mu) \rceil$ for achieving $(1-\epsilon_A)^N \leq \mu$. Hence, the statement follows. □

For the decision-type game, we need some machinery from the Bayesian hypothesis testing. Observe that the success probability of an inner adversary can be written as

$$\epsilon_A = \frac{1 + d_{\mathsf{TV}}(P_{A|U}(\cdot|0), P_{A|U}(\cdot|1))}{2},$$

where $P_{A|U}(\cdot|u)$ is the distribution of the inner adversary's output when the secret is u. When we evaluate the outer adversary's success probability, the exponential convergence is characterized by the Rényi divergence of order 1/2. The following lemma connects the total variation distance and the Rényi divergence of order 1/2.

Lemma 2. *For given distributions P and Q, we have*

$$d_{\mathsf{TV}}(P,Q)^2 \leq 1 - \exp(-D_{1/2}(P\|Q)).$$

Proof. For example, see [8, Proposition 5]. □

By using Lemma 2, we can derive the following upper bound on $N_{A,B}$ for the decision-type game.

Lemma 3 (Upper bound for $n = 1$). *Let G be a decision-type security game, and A be its inner adversary with success probability $\epsilon_A = (1+\delta)/2$ for $\delta \in (0, 1]$. Then, there exists an outer adversary B such that $\epsilon_{A,B} \geq 1 - \mu$ and*

$$N_{A,B} = \left\lceil \frac{2}{\delta^2} \ln(1/2\mu) \right\rceil. \tag{4}$$

Proof. We define the strategy of the outer adversary B as

$$b = \begin{cases} 0 & \text{if } P_{A^N|U}(a^N|0) \geq P_{A^N|U}(a^N|1) \\ 1 & \text{if } P_{A^N|U}(a^N|0) < P_{A^N|U}(a^N|1) \end{cases}$$

where $P_{A^N|U}(\cdot|u)$ is the distribution of N independent outputs $a_1, \ldots, a_N$ of the inner adversary for the secret u. Then, by using a standard technique of the Bayesian hypothesis testing (cf. [5, Section 11.9]), the error probability of the outer adversary can be bounded as

$$\begin{aligned}
\Pr[b \neq u] &= \frac{1}{2} \sum_{a^N} \min\left\{P_{A^N|U}(a^N|0), P_{A^N|U}(a^N|1)\right\} \\
&\leq \frac{1}{2} \sum_{a^N} \sqrt{P_{A^N|U}(a^N|0) \cdot P_{A^N|U}(a^N|1)} \\
&= \frac{1}{2} \exp\Big(-\frac{1}{2} D_{1/2}(P_{A^N|U}(\cdot|0) \| P_{A^N|U}(\cdot|1))\Big) \\
&= \frac{1}{2} \exp\Big(-\frac{N}{2} D_{1/2}(P_{A|U}(\cdot|0) \| P_{A|U}(\cdot|1))\Big).
\end{aligned}$$

Here, by noting $e^{-t} \geq 1 - t$, Lemma 2 implies

$$\delta^2 = d_{\mathsf{TV}}(P_{A|U}(\cdot|0), P_{A|U}(\cdot|1))^2 \leq D_{1/2}(P_{A|U}(\cdot|0)\|P_{A|U}(\cdot|1)).$$

Thus, we have

$$\Pr[b \neq u] \leq \frac{1}{2}\exp\left(-\frac{\delta^2 N}{2}\right).$$

This means that, in order to satisfy $\Pr[b \neq u] \leq \mu$, it suffices to take

$$N = \left\lceil \frac{2}{\delta^2}\ln(1/2\mu) \right\rceil,$$

which implies (4). □

We estimate the computational cost for implementing the outer adversary B in the above proof. We assume that B knows the conditional probability distributions $P_{A|U}(\cdot|0)$ and $P_{A|U}(\cdot|1)$. Given $a^N \in \{0,1\}^N$, B counts the number of 0's in a^N, denoted by N_0. Let $N_1 = N - N_0$. Then, B can compute the value $P_{A^N|U}(a^N|0)$ as $P_{A|U}(0|0)^{N_0} \cdot P_{A|U}(1|0)^{N_1}$. Also, $P_{A^N|U}(a^N|1)$ can be calculated similarly. The computation of B is for counting N_0, calculating the two probabilities, and comparing them. Thus, the computational complexity of B is $O(N)$. Even if we take into account the computational complexity of B, the bit security is affected by a constant that does not depend on security games.

It follows from the proof of Lemma 3 that the *Rényi advantage*

$$\mathsf{adv}_A^{\text{Renyi}} := D_{1/2}(P_{A|U}(\cdot|0)\|P_{A|U}(\cdot|1))$$

gives an upper bound for $n = 1$.

Lemma 4 (Upper bound for $n = 1$ with Rényi advantage). *Let G be a decision-type security game, and A be its inner adversary with the Rényi advantage with $\mathsf{adv}_A^{\text{Renyi}} > 0$. Then, there exists an outer adversary B such that $\epsilon_{A,B} \geq 1 - \mu$ and*

$$N_{A,B} = \left\lceil \frac{2}{\mathsf{adv}_A^{\text{Renyi}}}\ln(1/2\mu) \right\rceil. \tag{5}$$

From the above three lemmas, we can derive the following upper bound on the bit security.

Theorem 1. *Let G be an n-bit security game, and A be its inner adversary with success probability $\epsilon_A > 0$, running time T_A, and Rényi advantage $\mathsf{adv}_A^{\text{Renyi}} > 0$. Then, we have*

$$\mathrm{BS}_G^\mu \leq \begin{cases} \log_2 T_A + \log_2\left(\frac{1}{\epsilon_A}\right) + \log_2 \ln(1/\mu) + 1 & n > 1 \\ \log_2 T_A + 2\log_2\left(\frac{1}{2(\epsilon_A - 1/2)}\right) + \log_2 \ln(1/2\mu) + 2 & n = 1 \\ \log_2 T_A + \log_2\left(\frac{1}{\mathsf{adv}_A^{\text{Renyi}}}\right) + \log_2 \ln(1/2\mu) + 2 & n = 1 \end{cases}.$$

Proof. It directly follows from the definition of the bit security and the upper and lower bounds on $N_{A,B}$ in Lemmas 1, 3, and 4. □

Next, we derive a lower bound on the bit security. To that end, for a given inner adversary with success probability ϵ_A, we need to derive a lower bound on $N_{A,B}$ for arbitrary outer adversaries B. For the search-type game, the following bound can be derived from a simple union bound.

Lemma 5 (Lower bound for $n > 1$). *Let G be an n-bit security game, and A be its inner adversary with success probability ϵ_A. Then, any outer adversary B with $\epsilon_B \geq 1 - \mu$ must satisfy*

$$N_{A,B} \geq \frac{1-\mu}{\epsilon_A}.$$

Proof. Since ϵ_B is the probability that B successfully finds u at least once, by the union bound, we have $\epsilon_B \leq N_{A,B} \cdot \epsilon_A$, which implies the claim. □

For the decision-type game, deriving a lower bound on $N_{A,B}$ is more subtle. In fact, without further assumptions on the inner adversary to be discussed at the end of this section, it is not possible to derive a desirable lower bound in terms of the success probability ϵ_A of an inner adversary. Instead, we derive a lower bound in terms of the Rényi advantage as follows.

Lemma 6 (Lower bound for $n = 1$). *Let G be a 1-bit security game, and A be its inner adversary. Then, any outer adversary B with $\epsilon_B \geq 1 - \mu$ must satisfy*

$$N_{A,B} \geq \frac{\ln(1/(4\mu))}{\mathsf{adv}_A^{\mathrm{Renyi}}},$$

Proof. For any outer adversary B, we must have

$$\Pr[b \neq u] \geq \frac{1 - d_{\mathsf{TV}}(P_{A^N|U}(\cdot|0), P_{A^N|U}(\cdot|1))}{2}. \tag{6}$$

For two distributions P and Q, Lemma 2 implies

$$\begin{aligned} d_{\mathsf{TV}}(P,Q)^2 &\leq 1 - \exp(-D_{1/2}(P\|Q)) \\ &\leq \left(1 - \frac{1}{2}\exp(-D_{1/2}(P\|Q))\right)^2, \end{aligned}$$

i.e.,

$$1 - d_{\mathsf{TV}}(P,Q) \geq \frac{1}{2}\exp(-D_{1/2}(P\|Q)).$$

Thus, by applying this inequality to (6), we have

$$\begin{aligned} \Pr[b \neq u] &\geq \frac{1}{4}\exp(-D_{1/2}(P_{A^N|U}(\cdot|0)\|P_{A^N|U}(\cdot|1))) \\ &= \frac{1}{4}\exp(-ND_{1/2}(P_{A|U}(\cdot|0)\|P_{A|U}(\cdot|1))). \end{aligned}$$

Since $\Pr[b \neq u] \leq \mu$, it holds that

$$N \geq \frac{\ln(1/(4\mu))}{D_{1/2}(P_{A|U}(\cdot|0) \| P_{A|U}(\cdot|1))}.$$

□

From Lemma 5 and Lemma 6, we can derive the following implication on the bit security.

Theorem 2. *If an n-bit game G is not λ-bit secure, i.e.,* $\mathrm{BS}_G^\mu < \lambda$*, then there exists an inner adversary A for the game such that A runs in time* T_A *and satisfies*

$$\epsilon_A > \frac{T_A}{2^\lambda}(1-\mu)$$

for the search-type game $n > 1$*; and*

$$\mathsf{adv}_A^{\mathrm{Renyi}} = D_{1/2}(P_{A|U}(\cdot|0) \| P_{A|U}(\cdot|1)) > \frac{T_A}{2^\lambda} \cdot \ln(1/4\mu)$$

and

$$d_{\mathsf{HD}}(P_{A|U}(\cdot|0), P_{A|U}(\cdot|1)) > \min\left\{\frac{1}{\sqrt{2}}, \sqrt{\frac{T_A}{2^{\lambda+1}} \cdot \ln(1/4\mu)}\right\}.$$

for the decision-type game $n = 1$.

Proof. If G is not λ-bit secure, there exist an inner adversary A and an outer adversary B such that $N_{A,B} \cdot T_A < 2^\lambda$. Then, the bound for the search-type game follows from Lemma 5.

For the case that $n = 1$, Lemma 6 implies that $D_{1/2}(P_{A|U}(\cdot|0) \| P_{A|U}(\cdot|1)) > (T_A/2^\lambda) \cdot \ln(1/4\mu)$, and thus $d_{\mathsf{HD}}(P_{A|U}(\cdot|0), P_{A|U}(\cdot|1))^2 > \min\{1/2, x/2\}$ for $x = (T_A/2^\lambda) \cdot \ln(1/4\mu)$ by (3). □

Discussion

Theorem 1 roughly claims that for search-type games, if there is an adversary A with success probability ϵ_A and cost T_A, then the bit security cannot be larger than $\lambda \simeq \log_2(T_A/\epsilon_A)$; on the other hand, Theorem 2 roughly claims that if the best possible inner adversary A has success probability ϵ_A and cost T_A, then the bit security of $\lambda \simeq \log_2(T_A/\epsilon_A)$ is guaranteed. Thus, the upper bound and the lower bound essentially coincide.

For the decision-type game, the situation is more subtle. Theorems 1 and 2 show that the upper bound and the lower bound coincide in terms of the Rényi advantage. With the success probability, Theorem 1 claims that, if there exists an adversary A with success probability $\epsilon_A = (1+\delta)/2$ and cost T_A, then the bit security cannot be larger than $\lambda \simeq \log_2(T_A/\delta^2)$. By using the relation (1) between the total variation and the Hellinger distances, Theorem 2 guarantees that if the best possible inner adversary A has success probability $\epsilon_A = (1+\delta)/2$ and cost T_A, the bit security is guaranteed to be at least $\lambda \simeq \log_2(T_A/\delta)$. There is a gap of $\log_2(1/\delta)$ between the bounds. As a further illustration, let us consider an inner adversary given by $P_{A|U}(0|0) = \delta$, $P_{A|U}(1|0) = 1-\delta$, $P_{A|U}(0|1) = 0$, and $P_{A|U}(1|1) = 1$; this inner adversary makes no error when $u = 1$, and it makes an error most of the time, $1-\delta$, when $u = 0$. For this adversary, the advantage is given by

$$d_{\mathsf{TV}}(P_{A|U}(\cdot|0), P_{A|U}(\cdot|1)) = \delta.$$

On the other hand, the Rényi divergence/advantage is given by

$$\begin{aligned} D_{1/2}(P_{A|U}(\cdot|0)\|P_{A|U}(\cdot|1)) &= -\ln(1-\delta) \\ &= \delta + o(\delta). \end{aligned}$$

Thus, if this kind of inner adversary exists, we can only guarantee the bit security of $\lambda \simeq \log(T_A/\delta)$ as a function of possible advantage δ.

Let us consider *linear tests* against a PRG $g : \{0,1\}^\ell \to \{0,1\}^m$ (cf. [1,21]). It is known that they are powerful enough to give the best-known attack that yields the distinguishing advantage $\delta \geq 2^{-\ell/2}$ (See [1,7]). These tests output $a = 0$ and $a = 1$ with the same probability for the true random generator ($u = 1$). Thus, it seems reasonable to assume that the probability of each a given u is lower bounded as $P_{A|U}(a|u) \geq \beta$ for some $\beta > 0$; in the following, a class of inner adversaries satisfying such an assumption is termed, *β-balanced* adversaries.

When probabilities are bounded below, we can connect the total variation distance and the Rényi divergence.

Lemma 7. *For given distributions P and Q, we have*

$$D_{1/2}(P\|Q) \leq D(P\|Q) \leq 2\beta_Q^{-1} d_{\mathsf{TV}}(P,Q)^2,$$

where $\beta_Q = \min_{x\in\mathcal{X}^+} Q(x)$, $\mathcal{X}^+ = \{x : Q(x) > 0\}$, and $D(P\|Q) = \sum_x P(x)\log(P(x)/Q(x))$ is the KL-divergence.

Proof. The former inequality follows from the fact that the Rényi divergence is monotonically non-decreasing with respect to α and $D(P\|Q) = \lim_{\alpha\to 1} D_\alpha(P\|Q)$. For the latter inequality, see [11, Lemma 4.1]. □

Using Lemma 7, we can derive the following lower bound on the bit security against β-balanced adversaries.

Theorem 3. *If a 1-bit game G is not λ-bit secure against β-balanced adversaries, then there exists a β-balanced inner adversary A for the game such that A runs in time T_A and the success probability $\epsilon_A = (1+\delta)/2$ satisfies*

$$\delta^2 > \frac{\beta T_A}{2^{\lambda+1}} \cdot \ln\left(\frac{1}{4\mu}\right).$$

Proof. In the same manner as Theorem 2, Lemma 6 implies that $D_{1/2}(P_{A|U}(\cdot|0)\|P_{A|U}(\cdot|1)) > (T_A/2^\lambda)\cdot\ln(1/4\mu)$, which together with Lemma 7 and the β-balanced assumption imply the desired bound. □

Theorem 3 claims that, if the best possible advantage by β-balanced adversaries is δ, the bit security of $\lambda \simeq \log(\beta T_A/\delta^2)$ is guaranteed, which coincides with the upper bound for $\beta = \Omega(1)$.

4 Security Reductions

We present several security reductions of security games.

We give the following lemma used in the proofs.

Lemma 8. *Let A_0 and A_1 be distributions over $\{0,1\}$ such that $A_0(0) = \delta, A_0(1) = 1-\delta, A_1(0) = q\delta, A_1(1) = 1-q\delta$, where $0 \le \delta \le 1/32$ and $0 \le q\delta \le 1$. Then, $D_{1/2}(A_0\|A_1) \ge \phi(q)\cdot\delta$, where*

$$\phi(q) := (1-\sqrt{q})^2 - q/16.$$

Proof. By definition,

$$\begin{aligned}
D_{1/2}(A_0\|A_1) &= -2\ln\left(\sqrt{q\delta^2} + \sqrt{(1-\delta)(1-q\delta)}\right) \\
&= -\ln\left(q\delta^2 + (1-\delta)(1-q\delta) + 2\sqrt{(1-\delta)(1-q\delta)q\delta^2}\right) \\
&\ge -\ln\left(q\delta^2 + (1-\delta)(1-q\delta) + 2\sqrt{q}\delta\right) \\
&= -\ln\left(1 - (1+q)\delta + 2\sqrt{q}\delta + 2q\delta^2\right) \\
&= -\ln\left(1 - (1-\sqrt{q})^2\delta + 2q\delta^2\right) \\
&\ge (1-\sqrt{q})^2\delta - 2q\delta^2 \\
&\ge \left((1-\sqrt{q})^2 - q/16\right)\delta,
\end{aligned}$$

where the last inequality holds for $\delta \le 1/32$. □

4.1 Goldreich-Levin Hard-Core Predicate

For functions $f : \{0,1\}^n \to \{0,1\}^m$ and $h : \{0,1\}^n \to \{0,1\}$, the hard-core predicate game for f is a decision game with $X = (f(R), h(R))$ when $u = 0$, and $X = (f(R), U_1)$ otherwise, where R is the uniform distribution over $\{0,1\}^n$ and U_1 is the uniformly random bit.

We show that the Goldreich-Levin theorem [9,10] gives a tight reduction if adversaries for the hard-core predicate are restricted to be β-balanced for some constant $\beta > 0$. Namely, we assume that the adversary outputs each value with a not too small probability.

Theorem 4. *Let* $f : \{0,1\}^n \to \{0,1\}^m$ *be a* λ*-bit secure one-way function. Define* $g : \{0,1\}^{2n} \to \{0,1\}^{n+m}$ *as* $g(x,r) = (f(x), r)$. *Then, the function* $h : \{0,1\}^{2n} \to \{0,1\}$ *defined by* $h(x,r) = \sum_i x_i \cdot r_i \bmod 2$ *is a* $(\lambda - \alpha)$*-bit secure hard-core predicate for* g *against* β*-balanced adversaries, where* $\alpha = 2\log_2 n + 3\log_2 \lambda + \log_2(1/\beta) + \log_2 \ln(1/\mu) + O(1)$.

Proof. It was proved by Goldreich and Levin (cf. [9,10]) that for any inner adversary A for the hard-core predicate game with running time T_A and

$$\delta_A = 2 \cdot \Pr[A(f(Q,R)) = h(Q,R)] - 1 > 0,$$

where Q and R are uniform distributions over $\{0,1\}^n$, there is an adversary A' that runs in time $T_{A'} = O(n^2(\log_2(1/\delta_A))^3) \cdot T_A$ such that

$$\Pr[A(f(Q,R)) = (Q,R)] = \Omega(\delta_A^2).$$

Assume for contradiction that h is not $(\lambda - \alpha)$-bit secure hard-core for g against β-balanced adversaries. Then, by Theorem 3, there exists an inner adversary A with running time T_A such that the success probability for the hard-core predicate game is $\epsilon_A = (1 + \delta_A)/2$ for $\delta_A > \sqrt{\beta T_A \cdot \ln(1/4\mu)/2^{\lambda-\alpha+1}}$. It is well-known that the distinguisher A for the hard-core predicate can be used to construct a predictor of the value $h(x,r)$. By the Goldreich-Levin theorem, there is an inner adversary A' for the OWF game that runs in time $T_{A'} = O(n^2 \cdot \lambda^3) \cdot T_A$ with success probability $\epsilon_{A'} = \Omega(\beta T_A \cdot 2^{-(\lambda-\alpha)})$. It follows from Theorem 1 that the bit security of the OWF game is bounded above by $\log_2 T_{A'} + \log_2(1/\epsilon_{A'}) + \log_2 \ln(1/\mu) + 1$, which is at most

$$\lambda - \alpha + \log_2 O(n^2\lambda^3) + \log_2(1/\beta) + \log_2 \ln(1/\mu) + 1.$$

By choosing $\alpha = 2\log_2 n + 3\log_2 \lambda + \log_2(1/\beta) + \log_2 \ln(1/\mu) + O(1)$, f is not a λ-bit secure one-way function, a contradiction. Hence, the statement follows. □

If the β-balanced assumption is removed in Theorem 4, we cannot guarantee the existence of an inner adversary A with $\delta_A \simeq 2^{-\lambda/2}$. When the hard-core predicate is λ-bit secure against general adversaries, it might be attained by a "biased" inner adversary such that $\delta_A \simeq 2^{-\lambda}$. Then, the success probability of A' guaranteed by the Goldreich-Levin theorem would be $\Omega(2^{-2\lambda})$. Consequently, we can only guarantee that a 2λ-bit secure one-way function implies a λ-bit secure hard-core predicate. In this sense, it remains an open problem to prove if λ-bit secure one-way function implies λ-secure hard-core predicate in our framework. To that end, we may need a tight reduction that directly connects the Rényi advantage of predicting the hard-core to the success probability of inverting the one-way function.

4.2 PRG Implies OWF

Consider a pseudorandom generator $g : \{0,1\}^\ell \to \{0,1\}^m$. As noted in [7], since g is also a δ-*biased* generator (cf. [21]), the seed length ℓ must be at least

$2\log(1/\delta)$ for achieving the distinguishing advantage δ even for linear tests [1]. That is, it must be that $\delta \geq 2^{-\ell/2}$. We might deduce from this fact that the bit security of PRG needs to be half of OWF. We show that this is not the case in our framework. Namely, there would be a λ-bit secure PRG that is a λ-bit secure OWF but is not a $(\lambda + \omega(1))$-bit secure OWF.

Theorem 5. *If $g : \{0,1\}^\ell \to \{0,1\}^m$ is a λ-bit secure pseudorandom generator, then g is a $(\lambda - \alpha)$-bit secure one-way function for $\alpha = \max\{\log_2(1 + T_g) + \log_2(1/\phi(1/2)) + \log_2(\ln(1/2\mu)/(1-\mu)) + 2, \log_2(1+T_g) + \log_2 \ln(1/2\mu) + 14\}$, where T_g is the computational complexity for evaluating g.*

Proof. Suppose for contradiction that g is not a $(\lambda - \alpha)$-bit secure one-way function. Theorem 2 implies that there exists an inner adversary A that runs in T_A and has success probability $\epsilon_A > T_A(1-\mu)/2^{\lambda-\alpha}$. Also, it must be that $N_{A,B} \cdot T_A < 2^{\lambda-\alpha}$, implying that $T_A < 2^{\lambda-\alpha}$. Consider an inner adversary A' for the PRG game G such that, on input x, A' runs $A(x)$ to get a, and outputs 0 if $g(a) = x$, and 1 otherwise. For $u, b \in \{0,1\}$, let A_u be the probability distribution on the output of A' when $u \in \{0,1\}$ was chosen in the PRG game. Then, we have

$$A_0(0) = \epsilon_A, A_0(1) = 1 - \epsilon_A, A_1(0) \leq \frac{2^\ell}{2^m}\epsilon_A, A_1(1) \geq 1 - \frac{2^\ell}{2^m}\epsilon_A.$$

We apply Lemma 8 with $A_1(0) = q\epsilon_A$ and $A_1(1) = 1 - q\epsilon_A$ for some $q \leq 1/2$. Since $\phi(q)$ is monotonically decreasing on $[0, 1/2]$, we have

$$D_{1/2}(A_0||A_1) \geq \phi(q) \cdot \epsilon_A \geq \phi(1/2) \cdot \epsilon_A$$

as long as $\epsilon_A \leq 1/32$. By using Theorem 1,

$$\begin{aligned}\mathrm{BS}_G^\mu &\leq \log_2(T_A + T_g) + \log_2(1/\phi(1/2)\epsilon_A) + \log_2 \ln(1/2\mu) + 2 \\ &< \lambda - \alpha + \log_2(1 + T_g/T_A) + \log_2(1/\phi(1/2)) + \log_2(\ln(1/2\mu)/(1-\mu)) + 2 \\ &\leq \lambda.\end{aligned}$$

When $\epsilon_A > 1/32$, the success probability of A' is

$$\begin{aligned}\Pr[u = 0] \cdot A_0(0) + \Pr[u = 1] \cdot A_1(1) &\geq \frac{1}{2}\left(\epsilon_A + 1 - \frac{2^\ell}{2^m}\epsilon_A\right) \\ &\geq \frac{1}{2}\left(1 + \frac{\epsilon_A}{2}\right) \\ &> \frac{1}{2}\left(1 + \frac{1}{64}\right),\end{aligned}$$

where the second inequality follows from $m \geq \ell + 1$. By Theorem 1,

$$\begin{aligned}\mathrm{BS}_G^\mu &\leq \log_2(T_A + T_g) + 2\log_2(64) + \log_2 \ln(1/2\mu) + 2 \\ &< \lambda - \alpha + \log_2(1 + T_g/T_A) + \log_2 \ln(1/2\mu) + 14 \\ &\leq \lambda.\end{aligned}$$

In both cases, we have a contradiction. Hence, the statement follows. □

Next, we demonstrate that the bit security achieved in Theorem 5 is almost optimal. Specifically, we show that as long as considering pseudorandomness against β-balanced adversaries for constant $\beta > 0$, the PRG constructed from a λ-bit secure one-way permutation and the hard-core predicate is a $(\lambda - O(1))$-bit secure PRG. However, it is not a $(\lambda + \omega(1))$-bit secure OWF if the one-way permutation is not $(\lambda + 1)$-bit secure.

Theorem 6. *Let $f : \{0,1\}^n \to \{0,1\}^n$ be a λ-bit secure one-way permutation that is not $(\lambda + 1)$-bit secure one-way. Consider a function $g : \{0,1\}^{2n} \to \{0,1\}^{2n+1}$ defined by $g(x,r) = (f(x), r, h(x,r))$ and $h(x,r) = \sum_i x_i \cdot r_i \bmod 2$. Then, g is a $(\lambda - \alpha)$-bit secure pseudorandom generator against β-balanced adversaries, but is not a $(\lambda + \alpha')$-bit secure one-way function for $\alpha = 2\log_2 n + 3\log_2 \lambda + \log_2(1/\beta) + \log_2 \ln(1/\mu) + O(1)$ and $\alpha' = \log_2(1 + T_{f,h}) + \log_2(\ln(1/\mu)/(1-\mu)) + 2$, where $T_{f,h}$ is the computational complexity for evaluating f and h.*

Proof. First, we show that g is a PRG. Assume for contradiction that g is not a $(\lambda - \alpha)$-bit secure PRG against β-balanced adversaries. By Theorem 3, there exists a β-balanced inner adversary A for the PRG game of g that runs in T_A and has success probability $\epsilon_A = (1 + \delta_A)/2$ with $\delta_A > \sqrt{\beta T_A \ln(1/4\mu)/2^{\lambda-\alpha+1}}$. Since f is a permutation, the first $2n$ bits of g are distributed uniformly at random. Thus, the distinguisher A for the PRG g can work as a distinguisher for the hard-core predicate game of $h(x,r)$ for function $g'(x,r) = (f(x), r)$. By Theorem 4, as long as $\alpha = 2\log_2 n + 3\log_2 \lambda + \log_2(1/\beta) + \log_2 \ln(1/\mu) + O(1)$, f is not a λ-bit secure one-way function, a contradiction.

Next, we show that g is not a $(\lambda + \alpha')$-bit secure one-way function. Since f is not a $(\lambda + 1)$-bit secure one-way function, it follows from Theorem 2 that there is an inner adversary A for the OWF game of f that runs in time T_A and has success probability $\epsilon_A > T_A(1-\mu)/2^{\lambda+1}$. Consider an inner adversary A' for the OWF game of g that given (y, r, b), runs A on input y, and outputs (a, r) if A output a satisfying $y = f(a)$ and $h(a, r) = b$, and $\perp$ otherwise. Let $\epsilon_{A'}$ be the success probability of A' in the OWF game of g. Since f is a permutation, there is no $a \in \{0,1\}^n$ satisfying $f(a) = f(x)$ and $a \neq x$. Thus, A' succeeds in the OWF game of g whenever A outputs a satisfying $y = f(a)$. That is, $\epsilon_{A'} \geq \epsilon_A$. Theorem 1 implies that the bit security of g is at most

$$\begin{aligned}&\log_2(T_A + T_{f,h}) + \log_2(1/\epsilon_{A'}) + \log_2 \ln(1/\mu) + 1\\&< \lambda + \log_2(1 + T_{f,h}) + \log_2 \frac{\ln(1/\mu)}{(1-\mu)} + 2.\end{aligned}$$

□

4.3 IND-CPA Encryption Implies OW-CPA Encryption

For an encryption scheme, the one-way chosen-plaintext-attack (OW-CPA) game $G^{\text{ow}}_{A,B}$ is defined such that given a ciphertext of a randomly chosen message $m \in \mathcal{M}$, an inner adversary A tries to output the plaintext m. At any time during the game, A can query any message in $\mathcal{M}$ and receive its encrypted ciphertext.

It is well-known that IND-CPA security implies OW-CPA security if the message space is sufficiently large. We reveal the quantitative relationship between the two notions in our framework. Note that if we employ the "conventional" advantage-based argument, 2λ-bit IND-CPA security is required for achieving λ-bit OW-CPA security. The reason is that by assuming an attacker for λ-bit secure OW-CPA game with advantage $\epsilon_A \approx 2^{-\lambda}$, Theorem 1 only guarantees that the bit security of IND-CPA is at most $2\log_2(1/\epsilon_A) \approx 2\lambda$. We resolve this problem by exploiting the Rényi advantage.

Theorem 7. *If an encryption scheme with message space $\mathcal{M}$ has λ-bit secure IND-CPA security, with $|\mathcal{M}| \geq \max\{2^{\lambda-\alpha+4}/(1-\mu)+1, 65\}$, then it has $(\lambda-\alpha)$-bit secure OW-CPA security, where $\alpha = \log_2(1+2(T_{\text{samp}}+T_{\text{eq}})) + \max\{\log_2(\ln(1/2\mu)/(1-\mu))+3, \log_2\ln(1/2\mu)+8\}$, where T_{samp} is the computational complexity for sampling a message from $\mathcal{M}$ uniformly at random and T_{eq} is for checking the equality of given two messages in $\mathcal{M}$.*

Proof. Assume for contradiction that the scheme does not have $(\lambda-\alpha)$-bit secure OW-CPA security. Theorem 2 implies that there exists an inner adversary A with running time T_A and success probability $\epsilon_A > T_A(1-\mu)/2^{\lambda-\alpha}$. Consider an inner adversary A' for the IND-CPA game G^{IND} such that A' first chooses two different messages $m_0, m_1 \in \mathcal{M}$ uniformly at random and sends them to the challenger. Given the challenge ciphertext c for message m_u, A' runs A on input c. Oracle queries from A can be replied by querying them to the oracles of A'. If A outputs either m_0 or m_1, A' outputs the corresponding bit. Otherwise, A' outputs 1. The computational complexity of A' for running the IND-CPA game is at most $T_A + 2(T_{\text{samp}} + T_{\text{eq}})$. Let A_u be the probability distribution on the output of A' when $u \in \{0,1\}$ is chosen as the secret in G^{IND}. By definition, $A_0(0) = \epsilon_A$ and $A_0(1) = 1-\epsilon_A$. We note that $A_1(0)$ is not necessarily equal to 0 since A' may accidentally output m_0 even when the ciphertext of m_1 is sent to A'. Since the challenge ciphertext does not contain any information on m_0 and m_0 is randomly chosen from $\mathcal{M} \setminus \{m_1\}$ when $u=1$, the probability that A' outputs m_0 is at most $1/(|\mathcal{M}|-1)$. Hence, we have $A_1(0) = \epsilon$ and $A_1(1) = 1-\epsilon$ for some $\epsilon \leq 1/(|\mathcal{M}|-1)$. Suppose that $\epsilon_A \leq 1/32$. By Lemma 8, the Rényi advantage of A' satisfies

$$\mathsf{adv}^{\text{Renyi}}_{A'} = D_{1/2}(A_0 \| A_1) \geq \phi(q) \cdot \epsilon_A$$

for $q = \epsilon/\epsilon_A$. By assumption on $|\mathcal{M}|$,

$$q = \frac{\epsilon}{\epsilon_A} \leq \frac{2^{\lambda-\alpha}}{T_A(1-\mu)(|\mathcal{M}|-1)} \leq \frac{1}{16}.$$

Since $\phi(q) > 1/2$ for $q \le 1/16$, we have $\mathsf{adv}_{A'}^{\mathrm{Renyi}} \ge \phi(1/16) \cdot \epsilon_A > \epsilon_A/2$. Theorem 1 implies that

$$\begin{aligned}\mathrm{BS}_{G\mathrm{IND}}^{\mu} &\le \log_2(T_A + 2(T_{\mathrm{samp}} + T_{\mathrm{eq}})) + \log_2(2/\epsilon_A) + \log_2 \ln(1/2\mu) + 2 \\ &< \lambda - \alpha + \log_2(1 + 2(T_{\mathrm{samp}} + T_{\mathrm{eq}})) + \log_2(\ln(1/2\mu)/(1-\mu)) + 3 \\ &\le \lambda.\end{aligned}$$

When $\epsilon_A > 1/32$, the success probability of A' is

$$\Pr[u = 0] \cdot A_0(0) + \Pr[u = 1] \cdot A_1(1) \ge \frac{1}{2}(\epsilon_A + 1 - \epsilon) > \frac{1}{2}\left(1 + \frac{1}{64}\right).$$

Since $T_A < 2^{\lambda - \alpha}$, it follows from Theorem 1 that

$$\begin{aligned}\mathrm{BS}_{G\mathrm{IND}}^{\mu} &< \log_2(T_A + 2(T_{\mathrm{samp}} + T_{\mathrm{eq}})) + \log_2(64) + \log_2 \ln(1/2\mu) + 2 \\ &< \lambda - \alpha + \log_2(1 + 2(T_{\mathrm{samp}} + T_{\mathrm{eq}})) + \log_2 \ln(1/2\mu) + 8 \\ &\le \lambda.\end{aligned}$$

In both cases, we have a contradiction. □

In the above reduction, the IND-CPA adversary does not make a random guess if the OW-CPA adversary fails to recover the plaintext. This reduction is different from the traditional one.

4.4 DDH and CDH Problems

Let G be a polynomial-time group-generation algorithm that outputs a description of a cyclic group $\mathbb{G}$ of prime order p and a generator $g \in \mathbb{G}$. The Computational Diffie-Hellman (CDH) problem is to compute g^{xy} from (g^x, g^y) for random $x, y \in \mathbb{Z}_p$. The success probability of an inner adversary A for the CDH game of G is formally defined by

$$\epsilon_A^{\mathrm{cdh}} = \Pr\left[(\mathbb{G}, p, g) \leftarrow G; x, y \xleftarrow{R} \mathbb{Z}_p; a \leftarrow A(\mathbb{G}, p, g, g^x, g^y) : a = g^{xy}\right]$$

The Decisional Diffie-Hellman (DDH) problem is to distinguish (g^x, g^y, g^z) from (g^x, g^y, g^{xy}) for random $x, y, z \in \mathbb{Z}_p$. The success probability of A for the DDH game of G is defined by

$$\epsilon_A^{\mathrm{ddh}} = \Pr\left[\begin{matrix} u \xleftarrow{R} \{0,1\}; (\mathbb{G}, p, g) \leftarrow G; \\ x, y, z \xleftarrow{R} \mathbb{Z}_p; (g_0, g_1) = (g^{xy}, g^z) \end{matrix} : u \leftarrow A(\mathbb{G}, p, g, g^x, g^y, g_u)\right].$$

It is well-known that the DDH problem is reducible to the corresponding CDH problem. Quantitatively, we show that the bit security of the CDH problem is at least that of the DDH problem.

Theorem 8. *Let G be a group-generation algorithm of cyclic groups of order p. If the DDH game of G has λ bit security with $p \geq \max\{2^{\lambda-\alpha+4}/(1-\mu), 64\}$, then the CDH game of G has $(\lambda - \alpha)$ bit security, where $\alpha = \log_2(1 + T_{\text{eq}}) + \max\{\log_2(\ln(1/2\mu)/(1-\mu)) + 3, \log_2 \ln(1/2\mu) + 8\}$ and T_{eq} is the computational complexity for checking the equality of given two elements in G.*

Proof. Assume for contradiction that the CDH game is not $(\lambda - \alpha)$-bit secure. By Theorem 2, there exists an inner adversary A for the CDH game G^{CDH} that runs in time T_A and has success probability $\epsilon_A > T_A(1-\mu)/2^{\lambda-\alpha}$. Consider an inner adversary A' for the DDH game that, given $(\mathbb{G}, p, g, g^x, g^y, g_u)$, runs A on input $(\mathbb{G}, p, g, g^x, g^y)$ to obtain a. If $a = g_u$, A' outputs 0. Otherwise, A' outputs 1. Let A_u be the probability distribution on the output of A' when $u \in \{0, 1\}$ was chosen in the DDH game. By definition, $A_0(0) = \epsilon_A$ and $A_0(1) = 1 - \epsilon_A$. Since the probability $A_1(0)$ is bounded above by the probability that a randomly chosen z equals xy in the DDH game, we have $A_1(0) \leq 1/p$ and $A_1(1) \geq 1 - 1/p$. Suppose that $\epsilon_A \leq 1/32$. By Lemma 8, $D_{1/2}(A_0 \| A_1) \geq \phi(q) \cdot \epsilon_A$ for $q \leq 1/p\epsilon_A$. Since $p \geq 2^{\lambda-\alpha+4}/(1-\mu)$, we have

$$\frac{1}{p\epsilon_A} \leq \frac{1-\mu}{2^{\lambda-\alpha+4}} \cdot \frac{2^{\lambda-\alpha}}{T_A(1-\mu)} \leq \frac{1}{16}.$$

Hence, $\phi(q) > 1/2$. It follows from Theorem 1 that

$$\begin{aligned} \mathrm{BS}^{\mu}_{G^{\mathrm{DDH}}} &\leq \log_2(T_A + T_{\text{eq}}) + \log_2(2/\epsilon_A) + \log_2 \ln(1/2\mu) + 2 \\ &< \lambda - \alpha + \log_2(1 + T_{\text{eq}}) + \log_2(\ln(1/2\mu)/(1-\mu)) + 3 \\ &\leq \lambda. \end{aligned}$$

When $\epsilon_A > 1/32$, the success probability of A' is

$$\Pr[u = 0] \cdot A_0(0) + \Pr[u = 1] \cdot A_1(1) \geq \frac{1}{2}(\epsilon_A + 1 - 1/p) > \frac{1}{2}\left(1 + \frac{1}{64}\right).$$

Since $T_A < 2^{\lambda-\alpha}$, Theorem 1 implies that

$$\begin{aligned} \mathrm{BS}^{\mu}_{G^{\mathrm{DDH}}} &\leq \log_2(T_A + T_{\text{eq}}) + \log_2(64) + \log_2 \ln(1/2\mu) + 2 \\ &< \lambda - \alpha + \log_2(1 + T_{\text{eq}}) + \log_2 \ln(1/2\mu) + 8 \\ &\leq \lambda. \end{aligned}$$

In both cases, we have a contradiction. □

4.5 Distribution Approximation

We consider replacing probability distributions in security games. Let $G = (X, R, \{O_i\}_i)$ be a game for primitive Π. Suppose that a distribution ensemble $Q = (Q_\theta)_\theta$ over $(\Omega_\theta)_\theta$ is employed in G, where each distribution Q_θ is available in a black-box manner such that when some player queries θ, a sample from Q_θ

is replied. We denote the game by G^Q for clarity. We want to show that the bit security of Π is preserved when replacing the ensemble Q with an approximated distribution ensemble $P = (P_\theta)_\theta$ if Q_θ and P_θ are close enough each other. The question is how close P should be to Q.

Let $d(P, Q)$ be a divergence/distance on probability distributions. A divergence is said to be (β, γ)-*efficient* if it satisfies the following conditions:

1. Sub-additivity: For two distribution ensembles $(X_i)_i$ and $(Y_i)_i$ over the same finite support $\prod_i \Omega_i$,
$$d((X_i)_i, (Y_i)_i) \leq \sum_i \max_{a \in \prod_{j<i} \Omega_j} d\left((X_i|X_{<i} = a), (Y_i|Y_{<i} = a)\right),$$
where $X_{<i} = (X_1, \ldots, X_{i-1})$ and $Y_{<i} = (Y_1, \ldots, Y_{i-1})$.
2. Data processing inequality: For any two distributions P and Q and function f, $d(f(P), f(Q)) \leq d(P, Q)$.
3. (β, γ)-Pythagorean probability preservation: For two distribution ensembles $(X_i)_i$ and $(Y_i)_i$ over the same finite support $\prod_i \Omega_i$, if
$$d\left((X_i|X_{<i} = a_i), (Y_i|Y_{<i} = a_i)\right) \leq \beta$$
for all i and $a_i \in \prod_{j<i} \Omega_j$, then
$$d_{\mathsf{TV}}((X_i)_i, (Y_i)_i) \leq \gamma \cdot \left\| \left(\max_{a_i} d((X_i|X_{<i} = a_i), (Y_i|Y_{<i} = a_i) \right)_i \right\|_2.$$

The above is a generalization of λ-efficient divergence in [18,19] so that it also captures the Hellinger distance as a special case.

It is known that the *max-log* distance is $(1/3, 1)$-efficient [18]. Also, the Hellinger distance is $(1, \sqrt{2})$-efficient [26]. The following lemma follows from the proof of Lemma 1 in [26].

Lemma 9. *Let $Q = (Q_1, \ldots, Q_\ell)$ and $P = (P_1, \ldots, P_\ell)$ be probability distribution ensembles over a finite support $\prod_i \Omega_i$. Then,*
$$d_{\mathsf{HD}}(P, Q) \leq \sqrt{\ell} \cdot \max_{a_i \in \prod_{j<i} \Omega_j} d_{\mathsf{HD}}(P_i|a_i, Q_i|a_i).$$

We present a sufficient condition under which a distribution ensemble Q can be replaced with P without compromising bit security. Specifically, to preserve λ-bit security, two ensembles should be close enough in $(2^{-\lambda/2}, O(1))$-efficient divergences for search-type games and are close within $2^{-\lambda/2}$ in the Hellinger distance for decision-type games.

Theorem 9. *Let $Q = (Q_i)_i$ and $P = (P_i)_i$ be distribution ensembles over a finite support $\prod_i \Omega_i$.*

1. *If an n-bit security game G^Q with $n > 1$ is λ-bit secure and $d((P_i|P_{<i} = a_i), (Q_i|Q_{<i} = a_i)) \leq 2^{-\lambda/2}$ for (β, γ)-efficient divergence d with $\beta \geq 2^{-\lambda/2}$, then G^P is $(\lambda - \alpha)$-bit secure for $\alpha = \max\{2 \log_2(\gamma \cdot \sqrt{\ln(1/\mu)/(1-\mu)}/(1 - 2^{-\rho} - \mu)), \rho + \log_2(\ln(1/\mu)^2/(1-\mu)) + 1\}$ and $\rho > 0$.*

2. *If a 1-bit security game G^Q is λ-bit secure and $d_{\mathsf{HD}}((P_i|P_{<i} = a_i), (Q_i|Q_{<i} = a_i)) \leq 2^{-\lambda/2}$ for any i and $a_i \in \prod_{j<i} \Omega_j$, then G^P is $(\lambda - \alpha)$-bit secure for $\alpha = \max\{\log_2(\ln(1/2\mu)/\ln(1/4\mu)) + 3, \log_2 \ln(1/2\mu) + 6, 7\}$.*

Proof. First, we show the case that $n > 1$. Let $\delta = \max_{i,a_i} d((P_i|P_{<i} = a_i), (Q_i|Q_{<i} = a_i))$, which is at most $2^{-\lambda/2}$ by assumption. Suppose for contradiction that G^P is not $(\lambda-\alpha)$-bit secure. Theorem 2 implies that there exists an inner adversary A for G^P that runs in time T_A and has success probability $\epsilon_A^P > T_A(1-\mu)/2^{\lambda-\alpha}$. Let N^P be the number of invocations of A by the outer adversary B to achieve $\epsilon_{A,B}^P \geq 1-\mu$. By Lemma 1, N^P is at most $\lceil \ln(1/\mu)/\epsilon_A^P \rceil$. Now consider the success probability $\epsilon_{A,B}^Q$, where the probability distribution P is replaced with Q. Since the number of queries to the distribution ensemble during the inner game is at most T_A, we have

$$\left|\epsilon_{A,B}^P - \epsilon_{A,B}^Q\right| \leq d_{\mathsf{TV}}(P^{N^P}, Q^{N^P}) \leq \gamma \cdot \sqrt{N^P T_A \delta^2},$$

where the last inequality follows from the (β, γ)-Pythagorean probability preservation property of d. It holds that

$$\begin{aligned}
\epsilon_{A,B}^Q &\geq \epsilon_{A,B}^P - \gamma \cdot \sqrt{N^P T_A \delta^2} \\
&> 1 - \mu - \gamma \cdot \sqrt{\frac{\ln(1/\mu)}{\epsilon_A^P} \cdot \frac{\epsilon_A^P \cdot 2^{\lambda-\alpha}}{1-\mu} \cdot \frac{1}{2^\lambda}} \\
&= 1 - \mu - \gamma \cdot \sqrt{\frac{\ln(1/\mu)}{(1-\mu)2^\alpha}} \\
&\geq 2^{-\rho},
\end{aligned}$$

where the last inequality follows by the assumption on α. We can consider the pair of adversaries (A, B) as an inner adversary A' that achieves the success probability $\epsilon_{A'} > 2^{-\rho}$ with computational complexity $T_{A'} = N^P T_A$. Thus, by Theorem 1, the bit security of G^Q is bounded above by

$$\log_2(N^P T_A) + \rho + \log_2 \ln(1/\mu) + 1 < \lambda - \alpha + \rho + \log_2(\ln(1/\mu)^2/(1-\mu)) + 1,$$

which is less than λ by assumption on α. It contradicts the assumption that G^Q is λ-bit secure.

Next, we prove the second case. Let $\delta = \max_{i,a_i} d_{\mathsf{HD}}((P_i|P_{<i} = a_i), (Q_i|Q_{<i} = a_i)) \leq 2^{-\lambda/2}$. Suppose for contradiction that G^P is not $(\lambda-\alpha)$-bit secure. Theorem 2 implies that there exists an inner adversary A for G^P that runs in time T_A and satisfies

$$d_{\mathsf{HD}}(A_0^P, A_1^P) > \min\left\{\frac{1}{\sqrt{2}}, \sqrt{\frac{T_A}{2^{\lambda-\alpha+1}} \cdot \ln(1/4\mu)}\right\} := \omega^P,$$

where A_u^P is the probability distribution of the output of A under the condition that $u \in \{0, 1\}$ is chosen in G^P. We define A_0^Q and A_1^Q for G^Q similarly. Since the number of queries to distribution ensembles P/Q is at most T_A, it follows from Lemma 9 and the data processing inequality that for $u \in \{0,1\}$,

$$d_{\mathsf{HD}}(A_u^P, A_u^Q) \leq \sqrt{T_A} \cdot \delta \leq \sqrt{\frac{T_A}{2^\lambda}}.$$

By the triangle inequality, we have

$$\begin{aligned} d_{\mathsf{HD}}(A_0^P, A_1^P) &\leq d_{\mathsf{HD}}(A_0^P, A_0^Q) + d_{\mathsf{HD}}(A_0^Q, A_1^Q) + d_{\mathsf{HD}}(A_1^Q, A_1^P) \\ &\leq d_{\mathsf{HD}}(A_0^Q, A_1^Q) + 2\sqrt{\frac{T_A}{2^\lambda}}. \end{aligned}$$

Thus, $d_{\mathsf{HD}}(A_0^Q, A_1^Q) \geq \omega^P - 2\sqrt{T_A/2^\lambda}$.

Suppose that $\omega^P = \sqrt{T_A \ln(1/4\mu)/2^{\lambda-\alpha+1}}$. Then,

$$\begin{aligned} d_{\mathsf{HD}}(A_0^Q, A_1^Q) &\geq \sqrt{\frac{2\ln(1/2\mu)T_A}{2^\lambda}} \left(\sqrt{\frac{2^{\alpha-2}\ln(1/4\mu)}{\ln(1/2\mu)}} - \sqrt{\frac{2}{\ln(1/2\mu)}} \right) \\ &> \sqrt{\frac{2\ln(1/2\mu)T_A}{2^\lambda}} \end{aligned}$$

by assumption on α. Let $\mathsf{adv}_{A,Q}^{\text{Renyi}}$ be the Rényi advantage of A for the game G^Q. By (2), we have $\mathsf{adv}_{A,Q}^{\text{Renyi}} \geq 2d_{\mathsf{HD}}(A_0^Q, A_1^Q)^2 > 4\ln(1/2\mu)T_A/2^\lambda$. It follows from Theorem 1 that the bit security of G^Q is at most

$$\log_2 T_A + \log_2 \left(1/\mathsf{adv}_{A,Q}^{\text{Renyi}}\right) + \log_2 \ln(1/2\mu) + 2 < \lambda.$$

Next, suppose that $\omega^P = 1/\sqrt{2}$. We have the relation that $d_{\mathsf{TV}}(A_0^P, A_1^P) \geq d_{\mathsf{HD}}(A_0^P, A_1^P)^2 \geq (\omega^P)^2 = 1/2$. Thus, adversary A has success probability $\epsilon_A^P = (1 + d_{\mathsf{TV}}(A_0^P, A_1^P))/2 \geq 3/4$ for G^P. Since we assume that G^P is not $(\lambda - \alpha)$-bit secure, it must be that $N_{A,B} \cdot T_A < 2^{\lambda-\alpha}$, implying that $T_A < 2^{\lambda-\alpha}$. Since the Hellinger distance is $(1, \sqrt{2})$-efficient, we have

$$\left|\epsilon_A^P - \epsilon_A^Q\right| \leq d_{\mathsf{TV}}(P, Q) \leq \gamma \cdot \sqrt{T_A \cdot \delta^2} \leq \sqrt{\frac{2T_A}{2^\lambda}} < \sqrt{\frac{1}{2^{\alpha-1}}} \leq \frac{1}{8},$$

where the last inequality follows from $\alpha \geq 7$. Hence, $\epsilon_A^Q \geq 5/8$. By Theorem 1, the bit security of G^Q is at most

$$\log_2 T_A + \log_2 \ln(1/2\mu) + 6 < \lambda - \alpha + \log_2 \ln(1/2\mu) + 6,$$

which is less than λ by assumption on α.

In both cases, we have shown that G^Q is not λ-bit secure, contradicting the assumption. Hence, the statement follows. □

4.6 Hybrid Arguments

We show that a hybrid argument can be generally applied to decision games in our framework.

Theorem 10. *Let $H_1, \dots, H_{k+1}$ be distributions over the same finite alphabet. If H_i and H_{i+1} are λ-bit secure indistinguishable for all i, then H_1 and H_{k+1} are $(\lambda - \alpha)$-bit secure indistinguishable for $\alpha = 2\log_2 k + \max\{\log_2(1/2\mu) + 1, 3\}$.*

Proof. Suppose that H_1 and H_{k+1} are not $(\lambda - \alpha)$-bit secure indistinguishable. Theorem 2 implies that there exists an inner adversary A that runs in time T_A and satisfies

$$d_{\mathsf{HD}}(A_1, A_{k+1}) > x = \min\left\{\frac{1}{\sqrt{2}}, \sqrt{\frac{T_A}{2^{\lambda-\alpha+1}} \cdot \ln(1/4\mu)}\right\},$$

where A_i is the output distribution of A on input H_i. By the triangle inequality, we have

$$x < d_{\mathsf{HD}}(A_1, A_{k+1}) \le \sum_{i=1}^{k} d_{\mathsf{HD}}(A_i, A_{i+1}).$$

There must be some i such that $d_{\mathsf{HD}}(A_i, A_{i+1}) > x/k$. Let A^u be the output distribution of A when $u \in \{0, 1\}$ was chosen. By (2), the Rényi advantage of A for distinguishing A_i from A_{i+1} satisfies

$$\mathsf{adv}_A^{\mathrm{Renyi}} = D_{1/2}(A^0 \| A^1) \ge 2 d_{\mathsf{HD}}(A_i, A_{i+1})^2 > 2(x/k)^2.$$

By Theorem 1, the bit security $\mathrm{BS}^{\mu}_{i,i+1}$ for distinguish A_i from A_{i+1} satisfies

$$\mathrm{BS}^{\mu}_{i,i+1} < \log_2 T_A + 2\log_2(k/x) + \log_2(1/2\mu) + 1.$$

Suppose $x = 1/\sqrt{2}$. Since H_1 and H_{k+1} are not $(\lambda - \alpha)$-bit secure, we have $2^{\lambda-\alpha} > N_{A,B} \cdot T_A \ge T_A$. Thus, $\mathrm{BS}^{\mu}_{i,i+1} < \lambda - \alpha + 2\log_2 k + \log_2(1/2\mu) + 1 \le \lambda$. Suppose $x = \sqrt{(T_A/2^{\lambda-\alpha+1})\ln(1/4\mu)}$. Then,

$$\begin{aligned}\mathrm{BS}^{\mu}_{i,i+1} &< \log_2 T_A + 2\log_2 k - \log_2 T_A + \lambda - \alpha + 1 - \log_2(1/4\mu) + \log_2(1/2\mu) + 1 \\ &\le \lambda.\end{aligned}$$

In both cases, we have $\mathrm{BS}^{\mu}_{i,i+1} < \lambda$, which contradicts the assumption that H_i and H_{i+1} are λ-bit secure indistinguishable. □

Acknowledgements. The work of S.W. was supported in part by JSPS KAKENHI under Grant 20H02144.

References

1. Alon, N., Goldreich, O., Hastad, J., Peralta, R.: Simple construction of almost k-wise independent random variables. Random Struct. Algorithms **3**(3), 289–304 (1992)

2. Bai, S., Langlois, A., Lepoint, T., Stehlé, D., Steinfeld, R.: Improved security proofs in lattice-based cryptography: using the Rényi divergence rather than the statistical distance. In: Iwata, T., Cheon, J.H. (eds.) ASIACRYPT 2015. LNCS, vol. 9452, pp. 3–24. Springer, Heidelberg (2015). https://doi.org/10.1007/978-3-662-48797-6_1
3. Bernstein, D.J., Lange, T.: Non-uniform cracks in the concrete: the power of free precomputation. In: Sako, K., Sarkar, P. (eds.) ASIACRYPT 2013. LNCS, vol. 8270, pp. 321–340. Springer, Heidelberg (2013). https://doi.org/10.1007/978-3-642-42045-0_17
4. Bogdanov, A., Guo, S., Masny, D., Richelson, S., Rosen, A.: On the hardness of learning with rounding over small modulus. In: Kushilevitz, E., Malkin, T. (eds.) TCC 2016. LNCS, vol. 9562, pp. 209–224. Springer, Heidelberg (2016). https://doi.org/10.1007/978-3-662-49096-9_9
5. Cover, T.M., Thomas, J.A.: Elements of Information Theory, 2nd edn. Wiley, Hoboken (2006)
6. De, A., Trevisan, L., Tulsiani, M.: Time space tradeoffs for attacks against one-way functions and PRGs. In: Rabin, T. (ed.) CRYPTO 2010. LNCS, vol. 6223, pp. 649–665. Springer, Heidelberg (2010). https://doi.org/10.1007/978-3-642-14623-7_35
7. Dodis, Y., Steinberger, J.: Message authentication codes from unpredictable block ciphers. In: Halevi, S. (ed.) CRYPTO 2009. LNCS, vol. 5677, pp. 267–285. Springer, Heidelberg (2009). https://doi.org/10.1007/978-3-642-03356-8_16
8. Fuchs, C.A., van de Graaf, J.: Cryptographic distinguishability measures for quantum-mechanical states. IEEE Trans. Inf. Theory **45**(4), 1216–1227 (1999)
9. Goldreich, O.: The Foundations of Cryptography - Volume 1: Basic Techniques. Cambridge University Press, Cambridge (2001)
10. Goldreich, O., Levin, L.A.: A hard-core predicate for all one-way functions. In: Johnson, D.S. (ed.) Proceedings of the 21st Annual ACM Symposium on Theory of Computing, Seattle, Washington, USA, 14–17 May 1989, pp. 25–32. ACM (1989)
11. Götze, F., Sambale, H., Sinulis, A.: Higher order concentration for functions of weakly dependent random variables. Electron. J. Probab. **24**(85), 1–19 (2019)
12. Iwamoto, M., Shikata, J.: Information theoretic security for encryption based on conditional Rényi entropies. In: Padró, C. (ed.) ICITS 2013. LNCS, vol. 8317, pp. 103–121. Springer, Cham (2014). https://doi.org/10.1007/978-3-319-04268-8_7
13. Koblitz, N., Menezes, A.: Another look at non-uniformity. Groups Complex. Cryptol. **5**(2), 117–139 (2013)
14. Kowalczyk, L., Malkin, T., Ullman, J., Zhandry, M.: Strong hardness of privacy from weak traitor tracing. In: Hirt, M., Smith, A. (eds.) TCC 2016. LNCS, vol. 9985, pp. 659–689. Springer, Heidelberg (2016). https://doi.org/10.1007/978-3-662-53641-4_25
15. Langlois, A., Stehlé, D., Steinfeld, R.: GGHLite: more efficient multilinear maps from ideal lattices. In: Nguyen, P.Q., Oswald, E. (eds.) EUROCRYPT 2014. LNCS, vol. 8441, pp. 239–256. Springer, Heidelberg (2014). https://doi.org/10.1007/978-3-642-55220-5_14
16. Levin, L.A.: Randomness and non-determinism. J. Symb. Log. **58**(3), 1102–1103 (1993)
17. Matsuda, T., Takahashi, K., Murakami, T., Hanaoka, G.: Improved security evaluation techniques for imperfect randomness from arbitrary distributions. In: Lin, D., Sako, K. (eds.) PKC 2019. LNCS, vol. 11442, pp. 549–580. Springer, Cham (2019). https://doi.org/10.1007/978-3-030-17253-4_19

18. Micciancio, D., Walter, M.: Gaussian sampling over the integers: efficient, generic, constant-time. In: Katz, J., Shacham, H. (eds.) CRYPTO 2017. LNCS, vol. 10402, pp. 455–485. Springer, Cham (2017). https://doi.org/10.1007/978-3-319-63715-0_16
19. Micciancio, D., Walter, M.: On the bit security of cryptographic primitives. In: Nielsen, J.B., Rijmen, V. (eds.) EUROCRYPT 2018. LNCS, vol. 10820, pp. 3–28. Springer, Cham (2018). https://doi.org/10.1007/978-3-319-78381-9_1
20. Mironov, I.: Rényi differential privacy. In: 30th IEEE Computer Security Foundations Symposium, CSF 2017, Santa Barbara, CA, USA, 21–25 August 2017, pp. 263–275. IEEE Computer Society (2017)
21. Naor, J., Naor, M.: Small-bias probability spaces: efficient constructions and applications. SIAM J. Comput. **22**(4), 838–856 (1993)
22. Prest, T.: Sharper bounds in lattice-based cryptography using the Rényi divergence. In: Takagi, T., Peyrin, T. (eds.) ASIACRYPT 2017. LNCS, vol. 10624, pp. 347–374. Springer, Cham (2017). https://doi.org/10.1007/978-3-319-70694-8_13
23. Sason, I., Verdú, S.: f-divergence inequalities. IEEE Trans. Inf. Theory **62**(11), 5973–6006 (2016)
24. Takashima, K., Takayasu, A.: Tighter security for efficient lattice cryptography via the Rényi divergence of optimized orders. In: Au, M.-H., Miyaji, A. (eds.) ProvSec 2015. LNCS, vol. 9451, pp. 412–431. Springer, Cham (2015). https://doi.org/10.1007/978-3-319-26059-4_23
25. van Erven, T., Harremoës, P.: Rényi divergence and Kullback-Leibler divergence. IEEE Trans. Inf. Theory **60**(7), 3797–3820 (2014)
26. Yasunaga, K.: Replacing probability distributions in security games via Hellinger distance. In: Tessaro, S. (ed.) 2nd Conference on Information-Theoretic Cryptography (ITC 2021), volume 199 of Leibniz International Proceedings in Informatics (LIPIcs), Dagstuhl, Germany, pp. 17:1–17:15. Schloss Dagstuhl - Leibniz-Zentrum für Informatik (2021)

Giving an Adversary Guarantees (Or: How to Model Designated Verifier Signatures in a Composable Framework)

Ueli Maurer[1](✉), Christopher Portmann[2], and Guilherme Rito[1]

[1] Department of Computer Science, ETH Zürich, Zürich, Switzerland
{maurer,gteixeir}@inf.ethz.ch

[2] Concordium, Zürich, Switzerland
cp@concordium.com

Abstract. When defining a security notion, one typically specifies what dishonest parties cannot achieve. For example, communication is confidential if a third party cannot learn anything about the messages being transmitted, and it is authentic if a third party cannot impersonate the real (honest) sender. For certain applications, however, security crucially relies on giving dishonest parties certain capabilities. As an example, in Designated Verifier Signature (DVS) schemes, one captures that only the designated verifier can be convinced of the authenticity of a message by guaranteeing that any dishonest party can forge signatures which look indistinguishable (to a third party) from original ones created by the sender.

However, composable frameworks cannot typically model such guarantees as they are only designed to bound what a dishonest party can do. In this paper we show how to model such guarantees—that dishonest parties must have some capability—in the Constructive Cryptography framework (Maurer and Renner, ICS 2011). More concretely, we give the first composable security definitions for Multi-Designated Verifier Signature (MDVS) schemes—a generalization of DVS schemes.

The ideal world is defined as the intersection of two worlds. The first captures authenticity in the usual way. The second provides the guarantee that a dishonest party can forge signatures. By taking the intersection we have an ideal world with the desired properties.

We also compare our composable definitions to existing security notions for MDVS schemes from the literature. We find that only recently, 23 years after the introduction of MDVS schemes, sufficiently strong security notions were introduced capturing the security of MDVS schemes (Damgård et al., TCC 2020). As we prove, however, these notions are still strictly stronger than necessary.

C. Portmann—Work done while author was at ETH Zürich, Switzerland.

M. Tibouchi and H. Wang (Eds.): ASIACRYPT 2021, LNCS 13092, pp. 189–219, 2021.
https://doi.org/10.1007/978-3-030-92078-4_7

1 Introduction

1.1 Composable Security

In a nutshell, composable security frameworks define security by designing an ideal world and proving that the real world is indistinguishable [2,5,8,12,20,22,23,26]. Typically, one first designs an *ideal functionality*, which corresponds to the functionality one wishes to achieve. For example, if one wants confidential communication from Alice to Bob, then the ideal functionality allows Alice to input messages, Bob to read messages, and guarantees that Eve can only learn the length of the messages input by Alice. Eve could additionally be given extra capabilities that do not violate confidentiality, e.g. inputting messages. A simulator is then connected to this ideal functionality, covering the idealized inputs and outputs available to dishonest parties and providing "real" inputs and outputs to the environment (that should be indistinguishable from those of the real world). Let $\mathbf{S}$ denote an ideal functionality, and $\mathsf{sim}\mathbf{S}$ the ideal world consisting of $\mathbf{S}$ with some simulator sim attached. Since any (efficient) simulator $\mathsf{sim} \in \Omega$ is acceptable, one can alternatively view the ideal world as the set of all possible acceptable ideal worlds:

$$\boldsymbol{\mathcal{S}} = \{\mathsf{sim}\mathbf{S}\}_{\mathsf{sim}\in\Omega}. \tag{1.1}$$

A security proof then shows that the real world $\boldsymbol{\mathcal{R}}$ (also modeled as a set) is a subset of the ideal world $\boldsymbol{\mathcal{S}}$. Since sim covers the dishonest parties' interfaces of $\mathbf{S}$, it can only further limit the capabilities of dishonest parties. For example, an ideal functionality for confidentiality might allow a third party to change Alice's message, but if this is not possible in the real world, the simulator can disallow the environment to use that capability. This structure of the ideal world makes it impossible for traditional composable frameworks to provide *guarantees* about a dishonest party's capabilities, because these might be blocked by the simulator.

Some prior works using the Constructive Cryptography (CC) framework [14,23] have noted that the ideal world does not have to be structured as in Eq. (1.1). In particular, the simulator does not have to necessarily cover all dishonest parties' interfaces (or might not be present at all). This relaxed view of the ideal world allows one to define composable security notions capturing the security of schemes whose security could not be modeled by traditional composable frameworks. In this work we crucially exploit this to give the first composable security notions for Multi-Designated Verifier Signature schemes. We refer the interested reader to [3] to see how to model Digital Signature Schemes (DSS) in CC, and to [14] for an extended introduction to CC, in which some of the novel techniques used here were first applied.

1.2 MDVS Schemes

Designated Verifier Signature (DVS) schemes are a variant of DSS that allow a signer to sign messages towards a specific receiver, chosen (or *designated*) by the signer [9,11,13,16–19,27–30,32]. The goal of these schemes is to establish an *authentic* communication channel, say from a sender Alice to a receiver Bob, where the *authenticity* property is *exclusive* to the receiver Bob designated by Alice, i.e. Bob and only Bob can tell whether Alice actually sent some message authentically. In Multi-Designated Verifier Signature (MDVS) schemes [9,11, 13,16,32], multiple receivers may be designated verifiers for the same message, e.g. Alice signs a message so that both Bob and Charlie can verify that Alice generated the signature, but a third party Eve would not be convinced that Alice signed it. This should hold even if a verifier is dishonest, say Bob, and provides his secret keys to Eve. MDVS schemes achieve this by guaranteeing that Bob could forge signatures that would look indistinguishable to Eve from Alice's signatures—but Charlie could distinguish the two using his secret key, thus authenticity with respect to the designated verifiers is not violated.

MDVS schemes have numerous applications: from secure messaging (and in particular secure group messaging for the multi-verifier case) [11], to online auctions wherein all bidders place their binding-bids in a non-interactive way, and the highest bidder wins. In the case of online auctions a bidder Bob would then sign its bid to both the auctioneer Charlie and his bank Blockobank, and if Bob wins Charlie would then sign a document stating Bob is the winner of the auction; the winner could also be kept anonymous by having Charlie signing such document only with respect to Bob, its bank Blockobank and any other official entity needed to confirm Bob's ownership of the auctioned item.

While composable security notions for DSS are well understood [1,3,5,6], the literature on (M)DVS schemes provides only a series of different game-based security definitions—which we discuss in detail in Sect. 5—capturing a variety of properties that an MDVS scheme could possess. By defining the ideal world for an MDVS scheme in this work, we can compare the resulting composable definition to the game-based ones and determine which security properties are needed. It turns out that crucial properties for the security of MDVS schemes like consistency—all (honest) designated verifiers will either accept or reject the same signature—and security against any subset of dishonest verifiers were only introduced very recently [11].

1.3 Contributions

Providing Guarantees to Dishonest Parties. To capture that a dishonest party is guaranteed to have some capability, we introduce a new type of ideal world specification, which we sketch in this section. The first step consists in defining a set of ideal functionalities (called resources or resource specification in CC [22, 23]) that have the required property. For example, in the case of MDVS schemes, we want a dishonest receiver to be able to generate a valid signature. This corresponds to a channel in which both Alice (the honest sender) and Bob (the dishonest receiver) may insert messages. Thus anyone reading from that channel would not know if the message is from Alice or Bob. Let $\widehat{\boldsymbol{\mathcal{X}}}$ denote such a set. The ideal worlds we are interested in are those in which a dishonest receiver could achieve this property if they run an (explicit) forging algorithm π. Thus, the ideal world of interest is defined as

$$\boldsymbol{\mathcal{X}} = \left\{ \mathbf{X} : \pi\mathbf{X} \in \widehat{\boldsymbol{\mathcal{X}}} \right\}, \tag{1.2}$$

where $\pi\mathbf{X}$ denotes a resource $\mathbf{X}$ with the algorithm π being run at the dishonest receivers' interface of $\mathbf{X}$.

Similar techniques could be used to model ideal worlds for ring signatures [4, 27] or coercibility [22, 31].

Composable Security Notions for MDVS Schemes. We then use the technique described above to define composable security for MDVS schemes. For example, if one considers a fixed honest sender and a fixed set of designated verifiers (some of which may be dishonest), then an MDVS scheme is expected to achieve *authenticity* with respect to the honest verifiers, but this authenticity should be *exclusive* to them, meaning that any dishonest player should be able to generate a signature that would fool a third party Eve. Authenticity is captured in the usual way (see, e.g. [3]), as in Eq. (1.1), i.e. we define an authentic channel $\mathbf{A}$ from Alice to the honest verifiers, and the ideal world is given by a set

$$\boldsymbol{\mathcal{A}} = \{\mathsf{sim}\,\mathbf{A}\}_{\mathsf{sim} \in \Omega}\,. \tag{1.3}$$

The exclusiveness of the authenticity is defined with a (set of) ideal world(s) as in Eq. (1.2). Both properties are then achieved by taking the intersection of the two, namely by proving that for the real world $\boldsymbol{\mathcal{R}}$ we have

$$\boldsymbol{\mathcal{R}} \subseteq \boldsymbol{\mathcal{A}} \cap \boldsymbol{\mathcal{X}}.$$

Comparison With Existing Notions for MDVS. Now that the composable security notion is defined, we compare it to the game-based definitions from the literature. It turns out that only the most recent definitions from [11] are sufficient to achieve composable security.

More precisely, we prove reductions and a separation between our composable security definition and the games of [11]. Our statements imply the following:

- any MDVS scheme which is Correct, Consistent, Unforgeable and Off-The-Record (according to [11]) can be used to construct the ideal world for MDVS;
- there is an MDVS scheme which satisfies the composable definition, but which is not Off-The-Record (as defined in [11]).

1.4 Structure of This Paper

In Sect. 2 we start by introducing the concepts from CC [14, 20, 22, 23] that are needed to understand the framework. We also define *repositories* which are the resources we use in this work for communication between parties jointly running a protocol (see also [3]). In Sect. 3 we consider a setting in which the sender and designated receivers are fixed and publicly known. This allows us to define the ideal worlds and the corresponding composable security definition in a simpler setting. Also for simplicity, we only require that dishonest delegated verifiers have the ability to forge signatures, not third parties. We then prove that the security games from [11] are sufficient to imply composable security. In Sect. 4 we model the more general setting where the sender and designated receivers can be arbitrarily chosen. As before, we model composable security and prove that the security games from [11] are sufficient to achieve composable security in this setting as well. But we also prove a seperation between the Off-The-Record game from [11] and the composable security defintion, showing that this game is stronger than necessary. Note that in this section any dishonest party should be able to forge signatures, not only the dishonest designated verifiers. Finally, in Sect. 5 we discuss the literature related to MDVS schemes and some of the issues in previous security definitions.

2 Constructive Cryptography

The Constructive Cryptography (CC) framework [20,22] views cryptography as a resource theory: protocols construct new resources from existing (assumed) ones. For example, a CCA-secure encryption scheme constructs a confidential channel given a public key infrastructure and an insecure channel on which the ciphertext is sent [10]. The notion of resource construction is inherently composable: if a protocol π_1 constructs $\boldsymbol{\mathcal{R}}$ from $\boldsymbol{\mathcal{S}}$ and π_2 constructs $\boldsymbol{\mathcal{T}}$ from $\boldsymbol{\mathcal{S}}$, then running both protocols will construct $\boldsymbol{\mathcal{T}}$ given that one initially has access to $\boldsymbol{\mathcal{R}}$.[1]

In this section we first review the building blocks of CC in Sect. 2.1. We explain how security is defined in Sect. 2.2. Then in Sect. 2.3 we model a specific type of resources, namely repositories, which is an abstract model of communication. Throughout the rest of the paper, for any set of parties $\mathcal{S}$, we denote by $\mathcal{S}^H$ the partition of $\mathcal{S}$ containing all honest parties, and $\overline{\mathcal{S}^H}$ the partition containing all dishonest parties, such that $\mathcal{S} = \mathcal{S}^H \uplus \overline{\mathcal{S}^H}$. The set of all parties is denoted $\mathcal{P}$.

2.1 Resource Specifications, Converters, and Distinguishers

Resource. A *resource* is an interactive system shared by all parties, e.g. a channel or a key resource—and is akin to an ideal functionality in UC [5]. Each party can provide inputs and receive outputs from the resource. We use the term *interface* to denote specific subsets of the inputs and outputs, in particular, all the inputs and outputs available to a specific party are assigned to that party's interface. For example, an insecure channel **INS** allows all parties to input messages at their interface and read the contents of the channel. A confidential channel resource **CONF** shared between a sender Alice, a receiver Bob and an eavesdropper Eve allows Alice to input messages at her interface; it allows Eve to insert her own messages and it allows her to duplicate Alice's messages, but not to read them[2]; and it allows Bob to receive at his interface any of the messages inserted by Alice or Eve. As another example, an authenticated channel

[1] For a formal statement of the composition theorem used here we refer to [14,23].

[2] More precisely, the **CONF** channel only allows Eve to read the length of messages.

from Bob to Alice (**AUT**) allows Bob to send messages through the channel and allows Alice and Eve to read messages from the channel.

Formally, a resource is a random system [24,25], i.e. it is uniquely defined by a sequence of conditional probability distributions. For simplicity, however, we usually describe resources by pseudo-code.

If multiple resources $\{\mathbf{R}_i\}_{i=1}^n$ are simultaneously accessible, we write $\mathbf{R} = [\mathbf{R}_1, \ldots, \mathbf{R}_n]$, or alternatively $\mathbf{R} = [\mathbf{R}_i]_{i\in\{1,\ldots,n\}}$, for the new resource obtained by the parallel composition of all $\mathbf{R}_i$, i.e. $\mathbf{R}$ is a resource that provides each party with access to the (sub)resources $\mathbf{R}_i$.

Converter. A *converter* is an interactive system executed either locally by a single party or cooperatively by multiple parties. Its inputs and outputs are partitioned into an inside interface and an outside interface. The inside interface connects to (those parties' interfaces of) the available resources, resulting in a new resource. For instance, connecting a converter α to Alice's interface A of a resource $\mathbf{R}$ results in a new resource, which we denote by $\alpha^A\mathbf{R}$. The outside interface of the converter α is now the new A-interface of $\alpha^A\mathbf{R}$. Thus, a converter may be seen as a map between resources. Note that converters applied at different interfaces commute, i.e. $\beta^B\alpha^A\mathbf{R} = \alpha^A\beta^B\mathbf{R}$.

A protocol is given by a tuple of converters $\pi = (\pi_{P_i})_{P_i\in\mathcal{P}^H}$, one for each (honest) party $P_i \in \mathcal{P}^H$. Simulators are also given by converters. For any set $\mathcal{S}$ will often write $\pi^{\mathcal{S}}\mathbf{R}$ for $(\pi_{P_i})_{P_i\in\mathcal{S}}\mathbf{R}$. We also often drop the interface superscript and write just $\pi\mathbf{R}$ when it is clear from the context to which interfaces π connects.

For example, suppose Alice and Bob share an insecure channel **INS** and a single use authenticated channel from Bob to Alice **AUT** and suppose that Alice runs a converter enc and Bob runs a converter dec, and that these converters behave as follows: First, converter dec generates a public-secret key-pair $(\mathtt{pk}, \mathtt{sk})$ for Bob and sends $\mathtt{pk}$ over the single-use authenticated channel **AUT** to Alice. Each time a message m is input at the outside interface of enc, the converter uses Bob's public key $\mathtt{pk}$—which it received from **AUT**—to compute a ciphertext $c = Enc_{\mathtt{pk}}(m)$; it then sends this ciphertext over the insecure channel to Bob (via the inside interface of enc connected to **INS**). Each time Bob's decryption converter dec receives a ciphertext c from the **INS** channel, it uses Bob's secret key $\mathtt{sk}$ to decrypt c, obtaining a message $m = Dec_{\mathtt{sk}}(c)$, and if m is a valid plaintext, the converter then outputs m to Bob (via the outside interface of the converter). The real world of such a system is given by

$$\mathsf{dec}^B\mathsf{enc}^A[\mathbf{AUT}, \mathbf{INS}]. \tag{2.1}$$

Specification. Often one is not interested in a unique resource, but in a set of resources with common properties. For example, the confidential channel described above allows Eve to insert messages of her own. Yet, if she did not have this ability, the resulting channel would still be a confidential one. We call such a set a *resource specification* (or simply also a *resource*), and denote it with a bold calligraphic letter, e.g. a specification of confidential channels could be defined as

$$\boldsymbol{\mathcal{T}} = \left\{\mathsf{sim}^E \mathbf{CONF}\right\}_{\mathsf{sim} \in \Omega} . \tag{2.2}$$

where Ω is a set of converters (the simulators) that are applied at Eve's interface.[3]

Parallel composition of specifications $\boldsymbol{\mathcal{R}}$ and $\boldsymbol{\mathcal{S}}$, and composition of a converter α and a specification $\boldsymbol{\mathcal{R}}$ follow by applying the operations elementwise to the resources $\mathbf{R} \in \boldsymbol{\mathcal{R}}$ and $\mathbf{S} \in \boldsymbol{\mathcal{S}}$.

Distinguisher. To measure the distance between two resources we use the standard notion of a distinguisher, an interactive system $\mathbf{D}$ which interacts with a resource at all its interfaces, and outputs a bit 0 or 1. The distinguishing advantage for distinguisher $\mathbf{D}$ is defined as

$$\Delta^{\mathbf{D}}(\mathbf{R}, \mathbf{S}) := \Pr[\mathbf{DS} = 1] - \Pr[\mathbf{DR} = 1]$$

where $\mathbf{DR}$ and $\mathbf{DS}$ are the random variables over the output of $\mathbf{D}$ when it interacts with $\mathbf{R}$ and $\mathbf{S}$, respectively.

Relaxation. Typically one proves that the ability to distinguish between two resources is bounded by some function of the distinguisher, e.g. for any $\mathbf{D}$,

$$|\Delta^{\mathbf{D}}(\mathbf{R}, \mathbf{S})| \leq \varepsilon(\mathbf{D})$$

where $\varepsilon(\mathbf{D})$ might be the probability that $\mathbf{D}$ can win a game or solve some finite instance of a problem believed to be hard.[4]

This distance measure then naturally defines another type of specification, namely an ε-ball: for a resource specification $\boldsymbol{\mathcal{R}}$, the ε-ball around $\boldsymbol{\mathcal{R}}$ is given by

$$\boldsymbol{\mathcal{R}}^{\varepsilon} := \bigcup_{\mathbf{R} \in \boldsymbol{\mathcal{R}}} \{\mathbf{S} : \forall \mathbf{D}, |\Delta^{\mathbf{D}}(\mathbf{R}, \mathbf{S})| \leq \varepsilon(\mathbf{D})\}. \tag{2.3}$$

If one chooses a function $\varepsilon(\mathbf{D})$ which is small for a certain class of distinguishers $\mathbf{D}$—e.g. $\varepsilon(\mathbf{D})$ is small for all $\mathbf{D}$ that cannot be used to solve (a finite instance of) a problem believed to be hard, as described in Footnote 4—but potentially large for other $\mathbf{D}$, then we have a specification of resources that are indistinguishable (to the distinguishers in the chosen class) from (one of) those in $\boldsymbol{\mathcal{R}}$.

---

[3] The definition of the set Ω may depend on the context, e.g. whether one is interested in bounded run time, bounded memory, and whether one is making finite or asymptotic statements.

[4] Formally, one first finds an (efficient) reduction χ which constructs a solver $\mathbf{S} = \chi(\mathbf{D})$ from any distinguisher $\mathbf{D}$. Then one bounds the distance $|\Delta^{\mathbf{D}}(\mathbf{R}, \mathbf{S})|$ with a function of the probability that $\chi(\mathbf{D})$ succeeds is solving some problem, i.e., $\varepsilon(\mathbf{D}) := f(\Pr[\chi(\mathbf{D}) \text{ succeeds}])$ for an f that does not significantly alter the probability of success. Thus for any $\mathbf{D}$ that cannot be used to solve the problem, $|\Delta^{\mathbf{D}}(\mathbf{R}, \mathbf{S})|$ must be small.

Remark 1 (Finite vs. Asymptotic security statements). In this paper, rather than making asymptotic security statements (where one considers the limit $k \to \infty$ for security parameter k) we make a security statement for each possible $k \in \mathbb{N}$. Specifications, resources, converters and distinguishers are then defined for a fixed security parameter k. If needed, one can obtain the corresponding asymptotic statements by defining sequences of resources, converters and distinguishers and then making a statement about the limit behavior of these sequences when $k \to \infty$.

2.2 Composable Security

We now have all the elements needed to define a cryptographic construction.

Definition 1 (Cryptographic Construction [14,23]**).** *Let $\mathcal{R}$ and $\mathcal{S}$ be two resource specifications, and π be a protocol for $\mathcal{R}$. We say that π constructs $\mathcal{S}$ from $\mathcal{R}$ if*

$$\pi\mathcal{R} \subseteq \mathcal{S}. \tag{2.4}$$

For example, in the case of constructing the confidential channel described above, the real world is the singleton set with the element given in Eq. (2.1), and the ideal world is given by an ε-ball around the set of confidential channels given in Eq. (2.2), i.e. to prove security one would need to show that

$$\mathsf{dec}^B\mathsf{enc}^A\{[\mathbf{AUT}, \mathbf{INS}]\} \subseteq \left(\{\mathsf{sim}^E\mathbf{CONF}\}_{\mathsf{sim}\in\Omega}\right)^{\varepsilon}. \tag{2.5}$$

Equation (2.5) is equivalent to the more traditional notation of requiring the existence of a simulator sim such that for all $\mathbf{D}$,

$$|\Delta^{\mathbf{D}}(\mathsf{dec}^B\mathsf{enc}^A[\mathbf{AUT}, \mathbf{INS}], \mathsf{sim}^E\mathbf{CONF})| \leq \varepsilon(\mathbf{D}).$$

But the formulation in Definition 1 is more general and allows other types of ideal worlds to be defined than the specification obtained by appending a simulator at Eve's interface of the ideal resource and taking an ε-ball.

Remark 2 (Asymptotic Construction). As pointed out in Remark 1, specifications, resources, converters and distinguishers are defined for a fixed security parameter k. The specifications and converters in Definition 1 are then to be interpreted as being defined for a concrete security parameter k, and Eq. (2.4) is to be understood as a statement about a fixed k, i.e.

$$\pi_k\mathcal{R}_k \subseteq \mathcal{S}_k. \tag{2.6}$$

For simplicity we omit the security parameter whenever it is clear from the context, and thus will simply write as in Eq. (2.4). If one wishes to make an asymptotic security statement then one defines efficient families $\{\pi_k\}_{k\in\mathbb{N}}$, $\{\mathcal{R}_k\}_{k\in\mathbb{N}}$, $\{\mathcal{S}_k\}_{k\in\mathbb{N}}$ and shows that Eq. (2.6) holds asymptotically in k, meaning that there is a family $\vec{\varepsilon} := \{\varepsilon_k\}_{k\in\mathbb{N}}$ of ε-balls such that $\pi_k\mathcal{R}_k \subseteq (\mathcal{S}_k{}^{\varepsilon_k})$, and for any efficient family of distinguishers $\vec{\mathbf{D}} := \{\mathbf{D}_k\}_{k\in\mathbb{N}}$, the function $\vec{\varepsilon}(\vec{\mathbf{D}}) : \mathbb{N} \to \mathbb{R}$ defined as $\vec{\varepsilon}(\vec{\mathbf{D}})(k) := \varepsilon_k(\mathbf{D}_k)$ is negligible.

Remark 3 (Modeling different sets of (dis)honest parties). When one is interested in making security statements for different sets of (dis)honest parties it is not sufficient to make a single statement as in Definition 1. Instead, one makes a statement for each relevant set of (dis)honest parties. For example, let π be the protocol defining a converter π_i for each party $P_i \in \mathcal{P}$. For every relevant subset of honest parties $\mathcal{P}^H \subseteq \mathcal{P}$, letting $\mathcal{R}^{\mathcal{P}^H}$ and $\mathcal{S}^{\mathcal{P}^H}$ denote, respectively, the available resources' specifications—the real world—and the desired resources' specifications—the ideal world—one needs to prove that

$$\pi^{\mathcal{P}^H}\mathcal{R}^{\mathcal{P}^H} \subseteq \mathcal{S}^{\mathcal{P}^H},$$

where $\pi^{\mathcal{P}^H}\mathcal{R}^{\mathcal{P}^H}$ denotes the attachment of each converter π_i—run by honest party $P_i \in \mathcal{P}^H$ as ascribed by the protocol π—to $\mathcal{R}^{\mathcal{P}^H}$. In this paper, although we will make statements of this format, i.e. modeling different sets of (dis)honest parties, we will drop the superscript $\mathcal{P}^H$ from the notation of the converters and specifications, whenever clear from the context.

2.3 Access Restricted Repositories

We formalize communication between different parties as having access to a *repository* resource. More specifically, a repository consists of a set of registers and a single buffer containing register identifiers; a register is a pair $\texttt{reg} = (\texttt{id}, m)$, which includes the register's identifier $\texttt{id}$ (uniquely identifying the register among all repositories), and a message $m \in \mathcal{M}$ (where $\mathcal{M}$ is the message space of the repository[5]). Access rights to a repository are divided in three classes: *write access* allows a party to add messages to a repository, *read access* allows a party to read all the messages in a repository, and *copy access* allows a party to make duplicates of messages already existing in the repository (without necessarily being able to read the messages).[6] Let $\mathcal{P}$ be the set of all parties, and let $\mathcal{W} \subseteq \mathcal{P}$, $\mathcal{R} \subseteq \mathcal{P}$ and $\mathcal{C} \subseteq \mathcal{P}$ denote the parties with write, read and copy access to a repository **rep**, respectively. We will write ${}^{\mathcal{C}}\mathbf{rep}_{\mathcal{R}}^{\mathcal{W}}$ whenever it is needed to make the access permissions explicit. Though we may drop them and only write **rep** whenever clear from the context. For example, in the three party setting with sender Alice, receiver Bob and dishonest Eve, i.e. $\mathcal{P} = \{A, B, E\}$, the insecure channel mentioned in Sect. 2.1—which allows all parties to read and write—is given by $\mathbf{INS}_{\mathcal{P}}^{\mathcal{P}}$;[7] an authentic channel from Alice

[5] In analogy to Remark 1 we consider that a repository defined for security parameter k has message space $\mathcal{M}_k$; for a family of repositories one then considers a corresponding family of message spaces $\overrightarrow{\mathcal{M}} := \{\mathcal{M}_k\}_{k \in \mathbb{N}}$. Since most statements are made for a fixed parameter k, we usually omit k from the notation, writing $\mathcal{M}$ instead.

[6] Copy access is used to capture the capability that dishonest parties have for copying or resending (modifications of) whatever they see; modeling this capability is crucial for some of the security proofs.

[7] Since all parties can read and write, copying capabilities are redundant.

to Bob is given by ${}^{\{E\}}\mathbf{AUT}^{\{A\}}_{\{B,E\}}$; for fixed-length message spaces, the confidential channel mentioned in Sect. 2.1 is given by ${}^{\{E\}}\mathbf{CONF}^{\{A,E\}}_{\{B\}}$. The exact semantics of such an (atomic) repository are defined in Algorithm 1.

Algorithm 1. Repository ${}^{\mathcal{C}}\mathbf{rep}^{\mathcal{W}}_{\mathcal{R}}$ for the set of parties $\mathcal{P}$.

```
INITIALIZATION
  Buffer ← ∅

(P ∈ W)-WRITE(m ∈ M)
  id ← NEWREGISTER(m)
  Buffer ← id
  P-OUTPUT(id)

(P ∈ R ∪ C)-READBUFFER
  P-OUTPUT(Buffer)

(P ∈ R)-READREGISTER(id)
  P-OUTPUT(GETMESSAGE(id))

(P ∈ C)-COPYREGISTER(id)
  m ← GETMESSAGE(id)
  id' ← NEWREGISTER(m)
  Buffer ← id'
  P-OUTPUT(id')
```

Parties will typically have access to many repositories simultaneously, e.g. an authentic repository from Alice to Bob and one from Alice to Charlie. One could model this as providing all these (atomic) repositories in parallel to the players, i.e.

$$[{}^{\mathcal{C}_1}\mathbf{rep_1}^{\mathcal{W}_1}_{\mathcal{R}_1}, \ldots, {}^{\mathcal{C}_n}\mathbf{rep_n}^{\mathcal{W}_n}_{\mathcal{R}_n}]. \tag{2.7}$$

However, this would mean that to check for incoming messages, a party would need to check every possible atomic repository $\mathbf{rep}_i$, which could be inefficient if the number of atomic repositories is very high. Instead, we define a new resource **REP** which is identical to a parallel composition of the atomic repositories, except that it allows parties to efficiently check for incoming messages (rather than requiring parties to poll each atomic repository $\mathbf{rep_i}$ they have access to). Abusing notation, we denote such a resource as in Eq. (2.7), namely

$$\mathbf{REP} = [{}^{\mathcal{C}_1}\mathbf{rep_1}^{\mathcal{W}_1}_{\mathcal{R}_1}, \ldots, {}^{\mathcal{C}_n}\mathbf{rep_n}^{\mathcal{W}_n}_{\mathcal{R}_n}]. \tag{2.8}$$

The new resource **REP** allows every party with read or copy access to issue a single READBUFFER operation that returns a list of pairs, each pair containing a register's identifier and a label identifying the atomic repository in which the register was written. In addition, it provides single READREGISTER and COPYREGISTER operations which return the contents of the register with the given `id` and copy the register with the given `id`, respectively. WRITE operations for **REP** additionally have to specify the atomic repository for which the operation is meant. The exact semantics of **REP** are defined in Algorithm 2.

3 Modeling MDVS with Fixed Sender and Receivers

One can find multiple definitions of Multi-Designated Verifier Signature (MDVS) schemes in the literature [9,11,16,32]. In this paper, we define an MDVS Π

Algorithm 2. Repository $\mathbf{REP} = [{}^{\mathcal{C}_1}\mathbf{rep_1}^{\mathcal{W}_1}_{\mathcal{R}_1}, \ldots, {}^{\mathcal{C}_n}\mathbf{rep_n}^{\mathcal{W}_n}_{\mathcal{R}_n}]$ for a set of parties $\mathcal{P}$.

INITIALIZATION
  for each $\mathbf{rep_i} \in \mathbf{REP}$ **do**
    $\mathbf{rep_i}$-INITIALIZATION

$(P \in \mathcal{P})$-WRITE($\mathbf{rep_i}$, $m \in \mathcal{M}$)
Require: $(P \in \mathcal{W}_i)$
  id ← $\mathbf{rep_i}$-WRITE(m)
  P-OUTPUT(id)

$(P \in \mathcal{P})$-READBUFFER
  outputList ← $\emptyset$
  for each $\mathbf{rep_i} \in \mathbf{REP}$ **do**
    if $P \in \mathcal{R}_i \cup \mathcal{C}_i$ **then**
      for each id $\in$ $\mathbf{rep_i}$-READBUFFER **do**
        outputList ← (id, $\mathbf{rep_i}$)
  P-OUTPUT(outputList)

$(P \in \mathcal{P})$-READREGISTER(id)
Require: $P \in \mathcal{R}_i$ for id $\in$ $\mathbf{rep_i}$-READBUFFER
  m ← $\mathbf{rep_i}$-READREGISTER(id)
  P-OUTPUT(m)

$(P \in \mathcal{P})$-COPYREGISTER(id)
Require: $P \in \mathcal{C}_i$ for id $\in$ $\mathbf{rep_i}$-READBUFFER
  id′ ← $\mathbf{rep_i}$-COPYREGISTER(id)
  P-OUTPUT(id′)

as a 5-tuple $\Pi = (\mathit{Setup}, G_S, G_V, \mathit{Sign}, \mathit{Vfy})$ of Probabilistic Polynomial Time algorithms (PPTs), following [17]. *Setup* takes the security parameter as input, and produces public parameters (pp) and a master secret key (msk),

$$(\mathtt{pp}, \mathtt{msk}) \leftarrow \mathit{Setup}(1^k).$$

These are then used by G_S and G_V to generate pairs of public and secret keys for the signers and verifiers, respectively,

$$\begin{aligned} (\mathtt{spk}_1, \mathtt{ssk}_1) &\leftarrow G_S(\mathtt{pp}, \mathtt{msk}), \quad \ldots \quad (\mathtt{spk}_m, \mathtt{ssk}_m) \leftarrow G_S(\mathtt{pp}, \mathtt{msk}), \\ (\mathtt{vpk}_1, \mathtt{vsk}_1) &\leftarrow G_V(\mathtt{pp}, \mathtt{msk}), \quad \ldots \quad (\mathtt{vpk}_n, \mathtt{vsk}_n) \leftarrow G_V(\mathtt{pp}, \mathtt{msk}). \end{aligned}$$

Finally, the signing algorithm *Sign* requires the signer's secret key and the public keys of all the verifiers, and the verifying algorithm *Vfy* requires the signer's public key, the secret key of whoever is verifying and the public keys of all verifiers. For example suppose that party A is signing a message m for a set of verifiers $\mathcal{V}$ and that $B \in \mathcal{V}$ verifies the signature, then

$$\begin{aligned} \sigma &\leftarrow \mathit{Sign}(\mathtt{pp}, \mathtt{ssk}_A, \{\mathtt{vpk}_i\}_{i \in \mathcal{V}}, m) \\ b &\leftarrow \mathit{Vfy}(\mathtt{pp}, \mathtt{spk}_A, \mathtt{vsk}_B, \{\mathtt{vpk}\}_{i \in \mathcal{V}}, m, \sigma), \end{aligned}$$

where $b = 1$ if the verification succeeds and $b = 0$ otherwise.

In this section we consider a fixed sender A, a fixed set of receivers $\mathcal{R} = \{B_1, \ldots, B_n\}$ and one eavesdropper E that is neither sender nor receiver, and is always dishonest. The set of parties is then given by $\mathcal{P} = \{A, B_1, \ldots, B_n, E\}$. Furthermore, we assume that sender A always designates $\mathcal{R}$ as the set of designated receivers for the messages it sends. This means in particular that if all receivers are honest then E always learns when A sends a message (as no other party can send messages).

3.1 Real-World

To communicate, each party in $\mathcal{P}$ has access to an insecure repository $\mathbf{INS} := \mathbf{INS}_k$ (for a fixed security parameter k) to which everyone can read from and write to (recall Sect. 2.3). In addition, parties also have access to a *Key Generation Authority* (**KGA**), which generates and stores the parties' key pairs.[8] For a fixed security parameter k, the $\mathbf{KGA} := \mathbf{KGA}_k$ resource runs the *Setup* algorithm giving it the (implicit) parameter k, and then generates and stores all key pairs for the sender A and each receiver in $\mathcal{R}$, using G_S and G_V, respectively. Every honest party can then query their own public-secret key pair, the public parameters and everyone's public key at their own interface. Dishonest parties can additionally query the public-secret key pairs of any other dishonest party. The semantics of the **KGA** resource is defined in Algorithm 3.[9]

Algorithm 3. *Key Generation Authority* resource **KGA** for MDVS scheme $\Pi = (\mathit{Setup}, G_S, G_V, \mathit{Sign}, \mathit{Vfy})$ with a set of senders $\mathcal{S}$ $(= \mathcal{S}^H \uplus \overline{\mathcal{S}^H})$ and set of receivers $\mathcal{R}$ $(= \mathcal{R}^H \uplus \overline{\mathcal{R}^H})$. In the following, k is the implicitly defined security parameter (i.e. $\mathbf{KGA} := \mathbf{KGA}_k$), and $\overline{\mathcal{P}^H}$ the set of all dishonest parties.

INITIALIZATION
- Sign-Keys $\leftarrow \emptyset$
- Vfy-Keys $\leftarrow \emptyset$
- $(\mathtt{pp}, \mathtt{msk}) \leftarrow \Pi.\mathit{Setup}(1^k)$
- **for each** $A_i \in \mathcal{S}$ **do**
  - $(\mathtt{spk}_i, \mathtt{ssk}_i) \leftarrow \Pi.G_S(\mathtt{pp}, \mathtt{msk})$
  - Sign-Keys $\leftarrow (A_i, (\mathtt{spk}_i, \mathtt{ssk}_i))$
- **for each** $B_j \in \mathcal{R}$ **do**
  - $(\mathtt{vpk}_j, \mathtt{vsk}_j) \leftarrow \Pi.G_V(\mathtt{pp}, \mathtt{msk})$
  - Vfy-Keys $\leftarrow (B_j, (\mathtt{vpk}_j, \mathtt{vsk}_j))$

$(P \in \mathcal{P})$-PUBLICPARAMETERS
- P-OUTPUT(pp)

$(A_i \in \mathcal{S}^H)$-SIGNERKEYPAIR
- $(\mathtt{spk}_i, \mathtt{ssk}_i) \leftarrow$ Sign-Keys(A_i)
- A_i-OUTPUT$(\mathtt{spk}_i, \mathtt{ssk}_i)$

$(P \in \overline{\mathcal{P}^H})$-SIGNERKEYPAIR$(A_i \in \overline{\mathcal{S}^H})$
- $(\mathtt{spk}_i, \mathtt{ssk}_i) \leftarrow$ Sign-Keys(A_i)
- P-OUTPUT$(\mathtt{spk}_i, \mathtt{ssk}_i)$

$(P \in \mathcal{P})$-SIGNERPUBLICKEY$(A_i \in \mathcal{S})$
- $(\mathtt{spk}_i, \mathtt{ssk}_i) \leftarrow$ Sign-Keys(A_i)
- P-OUTPUT$(\mathtt{spk}_i)$

$(B_j \in \mathcal{R})$-VERIFIERKEYPAIR
- $(\mathtt{vpk}_j, \mathtt{vsk}_j) \leftarrow$ Vfy-Keys(B_j)
- B_j-OUTPUT$(\mathtt{vpk}_j, \mathtt{vsk}_j)$

$(P \in \overline{\mathcal{P}^H})$-VERIFIERKEYPAIR$(B_j \in \overline{\mathcal{R}^H})$
- $(\mathtt{vpk}_j, \mathtt{vsk}_j) \leftarrow$ Vfy-Keys(B_j)
- P-OUTPUT$(\mathtt{vpk}_j, \mathtt{vsk}_j)$

$(P \in \mathcal{P})$-VERIFIERPUBLICKEY$(B_j \in \mathcal{R})$
- $(\mathtt{vpk}_j, \mathtt{vsk}_j) \leftarrow$ Vfy-Keys(B_j)
- P-OUTPUT$(\mathtt{vpk}_j)$

The sender A runs a converter Snd (locally) and each receiver $B_j \in \mathcal{R}$ runs a converter Rcv (also locally). This means sender A can send messages by simply running its converter Snd, and each receiver can receive messages by simply running its converter Rcv.

[8] The purpose of having an explicit **KGA** resource is guaranteeing that receivers know their secret keys, which is crucial for being able to achieve the *exclusiveness of authenticity* guarantee of MDVS schemes [13,29].

[9] Algorithm 3 defines the behavior of **KGA** in the case of multiple senders, which will only be used in Sect. 4.

The Snd converter connects to **INS** and **KGA** at its inner interface, and has an outer interface that is identical to the interface of a repository for a party who is a writer, i.e. it provides a procedure WRITE which takes as input a label $\langle A_i \rightarrow \mathcal{V}\rangle$ defining the sender A_i and set of receivers $\mathcal{V}$ and a message $m \in \mathcal{M}$ to be signed. Snd then gets the necessary keys and public parameters from **KGA**, signs the input message m using the algorithm *Sign*, which outputs some signature $\sigma \in \mathcal{S}$, and then writes $(m, \sigma, (A_i, \mathcal{V}))$ into the insecure repository **INS**. For simplicity, since in this section the label is always $\langle A \rightarrow \mathcal{R}\rangle$ it is simply omitted. In addition, rather than making the Snd converter always write $(m, \sigma, (A, \mathcal{R}))$ tuples into **INS**, we omit $(A, \mathcal{R})$ and simply write (m, σ) pairs instead. The exact (simplified) semantics for converter Snd is given in Algorithm 4.

Algorithm 4. Snd converter for $A \in \mathcal{S}^H$.

```
(A ∈ S^H) WRITE(m ∈ M)
  pp ← A-PUBLICPARAMETERS
  (spk, ssk) ← A-SIGNERKEYPAIR
  for each B_l ∈ R do
      {vpk_l} ← A-VERIFIERPUBLICKEY(B_l)
  σ ← Π.Sign(pp, ssk, {vpk_l}_{B_l ∈ R}, m)
  id ← A-WRITE(m, σ)
  return id
```

Similarly to Snd, the Rcv converter connects to **KGA** and **INS** at its inner interfaces and provides the same outer interface as a repository for a party with read access, i.e. it gives access to two read operations, namely READBUFFER and READREGISTER. The behavior of Rcv for each such read operation is specified by means of a procedure with the same name (i.e. a READBUFFER and a READREGISTER procedure). The READBUFFER procedure first reads all tuples $(m, \sigma, (A_i, \mathcal{V}))$ written into **INS**—by issuing a READBUFFER operation to **INS** followed by a series of READREGISTER operations, one for each `id` returned by the first operation—and for each tuple satisfying $A_i = A$ and $\mathcal{V} = \mathcal{R}$, the converter verifies whether σ is a valid signature on m with respect to sender A and set of receivers $\mathcal{R}$. To this end, the Rcv converter first fetches all the public parameters and keys needed from **KGA**, and then checks if σ is a valid signature on m with respect to the public keys of the sender A and of each receiver in $\mathcal{R}$ using the *Vfy* algorithm defined by the underlying MDVS scheme Π. The converter then outputs a list of pairs—one for each register stored in **INS** containing a valid message-signature pair according to *Vfy* and with respect to A and $\mathcal{R}$—where each pair contains a register's `id` and a label $\langle A \rightarrow \mathcal{R}\rangle$. Since in this section the label is always the same, we simply omit it. The READREGISTER procedure of the Rcv converter receives as input the `id` of the register to be read; if the register contains a valid tuple (in the same sense as above) the procedure then outputs the message contained in the register. The exact (simplified) semantics for the Rcv converter is given in Algorithm 5.

Algorithm 5. Rcv converter for $B_j \in \mathcal{R}^H$.

```
(B_j ∈ R^H)-ReadBuffer
  return B_j-GetValidIds

(B_j ∈ R^H)-ReadRegister(id)
  if id ∈ B_j-GetValidIds then
      (m, σ) ← B_j-ReadRegister(id)
      return m

(B_j ∈ R^H)-GetValidIds          ▷ Local procedure. Operation not available at outside interface.
  pp ← B_j-PublicParameters
  (vpk_j, vsk_j) ← B_j-VerifierKeyPair
  spk ← B_j-SignerPublicKey(A)
  for each B_l ∈ R do
      {vpk_l} ← B_j-VerifierPublicKey(B_l)
  validIds ← ∅
  for each id ∈ B_j-ReadBuffer do
      (m, σ) ← B_j-ReadRegister(id)
      if Π.Vfy(pp, spk, vsk_j, {vpk_l}_{B_l∈R}, m, σ) then
          validIds ← id
  return validIds
```

In the case where the sender and all receivers are honest—i.e. $\mathcal{P}^H = \{A\} \cup \mathcal{R}^H$ with $\mathcal{R}^H = \mathcal{R}$—the real world specification is given by

$$\mathsf{Snd}^A \mathsf{Rcv}^{\mathcal{R}^H}\{[\mathbf{KGA}, \mathbf{INS}]\}, \tag{3.1}$$

where $\mathsf{Rcv}^{\mathcal{R}^H} = \mathsf{Rcv}^{B_1} \cdots \mathsf{Rcv}^{B_n}$ denotes all receiver converters run at the interfaces of $B_j \in \mathcal{R}^H$. This is illustrated in Fig. 1. As explained in Remark 3 in Sect. 2.2, if a party P is dishonest, then we simply remove their converter from Eq. (3.1) to get the corresponding real world.

3.2 Ideal-Worlds

Whether the sender is honest or dishonest completely changes the guarantees one wishes to give, and thus completely changes the ideal world. So we divide this in two subsections, the first models a dishonest sender and the second an honest sender. Recall that the third-party E is always dishonest.

Dishonest Sender. In case of a dishonest sender the only property the construction must capture is *consistency*, namely that all honest receivers in $\mathcal{R}^H$ get the same messages (for any $\mathcal{R}^H \neq \emptyset$). This means that even if all dishonest parties collude, including the sender A, the dishonest receivers $\overline{\mathcal{R}^H}$ and the third-party E, they are unable to generate confusion within the honest senders as to whether some message is authentic or not: either every receiver $B_j \in \mathcal{R}^H$ accepts a message as authentic or none does. A repository to which all honest receivers have read access captures this guarantee. Since dishonest parties may share secret keys with each other, any of them may have either read or write access. The repository we want to construct is then

$$\langle A \to \mathcal{R} \rangle_{\mathcal{R} \cup \{A,E\}}^{\overline{\mathcal{R}^H} \cup \{A,E\}},$$

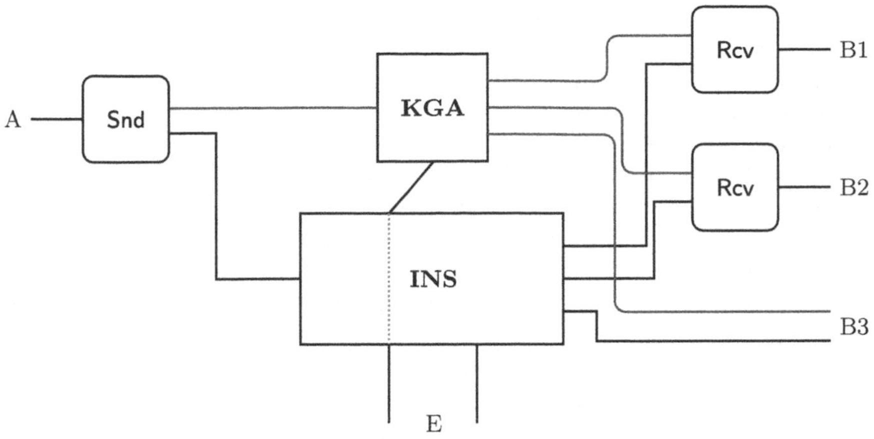

Fig. 1. Illustration of the real world system specified by Eq. (3.1) for the case where $\mathcal{R} = \{B1, B2, B3\}$, with $\mathcal{R}^H = \{B1, B2\}$.

where we have used $\langle \mathbf{A} \to \mathcal{R} \rangle$ as label to denote the repository. By considering a set of converters Ω[10] that could be run jointly at the dishonest parties' interfaces, one can then define the ideal world specification $\mathcal{C}_\Omega^{\text{Fix}}$ capturing consistency as

$$\mathcal{C}_\Omega^{\text{Fix}} := \left\{ \mathsf{sim}^{\overline{\mathcal{R}^H} \cup \{A,E\}} \left[\langle A \to \mathcal{R} \rangle_{\mathcal{R} \cup \{A,E\}}^{\overline{\mathcal{R}^H} \cup \{A,E\}} \right] \right\}_{\mathsf{sim} \in \Omega}. \tag{3.2}$$

Finally, we also want the ideal world to contain systems that are indistinguishable from the perfect ones defined above, so we put an ε-ball around the ideal resource.[11] The ideal world is then

$$\left(\mathcal{C}_\Omega^{\text{Fix}} \right)^\varepsilon .$$

Honest Sender. In the case of an honest sender, there are two properties that we expect from an MDVS scheme. The first is that the (honest) designated receivers can verify the *authenticity* of the message as coming from the actual sender A. The second is that this authenticity is *exclusive* to the designated receivers,[12] i.e. a third party E cannot be convinced that any message was sent

[10] We do not define Ω at this point, since in a finite setting there is no "good" and "bad" system (efficient or inefficient, negligible or non-negligible). Instead, in the theorem statement for a security proof we explicitly give the set Ω which is used, as the meaningfulness of the theorem will depend on the choice of this set.

[11] Like for Ω (see Footnote 10) we do not define acceptable ε here, but in a theorem statement for a security proof we explicitly give the one used.

[12] A third important property is *correctness*, but in our setting dishonest parties cannot delete the messages of honest parties, so correctness follows from authenticity and does not need to be considered separately.

by A, even if dishonest receivers leak all their secret keys to E.[13] To this end, MDVS schemes need to be such that every possible set of dishonest receivers can (cooperatively) come up with forged signatures that are indistinguishable from the real ones generated by A to the third-party E (who has access to the dishonest receivers' secret keys). Note, on the other hand, that honest designated receivers are not "fooled" by signatures forged by dishonest (designated) receivers; authenticity guarantees that honest designated receivers can verify whether it was really A signing a message or otherwise.

Authenticity is straightforward to capture: it essentially corresponds to a repository where only the sender can write, but everyone else can read. The only twist is that dishonest parties might be able to duplicate messages written by the sender A [3].[14] So the repository we wish to be constructed is given by

$$^{\overline{\mathcal{R}^H}\cup\{E\}}\langle A \to \mathcal{R}\rangle^{\{A\}}_{\mathcal{R}\cup\{E\}}.$$

As for consistency, by considering a set of converters Ω that could be run jointly at the dishonest parties' interfaces, one can then define the ideal world specification $\boldsymbol{\mathcal{A}}^{\text{Fix}}_{\Omega}$ capturing authenticity as

$$\boldsymbol{\mathcal{A}}^{\text{Fix}}_{\Omega} := \left\{\mathsf{sim}^{\overline{\mathcal{R}^H}\cup\{E\}}\left[^{\overline{\mathcal{R}^H}\cup\{E\}}\langle A \to \mathcal{R}\rangle^{\{A\}}_{\mathcal{R}\cup\{E\}}\right]\right\}_{\mathsf{sim}\in\Omega}. \tag{3.3}$$

Here too, we extend the ideal world to also contain systems that are indistinguishable from those in Eq. (3.3) by adding a ε-ball around the specification. The final ideal specification is thus

$$\left(\boldsymbol{\mathcal{A}}^{\text{Fix}}_{\Omega}\right)^{\varepsilon}.$$

Figure 2 illustrates the ideal world systems from the $\boldsymbol{\mathcal{A}}^{\text{Fix}}_{\Omega}$ specification.

Finally, the notion of *exclusiveness* of authenticity is captured in a world where there exists an (explicit) behavior π for the dishonest receivers that allows them to generate signatures that look just like fresh signatures to any third party E. This means that running π would result in a repository in which both the honest sender A and all the dishonest receivers in $\overline{\mathcal{R}^H}$ can write and E can read, namely[15]

$$\langle A \to \mathcal{R}\rangle^{\{A\}\cup\overline{\mathcal{R}^H}}_{\{E\}}. \tag{3.4}$$

As usual, we extend the specification by attaching a converter sim at the dishonest parties' interfaces. However, sim is not allowed to block or cover the write

[13] If all receivers are honest only A can send messages, and so in this case E just knows that A must be the one sending messages.

[14] They can do this either by creating a copy of a valid message-signature pair or by sending the same message but with a different signature.

[15] As one might note, the repository in Eq. (3.4) does not allow the honest designated receivers $\mathcal{R}^H$ to read. The reason for this is that the security statement does not concern them, so we remove them from the security statement. In fact, due to authenticity the honest designated receivers could distinguish signatures written by Alice or forged by the dishonest receivers.

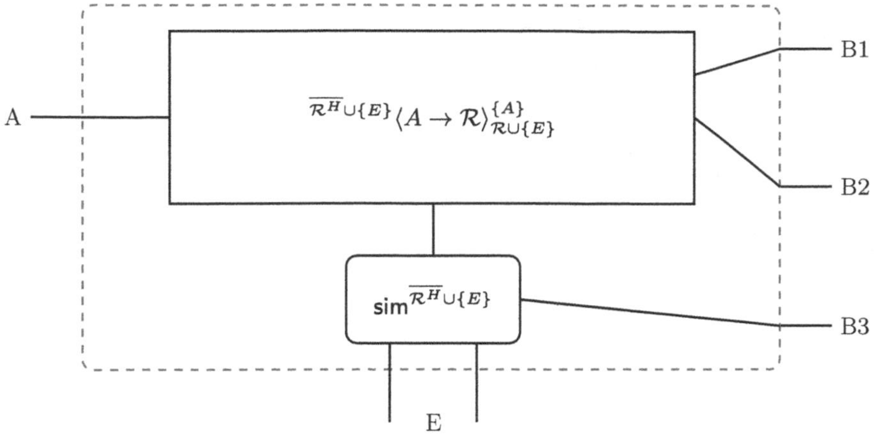

Fig. 2. Illustration of an ideal world system from the $\boldsymbol{\mathcal{A}}^{\text{Fix}}_{\Omega}$ specification (Eq. (3.3)) for the case where $\mathcal{R} = \{B1, B2, B3\}$, with $\mathcal{R}^H = \{B1, B2\}$.

ability at the interfaces of the parties in $\overline{\mathcal{R}^H}$, because we wish to *guarantee* that a dishonest receiver can write to the repository.[16] The specification providing the guarantee that E cannot distinguish real signatures (created by A) from fake ones (forged by the dishonest designated receivers) is given by

$$\widehat{\boldsymbol{\mathcal{X}}}^{\text{Fix}}_{\Omega} := \left\{\mathsf{sim}^{\{E\}}\left[\langle A \to \mathcal{R}\rangle^{\{A\}\cup\overline{\mathcal{R}^H}}_{\{E\}}\right]\right\}_{\mathsf{sim}\in\Omega}. \tag{3.5}$$

Figure 3 illustrates an ideal world system from $\widehat{\boldsymbol{\mathcal{X}}}^{\text{Fix}}_{\Omega}$. As stated above, there must exist a converter π that the dishonest receivers $\overline{\mathcal{R}^H}$ can run jointly to achieve a resource in the specification from Eq. (3.5). Since dishonest receivers could have run (and can run) π, a third party E cannot tell if the message was sent by them or by the honest sender A even when given access to the keys of all dishonest receivers (notice that E, being one of the dishonest parties, can query the **KGA** to obtain the secret keys of any dishonest receiver). Putting things together, the ideal world is defined as

$$\boldsymbol{\mathcal{X}}^{\text{Fix}}_{\Omega,\pi} := \left\{\mathbf{V} : \pi^{\overline{\mathcal{R}^H}}\bot^{\mathcal{R}^H}\mathbf{V} \in \widehat{\boldsymbol{\mathcal{X}}}^{\text{Fix}}_{\Omega}\right\}, \tag{3.6}$$

where $\bot^{\mathcal{R}^H}$ blocks the interfaces of all honest receivers $\mathcal{R}^H$.[17] Figure 4 illustrates a possible real world system in the $\boldsymbol{\mathcal{X}}^{\text{Fix}}_{\Omega,\pi}$ specification with a converter $\bot^{\mathcal{R}^H}$ blocking the interface of the (only) honest receiver B_1, and protocol $\pi^{\overline{\mathcal{R}^H}}$

[16] Traditional composable security frameworks require the simulator to cover all dishonest interfaces making it impossible to model Eq. (3.5).

[17] Note that the ideal specification in Eq. (3.6) does not follow the ideal-functionality-simulator paradigm, making it impossible to (directly) model the same thing in traditional composable frameworks.

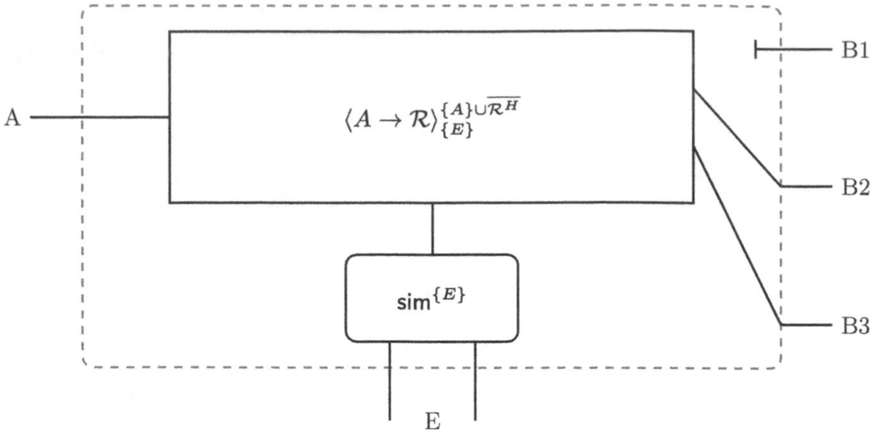

Fig. 3. Illustration of an ideal world system from the $\widehat{\boldsymbol{\mathcal{X}}}_{\Omega}^{\text{Fix}}$ specification (Eq. (3.5)) for the case where $\mathcal{R} = \{B1, B2, B3\}$, with $\mathcal{R}^H = \{B1\}$.

attached to the interfaces of the dishonest receivers (i.e. B_2 and B_3). Again, we put an ε-ball around Eq. (3.6), and define the ideal specification for the *exclusiveness* of authenticity to be

$$\left(\boldsymbol{\mathcal{X}}_{\Omega,\pi}^{\text{Fix}}\right)^{\varepsilon}.$$

Putting things together, the ideal world specification for the case of an honest sender is then given by

$$\boldsymbol{\mathcal{S}} = \left(\boldsymbol{\mathcal{A}}_{\Omega}^{\text{Fix}}\right)^{\varepsilon} \cap \left(\boldsymbol{\mathcal{X}}_{\Omega',\pi}^{\text{Fix}}\right)^{\varepsilon'}. \tag{3.7}$$

3.3 Reduction to Game-Based Security

We now compare our composable notions against the existing game-based security notions from the literature. The definitions of these game-based security notions can be found in the full version of this paper, together with full proofs of all the theorems below [21].

The first theorem shows that in the case of a dishonest sender, the advantage in distinguishing the real and ideal systems is upper bounded by the advantage in winning the consistency game.

Theorem 1. *When the sender $\mathcal{A}$ is dishonest, i.e. $\mathcal{P}^H = \mathcal{R}^H$, we find an explicit reduction system* $\mathbf{C}$ *and an explicit simulator* sim *such that for any $\Omega \supseteq \{\mathsf{sim}\}$:*

$$\boldsymbol{\mathcal{R}} \subseteq (\boldsymbol{\mathcal{C}}_{\Omega}^{\text{Fix}})^{Adv^{Cons}(\cdot\,\mathbf{C})} \tag{3.8}$$

where for any distinguisher $\mathbf{D}$, $Adv^{Cons}(\mathbf{DC})$ *is the advantage of* $\mathbf{D}' = \mathbf{DC}$ *(the distinguisher resulting from composing* $\mathbf{D}$ *and* $\mathbf{C}$*) in winning the Consistency game (see [21, Definition 3]).*

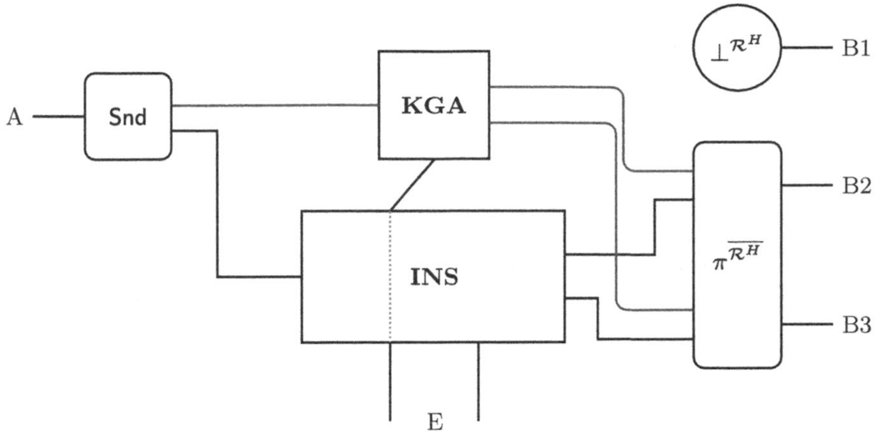

Fig. 4. Illustration of a possible real world system in the $\boldsymbol{\mathcal{X}}_{\Omega,\pi}^{\mathrm{Fix}}$ specification (Eq. (3.6)) for the case where $\mathcal{R} = \{B1, B2, B3\}$, with $\mathcal{R}^H = \{B1\}$. Converter $\perp^{\mathcal{R}^H}$ blocks B_1's interface; signature forgery protocol $\pi^{\overline{\mathcal{R}^H}}$ is attached to the interfaces of B_2 and B_3.

A proof of Theorem 1 is provided in the full version [21].

The second theorem shows that in the case of an honest sender, the advantage in distinguishing the real world from the ideal world for authenticity is upper bounded by the advantage in winning the unforgeability game and the correctness game.

Theorem 2. *When the sender is honest, i.e. for* $\mathcal{P}^H = \{A\} \cup \mathcal{R}^H$, *we find explicit reduction systems* $\mathbf{C}'$ *and* $\mathbf{C}$ *and an explicit simulator* sim *such that for any* $\Omega \supseteq \{\mathsf{sim}\}$*:*

$$\boldsymbol{\mathcal{R}} \subseteq (\boldsymbol{\mathcal{A}}_{\Omega}^{\mathrm{Fix}})^{Adv^{Unforg}(\cdot\,\mathbf{C}) + Adv^{Corr}(\cdot\,\mathbf{C}')} \tag{3.9}$$

where for any distinguisher $\mathbf{D}$, $Adv^{Unforg}(\mathbf{DC})$ *is the advantage of* $\mathbf{D}' = \mathbf{DC}$ *(the distinguisher resulting from composing* $\mathbf{D}$ *and* $\mathbf{C}$*) in winning the Unforgeability game (see [21, Definition 4]), and* $Adv^{Corr}(\mathbf{DC}')$ *is the advantage of* $\mathbf{D}'' = \mathbf{DC}'$ *in winning the Correctness game (see [21, Definition 2])*

A proof of Theorem 2 is provided in the full version [21].

In the third theorem we show that in the case of an honest sender, the advantage in distinguishing the real world from the ideal world for the exclusiveness of authenticity is bounded by the advantage in winning the Off-The-Record game.

Theorem 3. *When the sender is honest, i.e. for* $\mathcal{P}^H = \{A\} \cup \mathcal{R}^H$, *and for any signature forgery algorithm Forge suitable for the Off-The-Record security notion (see [21, Definition 5]), we find an explicit reduction system* $\mathbf{C}$ *and an explicit simulator* sim *such that for any* $\Omega \supseteq \{\mathsf{sim}\}$*:*

$$\boldsymbol{\mathcal{R}} \subseteq (\boldsymbol{\mathcal{X}}_{\Omega,\pi^{Forge}}^{\mathrm{Fix}})^{Adv^{OTR\text{-}Forge}(\cdot\,\mathbf{C})}, \tag{3.10}$$

where π^{Forge} is the converter running the Forge algorithm (see Algorithm 6), and for any distinguisher **D**, *$Adv^{OTR\text{-}Forge}(\mathbf{DC})$ is the advantage of $\mathbf{D}' = \mathbf{DC}$ (the distinguisher resulting from composing* **D** *and* **C***) in winning the Off-The-Record game with respect to the signature forgery algorithm Forge (see [21, Definition 5]).*

Algorithm 6. Converter π^{Forge} for set of (dishonest) parties $\overline{\mathcal{R}^H}$; π^{Forge} uses algorithm *Forge* to forge signatures, and is connected to a **KGA** and an insecure repository **INS**.

$(B_j \in \overline{\mathcal{R}^H})$-Write$(m \in \mathcal{M})$
  pp ← B_j-PublicParameters
  spk ← B_j-SignerPublicKey(A)
  for each $B_c \in \overline{\mathcal{R}^H}$ **do**
    $\{(\mathtt{vpk}_c, \mathtt{vsk}_c)\} \leftarrow B_j$-VerifierKeyPair$(B_c)$
  for each $B_l \in \mathcal{R}$ **do**
    $\{\mathtt{vpk}_l\} \leftarrow B_j$-VerifierPublicKey$(B_l)$
  $\sigma \leftarrow Forge(\mathtt{pp}, \mathtt{spk}, \{\mathtt{vpk}_l\}_{B_l \in \mathcal{R}}, \{\mathtt{vsk}_c\}_{B_c \in \overline{\mathcal{R}^H}}, m)$
  B_j-Output$(B_j$-Write$(m, \sigma))$

A proof of Theorem 3 is provided in the full version [21].

4 Modeling MDVS for Arbitrary Parties

In this section we model the security of MDVS schemes in the presence of multiple possible senders and multiple sets of receivers, which corresponds to a generalization of the models given in Sect. 3. Throughout this section, we denote by $\mathcal{S}$ the set of senders, and by $\mathcal{S}^H$ and $\overline{\mathcal{S}^H}$ the partitions of $\mathcal{S}$ corresponding to honest and dishonest senders. As before, $\mathcal{R}$, $\mathcal{R}^H$ and $\overline{\mathcal{R}^H}$ correspond to the set of all receivers, honest and dishonest receivers, respectively. Furthermore, we assume that $\mathcal{R}^H$, $\overline{\mathcal{R}^H}$, $\mathcal{S}^H$ and $\overline{\mathcal{S}^H}$ are all non-empty sets.

4.1 Real-World

The real world specification for this security model is similar to the one given in Sect. 3.1 for the fixed sender and fixed set of receivers case. However, in Sect. 3 we made a few simplifications in the description of converters Snd and Rcv namely, the fixed sender and a fixed set of receiver are hard-coded in the converters. In this section, the converters $\mathsf{Snd}^{\mathrm{Arb}}$ and $\mathsf{Rcv}^{\mathrm{Arb}}$ (see Algorithm 7 and Algorithm 8, respectively) allow the sender to specify the set of receivers for each message they send, and the $\mathsf{Rcv}^{\mathrm{Arb}}$ converters explicitly output the sender and the set of designated receivers. Moreover, the $\mathsf{Snd}^{\mathrm{Arb}}$ converter now attaches to each message-signature pair also the sender and set of receivers meant for that message-signature pair; the $\mathsf{Rcv}^{\mathrm{Arb}}$ converter then relies on this information to validate the authenticity of messages meant for the corresponding receiver. Apart from this, the real-world specification is as before: the $\mathsf{Snd}^{\text{Arb}}$ and $\mathsf{Rcv}^{\text{Arb}}$ converters connect to the **KGA** and to an insecure repository **INS**, and behave otherwise similarly to the Snd and Rcv converters. Since we assumed that $\mathcal{S}^H$ and $\mathcal{R}^H$ are non-empty sets, the real-world specification is then defined by

$$\mathsf{Snd}^{\text{Arb}^{\mathcal{S}^H}}\mathsf{Rcv}^{\text{Arb}^{\mathcal{R}^H}}\{[\mathbf{KGA}, \mathbf{INS}]\}, \tag{4.1}$$

as illustrated in Fig. 5.

Algorithm 7. $\mathsf{Snd}^{\text{Arb}}$ converter for $A_i \in \mathcal{S}^H$.

```
(A_i ∈ S^H)-WRITE(⟨A_i → V⟩, m ∈ M)
  pp ← A_i-PUBLICPARAMETERS
  (spk, ssk) ← A_i-SIGNERKEYPAIR
  for each B_l ∈ V do
      {vpk_l} ← A_i-VERIFIERPUBLICKEY(B_l)
  σ ← Π.Sign(pp, ssk, {vpk_l}_{B_l ∈ V}, m)
  id ← A_i-WRITE(m, σ, (A_i, V))
  return id
```

Algorithm 8. $\mathsf{Rcv}^{\text{Arb}}$ converter for $B_j \in \mathcal{R}^H$.

```
(B_j ∈ R^H)-READBUFFER
  return B_j-GETVALIDIDS

(B_j ∈ R^H)-READREGISTER(id)
  if (id, ⟨A_i → V⟩) ∈ B_j-GETVALIDIDS then
      (m, σ, (A_i, V)) ← B_j-READREGISTER(id)
      return m

(B_j ∈ R^H)-GETVALIDIDS        ▷ Local procedure. Operation not available at outside interface.
  pp ← B_j-PUBLICPARAMETERS
  (vpk_j, vsk_j) ← B_j-VERIFIERKEYPAIR
  validIds ← ∅
  for each (id, INS) ∈ B_j-READBUFFER do
      (m, σ, (A_i, V)) ← B_j-READREGISTER(id)
      if B_j ∈ V then
          spk_i ← B_j-SIGNERPUBLICKEY(A_i)
          for each B_l ∈ V do
              {vpk_l} ← B_j-VERIFIERPUBLICKEY(B_l)
          if Π.Vfy(pp, spk_i, vsk_j, {vpk_l}_{B_l ∈ V}, m, σ) then
              validIds ← (id, ⟨A_i → V⟩)
  return validIds
```

4.2 Ideal-Worlds

As aforementioned in Sect. 3.2, the guarantees given by the ideal world when a sender is honest are completely different from the ones when it is dishonest. However, since now we have both honest and dishonest senders at the same time,

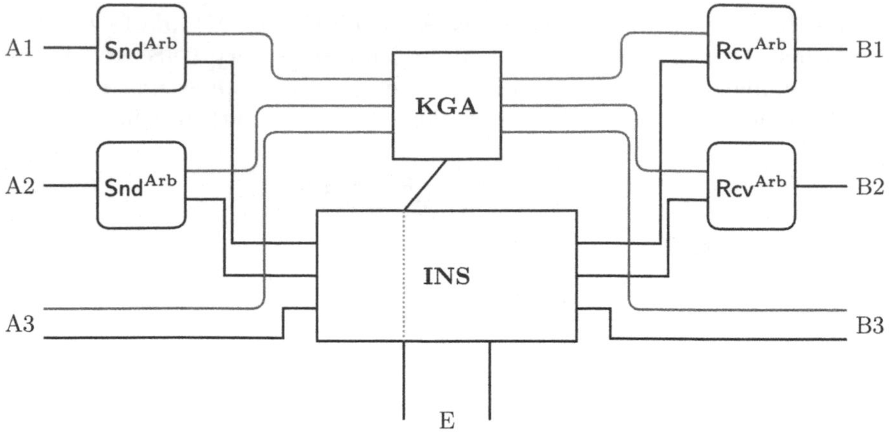

Fig. 5. Illustration of the real world system specified by Eq. (4.1) for the case where $\mathcal{S} = \{A1, A2, A3\}$ and $\mathcal{R} = \{B1, B2, B3\}$, with $\mathcal{S}^H = \{A1, A2\}$ and $\mathcal{R}^H = \{B1, B2\}$.

the ideal-world specification modeling the security of MDVS schemes consists of the intersection of only two (relaxed) specifications, one capturing the consistency and authenticity together $(\boldsymbol{\mathcal{CA}})^{\text{Arb}}_{\Omega}$,[18] and one capturing the exclusiveness of authenticity $\boldsymbol{\mathcal{X}}^{\text{Arb}}_{\Omega',\pi}$. The ideal world is then

$$\boldsymbol{\mathcal{S}} = \left((\boldsymbol{\mathcal{CA}})^{\text{Arb}}_{\Omega}\right)^{\varepsilon} \cap \left(\boldsymbol{\mathcal{X}}^{\text{Arb}}_{\Omega',\pi}\right)^{\varepsilon'}. \tag{4.2}$$

One key difference between the model we now introduce and the one from Sect. 3 is that we may have dishonest parties (other than Eve) that are neither sender nor designated receivers in this section, and we require exclusiveness of authenticity to hold with respect to them as well. So it is not sufficient that (any non-empty subset of) dishonest verifiers who have a secret verification key can forge signatures, parties with no secret verification key should also be able to forge.[19]

Consistency and Authenticity. As just mentioned, $(\boldsymbol{\mathcal{CA}})^{\text{Arb}}_{\Omega}$ models consistency and authenticity. More concretely, for dishonest senders $A_i \in \overline{\mathcal{S}^H}$, $(\boldsymbol{\mathcal{CA}})^{\text{Arb}}_{\Omega}$ includes the repository

$$\left[\langle A_i \to \mathcal{V}\rangle^{\overline{\mathcal{P}^H}}_{\mathcal{V}\cup\overline{\mathcal{P}^H}}\right]_{A_i\in\overline{\mathcal{S}^H},\mathcal{V}\subseteq\mathcal{R}},$$

18 As noted in Sect. 3, in our setting correctness follows from authenticity, so it does not need to be considered separately.

19 This could have been modeled in Sect. 3 by adding a second Eve, but we omitted it for simplicity.

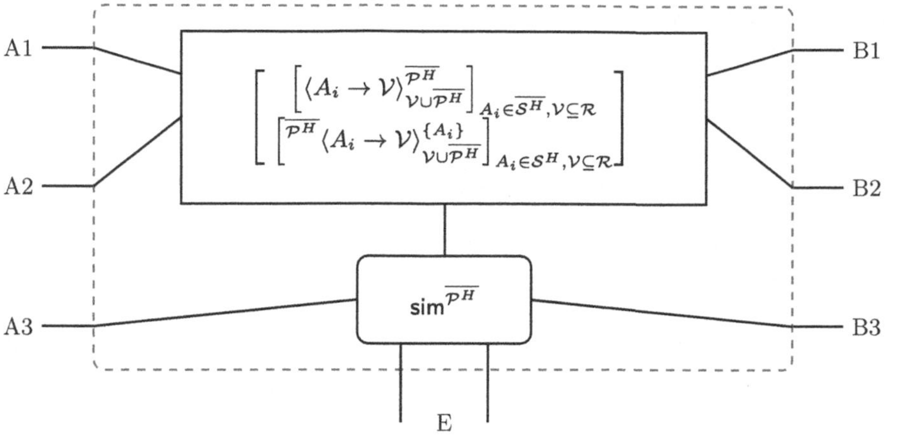

Fig. 6. Illustration of the ideal world system specified by Eq. (4.3) for the case where $\mathcal{S} = \{A1, A2, A3\}$, $\mathcal{R} = \{B1, B2, B3\}$, with $\mathcal{S}^H = \{A1, A2\}$ and $\mathcal{R}^H = \{B1, B2\}$.

which captures consistency, since all honest receivers have access to the same messages. And for honest senders $A_i \in \mathcal{S}^H$, $(\mathcal{CA})_\Omega^{\mathrm{Arb}}$ includes the repository

$$\left[{}^{\overline{\mathcal{P}^H}}\langle A_i \to \mathcal{V}\rangle_{\mathcal{V}\cup\overline{\mathcal{P}^H}}^{\{A_i\}}\right]_{A_i\in\mathcal{S}^H,\mathcal{V}\subseteq\mathcal{R}},$$

which captures authenticity, since only A_i can write. As before, a simulator sim is added at the interfaces of the dishonest parties, hence

$$(\mathcal{CA})_\Omega^{\mathrm{Arb}} := \left\{ \mathsf{sim}^{\overline{\mathcal{P}^H}} \begin{bmatrix} \left[\langle A_i \to \mathcal{V}\rangle_{\mathcal{V}\cup\overline{\mathcal{P}^H}}^{\overline{\mathcal{P}^H}}\right]_{A_i\in\overline{\mathcal{S}^H},\mathcal{V}\subseteq\mathcal{R}} \\ \left[{}^{\overline{\mathcal{P}^H}}\langle A_i \to \mathcal{V}\rangle_{\mathcal{V}\cup\overline{\mathcal{P}^H}}^{\{A_i\}}\right]_{A_i\in\mathcal{S}^H,\mathcal{V}\subseteq\mathcal{R}} \end{bmatrix} \right\}_{\mathsf{sim}\in\Omega}. \quad (4.3)$$

Figure 6 illustrates the ideal world systems from the $(\mathcal{CA})_\Omega^{\mathrm{Arb}}$ specification.

Exclusiveness of Authenticity. To model exclusiveness of authenticity, for honest senders $A_i \in \mathcal{S}^H$, we define a resource containing a repository where A_i and all dishonest parties (except Eve) can write and Eve can read, i.e.

$$\left[\langle A_i \to \mathcal{V}\rangle_{\{E\}}^{\{A_i\}\cup\overline{\mathcal{S}^H}\cup\overline{\mathcal{R}^H}}\right]_{A_i\in\mathcal{S}^H,\mathcal{V}\subseteq\mathcal{R}}.$$

This means that Eve does not know if the messages she sees are from Alice or another dishonest party—even those that are not designated verifiers can input messages.

In the arbitrary party setting, we also need to deal with the case of dishonest senders. Since we cannot exclude that by submitting forged signatures and seeing whether they are accepted, dishonest parties might learn something about the honest receivers' secret keys, we also include repositories where a dishonest party (Eve) can write and honest verifiers read,[20] namely

$$\left[\langle A_i \to \mathcal{V}\rangle^{\{E\}}_{\mathcal{V}^H}\right]_{A_i \in \overline{\mathcal{S}^H}, \mathcal{V} \subseteq \mathcal{R}}.$$

Like in the previous section, we want to guarantee that the ability of dishonest parties to write in the repositories for honest senders is preserved, so the simulator only covers Eve's interface.[21] We thus get a resource specification,

$$\widehat{\boldsymbol{\mathcal{X}}}^{\text{Arb}}_{\Omega} := \left\{ \quad \mathsf{sim}^{\{E\}} \quad \begin{bmatrix} \left[\langle A_i \to \mathcal{V}\rangle^{\{E\}}_{\mathcal{V}^H}\right]_{A_i \in \overline{\mathcal{S}^H}, \mathcal{V} \subseteq \mathcal{R}} \\ \left[\langle A_i \to \mathcal{V}\rangle^{\{A_i\} \cup \overline{\mathcal{S}^H} \cup \overline{\mathcal{R}^H}}_{\{E\}}\right]_{A_i \in \mathcal{S}^H, \mathcal{V} \subseteq \mathcal{R}} \end{bmatrix} \right\}. \tag{4.4}$$

As previously, our ideal world consists of all resources that when the interfaces of the honest designated verifiers on repositories with honest senders are covered and when the dishonest parties (excluding Eve) collude to run a forging protocol π result in a resource contained in $\widehat{\boldsymbol{\mathcal{X}}}^{\text{Arb}}_{\Omega}$, i.e. the ideal-world specification $\boldsymbol{\mathcal{X}}^{\text{Arb}}_{\Omega,\pi}$ is defined as

$$\boldsymbol{\mathcal{X}}^{\text{Arb}}_{\Omega,\pi} := \left\{ \mathbf{V} : \pi^{\overline{\mathcal{S}^H} \cup \overline{\mathcal{R}^H}} (\bot_{\text{Arb}})^{\mathcal{R}^H} \mathbf{V} \in \widehat{\boldsymbol{\mathcal{X}}}^{\text{Arb}}_{\Omega} \right\}, \tag{4.5}$$

where $\bot_{\text{Arb}}$ is the converter specified in Algorithm 9 which does not allow the receiver to verify the authenticity of messages input into any repository $\langle A_i \to \mathcal{V}\rangle$ with an honest sender (i.e. for which $A_i \in \mathcal{S}^H$).[22]

4.3 Reduction to Game-Based Security

We now compare our composable notions for arbitrary parties to the existing game-based security notions from the literature. Again, the definitions of these game-based security notions can be found in the full version of this paper, together with full proofs of all the theorems [21].

The first theorem in this section shows that that advantage in distinguishing the real world from the ideal world for authenticity and consistency is upper bounded by the advantage in winning the consistency, unforgeability and correctness games.

[20] Messages signed by a party with no knowledge of the signer's secret key will likely be recognized as forgeries, so we only need to consider the case where the sender is dishonest and the keys are shared. Furthermore, the distinguisher could in principle use any party's interface to submit these messages, but since it simplifies the presentation to only have the simulator at Eve's interface we only include Eve in the parties with write abilities.

[21] Traditional composable security frameworks require the simulator to cover all dishonest interfaces making it impossible to model Eq. (4.4).

[22] Note that the ideal specification in Eq. (4.5) does not follow the ideal-functionality-simulator paradigm, making it impossible to (directly) model the same thing in traditional composable frameworks.

Algorithm 9. $\perp_{\text{Arb}}$ converter for $B_j \in \mathcal{R}^H$.

```
(B_j ∈ R^H)-READBUFFER
  return B_j-GETVALIDIDS

(B_j ∈ R^H)-READREGISTER(id)
  if (id, ⟨A_i → V⟩) ∈ B_j-GETVALIDIDS then
     m ← B_j-READREGISTER(id)
     return m

(B_j ∈ R^H)-GETVALIDIDS        ▷ Local procedure. Operation not available at outside interface.
  validIds ← ∅
  for each (id, ⟨A_i → V⟩) ∈ B_j-READBUFFER do
     if A_i ∈ S̄^H then
        validIds ← (id, ⟨A_i → V⟩)
  return validIds
```

Theorem 4. *Consider a setting where* $\mathcal{R}^H$, $\overline{\mathcal{R}^H}$, $\mathcal{S}^H$ *and* $\overline{\mathcal{S}^H}$ *are all non-empty. We find an explicit reduction system* $\mathbf{C}'$*, an explicit simulator* sim *and explicit reduction systems* $\mathbf{C}$*,* $\mathbf{C}_{Cons}$ *and* $\mathbf{C}_{Unforg}$ *such that, for any* $\Omega \supseteq \{\mathsf{sim}\}$

$$\boldsymbol{\mathcal{R}} \subseteq \left((\boldsymbol{\mathcal{CA}})_{\Omega}^{\text{Arb}} \right)^{Adv^{Cons}(\cdot\,\mathbf{CC}_{Cons}) + Adv^{Unforg}(\cdot\,\mathbf{CC}_{Unforg}) + Adv^{Corr}(\cdot\,\mathbf{C}')}, \tag{4.6}$$

where for any distinguisher $\mathbf{D}$*,* $Adv^{Cons}(\mathbf{DCC}_{Cons})$*,* $Adv^{Unforg}(\mathbf{DCC}_{Unforg})$*, and* $Adv^{Corr}(\mathbf{DC}')$ *are, respectively, the advantages of* $\mathbf{D}' = \mathbf{DCC}_{Cons}$ *(the distinguisher resulting from composing* $\mathbf{D}$*,* $\mathbf{C}$ *and* $\mathbf{C}_{Cons}$*) in winning the Consistency game (see [21, Definition 3]), of* $\mathbf{D}'' = \mathbf{DCC}_{Unforg}$ *in winning the Unforgeability game (see [21, Definition 4]) and of* $\mathbf{D}''' = \mathbf{DC}'$ *in winning the Correctness game (see [21, Definition 2])*

A proof of Theorem 4 is provided in the full version [21].

In the second theorem we show that the advantage in distinguishing the real world from the ideal world for the exclusiveness of authenticity is bounded by the advantage in winning the Off-The-Record and Consistency games.

Theorem 5. *Consider a setting where* $\mathcal{R}^H$, $\overline{\mathcal{R}^H}$, $\mathcal{S}^H$ *and* $\overline{\mathcal{S}^H}$ *are all non-empty. For any signature forgery algorithm Forge suitable for the Off-The-Record security notion we find explicit reduction systems* $\mathbf{C}$ *and* $\mathbf{C}'$*, and an explicit simulator* sim *such that for any* $\Omega \supseteq \{\mathsf{sim}\}$*:*

$$\boldsymbol{\mathcal{R}} \subseteq (\boldsymbol{\mathcal{X}}_{\Omega,\pi^{Forge}}^{\text{Arb}})^{Adv^{OTR\text{-}Forge}(\cdot\,\mathbf{C}) + Adv^{Cons}(\cdot\,\mathbf{C}')}, \tag{4.7}$$

where π^{Forge} *is the converter running the Forge algorithm (see Algorithm 10), and for any for any distinguisher* $\mathbf{D}$*,* $Adv^{OTR\text{-}Forge}(\mathbf{DC})$ *and* $Adv^{Cons}(\mathbf{DC}')$ *are, respectively, the advantage of* $\mathbf{D}' = \mathbf{DC}$ *(the distinguisher resulting from composing* $\mathbf{D}$ *and* $\mathbf{C}$*) in winning the Off-The-Record game with respect to forgery algorithm Forge (see [21, Definition 5]), and the advantage of* $\mathbf{D}'' = \mathbf{DC}'$ *in winning the Consistency game (see [21, Definition 3]).*

A proof of Theorem 5 is provided in the full version [21].

Algorithm 10. π^{Forge} converter for set of (dishonest) parties $\overline{\mathcal{S}^H} \cup \overline{\mathcal{R}^H}$.

$(P \in \overline{\mathcal{S}^H} \cup \overline{\mathcal{R}^H})$-WRITE$(\langle A_i \to \mathcal{V}\rangle, m \in \mathcal{M})$
  pp ← P-PUBLICPARAMETERS
  $\mathtt{spk}_i$ ← P-SIGNERPUBLICKEY(A_i)
  for each $B_j \in \overline{\mathcal{V}^H}$ **do**
    $\{(\mathtt{vpk}_j, \mathtt{vsk}_j)\}$ ← P-VERIFIERKEYPAIR(B_j)
  for each $B_l \in \mathcal{V}$ **do**
    $\{\mathtt{vpk}_l\}$ ← P-VERIFIERPUBLICKEY(B_l)
  $\sigma \leftarrow Forge(\mathtt{pp}, \mathtt{spk}_i, \{\mathtt{vpk}_l\}_{B_l \in \mathcal{V}}, \{\mathtt{vsk}_c\}_{B_c \in \overline{\mathcal{V}^H}}, m)$
  P-OUTPUT$(P$-WRITE$(m, \sigma, (A_i, \mathcal{V})))$

Asymptotic Composable Security of MDVS. Analogously to Remark 2, for a security notion X, $Adv^{\mathsf{X}}(\overrightarrow{\mathbf{A}}) : \mathbb{N} \to \mathbb{R}$ denotes a function defined as $Adv^{\mathsf{X}}(\overrightarrow{\mathbf{A}})(k) := Adv^{\mathsf{X}}(\mathbf{A}_k)$. We say that a scheme satisfies X asymptotically if $Adv^{\mathsf{X}}(\overrightarrow{\mathbf{A}})$ is negligible on the security parameter k.

In the following, let $\Pi = (Setup, G_S, G_V, Sign, Vfy)$ be an MDVS scheme. The following corollaries, Corollary 1 and Corollary 2, follow from Theorem 4 and Theorem 5, respectively. These results state that any MDVS scheme Π that is asymptotically secure—according to asymptotic versions of [21, Definition 2], [21, Definition 3], [21, Definition 4], and [21, Definition 5]— and which is used as specified in Sect. 4.1 asymptotically constructs, from a real world specification $\boldsymbol{\mathcal{R}}$, the ideal world specification defined in Eq. 4.2 (see Remark 2). Note that, since we are making asymptotic construction statements, Ω and Ω' are both classes of efficient simulators (say non-uniform probabilistic polynomial time), and for any efficient family of distinguishers $\overrightarrow{\mathbf{D}}$, $\overrightarrow{\varepsilon}$ and $\overrightarrow{\varepsilon}'$ are both negligible functions (on the security parameter).

Corollary 1. *Consider a setting where $\mathcal{R}^H$, $\overline{\mathcal{R}^H}$, $\mathcal{S}^H$ and $\overline{\mathcal{S}^H}$ are all non-empty. If Π is asymptotically Correct (see [21, Definition 2]), Consistent (see [21, Definition 3]) and Unforgeable (see [21, Definition 4]), then $\boldsymbol{\mathcal{R}}$ asymptotically constructs $(\boldsymbol{\mathcal{CA}})^{\mathrm{Arb}}$.*

Corollary 2. *Consider a setting where $\mathcal{R}^H$, $\overline{\mathcal{R}^H}$, $\mathcal{S}^H$ and $\overline{\mathcal{S}^H}$ are all non-empty. If Π is asymptotically Off-The-Record (see [21, Definition 5]) and Consistent (see [21, Definition 3]), then $\boldsymbol{\mathcal{R}}$ asymptotically constructs $\boldsymbol{\mathcal{X}}^{\mathrm{Arb}}_{\pi^{Forge}}$, where π^{Forge} is the converter defined in Algorithm 10, running an algorithm Forge with respect to which Π is asymptotically Off-The-Record (i.e. no non-uniform probabilistic polynomial time adversary $\overrightarrow{\mathbf{A}}$ can win the Off-The-Record game of Π with respect to algorithm Forge with non-negligible advantage).*

4.4 Separation from Existing Game-Based Security Notions

The game-based security notion from [11] capturing the Off-The-Record security property of MDVS schemes (see [21, Definition 5]) is unnecessarily strong as for some MDVS schemes it allows the adversary to verify the validity of the challenge signatures, and thus allows it to trivially win the game. As hinted by our composable security notions, the main goal of the Off-The-Record security notion is capturing that a third party cannot tell whether a given signature is a valid one generated by the signer, or a forged one generated by dishonest receivers. The ability of a third party to generate signature replays—which might only be valid if the original signatures were already valid—does not violate any of the security properties that MDVS schemes intend to guarantee, and as such should not help in winning the corresponding security game. However, it does help in winning the Off-The-Record game from [11], meaning that this notion (i.e. the one from [11]) is unnecessarily strong.

Theorem 6. *Let* $\mathcal{P} = \{A_1, A_2, A_3, B_1, B_2, B_3, E\}$. *Consider any MDVS scheme* Π, *and let* $\varepsilon_{\Pi\text{-}4}$ *and* $\varepsilon_{\Pi\text{-}5}$ *denote the* ε*-balls (see Eq. (2.3)) given by, respectively, Theorem 4 and Theorem 5 for settings where* $\mathcal{R}^H$, $\overline{\mathcal{R}^H}$, $\mathcal{S}^H$ *and* $\overline{\mathcal{S}^H}$ *are all non-empty sets. Then there is a modified MDVS scheme* Π' *that is also secure as in each of these two theorems and for essentially the same* ε*-balls as* Π, *but such that for any suitable algorithm Forge for the Off-The-Record security notion (see [21, Definition 5]) there is an explicit and efficient adversary* $\mathbf{A}$ *such that*

$$Adv^{\Pi'\text{-}OTR\text{-}Forge}(\mathbf{A}) \geq 1 - \delta_{corr} - \delta_{auth},$$

where $Adv^{\Pi'\text{-}OTR\text{-}Forge}(\mathbf{A})$ *denotes the advantage of* $\mathbf{A}$ *in winning the Off-The-Record game for* Π' *with respect to the signature forgery algorithm Forge(see [21, Definition 5]),* δ_{corr} *is the probability that a single honestly generated signature does not verify correctly and* δ_{auth} *is the probability that a single forged signature is considered valid by the signature verification algorithm.*

A proof of Theorem 6 is provided in the full version [21].

5 Further Related Work

In [13], Jakobsson, Sako, and Impagliazzo introduce DVS and MDVS schemes and give two property-based security notions for the single designated verifier case. Their weaker notion is intended to capture essentially the same as our weaker exclusiveness of authenticity notion—if all receivers are honest, Eve learns that Alice is the one sending messages—whereas their stronger notion is intended to capture our stronger notion—even if all receivers are honest, Eve cannot tell if Alice sent any message. Unfortunately, the signature unforgeability notion considered—equivalent to Existential Unforgeability under No-Message Attacks (EUF-NMA)—is known to be too weak to allow for authentic communication.[23] Furthermore, the security notion capturing the exclusiveness of authenticity which is implicitly considered for the case of multiple receivers is

[23] Existential Unforgeability under Chosen Message Attacks (EUF-CMA)—a security notion known to be strictly stronger than EUF-NMA—is necessary for authentic communication, see [3,7].

also too weak, and in particular is not sufficient to achieve neither of our composable notions. This is so since simulating signatures requires secret information from every designated verifier, and thus if at least one of the verifiers is honest, doing so is not feasible.

In [29], Steinfeld, Bull, Wang and Pieprzyk introduce Universal Designated Verifier Signatures, wherein a signer can generate publicly verifiable signatures which can then be transformed into designated verifier ones (possibly by a distinct party not possessing the secret signing key). Although the security notions capturing the exclusiveness of authenticity property introduced in that paper are weak—in that they only meet the weaker notion we introduce in this paper—the proposed schemes meet our stronger notion for this property (for the single receiver case). On the other hand, the unforgeability notion considered in the paper is too weak: it does not suffice to achieve even our weaker composable security notion. Unfortunately, numerous subsequent works have considered the same unforgeability notion [16–19,30,32].

In [15], Krawczyk and Rabin introduce Chameleon signature schemes, which work by first using a chameleon hash function to hash a message and then using a normal signature scheme to sign the resulting hash. Chameleon hash functions are public key schemes which are collision-resistant for anyone not possessing the secret key, but which allow for efficient collision finding given the secret key. The intended use of these schemes is to provide the same guarantees as DVS schemes: a designated receiver first generates its chameleon hash function, and sends the corresponding public key to the signer; the signer then sends a signature on the message under the hash function provided by the receiver, which it can verify. Since the receiver knows the secret key of the chameleon hash function it sent to the signer, no one other than the receiver gets convinced that the signer signed any particular message. However, these schemes do not allow to achieve the exclusiveness of authenticity that our stronger composable notion captures: anyone with the public keys of the signer and of the chameleon hash function can verify whether a certain signature is a valid one (for some message), which implies that no third-party can feasibly forge signatures that are indistinguishable from real ones (or otherwise the signature scheme used by the signer is not unforgeable). Moreover, they also do not achieve our weaker notion, as dishonest receivers can only forge signatures once the signer signed a message.

In [27], Rivest, Shamir and Tauman mention that two party ring signatures are DVS schemes. Indeed, one can obtain a DVS scheme meeting our weaker composable notion for the case of a single receiver B by taking a ring signature scheme and using it to produce signatures for a ring composed by the signer A and by the intended (designated) receiver of that message, B.[24] But notice that, similarly to the case of Chameleon signature schemes, public keys are enough to verify signatures, implying that the DVS schemes yielded by ring signatures

[24] As one might note, the resulting DVS scheme can only meet our weaker composable notion if the underlying ring signature scheme meets the stronger Anonymity against Attribution Attacks [4, Definition 4].

can really only achieve our weaker security notion—where if both A and B are honest, E learns A is the signer. Furthermore, since any ring member can locally sign messages that are valid with respect to the entire ring, which is incompatible with the stronger authenticity requirement of MDVS schemes, ring signatures may only be used as DVS schemes for the case of a single receiver. Unfortunately, this went unnoticed in various prior works [9,16,18], which gave constructions of MDVS schemes based on ring signature schemes.

One could think that perhaps, to achieve our stronger notion for exclusiveness of authenticity—where a third party is not convinced that the signer signed some message even when all the designated receivers (and the signer) are honest—it suffices to guarantee that the validity of a signature can only be efficiently determined with the secret key given as input [28]. However, this is not the case. Consider for example, the case where the sender and the designated receivers share the signing key dsk of some (traditional) Digital Signature Scheme (DSS) (with the corresponding verification key dvk being publicly known), and where the MDVS signature σ_m for each message m also includes a signature $\sigma_m{}'$ under dsk on m. Then, while to verify the validity of an MDVS signature σ_m one may need the secret verification key for the MDVS scheme, by verifying the corresponding $\sigma_m{}'$ using dvk signature a third party already gets convinced, in the case where the sender and all the designated receivers are honest, that the really signer signed m. This same reasoning also explains why, in general, MAC schemes cannot be used per se as DVS schemes (in the stronger sense, captured by our stronger composable notion) for the two party case: it may not be feasible to simulate MAC schemes which look just like real ones.

References

1. Backes, M., Hofheinz, D.: How to break and repair a universally composable signature functionality. In: Zhang, K., Zheng, Y. (eds.) ISC 2004. LNCS, vol. 3225, pp. 61–72. Springer, Heidelberg (2004). https://doi.org/10.1007/978-3-540-30144-8_6
2. Backes, M., Pfitzmann, B., Waidner, M.: The reactive simulatability (RSIM) framework for asynchronous systems. Cryptology ePrint Archive, Report 2004/082 (2004). https://eprint.iacr.org/2004/082
3. Badertscher, C., Maurer, U., Tackmann, B.: On composable security for digital signatures. In: Abdalla, M., Dahab, R. (eds.) PKC 2018, Part I. LNCS, vol. 10769, pp. 494–523. Springer, Cham (2018). https://doi.org/10.1007/978-3-319-76578-5_17
4. Bender, A., Katz, J., Morselli, R.: Ring signatures: stronger definitions, and constructions without random oracles. In: Halevi, S., Rabin, T. (eds.) TCC 2006. LNCS, vol. 3876, pp. 60–79. Springer, Heidelberg (2006). https://doi.org/10.1007/11681878_4
5. Canetti, R.: Universally composable security: a new paradigm for cryptographic protocols. In: 42nd FOCS, pp. 136–145. IEEE Computer Society Press, October 2001. https://doi.org/10.1109/SFCS.2001.959888
6. Canetti, R.: Universally composable signatures, certification and authentication. Cryptology ePrint Archive, Report 2003/239 (2003). https://eprint.iacr.org/2003/239

7. Canetti, R.: Universally composable signature, certification, and authentication. In: 17th IEEE Computer Security Foundations Workshop (CSFW-17 2004), 28–30 June 2004, Pacific Grove, CA, USA, p. 219. IEEE Computer Society (2004). https://doi.org/10.1109/CSFW.2004.24. http://doi.ieeecomputersociety.org/10.1109/CSFW.2004.24
8. Canetti, R., Dodis, Y., Pass, R., Walfish, S.: Universally composable security with global setup. In: Vadhan, S.P. (ed.) TCC 2007. LNCS, vol. 4392, pp. 61–85. Springer, Heidelberg (2007). https://doi.org/10.1007/978-3-540-70936-7_4
9. Chow, S.S.M.: Multi-designated verifiers signatures revisited. Int. J. Netw. Secur. **7**(3), 348–357 (2008). http://ijns.jalaxy.com.tw/contents/ijns-v7-n3/ijns-2008-v7-n3-p348-357.pdf
10. Coretti, S., Maurer, U., Tackmann, B.: Constructing confidential channels from authenticated channels—public-key encryption revisited. In: Sako, K., Sarkar, P. (eds.) ASIACRYPT 2013, Part I. LNCS, vol. 8269, pp. 134–153. Springer, Heidelberg (2013). https://doi.org/10.1007/978-3-642-42033-7_8
11. Damgård, I., Haagh, H., Mercer, R., Nitulescu, A., Orlandi, C., Yakoubov, S.: Stronger security and constructions of multi-designated verifier signatures. In: Pass, R., Pietrzak, K. (eds.) TCC 2020, Part II. LNCS, vol. 12551, pp. 229–260. Springer, Cham (2020). https://doi.org/10.1007/978-3-030-64378-2_9
12. Hofheinz, D., Shoup, V.: GNUC: a new universal composability framework. J. Cryptol. **28**(3), 423–508 (2013). https://doi.org/10.1007/s00145-013-9160-y
13. Jakobsson, M., Sako, K., Impagliazzo, R.: Designated verifier proofs and their applications. In: Maurer, U. (ed.) EUROCRYPT 1996. LNCS, vol. 1070, pp. 143–154. Springer, Heidelberg (1996). https://doi.org/10.1007/3-540-68339-9_13
14. Jost, D., Maurer, U.: Overcoming impossibility results in composable security using interval-wise guarantees. In: Micciancio, D., Ristenpart, T. (eds.) CRYPTO 2020, Part I. LNCS, vol. 12170, pp. 33–62. Springer, Cham (2020). https://doi.org/10.1007/978-3-030-56784-2_2
15. Krawczyk, H., Rabin, T.: Chameleon signatures. In: NDSS 2000. The Internet Society, February 2000
16. Laguillaumie, F., Vergnaud, D.: Multi-designated verifiers signatures. In: Lopez, J., Qing, S., Okamoto, E. (eds.) ICICS 2004. LNCS, vol. 3269, pp. 495–507. Springer, Heidelberg (2004). https://doi.org/10.1007/978-3-540-30191-2_38
17. Laguillaumie, F., Vergnaud, D.: Designated verifier signatures: anonymity and efficient construction from any bilinear map. In: Blundo, C., Cimato, S. (eds.) SCN 2004. LNCS, vol. 3352, pp. 105–119. Springer, Heidelberg (2005). https://doi.org/10.1007/978-3-540-30598-9_8
18. Li, Y., Susilo, W., Mu, Y., Pei, D.: Designated verifier signature: definition, framework and new constructions. In: Indulska, J., Ma, J., Yang, L.T., Ungerer, T., Cao, J. (eds.) UIC 2007. LNCS, vol. 4611, pp. 1191–1200. Springer, Heidelberg (2007). https://doi.org/10.1007/978-3-540-73549-6_116
19. Lipmaa, H., Wang, G., Bao, F.: Designated verifier signature schemes: attacks, new security notions and a new construction. In: Caires, L., Italiano, G.F., Monteiro, L., Palamidessi, C., Yung, M. (eds.) ICALP 2005. LNCS, vol. 3580, pp. 459–471. Springer, Heidelberg (2005). https://doi.org/10.1007/11523468_38
20. Maurer, U.: Constructive cryptography – a new paradigm for security definitions and proofs. In: Mödersheim, S., Palamidessi, C. (eds.) TOSCA 2011. LNCS, vol. 6993, pp. 33–56. Springer, Heidelberg (2012). https://doi.org/10.1007/978-3-642-27375-9_3

21. Maurer, U., Portmann, C., Rito, G.: Giving an adversary guarantees (or: how to model designated verifier signatures in a composable framework). Cryptology ePrint Archive, Report 2021/1185 (2021). https://eprint.iacr.org/2021/1185
22. Maurer, U., Renner, R.: Abstract cryptography. In: Chazelle, B. (ed.) ICS 2011, pp. 1–21. Tsinghua University Press, January 2011
23. Maurer, U., Renner, R.: From indifferentiability to constructive cryptography (and back). In: Hirt, M., Smith, A. (eds.) TCC 2016, Part I. LNCS, vol. 9985, pp. 3–24. Springer, Heidelberg (2016). https://doi.org/10.1007/978-3-662-53641-4_1
24. Maurer, U.: Indistinguishability of random systems. In: Knudsen, L.R. (ed.) EUROCRYPT 2002. LNCS, vol. 2332, pp. 110–132. Springer, Heidelberg (2002). https://doi.org/10.1007/3-540-46035-7_8
25. Maurer, U., Pietrzak, K., Renner, R.: Indistinguishability amplification. In: Menezes, A. (ed.) CRYPTO 2007. LNCS, vol. 4622, pp. 130–149. Springer, Heidelberg (2007). https://doi.org/10.1007/978-3-540-74143-5_8
26. Pfitzmann, B., Waidner, M.: A model for asynchronous reactive systems and its application to secure message transmission. In: 2001 IEEE Symposium on Security and Privacy, pp. 184–200. IEEE Computer Society Press, May 2001. https://doi.org/10.1109/SECPRI.2001.924298
27. Rivest, R.L., Shamir, A., Tauman, Y.: How to leak a secret. In: Boyd, C. (ed.) ASIACRYPT 2001. LNCS, vol. 2248, pp. 552–565. Springer, Heidelberg (2001). https://doi.org/10.1007/3-540-45682-1_32
28. Saeednia, S., Kremer, S., Markowitch, O.: An efficient strong designated verifier signature scheme. In: Lim, J.-I., Lee, D.-H. (eds.) ICISC 2003. LNCS, vol. 2971, pp. 40–54. Springer, Heidelberg (2004). https://doi.org/10.1007/978-3-540-24691-6_4
29. Steinfeld, R., Bull, L., Wang, H., Pieprzyk, J.: Universal designated-verifier signatures. In: Laih, C.-S. (ed.) ASIACRYPT 2003. LNCS, vol. 2894, pp. 523–542. Springer, Heidelberg (2003). https://doi.org/10.1007/978-3-540-40061-5_33
30. Steinfeld, R., Wang, H., Pieprzyk, J.: Efficient extension of standard Schnorr/RSA signatures into universal designated-verifier signatures. In: Bao, F., Deng, R., Zhou, J. (eds.) PKC 2004. LNCS, vol. 2947, pp. 86–100. Springer, Heidelberg (2004). https://doi.org/10.1007/978-3-540-24632-9_7
31. Unruh, D., Müller-Quade, J.: Universally composable incoercibility. In: Rabin, T. (ed.) CRYPTO 2010. LNCS, vol. 6223, pp. 411–428. Springer, Heidelberg (2010). https://doi.org/10.1007/978-3-642-14623-7_22
32. Zhang, Y., Au, M.H., Yang, G., Susilo, W.: (Strong) multi-designated verifiers signatures secure against rogue key attack. In: Xu, L., Bertino, E., Mu, Y. (eds.) NSS 2012. LNCS, vol. 7645, pp. 334–347. Springer, Heidelberg (2012). https://doi.org/10.1007/978-3-642-34601-9_25

How to Build a Trapdoor Function from an Encryption Scheme

Sanjam Garg[1(✉)], Mohammad Hajiabadi[2], Giulio Malavolta[3], and Rafail Ostrovsky[4]

[1] University of California, Berkeley, Berkeley, USA
sanjamg@berkeley.edu
[2] University of Waterloo, Waterloo, Canada
[3] Max Planck Institute for Security and Privacy, Bochum, Germany
[4] University of California, Los Angeles, Los Angeles, USA

Abstract. In this work we ask the following question: Can we transform any encryption scheme into a trapdoor function (TDF)? Alternatively stated, can we make any encryption scheme randomness recoverable? We propose a generic compiler that takes as input any encryption scheme with pseudorandom ciphertexts and adds a trapdoor to invert the encryption, recovering also the random coins. This *universal TDFier* only assumes in addition the existence of a hinting pseudorandom generator (PRG). Despite the simplicity, our transformation is quite general and we establish a series of new feasibility results:

- The first identity-based TDF [Bellare et al. EUROCRYPT 2012] from the CDH assumption in pairing-free groups (or from factoring), thus matching the state of the art for identity-based encryption schemes. Prior works required pairings or LWE.
- The first collusion-resistant attribute-based TDF (AB-TDF) for all (NC^1, resp.) circuits from LWE (bilinear maps, resp.). Moreover, the first single-key AB-TDF from CDH. To the best of our knowledge, no AB-TDF was known in the literature (not even for a single key) from any assumption. We obtain the same results for predicate encryption.

As an additional contribution, we define and construct a *trapdoor garbling* scheme: A simulation secure garbling scheme with a hidden "trigger" that allows the evaluator to fully recover the randomness used by the garbling algorithm. We show how to construct trapdoor garbling from the DDH or LWE assumption with an interplay of key-dependent message (KDM) and randomness-dependent message (RDM) techniques.

S. Garg—Supported in part from DARPA/ARL SAFEWARE Award W911NF15C0210, AFOSR Award FA9550-15-1-0274, AFOSR Award FA9550-19-1-0200, AFOSR YIP Award, NSF CNS Award 1936826, DARPA and SPAWAR under contract N66001-15-C-4065, a Hellman Award and research grants by the Okawa Foundation, Visa Inc., and Center for Long-Term Cybersecurity (CLTC, UC Berkeley). The views expressed are those of the author and do not reflect the official policy or position of the funding agencies.

R. Ostrovsky—Supported by DARPA SPAWAR contract N66001-15-C-4065.

M. Tibouchi and H. Wang (Eds.): ASIACRYPT 2021, LNCS 13092, pp. 220–249, 2021.
https://doi.org/10.1007/978-3-030-92078-4_8

Trapdoor garbling allows us to obtain alternative constructions of (single-key) AB-TDFs with additional desirable properties, such as adaptive security (in the choice of the attribute) and projective keys. We expect trapdoor garbling to be useful in other contexts, e.g. in case where, upon successful execution, the evaluator needs to immediately verify that the garbled circuit was well-formed.

1 Introduction

Seminal results in 1970's laid the foundations of public-key cryptography by introducing the notion of trapdoor functions [14,35]. These are families of injective functions, where each function can be computed in the forward direction, but a randomly chosen function is one-way. Moreover, any function in the family can be efficiently inverted using the function's associated trapdoor key.

The historical interest in TDFs stems from this primitive being sufficient for CPA-secure public-key encryption (PKE) schemes. Recent results, however, have substantially changed this perspective, showing TDFs (or extensions thereof) enable many applications which are beyond the reach of traditional public-key encryption techniques [3,4,18,25,32]. Most notably, a recent result of Hohenberger, Koppula and Waters shows that TDFs generically imply the existence of CCA-secure PKE schemes [25], while whether or not CPA-secure PKE is sufficient is a long standing open problem. Also, recent advances in TDFs have led to many new feasibility results (e.g. rate-1 oblivious transfer) [18].

What makes trapdoor functions a strong primitive is its inversion property: The inversion algorithm recovers the entire input, in contrast to randomized PKE schemes where the decryption algorithm may not necessarily recover the encryption randomness. Such a property is crucially used in all the above applications, and in particular is the central ingredient of the recent result of Hohenberger et al. [25] for enforcing well-formedness of ciphertexts.

We now have constructions of TDFs from a range of specific assumptions, including factoring/QR/DCR [19,33], LWE/DDH [32], low-noise LPN [27], and CDH [20,21]. One limitation of these results is that they employ what appear to be ad-hoc techniques to obtain TDFs. Consequently, it is not clear whether and how these techniques will scale to obtain TDFs for more advanced primitives such as Identity-Based Encryption (IBE) or Attribute-Based Encryption (ABE). As we argue below, while TDFs for such advanced primitives will have additional applications, our knowledge of how these advanced TDFs may be realized is quite limited.

TDFs for Advanced Encryption. In this work, we are interested in realizing TDF notions for advanced encryption primitives, such as ABE or IBE. For example, under *Identity-Based TDFs* (IB-TDFs), one *deterministically* evaluates an input $x \in \{0,1\}^n$ as $\mathsf{Eval}(\mathsf{pp}, \mathsf{id}, x)$ to get an image y; an inverter with knowledge of $\mathsf{td}_{\mathsf{id}}$, a user secret key for identity id, may retrieve x as $\mathsf{Invert}(\mathsf{td}_{\mathsf{id}}, y)$. More generally, under *Attribute-Based TDFs* (AB-TDFs), one deterministically evaluates an input x relative to a public parameter pp and attribute α to get an image y; the value of x can be recovered from y by using a trapdoor key td_C for a circuit C where $C(\alpha) = 1$. Moreover, if $C(\alpha) = 0$, then even given td_C it should be computationally infeasible to recover x from y. This notion can be extended to allow many key corruptions, as in the standard ABE setting, or even to hide the attribute if $C(\alpha) = 0$, as in predicate encryption (PE).

Why TDFs for Advanced Encryption? In addition to being an interesting notion on its own, AB-TDFs enable applications that cannot be obtained using either TDFs or randomized ABE schemes alone. For example, while TDFs allow us to build CCA-secure PKE schemes [25], we do not know whether TDFs are sufficient for realizing stronger primitives, such as Designated-Verifier Non-Interactive Zero-Knowedge (DV-NIZK). On the other hand, the work of [31] shows that DV-NIZK can be realized using any single-key AB-TDFs or, more generally, under what they called single-key weak-function hiding ABE. At a high level, this latter notion requires that using sk_C to decrypt any (possibly malformed) ciphertext c with a public attribute x should reveal nothing beyond whether or not $C(x) = 1$. Any AB-TDF (or equivalently a randomness-recoverable ABE) by design has this property as one can decrypt and re-encrypt to reject all malformed ciphertexts.

Also, the direct usage of IB/AB-TDF can be beneficial: As shown in [5], they directly imply secure constructions of *deterministic* encryption [2,7] (lifted to the IBE/ABE settings) that allow users to publicly search over encrypted data while maintaining the maximum level of privacy possible. Another application of this class of primitives is the construction of *hedged* IBE/ABE [3,36] where the encryption algorithm is made resilient to the presence of low-quality randomness.

Assumptions Behind AB-TDFs/IB-TDFs. While single-key ABE can be built from any CPA-secure PKE, we do not have any constructions of (even) single-key AB-TDFs for general circuits. The closest result is the approach of [31], which shows that, assuming LWE, one can build an ABE scheme where the decryption algorithm recovers an "encoded" version of the underlying randomness, which nonetheless is sufficient for checking whether the ciphertext is well-formed (i.e. the LWE noise values sampled during encryption, as opposed to the encryption coins themselves). Even in the simpler IBE setting, the only known constructions of IB-TDFs (for the multi-key setting) are from pairings/LWE [5]. Recent advancements in the IBE landscape showed constructions from CDH/DDH [12,15,16], however it is currently not clear whether these assumptions are sufficient for constructing IB-TDFs.

Difficulties in Building AB-TDFs. Let us review the construction of single-key ABE from CPA-secure PKE, as a way to understand the underlying difficulties in realizing AB-TDFs. For circuits of size m, the public parameter $\mathsf{pp} := \{\mathsf{pk}_{i,b}\}_{i\in[m],b\in\{0,1\}}$ contains $2m$ public keys; a secret key for a circuit $C \in \{0,1\}^m$ is the sequence of secret keys $\{\mathsf{sk}_{i,C_i}\}$. To encrypt a message m relative to (pp, α) we garble the universal circuit which has $[\alpha, m]$ hardwired, and which on input C returns m if and only if $C(\alpha) = 1$. The resulting ciphertext consists of the garbled circuit as well as an encryption of the (i, b) label under $\mathsf{pk}_{i,b}$. Making the above scheme randomness recoverable encounters two major difficulties: (1) The random coins used to generate the garbled circuit during encryption should be kept private to ensure circuit privacy; and (2) The random coins used to encrypt the $2m$ labels should also be kept secret, since otherwise the security of the garbled circuit will be lost. Using a TDF (or equivalently a randomness recoverable PKE) to encrypt the labels does not get us too far either, because it will only allow us to recover half of the randomness used to encrypt the labels (and none of the coins used to garble the circuit).

The same obstacles emerge trying to extend the approach of [15,16] to get IB-TDFs: During encryption we generate a sequence of garbled circuits, and recovering the underlying random coins seems hopeless, as explained above.

1.1 Our Results

We propose a generic approach for building TDFs for advanced encryption functionalities. Our first contribution is the construction of a *universal TDFier*: Given any IBE/ABE/PE with pseudorandom ciphertexts, our compiler returns a secure IB/AB/P-TDF. Our transformation is insensitive to the exact security and functionality of the underlying encryption scheme: For example, if the base ABE is single-key (resp., collusion) secure for a function family F, then so is the resulting AB-TDFs. The only additional building block needed by our compiler is a hinting PRG [29]. More precisely, we prove the following theorem.

Theorem 1 (Informal). *If there exists a {PKE, IBE, ABE, PE} with pseudorandom ciphertext and a hinting PRG, then there exists a {TDF, IB-TDF, AB-TDF,P-TDF}. Moreover, if the hinting PRG is* robust, *the constructed scheme provides deterministic-encryption security.*

To complement our result, we define and construct hinting PRGs that satisfy (k, n)-robustness: The hinting PRG provides pseudorandomness even if the seed is not uniformly distributed, but is a (k, n)-source (i.e., the n-bit seed has at least k bits min-entropy). By tweaking the hinting-PRG construction of [29], we show the following.

Theorem 2 (Informal). *If the {CDH, LWE} problem is hard, then there exists a (k, n)-robust hinting PRG.*

One of the most surprising features of our compiler is its *simplicity*: Once all components are in place, our transformation adds a very small (conceptual and computational) overhead. Yet, it is quite *general.* It allows us to establish a new series of feasibility results, such as:

- The first IB-TDF from the CDH assumption in pairing-free groups (or under factoring), thus matching the state of the art for IBE schemes. Prior work [5] gave two specialized constructions from pairings and LWE, respectively.
- The first (collusion-resistant) {AB-TDF, P-TDF} for NC^1 circuits from bilinear maps. To the best of our knowledge, this is the first provably secure version of AB-TDF from any assumption.
- The first (collusion-resistant) {AB-TDF, P-TDF} for all circuits from the LWE assumption. We believe that there might already be a way to build

(many-key) AB-TDF for circuits from LWE, by using the techniques of [1,9] in the context of [5]. The resulting construction might be more efficient than our HPRG-based LWE-based one, but ours is generic.

As an added bonus, using our compiler, the public/secret keys of the resulting TDF are identical to that of the underlying encryption scheme. This means that the trapdoor functionality (i.e. the randomness recoverability) can be added to the encryption *after the fact*, without the need to redistribute keys, by just including some additional public parameters (which can be reused across multiple instances of the scheme).

Trapdoor Projective Garbled Circuits. We also initiate the study of randomness recoverability for garbled circuits. Our result is a new notion of *trapdoor garbled circuits*: Given a garbled circuit $\tilde{\mathsf{P}}$ and garbled labels $\{\ell_{i,b}\}$ produced for a circuit $\mathsf{P} : \{0,1\}^m \rightarrow \{0,1\}$ using randomness r, we require the following properties. (1) Randomness recoverability: For any x such that $\mathsf{P}(x) = 1$, given $(\tilde{\mathsf{P}}, \{\ell_{i,x_i}\})$ we can recover r; and (2) Privacy: We have simulation security against any input x such that $\mathsf{P}(x) = 0$. We note that a randomness recoverable single-key ABE (constructed from Theorem 1 above) allows one to build a trapdoor garbled circuit, but it will not be projective (i.e., one label for each input wire value). The projective property of garbled circuits is crucially used in many applications, and hence is a desirable feature to have. One of our main contributions is a construction of trapdoor garbling under standard assumptions.

Theorem 3 (Informal). *If the {DDH, LWE} problem is hard, then there exists a trapdoor (projective) garbling scheme for all circuits.*

Our scheme builds on an interplay of key-dependent message (KDM) and randomness-dependent message (RDM) techniques, which may be of independent interest. As an immediate application, we obtain a single-key AB-TDF that is simultaneously (1) adaptively secure (in the choice of the identity/attribute), (2) perfectly correct, and (3) has projective keys (i.e. one label for each input wire value).[1] We believe trapdoor garbling may find further applications in the future.

2 Technical Overview

In this section we give an overview of our techniques for building TDFs from advanced encryption schemes.

2.1 A Universal TDFier

Our construction of universal TDFier is quite simple and the best way to present it is to just describe the scheme. It builds on the mirroring technique of [20].

[1] Our generic conversion starting from any single-key ABE does not preserve property (1) and (3).

Before delving into the technical details, we recall the notion of a hinting PRG and we briefly define the security notion of (k, n)-robustness that is at the heart of our transformation.

Robust Hinting PRGs. The notion of hinting PRG [29] was introduced in the context of upgrading CPA-secure scheme into CCA-secure ones.[2] A hinting PRG, is a function that takes as input an n-bit seed and returns n-many ℓ-bit strings, for some polynomial $\ell = \ell(\lambda)$. A hinting PRG is required to satisfy an enhanced notion of pseudorandomness. In the security game, we define a 2-by-n matrix where the rows corresponding to the bit representation of the seed are populated with the outputs of the hinting PRG, whereas the other entries are sampled uniformly ℓ-bit strings. The requirement is that it is computationally hard to distinguish such 2-by-n matrix from a uniform one. Note that such a notion does not follow from the standard definition of pseudorandomness: The pseudorandom entries of the 2-by-n matrix give a "hint" about the input seed. Nevertheless, it was shown that such a notion can be achieved under standard assumptions, such as CDH or LWE [29].

In this work we are interested in a stronger notion of security that we call (k, n) robustness. Loosely speaking, we require that the above guarantee is retained even if the n-bit seed is not sampled uniformly, but rather from a distribution with k-bits of min entropy. We observe that the schemes in [29], which are in turn based on the constructions of chameleon encryption from [12,13,16,17,21], can be shown to satisfy (k, n)-robustness with some tweaking of the parameters and of the security analysis. Henceforth, we simply assume we are given a (k, n)-robust hinting PRG.

Universal TDFier. We are now ready to show how to add randomness recoverability to any encryption scheme (i.e. construction a TDF). We only require such an encryption to satisfy a mild structural property, which is usually referred to as *pseudorandom ciphertext*: Ciphertexts $c \in \mathsf{Enc}(\mathsf{pk}, \cdot)$ must be computationally indistinguishable from uniformly sampled bitstrings $\{0,1\}^{|c|}$. Our actual compiler will be slightly more general, allowing us to capture all ciphertext domains that form a (not necessarily Abelian) group, with efficiently samplable elements. This will allow us to capture a large class of encryption schemes and will significantly expand the scope of our compiler. However, for the sake of this overview we assume ciphertexts are indistinguishable from uniformly random strings.

We describe our universal TDFier for the simple case of PKE, which already contains the main ideas of our approach. We refer the reader to the main body for the generalization to IBE/ABE/PE. The key generation algorithm consists of sampling a key pair $(\mathsf{sk}, \mathsf{pk})$ of the input PKE, along with the public parameters $\mathsf{pp}_{\mathsf{HPRG}}$ of a (k, n)-robust hinting PRG and n random strings $r_i \xleftarrow{\$} \{0,1\}^{|c|}$. The index key of the TDF consists of

$$(\mathsf{pk}, \mathsf{pp}_{\mathsf{HPRG}}, r_1, \dots, r_n)$$

[2] Although there is some resemblance with our approach, we note that the compiled scheme of [29] is *not* randomness recoverable unless one starts with a randomness recoverable encryption scheme, which is tautological.

and the trapdoor is set to sk. On input some string $x \in \{0,1\}^n$, we define the evaluation algorithm of the TDF as follows. For all $i \in [n]$:

- If $x_i = 0$: Compute $y_i = \mathsf{Enc}(\mathsf{pk}, \$; z_i)$, where $z_i = \mathsf{HPRG.Eval}(\mathsf{pp}_{\mathsf{HPRG}}, x, i)$.
- If $x_i = 1$: Compute $y_i = \mathsf{Enc}(\mathsf{pk}, \$; z_i) \oplus r_i$, where $z_i = \mathsf{HPRG.Eval}(\mathsf{pp}_{\mathsf{HPRG}}, x, i)$.

Return the image $y = (y_1, \ldots, y_n)$. Here \$ denotes some distinguished string, which is instrumental to ensure correctness of the inversion. Given the trapdoor sk, one can recover the input x from an image $y = (y_1, \ldots, y_n)$ bit by bit, setting $x_i = 0$ if $\mathsf{Dec}(\mathsf{sk}, y_i) = \$$ and $x_i = 1$ otherwise. Setting \$ to be a large enough string, we can show that the scheme achieves perfect correctness with all but negligible probability, over the random choice of the index key.

Besides adding small overhead to the runtime of the encryption scheme (i.e. n evaluations of a hinting PRG and n calls to the encryption algorithm), the public/secret keys of the compiled scheme are identical to that of the underlying PKE, except for some additional public parameters $(\mathsf{pp}_{\mathsf{HPRG}}, r_1, \ldots, r_n)$. This means that we can take any encryption scheme (with pseudorandom ciphertexts) and add randomness recoverability almost for free.

Security Proof (Sketch). We provide a high-level idea of the proof strategy, to motivate the security requirements for the underlying building blocks. To prove CPA-security, we modify the distribution of the challenge image through a series of hybrids, which we summarize below.

- Hybrid 0: This is the original distribution.
- Hybrid 1: In this hybrid we compute the public parameters after the challenge ciphertext. More precisely, for all $i \in [n]$:
  - If $x_i = 0$: Compute $y_i = \mathsf{Enc}(\mathsf{pk}, \$; z_i)$, where $z_i = \mathsf{HPRG.Eval}(\mathsf{pp}_{\mathsf{HPRG}}, x, i)$. The set $r_i = y_i \oplus s_i$, where $s_i \xleftarrow{\$} \{0,1\}^{|\mathsf{c}|}$
  - If $x_i = 1$: Compute $y_i = s_i \xleftarrow{\$} \{0,1\}^{|\mathsf{c}|}$ and set $r_i = y_i \oplus \mathsf{Enc}(\mathsf{pk}, \$; z_i)$, where $z_i = \mathsf{HPRG.Eval}(\mathsf{pp}_{\mathsf{HPRG}}, x, i)$.

  This step is reminiscent of the mirroring technique from [20] and will allow us to later equivocate the challenge image. Note that so far the distribution did not change.
- Hybrid 2: In this hybrid we change the s_i (as defined above) to be encryptions of \$ with fresh random coins. Indistinguishability follows from the pseudorandomness of the ciphertexts of the encryption scheme. The effect of this change is to remove the "signal" of x in the challenge image: Regardless of the value of x_i, we always compute y_i as an encryption of \$ and r_i as $\mathsf{Enc}(\mathsf{pk}, \$) \oplus \mathsf{Enc}(\mathsf{pk}, \$)$. However we are not yet done: The usage of pseudorandom/truly random coins still contains some lingering information about x.
- Hybrid 3: In this hybrid we compute all ciphertexts for the challenge image with truly random coins. It is tempting to conclude that the indistinguishability follows from the pseudorandomness of the hinting PRG, however note

that x is not necessarily uniformly sampled.[3] Our final weapon to deploy is the notion of (k, n)-robustness of the hinting PRG: Provided that x has enough min-entropy, this step goes trough.
- Hybrid 4: In the last step we change all ciphetexts to encrypt 0 (padded to the appropriate length). Since they are all computed using truly random coins, we can now invoke the CPA-security of the encryption scheme.

The proof is concluded by observing that the image in the last hybrid has no pre-image.

2.2 Trapdoor Garbled Circuits and Single-Key ABE

We will now show an alternative way of building single-key AB-TDFs. We will start with a single-key ABE built from a CPA-secure PKE and garbled circuits and develop new techniques that will allow us to make this scheme randomness recoverable. This new approach has several advantages when compared with our generic transformation:

- The resulting AB-TDF is adaptively secure in the choice of the attribute string α.
- The resulting AB-TDF has projective keys, i.e. one labels per input wire.

Along the way, we define and construct a notion we call *trapdoor garbling*, which may be of independent interest.

An ABE scheme ABE is defined as follows. The public parameter $\mathsf{pp} := \{\mathsf{pk}_{i,b}\}$ consist of $2n$ public keys; the secret key for a circuit C is $\mathsf{sk}_C := \{\mathsf{sk}_{i,C_i}\}$. To encrypt a message m to an attribute α, we garble the universal circuit $\mathsf{P}[\alpha, m]$ (where $\mathsf{P}[\alpha, m](C) = m$ iff $C(\alpha) = 1$) to get $(\tilde{\mathsf{P}}, \{\mathsf{lb}_{i,b}\})$; we then output $\mathsf{ct} := (\tilde{\mathsf{P}}, \{\mathsf{PKE.Enc}(\mathsf{pk}_{i,b}, \mathsf{lb}_{i,b})\})$. Let ρ be the randomness used to garble $C[\alpha, m]$ and let $\{r_{i,b}\}$ be the randomness used to encrypt the labels $\{\mathsf{lb}_{i,b}\}$.

How to Make ABE Randomness Recoverable? Recall the two sources of randomness ρ, $\{r_{i,b}\}$ mentioned above. At first, one might think that recovering ρ would be too much to ask for, since otherwise the whole security of the garbled circuit is lost. We, however, notice that there is some wiggle room here: Only *legitimate* inverters—namely one who has sk_C where $C(\alpha) = 1$—need to be able to recover ρ, while security should hold against *illegitimate* inverters. This brings us to the notion of *trapdoor garbling*.

Trapdoor Garbling. We explain the idea of trapdoor garbling in the above context. Letting $(\tilde{\mathsf{P}}, \{\mathsf{lb}_{i,b}\})$ be as above, trapdoor garbling requires: (1) Randomness Recoverability: for any C such that $C(\alpha) = 1$, given $(\tilde{\mathsf{P}}, \{\mathsf{lb}_{i,C_i}\})$ one may efficiently recover ρ; we call this *trapdoor mode*; and (2) Security: for any

---

[3] One could define the security of the TDF to hold only for uniformly sampled inputs (i.e. one-wayness) however this precludes many interesting applications, such as deterministic and searchable encryption.

C such that $C(\alpha) = 0$ (which we call *security mode*), the pair $(\tilde{\mathsf{P}}, \{\mathsf{lb}_{i,C_i}\})$ can be simulated in the standard sense (and in particular without knowing m or α).

Realizing Trapdoor Garbling. Let us see the challenges involved in adding a trapdoor mode to Yao's garbling scheme. For Yao's scheme, the garbling randomness ρ may be split into (A) ρ_k: the coins used to generate all the underlying wire keys and (B) ρ_c: the coins used to generate the underlying ciphertexts for the garble tables. Yao's scheme guarantees coin recovery for neither case. Let Key be the set of all keys produced during the garbling algorithm (i.e., two keys per wire). Our first observation is that if the underlying secret-key encryption scheme $\mathsf{SKE} := (\mathsf{G}, \mathsf{Enc}, \mathsf{Dec})$ is randomness recoverable and that if a secret key is just the coins of G, then recovering *all* the keys in Key will enable recovering both ρ_k and ρ_c. We can recover ρ_k because a key is just the coins of G; and we can recover ρ_c because we can decrypt every ciphertext to recover the underlying coins. Now to recover Key in trapdoor mode, letting $k_{\mathsf{out},1}$ be the output-wire key for value 1, we simply add an encryption $\mathsf{SKE.Enc}(k_{\mathsf{out},1}, k)$ for any $k \in \mathsf{Key}$ to $\tilde{\mathsf{P}}$.[4] We will have randomness recoverability, but we have introduced key-dependent-message (KDM) circularity involving multiple keys (since $k_{\mathsf{out},1}$ encrypts all the keys in Key, and is in turn encrypted under those keys via a chain of "hops"). While we have multi-key KDM-secure SKE schemes, we have to make sure both Conditions (A) and (B) above hold. Fortunately, the DDH-based SKE schemes of Boneh et al. ($\mathsf{SKEBHHO}$) [10] and the LWE-based Dual-Regev's SKE scheme [22,34] provide both Conditions (A) and (B). For concreteness, under $\mathsf{SKEBHHO}$, a key is chosen as $s \xleftarrow{\$} \{0,1\}^n$; to encrypt $\mathsf{Enc}(s, g)$: we return $(g_1, \ldots, g_n, s \cdot \mathbf{g})$, where $\mathbf{g} := (g_1, \ldots, g_n) \xleftarrow{\$} \mathbb{G}^n$ and $s \cdot \mathbf{g} = \prod g_i^{s_i}$.[5] The proof of security is exactly like Yao's scheme [30,37], breaking the circularity using the underlying KDM-secure scheme.

ABE Made Randomness Recoverable? Unfortunately, we are not done yet, because in the ABE scheme we need to recover both ρ (the garbled circuit randomness) and $\{r_{i,b}\}$, the randomness used to encrypt the labels $\{\mathsf{lb}_{i,b}\}$ under $\{\mathsf{pk}_{i,b}\}$. Trapdoor garbling allows us to recover ρ, but we are left with recovering $\{r_{i,b}\}$. Even if the underlying PKE scheme is randomness recoverable, we can only recover half of $\{r_{i,b}\}$, those corresponding to the bits of C. Moreover, we cannot make $r_{i,0}$ and $r_{i,1}$ related (so to have either one reveal the other one) because the ABE security will be lost. So, it seems we are stuck here. To get around this, we augment the garbled circuit $\tilde{\mathsf{P}}$ even further! We now add to $\tilde{\mathsf{P}}$ an encryption of $\mathsf{SKEBHHO.Enc}(k_{\mathsf{out},1}, r_{i,b})$ for all i and b, where recall that

[4] In Yao's scheme [30,37], the key $k_{\mathsf{out},1}$ is put in the clear in $\tilde{\mathsf{P}}$ with the corresponding bit 1 for it; we do not put $k_{\mathsf{out},1}$ in the clear in $\tilde{\mathsf{P}}$, but rather we encrypt 1 under $k_{\mathsf{out},1}$ to assert the underlying recovered key corresponds to bit 1; similarly, we encrypt 0 under the output-wire key $k_{\mathsf{out},0}$ for bit 0.

[5] One might complain that the scheme is not randomness recoverable in a strict sense, in that the coins used to sample the group elements are not recovered. We note, however, that in our ABE application, these group elements $\mathbf{g}$ may be chosen during key-generation time and put in pp. We ignore these issues for simplicity.

$k_{\mathsf{out},1}$ is the output-wire key for bit 1. Doing so will indeed make the underlying ABE scheme randomness recoverable, but we have now introduced a much more complicated circularity, involving both KDM and RDM (randomness-dependent messaging) at the same time. In particular, (i) $\mathsf{pk}_{i,b}$ encrypts $\mathsf{lb}_{i,b}$ using coins $r_{i,b}$ and (ii) $r_{i,b}$ is encrypted under $k_{\mathsf{out},1}$; and (iii) $k_{\mathsf{out},1}$ is encrypted under $\mathsf{lb}_{i,b}$ (via a sequence of intermediate encryptions). We have RDM dependence because of (ii) and similarly we have KDM dependence. We now introduce a technique that will allow us to handle the above circularity, using a careful choice of encryption schemes. To make things more concrete, let us focus on a special case of the above circularity which nonetheless captures all the difficulties: (A) $\mathsf{pk}_{i,b}$ encrypts $k_{\mathsf{out},1}$ using coins $r_{i,b}$ and (B) $k_{\mathsf{out},1}$ encrypts $r_{i,b}$ using fresh coins (under the SKE scheme).

Handling RDM+KDM. Let $\mathsf{SKE} := (\mathsf{G}, \mathsf{Enc}, \mathsf{Dec})$ be an SKE scheme and $\mathsf{PKE} := (\mathsf{G}, \mathsf{Enc}, \mathsf{Dec})$ be a PKE scheme. We need security in the presence of

$$\mathsf{pk}, \mathsf{PKE.Enc}(\mathsf{pk}, s; r), \mathsf{SKE.Enc}(s, r), \tag{1}$$

where all the variables are chosen at random and that $\mathsf{SKE.Enc}$ uses fresh coins to encrypt. By having security, we mean semantic security against both pk and s. We give a technique that allows us to reduce RDM+KDM in the sense of Eq. 1 to KDM alone. Focusing on DDH, SKE will be $\mathsf{SKEBHHO}$ (see above) and PKE will be the dual version of $\mathsf{PKE}_{\mathrm{bhho}}$, where the roles of randomness and secret keys are swapped.

Let $|s| = n$. Let $\mathsf{PKE}_{\mathrm{bhho}}$ be the n-bit version of BHHO (defined below). We will define a dual version of n-bit BHHO, which we call $\mathsf{PKE}_{\mathrm{dbhho}}$, satisfying:

1. An encryption randomness under $\mathsf{PKE}_{\mathrm{dbhho}}$ is a secret key under $\mathsf{PKE}_{\mathrm{bhho}}$. Also, a secret key under $\mathsf{PKE}_{\mathrm{dbhho}}$ is an encryption randomness under $\mathsf{PKE}_{\mathrm{bhho}}$.
2. Looking at the PKE part of Eq. 1, we require

$$\mathsf{pk}_{\mathrm{dbhho}}, \mathsf{PKE}_{\mathrm{dbhho}}.\mathsf{Enc}(\mathsf{pk}_{\mathrm{dbhho}}, s; \mathsf{r}_{\mathrm{dbhho}}) \equiv \mathsf{pk}_{\mathrm{bhho}}, \mathsf{PKE}_{\mathrm{bhho}}.\mathsf{Enc}(\mathsf{pk}_{\mathrm{bhho}}, s; \mathsf{r}_{\mathrm{bhho}}), \tag{2}$$

where $(\mathsf{pk}_{\mathrm{dbhho}}, \mathsf{sk}_{\mathrm{dbhho}})$ is a key pair under $\mathsf{PKE}_{\mathrm{dbhho}}$, $\mathsf{sk}_{\mathrm{bhho}} := \mathsf{r}_{\mathrm{dbhho}}$, $\mathsf{pk}_{\mathrm{bhho}}$ is the corresponding public key for $\mathsf{sk}_{\mathrm{bhho}}$ under $\mathsf{PKE}_{\mathrm{bhho}}$ and $\mathsf{r}_{\mathrm{bhho}} := \mathsf{sk}_{\mathrm{dbhho}}$.

Instantiating Eq. 1 with $\mathsf{PKE}_{\mathrm{dbhho}}$, using Eq. 2, we may rewrite Eq. 1 as

$$\mathsf{pk}_{\mathrm{bhho}}, \mathsf{PKE}_{\mathrm{bhho}}.\mathsf{Enc}(\mathsf{pk}_{\mathrm{bhho}}, s; \mathsf{r}_{\mathrm{bhho}}), \mathsf{SKEBHHO.Enc}(s, \mathsf{sk}_{\mathrm{bhho}}), \tag{3}$$

where everything is chosen randomly. Since the randomness of $\mathsf{PKE}_{\mathrm{bhho}}.\mathsf{Enc}$ (i.e., $\mathsf{r}_{\mathrm{bhho}}$) never appears as a plaintext, Eq. 3 is secure by [10].[6]

We quickly review k-bit BHHO [10], where the secret key size is n. (In our ABE instantiation, k will be n, because we need to encrypt a secret key of the

[6] The result of [10] concerns a single PKE scheme; in our setting $\mathsf{SKEBHHO}$ is just the secret-key version of BHHO, and by choosing the public parameter to be the same across the two schemes, we will have cross KDM security.

SKE scheme.) We have a public parameter $\mathbf{g} := (g_1, \dots, g_n)$. The secret key of $\mathsf{PKE}_{\mathsf{bhho}}$ is $\mathsf{sk} \in \{0,1\}^n$ and the public key is $(\mathbf{g}, g_{\mathsf{pub}})$, where $g_{\mathsf{pub}} := \mathsf{sk} \cdot \mathbf{g}$. To encrypt k group elements $(g'_1, \dots, g'_k)$, sample k exponents $\mathbf{r} := (f_1, \dots, f_k)$ and set $\mathsf{ct} := (\mathbf{g}^{f_1}, g_{\mathsf{pub}}^{f_1} \cdot g'_1, \dots, \mathbf{g}^{f_k}, g_{\mathsf{pub}}^{f_k} \cdot g'_k)$.

Dual BHHO. We define k-bit $\mathsf{PKE}_{\mathrm{dbhho}}$ as follows: the secret key is k random exponents $(f_1, \dots, f_k)$ and the public key is $(\mathbf{g}, \mathbf{g}'_1, \dots, \mathbf{g}'_k) := (\mathbf{g}, \mathbf{g}^{f_1}, \dots, \mathbf{g}^{f_k})$, where $\mathbf{g}$ is as above. To encrypt k-group elements $(g'_1, \dots, g'_k)$, sample $s \xleftarrow{\$} \{0,1\}^n$ and return $(s \cdot \mathbf{g}, (s \cdot \mathbf{g}'_1) \times g'_1, \dots, (s \cdot \mathbf{g}'_k) \times g'_k)$.

Now notice that an encryption randomness under k-bit $\mathsf{PKE}_{\mathrm{dbhho}}$ is an n-bit string, a secret key for k-bit $\mathsf{PKE}_{\mathsf{bhho}}$. Also, a secret key for k-bit $\mathsf{PKE}_{\mathrm{dbhho}}$ is a tuple of k exponents, an encryption randomness for k-bit $\mathsf{PKE}_{\mathsf{bhho}}$. Finally, Eq. 2 may be verified by inspection. (See Lemma 5.)

For LWE we can do a similar trick, by plugging in Regev's PKE scheme [34] and Dual-Regev's secret-key scheme [22] in Eq. 1. While dual PKE/SKE Regev is known, we are the first to introduce Dual BHHO. We believe our RDM/KDM switching technique may find other applications in the future.

Back to the AB-TDF scheme, Eq. 1 may now be used to reduce RDM+KDM (created by encrypting ρ and $\{r_{i,b}\}$ under $k_{\mathsf{out},1}$) to a KDM-only setting. At this point, we can rely on the underlying KDM-secure schemes to argue security for the garbled circuit.

How is Adaptive Security Obtained? We now have a randomness-recoverable single-key ABE scheme. Unlike the construction in Sect. 2.1 which only provides selective security, we obtain adaptive security in the sense that the attribute α may be chosen based on the ABE public parameter. We get this exactly because of the same reason that single-key ABE constructed from CPA-secure PKE provides adaptive security in the choice of α. The difference in our setting is that (after the RDM+KDM to KDM reduction) we have KDM-dependency, but notice that the input wires for the corrupted circuit C are chosen *non-adaptively*; this is why we can use the KDM results as is. In other words, the adaptive choice of α, only specifies the circuit $\mathsf{P}[\alpha]$, but the input C to this circuit is chosen non-adaptively, and not after seeing $\tilde{\mathsf{P}}$.

2.3 Related Works

The work of Kitagawa et al. [28] shows a generic approach for constructing TDFs, starting from randomness-recoverable KDM-secure symmetric encryption and PKE with pseudorandom ciphertexts. We highlight the main conceptual and technical differences in the following.

- **Robustness:** The TDF from [28] is not robust, i.e. it does not offer deterministic-encryption security. This means that none of our results on deterministic IBE/ABE follows from their work. This is not just an artifact of the analysis, in fact there is a concrete attack[7] if one allows non-uniform

[7] We remark that this attack does not invalidate any claim made in [28], but rather exemplifies the separation between their approach and ours.

(but high-entropy) inputs: In their scheme, a domain point is of the form $(s, r_1, \ldots, r_n)$. Fixing a distribution where the first $n/2$ bits of s and the variables $(r_1, \ldots, r_{n/2})$ are fixed to 0, we obtain an image that contains

$$\mathsf{Enc}(\mathsf{pk}, 0; 0), \ldots, \mathsf{Enc}(\mathsf{pk}, 0; 0), \mathsf{Enc}(\mathsf{pk}, s_{n/2+1}; r_{n/2+1}), \ldots, \mathsf{Enc}(\mathsf{pk}, s_n; r_n)$$

which is easily distinguishable from uniform. The high-level issue (that our approach overcomes using robust hinting PRGs) is the *locality* of the output bits of the TDF.

- **Generality:** The work of [28] does not elaborate on more advanced primitives than TDFs. Although it appears to be likely that one could generalize their techniques to construct IB/AB-TDF, they would suffer from the above mentioned drawbacks. Furthermore, we view the connection of hinting PRGs with IB/AB-TDF as an important conceptual contribution of our work.
- **Assumptions:** Our work requires hinting PRGs, whereas [28] assumes randomness-recoverable KDM-secure symmetric encryption. These assumptions are not known to be equivalent: From hinting PRGs, one can build KDM-secure encryption, but it is not randomness recoverable.

Finally, we mention that [31] showed[8] a construction of trapdoor garbling (although with a different syntax) for NC^1 circuits, assuming CDH or LWE. Their approach does not appear to be extendable to all circuits, due to the reliance on information-theoretic secret-sharing.

3 Preliminaries

Notation. We use λ for the security parameter. We use $\stackrel{c}{\equiv}$ to denote computational indistinguishability and use $\equiv$ to denote two distributions are identical. For a distribution $\mathcal{S}$ we use $x \stackrel{\$}{\leftarrow} \mathcal{S}$ to mean x is sampled according to $\mathcal{S}$ and use $y \in \mathcal{S}$ to mean $y \in \sup(\mathcal{S})$, where sup denotes the support of a distribution. For a set S we overload the notation to use $x \stackrel{\$}{\leftarrow} \mathsf{S}$ to indicate that x is chosen uniformly at random from S. If $\mathsf{A}(x_1, \ldots, x_n)$ is a randomized algorithm, then $\mathsf{A}(a_1, \ldots, a_n)$, for deterministic inputs $a_1, \ldots, a_n$, denotes the random variable obtained by sampling random coins r uniformly at random and returning $\mathsf{A}(a_1, \ldots, a_n; r)$. We use $[n] := \{1, \ldots, n\}$ and $[i, i+s] := \{i, i+1, \ldots, i+s\}$. The min-entropy of a distribution $\mathcal{S}$ is defined as $\mathsf{H}_\infty(\mathcal{S}) \triangleq -\log(\max_{\mathsf{x}} \Pr[\mathcal{S} = \mathsf{x}])$. We call a distribution $\mathcal{S}$ a (k, n)-source if $\mathsf{H}_\infty(\mathcal{S}) \geq k$ and $\sup(\mathcal{S}) \subseteq \{0,1\}^n$. We recall the standard notion of statistical distance. Unless otherwise stated, we assume the length of a randomness value to a function is λ.

Definition 1 (Statistical Distance). *Let $\mathcal{X}$ and $\mathcal{Y}$ be two random variables over a finite set U. The statistical distance between $\mathcal{X}$ and $\mathcal{Y}$ is defined as*

$$\mathbb{SD}[\mathcal{X}, \mathcal{Y}] = \frac{1}{2} \sum_{u \in \mathsf{U}} |\Pr[\mathcal{X} = u] - \Pr[\mathcal{Y} = u]| .$$

[8] The scheme appears in Appendix D in an older version of the paper.

3.1 Standard Lemmas

We recall the Markov inequality.

Lemma 1 (Markov Inequality). *Let $\mathcal{X}$ be a non-negative random variable. Then, for all $\varepsilon > 0$:*

$$\Pr[\mathcal{X} \geq \varepsilon] \leq \frac{\mathsf{E}[\mathcal{X}]}{\varepsilon}$$

where $\mathsf{E}[\mathcal{X}]$ denotes the expected value of $\mathcal{X}$.

We recall the definition of universal hash and the leftover hash lemma [26].

Definition 2 (Universal Hash Functions). *An ensemble of functions $\mathcal{H} : \mathsf{X} \rightarrow \mathsf{Y}$ is called universal, if it holds for all $x \neq x' \in \mathsf{X}$ that*

$$\Pr_h [h(x) = h(x')] \leq 1/|\mathsf{Y}|$$

where $h \xleftarrow{\$} \mathcal{H}$.

Lemma 2 (Leftover Hash Lemma). *Let $\mathcal{X}$ be a random variable over X and $h : \mathsf{S} \times \mathsf{X} \rightarrow \mathsf{Y}$ be a universal hash function, where $|\mathsf{Y}| \leq 2^m$ for some $m > 0$. If $m \leq \mathsf{H}_\infty(\mathcal{X}) - 2\log\left(\frac{1}{\varepsilon}\right)$, then*

$$\mathbb{SD}[(h(\mathcal{S}, \mathcal{X}), \mathcal{S}), (\mathcal{U}, \mathcal{S})] \leq \varepsilon$$

where $\mathcal{S}$ is uniform over S and $\mathcal{U}$ is uniform over Y.

3.2 Standard TDFs

We recall the notion of trapdoor functions (TDFs).

Definition 3 (Trapdoor Functions). *Let $n = n(\lambda)$ be a polynomial. A family of trapdoor functions* (KeyGen, Eval, Invert) *with domain $\{0,1\}^n$ consists of the following algorithms.*

- $\mathsf{KeyGen}(1^\lambda)$: *On input the security parameter, the key generation algorithm returns the index key* ik *and the trapdoor* td.
- $\mathsf{Eval}(\mathsf{ik}, x)$: *On input the index key* ik *and an input string $x \in \{0,1\}^n$, the evaluation algorithm returns an image y.*
- $\mathsf{Invert}(\mathsf{td}, y)$: *On input a trapdoor* td *and an image y, the inversion algorithm returns a pre-image x.*

We require the following properties.

- *(Correctness) There exists a negligible function* negl *such that for all $\lambda \in \mathbb{N}$ it holds that*

$$\Pr_{(\mathsf{ik},\mathsf{td})} [\exists x \in \{0,1\}^n \ s.t.\ \mathsf{Invert}(\mathsf{td}, \mathsf{Eval}(\mathsf{ik}, x)) \neq x] = \mathsf{negl}(\lambda)$$

where the probability is taken over $(\mathsf{ik}, \mathsf{td}) \xleftarrow{\$} \mathsf{KeyGen}(1^\lambda)$.

– *(One-Wayness) There exists a negligible function* negl *such that for all* $\lambda \in \mathbb{N}$ *and all PPT adversaries* $\mathcal{A}$ *it holds that*

$$\Pr[\mathcal{A}(\mathsf{ik}, \mathsf{Eval}(\mathsf{ik}, x)) = x] = \mathsf{negl}(\lambda)$$

where $(\mathsf{ik}, \mathsf{td}) \xleftarrow{\$} \mathsf{KeyGen}(1^\lambda)$ *and* $x \xleftarrow{\$} \{0,1\}^n$.

3.3 Predicate Trapdoor Functions

In the following we define a generalized notion of TDFs, that we call predicate TDFs. A predicate TDF allows one to evaluate a function with respect to an attribute α and issue trapdoors for circuits C. The trapdoor td_C allows one to invert the function if and only if $C(\alpha) = 1$ and otherwise the input (as well as the attribute) is hard to recover. This notion generalizes identity-based TDFs [5] in the same way as functional encryption [11] generalizes identity-based [8] and attribute-based encryption [24]. We give a formal definition below.

Definition 4 (Predicate TDFs). *Let* $n = n(\lambda)$ *be a polynomial. A family of predicate TDFs* (Setup, KeyGen, Eval, Invert) *with domain* $\{0,1\}^n$ *consists of the following algorithms.*

- $\mathsf{Setup}(1^\lambda)$*: On input the security parameter, the setup algorithm returns a master secret key* msk *and some public parameters* pp.
- $\mathsf{KeyGen}(\mathsf{msk}, C)$*: On input the master secret key* msk *and a circuit* C*, the key generation algorithm returns a trapdoor* td_C.
- $\mathsf{Eval}(\mathsf{pp}, \alpha, x)$*: On input the public parameters* pp*, an attribute* α*, and an input string* $x \in \{0,1\}^n$*, the evaluation algorithm returns an image* y.
- $\mathsf{Invert}(\mathsf{td}_C, y)$*: On input a trapdoor* td_C *for a circuit* C *and an image* y*, the inversion algorithm returns a pre-image* x.

We require the following notion of correctness.

– *(Correctness) There exists a negligible function* negl *such that for all* $\lambda \in \mathbb{N}$ *it holds that*

$$\Pr_{(\mathsf{pp},\mathsf{msk})}[\exists(x, \alpha, C) \text{ s.t. } \mathsf{Invert}(\mathsf{KeyGen}(\mathsf{msk}, C), \mathsf{Eval}(\mathsf{pp}, \alpha, x)) \wedge C(\alpha) = 1] = \mathsf{negl}(\lambda)$$

where the probability is taken over $(\mathsf{pp}, \mathsf{msk}) \xleftarrow{\$} \mathsf{Setup}(1^\lambda)$.

Deterministic Security. We now define a strong notion of security for predicate TDFs, i.e. we require that evaluating the TDF over two inputs with enough min-entropy yields two computationally indistinguishable distributions. This is the natural generalization of the standard notion of security for deterministic encryption [7] and thus we refer to it as *deterministic security.* Note that the following definitions assume without loss of generality that the key generation algorithm is deterministic. This can always be enforced by drawing the random coins from a PRF applied to the input circuit C.

Definition 5 (Deterministic CPA Security). *A predicate TDF is (k, n)-CPA secure if there exists a negligible function* negl *such that for all $\lambda \in \mathbb{N}$, all PPT adversaries $\mathcal{A}$, any two (k, n)-sources $\mathcal{S}_0$ and $\mathcal{S}_1$, all pairs of attributes (α_0, α_1) it holds that*

$$\Pr\left[\mathcal{A}^{\mathsf{KeyGen}(\mathsf{msk},\cdot)}(\mathsf{pp}, \alpha_0, \alpha_1, \mathsf{Eval}(\mathsf{pp}, \alpha_b, x_b)) = b\right] - 1/2 = \mathsf{negl}(\lambda)$$

where $(\mathsf{pp}, \mathsf{msk}) \xleftarrow{\$} \mathsf{Setup}(1^\lambda)$, $b \xleftarrow{\$} \{0, 1\}$, $x_b \xleftarrow{\$} \mathcal{S}_b$, *and the adversary never queries the* KeyGen *oracle on some C such that $C(\alpha_0) = 1$ or $C(\alpha_1) = 1$.*

To draw an analogy to the standard public-key settings (i.e. encryption without randomness recovery) the above definition corresponds to the notion of one-sided security for predicate encryption (where the attribute is not hidden if $C(\alpha) = 1$). However, in our settings this seems to be the best-possible notion to achieve: Since the secret keys for accepting predicates are required to recover all random coins of the evaluation function, it is impossible to fully hide the attribute α if $C(\alpha) = 1$. This is because one can always try to recompute the ciphertext with a candidate attribute and see whether the result matches.

Selective vs Adaptive Security. We note that the definition as stated above captures the *selective* variant of security, where the challenge attributes are fixed ahead of times and prior to the adversary seeing the public parameters of the scheme. The stronger (and perhaps more natural) notion of *adaptive* security allows the adversary to choose the challenge attributes (α_0, α_1) depending on the public parameters of the scheme and possibly the answers of some queries to the KeyGen oracle. The formal definition is the same as Definition 5 modified in the natural way. We remark that any selectively secure scheme can be shown to be also adaptively secure although with an exponential decrease in the success probability of the reduction (via complexity leveraging).

4 Robust Hinting PRGs

A hinting pseudorandom generator (PRG) is a notion introduced in [29] and has since found several applications (e.g. [28,31]). Roughly speaking, it stretches the input n-bit seed into a $n \cdot \ell$-bit string. In the security game, the distinguisher is given a 2-by-n matrix where the entries corresponding to the seed are taken from the output of the hinting PRG and the others are uniformly sampled. The distinguisher has to tell this distribution apart from a uniformly random 2-by-n matrix. In this work we are interested in a stronger notion of hinting PRG where the seed is not required to be uniformly sampled, instead we only impose that it has high-enough min-entropy. We call this notion *robust* hinting PRG and we provide formal definitions in the following. We recall the syntax of hinting PRG [29].

Definition 6 (Hinting PRGs). *Let $n = n(\lambda)$ and $\ell = \ell(\lambda)$ be two polynomials. A family of hinting PRGs consists of the following algorithms.*

- $\mathsf{Setup}(1^\lambda)$: *On input the security parameter* 1^λ, *the setup algorithm returns the public parameters* pp.
- $\mathsf{Eval}(\mathsf{pp}, x, i)$: *On input the public parameters* pp, *an input string* $x \in \{0,1\}^n$, *and an index* i, *the evaluation algorithm returns an image* $y \in \{0,1\}^\ell$.

The security that we require is essentially identical to that of [29], except that we only require the seed to have high min-entropy, as opposed to be uniformly sampled. We name this notion (k, n)-robustness and we present a formal definition below.

Definition 7 (Robustness). *A hinting PRG* $(\mathsf{Setup}, \mathsf{Eval})$ *is* (k, n)*-robust if there exists a negligible function* negl *such that for all* $\lambda \in \mathbb{N}$, *all PPT adversaries* $\mathcal{A}$, *all* (k, n)*-sources* $\mathcal{S}$ *it holds that*

$$\Pr\left[\mathcal{A}\left(\mathsf{pp}, y_0^b, \begin{pmatrix} y_{1,0}^b, \dots, y_{n,0}^b \\ y_{1,1}^b, \dots, y_{n,1}^b \end{pmatrix}\right) = b\right] - 1/2 = \mathsf{negl}(\lambda)$$

where

- $\mathsf{pp} \xleftarrow{\$} \mathsf{Setup}(1^\lambda)$, $x \xleftarrow{\$} \mathcal{S}$, *and* $b \xleftarrow{\$} \{0,1\}$.
- $y_0^0 \xleftarrow{\$} \{0,1\}^\ell$ *and* $y_0^1 \leftarrow \mathsf{Eval}(\mathsf{pp}, x, 0)$.
- *For all* $i \in [n]$: $(y_{i,0}^0, y_{i,1}^0) \xleftarrow{\$} \{0,1\}^{2\ell}$, $y_{i,x_i}^1 \leftarrow \mathsf{Eval}(\mathsf{pp}, x, i)$ *and* $y_{i,x_i \oplus 1}^1 \xleftarrow{\$} \{0,1\}^\ell$.

In the full version we show how to instantiate robust hinting PRGs assuming the hardness of the CDH or the LWE problem.

5 A Universal TDFier

In the following we show how a generic compiler that takes as input any encryption scheme (that satisfies some mild structural properties) and makes it randomness recoverable, i.e. transforms it into a TDF. We call this scheme a *universal TDFier.*

5.1 One-Sided Predicate Encryption

We recall the notion of predicate encryption with one-sided security [23], which one of the most general derivations of the standard notion of public-key encryption.

Definition 8 (Predicate Encryption). *A family of one-sided predicate encryption schemes* $(\mathsf{Setup}, \mathsf{KeyGen}, \mathsf{Enc}, \mathsf{Dec})$ *consists of the following algorithms.*

- $\mathsf{Setup}(1^\lambda)$: *On input the security parameter, the setup algorithm returns a master secret key* msk *and some public parameters* pp.

- $\mathsf{KeyGen}(\mathsf{msk}, C)$: *On input the master secret key* msk *and a circuit* C, *the key generation algorithm returns a secret key* sk_C.
- $\mathsf{Enc}(\mathsf{pp}, \alpha, m)$: *On input the public parameters* pp, *an attribute* α, *and a message* m, *the evaluation algorithm returns a ciphertext* c.
- $\mathsf{Dec}(\mathsf{sk}_C, c)$: *On input a secret key* sk_C *for a circuit* C *and a ciphertext* c, *the decryption algorithm returns a message* m.

We require the following properties.

- *(Correctness) For all* $\lambda \in \mathbb{N}$, *all* $(\mathsf{pp}, \mathsf{msk})$ *in the support of* $\mathsf{Setup}(1^\lambda)$, *all messages* m, *all attributes* α, *all circuits* C *such that* $C(\alpha) = 1$, *and all* sk_C *in the support of* $\mathsf{KeyGen}(\mathsf{msk}, C)$, *it holds that*

$$\mathsf{Dec}(\mathsf{sk}_C, \mathsf{Enc}(\mathsf{pp}, \alpha, m)) = m.$$

- *(One-Sided CPA Security) There exists a negligible function* negl *such that for all* $\lambda \in \mathbb{N}$, *all PPT adversaries* $\mathcal{A}$, *and all pairs of attributes* (α_0, α_1) *it holds that*

$$\Pr\left[\mathcal{A}^{\mathsf{KeyGen}(\mathsf{msk},\cdot)}(c) = b \;\middle|\; \begin{array}{l} (\mathsf{pp}, \mathsf{msk}) \xleftarrow{\$} \mathsf{Setup}(1^\lambda) \\ (m_0, m_1) \leftarrow \mathcal{A}^{\mathsf{KeyGen}(\mathsf{msk},\cdot)}(\mathsf{pp}) \\ b \xleftarrow{\$} \{0,1\} \\ c \xleftarrow{\$} \mathsf{Enc}(\mathsf{pp}, \alpha_b, m_b) \end{array}\right] - 1/2 = \mathsf{negl}(\lambda)$$

where the adversary never queries the KeyGen *oracle on some* C *such that* $C(\alpha_0) = 1$ *or* $C(\alpha_1) = 1$.

We remark that we require the scheme to satisfy perfect correctness, which is the case for most natural candidates of predicate encryption schemes (we refer the reader to the full version for a detailed discussion). We also note that generic transformation from approximate to perfect correctness are known [6].

Pseudorandom Ciphertexts. We additionally require that the ciphertext space satisfies some group-like structural properties. More specifically, we require the existence of a (not necessarily Abelian) group $\mathbb{H}$ with group operation $\circ$ such that (i) all ciphertexts in the range of the encryption algorithm consist of elements of $\mathbb{H}$ and (ii) undecryptable ciphertexts are computationally indistinguishable from uniformly sampled elements in $\mathbb{H}$. We define this more formally below.

Definition 9 (Pseudorandom Ciphertexts). *A one-sided predicate encryption scheme* (Setup, KeyGen, Enc, Dec) *has pseudorandom ciphertexts if there exists a negligible function* negl *and a group* $\mathbb{H}$ *such that for all* $\lambda \in \mathbb{N}$, *all PPT adversaries* $\mathcal{A}$, *and attributes* α *it holds that*

$$\Pr\left[\mathcal{A}^{\mathsf{KeyGen}(\mathsf{msk},\cdot)}(c) = b \;\middle|\; \begin{array}{l} (\mathsf{pp}, \mathsf{msk}) \xleftarrow{\$} \mathsf{Setup}(1^\lambda) \\ m \leftarrow \mathcal{A}^{\mathsf{KeyGen}(\mathsf{msk},\cdot)}(\mathsf{pp}) \\ b \xleftarrow{\$} \{0,1\} \\ c \xleftarrow{\$} \mathsf{Enc}(\mathsf{pp}, \alpha, m) \text{ if } b = 0 \\ c \xleftarrow{\$} \mathbb{H} \text{ if } b = 1 \end{array}\right] - 1/2 = \mathsf{negl}(\lambda)$$

where the adversary never queries the KeyGen *oracle on some* C *such that* $C(\alpha) = 1$.

As an example, schemes that have ciphertexts indistinguishable from uniformly sampled bit strings satisfy this notion of security, since the set of all binary strings $\{0,1\}^p$ of length $p = p(\lambda)$ form a group with group operation $\oplus$. We will also consider schemes that have ciphertexts indistinguishable from uniformly sampled integers in $\mathbb{Z}_q^d$, with dimension $d = d(\lambda)$, where the group operation is the component-wise addition modulo q. Note that also a combination of both $\{0,1\}^p \times \mathbb{Z}_q^d$ satisfies this definition by defining the group operation canonically.

Selective vs Adaptive Security. As discussed before, we state the security definition in its selective variant, where the challenge attribute is fixed ahead of time. The definition can be extended to the adaptive settings canonically.

5.2 The Construction

In the following we present our compiler, which turns any one-sided predicate encryption scheme with pseudorandom ciphertexts into a predicate TDF for (k, n)-sources. The scheme is described below.

Construction 4 (Universal TDFier). *Let* $(\mathsf{PE.Setup}, \mathsf{PE.KeyGen}, \mathsf{PE.Enc}, \mathsf{PE.Dec})$ *be a one-sided predicate encryption scheme with pseudorandom ciphertexts over* $\mathbb{H}$ *with group operation* $\circ$, *and let* $(\mathsf{HPRG.Setup}, \mathsf{HPRG.Eval})$ *be a* (k, n)*-robust hinting PRG. Our scheme* $(\mathsf{Setup}, \mathsf{KeyGen}, \mathsf{Eval}, \mathsf{Invert})$ *is defined as follows.*

- $\mathsf{Setup}(1^\lambda)$: *Invoke* $(\mathsf{pp}_{\mathsf{PE}}, \mathsf{msk}) \xleftarrow{\$} \mathsf{PE.Setup}(1^\lambda)$ *and* $\mathsf{pp}_{\mathsf{HPRG}} \xleftarrow{\$} \mathsf{HPRG.Setup}(1^\lambda)$, *then sample* $(r_1, \dots, r_n) \xleftarrow{\$} \mathbb{H}^n$ *and a uniform* $u \xleftarrow{\$} \{0,1\}^{|C|+|\alpha|+3\lambda}$. *Set the public parameters of the scheme to be* $\mathsf{pp} := (\mathsf{pp}_{\mathsf{PE}}, \mathsf{pp}_{\mathsf{HPRG}}, r_1, \dots, r_n, u)$ *and the master secret key to* msk.
- $\mathsf{KeyGen}(\mathsf{msk}, C)$: *Return the trapdoor* $\mathsf{td}_C \leftarrow \mathsf{PE.KeyGen}(\mathsf{msk}, C)$.
- $\mathsf{Eval}(\mathsf{pp}, \alpha, x)$: *On input some* $x \in \{0,1\}^n$, *for all* $i \in [n]$, *proceed as follows.*
  - *If* $x_i = 0$: *Compute*
  $$d_i \leftarrow \mathsf{PE.Enc}(\mathsf{pp}_{\mathsf{PE}}, \alpha, u; z_i)$$
  where $z_i \leftarrow \mathsf{HPRG.Eval}(\mathsf{pp}_{\mathsf{HPRG}}, x, i)$. *Set* $c_i := d_i$.
  - *If* $x_i = 1$: *Compute*
  $$d_i \leftarrow \mathsf{PE.Enc}(\mathsf{pp}_{\mathsf{PE}}, \alpha, u; z_i)$$
  where $z_i \leftarrow \mathsf{HPRG.Eval}(\mathsf{pp}_{\mathsf{HPRG}}, x, i)$. *Set* $c_i := d_i \circ r_i$.

  Return the image $y := (c_1, \dots, c_n)$.
- $\mathsf{Invert}(\mathsf{td}_C, y)$: *On input some* $y \in \mathbb{H}^n$, *for all* $i \in [n]$, *proceed as follows: If* $u = \mathsf{Dec}(\mathsf{td}_C, c_i)$ *then set* $\tilde{x}_i := 0$, *else set* $\tilde{x}_i := 1$. *Return* $(\tilde{x}_1, \dots, \tilde{x}_n)$.

Before proceeding with the analysis of our scheme, we highlight two important facts about the compiled TDF.

1. The public parameters of the scheme consist of the public parameters of the encryption scheme $\mathsf{pp}_{\mathsf{PE}}$, together with some independently sampled strings $(\mathsf{pp}_{\mathsf{HPRG}}, r_1, \ldots, r_n, u)$.
2. The master secret key and the user-specific keys are identical to those of the underlying encryption scheme.

Taken together, these imply that the underlying (predicate) encryption scheme can be upgraded to TDF (or, equivalently, made randomness recoverable) *after the fact*: Users of an existing (predicate) encryption scheme can decide to upgrade it to a TDF without the need to update their public nor their secret keys. Instead they just need to add some public parameters (fixed once and for all) and modify their encryption/decryption procedure to achieve randomness recoverability. Alternatively, one can think of the above compiler as to add a *dual mode* to the encryption algorithm: Users are can choose whether they want to make their encryption randomness recoverable or not, without the need to change the public/secret keys of the scheme.

Correctness. We now show that the scheme as described above satisfies perfect correctness with all but negligible probability over the choice of the public parameters.

Theorem 5 (Correctness). *Let* (PE.Setup, PE.KeyGen, PE.Enc, PE.Dec) *be a one-sided predicate encryption with perfect correctness. Then Construction 4 satisfies correctness.*

Proof. We assume without loss of generality that the encryption algorithm of the one-sided predicate encryption scheme uses exactly λ-many bits of randomness. Recall that $\mathbb{H}$ is a bound on the ciphertext space of the scheme. Note that each secret key td_C defines a one-to-one mapping $\mathbb{H} \rightarrow P_C$, where the multiset P_C is populated by plaintexts (possibly with repeated elements). Define P to be the multiset that contains (possibly with repeated elements) all P_i for $i \in \left[2^{|C|}\right]$, where $|P| = |\mathbb{H}| \cdot 2^{|C|}$. Let $S_u \subseteq P$ be the subset of P where all entries of S_u are equal to u. In expectation, over the random choice of u, we have that

$$\mathsf{E}\left[|S_u|\right] = \frac{|P|}{2^{|u|}} = \frac{|\mathbb{H}| \cdot 2^{|C|}}{2^{|u|}}.$$

By Lemma 1, we have that

$$|S_u| \leq \frac{|\mathbb{H}| \cdot 2^{|C|} \cdot 2^{\lambda}}{2^{|u|}}$$

except with probability $2^{-\lambda}$, over the random choice of u. Define $T_u \subseteq \mathbb{H}$ to be the set of all pre-images of S_u. Note that

$$|T_u| \leq |S_u| \leq \frac{|\mathbb{H}| \cdot 2^{|C|} \cdot 2^{\lambda}}{2^{|u|}}.$$

Let R_u be the set such that for all $r \in R_u$ there exist ciphertexts $\mathsf{PE.Enc}(\mathsf{pp_{PE}}, \cdot, u)$ such that $\mathsf{PE.Enc}(\mathsf{pp_{PE}}, \cdot, u) \circ r \in T_u$. Note that there are at most $2^{|\alpha|} \cdot 2^{\lambda}$ many ciphertexts in the support of $\mathsf{PE.Enc}(\mathsf{pp_{PE}}, \cdot, u)$ and therefore we can bound

$$|R_u| \leq \frac{|\mathbb{H}| \cdot 2^{|C|} \cdot 2^{\lambda} \cdot 2^{|\alpha|} \cdot 2^{\lambda}}{2^{|u|}} = \frac{|\mathbb{H}| \cdot 2^{|C|+|\alpha|+2\lambda}}{2^{|u|}}$$

by a counting argument. Thus the probability that a uniformly chosen $r \xleftarrow{\$} \mathbb{H}$ belongs to R_u is at most

$$\Pr[r \in R_u] \leq \frac{|\mathbb{H}| \cdot 2^{|C|+|\alpha|+2\lambda}}{|\mathbb{H}| \cdot 2^{|u|}} = \frac{2^{|C|+|\alpha|+2\lambda}}{2^{|C|+|\alpha|+3\lambda}} = \frac{1}{2^{\lambda}}.$$

Note that a decryption error only happens whenever some r_i maps a valid encryption of u to some other encryption of u, i.e. $r \in R_u$. By a union bound, the probability that at least one of the elements $(r_1, \ldots, r_n)$ belong to such a set is also negligible. This concludes our proof. □

Security. We now turn to prove the deterministic CPA security of our scheme. Note that we restrict our analysis to the selective variant of the security definition.

Theorem 6 (CPA Security). *Let* $(\mathsf{PE.Setup}, \mathsf{PE.KeyGen}, \mathsf{PE.Enc}, \mathsf{PE.Dec})$ *be a one-sided predicate encryption scheme with pseudorandom ciphertexts over* $\mathbb{H}$ *with group operation* $\circ$*, and let* $(\mathsf{HPRG.Setup}, \mathsf{HPRG.Eval})$ *be a* (k, n)*-robust hinting PRG. Then Construction 4 satisfies selective* (k, n)*-CPA security.*

Proof. The proof proceeds by a series on hybrids where we gradually change the distribution of the public parameters and of the challenge ciphertext.

- Hybrid $\mathcal{H}_0$: This is the original experiment with the challenge bit b fixed to 0.
- Hybrid $\mathcal{H}_1$: In this hybrid we first compute the challenge ciphertext and then we set the values of $(r_1, \ldots, r_n)$ accordingly. More specifically, for all $i \in [n]$, we do the following:
  - If $x_i = 0$ compute $c_i \leftarrow \mathsf{PE.Enc}(\mathsf{pp_{PE}}, \alpha, u; z_i)$, then define $r_i := c_i \circ s_i$, where $s_i \xleftarrow{\$} \mathbb{H}$.
  - If $x_i = 1$ compute $c_i \xleftarrow{\$} \mathbb{H}$ and define $r_i := c_i \circ \mathsf{PE.Enc}(\mathsf{pp_{PE}}, \alpha_0, u; z_i)$.

  Since $\mathbb{H}$ is a group and in particular all elements of $\mathbb{H}$ have an inverse, the distribution induced by this hybrid is identical to the previous one and thus the change described here is only syntactical.
- Hybrids $\mathcal{H}_2 \ldots \mathcal{H}_{n+1}$: For all $i \in [2, n+1]$ we define $\mathcal{H}_i$ as the previous one, except for the following modification:
  - If $x_i = 0$ compute $c_i \leftarrow \mathsf{PE.Enc}(\mathsf{pp_{PE}}, \alpha_0, u; z_i)$, then define $r_i := c_i \circ s_i$, where $s_i \xleftarrow{\$} \mathsf{PE.Enc}(\mathsf{pp_{PE}}, \alpha_0, u)$.

  - If $x_i = 1$ compute $c_i \xleftarrow{\$} \mathsf{PE.Enc}(\mathsf{pp}_{\mathsf{PE}}, \alpha_0, u)$, then define the variable $r_i := c_i \circ \mathsf{PE.Enc}(\mathsf{pp}_{\mathsf{PE}}, \alpha_0, u; z_i)$.

  I.e. instead of sampling a random mask, we compute an encryption of u under the appropriate attribute using fresh random coins. Indistinguishability follows from a routine reduction against the (selective) pseudorandom ciphertexts of the one-sided predicate encryption scheme.
- Hybrid $\mathcal{H}_{n+2}$: In this hybrid we compute the challenge ciphertext and the setup using fresh random coins. More precisely, for all $i \in [n]$ we do the following:
  - If $x_i = 0$ compute $c_i \xleftarrow{\$} \mathsf{PE.Enc}(\mathsf{pp}_{\mathsf{PE}}, \alpha_0, u)$, then define $r_i := c_i \circ s_i$, where $s_i \xleftarrow{\$} \mathsf{PE.Enc}(\mathsf{pp}_{\mathsf{PE}}, \alpha_0, u)$.
  - If $x_i = 1$ compute $c_i \xleftarrow{\$} \mathsf{PE.Enc}(\mathsf{pp}_{\mathsf{PE}}, \alpha_0, u)$, then define $r_i := c_i \circ s_i$, where $s_i \xleftarrow{\$} \mathsf{PE.Enc}(\mathsf{pp}_{\mathsf{PE}}, \alpha_0, u)$.

  Note that the only difference between this hybrid and the previous one is that we use fresh coins instead of pseudorandom ones derived from applying the hinting PRG to x_0. Furthermore, note that the only information about x is encoded in the positions where we used truly random coins instead of pseudorandom. Since x_0 is a (k, n)-source, indistinguishability follows by a reduction against the (k, n)-robustness of the hinting PRG.
- Hybrid $\mathcal{H}_{n+3}$: In this hybrid we fix the challenge bit b to 1. Note that the challenge ciphertext does no longer depend on the input x so the only difference here is that we compute all ciphertexts as $\mathsf{PE.Enc}(\mathsf{pp}_{\mathsf{PE}}, \alpha_1, u)$ instead of $\mathsf{PE.Enc}(\mathsf{pp}_{\mathsf{PE}}, \alpha_0, u)$. Indistinguishability follows by a standard hybrid argument against the one-sided CPA security of the predicate encryption scheme.
- Hybrids $\mathcal{H}_{n+4} \dots \mathcal{H}_{2n+5}$: In these hybrids we undo the changes that we performed in the previous hybrids, except for switching the challenge bit. The indistinguishability arguments are identical. The final hybrid is the original experiment with b fixed to 1.

To summarize, we have that

$$\mathcal{H}_0 \equiv \mathcal{H}_1 \stackrel{c}{\equiv} \mathcal{H}_2 \stackrel{c}{\equiv} \dots \stackrel{c}{\equiv} \mathcal{H}_{n+1} \stackrel{c}{\equiv} \mathcal{H}_{n+2} \stackrel{c}{\equiv} \mathcal{H}_{n+3} \stackrel{c}{\equiv} \mathcal{H}_{n+4} \stackrel{c}{\equiv} \dots \stackrel{c}{\equiv} \mathcal{H}_{2n+4} \equiv \mathcal{H}_{2n+5}$$

which implies that the scheme is selective (k, n)-CPA secure. □

6 Trapdoor Garbled Circuits and Adaptive Single-Key AB-TDFs

The AB-TDF scheme in Sect. 5 is only selectively secure. In this section we show an alternative way of building single-key AB-TDFs, that provides adaptive security in the choice of the attribute α (i.e., α can be chosen adaptively based on the ABE public parameter). Along the way, we define a concept called trapdoor garbling, and show how to build it from DDH/LWE.

Adaptive Security for Single-Key AB-TDF. For simplicity, we will focus on one-wayness only (as opposed to deterministic-encryption security). Here the adversary after seeing pp can choose a circuit C and an attribute α satisfying $C(\alpha) = 0$, and is tasked with recovering a random $x \xleftarrow{\$} \{0,1\}^n$ from sk_C and $y := \mathsf{Eval}(\mathsf{pp}, \alpha, x)$.

6.1 Definition

Garbled circuits in a traditional sense allows one to garble a circuit $\mathsf{P} : \{0,1\}^m \rightarrow \{0,1\}$, so that a garbled circuit and a corresponding garbled label for an input x reveals nothing beyond $\mathsf{P}(x)$—in particular, the randomness used by the garbling algorithm as well as any possible circuit-hardcoded information should remain hidden. We introduce and realize a notion of garbled circuits which allows one to recover the randomness on specific garbled inputs. We define it for the *universal circuit* below.

Definition 10 (Trapdoor Garbling). *Let* $\mathsf{U}[\cdot,\cdot]$ *be a circuit that works as follows: the output of* $\mathsf{U}[s_1, s_2](C)$ *is* s_2 *if* $C(s_1) = 1$*, and is a special symbol* \$ *otherwise. We define a trapdoor garbling scheme* $\mathsf{GRB} = (\mathsf{Garble}, \mathsf{Eval}, \mathsf{Sim})$ *for* $\mathsf{U}[\cdot,\cdot] \colon \{0,1\}^m \rightarrow \{0,1\}^\kappa \cup \{\$\}$.

- $\mathsf{Garble}(1^\lambda, s_1, s_2; \rho)$*: On input the security parameter* 1^λ *and private hardcoded strings* s_1, s_2*, and randomness* ρ*, the garbling algorithm returns a garbled circuit* $\tilde{\mathsf{U}}$ *and a set of* m *pairs of labels* $\{\ell_{i,0}, \ell_{i,1}\}_{i \in [m]}$.
- $\mathsf{Eval}(\tilde{\mathsf{U}}, \{\ell_{i,C_i}\}_{i \in [m]})$*: On input a garbled circuit* $\tilde{\mathsf{U}}$ *and a set of labels* $\{\ell_{i,C_i}\}_{i \in [m]}$*, the evaluation algorithm returns an output string* $y \in \{0,1\}^\kappa \cup \{\$\}$.

We require the following properties.

- *(Correctness) For all* $\lambda \in \mathbb{N}$*, all* s_1*, all* $s_2 \in \{0,1\}^\kappa$*,* $C \in \{0,1\}^m$*, and garbling randomness* ρ*, letting* $(\tilde{\mathsf{U}}, \{\ell_{i,0}, \ell_{i,1}\}_{i \in [m]}) \xleftarrow{\$} \mathsf{Garble}(1^\lambda, s_1, s_2; \rho)$*:*
  - *if* $\mathsf{U}[s_1, s_2](C) = \$$*, then* $\mathsf{Eval}\left(\tilde{\mathsf{U}}, \{\ell_{i,x_i}\}_{i \in [m]}\right) = \$$
  - *else,* $\mathsf{Eval}\left(\tilde{\mathsf{U}}, \{\ell_{i,C_i}\}_{i \in [m]}\right) = (s_2, \rho)$.
- *(Simulation Security) For any "admissible" PPT adversary* $\mathcal{A}$*, the following holds. Letting* $((s_1, s_2, C), \mathsf{st}) \xleftarrow{\$} \mathcal{A}(1^\lambda)$*,* $\rho \xleftarrow{\$} \{0,1\}^*$*, and* $(\tilde{\mathsf{U}}, \{\ell_{i,0}, \ell_{i,1}\}_{i \in [m]}) = \mathsf{Garble}(1^\lambda, s_1, s_2; \rho)$*:*

$$\left(\mathsf{st}, \tilde{\mathsf{U}}, \{\ell_{i,C_i}\}_{i \in [m]}\right) \stackrel{c}{\equiv} \left(\mathsf{st}, \mathsf{Sim}\left(1^\lambda, |s_1|, |s_2|, \mathsf{U}[s_1, s_2](C)\right)\right).$$

We say $\mathcal{A}$ *is admissible if* $\mathsf{U}[s_1, s_2](C) = \$$*, where all strings are as above.*

6.2 Tools for Building Single-Key AB-TDFs

We show how to build single-key AB-TDFs from DDH/LWE. (All our results will also apply to the predicate-encryption setting.) Our techniques will implicitly also realize trapdoor garbling (Definition 10).

Definition 11 (Randomness Recoverable SKE). *We say* $\mathsf{SKE} := (\mathsf{G}, \mathsf{Enc}, \mathsf{Dec})$ *is randomness recoverable if (1) a key is chosen at random from* $\{0,1\}^n$ *for some* $n = n(\lambda)$*; and (2) given* k *and* $\mathsf{Enc}(k, m; r)$ *we can recover both* m *and* r.

Notation. We use the shorthand $\{a_{i,b}\}$ to mean $\{a_{i,b}\}_{i\in[m],b\in\{0,1\}}$.

We will now define and later realize an enhanced version of Yao's garbled circuits. Informally, this enhancement allows the recovery of the garbled circuits coins, in trapdoor mode (i.e., when we have labels corresponding to an input which makes the circuit evaluate to one). We explained the high-level idea in the introduction, and will now formalize it.

In the construction below, we assume the following for Yao's scheme for garbling single-bit output circuits:

Construction 7 (Enhanced Garbled Circuits). *We describe an enhanced way of garbling* $\mathsf{U}[\cdot,\cdot]$*, introduced in Definition 10. Let* $\mathsf{P}[\cdot]$ *be a circuit, where for* $\alpha \in \{0,1\}^k$ *and* $C \in \{0,1\}^m$*,* $\mathsf{P}[\alpha](C) = C(\alpha)$*. Let* $(\mathsf{Garble}, \mathsf{Eval})$ *be Yao's garbled-circuit scheme for* $\mathsf{P}[\cdot]$*, as described in [30, 37], with the following slight modification: Letting* $k_{\mathsf{out},0}$ *and* $k_{\mathsf{out},1}$ *be the keys for the two values of the output wire, instead of appending* $(k_{\mathsf{out},0}, 0)$ *and* $(k_{\mathsf{out},1}, 1)$ *to the garbled circuit, we append* $\mathsf{Enc}(k_{\mathsf{out},0}, 0)$ *and* $\mathsf{Enc}(k_{\mathsf{out},1}, 1)$ *to the garbled circuit (i.e., the values of* $k_{\mathsf{out},0}$ *and* $k_{\mathsf{out},1}$ *are not copied in the garbled circuit in the clear).*

- $\overline{\mathsf{Garble}}(\alpha, x)$*: Sample* $(\tilde{C}, \{\mathsf{lb}_{i,b}\}) \xleftarrow{\$} \mathsf{Garble}(\mathsf{P}, \alpha)$ *and let* $k_{\mathsf{out},1}$ *be output wire for bit value* 1*. Let* Key *be the set of all keys for the circuit wires (i.e., two keys for each wire), and let* $\mathsf{CT} = \{\mathsf{Enc}(k_{\mathsf{out},1}, x)\} \cup \{\mathsf{Enc}(k_{\mathsf{out},1}, k) : k \in \mathsf{Key} \setminus \{k_{\mathsf{out},1}\}\}$*. Let* $\widetilde{C_{\mathsf{en}}} := (\mathsf{CT}, \tilde{C})$*, and return* $(\widetilde{C_{\mathsf{en}}}, \{\mathsf{lb}_{i,b}\}_{i\in[m],b\in\{0,1\}})$.
- $\overline{\mathsf{Eval}}(\widetilde{C_{\mathsf{en}}}, \mathbf{lb})$*: Parse* $\widetilde{C_{\mathsf{en}}} := (\mathsf{CT}, \tilde{C})$*. Let* $b := \mathsf{Eval}(\tilde{C}, \mathbf{lb})$*. If* $b = 0$*, return* \$*; otherwise, letting* $k_{\mathsf{out},1}$ *be the key for the output wire, return* $(\mathsf{Dec}(k_{\mathsf{out},1}, \mathsf{CT}))$*, where* $\mathsf{Dec}(k_{\mathsf{out},1}, \mathsf{CT}) = \{\mathsf{Dec}(k_{\mathsf{out},1}, c) : c \in \mathsf{CT}\}$.

The following lemma shows that given an enhanced garbled circuit and a sequence of accepting labels, then in addition to x, we can recover the randomness used to garble the circuit.

Lemma 3 (Randomness Recoverability of the Enhanced Garbled Circuit). *Suppose* $\mathsf{SKE} := (\mathsf{G}, \mathsf{Enc}, \mathsf{Dec})$ *is randomness recoverable. Fix randomness* ρ *for* $\overline{\mathsf{Eval}}$ *and let* $(\widetilde{C_{\mathsf{en}}}, \{\mathsf{lb}_{i,b}\}) := \overline{\mathsf{Garble}}(\alpha, x; \rho)$*. Assuming* $\overline{\mathsf{Eval}}(\widetilde{C_{\mathsf{en}}}, \{\mathsf{lb}_{i,C_i}\}) = (x, \omega)$*, then given* ω *we can recover the original randomness* ρ.

Proof. Notice that ρ consist of two sources of randomness: (1) those used to generate the keys for the wires (i.e., the keys in set Key, Construction 7) and (2) the random coins used to encrypt the keys. Given $k_{\mathsf{out},1}$, we can recover all the keys in Key (since they are all encrypted under $k_{\mathsf{out},1}$) and hence by Definition 11 all random coins involving Source (1) are recovered. Having recovered all the keys in Key, by Definition 11 we can recover all the coins used to generate the ciphertexts. □

6.3 Single-Key AB-TDFs Construction

We now give the construction.

Construction 8 (Single-Key AB-TDF). *Let m and k be the size of the circuit and attribute.*

Ingredients. *A randomness recoverable secret-key encryption scheme* $\mathsf{SKE} = (\mathsf{G}, \mathsf{Enc}, \mathsf{Dec})$ *(Definition 11), a PKE scheme* $\mathsf{PKE} = (\mathsf{G}, \mathsf{Enc}, \mathsf{Dec})$ *and an enhanced Yao's garbling scheme* $(\overline{\mathsf{Garble}}, \overline{\mathsf{Eval}})$ *(Construction 7).*

Input to the TDF. *The input to a function is of the form* $(\mathbf{r}, \rho)$*, consisting of* $2n$ *randomness values* $\mathbf{r} := \{r_{i,b}\}$ *for* $\mathsf{PKE.Enc}$ *and a randomness string* ρ *for the garble function* $\overline{\mathsf{Garble}}(\mathsf{U}[\alpha, \mathbf{r}])$.

- $\mathsf{Setup}(1^\lambda)$: *for* $i \in [m]$ *and* $b \in \{0,1\}$: $(\mathsf{pk}_{i,b}, \mathsf{sk}_{i,b}) \xleftarrow{\$} \mathsf{PKE.G}(1^\lambda)$. *Let* $\mathsf{pp} := \{\mathsf{pk}_{i,b}\}_{i\in[m],b\in\{0,1\}}$ *and* $\mathsf{msk} := \{\mathsf{sk}_{i,b}\}_{i\in[m],b\in\{0,1\}}$.
- $\mathsf{KeyGen}(\mathsf{msk}, C)$: *output* $\mathsf{sk}_C := (C, \mathsf{sk}_{1,C_1}, \ldots, \mathsf{sk}_{m,C_m})$.
- $\mathsf{Eval}(\mathsf{pp}, \alpha, x)$: *parse* $x := (\mathbf{r} := \{r_{i,b}\}_{i\in[m],b\in\{0,1\}}, \rho)$. *Let* $(\tilde{C}, \mathbf{lb}) = \overline{\mathsf{Garble}}(\alpha, x; \rho)$, *and parse* $\mathbf{lb} := \{\mathsf{lb}_{i,b}\}_{i\in[m],b\in\{0,1\}}$. *Let* $\mathsf{ct}_{i,b} := \mathsf{PKE.Enc}(\mathsf{pk}_{i,b}, \mathsf{lb}_{i,b}; r_{i,b})$ *and return* $y := (\tilde{C}, \{\mathsf{ct}_{i,b}\})$.
- $\mathsf{Invert}(\mathsf{sk}_C, y)$: *Parse* $\mathsf{sk}_C := (C, \tilde{\mathsf{sk}}_1, \ldots, \tilde{\mathsf{sk}}_m)$ *and* $y := (\tilde{C}, \tilde{\mathsf{ct}}_1, \ldots, \tilde{\mathsf{ct}}_m)$ *and let* $\ell_i := \mathsf{PKE.Dec}(\tilde{\mathsf{sk}}_i, \tilde{\mathsf{ct}}_i)$ *for* $i \in [m]$. *Run* $\overline{\mathsf{Eval}}(\tilde{C}, \{\ell_i\})$; *if the output is* \$, *return* $\perp$; *otherwise, parsing the output* (x, ω), *return* (x, ρ) *where* ρ *is computed from* ω *as shown in Lemma 3.*

Lemma 4 (Correctness). *Assuming* $\mathsf{SKE} := (\mathsf{G}, \mathsf{Enc}, \mathsf{Dec})$ *is randomness recoverable (Definition 11), the resulting scheme PE-TDF in Construction 8 has perfect correctness (Definition 3).*

Proof. The proof follows because by Lemma 3 the enhanced version of Yao's garbled circuit is randomness recoverable (hence recovering ρ), and also all the random coins used to encrypt the labels (i.e., $\mathbf{r}$ in Construction 8) are outputted by the evaluation algorithm on an accepting sequence of garbled labels. □

Instantiating the Encryption Schemes in Construction 8. Construction 8 introduces a circularity: the labels of the garbled circuit are encrypted under a PKE scheme using randomness $\mathbf{r}$, and the underlying randomness $\mathbf{r}$ is hardwired into the circuit being garbled. We now show how to overcome this circularity in a provable way using the following instantiations: the underlying PKE scheme will be Dual-BHHO (which we call $\mathsf{PKE}_{\mathrm{dbhho}}$), while the secret-key encryption scheme is BHHO, adapted to the private-key setting.

Construction 9 (Private-Key BHHO). *Define* $\mathsf{SKE} = (\mathsf{SKE.G}, \mathsf{SKE.Enc}, \mathsf{SKE.Dec})$ *as follows:*

- $\mathsf{SKE.G}(1^\lambda)$: *return* $s \xleftarrow{\$} \{0,1\}^n$.
- $\mathsf{SKE.Enc}(s, g')$: *sample* $(g_1, \ldots, g_n) \xleftarrow{\$} \mathbb{G}$ *and return* $(g_1, \ldots, g_n, g' \times \Pi g_i^{s_i})$.
- $\mathsf{SKE.Dec}(s, \mathsf{ct})$: *parse* $\mathsf{ct} := (\mathbf{g}, g'')$; *return,* $g''/(s \cdot \mathbf{g})$.

Randomness Recoverability. For SKE of Construction 9, the encryption algorithm also samples n group elements, and one might complaint that we cannot necessarily recover the underlying coins used to generate these group elements. However, this fact can be handled by putting all these group elements in the public parameter pp of the TD-ABE scheme (Construction 8). In other words, the algorithm Setup of Construction 8 will include n group elements in pp for every private-key encryption that is going to be performed during Eval (more specifically, during $\overline{\mathsf{Garble}}$). We ignore this fact here, and we hereon assume these group elements are generated as part of each encryption.

We review the scheme of k-block BHHO, which outputs k ciphertexts each sampled under BHHO.

Construction 10 (k-block BHHO [10]**).** *We review the definition of the BHHO scheme* $\mathsf{PKE_{bhho}}$ *for encrypting k group elements.*

- $\mathsf{S}(1^\lambda)$: *Sample n random group elements* $\mathsf{pp} := \mathbf{g} := (g_1, \ldots, g_n)$, *where* $n \in \omega(\log p)$, *where* $p = |\mathbb{G}|$.
- $\mathsf{G}(\mathsf{pp})$: *On* $\mathsf{pp} := \mathbf{g}$, *return* $(\mathsf{pk}, \mathsf{sk} := s)$, *where* $s \xleftarrow{\$} \{0,1\}^n$ *and* $\mathsf{pk} := (\mathbf{g}, s \cdot \mathbf{g})$. *By abusing notation, we may sometimes write* $\mathsf{pk} = \mathsf{G}(\mathsf{pp}, \mathsf{sk})$.
- $\mathsf{Enc}(\mathsf{pk}, \mathbf{m} := (g'_1, \ldots, g'_k))$: *To encrypt* $\mathbf{m}$ *under* $\mathsf{pk} := (\mathbf{g}, g_{\mathsf{pk}})$, *sample a k-tuple randomness* $(r_1, \ldots, r_k) \xleftarrow{\$} \mathbb{Z}_p^k$ *and return* $\mathsf{ct} := (\mathbf{g}^{r_1}, g_{\mathsf{pk}}^{r_1} \cdot g'_1, \ldots, \mathbf{g}^{r_k}, g_{\mathsf{pk}}^{r_k} \cdot g'_k)$.
- $\mathsf{Dec}(\mathsf{sk}, \mathsf{ct})$: *Obvious.*

Construction 11 (k-block Dual BHHO). *Define* $\mathsf{PKE_{dbhho}} = (\mathsf{S}, \mathsf{G}, \mathsf{Enc}, \mathsf{Dec})$, *the k-block version of* DualBHHO, *as follows.*

- $\mathsf{S}(1^\lambda)$: Sample n random group elements $\mathsf{pp} := \mathbf{g} := (g_1, \ldots, g_n)$, where $n \in \omega(\log(|\mathbb{G}|))$.
- $\mathsf{G}(\mathbf{g})$: On $\mathsf{pp} := \mathbf{g}$, return $(\mathsf{pk}, \mathsf{sk})$, where $\mathsf{sk} := (r_1, \ldots, r_k) \xleftarrow{\$} \mathbb{Z}_p^k$ and $\mathsf{pk} := (\mathbf{g}, \mathbf{g}^{r_1}, \ldots, \mathbf{g}^{r_k})$. By abusing notation, we may sometimes write $\mathsf{pk} = \mathsf{G}(\mathsf{pp}, \mathsf{sk})$.
- $\mathsf{Enc}(\mathsf{pk}, g_m)$: To encrypt k group element $(g_1, \ldots, g_k)$ under $\mathsf{pk} := (\mathbf{g}, \mathbf{g}_1, \ldots, \mathbf{g}_k)$, sample randomness $s \xleftarrow{\$} \{0,1\}^n$ and return $\mathsf{ct} := (s \cdot \mathbf{g}, (s \cdot \mathbf{g}_1) \times g_1, \ldots, (s \cdot \mathbf{g}_k) \times g_k)$, where $s \cdot \mathbf{g} := \Pi g_i^{s_i}$.
- $\mathsf{Dec}(\mathsf{sk}, \mathsf{ct})$: parse $\mathsf{sk} := (r_1, \ldots, r_k)$ and $\mathsf{ct} := (g_1, g_2, \ldots, g_{k+1})$, then return $(g_2/(g_1)^{r_1}, \ldots, g_{k+1}/(g_1)^{r_k})$.

We now prove a technique for switching RDM+KDM security to KDM security. Recall that under $\mathsf{PKE_{dbhho}}$ the encryption randomness is a string $s \in \{0,1\}^n$, the same as a secret key for $\mathsf{PKE_{bhho}}$. Similarly, a secret key $(r_1, \ldots, r_k)$ under $\mathsf{PKE_{dbhho}}$ corresponds to encryption randomness for k-block $\mathsf{PKE_{bhho}}$. We give the following lemma, and will then discuss its usefulness.

Lemma 5 (RDM/KDM Switching Lemma). *Let* $\mathbf{m} = (m_1, \ldots, m_k)$ *be a sequence of k group elements, to be encrypted. Fix a public parameter* $\mathbf{g} := (g_1, \ldots, g_n)$ *across both* $\mathsf{PKE_{bhho}}$ *and* $\mathsf{PKE_{dbhho}}$. *Let*

– $\mathbf{r} := (r_1, \ldots, r_k) \in \mathbb{Z}_p^k$ *be a secret key under* $\mathsf{PKE}_{\mathrm{dbhho}}$ *and let* pk *be the corresponding public key;* $\mathsf{pk} := (\mathbf{g}, \mathbf{g}^{r_1}, \ldots, \mathbf{g}^{r_k})$.
– $s \in \{0,1\}^n$ *be a randomness value under* $\mathsf{PKE}_{\mathrm{dbhho}}$. *Also, let* pk' *be the corresponding BHHO public key under s:That is,* $\mathsf{pk}' := (\mathbf{g}, s \cdot \mathbf{g})$.

Up to "rearrangement of the terms":

$$\mathsf{pk}, \mathsf{Enc}_{\mathrm{dbhho}}(\mathsf{pk}, \mathbf{m}; s) = \mathsf{pk}', \mathsf{Enc}_{\mathsf{bhho}}(\mathsf{pk}', \mathbf{m}; \mathbf{r}),$$

where $=$ *indicates that the two distributions are identical.*

Usefulness of Lemma 5. Let SKE be the private-key BHHO scheme (Construction 9) and assume $|s| = n$. Then we can reduce a combination of RDM and KDM attacks into a solely KDM scenario.

$$\underbrace{\mathsf{pk}, \mathsf{Enc}_{\mathrm{dbhho}}(\mathsf{pk}, s; s'), \mathsf{SKE.Enc}(s, s')}_{\text{RDM+KDM}} \equiv \underbrace{\mathsf{pk}', \mathsf{Enc}_{\mathsf{bhho}}(\mathsf{pk}', s; \mathbf{r}), \mathsf{SKE.Enc}(s, s')}_{\text{KDM Only}} \tag{4}$$

where $s \xleftarrow{\$} \{0,1\}^n$, $\mathbf{r} \xleftarrow{\$} \mathbb{Z}_p^n$, $\mathsf{pk} := \mathsf{PKE}_{\mathrm{dbhho}}.\mathsf{G}(\mathsf{pp}, \mathbf{r})$, $s' \xleftarrow{\$} \{0,1\}^n$ and $\mathsf{pk}' := \mathsf{G}_{\mathsf{bhho}}(\mathsf{pp}, s')$. Notice that the randomness $\mathbf{r}$ in the righthand side is not used anywhere else in that side, so we do not have randomness dependency anymore.

Proof of Lemma 5. The proof follows easily by inspection. Letting $\mathbf{g} := (g_1, \ldots, g_n)$:

$$\mathsf{pk}, \mathsf{Enc}_{\mathrm{dbhho}}(\mathsf{pk}, \mathbf{m}; s) := \begin{pmatrix} g_1, g_2, \ldots, g_n \\ g_1^{r_1}, g_2^{r_1}, \ldots, g_n^{r_1} \\ \vdots \\ g_1^{r_k}, g_2^{r_k}, \ldots, g_n^{r_k} \end{pmatrix}, \begin{pmatrix} s \cdot \mathbf{g} \\ (s \cdot \mathbf{g})^{r_1} \cdot m_1 \\ \vdots \\ (s \cdot \mathbf{g})^{r_k} \cdot m_k \end{pmatrix}.$$

Thus, we may concisely write

$$\mathsf{pk}, \mathsf{Enc}_{\mathrm{dbhho}}(\mathsf{pk}, \mathbf{m}; s) := \begin{pmatrix} g_1, & g_2, \ldots, & g_n, & s \cdot \mathbf{g} \\ g_1^{r_1}, & g_2^{r_1}, \ldots, & g_n^{r_1}, & (s \cdot \mathbf{g})^{r_1} \cdot m_1 \\ & & \vdots & \\ g_1^{r_k}, & g_2^{r_k}, \ldots, & g_n^{r_k}, & (s \cdot \mathbf{g})^{r_k} \cdot m_k \end{pmatrix}, \tag{5}$$

Recall that $\mathsf{pk}' = (g_1, \ldots, g_n, s \cdot \mathbf{g})$, which is the first column of the matrix in Eq. 5. Thus, the matrix in Eq. 5 corresponds to $\mathsf{pk}', \mathsf{Enc}_{\mathsf{bhho}}(\mathsf{pk}', \mathbf{m}; \mathbf{r})$, up to obvious rearrangement of the terms. □

Lemma 6 (Adaptive Security for AB-TDF). *Assuming the DDH assumption holds. Instantiating Construction with* SKE *of Construction 9 and* PKE *of Construction 11 and an enhanced garbled circuit (Construction 7), the AB-TDF scheme of Construction 8 is single-key adaptively secure.*

Proof. Let $(\tilde{C}, \{\mathsf{lb}_{i,b}\})$ be the resulting garbled circuits and labels. Let

- $k_{1,0}, k_{1,1}, \ldots, k_{m,0}, k_{m,1}$ be the input labels of the garbled circuit (i.e., $\mathsf{lb}_{i,b} = k_{i,b}$), and let $\{\mathsf{pk}_{i,b}\}$ be the $2n$ pairs of public keys and secret keys used to encrypt the corresponding input label.
- Key be the set of all keys sampled during the garbled circuit construction (Construction 7).

Also, let $k_{\mathsf{out},0}$ and $k_{\mathsf{out},1}$ be the output-wire keys corresponding to bit values zero and one. Let $\mathsf{CT}_{\mathsf{all}}$ be the set of all ciphertexts in the image y. We may split $\mathsf{CT}_{\mathsf{all}}$ into three subsets:

1. $\mathsf{CT}_{\mathsf{all}1}$: label encryptions:

$$\mathsf{CT}_{\mathsf{all}1} : \{\mathsf{PKE}_{\mathrm{dbhho}}.\mathsf{Enc}(\mathsf{pk}_{i,b}, k_{i,b}; r_{i,b}) \colon i \in [m], b \in \{0,1\}\};$$

2. $\mathsf{CT}_{\mathsf{all}2}$: encryptions of the random coins $\{r_{i,b}\}$ used in Step 1. as well as the garbled circuit keys Key, made under $k_{\mathsf{out},1}$:

$$\mathsf{CT}_{\mathsf{all}2} := \{\mathsf{SKE}.\mathsf{Enc}(k_{\mathsf{out},1}, r_{i,b}) \colon i \in [m], b \in \{0,1\}\} \cup \{\mathsf{SKE}.\mathsf{Enc}(k_{\mathsf{out},1}, k) \colon k \in \mathsf{Key} \setminus \{k_{\mathsf{out},1}\}\}$$

   where all encryptions in $\mathsf{CT}_{\mathsf{all}2}$ use fresh randomness.
3. $\mathsf{CT}_{\mathsf{all}3}$: all intermediate key encryptions, as per Yao's garbled circuit construction (Construction 7).

Notice the RDM/KDM circularity involved between $\mathsf{CT}_{\mathsf{all}1}$ and $\mathsf{CT}_{\mathsf{all}2}$: $\mathsf{pk}_{i,b}$ are encrypting $k_{i,b}$ (which in turn encrypt $k_{\mathsf{out},1}$ via a sequence of hops), and the random coins used to encrypt $k_{i,b}$ under $\mathsf{pk}_{i,b}$ are encrypted under $k_{\mathsf{out},1}$.

We will now use Lemma 5 to reduce the above RDM+KDM dependency to KDM-dependency alone, at which point we can use the BHHO result to argue security for the garbled circuit.

Let $\mathbf{h}_{i,b} \xleftarrow{\$} \mathbb{Z}_p^k$ be the randomness used to generate $(\mathsf{pk}_{i,b}, \mathsf{sk}_{i,b})$, and note that this randomness is never encrypted in CT. Also, recall that $r_{i,b} \xleftarrow{\$} \{0,1\}^n$. By Lemma 5

$$\mathsf{PKE}_{\mathrm{dbhho}}.\mathsf{Enc}(\mathsf{pk}_{i,b}, k_{i,b}; r_{i,b}) := \mathsf{PKE}_{\mathrm{bhho}}.\mathsf{Enc}(\mathsf{pk}'_{i,b}, k_{i,b}; \mathbf{h}_{i,b}), \tag{6}$$

where $\mathsf{pk}'_{i,b} = \mathsf{PKE}_{\mathrm{bhho}}.\mathsf{G}(\mathsf{pp}, r_{i,b})$. In other words, $r_{i,b}$ is now the secret key of $\mathsf{pk}'_{i,b}$. With this in mind, we may write

$$\mathsf{CT}_{\mathsf{all}1} : \{\mathsf{PKE}_{\mathrm{bhho}}.\mathsf{Enc}(\mathsf{pk}'_{i,b}, k_{i,b}; \mathbf{h}_{i,b}) \colon i \in [m], b \in \{0,1\}\}. \tag{7}$$

Notice that $\mathsf{CT}_{\mathsf{all}2}$ is now encrypting the secret keys of $\mathsf{pk}'_{i,b}$, and thus we are in a KDM-only scenario.

Once having reduced RMD/KDM to KDM-only in the garbled circuits, the rest of the proof follows as in [30, 37]. □

Instantiation Using LWE. Instantiating Construction 8 with SKE which is dual-Regev's circularly-secure SKE scheme [22], with PKE which is Regev's PKE scheme [34] and an enhanced garbled circuit (Construction 7) based on SKE above, the AB-TDF scheme of Construction 8 is adaptively secure. The proof will be the same, since we can prove the RDM/KDM switching lemma (Lemma 5) based on these encryption schemes. See the full version for further details.

References

1. Alwen, J., Krenn, S., Pietrzak, K., Wichs, D.: Learning with rounding, revisited. In: Canetti, R., Garay, J.A. (eds.) CRYPTO 2013. LNCS, vol. 8042, pp. 57–74. Springer, Heidelberg (2013). https://doi.org/10.1007/978-3-642-40041-4_4
2. Bellare, M., Boldyreva, A., O'Neill, A.: Deterministic and efficiently searchable encryption. In: Menezes, A. (ed.) CRYPTO 2007. LNCS, vol. 4622, pp. 535–552. Springer, Heidelberg (2007). https://doi.org/10.1007/978-3-540-74143-5_30
3. Bellare, M., et al.: Hedged public-key encryption: how to protect against bad randomness. In: Matsui, M. (ed.) ASIACRYPT 2009. LNCS, vol. 5912, pp. 232–249. Springer, Heidelberg (2009). https://doi.org/10.1007/978-3-642-10366-7_14
4. Bellare, M., Hofheinz, D., Yilek, S.: Possibility and impossibility results for encryption and commitment secure under selective opening. In: Joux, A. (ed.) EUROCRYPT 2009. LNCS, vol. 5479, pp. 1–35. Springer, Heidelberg (2009). https://doi.org/10.1007/978-3-642-01001-9_1
5. Bellare, M., Kiltz, E., Peikert, C., Waters, B.: Identity-based (lossy) trapdoor functions and applications. In: Pointcheval, D., Johansson, T. (eds.) EUROCRYPT 2012. LNCS, vol. 7237, pp. 228–245. Springer, Heidelberg (2012). https://doi.org/10.1007/978-3-642-29011-4_15
6. Bitansky, N., Vaikuntanathan, V.: A note on perfect correctness by derandomization. In: Coron, J.-S., Nielsen, J.B. (eds.) EUROCRYPT 2017. LNCS, vol. 10211, pp. 592–606. Springer, Cham (2017). https://doi.org/10.1007/978-3-319-56614-6_20
7. Boldyreva, A., Fehr, S., O'Neill, A.: On notions of security for deterministic encryption, and efficient constructions without random oracles. In: Wagner, D. (ed.) CRYPTO 2008. LNCS, vol. 5157, pp. 335–359. Springer, Heidelberg (2008). https://doi.org/10.1007/978-3-540-85174-5_19
8. Boneh, D., Franklin, M.: Identity-based encryption from the weil pairing. In: Kilian, J. (ed.) CRYPTO 2001. LNCS, vol. 2139, pp. 213–229. Springer, Heidelberg (2001). https://doi.org/10.1007/3-540-44647-8_13
9. Boneh, D., et al.: Fully key-homomorphic encryption, arithmetic circuit ABE and compact garbled circuits. In: Nguyen, P.Q., Oswald, E. (eds.) EUROCRYPT 2014. LNCS, vol. 8441, pp. 533–556. Springer, Heidelberg (2014). https://doi.org/10.1007/978-3-642-55220-5_30
10. Boneh, D., Halevi, S., Hamburg, M., Ostrovsky, R.: Circular-secure encryption from decision Diffie-Hellman. In: Wagner, D. (ed.) CRYPTO 2008. LNCS, vol. 5157, pp. 108–125. Springer, Heidelberg (2008). https://doi.org/10.1007/978-3-540-85174-5_7
11. Boneh, D., Sahai, A., Waters, B.: Functional encryption: definitions and challenges. In: Ishai, Y. (ed.) TCC 2011. LNCS, vol. 6597, pp. 253–273. Springer, Heidelberg (2011). https://doi.org/10.1007/978-3-642-19571-6_16

12. Brakerski, Z., Lombardi, A., Segev, G., Vaikuntanathan, V.: Anonymous IBE, leakage resilience and circular security from new assumptions. In: Nielsen, J.B., Rijmen, V. (eds.) EUROCRYPT 2018. LNCS, vol. 10820, pp. 535–564. Springer, Cham (2018). https://doi.org/10.1007/978-3-319-78381-9_20
13. Cho, C., Döttling, N., Garg, S., Gupta, D., Miao, P., Polychroniadou, A.: Laconic oblivious transfer and its applications. In: Katz, J., Shacham, H. (eds.) CRYPTO 2017. LNCS, vol. 10402, pp. 33–65. Springer, Cham (2017). https://doi.org/10.1007/978-3-319-63715-0_2
14. Diffie, W., Hellman, M.E.: New directions in cryptography. IEEE Trans. Inf. Theory **22**(6), 644–654 (1976)
15. Döttling, N., Garg, S.: From selective IBE to full IBE and selective HIBE. In: Kalai, Y., Reyzin, L. (eds.) TCC 2017. LNCS, vol. 10677, pp. 372–408. Springer, Cham (2017). https://doi.org/10.1007/978-3-319-70500-2_13
16. Döttling, N., Garg, S.: Identity-based encryption from the Diffie-Hellman assumption. In: Katz, J., Shacham, H. (eds.) CRYPTO 2017. LNCS, vol. 10401, pp. 537–569. Springer, Cham (2017). https://doi.org/10.1007/978-3-319-63688-7_18
17. Döttling, N., Garg, S., Hajiabadi, M., Masny, D.: New constructions of identity-based and key-dependent message secure encryption schemes. In: Abdalla, M., Dahab, R. (eds.) PKC 2018. LNCS, vol. 10769, pp. 3–31. Springer, Cham (2018). https://doi.org/10.1007/978-3-319-76578-5_1
18. Döttling, N., Garg, S., Ishai, Y., Malavolta, G., Mour, T., Ostrovsky, R.: Trapdoor hash functions and their applications. In: Boldyreva, A., Micciancio, D. (eds.) CRYPTO 2019. LNCS, vol. 11694, pp. 3–32. Springer, Cham (2019). https://doi.org/10.1007/978-3-030-26954-8_1
19. Freeman, D.M., Goldreich, O., Kiltz, E., Rosen, A., Segev, G.: More constructions of lossy and correlation-secure trapdoor functions. In: Nguyen, P.Q., Pointcheval, D. (eds.) PKC 2010. LNCS, vol. 6056, pp. 279–295. Springer, Heidelberg (2010). https://doi.org/10.1007/978-3-642-13013-7_17
20. Garg, S., Gay, R., Hajiabadi, M.: New techniques for efficient trapdoor functions and applications. In: Ishai, Y., Rijmen, V. (eds.) EUROCRYPT 2019. LNCS, vol. 11478, pp. 33–63. Springer, Cham (2019). https://doi.org/10.1007/978-3-030-17659-4_2
21. Garg, S., Hajiabadi, M.: Trapdoor functions from the computational Diffie-Hellman assumption. In: Shacham, H., Boldyreva, A. (eds.) CRYPTO 2018. LNCS, vol. 10992, pp. 362–391. Springer, Cham (2018). https://doi.org/10.1007/978-3-319-96881-0_13
22. Gentry, C., Peikert, C., Vaikuntanathan, V.: Trapdoors for hard lattices and new cryptographic constructions. In: Ladner, R.E., Dwork, C. (eds.) 40th ACM STOC, Victoria, BC, Canada, 17–20 May 2008, pp. 197–206. ACM Press (2008)
23. Gorbunov, S., Vaikuntanathan, V., Wee, H.: Predicate encryption for circuits from LWE. In: Gennaro, R., Robshaw, M. (eds.) CRYPTO 2015. LNCS, vol. 9216, pp. 503–523. Springer, Heidelberg (2015). https://doi.org/10.1007/978-3-662-48000-7_25
24. Goyal, V., Pandey, O., Sahai, A., Waters, B.: Attribute-based encryption for fine-grained access control of encrypted data. In: Juels, A., Wright, R.N., De Capitani di Vimercati, S. (eds.) ACM CCS 2006, Alexandria, Virginia, USA, 30 October–3 November 2006, pp. 89–98. ACM Press (2006). Available as Cryptology ePrint Archive Report 2006/309

25. Hohenberger, S., Koppula, V., Waters, B.: Chosen ciphertext security from injective trapdoor functions. In: Micciancio, D., Ristenpart, T. (eds.) CRYPTO 2020. LNCS, vol. 12170, pp. 836–866. Springer, Cham (2020). https://doi.org/10.1007/978-3-030-56784-2_28
26. Impagliazzo, R., Levin, L.A., Luby, M.: Pseudo-random generation from one-way functions (extended abstracts). In: 21st ACM STOC, Seattle, WA, USA, 15–17 May 1989, pp. 12–24. ACM Press (1989)
27. Kiltz, E., Masny, D., Pietrzak, K.: Simple chosen-ciphertext security from low-noise LPN. In: Krawczyk, H. (ed.) PKC 2014. LNCS, vol. 8383, pp. 1–18. Springer, Heidelberg (2014). https://doi.org/10.1007/978-3-642-54631-0_1
28. Kitagawa, F., Matsuda, T., Tanaka, K.: CCA security and trapdoor functions via key-dependent-message security. In: Boldyreva, A., Micciancio, D. (eds.) CRYPTO 2019. LNCS, vol. 11694, pp. 33–64. Springer, Cham (2019). https://doi.org/10.1007/978-3-030-26954-8_2
29. Koppula, V., Waters, B.: Realizing chosen ciphertext security generically in attribute-based encryption and predicate encryption. In: Boldyreva, A., Micciancio, D. (eds.) CRYPTO 2019. LNCS, vol. 11693, pp. 671–700. Springer, Cham (2019). https://doi.org/10.1007/978-3-030-26951-7_23
30. Lindell, Y., Pinkas, B.: A proof of security of Yao's protocol for two-party computation. J. Cryptol. **22**(2), 161–188 (2009). https://doi.org/10.1007/s00145-008-9036-8
31. Lombardi, A., Quach, W., Rothblum, R.D., Wichs, D., Wu, D.J.: New constructions of reusable designated-verifier NIZKs. In: Boldyreva, A., Micciancio, D. (eds.) CRYPTO 2019. LNCS, vol. 11694, pp. 670–700. Springer, Cham (2019). https://doi.org/10.1007/978-3-030-26954-8_22
32. Peikert, C., Waters, B.: Lossy trapdoor functions and their applications. In: Ladner, R.E., Dwork, C. (eds.) 40th ACM STOC, Victoria, BC, Canada, 17–20 May 2008, pp. 187–196. ACM Press (2008)
33. Rabin, M.O.: Digital signatures and public key functions as intractable as factorization. Technical report MIT/LCS/TR-212, Massachusetts Institute of Technology, January 1979
34. Regev, O.: On lattices, learning with errors, random linear codes, and cryptography. In: Gabow, H.N., Fagin, R. (eds.) 37th ACM STOC, Baltimore, MA, USA, 22–24 May 2005, pp. 84–93. ACM Press (2005)
35. Rivest, R.L., Shamir, A., Adleman, L.M.: A method for obtaining digital signatures and public-key cryptosystems. Commun. Assoc. Comput. Mach. **21**(2), 120–126 (1978)
36. Rogaway, P., Shrimpton, T.: A provable-security treatment of the key-wrap problem. In: Vaudenay, S. (ed.) EUROCRYPT 2006. LNCS, vol. 4004, pp. 373–390. Springer, Heidelberg (2006). https://doi.org/10.1007/11761679_23
37. Yao, A.C.-C.: How to generate and exchange secrets (extended abstract). In: 27th FOCS, Toronto, Ontario, Canada, 27–29 October 1986, pp. 162–167. IEEE Computer Society Press (1986)

Beyond Software Watermarking: Traitor-Tracing for Pseudorandom Functions

Rishab Goyal[1(✉)], Sam Kim[2], Brent Waters[3,4], and David J. Wu[3]

[1] MIT, Cambridge, MA, USA
goyal@utexas.edu
[2] Stanford University, Stanford, CA, USA
skim13@cs.stanford.edu
[3] University of Texas at Austin, Austin, TX, USA
{bwaters,dwu4}@cs.utexas.edu
[4] NTT Research, Sunnyvale, CA, USA

Abstract. Software watermarking schemes allow a user to embed an identifier into a piece of code such that the resulting program is nearly functionally-equivalent to the original program, and yet, it is difficult to remove the identifier without destroying the functionality of the program. Such schemes are often considered for proving software ownership or for digital rights management. Existing constructions of watermarking have focused primarily on watermarking pseudorandom functions (PRFs).

In this work, we revisit the definitional foundations of watermarking, and begin by highlighting a major flaw in existing security notions. Existing security notions for watermarking only require that the identifier be successfully extracted from programs that preserve the *exact* input/output behavior of the original program. In the context of PRFs, this means that an adversary that constructs a program which computes a quarter of the output bits of the PRF or that is able to distinguish the outputs of the PRF from random are considered to be *outside* the threat model. However, in any application (e.g., watermarking a decryption device or an authentication token) that relies on PRF security, an adversary that manages to predict a quarter of the bits or distinguishes the PRF outputs from random would be considered to have defeated the scheme. Thus, existing watermarking schemes provide very little security

R. Goyal—Part of this work was done while at UT Austin and the Simons Institute for the Theory of Computing. Research supported in part by an IBM PhD fellowship and the Simons-Berkeley research fellowship.

S. Kim—Part of this work was done at the Simons Institute for the Theory of Computing. Research supported by NSF, DARPA, a grant from ONR, and the Simons Foundation.

B. Waters—Research supported by NSF CNS-1908611, a Simons Investigator award, and a Packard Foundation Fellowship.

D. J. Wu—Part of this work was done at the University of Virginia and while visiting the Simons Institute for the Theory of Computing. Research supported by NSF CNS-1917414, CNS-2045180, and a Microsoft Research Faculty Fellowship.

M. Tibouchi and H. Wang (Eds.): ASIACRYPT 2021, LNCS 13092, pp. 250–280, 2021.
https://doi.org/10.1007/978-3-030-92078-4_9

guarantee against realistic adversaries. None of the existing constructions of watermarkable PRFs would be able to extract the identifier from a program that only outputs a quarter of the bits of the PRF or one that perfectly distinguishes.

To address the shortcomings in existing watermarkable PRF definitions, we introduce a new primitive called a *traceable PRF*. Our definitions are inspired by similar definitions from public-key traitor tracing, and aim to capture a very robust set of adversaries: namely, any adversary that produces a useful distinguisher (i.e., a program that can break PRF security), can be traced to a specific identifier. We provide a general framework for constructing traceable PRFs via an intermediate primitive called *private linear constrained PRFs*. Finally, we show how to construct traceable PRFs from a similar set of assumptions previously used to realize software watermarking. Namely, we obtain a single-key traceable PRF from standard lattice assumptions and a fully collusion-resistant traceable PRF from indistinguishability obfuscation (together with injective one-way functions).

1 Introduction

Software watermarking is a mechanism for protecting against unauthorized redistribution of software. In a watermarking scheme, a user can embed some special information called a "mark" into a program such that the resulting program is nearly functionally-equivalent to the original one, and moreover, it is difficult for an adversary to remove the watermarking without destroying its input/output behavior. The majority of works studying cryptographic notions of watermarking have focused primarily on watermarking pseudorandom functions (PRFs) [CHN+16, BLW17, KW17, QWZ18, YAL+18, KW19, YAL+19, YAYX20]. Namely, the goal in each of these constructions is to embed an identifier (e.g., a user's name or a device id) into a PRF key such that (1) the marked key still preserves the input/output behavior of the original PRF; and (2) no efficient adversary is able to construct a key that both preserves the input/output behavior of the PRF on an ε-fraction of the domain and does not contain the identifier. The first requirement corresponds to "correctness" while the second corresponds to "unremovability."

The Limitations of Existing Definitions. While these correctness and unremovability requirements seem to capture an intuitive notion of what we might desire from a watermarking scheme, they fall short of capturing meaningful notions of security in many realistic settings. For instance, take a watermarkable PRF that is secure under the above notions, and consider an adversary that takes a marked circuit $C\colon \{0,1\}^n \to \{0,1\}^n$ and outputs a circuit C' that on input x, outputs the first $n/4$ bits of $C(x)$. Under existing definitions, mark-extraction is allowed to fail in this setting (since C' does *not* preserve the input/output behavior of the marked program). At the same time, C' still reveals substantial information about the original function and is often sufficient to compromise security of any

(a) Original (b) Encrypted (c) Recovered (pixel-level) (d) Recovered (block-level)

Fig. 1. Illustration of plaintext recovery using a PRF-based encryption scheme given a circuit that computes the leading $n/4$ bits of the PRF. Figure 1a shows the original image and Fig. 1b shows the image encrypted using a PRF in counter mode. Figures 1c and 1d shows the recovered image if the image is encrypted pixel-by-pixel and block-by-block, respectively, and the adversary has a circuit that computes the $n/4$ most significant bits of the PRF output.

cryptographic scheme that relies on the watermarked PRF. For instance, if the PRF is used to construct a symmetric encryption scheme, a circuit that outputs a quarter of the bits of the PRF completely breaks semantic security of the encryption scheme (see Fig. 1 for a visual example of this). However, even though C' suffices to completely break semantic security of the encryption scheme, the watermarking scheme *cannot* recover the mark from the compromised key.

The above example highlights a limitation in existing security notions for cryptographic watermarking: namely, the existing definition only allows for a restrictive (and unrealistic) set of adversarial strategies. Indeed, *none* of the existing constructions [CHN+16, BLW17, KW17, QWZ18, YAL+18, KW19, YAL+19, YAYX20] of software watermarking remain secure if we expand the set of admissible adversarial strategies to include the simple example described above. Existing watermarking constructions all take the approach of carefully embedding the identifier in the output of the function. Such an embedding critically exploits of the assumption that the adversary must preserve much of the exact input/output behavior of the original function, in which case, most of the original outputs (that embed the identifier) are also preserved. Consequently, if the adversary constructs a circuit that does not exactly preserve the input/output behavior, then the tracing algorithm cannot recover the embedded identifier.[1]

In cryptography, it is not only prudent, but oftentimes, essential for applications, to design expressive threat models that enable the broadest range of

[1] In some cases (e.g., [CHN+16]), the tracing algorithm can still *partially* recover the identity (e.g., a quarter of the bits) from a circuit that outputs a quarter the bits of each output. But this tracing algorithm can be defeated by an adversary which outputs a circuit that only distinguishes the output of the PRF (i.e., on input (x, y), output 1 if $\mathsf{Eval}(\mathsf{msk}, x) = y$ and 0 otherwise) or a circuit that computes the parity of the bits of the PRF output.

adversaries. Indeed, the very first formal security notions [GM84, GGM84] in cryptography carefully distinguished between the functionality requirements of a primitive and what the adversary would need to do to break it. In the case of semantic security [GM84], it sufficed for an adversary to *distinguish* between encryptions of two messages, and not that the adversary be able to *recover* the original message. In the case of PRFs [GGM84], it sufficed that the adversary could *distinguish* PRF evaluations from random as opposed to needing to *predict* the outputs of the PRF (and indeed, imposing such a restriction on the adversary would limit the usefulness of the primitive). In each of these examples, the adversary's objective is easier to achieve than emulating the exact functionality or semantic requirements of the primitive. This is the philosophy we take when designing our security definitions.

This Work. Our primary goals in this work are to highlight the deficiencies of existing security notions for cryptographic watermarking and to introduce a new security framework that better models our intuitive notions of security for a watermarking scheme. Our definitions are inspired by similar notions developed in the literature on traitor tracing [CFN94, BSW06, NWZ16, GKRW18, GKW18] and recent work on watermarking public-key cryptographic primitives [GKM+19]. We begin by introducing a new notion of a *traceable PRF* which both suffices to instantiate the existing applications of watermarkable PRFs and addresses the limitations of existing watermarkable PRF definitions and offers meaningful security guarantees in realistic scenarios (e.g., they can be used to construct traceable symmetric encryption schemes). We then show how to construct non-collusion-resistant traceable PRFs from private constrained PRFs [BLW17] and fully collusion-resistant traceable PRFs from indistinguishability obfuscation [BGI+01]. We note that the assumptions needed to instantiate both of our schemes match the assumptions needed to instantiate watermarkable PRFs. This means that our new primitives can be instantiated from the same assumptions as watermarkable PRFs, and yet, provide much stronger security guarantees.

1.1 Our Results

Our first contribution is a new security definition that better captures the security goals in watermarkable PRFs. Here, we start from the beginning by re-examining the original motivation for building watermarkable PRFs. The original intent of watermarking PRFs is to be able to give a user a marked implementation of a PRF (e.g., for use in a symmetric encryption or authentication scheme) such that if the user later on tries to replicate the PRF functionality, there is a way to *trace* the replicated program back to the user's original key. The question is what constitutes a "valid" attempt at replicating the functionality. In this work, we consider any program that violates the security of the PRF (i.e., is able to distinguish PRF outputs from random) to be a "valid" attack. This definition is in part inspired by security definitions proposed in the setting of traitor tracing by Nishmaki et al. [NWZ16] (and adopted by later papers [GKRW18, GKW18]). In the earlier definitions starting with [CFN94], the tracing algorithm was only required to work against adversarial decoders that could successfully decrypt and recover the original message in its entirety from a ciphertext. However, [NWZ16] observed that this definition can be too restrictive as it ruled out valid attacks that could extract *partial* information about the encrypted message (e.g., the first quarter of an encrypted video stream) or simply distinguished between different messages. Fortunately, most traitor tracing constructions developed under earlier definitions also remained secure under the strengthened definition. However, this does not appear to be the case for watermarkable PRFs.

Our Notion: Traceable PRFs. Since the functionality in this case is a PRF, a natural security notion is that if the adversary outputs any functionality that helps one break pseudorandomness (i.e., distinguish the outputs of the PRF from random), then it should be possible to trace the identity associated with the functionality. In this work, we require that the tracing algorithm succeeds against any distinguisher that can break *weak pseudorandomness* of the PRF. Specifically, any program that can distinguish the PRF outputs on *random* domain elements can be traced to one (or more) compromised keys. Observe that this not only captures adversarial strategies that preserve the exact input/output behavior of the PRF on an ε-fraction of the domain (as in the case of watermarking), but also the previous example of a program that outputs a quarter of the bits of the PRF. It also includes more general strategies such as a distinguisher circuit that outputs 1 if (x, y) is an input/output pair of the PRF and 0 otherwise. Under our definition, no efficient adversary can remove a mark from the program unless it produces a program that does not break weak pseudorandomness of the PRF.

It is natural to ask whether we could trace the embedded mark from *any* PRF distinguisher, such as a distinguisher that can adaptively choose the inputs rather than only seeing evaluations at random points. While this may seem more natural, a closer inspection shows that it is unsatisfiable. This is because under this definition, we can construct an untraceable PRF distinguisher by simply hardwiring a *single* PRF input-output pair (x, y) in the distinguisher. This distinguisher completely breaks pseudorandomness, but is untraceable as it contains no information about the PRF except a single input-output pair. It is crucial to observe that such a distinguisher is also useless for any adversarial applications of the PRF. This shows that the concept of traceability must be carefully defined to precisely capture the semantics of a "useful" distinguisher. We discuss this in more detail in Sect. 3.1. Our definition considers distinguishers for weak pseudorandomness, which means that the adversary's program necessarily contains information about the PRF on a noticeable fraction of the domain. We also note that this does *not* preclude a traceable PRF to satisfy pseudorandomness as a standalone primitive (and indeed, the constructions we propose in this work satisfy the usual notion of pseudorandomness). The restriction to distinguishers that break weak pseudorandomness is only in the definition of tracing security.

Traceable PRF Syntax. A traceable PRF scheme consists of four algorithms: Setup, KeyGen, Eval, and Trace. The Setup algorithm samples a PRF key msk and a tracing key tk that is used for tracing. The key-generation algorithm takes as input the PRF key msk and an identifier id and outputs a "marked" key $\mathsf{sk}_{\mathsf{id}}$. The evaluation algorithm Eval takes as input either the PRF key msk or an identity key $\mathsf{sk}_{\mathsf{id}}$ and implements PRF evaluation. We require that $\mathsf{Eval}(\mathsf{sk}_{\mathsf{id}}, \cdot)$ and $\mathsf{Eval}(\mathsf{msk}, \cdot)$ agree almost everywhere (i.e., on all but a negligible fraction of the domain). This property is the analog of the "correctness" or "functionality-preserving" property in the setting of watermarking schemes. Finally, there is a trace algorithm Trace that takes as input the tracing key tk and has *oracle* access to a distinguisher D, and outputs a set of compromised keys (if any). Our security requirement says that if the distinguisher D is able to break *weak pseudorandomness* of the PRF (i.e., distinguish the outputs of $\mathsf{Eval}(\mathsf{msk}, \cdot)$ at random points from those of a random function), then the tracing algorithm must successfully identify a set of compromised keys used to construct D. Similar to the corresponding notions in traitor tracing (and watermarking), we can consider several variations of our basic schema and requirements:

- **Collusion-resistance:** We say that a traceable PRF is fully collusion-resistant if an adversary who has an arbitrary number of identity keys $S = \{\mathsf{sk}_{\mathsf{id}_1}, \ldots, \mathsf{sk}_{\mathsf{id}_k}\}$ still cannot construct a useful distinguisher D where $\mathsf{Trace}^D(\mathsf{tk})$ does not output a non-empty set $T \subseteq S$.[2] We say that a scheme satisfies bounded (resp., Q-key) collusion resistance if security only holds against adversaries that compromise an a priori bounded number of keys (resp., at most Q keys). In this work, we show how to construct a single-key traceable PRF from standard lattice assumptions[3] and a fully collusion resistant traceable PRF from indistinguishability obfuscation (and injective one-way functions).
- **Public tracing vs. secret tracing:** We say that a traceable PRF supports public tracing if security holds even if the tracing key tk is public. Otherwise, we say the traceable PRF is in the secret tracing setting. Our basic single-key traceable PRF from lattices is secure in the secret-tracing setting, while our obfuscation-based construction is secure in the public-tracing setting.

We provide the full definition in Sect. 4.1.

Constructing Traceable PRFs. To construct traceable PRFs, we introduce an intermediate primitive of a *private linear constrained PRF.* This primitive can

[2] We cannot stipulate that $T = S$ since the adversary might not use every compromised key when constructing the distinguisher D. The tracing algorithm can only recover the keys the adversary actually uses.

[3] A traceable PRF bears many similarities with a *constrained* PRF [BW13,KPTZ13, BGI14], and all known constructions of collusion-resistant constrained PRFs for sufficiently complex constraints from standard lattice assumptions are secure only in the single-key setting [BV15]. Fully collusion-resistance constrained PRFs for general constraints are only known from indistinguishability obfuscation [BZ14] and one-way functions. Recent work has shown how to construct indistinguishability obfuscation from the combination of *multiple* standard assumptions [JLS21].

be viewed as a symmetric analog of a "private linear broadcast encryption" (PLBE) from [BSW06] and which has featured prominently in a number of subsequent traitor tracing constructions [GKSW10,NWZ16,GKW18]. First, recall that in a constrained PRF [BW13,KPTZ13,BGI14], the holder of the PRF master secret key msk can issue a constrained key sk_f for a constraint f such that the constrained key can be used to evaluate on only the inputs x that satisfy the constraint (i.e., the inputs x where $f(x) = 1$). Moreover, the value of the PRF at points x where $f(x) = 0$ remain pseudorandom even given sk_f.

A private linear constrained PRF is similar in spirit to a constrained PRF for a class of linear constraints.[4] In this case, the constrained keys are each associated with a κ-bit index $\mathsf{id} \in [0, 2^\kappa - 1]$. Every input in the domain is associated with a *private* index $t \in [0, 2^\kappa]$ and a constrained key for index id can be used to evaluate the PRF on all inputs whose index $t \leq \mathsf{id}$. In addition to the usual Setup (for sampling the PRF key), KeyGen (for issuing constrained keys), and Eval (for evaluating the PRF), there is a fourth algorithm Samp that is used to sample domain elements with a given index t together with the PRF evaluation at the sampled point. The sampling algorithm Samp can either be public-key algorithm (in which case we obtain a publicly-traceable PRF) or a secret-key algorithm (in which case we obtain a secretly-traceable PRF). Similar to a PLBE scheme, there are three main security requirements we require on a private linear constrained PRF:

- **Normal hiding:** A random domain element is computationally indistinguishable from a randomly-sampled domain element with index 0 (output by Samp), even given any collection of identity keys.
- **Identity hiding:** A randomly-sampled domain element with index i is computationally indistinguishable from a randomly-sampled domain element with index j, provided that the adversary does not have any identity keys for an index $\mathsf{id} \in [i, j-1]$.
- **Pseudorandomness:** The PRF evaluations on randomly-sampled domain elements with index 2^κ are computationally indistinguishable from uniform given any collection of identity keys.

Given a private linear constrained PRF satisfying the above properties, we can construct a traceable PRF using a similar type of transformation used to construct traitor tracing from PLBE. Namely, we can reduce the tracing problem to a "jump-finding" problem as follows. Let D be the decoder constructed by the adversary. By assumption, we assume that D is useful: namely, it breaks weak pseudorandomness of the encryption scheme. This means that D is able to distinguish the PRF evaluation at a randomly-sampled domain element from a uniformly random value with non-negligible advantage ε. By the normal hiding property, D must also have advantage ε when distinguishing evaluations at randomly-sampled points with index 0. Next, by the pseudorandomness property,

[4] As we describe more formally below, the "privacy" requirement refers to a property on the inputs to the PRF, and *not* the notion of constraint-privacy in the standard definition of a "private constrained PRF" from [BLW17].

the distinguishing advantage of D for randomly-sampled points with index 2^κ must be negligible. Thus, there must be a "jump" in the decoder's distinguishing advantage on domain elements on some index $0 < t < 2^\kappa$. By the identity-hiding property, such "jumps" can only occur on indices for which the adversary possesses an identity key. We can then identify these jumps (and correspondingly, the set of compromised keys) by either performing a linear scan over the identity space (when the identity space is polynomial) [BSW06, GKSW10, GKW18] or by using a jump-finding algorithm (when the identity space is exponential) [NWZ16].

Due to some technical differences between PLBE and private linear constrained PRFs, we actually have to run the tracing algorithm *twice* in our construction. Very briefly, the reason behind this requirement is that, unlike encryption systems where the distinguisher just receives a single ciphertext and has to output its guess, the distinguisher in the case of traceable PRFs receives a tuple consisting of *both* a random domain element together with its evaluation. Here, the distinguisher may stop working if it notices the tracer is changing the distribution used to sample the inputs (i.e., domain elements). This means that if the tracer only performs a single scan, such decoders may evade detection. Thus, we need to apply the underlying tracing algorithm twice to circumvent this issue. In the first scan, the tracer runs the scan with a consistent output distribution, and then it performs a second scan where the output distribution is random and essentially independent of the input distribution. We provide the full technical details in Sect. 4.2.

Constructing Private Linear Constrained PRFs. In this work, we describe two constructions of private linear constrained PRFs. The first construction gives a single-key private linear constrained PRF in the secret-tracing setting and can be instantiated from LWE while the second construction is a collusion-resistant private linear constrained PRF in the public-tracing setting. Interestingly, both of our constructions rely on a similar set of building blocks as those used for watermarkable PRFs. We give a high-level sketch of our main constructions here:

- **Single-key private linear constrained PRF.** Our first construction combines a private constrained PRF together with an authenticated encryption scheme with pseudorandom ciphertexts (such authentication encryption schemes can be based on one-way functions). Recall first that a private constrained PRF is a constrained PRF where the constrained key sk_f hides the associated constraint function f.
  Let ℓ be the bit-length of the ciphertexts in the authenticated encryption scheme, and let sk be the secret key of the authenticated encryption scheme. The domain of our PRF will be $\{0,1\}^\ell$, and a point with index $t \in [0, 2^\kappa]$ will be an authenticated encryption of t. A constrained key for an identity id consists of a private constrained key for the function $f_{\mathsf{sk},\mathsf{id}}$ where $f_{\mathsf{sk},\mathsf{id}}(x) = 0$ whenever x is a valid encryption under sk of some index $t' > \mathsf{id}$, and is 1 otherwise. The (secret-key) sampling algorithm will first encrypt the target

index t under sk and output the resulting ciphertext ct_t together with the PRF evaluation at ct_t.
At a high-level, the security proof relies on the fact that a private constrained PRF hides the constraint function, which in this particular case, means that it hides the secret key sk. Then, normal hiding and identity hiding follows from the fact that ciphertexts are pseudorandom, and pseudorandomness follows from constrained security of the underlying constrained PRF. We give the full description and analysis in Sect. 5.
- **Collusion-resistant private linear constrained PRF with public-tracing.** Our second construction gives a fully collusion resistant private linear constrained PRF that supports public tracing from indistinguishability obfuscation and injective one-way functions. By the recent breakthrough work of Jain et al. [JLS21], both assumptions hold assuming the existence of a PRG in NC^0 together with the LWE, LPN, and SXDH assumptions. The high-level idea is very similar to our secret-key scheme above. Namely, the domain elements are ciphertexts in a (puncturable) public-key encryption scheme [CHN+16], and the identity keys consist of an obfuscated program with the decryption key hard-wired within it. To publicly sample inputs/outputs of the PRF (needed for public tracing), we provide an obfuscated program with a (puncturable) PRF key hard-wired within. We provide the details and analysis in Sect. 6.

An Application: Secret-key Traitor Tracing. We note that our notion of traceable PRFs lends itself naturally to a secret-key traitor tracing scheme. For instance, we can take our encryption scheme to be standard nonce-based encryption with a PRF (i.e., to encrypt a message m, sample a random $r \leftarrow \{0,1\}^n$ and compute the ciphertext $\mathsf{ct} = (r, m \oplus \mathsf{PRF}(k, r))$. If we instantiate the underlying PRF with a traceable PRF, then the resulting scheme immediately gives a traitor tracing scheme. Namely, any decoder that is able to distinguish between the encryption of two messages m_0 and m_1 also necessarily is able to distinguish $\mathsf{PRF}(k, r)$ from uniformly random for a random choice of $r \leftarrow \{0,1\}^n$. The claim then follows by tracing security. We stress here that a similar notion would *not* follow if we replace PRF with a watermarkable PRF. Here, it is not clear how to translate a decoder D that is only able to distinguish between encryptions of two messages into an algorithm that is able to recover the full input/output behavior of the PRF on a noticeable fraction of the domain.

Comparison with Watermarkable PRFs. One distinction between traceable PRFs and watermarkable PRFs is that in our definition of a traceable PRF, the tracing key is sampled jointly with the PRF key. In classic definitions of watermarking, it is possible to have a single (fixed) tracing key for an entire family of PRFs. This means that it is possible to sample a PRF key and decide to mark it at a later point in time. As we discuss in Sect. 3.1, having a tracing key that depends on the PRF key is essential to realizing the strong security notions in a traceable PRF. In most practical scenarios, if one wanted to take advantage of watermarking for software protection, it seems reasonable for them to sample the PRF key together with the marked key(s). Thus this distinction does not seem significant in practice, and we believe that the stronger and meaningful security notions achieved by traceable PRFs makes it a far more suitable primitive than a watermarkable PRF in any realistic environment.

1.2 Related Work

Watermarking. Barak et al. [BGI+01,BGI+12] and Hopper et al. [HMW07] introduced the first rigorous mathematical frameworks for software watermarking that considered *arbitrary* adversarial strategies (i.e., the adversary is allowed to output an arbitrary circuit that preserves the input-output behavior of the original program). Cohen et al. [CHN+16] provided the first construction of a watermarking scheme for PRFs using indistinguishability obfuscation. Earlier works on watermarking [NSS99,YF11,Nis13] imposed additional restrictions on the adversary's capabilities. Several works have also studied watermarking public-key cryptographic primitives [CHN+16,BKS17,GKM+19,Nis20]. Here, the work of Goyal et al. [GKM+19] expanded watermarking security definitions (in the public-key setting) to include adversaries that are able to break the "semantics" of a scheme (as opposed to just the set of adversaries that preserve exact input/output behavior).

Traitor Tracing. The notion of traitor tracing was first proposed by Chor et al. [CFN94] for solving the piracy problem in broadcast systems. Since then, numerous relaxations have been studied in order to achieve short ciphertexts. Broadly these can be categorized as follows: schemes where the traceability guarantees hold as long as the adversary corrupts an a priori bounded number of users and schemes where the guarantees hold as long as the adversary's decoder succeeds with probability greater than an a priori threshold. The former relaxation leads to traitor tracing schemes in the bounded collusion setting where we have numerous constructions via combinatorial tools [CFN94,SW98,CFNP00,SSW01,PST06,BP08] as well as a variety of cryptographic assumptions [KD98,BF99,KY02a,KY02b,CPP05,ADM+07,FNP07, LPSS14,NWZ16,ABP+17]. The latter schemes are typically referred to as "threshold traitor tracing" [NP98,CFNP00,BN08]. In another line of work, [GKRW18] considered schemes with a relaxed tracing guarantee: namely, the tracing algorithm does not need to be succeed in all cases. Recently, there has been significant progress on constructing fully collusion-resistant compact traitor tracing schemes from standard lattice assumptions [GKW18,GKW19a]. Since then, a sequence of works has built new traitor tracing systems with more functionality from standard cryptographic assumptions [CVW+18,GQWW19, GKW19b,KW20].

2 Preliminaries

We write PPT to denote probabilistic polynomial-time. We denote the set of all positive integers up to n as $[n] := \{1, \ldots, n\}$. Throughout this paper, unless specified otherwise, all polynomials we consider are positive polynomials. For any finite set S, $x \leftarrow S$ denotes a uniformly random element x from the set S. Similarly, for any distribution $\mathcal{D}$, $x \leftarrow \mathcal{D}$ denotes an element x drawn from distribution $\mathcal{D}$. The distribution $\mathcal{D}^n$ is used to represent a distribution over vectors of n components, where each component is drawn independently from the distribution $\mathcal{D}$.

For (possibly randomized) algorithms $\mathcal{A}$ and D, we use the notation A^D to denote that algorithm $\mathcal{A}$ has oracle access to algorithm D. Here, if the algorithm D is stateless, then on each query made by $\mathcal{A}$ to D, the oracle responds with a randomly drawn sample from the corresponding output distribution. If the algorithm D is stateful, then whenever $\mathcal{A}$ queries the oracle D, it can choose to either suspend the current execution of the oracle D or to continue executing D while it maintains its state. If D terminates after receiving an input, then it sends the final output of the computation as its query response to $\mathcal{A}$.

Pseudorandom Generator. A pseudorandom generator $\mathsf{PRG}\colon \{0,1\}^\lambda \to \{0,1\}^\ell$ is secure if for every PPT adversary $\mathcal{A}$, there exists a negligible function $\mathsf{negl}(\cdot)$ such that

$$\Pr\left[\mathcal{A}(t_b) = b \ : \ \begin{array}{c} s \leftarrow \{0,1\}^\lambda, t_0 \leftarrow \mathsf{PRG}(s) \\ t_1 \leftarrow \{0,1\}^\ell, b \leftarrow \{0,1\} \end{array}\right] \leq \frac{1}{2} + \mathsf{negl}(\lambda).$$

3 Defining Traceable PRFs

In this section, we formally introduce our notion of a *traceable* PRF.

Syntax. A traceable PRF scheme, with input-output space $\mathcal{X} = \{\mathcal{X}_{\lambda,\kappa}\}_{\lambda,\kappa\in\mathbb{N}}$ and $\mathcal{Y} = \{\mathcal{Y}_{\lambda,\kappa}\}_{\lambda,\kappa\in\mathbb{N}}$[5], consists of the following four algorithms:

$\mathsf{Setup}(1^\lambda, 1^\kappa) \to (\mathsf{msk}, \mathsf{tk})$. The setup algorithm takes as input the security parameter λ, the "'identity space" parameter κ, and outputs a master PRF key msk and a tracing key tk.

$\mathsf{KeyGen}(\mathsf{msk}, \mathsf{id}) \to \mathsf{sk}_{\mathsf{id}}$. The key generation algorithm takes as input the master key and an identity $\mathsf{id} \in \{0,1\}^\kappa$. It outputs a secret key $\mathsf{sk}_{\mathsf{id}}$.

$\mathsf{Eval}(\mathsf{sk}, x) \to y$. The decryption algorithm takes as input a secret key sk (which could be the master key), input $x \in \mathcal{X}$, and outputs $y \in \mathcal{Y}$.

$\mathsf{Trace}^D(\mathsf{tk}, 1^z) \to T \subseteq \{0,1\}^\kappa$. The tracing algorithm has oracle access to a program D, it takes as input the tracing key tk, parameter z, and it outputs a set T of identities.

[5] Throughout the paper, we drop the dependence of spaces $\mathcal{X}_{\lambda,\kappa}$ and $\mathcal{Y}_{\lambda,\kappa}$ on security parameter λ and identity length parameter κ whenever clear from context.

Weak Pseudorandomness. Below we define the weak pseudorandomness property for traceable PRFs.

Definition 3.1 (Weak pseudorandomness). *A traceable PRF scheme* $\mathsf{Tr\text{-}PRF} = (\mathsf{Setup}, \mathsf{KeyGen}, \mathsf{Eval}, \mathsf{Trace})$ *satisfies weak pseudorandomness property if for every stateful PPT adversary* $\mathcal{A}$, *there exists a negligible function* $\mathsf{negl}(\cdot)$ *such that for all* $\lambda \in \mathbb{N}$, *the following holds*

$$\Pr\left[\mathcal{A}^{O_b(\mathsf{msk})} = b : \begin{array}{c} 1^\kappa \leftarrow \mathcal{A}(1^\lambda), b \leftarrow \{0,1\} \\ (\mathsf{msk}, \mathsf{tk}) \leftarrow \mathsf{Setup}(1^\lambda, 1^\kappa) \end{array}\right] \leq \frac{1}{2} + \mathsf{negl}(\lambda),$$

where the oracle $O_b(\mathsf{msk})$ *is defined as follows: if* $b = 0$, *then on each evaluation query made by adversary* $\mathcal{A}$, *the oracle samples random input* $x \leftarrow \mathcal{X}$ *and sends* $(x, \mathsf{Eval}(\mathsf{msk}, x))$ *to* $\mathcal{A}$; *otherwise, if* $b = 1$, *then on each evaluation query made by adversary* $\mathcal{A}$, *the oracle samples random input* $x \leftarrow \mathcal{X}$ *and sends* $(x, f(x))$ *to* $\mathcal{A}$ *where* $f : \mathcal{X} \rightarrow \mathcal{Y}$ *is a random function.*[6]

Key-similarity Property. Informally, the key-similarity property says that the marked key is functionally equivalent to the original unmarked key on all but a negligible fraction of inputs. Formally, we define the property as follows:

Definition 3.2 (Key similarity). *A traceable PRF scheme* $\mathsf{Tr\text{-}PRF} = (\mathsf{Setup}, \mathsf{KeyGen}, \mathsf{Eval}, \mathsf{Trace})$ *satisfies key-similarity if there exists a negligible function* $\mathsf{negl}(\cdot)$ *such that for all* $\lambda, \kappa \in \mathbb{N}$, *identity* $\mathsf{id} \in \{0,1\}^\kappa$, $(\mathsf{msk}, \mathsf{tk}) \leftarrow \mathsf{Setup}(1^\lambda, 1^\kappa)$, *the following holds*

$$\Pr\left[\mathsf{Eval}(\mathsf{msk}, x) \neq \mathsf{Eval}(\mathsf{sk}_{\mathsf{id}}, x) : \begin{array}{c} \mathsf{sk}_{\mathsf{id}} \leftarrow \mathsf{KeyGen}(\mathsf{msk}, \mathsf{id}) \\ x \leftarrow \mathcal{X} \end{array}\right] \leq \mathsf{negl}(\lambda).$$

We note that while the marked keys agree with the unmarked key almost everywhere, it may still be easy for an adversary to efficiently find a point on which they differ. Thus, we can consider a strengthening of the property called "key indistinguishability" which we introduce next.

Key-indistinguishability Property. Informally, the key-indistinguishability property states that it should be hard for any PPT adversary to *find* inputs where the marked key (for an identity of the adversary's choosing) disagrees with the unmarked key. Formally, we define key indistinguishability as follows:

Definition 3.3 (Key indistinguishability). *A traceable PRF scheme* $\mathsf{Tr\text{-}PRF} = (\mathsf{Setup}, \mathsf{KeyGen}, \mathsf{Eval}, \mathsf{Trace})$ *satisfies key indistinguishability if for every stateful PPT adversary* $\mathcal{A}$, *there exists a negligible function* $\mathsf{negl}(\cdot)$ *such that for all* $\lambda \in \mathbb{N}$, *the following holds*

$$\Pr\left[\mathsf{Eval}(\mathsf{msk}, x) \neq \mathsf{Eval}(\mathsf{sk}^*, x) : \begin{array}{c} 1^\kappa \leftarrow \mathcal{A}(1^\lambda), (\mathsf{msk}, \mathsf{tk}) \leftarrow \mathsf{Setup}(1^\lambda, 1^\kappa) \\ (x, \mathsf{idx}, \mathsf{id}^*) \leftarrow \mathcal{A}^{\mathsf{Eval}(\mathsf{msk}, \cdot), \mathsf{KeyGen}(\mathsf{msk}, \cdot)} \end{array}\right] \leq \mathsf{negl}(\lambda),$$

[6] Note that instead of actually sampling a random function, the challenger simulates it by sampling random input-output pairs on the fly and storing them in a table.

where sk^* *is defined as*

$$\mathsf{sk}^* = \begin{cases} \mathsf{sk}^{(\mathsf{idx})} & \text{if } \mathsf{idx} \neq \bot \\ \mathsf{sk}_{\mathsf{id}^*} \leftarrow \mathsf{KeyGen}(\mathsf{msk}, \mathsf{id}^*) & \text{otherwise}, \end{cases}$$

and $\mathsf{sk}^{(\ell)}$ *denotes the* ℓ^{th} *key* $\mathcal{A}$ *submits to the key-generation oracle.*

Remark 3.4 (Key similarity vs. key indistinguishability). It is easy to see that key indistinguishability is a *strictly stronger* property than key similarity. As a result, this property is only achievable in the *secret-tracing* setting. As we define more formally below, our tracing algorithm only has *oracle* access to the adversary's distinguishing circuit. If this tracing algorithm can be run publicly, then it must be the case that the tracing algorithm must be able to efficiently find *some* input where the unmarked key and the marked key differ. Otherwise, it cannot distinguish between the two keys given just oracle access to the evaluation algorithm.

In the full version of this paper [GKWW20], we also describe a weaker notion of key indistinguishability that we consider in some of our constructions.

Secure Tracing. The secure tracing property states that if any PPT adversary creates a successful PRF distinguisher with respect to a master key, then the tracing algorithm, when provided with the PRF distinguisher, outputs the identity of at least one corrupted secret key, while never outputting the identity of an uncorrupt secret key. We define secure tracing as follows:

Definition 3.5 (Secure tracing). *Let* $\mathsf{Tr\text{-}PRF} = (\mathsf{Setup}, \mathsf{KeyGen}, \mathsf{Eval}, \mathsf{Trace})$ *be a traceable PRF scheme. For any nonnegligible function* $\varepsilon(\cdot)$, *polynomial* $p(\cdot)$ *and PPT adversary* $\mathcal{A}$, *we define the tracing experiment* $\mathsf{ExptTPRF}^{\mathsf{Tr\text{-}PRF}}_{\mathcal{A},\varepsilon}(\lambda)$ *in Fig. 2. Based on* $\mathsf{ExptTPRF}^{\mathsf{Tr\text{-}PRF}}_{\mathcal{A},\varepsilon}$, *we define the following set of (probabilistic) events and their corresponding probabilities (which are a functions of* λ *and parameterized by* $\mathcal{A}, \varepsilon$*):*

- $\mathsf{Good\text{-}Dis}$: $\Pr\left[D^{O_b(\mathsf{msk})}(1^\lambda) = b \;:\; b \leftarrow \{0,1\}\right] \geq \frac{1}{2} + \varepsilon(\lambda)$,
  where the probability is taken over the coins of D, *and oracle* $O_b(\mathsf{msk})$ *is exactly as defined in Definition 3.1.*
  Intuitively, this says that a distinguisher D *is an* ε*-good distinguisher if* D *can break weak pseudorandomness of the underlying PRF with advantage* $\varepsilon = \varepsilon(\lambda)$.
  $\Pr\text{-}\mathsf{G\text{-}D}_{\mathcal{A},\varepsilon}(\lambda) = \Pr[\mathsf{Good\text{-}Dis}]$.
- $\mathsf{Cor\text{-}Tr}$: $T \neq \varnothing \wedge T \subseteq S_{\mathcal{ID}}$
  This event corresponds to the tracing algorithm successfully outputting one or more of the keys the adversary possesses.
  $\Pr\text{-}\mathsf{Cor\text{-}Tr}_{\mathcal{A},\varepsilon}(\lambda) = \Pr[\mathsf{Cor\text{-}Tr}]$.
- $\mathsf{Fal\text{-}Tr}$: $T \not\subseteq S_{\mathcal{ID}}$
  This event corresponds to the tracing algorithm outputting a key that the adversary did not request (i.e., falsely implicating an honest user).
  $\Pr\text{-}\mathsf{Fal\text{-}Tr}_{\mathcal{A},\varepsilon}(\lambda) = \Pr[\mathsf{Fal\text{-}Tr}]$.

Experiment $\mathsf{ExptTPRF}^{\mathsf{Tr\text{-}PRF}}_{\mathcal{A},\varepsilon}(\lambda)$

- $1^\kappa \leftarrow \mathcal{A}(1^\lambda)$.
- $(\mathsf{msk}, \mathsf{tk}) \leftarrow \mathsf{Setup}(1^\lambda, 1^\kappa)$.
- $D \leftarrow \mathcal{A}^{\mathsf{Eval}(\mathsf{msk},\cdot),\mathsf{KeyGen}(\mathsf{msk},\cdot),\mathsf{SplEval}(\mathsf{msk},\cdot,\cdot)}$.
- $T \leftarrow \mathsf{Trace}^D(\mathsf{tk}, 1^{1/\varepsilon(\lambda)})$.

Let $S_{\mathcal{ID}}$ be the set of identities queried by $\mathcal{A}$ to the key generation oracle $\mathsf{KeyGen}(\mathsf{msk},\cdot)$. Here, $\mathsf{SplEval}$ denotes a *special evaluation* algorithm that is defined as a randomized oracle algorithm that has msk hardwired, takes as input an identity $\mathsf{id} \in \{0,1\}^\kappa$, a string $x \in \mathcal{X}$, and outputs $y = \mathsf{Eval}(\mathsf{sk}_{\mathsf{id}}, x)$ where $\mathsf{sk}_{\mathsf{id}} \leftarrow \mathsf{KeyGen}(\mathsf{msk}, \mathsf{id})$. We discuss the rationale for this oracle in Remark 3.7.

Fig. 2. Experiment $\mathsf{ExptTPRF}$

A traceable PRF scheme Tr-PRF *(with secret-key tracing) is said to satisfy secure tracing property if for every PPT adversary $\mathcal{A}$, polynomial $q(\cdot)$, and non-negligible function $\varepsilon(\cdot)$, there exists a negligible function* $\mathsf{negl}(\cdot)$ *such that for all $\lambda \in \mathbb{N}$ satisfying $\varepsilon(\lambda) > 1/q(\lambda)$, the following two properties hold:*

$$\Pr\text{-}\mathsf{Fal\text{-}Tr}_{\mathcal{A},\varepsilon}(\lambda) \leq \mathsf{negl}(\lambda) \text{ and } \Pr\text{-}\mathsf{Cor\text{-}Tr}_{\mathcal{A},\varepsilon}(\lambda) \geq \Pr\text{-}\mathsf{G\text{-}D}_{\mathcal{A},\varepsilon}(\lambda) - \mathsf{negl}(\lambda).$$

Intuitively, the first property states that the tracing algorithm cannot falsely implicate an honest user with non-negligible probability and the second property requires that whenever D is a ε-good distinguisher, then the tracing algorithm correctly traces at least one corrupt user.

Remark 3.6 (Security for publicly-traceable PRFs). A traceable PRF scheme with public-tracing is defined identically to its secret-tracing counterpart, except now the adversary is additionally provided the tracing key tk in all of the security games. In the public-tracing setting, we require the scheme to satisfy weak pseudorandomness, key similarity, and the secure public tracing property (but not key indistinguishability; see Remark 3.4).

Remark 3.7 (Special evaluation oracle SplEval*).* In our tracing experiment, we allow an attacker to not only corrupt keys for different users, but also query for PRF evaluations under keys of *non-corrupt* users on inputs of the adversary's choosing. Although providing access to this "special evaluation" oracle SplEval is not necessary for applications of traceable PRFs to traitor tracing systems, we include this as part of our definition to cover a broader class of adversarial strategies. For instance, this definition captures adversaries that may passively observe interactions between honest users using their respective identity keys. Our definition says that even if the adversary can see (polynomially-many) such evaluations, they cannot construct a distinguisher that evades the tracing algorithm (nor can they cause the tracing algorithm to implicate one of the honest users). Thus, by allowing the adversary access to such an oracle, the definition provides security even against these much powerful adversaries.

Also, one could possibly have a seemingly stronger mechanism for capturing the special evaluation oracle where now it will be a stateful oracle and the adversary can ask the oracle to either sample (and store) a fresh key followed by evaluation with respect to the sampled key, or answer a evaluation query with respect to a previously-sampled key. Although this might seem like a stronger definition, this is not necessary since we can always assume without loss of generality that key generation algorithm is deterministic (by using a standard PRF for derandomization).

3.1 Note on Weak Pseudorandomness and Other Definitional Choices

In this section, we briefly discuss and motivate the definitional choices for our traceable PRF notion.

On Weak Pseudorandomness. In our definitional framework above, we focus on *weak pseudorandomness* as the target for both PRF security as well as the class of distinguishers against which we provide the tracing guarantee. There are a few technical reasons for the above choice. First, observe that it is impossible for a traceable PRF to be a secure PRF in the standard sense (i.e., appear pseudorandom on adversarially-chosen inputs) while also providing tracing guarantees against distinguishers that only break pseudorandomness in the standard sense. This is because in such a scenario, the adversary can construct an untraceable distinguisher by simply hardwiring a *single* PRF input-output pair (on a random input) and use that to claim that it is a valid distinguisher. Such a distinguisher can break the standard PRF game with advantage close to 1 by querying on its hard-wired input, and yet, no tracing algorithm can succeed here (since with overwhelming probability, the single input-output pair chosen by the adversary coincides with the real PRF evaluation on that input, and thus, cannot contain any information about an embedded identity).

Another possibility could be to allow the distinguisher to make arbitrary evaluation queries to the PRF, but the challenge point would still be chosen randomly. While this is a meaningful notion, this causes problems when defining publicly-traceable PRFs. Under this definition, the tracing algorithm would need the actual code of the distinguisher, as opposed to only requiring *oracle access* to the distinguisher. This is because under this definition, the tracing algorithm would need a way to respond to the distinguisher's evaluation queries (in order to use the distinguisher at tracing time). But if the distinguisher can make arbitrary PRF evaluation queries that the *public* tracing algorithm can answer, then the tracing algorithm can be used to break pseudorandomness. Consequently, this model is only achievable in the setting where the public tracing algorithm has access to the code of the distinguisher. In this work, we focus on settings where tracing can be done just given *black-box* access to the decoder. Note that if we restrict ourselves to weak pseudorandomness, then there is no inherent contradiction; namely, a public tracing key only needs to provide an ability to sample random input-output evaluations of the PRF. Using indistinguishability obfuscation, we can realize this by publishing an obfuscated program that can sample input-output evaluations from a *sparse* pseudorandom subset of the domain and which does not compromise standard pseudorandomness.

A third possibility is to consider secure tracing against distinguishers which only break weak pseudorandomness, while requiring the PRF to achieve (regular) pseudorandomness security. Although this is not impossible (and our current constructions can be shown to satisfy this property), we decided to simply consider weak pseudorandomness security for PRF security since that yields a *unified* definitional framework and sufficed for many applications. Basically our intuition here is to avoid *unevenness* between the target pseudorandomness security for PRF security and the class of distinguishers against which we provide secure traceability.

Joint Sampling of Tracing and PRF Keys. Lastly, our definitions assume that the tracing key is generated together with a PRF master key (via the Setup algorithm). That is, each PRF key is associated with a specific tracing key. An alternate definition could be to sample a *single* tracing key during the system setup, and then PRF keys could be sampled independent of the tracing key. This is the setting encountered in the context of watermarking PRFs [CHN+16]. However PRFs are a *symmetric-key* primitive. This means that in this scenario, the tracing algorithm would either need a description of the master PRF key to run the tracing algorithm, or the PRF setup must non-trivially depend on the tracing key itself. In the former case, it seems very restrictive since now the tracing party needs to know the full master key which may not be accessible in most applications. As to the latter case, it is not clear whether it provides any more functionality compared to our current definition. Therefore, we decided to consider a single joint setup for sampling the master PRF key as well as the tracing parameters as done in prior works on traitor tracing for public-key encryption systems [BSW06, NWZ16, GKRW18, GKW19a].

4 Traceable PRFs via Private Linear Constrained PRFs

In this section, we introduce an intermediate abstraction, that we call private linear constrained PRFs (PLCPRFs), towards building a traceable PRF scheme. This primitive mirrors the notion of private linear broadcast encryption (PLBE) [BSW06] from traitor tracing literature where PLBE was used as a useful abstraction for building general traitor tracing systems. We first present the syntax and security definitions for PLCPRFs, and later show that PLCPRFs lead to traceable PRFs.

4.1 Defining Private Linear CPRFs

Syntax. A private linear CPRF scheme with input-output space $\mathcal{X} = \{\mathcal{X}_{\lambda,\kappa}\}_{\lambda,\kappa\in\mathbb{N}}$ and $\mathcal{Y} = \{\mathcal{Y}_{\lambda,\kappa}\}_{\lambda,\kappa\in\mathbb{N}}$[7] consists of the following four algorithms:

$\mathsf{Setup}(1^\lambda, 1^\kappa) \to (\mathsf{msk}, \mathsf{tk})$. The setup algorithm takes as input the security parameter λ, the "identity space" parameter κ, and outputs a master PRF key msk and a tracing key tk.

$\mathsf{KeyGen}(\mathsf{msk}, \mathsf{id}) \to \mathsf{sk}_{\mathsf{id}}$. The key generation algorithm takes as input the master key and an identity $\mathsf{id} \in \{0,1\}^\kappa$. It outputs a secret key $\mathsf{sk}_{\mathsf{id}}$.[8]

$\mathsf{Eval}(\mathsf{sk}, x) \to y$. The decryption algorithm takes as input a secret key sk (which could be the master key), input $x \in \mathcal{X}$, and outputs $y \in \mathcal{Y}$.

$\mathsf{Samp}(\mathsf{tk}, t) \to (x, y)$. The sampling algorithm takes as input the tracing key tk, a threshold $t \in [0, 2^\kappa]$, and it outputs a input-output pair $(x, y) \in \mathcal{X} \times \mathcal{Y}$.

Key Similarity and Key Indistinguishability. We define key similarity and key indistinguishability for PLCPRFs to be identical to that for traceable PRFs as in Definitions 3.2 and 3.3.

Security. We now introduce some useful security properties for PLCPRFs that will be useful for constructing traceable PRFs. Intuitively, the properties can be stated as follows. The first property is called the *normal hiding* property which states that for any PPT adversary, it should be hard to distinguish whether an input string x is sampled uniformly at random from the full domain $\mathcal{X}$, or if it is sampled uniformly at random using the sample algorithm for threshold 0 (that is, as $(x, y) \leftarrow \mathsf{Samp}(\mathsf{tk}, 0)$). The second property is called the *identity hiding* property which states that an input string x should also hide the threshold t corresponding to which it is sampled as long as the adversary cannot trivially learn it by simply evaluating at x using its secret keys. Lastly, we define the *pseudorandomness* property which states that the PRF output on input strings sampled corresponding to threshold 2^κ are pseudorandom. Formally, we define each notion similar to the corresponding set of PLBE definitions from [BSW06, GKW18, GKW19a]. However, in our setting, we allow the adversary to make an *a priori unbounded* number of oracle queries, which will be essential to our construction of traceable PRFs from PLCPRFs. In the public-key setting, handling a single encryption query is sufficient to construct traitor tracing.

[7] As mentioned previously, we drop the dependence on λ, κ whenever clear from context.

[8] This could also be viewed as a "constrain" algorithm (in the language of constrained PRFs [BW13, KPTZ13, BGI14]), but there are some semantic differences. As such, we refer to this algorithm as a "key-generation" algorithm instead.

Definition 4.1 (Normal hiding). *A PLCPRF scheme is said to satisfy normal hiding if for every stateful PPT adversary $\mathcal{A}$, there exists a negligible function* $\mathsf{negl}(\cdot)$ *such that for every $\lambda \in \mathbb{N}$, the following holds:*

$$\Pr\left[\mathcal{A}^{\mathsf{S}(\cdot),\mathsf{E}(\cdot),\mathsf{K}(\cdot),\mathsf{SIE}(\cdot,\cdot)}(x_b) = b \;:\; \begin{array}{c} 1^\kappa \leftarrow \mathcal{A}(1^\lambda); (\mathsf{msk},\mathsf{tk}) \leftarrow \mathsf{Setup}(1^\lambda, 1^\kappa) \\ b \leftarrow \{0,1\};\; x_0 \leftarrow \mathcal{X} \\ (x_1, y_1) \leftarrow \mathsf{Samp}(\mathsf{tk}, 0) \end{array}\right] \le \frac{1}{2} + \mathsf{negl}(\lambda),$$

where the oracles $\mathsf{S},\mathsf{E},\mathsf{K},\mathsf{SIE}$ *are defined as follows:*

- $\mathsf{S}(\cdot) = \mathsf{Samp}(\mathsf{tk}, \cdot)$ *is the sampling oracle with* tk *hardwired,*
- $\mathsf{E}(\cdot) = \mathsf{Eval}(\mathsf{msk}, \cdot)$ *is the evaluation oracle with* msk *hardwired,*
- $\mathsf{K}(\cdot) = \mathsf{KeyGen}(\mathsf{msk}, \cdot)$ *is the key-generation oracle with* msk *hardwired, and*
- $\mathsf{SIE}(\cdot,\cdot)$ *is a randomized oracle that has* msk *hardwired, takes as input an identity* $\mathsf{id} \in \{0,1\}^\kappa$, *a string $x \in \mathcal{X}$, and outputs* $y = \mathsf{Eval}(\mathsf{sk}_{\mathsf{id}}, x)$ *where* $\mathsf{sk}_{\mathsf{id}} \leftarrow \mathsf{KeyGen}(\mathsf{msk}, \mathsf{id})$.

Definition 4.2 (Identity hiding). *A PLCPRF scheme is said to satisfy identity hiding if for every stateful PPT adversary $\mathcal{A}$, there exists a negligible function* $\mathsf{negl}(\cdot)$ *such that for every $\lambda \in \mathbb{N}$, the following holds:*

$$\Pr\left[\mathcal{A}^{\mathsf{S}(\cdot),\mathsf{E}(\cdot),\mathsf{K}(\cdot),\mathsf{SIE}(\cdot,\cdot)}(x) = b \;:\; \begin{array}{c} 1^\kappa \leftarrow \mathcal{A}(1^\lambda); (\mathsf{msk},\mathsf{tk}) \leftarrow \mathsf{Setup}(1^\lambda, 1^\kappa) \\ (t_0, t_1) \leftarrow \mathcal{A}^{\mathsf{S}(\cdot),\mathsf{E}(\cdot),\mathsf{K}(\cdot),\mathsf{SIE}(\cdot,\cdot)} \\ b \leftarrow \{0,1\};\; (x, y) \leftarrow \mathsf{Samp}(\mathsf{tk}, t_b) \end{array}\right] \le \frac{1}{2} + \mathsf{negl}(\lambda),$$

where the oracles are defined as in Definition 4.1, and $\mathcal{A}$ must not query oracle SIE *on the input-identity pair* (x, id) *where* $\mathsf{id} \in [t_0, t_1 - 1]$, *and each query* id *made by $\mathcal{A}$ to the key-generation oracle* K *must satisfy the condition that* $\mathsf{id} \notin [t_0, t_1 - 1]$.[9] *We say the PLCPRF scheme satisfies* selective *identity hiding if the adversary has to commit to its challenge identities (t_0, t_1) at the* beginning *of the game before it makes any oracle queries. Note that selective security implies adaptive security at the expense of a sub-exponential loss in the security reduction via a technique called complexity leveraging [BB04].*

Definition 4.3 (Pseudorandomness). *A PLCPRF scheme is said to satisfy pseudorandomness if for every stateful PPT adversary $\mathcal{A}$, there exists a negligible function* $\mathsf{negl}(\cdot)$ *such that for every $\lambda \in \mathbb{N}$, the following holds:*

$$\Pr\left[\mathcal{A}^{\mathsf{S}(\cdot),\mathsf{E}(\cdot),\mathsf{K}(\cdot),\mathsf{SIE}(\cdot,\cdot)}(x, y_b) = b \;:\; \begin{array}{c} 1^\kappa \leftarrow \mathcal{A}(1^\lambda); (\mathsf{msk},\mathsf{tk}) \leftarrow \mathsf{Setup}(1^\lambda, 1^\kappa) \\ b \leftarrow \{0,1\};\; (x, y_0) \leftarrow \mathsf{Samp}(\mathsf{tk}, 2^\kappa);\; y_1 \leftarrow \mathcal{Y} \end{array}\right] \le \frac{1}{2} + \mathsf{negl}(\lambda),$$

[9] Here and throughout, the κ-bit identities are interpreted as non-negative integers between 0 and $2^\kappa - 1$ for comparison.

where the oracles are defined as in Definition 4.1, $\mathcal{A}$ cannot query oracle SIE *on the input-identity pair* $(x, 2^\kappa)$*, and* $\mathcal{A}$ *cannot query the evaluation oracle* E *on input* x.

Remark 4.4 (Multi-challenge security). For security of PLCPRFs, we consider three properties (normal hiding, identity hiding, and pseudorandomness). Note that in each of Definitions 4.1 to 4.3, we consider a single-challenge variant which means that the adversary gets to see exactly one challenge element. For instance, in the normal hiding game it gets a single challenge x_b which is either a random input or an input sampled corresponding to threshold 0.

Consider a multi-challenge variant of these security properties where the adversary instead gets unbounded access to a challenge oracle, where the challenge oracle on each query provides a fresh sample from the corresponding challenge distribution. For instance, in the multi-challenge version of normal hiding, the adversary gets oracle access to a challenge oracle where on every query, the challenger provides a freshly sampled input x_b which is either a random input or an input sampled for threshold 0. (Here, the challenge bit b is chosen only once.) In our transformation provided in Sect. 4.2, we will rely on this multi-challenge variant of the security game. Note that single-challenge and multi-challenge definitions are equivalent since the adversary is given unbounded oracle access to the sampling oracle S in these games already. This follows from a standard hybrid argument.

Remark 4.5 (Security for publicly-sampleable PLCPRFs). Similar to that for traceable PRFs, a PLCPRF with public-sampleability is defined identically to its secret-key counterpart, except now the attacker is additionally provided the tracing key tk in all the security games.

Remark 4.6 (Single-key security). In some settings, we will consider private linear constrained PRFs where the security properties (Definitions 4.1 and 4.3) only hold against adversaries that can make a *single* key-generation query. We refer to such schemes as single-key private linear constrained PRFs. In the single-key setting, we also consider the *selective* notion of security where the adversary is required to commit to its key-generation query at the beginning of the security game (before making any oracle queries or in the case of the public-tracing setting, seeing the tracing key). Note that selective single-key security implies the standard adaptive single-key security at the expense of making a stronger sub-exponential hardness assumption via complexity leveraging [BB04].

4.2 Building Traceable PRFs

In this section, we show how to build a traceable PRF scheme from a private linear CPRF scheme. First, we recall the 'jump-finding' problem introduced in the work of Nishimaki et al. [NWZ16]. Later on, we describe our construction.

Definition 4.7 (Noisy jump finding problem *[NWZ16, Definition 3.6]***).** *The* $(N, q, \delta, \varepsilon)$*-jump-finding problem is defined as follows. An adversary chooses* *a set $C \subseteq [N]$ of q unknown points. Then, the adversary provides an oracle $P\colon [0,N] \to [0,1]_{\mathcal{R}}$ with the following properties:*

- $|P(N) - P(0)| \geq \varepsilon$.
- *For any $x, y \in [0,N]$ where $x < y$ and $[x+1, y] \cap C = \varnothing$, then $|P(y) - P(x)| < \delta$.*

*The $(N, q, \delta, \varepsilon)$-jump finding problem is to interact with the oracle P and output an element in C. In the $(N, q, \delta, \varepsilon)$-*noisy jump finding problem, *the oracle P is replaced with a randomized oracle $Q\colon [0,N] \to \{0,1\}$ where on input $x \in [0,N]$, $Q(x)$ outputs 1 with probability $P(x)$. A fresh independent draw is chosen for each query to $Q(x)$.*

Theorem 4.8 (Noisy jump finding algorithm *[NWZ16, Theorem 3.7]***).** *There is an efficient algorithm $\mathsf{QTrace}^Q(\lambda, N, q, \delta, \varepsilon)$ that runs in time $t = \mathsf{poly}(\lambda, \log N, q, 1/\delta)$ and makes at most t queries to Q that solves the $(N, q, \delta, \varepsilon)$-noisy-jump-finding problem whenever $\varepsilon > \delta(5 + 2(\lceil \log N - 1 \rceil)q)$. In particular, $\mathsf{QTrace}^Q(\lambda, N, q, \delta, \varepsilon)$ will output at least one element in C with probability $1 - \mathsf{negl}(\lambda)$ and will never output an element outside C. Moreover, any element x output by $\mathsf{QTrace}^Q(\lambda, N, q, \delta, \varepsilon)$ has the property that $P(x) - P(x-1) > \delta$, where $P(x) = \Pr[Q(x) = 1]$.*

Remark 4.9 (Relaxed non-intersection property [NWZ16, Remark 3.8]*).* The algorithm QTrace^Q in Theorem 4.8 succeeds in solving the $(N, q, \delta, \varepsilon)$-noisy-jump-finding problem even if the associated oracle P does not satisfy the second property in Definition 4.7: namely, there may exist x, y where $[x+1, y] \cap C = \varnothing$ and $|P(y) - P(x)| \geq \delta$. As long as the property holds for all pairs x, y queried by QTrace^Q, Theorem 4.8 applies.

Construction 4.10 (Traceable PRF). *Let* $\mathsf{PLCPRF} = (\mathsf{PL.Setup}, \mathsf{PL.KeyGen}, \mathsf{PL.Eval}, \mathsf{PL.Samp})$ *be a private linear CPRF scheme with input-output space $\mathcal{X}$ and $\mathcal{Y}$. Below we construct a traceable PRF scheme with identical input-output spaces. (Here we provide a transformation for PRF schemes with secret key tracing, but the construction can be easily extended to work in the public tracing setting if the special sampling algorithm in the underlying* PLCPRF *scheme is public key as well, that is tracing key* tk *is public).*

$\mathsf{Setup}(1^\lambda, 1^\kappa) \to (\mathsf{msk}, \mathsf{tk})$. *The setup algorithm runs the* PLCPRF *setup as* $(\mathsf{msk}, \mathsf{tk}) \leftarrow \mathsf{PL.Setup}(1^\lambda, 1^\kappa)$*, and outputs master secret-tracing key pair as* $(\mathsf{msk}, \mathsf{tk})$.

$\mathsf{KeyGen}(\mathsf{msk}, \mathsf{id}) \to \mathsf{sk}_{\mathsf{id}}$. *The key generation algorithm runs the* PLCPRF *key generation algorithm as* $\mathsf{sk}_{\mathsf{id}} \leftarrow \mathsf{PL.KeyGen}(\mathsf{msk}, \mathsf{id})$*, and outputs secret key* $\mathsf{sk}_{\mathsf{id}}$.

$\mathsf{Eval}(\mathsf{sk}, x) \to y$. *The evaluation algorithm runs the* PLCPRF *evaluation algorithm as* $y = \mathsf{PL.Eval}(\mathsf{sk}, x)$*, and outputs y.*

$\mathsf{Trace}^D(\mathsf{tk}, 1^z, q) \to T$. *The tracing algorithm runs the* QTrace *algorithm twice as* $T^{(\mathsf{real})} \leftarrow \mathsf{QTrace}^{Q_D^{(\mathsf{real})}}(\lambda, 2^\kappa, q, \delta, \varepsilon)$ *and* $T^{(\mathsf{rnd})} \leftarrow \mathsf{QTrace}^{Q_D^{(\mathsf{rnd})}}(\lambda, 2^\kappa, q, \delta, \varepsilon)$*, where $\delta = \varepsilon/(5 + 2\kappa q)$, $\varepsilon = 1/z$, and oracles $Q_D^{(\mathsf{real})}$ and $Q_D^{(\mathsf{rnd})}$ are described in Fig. 3. Finally, it outputs the set as* $T^{(\mathsf{real})} \cup T^{(\mathsf{rnd})}$.

On input $\tau \in [0, 2^\kappa]$, the oracle $Q_D^{(\mathsf{mode})}$ proceeds as follows:

- *Let* comp_τ *denote the comparison function that on input* inp*, outputs 1 if and only if* $\mathsf{inp} \geq \tau$.
- *Run the (stateful) oracle D, where on each query made by D the oracle Q_D samples an input-output pair as $(x, y) \leftarrow \mathsf{PL.Samp}(\mathsf{tk}, \tau)$. It samples a random output string $y' \leftarrow \mathcal{Y}$. If $\mathsf{mode} = \mathsf{real}$, it sends (x, y) as the query response to D. Otherwise, it sends (x, y') as the query response to D.*
- *Finally, D outputs a bit b, and oracle Q_D outputs the same bit b.*

Fig. 3. The distinguishing oracle $Q_D^{(\mathsf{mode})}$ for $\mathsf{mode} \in \{\mathsf{real}, \mathsf{rnd}\}$.

Remark 4.11 (Additional parameter q). Note that here the trace algorithm takes an additional parameter q. This is not an additional restriction since one could simply run the tracing algorithm increasingly with parameter q growing as successive powers of two as long as the tracing algorithm outputs an empty set. A similar approach was taken in prior works such as [NWZ16, GKW19b].

4.3 Security

In this section, we prove security of our construction. Formally, we prove the following.

Theorem 4.12 (Correctness). *If the PLCPRF scheme* $\mathsf{PLCPRF} = (\mathsf{PL.Setup}, \mathsf{PL.KeyGen}, \mathsf{PL.Eval}, \mathsf{PL.Samp})$ *satisfies the key-similarity (resp., key-indistinguishability) property (Definitions 3.2 and 3.3, respectively), then the scheme* $\mathcal{T} = (\mathsf{Setup}, \mathsf{KeyGen}, \mathsf{Eval}, \mathsf{Trace})$ *from Construction 4.10 also satisfies key-similarity (resp., key-indistinguishability).*

The above theorem follows directly from our construction. Next, we prove tracing security of our scheme.

Theorem 4.13 (Security). *If the scheme* $\mathsf{PLCPRF} = (\mathsf{PL.Setup}, \mathsf{PL.KeyGen}, \mathsf{PL.Eval}, \mathsf{PL.Samp})$ *satisfies normal hiding (Definition 4.1), identity hiding (Definition 4.2), and pseudorandomness (Definition 4.3) (resp., in the absence of* SIE *queries), then the scheme* $\mathcal{T} = (\mathsf{Setup}, \mathsf{KeyGen}, \mathsf{Eval}, \mathsf{Trace})$ *from Construction 4.10 is a secure traceable PRF scheme as per Definition 3.5 (resp., in the absence of* SIE *queries).*

We provide an overview of the security proof below and provide the full proof in the full version of this paper [GKWW20].

Proof Overview. We prove the theorem in two parts. First, we show that the false tracing probability is bounded by a negligible function. Next, we show the correct tracing probability is close to the probability of adversary outputting an ε-good distinguisher for some non-negligible ε.

We begin by introducing some notation for the overview. Fix some master secret-tracing key pair $(\mathsf{msk}, \mathsf{tk})$. Given any pirate distinguisher D and threshold $\tau \in [0, 2^\kappa]$, let

$$p^{\tau,D} = \Pr\left[D^{\mathsf{PL.Samp}(\mathsf{tk},\tau)}(1^\lambda) = 0\right] \text{ and } q^{\tau,D} = \Pr\left[D^{\widetilde{\mathsf{PL.Samp}}(\mathsf{tk},\tau)}(1^\lambda) = 0,\right]$$

where the oracle algorithm $\widetilde{\mathsf{PL.Samp}}$ is defined as the regular $\mathsf{PL.Samp}$ oracle algorithm, except the second tuple element (i.e., the output string) is sampled uniformly at random. Concretely, on each query to $\widetilde{\mathsf{PL.Samp}}(\mathsf{tk}, \tau)$, the oracle first samples $(x, y) \leftarrow \mathsf{PL.Samp}(\mathsf{tk}, \tau)$, $y' \leftarrow \mathcal{Y}$, and outputs (x, y') as the response. Here the probability is taken over the random coins of distinguisher D as well as the randomness used by the sample algorithm. Similarly, let

$$p^{\mathrm{nrml},D} = \Pr\left[D^{\mathsf{Real}(\mathsf{msk})}(1^\lambda) = 0\right], \text{ and } p^{\mathsf{rnd},D} = \Pr\left[D^{\mathsf{Rand}}(1^\lambda) = 0\right]$$

where oracle $\mathsf{Real}(\mathsf{msk})$ on each query, samples a random input $x \leftarrow \mathcal{X}$, and outputs $(x, \mathsf{Eval}(\mathsf{msk}, x))$ as the query response; whereas the oracle Rand is simulated by sampling by a random function $f : \mathcal{X} \to \mathcal{Y}$, and on each query, it samples a random input $x \leftarrow \mathcal{X}$, and outputs $(x, f(x)))$ as the query response. The above probabilities are also parameterized by the PLCPRF keys, but for simplicity of notation we do not include them as they are clear from context.

Now, suppose there exists a successful attacker $\mathcal{A}$. That is, $\mathcal{A}$ produces a distinguisher D^*, after making polynomially-many evaluation and key-generation queries, such that $p^{\mathrm{nrml},D^*} - p^{\mathsf{rnd},D^*} \geq 2\varepsilon$, and the tracing algorithm outputs either an empty set or an identity outside the set of identities queried by $\mathcal{A}$.[10] Let $\delta = \varepsilon/(5 + 2\kappa q)$ as used in the construction. Let γ^* denote the probability that the distinguisher D^* outputs 0 when given oracle access to a random function. Thus, we get that $p^{\mathrm{nrml},D^*} \geq \gamma^* + 2\varepsilon$. We first argue that it must also be the case that $p^{0,D^*} > \gamma^* + 2\varepsilon - \delta$, as otherwise we could use $\mathcal{A}$ to break the PLCPRF normal hiding property. Next, we also show that for any two thresholds $\tau_1 < \tau_2$, $p^{\tau_1,D^*} - p^{\tau_2,D^*} < \delta$ and $q^{\tau_2,D^*} - q^{\tau_1,D^*} < \delta$ as long as $\mathcal{A}$ does not make any key-generation query for an identity in the range $[\tau_1, \tau_2 - 1]$. This argument relies on the identity hiding property of the PLCPRFs. Next, we argue that $p^{2^\kappa,D^*} - q^{2^\kappa,D^*} < \delta$, as otherwise we could break the pseudorandomness security of the PLCPRFs. Lastly, we also argue that $q^{0,D^*} - p^{\mathsf{rnd},D^*} < \delta$, as otherwise we could break the PLCPRF normal hiding property. Combining these statements with the guarantees provided by the noisy jump finding algorithm (Theorem 4.8), we conclude that the tracing does not output an incorrect identity. □

[10] Recall that if D^* is a ε-good distinguisher, then we have the bound $\Pr\left[D^{*\mathcal{O}_b(\mathsf{msk})}(1^\lambda) = b \,:\, b \leftarrow \{0,1\}\right] \geq \varepsilon$. This can be rewritten as $p^{\mathrm{nrml},D^*} - p^{\mathsf{rnd},D^*} \geq 2\varepsilon$.

Remark 4.14 (Public-tracing and handling SIE *oracle queries).* In the proof of Theorem 4.13 above, we showed that Construction 4.10 gives a traceable PRF scheme with private tracing (which is secure in the absence of special evaluation oracle (SIE) queries), as long as the underlying PLCPRF scheme is privately-sampleable and secure in the absence of SIE queries. However, if the underlying PLCPRF scheme is either publicly-sampleable or secure in presence of SIE queries, or both, then the reduction algorithm described above easily extends to prove the construction described above to be publicly-traceable, or secure in presence of SIE queries, or both, respectively.

Remark 4.15 (Single-key security). In the proof of Theorem 4.13, the number of key-generation queries each of the reduction algorithms needs to make to the underlying private linear constrained PRF is equal to the number of key-generation queries the tracing adversary makes. Thus, if we have a single-key private linear constrained PRF (Remark 4.6), that implies a traceable PRF with security against adversaries that can only make a single key-generation query. In Sect. 5, we show how to construct a single-key private linear constrained PRF from standard lattice assumptions (using single-key private constrained PRFs) as a starting point. It is an open problem to construct a many-key (i.e., collusion-resistant) private linear constrained PRF (or a traceable PRF) from standard lattice assumptions. We can construct a fully collusion-resistant private linear constrained PRF from indistinguishability obfuscation and injective one-way functions (see Sect. 6).

5 Privately-Traceable Private Linear Constrained PRFs

In this section, we show how to construct a single-key private linear constrained PRF from a private constrained PRF (for general circuit constraints) and an authenticated encryption scheme. Together with Construction 4.10, this yields a single-key traceable PRF in the private-tracing setting (and without access to the SIE) from standard lattice assumptions (namely, on the sub-exponential hardness of LWE with a sub-exponential modulus-to-noise ratio). We define private constrained PRFs below and provide the formal definitions of authenticated encryption in the full version of this paper [GKWW20].

5.1 Private Constrained PRFs

Syntax. A private constrained PRF with input space $\mathcal{X}$, output-space $\mathcal{Y}$, and constraint family $\mathcal{F} = \{\mathcal{F}_{\lambda,\kappa}\}_{\lambda,\kappa \in \mathbb{N}}$ where $\mathcal{F}_{\lambda,\kappa} = \{f : \mathcal{X} \to \{0,1\}\}$ consists of the following algorithms:

$\mathsf{Setup}(1^\lambda, 1^\kappa) \to \mathsf{msk}$. The setup algorithm takes as input the security parameter λ and a constraint-family parameter κ and outputs a master PRF key msk.

$\mathsf{Constrain}(\mathsf{msk}, f) \to \mathsf{sk}_f$. The constrain algorithm takes as input the master secret key msk and a constraint $f \in \mathcal{F}_{\lambda,\kappa}$ and outputs a constrained key sk_f.

$\mathsf{Eval}(\mathsf{sk}, x) \to y$. The evaluation algorithm takes as input a secret key sk (which could be the master secret key msk) and an input $x \in \mathcal{X}$ and outputs a value $y \in \mathcal{Y}$.

Correctness and Security. We describe the correctness and security definitions for a private constrained PRF in the full version of this paper [GKWW20].

Instantiations. Private constrained PRFs (for general circuit constraints) satisfying the above properties can be built assuming sub-exponential hardness of LWE (with a sub-exponential modulus-to-noise ratio) [BTVW17, PS18].

5.2 Constructing a Private Linear Constrained PRF

We begin with a brief overview of our construction of a private linear constrained PRF. As discussed in Sect. 1.1, the domain of our PRF will be the ciphertext space $\{0,1\}^\ell$ for an authenticated encryption scheme with pseudorandom ciphertexts. A point corresponding to an index $t \in [0, 2^\kappa]$ (as would be output by the Samp algorithm) is an authenticated encryption of t. The PRF itself is implemented using a private constrained PRF, and the marked keys in our system correspond to a constrained key. Specifically, a marked key for an identity id consists of a constrained key for the function $f_{\mathsf{sk},\mathsf{id}}$ that has the secret key sk and the identity id hard-wired within in. The constraint $f_{\mathsf{sk},\mathsf{id}}$ has the property that $f_{\mathsf{sk},\mathsf{id}}(x) = 0$ whenever x is a valid encryption under sk of some index $t' > \mathsf{id}$, and is 1 otherwise.

At a high-level, the security proof relies on the fact that a private constrained PRF hides the constraint function, which in this particular case, means that it hides the secret key sk. Then, normal hiding and identity hiding follows from the fact that the ciphertexts in the underlying authenticated encryption scheme are pseudorandom, and pseudorandomness follows from constrained security of the underlying constrained PRF. We give our formal construction and security analysis below:

Construction 5.1 *(Private linear constrained PRF). Fix a security parameter λ and an identity-space parameter κ. Our private linear constrained PRF relies on the following ingredients:*

- *A symmetric encryption scheme* $(\mathsf{SE.Setup}, \mathsf{SE.Enc}, \mathsf{SE.Dec})$ *with key-space $\mathcal{K}$, message-space $\mathcal{M} = \{\mathcal{M}_\kappa\}_{\kappa \in \mathbb{N}}$ where $\mathcal{M}_\kappa = [0, 2^\kappa]$, and ciphertext space $\mathcal{C} = \{\mathcal{C}_{\lambda,\kappa}\}_{\lambda,\kappa \in \mathbb{N}}$. Suppose that $\mathcal{C}_{\lambda,\kappa} \subseteq \{0,1\}^\ell$ where $\ell = \ell(\lambda, \kappa)$.*
- *For a symmetric encryption key $k \in \mathcal{K}$ and a threshold $t \in [0, 2^\kappa]$, let $f_{k,t} \colon \{0,1\}^\ell \to \{0,1\}$ be the following predicate:*

> *On input* $\mathsf{ct} \in \{0,1\}^\ell$*:*
>
> 1. *Compute $t' \leftarrow$* $\mathsf{SE.Dec}(k, \mathsf{ct})$. *If* $\mathsf{SE.Dec}(k, \mathsf{ct})$ *does not have this form, output* 1.
> 2. *Output* 1 *if $t' \leq t$ and* 0 *otherwise.*

- *A private constrained PRF* $(\mathsf{PCPRF.Setup}, \mathsf{PCPRF.Eval}, \mathsf{PCPRF.Constrain})$ *with input space $\mathcal{X} = \{0,1\}^\ell$, output space $\mathcal{Y}$ and constraint family $\mathcal{F}_{\lambda,\kappa} = \{f_{k,t} \mid k \in \mathcal{K}, t \in [0, 2^\kappa]\}$.*

We construct a private linear constrained PRF with input space $\mathcal{X} = \{0,1\}^\ell$, *output space* $\mathcal{Y}$ *as follows:*

$\mathsf{Setup}(1^\lambda, 1^\kappa) \rightarrow (\mathsf{msk}, \mathsf{tk})$ *The setup algorithm samples a symmetric encryption key* $k \leftarrow \mathsf{SE.Setup}(1^\lambda, 1^\kappa)$ *and a private constrained PRF key* $\mathsf{pcprf.msk} \leftarrow \mathsf{PCPRF.Setup}(1^\lambda, 1^\kappa)$. *Then, it outputs* $\mathsf{msk} = \mathsf{tk} = (k, \mathsf{pcprf.msk})$.

$\mathsf{KeyGen}(\mathsf{msk}, \mathsf{id}) \rightarrow \mathsf{sk}_{\mathsf{id}}$. *The key-generation algorithm takes as input a master secret key* $\mathsf{msk} = (k, \mathsf{pcprf.msk})$ *and an identity* $\mathsf{id} \in [0, 2^\kappa]$ *and outputs* $\mathsf{sk}_{\mathsf{id}} \leftarrow \mathsf{PCPRF.Constrain}(\mathsf{pcprf.msk}, f_{k,\mathsf{id}})$.

$\mathsf{Eval}(\mathsf{sk}, x) \rightarrow y$. *The evaluation algorithm takes as input a secret key* sk *and an input* $x \in \{0,1\}^\ell$ *and output* $y \leftarrow \mathsf{PCPRF.Eval}(\mathsf{sk}, x)$.

$\mathsf{Samp}(\mathsf{tk}, t) \rightarrow (x, y)$. *The sampling algorithm takes as input the tracing key* $\mathsf{tk} = (k, \mathsf{pcprf.msk})$ *and a threshold* $t \in [0, 2^\kappa]$. *It computes* $x \leftarrow \mathsf{SE.Enc}(k, t)$ *and* $y \leftarrow \mathsf{PCPRF.Eval}(\mathsf{pcprf.msk}, x)$ *and outputs* (x, y).

As long as the underlying private constrained PRF PCPRF is single-key secure and the underlying authenticated encryption scheme is secure, Construction 5.1 is a single-key private linear constrained PRF (see Remarks 4.6 and 4.15 for a discussion of single-key security). We provide the proofs in the full version of this paper [GKWW20].

Theorem 5.2 (Key indistinguishability). *Suppose* PCPRF *satisfies correctness and single-key selective privacy, and that* SE *satisfies ciphertext integrity. Then, the private linear constrained PRF from Construction 5.1 satisfies single-key selective key indistinguishability where the adversary is only able to choose* $\mathsf{idx} = 1$ *(i.e., the adversary can only target the identity key* $\mathsf{sk}_{\mathsf{id}}$ *it requested).*

Theorem 5.3 (Single-key normal hiding). *Suppose* PCPRF *satisfies single-key selective privacy,* SE *is correct and satisfies ciphertext integrity and ciphertext pseudorandomness. Then, the private linear constrained PRF from Construction 5.1 satisfies selective single-key normal hiding security (without* SIE *queries).*

Theorem 5.4 (Single-key identity hiding). *Suppose* PCPRF *satisfies single-key selective privacy,* SE *is correct and satisfies ciphertext integrity and CPA-security. Then, the private linear constrained PRF from Construction 5.1 satisfies selective single-key identity hiding security (without* SIE *queries).*

Theorem 5.5 (Single-key pseudorandomness). *Suppose* PCPRF *satisfies constrained pseudorandomness and* SE *is correct and satisfies CPA-security. Then, the private linear constrained PRF from Construction 5.1 satisfies selective single-key pseudorandomness (without* SIE *queries).*

Instantiating Construction 5.1. Combining a private constrained PRF for circuit constraints [BTVW17, PS18] with an authenticated encryption scheme with pseudorandom ciphertexts (implied by any one-way function), we obtain a private linear constrained PRF from sub-exponential hardness of LWE with a sub-exponential modulus-to-noise ratio (by applying complexity leveraging [BB04] to the selectively secure construction above).

6 Publicly-Traceable Private Linear Constrained PRFs

In this section, we show how to construct a publicly-traceable private linear constrained PRF from indistinguishability obfuscation [BGI+01] together with a puncturable public-key encryption scheme [CHN+16]. We provide the formal definitions of these building blocks in the full version of this paper [GKWW20].

Our construction takes the same general approach as our previous construction based on private constrained PRFs in Sect. 5. Namely, the domain of the PRF is the ciphertext space for a sparse (puncturable) public-key encryption scheme with pseudorandom ciphertexts.[11] The special points associated with an index $t \in [0, 2^\kappa]$ used for tracing correspond to encryptions of t under the public-key encryption scheme. A marked key for an identity id consists of an obfuscated program that has both the decryption key hard-wired within it (needed to identify special points) as well as the master PRF key (in order to compute valid PRF evaluations on non-special points). Similarly, the public sampling algorithm consists of an obfuscated program with the master PRF key hard-wired and which takes an index t and randomness r, and samples an input-output pair for the PRF. In the security proof, we show that security holds as long as the public-key encryption scheme and the underlying PRF are *puncturable*, and the analysis is a standard application of the punctured programming paradigm of [SW14].

Construction 6.1 (Private linear constrained PRF with public tracing). *Fix a security parameter λ and an identity-space parameter κ. We rely on the following ingredients:*

- *A puncturable public-key encryption scheme* $(\mathsf{PE.Setup}, \mathsf{PE.Enc}, \mathsf{PE.Dec}, \mathsf{PE.Puncture})$ *with message space $\mathcal{M} = \{\mathcal{M}_\kappa\}_{\kappa \in \mathbb{N}}$ where $\mathcal{M}_\kappa = [0, 2^\kappa]$, and ciphertext space $\mathcal{C} = \{\mathcal{C}_{\lambda,\kappa}\}_{\lambda \in \mathbb{N}, \kappa \in \mathbb{N}}$, where $\mathcal{C}_{\lambda,\kappa} \subseteq \{0,1\}^\ell$ for some $\ell = \ell(\lambda, \kappa)$. Let $\rho = \rho(\lambda)$ be a bound on the number of bits of randomness* $\mathsf{PE.Enc}$ *takes.*
- *A length-doubling pseudorandom generator* $\mathsf{PRG} \colon \{0,1\}^\lambda \to \{0,1\}^{2\lambda}$.
- *A puncturable PRF*[12] $(\mathsf{PPRF.Setup}, \mathsf{PPRF.Eval}, \mathsf{PPRF.Puncture})$ *with domain $\{0,1\}^{\ell+2\lambda}$ and range $\mathcal{Y}$.*
- *An indistinguishability obfuscator $i\mathcal{O}$ for general circuits.*

We construct our private linear constrained PRF family with domain $\{0,1\}^{\ell+2\lambda}$ and range $\mathcal{Y}$ as follows (Figs. 4, 5):

$\mathsf{Setup}(1^\lambda, 1^\kappa) \to (\mathsf{msk}, \mathsf{tk})$. *Sample a public and secret key-pair* $(\mathsf{PE.pk}, \mathsf{PE.sk}) \leftarrow \mathsf{PE.Setup}(1^\lambda, 1^\kappa)$ *and a puncturable PRF key* $\mathsf{PPRF.msk} \leftarrow \mathsf{PPRF.Setup}(1^\lambda)$. *Let $P_{\mathsf{Samp}}[\mathsf{PE.pk}, \mathsf{PPRF.msk}]$ be the following program:*

[11] To implement the punctured programming ideas from [SW14] in the security analysis, we also adjoin a long pseudorandom string to the domain.

[12] A puncturable PRF is a constrained PRF (see Sect. 5.1) is a constrained PRF for the family of "puncturing" constraints $\mathcal{F} = \{f_x \colon \mathcal{X} \to \{0,1\} : x \in \mathcal{X}\}$ where $f_x(y) = 1$ if $x \neq y$ and 0 if $x = y$. They can be built directly from one-way functions [GGM84, BW13, KPTZ13, BGI14].

Hard-wired: *a* PE *public key* PE.pk *and a puncturable PRF key* PPRF.msk

Input: *an index* $t \in [0, 2^\kappa]$*, and randomness* $r \in \{0,1\}^{\rho+\lambda}$.

- *Parse* $r = r_0 \| r_1$ *where* $r_0 \in \{0,1\}^\rho$ *and* $r_1 \in \{0,1\}^\lambda$. *Compute* $\mathsf{ct} \leftarrow \mathsf{PE.Enc}(\mathsf{PE.pk}, t; r_0)$*, set* $z \leftarrow \mathsf{ct} \| \mathsf{PRG}(r_1) \in \{0,1\}^{\ell+2\lambda}$*, and output* $(z, \mathsf{PPRF.Eval}(\mathsf{PPRF.msk}, z))$.

Fig. 4. The program $P_{\mathsf{Samp}}[\mathsf{PE.pk}, \mathsf{PPRF.msk}]$

Hard-wired: *an identity* $\mathsf{id} \in \{0,1\}^\kappa$*, a* PE *secret key* PE.sk*, and a PRF key* PPRF.msk

Input: *an input* $x \in \{0,1\}^{\ell+2\lambda}$

- *Parse* x *as* $\mathsf{ct} \| x'$ *where* $\mathsf{ct} \in \{0,1\}^\ell$ *and* $x' \in \{0,1\}^{2\lambda}$. *Compute* $t' \leftarrow \mathsf{PE.Dec}(\mathsf{PE.sk}, \mathsf{ct})$. *If* $t' = \bot$*, output* $\mathsf{PPRF.Eval}(\mathsf{PPRF.msk}, x)$.
- *Otherwise, output* $\mathsf{PPRF.Eval}(\mathsf{PPRF.msk}, x)$ *if* $t' \leq \mathsf{id}$ *and* $\bot$ *if* $t' > \mathsf{id}$.

Fig. 5. The program $P_{\mathsf{Eval}}[\mathsf{id}, \mathsf{PE.sk}, \mathsf{PPRF.msk}]$

The setup algorithm outputs $\mathsf{msk} \leftarrow (\mathsf{PE.pk}, \mathsf{PE.sk}, \mathsf{PPRF.msk})$ *and* $\mathsf{tk} \leftarrow i\mathcal{O}(1^\lambda, P_{\mathsf{Samp}}[\mathsf{PE.pk}, \mathsf{PPRF.msk}])$. *Note that* $P_{\mathsf{Samp}}[\mathsf{PE.pk}, \mathsf{PPRF.msk}]$ *is padded to be the maximum size of all modified* P'_{Samp} *programs that appear in the security analysis.*

$\mathsf{KeyGen}(\mathsf{msk}, \mathsf{id}) \rightarrow \mathsf{sk}_{\mathsf{id}}$. *Let* $P_{\mathsf{Eval}}[\mathsf{id}, \mathsf{PE.sk}, \mathsf{PPRF.msk}]$ *be the following program:*

Output $\mathsf{sk}_{\mathsf{id}} \leftarrow i\mathcal{O}(1^\lambda, P_{\mathsf{Eval}}[\mathsf{id}, \mathsf{PE.sk}, \mathsf{PPRF.msk}])$. *Similar to* Setup*, the program* $P_{\mathsf{Eval}}[\mathsf{id}, \mathsf{PE.sk}, \mathsf{PPRF.msk}]$ *is padded to be the maximum size of all modified* P'_{Eval} *programs that appear in the security analysis.*

$\mathsf{Eval}(\mathsf{sk}, x) \rightarrow y$. *If the secret key* sk *has the form* $(\mathsf{PE.pk}, \mathsf{PE.sk}, \mathsf{PPRF.msk})$*, then output* $\mathsf{PPRF.Eval}(\mathsf{PPRF.msk}, x)$. *Otherwise, if* $\mathsf{sk}_{\mathsf{id}}$ *is a description of an obfuscated program, output* $\mathsf{sk}_{\mathsf{id}}(x)$.

$\mathsf{Samp}(\mathsf{tk}, t) \rightarrow (x, y)$. *Sample a random* $r \leftarrow \{0,1\}^{\rho+\lambda}$ *and output* $\mathsf{tk}(t, r)$.

Due to space limitations, we defer the formal theorem statements and their proofs to the full version of this paper [GKWW20].

References

[ABP+17] Agrawal, S., Bhattacherjee, S., Phan, D.H., Damien Stehlé, D., Yamada, S.: Efficient public trace and revoke from standard assumptions: extended abstract. In: ACM CCS, pp. 2277–2293 (2017)

[ADM+07] Abdalla, M., Dent, A.W., Malone-Lee, J., Neven, G., Phan, D.H., Smart, N.P.: Identity-based traitor tracing. In: Okamoto, T., Wang, X. (eds.) PKC 2007. LNCS, vol. 4450, pp. 361–376. Springer, Heidelberg (2007). https://doi.org/10.1007/978-3-540-71677-8_24

[BB04] Boneh, D., Boyen, X.: Secure identity based encryption without random oracles. In: Franklin, M. (ed.) CRYPTO 2004. LNCS, vol. 3152, pp. 443–459. Springer, Heidelberg (2004). https://doi.org/10.1007/978-3-540-28628-8_27

[BF99] Boneh, D., Franklin, M.: An efficient public key traitor tracing scheme. In: Wiener, M. (ed.) CRYPTO 1999. LNCS, vol. 1666, pp. 338–353. Springer, Heidelberg (1999). https://doi.org/10.1007/3-540-48405-1_22

[BGI+01] Barak, B., et al.: On the (im)possibility of obfuscating programs. In: Kilian, J. (ed.) CRYPTO 2001. LNCS, vol. 2139, pp. 1–18. Springer, Heidelberg (2001). https://doi.org/10.1007/3-540-44647-8_1

[BGI+12] Barak, B., et al.: On the (im)possibility of obfuscating programs. J. ACM **59**(2), 6 (2012)

[BGI14] Boyle, E., Goldwasser, S., Ivan, I.: Functional signatures and pseudorandom functions. In: Krawczyk, H. (ed.) PKC 2014. LNCS, vol. 8383, pp. 501–519. Springer, Heidelberg (2014). https://doi.org/10.1007/978-3-642-54631-0_29

[BKS17] Baldimtsi, F., Kiayias, A., Samari, K.: Watermarking public-key cryptographic functionalities and implementations. In: Nguyen, P., Zhou, J. (eds.) Information Security. ISC 2017. LNCS, vol. 10599, pp. 173–191. Springer, Cham (2017). https://doi.org/10.1007/978-3-319-69659-1_10

[BLW17] Boneh, D., Lewi, K., Wu, D.J.: Constraining pseudorandom functions privately. In: Fehr, S. (ed.) PKC 2017. LNCS, vol. 10175, pp. 494–524. Springer, Heidelberg (2017). https://doi.org/10.1007/978-3-662-54388-7_17

[BN08] Boneh, D., Naor, M.: Traitor tracing with constant size ciphertext. In: ACM CCS, pp. 501–510 (2008)

[BP08] Billet, O., Phan, D.H.: Efficient traitor tracing from collusion secure codes. In: Safavi-Naini, R. (ed.) ICITS 2008. LNCS, vol. 5155, pp. 171–182. Springer, Heidelberg (2008). https://doi.org/10.1007/978-3-540-85093-9_17

[BSW06] Boneh, D., Sahai, A., Waters, B.: Fully collusion resistant traitor tracing with short ciphertexts and private keys. In: Vaudenay, S. (ed.) EUROCRYPT 2006. LNCS, vol. 4004, pp. 573–592. Springer, Heidelberg (2006). https://doi.org/10.1007/11761679_34

[BTVW17] Brakerski, Z., Tsabary, R., Vaikuntanathan, V., Wee, H.: Private constrained PRFs (and more) from LWE. In: Kalai, Y., Reyzin, L. (eds.) TCC 2017. LNCS, vol. 10677, pp. 264–302. Springer, Cham (2017). https://doi.org/10.1007/978-3-319-70500-2_10

[BV15] Brakerski, Z., Vaikuntanathan, V.: Constrained key-homomorphic PRFs from standard lattice assumptions. In: Dodis, Y., Nielsen, J.B. (eds.) TCC 2015. LNCS, vol. 9015, pp. 1–30. Springer, Heidelberg (2015). https://doi.org/10.1007/978-3-662-46497-7_1

[BW13] Boneh, D., Waters, B.: Constrained pseudorandom functions and their applications. In: Sako, K., Sarkar, P. (eds.) ASIACRYPT 2013. LNCS, vol. 8270, pp. 280–300. Springer, Heidelberg (2013). https://doi.org/10.1007/978-3-642-42045-0_15

[BZ14] Boneh, D., Zhandry, M.: Multiparty key exchange, efficient traitor tracing, and more from indistinguishability obfuscation. In: Garay, J.A., Gennaro, R. (eds.) CRYPTO 2014. LNCS, vol. 8616, pp. 480–499. Springer, Heidelberg (2014). https://doi.org/10.1007/978-3-662-44371-2_27

[CFN94] Chor, B., Fiat, A., Naor, M.: Tracing traitors. In: Desmedt, Y.G. (ed.) CRYPTO 1994. LNCS, vol. 839, pp. 257–270. Springer, Heidelberg (1994). https://doi.org/10.1007/3-540-48658-5_25

[CFNP00] Chor, B., Fiat, A., Naor, M., Pinkas, B.: Tracing traitors. IEEE Trans. Inf. Theory **46**(3), 893–910 (2000)

[CHN+16] Cohen, A., Holmgren, J., Nishimaki, R., Vaikuntanathan, V., Wichs, D.: Watermarking cryptographic capabilities. In: STOC, pp. 1115–1127 (2016)

[CPP05] Chabanne, H., Phan, D.H., Pointcheval, D.: Public traceability in traitor tracing schemes. In: Cramer, R. (ed.) EUROCRYPT 2005. LNCS, vol. 3494, pp. 542–558. Springer, Heidelberg (2005). https://doi.org/10.1007/11426639_32

[CVW+18] Chen, Y., Vaikuntanathan, V., Waters, B., Wee, H., Wichs, D.: Traitor-tracing from LWE made simple and attribute-based. In: Beimel, A., Dziembowski, S. (eds.) TCC 2018. LNCS, vol. 11240, pp. 341–369. Springer, Cham (2018). https://doi.org/10.1007/978-3-030-03810-6_13

[FNP07] Fazio, N., Nicolosi, A., Phan, D.H.: Traitor tracing with optimal transmission rate. In: Garay, J.A., Lenstra, A.K., Mambo, M., Peralta, R. (eds.) ISC 2007. LNCS, vol. 4779, pp. 71–88. Springer, Heidelberg (2007). https://doi.org/10.1007/978-3-540-75496-1_5

[GGM84] Goldreich, O., Goldwasser, S., Micali, S.: How to construct random functions (extended abstract). In: FOCS, pp. 464–479 (1984)

[GKM+19] Goyal, R., Kim, S., Manohar, N., Waters, B., Wu, D.J.: Watermarking public-key cryptographic primitives. In: Boldyreva, A., Micciancio, D. (eds.) CRYPTO 2019. LNCS, vol. 11694, pp. 367–398. Springer, Cham (2019). https://doi.org/10.1007/978-3-030-26954-8_12

[GKRW18] Goyal, R., Koppula, V., Russell, A., Waters, B.: Risky traitor tracing and new differential privacy negative results. In: Shacham, H., Boldyreva, A. (eds.) CRYPTO 2018. LNCS, vol. 10991, pp. 467–497. Springer, Cham (2018). https://doi.org/10.1007/978-3-319-96884-1_16

[GKSW10] Garg, S., Kumarasubramanian, A., Sahai, A., Waters, B.: Building efficient fully collusion-resilient traitor tracing and revocation schemes. In: ACM CCS, pp. 121–130 (2010)

[GKW18] Goyal, R., Koppula, V., Waters, B.: Collusion resistant traitor tracing from learning with errors. In: STOC, pp. 660–670 (2018)

[GKW19a] Goyal, R., Koppula, V., Waters, B.: Collusion resistant traitor tracing from learning with errors. SIAM J. Comput. STOC18-94 (2019)

[GKW19b] Goyal, R., Koppula, V., Waters, B.: New approaches to traitor tracing with embedded identities. In: Hofheinz, D., Rosen, A. (eds.) TCC 2019. LNCS, vol. 11892, pp. 149–179. Springer, Cham (2019). https://doi.org/10.1007/978-3-030-36033-7_6

[GKWW20] Goyal, R., Kim, S., Waters, B., David, J.W.: Beyond software watermarking: traitor-tracing for pseudorandom functions. IACR Cryptol. ePrint Arch. **2020**, 316 (2020)

[GM84] Goldwasser, S., Micali, S.: Probabilistic encryption. J. Comput. Syst. Sci. **28**(2), 270–299 (1984)

[GQWW19] Goyal, R., Quach, W., Waters, B., Wichs, D.: Broadcast and trace with N^ε ciphertext size from standard assumptions. In: Boldyreva, A., Micciancio, D. (eds.) CRYPTO 2019. LNCS, vol. 11694, pp. 826–855. Springer, Cham (2019). https://doi.org/10.1007/978-3-030-26954-8_27

[HMW07] Hopper, N., Molnar, D., Wagner, D.: From weak to strong watermarking. In: Vadhan, S.P. (ed.) TCC 2007. LNCS, vol. 4392, pp. 362–382. Springer, Heidelberg (2007). https://doi.org/10.1007/978-3-540-70936-7_20

[JLS21] Jain, A., Lin, H., Sahai, A.: Indistinguishability obfuscation from well-founded assumptions (2021)

[KD98] Kurosawa, K., Desmedt, Y.: Optimum traitor tracing and asymmetric schemes. In: Nyberg, K. (ed.) EUROCRYPT 1998. LNCS, vol. 1403, pp. 145–157. Springer, Heidelberg (1998). https://doi.org/10.1007/BFb0054123

[KPTZ13] Kiayias, A., Papadopoulos, S., Triandopoulos, N., Zacharias, T.: Delegatable pseudorandom functions and applications. In: ACM CCS, pp. 669–684 (2013)

[KW17] Kim, S., Wu, D.J.: Watermarking cryptographic functionalities from standard lattice assumptions. In: Katz, J., Shacham, H. (eds.) CRYPTO 2017. LNCS, vol. 10401, pp. 503–536. Springer, Cham (2017). https://doi.org/10.1007/978-3-319-63688-7_17

[KW19] Kim, S., Wu, D.J.: Watermarking PRFs from lattices: stronger security via extractable PRFs. In: Boldyreva, A., Micciancio, D. (eds.) CRYPTO 2019. LNCS, vol. 11694, pp. 335–366. Springer, Cham (2019). https://doi.org/10.1007/978-3-030-26954-8_11

[KW20] Kim, S., Wu, D.J.: Collusion resistant trace-and-revoke for arbitrary identities from standard assumptions. In: Moriai, S., Wang, H. (eds.) ASIACRYPT 2020. LNCS, vol. 12492, pp. 66–97. Springer, Cham (2020). https://doi.org/10.1007/978-3-030-64834-3_3

[KY02a] Kiayias, A., Yung, M.: Traitor tracing with constant transmission rate. In: Knudsen, L.R. (ed.) EUROCRYPT 2002. LNCS, vol. 2332, pp. 450–465. Springer, Heidelberg (2002). https://doi.org/10.1007/3-540-46035-7_30

[KY02b] Kurosawa, K., Yoshida, T.: Linear code implies public-key traitor tracing. In: Naccache, D., Paillier, P. (eds.) PKC 2002. LNCS, vol. 2274, pp. 172–187. Springer, Heidelberg (2002). https://doi.org/10.1007/3-540-45664-3_12

[LPSS14] Ling, S., Phan, D.H., Stehlé, D., Steinfeld, R.: Hardness of k-LWE and applications in traitor tracing. In: Garay, J.A., Gennaro, R. (eds.) CRYPTO 2014. LNCS, vol. 8616, pp. 315–334. Springer, Heidelberg (2014). https://doi.org/10.1007/978-3-662-44371-2_18

[Nis13] Nishimaki, R.: How to watermark cryptographic functions. In: Johansson, T., Nguyen, P.Q. (eds.) EUROCRYPT 2013. LNCS, vol. 7881, pp. 111–125. Springer, Heidelberg (2013). https://doi.org/10.1007/978-3-642-38348-9_7

[Nis20] Nishimaki, R.: Equipping public-key cryptographic primitives with watermarking (or: a hole is to watermark). In: Pass, R., Pietrzak, K. (eds.) TCC 2020. LNCS, vol. 12550, pp. 179–209. Springer, Cham (2020). https://doi.org/10.1007/978-3-030-64375-1_7

[NP98] Naor, M., Pinkas, B.: Threshold traitor tracing. In: Krawczyk, H. (ed.) CRYPTO 1998. LNCS, vol. 1462, pp. 502–517. Springer, Heidelberg (1998). https://doi.org/10.1007/BFb0055750

[NSS99] Naccache, D., Shamir, A., Stern, J.P.: How to copyright a function? In: Imai, H., Zheng, Y. (eds.) PKC 1999. LNCS, vol. 1560, pp. 188–196. Springer, Heidelberg (1999). https://doi.org/10.1007/3-540-49162-7_14

[NWZ16] Nishimaki, R., Wichs, D., Zhandry, M.: Anonymous traitor tracing: how to embed arbitrary information in a Key. In: Fischlin, M., Coron, J.-S. (eds.) EUROCRYPT 2016. LNCS, vol. 9666, pp. 388–419. Springer, Heidelberg (2016). https://doi.org/10.1007/978-3-662-49896-5_14

[PS18] Peikert, C., Shiehian, S.: Privately constraining and programming PRFs, the LWE way. In: Abdalla, M., Dahab, R. (eds.) PKC 2018. LNCS, vol. 10770, pp. 675–701. Springer, Cham (2018). https://doi.org/10.1007/978-3-319-76581-5_23

[PST06] Phan, D.H., Safavi-Naini, R., Tonien, D.: Generic Construction of hybrid public key traitor tracing with full-public-traceability. In: Bugliesi, M., Preneel, B., Sassone, V., Wegener, I. (eds.) ICALP 2006. LNCS, vol. 4052, pp. 264–275. Springer, Heidelberg (2006). https://doi.org/10.1007/11787006_23

[QWZ18] Quach, W., Wichs, D., Zirdelis, G.: Watermarking PRFs under standard assumptions: public marking and security with extraction queries. In: Beimel, A., Dziembowski, S. (eds.) TCC 2018. LNCS, vol. 11240, pp. 669–698. Springer, Cham (2018). https://doi.org/10.1007/978-3-030-03810-6_24

[SSW01] Staddon, J., Stinson, D.R., Wei, R.: Combinatorial properties of frameproof and traceability codes. IEEE Trans. Inf. Theory **47**(3), 1042–1049 (2001)

[SW98] Stinson, D.R., Wei, R.: Combinatorial properties and constructions of traceability schemes and frameproof codes. SIAM J. Discret. Math. **11**(1), 41–53 (1998)

[SW14] Sahai, A., Waters, B.: How to use indistinguishability obfuscation: deniable encryption, and more. In: STOC, pp. 475–484 (2014)

[YAL+18] Yang, R., Au, M.H., Lai, J., Xu, Q., Yu, Z.: Unforgeable watermarking schemes with public extraction. In: Catalano, D., De Prisco, R. (eds.) SCN 2018. LNCS, vol. 11035, pp. 63–80. Springer, Cham (2018). https://doi.org/10.1007/978-3-319-98113-0_4

[YAL+19] Yang, R., Au, M.H., Lai, J., Xu, Q., Yu, Z.: Collusion resistant watermarking schemes for cryptographic functionalities. In: Galbraith, S.D., Moriai, S. (eds.) ASIACRYPT 2019. LNCS, vol. 11921, pp. 371–398. Springer, Cham (2019). https://doi.org/10.1007/978-3-030-34578-5_14

[YAYX20] Yang, R., Au, M.H., Yu, Z., Xu, Q.: Collusion resistant watermarkable PRFs from standard assumptions. In: Micciancio, D., Ristenpart, T. (eds.) CRYPTO 2020. LNCS, vol. 12170, pp. 590–620. Springer, Cham (2020). https://doi.org/10.1007/978-3-030-56784-2_20

[YF11] Yoshida, M., Fujiwara, T.: Toward digital watermarking for cryptographic data. IEICE Trans. **94-A**(1) (2011)

Batching Base Oblivious Transfers

Ian McQuoid(✉), Mike Rosulek, and Lawrence Roy

Oregon State University, Corvallis, USA
{mcquoidi,rosulekm,royl}@oregonstate.edu

Abstract. Protocols that make use of oblivious transfer (OT) rarely require just one instance. Usually, a batch of OTs is required—notably, when generating base OTs for OT extension. There is a natural way to optimize 2-round OT protocols when generating a batch, by reusing certain protocol messages across all instances. In this work we show that this batch optimization is error prone. We catalog many implementations and papers that have an incorrect treatment of this batch optimization, some of them leading to catastrophic leakage in OT extension protocols. We provide a full treatment of how to properly optimize recent 2-round OT protocols for the batch setting. Along the way we show several performance improvements to the OT protocol of McQuoid, Rosulek, and Roy (ACM CCS 2020). In particular, we show an extremely simple OT construction that may be of pedagogical interest.

1 Introduction

Oblivious transfer (OT) is a fundamental primitive for cryptographic protocols. It is well-known that OT cannot be constructed in a black-box way from symmetric-key primitives [IR90]. Nevertheless, it is possible to generate a large number of OTs from symmetric-key primitives and *a small number of "base OTs"*, thanks to an idea called **OT extension** [Bea96]. With OT extension, parties can generate many OT instances where the *marginal cost* of each instance involves only cheap symmetric-key operations. Modern OT extension protocols [IKNP03,KK13,ALSZ13,KOS15] can generate millions of OTs per second.

OT extension protocols require κ (*e.g.*, 128) base OTs, and yet most base-OT protocols in the literature are described in terms of a single OT instance. Obviously any single-instance OT protocol can be invoked κ times to produce base OTs; however, this overlooks the possibility of optimizations for the batch setting. In this work we provide a full treatment of the batch setting for recent leading OT protocols.

1.1 Overview of Our Results

Naïve Batching is Insecure. There is a natural way to optimize certain 2-round OT protocols for the batch setting. When the OT sender is first to speak, it is

Third author is supported by a DoE CSGF Fellowship.

M. Tibouchi and H. Wang (Eds.): ASIACRYPT 2021, LNCS 13092, pp. 281–310, 2021.
https://doi.org/10.1007/978-3-030-92078-4_10

Sender		Receiver
$a \leftarrow \mathsf{KA}.\mathcal{R}$		(input $c \in \{0,1\}$)
$A = \mathsf{KA}.\mathsf{msg}_1(a)$	$\xrightarrow{\quad A \quad}$	
		$b \leftarrow \mathsf{KA}.\mathcal{R}$
	$\xleftarrow{\tilde{B} = \Pi(B) \oplus c}$	$B = \mathsf{KA}.\mathsf{msg}_2(b, A)$
$M_0 := \mathsf{KA}.\mathsf{key}_1(a, \Pi^{-1}(\tilde{B}))$		$M_c = \mathsf{KA}.\mathsf{key}_2(b, A)$
$M_1 := \mathsf{KA}.\mathsf{key}_1(a, \Pi^{-1}(\tilde{B} \oplus 1))$		

Fig. 1. Our conceptually simple 1-of-2 random OT protocol, from instantiating [MRR20] with a new "programmable-once public function." $\Pi^{\pm}$ is an ideal permutation and KA is a 2-message key agreement whose "B-messages" are pseudorandom bit strings.

natural to reuse their protocol message for all OT instances in the batch. We call this method **naïve batching**.

We show that naïve batching is not guaranteed to be secure. Not only does naïve batching fail to achieve an appropriate security notion, but it is also demonstrably unsuitable as the base OTs for certain OT extension protocols. Specifically, we show a serious attack on the 1-out-of-N OT extension protocol of Orrù, Orsini, and Scholl [OOS17], when its base OTs are generated with naïve batching. Unfortunately, we find improper batching (including naïve batching) implemented in several protocol libraries [Rin, CMR, Kel20, Sma] and appearing in several papers [CO15, HL17, CSW20].

Proper Batching of Base OTs. We then give a complete treatment of how to correctly optimize leading OT protocols for the batch setting. Fortunately, it is simple and cheap to fix naïve batching, although the complete security analysis requires care. We show how to correctly optimize the recent OT protocol of McQuoid, Rosulek, and Roy [MRR20] (hereafter, MRR) for the batch setting. As we show, the Masny-Rindal protocol [MR19] is a special case of the MRR protocol, so our analysis applies to that protocol as well. A comparison of our batched-OT/base-OT protocol to existing work is shown in Table 1.

Other Improvements. We present several additional improvements to the OT protocol paradigm of McQuoid-Rosulek-Roy (MRR). The MRR protocol can provide 1-out-of-N random-OT, for essentially any N. Modern OT extension protocols require the base OTs to provide only 1-out-of-2 OT. Our optimizations to the MRR approach center around the special case of 1-out-of-2 OT[1] and specific properties of the batch setting.

- The MRR protocol revolves around an object called a **programmable-once public function (POPF)**. A POPF with domain $[N]$ leads to a protocol for 1-out-of-N OT. In introducing the concept of a POPF, MRR describe a

[1] Most of our improvements also apply to 1-out-of-N OT, for polynomial N.

Table 1. Comparison of m-instance random 1-of-2 OT protocols. "Exp" denotes exponentiations (f = fixed-base, v = variable-base, fM = fixed-base Montgomery, vM = variable-base Montgomery). "Com" denotes communication ($\mathbb{G}$ = one group element). PRO = programmable random oracle; ORO = observable random oracle; IC = ideal cipher.

Scheme	Assumption	Setup	Flows	Exp (Send/Receive)	Com (Send/Receive)
SimplestOT [CO15]	Gap-CDH	PRO	2	1f $(m+1)$v/mf mv	$1\mathbb{G}/m\mathbb{G}$
BlazingOT [CSW20]	CDH	ORO	3	1f $(m+1)$v/mf mv	$m\kappa + 1\mathbb{G}/2\kappa + m\mathbb{G}$
EndemicOT [MR19]	DDH	PRO	2	2mf 2mv/mf mv	$2m\mathbb{G}/2m\mathbb{G}$
EndemicOT [MR19]	iDDH	PRO	1	mf 2mv/mf mv	$m\mathbb{G}/2m\mathbb{G}$
Ours (MR)	ODH	PRO	1	2fM 2mvM/mfM mvM	$2\mathbb{G}/2m\mathbb{G}$
Ours (EKE)	ODH	IC	1	2fM 2mvM/mfM mvM	$2\mathbb{G}/m\mathbb{G}$
Ours (Feistel)	ODH	PRO	1	2fM 2mvM/mfM mvM	$2\mathbb{G}/m\mathbb{G}$

POPF with domain $\{0,1\}^*$, which is useful in some applications but overkill for the special case of 1-out-of-2 OT.
We show several improved POPF constructions for small domains (such as $N = 2$). One particularly interesting and new POPF is in the ideal random permutation model[2] and is inspired by the Even-Mansour block cipher construction [EM93]. When we instantiate MRR with this new POPF, we obtain an endemic OT protocol that is efficient, incredibly simple to describe, and may have pedagogical value as well (Fig. 1).

- The MRR protocol constructs OT from a POPF and a key agreement (KA) protocol. These two components must be compatible, and in [MRR20] it was shown how to make elliptic-curve Diffie-Hellman KA compatible with POPFs, by using hash-to-curve operations or Elligator [BHKL13] encoding steps. In this work, we present an alternative approach that avoids using either of these somewhat costly operations, based on a trick due to Möller [Möl04]. Möller-DHKA also avoids curve point addition, allowing us to use Montgomery ladders to multiply, which are more efficient. Adopting the Möller technique requires doubling the length of the sender's protocol message; however, in the batch setting it is exactly this sender's message that is reused across all OT instances in the batch, so the effect of doubling its size is minimal. In our performance benchmark, we found that the Möller technique affords up to a 36% increase in efficiency when batching OTs. This allows for UC secure constructions with comparable runtime to those with standalone security. See Table 2.

Finally, we show how our batch OT protocol can be used as the base OTs in **2-round** OT extension.

[2] The ideal random permutation model is like the random oracle model, except that all parties have access to a random permutation on $\{0,1\}^{2\kappa}$, *and its inverse!*.

Functionality $\mathcal{F}_{\text{batchEOT}}$

The functionality $\mathcal{F}_{\text{batchEOT}}$ is parameterized by the length of the OT strings ℓ and the number m of OTs in the batch. It interacts with two parties, a sender S and a receiver R via the following queries:

On input $(\text{READY}, (\tilde{r}_{1,0}, \tilde{r}_{1,1}, \ldots, \tilde{r}_{m,0}, \tilde{r}_{m,1}))$ from S, with $\tilde{r}_{i,c} \in \{0,1\}^\ell$:

- If S is corrupt, and there has been no previous READY command from S, then internally record $r_{i,c} = \tilde{r}_{i,c}$ for all $i \in [m]$, $c \in \{0,1\}$. Otherwise do nothing.

On input $(\text{READY}, (c_1, \ldots c_m) \in \{0,1\}^m, (\tilde{r}_1, \ldots, \tilde{r}_m))$ from R, with $\tilde{r}_i \in \{0,1\}^\ell$:

- Do nothing if there has been a previous READY query from R.
- Internally record $(c_1, \ldots c_m)$
- If R is corrupt, then internally record $r_{i,c_i} = \tilde{r}_i$ for each $i \in [m]$.

After receiving READY queries from both S and R:

- For all $i \in [m], c \in \{0,1\}$, if $r_{i,c}$ is not already defined, then sample $r_{i,c} \leftarrow \{0,1\}^\ell$.
- Output $(r_{1,c_1}, \ldots, r_{m,c_m})$ to R and $((r_{1,0}, r_{1,1}), \ldots, (r_{m,0}, r_{m,1}))$ to S.

Fig. 2. Ideal functionality for a size m batch of endemic 1-out-of-2 oblivious transfers, $\mathcal{F}_{\text{batchEOT}}$. Adapted from the endemic OT functionality of [MR19].

2 Preliminaries

Endemic OT. We use the security definitions for universally composable OT suggested by [MR19] (ideal functionality given in Fig. 2), which are a convenient middle-ground between random OT and chosen-message OT. An OT protocol results in outputs r_0, r_1 for the sender and r_c for the receiver (who has choice bit c). In **endemic OT**, a corrupt party may choose their own OT outputs, and all other OT outputs are chosen uniformly by the functionality. Hence, a corrupt sender can choose both r_0 and r_1. A corrupt receiver can choose r_c and the functionality will ensure that r_{1-c} is uniform. As shown in [MR19], OT extension protocols are secure if the base OTs satisfy this notion of endemic OT.

3 Problems with Naïve Batching

3.1 Naïve Batching

Consider any 2-round protocol for (endemic) OT, with the following syntax:

Sender		Receiver (input $c \in \{0,1\}$)
$s_S \leftarrow \{0,1\}^\kappa$		
$M_S = \mathsf{OT.msg}_S(s_S)$	$\xrightarrow{M_S}$	
		$s_R \leftarrow \{0,1\}^\kappa$
		$M_R = \mathsf{OT.msg}_R(s_R, M_S, c)$
	$\xleftarrow{M_R}$	
$(r_0, r_1) = \mathsf{OT.out}_S(s_S, M_R)$		$r_c = \mathsf{OT.out}_R(s_R, M_S, c)$

Where the four functions $\mathsf{OT}.\{\mathsf{msg}, \mathsf{out}\}_{\{S,R\}}$ are abstracted from the raw OT protocol. In such a protocol, the sender's message M_S is clearly independent of the receiver's influence. In many protocols M_S is additionally a message from a KA protocol, and it is well-known that a KA message can be reused for many KA instances, in certain circumstances. These observations suggest reusing the first OT protocol message in the following way, when generating a batch of m OTs:

Sender		Receiver (inputs $\{c_i\}_{i\in[m]}$)
$s_S \leftarrow \{0,1\}^\kappa$		
$M_S = \mathsf{OT}.\mathsf{msg}_S(s_S)$	$\xrightarrow{M_S}$	
		for $i \in [m]$:
		$s_{R,i} \leftarrow \{0,1\}^\kappa$
		$M_{R,i} = \mathsf{OT}.\mathsf{msg}_R(s_{R,i}, M_S, c_i)$
	$\xleftarrow{M_{R,1},\ldots,M_{R,m}}$	
for $i \in [m]$:		for $i \in [m]$:
$(r_{i,0}, r_{i,1}) = \mathsf{OT}.\mathsf{out}_S(s_S, M_{R,i})$		$r_{i,c_i} = \mathsf{OT}.\mathsf{out}_R(s_{R,i}, M_S, c_i)$

We call this protocol transformation **naïve batching**. All four component functions taken from the base OT protocol will be given the same (sub)session ID because they are treated as a single batch instance. They are reused in such a way that disallows for internal domain separation.

Lemma 1. *Naïve batching does **not** securely realize batch endemic OT (Fig. 2).*

Proof. The attack is simple: a corrupt receiver simply sends $M_{R,1} = \cdots = M_{R,m}$. As a result, the sender must compute $(r_{1,0}, r_{1,1}) = \cdots = (r_{m,0}, r_{m,1})$. There is no way for the simulator to influence the sender's output in this way in the ideal model, hence this constitutes an attack.

Why Not Trivially Patch this Attack? The attack is for the receiver to send the same OT response for all instances. We could simply tell the sender to abort if it receives any repeated OT responses.

However, the simple attack that we have described is only the tip of the iceberg. In all of the 2-round OT protocols that we consider, a corrupt receiver can induce more complicated correlations among the OT values. For example, a receiver can act honestly in the first OT instance to learn $r_{1,0}$. Then $r_{1,1}$ is unknown to the receiver. But there is a more sophisticated strategy for the receiver to force the ratio $r_{1,1}/r_{2,0}$ to be a certain value. (The details of this strategy are given in the full version of this paper, and depend on the details of a specific base OT protocol.)

Based on this kind of attack, one might wish to weaken the endemic OT functionality. Why not allow the simulator to specify these kinds of correlations in the ideal model? Even this will not work, because the attack is *perfectly* indistinguishable from honest behavior by the receiver. Thus, there is simply no way for the simulator to distinguish this kind of an attack (where the receiver must learn $r_{1,1}/r_{2,0}$) vs. honest behavior (where the receiver must learn $r_{2,0}$).

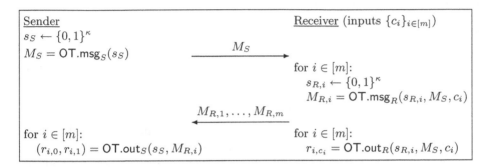

For these reasons, we believe there is no way to closely capture the security of naïve batching in a UC ideal functionality.

3.2 Implications for OT Extension

Since the main application for batch OTs is as base OTs for OT extension, it is natural to wonder whether the simple attack above jeopardizes the security of OT extension. It has been established that OT extension can be securely realized from base OTs with weakened security. For example, [CSW20] show that certain input-dependent aborts in the base OTs do not harm the security of OT extension.

We show that our simple attack on naïve batching indeed compromises security of some OT extension protocols. Specifically, we consider the protocol of Orrù, Orsini, and Scholl (OOS) [OOS17]. This OT extension protocol generates many instances of 1-out-of-2^t OT, where in each one the sender obtains $r_1, \ldots, r_{2^t}$ and the receiver learns only r_c, where c is an input. It will be convenient to consider c to be an element of $\{0,1\}^t$ in the natural way.

The OOS protocol is secure when the base OTs securely realize endemic batch OT; see [MR19] for details. However, it loses security when using naïve batching to generate its base OTs.

Lemma 2. *The OOS protocol [OOS17] is demonstrably insecure when its base OTs are instantiated via naïve batching.*

Proof. The complete details of OOS can be found in [OOS17]. We sketch the relevant details of their protocol here. Let Alice be the OOS sender (with no inputs), and Bob be the OOS receiver (with choice value $c_i \in \{0,1\}^t$ for the ith OT instance). The protocol proceeds as follows:

- The parties run m base OT instances, with Alice acting as receiver and Bob acting as sender. Bob obtains base-OT outputs $(k_{1,0}, k_{1,1}), \ldots, (k_{m,0}, k_{m,1})$. Alice's inputs and outputs are not relevant here.
- When extending to N OTs, Bob constructs two $N \times m$ matrices K and R as follows:

• The jth column of K is $\mathsf{PRG}(k_{j,0}) \oplus \mathsf{PRG}(k_{j,1})$.
• The ith row of R is $C(c_i)$ where $C : \{0,1\}^t \to \{0,1\}^m$ is a suitable binary error correcting code (the details of which are not relevant here).

Bob sends $K \oplus R$ to Alice.

These details of OOS are enough to understand the attack. A corrupt Alice will attack the base OTs (in the role of OT receiver as above) so that all $k_{i,0}$'s are the same and all $k_{i,1}$'s are the same. As a result, every column of K is identical. In other words, every *row* of K is either 0^m or 1^m.

Then the ith row of Bob's matrix $K \oplus R$ is either $C(c_i)$ or its complement. This means that if $c, c' \in \{0,1\}^t$ are any two choices for Bob whose codewords are not bitwise complements of each other, then Alice can distinguish between Bob having choice c vs c' in each extended OT. For some choices of C, learning $C(x)$ up to complement uniquely reveals x. This attack results in almost complete leakage of Bob's private input.

What if C is a Repetition Code? C is a binary error-correcting code, the simplest of which is the repetition code $C : \{0,1\} \to \{0,1\}^m$. This corresponds to the case of $t = 1$, and hence 1-out-of-2 OT extension. Specifically, instantiating OOS with a repetition code collapses it to the Keller-Orsini-Scholl 1-out-of-2 OT extension protocol (KOS) [KOS15].

In this case the only two codewords are 0^m and 1^m. Since these are bitwise complements of one another, it is not clear that our attack leads to any security problems. The rows of matrix R (encoding Bob's private input) are masked by either 0^m or 1^m, depending on a bit that is unknown to Alice. We are not sure whether a more sophisticated attack on the base OTs (even for a specific naïvely batched OT) can break KOS OT extension.

3.3 Problematic Batching Found in the Wild

Looking ahead, the fix for naïve batching is simple and essentially free (although the security analysis of the fix requires some care, as we show in the next sections). In Diffie-Hellman-based OT protocols, the OT outputs r_0, r_1 are computed by taking a (random oracle) hash of a Diffie-Hellman value. The fix is to include the OT index in that key derivation—*i.e.*, instead of $r_0 = H(sid, g^{ab})$, use $r_0 = H(sid, g^{ab}, \underline{i})$ in the ith OT instance in the batch. That way, even if all g^{ab} values are identical (or correlated strangely), the final OT values are independently random.

Given that both the attack and the fix are so simple, one may wonder whether this problem is well-known. In fact, we found problems related to OT batching in many libraries that implement malicious-secure OT extension.[3] We focus on the implications for the overall OT extension protocols, which are minor in most cases. However, the consequences would be more severe for developers that directly access the base-OT functionalities of these libraries.

- The `libote` OT extension library [Rin] implements Masny-Rindal [MR19] base OTs and applies naïve batching. The original Masny-Rindal paper considers only the single-instance setting and does not discuss security of the batch setting under naïve batching. In some configurations, the `libote` implementation of OOS indeed uses these naïvely batched base OTs, thus falling victim to our attack. Other configurations use a hybrid approach, first naïvely batching 128 base OTs, then using KOS to extend to 512 OTs, and using those 512 OTs as base for OOS. As mentioned above, we are not aware of any explicit attack on KOS extension, but our observations merely raise some concerns about its security with naïvely batched OTs.

[3] We notified the maintainers of these libraries about the issues and the suggested fix. By the time of writing, all maintainers have either already fixed or planned to fix their handling of batch OTs.

- The swanky MPC library [CMR] implements the Chou-Orlandi protocol and reuses the sender's message, but uses good domain separation in key derivation.[4] However, it allows the sender's protocol message to be reused across several batches, while the domain separation is local to the batch! In other words, parties could execute two batches of OTs, and the receiver could cause the batches to produce identical outputs, by replaying its protocol messages. In this library's implementation of OT extension, they first apply the transformation in [MR19] from endemic OT to uniform-message OT on the base OTs. This prevents the receiver from forcing OT extension to operate on identical base OTs. If not for this additional step, even KOS OT extension would leak information across different batches. As it is, only the XOR of PRG seeds is leaked under our attack on naïve batching, which is unlikely to lead to a concrete attack.
- The mp-spdz [Kel20] and scale-mamba [Sma] library implementations of OT use naïve batching of Chou-Orlandi base OTs. These libraries implement only KOS and not OOS, and therefore we know of no concrete attack against their OT extension.

We have also identified problematic handling of OT batching in several papers:

- The Chou-Orlandi OT protocol [CO15] explicitly considers the batch setting and uses naïve batching to achieve it. As such, the protocol as written is not suitable as the base OT for certain OT extensions.
- Since security flaws (unrelated to batching) were discovered in the Chou-Orlandi protocol, several works have attempted to address and repair them. Of those works, both [HL17] and [CSW20] explicitly consider the batch setting. The paper of Hauck & Loss [HL17] maintains the naïve batching of the original.
- The "Blazing OT" construction of Canetti, Sarkar, and Wang [CSW20] does not technically use naïve batching, since it introduces a joint consistency check across all instances in the batch. However, the key derivation in their base OTs does *not* include the OT index. This means that the attack in Lemma 1 has the intended effect: causing all OT instances to give identical output. The paper only considers a combined protocol with batched Chou-Orlandi base OTs and KOS OT extension, and as such we are not aware of an explicit attack on their final OT extension protocol. However, their security analysis does not seem to acknowledge the possibility of all base OTs giving identical outputs.

We found one instance of totally correct batching, in the implementation of Chou-Orlandi OT in emp-toolkit [WMK16], despite naïve batching being described in the paper.

[4] The authors explicitly justify their correct key derivation as a bug in the Chou-Orlandi paper, and reference the attack in which all base OTs generate identical output. See chou_orlandi.rs.

4 Properly Batching OTs

In this section we describe how to repair naïve batching. We focus on the McQuoid-Rosulek-Roy (MRR) protocol [MRR20] since it subsumes the Masny-Rindal protocol, while the Chou-Orlandi protocol does not achieve UC security. As we saw, the main problem is that a corrupt receiver can force correlations among the OT outputs in different instances—even causing some OT values to be equal. The solution is to enforce "domain separation" among the different instances. Intuitively, parties should hash each instance's OT outputs under a random oracle, with domain separation (*i.e.*, include the index of that instance in the hash).

However, proving the security of this change requires some care. For example, we cannot prove security merely from the single-instance security of the OT protocol, since the single-instance protocol is not being used correctly. Instead, we must use some known structure of the protocol. The MRR protocol derives its outputs from its underlying KA protocol, and we require stronger properties from that KA. The KA must accept an extra "tag" argument, so that even if the KA messages are identical, the resulting keys will be different under different tags.

4.1 Tagged KA

A **tagged KA** is identical in syntax to a traditional KA, except that the $\mathsf{KA.key}_1$ and $\mathsf{KA.key}_2$ algorithms take an additional tag argument. Correctness is that for all $a, b \in \mathsf{KA}.\mathcal{R}$ and all tags τ:

$$\mathsf{KA.key}_1(a, \mathsf{KA.msg}_2(b, \mathsf{KA.msg}_1(a)), \tau) = \mathsf{KA.key}_2(b, \mathsf{KA.msg}_1(a), \tau)$$

Looking ahead to our batch OT protocol, we will let the tag τ be the index of the OT instance (*e.g.*, OT instance 1, 2, 3, ...).

Intuitively, we will require that KA outputs under different tags appear independently random. This should hold not only when the KA protocol messages are identical, but also when the KA messages (*e.g.*, $\mathsf{KA.msg}_2$) are correlated, since we previously observed (Sect. 3) that the adversary could induce arbitrary correlations across OT/KA instances. This definition may be of independent interest—specifically, in scenarios where KA protocol messages are reused.

Definition 3. *A tagged KA protocol is* ***tag-non-malleable*** *if a session with tag* τ^* *is secure, even against an eavesdropper that has oracle access to* $\mathsf{KA.key}_1(a, \cdot, \cdot)$*, provided the eavesdropper never queries the oracle on tag* τ^**. Formally, the following distributions are indistinguishable, for all* τ^* *and every PPT* $\mathcal{A}$ *that never queries its oracle with second argument* τ^**:*

$a, b \leftarrow \mathsf{KA}.\mathcal{R}$ $M_1 = \mathsf{KA.msg}_1(a)$ $M_2 = \mathsf{KA.msg}_2(b, M_1)$ $K = \mathsf{KA.key}_1(a, M_2, \tau^*)$ return $\mathcal{A}^{\mathsf{KA.key}_1(a,\cdot,\cdot)}(M_1, M_2, K)$	$a, b \leftarrow \mathsf{KA}.\mathcal{R}$ $M_1 = \mathsf{KA.msg}_1(a)$ $M_2 = \mathsf{KA.msg}_2(b, M_1)$ $K \leftarrow \mathsf{KA}.\mathcal{K}$ return $\mathcal{A}^{\mathsf{KA.key}_1(a,\cdot,\cdot)}(M_1, M_2, K)$

Like [MRR20], we also require the KA protocol to satisfy the following randomness property:

Definition 4. *A key agreement protocol has* ***strongly random responses*** *if the honest output of* $\mathsf{KA.msg}_2$ *is indistinguishable from random, even to an adversary who (perhaps maliciously) generated* M_1*. Formally, for all polynomial time* $\mathcal{A}$*, the following distributions are indistinguishable:*

$(M_1, state) \leftarrow \mathcal{A}()$ $b \leftarrow \mathsf{KA}.\mathcal{R}$ $M_2 = \mathsf{KA.msg}_2(b, M_1)$ return $(state, M_2)$	$(M_1, state) \leftarrow \mathcal{A}()$ $M_2 \leftarrow \mathsf{KA}.\mathcal{M}$ return $(state, M_2)$

4.2 Programmable-Once Public Functions

The MRR protocol uses a primitive called programmable-once public functions (POPFs). We introduce definitions for POPF here, which slightly differ from the original definitions. We have specialized the definitions for the case of 1-out-of-2 OT[5]—[MRR20] define POPFs in a way that is useful for 1-out-of-N OT (with exponential N) and also password-authenticated key exchange. In the original POPF definitions, a simulator simulated the random oracle setup in the service of a single POPF instance; in our batch setting there will be many POPF instances, thus we must adapt the definitions to explicitly allow simulation of multiple POPFs in a non-interfering way.

Definition 5. *A* ***1-weak random oracle*** *is a function* $F\colon \mathcal{N} \to \mathcal{O}$ *such that the following two distributions are indistinguishable,*

$x \leftarrow \mathcal{N}$ $y := F(x)$ return x, y	$x \leftarrow \mathcal{N}$ $y \leftarrow \mathcal{O}$ return x, y

when the adversary does not have access to F *other than through these experiments.*

Note that F is only allowed to be used once this definition. This makes it an extremely weak property—it's even satisfied by universal hashes.

Definition 6 (Syntax). *A* ***batch 2-way programmable-once public function (batch 2-POPF)*** *consists of algorithms:*

- $\mathsf{Eval}: \mathcal{M} \times \{0,1\} \to \mathcal{N}$
- $\mathsf{Program}: \{0,1\} \times \mathcal{N} \to \mathcal{M}$

[5] All of the POPFs in this paper have straightforward generalizations to the 1-out-of-N case, for polynomial N, and some to exponential N as well, but we restrict ourselves to the 1-out-of-2 case for simplicity.

Both algorithms access some local setup $\mathbb{H}$*—depending on the instantiation,* $\mathbb{H}$ *could consist of common reference strings, random oracles, ideal ciphers, etc. All parties (adversaries) may access the setup directly as well, although it is local to a single instance of the batch 2-POPF. The setup may be stateful (e.g., the "lazy" formulation of a random oracle, which samples outputs on the fly).*

A 2-POPF must also include alternative local setups, which are used in different security definitions:

- $\mathbb{H}_{\mathsf{HSim}}$ *must provide the same interface as* $\mathbb{H}$ *as well as an additional method* $\mathsf{HSim}\colon \mathcal{N} \times \mathcal{N} \to \mathcal{M}$.
- $\mathbb{H}_{\mathsf{Extract}}$ *must provide the same interface as* $\mathbb{H}$ *as well as an additional method* $\mathsf{Extract}\colon \mathcal{M} \to \{0,1\}$. $\mathsf{Extract}$ *must not modify the private state of* $\mathbb{H}_{\mathsf{Extract}}$.

We write $\mathcal{A}^{\mathbb{H}}$ to denote an algorithm $\mathcal{A}$ with oracle access to all methods provided by the setup $\mathbb{H}$.

Definition 7 (Correctness). *A batch 2-POPF satisfies* **correctness** *if* $\mathsf{Eval}(\phi, x^*) = y^*$ *with all but negligible probability, whenever* $\phi \leftarrow \mathsf{Program}(x^*, y^*)$.

Definition 8 (Security). *A batch 2-POPF is* **secure** *if it satisfies the following properties:*

1. **Indistinguishable Local Setups:** *The local setups* $\mathbb{H}$, $\mathbb{H}_{\mathsf{HSim}}$ *and* $\mathbb{H}_{\mathsf{Extract}}$ *all implement a common interface. The setups must be indistinguishable to an adversary that only queries on this interface. Formally, if* $\mathcal{A}$ *is a polynomial-time algorithm that only queries its setup on the interface of* $\mathbb{H}$ *then the following probabilities are negligibly close:*

$$\Pr[\mathcal{A}^{\mathbb{H}}() = 1]; \qquad \Pr[\mathcal{A}^{\mathbb{H}_{\mathsf{HSim}}}() = 1]; \qquad \Pr[\mathcal{A}^{\mathbb{H}_{\mathsf{Extract}}}() = 1]$$

2. **Honest Simulation:** *Any* ϕ *that is generated honestly as* $\phi \leftarrow \mathsf{Program}(x^*, y^*)$, *with* y^* *chosen uniformly, is indistinguishable from* ϕ *generated via the* HSim *algorithm of* $\mathbb{H}_{\mathsf{HSim}}$. *Since* HSim *does not have a "preferred" input* x^*, *this establishes that an honestly generated* ϕ *hides the* x^* *on which it was programmed.*
Formally, define the following functions:

```
REAL_PHI(x* ∈ {0,1}, 𝔇):
  (s, y*) ← 𝔇
  φ ← Program(x*, y*)
  r_0 := Eval(φ, 0)
  r_1 := Eval(φ, 1)
  return s, φ, r_0, r_1
```

```
SIM_PHI(x* ∈ {0,1}, 𝔇):
  (s, y*) ← 𝔇
  r_{x*} := y*
  r_{1−x*} ← 𝒩
  φ ← HSim(r_0, r_1)
  return s, φ, r_0, r_1
```

Then for all polynomial time $\mathcal{A}$,

$$\Pr[\mathcal{A}^{\mathbb{H}_{\mathsf{HSim}}, \text{REAL\_PHI}}() = 1] - \Pr[\mathcal{A}^{\mathbb{H}_{\mathsf{HSim}}, \text{SIM\_PHI}}() = 1]$$

is negligible. Here we restrict $\mathcal{A}$ to always query with $\mathfrak{D}$ a distribution over $\{0,1\}^* \times \mathcal{N}$ such that the marginal distribution of y^* is indistinguishable from the uniform distribution over $\mathcal{N}$. The other component s appears for technical reasons; the reader can think of it as the coins used to sample y^*.
Note that SIM_PHI *calls the* HSim *method of the local setup, and that $\mathcal{A}$ may even query the* HSim *method (both the real and ideal experiments use $\mathbb{H}_{HSim}$).*

3. **Uncontrollable Outputs:** *For any ϕ generated by the adversary, the* Extract *method of $\mathbb{H}_{\mathsf{Extract}}$ can identify an input x^* such that the adversary has no control over $\mathsf{Eval}(\phi, 1-x^*)$. We say that $\mathsf{Eval}(\phi, 1-x^*)$ is beyond the adversary's control if $F(\mathsf{Eval}(\phi, 1-x^*))$ is indistinguishable from random, for any 1-weak-RO F.*[6]
Formally, the following distributions must be indistinguishable for all polynomial-time $\mathcal{A}_1, \mathcal{A}_2$ and all 1-weak-RO F:

$(\phi, state) \leftarrow \mathcal{A}_1^{\mathbb{H}_{\mathsf{Extract}}}()$	$(\phi, state) \leftarrow \mathcal{A}_1^{\mathbb{H}_{\mathsf{Extract}}}()$
$x^* := \mathsf{Extract}(\phi)$	
$r := F(\mathsf{Eval}(\phi, 1-x^*))$	$r \leftarrow \mathcal{N}$
return $\mathcal{A}_2^{\mathbb{H}_{\mathsf{Extract}}}(state, r)$	return $\mathcal{A}_2^{\mathbb{H}_{\mathsf{Extract}}}(state, r)$

As above, the left distribution calls the Extract *method of the $\mathbb{H}_{\mathsf{Extract}}$ setup, and the adversary may query this method as well. Note that $\mathcal{A}$ does not have any access to F beyond the one call provided by this experiment.*

The reader may be curious why we forced y^* to be sampled inside Honest Simulation, instead of letting the adversary choose it like in [MRR20]. The answer is that otherwise an ideal cipher would not be a POPF. An adversary could have already run $\mathsf{Program}(0, y^*)$ earlier, and because for each x there is a bijection between values of y and ϕ, a call to $\mathsf{HSim}(y^*, r_1)$ would be forced to return the same ϕ as before. Ideal ciphers were used as a motivating example for POPFs in [MRR20], so this is clearly a mistake. Ideal ciphers satisfy our new definition (Sect. 5.1).

4.3 The Batch OT Protocol

In Fig. 3 we present the batch variant of the OT protocol of [MRR20]. The protocol is essentially the naïve batching of the single-instance protocol, except we use a tagged KA and use different tags for each KA output.

Theorem 9. *When instantiated with a secure batch POPF and a tag-non-malleable KA scheme (Definition 3) with strongly random responses (Definition 4), the OT protocol in Fig. 3 is a UC secure batch endemic OT (Fig. 2), if the POPF's output satisfies $\mathcal{N} = \mathsf{KA}.\mathcal{M}_2$.*

[6] There are 1-weak ROs whose outputs can be distinguished from random when inputs are chosen in a certain adversarial way. Hence, requiring the RO outputs to remain random is a way of requiring that these values are not chosen in an adversarial way.

Sender		Receiver (with input $\{c_i\}_{i\in[m]}$)
$a \leftarrow \mathsf{KA}.\mathcal{R}$		
$M_S = \mathsf{KA}.\mathsf{msg}_1(a)$	$\xrightarrow{M_S}$	for $i \in [m]$:
		$b_i \leftarrow \mathsf{KA}.\mathcal{R}$
		$M_{R,i} := \mathsf{KA}.\mathsf{msg}_2(b_i, M_S)$
	$\xleftarrow{\phi_1, \ldots, \phi_m}$	$\phi_i := \mathsf{Program}(c_i, M_{R,i})$
for $i \in [m]$:		
for $j \in \{0,1\}$:		for $i \in [m]$:
$r_{i,j} = \mathsf{KA}.\mathsf{key}_1(a, \mathsf{Eval}(\phi_i, j), i \parallel j)$		$r_{i,c_i} = \mathsf{KA}.\mathsf{key}_2(b_i, M_S, i \parallel c_i)$

Fig. 3. Our m-batch 1-of-2 oblivious transfer protocol.

Proof. Correctness of the POPF and KA clearly show that the protocol is correct in the case where both parties are honest. When both parties are corrupt, the simulator has direct access to both parties and can simulate the real protocol by just running it. This leaves the two interesting cases, where one party is malicious and the other is honest. We prove each case by giving first a simulator, then a sequence of hybrids showing indistinguishability. The hybrids start from the real world and end at the ideal world: the simulator composed with an ideal batch endemic OT.

Simulator for Malicious Sender: The simulator uses $\mathbb{H}_{\mathsf{HSim}}$ instead of $\mathbb{H}$ to implement the local setup. It then waits until the sender provides its protocol message M_S. It creates fresh random values $b_{i,j} \in \mathsf{KA}.\mathcal{R}$ for $i \in [m], j \in \{0,1\}$, then computes the KA messages $M_{i,j} = \mathsf{KA}.\mathsf{msg}_2(b_{i,j}, M_S)$. Then it chooses $\phi_i \leftarrow \mathsf{HSim}(M_{i,0}, M_{i,1})$ and sends $\phi_1, \ldots, \phi_m$ as the simulated protocol message from the honest receiver. Finally, it submits $r_{i,j} = \mathsf{KA}.\mathsf{key}_2(b_{i,j}, M_S, i \parallel j)$ to the ideal functionality, for $i \in [m]$ and $j \in \{0,1\}$ (as the endemic OT values).

Sequence of Hybrids for Malicious Sender: Starting at the real interaction between malicious sender and honest receiver:

1. Replace local setup $\mathbb{H}$ with $\mathbb{H}_{\mathsf{HSim}}$. This change is indistinguishable by the Indistinguishable Local Setups property of the POPF.
2. Change how ϕ_i is generated:

   replace
   $$\begin{array}{|l|}\hline b_i \leftarrow \mathsf{KA}.\mathcal{R} \\ M_{R,i} = \mathsf{KA}.\mathsf{msg}_2(b_i, M_S) \\ \phi_i \leftarrow \mathsf{Program}(c_i, M_{R,i}) \\ \hline \end{array}$$
   with
   $$\begin{array}{|l|}\hline b_i \leftarrow \mathsf{KA}.\mathcal{R} \\ M_{i,c_i} = \mathsf{KA}.\mathsf{msg}_2(b_i, M_S) \\ M_{i,1-c_i} \leftarrow \mathsf{KA}.\mathcal{M} \\ \phi_i \leftarrow \mathsf{HSim}(M_{i,0}, M_{i,1}) \\ \hline \end{array}$$

   This is indistinguishable by the Honest Simulation property. Recall that this property requires b_i, M_{i,c_i} to come from a distribution $\mathfrak{D}$ over $\{0,1\}^* \times \mathcal{N}$ where the marginal distribution of the second element is indistinguishable from uniform. This holds because KA has strongly random responses.
3. Change how $M_{i,1-c_i}$ is sampled:

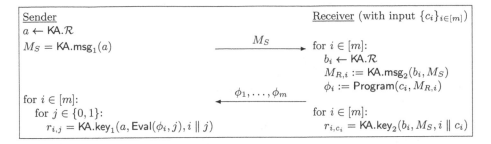

$$\text{replace} \boxed{\begin{array}{l} b_i \leftarrow \mathsf{KA}.\mathcal{R} \\ M_{i,c_i} = \mathsf{KA}.\mathsf{msg}_2(b_i, M_S) \\ M_{i,1-c_i} \leftarrow \mathsf{KA}.\mathcal{M} \\ \phi_i \leftarrow \mathsf{HSim}(M_{i,0}, M_{i,1}) \end{array}} \text{ with } \boxed{\begin{array}{l} b_{i,0}, b_{i,1} \leftarrow \mathsf{KA}.\mathcal{R} \\ M_{i,0} = \mathsf{KA}.\mathsf{msg}_2(b_{i,0}, M_S) \\ M_{i,1} = \mathsf{KA}.\mathsf{msg}_2(b_{i,1}, M_S) \\ \phi_i \leftarrow \mathsf{HSim}(M_{i,0}, M_{i,1}) \end{array}}$$

Later references to b_i become references to b_{i,c_i}. This is indistinguishable because KA has strongly random responses.

This final hybrid describes the ideal world. The receiver's inputs c_i are not used to simulate protocol messages to the sender; they are used only to determine which $r_{i,j} \stackrel{\text{def}}{=} \mathsf{KA}.\mathsf{key}_2(b_{i,j}, M_S)$ the receiver takes as output. In the ideal world the simulator sends identically defined $r_{i,j}$ to the ideal functionality, which uses the receiver's c_i inputs to determine which ones to deliver as the receiver's output.

Simulator for Malicious Receiver: The simulator uses $\mathbb{H}_{\mathsf{Extract}}$ instead of $\mathbb{H}$ to implement the local setup. It generates M_S in the same way as an honest sender and sends it to the corrupted receiver. When the receiver provides $\phi_1, \ldots, \phi_m$, the simulator runs $c_i = \mathsf{Extract}(\phi_i)$ for all $i \in [m]$, and submits them to the ideal functionality. It also computes $r_{i,c_i} = \mathsf{KA}.\mathsf{key}_1(a, \mathsf{Eval}(\phi_i, c_i), i \parallel c_i)$, and submits these to the ideal functionality as well (as the endemic OT values).

Sequence of Hybrids for Malicious Receiver

1. Replace local setup $\mathbb{H}$ with $\mathbb{H}_{\mathsf{Extract}}$, an indistinguishable change.
2. Rearrange how $r_{i,j}$ are computed:

$$\text{replace} \boxed{\begin{array}{l} \text{for } j \in \{0,1\}: \\ \quad r_{i,j} = \mathsf{KA}.\mathsf{key}_1(a, \mathsf{Eval}(\phi_i, j), i \parallel j) \end{array}}$$

$$\text{with} \boxed{\begin{array}{l} c_i \leftarrow \mathsf{Extract}(\phi_i) \\ r_{i,c_i} = \mathsf{KA}.\mathsf{key}_1(a, \mathsf{Eval}(\phi_i, c_i), i \parallel c_i) \\ r_{i,1-c_i} = \mathsf{KA}.\mathsf{key}_1(a, \mathsf{Eval}(\phi_i, 1-c_i), i \parallel 1-c_i) \end{array}}$$

   This is indistinguishable because running Extract has no effect on the local setup's internal state.
3. For each $i \in [m]$ and $j \in \{0,1\}$, create an oracle $F_{i,j} = y \mapsto \mathsf{KA}.\mathsf{key}_1(a, y, i \parallel j)$. Then rewrite the computation of $r_{i,j}$ in terms of these oracles as $r_{i,j} = F_{i,j}(\mathsf{Eval}(\phi_i, j))$. In Lemma 10 we show that every oracle $F_{i,j}$ is a 1-weak random oracle.
4. Change how $r_{i,1-c_i}$ is chosen:

$$\text{replace} \boxed{\begin{array}{l} c_i \leftarrow \mathsf{Extract}(\phi_i) \\ r_{i,c_i} = F_{i,c_i}(\mathsf{Eval}(\phi_i, c_i)) \\ r_{i,1-c_i} = F_{i,c_i-1}(\mathsf{Eval}(\phi_i, 1-c_i)) \end{array}} \text{ with } \boxed{\begin{array}{l} c_i \leftarrow \mathsf{Extract}(\phi_i) \\ r_{i,c_i} = F_{i,c_i}(\mathsf{Eval}(\phi_i, c_i)) \\ r_{i,1-c_i} \leftarrow \mathsf{KA}.\mathcal{K} \end{array}}$$

   This change is indistinguishable by the Uncontrollable Outputs property. Since each $F_{i,j}$ is a 1-weak RO, we can apply the Uncontrollable Outputs property once for each i to make the change described here.

This final hybrid describes the ideal world. After seeing the receiver's protocol message, the simulator extracts c_i values and also computes values r_{i,c_i} which will be part of the sender's output. The other OT values in the sender's output ($r_{i,1-c_i}$) are sampled uniformly, just as in the ideal world.

Lemma 10. *For any tag-non-malleable key agreement KA with strongly random responses, and for any set of tags $\mathcal{T}$, the following distribution outputs a key agreement message and a collection of $|\mathcal{T}|$ weak random oracles from $\mathsf{KA}.\mathcal{M}_2$ to $\mathsf{KA}.\mathcal{K}$.*

$$\boxed{\begin{array}{l} a \leftarrow \mathsf{KA}.\mathcal{R} \\ M_S := \mathsf{KA.msg}_1(a) \\ \text{for } \tau \in \mathcal{T}: \\ \quad F_\tau := x \mapsto \mathsf{KA.key}_1(a, x, \tau) \\ \text{return } M_S, \{F_\tau\}_{\tau \in \mathcal{T}} \end{array}}$$

Proof. We need to show that every F_τ is a weak random oracle. We describe a sequence of hybrids starting from the real weak random oracle distribution and ending at random.

1. Sample the input x and compute y early, when the oracle F_τ is created, rather than when the weak RO experiment is run.
2. Instead of sampling $x \leftarrow \mathsf{KA}.\mathcal{M}_2$, sample $b \leftarrow \mathsf{KA}.\mathcal{R}$ and set $x = \mathsf{KA.msg}_2(b, M_S)$. This is indistinguishable by the strongly random responses property of KA.
3. We are now computing $y = \mathsf{KA.key}_1(a, x, \tau)$ for a random KA message x, then giving oracle access to $\mathsf{KA.key}_1(a, x', \tau')$ (from the other oracles $F_{\tau'}$), but only for $\tau' \neq \tau$. This is exactly the same as the real distribution for a tag-non-malleable KA, so it is indistinguishable to switch to the random distribution by randomly sampling $y \leftarrow \mathsf{KA}.\mathcal{K}$ instead.
4. Use strongly random responses again, to sample $x \leftarrow \mathsf{KA}.\mathcal{M}_2$ and remove b.
5. Delay the sampling of x, y until the 1-weak RO distribution is run.

Our protocol considers an underlying KA with sequential messages. Yet Diffie-Hellman-based KA protocols have independent messages that can be sent in any order. We call such a KA protocol **1-flow**, where $\mathsf{KA.msg}_2(b)$ is independent of M_S. When the KA is 1-flow, the OT protocol can also be made 1-flow by sending both messages in parallel.

Theorem 11. *Our OT protocol (Fig. 3) becomes a 1-flow UC secure batch endemic OT when KA is 1-flow.*

Proof. This theorem largely the same as Theorem 9 from the previous one, but with key changes. In the 1-flow instance, the adversary may rush the other party, requiring them to send their message first before responding. For malicious receiver the adversary already went last, but it's different for malicious sender.

When the sender is corrupt, the simulator instead generates $\phi_1, \ldots, \phi_m$ with HSim before receiving M_S, as each of the receiver's messages from the key agreement may now be sampled independently of the sender's. The hybrid proof continues as before, after replacing $\mathsf{KA.msg}_2(b, M_S)$ with $\mathsf{KA.msg}_2(b)$.

5 New/Improved POPF Constructions

In this section, we describe several suitable POPF constructions for the batch OT protocol.

5.1 Ideal Cipher (EKE)

$\mathcal{M} := \mathcal{N}$

<u>Program(x, y):</u>
  return $E(x, y)$

<u>Eval(ϕ, x):</u>
  return $E^{-1}(x, \phi)$

$\mathbb{H}$

$T :=$ empty list
<u>$E(x, y)$:</u>
  if $\exists \phi.\, (x, y, \phi) \in T$:
    return ϕ
  $\phi \leftarrow \mathcal{M}$
  append (x, y, ϕ) to T
  return ϕ
<u>$E^{-1}(x, \phi)$:</u>
  if $\exists y.\, (x, y, \phi) \in T$:
    return y
  $y \leftarrow \mathcal{N}$
  append (x, y, ϕ) to T
  return y

$\mathbb{H}_{\mathsf{HSim}}$

$T := \{\}$
// E and E^{-1} are same as in $\mathbb{H}$
<u>HSim(r_0, r_1):</u>
  if $\exists x, \phi.\, (x, r_x, \phi) \in T$:
    return $\perp$
  $\phi \leftarrow \mathcal{M}$
  append $(0, r_0, \phi)$ to T
  append $(1, r_1, \phi)$ to T
  return ϕ

$\mathbb{H}_{\mathsf{Extract}}$

$T := \{\}$
// E and E^{-1} are same as in $\mathbb{H}$
<u>Extract(ϕ):</u>
  find first $(x^*, y^*, \phi) \in T$:
    return x^*
  if none exist:
    return 0

Fig. 4. Batch 2-POPF based on an ideal cipher.

Our first POPF is inspired by the EKE password-authenticated key exchange protocol of Bellovin & Merritt [BM92]. POPF was created as a generalization of an ideal cipher in the EKE protocol, and it is no surprise that in fact an ideal cipher is a POPF. The full definition is in Fig. 4. We are not aware of prior work pointing out the connection between EKE and oblivious transfer. But it is easy to see that an ideal cipher is useful for OT: the adversary can know the trapdoor to at most one of $E^{-1}(0, \phi)$ and $E^{-1}(1, \phi)$.

The local setup $\mathbb{H}$ is simply an ideal cipher. Actually, we have defined $\mathbb{H}$ in a way that is indistinguishable from an ideal cipher—it chooses oracle responses uniformly, instead guaranteeing that each $E(x, \cdot)$ is a permutation. By a standard

PRF/PRP switching lemma, the difference is indistinguishable, and this choice makes the description of $\mathbb{H}$ simpler. $\mathbb{H}_{\mathsf{HSim}}$ is similar to $\mathbb{H}$, but it programs E^{-1} so that $\mathsf{Eval}(\phi, i) = r_i$, to satisfy the honest simulation property.

In $\mathbb{H}_{\mathsf{Extract}}$, $\mathsf{Extract}(\phi)$ finds the first ideal cipher call that produced ϕ—either as the input to an E^{-1} query or the output of an E query. The idea is that once ϕ has appeared in some ideal cipher query, future forward queries to E give output ϕ only with negligible probability. Hence, all future calls that involve ϕ must be of the form $E^{-1}(\cdot, \phi)$, meaning that the adversary has no control over the outputs of these queries (which are outputs of Eval). This is precisely the property needed for a POPF.

Theorem 12. *Figure 4 defines a secure and correct batch 2-POPF with all distinguisher advantages except for Uncontrollable Outputs bounded by* $O\left(\frac{q^2}{|\mathcal{N}|}\right)$, *when the adversary makes q ideal cipher lookups. Uncontrollable Outputs instead has advantage bounded by* $q\,\mathrm{Adv}(wRO) + O\left(\frac{q^2}{|\mathcal{N}|}\right)$, *where* $\mathrm{Adv}(wRO)$ *is the distinguisher advantage against the 1-weak RO F.*

Proof. We have deferred the security proofs for the POPF constructions to the full version of this work.

5.2 Even-Mansour POPF

In [MRR20] the authors construct a POPF with a 2-round Feistel cipher. Intuitively, a POPF generalizes an ideal cipher, but is strictly weaker. So, while an 8-round Feistel cipher is indifferentiable from an ideal cipher, a 2-round Feistel cipher suffices for a POPF. Similarly, we suggest a POPF based on the Even-Mansour [EM93] construction. While the Even-Mansour construction is not an ideal cipher unless many rounds are added [DSST17], a single round suffices for a POPF.

The construction (Fig. 5) is similar to the Ideal Cipher POPF, but with a few changes. The local setup $\mathbb{H}$ is not an ideal cipher, but a simpler ideal random permutation. In the ideal cipher POPF, every query to the oracles included the x-value (as the key of the cipher). In this Even-Mansour POPF the value x is used only by xor'ing with the ideal permutation output—it is not directly available to the simulator (in $\mathsf{Extract}$).

To deal with this challenge, we observe that x can be inferred by the simulator given ϕ. The only situation where x is ambiguous given ϕ is when $\Pi(y_1) \oplus x_1 = \phi = \Pi(y_2) \oplus x_2$ for distinct bits x_1, x_2. This event implies $\Pi(y_1) \oplus \Pi(y_2) = x_1 \oplus x_2 = 1$, which is negligibly likely for forward queries to Π. This turns out to be enough for the simulator to extract. The construction generalizes to strings x which are significantly shorter than the ideal permutation output.

Theorem 13. *Figure 5 defines a secure and correct batch 2-POPF where the distinguisher advantage is* $O(q^2 2^{-\alpha})$ *when the adversary makes q ideal permutation lookups, except for Uncontrollable Outputs which allows an additional advantage of* $q\,\mathrm{Adv}(wRO)$.

Proof. We have deferred this proof to the full version of this work.

$\mathcal{M} := \mathcal{N} := \{0,1\}^\alpha$

```
Program(x, y):
  return Π(y) ⊕ x

Eval(φ, x):
  return Π^{-1}(φ ⊕ x)
```

```
ℍ
T := empty list
Π(u):
  if ∃v. (u, v) ∈ T:
    return v
  v ← {0,1}^α
  append (u, v) to T
  return v
Π^{-1}(v):
  if ∃u. (u, v) ∈ T:
    return u
  u ← {0,1}^α
  append (u, v) to T
  return u
```

```
ℍ_HSim
T := empty list
// E and E^{-1} are same as in ℍ
HSim(r_0, r_1):
  if ∃x, φ. (r_x, φ ⊕ x) ∈ T:
    return ⊥
  φ ← {0,1}^α
  append (r_0, φ ⊕ 0) to T
  append (r_1, φ ⊕ 1) to T
  return φ
```

```
ℍ_Extract
T := empty list
// E and E^{-1} are same as in ℍ
Extract(φ):
  find first (y*, φ ⊕ x*) ∈ T:
    return x*
  if none exist:
    return 0
```

Fig. 5. Batch 2-POPF based on an ideal permutation.

5.3 Masny-Rindal POPF

This next POPF is inspired by the OT construction of Masny and Rindal [MR19]. Using this POPF in the context of Fig. 3 we see that the Masny-Rindal OT protocol for 1-out-of-2 OT[7] is then a specific instance of our protocol. The description of the POPF can be found in Fig. 6.

The local setup $\mathbb{H}$ consists of two random oracles H_0, H_1 whose outputs are a group $\mathbb{G}$. In the resulting OT protocol, the KA scheme must have protocol messages that reside in this group. $\mathbb{H}_{\mathsf{HSim}}$ is similar to $\mathbb{H}$, but it also tracks the values r_0, r_1 that have been given to $\mathsf{HSim}(R)$. To satisfy the honest simulation property, it further programs the random oracles H_x to be consistent:

$$\mathsf{Eval}(\phi, x) = s_x \cdot H_x(s_{1-x}) = s_x \cdot (s_x)^{-1} \cdot r_x = r_x.$$

$\mathbb{H}_{\mathsf{Extract}}$ is also very similar to $\mathbb{H}$, but it also tracks chronological order of the oracle queries. $\mathsf{Extract}(\phi)$, upon seeing $\phi = (s_0, s_1)$, checks if s_{1-x^*} was a query

[7] Generalizing to 1-out-of-N for polynomial N works the same as in [MR19].

$\mathcal{M} := \mathbb{G}^2$

Program(x, y):
- $s_{1-x} \leftarrow \mathbb{G}$
- $s_x = y \cdot (H_x(s_{1-x}))^{-1}$
- return (s_0, s_1)

Eval$((s_0, s_1), x)$:
- return $s_x \cdot H_x(s_{1-x})$

$\mathbb{H}$

record calls in a transcript T

$H_x(u)$:
- if $\exists v. (v \leftarrow H_x(u)) \in T$:
  - return v
- $v \leftarrow \mathbb{G}$
- return v

$\mathbb{H}_{\mathsf{HSim}}$

record calls in a transcript T

$U :=$ empty assoc. array

$H_x(u)$:
- if $\exists v. (v \leftarrow H_x(u)) \in T$:
  - return v
- if $U[x, u]$ defined:
  - return $U[x, u]$
- $v \leftarrow \mathbb{G}$
- return v

HSim(r_0, r_1):
- $\phi = (s_0, s_1) \leftarrow \mathcal{M}$
- $U[0, s_1] := s_0^{-1} \cdot r_0$
- $U[1, s_0] := s_1^{-1} \cdot r_1$
- return ϕ

$\mathbb{H}_{\mathsf{Extract}}$

record calls in a transcript T

// H_x is the same as in $\mathbb{H}$

Extract$((s_0, s_1))$:
- find first query $H_{x^*}(s_{1-x^*})$ in T:
  - return x^*
- if none exist:
  - return 0

Fig. 6. Batch 2-POPF based on the OT construction of Masny-Rindal [MR19]. Here $H_0, H_1 : \mathbb{G} \to \mathbb{G}$ are random oracles, and $(\mathbb{G}, \cdot)$ is a group.

to the random oracle H_{x^*}, for either $x^* \in \{0, 1\}$. Extract(ϕ) then chooses the first query (chronologically) and returns the associated x^*, or chooses x^* arbitrarily to be 0 if neither call was made. As in the original proof in [MR19] the main idea is that for the adversary to program ϕ, they need to query on one of the two s_x values to find the other, unless the "other" is sampled independently, in which case the adversary fails to program.

Theorem 14. *Figure 6 defines a secure and correct batch 2-POPF with all distinguisher advantages except for Uncontrollable Outputs bounded by* $O\left(\frac{q^2}{|\mathbb{G}|}\right)$ *when the adversary makes q queries to the random oracles. Uncontrollable Outputs instead has advantage bounded by* $\frac{q^2-q+2}{2}\,\mathrm{Adv}(wRO) + O\left(\frac{q^2}{|\mathbb{G}|}\right)$.

Proof. We have deferred this proof to the full version of this work.

5.4 Streamlined Feistel POPF

[MRR20] propose a POPF based on 2-round Feistel, in which the ϕ value is 3κ bits longer than the underlying value from $\mathcal{N}$. We present an alternative

```
𝒩 := 𝔾
ℳ := 𝔾 × 𝔽

Program(x, y):
  u ← 𝔽
  t := H(x, u)^{-1} · y
  s := u − ι(t)x
  return s, t

Eval((s, t), x):
  return H(x, ι(t)x + s) · t
```

```
ℍ
record calls in a transcript T
H(x, u):
  if ∃v. (v ← H(x, u)) ∈ T:
    return v
  v ← 𝔾
  return v
```

```
ℍ_HSim
record calls in a transcript T
U := empty assoc. array
H(x, u):
  if ∃v. (v ← H(x, u)) ∈ T:
    return v
  if U[x, u] defined:
    return U[x, u]
  v ← 𝔾
  return v
HSim(r_0, r_1):
  (s, t) ← 𝔾 × 𝔽
  U[0, ι(t) 0 + s] := r_0 · t^{-1}
  U[1, ι(t) 1 + s] := r_1 · t^{-1}
  return (s, t)
```

```
ℍ_Extract
record calls in a transcript T
// H is the same as in ℍ
Extract((s, t)):
  find first query H(x*, ι(t)x* + s):
    return x*
  if none exist:
    return 0
```

Fig. 7. Variant of the Feistel POPF in [MRR20], where one random oracle has been replaced with multiplication in a finite field $\mathbb{F}$. ι is an injection with an efficient left inverse ι^{-1}, i.e., $\forall t.\, \iota^{-1}(\iota(t)) = t$.

construction (Fig. 7) that improves on this when $\mathbb{G} = \mathcal{N}$ can be represented with less than 3κ bits. This is useful because elliptic curve points usually can be represented with 2κ bits.

As with [MRR20], we need $\mathcal{N}$ to be a group $\mathbb{G}$, and the local setup $\mathbb{H}$ is a hash function H mapping into $\mathbb{G}$. However, instead of a second random oracle $H'(x, T)$, we use an injection ι from $\mathbb{G}$ into a finite field $\mathbb{F}$. The hash call $H'(x, T)$ in one of the Feistel rounds is then replaced with multiplication $\iota(T)x$. ι is required to have an efficiently computable left inverse ι^{-1}.

These changes eliminate the main bad event in the security proof of [MRR20], which occurs when the adversary manages to delay making the H' query, which the simulator needs to see in order to find what T the adversary chose, until after the simulator needs to use T to program H. The simulator can now find T directly using ι^{-1}.

Theorem 15. *The streamlined Feistel POPF in Fig. 7 is a secure and correct batch 2-POPF. The distinguisher advantage is* $O\left(\frac{q^2}{|\mathbb{G}|}\right)$ *when the adversary makes* q *ideal permutation lookups, except for Uncontrollable Outputs which allows an additional advantage of* $\frac{q^2-q+2}{2}\,\mathrm{Adv}(wRO)$.

Proof. We have deferred this proof to the full version of this work.

The original 2-round Feistel POPF in [MRR20] also satisfies our new definitions. We omit the proof because it is substantially similar to the proof of Theorem 15, just preserving a few more ideas from [MRR20].

6 Suitable Key Agreement Choices

Our batched OT protocol requires a tagged KA in which the receiver's protocol messages are indistinguishable from the uniform distribution over the domain of the POPF (outputs of Eval). In this section we discuss several choices for KA, including one not considered in [MRR20] but which is well-suited to the batch setting.

The main challenge is that traditional DHKA on an elliptic curve is not enough. Under the usual encoding (the x-coordinate), points on the curve are easily distinguishable from random strings, while it is more natural to define a POPF operating on strings. Hence, some care is involved in making the POPF and KA compatible.

6.1 Curve Mappings

In [MRR20], the authors suggest two ways to achieve compatibility between POPF and KA over elliptic curves.

One choice is to ensure that the KA protocol messages are uniform *bit strings*. This can be done using the Elligator technique of [BHKL13] to encode curve elements. Elligator is an injective and efficiently invertible function ι from $\{0,1\}^\kappa$ to a large subset of the elliptic curve. If some party wishes to make their KA protocol message a uniform string, they simply sample from points in the image of ι. This is achieved in practice by re-sampling a DH scalar until the resulting curve point is in $\iota(\{0,1\}^\kappa)$. If the range of ι is a large fraction of the elliptic curve, then the expected number of re-samples is small. See Fig. 8 for a formal description of tagged Elligator ECDHKA.

Another choice is to ensure that the POPF Eval function only outputs values on the curve. In the POPF construction of [MRR20] this can be achieved by instantiating a random oracle that gives outputs in the curve.

These techniques incur nontrivial computational overhead. The Elligator approach requires resampling each curve element some constant number of times on average. The state-of-the-art techniques for hashing-to-curve [BCI10, FFS+10, TK17] have cost roughly 25% that of a scalar multiplication on the curve, and the POPF requires at least 2 hash-to-curve operations per party.

Sender (tag τ)		Receiver (tag τ)
		do:
$a \leftarrow \mathbb{F}_p$		$b \leftarrow \mathbb{F}_p$
$A = aG$		$B = bG$
	A $\longrightarrow$	while $B \notin \iota(\{0,1\}^\kappa)$
	$\tilde{B} = \iota^{-1}(B)$ $\longleftarrow$	
return $H(a \cdot \iota(\tilde{B}), \tau)$		return $H(bA, \tau)$

Fig. 8. Tagged Elligator ECDHKA. G is a generator of the curve and ι is the injective Elligator mapping of [BHKL13].

6.2 Möller Variant of ECDHKA

We now suggest a more efficient approach that is well suited for the batch setting. Before continuing, let us give a brief review of elliptic curves. For the remainder of this section, we will consider curves over prime fields with order larger than 3. Further results and descriptions can be found in Silverman [Sil09].

Definition 16. *An **elliptic curve** $E_{a,b}$ over a field $\mathbb{F}_p$ is defined by a congruence of the form $Y^2 = X^3 + aX + b$ parameterized by elements $a, b \in F_p$ such that $4a^3 + 27b^2 \neq 0$. The elements of $E_{a,b}$ are given by tuples (X, Y) satisfying the congruence along with a neutral element $\mathcal{O}$, the **point at infinity**.*

We may equip this set with a group law called the chord-and-tangent law such that we arrive at a commutative group where the usual Diffie-Hellman problems are believed to be hard.

Definition 17. *Given an elliptic curve $E_{a,b}$ over a field $\mathbb{F}_p$ and $c \in \mathbb{F}_p$, we may consider the elliptic curve $E'_c : cY^2 = X^3 + aX + b$. If c is a quadratic residue in $\mathbb{F}_p$ then E' is isomorphic to E, otherwise, E' is called the (quadratic) **twist** of E.*

As a twist of a given curve is unique up to isomorphism, we may consider, singly, a primary curve and its twist curve. It follows from the definition that any $x \in \mathbb{F}_p$ is the abscissa (x-coordinate) of a point on E or of a point on the twist E'.

Lemma 18. *Let $c \neq 0$ be a quadratic non-residue in the field $\mathbb{F}_p$, and let $E_{a,b}$ be an elliptic curve over $\mathbb{F}_p$ with twist E'_c. Then for every $x \in \mathbb{F}_p$:*

1. *If $x^3 + ax + b$ is a non-zero quadratic residue, then $(x, \pm\sqrt{x^3 + ax + b})$ are points on $E_{a,b}$. Furthermore, $(x^3 + ax + b)/c$ is a quadratic non-residue and x is not the abscissa of any point on E'_c*
2. *If $x^3 + ax + b$ is a quadratic non-residue, then x is not a point on $E_{a,b}$. Furthermore, $(x^3 + ax + b)/c$ is a quadratic residue and $(x, \pm\sqrt{(x^3 + ax + b)/c})$ are points on E'_c.*
3. *If $x^3 + ax + b = 0$, then $(x, 0)$ is a point on $E_{a,b}$ and E'_c.*

This idea is of importance as for many curves and applications; only the abscissa of a point is needed. This means that we can work with bitstrings using the implicit mapping defined above.

Furthermore, there are a similar number of points on the twist as there are on the curve. If one were to toss a coin $b \leftarrow \{0,1\}$, and then sample an x-coordinate of a random curve point (if $b = 0$) or a random twist point (if $b = 1$), the result would be statistically close to the uniform distribution on the set of bitstrings.

Lemma 19 ([CFGP06, Corollary 11]). *Given a curve $E_{a,b}$ and its twist E'_c over $\mathbb{F}_p$, where $2^q - p < 2^{q/2}$ (i.e., p is very close to a power of 2), the following distribution is indistinguishable from the uniform distribution in $\{0,1\}^q$*

$$\mathcal{D} = \{\beta \leftarrow \{0,1\}, x_0 \leftarrow [E_{a,b}]_{abscissa}, x_1 \leftarrow [E'_c]_{abscissa} : K = x_\beta\},$$

with statistical distance

$$\delta = \frac{1}{2}\sum_{x \in \mathbb{F}_p} \left| \Pr_{K \leftarrow \mathbb{F}_{2^q}}[K = x] - \Pr_{K \leftarrow \mathcal{D}}[K = x] \right| \leq \frac{1+\sqrt{2}}{2^{q/2}}.$$

This suggests the key agreement approach in Fig. 9. The receiver will sample an x-coordinate as above. The sender cannot anticipate the receiver's choice, so she prepares a DH message on both the curve and the twist, then chooses the correct one to compute the final key. Lemma 19 establishes that the receiver's KA message is statistically indistinguishable from the uniform distribution on strings.

Note that the sender sends two curve/twist elements instead just one as in standard DHKA. However, in batched OT it is exactly this sender message that is reused across all OT instances. Hence a slight increase in its size has minimal effect on the overall OT protocol's efficiency.

Similar approaches to representation have been used in the context of PAKE [BMN01], pseudo-random permutations [Kal91], authenticated key exchange [CFGP06], and by Möller [Möl04] in the context of ElGamal.

6.3 Curve Choice and Security

We now discuss the security of the Möller variant (tagged) KA protocol. The choice of curve must satisfy the following

- The finite field must have order at least $2^q - 2^{q/2}$.
- The curve and its twist must be cryptographically secure.
- The curve and its twist must be cyclic.

More specifically, we need a security property similar to the **oracle Diffie-Hellman (ODH)** assumption [ABR01]. That definition is as follows:

Definition 20 ([ABR01])**.** *Let $\mathbb{G}$ be a cyclic group of order n, with generator g, and let $H : \{0,1\}^* \to \{0,1\}^\ell$ be a hash function. Then the* ***oracle Diffie-Hellman (ODH)*** *assumption holds in $\mathbb{G}$ with respect to H if the following distributions are indistinguishable, for all $\mathcal{A}$ that do not query their oracle at bg.*

Sender (tag τ)		Receiver (tag τ)
$a_0 \leftarrow [n]$		$b \leftarrow [n]$
$a_1 \leftarrow [n]$		$\beta \leftarrow \{0,1\}$
$A_0 = a_0 G_0$		$B = bG_\beta$
$A_1 = a_1 G_1$	$\xrightarrow{A_0, A_1}$	
	$\xleftarrow{B_{\text{abscissa,sign}}}$	
if B on the curve:		
$\beta = 0$		
else: $\beta = 1$		
return $H(a_\beta \cdot B, \tau)$		return $H(b \cdot A_\beta, \tau)$

Fig. 9. Möller tagged ECDHKA. G_0 is a generator of the curve and G_1 is a generator of its twist.

$a, b \leftarrow [n]$	$a, b \leftarrow [n]$
def $\mathcal{H}_a(X) = H(aX)$	def $\mathcal{H}_a(X) = H(aX)$
$K = H(abg)$	$K \leftarrow \{0,1\}^\ell$
return $\mathcal{A}^{\mathcal{H}_a}(ag, bg, K)$	return $\mathcal{A}^{\mathcal{H}_a}(ag, bg, K)$

Our applications require a variant of ODH where the hash function H takes an additional *tag* argument:

Definition 21. *Let $\mathbb{G}$ be a cyclic group of order n, with generator g, and let $H : \{0,1\}^* \times \{0,1\}^* \to \{0,1\}^\ell$ be a hash function. Then the* ***tagged oracle Diffie-Hellman (TODH)*** *assumption holds in $\mathbb{G}$ with respect to H if the following distributions are indistinguishable, for all tags τ^* and all $\mathcal{A}$ that do not query their oracle with second argument τ^*:*

$a, b \leftarrow [n]$	$a, b \leftarrow [n]$
def $\mathcal{H}_a(X, \tau) = H(aX, \tau)$	def $\mathcal{H}_a(X, \tau) = H(aX, \tau)$
$K = H(abg, \tau^*)$	$K \leftarrow \{0,1\}^\ell$
return $\mathcal{A}^{\mathcal{H}_a}(ag, bg, K)$	return $\mathcal{A}^{\mathcal{H}_a}(ag, bg, K)$

In [ABR01] the authors show that standard ODH is secure in the generic group model when H is a random oracle. This proof is easily adapted to the new TODH assumption as well.

Proposition 22. *Möller tagged DHKA (Fig. 9) satisfies tag nonmalleability (Definition 3) if the TODH assumption holds in both the curve and its twist.*

A further small optimization is possible for Montgomery curves. The multiplication algorithm only depends on the x-coordinate of its input and is uniform for both the curve and its twist, in the sense that the usual multiplication algorithm for the curve also correctly multiplies in the twist if the input is on the twist. So if the sender in Fig. 9 chooses $a_0 = a_1$ then there is no need to check

Sender		Receiver (with input $\{c_i\}_{i\in[N]}$)
$\phi_1 \ldots \phi_\kappa \leftarrow$ Base OT Receiver	$\xrightarrow{\phi_1,\ldots,\phi_\kappa}$	$M_S, \{r_{i,j}\} \leftarrow$ Base OT Sender
		$\{u^i\} \leftarrow$ OT Extension Receiver
		chal := $H(\{\phi_i\}, M_S, \{u^i\})$
$r_{i,c_i} \leftarrow$ Base OT Receiver	$\xleftarrow{M_S, \{u^i\}, \text{resp}}$	resp $\leftarrow$ OT Extension Receiver
chal := $H(\{\phi_i\}, M_S, \{u^i\})$		
check that resp answers chal		
$\{r'_{i,j}\}_{i,j} \leftarrow$ OT Extension Sender		$\{r'_{i,c_i}\}_i \leftarrow$ OT Extension Receiver
return $\{r'_{i,j}\}_{i\in[N],j\in\{0,1\}}$		return $\{r'_{i,c_i}\}_{i\in[N]}$

Fig. 10. Sketch of the composition of our batch OT protocol with the KOS OT extension protocol, in 2 rounds.

whether the receiver's B is on the curve or twist. Instead, the sender simply multiplies B without any checking. However, security of this optimization requires that a kind of TODH assumption hold for the curve and twist jointly (instead of separately/independently for the curve and for the twist).

Instantiation. When creating a concrete instantiation of Möller ECDHKA, we chose to use Curve25519 [Ber06]. The main reasons for this choice were:

1. The base field $\mathbb{F}_p$ is of prime order $2^{255} - 19 > 2^{255} - 2^{255/2}$.
2. Curve25519 is explicitly designed to have a twist that is as secure as the curve itself.
3. Curve25519 can take full advantage of Montgomery Ladders for scalar multiplication which allows us to use only the abscissa in computations.
4. Curve25519 and its twist have large prime subgroups of size $\#E/8$ and $\#E'_c/4$.

Curve25519 also provides additional evidence for the security of the above optimization of setting $a_0 = a_1$, because [Ber06] recommends not checking whether a given point is on the curve or twist before performing scalar multiplication. This optimization is why Curve25519 was chosen to have a secure twist, and in fact the reference implementation does not check if an elliptic curve point is on the curve. This requires a similar additional security assumption to our optimization because it uses the same key for both the curve and its twist.

7 2-Round Endemic OT Extension

When our protocol is used for base OTs, we can achieve a 2-round Endemic OT extension protocol if the Fiat-Shamir heuristic is used. First, recall that our batch OT protocol is 1-flow when instantiated with a 1-flow KA protocol, *e.g.*, any Diffie-Hellman-based KA protocol. This gives us the flexibility to send base OT messages in any order.

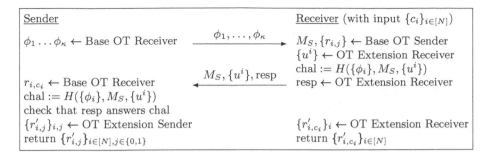

Second, we summarize the 1-out-of-2 OT extension protocol of [KOS15]:

- The parties perform base OTs
- The receiver (who is base OT sender) sends data as in all IKNP-based [IKNP03] extension protocols.
- To protect against a malicious receiver, the sender gives a random challenge
- The receiver sends a response to this challenge, which the sender checks.

We can order the messages of the base OTs so that the receiver can send their IKNP data along with their base OT sender message. Additionally, we can collapse the malicious consistency check using the Fiat-Shamir heuristic, since the sender's challenge is random. The resulting OT extension protocol is sketched in Fig. 10.

In related work, [CSW20] show how to use the Chou-Orlandi base OT protocol to achieve 3-round OT extension. This is inevitable since their base OTs already require 3 rounds. [BCG19] show a 2-round OT extension protocol based on newer "silent OT" techniques. Note however that both these papers achieve chosen message OT, while Fig. 10 only achieves endemic OT and would require a third round to derandomize the sender's messages.

8 Performance Evaluation

In this section, we will explore the concrete performance benchmarks of multiple instantiations of the protocol in Fig. 3.

8.1 Implementation Details

We implemented[8] our protocol inside the `libote` OT extension library [Rin], modifying the library to use Rijndael-256 [DR99,BÖS11] to instantiate an ideal cipher and `libsodium` [Den20] to implement elliptic curve operations. The library uses Blake2 [ANWW13] to instantiate a random oracle. We then tested the protocols on a machine running on an Intel Xeon E5-2699 v3 CPU, without assembly optimizations or multi-threading. For benchmarking, each protocol was run in a batch of 128 OTs for two settings of simulated latency and bandwidth limiting. The two settings are meant to shed light on the LAN vs WAN environments that these protocols may run in. The number of OTs to run was chosen to provide a realistic setting in the case of 128 base OTs as is common in OT extension.

We compared the following implementations:

- Chou-Orlandi (Simplest OT).
- Naor-Pinkas OT
- Masny-Rindal (Endemic OT), with and without reusing the sender's message. This protocol uses hash-to-curve operations.

[8] Source code is at https://github.com/Oreko/popfot-implementation.

Table 2. Running time to generate a batch of 128 OT instances. We report the average of 100 trials for each experiment.

Protocol	Security	Sender (ms)	Receiver (ms)
0.1 ms latency, 10000 Mbps bandwidth cap			
Simplest OT [CO15] (Sender-reuse)	Standalone	35	17
Naor-Pinkas OT [NP01] (Sender-reuse)	Standalone	43	34
Endemic OT [MR19] (No reuse)	UC	79	42
Endemic OT (Sender-reuse)	UC	62	37
Ours (Field Feistel POPF Fig. 7—DHKA)	UC	80	40
Ours (Field Feistel POPF—Möller DHKA)	UC	50	27
Ours (MR POPF Fig. 6—Möller DHKA)	UC	48	27
Ours (EKE POPF Fig. 4—Möller DHKA)	UC	50	25
30 ms latency, 100 Mbps bandwidth cap			
Simplest OT [CO15] (Sender-reuse)	Standalone	105	111
Naor-Pinkas OT [NP01] (Sender-reuse)	Standalone	101	107
Endemic OT [MR19] (No reuse)	UC	161	53
Endemic OT (Sender-reuse)	UC	137	53
Ours (Field Feistel POPF Fig. 7—DHKA)	UC	155	47
Ours (Field Feistel POPF—Möller DHKA)	UC	128	44
Ours (MR POPF Fig. 6—Möller DHKA)	UC	128	44
Ours (EKE POPF Fig. 4—Möller DHKA)	UC	128	44

- Our protocol instantiated with Möller's DHKA and various POPFs presented in Sect. 5. Because the messages from Möller's scheme are uniformly random bit strings, our POPFs avoid the hash-to-curve operations that are needed in [MR19]. We did not evaluate the Even-Mansour POPF (Fig. 5) since its performance would be identical to the EKE POPF (Fig. 4) when Rijndael is used to instantiate both the ideal cipher and ideal permutation.
- Our protocol with traditional DHKA, and all POPF instantiations excluding EKE and Masny-Rindal. We did not implement the EKE POPF using DHKA; however, this might be possible using Elligator or a similar mapping to construct an ideal cipher on a subset of the curve points. We did not implement our protocol with Masny-Rindal POPF as it would be nearly identical to the Masny-Rindal protocol.

8.2 Results and Discussion

The performance benchmarks can be found in Table 2 for both settings.

As we would expect, when comparing the three instances of Masny-Rindal OT, each with their own improvement, we see a marked increase in efficiency. Specifically, reusing the sender's message reduced the total time spent by both parties by 18%/11% in the low latency and high bandwidth setting/the high latency and low bandwidth setting, respectively. Moving to Möller's KA caused an additional 24%/9% improvement, respectively, for the Masny-Rindal construction. On average, for the three protocols with both DHKA and Möller DHKA versions (Masny-Rindal and the Feistel POPF) we saw an improvement of 31%/12%, respectively, when moving to Möller's KA.

As expected, the Simplest OT protocol outperforms our instantiations for the sender since it uses fewer exponentiations in the group. One point to take note of in the evaluation data is the large gap in the performance for the receiver between the Naor-Pinkas and Simplest/Blazing OT constructions and the POPF and Masny-Rindal constructions in the high latency/low bandwidth setting. This is due to the different flow requirements between the two sets of protocols. Simplest OT and Naor-Pinkas constructions all require an additional flow (or two) which, in the WAN setting, will accrue more time for the party which needs to wait. It then follows that the advantages of our protocol over Simplest OT is our UC security and round/flow complexity.

References

[ABR01] Abdalla, M., Bellare, M., Rogaway, P.: The oracle Diffie-Hellman assumptions and an analysis of DHIES. In: Naccache, D. (ed.) CT-RSA 2001. LNCS, vol. 2020, pp. 143–158. Springer, Heidelberg (2001). https://doi.org/10.1007/3-540-45353-9_12

[ALSZ13] Asharov, G., Lindell, Y., Schneider, T., Zohner, M.: More efficient oblivious transfer and extensions for faster secure computation. In: Sadeghi, A.-R., Gligor, V.D., Yung, M., (eds.) ACM CCS 2013, pp. 535–548. ACM Press, November 2013

[ANWW13] Aumasson, J.-P., Neves, S., Wilcox-O'Hearn, Z., Winnerlein, C.: BLAKE2: simpler, smaller, fast as MD5. In: Jacobson, M., Locasto, M., Mohassel, P., Safavi-Naini, R. (eds.) ACNS 2013. LNCS, vol. 7954, pp. 119–135. Springer, Heidelberg (2013). https://doi.org/10.1007/978-3-642-38980-1_8

[BCG19] Boyle, E., et al.: Efficient two-round OT extension and silent non-interactive secure computation. In: Cavallaro, L., Kinder, J., Wang, X., Katz, J. (eds.) ACM CCS 2019, pp. 291–308. ACM Press, November 2019

[BCI10] Brier, E., Coron, J.-S., Icart, T., Madore, D., Randriam, H., Tibouchi, M.: Efficient indifferentiable hashing into ordinary elliptic curves. In: Rabin, T. (ed.) CRYPTO 2010. LNCS, vol. 6223, pp. 237–254. Springer, Heidelberg (2010). https://doi.org/10.1007/978-3-642-14623-7_13

[Bea96] Beaver, D.: Correlated pseudorandomness and the complexity of private computations. In: 28th ACM STOC, pp. 479–488. ACM Press, May 1996

[Ber06] Bernstein, D.J.: Curve25519: new Diffie-Hellman speed records. In: Yung, M., Dodis, Y., Kiayias, A., Malkin, T. (eds.) PKC 2006. LNCS, vol. 3958, pp. 207–228. Springer, Heidelberg (2006). https://doi.org/10.1007/11745853_14

[BHKL13] Bernstein, D.J., Hamburg, M., Krasnova, A., Lange, T.: Elligator: elliptic-curve points indistinguishable from uniform random strings. In: Sadeghi, A.-R., Gligor, V.D., Yung, M. (eds.) ACM CCS 2013, pp. 967–980. ACM Press, November 2013

[BM92] Bellovin, S.M., Merritt, M.: Encrypted key exchange: password-based protocols secure against dictionary attacks. In: 1992 IEEE Symposium on Security and Privacy, pp. 72–84. IEEE Computer Society Press, May 1992

[BMN01] Boyd, C., Montague, P., Nguyen, K.: Elliptic curve based password authenticated key exchange protocols. In: Varadharajan, V., Mu, Y. (eds.) ACISP 2001. LNCS, vol. 2119, pp. 487–501. Springer, Heidelberg (2001). https://doi.org/10.1007/3-540-47719-5_38

[BÖS11] Bos, J.W., Özen, O., Stam, M.: Efficient hashing using the AES instruction set. In: Preneel, B., Takagi, T. (eds.) CHES 2011. LNCS, vol. 6917, pp. 507–522. Springer, Heidelberg (2011). https://doi.org/10.1007/978-3-642-23951-9_33

[CFGP06] Chevassut, O., Fouque, P.-A., Gaudry, P., Pointcheval, D.: The twist-augmented technique for key exchange. In: Yung, M., Dodis, Y., Kiayias, A., Malkin, T. (eds.) PKC 2006. LNCS, vol. 3958, pp. 410–426. Springer, Heidelberg (2006). https://doi.org/10.1007/11745853_27

[CMR] Carmer, B., Malozemoff, A.J., Rosen, M.: Swanky: a suite of rust libraries for secure multi-party computation. https://github.com/GaloisInc/swanky

[CO15] Chou, T., Orlandi, C.: The simplest protocol for oblivious transfer. In: Lauter, K., Rodríguez-Henríquez, F. (eds.) LATINCRYPT 2015. LNCS, vol. 9230, pp. 40–58. Springer, Cham (2015). https://doi.org/10.1007/978-3-319-22174-8_3

[CSW20] Canetti, R., Sarkar, P., Wang, X.: Blazing fast OT for three-round UC OT extension. In: Kiayias, A., Kohlweiss, M., Wallden, P., Zikas, V. (eds.) PKC 2020. LNCS, vol. 12111, pp. 299–327. Springer, Cham (2020). https://doi.org/10.1007/978-3-030-45388-6_11

[Den20] Denis, F.: The sodium cryptography library, November 2020

[DR99] Daemen, J., Rijmen, V.: AES proposal: Rijndael (1999)

[DSST17] Dai, Y., Seurin, Y., Steinberger, J., Thiruvengadam, A.: Indifferentiability of iterated Even-Mansour ciphers with non-idealized key-schedules: five rounds are necessary and sufficient. In: Katz, J., Shacham, H. (eds.) CRYPTO 2017. LNCS, vol. 10403, pp. 524–555. Springer, Cham (2017). https://doi.org/10.1007/978-3-319-63697-9_18

[EM93] Even, S., Mansour, Y.: A construction of a cipher from a single pseudorandom permutation. In: Imai, H., Rivest, R.L., Matsumoto, T. (eds.) ASIACRYPT 1991. LNCS, vol. 739, pp. 210–224. Springer, Heidelberg (1993). https://doi.org/10.1007/3-540-57332-1_17

[FFS+10] Farashahi, R.R., Fouque, P.-A., Shparlinski, I.E., Tibouchi, M., Felipe Voloch, J.: Indifferentiable deterministic hashing to elliptic and hyperelliptic curves. Cryptology ePrint Archive, Report 2010/539 (2010). http://eprint.iacr.org/2010/539

[HL17] Hauck, E., Loss, J.: Efficient and universally composable protocols for oblivious transfer from the CDH assumption. Cryptology ePrint Archive, Report 2017/1011 (2017). http://eprint.iacr.org/2017/1011

[IKNP03] Ishai, Y., Kilian, J., Nissim, K., Petrank, E.: Extending oblivious transfers efficiently. In: Boneh, D. (ed.) CRYPTO 2003. LNCS, vol. 2729, pp. 145–161. Springer, Heidelberg (2003). https://doi.org/10.1007/978-3-540-45146-4_9

[IR90] Impagliazzo, R., Rudich, S.: Limits on the provable consequences of one-way permutations. In: Goldwasser, S. (ed.) CRYPTO 1988. LNCS, vol. 403, pp. 8–26. Springer, New York (1990). https://doi.org/10.1007/0-387-34799-2_2

[Kal91] Kaliski, B.S., Jr.: One-way permutations on elliptic curves. J. Cryptol. **3**(3), 187–199 (1991)

[Kel20] Keller, M.: MP-SPDZ: a versatile framework for multi-party computation. Cryptology ePrint Archive, Report 2020/521 (2020). https://eprint.iacr.org/2020/521

[KK13] Kolesnikov, V., Kumaresan, R.: Improved OT extension for transferring short secrets. In: Canetti, R., Garay, J.A. (eds.) CRYPTO 2013. LNCS, vol. 8043, pp. 54–70. Springer, Heidelberg (2013). https://doi.org/10.1007/978-3-642-40084-1_4

[KOS15] Keller, M., Orsini, E., Scholl, P.: Actively secure OT extension with optimal overhead. In: Gennaro, R., Robshaw, M. (eds.) CRYPTO 2015. LNCS, vol. 9215, pp. 724–741. Springer, Heidelberg (2015). https://doi.org/10.1007/978-3-662-47989-6_35

[Möl04] Möller, B.: A public-key encryption scheme with pseudo-random ciphertexts. In: Samarati, P., Ryan, P., Gollmann, D., Molva, R. (eds.) ESORICS 2004. LNCS, vol. 3193, pp. 335–351. Springer, Heidelberg (2004). https://doi.org/10.1007/978-3-540-30108-0_21

[MR19] Masny, D., Rindal, P.: Endemic oblivious transfer. In: Cavallaro, L., Kinder, J., Wang, X., Katz, J. (eds.) ACM CCS 2019, pp. 309–326. ACM Press, November 2019

[MRR20] McQuoid, I., Rosulek, M., Roy, L.: Minimal symmetric PAKE and 1-out-of-N OT from programmable-once public functions. In: Ligatti, J., Ou, X., Katz, J., Vigna, G. (eds.) ACM CCS 2020, pp. 425–442. ACM Press, November 2020

[NP01] Naor, M., Pinkas, B.: Efficient oblivious transfer protocols. In: Rao Kosaraju, S. (ed.) 12th SODA, pp. 448–457. ACM-SIAM, January 2001

[OOS17] Orrù, M., Orsini, E., Scholl, P.: Actively secure 1-out-of-N OT extension with application to private set intersection. In: Handschuh, H. (ed.) CT-RSA 2017. LNCS, vol. 10159, pp. 381–396. Springer, Cham (2017). https://doi.org/10.1007/978-3-319-52153-4_22

[Rin] Rindal, P.: libOTe: an efficient, portable, and easy to use Oblivious Transfer Library. https://github.com/osu-crypto/libOTe

[Sil09] Silverman, J.H.: The Arithmetic of Elliptic Curves, vol. 106. Springer, New York (2009). https://doi.org/10.1007/978-0-387-09494-6

[Sma] Nigel Smart. SCALE-MAMBA: Secure computation algorithms from LEuven, multiparty algorithms basic argot. https://homes.esat.kuleuven.be/~nsmart/SCALE/

[TK17] Tibouchi, M., Kim, T.: Improved elliptic curve hashing and point representation. Des. Codes Cryptogr. **82**, 161–177 (2017)

[WMK16] Wang, X., Malozemoff, A.J., Katz, J.: EMP-toolkit: efficient multiparty computation toolkit (2016). https://github.com/emp-toolkit

Algebraic Adversaries in the Universal Composability Framework

Michel Abdalla[1,2](✉), Manuel Barbosa[3], Jonathan Katz[4], Julian Loss[5], and Jiayu Xu[6]

[1] DIENS, École normale supérieure, CNRS, PSL University, Paris, France
[2] DFINITY, Zürich, Switzerland
[3] University of Porto (FCUP) and INESC TEC, Porto, Portugal
mbb@fc.up.pt
[4] University of Maryland, College Park, USA
[5] CISPA Helmholtz Center for Information Security, Saarbrücken, Germany
[6] Algorand, Boston, USA
jiayux@uci.edu

Abstract. The algebraic-group model (AGM), which lies between the generic group model and the standard model of computation, provides a means by which to analyze the security of cryptosystems against so-called *algebraic* adversaries. We formalize the AGM within the framework of universal composability, providing formal definitions for this setting and proving an appropriate composition theorem. This extends the applicability of the AGM to more-complex protocols, and lays the foundations for analyzing algebraic adversaries in a composable fashion. Our results also clarify the meaning of composing proofs in the AGM with other proofs and they highlight a natural form of independence between idealized groups that seems inherent to the AGM and has not been made formal before—these insights also apply to the composition of game-based proofs in the AGM. We show the utility of our model by proving several important protocols universally composable for algebraic adversaries, specifically: (1) the Chou-Orlandi protocol for oblivious transfer, and (2) the SPAKE2 and CPace protocols for password-based authenticated key exchange.

1 Introduction

Security proofs are often carried out in idealized models that seek to capture certain classes of adversarial behavior. Examples include the random-oracle model [9], in which the attacker is assumed to treat a hash function as an ideal random function; the ideal-cipher model, in which the attacker is assumed to treat a block cipher as an ideal keyed permutation; and the generic-group model (GGM) [29,30], where the attacker is assumed to treat group elements as abstract identifiers and group operations as black-box operations on those identifiers.

J. Loss—Work done while at the University of Maryland.

J. Xu—Work done while at George Mason University.

M. Tibouchi and H. Wang (Eds.): ASIACRYPT 2021, LNCS 13092, pp. 311–341, 2021.
https://doi.org/10.1007/978-3-030-92078-4_11

Cryptographers continually seek to refine these models, making them more expressive so they capture larger classes of algorithms and thus come closer to modeling adversaries performing arbitrary computation. With this motivation in mind, Fuchsbauer et al. [19] (based on ideas of Abdalla et al. [4]) proposed the *algebraic-group model* (AGM) as a more expressive version of the GGM. Roughly, the AGM considers *algebraic* adversaries that compute group elements via a sequence of "generic" group operations, but which—in contrast to the GGM—are allowed to utilize the *actual bitstrings* representing group elements in the course of their computation. This model is strictly stronger than the GGM; for example, index-calculus algorithms that apply to certain classes of groups are algebraic and hence allowed in the AGM, even though they are ruled out in the GGM by known lower bounds on the hardness of the discrete-logarithm problem in that model. The AGM has been used to show equivalence of various number-theoretic assumptions [6,7,19] and to prove security of SNARKs [17,19,27] and blind signatures [20]. An extension called the *strong* AGM has recently been used to prove hardness of the repeated squaring assumption underlying timed commitments and related primitives [24].

Notably, none of the aforementioned results provide any guarantees of security under composition with other protocols (whether proven secure in the AGM or not). Here, we lay the foundations for a composable treatment of algebraic adversaries by formalizing the AGM within the framework of *universal composability* (UC) [13] and proving a corresponding composition theorem. This involves not only formalizing a number of subtle issues related to the AGM itself (which may be of independent interest for subsequent work in the AGM), but also making a number of careful design decisions in defining what algebraic adversaries mean in the UC framework, in part to ensure that a suitable composition theorem holds. We discuss this in more detail in the following section.

We demonstrate the utility of our model by proving several important protocols universally composable for algebraic adversaries. Specifically, we prove security of (1) the Chou-Orlandi protocol for oblivious transfer [18], and (2) the SPAKE2 and CPace protocols for password-based authenticated key exchange [5,22] in our model. We describe these results further in Sect. 1.2.

1.1 Defining the AGM Within the UC Framework

We first define some notation and terminology related to the AGM that suffices to understand the discussion that follows. (Our treatment here is deliberately informal, and we refer the reader to Sect. 2 for technical details.) Fix a group $\mathbb{G}$. An *algebraic representation* of $h \in \mathbb{G}$ with respect to a list of elements $g_1, \ldots, g_n \in \mathbb{G}$ is a tuple $(x_1, \ldots, x_n) \in \mathbb{Z}^n$ with $h = \prod_i g_i^{x_i}$. Roughly speaking, the AGM considers adversaries that are *algebraic* (with respect to $\mathbb{G}$), meaning that if an adversary $\mathcal{A}$ outputs a group element $h \in \mathbb{G}$, then $\mathcal{A}$ must also output an algebraic representation of h with respect to the set of group elements (which we call a *base*) that $\mathcal{A}$ has been given as input thus far.

We generalize the AGM to the standard UC framework by restricting our attention to algebraic attackers.[1] While this is a natural idea, it involves dealing with a number of subtle technical issues. First of all, to make this notion meaningful it is not sufficient to restrict the adversary to be algebraic; rather, we require the *environment* to be algebraic as well. Moreover, in order for composition to possibly hold, we must also require the *simulator* used in proving security to be algebraic. That is, in the *UC-AGM* a protocol π securely realizes a functionality $\mathcal{F}$ if, for any efficient algebraic adversary $\mathcal{A}$, there is an efficient algebraic simulator $\mathcal{S}$ such that no efficient algebraic environment can distinguish the execution of $\mathcal{A}$ with π from the execution of $\mathcal{S}$ with $\mathcal{F}$. Under this definition, we can indeed prove that a UC-style composition theorem holds in the UC-AGM.

Our definition of an algebraic algorithm makes a distinction between adversarial entities (real and ideal world adversaries and environments) and non-adversarial entities (uncorrupted protocol participants and ideal functionalities). In the real world, we require the adversary to behave algebraically when it delivers group elements to uncorrupted participants and to ideal functionalities (when the proof is carried out in a hybrid real-world); moreover, we also require the environment to behave algebraically when it delivers group elements to the adversary, but not the converse. Algebraic behavior is defined within the context of a UC-AGM proof by specifying what set of group elements occurring during the protocol execution in the real-world must be used by the environment and by the adversary as a base for the provided group element representations. When this is the empty set, we recover the standard UC framework. The natural definition for this set is to include in it *all* the group elements that are produced by non-adversarial entities.

Formally, the quantification of the UC-emulation notion is subtle. As in UC, we require for all adversaries $\mathcal{A}$, the existence of a simulator $\mathcal{S}$, such that for all enviroments $\mathcal{Z}$ the real and ideal worlds are indistinguishable. However, the simulator is only required to work if the pair $(\mathcal{A}, \mathcal{Z})$ satisfies the algebraic restrictions specified in the real world. Intuitively, the extra power of the simulator comes from the fact that $\mathcal{Z}$ is bound to behave algebraically when interacting with $\mathcal{A}$ and, furthermore, that $\mathcal{A}$ will also behave algebraically if the simulator runs it internally. A caveat is that the simulator must also ensure that $(\mathcal{S}, \mathcal{Z})$ satisfy the algebraic restrictions in the ideal world. However, in the most common case when the simulator is interacting with an ideal functionality, if this interaction does not involve group elements, then the algebraic requirement is not a restriction on the simulation strategy (this is the case in all our proofs for concrete protocols).

[1] One can consider formalizing the AGM within the UC framework by introducing a functionality $\mathcal{F}_{\mathsf{AGM}}$ that "forces" arbitrary algorithms to behave algebraically by registering group elements and their representations in a central repository. This has a number of disadvantages that we discuss in the full version [3]. Our approach is closer to the spirit of the AGM, which idealizes groups by quantifying over restricted classes of adversaries.

The UC AGM composition theorem then states, as expected, that $\rho^\pi \sim \rho^\mathcal{F}$ if $\pi \sim \mathcal{F}$. Again the quantification is subtle. The composition theorem guarantees only hold if we restrict our quantification to match the emulation guarantee provided by π: i.e., we have that $\rho^\pi \sim \rho^\mathcal{F}$ with respect to pairs $(\mathcal{A}, \mathcal{Z})$ that adhere to the base B_π when interacting with machines in π. Note that this means, in particular, that the attacker cannot use group elements produced in ρ when attacking π, unless it is able to provide a representation according to B_π.

The companion UC AGM transitivity theory further highlights a natural notion of independence between UC AGM proofs. Suppose that $\rho^\mathcal{F}$ is known to UC AGM emulate some functionality $\mathcal{G}$. Transitivity intuitively implies that $\rho^\pi \sim \mathcal{G}$ if $\rho^\pi \sim \rho^\mathcal{F}$. We show that this is the case also in the UC AGM setting, if we restrict the quantification over $(\mathcal{A}, \mathcal{Z})$ to those attackers that independently meet the AGM restrictions imposed by the proofs of both π and ρ. This means providing algebraic decompositions to parties executing π with respect to a base B_π defined in the proof of π and, similarly, respecting the algebraic base B_ρ when interacting with parties executing ρ. This restriction means that AGM UC composition works as expected for protocols that operate on groups that can be assumed to be *independent.*

In Sect. 2.3 we give full technical details and also show that proofs in the UC AGM naturally compose with proofs in the plain UC model; as expected, the composed protocols can only be shown to be secure in the UC AGM setting. We also show that the standard approach of writing UC proofs wrt to a dummy adversary still applies in the UC AGM setting.

Discussion. Our theorems show that one should be very careful when composing proofs in the AGM, and not only in the UC setting. For example, when composing game-based reductions carried out in the AGM, the same issues arise. Intuitively, composition can only be guaranteed when the AGM assumptions do not interact badly with each-other, i.e., interacting with one protocol does not allow an attacker to override the extractability assumption that is being captured by the AGM in the proof of another protocol. In practice this seems to imply excluding attackers that take group elements from one protocol and use them to attack another protocol (unless of course the algebraic construction of those elements can be explained with respect to the set of bases defined by the target protocol alone).

Interestingly, in recent independent work Kerber, Kiayias and Kohlweiss [25] encouter a manifestation of the same problem in the constructive cryptography framework. In this work, the authors propose a general notion of proofs wrt to knowledge assumptions, which generalizes the AGM: adversaries provide the relevant extractable information when interacting with the protocol. Their goal is to study the composition of protocols that rely on different knowledge assumptions. It is beyond the scope of this paper to make a detailed comparison, since the approaches rely on different compositional frameworks and have different goals, but it is clear that the same restrictions must be imposed in the composition theorem to enable a proof; quoting from the paper: "*Care must be taken that knowledge stemming from one knowledge assumption does not give an advantage in another... we conjecture that multiple instances with the AGM with independently sampled groups are sufficiently independent.*"

To conclude, we do not see the restrictions in the UC AGM composition theorems as a limitation of our work, but rather as a limitation inherent to proofs in idealized models—for example, it is easy to establish a parallel with the random oracle model in the UC setting, where the need for independent RO instances is well known [16]. On the contrary, we believe that an important contribution of our work is to clarify what this limitation means for proofs in the AGM. To overcome these limitations, and similarly to proofs in the random-oracle model, one can prove multiple protocol executions secure simultaneously. At the very least, it is important to ensure that AGM UC proofs are carried out with respect to multi-session ideal functionalities, so that multiple executions of the same protocol can be guaranteed to compose securely. We adopt this approach in our proofs. Another option is to strengthen the proofs of each protocol to consider a global/shared source of bases along with a more powerful composition theorem, similarly to UC with global functionalities. We leave exploring this option as an interesting and important direction for future work.

1.2 Proofs of Security in the UC-AGM

In addition to defining the UC-AGM framework, we also show that several important protocols from the literature—which were previously lacking full proofs of security in the UC framework—can be proven secure in our model.

The Chou-Orlandi Protocol. Chou and Orlandi [18] proposed a simple and elegant protocol for oblivious transfer and claimed that it was universally composable (with adaptive corruptions) under a suitable assumption in the random-oracle model. Unfortunately, subsequent works [11,21,23] uncovered several problems with their proof. While these subsequent works also showed how to address some of these issues, and/or presented modified protocols that could be proven secure, there seems to be no way of proving the original Chou-Orlandi protocol universally composable, even in the random-oracle model.

We show that the original Chou-Orlandi protocol can be proven secure in the UC-AGM, based on the discrete-logarithm assumption in the random-oracle model. We refer to Sect. 3 for a high-level view of the proof and further details.

The SPAKE2 and CPace Protocols. SPAKE2 [5] and CPace [22] have attracted a lot of interest recently due to their consideration for standardization by the IETF. The selection process explicitly considered whether these protocols were universally composable, which turned out to be a surprisingly difficult question to answer.[2]

Abdalla et al. [2] recently proved that these protocols are universally composable with respect to a *relaxed* version of the standard functionality for password-based authenticated key exchange (PAKE) that, roughly speaking, allows the

[2] For a review of the security proofs available for both protocols at the time, see https://mailarchive.ietf.org/arch/msg/cfrg/47pnOSsrVS8uozXbAuM-alEk0-s.

adversary to delay its password guess for a session until an arbitrary time after that session ends. The full implications of relying on that relaxed functionality are unclear; in particular, although Abdalla et al. [2] showed that adding a key-confirmation step lifts a UC PAKE protocol to one that provides explicit entity authentication, we do not know if this is the case when we start from a PAKE protocol that only realizes the relaxed PAKE functionality.

In this work, we improve upon these results by showing that both SPAKE2 and CPace are universally composable with respect to the *original* PAKE functionality [15] when we restrict our attention to algebraic adversaries. Interestingly, our proofs are significantly simpler than those of Abdalla et al. [2], since the simulator in our case can leverage the fact that the adversary is algebraic to directly extract password guesses, rather than performing an indirect extraction using the random oracle.

In addition, we also demonstrate that an important variant of SPAKE2, known as SPAKE1, is secure in the UC-AGM. SPAKE1, in contrast to SPAKE2, does not include the password as input to the final key-derivation function, and thus may be advantageous relative to SPAKE2 with regard to side-channel attacks targeting the key-derivation step. Prior to this work, SPAKE1 was not known to satisfy the standard notions of security for game-based and UC PAKE. In particular, it was not known to guarantee even the weaker notion of forward secrecy, in which the attacker can only learn passwords for sessions in which it played the role of a passive eavesdropper.

1.3 Related Work

We are not aware of any prior work modeling algebraic adversaries in the UC framework, however a few works have considered generic groups and other idealized models in that setting. Larangeira and Tanaka [26] analyze universally composable non-committing encryption schemes in the GGM and the generic-ring model (GRM). However, they leave the modeling of the GGM/GRM in the UC framework informal, and in particular do not prove that composition holds in their setting. Bradley et al. [10] prove security of a strong asymmetric PAKE protocol against a generic-group adversary in the UC framework, but their treatment is also informal; in particular, their protocol is split into an "offline part" and an "online part," with the GGM used only in the former, and it is unclear how these two parts are defined for general protocols or what the implications are for composition. Naor et al. [28] model generic-group adversaries in the UC framework by introducing a generic-group functionality $\mathcal{F}_{\mathsf{GGM}}$ in a way similar in spirit to the approach involving the $\mathcal{F}_{\mathsf{AGM}}$ functionality described earlier that we ultimately rejected. A similar approach was followed in [8] for the analysis of time-lock puzzles in the UC setting.

1.4 Overview of the Paper

Section 2 introduces the UC-AGM model. Section 3 then presents a proof of the Chou-Orlandi protocol in the UC-AGM. Next, Sect. 4 proves security of

SPAKE1, SPAKE2, and CPace in the new model. The full version [3] includes detailed proofs for theorems in Sects. 2 to 4.

2 Defining Algebraic Adversaries in the UC Framework

In this section, we introduce the UC-AGM framework that incorporates algebraic adversaries into the UC framework. We provide a brief overview of the UC framework [13] in Sect. 2.1; for a more detailed description, see the full version of this paper [3]. In Sect. 2.2 we formally define algebraic adversaries and introduce the notation of AGM-emulation that underlies the UC-AGM. We also show there that, analogous to the UC framework, it suffices to consider "algebraically dummy" adversaries when proving AGM-emulation. We prove a composition theorem for the UC-AGM in Sect. 2.3.

For simplicity, our treatment of the UC-AGM is based on the so-called simplified UC framework [13, Section 2] where the number of parties, their identities, program code, and connectivity are all fixed in advance. In the full version [3] we explain how the UC-AGM can be extended to the full UC framework.

2.1 Overview of the UC Framework

A *protocol* consists of a number of machines (or parties) with unique identities, each of which represents some computational entity. Protocol machines communicate with each other via messages labeled input or subroutine-output. In an *execution of the protocol*, two additional machines (whose identities are distinct from any protocol machines) are added: the *environment* $\mathcal{E}$ and the *adversary* $\mathcal{A}$. (Below we assume that $\mathcal{E}$ has identity 0 and $\mathcal{A}$ has identity 1.) The environment $\mathcal{E}$ can send input messages to $\mathcal{A}$ and a subset of the protocol machines (called *main machines*), and protocol machines can send subroutine-output messages to $\mathcal{E}$; the adversary $\mathcal{A}$ can send backdoor messages to $\mathcal{E}$ and all protocol machines, and receive backdoor messages from all protocol machines.

The notion of *UC emulation* involves two protocols, π and ϕ. We say that π emulates ϕ if for any efficient adversary $\mathcal{A}$ in an execution of π, there is an efficient adversary (called the *simulator*) $\mathcal{S}$ in an execution of ϕ that "simulates" the environment's view, in the sense that no efficient environment can distinguish an execution of π with $\mathcal{A}$ from an execution of ϕ with $\mathcal{S}$. A particularly important example of UC emulation is *realizing an ideal functionality*, in which the emulated protocol $\text{IDEAL}_{\mathcal{F}}$ consists of an incorruptible *ideal functionality* $\mathcal{F}$, and the main machines are dummy parties that simply pass messages between the ideal functionality and the environment.

2.2 UC Emulation in the Algebraic Group Model

In this work we put forth a notion of UC emulation (called *AGM-emulation*) in which the adversary is restricted to be algebraic. To this end, we first introduce the concept of *algebraic adversaries* [19]. At a high level, an algebraic adversary has an additional auxiliary tape on which it writes the representation of any group element it outputs on (some of) its other tapes.[3] We assume for simplicity that the group $\mathcal{G} = (\mathbb{G}, g, p)$ under consideration is cyclic with known order p, though neither of these assumptions is essential.

Definition 1. *Suppose an execution of protocol π involves protocol machines sending elements in group $\mathcal{G} = (\mathbb{G}, g, p)$ (henceforce "protocol π involves group $\mathcal{G}$").[4] A pair of environment $\mathcal{E}$ and adversary $\mathcal{A}$ (in π's execution) is $(\mathcal{G}, \pi)$-*algebraic *if it satisfies the following:*

(1) $\mathcal{A}$ has a special output tape called the algebraic tape*;*
(2) Whenever $\mathcal{A}$ sends $(\mathsf{backdoor}, m)$ *to some protocol machine, where m contains some $\mathbf{X} \in \mathbb{G}$, then either (1) $\mathcal{A}$ also writes an* algebraic representation *of $\mathbf{X}$ on its algebraic tape, or (2) $\mathcal{A}$ has previously received such representation from $\mathcal{E}$; where the algebraic representation of $\mathbf{X}$ is a list $\Lambda = [(\mathbf{X}_1, \lambda_1), \ldots, (\mathbf{X}_k, \lambda_k)]$ (where $\mathbf{X}_1, \ldots, \mathbf{X}_k \in \mathbb{G}$ and $\lambda_1, \ldots, \lambda_k \in \mathbb{Z}_p$) such that $\mathbf{X} = \mathbf{X}_1^{\lambda_1} \cdots \mathbf{X}_k^{\lambda_k}$, and $\mathbf{X}_1, \ldots, \mathbf{X}_k$ is the ordered list of group elements in messages $\mathcal{E}$ and/or $\mathcal{A}$ has received up to that point in the execution of π.*

We stress that it is necessary to separate the algebraic tape from the other tapes of $\mathcal{A}$ so that, for example, the message m itself does not contain an algebraic representation of $\mathbf{X}$. When clear from the context, we will drop $\mathcal{G}$ and π, and simply say that the environment/adversary is "algebraic."

We note that when considering static corruptions, the adversary runs the corrupt parties internally and hence messages produced by corrupt parties are subject to the restrictions above. The model for adaptive corruptions is the obvious one. Non-corrupt parties compute group elements honestly. So, if no secure erasure is assumed, the representations of any group elements computed by non-corrupt parties are part of their state when they are corrupted (and are given to the adversary). If we assume secure erasure, then any such state will not be available, and so any group elements that are part of a non-corrupt party's state will not have their representations available; in this case they must be added to the adversary's basis.

AGM Emulation. We could now consider standard UC emulation restricted to algebraic adversaries and environments. However, looking ahead, in order for composition to hold we will want the simulator to be algebraic as well.

[3] Formally, we assume an encoding of group elements that distinguishes them from arbitrary strings. This can be done by simply prefixing any group element with a 0 and any other string (not necessarily representing a group element) with a 1. Following prior work [19], we use bold capital letters to denote group elements (except for the generator g).

[4] Formally, we consider protocols having access to a $\mathcal{F}_{\text{CRS}}$ functionality, where $\mathcal{F}_{\text{CRS}}$ runs a group-generation algorithm to obtain $\mathcal{G}$ (and possibly additional group elements), and then sends $\mathcal{G}$ (and any other elements) to parties that request it. Note that the protocol may use other groups, but we only require the adversary to be algebraic with respect to $\mathcal{G}$.

Definition 2. *Suppose protocols π and ϕ involve the same group $\mathcal{G}$. We say that* π $\mathcal{G}$-AGM emulates ϕ *if the following holds: for any efficient adversary $\mathcal{A}$, there is an efficient adversary $\mathcal{S}$ (called the* simulator*) such that: for any efficient $\mathcal{E}$ such that $(\mathcal{E}, \mathcal{A})$ are $(\mathcal{G}, \pi)$-algebraic, we have that $(\mathcal{E}, \mathcal{S})$ are $(\mathcal{G}, \phi)$-algebraic, and*

$$\text{EXEC}_{\phi,\mathcal{S},\mathcal{E}} \approx \text{EXEC}_{\pi,\mathcal{A},\mathcal{E}},$$

where $\text{EXEC}_{\pi,\mathcal{A},\mathcal{E}}$ *denotes environment $\mathcal{E}$'s view in π's execution with adversary $\mathcal{A}$.*

Above, we write $\approx$ to denote generic computational indistinguishability. This may refer to either asymptotic indistinguishability, in which case a security parameter is introduced as well, or concrete indistinguishability, in which case we write $\approx_\epsilon$ to denote that the distinguishing advantage is bounded by ϵ.

Definition 3. *Protocol* π $\mathcal{G}$-AGM realizes *ideal functionality $\mathcal{F}$ if π $\mathcal{G}$-AGM emulates* $\text{IDEAL}_{\mathcal{F}}$*, the ideal protocol for $\mathcal{F}$.*

AGM Emulation with Respect to a Sub-protocol. Our definitions of algebraic adversary and environment can be easily extended to the setting where the adversary/environment is restricted within a sub-protocol, namely it can only use group elements in received from *parties in this sub-protocol* as its basis for algebraic representation.

Definition 4. *Suppose protocol ρ^π involves group $\mathcal{G}$, and π is a sub-protocol of ρ^π. A pair of environment $\mathcal{E}$ and adversary $\mathcal{A}$ (in ρ^π's execution) is $(\mathcal{G}, \pi)$-*algebraic *if it satisfies the following:*

(1) $\mathcal{A}$ has a special output tape called the algebraic tape*;*
(2) Whenever $\mathcal{A}$ sends (backdoor, m) *to some protocol machine, where m contains some $\mathbf{X} \in \mathbb{G}$, then either (1) $\mathcal{A}$ also writes an* algebraic representation (with respect to π) *of $\mathbf{X}$ on its algebraic tape, or (2) $\mathcal{A}$ has previously received such representation from $\mathcal{E}$; where the algebraic representation of $\mathbf{X}$ is a list $\Lambda = [(\mathbf{X}_1, \lambda_1), \ldots, (\mathbf{X}_k, \lambda_k)]$ (where $\mathbf{X}_1, \ldots, \mathbf{X}_k \in \mathbb{G}$ and $\lambda_1, \ldots, \lambda_k \in \mathbb{Z}_p$) such that $\mathbf{X} = \mathbf{X}_1^{\lambda_1} \cdots \mathbf{X}_k^{\lambda_k}$, and $\mathbf{X}_1, \ldots, \mathbf{X}_k$ is the ordered list of group elements in messages $\mathcal{E}$ and/or $\mathcal{A}$ have received up to that point* from either the environment or protocol machines in π, that is, excluding protocol machines in $\rho^\pi \setminus \pi$. *(For the formal definition of a "sub-protocol," see the full version [3].)*

Clearly, Definition 1 can be viewed as Definition 4 in the special case that $\rho^\pi = \pi$. Note that now we can talk about AGM emulation *with respect to a sub-protocol*, i.e., protocol ρ^π $(\mathcal{G}, \pi, \phi)$-AGM emulates ρ^ϕ, where the environment/adversary pair is restricted by the sub-protocol π, and the environment/simulator pair is restricted by the sub-protocol ϕ. The formal definition exactly follows Definition 2.

The Algebraically Dummy Adversary. Similar to the standard UC framework, we can also define a notion of dummy adversary here; this will be usful in our protocol analyses in the later sections. Recall that in the standard UC framework, the dummy adversary is one that merely passes messages to and from the environment. However, in our setting, the environment might send some algebraic representations to the adversary, which we do not want the protocol parties to receive. Hence, we define the *algebraically dummy adversary* as dropping these algebraic representations.

Definition 5. *Suppose protocol π involves group $\mathcal{G}$. An adversary $\mathcal{D}$ (in π's execution) is* $(\mathcal{G}, \pi)$-algebraically dummy *if it satisfies the following: for any message* $(\mathsf{backdoor}, m)$ *sent from some identity $ID \neq 0$ (i.e., from some protocol machine), it sends* $(\mathsf{backdoor}, (ID, m))$ *to the environment $\mathcal{E}$; for any message* $(\mathsf{input}, (ID, m))$ *sent from $\mathcal{E}$, it sends* $(\mathsf{backdoor}, m)$ *to identity ID, except that if m contains $\mathbf{X} \in \mathbb{G}$ and its algebraic representation Λ, then $\mathcal{A}$ sends* $(\mathsf{backdoor}, m')$ *to identity ID instead, where m' is m with Λ deleted.*

Since $\mathcal{D}$ does not write anything on its algebraic tape, for $(\mathcal{E}, \mathcal{D})$ to be algebraic, $\mathcal{E}$ must send all necessary algebraic representations to $\mathcal{D}$. To simplify notations, we may say "$\mathcal{E}$ is algebraic" in this case.

Now we can define AGM emulation with respect to the dummy adversary:

Definition 6. *Suppose protocols π and ϕ involve the same group $\mathcal{G}$. π* $\mathcal{G}$-AGM emulates ϕ with respect to the dummy adversary *if the following holds: there is an efficient simulator $\mathcal{S}$ such that: for any efficient and $(\mathcal{G}, \pi)$-algebraic environment $\mathcal{E}$, we have that $(\mathcal{E}, \mathcal{S})$ are $(\mathcal{G}, \phi)$-algebraic, and*

$$\mathrm{EXEC}_{\phi,\mathcal{S},\mathcal{E}} \approx \mathrm{EXEC}_{\pi,\mathcal{D},\mathcal{E}},$$

where $\mathcal{D}$ is the $(\mathcal{G}, \pi)$-algebraically dummy adversary.

Similar to the standard UC framework, we can show that emulation is equivalent to emulation with respect to the dummy adversary. This simplifies protocol analysis, since from now on we can simply assume that the adversary is algebraically dummy.

Theorem 1. *Suppose protocols π and ϕ involve the same group $\mathcal{G}$. Then π $\mathcal{G}$-AGM emulates ϕ (as in Definition 2) iff π $\mathcal{G}$-AGM emulates ϕ with respect to the dummy adversary (as in Definition 6).*

The proof is tedious and is therefore deferred to the full version [3].

2.3 Composition in the UC-AGM

The Composition Theorem. We are now ready to prove the composition theorem in our UC-AGM framework:

Theorem 2. *Suppose protocols π and ϕ involve the same group $\mathcal{G}$, such that ϕ is a sub-protocol of ρ^ϕ, π $\mathcal{G}$-AGM emulates ϕ, and π is identity-compatible with ρ^ϕ and ϕ. Then ρ^π (ρ^ϕ with its sub-protocol ϕ replaced with π) $(\mathcal{G}, \pi, \phi)$-AGM emulates ρ^ϕ. (For formal definitions of "identity-compatibility" and "sub-protocol replacement", see the full version [3])*

Proof. Let $\mathcal{D}_\pi$ be the algebraically dummy adversary in an execution of π. Since π $\mathcal{G}$-AGM emulates ϕ, we know that there is an efficient simulator $\mathcal{S}_\pi$ such that: for any efficient and $(\mathcal{G}, \pi)$-algebraic environment $\mathcal{E}_\pi$, we have that $(\mathcal{E}_\pi, \mathcal{S}_\pi)$ are $(\mathcal{G}, \phi)$-algebraic, and

$$\mathrm{EXEC}_{\phi,\mathcal{S}_\pi,\mathcal{E}_\pi} \approx \mathrm{EXEC}_{\pi,\mathcal{D}_\pi,\mathcal{E}_\pi}.$$

Let $\rho = \rho^\phi \setminus \phi$, i.e., ρ is the "caller" part of ρ^π.

Construction of Simulator $\mathcal{S}$. By Theorem 1, it suffices to consider the $(\mathcal{G}, \pi)$-algebraically dummy adversary $\mathcal{D}$ in an execution of ρ^π. We construct a simulator $\mathcal{S}$ (in an execution of ρ^ϕ) which simulates $\mathcal{E}$'s view for any efficient and $(\mathcal{G}, \pi)$-algebraic environment $\mathcal{E}$. $\mathcal{S}$ essentially "combines" $\mathcal{D}$ and $\mathcal{S}_\pi$. Concretely, $\mathcal{S}$ works as follows:

1. On message $(\mathsf{input}, (ID, m_0))$ from identity 0 (recall that this means that $\mathcal{E}$ instructs $\mathcal{S}$ to send message m_0 to the protocol party with identity ID), $\mathcal{S}$ checks if there is a machine in ϕ with identity ID.
   (a) If so, then $\mathcal{S}$ activates $\mathcal{S}_\pi$ with input $(\mathsf{input}, (ID, m_0))$ (as from the environment), and follows $\mathcal{S}_\pi$'s instruction until the activation of $\mathcal{S}_\pi$ completes.
   (b) Otherwise, i.e., ID is the identity of a machine in ρ, $\mathcal{S}$ parses $m_0 = (m_0', \Lambda)$ (where Λ is the algebraic representations of the group elements in m_0') and sends $(\mathsf{backdoor}, m_0')$ to ID, and writes Λ on its algebraic tape.
2. On message $(\mathsf{backdoor}, m_1)$ from some identity $ID \neq 0$ (i.e., from a protocol party), $\mathcal{S}$ checks if there is a machine in ϕ with identity ID.
   (a) If so, then $\mathcal{S}$ activates $\mathcal{S}_\pi$ with input $(\mathsf{backdoor}, m_1)$ (as from ID), and follows $\mathcal{S}_\pi$'s instruction until the activation of $\mathcal{S}_\pi$ completes.
   (b) Otherwise, i.e., ID is the identity of a machine in ρ, $\mathcal{S}$ sends $(\mathsf{backdoor}, m_1)$ to identity 0 (i.e., to $\mathcal{E}$).

Analysis of Simulator $\mathcal{S}$. It is straightforward to see that if $\mathcal{S}_\pi$ is efficient, then $\mathcal{S}$ is also efficient. We now show that $(\mathcal{E}, \mathcal{S})$ are $(\mathcal{G}, \phi)$-algebraic. Recall that $(\mathcal{E}, \mathcal{S})$ are $(\mathcal{G}, \phi)$-algebraic iff whenever $\mathcal{S}$ sends $(\mathsf{backdoor}, m)$ to identity $ID \neq 1$, it also writes on its algebraic tape the algebraic representations (w.r.t. ϕ) of all group elements in m. According to the description of $\mathcal{S}$ above, $\mathcal{S}$ sends $\mathsf{backdoor}$ messages to identity $ID \neq 1$ in step 1(b) only; in this case $\mathcal{S}$ writes the algebraic representation Λ on its algebraic tape, so $\mathcal{E}$ is $(\mathcal{G}, \pi)$-algebraic implies that $(\mathcal{E}, \mathcal{S})$ are $(\mathcal{G}, \phi)$-algebraic.

Moreover, $\mathcal{S}$ plays the role of an $(\mathcal{G}, \pi)$-*algebraic* environment when activating $\mathcal{S}_\pi$ with message $(\mathsf{input}, (ID, m_0))$. This is because $\mathcal{S}$ copies $\mathcal{E}$'s message payload

m_0, so $\mathcal{E}$ is $(\mathcal{G}, \pi)$-algebraic implies that m_0 contains the algebraic representations (w.r.t. π) of its all group elements.

Next we show the validity of $\mathcal{S}$. We construct another environment $\mathcal{E}_\pi$, which aims to distinguish between π's execution with $\mathcal{D}$ and ϕ's execution with $\mathcal{S}_\pi$. $\mathcal{E}_\pi$ simulates instances of $\mathcal{E}$ and runs the codes of ρ and $\mathcal{S}$ locally, and essentially "combines" $\mathcal{E}$, ρ, and $\mathcal{S}$. Concretely, $\mathcal{E}_\pi$, on initial input z, activates $\mathcal{E}$ with initial input z. Then $\mathcal{E}_\pi$ works as follows:

1. When $\mathcal{E}$ completes this activation,
   (a) If $\mathcal{E}$ halts with some output, then $\mathcal{E}_\pi$ also halts with the same output.
   (b) If $\mathcal{E}$ generates an outgoing message (input, m_0) to some identity ID such that there is a machine $\mu \in \rho$ with identity ID, then $\mathcal{E}_\pi$ runs the code of μ on message (input, m_0). When μ halts, $(*)$
      i If μ generates an outgoing message $(\mathsf{subroutine\text{-}output}, m_1)$ to identity 0, then $\mathcal{E}_\pi$ activates $\mathcal{E}$ with message $(\mathsf{subroutine\text{-}output}, m_1)$ (as from ID) and jumps to the beginning of this step.
      ii If μ generates an outgoing message $(\mathsf{backdoor}, m_1)$ to identity 1, then $\mathcal{E}_\pi$ runs the code of $\mathcal{S}$ on message $(\mathsf{backdoor}, m_1)$.
      iii If μ generates an outgoing message (input, m_1) to identity ID', which is the identity of a machine $\mu' \in \rho$, then $\mathcal{E}_\pi$ runs the code of μ' on input (input, m_1) and jumps to $(*)$ (with μ replaced by μ').
      iv If μ generates an outgoing message (input, m_1) to identity ID', which is the identity of a machine in ϕ/π, then $\mathcal{E}_\pi$ sends (input, m_1) to identity ID'.
   (c) If $\mathcal{E}$ generates an outgoing message $(\mathsf{input}, (ID, m_0))$ to identity 1, then $\mathcal{E}_\pi$ runs the code of $\mathcal{S}$ on message $(\mathsf{input}, (ID, m_0))$.
2. When $\mathcal{S}$ halts (as in case (b)ii or (c) in step 1; recall that $\mathcal{S}$ is a piece of code run by $\mathcal{E}$ itself),
   (a) If $\mathcal{S}$ generates an outgoing message $(\mathsf{backdoor}, m_2)$ to identity 0, then $\mathcal{E}_\pi$ activates $\mathcal{E}$ with message $(\mathsf{backdoor}, m_2)$ and jumps to step 1.
   (b) If $\mathcal{S}$ generates an outgoing message $(\mathsf{backdoor}, m_2)$ to identity ID, which is the identity of a machine $\mu \in \rho$, then $\mathcal{E}_\pi$ runs the code of μ on message (input, m_2) and jumps to $(*)$.
   (c) If $\mathcal{S}$ activates $\mathcal{S}_\pi$[5] with message $(\mathsf{input}, (ID, m_2))$, then $\mathcal{E}_\pi$ sends $(\mathsf{input}, (ID, m_2))$ to identity 1 (i.e., to $\mathcal{D}_\pi$ or $\mathcal{S}_\pi$).
3. On message $(\mathsf{backdoor}, (ID, m_3))$ from identity 1, $\mathcal{E}_\pi$ runs the code of $\mathcal{S}$ on message $(\mathsf{backdoor}, (ID, m_3))$ (as from $\mathcal{S}_\pi$) and jumps to step 2.
4. On message $(\mathsf{backdoor}, m_3)$ from some identity $ID \neq 1$ (i.e., from a machine in ϕ or π) aimed at some identity ID',
   (a) If there is a machine $\mu' \in \rho$ with identity ID', then $\mathcal{E}_\pi$ runs the code of μ' on message (input, m_3) and jumps to $(*)$ (with μ replaced by μ').
   (b) Otherwise, i.e., if ID' is an external identity, then $\mathcal{E}_\pi$ activates $\mathcal{E}$ with message $(\mathsf{backdoor}, m_3)$ (as from ID) and jumps to step 1.

[5] Note that this $\mathcal{S}_\pi$ is an imaginary machine supposed to run inside $\mathcal{S}$, whereas the "actual" $\mathcal{S}_\pi$ is the simulator in the execution of ϕ. Same with step 3 below.

It is straightforward to see that if $\mathcal{E}$ is efficient, then $\mathcal{E}_\pi$ is also efficient. Also, $\mathcal{E}_\pi$ perfectly simulates an instance of $\mathcal{D}$ in π's execution, and an instance of $\mathcal{S}_\pi$ in ϕ's execution, i.e.,

$$\text{EXEC}_{\pi,\mathcal{D}_\pi,\mathcal{E}_\pi} = \text{EXEC}_{\rho^\pi,\mathcal{D},\mathcal{E}}, \quad \text{and} \quad \text{EXEC}_{\phi,\mathcal{S}_\pi,\mathcal{E}_\pi} = \text{EXEC}_{\rho^\phi,\mathcal{S},\mathcal{E}}.$$

Next we claim that if $\mathcal{E}$ is $(\mathcal{G},\pi)$-algebraic, then $\mathcal{E}_\pi$, as the environment in an execution of π, is also $(\mathcal{G},\pi)$-algebraic. Recall that $\mathcal{E}_\pi$ is $(\mathcal{G},\pi)$-algebraic iff whenever it sends (input, m) to identity 1, m contains the algebraic representations (w.r.t. π) of its all group elements. According to the description of $\mathcal{E}_\pi$ above, $\mathcal{E}_\pi$ sends input messages to identity 1 in step 2(c) only. The message payload m_2 is copied from $\mathcal{S}$'s message aimed at $\mathcal{S}_\pi$; we have argued above that $\mathcal{S}$ plays the role of a $(\mathcal{G},\pi)$-algebraic environment while communicating with $\mathcal{S}_\pi$, which implies that m_2 contains the algebraic representations (w.r.t. π) of its all group elements.

Since $\mathcal{E}_\pi$ is both efficient and $(\mathcal{G},\pi)$-algebraic, by the definition of $\mathcal{S}_\pi$, we have that

$$\text{EXEC}_{\phi,\mathcal{S}_\pi,\mathcal{E}_\pi} \approx \text{EXEC}_{\pi,\mathcal{D}_\pi,\mathcal{E}_\pi}.$$

Combining the three results above, we conclude that

$$\text{EXEC}_{\rho^\phi,\mathcal{S},\mathcal{E}} \approx \text{EXEC}_{\rho^\pi,\mathcal{D},\mathcal{E}},$$

completing the proof. □

Transitivity of AGM-emulation. The following theorem is straightforward to prove, similarly to the standard UC framework.

Theorem 3. *Suppose protocols π, π', ϕ involve the same group $\mathcal{G}$, such that π $\mathcal{G}$-AGM emulates π' and π' $\mathcal{G}$-AGM emulates ϕ. Then π $\mathcal{G}$-AGM emulates ϕ.*

Proof. Our goal is to give a simulator $\mathcal{S}$ such that $\text{EXEC}_{\phi,\mathcal{S},\mathcal{E}} \approx \text{EXEC}_{\pi,\mathcal{A},\mathcal{E}}$ when $(\mathcal{A},\mathcal{E})$ are $(\mathcal{G},\pi)$-algebraic. Furthermore, $(\mathcal{S},\mathcal{E})$ must be $(\mathcal{G},\phi)$-algebraic.

By assumption, since π AGM-emulates π', there is an efficient algebraic adversary $\mathcal{A}'$ such that $\text{EXEC}_{\pi',\mathcal{A}',\mathcal{E}} \approx \text{EXEC}_{\pi,\mathcal{A},\mathcal{E}}$ when $(\mathcal{A},\mathcal{E})$ are $(\mathcal{G},\pi)$ algebraic. Furthermore, $(\mathcal{A}',\mathcal{E})$ are $(\mathcal{G},\pi')$-algebraic.

Moreover, since π' AGM-emulates ϕ, there is an efficient algebraic adversary $\mathcal{S}$ such that $\text{EXEC}_{\phi,\mathcal{S},\mathcal{E}} \approx \text{EXEC}_{\pi',\mathcal{A}',\mathcal{E}}$ when $(\mathcal{A}',\mathcal{E})$ are $(\mathcal{G},\pi')$-algebraic. Furthermore, $(\mathcal{S},\mathcal{E})$ are $(\mathcal{G},\phi)$-algebraic. This implies that $\mathcal{S}$ is the required simulator, which concludes the proof. □

In the standard UC framework, the guarantees given by the UC composition theorem can be plugged in as hypothesis of the transitivity theorem, which allows deriving a natural corollary when ϕ is an ideal functionality. Intuitively, in the standard UC setting, composition allows us to derive that ρ^{π} emulates $\rho^{\mathcal{F}}$, when π emulates $\mathcal{F}$. If, in turn $\rho^{\mathcal{F}}$ has been shown to emulate $\mathcal{F}'$, then transitivity yields that ρ^{π} emulates $\mathcal{F}'$.

However, this is not the case in the UC AGM setting. The composition theorem guarantees that ρ^{π} emulates $\rho^{\mathcal{F}}$ with respect to $(\mathcal{G}, \pi)$-algebraic attackers, rather than $(\mathcal{G}, \rho^{\pi})$-algebraic attackers. This means that, in order to plug-in composition results with transitivity to obtain a result for ideal functionality emulation, we require a refined theorem that considers the specific case of composed protocols.

Theorem 4. *Suppose protocols $\rho^{\mathcal{F}}$, π and ideal functionalities $\mathcal{F}$, $\mathcal{F}'$ involve the same group $\mathcal{G}$, such that:*

1. $\text{IDEAL}_{\mathcal{F}}$ *is a sub-protocol of* $\rho^{\mathcal{F}}$,
2. *the π protocol $(\mathcal{G}, \pi)$-AGM realizes $\mathcal{F}$,*
3. *the $\rho^{\mathcal{F}}$ protocol $(\mathcal{G}, \rho)$-AGM realizes $\mathcal{F}'$, and*
4. *π is identity-compatible with $\rho^{\mathcal{F}}$ and* $\text{IDEAL}_{\mathcal{F}}$.

Then the instantiated protocol ρ^{π} *AGM realizes $\mathcal{F}'$ with respect to attackers that are* both $(\mathcal{G}, \rho)$- and $(\mathcal{G}, \pi)$-*algebraic.*

Proof (Sketch). To prove this statement we need to recall the structure of the simulator for ρ^{π} that is implied by the composition theorem; here we will call it $\mathcal{A}'$ consistently with the transitivity theorem proof.

This simulator runs $\mathcal{A}$ internally and, when $\mathcal{A}$ communicates with machines executing π, it uses the simulator $\mathcal{S}_{\pi}$ as a *translator* that communicates to $\mathcal{F}$ instead. On the other hand, communications between $\mathcal{A}$ and parties executing ρ are just passed along.

Note that, to use this simulator we need to apply the composition theorem, which means that $(\mathcal{A}, \mathcal{E})$ must be $(\mathcal{G}, \pi)$ algebraic; this is guaranteed by the stronger restriction that attackers are both $(\mathcal{G}, \rho)$ *and* $(\mathcal{G}, \pi)$ algebraic.

At this point we can now follow the same strategy adopted in the proof of the transitivity theorem: simulator $\mathcal{A}'$ is used as an attacker against $\rho^{\mathcal{F}}$. The crucial observation now is that, this simulator guarantees that, if $(\mathcal{A}, \mathcal{E})$ are $(\mathcal{G}, \pi)$ algebraic *and* $(\mathcal{G}, \rho)$ algebraic, then $(\mathcal{A}', \mathcal{E})$ is also $(\mathcal{G}, \rho)$ algebraic. This is because communications with ρ are just passed along between $\mathcal{A}$ and ρ.

We can now apply the hypothesis that the $\rho^{\mathcal{F}}$ protocol $(\mathcal{G}, \rho)$-AGM realizes $\mathcal{F}'$ and take simulator $\mathcal{S}$ implied by this hypothesis to conclude the proof. □

Extension to the Full UC Framework and Relation to UC Proofs. In the full version [3] we explain how our treatment here can be extended to the full UC framework, which models fully dynamic and evolving distributed computing systems.

UC Emulation Implies AGM Emulation. For completeness, we note that UC emulation implies AGM emulation whenever the algebraic restriction on the simulator is moot. To see this, fix protocols π, ϕ where π UC emulates ϕ and ϕ

does not impose any algebraic restriction on $\mathcal{S}$. Any efficient algebraic environment $\mathcal{E}$ is in particular an efficient environment, so there is an efficient simulator $\mathcal{S}$ for which $\text{EXEC}_{\phi,\mathcal{S},\mathcal{E}} \approx \text{EXEC}_{\pi,\mathcal{D},\mathcal{E}}$ holds for any efficient algebraic environment $\mathcal{E}$. Furthermore, $\mathcal{S}$ is trivially algebraic since there is no such requirement when interacting with ϕ.

In the full version [3] we discuss in detail how UC AGM proofs compose with stronger standard UC emulation results, and further clarify the implications of the UC AGM composition theorems. The discussion also clarifies what happens in the setting where different groups are used by different protocols.

We finally note that the fact that we refer to protocols that use the same group in our theorems because this is the more problematic case, and it serves to highlight the limitations to composition in the AGM. All our results carry without change to the case where different groups are used; in this case excluding attacks that prevent using group elements occurring in one protocol in an attack against another protocol, unless a representation can be provided, seems less of a limitation.

3 Analysis of the Chou-Orlandi Protocol

In this section, we analyze the security of the Chou-Orlandi protocol for oblivious transfer in the UC-AGM. For convenience, we present the standard OT functionality $\mathcal{F}_{\text{OT}}$ in Fig. 1. We describe the Chou-Orlandi protocol Π_{CO} in Fig. 2. All messages sent in the protocol are via a message authentication functionality $\mathcal{F}_{\text{AUTH}}$, as presented in [13].

We now turn toward proving security of the protocol. In the following, we denote S and R as the sender and the receiver in protocol Π_{CO}, respectively. We describe a simulator Sim_{CO} for Π_{CO} by considering the different options for the order of corruptions. We assume that the simulator immediately aborts if it obtains syntactically ill-formed messages from a corrupted party as part of Π_{CO}. We first give an outline of the proof.

Proof Intuition. Roughly speaking, our proof must overcome two main challenges from the original work of Chou and Orlandi. The first is how to simulate the internal state of parties upon adaptive corruption. Namely, in Chou and Orlandi's proof, there seems to be no way of explaining the secret exponent x chosen by R if S is statically corrupted and can send an arbitrary group element $\mathbf{A}$ in Step 1 for which R does not know the discrete logarithm y. This issue is easily resolved using the AGM, as the simulator always learns the exponent y from the algebraic coefficients provided for $\mathbf{A}$.

The second issue in their proof comes from an improperly defined $\mathcal{F}_{\text{OT}}$ functionality. Roughly speaking, their version of this functionality does not notify S upon R obtaining the message m_b. If the corrupted R never makes the query for one of the keys k_b to H then the simulator cannot extract the correct bit and complete the simulation of the protocol. Note that this issue cannot be overcome by the simulator naively completing the simulation before R makes this query

Functionality $\mathcal{F}_{\mathrm{OT}}$

- On input $(\mathsf{receive}, sid, b)$ where $b \in \{0,1\}$ from R do: if no message of the form $(\mathsf{receive}, sid, b), b \in \{0,1\}$ has been stored, store $(\mathsf{receive}, sid, b)$. Output $(\mathsf{receive}, sid)$ to $\mathcal{S}$.
- On input $(\mathsf{send}, sid, m_0, m_1)$ where $m_0, m_1 \in \{0,1\}^\ell$ from S do: if no message of the form $(\mathsf{send}, sid, m_0, m_1)$ has been stored, store $(\mathsf{send}, sid, m_0, m_1)$. Output (send, sid) to $\mathcal{S}$.

Adversary $\mathcal{S}$:

- On input $(\mathsf{receive}, sid, b)$ where $b \in \{0,1\}$ from $\mathcal{S}$ do: if no message of the form $(\mathsf{receive}, sid, b), b \in \{0,1\}$ has been stored, store $(\mathsf{receive}, sid, b)$.
- On input $(\mathsf{send}, sid, m_0, m_1)$ where $m_0, m_1 \in \{0,1\}^\ell$ from $\mathcal{S}$ do: if no message of the form $(\mathsf{send}, sid, m_0, m_1)$ has been stored, store $(\mathsf{send}, sid, m_0, m_1)$.
- On input $(\mathsf{deliver}, sid, R)$ from $\mathcal{S}$: if both $(\mathsf{receive}, sid, b)$ and $(\mathsf{send}, sid, m_0, m_1)$ have previously been stored, do:
  - If R is honest: output $(\mathsf{output}, sid, m_b)$ to R.
  - If R is corrupted: output $(\mathsf{output}, sid, m_b)$ to $\mathcal{S}$.

  Otherwise, output $\perp$ to $\mathcal{S}$.
- On input $(\mathsf{deliver}, sid, S)$ from $\mathcal{S}$, if $(\mathsf{output}, sid, m_b)$ was previously output (to R or to $\mathcal{S}$) and S is honest, output (output, sid) to S. Otherwise, output $\perp$ to $\mathcal{S}$.

Fig. 1. Functionality for 1-out-of-2 OT

Protocol Π_{CO}

- **Step 1:** Upon receiving input $(\mathsf{send}, sid, m_0, m_1)$, S samples $y \leftarrow \mathbb{Z}_p$ and computes $\mathbf{A} := g^y, \mathbf{B} := g^{y^2}$. It sends $\mathbf{A}$ to R via $\mathcal{F}_{\mathrm{AUTH}}$.
- **Step 2:** Upon receiving input $(\mathsf{receive}, sid, b)$ and $\mathbf{A} \in \mathbb{G}$ from S, R samples $x \leftarrow \mathbb{Z}_p$ and computes $\mathbf{U} := \mathbf{A}^b g^x$. It sends $\mathbf{U}$ to S via $\mathcal{F}_{\mathrm{AUTH}}$.
- **Step 3:** Upon receiving $\mathbf{U}$ from R, S computes $k_b := H(\mathbf{A}, \mathbf{U}^y \mathbf{B}^{-b-1}), e_b := m_b \oplus k_b$ for $b \in \{0,1\}$. It sends e_0, e_1 to R via $\mathcal{F}_{\mathrm{AUTH}}$ and outputs (output, sid).
- **Step 4:** Upon receiving e_0, e_1 from S, R computes $k_{b^*} := H(\mathbf{A}, \mathbf{A}^x), m_{b^*} := e_{b^*} \oplus k_{b^*}$ for $b^* \in \{0,1\}$. It outputs $(\mathsf{output}, sid, m_{b^*})$.

Fig. 2. The Chou-Orlandi OT protocol.

by prompting the message (output, sid) from $\mathcal{F}_{\mathrm{OT}}$ to S prematurely via a query on some arbitrary b. The reason is that $\mathcal{E}$ can always make the opposite query to H, i.e., for k_{1-b}, with probability 1 after the simulation is complete. In this case, there is no way to obtain m_{1-b} from $\mathcal{F}_{\mathrm{OT}}$ again, since $\mathcal{S}$ already had to make the query in order to force (output, sid) being output to $\mathcal{E}$. Both of these issues can be overcome when requiring that the environment $\mathcal{E}$ be algebraic. In this case, y

is revealed when the corrupted S sends it in Step 1. For the issue of extraction, $\mathcal{S}$ observes that R either sends $\mathbf{U} := \mathbf{A}^b g^x$ as specified by the protocol, or sends $\mathbf{U} := g^x$ that does not satisfy this format. In the either case, $\mathcal{S}$ can safely carry out the extraction according to either b or an arbitrary bit (in case $\mathbf{U}$ is not of the specified format). The only way for $\mathcal{E}$ to distinguish the simulation from the real world is by making a query from which a discrete logarithm instance can be solved (using algebraic coefficients provided by $\mathcal{E}$ as part of that query to H).

Let g denote a generator for a cyclic group $\mathbb{G}$ of prime order q and let DL denote the problem of computing a when given a random element $\mathbf{A} = g^a$ in $\mathbb{G}$. Moreover, denote $\mathsf{Adv}^{\mathsf{DL}}_{\mathcal{B}} := \Pr[a' = a \mid a' \leftarrow \mathcal{B}(g^a)]$ the advantage of adversary $\mathcal{B}$ in solving DL. Then Theorem 5 shows that the Π_{CO} protocol for oblivious transfer AGM realizes $\mathcal{F}_{\mathrm{OT}}$.

Theorem 5. *Π_{CO} UC-realizes $\mathcal{F}_{\mathrm{OT}}$ in the $\mathcal{F}_{\mathsf{RO}}$-hybrid model under adaptive corruptions. More precisely, there exists an algebraic simulator $\mathsf{Sim}_{\mathsf{CO}}$ for the algebraically dummy adversary $\mathcal{D}$ such that, for every algebraic environment $\mathcal{E}$ that makes at most q_H queries to $\mathcal{F}_{\mathsf{RO}}$, there exist attackers $\mathcal{B}_1$ and $\mathcal{B}_2$ running in roughly the same time as $\mathcal{E}$, such that $\mathrm{EXEC}_{\mathcal{F}_{\mathrm{OT}},\mathcal{S},\mathcal{E}} \approx_\epsilon \mathrm{EXEC}_{\Pi_{\mathsf{CO}},\mathcal{D},\mathcal{E}}$, with*

$$\epsilon \leq q_H \cdot (\mathsf{Adv}^{\mathsf{DL}}_{\mathcal{B}_1} + \mathsf{Adv}^{\mathsf{DL}}_{\mathcal{B}_2}).$$

Proof. The simulator $\mathsf{Sim}_{\mathsf{CO}}$ is as follows:

S is corrupted before Step 1.

- **R is corrupted before Step 2.** In this case, there is nothing for $\mathsf{Sim}_{\mathsf{CO}}$ to simulate.
- **R is corrupted between Step 2 and 4.** In this case, R has received $\mathbf{A} \in \mathbb{G}$ from S (but has not yet received e_0, e_1). In addition, $\mathsf{Sim}_{\mathsf{CO}}$ learns $y \in \mathbb{Z}_p$ s.t. $\mathbf{A} = g^y$. $\mathsf{Sim}_{\mathsf{CO}}$ samples $u \leftarrow \mathbb{Z}_p$ and computes $\mathbf{U} := g^u$, which it sends to S. When R becomes corrupted, $\mathsf{Sim}_{\mathsf{CO}}$ learns b and sets $x := u - yb$. It outputs (b, x) to $\mathcal{E}$. In addition, it simulates the random oracle H as described in the next subcase.
- **R is corrupted after Step 4.** In this case, R receives $\mathbf{A} \in \mathbb{G}$ at Step 2 and e_0, e_1 at Step 4. In addition, $\mathsf{Sim}_{\mathsf{CO}}$ learns $y \in \mathbb{Z}_p$ s.t. $\mathbf{A} = g^y$. $\mathsf{Sim}_{\mathsf{CO}}$ samples $u \leftarrow \mathbb{Z}_p$ and computes $\mathbf{U} := g^u$, which it sends to S. To program H, when $\mathcal{E}$ queries H on input $(\mathbf{I}, \mathbf{J})$ (together with the algebraic representations of $\mathbf{I}, \mathbf{J}$), $\mathsf{Sim}_{\mathsf{CO}}$ does as follows.
  - It first checks whether $H[\mathbf{I}, \mathbf{J}] \neq \perp$. In this case, it returns $H[\mathbf{I}, \mathbf{J}]$. Thus, assume in the following that $\mathcal{E}$ queries H on some input for the first time. In addition, for any fresh query $\mathbf{I}, \mathbf{J}$, assume that $\mathsf{Sim}_{\mathsf{CO}}$ sets $H[\mathbf{I}, \mathbf{J}]$ to the value it returns.
  - If the query is of the form $H(g^y, \mathbf{U}^y g^{y^2(b-1)})$ for $b \in \{0, 1\}$, $\mathsf{Sim}_{\mathsf{CO}}$ sets $k_b \leftarrow \{0, 1\}^\kappa$. It returns k_b.
  - Otherwise $\mathsf{Sim}_{\mathsf{CO}}$ samples $k \leftarrow \{0, 1\}^\kappa$ and returns k.
  - After observing both $\mathbf{A}$ and $\mathbf{U}$ in the protocol, $\mathsf{Sim}_{\mathsf{CO}}$ also retroactively checks whether it has previously set $H[g^y, \mathbf{U}^y g^{y^2(b-1)}]$. If so, it sets $k_b := H[g^y, \mathbf{U}^y g^{y^2(b-1)}]$.

Upon having received e_0, e_1 from S, $\mathsf{Sim}_{\mathsf{CO}}$ samples $m_0, m_1 \leftarrow \{0,1\}^\kappa$. For all $b \in \{0,1\}$ for which $k_b = \perp$ at this point, it sets $k_b \leftarrow \{0,1\}^\kappa$ and programs $H[g^y, \mathbf{U}^y g^{y^2(b-1)}] = k_b$ (it does not resample k_b in case it has already been defined). It then sets $m_0 := e_0 \oplus k_0, m_1 := e_1 \oplus k_1$ and inputs $(\mathsf{send}, sid, m_0, m_1)$ and $(\mathsf{deliver}, sid, R)$ to $\mathcal{F}_{\mathrm{OT}}$. This prompts the output $(\mathsf{output}, sid, m_b)$ to the honest R, since R has previously input $(\mathsf{receive}, sid, b)$ to $\mathcal{F}_{\mathrm{OT}}$. When R is corrupted, $\mathsf{Sim}_{\mathsf{CO}}$ learns b and sets $x := u - yb \pmod q$. It outputs (b, x, m_b) to $\mathcal{E}$.

S is corrupted between Step 1 and Step 3. To simulate the behaviour of S, $\mathsf{Sim}_{\mathsf{CO}}$ samples $y \leftarrow \mathbb{Z}_p$ and computes $\mathbf{A} := g^y, \mathbf{B} := g^{y^2}$. It sends $\mathbf{A}$ to R. When S is corrupted, $\mathsf{Sim}_{\mathsf{CO}}$ learns m_0, m_1. It outputs (y, m_0, m_1) to $\mathcal{E}$.

- **R is corrupted before Step 2.** In this case, $\mathsf{Sim}_{\mathsf{CO}}$ only needs to simulate H before S becomes corrupted (afterwards, both parties are corrupt and there is nothing to simulate). When R sends $\mathbf{U}$ in Step 2, $\mathsf{Sim}_{\mathsf{CO}}$ learns u, v s.t. $\mathbf{U} = g^u \mathbf{A}^v$. $\mathsf{Sim}_{\mathsf{CO}}$ now proceeds to simulate H exactly as in the case where S is corrupted before Step 1, except that it aborts if it ever sets both $k_0, k_1 \neq \perp$. As in the case where the Sender is corrupted before Step 1, $\mathsf{Sim}_{\mathsf{CO}}$'s simulation is indeed efficient, since it knows y and can hence check the necessary relations in the exponent of $\mathbf{U}$.

  Claim. $\mathsf{Sim}_{\mathsf{CO}}$ does not abort except with probability $\frac{1}{q_H}\mathsf{Adv}^{\mathsf{DL}}_{\mathcal{B}_1}$, where $\mathcal{B}_1$ is an adversary that runs in roughly the same time as $\mathcal{E}$.

  Proof. $\mathsf{Sim}_{\mathsf{CO}}$ aborts in this case only if the adversary queries $g^y, \mathbf{U}^y g^{y^2)}$, as it queries both $g^y, \mathbf{U}^y g^{y^2(b-1)}$ for both $b = 0, b = 1$ to H by assumption. In this case, we can construct $\mathcal{B}_1$ as follows. On input a discrete logarithm challenge $\mathbf{A} = g^y$ in game DL, $\mathcal{B}_1$ samples $i \in [q_H]$ uniformly at random and runs $\mathcal{E}$. It simulates the behavior of $\mathsf{Sim}_{\mathsf{CO}}$ by sending the element $\mathbf{A}$ in Step 1. If $\mathcal{E}$ corrupts R, $\mathcal{B}_1$ aborts. When $\mathcal{E}$ (controlling R) queries H on input $\mathbf{A}, \mathbf{J}$, $\mathsf{Sim}_{\mathsf{CO}}$ learns coefficients a, b s.t. $\mathbf{J} = g^a \mathbf{A}^b$. If $\mathbf{J} = \mathbf{A}$, and $v = 0$, then $\mathcal{B}_1$ sets $k_b \leftarrow \{0,1\}^\kappa$ and programs $H[\mathbf{I}, \mathbf{J}] = k_b$. For the i-th such query for which $v \neq 0$, $\mathcal{B}$ solves the equation $(1+v) \cdot y^2 + (u-b) \cdot y - a = 0 \pmod q$ for y, and outputs y. (Note that this yields the correct solution in case the i-th query is of the form $g^y, \mathbf{U}^y g^{y^2)}$). Since $\mathcal{B}_1$ guesses q correctly with probability at least $\frac{1}{q_H}$ and perfectly simulates the behavior of $\mathsf{Sim}_{\mathsf{CO}}$ up that point perfectly, the claim follows. □

- **R is corrupted between Steps 2 and 4.** In this case, the simulation for R can be carried out as in the case where S is corrupted before Step 1.
- **R is corrupted after Step 4.** In this case, R receives e_0, e_1 from the corrupted sender S at Step 4. The only difference to the case where S is corrupted before Step 1 is that $\mathsf{Sim}_{\mathsf{CO}}$ knows $y \in \mathbb{Z}_p$ s.t. $\mathbf{A} = g^y$ from sampling it in the first part of the simulation (rather than learning it from the algebraic coefficients output by the corrupted S).

S is corrupted after Step 3. To simulate the behaviour of S, in Step 1, $\mathsf{Sim}_{\mathsf{CO}}$ samples $y \leftarrow \mathbb{Z}_p$ and computes $\mathbf{A} := g^y, \mathbf{B} := g^{y^2}$. It sends $\mathbf{A}$ to R.

- R **is corrupted before Step 2.** When R sends $\mathbf{U} \in \mathbb{G}$ to S, $\mathsf{Sim}_{\mathsf{CO}}$ checks whether the algebraic coefficients provided by R are such that $\mathbf{U} = \mathbf{A}^b g^x$ for some $b \in \{0,1\}, x \in \mathbb{Z}_p$.
  - If so, $\mathsf{Sim}_{\mathsf{CO}}$ inputs $(\mathsf{receive}, sid, b)$ and then $(\mathsf{deliver}, sid, R)$ to $\mathcal{F}_{\mathrm{OT}}$.
  - Otherwise, $\mathsf{Sim}_{\mathsf{CO}}$ samples $b \leftarrow \{0,1\}, x \leftarrow \mathbb{Z}_p$ and inputs $(\mathsf{receive}, sid, b)$ and then $(\mathsf{deliver}, sid, R)$ to $\mathcal{F}_{\mathrm{OT}}$.

  Either case prompts the output $(\mathsf{output}, sid, m_b)$ to $\mathsf{Sim}_{\mathsf{CO}}$, since S is honest at this point and has previously input $(\mathsf{send}, sid, m_0, m_1)$ to $\mathcal{F}_{\mathrm{OT}}$. To simulate H on input $(\mathbf{I}, \mathbf{J})$, $\mathsf{Sim}_{\mathsf{CO}}$ does as follows.
  - It first checks whether $H[\mathbf{I}, \mathbf{J}] \neq \bot$. In this case, it returns $H[\mathbf{I}, \mathbf{J}]$. Thus, assume in the following that H is queried on some input for the first time. In addition, for any fresh query $\mathbf{I}, \mathbf{J}$, assume that $\mathsf{Sim}_{\mathsf{CO}}$ sets $H[\mathbf{I}, \mathbf{J}]$ to the value it returns.
  - For any query to H, $\mathsf{Sim}_{\mathsf{CO}}$ checks whether it is of the form $H(g^y, g^{y^2}, \mathbf{U}^y g^{y^2(b-1)})$ for $b \in \{0,1\}$, (i.e., it checks with respect to both $b = 0$ *and* $b = 1$). If any queries have been made before $\mathbf{U}$ was set by the corrupted R, $\mathsf{Sim}_{\mathsf{CO}}$ also checks whether they have this format.
    - * If not, it samples $k \leftarrow \{0,1\}^\kappa$ and returns k.
    - * Otherwise, if $\mathsf{Sim}_{\mathsf{CO}}$ has previously set $e_b \neq \bot$ (see below) it sets $k_b := e_b \oplus m_b$. Else, it sets $k_b \leftarrow \{0,1\}^\kappa$. It returns k_b.
  - If during this process, $\mathsf{Sim}_{\mathsf{CO}}$ ever sets both $k_0, k_1 \neq \bot$, it aborts.

  In Step 3, $\mathsf{Sim}_{\mathsf{CO}}$ samples $e_0, e_1 \leftarrow \{0,1\}^\kappa$ and sends them to R. After $\mathsf{Sim}_{\mathsf{CO}}$ performs Step 3 of the protocol, $\mathsf{Sim}_{\mathsf{CO}}$ inputs $(\mathsf{deliver}, sid, S)$ to $\mathcal{F}_{\mathrm{OT}}$ which prompts the output (output, sid) to S. Once S is corrupted (after Step 3), $\mathsf{Sim}_{\mathsf{CO}}$ learns m_0, m_1. It outputs (y, m_0, m_1) to $\mathcal{E}$.
- R **is corrupted between Step 2 and Step 4.** In this case, the simulation for R can be carried out as in the case where S is corrupted before Step 1. In addition, after S performs Step 3 of the protocol, $\mathsf{Sim}_{\mathsf{CO}}$ inputs $(\mathsf{receive}, sid, b), (\mathsf{deliver}, sid, S)$ to $\mathcal{F}_{\mathrm{OT}}$ (in this order). This prompts the output (output, sid) to S, since S is honest at this point and thus has input $(\mathsf{send}, sid, m_0, m_1)$ to $\mathcal{F}_{\mathrm{OT}}$. Moreover, $\mathsf{Sim}_{\mathsf{CO}}$ aborts upon setting both $k_0, k_1 \neq \bot$.
- R **is corrupted after Step 4.** Same as previous case, except that $\mathsf{Sim}_{\mathsf{CO}}$ does not have to abort if R is corrupted after S.

The proof of the following claim is almost identical to the one given for the case where S is corrupted between Step 1 and Step 3.

Claim. $\mathsf{Sim}_{\mathsf{CO}}$ does not abort in case the sender is corrupted after Step 3 except with probability $\frac{1}{q_H}\mathsf{Adv}^{\mathsf{DL}}_{\mathcal{B}_2}$, and $\mathcal{B}_2$ runs in roughly the same time as $\mathcal{E}$.

As long as $\mathsf{Sim}_{\mathsf{CO}}$ does not abort, it perfectly simulates the behavior of a party in Π_{CO}, as all outputs of the random oracle H are uniformly distributed in this case from the view of $\mathcal{E}$. Moreover, $\mathsf{Sim}_{\mathsf{CO}}$ can consistently simulate the view of $\mathcal{E}$. Finally, it is easy to see that all $\mathsf{Sim}_{\mathsf{CO}}$ can output algebraic representations of all elements that it outputs relative to group elements it receives as input, and hence $\mathsf{Sim}_{\mathsf{CO}}$ is algebraic. This concludes the proof. □

4 Analysis of PAKE Protocols: SPAKE2 and CPace

In this section we analyze the UC security of PAKE protocols SPAKE2 and CPace in the algebraic group model. We show that, modeling the hash functions used by these protocols as random oracles, they both achieve full UC security. The proofs are simpler than the ones we encountered in the literature for the UC and game-based security of the same protocols and they are based on standard (non-interactive) assumptions (we do not need *gap* assumptions). We use the standard definition of $\mathcal{F}_{\mathsf{pwKE}}$ from [2,15] supporting multiple sessions Fig. 3.

Remark. Throughout the paper we present the simulators as running their own instances of the random oracle functionality used by the protocols, which means that we assume that the random oracle is local to the protocol [14]. However, in this section, we make it clear that none of the given simulators needs to program the random oracle functionality and, in the case of the SPAKE2 protocol, it does not even need to know which adversarial queries were made to the random oracle. These observations indicate that our proofs of security may carry over to a setting with global random oracle as in [12,16]. Providing a full formalization of the referred works in the AGM is beyond the scope of this paper; however, we believe that our formal approach will carry naturally to extensions of UC with global functionalities.

Remark. The SPAKE2 simulator does not need to program the common reference string and the CPace protocol does not use one (in addition to the group description). We also show for both protocols that the simulators are algebraic. This means that the UC-AGM composition applies to both protocols.

4.1 SPAKE2

Figure 4 shows a SPAKE2 protocol execution between an user U and a server S. SPAKE2 is a two-pass protocol, where we assume the user plays the role of the initiator and the server that of the responder.

Let SqDH denote the problem of computing g^{a^2}, when given a random element $\mathbf{A} = g^a$ in $\mathbb{G}$, and $\mathsf{Adv}_{\mathcal{B}}^{\mathsf{SqDH}}$ the probability that attacker $\mathcal{B}$ succeeds in solving this problem. Theorem 6 shows that SPAKE2 AGM realizes $\mathcal{F}_{\mathsf{pwKE}}$ assuming that SqDH and the discrete-logarithm problems are hard in $\mathbb{G}$.

Theorem 6. *SPAKE2 AGM-emulates $\mathcal{F}_{\mathsf{pwKE}}$ in the $(\mathcal{F}_{\mathsf{RO}}, \mathcal{F}_{\mathsf{CRS}})$-hybrid model under static corruptions. More precisely, there exists an algebraic simulator $\mathcal{S}$ for the (algebraic) dummy adversary $\mathcal{D}$ such that, for every efficient algebraic environment $\mathcal{E}$ creating at most q_S sessions and placing at most q_{H} queries to the random oracle, there exist attackers $\mathcal{B}_1^1$, $\mathcal{B}_1^2$, and $\mathcal{B}_2$ running in roughly the same time as $\mathcal{E}$ such that $\mathrm{EXEC}_{\mathsf{pwKE},\mathcal{S},\mathcal{E}} \approx_\epsilon \mathrm{EXEC}_{\mathrm{SPAKE2},\mathcal{D},\mathcal{E}}$, where*

$$\epsilon \le \mathsf{Adv}_{\mathcal{B}_1^1}^{\mathsf{DL}} + \mathsf{Adv}_{\mathcal{B}_1^2}^{\mathsf{DL}} + q_{\mathrm{H}} \cdot \mathsf{Adv}_{\mathcal{B}_2}^{\mathsf{SqDH}} + \frac{q_S + 1}{q}.$$

Functionality $\mathcal{F}_{\mathsf{pwKE}}$

Upon receiving a query ($\mathsf{NewSession}, sid, P, P', \mathsf{pw}, \mathrm{role}$) **from party** P**:**
Ignore this query if record $(sid, P, \cdot, \cdot, \cdot)$ already exists. Otherwise, record $(sid, P, P', \mathsf{pw}, \mathrm{role})$ marked fresh and send ($\mathsf{NewSession}, sid, P, P', \mathrm{role}$) to $\mathcal{S}$.

Upon receiving a query ($\mathsf{TestPwd}, sid, P, \mathsf{pw}^*$) **from** $\mathcal{S}$**:**
If $\exists$ a fresh record $(sid, P, P', \mathsf{pw}, \cdot)$ then:
- If $\mathsf{pw}^* = \mathsf{pw}$ then mark it $\mathsf{compromised}$ and return "correct guess";
- If $\mathsf{pw}^* \neq \mathsf{pw}$ then mark it $\mathsf{interrupted}$ and return "wrong guess".

Upon receiving a query ($\mathsf{NewKey}, sid, P, K^*$) **from** $\mathcal{S}$**:**
If $\exists$ a record $(sid, P, P', \mathsf{pw}, \mathrm{role})$ not marked $\mathsf{completed}$ then do:
- If the record is $\mathsf{compromised}$, or either P or P' is corrupted, then set $K := K^*$.
- If the record is fresh and $\exists$ a $\mathsf{completed}$ record $(sid, P', P, \mathsf{pw}, \mathrm{role}', K')$ with $\mathrm{role}' \neq \mathrm{role}$ that was fresh when P' output (sid, K'), then set $K := K'$.
- In all other cases pick K uniformly at random.

Finally, append K to record $(sid, P, P', \mathsf{pw}, \mathrm{role})$, mark it $\mathsf{completed}$, and output (sid, K) to P.

Fig. 3. The password-based key-exchange functionality $\mathcal{F}_{\mathsf{pwKE}}$.

User		Server
	$sid, U, S, \mathsf{pw} \in \mathcal{P}, \mathsf{crs} = (\mathbb{G}, M, N)$	
$x \twoheadleftarrow \mathbb{Z}_q$		$y \twoheadleftarrow \mathbb{Z}_q$
$X \leftarrow g^x$		$Y \leftarrow g^y$
$X^\star \leftarrow X \cdot M^{\mathsf{pw}}$	$\xrightarrow{X^\star}$	$X \leftarrow X^\star / M^{\mathsf{pw}}$
$Y \leftarrow Y^\star / N^{\mathsf{pw}}$	$\xleftarrow{Y^\star}$	$Y^\star \leftarrow Y \cdot N^{\mathsf{pw}}$
$K \leftarrow \mathrm{H}(sid, U, S, X^\star, Y^\star, \mathsf{pw}, Y^x)$		$K \leftarrow \mathrm{H}(sid, U, S, X^\star, Y^\star, \mathsf{pw}, X^y)$

Fig. 4. The SPAKE2 protocol [5]. The CRS includes the group description $\mathbb{G}$, where $|\mathbb{G}| = q$ and two group elements $M, N \in \mathbb{G}$ sampled uniformly at random.

Note, that the DL problem and the SqDH problems are equivalent when we consider algebraic attackers, so the theorem follows with a reduction to the DL problem even if the proof relies on an apparently stronger assumption.

We also remark that the structure of this proof is much simpler than the proof that SPAKE2 satisfies relaxed UC PAKE security [2]. This is because, in the AGM, the password guessing event can be detected directly by the simulator (and hence by the reductions) and one does not need to rely on the random oracle to extract passwords in active attacks.

We give a sketch of the proof and provide the full proof in the full version [3].

SIMULATOR $\mathcal{S}$ for SPAKE2

proc INITIALIZE()

Get CRS=$(\mathbf{M}, \mathbf{N})$

On input (NewSession, sid, P, P', role) from $\mathcal{F}_{\mathsf{pwKE}}$

If $\neg(\pi_P^{sid} = \perp)$ discard input.
If role = init
  $x \twoheadleftarrow \mathbb{Z}_q$; $\mathbf{X}^\star \leftarrow \mathbf{M}^x$; $\pi_P^{sid} \leftarrow (x, (P, P', sid, \mathbf{X}^\star, \perp), \perp, \text{init})$
  Send SENDINIT$(P, P', sid, \mathbf{X}^\star)$ to $\mathcal{E}$
Else
  $y \twoheadleftarrow \mathbb{Z}_q$; $\mathbf{Y}^\star \leftarrow \mathbf{N}^y$; $\pi_P^{sid} \leftarrow (y, (P', P, sid, \perp, \mathbf{Y}^\star), \perp, \text{resp})$

On message SENDINIT$(P, P', sid, (\mathbf{X}^\star, \mathsf{alg}))$ from $\mathcal{E}$

Ignore if $\pi_{P'}^{sid} \neq (y, (P, P', sid, \perp, \mathbf{Y}^\star), \perp, \text{resp})$
(A unique $\pi_{P'}^{sid}$ satisfies the above check for some y and $\mathbf{Y}^\star$)
$K \twoheadleftarrow \mathcal{K}$
(Can't interrupt passive sessions so $\mathcal{F}$ sets $=K$ at output)
If $\pi_P^{sid} = (\cdot, (P, P', sid, \mathbf{X}^\star, \perp), \perp, \text{init})$ Jump to COMPLETE
(First check whether $\mathbf{X}^\star$ was constructed as per protocol)
If $\mathsf{alg} = [(g, x); (\mathbf{M}, \mathsf{pw})]$
  Query (TestPwd, sid, P', pw) to $\mathcal{F}_{\mathsf{pwKE}}$
  If $\mathcal{F}_{\mathsf{pwKE}}$ responds with "correct guess"
    $Y \leftarrow \mathbf{Y}^\star / \mathbf{N}^{\mathsf{pw}}$; $K \leftarrow \mathrm{H}(P, P', sid, \mathbf{X}^\star, \mathbf{Y}^\star, \mathsf{pw}, Y^x)$
(Interrupt all other sessions so independent key is set)
Else Query (TestPwd, $sid, P', \perp$) to $\mathcal{F}_{\mathsf{pwKE}}$
COMPLETE: Send SENDRESP$(P', P, sid, \mathbf{Y}^\star)$ to $\mathcal{E}$
  $\pi_{P'}^{sid} \leftarrow (y, (P, P', sid, \mathbf{X}^\star, \mathbf{Y}^\star), K, \text{resp})$
  Query (NewKey, sid, P', K) to $\mathcal{F}_{\mathsf{pwKE}}$

On message SENDRESP$(P', P, sid, (\mathbf{Y}^\star, \mathsf{alg}))$ from $\mathcal{E}$

Ignore if $\pi_P^{sid} \neq (x, (P, P', sid, \mathbf{X}^\star, \perp), \perp, \text{init})$
(A unique π_P^{sid} satisfies the above check for some x and $\mathbf{X}^\star$)
$K \twoheadleftarrow \mathcal{K}$
(Can't interrupt passive sessions so $\mathcal{F}$ sets $=K$ at output)
If $\pi_{P'}^{sid} = (\cdot, (P, P', sid, \mathbf{X}^\star, \mathbf{Y}^\star), \cdot, \text{resp})$ Jump to COMPLETE
(First check whether $\mathbf{Y}^\star$ was constructed as per protocol)
If $\mathsf{alg} = [(g, y); (\mathbf{N}, \mathsf{pw})]$
  Query (TestPwd, sid, P, pw) to $\mathcal{F}_{\mathsf{pwKE}}$
  If $\mathcal{F}_{\mathsf{pwKE}}$ responds with "correct guess"
    $X \leftarrow \mathbf{X}^\star / \mathbf{M}^{\mathsf{pw}}$; $K \leftarrow \mathrm{H}(P, P', sid, \mathbf{X}^\star, \mathbf{Y}^\star, \mathsf{pw}, X^y)$
(Interrupt all other sessions so independent key is set)
Else Query (TestPwd, $sid, P, \perp$) to $\mathcal{F}_{\mathsf{pwKE}}$
COMPLETE: $\pi_P^{sid} \leftarrow (x, (P, P', sid, \mathbf{X}^\star, \mathbf{Y}^\star), K, \text{init})$
  Query (NewKey, sid, P, K) to $\mathcal{F}_{\mathsf{pwKE}}$

Fig. 5. The operation of the SPAKE2 simulator. The simulator does not need to observe adversarial random oracle queries nor program either of the random oracle or the CRS.

Proof (Sketch). Simulator $\mathcal{S}$ is shown in Fig. 5. Recall that, whenever the dummy adversary is instructed to deliver a group element to an uncorrupted party, it will output on its auxiliary tape the algebraic representation of that element with respect to group elements that appear in the view of the environment. In this case, the bases for such representations include $\mathbf{M}$, $\mathbf{N}$ and any messages $\mathbf{X}^\star$ or $\mathbf{Y}^\star$ produced by an uncorrupted party.

Simulation Strategy. The simulator generates all messages of uncorrupted parties by raising either $\mathbf{M}$ or $\mathbf{N}$ to a random exponent. It does so because it does not know the corresponding password. The distribution of such messages is identical to those produced by honest parties in the real world, which are of the form $g^x\mathbf{M}^{\mathsf{pw}}$ or $g^y\mathbf{N}^{\mathsf{pw}}$. The simulator then keeps track of whether the adversary is launching a passive attack or an active attack: where the former means that there exists another simulated session with a consistent view. All passively attacked sessions are not interrupted by the simulator, which means that $\mathcal{F}_{\mathsf{pwKE}}$ will choose independent keys at the associated dummy parties' outputs.

For actively attacked sessions, the simulator checks if the delivered message was constructed as per the protocol and, if so, it extracts the password. All malformed messages cause the simulator to interrupt the session in the functionality by calling TestPw with $\mathsf{pw} = \perp$. For well formed messages, the simulator queries TestPw on the extracted password and, if the password is correct, computes the correct key: this is possible because, even though the simulator does not know the correct exponent implicit in the simulated honest party's state, it knows the algebraic decomposition of the delivered message and this is well formed (this means it can compute the key as the adversary would). If the password is incorrect, the simulator generates a totally random key (this is ignored by the functionality if there are no corrupt parties involved in the session, but it is relevant otherwise as we discuss below).

The simulation is perfect for all sessions with well-formed messages and correct password guesses. It looks perfect for all other sessions, unless the attacker can query the random oracle on the group element that such a session would compute in the real world. Our proof shows that any such query can, with overwhelming probability, be used to solve the SqDH problem. Two important observations for the proof: i. the simulator never uses the random exponents it generates for the honest party messages to perform any computation; and ii. the simulator never constructs any group element for which it cannot provide an algebraic decomposition to bases g, $\mathbf{M}$ and $\mathbf{N}$. The second observation guarantees that our simulator is an algebraic adversary as required by the composition theorem in Sect. 2.

Corrupt Parties. Figure 5 does not show explicitly the simulator's handling of sessions involving corrupt parties. In this case, the environment tells the simulator what the corrupt party should be doing, and the simulator does not keep the state of the corrupt party. Moreover, any group elements transmitted by the corrupt party come with their algebraic decomposition as above. Our simulator is structured to handle this case identically to the setting where the uncorrupted party is actively attacked while interacting with another uncorrupted party; we explain why this is the case in the detailed version of the proof provided in the full version [3]. The proof below covers this scenario as a particular case.

Proof of Simulator Correctness. From this point on we consider only interactions involving uncorrupted parties. The first observation we make is that the distribution of the protocol messages produced by the simulator is identical to that occurring in the real world, even though they are constructed differently. It therefore remains to prove that the outputs of the ideal functionality match the distribution of the parties' outputs in the real world. We observe that the real and ideal worlds are identical until bad, where *bad* is defined as the event that a secret key that is selected uniformly at random by the functionality at the output of an uncorrupted party is inconsistent with the answer given by H to the adversary. This is because in all other cases the simulator programs the output of the ideal functionality consistently with the real world. This means formally that, for $\epsilon = \Pr[\text{EXEC}_{\mathsf{pwKE},\mathcal{S},\mathcal{E}} \Rightarrow \mathsf{bad}]$, we have

$$\text{EXEC}_{\mathsf{pwKE},\mathcal{S},\mathcal{E}} \approx_\epsilon \text{EXEC}_{\text{SPAKE2},\mathcal{D},\mathcal{E}}$$

More precisely, we define event bad as the existence within the set of queries placed by $\mathcal{E}$ to the random oracle of a query $(sid, P, P', \mathbf{X}^\star, \mathbf{Y}^\star, \mathsf{pw}, \mathbf{Z})$ that is *consistent* with the trace of a session at an uncorrupted party, which accepted after a passive attack or after an active attack where the simulator did not place a correct TestPw query. We define now these conditions formally.

We say a random oracle query $(sid, P, P', \mathbf{X}^\star, \mathbf{Y}^\star, \mathsf{pw}, \mathbf{Z})$ is *consistent* with an initiator session π_P^{sid} if this instance was created following a NewSession query by $\mathcal{E}$ using pw and $\pi_P^{sid} = (\cdot, (P, P', \mathbf{X}^\star, \mathbf{Y}^\star), \cdot, \mathsf{init})$. Similarly, the condition for responder session $\pi_{P'}^{sid}$ is $\pi_{P'}^{sid} = (\cdot, (P, P', \mathbf{X}^\star, \mathbf{Y}^\star), \cdot, \mathsf{resp})$. Note that the order of party identities in the trace determines the role of the party.

We say an initiator session π_P^{sid} *accepted after a passive attack* if it completed following a $\text{SendResp}(P', P, sid, (\mathbf{Y}^\star, \mathsf{alg}))$ message from $\mathcal{E}$, when $\pi_{P'}^{sid} = (\cdot, (P, P', sid, \mathbf{X}^\star, \mathbf{Y}^\star), \cdot, \text{resp})$. We say a responder session $\pi_{P'}^{sid}$ *accepted after a passive attack* if it completed following a $\text{SendInit}(P, P', sid, (\mathbf{X}^\star, \mathsf{alg}))$ message from $\mathcal{E}$, when $\pi_P^{sid} = (\cdot, (P, P', sid, \mathbf{X}^\star, \mathbf{Y}^\star), \cdot, \text{init})$. All other sessions are considered to be *under active attack*.

We reduce the probability of bad to SqDH. Intuitively, our reduction embeds the SqDH challenge $\mathbf{A}$ in the global parameters ($\mathbf{M} = \mathbf{A}, \mathbf{N} = \mathbf{A}^\delta$) for δ sampled uniformly at random from $\mathbb{Z}_q^\star$ (this accounts for the $1/q$ term in the theorem statement). Suppose bad is first set for a random oracle entry that is consistent with a session accepted by an initiator session. The attacker delivered a message $\mathbf{Y}^\star$ and an algebraic representation that we can see as $[(a, g), (b, \mathbf{M}), (c, \mathbf{N})]$. The reduction can transform this algebraic representation into $[(a, g), (b+\delta c, \mathbf{A})]$. Let $\mathsf{CDH}(\mathbf{A}, \mathbf{B}) = g^{ab}$ for $\mathbf{A} = g^a$ and $\mathbf{B} = g^b$. This means that any problematic random oracle query will include a group element of the form

$$\mathbf{Z} = \mathsf{CDH}(\mathbf{A}^{x-\mathsf{pw}}, g^a \mathbf{A}^{b+\delta(c-\mathsf{pw})}) = \mathsf{CDH}(\mathbf{A}^{x-\mathsf{pw}}, g^a) \cdot \mathsf{CDH}(\mathbf{A}^{x-\mathsf{pw}}, \mathbf{A}^{b+\delta(c-\mathsf{pw})})$$

where x was chosen by the reduction following the simulator code. Since the reduction can compute the first factor, we can recover

$$\mathsf{CDH}(\mathbf{A},\mathbf{A})^{(x-\mathsf{pw})(b+\delta(c-\mathsf{pw}))}$$

which means that the required SqDH solution can be recovered when $(x-\mathsf{pw})(b+\delta(c-\mathsf{pw}))\neq 0$. The case of responders is similar, but we can only recover the SqDH result provided $\delta(y-\mathsf{pw})(b+\delta c-\mathsf{pw})\neq 0$.

The detailed proof given the full version [3] bounds the probability that our reduction strategy fails using a statistical term and reductions $\mathcal{B}_1^1$ and $\mathcal{B}_1^2$ to the discrete logarithm problem. Once this possibility is excluded, we can reduce the probability of bad to SqDH. The detailed proof also includes the code for the algorithm $\mathcal{B}_2$ that breaks SqDH if the bad event occurs. In this case, we know that the random oracle table will contain a solution to SqDH if the event bad has occurred. When the experiment terminates, $\mathcal{B}_2$ therefore samples a random oracle query uniformly at random[6] and looks for a consistent session. It could find one or two consistent sessions, where the latter case corresponds to a passive attack with matching passwords on both sides. In any case, it computes a candidate SqDH value using the appropriate initiator or responder-side formula we described above. If the randomly selected random oracle entry was the first to cause the bad event, the algorithm solves SqDH. This accounts for the q_H multiplicative loss in the theorem statement. □

Remark. The above proof strategy can be used almost without change for an alternative version of the protocol that does not include the password pw in the input to the key derivation hash. This has practical advantages, as the password need not be kept in memory after computing the outgoing message. This version of the protocol was introduced as SPAKE1 in [5], and it was previously not known that this protocol could achieve forward secrecy or UC security. The only point where the current proof would need to be modified is in the final computation of the SqDH solution: in the particular case of a passive attack there now could be two protocol instances at P and P' with different passwords, but matching the same random oracle entry. In this case, the reduction would toss a coin and choose one of them at random to fix the password used to compute the SqDH solution. This adds only a factor of 2 to the final reduction step.

Furthermore, the same proof applies to both protocols when we can rely on a DDH oracle to the fixed basis $\mathbf{A}$ to look for the offending random oracle entry. In this case, we get a tight reduction to *Strong* SqDH for both protocols, i.e., the strong DH assumption adapted to the computation of g^{a^2}. Finally, the proof also applies to variants of the protocol discussed in [1], whereby the CRS is defined as $(M, N=M)$, or when the CRS is simply the group description and $(M,N)=\mathrm{H}(sid,U,S)$ and H is modeled as a random oracle.

[6] This step could be replaced with a search for a consistent entry using a DDH oracle to the fixed basis $\mathbf{A}$, resulting in a tighter reduction to Strong SqDH where the q_H factor disappears.

4.2 CPace

Figure 6 shows a CPace protocol execution between an user U and a server S. CPace is a two-pass protocol, where we assume the user plays the role of the initiator and the server that of the responder. We give a sketch of the proof here and provide the complete proof in the full version [3].

User		Server
	$sid, U, S, \mathsf{pw} \in \mathcal{P}, \mathsf{crs} = (\mathbb{G})$	
$G \leftarrow \mathrm{H}_1(sid, U, S, \mathsf{pw})$		$G \leftarrow \mathrm{H}_1(sid, U, S, \mathsf{pw})$
$x \twoheadleftarrow \mathbb{Z}_q$		$y \twoheadleftarrow \mathbb{Z}_q$
$X \leftarrow G^x$	$\xrightarrow{X}$	Abort if $X = \mathbf{1}$
Abort if $Y = \mathbf{1}$	$\xleftarrow{Y}$	$Y \leftarrow G^y$
$K \leftarrow \mathrm{H}_2(sid, X, Y, Y^x)$		$K \leftarrow \mathrm{H}_2(sid, X, Y, X^y)$

Fig. 6. The CPace protocol [22]. CRS includes the group description $\mathbb{G}$ s.t. $|\mathbb{G}| = q$.

Let InvCDH denote the problem of computing $g^{1/a}$ when given a random element $\mathbf{A} = g^a$ in $\mathbb{G}$ and let $\mathsf{Adv}_{\mathcal{B}}^{\mathsf{InvCDH}}$ denote the probability that attacker $\mathcal{B}$ solves this problem. Theorem 7 shows that CPace AGM realizes $\mathcal{F}_{\mathsf{pwKE}}$ if InvCDH is hard in $\mathbb{G}$.

Theorem 7. *CPace AGM-emulates $\mathcal{F}_{\mathsf{pwKE}}$ under static corruptions, in a hybrid model with the random oracle functionality. More precisely, there exists an algebraic simulator $\mathcal{S}$ for the (algebraic) dummy adversary $\mathcal{D}$ such that, for every efficient algebraic environment $\mathcal{E}$ creating at most q_S sessions, querying H_1 at most q_{H_1} times and querying H_2 at most q_{H_2} times, there exists $\mathcal{B}_{\ell_1,\ell_2}$ running in roughly the same time as $\mathcal{E}$ such that $\mathrm{EXEC}_{\mathsf{pwKE},\mathcal{S},\mathcal{E}} \approx_\epsilon \mathrm{EXEC}_{\mathrm{CPACE},\mathcal{D},\mathcal{E}}$, where*

$$\epsilon \leq q_{\mathrm{H}_1} \cdot q_{\mathrm{H}_2} \cdot \mathsf{Adv}_{\mathcal{B}_{\ell_1,\ell_2}}^{\mathsf{InvCDH}}() + \frac{q_{\mathrm{H}_1}^2 + q_S}{q}.$$

Note that the InvCDH problem is equivalent to the DL problem when we consider algebraic attackers, so the theorem follows with a reduction to the DL problem even if the proof relies on this apparently stronger assumption.

Proof. (Sketch) Simulator $\mathcal{S}$ is shown in Fig. 7. The simulation strategy here is identical to that we adopt for the SPAKE2 proof, with the caveat that the simulator must learn the environment's queries to H_1 in order to extract the password in an active attack. (In this case, the bases for the algebraic representations of adversarially constructed messages include the outputs of the random oracle H_1 and any messages $\mathbf{X}$ or $\mathbf{Y}$ produced by an uncorrupted party.) Also

SIMULATOR $\mathcal{S}$ for CPace

proc $H_1(sid, P, P', \mathsf{pw})$ (non-repeat queries)

$r \twoheadleftarrow \mathbb{Z}_q$; $\mathbf{G} \leftarrow g^r$; $T_1[sid, P, P', \mathsf{pw}] \leftarrow \mathbf{G}$; return $\mathbf{G}$

Simulator aborts if at any point T_1 is non-injective.

On input $(\mathsf{NewSession}, sid, P, P', \mathrm{role})$ from $\mathcal{F}_{\mathsf{pwKE}}$

If $\neg(\pi_P^{sid} = \perp)$ discard input.

If role = init

  $\hat{x} \twoheadleftarrow \mathbb{Z}_q^*$; $\mathbf{X} \leftarrow g^{\hat{x}}$

  $\pi_P^{sid} \leftarrow (\hat{x}, (P, P', sid, \mathbf{X}, \perp), \perp, \mathrm{init})$

  Send SENDINIT$(P, P', sid, \mathbf{X})$ to $\mathcal{D}$

Else $\hat{y} \twoheadleftarrow \mathbb{Z}_q^*$; $\mathbf{Y} \leftarrow g^{\hat{y}}$

  $\pi_P^{sid} \leftarrow (\hat{y}, (P', P, sid, \perp, \mathbf{Y}), \perp, \mathrm{resp})$

On message SENDINIT$(P, P', sid, (\mathbf{X}, \mathsf{alg}) \neq \mathbf{1})$ from $\mathcal{E}$ via $\mathcal{D}$

Ignore if $\pi_{P'}^{sid} \neq (\hat{y}, (P, P', sid, \perp, \mathbf{Y}), \perp, \mathrm{resp})$

(A unique $\pi_{P'}^{sid}$ satisfies the above check for some $\hat{y}$ and $\mathbf{Y}$)

$K \twoheadleftarrow \mathcal{K}$

(Can't interrupt passive sessions so $\mathcal{F}$ sets $=K$ at output)

If $\pi_P^{sid} = (\cdot, (P, P', sid, \mathbf{X}, \perp), \perp, \mathrm{init})$ Jump to COMPLETE

(First check whether $\mathbf{X}$ was constructed as per protocol)

If $\mathsf{alg} = [(\mathbf{G}, x))] \wedge (sid, P, P', \mathsf{pw}, \mathbf{G}) \in T_1$

  Query $(\mathsf{TestPwd}, sid, P', \mathsf{pw})$ to $\mathcal{F}_{\mathsf{pwKE}}$

  If $\mathcal{F}_{\mathsf{pwKE}}$ responds with "correct guess" Then $K \leftarrow H_2(sid, \mathbf{X}, \mathbf{Y}, \mathbf{Y}^x)$

(Interrupt all other non-passive sessions.)

Else Query $(\mathsf{TestPwd}, sid, P', \perp)$ to $\mathcal{F}_{\mathsf{pwKE}}$

COMPLETE: Send SENDRESP$(P', P, sid, \mathbf{Y})$ to $\mathcal{D}$

  $\pi_{P'}^{sid} \leftarrow (\perp, (P, P', sid, \mathbf{X}, \mathbf{Y}), K, \mathrm{resp})$

  Query $(\mathsf{NewKey}, sid, P', K)$ to $\mathcal{F}_{\mathsf{pwKE}}$

On message SENDRESP$(P', P, sid, (\mathbf{Y}, \mathsf{alg}) \neq \mathbf{1})$ from $\mathcal{E}$ via $\mathcal{D}$

Ignore if $\pi_P^{sid} \neq (\hat{x}, (P, P', sid, \mathbf{X}, \perp), \perp, \mathrm{init})$

(A unique π_P^{sid} satisfies the above check for some $\hat{x}$ and $\mathbf{X}$)

$K \twoheadleftarrow \mathcal{K}$

(Can't interrupt passive sessions so $\mathcal{F}$ sets $=K$ at output)

If $\pi_{P'}^{sid} = (\cdot, (P, P', sid, \mathbf{X}, \mathbf{Y}), \cdot, \mathrm{resp})$ Jump to COMPLETE

(First check whether $\mathbf{Y}$ was constructed as per protocol)

If $\mathsf{alg} = [(\mathbf{G}, y)] \wedge (sid, P, P', \mathsf{pw}, \mathbf{G}) \in T_1$

  Query $(\mathsf{TestPwd}, sid, P, \mathsf{pw})$ to $\mathcal{F}_{\mathsf{pwKE}}$

  If $\mathcal{F}_{\mathsf{pwKE}}$ responds with "correct guess" Then $K \leftarrow H_2(sid, \mathbf{X}, \mathbf{Y}, \mathbf{X}^y)$

(Interrupt all other non-passive sessions.)

Else Query $(\mathsf{TestPwd}, sid, P, \perp)$ to $\mathcal{F}_{\mathsf{pwKE}}$

COMPLETE: $\pi_P^{sid} \leftarrow (\perp, (P, P', sid, \mathbf{X}, \mathbf{Y}), K, \mathrm{init})$

  Query $(\mathsf{NewKey}, sid, P, K)$ to $\mathcal{F}_{\mathsf{pwKE}}$

Fig. 7. The operation of the CPace simulator. The simulator needs to observe adversarial random oracle queries on H_1 but not on H_2, and it does not need to program either of the random oracles. T_1 is initially empty.

here the simulator never generates any group element for which it cannot give an algebraic decomposition with respect to base g, and hence it is an algebraic adversary. The handling of corrupt parties is also the same.

Proof of Simulator Correctness. This part of the proof is also similar in structure to that of SPAKE2. We first eliminate some corner cases, where the distribution of real world and the ideal world views do not match, but are straightforward to bound using a statistical term; this includes collisions at the random oracle output. We then conclude that the real and ideal worlds are identical until bad, where *bad* is defined as the existence within the set of queries placed by $\mathcal{E}$ to H_2 of a query $(sid, \mathbf{X}, \mathbf{Y}, \mathbf{Z})$ that is *consistent* with the trace of a session at an uncorrupted party, which accepted after a passive attack or after an active attack where the simulator did not place a correct TestPw query. We define now these conditions formally.

We say an H_2 query $(sid, \mathbf{X}, \mathbf{Y}, \mathbf{Z})$ is *consistent* with an initiator session π_P^{sid} if $\pi_P^{sid} = (\cdot, (\cdot, \cdot, \mathbf{X}, \mathbf{Y}), \cdot, \mathsf{init})$. Similarly, the condition for responder session $\pi_{P'}^{sid}$ is $\pi_{P'}^{sid} = (\cdot, (\cdot, \cdot, \mathbf{X}, \mathbf{Y}), \cdot, \mathsf{resp})$. We say an initiator session π_P^{sid} *accepted after a passive attack* if it completed following a $\textsc{SendResp}(P', P, sid, (\mathbf{Y}, \mathsf{alg}))$ message from $\mathcal{E}$, when $\pi_{P'}^{sid} = (\cdot, (P, P', sid, \mathbf{X}, \mathbf{Y}), \cdot, \mathrm{resp})$. Responder session $\pi_{P'}^{sid}$ *accepted after a passive attack* if it completed after a $\textsc{SendInit}(P, P', sid, (\mathbf{X}, \mathsf{alg}))$ message from $\mathcal{E}$, when $\pi_P^{sid} = (\cdot, (P, P', sid, \mathbf{X}, \mathbf{Y}), \cdot, \mathrm{init})$. All other sessions are considered to be *under active attack.* Finally, we say a T_1 entry of the form $(sid, P, P', \mathsf{pw})$ is *consistent* with an initiator (resp. responder) instance, if that instance was initialized by the environment in a $\textsc{NewSession}$ query with $(sid, P, P', \mathsf{pw}, \mathsf{init})$ (resp. $(sid, P', P, \mathsf{pw}, \mathsf{resp})$).

We bound the probability of bad in the ideal world using a sequence of games.

Guessing the RO Entries that Cause bad. We modify ideal world as follows: sample (ℓ_1, ℓ_2) uniformly at random in $[q_{H_1}] \times [q_{H_2}]$. Then, if bad first occurs due to the i-th H_2 query such that $i \neq \ell_2$, abort. Furthermore, if the offending T_1 entry (i.e., the T_1 unique entry consistent with the session where the bad event was detected) is not the ℓ_1-th one, abort. Clearly, we can still bound the probability of bad in the previous game with the pessimistic bound $q_{H_1} \cdot q_{H_2} \cdot \Pr[\mathsf{bad}]$, where we only check for bad if the experiment has not aborted. We give in the full version [3] a reduction $\mathcal{B}_{\ell_1,\ell_2}$ that solves the InvCDH problem whenever bad occurs in this modified game.

Final Reduction. The reduction strategy is as follows. The generator returned by H_1 for the problematic session associated with the ℓ_2-th password query is programmed to be $\mathbf{A}$, the InvCDH problem instance. All messages generated by uncorrupted parties are generated as $g^{\hat{x}}$ or $g^{\hat{y}}$. All random oracle queries consistent with a session with trace $(\mathbf{X}, \mathbf{Y})$ and generator $\mathbf{A}$ include the key element $\mathbf{Z}$ satisfying the following equation:

$$\mathbf{Z} = \mathbf{X}^{\mathsf{dlog}_{\mathbf{A}}(\mathbf{Y})} = \mathbf{Y}^{\mathsf{dlog}_{\mathbf{A}}(\mathbf{X})} = \mathbf{A}^{(\mathsf{dlog}_{\mathbf{A}}(\mathbf{X}) \cdot \mathsf{dlog}_{\mathbf{A}}(\mathbf{Y}))}$$

Observing that $\mathsf{dlog}_{\mathbf{A}}(\mathbf{X}) = \mathsf{dlog}_g(\mathbf{X})/\mathsf{dlog}_g(\mathbf{A})$ the equation can be re-written as:

$$\mathbf{Z} = g^{\frac{\mathsf{dlog}_g(\mathbf{X})\cdot\mathsf{dlog}_g(\mathbf{Y})}{\mathsf{dlog}_g\mathbf{A}}}$$

In the simplest case of a passive attack, it is immediate that we recover the solution to the InvCDH problem if $\hat{x}\cdot\hat{y} \neq 0$, which we know to be the case.

Now let us suppose the problematic case occurs with an actively attacked initiator session. Then we know that $\mathbf{Y} = g^{\alpha}\mathbf{A}^{\beta}$ and $\alpha \neq 0$; otherwise this would be a correct password guess and the bad event could never have occurred for this session—recall the experiment would have aborted if H_1 did not program $\mathbf{A}$ as the output for the password associated with this session. We can therefore refine the equation above to:

$$\mathbf{Z} = g^{\frac{\hat{x}\cdot(\alpha+\beta\cdot\mathsf{dlog}_g(\mathbf{A}))}{\mathsf{dlog}_g\mathbf{A}}} = g^{\frac{\hat{x}\cdot\alpha}{\mathsf{dlog}_g\mathbf{A}}+\hat{x}\cdot\beta}$$

Again, the InvCDH solution can be recovered, as long as $\hat{x} \neq 0$. The responder session case is identical. □

Remark. As in the proof of SPAKE2, we could eliminate the q_{H_2} factor in the reduction by using a DDH oracle to the fixed basis $\mathbf{A}$ to detect which of the entries in H_2 is consistent with the bad event; however, we would still be guessing the problematic H_1 query in order to program the hard problem instance, and the q_{H_1} factor would remain.

Remark. In the proofs for SPAKE2 and CPace, we have seen that it is possible to have tighter reductions to a stronger gap assumption that excludes the need to guess an entry in the key derivation random oracle. However, we should also mention that in the algebraic group model, the gap versions of the SqDH and InvCDH assumptions are actually equivalent to the standard versions, provided that the reduction is able to give algebraic decompositions of all the elements queried to the DDH oracle. This is the case in our proofs, provided that the attacker is also required to give algebraic decompositions of the group elements it queries to the random oracle. Note that this is a requirement for algebraic environments in the UC AGM model, as explained in Sect. 2. The take away from this discussion is that our proof of SPAKE2 implies a tight reduction to SqDH in the algebraic group model for both SPAKE1 and SPAKE2 (SPAKE1 is the variant that does not include pw in the key derivation hash). The CPace proof implies a reduction to InvCDH in the AGM with a loss of q_{H_1}.

References

1. Abdalla, M., Barbosa, M.: Perfect forward security of SPAKE2. Cryptology ePrint Archive, Report 2019/1194 (2019). https://eprint.iacr.org/2019/1194

2. Abdalla, M., Barbosa, M., Bradley, T., Jarecki, S., Katz, J., Xu, J.: Universally composable relaxed password authenticated key exchange. In: Micciancio, D., Ristenpart, T. (eds.) CRYPTO 2020, Part I. LNCS, vol. 12170, pp. 278–307. Springer, Cham (2020). https://doi.org/10.1007/978-3-030-56784-2_10
3. Abdalla, M., Barbosa, M., Katz, J., Loss, J., Xu, J.: Algebraic adversaries in the universal composability framework. Cryptology ePrint Archive, Report 2021/3878 (2021). https://ia.cr/2021/3878
4. Abdalla, M., Benhamouda, F., MacKenzie, P.: Security of the J-PAKE password-authenticated key exchange protocol. In: 2015 IEEE Symposium on Security and Privacy, pp. 571–587. IEEE (2015)
5. Abdalla, M., Pointcheval, D.: Simple password-based encrypted key exchange protocols. In: Menezes, A. (ed.) CT-RSA 2005. LNCS, vol. 3376, pp. 191–208. Springer, Heidelberg (2005). https://doi.org/10.1007/978-3-540-30574-3_14
6. Auerbach, B., Giacon, F., Kiltz, E.: Everybody's a target: scalability in public-key encryption. In: Canteaut, A., Ishai, Y. (eds.) EUROCRYPT 2020, Part III. LNCS, vol. 12107, pp. 475–506. Springer, Cham (2020). https://doi.org/10.1007/978-3-030-45727-3_16
7. Bauer, B., Fuchsbauer, G., Loss, J.: A classification of computational assumptions in the algebraic group model. In: Micciancio, D., Ristenpart, T. (eds.) CRYPTO 2020, Part II. LNCS, vol. 12171, pp. 121–151. Springer, Cham (2020). https://doi.org/10.1007/978-3-030-56880-1_5
8. Baum, C., David, B., Dowsley, R., Nielsen, J.B., Oechsner, S.: TARDIS: a foundation of time-lock puzzles in UC. In: Canteaut, A., Standaert, F.-X. (eds.) EUROCRYPT 2021. LNCS, vol. 12698, pp. 429–459. Springer, Cham (2021). https://doi.org/10.1007/978-3-030-77883-5_15. Cryptology ePrint Archive, Report 2020/537, https://ia.cr/2020/537
9. Bellare, M., Rogaway, P.: Random oracles are practical: a paradigm for designing efficient protocols. In: ACM Conference on Computer and Communications Security, pp. 62–73. ACM Press (1993)
10. Bradley, T., Jarecki, S., Xu, J.: Strong asymmetric PAKE based on trapdoor CKEM. In: Boldyreva, A., Micciancio, D. (eds.) CRYPTO 2019, Part III. LNCS, vol. 11694, pp. 798–825. Springer, Cham (2019). https://doi.org/10.1007/978-3-030-26954-8_26
11. Byali, M., Patra, A., Ravi, D., Sarkar, P.: Fast and universally-composable oblivious transfer and commitment scheme with adaptive security. Cryptology ePrint Archive, Report 2017/1165 (2017). https://eprint.iacr.org/2017/1165
12. Camenisch, J., Drijvers, M., Gagliardoni, T., Lehmann, A., Neven, G.: The wonderful world of global random oracles. In: Nielsen, J.B., Rijmen, V. (eds.) EUROCRYPT 2018, Part I. LNCS, vol. 10820, pp. 280–312. Springer, Cham (2018). https://doi.org/10.1007/978-3-319-78381-9_11
13. Canetti, R.: Universally composable security: a new paradigm for cryptographic protocols. In: 42nd Annual Symposium on Foundations of Computer Science (FOCS), pp. 136–145. IEEE (2001)
14. Canetti, R., Dodis, Y., Pass, R., Walfish, S.: Universally composable security with global setup. In: Vadhan, S.P. (ed.) TCC 2007. LNCS, vol. 4392, pp. 61–85. Springer, Heidelberg (2007). https://doi.org/10.1007/978-3-540-70936-7_4
15. Canetti, R., Halevi, S., Katz, J., Lindell, Y., MacKenzie, P.: Universally composable password-based key exchange. In: Cramer, R. (ed.) EUROCRYPT 2005. LNCS, vol. 3494, pp. 404–421. Springer, Heidelberg (2005). https://doi.org/10.1007/11426639_24

16. Canetti, R., Jain, A., Scafuro, A.: Practical UC security with a global random oracle. In: ACM Conference on Computer and Communications Security (CCS), pp. 597–608. ACM Press (2014)
17. Chiesa, A., Hu, Y., Maller, M., Mishra, P., Vesely, N., Ward, N.: Marlin: preprocessing zkSNARKs with universal and updatable SRS. In: Canteaut, A., Ishai, Y. (eds.) EUROCRYPT 2020, Part I. LNCS, vol. 12105, pp. 738–768. Springer, Cham (2020). https://doi.org/10.1007/978-3-030-45721-1_26
18. Chou, T., Orlandi, C.: The simplest protocol for oblivious transfer. In: Lauter, K., Rodríguez-Henríquez, F. (eds.) LATINCRYPT 2015. LNCS, vol. 9230, pp. 40–58. Springer, Cham (2015). https://doi.org/10.1007/978-3-319-22174-8_3
19. Fuchsbauer, G., Kiltz, E., Loss, J.: The algebraic group model and its applications. In: Shacham, H., Boldyreva, A. (eds.) CRYPTO 2018, Part II. LNCS, vol. 10992, pp. 33–62. Springer, Cham (2018). https://doi.org/10.1007/978-3-319-96881-0_2
20. Fuchsbauer, G., Plouviez, A., Seurin, Y.: Blind schnorr signatures and signed elgamal encryption in the algebraic group model. In: Canteaut, A., Ishai, Y. (eds.) EUROCRYPT 2020, Part II. LNCS, vol. 12106, pp. 63–95. Springer, Cham (2020). https://doi.org/10.1007/978-3-030-45724-2_3
21. Genç, Z.A., Iovino, V., Rial, A.: The simplest protocol for oblivious transfer revisited. Cryptology ePrint Archive, Report 2017/370 (2017). http://eprint.iacr.org/2017/370
22. Haase, B., Labrique, B.: AuCPace: efficient verifier-based PAKE protocol tailored for the IIoT. IACR Trans. Cryptogr. Hardw. Embed. Syst. **2019**(2), 1–48 (2019). https://tches.iacr.org/index.php/TCHES/article/view/7384
23. Hauck, E., Loss, J.: Efficient and universally composable protocols for oblivious transfer from the CDH assumption. Cryptology ePrint Archive, Report 2017/1011 (2017). http://eprint.iacr.org/2017/1011
24. Katz, J., Loss, J., Xu, J.: On the security of time-locked puzzles and timed commitments. Cryptology ePrint Archive, Report 2020/730 (2020). https://eprint.iacr.org/2020/730
25. Kerber, T., Kiayias, A., Kohlweiss, M.: Composition with knowledge assumptions. Cryptology ePrint Archive, Report 2021/165 (2021). https://eprint.iacr.org/2021/165
26. Larangeira, M., Tanaka, K.: Programmability in the generic ring and group models. J. Internet Serv. Inf. Secur. **1**(2/3), 57–73 (2011)
27. Maller, M., Bowe, S., Kohlweiss, M., Meiklejohn, S.: Sonic: zero-knowledge SNARKs from linear-size universal and updatable structured reference strings. In: ACM Conference on Computer and Communications Security (CCS), pp. 2111–2128. ACM Press (2019)
28. Naor, M., Paz, S., Ronen, E.: CRISP: Compromise resilient identity-based symmetric PAKE. Cryptology ePrint Archive, Report 2020/529 (2020). https://eprint.iacr.org/2020/529
29. Nechaev, V.I.: Complexity of a determinate algorithm for the discrete logarithm. Math. Notes **55**(2), 165–172 (1994)
30. Shoup, V.: Lower bounds for discrete logarithms and related problems. In: Fumy, W. (ed.) EUROCRYPT 1997. LNCS, vol. 1233, pp. 256–266. Springer, Heidelberg (1997). https://doi.org/10.1007/3-540-69053-0_18

Symmetric-Key Constructions

Luby-Rackoff Backwards with More Users and More Security

Srimanta Bhattacharya[1(✉)] and Mridul Nandi[2]

[1] SIAS, KREA University, Sri City, India
[2] Indian Statistical Institute, Kolkata, India
mridul@isical.ac.in

Abstract. It is known, from the work of Dai *et al.* (in CRYPTO'17), that the PRF advantage of XORP (bitwise-xor of two outputs of n-bit random permutations with domain separated inputs), against an adversary making q queries, is about $q/2^n$ for $q \leq 2^{n-5}$. The same bound can be easily shown to hold for $\mathsf{XORP}[k]$ (bitwise-xor of k outputs n-bit pseudorandom random permutations with domain separated inputs), for $k \geq 3$. In this work, we first consider multi-user security of $\mathsf{XORP}[3]$. We show that the multi-user PRF advantage of $\mathsf{XORP}[3]$ is about $\sqrt{uq_{\max}}/2^n$ for all $q_{\max} \leq 2^n/12$, where u is the number of users and $q_{\max}$ is the maximum number of queries the adversary can make to each user. In the multi-user setup, this implies that $\mathsf{XORP}[3]$ gives security for $O(2^n)$ users even allowing almost $O(2^n)$ queries to each user. This also indicates significant improvement in the single-user setup (*i.e.*, when $u = 1$), where the distinguishing advantage of the adversary even after making $O(2^n)$ queries is $O(\frac{1}{\sqrt{2^n}})$, *i.e.*, negligible. Subsequently, we consider a simple efficient variant of $\mathsf{XORP}[3]$ in which we use five calls to produce $2n$ bit output (instead of six calls in the case of $\mathsf{XORP}[3]$). This variant also achieves similar level of security. As an immediate application, we can construct a variant of block cipher based counter mode which provides much higher security (both in the single-user and the multi-user setup) compared to the security of the encryption part of GCM at the cost of efficiency.

Keywords: Random permutation · PRF security · Multi-user security · χ^2 method · XOR construction

1 Introduction

LUBY-RACKOFF BACKWARDS. *Pseudorandom functions* (PRFs) are important cryptographic primitives. Construction of PRFs using other primitives is an intriguing problem in cryptography. In the context of symmetric-key cryptography, construction of PRFs from *pseudorandom permutations* (PRPs) is commonly termed "Luby-Rackoff Backwards" [BKR98].[1]

[1] In reference to the seminal work by Luby and Rackoff ([LR88]) who considered the converse problem and showed how to construct a PRP from a PRF.

S. Bhattacharya—The work was carried out when the author was affiliated with the Indian Statistical Institute, Kolkata.

M. Tibouchi and H. Wang (Eds.): ASIACRYPT 2021, LNCS 13092, pp. 345–375, 2021.
https://doi.org/10.1007/978-3-030-92078-4_12

A potential drawback of block ciphers (modeled as a PRP) is that they merely achieve *birthday bound* security, *i.e.*, a block cipher becomes distinguishable from a PRF when it is queried $O(2^{n/2})$ times, where n is the block size. Achieving security *beyond the birthday bound* (BBB) is very much desirable but non-trivial. Bellare, Krovetz, and Rogaway ([BKR98]) and Hall, Wagner, Kelsey, and Schneier ([HWKS98]) initiated the study of constructions of good PRFs from block ciphers with BBB security. Since then the problem has received a lot of attention and at present, it is an intensely investigated area of research.

Different constructions have been proposed in the literature that achieve varying level of BBB security. A particularly simple construction which we refer to as the XORP construction, has received much attention in this context. Given an n-bit random permutation RP, the construction is given by $\mathsf{XORP} : \{0,1\}^{n-1} \to \{0,1\}^n$; $\mathsf{XORP}(x) = \mathsf{RP}(0\|x) \oplus \mathsf{RP}(1\|x)$.

In a generalized version of XORP, denoted by $\mathsf{XORP}[k]$, xor of k independent n-bit random permutations is considered (though in this work, we will consider its domain separated version). Lucks [Luc00] showed BBB security for $\mathsf{XORP}[k]$ for all $k \geq 2$. More precisely, he showed that the construction is secure up to $O(2^{\frac{kn}{k+1}})$ queries. This was further improved in a sequence of papers [BI99,CLP14,Pat10,Pat08,DHT17]. In particular, in [DHT17], it was shown that the PRF advantage of an adversary making at most q queries to the XORP construction is at most $\frac{q}{2^n} + 3(\frac{q}{2^n})^{1.5}$ indicating that XORP is secure up to $O(2^n)$ queries.

On the other hand, Mennink *et al.* [MP15] showed a reduction proving that the security of $\mathsf{XORP}[k]$ can be reduced to that of XORP for any $k \geq 3$. Hence, $\mathsf{XORP}[k]$ also achieves n-bit security. So, to begin with, PRF security of $\mathsf{XORP}[k]$ for $k \geq 2$ looks settled. But we show that further improvement is possible (in terms of the distinguishing advantage of the adversary) even in the case of $\mathsf{XORP}[3]$. Consideration of XORP (or its general version $\mathsf{XORP}[k]$) is important since it has been used to obtain some constructions achieving BBB (or sometimes almost full) security (e.g., CENC [Iwa06,BN18c], PMAC_Plus [Yas11], and ZMAC [IMPS17]).

MULTI-USER SECURITY. In the multi-user PRF setting of $\mathsf{XORP}[k]$, the adversary can query multiple independent random functions in the ideal world or multiple independent $\mathsf{XORP}[k]$'s (by independent choice of underlying random permutation) in the *real world*. In the present-day scenario, multi-user security (first considered in [BBM00] in the context of public-key cryptography) of a cryptographic primitive is a prudent goal to achieve. Perhaps, due to the large scale deployment of primitives over the internet it deserves more urgent attention. Quite a few recent works ([BT16,HTT18,BHT18,HT17,ML15]) have addressed this area.

MULTI USER SECURITY OF $\mathsf{XORP}[k]$. To motivate its significance in a concrete manner let us further investigate the multi-user security of $\mathsf{XORP}[k]$. Until now, the best single-user PRF advantage for $\mathsf{XORP}[k]$ is $q/2^n$ for any $k \geq 2$ (ignoring the other lower order terms). By using standard hybrid reduction, multi-user PRF bound of $\mathsf{XORP}[k]$ is $uq_{max}/2^n$, where u is the number of users and q_{max}

is the maximum number of queries per user. When we use AES (so $n = 128$) as the underlying block cipher, we have to limit u and q_{max} such that $uq_{max} \leq 2^{96}$ if we tolerable distinguishing advantage is at most 2^{-32}. Even though the limit is reasonable for the time being, it may be a concern as the number of users as well as amount of usage of the internet is growing at a huge pace. One option to boost the security is to increase the block size n. Unfortunately, AES does not support block size other than 128[2]. The other option could be to come up with some construction which provides stronger security. In this work, we investigate the second option.

1.1 Our Contribution

In this paper, we investigate the multi-user PRF security of $\mathsf{XORP}[3]$ construction. We show that, for any adversary, making at most q_{max} queries to any user, the multi-user PRF advantage for $\mathsf{XORP}[3]$ is at most $20\sqrt{uq_{max}}/2^n$, where u is the number of users and $q_{max} \leq 2^n/12$. The result shows that $\mathsf{XORP}[3]$ can be simultaneously used by $O(2^n)$ users even after allowing the adversary to make almost $O(2^n)$ queries to each user (provided the keys, *i.e.* the underlying random permutations of $\mathsf{XORP}[3]$ are chosen independently by each user); though in practice the random permutation should be instantiated with a block cipher with sufficiently long key (see [ML15]). For a single user, *i.e.*, when $u = 1$, the result says that even if the adversary is allowed to query almost all inputs of the block cipher, its distinguishing advantage is $O\left(\frac{1}{\sqrt{2^n}}\right)$, which is negligible in n. To the best of our knowledge, this is the first result (in the standard model) showing negligible advantage for an adversary that is allowed to query almost the entire domain.

We also analyze the single-user PRF security of a simple variant of $\mathsf{XORP}[3]$, which we denote as $\mathsf{XORP}'[3]$. This construction makes 5 calls to the underlying block cipher (instead of 6 in case of $\mathsf{XORP}[3]$) to generate 2 output blocks. Even with a saving in the number of block cipher calls we show that the PRF security of $\mathsf{XORP}'[3]$ is very similar to that of $\mathsf{XORP}[3]$. In particular, we show that the PRF advantage of the construction is bounded by $\frac{5\sqrt{q}}{N} + \frac{256q}{N^2} + \frac{8192q}{N^{\frac{3}{2}}}$. Though we have analyzed the single-user case for the sake of simplicity, multi-user PRF security of $\mathsf{XORP}'[3]$ can be analyzed in the same way as that of $\mathsf{XORP}[3]$.

In order to emphasize our contribution further, we mention that multi-user PRF advantage of $\mathsf{XORP}[2]$ (obtained in [HS20] using the χ^2 method) and $\mathsf{XORP}'[2]$ (obtained in [Cog18] using Patarin's Mirror theory) are at most $O\left(\frac{\sqrt{n}q}{2^n}\right)$ and $O\left(\frac{q}{2^n}\right)$, where q is the total number of queries made to all the users.

1.2 Our Technique

We use the χ^2 method, introduced in [DHT17], which has of late emerged as a potent tool for bounding *statistical distance* between two joint distributions.

[2] However, Rijndael has variants with larger block sizes.

Though relatively new, it has so far been effectively applied in quite a few other works ([BN18c, BN18a, CLL19, Men19, GM20]). Although its application to bound PRF advantage of an adversary for $\mathsf{XORP}[k]$ is not novel, in the present case of $\mathsf{XORP}[3]$ and $\mathsf{XORP}'[3]$, the analyses become significantly intricate. In the case of $\mathsf{XORP}[3]$, we need to handle the multi-user scenario with subtle but important adjustments. On the other hand, in case of $\mathsf{XORP}'[3]$, calculations are quite involved. However, as discussed above, by applying this method we get significantly better bounds than the existing ones. We give technical description of the χ^2 method in Sect. 2.3.

2 Preliminaries

2.1 Notation

In this paper, we denote 2^n by N. We fix $\mathcal{G}$ to be the group $\mathbb{F}_2^n$, and denote the group addition (*i.e.*, bit-wise $\mathtt{xor}$) by $+$. For an element $\mathsf{g} \in \mathcal{G}$ and a subset $\mathcal{H} \in \mathcal{G}$, we denote by $\mathsf{g} + \mathcal{H}$ the subset $\{\mathsf{g} + \mathsf{h} | \mathsf{h} \in \mathcal{H}\}$. Sometimes (will be clear from context) we will term the elements of $\mathcal{G}$ as *blocks.*[3]

For a positive integer s, we denote an s-tuple $(\mathsf{x}_1, \ldots, \mathsf{x}_s)$ as x^s; however, when the value of s is clear from the context we will drop it (for notational simplicity) and denote the tuple as x. Also, when a sequence x^s is partitioned into subsequences (in a way that will be appropriately specified), we will denote the i-th subsequence by $\widehat{\mathsf{x}}_i$. Moreover, by slightly abusing the notation we will denote by $(\mathsf{x}^s \setminus \widehat{\mathsf{x}}_i)$ the subsequence of x^s formed (maintaining the same order of x^s) by removing the elements of $\widehat{\mathsf{x}}_i$.

For a random variable X, we write $\mathbf{Pr}_{\mathsf{X}}$ to denote the probability distribution (or function) corresponding to X. Sample space of a random variable X is a set Ω so that $\mathbf{Pr}_{\mathsf{X}}(\Omega) = 1$. Support of X is the sample space Ω of X so that for all $x \in \Omega$, $\mathbf{Pr}_{\mathsf{X}}(\mathsf{x}) > 0$. Given a set $\mathcal{S}$ and the tuple $\mathsf{X}^s := (\mathsf{X}_1, \ldots, \mathsf{X}_s)$, we will write $\mathsf{X}_1, \ldots, \mathsf{X}_s \leftarrow\!\!\$\, \mathcal{S}$ to mean that X_i's are sampled uniformly and independently from the set $\mathcal{S}$. Moreover, these are also independent with all other previously sampled random variables in the context. A sample, *i.e.*, a particular realization of X^s will be denoted by $\mathsf{x}^s := (\mathsf{x}_1, \ldots, \mathsf{x}_s)$.

With and Without Replacement. Let $\mathcal{S}$ be a set of size M and s be a positive integer. To distinguish between *with replacement* (WR) sampling and *without replacement* (WOR) sampling (when they appear in the same context) we write $\mathsf{X}_1, \ldots, \mathsf{X}_s \leftarrow_{\mathrm{wr}} \mathcal{S}$ to represent that $\mathsf{X}_1, \ldots, \mathsf{X}_s$ are chosen randomly in WR manner from $\mathcal{S}$ (*i.e.*, $\mathsf{X}_1, \ldots, \mathsf{X}_s \leftarrow\!\!\$\, \mathcal{S}$), and we write $\mathsf{X}_1, \ldots, \mathsf{X}_s \leftarrow_{\mathrm{wor}} \mathcal{S}$ to mean that X_i's are randomly sampled in WOR manner from the set $\mathcal{S}$. Let

$$\mathcal{S}^{\underline{s}} = \{(\mathsf{x}_1, \ldots, \mathsf{x}_s) : \mathsf{x}_i\text{'s are distinct elements of } \mathcal{S}\}$$

[3] We do not reserve the term 'block' solely for this purpose. However, its presence in other contexts will not create any ambiguity.

be the set of all block-wise distinct (*i.e.*, the elements of the tuple are distinct) s-tuples of blocks. Note that $|\mathcal{S}^{\underline{s}}| = M(M-1)\cdots(M-s+1)$. We use shorthand notation $M^{\underline{s}} := M(M-1)\cdots(M-s+1)$. In this notation, a WOR sample X^s is chosen uniformly from $\mathcal{S}^{\underline{s}}$. In other words,

$$\mathbf{Pr}[\mathsf{X}^s = \mathsf{a}^s] = \frac{1}{|\mathcal{S}|^{\underline{s}}}, \text{ for all } \mathsf{a}^s \in \mathcal{S}^{\underline{s}}.$$

So, $\mathcal{S}^{\underline{s}}$ is the support of X^s.

Definition 1 (Random Set). *A subset $\mathcal{V}_r \subseteq \mathcal{G}$ of size r is called a random r-set if it is chosen uniformly from the set of all r sized subsets of $\mathcal{G}$. Thus, for every $\mathcal{V} \subseteq \mathcal{G}$, with $|\mathcal{V}| = r$,*

$$\mathbf{Pr}[\mathcal{V}_r = \mathcal{V}] = \binom{N}{r}^{-1}.$$

Throughout the paper we denote a random r-set in $\mathcal{G}$ as $\mathcal{V}_r$. A random r-set can be constructed by drawing a random WOR sample, *i.e.*, $\mathcal{V}_r = \{\mathsf{X}_1, \ldots, \mathsf{X}_r\}$, where $(\mathsf{X}_1, \ldots, \mathsf{X}_r) \leftarrow_{\text{wor}} \mathcal{G}$. Note that the complement set $\mathcal{G} \setminus \mathcal{V}_r$ is a random $(N-r)$-set. We will require the following estimate from [BN18c].

Lemma 1 ([BN18c]). *If $2w < N$ then $1 - \frac{(N-r)^{\underline{w}}}{N^{\underline{w}}} \leq \frac{2rw}{N}$.*

2.2 Adversary and Advantage

Here, we recall the notion of adversarial advantage in the context of a generic *indistinguishability game*. An *oracle adversary* or *oracle distinguisher* $\mathcal{A}$ is an *oracle algorithm* that interacts with an *oracle* $\mathcal{O}$ through a set of (potentially adaptive) queries and responses. Finally, it returns a bit $b \in \{0,1\}$. We express this as $\mathcal{A}^{\mathcal{O}} \rightarrow b$. In an *indistinguishability game*, $\mathcal{A}$ interacts with two oracles $\mathcal{O}_1$ and $\mathcal{O}_2$. The goal of $\mathcal{A}$ is to distinguish between $\mathcal{O}_1$ and $\mathcal{O}_2$ only from the corresponding queries and responses. The *advantage* of the adversary in this game, denoted $\mathsf{Adv}_{\mathcal{A}}(\mathcal{O}_1, \mathcal{O}_2)$, is given by

$$\mathsf{Adv}^{\text{dist}}_{\mathcal{O}_1,\mathcal{O}_2}(\mathcal{A}) := |\mathbf{Pr}[\mathcal{A}^{\mathcal{O}_1} \rightarrow 1] - \mathbf{Pr}[\mathcal{A}^{\mathcal{O}_2} \rightarrow 1]|,$$

where the probabilities are taken over the random coins of $\mathcal{A}, \mathcal{O}_1$, and $\mathcal{O}_2$.

PSEUDORANDOM FUNCTION (PRF) is a very important cryptographic primitive. For example, while analyzing *message authentication code* (MAC), we mostly study *PRF security* as it is a stronger notion than MAC. It has also been used to define *encryption schemes, authenticated encryptions* and other cryptographic algorithms. PRF security is quantified by *PRF advantage*. Below we describe the PRF advantage of a *keyed function* which is relevant for this work.

Let m and n be positive integers. Let $\mathsf{Func}_{m\rightarrow n}$ is the set of all functions from $\{0,1\}^m$ to $\{0,1\}^n$, and let $\mathsf{RF}_{m\rightarrow n} \leftarrow_{\$} \mathsf{Func}_{m\rightarrow n}$, *i.e.*, $\mathsf{RF}_{m\rightarrow n}$ is a function chosen uniformly at random from $\mathsf{Func}_{m\rightarrow n}$. Also, let $\mathcal{K}$ be a finite set, termed the *key space*. Given a function $f : \mathcal{K} \times \{0,1\}^m \to \{0,1\}^n$, for every $\mathsf{k} \in \mathcal{K}$, we denote by f_{k} the function (also termed a *keyed function*) $f(\mathsf{k},\cdot) \in \mathsf{Func}_{m\to n}$. The PRF advantage of an oracle adversary $\mathcal{A}$ against f is defined as follows.

Definition 2 (PRF advantage). *Let $f : \mathcal{K} \times \{0,1\}^m \to \{0,1\}^n$ be a function and $\mathcal{A}$ be a distinguisher. Then the PRF advantage of $\mathcal{A}$ against f is defined as*

$$\mathbf{Adv}_f^{\mathrm{prf}}(\mathcal{A}) := \mathsf{Adv}^{\mathrm{dist}}_{f,RF}(\mathcal{A}) = |\mathbf{Pr}[\mathcal{A}^{f_{\mathsf{K}}} \to 1 \ : \ \mathsf{K} \leftarrow_{\$} \mathcal{K}] - \mathbf{Pr}[\mathcal{A}^{RF_{m\to n}} \to 1]|.$$

PRP ADVANTAGE is defined in an analogous manner. Here, instead of a random function oracle the adversary $\mathcal{A}$ interacts with a random permutation oracle $\mathsf{RP}_n \leftarrow_{\$} \mathsf{Perm}_n$, where Perm_n is the set of all permutations on $\{0,1\}^n$. PRP advantage is relevant in the context of a *block cipher* which is modeled as a *pseudorandom permutation*. More formally, an n-bit block cipher is a function $e : \mathcal{K} \times \{0,1\}^n \to \{0,1\}^n$ such that for all $\mathsf{K} \in \mathcal{K}$, $e_{\mathsf{K}} := e(\mathsf{K},\cdot)$ is a permutation on $\{0,1\}^n$. The PRP advantage of $\mathcal{A}$ against e is defined as

$$\mathbf{Adv}_e^{\mathrm{prp}}(\mathcal{A}) = \mathsf{Adv}^{\mathrm{dist}}_{e,\mathsf{RP}}(\mathcal{A}) = |\mathbf{Pr}[\mathcal{A}^{e_{\mathsf{K}}} \to 1 \ : \ \mathsf{K} \leftarrow_{\$} \mathcal{K}] - \mathbf{Pr}[\mathcal{A}^{\mathsf{RP}_n} \to 1]|.$$

We write $\mathbf{Adv}_f^{\mathrm{prf}}(q,t) = \max_{\mathcal{A}} \mathbf{Adv}_f^{\mathrm{prf}}(\mathcal{A})$ where maximum is taken over all adversaries making at most q queries and runs in time t. We similarly define $\mathbf{Adv}_f^{\mathrm{prp}}(q,t)$ for PRP advantage.

Since we are concerned with information theoretic security (with the only restriction that the adversary makes total q queries), w.l.o.g we assume that the adversary is deterministic and does not repeat its queries.

When $\mathcal{A}$ is interacting with $\mathsf{RF}_{m\to n}$, the outputs follow uniform and independent distributions over $\{0,1\}^n$ which we denote as $\mathsf{U}_1,\ldots,\mathsf{U}_q \leftarrow_{\$} \{0,1\}^n$. Similarly, $\mathsf{X}_1,\ldots,\mathsf{X}_q$ denote the outputs of f_{K} where $\mathsf{K} \leftarrow_{\$} \mathcal{K}$. We denote the probability distributions associated to $\mathsf{U}_1,\ldots,\mathsf{U}_q$ and $\mathsf{X}_1,\ldots,\mathsf{X}_q$ by $\Pr_{\mathsf{U}}$ and $\Pr_{\mathsf{X}}$ respectively. Thus,

$$\mathbf{Adv}_f^{\mathrm{prf}}(\mathcal{A}) = |\mathbf{Pr}_{\mathsf{X}}(\mathcal{E}) - \mathbf{Pr}_{\mathsf{U}}(\mathcal{E})|, \tag{1}$$

where $\mathcal{E}$ is the set of all q-tuple responses $\mathsf{x}^q = (\mathsf{x}_1,\ldots,\mathsf{x}_q) \in (\{0,1\}^n)^q$ at which $\mathcal{A}$ returns 1. It is well known that the statistical distance between the distributions $\mathbf{Pr}_{\mathsf{X}}$ and $\mathbf{Pr}_{\mathsf{U}}$ is given by

$$\|\mathbf{Pr}_{\mathsf{U}} - \mathbf{Pr}_{\mathsf{X}}\| \stackrel{\mathrm{def}}{=} \frac{1}{2} \sum_{\mathsf{x}^q \in (\{0,1\}^n)^q} |\mathbf{Pr}_{\mathsf{X}}(\mathsf{x}^q) - \mathbf{Pr}_{\mathsf{U}}(\mathsf{x}^q)| = \max_{\mathcal{E} \subseteq (\{0,1\}^n)^q} (\mathbf{Pr}_{\mathsf{X}}(\mathcal{E}) - \mathbf{Pr}_{\mathsf{U}}(\mathcal{E})). \tag{2}$$

MULTI-USER PRF ADVANTAGE is a generalization of the PRF advantage of a keyed function to the multi-user scenario. Let u be the number of users denoted by the elements of $[u]$. With a keyed function $f : \mathcal{K} \times \{0,1\}^m \to \{0,1\}^n$, we associate its multi-user extension $f^{(u)} : \mathcal{K}^u \times [u] \times \{0,1\}^m \to \{0,1\}^n$ mapping (k^u, i, x) to $f_{\mathsf{k}_i}(x)$, for all $\mathsf{k}^u \in \mathcal{K}^u, i \in [u]$. Let RF denote the random function from $[u] \times \{0,1\}^m$ to $\{0,1\}^n$. We define the multi-user advantage against f for u users as

$$\mathbf{Adv}_f^{\mathrm{mu\text{-}prf}}(u, q_{\max}, q, t) = \max_{\mathcal{A}} \mathsf{Adv}^{\mathrm{dist}}_{f^{(u)},\mathsf{RF}}(\mathcal{A}),$$

where the maximum is taken over all adversaries $\mathcal{A}$ that run in time t making at most $q_{\max}$ queries to each user and q queries altogether to all users. To simplify our analysis, w.l.o.g. we allow $\mathcal{A}$ to make exactly q_{max} queries to each user in $[u]$. Indeed, this can only increase $\mathcal{A}$'s advantage which we are going to upper bound. So, with this convention, we have $q = u \times q_{max}$. Also, following the same considerations made for the single-user case we assume, w.l.o.g, that $\mathcal{A}$ makes distinct queries to individual users.

2.3 χ^2 Method

Given a set Ω, let $\mathsf{X}^q := (\mathsf{X}_1, \ldots, \mathsf{X}_q)$ and $\mathsf{Z}^q := (\mathsf{Z}_1, \ldots, \mathsf{Z}_q)$ be two random vectors distributed over $\Omega^q = \Omega \times \cdots \times \Omega$ (q times) according to the distributions $\Pr_{\mathsf{X}}$ and $\Pr_{\mathsf{Z}}$ respectively. In what follows, we will require the following conditional distributions.

$$\mathbf{Pr}_{\mathsf{X}|\mathsf{x}^{i-1}}(\mathsf{x}_i) := \mathbf{Pr}[\mathsf{X}_i = \mathsf{x}_i \mid \mathsf{X}_1 = \mathsf{x}_1, \ldots, \mathsf{X}_{i-1} = \mathsf{x}_{i-1}],$$
$$\mathbf{Pr}_{\mathsf{Z}|\mathsf{x}^{i-1}}(\mathsf{x}_i) := \mathbf{Pr}[\mathsf{Z}_i = \mathsf{x}_i \mid \mathsf{Z}_1 = \mathsf{x}_1, \ldots, \mathsf{Z}_{i-1} = \mathsf{x}_{i-1}].$$

When $i = 1$, $\mathbf{Pr}_{\mathsf{X}|\mathsf{x}^{i-1}}(\mathsf{x}_1)$ represents $\mathbf{Pr}[X_1 = \mathsf{x}_1]$. Similarly, for $\mathbf{Pr}_{\mathsf{Z}|\mathsf{x}^{i-1}}(\mathsf{x}_1)$. Let $\mathsf{x}^{i-1} \in \Omega^{i-1}$, $i \geq 1$. The χ^2-distance between these two conditional probability distributions is defined as

$$\chi^2(\mathbf{Pr}_{\mathsf{X}|\mathsf{x}^{i-1}}, \mathbf{Pr}_{\mathsf{Z}|\mathsf{x}^{i-1}}) := \sum_{x_i \in \Omega} \frac{(\mathbf{Pr}_{\mathsf{X}|\mathsf{x}^{i-1}}(\mathsf{x}_i) - \mathbf{Pr}_{\mathsf{Z}|\mathsf{x}^{i-1}}(\mathsf{x}_i))^2}{\mathbf{Pr}_{\mathsf{Z}|\mathsf{x}^{i-1}}(\mathsf{x}_i)}, \tag{3}$$

with the assumption that the support of the distribution $\mathbf{Pr}_{\mathsf{X}|\mathsf{x}^{i-1}}$ be contained within the support of the distribution $\mathbf{Pr}_{\mathsf{Z}|\mathsf{x}^{i-1}}$. Further, when the distributions $\mathbf{Pr}_{\mathsf{X}|\mathsf{x}^{i-1}}$ and $\mathbf{Pr}_{\mathsf{Z}|\mathsf{x}^{i-1}}$ are clear from the context we will use the notation $\chi^2(\mathsf{x}^{i-1})$ for $\chi^2(\mathbf{Pr}_{\mathsf{X}|\mathsf{x}^{i-1}}, \mathbf{Pr}_{\mathsf{Z}|\mathsf{x}^{i-1}})$. Then the crux of the χ^2 method is the following theorem from [DHT17] (see also [BN18b]).

Theorem 1 ([DHT17]). *Following the notation as above and suppose the support of the distribution $\mathbf{Pr}_{\mathsf{X}|\mathsf{x}^{i-1}}$ is contained within the support of the distribution $\mathbf{Pr}_{\mathsf{Z}|\mathsf{x}^{i-1}}$ for all x^{i-1}, then*

$$\|\mathbf{Pr}_{\mathsf{X}} - \mathbf{Pr}_{\mathsf{Z}}\| \leq \left(\frac{1}{2} \sum_{i=1}^{q} \mathbf{Ex}[\chi^2(X^{i-1})] \right)^{\frac{1}{2}}, \tag{4}$$

where for each i, the expectation is over the $(i-1)$-th marginal distribution of $\mathbf{Pr}_{\mathsf{X}}$.

3 Multi-user PRF Security of XORP[3]

In this section, we analyze the multi-user PRF security of $\mathsf{XORP}[3](x)$. Formally, the output of $\mathsf{XORP}[3]$ is given by $\mathsf{XORP}[3](x) := \mathsf{RP}(x\|00) \oplus \mathsf{RP}(x\|01) \oplus$

$\mathsf{RP}(x\|10)$, where RP is an n-bit random permutation and $x \in \{0,1\}^{n-2}$. In the multi-user setting of $\mathsf{XORP}[3]$, we let $\mathscr{A}$ to interact with u users $[u] : \{1,\ldots,u\}$. In the real world, each of the u users holds an independent copy of the underlying random permutation RP. In the ideal world, there is a random function $\mathsf{RF} : [u] \times \{0,1\}^{n-2} \rightarrow \{0,1\}^n$. We allow $\mathscr{A}$ to make total q queries of the form (u_i, x_i) with $u_i \in [u], \mathsf{x}_i \in \{0,1\}^{n-2}$ for $i \in [q]$. Repeating our assumptions for multi-user security in this setting we have *(i)* For all $v \in [u]$ if $(v, \mathsf{x}_i), (v, \mathsf{x}_j)$ are two queries then $\mathsf{x}_i \neq \mathsf{x}_j$ *(ii)* For all $v \in [u]$ the number of queries of the form (v, x) is q_{max}. So, we have $q = u \times q_{max}$.

Let the transcript of replies be $\mathsf{P} := (\mathsf{P}_1,\ldots,\mathsf{P}_q)$ when $\mathscr{A}$ is interacting in the real world and $\mathsf{R} := (\mathsf{R}_1,\ldots,\mathsf{R}_q)$ when it is interacting in the ideal world, where $\mathsf{P}_i, \mathsf{R}_i \in \mathcal{G}$ are the replies to the i-th query. Therefore, here our goal is to upper bound $\|\mathbf{Pr}_\mathsf{P} - \mathbf{Pr}_\mathsf{R}\|$. Here, it is important to observe that the q_{max} replies given by any user is distributed independently of the other replies. For example, suppose w.l.o.g. that user 1's reply is the sequence $(\mathsf{P}_1,\ldots,\mathsf{P}_{q_{max}})$. Then $(\mathsf{P}_1,\ldots,\mathsf{P}_{q_{max}})$ is independent of $(\mathsf{P}_{q_{max}+1},\ldots,\mathsf{P}_q)$. Indeed, this follows from the fact that each user in $[u]$ holds an independent copy of RP.

Now, there is a subtle technical difficulty involved while working with the distributions $\mathbf{Pr}_\mathsf{P}$ and $\mathbf{Pr}_\mathsf{R}$ in the setting of the χ^2-method. The difficulty arises because user U_i for the i-th query is not completely dependent on i. We will highlight and elaborate more on the issue at the appropriate place in our proof of Theorem 2 (see the discussion immediately following (7)).

In order to overcome the difficulty, we reorder the samples P and R to get new samples S and U respectively. In S, P_i's are grouped into a sequence of u blocks, where each block comprises of q_{max} P_i's output by the same user; similarly for the distribution U (though we note that R and U are the same, because any reordering of a sequence of q outputs of a random function is identical to itself).[4] Now it is easy to see that in S and U each $i \in [q]$ uniquely identifies $U_i \in [u]$. In Fig. 1, we present a precise description of the samples U and S together with a formal explanation presented below.

For $i \in [u]$, let $\mathrm{I}_i := \{(i-1)q_{max} + j : j \in [q_{max}]\}$. So, the sequence $(\mathrm{I}_i)_{i\in[u]}$ partitions $[q]$. Let $\mathsf{U} := (\mathsf{U}_1, \mathsf{U}_2, \ldots, \mathsf{U}_q)$, be a WR or with replacement sample (represented as a tuple) of size q, each U_i is sampled from $\mathcal{G}$ uniformly and independently. In other words, we have $\mathsf{U} \leftarrow_\$ \mathcal{G}^q$. On the other hand, the sample $\mathsf{S} := (\mathsf{S}_1, \mathsf{S}_2, \ldots, \mathsf{S}_q)$ is generated (as described in Fig. 1) as follows. First, for each $i \in [u]$, a WOR or without replacement sample $\widehat{\mathsf{T}}_i = (\mathsf{T}_{j,k} : j \in \mathrm{I}_i, k \in [3])$ of size $3q_{max}$ is generated, where $\widehat{\mathsf{T}}_i$ is independent of $\widehat{\mathsf{T}}_j$ for each $1 \leq j \leq i-1$.

---

[4] It is not difficult to conceive a bijection between P and S effected by the reordering described here (since R and U are identical we only focus on P and S). Indeed, for this purpose one can consider an extended transcript $\mathsf{P}' := ((\mathsf{P}_1, U_1), \ldots, (\mathsf{P}_q, U_q))$ which also contains the user U_i associated with the i-th query, and subsequently express the bijection in an explicit manner. However, we will not do that here in order to reduce notational complexity. More so, because we will not refer to this bijection in the subsequent discussion.

Then for each $\ell \in [q]$, S_ℓ is computed as

$$\mathsf{S}_\ell = \mathsf{T}_{\ell,1} + \mathsf{T}_{\ell,2} + \mathsf{T}_{\ell,3}.$$

So both U and S have the same sample space $\mathcal{G}^q$, and since they are permutations of R and P respectively, we note that

$$\|\mathbf{Pr}_{\mathsf{S}} - \mathbf{Pr}_{\mathsf{U}}\| = \|\mathbf{Pr}_{\mathsf{P}} - \mathbf{Pr}_{\mathsf{R}}\| \tag{5}$$

Here it can be noted that the reordering works in the case of XORP[3] because the distribution of the output of any query does not depend on the input value in both worlds. Moreover, we assumed with no loss of advantage for the adversary, the number of queries to each user is constant (maximum allowed for each user).

Random Experiment for U	Random Experiment for S
$\mathsf{U} := (\mathsf{U}_i : i \in [q]) \xleftarrow{\text{wr}} \mathcal{G}$	**for** $1 \le i \le u$
return U	$\quad \widehat{\mathsf{T}}_i := (\mathsf{T}_{j,k} : j \in [\mathrm{I}_i], k \in [3]) \xleftarrow{\text{wor}} \mathcal{G}$
	// $\widehat{\mathsf{T}}_i$ is sampled independent of $\widehat{\mathsf{T}}_j$, $1 \le j \le i-1$
	for $1 \le \ell \le q$
	$\quad \mathsf{S}_\ell = \mathsf{T}_{\ell,1} + \mathsf{T}_{\ell,2} + \mathsf{T}_{\ell,3}$
	return $\mathsf{S} := (\mathsf{S}_\ell : \ell \in [q])$

Fig. 1. Description of sampling methods of random variables U, S.

Now, we state our main theorem which provides an upper bound on the statistical distance $\|\mathbf{Pr}_{\mathsf{S}} - \mathbf{Pr}_{\mathsf{U}}\|$. The theorem shows that the sample S is very close to the uniform sample U even though it is computed from a non-uniform sample.

Theorem 2 (Pseudorandomness of S). *Let* U *and* S *be the random vectors as described in Fig. 1. Then, for all* $q_{max} \le N/12$

$$\|\mathbf{Pr}_{\mathsf{S}} - \mathbf{Pr}_{\mathsf{U}}\| \le \frac{20\sqrt{uq_{max}}}{N}$$

We postpone the proof to Sect. 3.4.

3.1 Application to Single-User PRF Security of XORP[3]

We now describe the cryptographic implications of the result from Theorem 2. Let us define XORP[3] construction based on a single keyed n-bit block cipher $e : \mathcal{K} \times \{0,1\}^n \to \{0,1\}^n$ with key-space $\mathcal{K}$. For $x \in \{0,1\}^{n-2}$ and $\mathsf{k} \in \mathcal{K}$, we define

$$\mathsf{XORP}_e[3](\mathsf{k}, x) = e_{\mathsf{k}}(x\|00) \oplus e_{\mathsf{k}}(x\|01) \oplus e_{\mathsf{k}}(x\|10) \tag{6}$$

Using the hybrid argument we can replace e by a random permutation at the cost of PRP advantage. Then we can apply our result to get the following corollary.

Corollary 1. *For all* $q \leq 2^n/12$,

$$\mathbf{Adv}^{\mathrm{prf}}_{\mathsf{XORP}_e[3]}(q, t) \leq \mathbf{Adv}^{\mathrm{prp}}_{e}(3q, t') + \frac{20\sqrt{q}}{2^n}$$

where $t' \approx t + 3q$.

The above corollary is a simple hybrid argument where we replace the underlying block cipher e by a random permutation. We note that outputs of a random permutation for distinct inputs is exactly a WOR or without replacement sample and hence we apply Theorem 2.

3.2 Application to Multi-user PRF Security of XORP[3]

Similarly, we state multi-user security of XORP construction.

$$\mathbf{Adv}^{\mathrm{mu\_prf}}_{\mathsf{XORP}_e[3]}(u, q_{\max}, q, t) \leq \mathbf{Adv}^{\mathrm{mu\text{-}prp}}_{e}(u, 3q_{\max}, t') + \frac{20\sqrt{uq_{\max}}}{N}$$

where u denotes the number of users.

3.3 Application to Counter Mode Encryption

Parity method encryption scheme introduced by Bellare-Goldreich-Krawczyk in [BGK99] is a probabilistic encryption scheme based on a pseudorandom function. Let $F_{\mathsf{K}} : \{0,1\}^n \to \{0,1\}^n$ be a pseudorandom function. Then for message $\mathsf{m} \in \{0,1\}^n$ and randomness $\mathsf{r}^t := (\mathsf{r}_1, \ldots, \mathsf{r}_t) \in (\{0,1\}^n)^t$, the ciphertext of the parity method encryption scheme is given by $(\mathsf{r}^t, F_{\mathsf{K}}(\mathsf{r}_1) \oplus \cdots \oplus F_{\mathsf{K}}(\mathsf{r}_t) \oplus \mathsf{m})$. For all $q \leq N/(e^2t)$, the PRF-advantage of this construction is shown to be $O(q^2/N^t) + O(q^3/N^{3t/2})$ for even t and $O(q^2/N^t) + O(q^4/N^{2t})$ for odd t. Thus, for $t = 2$, the construction achieves n-bit security and for $t = 4$, it achieves beyond n-bit security. However, the construction requires a pseudorandom function and random coins.

Counter mode encryption is a practical alternative to the above scheme. In counter mode encryption, we replace the random coins by some nonce (which does not repeat over all executions). More precisely, for nonce N and message m, the ciphertext of the counter mode encryption is $(\mathsf{N}, F_{\mathsf{K}}(\mathsf{N}) \oplus \mathsf{m})$. If the nonce does not repeat then the security of the encryption relies on the PRF security of F_{K}.

As the counter mode is quite popular and has wide applications, the multi-user security of the counter mode is also of considerable significance. Now, XORP[3], which uses pseudorandom permutations, can be seen to be the following counter mode encryption scheme.

Let s be the size of the counter (maximum message length is at most $n2^s$).

1. Given a message $\mathsf{m} = (\mathsf{m}_1, \ldots, \mathsf{m}_\ell) \in \{0,1\}^{n\ell}$, and a nonce $\mathsf{N} \in \{0,1\}^{n-s-2}$, we define $\mathsf{x}_{i,j} = \mathsf{N} \| \langle j \rangle_2 \| \langle i \rangle_s$, for all $j \in [3], i \in [\ell]$.
2. Let $\mathsf{z}_i = e_\mathsf{K}(\mathsf{x}_{i,1}) \oplus e_\mathsf{K}(\mathsf{x}_{i,2}) \oplus e_\mathsf{K}(\mathsf{x}_{i,3})$ for all $i \in [\ell]$.
3. The ciphertext is defined as $(\mathsf{N}, \mathsf{z}_1 \oplus \mathsf{m}_1, \ldots, \mathsf{z}_\ell \oplus \mathsf{m}_\ell)$.

The multi-user PRF security of the above encryption scheme is the same as the multi-user PRF security of XORP[3]. More precisely, the u-user privacy advantage of the counter mode encryption scheme (provided the nonce does not repeat) for an adversary making *(i)* at most $q_{\max}$ queries to each user, *(ii)* maximum number of message blocks is at most ℓ, and *(iii)* total q queries made to all users is given by (following the same hybrid argument as before)

$$\mathbf{Adv}_e^{\text{mu-prp}}(u, 3\ell q, t') + \frac{20\sqrt{u q_{max}}}{N}$$

.

3.4 Proof of Theorem 2

First, in Fig. 2, we describe the extended random variables X and Y which extends S and U respectively. Here, by extension we mean that S and U are marginal random variables of X and Y respectively. Note that in line 7 of the random experiment for Y, the execution following **else** will not be required in our paper. It is kept only for the sake of the completeness of the definition. We will formally show this in Claim 1.

Random Experiment for X

1 : **for** $1 \le i \le u$
2 : $\quad \widehat{\mathsf{T}}_i := (\mathsf{T}_{j,k} : j \in [\mathrm{I}_i], k \in [3]) \xleftarrow{\text{wor}} \mathcal{G}$
$\qquad$ // $\widehat{\mathsf{T}}_i$ **is independent of** $\widehat{\mathsf{T}}_\ell, 1 \le \ell \le i-1$
3 : **for** $1 \le i \le q$
4 : $\quad \mathsf{S}_i = \mathsf{T}_{i,1} + \mathsf{T}_{i,2} + \mathsf{T}_{i,3}$
5 : $\quad \mathsf{X}_i = (\mathsf{T}_{i,1}, \mathsf{T}_{i,2}, \mathsf{S}_i)$
6 : **return** $\mathsf{X} := (\mathsf{X}_i : i \in [q])$

Random Experiment for Y

1 : **for** $1 \le i \le u$
2 : $\quad$ **initialize** $\mathcal{S}_i^0 = \mathcal{G}$
3 : $\quad$ **for** $j \in \mathrm{I}_i$
4 : $\qquad k = j - (i-1)q_{max}$
5 : $\qquad \mathsf{U}_j \xleftarrow{\$} \mathcal{G}$
6 : $\qquad \mathcal{n}_j = \{(\mathsf{v}_1, \mathsf{v}_2) |$
$\qquad\qquad \mathsf{v}_1, \mathsf{v}_2, \mathsf{U}_j + \mathsf{v}_1 + \mathsf{v}_2 \in \mathcal{S}_i^{k-1},$
$\qquad\qquad \mathsf{U}_j + \mathsf{v}_1 + \mathsf{v}_2, \mathsf{v}_1, \mathsf{v}_2 \text{ distinct}\}$
7 : $\qquad$ **if** $\mathcal{n}_j \neq \emptyset$ **then** $(\mathsf{V}_{j,1}, \mathsf{V}_{j,2}) \xleftarrow{\$} \mathcal{n}_j$
8 : $\qquad$ **else** $(\mathsf{V}_{j,1}, \mathsf{V}_{j,2}) = (0, 0)$
9 : $\qquad \mathsf{Y}_j = (\mathsf{V}_{j,1}, \mathsf{V}_{j,2}, \mathsf{U}_j)$
10 : $\qquad \mathcal{S}_i^k = \mathcal{S}_i^{k-1} \setminus \{\mathsf{V}_{j,1}, \mathsf{V}_{j,2},$
11 : $\qquad\qquad \mathsf{V}_{j,3} := \mathsf{U}_j + \mathsf{V}_{j,1} + \mathsf{V}_{j,2}\}$
12 : **return** $\mathsf{Y} := (\mathsf{Y}_1, \ldots, \mathsf{Y}_q)$

Fig. 2. X and Y are extended random variables of S and U respectively.

Claim 1. *In the Random Experiment for* Y *(in Fig. 2),* $\mathcal{N}_j \neq \emptyset$ *holds for all* j. *Therefore, line 8 (following* **else***) never executes.*

Proof of claim. Without loss of generality first we fix user i. Then it is sufficient to show that for any $\mathsf{u}_j \in \mathcal{G}$, we can choose distinct $\mathsf{v}_1, \mathsf{v}_2 \in \mathcal{S}_i^{k-1}$ such that $\mathsf{u}_j + \mathsf{v}_1 + \mathsf{v}_2 \in \mathcal{S}_i^{k-1} \setminus \{\mathsf{v}_1, \mathsf{v}_2\}$ for $k \leq q_{max}$. To do this, we fix $\mathsf{u}_j \in \mathcal{G}$. Note that the distinctness of $\mathsf{v}_1, \mathsf{v}_2, \mathsf{u}_j + \mathsf{v}_1 + \mathsf{v}_2$ is equivalent to the distinctness of $\mathsf{v}_1, \mathsf{v}_2, \mathsf{u}_j$. Now, we choose v_1 arbitrarily from the set $\mathcal{S}_i^{k-1} \setminus \{\mathsf{u}_j\}$. This is clearly possible as we have that $|\mathcal{S}_i^{k-1} \setminus \{\mathsf{u}_j\}| \geq N - 3(k-1) > N - 3q_{max} \geq \frac{3N}{4}$, since $q_{max} \leq \frac{N}{12}$ by our assumption. Next, we choose v_2 arbitrarily from the set $\mathcal{D} = \mathcal{S}_i^{k-1} \setminus \{\{\mathsf{u}_j, \mathsf{v}_1\} \cup \{(\mathsf{u}_j + \mathsf{v}_1) + \{\mathcal{G} \setminus \mathcal{S}_i^{k-1}\}\}\}$. This is also possible since $|\mathcal{D}| \geq N - (2 \times 3(k-1) + 2) > N - 6q_{max} \geq \frac{N}{2}$. Then it is easy to see that, for the given u_j, the choice of v_1 and v_2 satisfies the desired condition. ■

Let $\mathcal{C} = \mathcal{G}^3$ denote the set of all 3-tuples of $\mathcal{G}$. To understand the probability distributions of the random vectors X and Y and their supports we consider the following involution (a permutation with self inverse) ρ over the set $\mathcal{C}$ mapping $(\mathsf{x}_1, \mathsf{x}_2, \mathsf{x}_3)$ to $(\mathsf{x}_1, \mathsf{x}_2, \mathsf{x}_1 + \mathsf{x}_2 + \mathsf{x}_3)$.

We extend the definition of the mapping ρ to a mapping ρ^* which is defined over $\mathcal{C}^c$ for any c. Formally, we define $\rho^*(\mathsf{z}_1, \ldots, \mathsf{z}_c) := (\rho(\mathsf{z}_1), \ldots, \rho(\mathsf{z}_c))$. From the random experiments, it is trivial to see that

$$\rho(\mathsf{X}_i) = \mathsf{T}_i := (\mathsf{T}_{i,1}, \mathsf{T}_{i,2}, \mathsf{T}_{i,3}) \qquad \rho(\mathsf{Y}_i) = \mathsf{V}_i := (\mathsf{V}_{i,1}, \mathsf{V}_{i,2}, \mathsf{V}_{i,3})$$

where $\mathsf{V}_{i,3} = \mathsf{U}_i + \mathsf{V}_{i,1} + \mathsf{V}_{i,2}$. So, for every $i \in [q]$, $\rho^*(\mathsf{X}^i) = \mathsf{T}^i$ and $\rho^*(\mathsf{Y}^i) = \mathsf{V}^i$. In other words, the random variables X and Y are equivalent to the random variables T and $\mathsf{V} := ((\mathsf{V}_{i,1}, \mathsf{V}_{i,2}, \mathsf{V}_{i,3}), i \in [q])$ respectively. More precisely, in the first case, for each $i \in [u]$, we first have WOR sample $\widehat{\mathsf{T}}_i$ and then define $\widehat{\mathsf{X}}_i$ by applying ρ on each block. Whereas, in the second case, for each $i \in [u]$, we first sample $\widehat{\mathsf{Y}}_i$ (extending a WR sample $\widehat{\mathsf{U}}_i$) and then we define $\widehat{\mathsf{V}}_i$ by applying ρ on each block. However, $\widehat{\mathsf{V}}_i$ behaves like a WOR sample (though it is not perfect WOR sample, it would have same support as a WOR sample). So for every $i \in [u]$ and every $j \in [q_{max}]$, the support of $\widehat{\mathsf{T}}_i^j$ (as well as $\widehat{\mathsf{V}}_i^j$) is the set

$$\widehat{\Gamma}_i^j := \{((\mathsf{a}_{i',1}, \mathsf{a}_{i',2}, \mathsf{a}_{i',3}) : i' \in [j]) : \mathsf{a}'_{i',k}s \text{ are distinct for all } i' \in [j], k \in [3]\}.$$

Hence, the support of $\widehat{\mathsf{X}}_i^j$ (as well as $\widehat{\mathsf{Y}}_i^j$), denoted as $\widehat{\Omega}_i^j$, would be the set of all such $3j$ tuples

$$\widehat{\Omega}_i^j := \{(\mathsf{x}_{i',j} : i' \in [j], k \in [3]) \in \mathcal{G}^{3i} : ((\mathsf{a}_{i',1}, \mathsf{a}_{i',2}, \mathsf{a}_{i',3}) : i' \in [j]) \in \widehat{\Gamma}_i^j$$
$$\rho(\mathsf{a}_{i',1}, \mathsf{a}_{i',2}, \mathsf{a}_{i',3}) = (\mathsf{x}_{i',1}, \mathsf{x}_{i',2}, \mathsf{x}_{i',3})\}.$$

Therefore, the support of vectors X and Y is given by $\Omega = (\widehat{\Omega}_i^{q_{max}} | i \in [u])$.

Next, for a fixed $i \in [q]$ let $i = (j-1)q_{max} + k,\ j \in [u], k \in [q_{max}]$. Then it follows that $\mathsf{X}_i = \widehat{\mathsf{X}}_{j,k} \in \widehat{\mathsf{X}}_j^k$. Then for every $\mathsf{x}^i \in \Omega^i$, the conditional probability for X can be expressed as

$$\begin{aligned}
\mathbf{Pr}_{\mathsf{X}}(\mathsf{x}_i \mid \mathsf{x}^{i-1}) &\stackrel{\text{def}}{=} \mathbf{Pr}[\mathsf{X}_i = \mathsf{x}_i \mid \widehat{\mathsf{X}}_j^{k-1} = \widehat{\mathsf{x}}_j^{k-1}, (\mathsf{X}^{i-1} \setminus \widehat{\mathsf{X}}_j) = (\mathsf{x}^{i-1} \setminus \widehat{\mathsf{x}}_j^{k-1})] \\
&= \mathbf{Pr}[\widehat{\mathsf{X}}_{j,k} = \widehat{\mathsf{x}}_{j,k} \mid \widehat{\mathsf{X}}_j^{k-1} = \widehat{\mathsf{x}}_j^{k-1}], \qquad (7) \\
&\quad \text{since } \widehat{\mathsf{X}}_j \text{ is independent of } (\mathsf{X}^{i-1} \setminus \widehat{\mathsf{X}}_j) \\
&= \mathbf{Pr}[\widehat{\mathsf{T}}_{j,k} = \widehat{\mathsf{t}}_{j,k} \mid \widehat{\mathsf{T}}_j^{k-1} = \widehat{\mathsf{t}}_j^{k-1}] \\
&= \frac{1}{(N - 3(k-1))_{\underline{3}}}. \qquad (8)
\end{aligned}$$

Here, we take a small but important detour in our proof to explain the technical issue involving the distributions $\mathbf{Pr}_{\mathsf{P}}$ and $\mathbf{Pr}_{\mathsf{R}}$ mentioned in the beginning. Note that in (7) the independence of $\widehat{\mathsf{X}}_j$ from $(\mathsf{X}^{i-1} \setminus \widehat{\mathsf{X}}_j)$ follows because the user number u_i is completely determined by i. This is not the case for the original distribution $\mathbf{Pr}_{\mathsf{P}}$. Indeed, for this distribution $\mathscr{A}$ can make adaptive choice of user u_i for the i-th query based on all the previous queries, and hence P_i may depend on the entire P^{i-1}. By reordering P into S (and correspondingly X) we make u_i completely determined by i, and hence the independence of $\widehat{\mathsf{X}}_j$ from $(\mathsf{X}^{i-1} \setminus \widehat{\mathsf{X}}_j)$. Similar observation holds in (9) corresponding to the reordering of the distribution R into U (and subsequently into Y).

Now, we introduce some notations for the random experiment Y.

For all $i \in [q]$, let us denote $\mathsf{u}_i = \mathsf{x}_{i,3}$, *i.e.*, $\mathsf{x}_i = (\mathsf{x}_{i,1}, \mathsf{x}_{i,2}, \mathsf{u}_i)$. As before, let $\rho(\mathsf{x}_{i'}) = \mathsf{t}_{i'}$ for every $i' \in [i]$. So, $\mathsf{t}_{i',j}$'s are distinct. Now, we define the two crucial sets for our analysis. For $j \in [u], k \in [q_{max}]$ let us denote

$$\mathcal{S}_j^k = \mathcal{G} \setminus \{\mathsf{t}_{\ell,p} : \ell \in [\mathrm{I}_j], p \in [3]\}, \text{ with } \mathcal{S}_j^0 = \mathcal{G},$$
$$\mathcal{N}^{\mathsf{u}_i}(\widehat{\mathsf{x}}_j^{k-1}) := \{\mathsf{v}_1, \mathsf{v}_2 \in \mathcal{S}_j^{k-1} : \mathsf{u}_i + \mathsf{v}_1 + \mathsf{v}_2 \in \mathcal{S}_j^{k-1} \text{ and } \mathsf{v}_1, \mathsf{v}_2, \mathsf{u}_i \text{ distinct}\}.$$

As noted earlier in Claim 1, the condition that $\mathsf{v}_1, \mathsf{v}_2, \mathsf{u}_i$ are distinct is equivalent to the condition that $\mathsf{v}_1, \mathsf{v}_2, \mathsf{v}_1 + \mathsf{v}_2 + \mathsf{u}_i$ are distinct.

Now, for $\mathsf{U}_i = \mathsf{u}_i$ and $\widehat{\mathsf{Y}}_j^{k-1} = \widehat{\mathsf{x}}_j^{k-1}$, the set $\mathcal{N}_i$ and the set $\mathcal{S}_j^k$ (defined in the line 5 and line 9 of the random experiment of Y in Fig. 2) is exactly the same as the set $\mathcal{N}^{u_i}(\widehat{\mathsf{x}}_j^{k-1})$ and $\mathcal{S}_j^k$ defined above. It is easy to observe the following:

– If $\widehat{\mathsf{x}}_j^{k-1} \in \widehat{\Omega}_j^{k-1}$ then the set $\mathcal{N}^{\mathsf{u}_i}(\widehat{\mathsf{x}}_j^{k-1})$ is nonempty as $\mathsf{x}_{i,1}, \mathsf{x}_{i,2} \in \mathcal{N}^{\mathsf{u}_i}(\widehat{\mathsf{x}}_j^{k-1})$.

Recall that in Claim 1 we have already justified that the set $\mathcal{N}_i$ is non-empty (and hence line 8 of the Random Experiment for Y is never executed) using a different argument. Now, we compute the conditional probability on the support of Y.

Claim 2. *Let $i = (j-1)q_{max} + k$, with $i \in [q], j \in [u], k \in [q_{max}]$. Then for all $\mathsf{x}^i \in \Omega^i$ we have,*

$$\mathbf{Pr}_{\mathsf{Y}}(\mathsf{x}_i \mid \mathsf{x}^{i-1}) \stackrel{\text{def}}{=} \mathbf{Pr}[\mathsf{Y}_i = \mathsf{x}_i \mid \mathsf{Y}^{i-1} = \mathsf{x}^{i-1}] = \frac{1}{N} \times \frac{1}{|\mathcal{N}^{\mathsf{u}_i}(\widehat{\mathsf{x}}_j^{k-1})|}.$$

Proof of claim. First, note that $\mathsf{x}^{i-1} \in \Omega^{i-1}$, and $\mathcal{N}^{\mathsf{u}_i}(\widehat{\mathsf{x}}_j^{k-1})$ cannot be the empty set as $\mathsf{x}_{i,1}, \mathsf{x}_{i,2} \in \mathcal{N}^{\mathsf{u}_i}(\widehat{\mathsf{x}}_j^{k-1})$. So,

$$\begin{aligned}
\mathbf{Pr}_{\mathsf{Y}}(\mathsf{x}_i \mid \mathsf{x}^{i-1}) &\stackrel{\text{def}}{=} \mathbf{Pr}[\mathsf{Y}_i = \mathsf{x}_i \mid \mathsf{Y}^{i-1} = \mathsf{x}^{i-1}] \\
&= \mathbf{Pr}[\widehat{\mathsf{Y}}_{j,k} = \widehat{\mathsf{x}}_{j,k} \mid \widehat{\mathsf{Y}}_j^{k-1} = \widehat{\mathsf{x}}_j^{k-1}, (\mathsf{Y}^{i-1} \setminus \widehat{\mathsf{Y}}_j^{k-1}) = (\mathsf{x}^{i-1} \setminus \widehat{\mathsf{x}}_j^{k-1})], \quad (9) \\
&\quad \text{(since } (\mathsf{Y}^{i-1} \setminus \widehat{\mathsf{Y}}_j^{k-1}) \text{ is independent of } \widehat{\mathsf{Y}}_j^{k-1} \text{ and } \widehat{\mathsf{Y}}_{j,k}) \\
&= \mathbf{Pr}[\widehat{\mathsf{Y}}_{j,k} = \widehat{\mathsf{x}}_{j,k} \mid \widehat{\mathsf{Y}}_j^{k-1} = \widehat{\mathsf{x}}_j^{k-1}] \\
&= \mathbf{Pr}[\mathsf{U}_i = \mathsf{u}_i \mid \widehat{\mathsf{Y}}_j^{k-1} = \widehat{\mathsf{x}}_j^{k-1}] \times \mathbf{Pr}[(\mathsf{V}_{i,1}, \mathsf{V}_{i,2}) = (\mathsf{x}_{i,1}, \mathsf{x}_{i,2}) \mid \\
&\quad \mathsf{U}_i = \mathsf{u}_i \wedge \widehat{\mathsf{Y}}_j^{k-1} = \widehat{\mathsf{x}}_j^{k-1}] \\
&= \frac{1}{N} \times \frac{1}{|\mathcal{n}^{\mathsf{u}_i}(\widehat{\mathsf{x}}_j^{k-1})|}. \quad (10)
\end{aligned}$$

The last equality follows from the definition of sampling of U_i and $(\mathsf{V}_{i,1}, \mathsf{V}_{i,2})$. ■

We now apply the χ^2 method to X and Y.

$$\begin{aligned}
\chi^2(\mathsf{x}^{i-1}) &:= \sum_{\mathsf{x}_i} \frac{(\mathbf{Pr}_{\mathsf{X}}(\mathsf{x}_i|\widehat{\mathsf{x}}_j^{k-1}) - \mathbf{Pr}_{\mathsf{Y}}(\mathsf{x}_i|\widehat{\mathsf{x}}_j^{k-1}))^2}{\mathbf{Pr}_{\mathsf{Y}}(\mathsf{x}_i|\widehat{\mathsf{x}}_j^{k-1})} \\
&=_{(a)} \sum_{\mathsf{x}_i = (\mathsf{x}_{i,1}, \mathsf{x}_{i,2}, \mathsf{u}_i)} \frac{\left(\frac{1}{(N-3(k-1))^{\underline{3}}} - \frac{1}{N|\mathcal{n}^{\mathsf{u}_i}(\widehat{\mathsf{x}}_j^{k-1})|}\right)^2}{\frac{1}{N|\mathcal{n}^{\mathsf{u}_i}(\widehat{\mathsf{x}}_j^{k-1})|}} \\
&=_{(b)} C \times \sum_{\mathsf{u}_i} \sum_{(\mathsf{x}_{i,1}, \mathsf{x}_{i,2})} \frac{\left(|\mathcal{n}^{\mathsf{u}_i}(\widehat{\mathsf{x}}_j^{k-1})| - D\right)^2}{|\mathcal{n}^{\mathsf{u}_i}(\widehat{\mathsf{x}}_j^{k-1})|} \\
&=_{(c)} C \times \sum_{\mathsf{u}_i} \left(|\mathcal{n}^{\mathsf{u}_i}(\widehat{\mathsf{x}}_j^{k-1})| - D\right)^2, \quad (11)
\end{aligned}$$

where $C = \frac{N}{((N-3(k-1))^{\underline{3}})^2}$, and $D = \frac{(N-3(k-1))^{\underline{3}}}{N}$. The equality (a) follows by plugging the conditional probabilities derived in (8) and (10). The expression on the r.h.s. of (b) is obtained by algebraic simplification. The equation (c) follows from the observation that

(1) $\frac{\left(|\mathcal{n}^{\mathsf{u}_i}(\widehat{\mathsf{x}}_j^{k-1})| - D\right)^2}{|\mathcal{n}^{\mathsf{u}_i}(\widehat{\mathsf{x}}_j^{k-1})|}$ is functionally independent of $(\mathsf{x}_{i,1}, \mathsf{x}_{i,2})$,

and (2) for each u_i, the number of choices of $(\mathsf{x}_{i,1}, \mathsf{x}_{i,2})$ is $|\mathcal{n}^{\mathsf{u}_i}(\widehat{\mathsf{x}}_j^{k-1})|$.

Next, in order to apply Theorem 1, we compute $\mathbf{Ex}[\chi^2(\mathsf{X}^{i-1})]$ which (from (11)) is given by

$$C \times \sum_{\mathsf{u}_i} \mathbf{Ex}[(|\mathcal{n}^{\mathsf{u}_i}(\widehat{\mathsf{X}}_j^{k-1})| - D)^2].$$

Note that $|\mathcal{n}^{\mathsf{u}_i}(\widehat{\mathsf{x}}_j^{k-1})|$ is a function of $\widehat{\mathsf{x}}_j^{k-1}$, and so, it is also a function of $\widehat{\mathsf{t}}_j^{k-1}$. When $\widehat{\mathsf{x}}_j^{k-1}$ is sampled according to $\widehat{\mathsf{X}}_j^{k-1}$, $\widehat{\mathsf{t}}_j^{k-1}$ would be sampled according to $\widehat{\mathsf{T}}_j^{k-1}$ (WOR sample).

For notational simplicity, let $r = N - 3(k-1)$ and $r' = N - r = 3(k-1)$. Note that $D = \frac{r^{\underline{3}}}{N}$. Also, let

$$\mathcal{V}_r = \mathcal{G} \setminus \{\mathsf{T}_{\ell,p} : \ell \in \mathrm{I}_j, \ell \leq i, p \in [3]\},$$

which is a random r-set in $\mathcal{G}$. Then the set $\mathcal{N}^{\mathsf{u}_i}(\widehat{\mathsf{x}}_j^{k-1})$ is same as the set

$$\{\mathsf{v}_1, \mathsf{v}_2 \in \mathcal{V}_r : \mathsf{u}_i + \mathsf{v}_1 + \mathsf{v}_2 \in \mathcal{V}_r, \text{ and } \mathsf{u}, \mathsf{v}_1, \mathsf{v}_2 \text{ distinct}\}.$$

We denote the size of the set by $\mathbf{N}_r^{\mathsf{u}_i}$. Then we have

$$\mathbf{Ex}[\chi^2(\mathsf{X}^{i-1})] = C \times \sum_{u_i} \mathbf{Ex}[(\mathbf{N}_r^{\mathsf{u}_i} - D)^2]. \tag{12}$$

Next, we apply the following core lemma (its proof is postponed to Sect. 3.5) to get an upper bound on the r.h.s. of (12).

Lemma 2 (core lemma for XORP). *Let C, r, r' be defined as above, where $r' \leq \frac{N}{4}$. Then for every $\mathsf{b} \in \mathcal{G}$, we have*

$$\mathbf{Ex}[\mathbf{N}_r^{\mathsf{b}}] = \frac{r^{\underline{3}}}{N}, \quad \text{and } \mathbf{Ex}[(\mathbf{N}_r^{\mathsf{b}} - \frac{r^{\underline{3}}}{N})^2] \leq \frac{1}{C}\left(\frac{576}{N^3} + \frac{4^8(r')^3}{27N^6}\right). \tag{13}$$

Subsequently, for $r' \leq \frac{N}{4}$ we have

$$\mathbf{Ex}[\chi^2(\mathsf{X}^{i-1})] \leq \frac{576}{N^2} + \frac{4^8(r')^3}{27N^5}.$$

Now, we continue to bound the statistical distance between X and Y using the χ^2-method as follows. Since $q_{max} \leq N/12$, we have $r' \leq N/4$ (a required condition for our core lemma). Therefore

$$\begin{aligned}
\|\mathbf{Pr}_{\mathsf{X}} - \mathbf{Pr}_{\mathsf{Y}}\| &\leq \left(\frac{1}{2}\sum_{i=1}^{q} \mathbf{Ex}[\chi^2(\mathsf{X}^{i-1})]\right)^{\frac{1}{2}} \\
&= \left(\frac{1}{2}\sum_{j=1}^{u}\sum_{k=1}^{q_{max}} \mathbf{Ex}[\chi^2(\mathsf{X}^{k-1})]\right)^{\frac{1}{2}} \\
&\leq \left(\sum_{j=1}^{u}\sum_{k=1}^{q_{max}} \frac{288}{N^2} + \frac{4^8(r')^3}{54N^5}\right)^{\frac{1}{2}} \\
&\leq \left(\sum_{j=1}^{u}\sum_{k=1}^{q_{max}} \frac{288}{N^2} + \frac{4^8(k-1)^3}{2N^5}\right)^{\frac{1}{2}} \quad \text{, since } r' = 3(k-1) \\
&\leq \left(\sum_{j=1}^{u} \frac{288 q_{max}}{N^2} + \frac{4^7 {q_{max}}^4}{2N^5}\right)^{\frac{1}{2}}
\end{aligned}$$

$$\leq \left(\frac{288uq_{max}}{N^2} + \frac{4^7 u{q_{max}}^4}{2N^5}\right)^{\frac{1}{2}}$$
$$\leq \frac{12\sqrt{2uq_{max}}}{N} + \frac{64\sqrt{2uq_{max}}^2}{N^{\frac{5}{2}}}.$$
$$\leq \frac{12\sqrt{2uq_{max}}}{N}(1 + 6/(12)^{1.5}) \text{ , since } q_{max} \leq N/12$$
$$\leq \frac{20\sqrt{uq_{max}}}{N}.$$

Therefore, we finally have

$$\|\mathbf{Pr}_{\mathsf{Q}} - \mathbf{Pr}_{\mathsf{S}}\| \leq \|\mathbf{Pr}_{\mathsf{X}} - \mathbf{Pr}_{\mathsf{Y}}\| \leq \frac{20\sqrt{uq_{max}}}{N}.$$ ■

3.5 Proof of Lemma 2

Let r, N be positive integers such that $r' = N - r \leq \frac{N}{4}$. Let $\mathcal{G}$ be a group of size N, and $\mathcal{V}_r$ be a random r-set in $\mathcal{G}$.

Definition 3. *For* $\mathsf{u} \in \mathcal{G}$ *we associate a random variable* $\mathbf{N}_r^{\mathsf{u}}$ *defined as the size of the following set*

$$n_r^{\mathsf{u}} := \{\mathsf{g}_1 \neq \mathsf{g}_2 \in \mathcal{V}_r : \mathsf{u} + \mathsf{g}_1 + \mathsf{g}_2 \in \mathcal{V}_r, \mathsf{g}_1 \neq \mathsf{u} \neq \mathsf{g}_2.\}$$

We would like to note that $\mathbf{N}_r^{\mathsf{u}}$ as defined above is equivalent to the previous definition since $\mathcal{V}_r$ is a random r'-set. We represent $\mathbf{N}_r^{\mathsf{u}}$ as a sum of indicator random variables. To do so we define the set $\mathcal{G}_{\mathsf{u}}$ of tuples of distinct elements of $\mathcal{G}$ as

$$\mathcal{G}_{\mathsf{u}} = \{(\mathsf{g}_1, \mathsf{g}_2) | \mathsf{g}_1 \neq \mathsf{g}_2 \in \mathcal{G} \setminus \{\mathsf{u}\}\}.$$

So, $|\mathcal{G}_{\mathsf{u}}| = (N-1)(N-2)$. Then we have

$$\mathbf{N}_r^{\mathsf{u}} = \sum_{\mathsf{g} \in \mathcal{G}_{\mathsf{u}}} \mathtt{I}_{\mathsf{g}}, \tag{14}$$

where, for $\mathsf{g} = (\mathsf{g}_1, \mathsf{g}_2)$, the indicator random variable $\mathtt{I}_{\mathsf{g}}$ is defined as

$$\mathtt{I}_{\mathsf{g}} = \begin{cases} 1 \text{ if } \mathsf{g}_1, \mathsf{g}_2, \mathsf{u} + \mathsf{g}_1 + \mathsf{g}_2 \in \mathcal{V}_r, \text{ and } \mathsf{g}_1 \neq \mathsf{u} \neq \mathsf{g}_2 \\ 0 \text{ otherwise.} \end{cases}$$

We note that $\mathsf{g}_1, \mathsf{g}_2, \mathsf{u} + \mathsf{g}_1 + \mathsf{g}_2$ are distinct elements of $\mathcal{G}$ since $\mathsf{g}_1 \neq \mathsf{u} \neq \mathsf{g}_2$. So, the number of r-sets that contain the three distinct elements $\mathsf{g}_1, \mathsf{g}_2, \mathsf{u} + \mathsf{g}_1 + \mathsf{g}_2$ is exactly $\binom{N-3}{r-3}$. Thus,

$$\mathbf{Ex}[\mathtt{I}_{\mathsf{g}}] = \mathbf{Pr}[\{\mathsf{g}_1, \mathsf{g}_2, \mathsf{u} + \mathsf{g}_1 + \mathsf{g}_2\} \subseteq \mathcal{V}_r] = \frac{\binom{N-3}{r-3}}{\binom{N}{r}} = \frac{r^{\underline{3}}}{N^{\underline{3}}}. \tag{15}$$

By using the linearity of expectation, we have

$$\begin{aligned}\mathbf{Ex}[\mathbf{N}_r^{\mathsf{u}}] &= \sum_{\mathsf{g}\in\mathcal{G}_{\mathsf{u}}} \mathbf{Ex}[\mathtt{I}_{\mathsf{g}}] \\ &= \sum_{\mathsf{g}\in\mathcal{G}_{\mathsf{u}}} \frac{r^{\underline{3}}}{N^{\underline{3}}} = |\mathcal{G}_{\mathsf{u}}| \times \frac{r^{\underline{3}}}{N^{\underline{3}}} = \frac{r^{\underline{3}}}{N}.\end{aligned}$$

Now, we compute the second part of the lemma which gives a bound on the variance of $\mathbf{N}_r^{\mathsf{u}}$. Since $\mathbf{N}_r^{\mathsf{u}}$ is sum of indicator random variables, we can write

$$\begin{aligned}\mathbf{Var}[\mathbf{N}_r^{\mathsf{u}}] &= \mathbf{Var}[\sum_{\mathsf{g}\in\mathcal{G}_{\mathsf{u}}} \mathtt{I}_{\mathsf{g}}] \\ &= \sum_{\mathsf{g}\in\mathcal{G}_{\mathsf{u}}} \mathbf{Var}[\mathtt{I}_{\mathsf{g}}] + \sum_{\mathsf{g}\neq\mathsf{g}'\in\mathcal{G}_{\mathsf{u}}} \mathbf{Cov}(\mathtt{I}_{\mathsf{g}}, \mathtt{I}_{\mathsf{g}'}).\end{aligned}$$

For the sake of notational simplicity, we denote the set $\{\mathsf{g}_1, \mathsf{g}_2, \mathsf{u}+\mathsf{g}_1+\mathsf{g}_2\}$ as $\mathcal{S}_{\mathsf{u}}^{\mathsf{g}}$ for every $\mathsf{g} \in \mathcal{G}_{\mathsf{u}}$. In (15), we have shown that $\mathbf{Ex}[\mathtt{I}_{\mathsf{g}}] = \frac{r^{\underline{3}}}{N^{\underline{3}}}$. As $\mathtt{I}_{\mathsf{g}}$ is a $0-1$ random variable, $\mathbf{Ex}[\mathtt{I}_{\mathsf{g}}^2] = \mathbf{Ex}[\mathtt{I}_{\mathsf{g}}]$. Thus,

$$\begin{aligned}\mathbf{Var}[\mathtt{I}_{\mathsf{g}}] &= \mathbf{Ex}[\mathtt{I}_{\mathsf{g}}^2] - \mathbf{Ex}[\mathtt{I}_{\mathsf{g}}]^2 \\ &= \mathbf{Ex}[\mathtt{I}_{\mathsf{g}}](1-\mathbf{Ex}[\mathtt{I}_{\mathsf{g}}]) \\ &= \frac{r^{\underline{3}}}{N^{\underline{3}}} \times \left(1 - \frac{r^{\underline{3}}}{N^{\underline{3}}}\right). \end{aligned} \tag{16}$$

Therefore,

$$\begin{aligned}\sum_{\mathsf{g}\in\mathcal{G}_{\mathsf{u}}} \mathbf{Var}[\mathtt{I}_{\mathsf{g}}] &= |\mathcal{G}_{\mathsf{u}}| \times \frac{r^{\underline{3}}}{N^{\underline{3}}} \times \left(1 - \frac{r^3}{N^3}\right) \\ &\leq \frac{6r^2(r-1)(r-2)}{N^2} \text{ by employing Lemma 1.}\end{aligned} \tag{17}$$

Considering $r' \leq \frac{N}{4} < \frac{3N}{4} \leq r$, here we settle for a weaker bound which is sufficient for our purpose.

Now, we compute the covariance term. Note that $\mathtt{I}_{\mathsf{g}}\mathtt{I}_{\mathsf{g}'} = 1$ if and only if $\mathcal{S}_{\mathsf{u}}^{\mathsf{g}} \cup \mathcal{S}_{\mathsf{u}}^{\mathsf{g}'} \subseteq \mathcal{V}_r$. So,

$$\mathbf{Ex}[\mathtt{I}_{\mathsf{g}}\mathtt{I}_{\mathsf{g}'}] = \mathbf{Pr}[\mathcal{S}_{\mathsf{u}}^{\mathsf{g}} \cup \mathcal{S}_{\mathsf{u}}^{\mathsf{g}'} \subseteq \mathcal{V}_r] = \frac{r^{\underline{w}}}{N^{\underline{w}}},$$

where $w = |\mathcal{S}_{\mathsf{u}}^{\mathsf{g}} \cup \mathcal{S}_{\mathsf{u}}^{\mathsf{g}'}|$. Here, it is not difficult to see that the possible values taken by w are $3, 5$, and 6. Indeed, for $w = 4$ it is necessary to have $|\mathcal{S}_{\mathsf{u}}^{\mathsf{g}} \cap \mathcal{S}_{\mathsf{u}}^{\mathsf{g}'}| = 2$. But this implies $\mathcal{S}_{\mathsf{u}}^{\mathsf{g}} = \mathcal{S}_{\mathsf{u}}^{\mathsf{g}'}$ (since any two elements of $\mathcal{S}_{\mathsf{u}}^{\mathsf{g}}$ or $\mathcal{S}_{\mathsf{u}}^{\mathsf{g}'}$ determines the third element), which violates the fact that $w = 4$.

Accordingly, we can partition the sum of covariances as follows.

$$\sum_{\mathsf{g} \neq \mathsf{g}' \in \mathcal{G}_{\mathsf{u}}} \mathbf{Cov}(\mathtt{I}_{\mathsf{g}}, \mathtt{I}_{\mathsf{g}'}) = \sum_{w \in \{3,5,6\}} \sum_{\substack{\mathsf{g} \neq \mathsf{g}' \in \mathcal{G}_{\mathsf{u}} \\ |\mathcal{S}_{\mathsf{u}}^{\mathsf{g}} \cup \mathcal{S}_{\mathsf{u}}^{\mathsf{g}'}| = w}} \mathbf{Cov}(\mathtt{I}_{\mathsf{g}}, \mathtt{I}_{\mathsf{g}'}). \tag{18}$$

Now, we consider the three possible cases according to the value of w.

Case $w = 3$: In this case, we have

$$|\{(\mathsf{g}, \mathsf{g}')|\ \mathsf{g} \neq \mathsf{g}' \in \mathcal{G}_{\mathsf{u}},\ |\mathcal{S}_{\mathsf{u}}^{\mathsf{g}} \cup \mathcal{S}_{\mathsf{u}}^{\mathsf{g}'}| = 3\}| = 5(N-1)(N-2).$$

To arrive at the above expression note that the choice of $\mathsf{g} = (\mathsf{g}_1, \mathsf{g}_2)$ can be made in $(N-1)(N-2)$ ways (since $\mathsf{u} \notin \{\mathsf{g}_1, \mathsf{g}_2\}$). Now, after fixing g the potential number of ordered choices for $\mathsf{g}' = (\mathsf{g}_1', \mathsf{g}_2')$ from the elements of $\mathcal{S}_{\mathsf{u}}^{\mathsf{g}}$ can be seen to be 6. Finally, from these 6 choices we discount the choice $(\mathsf{g}_1', \mathsf{g}_2') = (\mathsf{g}_1, \mathsf{g}_2)$.

Now, since $w = 3$, we have

$$\begin{aligned} \mathbf{Cov}(\mathtt{I}_{\mathsf{g}}, \mathtt{I}_{\mathsf{g}'}) &= \mathbf{Ex}[\mathtt{I}_{\mathsf{g}}\mathtt{I}_{\mathsf{g}'}] - \mathbf{Ex}[\mathtt{I}_{\mathsf{g}}]\mathbf{Ex}[\mathtt{I}_{\mathsf{g}'}] \\ &= \frac{r^{\underline{3}}}{N^{\underline{3}}} - \left(\frac{r^{\underline{3}}}{N^{\underline{3}}}\right)^2 \\ &= \frac{r^{\underline{3}}}{N^{\underline{3}}} \times \left(1 - \frac{r^{\underline{3}}}{N^{\underline{3}}}\right) \end{aligned}$$

Therefore, similar to (17) we get

$$\sum_{\substack{\mathsf{g} \neq \mathsf{g}' \in \mathcal{G}_{\mathsf{u}} \\ |\mathcal{S}_{\mathsf{u}}^{\mathsf{g}} \cup \mathcal{S}_{\mathsf{u}}^{\mathsf{g}'}| = 3}} \mathbf{Cov}(\mathtt{I}_{\mathsf{g}}, \mathtt{I}_{\mathsf{g}'}) \leq \frac{30r^2(r-1)(r-2)}{N^2} \tag{19}$$

Case $w = 5$: Here, we have

$$|\{(\mathsf{g}, \mathsf{g}')|\ \mathsf{g} \neq \mathsf{g}' \in \mathcal{G}_{\mathsf{u}},\ |\mathcal{S}_{\mathsf{u}}^{\mathsf{g}} \cup \mathcal{S}_{\mathsf{u}}^{\mathsf{g}'}| = 5\}| = 9(N-1)(N-2)(N-4).$$

To justify the above expression, observe that after fixing g in $(N-1)(N-2)$ ways the common element between the sets $\mathcal{S}_{\mathsf{u}}^{\mathsf{g}}$and $\mathcal{S}_{\mathsf{u}}^{\mathsf{g}'}$can be determined in $3 \times 3 = 9$ ways (note that in this case we necessarily have $|\mathcal{S}_{\mathsf{u}}^{\mathsf{g}} \cap \mathcal{S}_{\mathsf{u}}^{\mathsf{g}'}| = 1$). Following this, one of the two remaining elements of $\mathcal{S}_{\mathsf{u}}^{\mathsf{g}'}$can be chosen (from outside of the set $\mathcal{S}_{\mathsf{u}}^{\mathsf{g}} \cup \{\mathsf{u}\}$) in $N-4$ ways. This fixes g'.

Next, for $w = 5$ we have

$$\mathbf{Cov}(\mathtt{I}_{\mathsf{g}}, \mathtt{I}_{\mathsf{g}'}) = \mathbf{Ex}[\mathtt{I}_{\mathsf{g}}\mathtt{I}_{\mathsf{g}'}] - \mathbf{Ex}[\mathtt{I}_{\mathsf{g}}]\mathbf{Ex}[\mathtt{I}_{\mathsf{g}'}] = \frac{r^{\underline{5}}}{N^{\underline{5}}} - \left(\frac{r^{\underline{3}}}{N^{\underline{3}}}\right)^2.$$

Therefore,

$$\sum_{\substack{\mathsf{g}\neq\mathsf{g}'\in\mathcal{G}_{\mathsf{u}}\\ |\mathcal{S}_{\mathsf{u}}^{\mathsf{g}}\cup\mathcal{S}_{\mathsf{u}}^{\mathsf{g}'}|=5}} \mathbf{Cov}(\mathtt{I}_{\mathsf{g}},\mathtt{I}_{\mathsf{g}'}) = 9(N-1)(N-2)(N-4)\left(\frac{r^{\underline{5}}}{N^{\underline{5}}}-\left(\frac{r^{\underline{3}}}{N^{\underline{3}}}\right)^2\right) \tag{20}$$

<u>**Case $w=6$:**</u> In this case, the sets $\mathcal{S}_{\mathsf{u}}^{\mathsf{g}}$and $\mathcal{S}_{\mathsf{u}}^{\mathsf{g}'}$are necessarily disjoint. Ensuring this condition the choice of $\mathsf{g}_1,\mathsf{g}_2,\mathsf{g}_1'$ can be made (following similar argument as in the $w=5$ case) in $(N-1)(N-2)(N-4)$ ways. Now, letting $\mathcal{S}:=\mathcal{S}_{\mathsf{u}}^{\mathsf{g}}\cup\{\mathsf{u},\mathsf{g}_1'\}$, it can be seen that the choice of g_2' should be made from outside of the set $\mathcal{S}\cup\{\mathsf{u}+\mathsf{g}_1'+\mathsf{s}|\mathsf{s}\in\mathcal{S}\}$ which has cardinality 8. Therefore, we have the following.

$$|\{(\mathsf{g},\mathsf{g}')|\ \mathsf{g}\neq\mathsf{g}'\in\mathcal{G}_{\mathsf{u}},\ |\mathcal{S}_{\mathsf{u}}^{\mathsf{g}}\cup\mathcal{S}_{\mathsf{u}}^{\mathsf{g}'}|=6\}|=(N-1)(N-2)(N-4)(N-8).$$

So, for $w=6$ we have

$$\sum_{\substack{\mathsf{g}\neq\mathsf{g}'\in\mathcal{G}_{\mathsf{u}}\\ |\mathcal{S}_{\mathsf{u}}^{\mathsf{g}}\cup\mathcal{S}_{\mathsf{u}}^{\mathsf{g}'}|=6}} \mathbf{Cov}(\mathtt{I}_{\mathsf{g}},\mathtt{I}_{\mathsf{g}'}) = (N-1)(N-2)(N-4)(N-8)\left(\frac{r^{\underline{6}}}{N^{\underline{6}}}-\left(\frac{r^{\underline{3}}}{N^{\underline{3}}}\right)^2\right) \tag{21}$$

Next, to express the upper bound on $\mathbf{Var}[\sum_{\mathsf{g}\in\mathcal{G}_{\mathsf{u}}}\mathtt{I}_{\mathsf{g}}]$ in terms of r' we consider the sum of (17) and (19) together and (20) and (21) together.

$$\begin{aligned} C\times(\sum_{\mathsf{g}\in\mathcal{G}_{\mathsf{u}}}\mathbf{Var}[\mathtt{I}_{\mathsf{g}}]+\sum_{\substack{\mathsf{g}\neq\mathsf{g}'\in\mathcal{G}_{\mathsf{u}}\\ |\mathcal{S}_{\mathsf{u}}^{\mathsf{g}}\cup\mathcal{S}_{\mathsf{u}}^{\mathsf{g}'}|=3}}\mathbf{Cov}(\mathtt{I}_{\mathsf{g}},\mathtt{I}_{\mathsf{g}'})) &\leq \frac{N}{(r^{\underline{3}})^2}\times\frac{36r^2(r-1)(r-2)}{N^2}\\ &=\frac{36}{N(r-1)(r-2)}\\ &\leq\frac{576}{N^3} \end{aligned} \tag{22}$$

The last inequality follows from $(r-2)\geq\frac{N}{4}$. Suppressing the simplification, we get

$$\begin{aligned} C\times(\sum_{\substack{\mathsf{g}\neq\mathsf{g}'\in\mathcal{G}_{\mathsf{u}}\\ |\mathcal{S}_{\mathsf{u}}^{\mathsf{g}}\cup\mathcal{S}_{\mathsf{u}}^{\mathsf{g}'}|=5}}\mathbf{Cov}(\mathtt{I}_{\mathsf{g}},\mathtt{I}_{\mathsf{g}'}))+\sum_{\substack{\mathsf{g}\neq\mathsf{g}'\in\mathcal{G}_{\mathsf{u}}\\ |\mathcal{S}_{\mathsf{u}}^{\mathsf{g}}\cup\mathcal{S}_{\mathsf{u}}^{\mathsf{g}'}|=6}}\mathbf{Cov}(\mathtt{I}_{\mathsf{g}},\mathtt{I}_{\mathsf{g}'})) &\leq \frac{N}{(r^{\underline{3}})^2}\times(\frac{r^{\underline{3}}}{N^{\underline{3}}})\times\left(\frac{12N(r')^3}{(N-3)(N-5)}\right)\\ &\leq\frac{4^8(r')^3}{27N^6}. \end{aligned} \tag{23}$$

For the last inequality note that $(r-2)>\frac{N}{4}$ and $(N-5)>\frac{3N}{4}$ for $N\geq 32$. So, we have $r(r-1)(r-2)>(\frac{N}{4})^3$, and $(N-1)(N-2)(N-3)(N-5)>(\frac{3N}{4})^4$. Hence, the upper bound.

Therefore, finally we get

$$\begin{aligned}\mathbf{Ex}[\chi^2(X^{i-1})] &= C \times \sum_{u_i} \mathbf{Ex}[(\mathbf{N}_r^{u_i} - D)^2] \\ &= C \times \sum_{u_i} \mathbf{Var}[\mathbf{N}_r^{u_i}] \\ &= \sum_{u_i} C \times \mathbf{Var}[\mathbf{N}_r^{u_i}] \\ &\leq \frac{576}{N^2} + \frac{4^8(r')^3}{27N^5}. \end{aligned} \tag{24}$$

■

4 An Efficient Variant of XORP[3]

In this section, we consider an efficient version of XORP[3], which we term XORP′[3]. Formally, given an n-bit random permutation RP and an input $x \in \{0,1\}^{n-3}$, the output of XORP′[3] is given by

$$\mathsf{RP}(x\|000) \oplus \mathsf{RP}(x\|001) \oplus \mathsf{RP}(x\|010) \parallel \mathsf{RP}(x\|000) \oplus \mathsf{RP}(x\|101) \oplus \mathsf{RP}(x\|110).$$

So, for $2n$-bit output XORP′[3] makes 5 calls to the underlying random permutation RP - a saving of one call compared to XORP[3].

In Theorem 3, which is our main result of this section, we bound the total variation between the probability distributions of the random vectors S and U defined over the same sample space $\mathcal{G}^{2q}$. The formal description of these random variables is given in Fig. 3. The random vector

$$\mathsf{U} := (\mathsf{U}_{1,1}, \mathsf{U}_{1,2}, \mathsf{U}_{2,1}, \mathsf{U}_{2,2}, \ldots, \mathsf{U}_{q,1}, \mathsf{U}_{q,2})$$

is a WR sample (represented as a vector) of size $2q$, each $\mathsf{U}_{i,j}$ is sampled from $\mathcal{G}$. Whereas,

$$\mathsf{S} := (\mathsf{S}_{1,1}, \mathsf{S}_{1,2}, \mathsf{S}_{2,1}, \mathsf{S}_{2,2}, \ldots, \mathsf{S}_{q,1}, \mathsf{S}_{q,2})$$

is generated (as described in Fig. 3) from a WOR sample

$$\mathsf{T} := (\mathsf{T}_{1,1}, \mathsf{T}_{1,2}, \ldots, \mathsf{T}_{1,5}, \mathsf{T}_{2,1}, \mathsf{T}_{2,2}, \ldots, \mathsf{T}_{2,5}, \ldots, \mathsf{T}_{q,1}, \mathsf{T}_{q,2}, \ldots, \mathsf{T}_{q,5})$$

of size $5q$, each $\mathsf{T}_{i,j}$ is sampled from $\mathcal{G}$. More precisely, $\mathsf{S}_{i,j} = \mathsf{T}_{i,1} + \mathsf{T}_{i,2j} + \mathsf{T}_{i,2j+1}$ for all $1 \leq i \leq q, 1 \leq j \leq 2$. So both U and S have the same sample space $\mathcal{G}^{2q}$.

Now, we state our main theorem which provides an upper bound on the total variation between U and S. In other words, it shows the distribution of S is very close to uniform even though it is computed from a non-uniform distribution.

Theorem 3 (Pseudorandomness of S). *Let* U *and* S *be the random vectors as described in Fig. 3. Then, for all* $q \leq N/8$,

$$\|\mathbf{Pr}_{\mathsf{S}} - \mathbf{Pr}_{\mathsf{U}}\| \leq \frac{5\sqrt{q}}{N} + \frac{256q}{N^2} + \frac{8192q}{N^{\frac{3}{2}}}$$

Clearly, the PRF advantage of the above construction (when block cipher is replaced by a random permutation) is at most $\frac{5\sqrt{q}}{2^n} + \frac{256q}{2^{2n}} + \frac{8192q}{2^{\frac{3n}{2}}}$ for all $q \leq 2^{n-3}$.

Random Experiment for U	Random Experiment for S
$\mathsf{U} := (\mathsf{U}_{i,j} : i \in [q], j \in [2]) \xleftarrow{\text{wr}} \mathcal{G}$	$\mathsf{T} := (\mathsf{T}_{i,j} : i \in [q], j \in [5]) \xleftarrow{\text{wor}} \mathcal{G}$
return U	**for** $1 \le i \le q$
	for $1 \le j \le 2$
	$\mathsf{S}_{i,j} = \mathsf{T}_{i,1} + \mathsf{T}_{i,2j} + \mathsf{T}_{i,2j+1}$
	return $\mathsf{S} := (\mathsf{S}_{i,j} : i \in [q], j \in [2])$

Fig. 3. Description of sampling methods of random variables U, S.

4.1 Proof of Theorem 3

Proof will follow in a similar path as the proof of XORP[3]. First, in Fig. 4, we describe the extended random variables X and Y which extends S and U respectively. Here, by extension we mean that S and U are marginal random variables of X and Y respectively. By using similar argument as in Claim 1, which we do not present due to lack of space, we can show that the set $\mathcal{N}_i$ is always non-empty. Hence, execution of the part following **else** in line 5 of the Random Experiment for Y will never happen. It is kept only for the sake of the completeness of the definition.

Random Experiment for X

$\mathsf{T} = (\mathsf{T}_{i,j} : i \in [q], j \in [5]) \xleftarrow{\text{wor}} \mathcal{G}$
for $1 \le i \le q$
  for $1 \le j \le 2$
    $\mathsf{S}_{i,j} = \mathsf{T}_{i,1} + \mathsf{T}_{i,2j} + \mathsf{T}_{i,2j+1}$
    $\mathsf{X}_i = (\mathsf{S}_{i,1}, \mathsf{S}_{i,2}, \mathsf{T}_{i,1}, \mathsf{T}_{i,2}, \mathsf{T}_{i,4})$
  $\mathsf{S}_i = (\mathsf{S}_{i,1}, \ldots, \mathsf{S}_{i,w})$
return $\mathsf{X} := (\mathsf{X}_1, \ldots, \mathsf{X}_q)$

Random Experiment for Y

1 : **initialize** $\mathcal{S}_0 = \mathcal{G}$
2 : **for** $1 \le i \le q$
3 : $\mathsf{U}_i := (\mathsf{U}_{i,1}, \mathsf{U}_{i,2}) \xleftarrow{\$} \mathcal{G}$
4 : $\mathcal{N}_i = \{(\mathsf{v}_1, \mathsf{v}_2, \mathsf{v}_3) \mid \mathsf{v}_1, \mathsf{v}_2, \mathsf{v}_3,$
    $\mathsf{U}_{i,1} + \mathsf{v}_1 + \mathsf{v}_2, \mathsf{U}_{i,2} + \mathsf{v}_1 + \mathsf{v}_3 \subseteq \mathcal{S}_{i-1},$
    and distinct$\}$
5 :   **if** $\mathcal{N}_i \neq \emptyset$ **then** $(\mathsf{V}_{i,1}, \mathsf{V}_{i,2}, \mathsf{V}_{i,3}) \xleftarrow{\$} \mathcal{N}_i$
    else $(\mathsf{V}_{i,1}, \mathsf{V}_{i,2}, \mathsf{V}_{i,3}) = (0, 0, 0)$
6 : $\mathsf{Y}_i = (\mathsf{U}_{i,1}, \mathsf{U}_{i,2}, \mathsf{V}_{i,1}, \mathsf{V}_{i,2}, \mathsf{V}_{i,3})$
7 : $\mathcal{S}_i = \mathcal{S}_{i-1} \setminus \{\mathsf{V}_{i,1}, \mathsf{V}_{i,2}, \mathsf{V}_{i,3},$
    $\mathsf{U}_{i,1} + \mathsf{V}_{i,1} + \mathsf{V}_{i,2}, \mathsf{U}_{i,2} + \mathsf{V}_{i,1} + \mathsf{V}_{i,3}\}$
8 : **return** $\mathsf{Y} := (\mathsf{Y}_1, \ldots, \mathsf{Y}_q)$

Fig. 4. X and Y are extended random variables of S and U respectively.

Let $\mathcal{C} = \mathcal{G}^5$ denote the set of all 5-tuples of $\mathcal{G}$. To understand the probability distributions $\mathbf{Pr}_{\mathsf{X}}$ and $\mathbf{Pr}_{\mathsf{Y}}$ of the random vectors X and Y (respectively), and their supports we consider the following permutation ρ over the set $\mathcal{C}$ which maps the tuple $(\mathsf{x}_1, \ldots, \mathsf{x}_5)$ to $(\mathsf{x}_1+\mathsf{x}_2+\mathsf{x}_3, \mathsf{x}_1+\mathsf{x}_4+\mathsf{x}_5, \mathsf{x}_1, \mathsf{x}_2, \mathsf{x}_4)$. It is easy to see that ρ is a permutation and $\rho^{-1}(\mathsf{x}'_1, \mathsf{x}'_2, \ldots, \mathsf{x}'_5) = (\mathsf{x}'_3, \mathsf{x}'_4, \mathsf{x}'_1+\mathsf{x}'_3+\mathsf{x}'_4, \mathsf{x}'_5, \mathsf{x}'_2+\mathsf{x}'_3+\mathsf{x}'_5)$. We extend the definition of ρ over $\mathcal{C}^c$ for any c as $\rho^*(\mathsf{z}_1, \ldots, \mathsf{z}_c) = (\rho(\mathsf{z}_1), \ldots, \rho(\mathsf{z}_c))$. From the random experiments, it is trivial to see that

1. $\rho(\mathsf{X}_i) = \mathsf{T}_i := (\mathsf{T}_{i,1}, \ldots, \mathsf{T}_{i,5})$ and
2. $\rho(\mathsf{Y}_i) = \mathsf{V}_i := (\mathsf{V}_{i,1}, \mathsf{V}_{i,2}, \mathsf{U}_{i,1} + \mathsf{V}_{i,1} + \mathsf{V}_{i,2}, \mathsf{V}_{i,3}, \mathsf{U}_{i,2} + \mathsf{V}_{i,1} + \mathsf{V}_{i,3})$.

So, for every $i \leq q$, $\rho^*(\mathsf{X}^i) = \mathsf{T}^i$ and $\rho^*(\mathsf{Y}^i) = \mathsf{V}^i$. In other words, the random variables X and Y are equivalent to T and $\mathsf{V} := (\mathsf{V}_{i,j}, i \in [q], j \in [5])$ respectively. In the first case, we first sample T and then define X by applying ρ^{-1} on each block. Whereas, in the second case, we first sample Y and then we define V by applying ρ on each block. So, for every i, the support of T^i is the set of all block-wise distinct tuples $(\mathsf{a}_{i',j} : i' \in [i], j \in [w])$. Hence, the support of X^i, denoted as Ω_i, would be the set of all such iw tuples

$$\Omega_i := \{(\mathsf{x}_{i',j} : i' \in [i], j \in [w]) \in \mathcal{G}^{iw} : (\mathsf{a}_{i',j} : i' \in [i], j \in [5]) \text{ is block-wise distinct}\},$$

where $\rho(\mathsf{x}_{i'}) = \mathsf{a}_{i'} := (\mathsf{a}_{i',j} : j \in [5])$ for all i'. In fact, for every $\mathsf{x}^i \in \Omega_i$, the conditional probability for X can be expressed as

$$\begin{aligned} \mathbf{Pr}_{\mathsf{X}}(\mathsf{x}_i \mid \mathsf{x}^{i-1}) &\stackrel{\text{def}}{=} \Pr[\mathsf{X}_i = \mathsf{x}_i \, | \mathsf{X}^{i-1} = \mathsf{x}^{i-1}] \\ &= \Pr[\mathsf{T}_i = \mathsf{t}_i \, | \mathsf{T}^{i-1} = \mathsf{t}^{i-1}] \\ &= \frac{1}{(N - 5(i-1))^{\underline{5}}}. \end{aligned} \quad (25)$$

Now, we are going to argue that the support of Y^i contains Ω_i for all i. First, for all $(\mathsf{x}_1, \ldots, \mathsf{x}_i) \in \Omega_i$, let us denote $\mathsf{u}_i := (\mathsf{u}_{i,1}, \mathsf{u}_{i,2}) = (\mathsf{x}_{i,1}, \mathsf{x}_{i,2})$. Next, let $\mathsf{x}^i = (\mathsf{x}_1, \ldots, \mathsf{x}_i) \in \Omega_i$ be a fixed i-tuple of blocks with $\mathsf{x}_i = (\mathsf{u}_i, \mathsf{x}_{i,3}, \mathsf{x}_{i,4}, \mathsf{x}_{i,5})$. As before, let $\rho(\mathsf{x}_{i'}) = \mathsf{t}_{i'}$ for every $i' \in [i]$. So, $\mathsf{t}_{i',j}$'s are distinct. Next, we define the following set

$$\begin{aligned} \mathcal{N}^{\mathsf{u}_i}(\mathsf{x}^{i-1}) := \{(\mathsf{v}_1, \mathsf{v}_2, \mathsf{v}_3) : \mathsf{v}_1, \mathsf{v}_2, \mathsf{v}_3, \mathsf{u}_{i,1} + \mathsf{v}_1 + \mathsf{v}_2, \mathsf{u}_{i,2} + \mathsf{v}_1 + \mathsf{v}_3 \in \mathcal{S}_{i-1} \text{ ,and} \\ \mathsf{v}_1, \mathsf{v}_2, \mathsf{v}_3, \mathsf{u}_{i,1} + \mathsf{v}_1 + \mathsf{v}_2, \mathsf{u}_{i,2} + \mathsf{v}_1 + \mathsf{v}_3 \text{ distinct}\}, \end{aligned}$$

where $\mathcal{S}_{i-1} = \mathcal{G} \setminus \{\mathsf{t}_{i',j} : i' < i, j \in [5]\}$. Given that $\mathsf{U}_i = \mathsf{u}_i$ and $\mathsf{Y}^{i-1} = \mathsf{x}^{i-1}$, the set $\mathcal{N}_i$ (defined in the line 4 of the random experiment of Y in Fig. 4) is exactly the same as the set $\mathcal{N}^{\mathsf{u}_i}(\mathsf{x}^{i-1})$ defined above. It is easy to observe the following:

If $\mathsf{x}^i \in \Omega_i$ then the set $\mathcal{N}^{\mathsf{u}_i}(\mathsf{x}^{i-1})$ is nonempty as $\mathsf{x}_{i,3}, \mathsf{x}_{i,4}, \mathsf{x}_{i,5} \in \mathcal{N}^{\mathsf{u}_i}(\mathsf{x}^{i-1})$,

and $\mathsf{x}^i \in \Omega_i$ is indeed in the support of Y^i. Now, we have the following claim on the support of Y.[5]

Claim 3. *For all* $\mathsf{x}^i \in \Omega_i$*,*

$$\mathbf{Pr}_{\mathsf{Y}}(\mathsf{x}_i \mid \mathsf{x}^{i-1}) \stackrel{\text{def}}{=} \Pr[\mathsf{Y}_i = \mathsf{x}_i \mid \mathsf{Y}^{i-1} = \mathsf{x}^{i-1}] = \frac{1}{N^2} \times \frac{1}{|\mathcal{N}^{\mathsf{u}_i}(\mathsf{x}^{i-1})|}.$$

[5] As noted in the beginning of this proof, $\mathcal{N}_i$ can be shown to be non-empty by an argument similar to Claim 1.

Proof of claim. First, note that $\mathsf{x}^{i-1} \in \Omega_{i-1}$, and $\mathcal{N}^{\mathsf{u}_i}(\mathsf{x}^{i-1})$ cannot be the empty set as $\mathsf{x}_{i,3}, \mathsf{x}_{i,4}, \mathsf{x}_{i,5} \in \mathcal{N}^{\mathsf{u}_i}(\mathsf{x}^{i-1})$. So,

$$\begin{aligned}\mathbf{Pr}_{\mathsf{Y}}(\mathsf{x}_i \mid \mathsf{x}^{i-1}) &\stackrel{\text{def}}{=} \Pr[\mathsf{Y}_i = \mathsf{x}_i \mid \mathsf{Y}^{i-1} = \mathsf{x}^{i-1}] \\ &= \Pr[\mathsf{U}_i = \mathsf{u}_i \mid \mathsf{Y}^{i-1} = \mathsf{x}^{i-1}] \times \Pr[(\mathsf{V}_{i,1}, \mathsf{V}_{i,2}, \mathsf{V}_{i,3}) = (\mathsf{x}_{i,3}, \mathsf{x}_{i,4}, \mathsf{x}_{i,5}) \mid \\ &\quad \mathsf{U}_i = \mathsf{u}_i \wedge \mathsf{Y}^{i-1} = \mathsf{x}^{i-1}] \\ &= \frac{1}{N^2} \times \frac{1}{|\mathcal{N}^{\mathsf{u}_i}(\mathsf{x}^{i-1})|}, \qquad (26)\end{aligned}$$

where the last equality follows from the definition of sampling of U_i and $(\mathsf{V}_{i,1}, \mathsf{V}_{i,2}, \mathsf{V}_{i,3})$ in the Random Experiment for Y (see Fig. 4). ■

We now apply the χ^2 method to X and Y.

$$\begin{aligned}\chi^2(\mathsf{x}^{i-1}) &:= \sum_{\mathsf{x}_i} \frac{(\mathbf{Pr}_{\mathsf{X}}(\mathsf{x}_i|\mathsf{x}^{i-1}) - \mathbf{Pr}_{\mathsf{Y}}(\mathsf{x}_i|\mathsf{x}^{i-1}))^2}{\mathbf{Pr}_{\mathsf{Y}}(\mathsf{x}_i|\mathsf{x}^{i-1})} \\ &=_{(a)} \sum_{\mathsf{x}_i = (\mathsf{u}_i, \mathsf{x}_{i,3}, \mathsf{x}_{i,4}, \mathsf{x}_{i,5})} \frac{\left(\frac{1}{(N-5(i-1))^{\underline{5}}} - \frac{1}{N^2 |\mathcal{N}^{\mathsf{u}_i}(\mathsf{x}^{i-1})|}\right)^2}{\frac{1}{N^2 |\mathcal{N}^{\mathsf{u}_i}(\mathsf{x}^{i-1})|}} \\ &=_{(b)} C \times \sum_{\mathsf{u}_i} \sum_{(\mathsf{x}_{i,3}, \mathsf{x}_{i,4}, \mathsf{x}_{i,5})} \frac{\left(|\mathcal{N}^{\mathsf{u}_i}(\mathsf{x}^{i-1})| - D\right)^2}{|\mathcal{N}^{\mathsf{u}_i}(\mathsf{x}^{i-1})|} \\ &=_{(c)} C \times \sum_{\mathsf{u}_i} \left(|\mathcal{N}^{\mathsf{u}_i}(\mathsf{x}^{i-1})| - D\right)^2, \qquad (27)\end{aligned}$$

where $C = \frac{N^2}{((N-5(i-1))^{\underline{5}})^2}$, and $D = \frac{(N-5(i-1))^{\underline{5}}}{N^2}$. The equality (a) follows by plugging the conditional probabilities derived in (25) and (26). The expression on the r.h.s. of (b) is obtained by algebraic simplification. The equation (c) follows from the observation that $\frac{\left(|\mathcal{N}^{\mathsf{u}_i}(\mathsf{x}^{i-1})| - D\right)^2}{|\mathcal{N}^{\mathsf{u}_i}(\mathsf{x}^{i-1})|}$ is functionally independent of $(\mathsf{x}_{i,3}, \mathsf{x}_{i,4}, \mathsf{x}_{i,5})$, and for each u_i, the number of choices of $(\mathsf{x}_{i,3}, \mathsf{x}_{i,4}, \mathsf{x}_{i,5})$ is $|\mathcal{N}^{\mathsf{u}_i}(\mathsf{x}^{i-1})|$. Next, in order to apply Theorem 1, we compute $\mathbf{Ex}[\chi^2(\mathsf{X}^{i-1})]$ which (from (27)) is given by

$$C \times \sum_{\mathsf{u}_i} \mathbf{Ex}[\left(|\mathcal{N}^{\mathsf{u}_i}(\mathsf{X}^{i-1})| - D\right)^2].$$

Note that $|\mathcal{N}^{\mathsf{u}_i}(\mathsf{x}^{i-1})|$ is a function of x^{i-1}, and so, it is also a function of t^{i-1}. When x^{i-1} is sampled according to X^{i-1}, t^{i-1} would be sampled according to T^{i-1} (WOR sample).

For notational simplicity, let $r = N - 5(i-1)$ and $r' = N - r = 5(i-1)$. Also, let $\mathcal{V}_r = \mathcal{G} \setminus \{\mathsf{T}_{i',j} : i' \in [i-1], j \in [5]\}$ which is a random r-set in $\mathcal{G}$. Then the set $\mathcal{N}^{\mathsf{u}_i}(\mathsf{X}^{i-1})$ is same as the set

$$\{(\mathsf{v}_1, \mathsf{v}_2, \mathsf{v}_3) : \mathsf{v}_1, \mathsf{v}_2, \mathsf{v}_3, \mathsf{u}_{i,1} + \mathsf{v}_1 + \mathsf{v}_2, \mathsf{u}_{i,2} + \mathsf{v}_1 + \mathsf{v}_3 \in \mathcal{V}_r,$$

$$\mathsf{v}_1, \mathsf{v}_2, \mathsf{v}_3, \mathsf{u}_{i,1} + \mathsf{v}_1 + \mathsf{v}_2, \mathsf{u}_{i,1} + \mathsf{v}_1 + \mathsf{v}_3 \text{ distinct}\}$$

We denote the size of the set by $\mathbf{N}_r^{\mathsf{u}_i}$. Then we have

$$\begin{aligned}\mathbf{Ex}[\chi^2(\mathsf{X}^{i-1})] &= C \times \sum_{\mathsf{u}_i} \mathbf{Ex}[(\mathbf{N}_r^{\mathsf{u}_i} - D)^2] \\ &= C \times \sum_{\mathsf{u}_i} \left(\mathbf{Ex}[(\mathbf{N}_r^{\mathsf{u}_i} - \mathbf{Ex}[\mathbf{N}_r^{\mathsf{u}_i}])^2] + (\mathbf{Ex}[\mathbf{N}_r^{\mathsf{u}_i}] - D)^2\right) \\ &= \sum_{\mathsf{u}_i} C \times \mathbf{Var}[\mathbf{N}_r^{\mathsf{u}_i}] + \sum_{\mathsf{u}_i} C \times (\mathbf{Ex}[\mathbf{N}_r^{\mathsf{u}_i}] - D)^2. \qquad (28)\end{aligned}$$

Next, we apply the following lemma to get an upper bound on the r.h.s. of (28).

Lemma 3. *For every* $\mathsf{u} \in \mathcal{G}^2$, *we have*

$$C \times (\mathbf{Ex}[\mathbf{N}_r^{\mathsf{u}}] - D)^2 \leq \frac{25}{N^4},$$

$$C \times \mathbf{Var}[\mathbf{N}_r^{\mathsf{u}}] \leq \frac{2^{14} r'}{N^6} + \frac{2^{24} r'}{N^5} \text{ for } N \geq 100.$$

Subsequently, when $N \geq 100$ *and* $r' \leq \frac{5N}{8}$ *we have*

$$\mathbf{Ex}[\chi^2(\mathsf{X}^{i-1})] \leq \frac{2^{14} r'}{N^4} + \frac{2^{24} r'}{N^3} + \frac{25}{N^2}.$$

We defer the proof of the lemma to Sect. 4.2.

Finally, from Theorem 1 and Lemma 3, we get

$$\begin{aligned}\|\mathbf{Pr}_{\mathsf{S}} - \mathbf{Pr}_{\mathsf{U}}\| &\leq \|\mathbf{Pr}_{\mathsf{X}} - \mathbf{Pr}_{\mathsf{Y}}\| \qquad (29)\\ &\leq \left(\frac{1}{2}\sum_{i=1}^{q} \mathbf{Ex}[\chi^2(\mathsf{X}^{i-1})]\right)^{\frac{1}{2}} \\ &\leq \left(\sum_{i=1}^{q} \frac{25}{N^2} + \frac{4^7 r'}{N^4} + \frac{2^{24} r'}{N^3}\right)^{\frac{1}{2}} \quad \text{since } r' = 5(i-1) \leq 5q \leq 5N/8 \\ &\leq \left(\sum_{i=1}^{q} \frac{25}{N^2} + \frac{4^7 5(i-1)}{N^4} + \frac{2^{24} 5(i-1)}{N^3}\right)^{\frac{1}{2}} \quad \text{since } r' = 5(i-1) \\ &\leq \left(\frac{25q}{N^2} + \frac{4^8 q^2}{N^4} + \frac{2^{26} q^2}{N^3}\right)^{\frac{1}{2}} \\ &\leq \frac{5\sqrt{q}}{N} + \frac{256q}{N^2} + \frac{8192q}{N^{\frac{3}{2}}} \quad \text{for } N \geq 100. \qquad (30)\end{aligned}$$

■

4.2 Proof of Lemma 3

Let r, N be positive integers such that $r' = N - r \leq \frac{5N}{8}$. Let $\mathcal{G}$ be a group of size N, and $\mathcal{V}_r$ be a random r-set in $\mathcal{G}$. For $\mathsf{u} = (\mathsf{u}_1, \mathsf{u}_2) \in \mathcal{G}^2$ we associate a random variable $\mathbf{N}_r^{\mathsf{u}}$ defined as the size of the following set

$$\mathcal{N}_r^{\mathsf{u}} := \{(\mathsf{g}_1, \mathsf{g}_2, \mathsf{g}_3) \in \mathcal{G}^3 : \mathsf{g}_1, \mathsf{g}_2, \mathsf{g}_3, \mathsf{u}_1 + \mathsf{g}_1 + \mathsf{g}_2, \mathsf{u}_2 + \mathsf{g}_1 + \mathsf{g}_3 \in \mathcal{V}_r,$$
$$\mathsf{g}_1, \mathsf{g}_2, \mathsf{g}_3, \mathsf{u}_1 + \mathsf{g}_1 + \mathsf{g}_2, \mathsf{u}_2 + \mathsf{g}_1 + \mathsf{g}_3 \text{ distinct.}\}$$

We represent $\mathbf{N}_r^{\mathsf{u}}$ as a sum of indicator random variables. To do so we define the set $\mathcal{G}_{\mathsf{u}}$ of tuples of distinct elements of $\mathcal{G}$ as

$$\mathcal{G}_{\mathsf{u}} = \{(\mathsf{g}_1, \mathsf{g}_2, \mathsf{g}_3) : \mathsf{g}_1, \mathsf{g}_2, \mathsf{g}_3, \mathsf{u}_1 + \mathsf{g}_1 + \mathsf{g}_2, \mathsf{u}_2 + \mathsf{g}_1 + \mathsf{g}_3 \in \mathcal{G},$$
$$\mathsf{g}_1, \mathsf{g}_2, \mathsf{g}_3, \mathsf{u}_1 + \mathsf{g}_1 + \mathsf{g}_2, \mathsf{u}_2 + \mathsf{g}_1 + \mathsf{g}_3 \text{ distinct}\}.$$

Let $|\mathcal{G}_{\mathsf{u}}| = N_{\mathsf{u}}$. Then we have the following claim.

Claim 4 $N_{\mathsf{u}} \leq (N-1)(N-2)(N-3)$.

Proof of claim. It may be observed that for fixed u, $\mathsf{g}_1 \notin \{\mathsf{u}_1, \mathsf{u}_2\}$. Otherwise, either $\mathsf{u}_1 + \mathsf{g}_1 + \mathsf{g}_2 = \mathsf{g}_2$ or $\mathsf{u}_2 + \mathsf{g}_1 + \mathsf{g}_3 = \mathsf{g}_3$ which contradicts the distinctness requirement. Discounting for the fact $\mathsf{u}_1, \mathsf{u}_2$ may be equal we get that the number of choices for g_1 is at most $(N-1)$. Similarly, we have that $\mathsf{g}_2 \notin \{\mathsf{u}_1, \mathsf{g}_1\}$ and $\mathsf{g}_3 \notin \{\mathsf{g}_1, \mathsf{g}_2, \mathsf{u}_1 + \mathsf{g}_1 + \mathsf{g}_2\}$. Hence, the claim follows. ■

Next, we have

$$\mathbf{N}_r^{\mathsf{u}} = \sum_{\mathsf{g} \in \mathcal{G}_{\mathsf{u}}} \mathtt{I}_{\mathsf{g}}, \tag{31}$$

where, for $\mathsf{g} = (\mathsf{g}_1, \mathsf{g}_2, \mathsf{g}_3) \in \mathcal{G}_{\mathsf{u}}$, the indicator random variable $\mathtt{I}_{\mathsf{g}}$ is defined as follows.

$$\mathtt{I}_{\mathsf{g}} = \begin{cases} 1 \text{ if } \mathsf{g}_1, \mathsf{g}_2, \mathsf{g}_3, \mathsf{u}_1 + \mathsf{g}_1 + \mathsf{g}_2, \mathsf{u}_2 + \mathsf{g}_1 + \mathsf{g}_3 \in \mathcal{V}_r \text{ and distinct,} \\ 0 \text{ otherwise.} \end{cases}$$

So, we have

$$\begin{aligned} \mathbf{Ex}[\mathtt{I}_{\mathsf{g}}] &= \mathbf{Pr}[\{\mathsf{g}_1, \mathsf{g}_2, \mathsf{g}_3, \mathsf{u}_1 + \mathsf{g}_1 + \mathsf{g}_2, \mathsf{u}_2 + \mathsf{g}_1 + \mathsf{g}_3 \in \mathcal{V}_r\} \subseteq \mathcal{V}_r] \\ &= \frac{\binom{N-5}{r-5}}{\binom{N}{r}} \\ &= \frac{r^{\underline{5}}}{N^{\underline{5}}}. \end{aligned} \tag{32}$$

By using the linearity of expectation, we have

$$\mathbf{Ex}[\mathbf{N}_r^{\mathsf{u}}] = \sum_{\mathsf{g} \in \mathcal{G}_{\mathsf{u}}} \mathbf{Ex}[\mathtt{I}_{\mathsf{g}}]$$

$$= \sum_{\mathtt{g} \in \mathcal{G}_{\mathsf{u}}} \frac{r^{\underline{5}}}{N^{\underline{5}}}$$

$$\leq \frac{r^{\underline{5}}}{N(N-4)} \text{ using Claim 4.}$$

Therefore, plugging in the values of C and D we have

$$\begin{aligned} C \times (\mathbf{Ex}[\mathbf{N}_r^{\mathsf{u}}] - D)^2 &\leq \frac{N^2}{(r^{\underline{5}})^2} \times \left(\frac{r^{\underline{5}}}{N(N-4)} - \frac{r^{\underline{5}}}{N^2} \right)^2 \\ &\leq \frac{16}{N^2(N-4)^2} \\ &\leq \frac{25}{N^4} \text{ for } N \geq 20. \end{aligned} \tag{33}$$

Now, we compute the variance using the following relation.

$$\mathbf{Var}[\sum_{\mathtt{g} \in \mathcal{G}_{\mathsf{u}}} \mathtt{I}_{\mathtt{g}}] = \sum_{\mathtt{g} \in \mathcal{G}_{\mathsf{u}}} \mathbf{Var}[\mathtt{I}_{\mathtt{g}}] + \sum_{\mathtt{g} \neq \mathtt{g}' \in \mathcal{G}_{\mathsf{u}}} \mathbf{Cov}(\mathtt{I}_{\mathtt{g}}, \mathtt{I}_{\mathtt{g}'}). \tag{34}$$

For the sake of notational simplicity, for every $\mathtt{g} \in \mathcal{G}_{\mathsf{u}}$, we denote the set $\{\mathtt{g}_1, \mathtt{g}_2, \mathtt{g}_3, \mathsf{u}_1 + \mathtt{g}_1 + \mathtt{g}_2, \mathsf{u}_2 + \mathtt{g}_1 + \mathtt{g}_3\}$ as $\mathcal{S}_{\mathsf{u}}^{\mathtt{g}}$. In (32), we have obtained $\mathbf{Ex}[\mathtt{I}_{\mathtt{g}}] = \frac{r^{\underline{5}}}{N^{\underline{5}}}$. As $\mathtt{I}_{\mathtt{g}}$ is a $0-1$ random variable, $\mathbf{Ex}[\mathtt{I}_{\mathtt{g}}^2] = \mathbf{Ex}[\mathtt{I}_{\mathtt{g}}]$. Thus,

$$\begin{aligned} \mathbf{Var}[\mathtt{I}_{\mathtt{g}}] &= \mathbf{Ex}[\mathtt{I}_{\mathtt{g}}^2] - \mathbf{Ex}[\mathtt{I}_{\mathtt{g}}]^2 \\ &= \mathbf{Ex}[\mathtt{I}_{\mathtt{g}}](1 - \mathbf{Ex}[\mathtt{I}_{\mathtt{g}}]) \\ &= \frac{r^{\underline{5}}}{N^{\underline{5}}} \times \left(1 - \frac{r^{\underline{5}}}{N^{\underline{5}}}\right) \qquad (35) \\ &\leq \frac{r^{\underline{5}}}{N^{\underline{5}}} \times \frac{10r'}{N} \text{ using Lemma 1.} \qquad (36) \end{aligned}$$

Therefore, by using the estimate of N_{u} from Claim 4 we get

$$\begin{aligned} C \times \sum_{\mathtt{g} \in \mathcal{G}_{\mathsf{u}}} \mathbf{Var}[\mathtt{I}_{\mathtt{g}}] &= \frac{N^2}{(r^{\underline{5}})^2} \times N_{\mathsf{u}} \times \frac{r^{\underline{5}}}{N^{\underline{5}}} \times \frac{10r'}{N}. \\ &\leq \frac{2^{14}r'}{N^6} \text{ for } N \geq 16. \end{aligned} \tag{37}$$

Now, we compute the covariance term of (34). Note that $\mathtt{I}_{\mathtt{g}}\mathtt{I}_{\mathtt{g}'} = 1$ if and only if $\mathcal{S}_{\mathsf{u}}^{\mathtt{g}} \cup \mathcal{S}_{\mathsf{u}}^{\mathtt{g}'} \subseteq \mathcal{V}_r$. So,

$$\mathbf{Ex}[\mathtt{I}_{\mathtt{g}}\mathtt{I}_{\mathtt{g}'}] = \mathbf{Pr}[\mathcal{S}_{\mathsf{u}}^{\mathtt{g}} \cup \mathcal{S}_{\mathsf{u}}^{\mathtt{g}'} \subseteq \mathcal{V}_r] = \frac{r^{\underline{\ell}}}{N^{\underline{\ell}}},$$

where $\ell = |\mathcal{S}_{\mathsf{u}}^{\mathsf{g}} \cup \mathcal{S}_{\mathsf{u}}^{\mathsf{g}'}|$. Here, it is not difficult to observe that $\ell \in \{5, 6, 7, 8, 9, 10\}$.

Accordingly, we can partition the sum of covariances as follows.

$$\begin{aligned}\sum_{\mathsf{g} \neq \mathsf{g}' \in \mathcal{G}_{\mathsf{u}}} \mathbf{Cov}(\mathtt{I}_{\mathsf{g}}, \mathtt{I}_{\mathsf{g}'}) &= \sum_{\ell \in \{5,6,7,8,9,10\}} \sum_{\substack{\mathsf{g} \neq \mathsf{g}' \in \mathcal{G}_{\mathsf{u}} \\ |\mathcal{S}_{\mathsf{u}}^{\mathsf{g}} \cup \mathcal{S}_{\mathsf{u}}^{\mathsf{g}'}| = \ell}} \mathbf{Cov}(\mathtt{I}_{\mathsf{g}}, \mathtt{I}_{\mathsf{g}'}) \\ &= \sum_{\ell \in \{5,6,7,8,9,10\}} \Delta_{\ell}^{\mathsf{u}} \mathsf{COV}_{\ell},\end{aligned} \tag{38}$$

where

$$\Delta_{\ell}^{\mathsf{u}} = |\{(\mathsf{g}, \mathsf{g}') \in \mathcal{G}_{\mathsf{u}} \times \mathcal{G}_{\mathsf{u}} | \mathsf{g} \neq \mathsf{g}', |\mathcal{S}_{\mathsf{u}}^{\mathsf{g}} \cup \mathcal{S}_{\mathsf{u}}^{\mathsf{g}'}| = \ell\}|,$$

and

$$\begin{aligned}\mathsf{COV}_{\ell} &= \frac{r^{\underline{\ell}}}{N^{\underline{\ell}}} - \left(\frac{r^{\underline{5}}}{N^{\underline{5}}}\right)^2 \\ &= \left(\frac{r^{\underline{5}}}{N^{\underline{5}}}\right)\left(\frac{(r-5)\dots(r-\ell+1)}{(N-5)\dots(N-\ell+1)} - \frac{r^{\underline{5}}}{N^{\underline{5}}}\right) \\ &= \left(\frac{r^{\underline{5}}}{N^{5}}\right) \times \Gamma_{\ell},\end{aligned}$$

where $\Gamma_{\ell} = \left(\frac{(r-5)\dots(r-\ell+1)}{(N-5)\dots(N-\ell+1)} - \frac{r^{\underline{5}}}{N^{\underline{5}}}\right)$. Therefore,

$$\begin{aligned}C \times \mathsf{COV}_{\ell} &= \frac{N}{r^{\underline{5}}(N-1)^{\underline{4}}} \times \Gamma_{\ell} \\ &\leq \frac{1024}{N^8} \times \Gamma_{\ell} \quad \text{for } N \geq 16.\end{aligned} \tag{39}$$

Now, we estimate the order of magnitude of $\Delta_{\ell}^{\mathsf{u}}$ and Γ_{ℓ} for different values of ℓ through the following claims.

Claim 5. *With the notations mentioned above we have the following upper bounds.*

1. $\Delta_5^{\mathsf{u}} \leq 40 N_{\mathsf{u}}$,
2. $\Delta_6^{\mathsf{u}} \leq 600 N_{\mathsf{u}}$,
3. $\Delta_7^{\mathsf{u}} \leq 600 N N_{\mathsf{u}}$,
4. $\Delta_8^{\mathsf{u}} \leq 200 N N_{\mathsf{u}}$,
5. $\Delta_9^{\mathsf{u}} \leq 25 N^2 N_{\mathsf{u}}$,
6. $\Delta_{10}^{\mathsf{u}} = (N^3 - cN^2) N_{\mathsf{u}}$ *for some* c *with* $10 \leq c \leq 36$ *and* $N \geq 15$.

Proof of claim. Below, we provide case by case justification of the above claim, although with significant compromise on the accuracy of the constants as our primary focus is on the order of magnitude of the considered variables. In each case, *i.e.* for $\ell \in \{5, 6, 7, 8, 9, 10\}$, we fix some $\mathsf{g} \in \mathcal{G}_{\mathsf{u}}$ and consider the number of $\mathsf{g}' \in \mathcal{G}_{\mathsf{u}}$ for which $|\mathcal{S}_{\mathsf{u}}^{\mathsf{g}} \cap \mathcal{S}_{\mathsf{u}}^{\mathsf{g}'}| = \ell$, and then the final expression of $\Delta_{\ell}^{\mathsf{u}}$ is obtained by multiplying with the cardinality (N_{u}) of $\mathcal{G}_{\mathsf{u}}$ (*i.e.*, the number of g). Here note that $\mathsf{u} = (\mathsf{u}_1, \mathsf{u}_2)$ is already fixed.

1. In this case, we have $\mathcal{S}_{\mathsf{u}}^{\mathbf{g}} = \mathcal{S}_{\mathsf{u}}^{\mathbf{g}'}$. Now, with $\mathbf{g}$ fixed, $\mathbf{g}_1', \mathbf{g}_2'$ can be fixed by the elements of $\mathcal{S}_{\mathsf{u}}^{\mathbf{g}}$ in at most $5 \times 4 = 20$ ways. Not all such choices will be valid (because for some of them $\mathbf{g}_1' + \mathbf{g}_2' + \mathsf{u}_1 \notin \mathcal{S}_{\mathsf{u}}^{\mathbf{g}}$). For each valid choice of $\mathbf{g}_1', \mathbf{g}_2'$ there are at most 2 choices of $\mathbf{g}_3'$ (indeed $\mathbf{g}_3' \in \mathcal{S}_{\mathsf{u}}^{\mathbf{g}} \setminus \{\mathbf{g}_1', \mathbf{g}_2', \mathbf{g}_1' + \mathbf{g}_2' + \mathsf{u}_1\}$). So, $\Delta_5^{\mathsf{u}} \leq 40 N_{\mathsf{u}}$.
2. In this case, 4 elements of $\mathcal{S}_{\mathsf{u}}^{\mathbf{g}}$ can be chosen in 5 ways. These 4 elements can be assigned to the 4 elements of $\mathcal{S}_{\mathsf{u}}^{\mathbf{g}'}$ in at most $5 \times 4 \times 3 \times 2 = 120$ ways. This fixes the tuple $\mathbf{g}'$. So, $\Delta_6^{\mathsf{u}} \leq 120 \times 5 \times N_{\mathsf{u}} = 600 N_{\mathsf{u}}$.
3. Here, 3 elements of $\mathcal{S}_{\mathsf{u}}^{\mathbf{g}}$ can be chosen in 10 ways. The chosen elements can be assigned to 3 elements of $\mathcal{S}_{\mathsf{u}}^{\mathbf{g}'}$ in $5 \times 4 \times 3 = 60$ ways. Fixing any of the remaining 2 elements of $\mathcal{S}_{\mathsf{u}}^{\mathbf{g}'}$ can be done in at most N ways. This fixes the tuple $\mathbf{g}'$. So, we have $\Delta_7^{\mathsf{u}} \leq 600 N N_{\mathsf{u}}$.
4. Following an argument quite similar to the above, we get that $\Delta_8^{\mathsf{u}} \leq 200 N N_{\mathsf{u}}$.
5. In this case, the two sets $\mathcal{S}_{\mathsf{u}}^{\mathbf{g}}$ and $\mathcal{S}_{\mathsf{u}}^{\mathbf{g}'}$ intersect in a single element. This can happen in 25 possible ways and fixing any two from $\{\mathbf{g}_1', \mathbf{g}_2', \mathbf{g}_3'\} \setminus \mathcal{S}_{\mathsf{u}}^{\mathbf{g}}$ fixes the remaining one (among $\{\mathbf{g}_1', \mathbf{g}_2', \mathbf{g}_3'\}$) if it is already not in $\mathcal{S}_{\mathsf{u}}^{\mathbf{g}'}$. Now, the two elements can be fixed in at most N^2 number of ways. So, the claim for this case is established.
6. In this case, the sets $\mathcal{S}_{\mathsf{u}}^{\mathbf{g}}$ and $\mathcal{S}_{\mathsf{u}}^{\mathbf{g}'}$ are disjoint. So, for fixed $\mathbf{g}$ the number of choices of $\mathbf{g}_i'$ is $N - d_i$, for integers $d_i, 1 \leq i \leq 3$. Now, $d_1 = |\mathcal{S}_{\mathsf{u}}^{\mathbf{g}} \cup \{\mathsf{u}_1, \mathsf{u}_2\}|$. So, $5 \leq d_1 \leq 7$. Similarly, (conditioned on the choice of $\mathbf{g}_1'$) we have that $d_2 = |\mathcal{S}_{\mathsf{u}}^{\mathbf{g}} \cup \{\mathsf{u}_1, \mathbf{g}_1'\} \cup \mathsf{u}_1 + \mathbf{g}_1' + \mathcal{S}_{\mathsf{u}}^{\mathbf{g}}|$. From this it follows that $5 \leq d_2 \leq 12$. Finally, following similar argument, and compromising on accuracy it follows that (conditioned on the choice of $\mathbf{g}_1'$ and $\mathbf{g}_2'$) $5 \leq d_3 \leq 17$. So, for this case, the possible number of choices of $\mathbf{g}'$ for fixed $\mathbf{g}$ is $(N - d_1)(N - d_2)(N - d_3)$ which is $(N^3 - cN^2)$ for some $10 \leq c \leq 36$ and $N \geq 15$. ■

Claim 6

$$\Gamma_\ell \leq \frac{10r'}{N}$$

for $\ell \in \{5, 6, 7, 8\}$

Proof of claim. This (weaker) bound follows from Lemma 1. ■

Claim 7

$$\Delta_9^{\mathsf{u}} \Gamma_9 + \Delta_{10}^{\mathsf{u}} \Gamma_{10} \leq 720 r' N^3,$$

for $N \geq 100$

Proof of claim. Here we use the estimates of Δ_9^{u} and Δ_{10}^{u} from Claim 5 with $N_{\mathsf{u}} \leq N^3$. Also, we suppress the tedious calculation (verified using symbolic algebra package) and get the final upper bound $720 r' N^3$ for $N \geq 100$. ■

Next, using the estimates form Claim 5, Claim 6, and Claim 7 together with (39) and $N_{\mathsf{u}} \leq N^3$ we get the following upper bound on the r.h.s. of (38).

$$C \times \sum_{\mathbf{g} \neq \mathbf{g}' \in \mathcal{G}_{\mathsf{u}}} \mathbf{Cov}(\mathtt{I}_{\mathbf{g}}, \mathtt{I}_{\mathbf{g}'}) = C \times \sum_{\ell \in \{5,6,7,8,9,10\}} \Delta_\ell^{\mathsf{u}} \mathsf{cov}_\ell$$

$$
\begin{aligned}
&\leq \frac{1024}{N^8} \times \sum_{\ell \in \{5,6,7,8,9,10\}} \Delta_\ell^{\mathsf{u}} \Gamma_\ell \\
&\leq \frac{1024}{N^8} \times \left(640N^3 \times \frac{10r'}{N} + 800N^4 \times \frac{10r'}{N} + 720r'N^3\right) \\
&\leq \frac{1024}{N^8} \times (6400r'N^2 + 8000r'N^3 + 720r'N^3) \\
&\leq \frac{2^{24}r'}{N^5} \text{ for } N \geq 100. \qquad (40)
\end{aligned}
$$

Finally, using (33),(37), and (40) the r.h.s. of (28) yields

$$
\begin{aligned}
\mathbf{Ex}[\chi^2(\mathsf{X}^{i-1})] &\leq \sum_{\mathsf{u}} \frac{25}{N^4} + \frac{2^{14}r'}{N^6} + \frac{2^{24}r'}{N^5} \\
&= \frac{25}{N^2} + \frac{2^{14}r'}{N^4} + \frac{2^{24}r'}{N^3} \text{ for } N \geq 100. \qquad (41)
\end{aligned}
$$

■

5 Conclusion

In this paper, we have demonstrated much stronger PRF security gurarantee of a block cipher based PRF construction termed $\mathsf{XORP}[3]$ in the multi-user and single-user setting. With the choice of a sufficiently secure block cipher, the construction allows simultaneous (independent) use by $O(2^n)$ users even when the adversary makes almost $O(2^n)$ many queries to each user. In the single-user scenario our result implies $O\left(1/\sqrt{2^n}\right)$, *i.e.*, negligible distinguishing advantage for an adversary even allowing it to make almost $O(2^n)$ many queries. We have also considered an efficient version of $\mathsf{XORP}[3]$, termed $\mathsf{XORP}'[3]$ which uses less number of block cipher calls but achieves same level of security. We have also shown an application of our result to counter mode encryption. In the end, we invite the reader to investigate whether the variant $\mathsf{XORP}'[3]$ can be further extended to achieve still better security/ efficiency.

Acknowledgement. We are indebted to all the reviewers, Dr. Akinori Hoshoyamada, and Mr. Abishanka Saha for carefully going through the manuscript, pointing out technical and editorial issues, and suggesting modifications leading to the final version.

The research was supported by the project "Study and Analysis of IoT Security" under Government of India at R.C.Bose Centre for Cryptology and Security, Indian Statistical Institute, Kolkata.

References

[BBM00] Bellare, M., Boldyreva, A., Micali, S.: Public-key encryption in a multi-user setting: security proofs and improvements. In: Preneel, B. (ed.) EUROCRYPT 2000. LNCS, vol. 1807, pp. 259–274. Springer, Heidelberg (2000). https://doi.org/10.1007/3-540-45539-6_18

[BGK99] Bellare, M., Goldreich, O., Krawczyk, H.: Stateless evaluation of pseudorandom functions: security beyond the birthday barrier. In: Wiener, M. (ed.) CRYPTO 1999. LNCS, vol. 1666, pp. 270–287. Springer, Heidelberg (1999). https://doi.org/10.1007/3-540-48405-1_17

[BHT18] Bose, P., Hoang, V.T., Tessaro, S.: Revisiting AES-GCM-SIV: multi-user security, faster key derivation, and better bounds. In: Nielsen, J.B., Rijmen, V. (eds.) EUROCRYPT 2018. LNCS, vol. 10820, pp. 468–499. Springer, Cham (2018). https://doi.org/10.1007/978-3-319-78381-9_18

[BI99] Bellare, M., Impagliazzo, R.: A tool for obtaining tighter security analyses of pseudorandom function based constructions, with applications to PRP to PRF conversion. IACR Cryptology ePrint Archive 1999, 24 (1999)

[BKR98] Bellare, M., Krovetz, T., Rogaway, P.: Luby-Rackoff backwards: increasing security by making block ciphers non-invertible. In: Nyberg, K. (ed.) EUROCRYPT 1998. LNCS, vol. 1403, pp. 266–280. Springer, Heidelberg (1998). https://doi.org/10.1007/BFb0054132

[BN18a] Bhattacharya, S., Nandi, M.: Full indifferentiable security of the Xor of two or more random permutations using the χ^2 method. In: Nielsen, J.B., Rijmen, V. (eds.) EUROCRYPT 2018. LNCS, vol. 10820, pp. 387–412. Springer, Cham (2018). https://doi.org/10.1007/978-3-319-78381-9_15

[BN18b] Bhattacharya, S., Nandi, M.: A note on the chi-square method: a tool for proving cryptographic security. Cryptogr. Commun. **10**(5), 935–957 (2018). https://doi.org/10.1007/s12095-017-0276-z

[BN18c] Bhattacharya, S., Nandi, M.: Revisiting variable output length XOR pseudorandom function. IACR Trans. Symmetric Cryptol. **2018**(1), 314–335 (2018)

[BT16] Bellare, M., Tackmann, B.: The multi-user security of authenticated encryption: AES-GCM in TLS 1.3. In: Robshaw, M., Katz, J. (eds.) CRYPTO 2016. LNCS, vol. 9814, pp. 247–276. Springer, Heidelberg (2016). https://doi.org/10.1007/978-3-662-53018-4_10

[CLL19] Choi, W., Lee, B., Lee, J.: Indifferentiability of truncated random permutations. In: Galbraith, S.D., Moriai, S. (eds.) ASIACRYPT 2019. LNCS, vol. 11921, pp. 175–195. Springer, Cham (2019). https://doi.org/10.1007/978-3-030-34578-5_7

[CLP14] Cogliati, B., Lampe, R., Patarin, J.: The indistinguishability of the XOR of k permutations. In: Cid, C., Rechberger, C. (eds.) FSE 2014. LNCS, vol. 8540, pp. 285–302. Springer, Heidelberg (2015). https://doi.org/10.1007/978-3-662-46706-0_15

[Cog18] Cogliati, B.: Tweaking a block cipher: multi-user beyond-birthday-bound security in the standard model. Des. Codes Crypt. **86**(12), 2747–2763 (2018). https://doi.org/10.1007/s10623-018-0471-8

[DHT17] Dai, W., Hoang, V.T., Tessaro, S.: Information-theoretic indistinguishability via the chi-squared method. In: Katz, J., Shacham, H. (eds.) CRYPTO 2017. LNCS, vol. 10403, pp. 497–523. Springer, Cham (2017). https://doi.org/10.1007/978-3-319-63697-9_17

[GM20] Gunsing, A., Mennink, B.: The summation-truncation hybrid: reusing discarded bits for free. In: Micciancio, D., Ristenpart, T. (eds.) CRYPTO 2020. LNCS, vol. 12170, pp. 187–217. Springer, Cham (2020). https://doi.org/10.1007/978-3-030-56784-2_7

[HS20] Hoang, V.T., Shen, Y.: Security of streaming encryption in Google's Tink library. In: Proceedings of the 2020 ACM SIGSAC Conference on Computer and Communications Security, pp. 243–262 (2020)

[HT17] Hoang, V.T., Tessaro, S.: The multi-user security of double encryption. In: Coron, J.-S., Nielsen, J.B. (eds.) EUROCRYPT 2017. LNCS, vol. 10211, pp. 381–411. Springer, Cham (2017). https://doi.org/10.1007/978-3-319-56614-6_13

[HTT18] Hoang, V.T., Tessaro, S., Thiruvengadam, A.: The multi-user security of GCM, revisited: tight bounds for nonce randomization. In: CCS 2018, pp. 1429–1440. ACM (2018)

[HWKS98] Hall, C., Wagner, D., Kelsey, J., Schneier, B.: Building PRFs from PRPs. In: Krawczyk, H. (ed.) CRYPTO 1998. LNCS, vol. 1462, pp. 370–389. Springer, Heidelberg (1998). https://doi.org/10.1007/BFb0055742

[IMPS17] Iwata, T., Minematsu, K., Peyrin, T., Seurin, Y.: ZMAC: a fast tweakable block cipher mode for highly secure message authentication. IACR Cryptology ePrint Archive 2017, 535 (2017)

[Iwa06] Iwata, T.: New blockcipher modes of operation with beyond the birthday bound security. In: Robshaw, M. (ed.) FSE 2006. LNCS, vol. 4047, pp. 310–327. Springer, Heidelberg (2006). https://doi.org/10.1007/11799313_20

[LR88] Luby, M., Rackoff, C.: How to construct pseudorandom permutations from pseudorandom functions. SIAM J. Comput. **17**(2), 373–386 (1988)

[Luc00] Lucks, S.: The sum of PRPs is a secure PRF. In: Preneel, B. (ed.) EUROCRYPT 2000. LNCS, vol. 1807, pp. 470–484. Springer, Heidelberg (2000). https://doi.org/10.1007/3-540-45539-6_34

[Men19] Mennink, B.: Linking Stam's bounds with generalized truncation. In: Matsui, M. (ed.) CT-RSA 2019. LNCS, vol. 11405, pp. 313–329. Springer, Cham (2019). https://doi.org/10.1007/978-3-030-12612-4_16

[ML15] Mouha, N., Luykx, A.: Multi-key security: the even-Mansour construction revisited. In: Gennaro, R., Robshaw, M. (eds.) CRYPTO 2015. LNCS, vol. 9215, pp. 209–223. Springer, Heidelberg (2015). https://doi.org/10.1007/978-3-662-47989-6_10

[MP15] Mennink, B., Preneel, B.: On the XOR of multiple random permutations. In: Malkin, T., Kolesnikov, V., Lewko, A.B., Polychronakis, M. (eds.) ACNS 2015. LNCS, vol. 9092, pp. 619–634. Springer, Cham (2015). https://doi.org/10.1007/978-3-319-28166-7_30

[Pat08] Patarin, J.: A proof of security in $O(2^n)$ for the Xor of two random permutations. In: Safavi-Naini, R. (ed.) ICITS 2008. LNCS, vol. 5155, pp. 232–248. Springer, Heidelberg (2008). https://doi.org/10.1007/978-3-540-85093-9_22

[Pat10] Patarin, J.: Introduction to mirror theory: analysis of systems of linear equalities and linear non equalities for cryptography. Cryptology ePrint Archive, Report 2017/287 (2010). http://eprint.iacr.org/2010/287

[Yas11] Yasuda, K.: A new variant of PMAC: beyond the birthday bound. In: Rogaway, P. (ed.) CRYPTO 2011. LNCS, vol. 6841, pp. 596–609. Springer, Heidelberg (2011). https://doi.org/10.1007/978-3-642-22792-9_34

Double-Block-Length Hash Function for Minimum Memory Size

Yusuke Naito[1(✉)], Yu Sasaki[2], and Takeshi Sugawara[3]

[1] Mitsubishi Electric Corporation, Kanagawa, Japan
Naito.Yusuke@ce.MitsubishiElectric.co.jp
[2] NTT Social Informatics Laboratories, Tokyo, Japan
yu.sasaki.sk@hco.ntt.co.jp
[3] The University of Electro-Communications, Tokyo, Japan
sugawara@uec.ac.jp

Abstract. Sharing a common primitive for multiple functionalities is essential for lightweight cryptography, and NIST's lightweight cryptography competition (LWC) considers the integration of hashing to AEAD. While permutations are natural primitive choices in such a goal, for design diversity, it is interesting to investigate how small block-cipher (BC) based and tweakable block-cipher (TBC) based schemes can be. Double-block-length (DBL) hash function modes are suitable to ensure the same security level for AEAD and hashing, but hard to achieve a small memory size. Romulus, a TBC-based finalist in NIST LWC, introduced the DBL hashing scheme Romulus-H, but it requires $3n + k$ bits of memory using an underlying primitive with an n-bit block and a k-bit (twea)key. Even the smallest DBL modes in the literature require $2n + k$ bits of memory. Addressing this issue, we present new DBL modes EXEX-NI and EXEX-I achieving $(n + k)$-bit state size, i.e., no extra memory in addition to $n + k$ bits needed within the primitive. EXEX-NI is indifferentiable from a random oracle up to $n - \log n$ bits. By instantiating it with SKINNY, we can provide hashing to Romulus with zero memory overhead. EXEX-I is an optimized mode with collision resistance. We finally compare the hardware performances of EXEX-NI, EXEX-I, and Romulus-H with SKINNY-128-384. EXEX-NI and EXEX-I achieve the circuit-area reduction by 2,000+ GE, yielding the total areas being smaller than 70% of that of Romulus-H.

Keywords: Double-block-length hash · Lightweight cryptography · Low memory · Indifferentiability · Collision resistance · Tweakable block cipher

1 Introduction

Lightweight cryptography receives great attention in the field of symmetric-key cryptography. The National Institute of Standards and Technology (NIST) is now organizing a competition (NIST LWC) to standardize lightweight authenticated encryption with associated data (AEAD) schemes [29]. In particular, it

M. Tibouchi and H. Wang (Eds.): ASIACRYPT 2021, LNCS 13092, pp. 376–406, 2021.
https://doi.org/10.1007/978-3-030-92078-4_13

is the final year of the competition, at the time of writing, and new knowledge on lightweight AEAD schemes is highly important. Sharing a common primitive for multiple functionalities is important for reducing hardware/software costs; it is an essential idea behind AEAD schemes that simultaneously realize both encryption and message authentication. For even higher efficiency, NIST LWC considers the integration of yet another functionality into AEAD: a hashing scheme.

Efficient integration of AEAD and hashing is a challenging task. Using a secret key is the central difference between AEAD and hashing, which results in different security levels for a given state size. Intuitively, to ensure the same level of security, hashing schemes require a larger state than AEAD schemes in order to resist collision attacks based on the birthday paradox. A naive approach to compensate for this difference is to use a larger primitive for hashing, but using a larger primitive for the optional functionality in NIST LWC is unreasonable for lightweight implementation. Compared to block ciphers (BCs) and tweakable block ciphers (TBCs), cryptographic permutations seem more suitable to support both AEAD and hashing by using the duplex construction for AEAD [5] and the sponge construction for hashing [4].

NIST LWC has recently proceeded into the final stage by selecting 10 schemes as finalists [30], where 6 of them are permutation-based schemes, and the rest have diversity; a BC-based scheme, a TBC-based scheme, a stream cipher-based scheme, and a keyed permutation-based scheme. Among the 10 finalists, the 4 schemes support both AEAD and hashing, and all of them adopt the duplex and the sponge constructions. NIST explicitly states that they consider design diversity during the selection [31], and exploring an efficient realization of hashing in other constructions is an important research challenge. The design team of the TBC-based scheme Romulus [12] has recently announced a hashing scheme called Romulus-H [13], which is an MDPH hashing mode [24] instantiated with SKINNY-128-384 [3] used in Romulus AEAD. This is an interesting direction, and the goal of this paper is to explore an optimal construction with respect to the memory size to realize a hashing scheme based on a BC or a TBC, particularly to satisfy the design requirements for NIST LWC.

We begin by recalling NIST's requirements for hash functions: (1) cryptanalytic attacks to find a collision, a second preimage, and a preimage shall require at least 2^{112} computations and (2) length extension attacks should be prevented. For example, if part of the message is a secret key, constructing a hash value corresponding to another message under the same key should be infeasible.

DBL Modes. Double block length (DBL) hashing modes construct a $2n$-bit hash function from an n-bit block cipher.[1] Given that hashing schemes require a larger state than AEAD schemes, DBL modes are very suitable to support both AEAD and hashing schemes by BCs. Moreover, NIST LWC requires at least

[1] Instead of BCs, TBCs can be used in DBL. Hashing modes replace a key with some public value, hence BCs with a k-bit key and TBCs with a k'-bit key and a t-bit tweak generally play the same role as long as $k = k' + t$. For sake of simplicity, we denote underlying primitives by BCs.

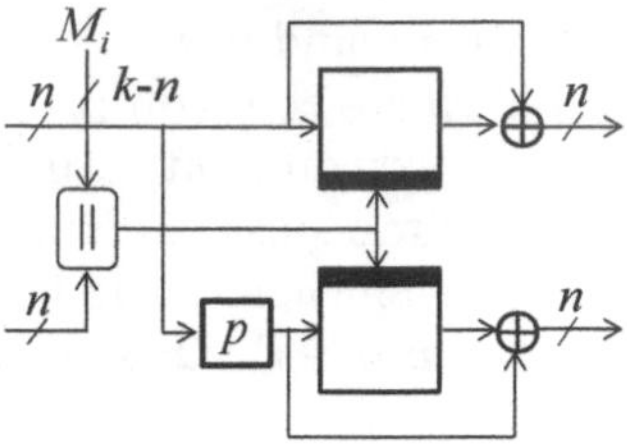

Fig. 1. Hirose's DBL CF. p is a permutation without fixed points.

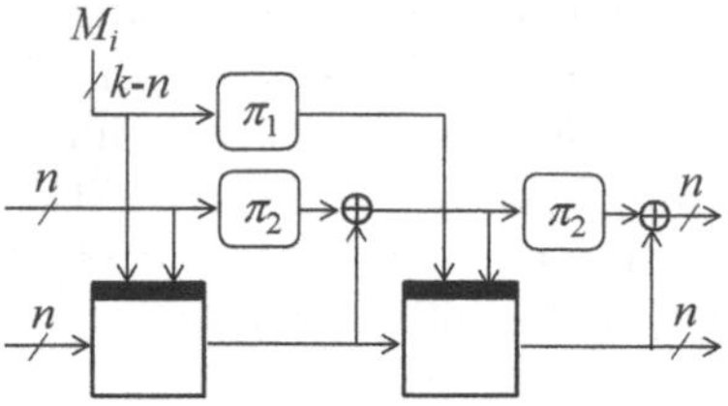

Fig. 2. EXEX CF. π_1 (resp. π_2) is an $(k-n)$-bit (resp. n-bit) linear function.

112-bit security for a hashing scheme, while most of the existing lightweight BCs and TBCs have a block size of 128 bits or shorter, which makes it natural to design a 256-bit hashing scheme from a 128-bit BC. Apart from NIST LWC, DBL modes are motivated by a practical demand; one may want to implement a 256-bit hash function from AES (128-bit block and a 128-bit or a 256-bit key) instead of implementing SHA-256 that has a completely different structure.

A popular approach to design DBL modes is to first design a DBL compression function (CF), which is then converted to a hash function (HF) by the Merkle-Damgård domain extension [9,21]. There are many such modes, including MDC-2, MDC-4 [7], Tandem-DM, and Abreast-DM [16]. Hirose's DBL construction [10] is one of the most widely known DBL CFs, which is depicted in Fig. 1. Besides, many DBL constructions have been proposed for different goals, e.g., for improving security [1,18,24], relaxing the key size limitation for underlying BCs [17,20], etc. In particular, there is a line of research works for reducing the required memory size, which determines the overall hardware cost in lightweight implementation. The goal of this paper is to optimize the memory size, and we explain below the previous works in this direction.

With an underlying BC having an n-bit block and a k-bit key, Hirose's DBL CF requires a $(3n+k)$-bit state. Bogdanov et al. proposed a lightweight hash function for RFID tags by instantiating Hirose's construction with a lightweight block cipher PRESENT [6]. Notably, they pointed out that the feed-forward operation in Hirose's DBL construction increases the memory size. Naito's MDPH, the mode used in Romulus-H, also requires a $(3n+k)$-bit state because it is an extension of Hirose's CF; MDPH replaces the standard Merkle-Damgård domain extension with Merkle-Damgård-Permutation (MDP) domain extension [11], thereby providing indifferentiability (from a random oracle) [19].

Özen and Stam broke the $(3n+k)$-bit barrier by proposing a synthetic approach to achieving the $(2n+k)$-bit state size [32]. Their generic construction includes Hirose's DBL CF without the feed-forward, which enables to reduce the state size to $2n+k$ bits. This is an interesting approach because the omission of the feed-forward makes the CF vulnerable, while the security (collision resistance) is guaranteed as a whole HF. Naito followed the same approach [23], and designed another mode achieving $2n+k$ bits of memory in which the CF is Hirose's construction without feed-forward, while the security

Table 1. Comparison of DBL modes. $-\epsilon$ denotes that security is lost by a factor of $\log n$. coll resp. indiff denote the collision resistance resp. the indifferentiability.

Scheme	Memory	Security in bits	Security goal	#BC calls	Message length	Key length	Parallel	Omit KSF^{-1}	Ref.
Tandem-DM	$3n+k$	n	coll	2	$k-n$	$n<k$	Yes	No	[16]
Abreast-DM	$3n+k$	n	coll	2	$k-n$	$2n \le k$	Yes	No	[16]
MDC-2	$3n+k$	$3n/5-\epsilon$	coll	2	n	$n \le k$	Yes	No	[7]
MDC-4	$3n+k$	$5n/8-\epsilon$	coll	4	n	$n \le k$	Yes	No	[7]
Mennink	$4n+k$	$n-\epsilon$	coll	3	n	$n \le k$	Yes	No	[20]
MJH	$5n+k$	$n-\epsilon$	coll	2	n	$n \le k$	Yes	No	[17]
Hirose	$3n+k$	n	coll	2	$k-n$	$n<k$	Yes	No	[10]
MDPH†	$3n+k$	$n-\epsilon$	indiff	2	$k-n$	$n<k$	Yes	No	[13, 24]
Özen-Stam	$2n+k$	$n-\epsilon$	coll	2	$k-n$	$n<k$	Yes	No	[32]
Naito‡	$2n+k$	n	indiff	2	$k-n$	$2n \le k$	Yes	No	[23]
EXEX-NI‡	$n+k$	$n-\epsilon$	indiff	2	$k-n$	$2n \le k$	No	Yes	Ours
EXEX-I	$n+k$	$n-\epsilon$	coll	2	$k-n$	$n<k$	No	Yes	Ours

†The mode used in Romulus-H. ‡Requires 2 additional BC calls.

(indifferentiability) for the HF is guaranteed by replacing the domain extension. Naito's mode imposes a stronger requirement on the underlying BC with $k \ge 2n$.

The memory size of existing DBL modes, along with their security and other associated parameters, is compared in Table 1. The smallest memory size in the literature is $2n+k$ bits by Özen-Stam [32] and Naito [23]. The collision resistance may not be sufficient to prevent the length extension attack, one of the requirements in NIST LWC, while indifferentiability suffices to prevent it. The lack of indifferentiability does not immediately imply that the length extension attack is feasible; however, the standard Merkle-Damgård domain extension is known to be vulnerable against the length extension attack.

Our Contributions. In this paper, we present new DBL hash function modes EXEX-NI (NI for <u>n</u>ested <u>i</u>terated) and EXEX-I (I for <u>i</u>terated) achieving $(n+k)$-bit state size using an underlying primitive having an n-bit block and a k-bit key. This is the smallest as compared in Table 1, and is optimal because we need $n+k$ bits just for implementing the BC. EXEX-NI and EXEX-I also accept a TBC of an n-bit block, a k'-bit key, and a t-bit tweak such that $k = k' + t$. Their instantiations with SKINNY can be efficient alternatives to Romulus-H; our modes provide hashing to Romulus (AEAD) with zero memory overhead.

Designing DBL modes with a small memory size is challenging. We first observe that many existing DBL modes call the underlying BC at least twice, and the results of the first BC call (or the value after the feed-forward) are stored on the memory, which will be used as a half of the compression function output after the second BC call. Our idea is to save such a memory. Namely, we use the result of the first BC call to compute an input to the second BC call, as shown in Fig. 2.[2] In this way, all the memory is always actively used to compute

[2] Linear dependency between the message and the key does not degrade security. Intuitively, previous block-cipher's output spreads to next block-cipher's key. This makes two keys different, and block-cipher's outputs become different random strings.

both BC calls, which enables us to reduce the memory size to $n + k$ bits. As a natural consequence of serialization, the new CF cannot run these consecutive BCs in parallel (see "Parallel" in Table 1), however, that has a negligible impact on low-area implementations.

Due to the strictly restricted memory size, we adopt the same approach as Özen-Stam and Naito that use a vulnerable CF [23,32], which actually allows an attacker to easily find a preimage of the CF. This implies that there exists a preimage attack on HF by using the meet-in-the-middle approach with $O(2^n)$ computational cost, though the digest size is $2n$ bits. As required in NIST LWC, not all practical usage require higher security for the preimage resistance than the collision resistance.[3] EXEX-NI and EXEX-I are suitable for such demand. We prove the security of EXEX-NI with respect to indifferentiability up to $n - \log n$ bits, which ensures that EXEX-NI resists the length-extension attacks. Recall that NIST LWC requires 112-bit security. This can be satisfied by using a 128-bit BC or a 128-bit TBC, say AES or SKINNY-128, even by considering the security loss of $\log n$ bits. We believe that EXEX-NI is an attractive design, especially as an alternative to the MDPH mode in Romulus-H.

As mentioned above, our CF is invertible. In contrast, to design an indifferentiable HF, we need a non-invertible function somewhere in the computation. In EXEX-NI, we fill this gap by using Coron et al.'s NMAC hash [8]: we add a special finalization function with 2 BC calls, making the finalization function non-invertible with a constant-time overhead. EXEX-NI requires an underlying BC to support the key size $k \geq 2n$, and the requirement can be satisfied by many existing BC designs, e.g., by AES-256 and SKINNY-128-256.

Although it is required in NIST LWC, we observe that resisting the length-extension attack may be unnecessary in practice. This is because all the NIST LWC candidates support an AEAD scheme, thus keyed computations such as MACs can be done by using the AEAD scheme. This motivates us to consider relaxing the security goal to the collision resistance rather than the indifferentiability. EXEX-I is a design for this purpose. EXEX-I does not require the finalization function, which reduces the number of BC calls by 2. This has a significant impact on the performance for short messages. Moreover, the requirement of the key size of the underlying BC is relaxed compared to EXEX-NI.

As shown in Fig. 2, we prove the security of EXEX-NI and EXEX-I by assuming that some part of the key state can be updated by using any linear functions π_1 and π_2, which allows us interesting optimization regarding on-the-fly key scheduling (see "Omit KSF^{-1}" in Table 1). This idea was first introduced by Naito et al. [26] and known to reduce the hardware cost when a key schedule function (and a tweak schedule function) of the underlying BC is a state-wise linear update, which is particularly useful when the underlying BC is SKINNY. In short, by setting π_1 and π_2 to the key schedule function (KSF), the updated key state during the computation of BC can immediately be used to compute the next BC without applying the KSF^{-1}.

[3] HMAC [28] and Hash-then-MAC [15] are example use-cases whose security is reduced to coll of the hashing scheme, thus does not require higher security level than coll.

Table 2. Comparison between EXEX and the sponge construction. A check mark ✓ shows that the target mode is advantageous.

Modes	Sponge	EXEX
Base primitive	Permutation	BC or TBC
Memory size for modes	$n + k$	$n + k$
Number of primitive calls	1	2
Construction simplicity	✓	—
Proof simplicity	✓	—
Memory size with TI	—	✓
Backward compatibility with AES	—	✓

We finally compare the hardware performances of EXEX-NI, EXEX-I, and Romulus-H by instantiating them with SKINNY-128-384 and implementing them with the same design policy. Thanks to the smaller memory size and the optimized tweakey-schedule implementation, EXEX-NI and EXEX-I achieved the circuit-area reduction by 2,000+ GE, yielding the total areas being smaller than 70% of that of the Romulus-H.

Related Work. It is well-known that permutation-based schemes (the sponge construction) provide an excellent hardware performance. Although BC-based and TBC-based hashing schemes are important with respect to the design diversity, it is still interesting to compare the performance of those schemes.

Memory sizes for the sponge construction and EXEX are the same to achieve the same rate under the same security level. The sponge construction is advantageous with respect to the number of primitive calls, design simplicity, and proof simplicity, though the number of primitive calls is a low-priority criterion for small implementations. EXEX is advantageous with respect to other metrics. First, TBC-based designs are advantageous with masking countermeasures against side-channel attack, as discussed in [25]. Second, it has backward compatibility with AES. Many microprocessors have AES accelerators and EXEX provides efficient hashing to them. The comparison is summarized in Table 2. Overall, EXEX is competitive with the key performance metric memory size and offers new options for implementers depending on the criteria of their choice.

Outline. Section 2 introduces notations and fundamentals. Section 3 shows our general approach to obtain DBL HF only with $n + k$-bit memory. Section 4 shows our higher-security variant EXEX-NI that satisfies the requirements in NIST LWC, followed by its proof in Sect. 5. Section 6 shows our rigorously optimized variant EXEX-I that compromises the security goal to collision resistance but provides better performance, particularly for short messages. Finally, we make a hardware performance comparison by implementing EXEX-NI, EXEX-I, and Romulus-H instantiated with SKINNY-128-384 in Sect. 7. Section 8 is the conclusion.

2 Preliminaries

Notation. Let $\{0,1\}^*$ be the set of all bit strings. Let λ be an empty string, and $\emptyset$ an empty set. For an integer $n \geq 0$, $\{0,1\}^n$ be the set of all n-bit strings, and $(\{0,1\}^n)^*$ be the set of all strings whose bit lengths are multiples of n. For an integer $i > 0$, let $[i]$ be the set of positive integers less than or equal to i. For an $m\ell$-bit string M, we write its partition into m-bit strings as $(M_1, M_2, \ldots, M_\ell) \xleftarrow{m} M$. For integers r, s with $0 \leq s \leq r$ and an r-bit string X, the most (resp. least) significant s bits of X is denoted by $[X]^s$ (resp. $[X]_s$). For a bit string Y, $X \leftarrow Y$ means that Y is assigned to X. $X \xleftarrow{\$} \mathcal{X}$ means that an element is sampled uniformly at random from a finite set $\mathcal{X}$ and is assigned to X. $\mathcal{Y} \leftarrow \mathcal{X}$ means that a finite set $\mathcal{X}$ is assigned to $\mathcal{Y}$, and $\mathcal{Y} \xleftarrow{\cup} \mathcal{X}$ means that $\mathcal{Y} \leftarrow \mathcal{X} \cup \mathcal{Y}$.

Security Definition of Hash Function. Our proofs are given in the ideal cipher model. For positive integers k and n, let E be (an encryption function of) a BC having a k-bit key and an n-bit plaintext block, which is a set of n-bit permutations indexed by keys. The decryption function of E is denoted by $D : \{0,1\}^k \times \{0,1\}^n \to \{0,1\}^n$. $\mathsf{BC}(k,n)$ denotes the set of all BCs with k-bit keys and n-bit blocks. An ideal cipher is defined as $E \xleftarrow{\$} \mathsf{BC}(k,n)$. In the ideal cipher model, an adversary has access to E and D.

Let $\mathsf{H}^E : \{0,1\}^* \to \{0,1\}^{2n}$ be a DBL hash function using a BC E. We define security notions for H^E.

Preimage Security. In the security game, a computationally unbounded adversary $\mathbf{A}$ is given oracle access to (E, D), where $E \xleftarrow{\$} \mathsf{BC}(k,n)$. The goal of $\mathbf{A}$ is to find a massage M of a given hash value H. The advantage function of an adversary $\mathbf{A}$ is defined as $\mathsf{Adv}^{\mathsf{pre}}_{\mathsf{H},H}(\mathbf{A}) = \mathsf{Pr}\left[\mathsf{H}^E(M) = H : M \leftarrow \mathbf{A}^{E,D}(H)\right]$, where the probabilities are taken over $\mathbf{A}$, H, and E.

Collision Security. In the security game, a computationally unbounded adversary $\mathbf{A}$ is given oracle access to (E, D), where $E \xleftarrow{\$} \mathsf{BC}(k,n)$. The goal of $\mathbf{A}$ is to find a pair of messages M and M' such that the hash values are equal. The advantage function of an adversary $\mathbf{A}$ is defined as $\mathsf{Adv}^{\mathsf{coll}}_{\mathsf{H}}(\mathbf{A}) = \mathsf{Pr}\left[\mathsf{H}^E(M) = \mathsf{H}^E(M') : (M, M') \leftarrow \mathbf{A}^{E,D}, M \neq M'\right]$, where the probabilities are taken over $\mathbf{A}$ and E.

Indifferentiability from a Random Oracle. The indifferentiability of H^E from a random oracle is indistinguishability between H^E (in the ideal cipher model) and a random oracle. $\mathsf{Func}(*, 2n)$ denotes the set of all functions from $\{0,1\}^*$ to $\{0,1\}^{2n}$, and a random oracle is defined as $\mathcal{RO} \xleftarrow{\$} \mathsf{Func}(*, 2n)$.

In the security game, an adversary $\mathbf{A}$ tries to distinguish a real world from an ideal world. $\mathbf{A}$ has access to a hash oracle L, an encryption oracle R_E, and a decryption oracle R_D. In the real world, these oracles are $(L, R_E, R_D) = (\mathsf{H}^E, E, D)$, where $E \xleftarrow{\$} \mathsf{BC}(k,n)$. In the ideal world, these oracles are $(L, R_E, R_D) = (\mathcal{RO}, \mathsf{S}_E^{\mathcal{RO}}, \mathsf{S}_D^{\mathcal{RO}})$, where $\mathcal{RO} \xleftarrow{\$} \mathsf{Func}(*, 2n)$, and $\mathsf{S}_E^{\mathcal{RO}}$ and

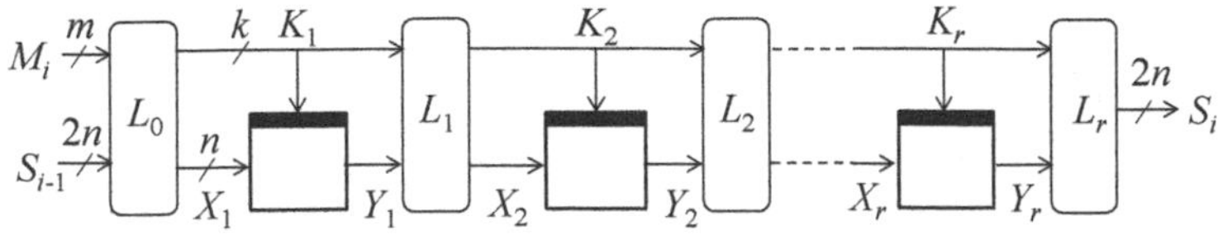

Fig. 3. GLMCF^E: a general construction for low-memory compression function.

$\mathsf{S}_D^{\mathcal{RO}}$ are simulators with access to $\mathcal{RO}$. After the interaction, **A** outputs a decision bit in $\{0,1\}$. An output of an adversary **A** with access to oracles L, R_E, R_D is denoted by $\mathbf{A}^{L,R_E,R_D}$. For a simulator $\mathsf{S}^{\mathcal{RO}} = (\mathsf{S}_E^{\mathcal{RO}}, \mathsf{S}_D^{\mathcal{RO}})$, the advantage function of an adversary **A** is defined as $\mathsf{Adv}_{\mathsf{H},\mathsf{S}}^{\mathsf{indiff}}(\mathbf{A}) = \Pr\left[\mathbf{A}^{\mathsf{H}^E,E,D} = 1\right] - \Pr\left[\mathbf{A}^{\mathcal{RO},\mathsf{S}_E^{\mathcal{RO}},\mathsf{S}_D^{\mathcal{RO}}} = 1\right]$, where the probabilities are taken over **A**, E, $\mathcal{RO}$, and S. H^E is indifferentiable from a random oracle if for any adversary **A**, there exists a simulator S such that the advantage function is upper-bounded by a negligible probability. In this paper, we call queries to L, R_E, and R_D hash queries, encryption queries, and decryption queries, respectively.

3 Conditions for Secure Low Memory DBL Hash Designs

In this section, we approach to DBL hash functions with the smallest memory size, which uses a block cipher $E : \{0,1\}^k \times \{0,1\}^n \to \{0,1\}^n$ and uses a memory of $k+n$ bits. We first introduce a generic framework to construct a CF in Sect. 3.1. We then derive conditions for parameters to resist collision attacks in Sect. 3.2. We show that such a CF is always invertible, thus requires additional effort to be indifferentiable in Sect. 3.3. Finally, a generic framework to construct a HF is introduced in Sect. 3.4.

3.1 Generic Construction of Low-Memory DBLCF

To design a DBL hash function with a $(k+n)$-bit memory, we need to design a CF with a $(k+n)$-bit memory. In this subsection, we introduce GLMCF^E: a generic construction of the low-memory CF with a block cipher E, which is depicted in Fig. 3.

Let m be the bit-length of a message block. GLMCF^E takes as input a $2n$-bit state value S_{i-1} and an m-bit message M_i, and generates a $2n$-bit output S_i. GLMCF^E calls a BC with n-bit block and a k-bit key, denoted by E. E can be called multiple times even under the restriction of $(k+n)$-bit memory if all E calls are sequentially processed. At this stage, we do not fix the number of calls of E, and let r be this number. Since E uses the entire $k+n$ bits, we cannot carry anything over the E call. This restricts the design of GLMCF^E to be an iteration of a linear function L_i and E. Namely, we first apply a linear function L_0 to map a $(2n+m)$-bit state to a $(k+n)$-bit state. Then, the state is updated to another $(k+n)$-bit state by E and linear function L_1. This is iterated r times

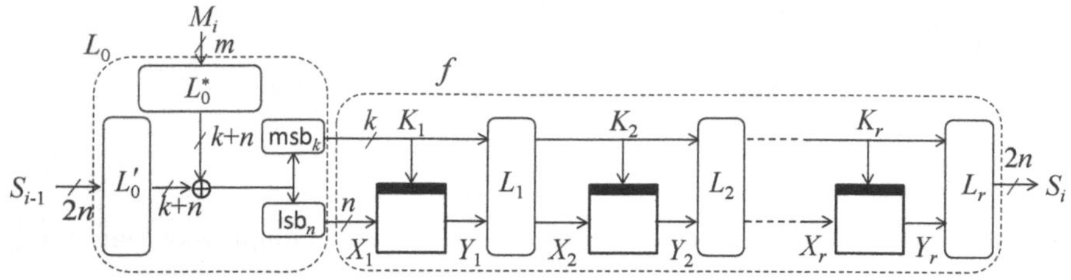

Fig. 4. Another formulation of GLMCF^E. msb_k (resp. lsb_n) returns the most (resp. least) significant k (resp. n) bits of the input.

to apply BC r times. Lastly, the $(k+n)$-bit state is transformed to $2n$-bit output by a linear function L_r. At this stage, we do not make any assumption on m, thus L_0 can be either an expanding or a contracting function and L_r can be its opposite.

The formal description is as follows. Let $L_0 : \{0,1\}^{2n} \times \{0,1\}^m \rightarrow \{0,1\}^k \times \{0,1\}^n$, $L_1 : \{0,1\}^k \times \{0,1\}^n \rightarrow \{0,1\}^k \times \{0,1\}^n, \ldots, L_{r-1} : \{0,1\}^k \times \{0,1\}^n \rightarrow \{0,1\}^k \times \{0,1\}^n$, and $L_r : \{0,1\}^k \times \{0,1\}^n \rightarrow \{0,1\}^{2n}$ be linear functions. We give the procedure of $\mathsf{GLMCF}^E : \{0,1\}^{2n} \times \{0,1\}^m \rightarrow \{0,1\}^{2n}$.

- $\mathsf{GLMCF}^E(S_{i-1}, M_i)$
  1. $(K_1, X_1) \leftarrow L_0(S_{i-1}, M_i)$
  2. **for** $j = 1, \ldots, r-1$ **do** $Y_j \leftarrow E(K_j, X_j)$; $(K_{j+1}, X_{j+1}) \leftarrow L_j(K_j, Y_j)$
  3. $Y_r \leftarrow E(K_r, X_r)$; $S_i \leftarrow L_r(K_r, Y_r)$; **return** S_i

3.2 Conditions of m, k, and n for n-bit Collision Resistance

Now we are lifting the CF to a HF. Suppose that a DBL HF is constructed by iteratively applying GLMCF^E, which is denoted by $i\mathsf{GLMCF}^E$. For sake of simplicity, an input message M is in $(\{0,1\}^m)^*$. Let IV be a $2n$-bit constant.

- $i\mathsf{GLMCF}^E(M)$
  1. $(M_1, M_2, \ldots, M_\ell) \xleftarrow{m} M$; $S_0 \leftarrow IV$
  2. **for** $i = 1, \ldots, \ell$ **do** $S_i \leftarrow \mathsf{GLMCF}^E(S_{i-1}, M_i)$
  3. **return** S_ℓ

First, the construction needs to satisfy $n \leq k$. In fact, if $n > k$, n-bit security cannot be ensured due to the birthday attack on the $(n+k)$-bit state.

Second, the construction needs to satisfy $k - n \geq m$. In fact, there is an attack that breaks the collision security on $i\mathsf{GLMCF}^E$ with $O(2^{(k+n-m)/2})$ complexity, which we discuss in this section. In this attack, we split the linear function L_0 in GLMCF^E into two linear functions $L'_0 : \{0,1\}^{2n} \rightarrow \{0,1\}^{k+n}$ and $L^*_0 : \{0,1\}^m \rightarrow \{0,1\}^{k+n}$ that satisfy $L_0(S_{i-1}, M_i) = L'_0(S_{i-1}) \oplus L^*_0(M_i)$. L^*_0 must be injective, otherwise one can trivially find a collision. The compression function with some formulation is given in Fig. 4, where $f : \{0,1\}^{n+k} \rightarrow \{0,1\}^{2n}$ is a composed function covering from the first BC to the last linear function L_r. The security bound is given in the following lemma.

Lemma 1. *Let f be an ideal function. For any $S_i \in \{0,1\}^{2n}$, there exists an adversary* $\mathbf{A}$ *making* $Q \cdot \max\{1, \lceil n/m \rceil\}$ *queries to* f *such that* $\mathsf{Adv}^{\mathsf{coll}}_{i\mathsf{GLMCF}}(\mathbf{A}) = \Omega\left(\frac{Q^2}{2^{k+n-m}}\right)$.

Proof. We define an adversary $\mathbf{A}$ that finds a collision of $i\mathsf{GLMCF}^E$ where f is ideal. Let $u := \lceil n/m \rceil$.

1. For $j = 1, \ldots, Q$ do the following steps.
   (a) Select a j-th message $(M_1^{(j)} \| \cdots \| M_u^{(j)})$ that is distinct from all previous messages $(M_1^{(1)} \| \cdots \| M_u^{(1)}), \ldots, (M_1^{(j-1)} \| \cdots \| M_u^{(j-1)})$.
   (b) Calculate the u-th state denoted by $S_u^{(j)}$ for the message $(M_1^{(j)} \| \cdots \| M_u^{(j)})$ by making queries to f.
   (c) For each $j' \in [j-1]$, check if there exist message blocks $M_{u+1}^{(j)}$ and $M_{u+1}^{(j')}$ such that $L'_0(S_u^{(j)}) \oplus L^*_0(M_{u+1}^{(j)}) = L'_0(S_u^{(j')}) \oplus L^*_0(M_{u+1}^{(j')})$ which causes a collision at the $(u+1)$-th CF call.
   (d) If such an index j' exists then $M \leftarrow (M_1^{(j)} \| \cdots \| M_u^{(j)} \| M_{u+1}^{(j)})$, $M' \leftarrow (M_1^{(j')} \| \cdots \| M_u^{(j')} \| M_{u+1}^{(j')})$, and go to Step 3.
2. Choose messages $M \xleftarrow{\$} \{0,1\}^m$ and $M' \xleftarrow{\$} \{0,1\}^m$.
3. Return (M, M').

The number of choices of the XOR value $L^*_0(M_{u+1}^{(j)}) \oplus L^*_0(M_{u+1}^{(j')})$ is 2^m. Hence, for each pair (j, j'), the probability that there exist message blocks $M_{u+1}^{(j)}$ and $M_{u+1}^{(j')}$ such that $L'_0(S_u^{(j)}) \oplus L^*_0(M_{u+1}^{(j)}) = L'_0(S_u^{(j')}) \oplus L^*_0(M_{u+1}^{(j')})$ is $\Omega(1/2^{k+n-m})$. By summing the probability for each pair, we have $\mathsf{Adv}^{\mathsf{coll}}_{i\mathsf{GLMCF}^E}(\mathbf{A}) = \Omega(Q^2/2^{k+n-m})$. □

To ensure n-bit security against the collision attack, $k + n - m \geq 2n$, which results in $k - n \geq m$. This implies that m can take any value between $k - n$ and 1. The memory size is $k+n$ bits for any m, while the number of bits processed in each invocation of GLMCF^E decreases when m becomes small. In the rest of the paper, we fix $k - n = m$, which is the optimal choice in terms of the performance under the restriction of the $(k+n)$-bit memory.

3.3 Conditions for Indifferentiability: Invertibility of GLMCF

The conditions in Sect. 3.2 were derived for the collision resistance, which is insufficient for the indifferentiability (to ensure resistance against length-extension attacks required by NIST). Towards indifferentiable constructions, we first show that one can break the preimage security of GLMCF^E, where E is an ideal cipher.

Lemma 2. *Fix r. For any $S_i \in \{0,1\}^{2n}$, there exists an adversary* $\mathbf{A}$ *making r queries such that* $\mathsf{Adv}^{\mathsf{pre}}_{\mathsf{GLMCF}^E, S_i}(\mathbf{A}) = 1$.

Proof. We define an adversary $\mathbf{A}$ that finds a preimage of a value S_i.

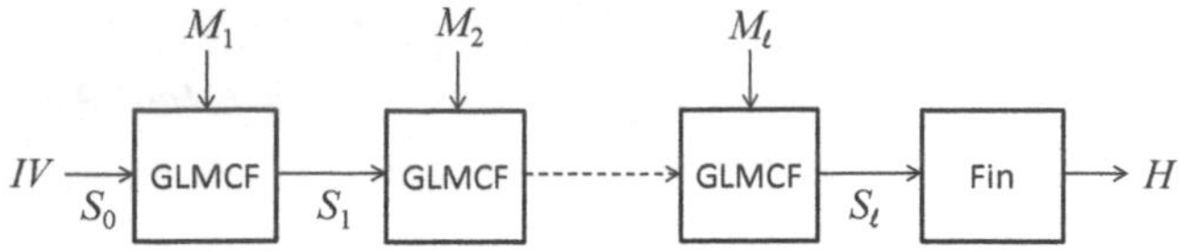

Fig. 5. Hash function GLMHF.

1. Find (K_r, Y_r) s.t. $S_i = L_r(K_r, Y_r)$; $X_r \leftarrow D(K_r, Y_r)$
2. **for** $j = r-1, \ldots, 1$ **do**
   Find (K_j, Y_j) s.t. $(K_{j+1}, X_{j+1}) = L_j(K_j, Y_j)$; $X_j \leftarrow D(K_j, Y_j)$
3. Find (S_{i-1}, M_i) s.t. $(K_1, X_1) = L_0(S_{i-1}, M_i)$; Return (S_{i-1}, M_i)

Since $L_0, L_1, \ldots, L_r$ are linear functions, for each $j = 0, 1, \ldots, r$, given an output of L_j, one can easily find the input. Hence, the adversary finds a preimage (M_i, S_{i-1}) by r queries. □

This analysis shows that only with $(k+n)$-bit memory satisfying $k - n = m$, GLMCF^E is easily invertible. To obtain an indifferentiable HF, we need a non-invertible part somewhere in HF.

3.4 Generic Construction of Low Memory DBL HF

The analysis in Sect. 3.3 motivates us to introduce a non-invertible finalization function $\mathsf{Fin} : \{0,1\}^{2n} \rightarrow \{0,1\}^{2n}$. Here, we define $\mathsf{GLMHF} : \{0,1\}^* \rightarrow \{0,1\}^{2n}$, a generic construction of low memory hash function using the compression function GLMCF^E and a finalization function Fin. Let $\mathsf{pad} : \{0,1\}^* \rightarrow (\{0,1\}^m)^*$ be an injective padding function.

- $\mathsf{GLMHF}^{E,\mathsf{Fin}}(M)$
  1. $(M_1, M_2, \ldots, M_\ell) \xleftarrow{m} \mathsf{pad}(M)$; $S_0 \leftarrow IV$
  2. **for** $i = 1, \ldots, \ell$ **do** $S_i \leftarrow \mathsf{GLMCF}^E(S_{i-1}, M_i)$
  3. $H \leftarrow \mathsf{Fin}(S_\ell)$; **return** H

Note that IV is a $2n$-bit constant. Figure 5 shows the structure of GLMHF. In the next section, we propose EXEX-NI by specifying details in GLMHF.

4 EXEX-NI: Low Memory Indifferentiable DBL HF

In this section, we specify every details of the general framework introduced in Sect. 3. In particular, a compression function EXEX and our indifferentiable DBF mode EXEX-NI are defined in Sect 4.1. An overview of its indifferentiability is given in Sect. 4.2 and Sect. 4.3.

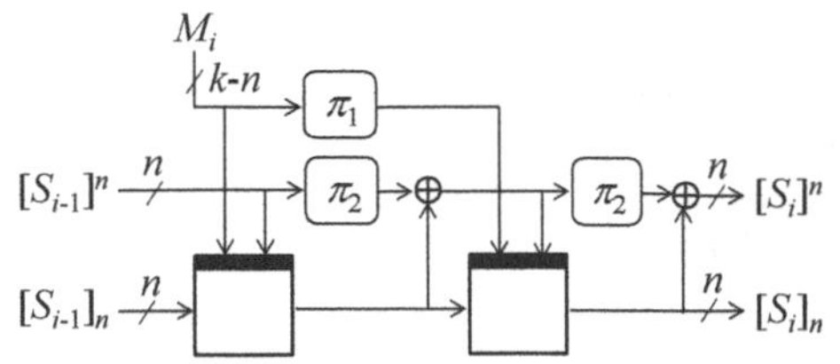

Fig. 6. Compression function EXEX. The figure shows the structure of the CF block $S_{i-1} \xrightarrow{M_i} S_i$ in the proof of Theorem 1.

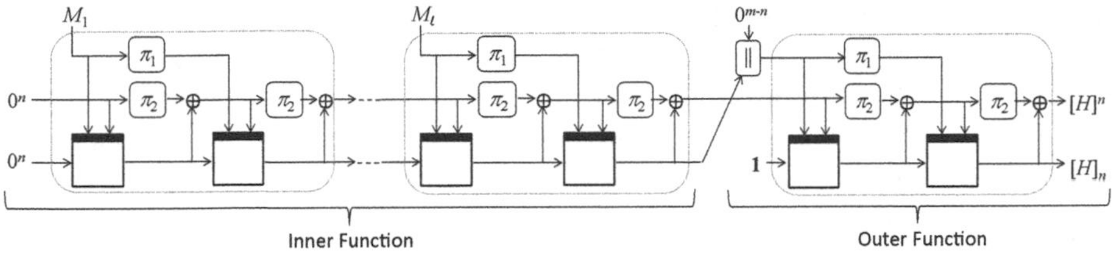

Fig. 7. Hash function EXEX-NI. The inner function of this figure shows the structure of the path $0^{2n} \xrightarrow{M_1 \| M_2 \| \cdots \| M_\ell} S_\ell$ in the proof of Theorem 1.

4.1 Specifications of EXEX and EXEX-NI

To realize our modes using GLMCF^E, we should specify the number of E calls r and the linear functions $L_0, \ldots, L_r$. Choosing the same linear function for L_0 to L_{r-1} is a reasonable decision considering implementation efficiency. In each invocation of GLMCF^E, the $2n$-bit state (chaining values) must be updated non-linearly. For this purpose, we XOR BC's output to the least significant n bits of the key state. To provide $2n$-bit entropy from BC's output, we set $r = 2$.[4]

We can prove security only with the above configuration, but in addition, we assume that the $(k-n)$-bit and the remaining n-bit key states are independently updated by any linear function π_1 and π_2. As shown by Naito et al. [26], a proof over π_1 and π_2 provides a certain optimization of the memory size when a key (and a tweak) schedule function of E is a state-wise linear update, which is particularly useful for SKINNY. The intuition behind is that k bits of memory for the key state is updated by a key schedule function inside E, thus starting the next E with the state after the key schedule function is more efficient. Indeed, if the next E takes as input the key state before the key schedule function, the k bits of memory must be reproduced by computing the inverse of the key schedule function. We will discuss this optimization later in Sect. 7. Note that π_1 and π_2

[4] For an EXEX-based hash function with $r = 1$ (single BC call), one can easily found a collision with $O(2^{n/2})$ complexity: Choosing distinct $2^{n/2}$ single-block messages, a collision of the BC outputs occurs with non-negligible probability, yielding a collision on the internal state. Note that when the linear layers of GLMCF^E are arbitrary, attacking GLMCF^E with $r = 1$ is non-trivial and an open problem.

can also be the identity map, hence if E does not have such a structure, we use the identity map to avoid having extra computations.

EXEX^E uses a BC $E : \{0,1\}^k \times \{0,1\}^n \to \{0,1\}^n$ with $k > n$. Let $m = k - n$. The formal definition of $\mathsf{EXEX}^E : \{0,1\}^{2n} \times \{0,1\}^m \to \{0,1\}^{2n}$ is given below, which is also depicted in Fig. 6.

- $\mathsf{EXEX}^E(S_{i-1}, M_i)$:
  1. $Y \leftarrow E(M_i \| [S_{i-1}]^n, [S_{i-1}]_n)$; $K \leftarrow \pi_1(M_i) \| (\pi_2([S_{i-1}]^n) \oplus Y)$;
  2. $[S_i]_n \leftarrow E(K, Y)$; $[S_i]^n \leftarrow \pi_2([K]_n) \oplus [S_i]_n$; return S_i

We next define a $\mathsf{EXEX\text{-}NI} : \{0,1\}^* \to \{0,1\}^{2n}$. Let $\mathsf{pad} : \{0,1\}^* \to (\{0,1\}^m)^*$ be an injective padding function, e.g., one-zero padding $\mathsf{pad}(M) = M \| 10^w$ where $w = m - 1 - |M| \bmod m$. We realize Fin in GLMHF by reusing EXEX to save the memory size. The nested-iterated construction enables us to achieve it. Let $\mathbf{i}$ be an n-bit representation of a positive integer i, e.g., $\mathbf{1} = 0^{n-1}1$. The definition is given below, which is also depicted in Fig. 7.

- $\mathsf{EXEX\text{-}NI}^E(M)$:
  1. $S_0 \leftarrow 0^{2n}$; $M_1, M_2, \cdots, M_\ell \xleftarrow{m} \mathsf{pad}(M)$
  2. for $i = 1, \ldots, \ell$ do $S_i \leftarrow \mathsf{EXEX}^E(S_{i-1}, M_i)$ // Inner Function
  3. $H \leftarrow \mathsf{EXEX}^E([S_\ell]^n \| \mathbf{1}, 0^{m-n} \| [S_\ell]_n)$ // Outer Function
  4. return H

4.2 Indifferentiability of EXEX-NI

We give an upper-bound of the indifferentiability of EXEX-NI below.

Theorem 1. *Let μ be any positive integer. There exists a simulator S such that for any adversary $\mathbf{A}$ running in time t and making q hash queries with σ BC calls in total and p encryption or decryption queries,*

$$\mathsf{Adv}^{\mathsf{indiff}}_{\mathsf{EXEX\text{-}NI},\mathsf{S}}(\mathbf{A}) \leq 2^{n+2} \cdot \binom{3Q}{\mu} \cdot \left(\frac{1}{2^n - 3Q}\right)^{\mu} + \frac{6\mu Q + 19Q}{2^n - 3Q} + \frac{22Q^2}{(2^n - 3Q)^2},$$

where $Q = \sigma + p$. S runs in time $t + O(p)$ and makes at most p queries.

We next study the upper-bound.

- Putting $\mu = n$ and using Stirling's approximation ($x! \geq (x/e)^x$ for any x), we have $\mathsf{Adv}^{\mathsf{indiff}}_{\mathsf{EXEX\text{-}NI},\mathsf{S}}(\mathbf{A}) \leq 4 \cdot \left(\frac{3eQ}{n(2^n - 2Q)}\right)^n + \frac{6nQ + 19Q}{2^n - 3Q} + \frac{22Q^2}{(2^n - 3Q)^2}$. The upper-bound ensures that EXEX-NI is indifferentiable from a random oracle up to $O(2^n/n)$ query complexity.
- Consider a BC with $n = 128$. In this case, putting $\mu = 17$ and using Stirling's approximation, $\mathsf{Adv}^{\mathsf{indiff}}_{\mathsf{EXEX\text{-}NI},\mathsf{S}}(\mathbf{A}) \leq \left(\frac{97Q}{2^{128} - 3Q}\right)^{17} + \frac{121Q}{2^{128} - 3Q} + \frac{22Q^2}{(2^{128} - 3Q)^2}$. The upper-bound is less than $1/2$ as long as $Q \leq 2^{118}$. Thus, EXEX-NI is indifferentiable from a random oracle up to 2^{118} query complexity.

4.3 Overview of the Proof of Theorem 1

We briefly describe the proof of Theorem 1 along with some definitions. We give the full proof in Sect. 5. The goal of this proof is to construct a simulator $\mathsf{S} = (\mathsf{S}_E, \mathsf{S}_D)$ such that the real-world oracles are indistinguishable from the ideal-world oracles up to $O(2^n/n)$ query complexity. The real-world oracles are $(L, R_E, R_D) = (\mathsf{EXEX\text{-}NI}^E, E, D)$, and the ideal-world oracles are $(L, R_E, R_D) = (\mathcal{RO}, \mathsf{S}_E^{\mathcal{RO}}, \mathsf{S}_D^{\mathcal{RO}})$.

Firstly, we give several definitions to explain an outline of our simulator.

Definition 1 (query-response of R_E/R_D). *An encryption (resp. decryption) query is denoted by $(K, X) \in \{0,1\}^k \times \{0,1\}^n$ (resp. $(K, Y) \in \{0,1\}^k \times \{0,1\}^n$) and the response is denoted by $Y \in \{0,1\}^n$ (resp. $X \in \{0,1\}^n$). Hence, $Y = R_E(K, X)$ and $X = R_D(K, Y)$. Let $\mathcal{L}_{\mathsf{qr}}$ be a set of tuples (K, X, Y) of R_E or R_D. A tuple in $\mathcal{L}_{\mathsf{qr}}$ is called R block.*

Definition 2 (block). *A CF block is a tuple (S_{i-1}, M_i, S_i) which is defined by two R blocks with the relation $S_i = \mathsf{EXEX}^{R_E}(S_{i-1}, M_i)$. The CF block is denoted by $S_{i-1} \xrightarrow{M_i} S_i$ (see Fig. 6). $\mathcal{L}_{\mathsf{block}}$ is a set of all CF blocks obtained from $\mathcal{L}_{\mathsf{qr}}$.*

Definition 3 (Path). *A path is a CF block or a concatenation of CF blocks which start from the initial value 0^{2n}. For a sequence of CF blocks $0^{2n} \xrightarrow{M_1} S_1, S_1 \xrightarrow{M_2} S_2, \dots, S_{\ell-1} \xrightarrow{M_\ell} S_\ell$, we denote the concatenation by $0^{2n} \xrightarrow{M_1\|M_2\|\cdots\|M_\ell} S_\ell$. Hence, the path represents the inner function of $\mathsf{EXEX\text{-}NI}^{R_E}(M_1\|M_2\|\cdots\|M_\ell)$ (see Fig. 7). $\mathcal{L}_{\mathsf{path}}$ is a set of all paths obtained from $\mathcal{L}_{\mathsf{block}}$.*

Definition 4. *For a path $0^{2n} \xrightarrow{M} S$ and an input (K, X) to R_E, if (K, X) is the first R block at the next CF block, i.e., $S = [K]_n\|X$, then the relation is denoted by $S \overset{in}{\rightsquigarrow} (K, X)$. If (K, X) is the input of the first R block at the outer function connected with the path $0^{2n} \xrightarrow{M} S$, i.e., $[K]_{2n} = [S]_n\|[S]^n$, $X = \mathbf{1}$, and $[K]^{m-n} = 0^{m-n}$, then the relation is denoted by $S \overset{out}{\rightsquigarrow} (K, X)$. We abuse the notation for a CF block $S' \xrightarrow{M'} H$, i.e., if $[S']_n = \mathbf{1}$, $S = [S']^n\|[M']_n$, and $[M']^{m-n} = 0^{m-n}$ then the relation is denoted by $S \overset{out}{\rightsquigarrow} (S', M')$.*

We next specify a relation between L and R_E in the real world. In the real world, for each query M, the response $L(M)$ is defined as $L(M) = \mathsf{EXEX\text{-}NI}^{R_E}(M)$ where $R_E = E$, thus the following relation is satisfied.

$$\forall\left(0^{2n} \xrightarrow{M} S\right) \in \mathcal{L}_{\mathsf{path}}, \left(S' \xrightarrow{M'} H\right) \in \mathcal{L}_{\mathsf{block}}$$
$$\text{s.t. } S \overset{out}{\rightsquigarrow} (S', M') : L(M) = H. \qquad (1)$$

On the other hand, in the ideal world, $L = \mathcal{RO}$ is a monolithic function. We thus need to construct a simulator $\mathsf{S}^{\mathcal{RO}} = (\mathsf{S}_E^{\mathcal{RO}}, \mathsf{S}_D^{\mathcal{RO}})$ so that Eq. (1) is satisfied and the simulator behaves like an ideal cipher.

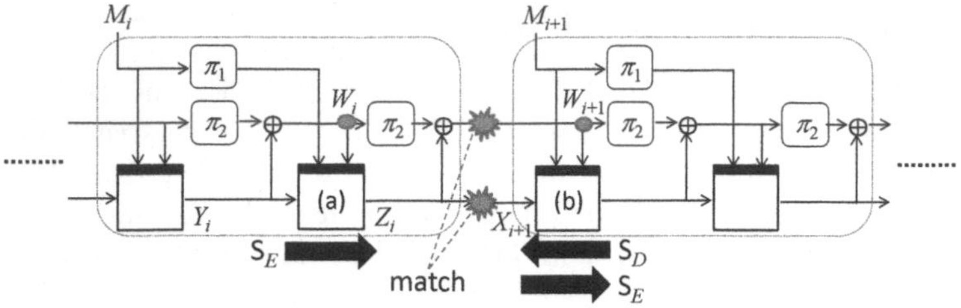

Fig. 8. Collision event E1. The R block (a) (resp. (b)) is defined by S_E (resp. S_E or S_D). The R block (b) by S_E is defined before the R block (a).

We explain an outline of our simulator. For each query to $\mathsf{S}_E/\mathsf{S}_D$, to behave like an ideal cipher, the response is defined by lazy sampling.[5] In addition, in order to ensure the relation in Eq. (1), the simulator keeps paths in a table $\mathcal{T}_{path}$ that are constructed from R blocks. Specifically, for each tuple (K, X, Y) defined by S_E, if there exists a path $\left(0^{2n} \xrightarrow{M'} S'\right) \in \mathcal{T}_{path}$ such that $S' \overset{in}{\rightsquigarrow} (K, X)$, then a new path $\left(0^{2n} \xrightarrow{M} S\right)$ is added to $\mathcal{T}_{path}$, which is defined by appending the CF block $\left(S' \xrightarrow{M^*} S\right)$ having the R block (K, X, Y) to $\left(0^{2n} \xrightarrow{M'} S'\right)$, where $M = M' \| M^*$. Since the new path represents an inner function with the input M, S_E defines a CF block corresponding to the outer function by using $\mathcal{RO}(M)$. That ensures the relation in Eq. (1) as long as the following events do not occur.

E1: For a path $\left(0^{2n} \xrightarrow{M} S\right) \in \mathcal{L}_{\mathsf{path}}$, there exists an i-th CF block defined by S_E such that the $(i+1)$-th CF block is defined by S_D or defined by S_E before the i-th CF block. The collision event is depicted in Fig. 8. In this event, if the CF blocks from the $(i+2)$-th to the last (in the outer function) are already defined, then S_E cannot obtain the message M when defining the last CF block. Thus, Eq. (1) cannot be satisfied.

E2: When the path $\left(0^{2n} \xrightarrow{M} S\right) \in \mathcal{L}_{\mathsf{path}}$ is defined, the last CF block (in the outer function) is already defined. In this event, S_E cannot obtain the message M when defining the last CF block. Thus, Eq. (1) cannot be satisfied.

E3: There exist collision paths $\left(0^{2n} \xrightarrow{M} S\right), \left(0^{2n} \xrightarrow{M^\dagger} S^\dagger\right) \in \mathcal{L}_{\mathsf{path}}$ such that $S = S^\dagger$. In this case, $\mathcal{RO}(M) \neq \mathcal{RO}(M^\dagger)$ is satisfied with a high probability (on the other hand, $\mathsf{EXEX\text{-}NI}^E(M) = \mathsf{EXEX\text{-}NI}^E(M^\dagger)$ is satisfied in the real world). In this event, Eq. (1) cannot be satisfied.

Assume that the above events do not occur. By $\neg$E1, for any path $\left(0^{2n} \xrightarrow{M} S\right)$, the internal CF blocks are defined in order from the first to the last. Since

[5] For a query (K, X) (resp. (K, Y)) to S_E (resp. S_D), the response Y (resp. X) is chosen uniformly at random from $\{0, 1\}^n$ excluding previous ciphertext (resp. plaintext) blocks associated with the key K.

no collision path exists by $\neg$E3, S can obtain the message M leading to S. By $\neg$E2, the path is defined before the R block in the outer function, thus the simulator can define the R block by using $\mathcal{RO}(M)$ so that Eq. (1) is satisfied. Thus, we have the indifferentiable bound by summing the upper-bounds of the probabilities for these events.

First, we analyze the event E1 by using Fig. 8. If the R block (b) defined by S_D before (a), then using the multi-collision technique for W_i, the number of the R block (b) resulting in the W_i value can be n, that is, the number of candidates for X_{i+1} is at most n. Thus, for each R block (a), the probability that E1 occurs is at most $O(n/2^n)$. Similarly, if the R block (b) is defined by S_D after (a), then using the multi-collision technique for W_{i+1}, for each R block (b), the probability that E1 occurs is at most $O(n/2^n)$. If the R block (b) is defined by S_E before (a), then by the randomnesses of Y_i and Z_i, the probability that the R block (a) connects with one of candidates for the R block (b) is $O(Q/2^{2n})$. Using the upper-bounds, we have $\Pr[\mathsf{E1}] \leq O(nQ/2^n)$.

Second, we analyze E2. For each path $\left(0^{2n} \xrightarrow{M} S\right) \in \mathcal{L}_{\mathsf{path}}$, since S is a $2n$-bit (almost) random value by two R blocks, the probability that S hits some R block (in the outer function) is at most $O(Q/2^{2n})$. Hence, we have $\Pr[\mathsf{E2}] \leq O(Q^2/2^{2n})$.

Third, we analyze E3. For a path $\left(0^{2n} \xrightarrow{M} S\right)$, since S is a $2n$-bit (almost) random value by two R blocks, the probability that there exists a collision path $\left(0^{2n} \xrightarrow{M^\dagger} S^\dagger\right)$ with $S = S^\dagger$ is at most $O(Q/2^{2n})$. Hence, we have $\Pr[\mathsf{E3}] \leq O(Q^2/2^{2n})$.

Finally, by these upper-bounds, we have the indifferentiable bound $O(nQ/2^n)$.

5 Proof of Theorem 1

In this proof, for the sake of simplicity, the padding function pad in EXEX-NI is omitted. Hence, an adversary **A** makes hash queries whose lengths are multiples of m. Since **A** can select any padding rule, this setting does not reduce the advantage of **A**.

This proof considers three games. Game 0 is the real world, Game 1 is defined later, and Game 2 is the ideal world. In each game, an adversary **A** interacts with three oracles (L, R_E, R_D). L is a hash oracle, R_E is an encryption oracle, and R_D is a decryption oracle.

In the following analysis, we use Definitions 1, 2, 3, and 4 in Subsect. 4.3.

5.1 Simulator

We define a simulator $\mathsf{S}^{\mathcal{RO}} = (\mathsf{S}_E^{\mathcal{RO}}, \mathsf{S}_D^{\mathcal{RO}})$, where $\mathsf{S}_E^{\mathcal{RO}} : \{0,1\}^k \times \{0,1\}^n \rightarrow \{0,1\}^n$ simulates an encryption oracle E, and $\mathsf{S}_D^{\mathcal{RO}} : \{0,1\}^k \times \{0,1\}^n \rightarrow \{0,1\}^n$ simulates a decryption oracle D. In the real world, for a hash query, the response is defined by using E via the EXEX-NI structure, thus the relation in Eq. (1) is

Algorithm 1. Simulator $\mathsf{S}^{\mathcal{RO}} = (\mathsf{S}_E^{\mathcal{RO}}, \mathsf{S}_D^{\mathcal{RO}})$

Simulator $\mathsf{S}_E^{\mathcal{RO}}(K, X)$

if $\mathsf{E}(K,X) \neq \lambda$ **then return** $\mathsf{E}(K,X)$
$Y \xleftarrow{\$} \{0,1\}^n \backslash \mathsf{E}(K,*)$; $\mathsf{E}(K,X) \leftarrow Y$; $\mathsf{D}(K,Y) \leftarrow X$
$X_2 \leftarrow Y$; $K_2 \leftarrow \pi_1([K]^m)\|(\pi_2([K]_n) \oplus Y)$
if $\mathsf{E}(K_2, X_2) = \lambda$ **then**
  $Y_2 \xleftarrow{\$} \{0,1\}^n \backslash \mathsf{E}(K_2,*)$; $\mathsf{E}(K_2,X_2) \leftarrow Y_2$; $\mathsf{D}(K_2,Y_2) \leftarrow X_2$
end if
$Y_2 \leftarrow \mathsf{E}(K_2, X_2)$; $Y_0 \leftarrow X$; $K_0 \leftarrow \pi_1^{-1}([K]^m)\|\pi_2^{-1}([K]_n \oplus X)$
if $\mathsf{D}(K_0, Y_0) = \lambda$ **then**
  $X_0 \xleftarrow{\$} \{0,1\}^n \backslash \mathsf{D}(K_0,*)$; $\mathsf{E}(K_0,X_0) \leftarrow Y_0$; $\mathsf{D}(K_0,Y_0) \leftarrow X_0$
end if
if $\exists\left(0^{2n} \xrightarrow{M'} S'\right) \in \mathcal{T}_{path}$ s.t. $S' \overset{in}{\rightsquigarrow} (K,X)$ **then**
  $M \leftarrow M'\|[K]^m$; $S \leftarrow \left(\pi_2([K_2]_n) \oplus Y_2\right)\|Y_2$; $\mathcal{T}_{path} \xleftarrow{\cup} \left(0^{2n} \xrightarrow{M} S\right)$
  $H \leftarrow \mathcal{RO}(M)$; $K_1' \leftarrow 0^{m-n}\|[S]_n\|[S]^n$; $X_1' \leftarrow \mathbf{1}$
  $Y_2' \leftarrow [H]_n$; $K_2' \leftarrow \pi_1([K_1']^m)\|\pi_2^{-1}([H]^n \oplus [H]_n)$; $X_2' \leftarrow [K_2']_n \oplus \pi_2([K_1']_n)$
  $Y_1' \leftarrow X_2'$; **if** $Y_1' \in \mathsf{E}(K_1',*)$ **then abort**
  $\mathsf{E}(K_1',X_1') \leftarrow Y_1'$; $\mathsf{D}(K_1',Y_1') \leftarrow X_1'$; **if** $Y_2' \in \mathsf{E}(K_2',*)$ **then abort**
  $\mathsf{E}(K_2',X_2') \leftarrow Y_2'$; $\mathsf{D}(K_2',Y_2') \leftarrow X_2'$
end if
return $\mathsf{E}(K,X)$

Simulator $\mathsf{S}_D^{\mathcal{RO}}(K, Y)$

if $\mathsf{D}(K,Y) \neq \lambda$ **then return** $\mathsf{D}(K,Y)$
$X \xleftarrow{\$} \{0,1\}^n \backslash \mathsf{D}(K,*)$; $\mathsf{E}(K,X) \leftarrow Y$; $\mathsf{D}(K,Y) \leftarrow X$
return $\mathsf{D}(K,Y)$

satisfied. On the other hand, in the ideal world, for a hash query, the hash value is defined by a monolithic random function $\mathcal{RO}$. Hence, the goal of a simulator is to simulate an ideal cipher so that the query-responses of $\mathcal{RO}$ and of S satisfy the relation in Eq. (1).

S is defined in Algorithm 1. S keeps R blocks in lists E and D whose entries are initially empty strings. If an R block (K,X,Y) is defined where $\mathsf{S}_E(K,X) = Y$ or $\mathsf{S}_D(K,Y) = X$, then Y is stored in $\mathsf{E}(K,X)$ and X is stored in $\mathsf{D}(K,Y)$. S also keeps paths in $\mathcal{T}_{path}$, which initially keeps only a path $0^{2n} \xrightarrow{\lambda} 0^{2n}$. For $K \in \{0,1\}^k$, let $\mathsf{E}(K,*) = \{\mathsf{E}(K,X) | X \in \{0,1\}^n \wedge \mathsf{E}(K,X) \neq \lambda\}$ a set of all entries associated with K in E and $\mathsf{D}(K,*) = \{\mathsf{D}(K,Y) | Y \in \{0,1\}^n \wedge \mathsf{D}(K,Y) \neq \lambda\}$ a set of all entries associated with K in D. For a query (K,X) to S_E, two ciphertext blocks Y, Y_2 and a plaintext block X_0 are defined, where the three tuples $(K_0,X_0,Y_0), (K,X,Y), (K_2,X_2,Y_2)$ offer two CF blocks: the first (resp. second) CF block consists of (K_0,X_0,Y_0) and (K,X,Y) (resp. (K,X,Y) and (K_2,X_2,Y_2)). See Fig. 9. If there exists a path $\left(0^{2n} \xrightarrow{M'} S'\right) \in \mathcal{T}_{path}$ such that $S' \overset{in}{\rightsquigarrow} (K,X)$, then a new path $\left(0^{2n} \xrightarrow{M} S\right)$ is defined by appending the CF

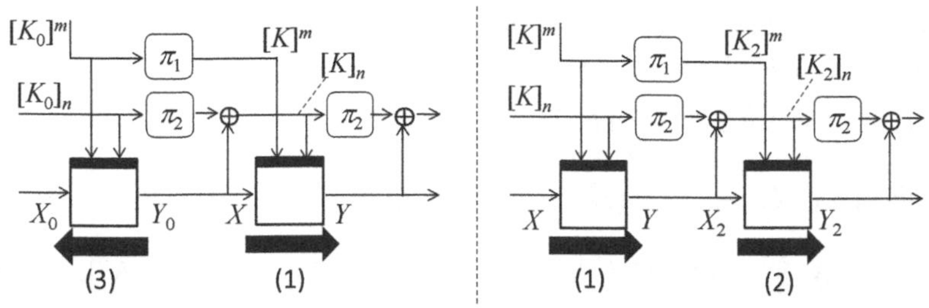

Fig. 9. Structures of R blocks defined by S_E. The R block (1) is defined by a forward operation, then the R block (2) is defined by a forward operation and the R block (3) is defined by an inverse operation.

block with (K, X, Y) and (K_2, X_2, Y_2) to the path, and is added to $\mathcal{T}_{path}$. To ensure the relation in Eq. (1), R blocks (K_1', X_1', Y_1') and (K_2', X_2', Y_2') in the outer function that are connected with the path are defined by using $\mathcal{RO}(M)$. Since Y_1' and Y_2' are defined by $\mathcal{RO}$, there is a case that $\mathsf{E}(K_1', X_1')$ or $\mathsf{E}(K_2', X_2')$ is already defined, which does not occur in the real world. If this case occurs, then S aborts.

For each encryption query, S_E makes a query to $\mathcal{RO}$ at most once. Hence, the number of queries to $\mathcal{RO}$ is at most p. Regarding the running time, for each query, the number of steps of S is a constant. Hence, the running time is $t+O(p)$.

In S_E, we call the operations to define Y, Y_2, Y_1', and Y_2' "forward operations", and the operation to define X_0 "inverse operation". In S_D, we call the operation to define X "inverse operation".

5.2 Main Part of the Proof

Structure of the Proof. As mentioned above, this proof consists of three games, Game 0, Game 1, and Game 2. Let Gi be oracles in Game i. These oracles are defined as follows: Game 0: $G0 := (L, R_E, R_D) = (\mathsf{EXEX\text{-}NI}^E, E, D)$; Game 1: $G1 := (L, R_E, R_D) = (\mathsf{EXEX\text{-}NI}^{\mathsf{S}_E}, \mathsf{S}_E^{\mathcal{RO}}, \mathsf{S}_D^{\mathcal{RO}})$; Game 2: $G2 := (L, R_E, R_D) = (\mathcal{RO}, \mathsf{S}_E^{\mathcal{RO}}, \mathsf{S}_D^{\mathcal{RO}})$. Game 1 is a middle game between the real world (Game 0) and the ideal world (Game 2): for each hash query, the response is defined by using S_E via the structure of $\mathsf{EXEX\text{-}NI}$. In the following proof, in Game 2, after finishing all queries by $\mathbf{A}$, the procedure of $\mathsf{EXEX\text{-}NI}^{\mathsf{S}_E^{\mathcal{RO}}}(M)$ is performed for all hash queries M. Note that the additional procedure does not reduce the advantage of $\mathbf{A}$.

Bad Events and Definitions. We next define bad events in Game 1 and Game 2. Let $\mathcal{Q}_F$ (resp. $\mathcal{Q}_I$) be a list of R blocks defined by forward (resp. inverse) operations in S. Let $q_F = |\mathcal{Q}_F|$ and $q_I = |\mathcal{Q}_I|$. We assume that after an

R block (K, X, Y) is stored in $\mathcal{Q}_F$ (resp. $\mathcal{Q}_I$), the R block is not stored in $\mathcal{Q}_I$ (resp. $\mathcal{Q}_F$). Note that $\mathcal{L}_{\mathsf{block}} = \mathcal{Q}_F \cup \mathcal{Q}_I$ is satisfied.

- $\mathsf{mcoll_F}$: $\exists (K_1, X_1, Y_1), \ldots, (K_\mu, X_\mu, Y_\mu) \in \mathcal{Q}_F$ s.t. $\pi_2([K_1]_n) \oplus Y_1 = \cdots = \pi_2([K_\mu]_n) \oplus Y_\mu$.
- $\mathsf{mcoll_I}$: $\exists (K_1, X_1, Y_1), \ldots, (K_\mu, X_\mu, Y_\mu) \in \mathcal{Q}_I$ s.t. $[K_1]_n \oplus X_1 = \cdots = [K_\mu]_n \oplus X_\mu$.
- $\mathsf{hit_{FI}}$: $\exists (K, X, Y) \in \mathcal{Q}_F, (K', X', Y') \in \mathcal{Q}_I$ s.t. $\pi_2([K]_n) \oplus Y = [K']_n \wedge Y = X'$.
- $\mathsf{hit_{IV}}$: $(\exists (K, X, Y) \in \mathcal{Q}_F$ s.t. $Y = 0^n \vee Y = \mathbf{1}) \vee (\exists (K, X, Y) \in \mathcal{Q}_I$ s.t. $X = 0^n \vee X = \mathbf{1})$.
- $\mathsf{hit_{XY}}$: $\exists (K, X, Y) \in \mathcal{Q}_F \cup \mathcal{Q}_I$ s.t. $X = Y$.
- coll: $\exists \left(0^{2n} \xrightarrow{M} S\right), \left(0^{2n} \xrightarrow{M'} S'\right) \in \mathcal{L}_{path}$ s.t. $M \neq M' \wedge S = S'$.
- $\mathsf{hit_{Path}}$: $\exists \left(0^{2n} \xrightarrow{M} S\right) \in \mathcal{L}_{\mathsf{path}}, (K, X, Y) \in \mathcal{Q}_F$ s.t. $S = [K]_n \| X$ or $[S]_n \| [S]^n = [K]_{2n}$, and the path is defined after the R block.
- Ecoll: S aborts.

For an event e, the event in Game 1 (resp. Game 2) is denoted by e^1 (resp. e^2). Let $\mathsf{bad}^1 := \mathsf{mcoll}_\mathsf{F}^1 \vee \mathsf{mcoll}_\mathsf{I}^1 \vee \mathsf{hit}_\mathsf{FI}^1 \vee \mathsf{hit}_\mathsf{IV}^1 \vee \mathsf{hit}_\mathsf{XY}^1 \vee \mathsf{coll}^1 \vee \mathsf{hit}_\mathsf{Path}^1$. Let $\mathsf{bad}^2 := \mathsf{mcoll}_\mathsf{F}^2 \vee \mathsf{mcoll}_\mathsf{I}^2 \vee \mathsf{hit}_\mathsf{FI}^2 \vee \mathsf{hit}_\mathsf{IV}^2 \vee \mathsf{hit}_\mathsf{XY}^2 \vee \mathsf{coll}^2 \vee \mathsf{hit}_\mathsf{Path}^2 \vee \mathsf{Ecoll}^2$.

Remark 1. For the overview in Sec. 4.3, $\mathsf{hit_{FI}}$ and $\mathsf{hit_{Path}}$ (first condition) correspond to E1, $\mathsf{hit_{Path}}$ (second condition) corresponds to E2, t coll corresponds to E3, and $\mathsf{mcoll_F}$ and $\mathsf{mcoll_I}$ correspond to the multi-collision technique used in the analysis of E1. Note that $\mathsf{hit_{IV}}$, $\mathsf{hit_{XY}}$, and Ecoll are not discussed in the overview. The following analyses show that these probabilities are negligible as long as other events do not occur.

Upper-Bounding the Advantage Function. To upper-bound the advantage, we use the following lemmas.

Lemma 3. *Let* $\left(0^{2n} \xrightarrow{M} S\right) \in \mathcal{L}_{\mathsf{path}}$ *be a path with* ℓ *CF blocks (i.e.,* 2ℓ *R blocks). In both Game 1 and Game 2, for any* $i \in [2\ell]$*, the* i*-th* R *block is defined by forward operations and is defined after the* $(i-1)$*-th* R *block as long as* $(\mathsf{hit_{FI}} \vee \mathsf{hit_{IV}} \vee \mathsf{hit_{XY}} \vee \mathsf{hit_{Path}})$ *does not occur.*

Lemma 4. *For* $V \in \{0,1\}^{2n}$ *and* $\left(0^{2n} \xrightarrow{M} S\right) \in \mathcal{L}_{\mathsf{path}}$ *such that* V *is given before the path is defined, we have* $\Pr[S = V] \leq 1/(2^n - 3Q)^2$ *as long as* $(\mathsf{hit_{FI}} \vee \mathsf{hit_{IV}} \vee \mathsf{hit_{XY}} \vee \mathsf{hit_{Path}})$ *does not occur.*

Lemma 5. $\Pr[\mathbf{A}^{G0} = 1] = \Pr[\mathbf{A}^{G1} = 1 \mid \neg\mathsf{Ecoll}^1]$.

Lemma 6. $\Pr[\mathbf{A}^{G1} = 1 \mid \neg\mathsf{bad}^1 \wedge \neg\mathsf{Ecoll}^1] = \Pr[\mathbf{A}^{G2} = 1 \mid \neg\mathsf{bad}^2]$.

Lemma 3 is used in the proofs of Lemmas 4 and 6 and in the analyses of the bad events. Lemma 4 is used in the analyses of the bad events. Using Lemmas 5 and 6, we have the following in equation[6]

$$\mathsf{Adv}^{\mathsf{indiff}}_{\mathsf{H,S}}(\mathbf{A}) \leq \mathsf{Pr}[\mathsf{bad}^1 \mid \neg\mathsf{Ecoll}^1] + \mathsf{Pr}[\mathsf{bad}^2],$$

where

$$\begin{aligned}\mathsf{Pr}[\mathsf{bad}^1 \mid \neg\mathsf{Ecoll}^1] \leq\ & \mathsf{Pr}[\mathsf{mcoll}^1_{\mathsf{F}} \mid \neg\mathsf{Ecoll}^1] + \mathsf{Pr}[\mathsf{mcoll}^1_{\mathsf{I}} \mid \neg\mathsf{Ecoll}^1] \\ &+ \mathsf{Pr}[\mathsf{hit}^1_{\mathsf{FI}} \mid \neg\mathsf{mcoll}^1_{\mathsf{F}} \wedge \neg\mathsf{mcoll}^1_{\mathsf{I}} \wedge \neg\mathsf{Ecoll}^1] \\ &+ \mathsf{Pr}[\mathsf{hit}^1_{\mathsf{IV}} \mid \neg\mathsf{Ecoll}^1] + \mathsf{Pr}[\mathsf{hit}^1_{\mathsf{XY}} \mid \neg\mathsf{Ecoll}^1] \\ &+ \mathsf{Pr}[\mathsf{coll}^1 \mid \neg\mathsf{hit}^1_{\mathsf{IV}} \wedge \neg\mathsf{hit}^1_{\mathsf{FI}} \wedge \neg\mathsf{hit}^1_{\mathsf{XY}} \wedge \neg\mathsf{hit}^1_{\mathsf{Path}} \wedge \neg\mathsf{Ecoll}^1] \\ &+ \mathsf{Pr}[\mathsf{hit}^1_{\mathsf{Path}} \mid \neg\mathsf{hit}^1_{\mathsf{IV}} \wedge \neg\mathsf{hit}^1_{\mathsf{FI}} \wedge \neg\mathsf{hit}^1_{\mathsf{XY}} \wedge \neg\mathsf{Ecoll}^1],\end{aligned}$$

and

$$\begin{aligned}\mathsf{Pr}[\mathsf{bad}^2] \leq\ & \mathsf{Pr}[\mathsf{mcoll}^2_{\mathsf{F}}] + \mathsf{Pr}[\mathsf{mcoll}^2_{\mathsf{I}}] + \mathsf{Pr}[\mathsf{hit}^2_{\mathsf{FI}} \mid \neg\mathsf{mcoll}^2_{\mathsf{F}} \wedge \neg\mathsf{mcoll}^2_{\mathsf{I}}] \\ &+ \mathsf{Pr}[\mathsf{hit}^2_{\mathsf{IV}}] + \mathsf{Pr}[\mathsf{hit}^2_{\mathsf{XY}}] + \mathsf{Pr}[\mathsf{coll}^2 \mid \neg\mathsf{hit}^2_{\mathsf{IV}} \wedge \neg\mathsf{hit}^2_{\mathsf{FI}} \wedge \neg\mathsf{hit}^2_{\mathsf{XY}} \wedge \neg\mathsf{hit}^2_{\mathsf{Path}}] \\ &+ \mathsf{Pr}[\mathsf{hit}^2_{\mathsf{Path}} \mid \neg\mathsf{hit}^2_{\mathsf{IV}} \wedge \neg\mathsf{hit}^2_{\mathsf{FI}} \wedge \neg\mathsf{hit}^2_{\mathsf{XY}}] + \mathsf{Pr}[\mathsf{Ecoll}^2 \mid \neg\mathsf{hit}^2_{\mathsf{Path}}].\end{aligned}$$

These upper-bounds are given in the following, which gives

$$\mathsf{Adv}^{\mathsf{indiff}}_{\mathsf{H,S}}(\mathbf{A}) \leq 2^{n+2} \cdot \binom{3Q}{\mu} \cdot \left(\frac{1}{2^n - 3Q}\right)^{\mu} + \frac{6\mu Q + 19Q}{2^n - 3Q} + \frac{22Q^2}{(2^n - 3Q)^2}.$$

Upper-Bounding $\mathsf{Pr}[\mathsf{mcoll}^1_{\mathsf{F}} \mid \neg\mathsf{Ecoll}^1]$**.** For each $(K, X, Y) \in \mathcal{Q}_F$, since Y is chosen uniformly at random from at least $2^n - 3Q$ elements in $\{0,1\}^n$, for some $V \in \{0,1\}^n$, we have $\mathsf{Pr}[\pi_2([K]_n) \oplus Y = V] \leq 1/(2^n - 3Q)$. Hence, we have $\mathsf{Pr}[\mathsf{mcoll}^1_{\mathsf{F}} \mid \neg\mathsf{Ecoll}^1] \leq 2^n \cdot \binom{q_F}{\mu} \cdot \left(\frac{1}{2^n - 3Q}\right)^{\mu}$.

[6] The inequation is obtained by

$$\begin{aligned}&\mathsf{Adv}^{\mathsf{indiff}}_{\mathsf{H,S}}(\mathbf{A}) = \Pr[\mathbf{A}^{G0} = 1] - \Pr[\mathbf{A}^{G2} = 1] = \Pr[\mathbf{A}^{G1} = 1 \mid \neg\mathsf{Ecoll}^1] - \Pr[\mathbf{A}^{G2} = 1] \\ &\leq \left(\Pr[\mathbf{A}^{G1} = 1 \wedge \mathsf{bad}^1 \mid \neg\mathsf{Ecoll}^1] + \Pr[\mathbf{A}^{G1} = 1 \wedge \neg\mathsf{bad}^1 \mid \neg\mathsf{Ecoll}^1]\right) \\ &\qquad - \left(\Pr[\mathbf{A}^{G2} = 1 \wedge \mathsf{bad}^2] + \Pr[\mathbf{A}^{G2} = 1 \wedge \neg\mathsf{bad}^2]\right) \\ &= \Big(\Pr[\mathbf{A}^{G1} = 1 \mid \mathsf{bad}^1 \wedge \neg\mathsf{Ecoll}^1] \cdot \mathsf{Pr}[\mathsf{bad}^1 \mid \neg\mathsf{Ecoll}^1] \\ &\quad + \underbrace{\Pr[\mathbf{A}^{G1} = 1 \mid \neg\mathsf{bad}^1 \wedge \neg\mathsf{Ecoll}^1]}_{=\mathsf{Pr}[\mathbf{A}^{G2}=1 \mid \neg\mathsf{bad}^2]} \cdot \underbrace{\mathsf{Pr}[\neg\mathsf{bad}^1 \mid \neg\mathsf{Ecoll}^1]}_{=1-\mathsf{Pr}[\mathsf{bad}^1 \mid \neg\mathsf{Ecoll}^1]}\Big) \\ &\qquad - \left(\Pr[\mathbf{A}^{G2} = 1 \mid \mathsf{bad}^2] \cdot \mathsf{Pr}[\mathsf{bad}^2] + \Pr[\mathbf{A}^{G2} = 1 \mid \neg\mathsf{bad}^2] \cdot \mathsf{Pr}[\neg\mathsf{bad}^2]\right) \\ &= \left(\Pr[\mathbf{A}^{G1} = 1 \mid \mathsf{bad}^1 \wedge \neg\mathsf{Ecoll}^1] - \Pr[\mathbf{A}^{G2} = 1 \mid \neg\mathsf{bad}^2]\right) \cdot \mathsf{Pr}[\mathsf{bad}^1 \mid \neg\mathsf{Ecoll}^1] \\ &\qquad + \left(\Pr[\mathbf{A}^{G2} = 1 \mid \neg\mathsf{bad}^2] - \Pr[\mathbf{A}^{G2} = 1 \mid \mathsf{bad}^2]\right) \cdot \mathsf{Pr}[\mathsf{bad}^2] \\ &\leq \mathsf{Pr}[\mathsf{bad}^1 \mid \neg\mathsf{Ecoll}^1] + \mathsf{Pr}[\mathsf{bad}^2].\end{aligned}$$

Upper-Bounding $\mathsf{Pr}[\mathsf{mcoll}_\mathsf{F}^2]$**.** By the same analysis as $\mathsf{Pr}[\mathsf{mcoll}_\mathsf{F}^1 \mid \neg\mathsf{Ecoll}^1]$, we have $\mathsf{Pr}[\mathsf{mcoll}_\mathsf{F}^2] \leq 2^n \cdot \binom{q_F}{\mu} \cdot \left(\frac{1}{2^n-3Q}\right)^\mu$.

Upper-Bounding $\mathsf{Pr}[\mathsf{mcoll}_\mathsf{I}^1 \mid \neg\mathsf{Ecoll}^1]$**.** For each $(K, X, Y) \in \mathcal{Q}_I$, since X is chosen uniformly at random from at least $2^n - 3Q$ elements in $\{0,1\}^n$, for some $V \in \{0,1\}^n$, we have $\mathsf{Pr}[[K]_n \oplus X = V] \leq 1/(2^n - 3Q)$. Hence, we have $\mathsf{Pr}[\mathsf{mcoll}_\mathsf{I}^1 \mid \neg\mathsf{Ecoll}^1] \leq 2^n \cdot \binom{q_I}{\mu} \cdot \left(\frac{1}{2^n-3Q}\right)^\mu$.

Upper-Bounding $\mathsf{Pr}[\mathsf{mcoll}_\mathsf{I}^2]$**.** By the same analysis as $\mathsf{Pr}[\mathsf{mcoll}_\mathsf{I}^1 \mid \neg\mathsf{Ecoll}^1]$, we have $\mathsf{Pr}[\mathsf{mcoll}_\mathsf{I}^2] \leq 2^n \cdot \binom{q_I}{\mu} \cdot \left(\frac{1}{2^n-3Q}\right)^\mu$.

Upper-Bounding $\mathsf{Pr}[\mathsf{hit}_\mathsf{FI}^1 \mid \neg\mathsf{mcoll}_\mathsf{F}^1 \wedge \neg\mathsf{mcoll}_\mathsf{I}^1 \wedge \neg\mathsf{Ecoll}^1]$**.** For R blocks (K, X, Y) and (K', X', Y'), if (K', X', Y') is defined after (K, X, Y), then the relation is denoted by $(K, X, Y) \lhd (K', X', Y')$. We consider the following two cases.

- $\mathsf{hit}_{\overleftarrow{\mathsf{FI}}}^1$: $\exists (K, X, Y) \in \mathcal{Q}_F, (K', X', Y') \in \mathcal{Q}_I$ s.t. $(K, X, Y) \lhd (K', X', Y') \wedge \pi_2([K]_n) \oplus Y = [K']_n \wedge Y = X'$.
- $\mathsf{hit}_{\overrightarrow{\mathsf{FI}}}^1$: $\exists (K, X, Y) \in \mathcal{Q}_F, (K', X', Y') \in \mathcal{Q}_I$ s.t. $(K', X', Y') \lhd (K, X, Y) \wedge \pi_2([K]_n) \oplus Y = [K']_n \wedge Y = X'$.

We analyze $\mathsf{hit}_{\overleftarrow{\mathsf{FI}}}^1$. For an input (K', Y') in $\mathcal{Q}_I$, by $\neg\mathsf{mcoll}_\mathsf{F}^1$, the number of tuples $(K, X, Y) \in \mathcal{Q}_F$ such that $\pi_2([K]_n) \oplus Y = [K']_n$ is satisfied is at most $\mu - 1$, thus the probability that X' equals one of the $(\mu - 1)$ ciphertext blocks is at most $(\mu - 1)/(2^n - 3Q)$. Summing the probability for each element in $\mathcal{Q}_I$, we have $\mathsf{Pr}[\mathsf{hit}_{\overleftarrow{\mathsf{FI}}}^1 \mid \neg\mathsf{mcoll}_\mathsf{F}^1 \wedge \neg\mathsf{mcoll}_\mathsf{I}^1 \wedge \neg\mathsf{Ecoll}^1] \leq (\mu - 1)q_I/(2^n - 3Q)$.

For $\mathsf{hit}_{\overrightarrow{\mathsf{FI}}}^1$, the analysis is the same as that of $\mathsf{hit}_{\overleftarrow{\mathsf{FI}}}^1$. Using the condition $\neg\mathsf{mcoll}_\mathsf{I}^1$, we have $\mathsf{Pr}[\mathsf{hit}_{\overrightarrow{\mathsf{FI}}}^1 \mid \neg\mathsf{mcoll}_\mathsf{F}^1 \wedge \neg\mathsf{mcoll}_\mathsf{I}^1 \wedge \neg\mathsf{Ecoll}^1] \leq (\mu - 1)q_F/(2^n - 3Q)$.

By $q_F + q_I \leq 3Q$, we have $\mathsf{Pr}[\mathsf{hit}_\mathsf{FI}^1 \mid \neg\mathsf{mcoll}_\mathsf{F}^1 \wedge \neg\mathsf{mcoll}_\mathsf{I}^1 \wedge \neg\mathsf{Ecoll}^1] \leq \frac{3(\mu-1)Q}{2^n-3Q}$.

Upper-Bounding $\mathsf{Pr}[\mathsf{hit}_\mathsf{FI}^2 \mid \neg\mathsf{mcoll}_\mathsf{F}^2 \wedge \neg\mathsf{mcoll}_\mathsf{I}^2]$**.** As the analysis of $\mathsf{Pr}[\mathsf{hit}_\mathsf{FI}^1 \mid \neg\mathsf{mcoll}_\mathsf{F}^1 \wedge \neg\mathsf{mcoll}_\mathsf{I}^1 \wedge \neg\mathsf{Ecoll}^1]$, using the conditions $\neg\mathsf{mcoll}_\mathsf{F}^2$ and $\neg\mathsf{mcoll}_\mathsf{I}^2$, we have $\mathsf{Pr}[\mathsf{hit}_\mathsf{FI}^2 \mid \neg\mathsf{mcoll}_\mathsf{F}^2 \wedge \neg\mathsf{mcoll}_\mathsf{I}^2] \leq \frac{3(\mu-1)Q}{2^n-3Q}$.

Upper-Bounding $\mathsf{Pr}[\mathsf{hit}_\mathsf{IV}^1 \mid \neg\mathsf{Ecoll}^1]$ For each $(K, X, Y) \in \mathcal{Q}_F$ (resp. $(K, X, Y) \in \mathcal{Q}_I$), Y (resp. X) is chosen uniformly at random from at least $2^n - 3Q$ elements in $\{0,1\}^n$. Thus, we have $\mathsf{Pr}[\mathsf{hit}_\mathsf{IV}^1 \mid \neg\mathsf{Ecoll}^1] \leq \frac{6Q}{2^n-3Q}$.

Upper-Bounding $\mathsf{Pr}[\mathsf{hit}_\mathsf{IV}^2]$**.** The analysis is the same as that of $\mathsf{Pr}[\mathsf{hit}_\mathsf{IV}^1 \mid \neg\mathsf{Ecoll}^1]$. We have $\mathsf{Pr}[\mathsf{hit}_\mathsf{IV}^2] \leq \frac{6Q}{2^n-3Q}$.

Upper-Bounding $\mathsf{Pr}[\mathsf{hit}_\mathsf{XY}^1 \mid \neg\mathsf{Ecoll}^1]$**.** For each $(K, X, Y) \in \mathcal{Q}_F$ (resp. $(K, X, Y) \in \mathcal{Q}_I$), Y (resp. X) is chosen uniformly at random from at least $2^n - 3Q$ elements in $\{0,1\}^n$. Thus, we have $\mathsf{Pr}[\mathsf{hit}_\mathsf{XY}^1 \mid \neg\mathsf{Ecoll}^1] \leq \frac{3Q}{2^n-3Q}$.

Upper-Bounding $\mathsf{Pr}[\mathsf{hit}_\mathsf{XY}^2]$**.** The analysis is the same as that of $\mathsf{Pr}[\mathsf{hit}_\mathsf{IV}^1 \mid \neg\mathsf{Ecoll}^1]$. We have $\mathsf{Pr}[\mathsf{hit}_\mathsf{XY}^2] \leq \frac{3Q}{2^n-3Q}$.

Upper-Bounding $\Pr[\mathsf{coll}^1 \mid \neg\mathsf{hit}^1_{\mathsf{IV}} \wedge \neg\mathsf{hit}^1_{\mathsf{FI}} \wedge \neg\mathsf{hit}^1_{\mathsf{XY}} \wedge \neg\mathsf{hit}^1_{\mathsf{Path}} \wedge \neg\mathsf{Ecoll}^1]$**.** Assume that $(\mathsf{hit}^1_{\mathsf{IV}} \vee \mathsf{hit}^1_{\mathsf{FI}} \vee \mathsf{hit}^1_{\mathsf{XY}} \vee \mathsf{hit}^1_{\mathsf{Path}} \vee \mathsf{Ecoll}^1)$ is not satisfied. Fix a path $\left(0^{2n} \xrightarrow{M} S\right) \in \mathcal{L}_{\mathsf{path}}$, and assume that coll^1 has not occurred before the path. Then, for each path $\left(0^{2n} \xrightarrow{M'} S'\right) \in \mathcal{L}_{\mathsf{path}}$ that was defined before $\left(0^{2n} \xrightarrow{M} S\right)$, we have $\Pr[S = S'] \leq 1/(2^n - 3Q)^2$ by Lemma 4. Summing the probability for each pair of paths where $|\mathcal{L}_{\mathsf{path}}| \leq 2Q$, we have $\Pr[\mathsf{coll}^1 \mid \neg\mathsf{hit}^1_{\mathsf{IV}} \wedge \neg\mathsf{hit}^1_{\mathsf{FI}} \wedge \neg\mathsf{hit}^1_{\mathsf{XY}} \wedge \neg\mathsf{hit}^1_{\mathsf{Path}} \wedge \neg\mathsf{Ecoll}^1] \leq \binom{2Q}{2} \cdot \frac{1}{(2^n-3Q)^2} \leq \frac{2Q^2}{(2^n-3Q)^2}$.

Upper-Bounding $\Pr[\mathsf{coll}^2 \mid \neg\mathsf{hit}^2_{\mathsf{IV}} \wedge \neg\mathsf{hit}^2_{\mathsf{FI}} \wedge \neg\mathsf{hit}^2_{\mathsf{XY}} \wedge \neg\mathsf{hit}^2_{\mathsf{Path}}]$**.** The analysis is the same as that of $\Pr[\mathsf{coll}^1 \mid \neg\mathsf{hit}^1_{\mathsf{IV}} \wedge \neg\mathsf{hit}^1_{\mathsf{FI}} \wedge \neg\mathsf{hit}^1_{\mathsf{XY}} \wedge \neg\mathsf{hit}^1_{\mathsf{Path}} \wedge \neg\mathsf{Ecoll}^1]$. By Lemma 4, we have $\Pr[\mathsf{coll}^2 \mid \neg\mathsf{hit}^2_{\mathsf{IV}} \wedge \neg\mathsf{hit}^2_{\mathsf{FI}} \wedge \neg\mathsf{hit}^2_{\mathsf{XY}} \wedge \neg\mathsf{hit}^2_{\mathsf{Path}}] \leq \frac{2Q^2}{(2^n-3Q)^2}$.

Upper-Bounding $\Pr[\mathsf{hit}^1_{\mathsf{Path}} \mid \neg\mathsf{hit}^1_{\mathsf{IV}} \wedge \neg\mathsf{hit}^1_{\mathsf{FI}} \wedge \neg\mathsf{hit}^1_{\mathsf{XY}} \wedge \neg\mathsf{Ecoll}^1]$**.** Fix $\left(0^{2n} \xrightarrow{M} S\right) \in \mathcal{L}_{\mathsf{path}}$ and $(K, X, Y) \in \mathcal{Q}_F$ such that $\mathsf{hit}^1_{\mathsf{Path}}$ has not occurred and the R block was defined before the path is defined. By Lemma 4, we have $\Pr[S = [K]_n \| X] \leq 1/(2^n - 3Q)^2$ and $\Pr[[S]_n \| [S]^n = [K]_{2n}] \leq 1/(2^n - 3Q)^2$. Summing the probabilities for each path and R block, we have $\Pr[\mathsf{hit}^1_{\mathsf{Path}} \mid \neg\mathsf{hit}^1_{\mathsf{IV}} \wedge \neg\mathsf{hit}^1_{\mathsf{FI}} \wedge \neg\mathsf{hit}^1_{\mathsf{XY}} \wedge \neg\mathsf{Ecoll}^{\prime}] \leq 2Q \cdot 2Q \cdot \frac{2}{(2^n-3Q)^2} \leq \frac{8Q^2}{(2^n-3Q)^2}$.

Upper-Bounding $\Pr[\mathsf{hit}^2_{\mathsf{Path}} \mid \neg\mathsf{hit}^2_{\mathsf{IV}} \wedge \neg\mathsf{hit}^2_{\mathsf{FI}} \wedge \neg\mathsf{hit}^2_{\mathsf{XY}}]$**.** The analysis is the same as that of $\Pr[\mathsf{hit}^1_{\mathsf{Path}} \mid \neg\mathsf{hit}^1_{\mathsf{IV}} \wedge \neg\mathsf{hit}^1_{\mathsf{FI}} \wedge \neg\mathsf{hit}^1_{\mathsf{XY}} \wedge \neg\mathsf{Ecoll}^1]$. Thus we have $\Pr[\mathsf{hit}^2_{\mathsf{Path}} \mid \neg\mathsf{hit}^2_{\mathsf{IV}} \wedge \neg\mathsf{hit}^2_{\mathsf{FI}} \wedge \neg\mathsf{hit}^2_{\mathsf{XY}}] \leq \frac{8Q^2}{(2^n-3Q)^2}$.

Upper-Bounding $\Pr[\mathsf{Ecoll}^2 \mid \neg\mathsf{hit}^2_{\mathsf{Path}}]$**.** For each process of $\mathsf{S}_E^{\mathcal{RO}}(K, X)$, if there exists a path $\left(0^{2n} \xrightarrow{M'} S'\right) \in \mathcal{T}_{path}$ s.t. $S' \overset{in}{\rightsquigarrow} (K, X)$, then by $\neg\mathsf{hit}^2_{\mathsf{Path}}$, $\mathsf{E}[K'_1, *] = \lambda$ and $\mathsf{E}[K'_2, *] = \lambda$ are satisfied. On the other hand, there is a case that $K'_1 = K'_2$ and $X'_1 \neq X'_2$ are satisfied, but $Y'_1 = Y'_2$ is satisfied. For each path, the collision probability is $1/2^n$, since Y'_1 and Y'_2 are defined by $\mathcal{RO}$. We thus have $\Pr[\mathsf{Ecoll}^2 \mid \mathsf{hit}^2_{\mathsf{Path}}] \leq \frac{Q}{2^n}$.

5.3 Proof of Lemma 3

Consider Game j where $j \in [2]$. Assume that $(\mathsf{hit}^j_{\mathsf{FI}} \vee \mathsf{hit}^j_{\mathsf{IV}} \vee \mathsf{hit}^j_{\mathsf{XY}} \vee \mathsf{hit}^j_{\mathsf{Path}})$ does not occur. Consider a path $\left(0^{2n} \xrightarrow{M} S\right) \in \mathcal{L}_{\mathsf{path}}$ with ℓ CF block (2ℓ R blocks). By the definition of S_E, after an R block is defined by a forward operation, the next R block is immediately defined by a forward operation, and the former R block is defined by an inverse operation. All R blocks in the path are defined by forward operations by $\neg\mathsf{hit}^j_{\mathsf{FI}}$ and $\neg\mathsf{hit}^j_{\mathsf{IV}}$, and for each $i \in [2\ell - 1]$, the $(i + 1)$-th R block in the path is defined after the i-th R block by $\neg\mathsf{hit}^j_{\mathsf{XY}}$ and $\neg\mathsf{hit}^j_{\mathsf{Path}}$.

5.4 Proof of Lemma 4

Consider Game j where $j \in [2]$. Assume that $(\mathsf{hit}^j_{\mathsf{FI}} \vee \mathsf{hit}^j_{\mathsf{IV}} \vee \mathsf{hit}^j_{\mathsf{XY}} \vee \mathsf{hit}^j_{\mathsf{Path}})$ does not occur. Fix a value $V \in \{0, 1\}^{2n}$. For a path $\left(0^{2n} \xrightarrow{M} S\right) \in \mathcal{L}_{\mathsf{path}}$, by

Lemma 3, the last CF block in the path consists of two R blocks defined by forward operations and the outputs are differently sampled. Since the outputs are chosen uniformly at random from at least $2^n - 3Q$ elements in $\{0,1\}^n$, we have $\mathsf{Pr}[S = V] \leq 1/(2^n - 3Q)^2$.

5.5 Proof of Lemma 5

Since outputs of $\mathcal{RO}$ are chosen uniformly at random from $\{0,1\}^{2n}$, a collision occurs in entries with the same key. In other words, S behaves as an ideal cipher if and only if such collision does not occur, i.e., $\mathsf{Ecoll}^1 = \mathsf{false}$. Thus, we have $\Pr[\mathbf{A}^{G0} = 1] = \Pr[\mathbf{A}^{G1} = 1 \mid \neg\mathsf{Ecoll}_1]$.

5.6 Proof of Lemma 6

We show that $\mathsf{Pr}[\mathbf{A}^{G1} = 1 \mid \neg\mathsf{bad}^1 \wedge \neg\mathsf{Ecoll}^1] = \mathsf{Pr}[\mathbf{A}^{G2} = 1 \mid \neg\mathsf{bad}^2]$ (Game 1 and Game 2 are indistinguishable). In this proof, we need to show that the structural difference of L gives no advantage to $\mathbf{A}$. The difference is: $L = \mathsf{EXEX\text{-}NI}^{R_E}$ (Game 1) and $L = \mathcal{RO}$ (Game 2), thus with the following two points, the equivalence is ensured.

1. In Game 1, for any hash query M, the response is equal to $\mathcal{RO}(M)$.
2. In Game 2, L and R are consistent as in Game 1 with respect to the structure of EXEX-NI, that is, for any $\left(0^{2n} \xrightarrow{M} S\right) \in \mathcal{L}_{path}$, $\left(S' \xrightarrow{M'} H\right) \in \mathcal{L}_{block}$ such that $S \overset{out}{\rightsquigarrow} (S', M')$, $H = L(M)$ is satisfied.

The following lemma ensures these two points. Hence, we have

$$\mathsf{Pr}[\mathbf{A}^{G1} = 1 \mid \neg\mathsf{bad}_1 \wedge \neg\mathsf{Ecoll}^1] = \mathsf{Pr}[\mathbf{A}^{G2} = 1 \mid \neg\mathsf{bad}_2].$$

Lemma 7. *In Game j $(= 1, 2)$, the following is satisfied as long as* bad^j *does not occur:* $\forall\left(0^{2n} \xrightarrow{M} S\right) \in \mathcal{L}_{\mathsf{path}}, \left(S' \xrightarrow{M'} H\right) \in \mathcal{L}_{\mathsf{block}}$ *s.t.* $S \overset{out}{\rightsquigarrow} (S', M')$*:* $H = \mathcal{RO}(M)$.

Proof (Lemma 7). In Game j $(j = 1, 2)$, for a path $\left(0^{2n} \xrightarrow{M} S\right) \in \mathcal{L}_{\mathsf{path}}$ and a CF block $\left(S' \xrightarrow{M'} H\right) \in \mathcal{L}_{\mathsf{block}}$ such that $S \overset{out}{\rightsquigarrow} (S', M')$, by $\neg\mathsf{hit}^j_{\mathsf{Path}}$, the CF block $\left(S' \xrightarrow{M'} H\right)$ is defined after the path $\left(0^{2n} \xrightarrow{M} S\right) \in \mathcal{L}_{\mathsf{path}}$ is defined. By Lemma 3, all R blocks in the path are defined by forward operations in order from the first to the last. By $\neg\mathsf{coll}^j$, there is no collision path leading to S. Thus, by the definition of S_E, H is defined as $H = \mathcal{RO}(M)$. □

6 EXEX-I: Low Memory Collision Resistant DBL HF

In this section, we consider relaxing the security goal to the collision resistance rather than the indifferentiability. We design EXEX-I in Sect. 6.1. An overview of its collision resistance is given in Sect. 6.2.

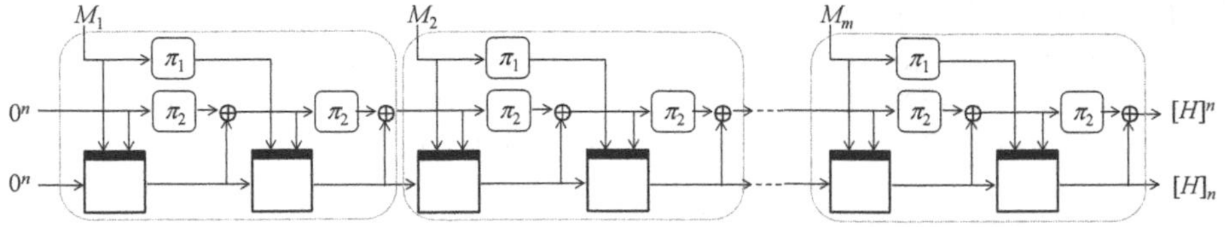

Fig. 10. Hash function EXEX-I.

6.1 Specification of EXEX-I

Like EXEX-NI, we design EXEX-I by iterating EXEX defined in Sect. 4.1, but unlike EXEX-NI, we relax the security goal to be collision resistance. The change of the security goal enables us to remove the outer function of EXEX-NI, which was introduced to achieve indifferentiability. Removal of the outer function relaxes the condition for the key length and improves the efficiency.

We define EXEX-I : $\{0,1\}^* \to \{0,1\}^{2n}$. Let pad : $\{0,1\}^* \to (\{0,1\}^m)^*$ be an injective padding function, e.g., one-zero padding $\mathsf{pad}(M) = M \| 10^w$ where $w = m - 1 - |M| \bmod m$. The construction of EXEX-I is depicted in Fig. 10.

- EXEX-$\mathsf{I}^E(M)$:
  1. $S_0 \leftarrow 0^{2n}$; $M_1, M_2, \cdots, M_\ell \xleftarrow{m} \mathsf{pad}(M)$
  2. for $i = 1, \ldots, \ell$ do $S_i \leftarrow \mathsf{EXEX}^E(S_{i-1}, M_i)$
  3. return S_ℓ

6.2 Collision Resistance of EXEX-I

The following gives an upper-bound for the collision resistance of EXEX-I.

Theorem 2. *Let μ be any positive integer. For any adversary* $\mathbf{A}$ *making Q queries, we have*

$$\mathsf{Adv}^{\mathsf{coll}}_{\mathsf{EXEX\text{-}I}}(\mathbf{A}) \leq \frac{0.5Q^2}{(2^n - 3Q)^2} + \frac{3\mu Q + 3Q}{2^n - 3Q} + 2^n \cdot \binom{3Q}{\mu} \cdot \left(\frac{1}{2^n - 3Q}\right)^\mu.$$

EXEX-I is equal to the inner function of EXEX-NI. Since a collision of the inner function breaks the indifferentiability of EXEX-NI, the proof of the collision resistance of EXEX-I is equal to (some part of) the proof of the indifferentiability of EXEX-NI. Using the proof, we can show that EXEX-I is collision resistant up to the bound given in the theorem.

7 Hardware Performance Evaluation

We compare the hardware performances of EXEX-NI, EXEX-I, and Romulus-H under the same design policy. We instantiate the candidates with

SKINNY-128-384 used in the first literature on Romulus-H [13].[7] All the instantiations achieve the same data rate, i.e., processing a 256-bit message block with two TBC calls. EXEX-NI and EXEX-I can choose SKINNY-128-256 for an even smaller implementation, which we will discuss later in Sect. 7.4.

7.1 SKINNY-128-384 Implementation

The baseline design is Naito et al.'s conventional SKINNY-128-384 implementation [25] based on the common byte-serial architecture [3]. The state array is a 128-bit register arranged in a 2-dimensional array, which integrates the linear operations, i.e., MixColumns and ShiftRows. It finishes the round function in 21 cycles, and the entire SKINNY-128-384 in 1,176 ($=21 \times 56$) cycles. We use a scan flip-flop, a special-purpose register with a built-in 2-way selector, for efficiently implementing the 2-dimensional array [3,25].

The 384-bit tweakey comprises independently scheduled 128-bit chunks, referred to as TK_1, TK_2, and TK_3 hereafter. We assign TK_1 for storing the state mixed with TBC outputs and $\mathsf{TK}_2||\mathsf{TK}_3$ for storing 256-bit message blocks. By following the baseline implementation, we again use the 2-dimensional arrays for storing the tweakey, namely the TK_1, TK_2, and TK_3 arrays. Those arrays efficiently realize a serial byte scanning and the byte-wise permutation for the tweakey schedule [25][8].

7.2 Hardware Implementation of EXEX-NI and EXEX-I

We decompose EXEX-NI into the four operations as shown in Fig. 11-(left): (C1) a TBC call, (C2) transferring a TBC output to TK_1, (C3) feeding a 256-bit new message block to $\mathsf{TK}_2||\mathsf{TK}_3$, and (C4) organizing data for the nested processing. The circuit in Fig. 11-(right) implements the four basic operations and can hash a long message by dispatching the operations in an appropriate order. Starting from the baseline SKINNY-128-384 implementation, we added some 8-bit selector, XOR, and AND gates for managing data transmission between the arrays to support the (C2) and (C4) operations. The EXEX-I implementation is the EXEX-NI implementation without the (C4) operation, and we can remove some gates from the datapath in Fig. 11-(right).

π_1 and π_2 for Tweakey Schedule. We use the linear operations π_1 and π_2 (see Fig. 7) to achieve better performance by eliminating the inverse tweakey schedule. A lightweight TBC implementation commonly uses an on-the-fly tweakey schedule to avoid storing the round keys. As a drawback, we lose the original tweakey by updating it in place, which is a problem for a mode of operation that uses the same tweakey in the following operations. The previous SKINNY-128-384

[7] In the updates for the NIST LWC final round, the Romulus team decided to use a reduced-round variant called SKINNY-128-384+. We discuss the impact of this change in Sect. 7.4.

[8] For efficiency, we remove a built-in arithmetic counter in the previous tweakey arrays needed for an AEAD mode of operation [25].

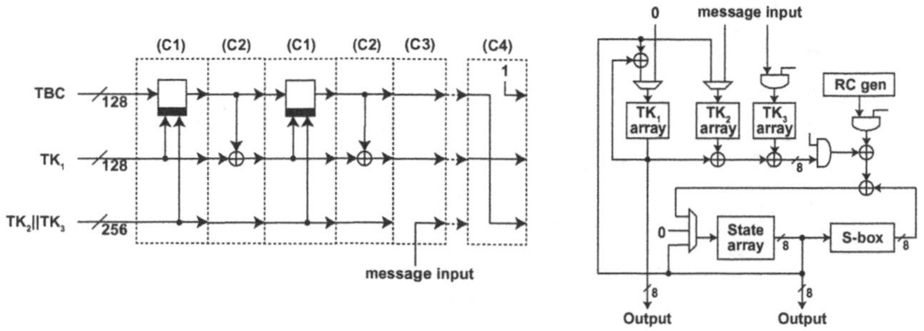

Fig. 11. (Left) Decomposition of EXEX-NI into basic operations and (Right) the datapath architecture realizing those operations

implementation addressed this issue by integrating the inverse tweakey schedule in the tweakey arrays at the cost of additional hardware resources [25].

A more sophisticated approach is integrating the tweakey schedule into a mode of operation so that we can continue without recovering the original tweakey [26]. EXEX-NI and EXEX-I support this optimization by assigning π_1 as TK_1's schedule and assigning π_2 as TK_2's and TK_3's schedule combined. As a result, by skipping the inverse operation after an on-the-fly key schedule, the (C2) operation implicitly executes π_2 and π_3 after a TBC call. This allows us to remove the circuits for the inverse tweakey operations from the tweakey arrays.[9]

7.3 Hardware Implementation of Romulus-H

Our Romulus-H design is based on the same SKINNY-128-384 implementation and has a similar architecture and components (the state and tweakey arrays). Romulus-H needs additional 2×128 bits of memory, and we realize them using a set of 128-bit shift registers, namely SR_0 and SR_1.

We decompose Romulus-H into several basic operations in Fig. 12-(left): (D1) a TBC call, (D2) processing the first TBC output, (D3) processing the second TBC output, and (D4) feeding a 256-bit new message block to $TK_2||TK_3$. Figure 12-(left) also illustrates how we manage data between the memory elements: we use SR_0 for storing the previous TBC input for feed-forward and use SR_1 for preserving a derivative of the first TBC call during the second one.

Figure 12-(right) shows the corresponding datapath. The major additions to the baseline SKINNY-128-384 implementation are SR_0 and SR_1 implemented as simple 8-bit width and 16-stage shift registers. We also added some 8-bit logic gates for enabling data transmission between the memory elements.

[9] The conventional TK_1–TK_3 arrays integrates circuits for inverse tweakey operations (the inverse LFSRs and inverse byte permutation) [25]. We remove these circuits along with selectors for switching between the datapaths. These circuits are intact in our Romulus-H implementation because it requires the inverse operations.

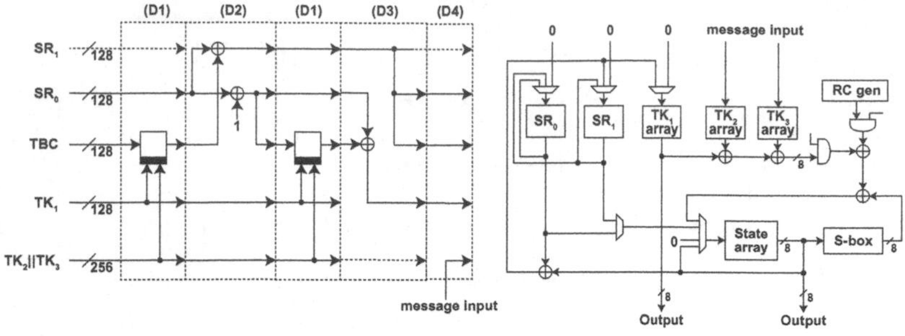

Fig. 12. (Left) Decomposition of Romulus-H into basic operations and (Right) the datapath architecture realizing those operations

7.4 Performance Evaluation and Comparison

Implementation and Evaluation Procedure. We implement the designs at the register-transfer level; we explicitly instantiate the standard cells only for the scan flip-flops [22]. We synthesize the designs using Synopsys Design Compiler with the NanGate 45-nm standard cell library [27]. Table 3 summarizes the circuit areas of our EXEX-NI, EXEX-I, and Romulus-H implementations in NAND gate equivalent (GE), along with its breakdown to major components that we preserved during the synthesis.

Comparison. The EXEX-NI and EXEX-I implementations are smaller than that of Romulus-H, as shown in Table 3. More specifically, the EXEX-NI implementation is smaller by 2,262 GE and is only 68% of the Romulus-H implementation. The main reason is the memory sizes: Romulus-H's additional memory, implemented as the shift registers SR_0 and SR_1, consumes roughly 1,500 GE, as shown in Table 3.[10] Another reason is the inverse tweakey schedule we discussed in Sect. 7.2. Eliminating the inverse tweakey schedule makes each tweakey array smaller by roughly 250 GE, resulting in the total reduction of 750 GE. The difference between the EXEX-NI and EXEX-I implementations is only 48 GE that corresponds to several 8-bit width logic gates for the (C4) operation; EXEX-I's main advantage is speed. The S-box circuit, composed of eight XORs and NORs, occupies roughly 30 GE which is negligible compared to the registers.

Missing Parallelism. The conventional schemes including Romulus-H can run up to two TBCs in parallel, which is impossible with EXEX-NI and EXEX-I that serializes the consecutive TBCs for smaller memory. Missing parallelism has a negligible impact on lightweight implementations because parallel execution needs double the hardware resources. On the other hand, in high-speed implementation with sufficiently many resources available, Romulus-H and other conventional schemes can have higher efficiency (i.e., throughput/area) by pipelining the consecutive TBCs.

[10] The per-bit cost of SR_0 and SR_1 is smaller than those of the state/tweakey arrays because SR_0 and SR_1 use a simple flip-flop instead of a scan flip-flop.

Table 3. Circuit-area comparison of EXEX-NI, EXEX-I, and Romulus-H instantiated with SKINNY-128-384 in gate-equivalent (GE)

Target	Total	State array	TK_1 array	TK_2 array	TK_3 array	SR_0	SR_1
EXEX-NI	4,755	1,078	1,007	1,019	1,019	–	–
EXEX-I	4,707	1,077	1,007	1,019	1,019	–	–
Romulus-H	7,017	1,078	1,231	1,270	1,271	743	743

Further optimization. We can implement EXEX-NI even smaller at the cost of speed by choosing a TBC with a smaller tweakey. If we instantiate EXEX-NI with SKINNY-128-256 instead of SKINNY-128-384, we can eliminate the TK_3 array and save roughly 1,000 GE, and the total circuit will be approximately 3,700 GE. Meanwhile, this modification comes at the cost of speed: the data rate is roughly halved because we can process only a 128-bit message block with a pair of TBC calls.

EXEX-NI and EXEX-I enjoy the conventional Romulus-H optimizations proposed by the Romulus team [13,14]. The first optimization is to reduce the round number considering SKINNY's large security margin [13], i.e., SKINNY-128-384+. It will speed up each TBC call but its impact to area should be limited. Another optimization is to virtually reduce the tweakey size by using message blocks stuffed with zeros. For example, if we limit the message size to 128 bits in our tweakey configuration, the input to TK_3 becomes always zero, and we can replace the TK_3 array with a constant-value generator, which makes the circuit area similar to those instantiated with SKINNY-128-256.

8 Conclusion

In this paper, we proposed two DBL hash modes achieving minimum memory size. When an underlying BC supports an n-bit block and a k-bit key, our modes only require $n + k$-bit memory, which improves the previous smallest results of $2n + k$-bit memory. EXEX-NI mode is indifferentiable up to $n - \log n$ bits. Its instantiation with SKINNY-128 can be an efficient alternative to Romulus-H; our mode satisfies all the requirements in NIST LWC and provides hashing to Romulus with zero memory overhead, which significantly reduces the memory size of $3n + k$ bits for Romulus-H. EXEX-I mode focuses on the fact that indifferetiability may be unnecessary to be integrated with AEAD schemes, and we rigorously optimized its efficiency by focusing on the collision resistance.

There are several possible research directions, which includes relaxing the key size limitation $k \geq 2n$ of EXEX-NI, finding an attack rigorously matching the bound, a new mode without security loss of $\log n$ bits, integrated implementations of AEAD and hashing schemes. Application of our modes to the BC-based NIST finalist GIFT-COFB [2] is also interesting because it does not support hashing. Its underlying cipher GIFT128 supports $n = 128$ and $k = 128$, thus the block size fits perfectly, while the key size does not. Modifying GIFT128 to support a 256-bit key or 128-bit tweak is an interesting challenge.

References

1. Armknecht, F., Fleischmann, E., Krause, M., Lee, J., Stam, M., Steinberger, J.: The preimage security of double-block-length compression functions. In: Lee, D.H., Wang, X. (eds.) ASIACRYPT 2011. LNCS, vol. 7073, pp. 233–251. Springer, Heidelberg (2011). https://doi.org/10.1007/978-3-642-25385-0_13
2. Banik, S., et al.: GIFT-COFB v1.0. Submitted to NIST LWC (2019)
3. Beierle, C., et al.: The SKINNY family of block ciphers and its low-latency variant MANTIS. In: Robshaw, M., Katz, J. (eds.) CRYPTO 2016. LNCS, vol. 9815, pp. 123–153. Springer, Heidelberg (2016). https://doi.org/10.1007/978-3-662-53008-5_5
4. Bertoni, G., Daemen, J., Peeters, M., Van Assche, G.: On the indifferentiability of the sponge construction. In: Smart, N. (ed.) EUROCRYPT 2008. LNCS, vol. 4965, pp. 181–197. Springer, Heidelberg (2008). https://doi.org/10.1007/978-3-540-78967-3_11
5. Bertoni, G., Daemen, J., Peeters, M., Van Assche, G.: Duplexing the sponge: single-pass authenticated encryption and other applications. In: Miri, A., Vaudenay, S. (eds.) SAC 2011. LNCS, vol. 7118, pp. 320–337. Springer, Heidelberg (2012). https://doi.org/10.1007/978-3-642-28496-0_19
6. Bogdanov, A., Leander, G., Paar, C., Poschmann, A., Robshaw, M.J.B., Seurin, Y.: Hash functions and RFID tags: mind the gap. In: Oswald, E., Rohatgi, P. (eds.) CHES 2008. LNCS, vol. 5154, pp. 283–299. Springer, Heidelberg (2008). https://doi.org/10.1007/978-3-540-85053-3_18
7. Brachtl, B.O., et al.: Data authentication using modification detection codes based on a public one way encryption function. U. S. Patent #4,908,861, March 1990
8. Coron, J.-S., Dodis, Y., Malinaud, C., Puniya, P.: Merkle-Damgård revisited: how to construct a hash function. In: Shoup, V. (ed.) CRYPTO 2005. LNCS, vol. 3621, pp. 430–448. Springer, Heidelberg (2005). https://doi.org/10.1007/11535218_26
9. Damgård, I.B.: A design principle for hash functions. In: Brassard, G. (ed.) CRYPTO 1989. LNCS, vol. 435, pp. 416–427. Springer, New York (1990). https://doi.org/10.1007/0-387-34805-0_39
10. Hirose, S.: Some plausible constructions of double-block-length hash functions. In: Robshaw, M. (ed.) FSE 2006. LNCS, vol. 4047, pp. 210–225. Springer, Heidelberg (2006). https://doi.org/10.1007/11799313_14
11. Hirose, S., Park, J.H., Yun, A.: A simple variant of the Merkle-Damgård scheme with a permutation. In: Kurosawa, K. (ed.) ASIACRYPT 2007. LNCS, vol. 4833, pp. 113–129. Springer, Heidelberg (2007). https://doi.org/10.1007/978-3-540-76900-2_7
12. Iwata, T., Khairallah, M., Minematsu, K., Peyrin, T.: Duel of the titans: the romulus and remus families of lightweight AEAD algorithms. IACR Trans. Symmetric Cryptol. **2020**(1), 43–120 (2020)
13. Iwata, T., Khairallah, M., Minematsu, K., Peyrin, T.: New results on romulus. In: NIST Lightweight Cryptography Workshop 2020 (2020). https://csrc.nist.gov/CSRC/media/Events/lightweight-cryptography-workshop-2020/documents/papers/new-results-romulus-lwc2020.pdf

14. Iwata, T., Khairallah, M., Minematsu, K., Peyrin, T.: Romulus for Round 3 (2020). https://csrc.nist.gov/CSRC/media/Projects/lightweight-cryptography/documents/round-2/status-update-sep2020/Romulus-for-Round-3.pdf
15. Khurana, D.: MACs and collision-resistance (section 6.3 hash-then-MAC) (2020). https://courses.physics.illinois.edu/cs498ac3/fa2020/Files/Lecture_6_Scribe.pdf
16. Lai, X., Massey, J.L.: Hash functions based on block ciphers. In: Rueppel, R.A. (ed.) EUROCRYPT 1992. LNCS, vol. 658, pp. 55–70. Springer, Heidelberg (1993). https://doi.org/10.1007/3-540-47555-9_5
17. Lee, J., Stam, M.: MJH: a faster alternative to MDC-2. In: Kiayias, A. (ed.) CT-RSA 2011. LNCS, vol. 6558, pp. 213–236. Springer, Heidelberg (2011). https://doi.org/10.1007/978-3-642-19074-2_15
18. Lee, J., Stam, M., Steinberger, J.: The collision security of tandem-DM in the ideal cipher model. In: Rogaway, P. (ed.) CRYPTO 2011. LNCS, vol. 6841, pp. 561–577. Springer, Heidelberg (2011). https://doi.org/10.1007/978-3-642-22792-9_32
19. Maurer, U., Renner, R., Holenstein, C.: Indifferentiability, impossibility results on reductions, and applications to the random oracle methodology. In: Naor, M. (ed.) TCC 2004. LNCS, vol. 2951, pp. 21–39. Springer, Heidelberg (2004). https://doi.org/10.1007/978-3-540-24638-1_2
20. Mennink, B.: Optimal collision security in double block length hashing with single length key. In: Wang, X., Sako, K. (eds.) ASIACRYPT 2012. LNCS, vol. 7658, pp. 526–543. Springer, Heidelberg (2012). https://doi.org/10.1007/978-3-642-34961-4_32
21. Merkle, R.C.: One way hash functions and DES. In: Brassard, G. (ed.) CRYPTO 1989. LNCS, vol. 435, pp. 428–446. Springer, New York (1990). https://doi.org/10.1007/0-387-34805-0_40
22. Moradi, A., Poschmann, A., Ling, S., Paar, C., Wang, H.: Pushing the limits: a very compact and a threshold implementation of AES. In: Paterson, K.G. (ed.) EUROCRYPT 2011. LNCS, vol. 6632, pp. 69–88. Springer, Heidelberg (2011). https://doi.org/10.1007/978-3-642-20465-4_6
23. Naito, Y.: Indifferentiability of double-block-length hash function without feed-forward operations. In: Pieprzyk, J., Suriadi, S. (eds.) ACISP 2017. LNCS, vol. 10343, pp. 38–57. Springer, Cham (2017). https://doi.org/10.1007/978-3-319-59870-3_3
24. Naito, Y.: Optimally indifferentiable double-block-length hashing without post-processing and with support for longer key than single block. In: Schwabe, P., Thériault, N. (eds.) LATINCRYPT 2019. LNCS, vol. 11774, pp. 65–85. Springer, Cham (2019). https://doi.org/10.1007/978-3-030-30530-7_4
25. Naito, Y., Sasaki, Yu., Sugawara, T.: Lightweight authenticated encryption mode suitable for threshold implementation. In: Canteaut, A., Ishai, Y. (eds.) EUROCRYPT 2020. LNCS, vol. 12106, pp. 705–735. Springer, Cham (2020). https://doi.org/10.1007/978-3-030-45724-2_24
26. Naito, Y., Sasaki, Y., Sugawara, T.: LM-DAE: low-memory deterministic authenticated encryption for 128-bit security. IACR Trans. Symmetric Cryptol. **2020**(4), 1–38 (2020)
27. NanGate: NanGate FreePDK45 Open Cell Library. https://si2.org/open-cell-library/ (2021). Accessed 22 May 2021
28. NIST: The Keyed-Hash Message Authentication Code (HMAC). FIPS PUB 198–1 (2008)
29. NIST: Submission Requirements and Evaluation Criteria for the Lightweight Cryptography Standardization Process (2018). https://csrc.nist.gov/Projects/lightweight-cryptography

30. NIST: Lightweight Cryptography Standardization: Finalists Announced (2021). https://csrc.nist.gov/News/2021/lightweight-crypto-finalists-announced
31. NIST: Status Report on the Second Round of the NIST Lightweight Cryptography Standardization Process (2021). https://csrc.nist.gov/publications/detail/nistir/8369/final
32. Özen, O., Stam, M.: Another glance at double-length hashing. In: Parker, M.G. (ed.) IMACC 2009. LNCS, vol. 5921, pp. 176–201. Springer, Heidelberg (2009). https://doi.org/10.1007/978-3-642-10868-6_11

Toward a Fully Secure Authenticated Encryption Scheme from a Pseudorandom Permutation

Wonseok Choi(✉), Byeonghak Lee(✉), Jooyoung Lee(✉), and Yeongmin Lee

KAIST, Daejeon, Korea
{krwioh,lbh0307,hicalf,dudals4780}@kaist.ac.kr

Abstract. In this paper, we propose a new block cipher-based authenticated encryption scheme, dubbed the Synthetic Counter with Masking (SCM) mode. SCM follows the NSIV paradigm proposed by Peyrin and Seurin (CRYPTO 2016), where a keyed hash function accepts a nonce N with associated data and a message, yielding an authentication tag T, and then the message is encrypted by a counter-like mode using both T and N. Here we move one step further by *encrypting nonces*; in the encryption part, the inputs to the block cipher are determined by T, counters, and an encrypted nonce, and all its outputs are also masked by an (additional) encrypted nonce, yielding keystream blocks.

As a result, we obtain, for the first time, a block cipher-based authenticated encryption scheme of rate 1/2 that provides n-bit security with respect to the query complexity (ignoring the influence of message length) in the nonce-respecting setting, and at the same time guarantees graceful security degradation in the faulty nonce model, when the underlying n-bit block cipher is modeled as a secure pseudorandom permutation. Seen as a slight variant of GCM-SIV, SCM is also parallelizable and inverse-free, and its performance is still comparable to GCM-SIV.

Keywords: Authenticated encryption · Beyond-birthday-bound security · Nonce-misuse resistance · Graceful degradation · Block cipher

1 Introduction

Authenticated Encryption. Authenticated encryption (AE) aims at achieving the two fundamental security goals of symmetric key cryptography, namely, the confidentiality and the authenticity of data. With a significant amount of research in this area, we now have a rich set of general-purpose AE schemes, some already standardized (e.g., GCM [21] and CCM [27]) and some expected to be adopted by new applications and standards (e.g., the CAESAR finalists

J. Lee—This work was supported by Institute for Information & communications Technology Planning & Evaluation(IITP) grant funded by the Korea government (MSIT) (No. 2019-0-01343, Regional strategic industry convergence security core talent training business).

M. Tibouchi and H. Wang (Eds.): ASIACRYPT 2021, LNCS 13092, pp. 407–434, 2021.
https://doi.org/10.1007/978-3-030-92078-4_14

COLM [1], Ascon [8], Deoxys II [18], OCB [20], ACORN [28], and AEGIS-128 [29]). Such AE schemes are built on top of various cryptographic primitives such as permutations and (tweakable) block ciphers. Most of recent constructions accept associated data (AD), which are authenticated but not encrypted. In this paper, we will also consider AE schemes with associated data.

NONCE-MISUSE RESISTANCE. Nonces or initial vectors (IVs) are used in most encryption schemes in order to guarantee the variability of the ciphertext. In particular, nonces will guarantee stronger security in the authentication part than deterministic constructions when they are never reused. On the other hand, only a single nonce repetition can completely break the security of the scheme. For example, GCM leaks its hash key as soon as a single nonce is used twice. However, it might be challenging to maintain the uniqueness of the nonce in certain environments, for example, in a stateless device where good quality randomness is not available. A faulty implementation of the AE scheme might also repeat nonces. For this reason, there has been a considerable amount of research on the design of AE schemes achieving nonce-misuse resistance.

Rogaway and Shrimpton [26] formalized the notion of misuse-resistant AE (MRAE) and proposed a method of turning a deterministic AE scheme into a nonce-based MRAE scheme. In this way, nonce repetitions do not affect the overall security of the scheme as long as a triple of nonce, AD and message values is not repeated. MRAE schemes include EAX [2], SIV [26], AEZ [12], and GCM-SIV [11]. Later, this notion has been refined by viewing the adversarial distinguishing advantage as a function of the maximum number of multicollisions in nonce values (amongst all encryption queries) [25]. Recently, Dutta et al. [9] introduced the *faulty nonce model*; an adversarial query is called a *faulty query* if there exists a previous query with the same nonce. Here, the adversarial distinguishing advantage is analyzed as a function of the number of faulty queries. They also proposed a new MAC scheme, dubbed nEHtM, and showed that it enjoys graceful degradation of security in this model. The two models of nonce misuse above seem to complement each other; when an m-multicollsion of a single nonce happens, it implies that there have been at least $m-1$ faulty queries, while any number of faulty queries can be made by multicollisions of nonces with small multiplicities.

BIRTHDAY AND BEYOND-BIRTHDAY SECURITY. Most block cipher-based AE modes provide only the birthday-bound security (with respect to the size of the underlying primitive). For example, if an AE mode is based on a 128-bit block cipher such as AES, then it would guarantee only up to 64-bit security, whereas this bound might not be sufficient in defense-in-depth applications where higher security is required.

Some AE schemes enjoy beyond-birthday-bound security. Iwata [14] proposed the CIP AE mode of rate 4/9 (for the default parameters) and $2n/3$-bit security, and Iwata and Minematsu [15] proposed a variant of GCM-SIV of rate 1/4 and $2n/3$-bit security. Bose et al. [4] proved n-bit security of AES-GCM-SIV in the ideal cipher model. However, in this stronger model, its provable security would not be called "full" since the underlying ideal primitive accepts $(n+\kappa)$-bit inputs,

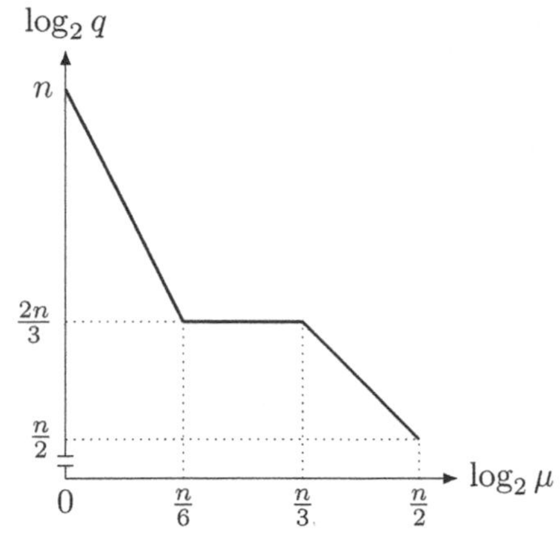

Fig. 1. Security of SCM in terms of the threshold number of encryption queries q as a function of the number of faulty queries μ.

where κ denotes the key size. Assuming the multi-user security of AES in the standard model, Iwata and Seurin [17] proved $3n/4$-bit security of AES-GCM-SIV. The mGCM mode [3] achieves almost n-bit security with reasonable efficiency (of rate around $1/2$) in the standard model, while it is vulnerable to nonce misuse.

When it comes to *tweakable* block cipher-based constructions (for simplicity, assuming that the underlying tweakable block cipher uses n-bit tweaks), SCT [25] provides n-bit security in the nonce-respecting setting, while its integrity falls down to the birthday bound as soon as a nonce is repeated. Iwata et al. proposed ZAE [16], which is a deterministic AE scheme providing n-bit security.

The focus of this paper is put on the construction of (conventional) block cipher-based *nonce-misuse resistant* AE schemes with almost n-bit security and reasonable efficiency assuming the *pseudorandomness* of the underlying block cipher in the single-user setting. One of the advantages of block cipher-based schemes is that it can be instantiated with a widely-used block cipher such as AES. Due to AES-NI instructions, and a considerable amount of research on efficient implementation of AES, AES-based schemes are usually faster than tweakable block cipher-based ones. On the other hand, compared to using an n-bit tweakable block cipher, it seems more challenging to achieve the same level of security using an n-bit conventional block cipher with a weaker security assumption.

1.1 Our Contribution

We propose the Synthetic Counter with Masking (SCM) mode, which turns a block cipher into a nonce-based authenticated encryption scheme. SCM follows the NSIV paradigm proposed by Peyrin and Seurin in CRYPTO 2016 [25], where a keyed hash function accepts a nonce N with associated data and a message, yielding an authentication tag T, and then the message is encrypted by a counter-

Table 1. Comparison of SCM with existing AE modes. NR (resp. NM) represents the nonce-respecting setting (resp. the nonce-misuse setting).

AEAD	Assumption	Rate	Security		Graceful degradation	Reference
			NR	NM		
GCM	PRF	1/2	$n/2$	–	✗	[21]
OCB3	PRP	1	$n/2$	–	✗	[19]
mGCM	PRP	1/2	n	–	✗	[3]
GCM-SIV	PRF	1/2	$n/2$	$n/2$	✓	[11]
CWC+	PRP	1/2	$3n/4$	$n/2^{\dagger}$	✓†	[9]
AES-GCM-SIV	muPRP	1/2	$3n/4$	$n/2$	✓	[17]
AES-GCM-SIV‡	ICM	1/2	n	$n/2$	✓	[4]
SCM	PRP	1/2	n	$n/2$	✓	This work
ΘCB	TPRP	1	n	–	✗	[19]
SCT	TPRP	1/2	n	$n/2$	✗	[25]
ZAE	TPRP	2/3	n	n	✓	[16]

† Authenticity only. CWC+ does not provide privacy in the nonce-misuse setting.
‡ A variant of AES-GCM-SIV with the key derivation function modified.

like mode using both T and N. Here we move one step further by *encrypting nonces*: from a secret key and a nonce, three encrypted nonces Δ, Δ' and Δ'' are computed. The authentication tag T is defined by a variant of nEHtM [9] using Δ''. More precisely, for an associated data A and a message M,

$$T = E_{K'}(H_{K_h}(A, M) \oplus (N \parallel 00)) \oplus \Delta''.$$

The i-th keystream block $Z[i]$ is defined as

$$Z[i] = E_K(T \oplus 2^{i-1}\Delta) \oplus \Delta',$$

which is xored to the corresponding message block. We prove that if H is a δ-almost XOR universal hash function with $\delta \approx \frac{1}{2^n}$, if E is a secure block cipher, and if the maximum length of encryption queries is sufficiently small, then SCM is secure up to $O(2^n)$ encryption and decryption queries in the nonce-respecting setting. Even if nonces are repeated, SCM is secure up to the birthday bound, enjoying graceful security degradation in the faulty nonce model. Figure 1 shows the security bounds of SCM in terms of the threshold number of encryption queries q as a function of the number of faulty queries μ ignoring the maximum message length. The influence of μ to the threshold number of decryption queries is negligible as seen in Theorem 1 (with $L = n$).

Table 1 compares SCM to well-known AE schemes based on (tweakable) block ciphers. For simplicity of comparison, we assume that the underlying tweakable block cipher uses n-bit tweaks. To the best of our knowledge, SCM is the first block cipher-based nonce-misuse resistant AE scheme of rate 1/2 that provides n-bit security in the nonce-respecting setting when the underlying n-bit block cipher is modeled as a pseudorandom permutation. Seen as a slight variant of GCM-SIV, SCM is also parallelizable and inverse-free.

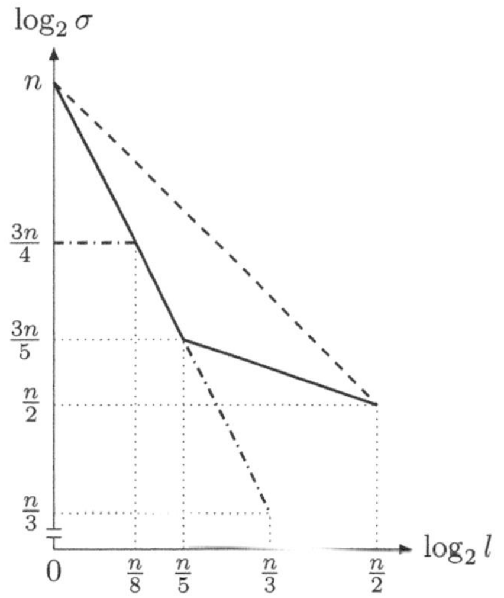

Fig. 2. The threshold number of the total length of the encryption queries σ as a function of l, where the number of faulty queries μ is fixed as a small constant. The solid line is the bound for SCM, while the dashed (resp. dash-dotted) line is the bound for AES-GCM-SIV in the ideal cipher (resp. multi-user PRP) model.

Figure 2 compares the influence of the maximum message length l to the threshold number of the total length of the encryption queries σ for SCM and AES-GCM-SIV, where we distinguish two different models in which AES-GCM-SIV has been analyzed. When security bounds are not represented by only σ and l, we use a (loose) bound $q \leq \sigma$. We see that SCM provides stronger bounds than AES-GCM-SIV in the standard model. We note that GCM, OCB3 and GCM-SIV are secure when $\sigma \ll 2^{\frac{n}{2}}$, while all the tweakble cipher-based constructions ΘCB, SCT, and ZAE are secure when $\sigma \ll 2^n$, all regardless of the maximum message length. In [9], CWC+ has been proved to be secure up to $2^{\frac{2n}{3}}$ block cipher queries, while one can obtain a stronger bound using recent results [3,6]. Even with this improvement, its security does not go beyond $2^{\frac{3n}{4}}$ (in terms of σ).

Being nonce-misuse resistant, SCM provides beyond-birthday-bound security as long as $\mu l \ll 2^{n/2}$, and it can be seen as optimal when μ and l are small enough. This property is practically relevant for a certain case, where data is broken into small parts, and they are encrypted with different nonces. For example, in the TLS network protocol, the maximum transmission unit (MTU) is typically set to 1500B, and each fragment is encrypted with a different nonce using its sequence number.

Table 2 compares SCM using POLYVAL[1] [10] as a universal hash function to existing AE schemes in terms of efficiency. In this comparison, we focus on the AE schemes whose reference codes are publicly available (except ZAE). The efficiency

[1] POLYVAL is a universal hash function used in AES-GCM-SIV.

Table 2. Performance comparison of SCM to various AE schemes. Throughput is measured in cycles per byte.

Mode	Cipher	Message			Reference
		1 KB	4 KB	64 KB	
ChaCha20-Poly1305	–	2.17	1.55	1.47	[22]
GCM	AES-128	1.23	0.63	0.56	[21]
AES-GCM-SIV	AES-128	1.57	0.89	0.81	[17]
Deoxys-I ($\approx \Theta$CB)	Deoxys-BC-256	1.38	0.91	0.77	[18]
Deoxys-II ($\approx$ SCT)	Deoxys-BC-256	2.19	1.68	1.52	[18]
ZAE	Deoxys-BC-256	$\geq$1.94	$\geq$1.41	$\geq$1.25	[16]
SCM	AES-128	0.94	0.86	0.83	This work

of ZAE has been only approximately estimated based on the speed of Deoxys-BC-256 in counter mode (as done in [16]), so the number in Table 2 should be understood as rough lower bounds. The implementations of ChaCha20-Poly1305, GCM, and AES-GCM-SIV are taken from BoringSSL[2] and those of Deoxys-I and Deoxys-II are taken from SUPERCOP[3]. Our experiments are done in the Skylake microarchitecture (i7-6700 CPU@4.20 GHz) which supports PCLMUL, AVX, SSE, and AES instructions, using GCC 7.4.0 with optimization level -O2.

Although SCM requires four block cipher calls to encrypt nonces at the beginning of every encryption, our implementation shows that it does not slow down the overall efficiency since it can be done in parallel with the encryption of the hash output. We see that SCM is comparable to AES-GCM-SIV.

Overview of the Proof. Our security proof takes a modular approach; SCM$[H, E]$ (based on a keyed hash function H and a block cipher E) is decomposed into a MAC scheme and an encryption scheme, denoted SCM.MAC$[H, E]$ and SCM.PRNG$[E]$, respectively. We first prove that if both SCM.MAC$[H, E]$ and SCM.PRNG$[E]$ are secure, then SCM$[H, E]$ is also secure (Lemma 5), where we need to slightly modify the security model for the encryption part; it takes as input a random tag T (which can be seen as an initial vector), and T is also given to the adversary.

The underlying MAC scheme is similar to the nonce-based enhanced hash-then-mask MAC (nEHtM), whose security has been recently proved up to $2^{\frac{3n}{4}}$ MAC queries [6]. The main difference of SCM.MAC from nEHtM is that the "encrypted mask" $E_K(N)$ used in nEHtM is replaced by $E_K(N\|00) \oplus E_K(N\|11)$ using an $(n-2)$-bit nonce N, which can be seen as $\rho(N)$ for a truly random function ρ. At the cost of an additional block cipher call, SCM.MAC$[H, E]$ is secure up to 2^n MAC queries when H is a δ-almost XOR universal with $\delta \approx \frac{1}{2^n}$ (Lemma 6).

[2] https://boringssl.googlesource.com/boringssl.
[3] https://bench.cr.yp.to/supercop.html.

The pseudorandomness of $\mathsf{SCM.PRNG}[E]$ is analyzed by two different approaches. When the number of faulty queries μ is relatively large, we use Mirror theory in a refined form as given in [6] (and restated in Lemma 3). In Lemma 7, we prove that $\mathsf{SCM.PRNG}[E]$ is pseudorandom up to $2^{\frac{2n}{3}}$ queries, enjoying graceful security degradation as μ increases.

When μ is small, for example, in the nonce-respecting setting, one can expect even stronger security. In such cases, we make the adversary *non-adaptive* by allowing it to repeat each nonce exactly μ times. In this setting, we can use the χ^2-method as restated in Lemma 2, and its interpretation in terms of Mirror theory as given in Lemma 4. All the bounds contain the sum-of-squares and sum-of-cubes of component sizes in the graph representation of the transcript, and it is the most challenging part of the proof to upper bound their expectation (Lemma 10 and 12). Finally, we apply the expectation method to prove the security of $\mathsf{SCM.PRNG}[E]$ up to 2^n queries in the nonce-respecting setting (Lemma 8).

2 Preliminaries

2.1 Notation

In all of the following, we fix a positive integer n such that $n \geq 3$. We denote 0^n (i.e., n-bit string of all zeros) by $\mathbf{0}$. The set $\{0,1\}^n$ is sometimes regarded as a set of integers $\{0,1,\ldots,2^n-1\}$ by converting an n-bit string $a_{n-1}\cdots a_1a_0 \in \{0,1\}^n$ to an integer $a_{n-1}2^{n-1}+\cdots+a_12+a_0$. We also identify $\{0,1\}^n$ with a finite field $\mathbf{GF}(2^n)$ with 2^n elements, assuming that 2 cyclically generates all the nonzero elements of $\mathbf{GF}(2^n)$. We write $\{0,1\}^*$ to denote the set of all binary strings including the empty string. For $X \in \{0,1\}^*$, $|X|$ denotes its length. For a nonnegative integer s and a string $X \in \{0,1\}^*$ such that $|X| \leq s$, $\mathsf{msb}_s(X)$ denotes the s most significant bits of X. For a positive integer q, we write $[q] = \{1,\ldots,q\}$.

Given a non-empty finite set $\mathcal{X}$, $x \leftarrow_\$ \mathcal{X}$ denotes that x is chosen uniformly at random from $\mathcal{X}$. The set of all functions from $\mathcal{X}$ to $\mathcal{Y}$ is denoted $\mathsf{Func}(\mathcal{X},\mathcal{Y})$, and the set of all permutations of $\mathcal{X}$ is denoted $\mathsf{Perm}(\mathcal{X})$. The set of all permutations of $\{0,1\}^n$ is simply denoted $\mathsf{Perm}(n)$. The set of all sequences that consist of b pairwise distinct elements of $\mathcal{X}$ is denoted $\mathcal{X}^{*b}$. For integers $1 \leq b \leq a$, we will write $(a)_b = a(a-1)\cdots(a-b+1)$ and $(a)_0 = 1$ by convention. If $|\mathcal{X}| = a$, then $(a)_b$ becomes the size of $\mathcal{X}^{*b}$.

When two sets $\mathcal{X}$ and $\mathcal{Y}$ are disjoint, their (disjoint) union is denoted $\mathcal{X} \sqcup \mathcal{Y}$. For a set $\mathcal{X} \subset \{0,1\}^n$ and $\lambda \in \{0,1\}^n$, we will write $\mathcal{X} \oplus \lambda = \{x \oplus \lambda : x \in \mathcal{X}\}$. For a graph $\mathcal{G} = (\mathcal{V},\mathcal{E})$, we will interchangeably write $|\mathcal{V}|$ and $|\mathcal{G}|$ for the number of vertices of $\mathcal{G}$.

2.2 Security Notions

Almost Xor Universal Hash Functions. Let $\delta > 0$, and let $H : \mathcal{K}_h \times \mathcal{M} \rightarrow \mathcal{X}$ be a keyed function for three non-empty sets $\mathcal{K}_h$, $\mathcal{M}$, and $\mathcal{X}$. H is said to be *δ-almost XOR universal* (AXU) if for any distinct $M, M' \in \mathcal{M}$ and $X \in \mathcal{X}$,

$$\Pr\left[K_h \leftarrow_\$ \mathcal{K}_h : H_{K_h}(M) \oplus H_{K_h}(M') = X\right] \leq \delta.$$

PRPs. Let $E : \mathcal{K} \times \{0,1\}^n \rightarrow \{0,1\}^n$ be a keyed permutation with key space $\mathcal{K}$, where $E(K,\cdot)$ is a permutation for each $K \in \mathcal{K}$. We will denote $E_K(X)$ for $E(K,X)$. A (q,t)-distinguisher against E is an algorithm $\mathcal{D}$ with oracle access to an n-bit permutation and its inverse, making at most q oracle queries, running in time at most t, and outputting a single bit. The advantage of $\mathcal{D}$ in breaking the PRP-security of E, i.e., in distinguishing E from a uniform random permutation $\pi \leftarrow_\$ \mathsf{Perm}(n)$, is defined as

$$\mathsf{Adv}_E^{\mathsf{prp}}(\mathcal{D}) = \left|\Pr\left[K \leftarrow_\$ \mathcal{K} : \mathcal{D}^{E_K, E_K^{-1}} = 1\right] - \Pr\left[\pi \leftarrow_\$ \mathsf{Perm}(n) : \mathcal{D}^{\pi,\pi^{-1}} = 1\right]\right|.$$

We define $\mathsf{Adv}_E^{\mathsf{prp}}(q,t)$ as the maximum of $\mathsf{Adv}_E^{\mathsf{prp}}(\mathcal{D})$ over all (q,t)-distinguishers against E.

Nonce-based MACs. Given four non-empty sets $\mathcal{K}$, $\mathcal{N}$, $\mathcal{M}$, and $\mathcal{T}$, a nonce-based MAC with key space $\mathcal{K}$, nonce space $\mathcal{N}$, message space $\mathcal{M}$ and tag space $\mathcal{T}$ is a function $F : \mathcal{K} \times \mathcal{N} \times \mathcal{M} \rightarrow \mathcal{T}$. Stated otherwise, it is a keyed function whose domain is a cartesian product $\mathcal{N} \times \mathcal{M}$. We will sometimes write $F_K(N,M)$ to denote $F(K,N,M)$.

For $K \in \mathcal{K}$, let Auth_K be the MAC oracle which takes as input a pair $(N,M) \in \mathcal{N} \times \mathcal{M}$ and returns $F_K(N,M)$, and let Ver_K be the verification oracle which takes as input a triple $(N,M,T) \in \mathcal{N} \times \mathcal{M} \times \mathcal{T}$ and returns $\top$ ("accept") if $F_K(N,M) = T$, and $\perp$ ("reject") otherwise. We assume that an adversary makes queries to the two oracles Auth_K and Ver_K for a secret key $K \in \mathcal{K}$. A MAC query (N,M) made by an adversary is called a *faulty query* if the adversary has already queried to the MAC oracle with the same nonce but with a different message. For example, if the i-th query is denoted by (N_i,M_i) and there are four distinct queries, (N_i,M_i) for $i \in [4]$ such that $N_1 \neq N_2 = N_3 = N_4$, the third and the fourth queries are faulty and the number of faulty queries is two.

In this work, we will consider the MAC security of F using the advantage of an adversary trying to distinguish the real world $(\mathsf{Auth}_K, \mathsf{Ver}_K)$ and the ideal world. The ideal world oracles are $(\mathsf{Rand}, \mathsf{Rej})$, where Rand returns an independent random value (instantiating a truly random function) and Rej always returns $\perp$ for every verification query. A (μ,q,v,t)-distinguisher against the MAC security of F is an algorithm $\mathcal{D}$ with oracle access to $\mathsf{Auth}_K/\mathsf{Rand}$ and $\mathsf{Ver}_K/\mathsf{Rej}$, making at most q MAC queries to its first oracle with at most μ faulty queries and at most v verification queries to its second oracle, and running in time at most t. We assume that $\mathcal{D}$ does not make a verification query by reusing any previous MAC query. We define

$$\mathsf{Adv}_F^{\mathsf{mac}}(\mu,q,v,t) = \max_{\mathcal{D}}\left(\Pr\left[K \leftarrow_\$ \mathcal{K} : \mathcal{D}^{\mathsf{Auth}_K, \mathsf{Ver}_K} = 1\right] - \Pr\left[\mathcal{D}^{\mathsf{Rand},\mathsf{Rej}} = 1\right]\right),$$

where the maximum is taken over all (μ,q,v,t)-distinguishers $\mathcal{D}$. When we consider information theoretic security, we will drop the parameter t.

NONCE-BASED AE SCHEMES. Given four non-empty sets $\mathcal{K}$, $\mathcal{N}$, $\mathcal{A}$ and $\mathcal{M}$, a nonce-based authenticated encryption (AE) scheme is a tuple

$$\Pi = (\mathcal{K}, \mathcal{N}, \mathcal{A}, \mathcal{M}, \mathsf{Enc}, \mathsf{Dec}),$$

where Enc and Dec are called encryption and decryption algorithms, respectively. The encryption algorithm Enc takes as input a key $K \in \mathcal{K}$, a nonce $N \in \mathcal{N}$, an associated data $A \in \mathcal{A}$, and a message $M \in \mathcal{M}$, and outputs a ciphertext $C \in \{0,1\}^*$. The decryption algorithm Dec takes as input a tuple $(K, N, A, C) \in \mathcal{K} \times \mathcal{N} \times \mathcal{A} \times \{0,1\}^*$, and outputs either a message $M \in \mathcal{M}$ or a special symbol $\perp$. We require that

$$\mathsf{Dec}(K, N, A, \mathsf{Enc}(K, N, A, M)) = M$$

for any tuple $(K, N, A, M) \in \mathcal{K} \times \mathcal{N} \times \mathcal{A} \times \mathcal{M}$. We will write $\mathsf{Enc}_K(N, A, M)$ and $\mathsf{Dec}_K(N, A, C)$ to denote $\mathsf{Enc}(K, N, A, M)$ and $\mathsf{Dec}(K, N, A, C)$, respectively.

The goal of an adversary $\mathcal{D}$ against the nonce-based AE security of Π is to distinguish the real world $(\mathsf{Enc}_K, \mathsf{Dec}_K)$ (using a random key K, unknown to $\mathcal{D}$) and the ideal world. The ideal world oracles are $(\mathsf{Rand}, \mathsf{Rej})$, where Rand returns an independent random string of length $|\mathsf{Enc}_K(N, A, M)|$ and Rej always returns $\perp$ for every decryption query. We assume that $\mathcal{D}$ does not make a decryption query by reusing any previous encryption query. The advantage of $\mathcal{D}$ breaking the nAE-security of Π is defined as

$$\mathsf{Adv}_{\Pi}^{\mathsf{nAE}}(\mathcal{D}) = \left|\Pr\left[K \leftarrow_\$ \mathcal{K} : \mathcal{D}^{\mathsf{Enc}_K, \mathsf{Dec}_K} = 1\right] - \Pr\left[\mathcal{D}^{\mathsf{Rand}, \mathsf{Rej}} = 1\right]\right|.$$

A $(\mu, q, v, \sigma, l, t)$-adversary against the nonce-based AE security of Π is an algorithm that makes at most q encryption queries to its first oracle with at most μ faulty queries (using repeated nonces) and at most v decryption queries to its second oracle, and running in time at most t, where the length of each encryption/decryption query is at most l blocks of n bits, and the total length of the encryption queries (nonce excluded) is at most σ blocks of n bits. When $\mu = 0$, we say that $\mathcal{D}$ is nonce-respecting, otherwise $\mathcal{D}$ is said nonce-misusing. However, the adversary is allowed to repeat nonces in its Dec oracle. We define $\mathsf{Adv}_{\Pi}^{\mathsf{nAE}}(\mu, q, v, \sigma, l, t)$ as the maximum of $\mathsf{Adv}_{\Pi}^{\mathsf{nAE}}(\mathcal{D})$ over all $(\mu, q, v, \sigma, l, t)$-adversaries $\mathcal{D}$ against Π. When we consider information theoretic security, we will drop the parameter t.

2.3 Coefficient-H Technique

We will use Patarin's coefficient-H technique, more precisely, its refinement called the *expectation method* [13]. The goal of this technique is to upper bound the adversarial distinguishing advantage between a real construction and its ideal counterpart. In the real and the ideal worlds, an information-theoretic adversary $\mathcal{D}$ is allowed to make queries to certain oracles (with the same oracle interfaces), denoted $\mathcal{O}_{\mathsf{real}}$ and $\mathcal{O}_{\mathsf{ideal}}$, respectively. The interaction between the adversary $\mathcal{D}$ and the oracle determines a "transcript"; it contains all the information obtained by $\mathcal{D}$ during the interaction. We call a transcript τ *attainable* if the probability of obtaining τ in the ideal world is non-zero. We also denote T_{id} (resp. T_{re}) the probability distribution of the transcript τ induced by the ideal world (resp. the real world). By extension, we use the same notation to denote a random variable distributed according to each distribution.

We partition the set of attainable transcripts Γ into a set of "good" transcripts Γ_{good} such that the probabilities to obtain some transcript $\tau \in \Gamma_{\mathsf{good}}$ are close in the real world and the ideal world, and a set Γ_{bad} of "bad" transcripts such that the probability to obtain any $\tau \in \Gamma_{\mathsf{bad}}$ is small in the ideal world. The lower bound in the ratio of the probabilities to obtain a good transcript in both worlds will be given as a function of τ, and we will take its expectation. The expectation method is summarized in the following lemma.

Lemma 1. *Let $\Gamma = \Gamma_{\mathsf{good}} \sqcup \Gamma_{\mathsf{bad}}$ be a partition of the set of attainable transcripts, where there exists a non-negative function $\varepsilon_1(\tau)$ such that for any $\tau \in \Gamma_{\mathsf{good}}$,*

$$\frac{\Pr\left[\mathsf{T}_{\text{re}} = \tau\right]}{\Pr\left[\mathsf{T}_{\text{id}} = \tau\right]} \geq 1 - \varepsilon_1(\tau),$$

and there exists ε_2 such that $\Pr[\mathsf{T}_{\text{id}} \in \Gamma_{\mathsf{bad}}] \leq \varepsilon_2$. Then for any adversary $\mathcal{D}$,

$$\left|\Pr\left[\mathcal{D}^{\mathcal{O}_{\mathsf{real}}} = 1\right] - \Pr\left[\mathcal{D}^{\mathcal{O}_{\mathsf{ideal}}} = 1\right]\right| \leq \mathsf{Ex}\left[\varepsilon_1(\tau)\right] + \varepsilon_2,$$

where the expectation is taken over the distribution T_{id} in the ideal world.

We refer to [13] for the proof of Lemma 1.

2.4 Sampling with Replacement Using a Random Permutation

Xoring the outputs of a random permutation is a simple way of generating pseudorandom samples using a random permutation. A random permutation can be viewed as a random sampling *without replacement*.

Fix positive integers $w_1, \ldots, w_r \geq 2$. Let $\sigma = \sum_{i \in [r]} w_i$, and let

$$\mathsf{T} = (T_{i,j})_{i \in [r], j \in [w_i]} = (T_{1,1}, \cdots, T_{1,w_1}, T_{2,1}, \cdots, T_{2,w_2}, \cdots, T_{r,1}, \cdots, T_{r,w_r})$$

be a sequence sampled from $(\{0,1\}^n)^{*\sigma}$ uniformly at random (i.e., by random sampling without replacement). Let

$$\begin{aligned} \mathsf{S} &= (T_{i,j} \oplus T_{i,w_i})_{i \in [r], j \in [w_i - 1]} \\ &= (T_{1,1} \oplus T_{1,w_1}, \cdots, T_{1,w_1-1} \oplus T_{1,w_1}, \cdots, T_{r,1} \oplus T_{r,w_r}, \cdots, T_{r,w_r-1} \oplus T_{r,w_r}) \end{aligned}$$

Using the χ^2-method, Bhattacharya and Nandi [3] proved the pseudorandomness of S as follows.

Lemma 2. *Let* S *be a sequence sampled as described above, and let* R *be a sequence sampled from* $(\{0,1\}^n)^{\sigma-r}$ *uniformly at random.*[4] *Then we have*

$$\|\mathsf{S}-\mathsf{R}\| \le \left(\frac{4\sigma}{2^{2n}}\sum_{i=1}^{r} w_i^3\right)^{\frac{1}{2}} + \sum_{i=1}^{r}\frac{w_i(w_i-1)}{2^{n+1}}. \tag{1}$$

For an integer $w \ge 2$*, let* $w_i = w$ *for* $i \in 1,\ldots,r$*. Then we have*

$$\|\mathsf{S}-\mathsf{R}\| \le \frac{\sqrt{2}rw^2}{2^n} + \frac{w(w-1)r}{2^{n+1}}. \tag{2}$$

We note that (2) is simply a restatement of Theorem 2 in [3], and (1) can also be derived from the proof of the theorem (see page 327 in [3]).

2.5 Mirror Theory

Mirror theory [23,24] is one of the main tools for our security proof, whose goal is to systematically estimate the number of solutions to a system of equations. Mirror theory is later generalized to *extended* Mirror theory [7,9], by including non-equations in the system.

A system of equations and non-equations can be represented by a graph. Each vertex corresponds to an n-bit *distinct* unknowns. By abuse of notation, we will identify the vertices with the values assigned to them. We distinguish two types of edges, namely, $=$-labeled edges and $\neq$-labeled edges that correspond to equations and non-equations, respectively. So we consider a graph $\mathcal{G} = (\mathcal{V}, \mathcal{E}^{=} \sqcup \mathcal{E}^{\neq})$, where $\mathcal{E}^{=}$ and $\mathcal{E}^{\neq}$ denote the set of $=$-labeled edges and the set of $\neq$-labeled edges, respectively. Then $\mathcal{G}$ can be seen as a superposition of two subgraphs $\mathcal{G}^{=} \stackrel{\text{def}}{=} (\mathcal{V}, \mathcal{E}^{=})$ and $\mathcal{G}^{\neq} \stackrel{\text{def}}{=} (\mathcal{V}, \mathcal{E}^{\neq})$.

We will define *label functions* $\lambda : \mathcal{E}^{=} \rightarrow \{0,1\}^n$ and $\lambda' : \mathcal{E}^{\neq} \rightarrow \{0,1\}^n$. If two vertices P and Q are adjacent by an $=$-labeled (resp. $\neq$-labeled) edge and $\lambda(P,Q) = c$ (resp. $\lambda'(P,Q) = c$) for some $c \in \{0,1\}^n$, then it would mean that $P \oplus Q = c$ (resp. $P \oplus Q \neq c$). We will write $h(\mathcal{G},\lambda,\lambda')$ to denote the number of solutions to $(\mathcal{G},\lambda,\lambda')$ such that all the vertices take different values in $\{0,1\}^n$. When there is no $\neq$-labeled edge, we will simply write $h(\mathcal{G},\lambda)$.

Throughout this paper, we will consider a graph $\mathcal{G}$ such that $\mathcal{G}^{=}$ has no cycle. In this case, $\mathcal{G}^{=}$ is decomposed into its connected components, all of which are trees; let

$$\mathcal{G}^{=} = \mathcal{C}_1 \sqcup \mathcal{C}_2 \sqcup \cdots \sqcup \mathcal{C}_r \sqcup \mathcal{D} \tag{3}$$

for some $r \ge 0$, where $\mathcal{C}_i$ denotes a component of size at least 2, and $\mathcal{D}$ denotes the set of *isolated* vertices. Any pair of distinct vertices P and Q in the same component are connected by a unique trail,[5] say,

$$P = P_0 - P_1 - \cdots - P_s = Q.$$

[4] We will view S and R as random variables, and also write them to denote their probability distributions.

[5] A trail is a walk in which all edges are distinct.

In this case, we define

$$\bar{\lambda}(P,Q) \stackrel{\text{def}}{=} \sum_{i=0}^{r-1} \lambda(P_i, P_{i+1}).$$

By defining $\bar{\lambda}(P,Q) = \perp$ for any pair of vertices P and Q contained in different components, $\bar{\lambda}$ is defined on $\mathcal{V}^{*2}$, extending λ. For $\mathcal{G} = (\mathcal{V}, \mathcal{E}^= \cup \mathcal{E}^{\neq})$, let

$$\mathcal{L}(\mathcal{G}) \stackrel{\text{def}}{=} \mathsf{Func}(\mathcal{E}^=, \{0,1\}^n) \times \mathsf{Func}(\mathcal{E}^{\neq}, \{0,1\}^n).$$

We call $(\lambda, \lambda') \in \mathcal{L}(\mathcal{G})$ *bad* if one of the following conditions holds:

- there exists $(P,Q) \in \mathcal{V}^{*2}$ such that $\bar{\lambda}(P,Q) = \mathbf{0}$;
- there exists $(P,Q) \in \mathcal{E}^{\neq}$ such that $\bar{\lambda}(P,Q) = \lambda'(P,Q)$.

Note that $h(\mathcal{G}, \lambda, \lambda') = 0$ if (λ, λ') is bad. Let $\mathcal{L}_{\mathsf{bad}}(\mathcal{G})$ denote the set of the bad label functions in $\mathcal{L}(\mathcal{G})$. When $(\lambda, \lambda') \notin \mathcal{L}_{\mathsf{bad}}(\mathcal{G})$, we can lower bound $h(\mathcal{G}, \lambda, \lambda')$ using the extended Mirror theory as follows.

Lemma 3. *For positive integers q and v, let $\mathcal{G} = (\mathcal{V}, \mathcal{E}^= \cup \mathcal{E}^{\neq})$ be a graph such that $\mathcal{G}^=$ has no cycle, $|\mathcal{V}| \leq 2^n$, $|\mathcal{E}^=| = q$, and $|\mathcal{E}^{\neq}| = v$. Suppose that $\mathcal{G}^=$ is decomposed into its connected components as in (3). Let $w_i = |\mathcal{C}_i|$ for $i = 1, \ldots, r$, and let $\sigma = \sum_{i=1}^{r} w_i$. Then, for any $(\lambda, \lambda') \notin \mathcal{L}_{\mathsf{bad}}(\mathcal{G})$, we have*

$$\frac{h(\mathcal{G}, \lambda, \lambda')}{(2^n)_{|\mathcal{V}|}} \geq \frac{1}{2^{qn}} \left(1 - \frac{\sigma^2}{2^{2n}} \sum_{i=1}^{r} w_i^2 - \frac{2v}{2^n} \right).$$

The proof of Lemma 3 is given in the full version [5].

From the definition of S and R (given in Sect. 2.4), (1) can be rephrased in terms of Mirror theory as follows.

Lemma 4. *For positive integers q and v, let $\mathcal{G} = (\mathcal{V}, \mathcal{E}^= \cup \mathcal{E}^{\neq})$ be a graph such that $\mathcal{G}^=$ has no cycle, $|\mathcal{E}^=| = q$, and $\mathcal{E}^{\neq} = \emptyset$. Suppose that $\mathcal{G}^=$ is decomposed into its connected components as in (3). Let $w_i = |\mathcal{C}_i|$ for $i = 1, \ldots, r$, and let $\sigma = \sum_{i=1}^{r} w_i$. Then we have*

$$\frac{1}{2} \sum_{\lambda \in \mathsf{Func}(\mathcal{E}^=, \{0,1\}^n)} \left| \frac{h(\mathcal{G}, \lambda)}{(2^n)_{|\mathcal{V}|}} - \frac{1}{2^{qn}} \right| \leq \left(\frac{4\sigma}{2^{2n}} \sum_{i=1}^{r} w_i^3 \right)^{\frac{1}{2}} + \sum_{i=1}^{r} \frac{w_i(w_i - 1)}{2^{n+1}}.$$

3 The SCM Authenticated Encryption Mode

The SCM AE mode is built on top of a keyed hash function $H : \mathcal{K}_h \times (\{0,1\}^* \times \{0,1\}^*) \rightarrow \{0,1\}^n$ and a block cipher $E : \mathcal{K}_b \times \{0,1\}^n \rightarrow \{0,1\}^n$. Formally, the SCM mode based on H and E is

$$\mathsf{SCM}[H, E] = (\mathcal{K}, \mathcal{N}, \mathcal{A}, \mathcal{M}, \mathsf{SCM.ENC}, \mathsf{SCM.DEC})$$

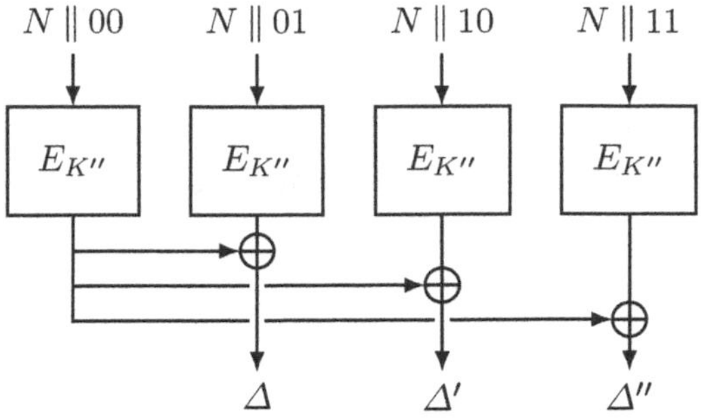

(a) Encrypting a nonce.

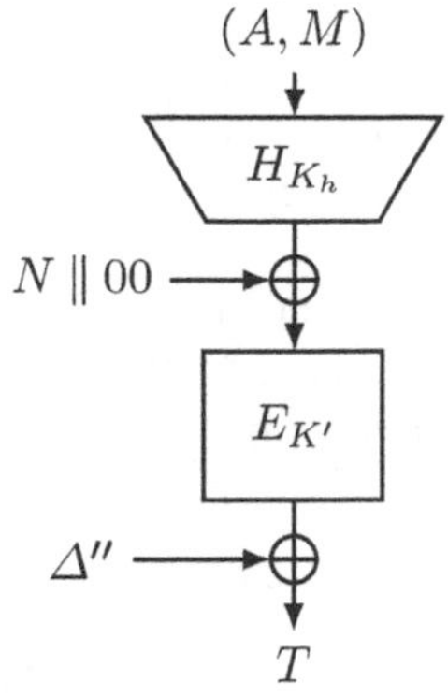

(b) Computing a tag.

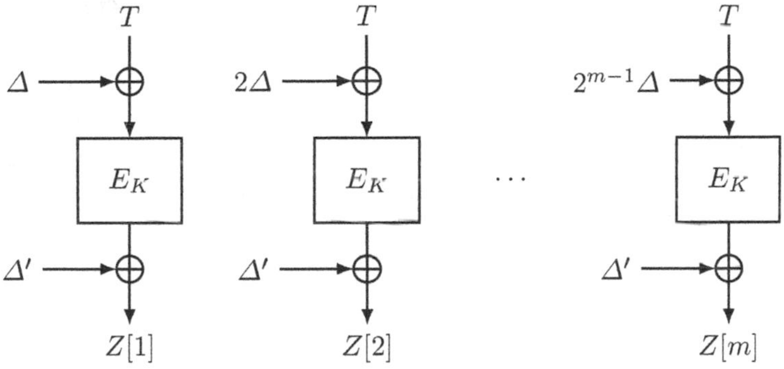

(c) Generating a keystream.

Fig. 3. The SCM mode based on H and E using a key (K_h, K, K', K'').

where $\mathcal{K} = \mathcal{K}_h \times \mathcal{K}_b \times \mathcal{K}_b \times \mathcal{K}_b$, $\mathcal{N} = \{0,1\}^{n-2}$, $\mathcal{A} = \mathcal{M} = \{0,1\}^*$, and SCM.ENC and SCM.DEC are deterministic algorithms. Given a key $(K_h, K, K', K'') \in \mathcal{K}$, a nonce $N \in \mathcal{N}$ and a message $M \in \mathcal{M}$ with associated data $A \in \mathcal{A}$,[6] $\mathsf{SCM}[H,E]_{K_h,K,K',K''}$ generates Δ, Δ' and Δ'', where

$$\begin{aligned}\Delta &= E_{K''}(N \,\|\, 00) \oplus E_{K''}(N \,\|\, 01),\\ \Delta' &= E_{K''}(N \,\|\, 00) \oplus E_{K''}(N \,\|\, 10),\\ \Delta'' &= E_{K''}(N \,\|\, 00) \oplus E_{K''}(N \,\|\, 11).\end{aligned}$$

Then the tag T is defined as

$$T = E_{K'}(H_{K_h}(A, M) \oplus (N \,\|\, 00)) \oplus \Delta''.$$

Let $M = M[1] \,\|\, M[2] \,\|\, \ldots \,\|\, M[m]$ for a positive integer m, where $|M[\alpha]| = n$ for $\alpha = 1, \ldots, m-1$, and $0 < M[m] \leq n$. Then, for $\alpha = 1, \ldots, m$, the α-th keystream block $Z[\alpha]$ is defined as

[6] We assume that either $|A| > 0$ or $|M| > 0$.

$$Z[\alpha] = E_K(T \oplus 2^{\alpha-1}\Delta) \oplus \Delta',$$

where the last block is truncated so that $|Z[m]| = |M[m]|$. The keystream $Z = Z[1] \parallel Z[2] \parallel \ldots \parallel Z[m]$ is xored to the message M, producing the corresponding ciphertext $C = M \oplus Z$ (see Fig. 3).

As shown in Fig. 4, SCM.ENC and SCM.DEC can be described using the underlying MAC scheme and the PRNG, denoted SCM.MAC and SCM.PRNG, respectively.

4 Security of SCM

The nAE-security of SCM is summarized by the following theorem.

Theorem 1. *Let $\delta > 0$, let $H : \mathcal{K}_h \times (\{0,1\}^* \times \{0,1\}^*) \to \{0,1\}^n$ be a δ-AXU function, and let $E : \mathcal{K}_b \times \{0,1\}^n \to \{0,1\}^n$ be a block cipher. Then for nonnegative integers μ, q, v, σ, l, t such that $q + v \leq 2^{n-3}$, and for any positive integer L, we have*

$$\begin{aligned}\mathsf{Adv}^{\mathsf{nAE}}_{\mathsf{SCM}[H,E]}(\mu, q, v, \sigma, l, t) \leq \min\left\{\frac{8q(\mu+1)^2l^2}{2^n}, \frac{4\sigma^3 l + 2\sigma^2\mu^2 l^2}{2^{2n}} + \frac{8\sigma l + 4\mu^2 l^2}{2^n}\right\}\\ + \frac{16\mu^4}{2^{2n}} + \frac{\mu^2}{2^n} + 4\mu^2\delta + \frac{4v}{2^n} + (2L+1)v\delta\\ + 2^n\left(\frac{e\mu^2}{L2^n}\right)^L + \frac{(16\sqrt{2}+6)(q+v)}{2^n}\\ + 3\mathsf{Adv}^{\mathsf{prp}}_E(5q + 5v + \sigma + vl, t + t'),\end{aligned}$$

where t' is the time complexity necessary to compute E for $5q+5v+\sigma+vl$ times.

Remark 1. When $L = n$ and $\mu \leq 2^{\frac{n}{2}}$, we have $2^n\left(\frac{e\mu^2}{L2^n}\right)^L \leq \left(\frac{2e}{n}\right)^n$, which is close to 0 for a sufficiently large n.

4.1 Proof of Theorem 1

Fix a $(\mu, q, v, \sigma, l, t)$-adversary $\mathcal{D}$ against $\mathsf{SCM}[H, E]$. Up to the prp-security of E, keyed permutations E_K, $E_{K'}$, and $E_{K''}$ can be replaced by truly random permutations π, π', and π'', respectively. Precisely, the cost of this replacement is upper bounded by

$$3\mathsf{Adv}^{\mathsf{prp}}_E(5q + 5v + \sigma + vl, t + t') \tag{4}$$

since $\mathcal{D}$ makes at most $5q + 5v + \sigma + vl$ block cipher queries.

Furthermore, by Lemma 2 (with $w = 4$ and $r = q + v$ in (2)), $\pi''(\cdot \parallel 00) \oplus \pi''(\cdot \parallel 01)$, $\pi''(\cdot \parallel 00) \oplus \pi''(\cdot \parallel 10)$ and $\pi''(\cdot \parallel 00) \oplus \pi''(\cdot \parallel 11)$ (used to encrypt nonces) can be replaced by three independent random functions ρ, ρ', and ρ'', respectively, at the cost of

$$\frac{(16\sqrt{2}+6)(q+v)}{2^n}. \tag{5}$$

SCM.MAC$[H, E]$

Input: $(K_h, K', K'') \in \mathcal{K}_h \times \mathcal{K}_b \times \mathcal{K}_b$, $N \in \mathcal{N}$, A, $M \in \{0,1\}^*$
Output: $T \in \{0,1\}^n$
$\Delta'' \leftarrow E_{K''}(N \,\|\, 00) \oplus E_{K''}(N \,\|\, 11)$
$X \leftarrow H_{K_h}(A, M) \oplus (N \,\|\, 00)$
$T \leftarrow E_{K'}(X) \oplus \Delta''$
return T

SCM.PRNG$[E]$

Input: $(K, K'') \in \mathcal{K}_b \times \mathcal{K}_b$, $N \in \mathcal{N}$, $T \in \{0,1\}^n$, m: nonnegative integer
Output: $Z \in \{0,1\}^*$
$\Delta \leftarrow E_{K''}(N \,\|\, 00) \oplus E_{K''}(N \,\|\, 01)$
$\Delta' \leftarrow E_{K''}(N \,\|\, 00) \oplus E_{K''}(N \,\|\, 10)$
for $i = 1, \ldots, m$ **do**
  $X[i] \leftarrow T \oplus 2^{i-1}\Delta$
  $Z[i] \leftarrow E_K(X[i]) \oplus \Delta'$
$Z \leftarrow Z[1] \,\|\, \cdots \,\|\, Z[m]$
return Z

SCM.ENC$[H, E]$

Input: $(K_h, K, K', K'') \in \mathcal{K}$, $N \in \mathcal{N}$, $A \in \mathcal{A}$, $M \in \mathcal{M}$
Output: $C \in \{0,1\}^*$, $T \in \{0,1\}^n$
$T \leftarrow \mathsf{SCM.MAC}[H, E]_{K_h, K', K''}(N, A, M)$
$m \leftarrow \lceil |M|/n \rceil$
$Z \leftarrow \mathsf{SCM.PRNG}[E]_{K, K''}(N, T, m)$
$Z \leftarrow \mathsf{msb}_{|M|}(Z)$
$C \leftarrow M \oplus Z$
return (C, T)

SCM.DEC$[H, E]$

Input: $(K_h, K, K', K'') \in \mathcal{K}$, $N \in \mathcal{N}$, $A \in \mathcal{A}$, $C \in \{0,1\}^*$, $T \in \{0,1\}^n$
Output: $M \in \mathcal{M}$ or $\bot$
$m \leftarrow \lceil |C|/n \rceil$
$Z \leftarrow \mathsf{SCM.PRNG}[E]_{K, K''}(N, T, m)$
$Z \leftarrow \mathsf{msb}_{|C|}(Z)$
$M \leftarrow C \oplus Z$
$T' \leftarrow \mathsf{SCM.MAC}[H, E]_{K_h, K', K''}(N, A, M)$
if $T \neq T'$ **then**
  return $\bot$
else
  return M

Fig. 4. Description of the SCM mode in pseudocode.

The resulting construction (using independent random permutations π and π', and three independent random functions ρ, ρ', and ρ'') will be denoted $\mathsf{SCM}^*[H]$.

Similarly to $\mathsf{SCM}[H,E]$, $\mathsf{SCM}^*[H]$ uses two subprocedures $\mathsf{SCM.MAC}^*[H]$ and $\mathsf{SCM.PRNG}^*$; $\mathsf{SCM.MAC}^*[H]$ takes as input a nonce $N \in \{0,1\}^{n-2}$ and a message $M \in \{0,1\}^*$ with associated data $A \in \{0,1\}^*$, and returns the tag T, where

$$T \overset{\text{def}}{=} \rho'(N) \oplus \pi'(H_{K_h}(A,M) \oplus (N \,\|\, 00)).$$

On the other hand, $\mathsf{SCM.PRNG}^*$ takes as input a nonce $N \in \{0,1\}^{n-2}$, a tag $T \in \{0,1\}^n$ and a nonnegative integer m such that $m \leq l$, and returns a keystream $Z = Z[1] \,\|\, \dots \,\|\, Z[m]$ and T, where

$$Z[\alpha] \overset{\text{def}}{=} \pi(T \oplus 2^{\alpha-1}\rho(N)) \oplus \rho'(N)$$

for $\alpha = 1, \dots, m$.

For our security proof, we consider a slightly modified variant of $\mathsf{SCM.PRNG}^*$, denoted $\mathsf{SCM.PRNG}^\#$, that takes as input a nonce $N \in \{0,1\}^{n-2}$ and a nonnegative integer m such that $m \leq l$, and returns $\mathsf{SCM.PRNG}^*_{\pi,\rho,\rho'}(N,T,m)$ and T, where T is chosen uniformly at random from $\{0,1\}^n$. For an adversary $\mathcal{B}$ making oracle queries to $\mathsf{SCM.PRNG}^\#$, its distinguishing advantage is defined as

$$\mathsf{Adv}^{\mathsf{prg}}_{\mathsf{SCM.PRNG}^\#}(\mathcal{B}) \overset{\text{def}}{=} \left|\Pr\left[\mathcal{B}^{\mathsf{SCM.PRNG}^\#} = 1\right] - \Pr\left[\mathcal{B}^{\$} = 1\right]\right|$$

where the ideal oracle \$ takes as input N and m, and returns a tuple of a random nm-bit string and a random n-bit string. Note that \$ is a sampling that returns a fresh random value for every redundant query.[7]

A (μ, q, σ, l)-adversary against $\mathsf{SCM.PRNG}^\#$ is an (information-theoretic) algorithm that makes at most q queries with at most μ faulty queries (using repeated nonces), where $m \leq l$ for every query, and the sum of m over all the queries is at most σ. Then we define $\mathsf{Adv}^{\mathsf{prg}}_{\mathsf{SCM.PRNG}^\#}(\mu, q, \sigma, l)$ as the maximum of $\mathsf{Adv}^{\mathsf{prg}}_{\mathsf{SCM.PRNG}^\#}(\mathcal{B})$ over all (μ, q, σ, l)-adversaries $\mathcal{B}$ against $\mathsf{SCM.PRNG}^\#$. With this notion of security, we can prove the following lemma.

Lemma 5. *Let $\delta > 0$, let $H : \mathcal{K}_h \times (\{0,1\}^* \times \{0,1\}^*) \mapsto \{0,1\}^n$ be a δ-AXU function. Then for nonnegative integers μ, q, v, σ, l, we have*

$$\mathsf{Adv}^{\mathsf{nAE}}_{\mathsf{SCM}^*[H]}(\mu, q, v, \sigma, l) \leq \mathsf{Adv}^{\mathsf{mac}}_{\mathsf{SCM.MAC}^*[H]}(\mu, q, v) + \mathsf{Adv}^{\mathsf{prg}}_{\mathsf{SCM.PRNG}^\#}(\mu, q, \sigma, l)$$

The MAC security of $\mathsf{SCM.MAC}^*[H]$ is proved as follows.

Lemma 6. *Let $\delta > 0$, and let $H : \mathcal{K} \times (\{0,1\}^* \times \{0,1\}^*) \mapsto \{0,1\}^n$ be a δ-AXU hash function. For nonnegative integers μ, q, v, such that $q + v \leq 2^{n-3}$ and for any positive integer L, we have*

$$\mathsf{Adv}^{\mathsf{mac}}_{\mathsf{SCM.MAC}^*[H]}(\mu, q, v) \leq \frac{16\mu^4}{2^{2n}} + \frac{\mu^2}{2^n} + 4\mu^2\delta + \frac{4v}{2^n} + (2L+1)v\delta + 2^n\left(\frac{e\mu^2}{L2^n}\right)^L.$$

[7] This property might allow an adversary to distinguish $\mathsf{SCM.PRNG}^\#$ and \$ by making redundant queries, and this aspect will be taken into account in Lemma 7 and 8.

We remark that the proof of Lemma 5 is similar to the NSIV composition Lemma by Peyrin and Seurin [25], and the proof of Lemma 6 is similar to the security proof of nEHtM by Choi et al. [6]. The proofs of Lemma 5 and 6 are given in the full version [5].

The following lemmas upper bound the adversarial distinguishing advantage against $\mathsf{SCM.PRNG}^{\#}$ using two different approaches.

Lemma 7. *For nonnegative integers μ, q, σ, and l, we have*

$$\mathsf{Adv}^{\mathsf{prg}}_{\mathsf{SCM.PRNG}^{\#}}(\mu, q, \sigma, l) \leq \frac{4\sigma^3 l + 2\sigma^2\mu^2 l^2}{2^{2n}} + \frac{8\sigma l + 4\mu^2 l^2}{2^n}.$$

Lemma 8. *For nonnegative integers μ, q, σ, and l, we have*

$$\mathsf{Adv}^{\mathsf{prg}}_{\mathsf{SCM.PRNG}^{\#}}(\mu, q, \sigma, l) \leq \frac{8q(\mu+1)^2 l^2}{2^n}.$$

The proof of Theorem 1 is complete by (4), (5), Lemma 5, 6, 7 and 8.

4.2 Proof of Lemma 7

Let $\mathcal{D}$ be a (μ, q, σ, l)-adversary against the pseudorandomness of $\mathsf{SCM.PRNG}^{\#}$, assuming that $\mathcal{D}$ makes exactly q encryption queries without loss of generality. At the end of the interaction, $\mathcal{D}$ will be given $\Delta_i =^{\text{def}} \rho(N_i)$, $i = 1, \ldots, q$, for free. In the ideal world, dummy masks Δ_i will be defined by an independent random function $\rho : \mathcal{N} \rightarrow \{0,1\}^n$, and given to $\mathcal{D}$. Then the transcript is defined as

$$\tau \stackrel{\text{def}}{=} (N_i, m_i, \Delta_i, T_i, Z_i[1] \parallel \cdots \parallel Z_i[m_i])_{i \in [q]}.$$

From this transcript, one can fix $X_i = X_i[1] \parallel \ldots \parallel X_i[m_i]$, where

$$X_i[\alpha] \stackrel{\text{def}}{=} T_i \oplus 2^{\alpha-1}\Delta_i$$

for $i \in [q]$ and $\alpha \in [m_i]$. Let

$$\mathcal{N}_m = \{N_1, \ldots, N_q\},$$
$$\mathcal{V} = \{\pi(X_i[\alpha]) : i \in [q], \alpha \in [m_i]\}.$$

For $N \in \mathcal{N}_m$, let

$$\mathcal{V}_N \stackrel{\text{def}}{=} \{\pi(X_i[\alpha]) : N_i = N, i \in [q], \alpha \in [m_i]\}.$$

For simplicity of notation, we rename the elements of $\mathcal{V}_N$, writing

$$\mathcal{V}_N = \{V_N[1], \ldots, V_N[s_N]\},$$

where s_N is the sum of m_i over all $i \in [q]$ such that $N_i = N$. The following bound will be useful in our security proof.

Property 1. $\sum_{N\in\mathcal{N}_m} s_N^2 \leq 2\sigma l + \mu^2 l^2$.

Proof. Let $\mathcal{F}$ denote the index set of faulty queries, namely,

$$\mathcal{F} = \{i \in [q] : N_i = N_j \text{ for some } j \text{ such that } j < i\}.$$

Since $\sum_{i\in[q]\setminus\mathcal{F}}(s_{N_i} - m_i) \leq \mu l$, we have

$$\sum_{N\in\mathcal{N}_m} s_N^2 = \sum_{i\in[q]\setminus\mathcal{F}} (m_i + (s_{N_i} - m_i))^2$$
$$\leq \sum_{i\in[q]\setminus\mathcal{F}} (2m_i s_{N_i} + (s_{N_i} - m_i)^2) \leq 2\sigma l + \mu^2 l^2. \quad \square$$

For $V_N[\alpha] \in \mathcal{V}_N$ such that $V_N[\alpha] = \pi(X_i[\beta])$, let $W_N[\alpha]$ denote the corresponding keysteam block $Z_i[\beta]$. This means that $W_N[\alpha] = V_N[\alpha] \oplus \rho'(N)$. A transcript τ is defined as *bad* if one of the following conditions holds.

- $\mathsf{bad}_1 \Leftrightarrow \bigvee_{t\geq 1} \mathsf{bad}_1[t]$, where $\mathsf{bad}_1[t]$ if and only if there exist $(N[i])_{i\in[t]} \in \mathcal{N}_m^{*t}$, $(\alpha_i)_{i\in[t]}$ and $(\beta_i)_{i\in[t]}$ such that $\alpha_i \neq \beta_i$ and
$$V_{N[i]}[\beta_i] = V_{N[i+1]}[\alpha_{i+1}]$$
for $i = 1, \ldots, t$, with indices taken modulo t;
- $\mathsf{bad}_2 \Leftrightarrow \bigvee_{t\geq 1} \mathsf{bad}_2[t]$, where $\mathsf{bad}_2[t]$ if and only if there exist $(N[i])_{i\in[t]} \in \mathcal{N}_m^{*t}$, $(\alpha_i)_{i\in[t]}$ and $(\beta_i)_{i\in[t]}$ such that $\alpha_i \neq \beta_i$ and
$$V_{N[i]}[\beta_i] = V_{N[i+1]}[\alpha_{i+1}]$$
for $i = 1, \ldots, t-1$, and
$$\sum_{i=1}^{t} (W_{N[i]}[\beta_i] \oplus W_{N[i]}[\alpha_i]) = \mathbf{0}.$$

The probability of each bad event (in the ideal world) is upper bounded as follows.

Lemma 9. $\Pr[\mathsf{bad}_1 \vee \mathsf{bad}_2] \leq \frac{8\sigma l + 4\mu^2 l^2}{2^n}$.

Sketch of Proof. For a fixed $t \geq 1$, consider $(N[i])_{i\in[t]} \in \mathcal{N}_m^{*t}$, $(\alpha_i)_{i\in[t]}$ and $(\beta_i)_{i\in[t]}$. The number of possibilities for such sequences is upper bounded by $\left(\sum_{N\in\mathcal{N}_m} s_N^2\right)^t$. Suppose that $V_{N[i]}[\beta_i]$ and $V_{N[i+1]}[\alpha_{i+1}]$ are defined by the γ-th block of the j-th query and the δ-th block of the k-th query, respectively. Then the equation $V_{N[i]}[\beta_i] = V_{N[i+1]}[\alpha_{i+1}]$ is equivalent to

$$T_j \oplus 2^{\gamma-1}\Delta_j = T_k \oplus 2^{\delta-1}\Delta_k.$$

In this way, $\mathsf{bad}_1[t]$ defines t equations, where we focus on $t+1$ random variables, namely, all the Δ-values and the T-value for the last query (with the other T-values fixed). From the $2^{(t+1)n}$ possible values for these variables, one can always find out 2^n solutions to this system of equations. Therefore, the system of equations holds with probability $\frac{1}{2^{tn}}$. Then, by Property 1, we have

$$\Pr[\mathsf{bad}_1] \le \sum_{t=1}^{\infty} \Pr[\mathsf{bad}_1[t]] \le \sum_{t=1}^{\infty} \frac{(2\sigma l + \mu^2 l^2)^t}{2^{tn}},$$

and hence, $\Pr[\mathsf{bad}_1] \le \frac{4\sigma l + 2\mu^2 l^2}{2^n}$ since

$$\sum_{t=1}^{\infty} \left(\frac{2\sigma l + \mu^2 l^2}{2^n}\right)^t \le \frac{4\sigma l + 2\mu^2 l^2}{2^n}$$

if $\frac{2\sigma l+\mu^2 l^2}{2^n} \le \frac{1}{2}$, and $\frac{4\sigma l+2\mu^2 l^2}{2^n} > 1$ otherwise. With a similar argument to the analysis of bad_1, we can also prove that $\Pr[\mathsf{bad}_2] \le \frac{4\sigma l+2\mu^2 l^2}{2^n}$, which completes the proof. □

If a transcript is not bad, then it will be called a *good* transcript. For a good transcript τ, we make some noteworthy observations as follows.

1. Distinct pairs $(i,\alpha) \in [q] \times [m_i]$ and $(j,\beta) \in [q] \times [m_j]$ such that $N_i = N_j$ correspond to distinct elements of $\mathcal{V}_{N_i} (= \mathcal{V}_{N_j})$ since otherwise we have $\mathsf{bad}_1[1]$. Therefore, we have $|\mathcal{V}_N| = s_N$ for any $N \in \mathcal{N}_m$.
2. For any pair of distinct nonces N and N', $|\mathcal{V}_N \cap \mathcal{V}_{N'}| \le 1$ since otherwise we have $\mathsf{bad}_1[1] \vee \mathsf{bad}_1[2]$.
3. Assuming $\neg(\mathsf{bad}_1[1] \vee \mathsf{bad}_1[2])$, for each nonce $N \in \mathcal{N}_m$, we can define a tree $\mathcal{T}_N = (\mathcal{V}_N, \mathcal{E}_N^{=})$, and a label function λ_N on $\mathcal{E}_N^{=}$, where any vertex $V_N[\alpha]$ such that $\alpha \ge 2$ is connected with $V_N[1]$, and

$$\lambda_N(V_N[1], V_N[\alpha]) \stackrel{\text{def}}{=} W_N[1] \oplus W_N[\alpha].$$

   We define a graph $\mathcal{G}_\tau = (\mathcal{V}, \mathcal{E}^{=})$ and a label function $\lambda : \mathcal{E}^{=} \to \{0,1\}^n$ as the union of $\mathcal{T}_N$ and the union of λ_N over all nonces in $\mathcal{N}_m$, respectively. Then,
   (a) there is no cycle in $\mathcal{G}_\tau$ since otherwise we have bad_1;
   (b) there is no pair of two vertices P and Q such that $\bar{\lambda}(P,Q) = \mathbf{0}$ since otherwise have bad_2.

Due to the above properties, we can apply Lemma 3 to $\mathcal{G}_\tau$ when τ is a good transcript. Let $\mathsf{Comp}(\mathcal{G}_\tau)$ denote the set of connected components of $\mathcal{G}_\tau$. We will lower bound the probability of obtaining the good transcript τ in the real world by the following steps.

1. Since the number of distinct nonces used in τ is $|\mathcal{N}_m|$, the probability that a random function ρ realizes (Δ_i) is $\frac{1}{2^{|\mathcal{N}_m|n}}$.
2. The probability that a random sampling realizes (T_i) is $\frac{1}{2^{qn}}$.

3. The number of possible assignments of distinct values to the vertices of $\mathcal{G}_\tau$ is lower bounded by

$$\frac{(2^n)_{|\mathcal{V}|}}{2^{|\mathcal{E}^=|n}}\left(1-\frac{\sigma^2}{2^{2n}}\sum_{\mathcal{C}\in\mathsf{Comp}(\mathcal{G}_\tau)}|\mathcal{C}|^2\right)$$

by Lemma 3 with $|\mathcal{E}^{\neq}|=0$. The probability that a random permutation π realizes each assignment is $1/(2^n)_{|\mathcal{V}|}$.
4. The above assignment uniquely determines $\rho'(N)$ for any $N\in\mathcal{N}_m$ (without any contradiction), and the probability that a random function ρ' realizes each assignment is $\frac{1}{2^{|\mathcal{N}_m|n}}$.

Therefore, we have

$$\Pr\left[\mathsf{T}_{\mathsf{re}}=\tau\right]\geq\frac{1}{2^{(q+2|\mathcal{N}_m|+|\mathcal{E}^=|)n}}\left(1-\frac{\sigma^2}{2^{2n}}\sum_{\mathcal{C}\in\mathsf{Comp}(\mathcal{G}_\tau)}|\mathcal{C}|^2\right).$$

Since $\Pr\left[\mathsf{T}_{\mathsf{id}}=\tau\right]=\frac{1}{2^{(q+2|\mathcal{N}_m|+|\mathcal{E}^=|)n}}$, we have

$$\frac{\Pr\left[\mathsf{T}_{\mathsf{re}}=\tau\right]}{\Pr\left[\mathsf{T}_{\mathsf{id}}=\tau\right]}\geq 1-\frac{\sigma^2}{2^{2n}}\cdot\varepsilon(\tau), \tag{6}$$

where

$$\varepsilon(\tau)\stackrel{\text{def}}{=}\sum_{\mathcal{C}\in\mathsf{Comp}(\mathcal{G}_\tau)}|\mathcal{C}|^2.$$

We define $\bar{\varepsilon}$ by extending the domain of ε to Γ; $\bar{\varepsilon}(\tau)=\varepsilon(\tau)$ if τ is good, and $\bar{\varepsilon}(\tau)=0$ otherwise.

Lemma 10. *If* $\sum_{N\in\mathcal{N}_m}s_N^2\leq 2^{n-1}$, *then*

$$\mathsf{Ex}\left[\bar{\varepsilon}\right]\leq 4\sigma l+2\mu^2l^2,$$

where the expectation is taken over the distribution T_{id} *in the ideal world.*

Proof. We define a random variable S over Γ such that $S(\tau)\geq\bar{\varepsilon}(\tau)$ for any attainable transcript τ.

- For $(N,N')\in\mathcal{N}^{*2}$, we define a random variable $I_{N,N'}:\Gamma\rightarrow\{0,1\}$. For $\tau\in\Gamma$, $I_{N,N'}(\tau)=1$ if, for a positive integer t, there exists $(N[0],\ldots,N[t])\in{\mathcal{N}_m}^{*(t+1)}$ such that $N[0]=N$, $N[t]=N'$, and $\mathcal{V}_{N[i]}\cap\mathcal{V}_{N[i+1]}\neq\emptyset$ for $i=0,\ldots,t-1$; $I_{N,N'}(\tau)=0$ otherwise.
- For $N\in\mathcal{N}$, we define a random variable $\bar{s}_N$ on Γ; for $\tau\in\Gamma$, $\bar{s}_N(\tau)=s_N$ if $N\in\mathcal{N}_m$, and $\bar{s}_N(\tau)=0$ otherwise.
- Finally, let

$$S\stackrel{\text{def}}{=}\sum_{N\in\mathcal{N}}\bar{s}_N^2+\sum_{(N,N')\in\mathcal{N}^{*2}}\bar{s}_N\bar{s}_{N'}I_{N,N'}.$$

Then for a good transcript τ, we have

$$S(\tau) = \sum_{N \in \mathcal{N}_m} s_N^2 + \sum_{(N,N') \in \mathcal{N}_m^{*2}} s_N s_{N'} I_{N,N'}.$$

Suppose that $\mathcal{N}_m = \{N_1, N_2\}$. If $\mathcal{T}_{N_1}$ and $\mathcal{T}_{N_2}$ are distinct components (i.e., $I_{N_1,N_2} = 0$), then $\sum_{\mathcal{C} \in \mathsf{Comp}(\mathcal{G}_\tau)} |\mathcal{C}|^2 = s_{N_1}^2 + s_{N_2}^2$, and otherwise,

$$\sum_{\mathcal{C} \in \mathsf{Comp}(\mathcal{G}_\tau)} |\mathcal{C}|^2 \le (s_{N_1} + s_{N_2})^2 = s_{N_1}^2 + s_{N_2}^2 + I_{N_1,N_2} s_{N_1} s_{N_2} + I_{N_2,N_1} s_{N_2} s_{N_1}.$$

By generalizing this observation, we have

$$\sum_{\mathcal{C} \in \mathsf{Comp}(\mathcal{G}_\tau)} |\mathcal{C}|^2 \le S(\tau).$$

Any attainable transcript τ is partitioned as $\tau = (\tau_1, \tau_2)$, where

$$\tau_1 = (N_i, m_i, T_i, Z_i[1] \parallel \cdots \parallel Z_i[m_i])_{i \in [q]},$$
$$\tau_2 = (\Delta_i)_{i \in [q]}.$$

A set of partial transcripts τ_1 (resp. τ_2) obtained from attainable transcripts will be denoted Γ_1 (resp. Γ_2). Let T_1 and T_2 denote the marginal distributions of τ_1 and τ_2, respectively, in the ideal world. So the joint probability distribution of T_1 and T_2 becomes T_{id}.

First, fix $\tau_1 \in \Gamma_1$. Then it determines $\mathcal{N}_m$. So we have

$$S = \sum_{N \in \mathcal{N}_m} s_N^2 + \sum_{(N,N') \in \mathcal{N}_m^{*2}} s_N s_{N'} I_{N,N'}.$$

For distinct nonces $N, N' \in \mathcal{N}_m$ and for a positive integer t, let

$$\mathcal{P}_t(N, N') \stackrel{\text{def}}{=} \left\{ (N[0], \ldots, N[t]) \in {\mathcal{N}_m}^{*(t+1)} : N[0] = N, N[t] = N' \right\}.$$

Then, we have

$$\begin{aligned}
\mathsf{Ex}_{\mathsf{T}_2}[I_{N,N'}] &\le \sum_{t=1}^{|\mathcal{N}_m|-1} \sum_{(N[0],\ldots,N[t]) \in \mathcal{P}_t(N,N')} \Pr\left[\bigwedge_{i=0}^{t-1} (\mathcal{V}_{N[i]} \cap \mathcal{V}_{N[i+1]} \neq \emptyset) \right] \\
&\le \sum_{t=1}^{|\mathcal{N}_m|-1} \sum_{(N[0],\ldots,N[t]) \in \mathcal{P}_t(N,N')} \prod_{i=0}^{t-1} \frac{s_{N[i]} s_{N[i+1]}}{2^n} \\
&\le \sum_{t=1}^{\infty} \frac{s_N s_{N'}}{2^n} \left(\frac{\sum_{N'' \in \mathcal{N}_m} s_{N''}^2}{2^n} \right)^{t-1} \le \frac{2 s_N s_{N'}}{2^n},
\end{aligned}$$

where the expectation is taken over the distribution T_2. By Property 1, we have

$$\begin{aligned}
\mathsf{Ex}_{\mathsf{T}_2}[S] &= \sum_{N\in\mathcal{N}_m} s_N^2 + \sum_{(N,N')\in(\mathcal{N}_m)^{*2}} s_N s_{N'} \mathsf{Ex}_{\mathsf{T}_2}[I_{N,N'}] \\
&\le \sum_{N\in\mathcal{N}_m} s_N^2 + \sum_{(N,N')\in(\mathcal{N}_m)^{*2}} \frac{2s_N^2 s_{N'}^2}{2^n} \\
&\le \sum_{N\in\mathcal{N}_m} s_N^2 + \sum_{N\in\mathcal{N}_m} s_N^2 \left(\frac{\sum_{N'\in\mathcal{N}_m} 2s_{N'}^2}{2^n}\right) \\
&\le \sum_{N\in\mathcal{N}_m} 2s_N^2 \le 4\sigma l + 2\mu^2 l^2,
\end{aligned}$$

where the expectation is also taken over the distribution of T_2. Since the above inequality holds for any $\tau_1 \in \Gamma_1$, we also have $\mathsf{Ex}[S] \le 4\sigma l + 2\mu^2 l^2$. The proof is complete since $\mathsf{Ex}[\bar{\varepsilon}] \le \mathsf{Ex}[S]$. □

By Lemma 1, 9 and 10, and (6), we have

$$\mathsf{Adv}^{\mathsf{prg}}_{\mathsf{SCM.PRNG}^{\#}}(\mu, q, \sigma, l) \le \frac{4\sigma^3 l + 2\sigma^2\mu^2 l^2}{2^{2n}} + \frac{8\sigma l + 4\mu^2 l^2}{2^n},$$

where the right-hand side of the above inequality is greater than 1 when $2^{n-1} < \sum_{N\in\mathcal{N}_m} s_N^2$ by Property 1.

4.3 Proof of Lemma 8

Let $\mathcal{D}$ be a (μ, q, σ, l)-adversary against the pseudorandomness of $\mathsf{SCM.PRNG}^{\#}$. By giving more power to $\mathcal{D}$, we will assume that $\mathcal{D}$ makes exactly $\mu + 1$ queries for each nonce, whose length is exactly l blocks of n bits, using exactly q distinct nonces. Since $\mathcal{D}$ makes the maximum number of queries for each nonce, and since each nonce is fed to random functions ρ and ρ', generating independent masks, we can assume that $\mathcal{D}$ is *non-adapative* using a fixed set of q distinct nonces. The set of nonces will be denoted $\mathcal{N}_m = \{N_1, \dots, N_q\}$.

At the end of the interaction, $\mathcal{D}$ will be given $\Delta_i =^{\text{def}} \rho(N_i)$, $i \in [q]$, for free. In the ideal world, dummy masks Δ_i will be defined by an independent random function $\rho : \mathcal{N} \to \{0,1\}^n$, and given to $\mathcal{D}$. Then the transcript is defined as

$$\tau \stackrel{\text{def}}{=} (N_i, \Delta_i, T_i, Z_i[1] \,\|\, \cdots \,\|\, Z_i[l])_{i\in[\bar{q}]},$$

where $\bar{q} = (\mu + 1)q$. For our security proof, we will partition this transcript as $\tau = (\tau', \tau'')$, where

$$\begin{aligned}
\tau' &\stackrel{\text{def}}{=} (N_i, \Delta_i, T_i)_{i\in[\bar{q}]}\,, \\
\tau'' &\stackrel{\text{def}}{=} (Z_i[1] \,\|\, \dots \,\|\, Z_i[l])_{i\in[\bar{q}]}\,.
\end{aligned}$$

A set of partial transcripts τ' (resp. τ'') obtained from attainable transcripts will be denoted Γ' (resp. Γ''). Let T' and T'' denote the marginal distributions of τ' and τ'', respectively, in the ideal world. We note that T' and T'' are independent.

For $i \in [\bar{q}]$ and $\alpha \in [l]$, one can fix $X_i = X_i[1] \parallel \ldots \parallel X_i[l]$, where $X_i[\alpha] = T_i \oplus 2^{\alpha-1}\Delta_i$. Let

$$\mathcal{V} = \{\pi(X_i[\alpha]) : i \in [\bar{q}], \alpha \in [l]\}.$$

For $N \in \mathcal{N}_m$, let

$$\mathcal{V}_N = \{\pi(X_i[\alpha]) : N_i = N, i \in [\bar{q}], \alpha \in [l]\}.$$

For simplicity of notation, we rename the elements of $\mathcal{V}_N$, writing

$$\mathcal{V}_N = \{V_N[1], \ldots, V_N[s]\},$$

where $s = (\mu + 1)l$. For $V_N[\alpha] \in \mathcal{V}_N$ such that $V_N[\alpha] = \pi(X_i[\beta])$, let $W_N[\alpha]$ denote the corresponding keysteam block $Z_i[\beta]$. This means that $W_N[\alpha] = V_N[\alpha] \oplus \rho'(N)$. We note that $\mathcal{V}_N$ and $\mathcal{V}$ are defined only by τ'. We will call a partial transcript τ' *bad* if the following condition holds.

- $\mathsf{bad} \Leftrightarrow \bigvee_{t\geq 1} \mathsf{bad}[t]$, where $\mathsf{bad}[t]$ if and only if there exist $(N[i])_{i\in[t]} \in \mathcal{N}_m^{*t}$, $(\alpha_i)_{i\in[t]}$ and $(\beta_i)_{i\in[t]}$ such that $\alpha_i \neq \beta_i$ and
$$V_{N[i]}[\beta_i] = V_{N[i+1]}[\alpha_{i+1}]$$
for $i = 1, \ldots, t$, with indices taken modulo t.

The subset of bad parts τ' in Γ' will be denoted Γ'_{bad}. Similarly to Lemma 9, we can prove the following lemma.

Lemma 11. $\Pr[\mathsf{T}' \in \Gamma'_{\mathsf{bad}}] \leq \frac{2q(\mu+1)^2l^2}{2^n}$.

We will call $\tau = (\tau', \tau'')$ a *good* transcript if τ' is not bad. Given a good transcript τ, we can define a tree $\mathcal{T}_N = (\mathcal{V}_N, \mathcal{E}_N^{=})$, and a label function λ_N on $\mathcal{E}_N^{=}$ for each nonce $N \in \mathcal{N}_m$, where any vertex $V_N[\alpha]$ such that $\alpha \geq 2$ is connected with $V_N[1]$, and

$$\lambda_N(V_N[1], V_N[\alpha]) \stackrel{\text{def}}{=} W_N[1] \oplus W_N[\alpha].$$

We also define a graph $\mathcal{G}_{\tau'} = (\mathcal{V}, \mathcal{E}^{=})$ and a label function $\lambda : \mathcal{E}^{=} \rightarrow \{0,1\}^n$ as the union of $\mathcal{T}_N$ and the union of λ_N over all nonces in $\mathcal{N}$, respectively. We note that $\mathcal{G}_{\tau'}$ is determined only by τ' (independent of τ''). We also see that there is no cycle in $\mathcal{G}_{\tau'}$ since otherwise we have bad. Similarly to the proof of Lemma 7, we have

$$\Pr[\mathsf{T}_{\mathsf{re}} = \tau] = \frac{1}{2^{(\bar{q}+2q)n}} \cdot \frac{h(\mathcal{G}_{\tau'}, \lambda)}{(2^n)_{|\mathcal{V}|}},$$
$$\Pr[\mathsf{T}_{\mathsf{id}} = \tau] = \frac{1}{2^{(q+\bar{q}+\bar{q}l)n}} = \frac{1}{2^{(|\mathcal{E}^{=}|+\bar{q}+2q)n}},$$

since $|\mathcal{E}^{=}| = \bar{q}l - q$. Therefore, we have

$$\begin{aligned}\|\mathsf{T}_{\mathsf{re}} - \mathsf{T}_{\mathsf{id}}\| &= \frac{1}{2}\sum_{\tau} |\Pr[\mathsf{T}_{\mathsf{re}} = \tau] - \Pr[\mathsf{T}_{\mathsf{id}} = \tau]| \\ &\leq \frac{1}{2}\Pr[\mathsf{T}' \in \Gamma'_{\mathsf{bad}}] + \frac{1}{2}\sum_{\tau' \notin \Gamma'_{\mathsf{bad}}}\sum_{\tau'' \in \Gamma''} |\Pr[\mathsf{T}_{\mathsf{re}} = \tau] - \Pr[\mathsf{T}_{\mathsf{id}} = \tau]| \\ &= \frac{q(\mu+1)^2 l^2}{2^n} + \frac{1}{2}\sum_{\tau' \notin \Gamma'_{\mathsf{bad}}}\sum_{\tau'' \in \Gamma''} \frac{1}{2^{(\bar{q}+2q)n}}\left|\frac{h(\mathcal{G}_{\tau'}, \lambda)}{(2^n)_{|\mathcal{V}|}} - \frac{1}{2^{|\mathcal{E}^{=}|n}}\right|. \quad (7)\end{aligned}$$

For each $\lambda \in \mathcal{L}(\mathcal{G}_{\tau'})$ (which is the set of all possible label functions on $\mathcal{G}_{\tau'}$), the number of partial transcripts τ'' yielding λ is exactly 2^{qn} since one can arbitrarily choose $W_N[1]$ for each $N \in \mathcal{N}_m$. Therefore, for a fixed $\tau' \notin \Gamma'_{\mathsf{bad}}$, we have

$$\begin{aligned}\frac{1}{2}\sum_{\tau'' \in \Gamma''}\left|\frac{h(\mathcal{G}_{\tau'}, \lambda)}{(2^n)_{|\mathcal{V}|}} - \frac{1}{2^{|\mathcal{E}^{=}|n}}\right| &= \frac{1}{2}\sum_{\lambda \in \mathcal{L}(\mathcal{G}_{\tau'})} 2^{qn}\left|\frac{h(\mathcal{G}_{\tau'}, \lambda)}{(2^n)_{|\mathcal{V}|}} - \frac{1}{2^{|\mathcal{E}^{=}|n}}\right| \\ &\leq 2^{qn} \cdot \varepsilon(\tau')\end{aligned}$$

where

$$\varepsilon(\tau') \stackrel{\text{def}}{=} \left(\frac{4\bar{q}l}{2^{2n}} \sum_{\mathcal{C} \in \mathsf{Comp}(\mathcal{G}_{\tau'})} |\mathcal{C}|^3\right)^{\frac{1}{2}} + \sum_{\mathcal{C} \in \mathsf{Comp}(\mathcal{G}_{\tau'})} \frac{|\mathcal{C}|^2}{2^{n+1}} \quad (8)$$

by Lemma 4 with $\sigma \leq \bar{q}l$, where $\mathsf{Comp}(\mathcal{G}_{\tau'})$ denotes the set of connected components of $\mathcal{G}_{\tau'}$. We define $\bar{\varepsilon}$ by extending the domain of ε to Γ'; $\bar{\varepsilon}(\tau') = \varepsilon(\tau')$ if $\tau' \in \Gamma' \backslash \Gamma'_{\mathsf{bad}}$, and $\bar{\varepsilon}(\tau') = 0$ otherwise. By (7) and (8), we have

$$\|\mathsf{T}_{\mathsf{re}} - \mathsf{T}_{\mathsf{id}}\| \leq \frac{q(\mu+1)^2 l^2}{2^n} + \mathsf{Ex}_{\mathsf{T}'}[\bar{\varepsilon}], \quad (9)$$

where the expectation is taken over the distribution T'.

Lemma 12. *If* $q(\mu+1)^2 l^2 \leq 2^{n-1}$, *then*

$$\mathsf{Ex}_{\mathsf{T}'}[\bar{\varepsilon}] \leq \frac{7q(\mu+1)^2 l^2}{2^n}.$$

Proof. We define some random variables to upper bound $\bar{\varepsilon}$ as follows.

- For $(N, N') \in \mathcal{N}_m{}^{*2}$, we define a random variable $I_{N,N'} : \Gamma' \to \{0, 1\}$. For $\tau' \in \Gamma'$, $I_{N,N'}(\tau') = 1$ if, for a positive integer t, there exists

$$(N[0], \ldots, N[t]) \in \mathcal{N}_m{}^{*(t+1)}$$

  such that $N[0] = N$, $N[t] = N'$, and $\mathcal{V}_{N[i-1]} \cap \mathcal{V}_{N[i]} \neq \emptyset$ for $i \in [t]$; $I_{N,N'}(\tau') = 0$ otherwise. If $\tau = (\tau', \tau'')$ is good, and $I_{N,N'}(\tau') = 1$, then two trees $\mathcal{T}_N$ and $\mathcal{T}_{N'}$ are in the same component of $\mathcal{G}_{\tau'}$.

- For $(N, N', N'') \in \mathcal{N}_m{}^{*3}$, we define a random variable $J_{N,N',N''} : \Gamma' \to \{0,1\}$. For $\tau' \in \Gamma'$, $J_{N,N',N''}(\tau') = 1$ if, for integers $t \geq 1$ and $t' \geq 0$, there exist two sequences of nonces

$$(N[0], \ldots, N[t]) \in \mathcal{N}_m{}^{*(t+1)},$$

$$(N'[0], \ldots, N'[t']) \in \mathcal{N}_m{}^{*(t'+1)}$$

such that $N[0] = N$, $N[t] = N''$, $N'[t'] = N'$, $\mathcal{V}_{N[i-1]} \cap \mathcal{V}_{N[i]} \neq \emptyset$ for $i \in [t]$, $\mathcal{V}_{N'[i-1]} \cap \mathcal{V}_{N'[i]} \neq \emptyset$ for $i \in [t']$, and

$$\{N[0], \ldots, N[t]\} \cap \{N'[0], \ldots, N'[t']\} = \{N'[0]\};$$

$J_{N,N',N''}(\tau') = 0$ otherwise. If $\tau = (\tau', \tau'')$ is good, and $J_{N,N',N''}(\tau') = 1$, then three trees $\mathcal{T}_N$, $\mathcal{T}_{N'}$ and $\mathcal{T}_{N''}$ are in the same component of $\mathcal{G}_{\tau'}$.
- Let

$$S(\tau') \stackrel{\text{def}}{=} qs^2 + \sum_{(N,N') \in \mathcal{N}_m{}^{*2}} s^2 I_{N,N'}(\tau'),$$

$$T(\tau') \stackrel{\text{def}}{=} qs^3 + 3 \sum_{(N,N') \in \mathcal{N}_m{}^{*2}} s^3 I_{N,N'}(\tau') + \sum_{(N,N',N'') \in \mathcal{N}_m{}^{*3}} s^3 J_{N,N',N''}(\tau').$$

Then for any $\tau' \in \Gamma' \backslash \Gamma'_{\mathsf{bad}}$, we have

$$\sum_{\mathcal{C} \in \mathsf{Comp}(\mathcal{G}_{\tau'})} |\mathcal{C}|^2 \leq S(\tau'), \qquad \sum_{\mathcal{C} \in \mathsf{Comp}(\mathcal{G}_{\tau'})} |\mathcal{C}|^3 \leq T(\tau'). \tag{10}$$

For any $\tau' \in \Gamma'$, let $\tau' = (\tau_1, \tau_2)$, where $\tau_1 = (N_i, T_i)_{i \in [\bar{q}]}$ and $\tau_2 = (\Delta_i)_{i \in [\bar{q}]}$. A set of partial transcripts τ_1 (resp. τ_2) obtained from the transcripts in Γ' will be denoted Γ_1 (resp. Γ_2). Let T_1 and T_2 denote the marginal distributions of τ_1 and τ_2, respectively, in the ideal world.

Similarly to the proof of Lemma 10, we have $\mathsf{Ex}_{\mathsf{T}_2}[I_{N,N'}] = \frac{2s^2}{2^n}$ for any $\tau_1 \in \Gamma_1$, and hence,

$$\mathsf{Ex}_{\mathsf{T}'}[S] \leq 2q(\mu + 1)^2 l^2. \tag{11}$$

The next goal is to upper bound $\mathsf{Ex}_{\mathsf{T}'}[T]$; we fix $\tau_1 \in \Gamma_1$. For distinct nonces $N, N', N'' \in \mathcal{N}_m$, integers $t \geq 1$ and $t' \geq 0$, the number of sequences $(N[i]) \in \mathcal{N}_m{}^{*(t+1)}$ and $(N'[i]) \in \mathcal{N}_m{}^{*(t'+1)}$ such that $N[0] = N$, $N[t] = N''$, $N'[0] = N[j]$ for some $j \in \{0, \ldots, t\}$, and $N'[t'] = N'$ is at most $(t+1)q^{t+t'-2}$, where it cannot be the case that both $t = 1$ and $t' = 0$. For each of such sequences, we have $\mathcal{V}_{N[i-1]} \cap \mathcal{V}_{N[i]} \neq \emptyset$ for $i \in [t]$, and $\mathcal{V}_{N'[i-1]} \cap \mathcal{V}_{N'[i]} \neq \emptyset$ for $i \in [t']$ with probability at most $\left(\frac{s^2}{2^n}\right)^{t+t'}$. Therefore, we have

$$\begin{aligned}
\mathsf{Ex}_{\mathsf{T}_2}[J_{N,N',N''}] &\leq \sum_{t'=1}^{\infty} \left(2q^{t'-1} \left(\frac{s^2}{2^n}\right)^{t'+1} \right) + \sum_{t=2}^{\infty} \sum_{t'=0}^{\infty} \left((t+1) q^{t+t'-2} \left(\frac{s^2}{2^n}\right)^{t+t'} \right) \\
&\leq \frac{4s^4}{2^{2n}} + \frac{s^4}{2^{2n}} \sum_{t=0}^{\infty} \left((t+3) \left(\frac{qs^2}{2^n}\right)^t \sum_{t'=0}^{\infty} \left(\frac{qs^2}{2^n}\right)^{t'} \right) \leq \frac{20s^4}{2^{2n}},
\end{aligned}$$

where the expectation is taken over the distribution T_2 and the last inequality holds since $qs^2 \leq 2^{n-1}$. By (10) and since $\mathsf{Ex}_{\mathsf{T}_2}[I_{N,N'}] \leq \frac{2s^2}{2^n}$, we have

$$\mathsf{Ex}_{\mathsf{T}_2}[T] \leq qs^3 + \frac{6q^2s^5}{2^n} + \frac{20q^3s^7}{2^{2n}} \leq 9qs^3 = 9q(\mu+1)^3l^3$$

where the expectation is also taken over the distribution T_2. Since the above inequality holds for any $\tau_1 \in \Gamma_1$, we have

$$\mathsf{Ex}_{\mathsf{T}'}[T] \leq 9q(\mu+1)^3l^3. \tag{12}$$

By (8), (10), (11), (12) and Jensen's inequality, we have

$$\begin{aligned}\mathsf{Ex}_{\mathsf{T}'}[\bar{\varepsilon}] &\leq \left(\frac{4\bar{q}l\mathsf{Ex}_{\mathsf{T}'}[T]}{2^{2n}}\right)^{\frac{1}{2}} + \frac{\mathsf{Ex}_{\mathsf{T}'}[S]}{2^{n+1}} \\ &\leq \left(\frac{36q^2(\mu+1)^4l^4}{2^{2n}}\right)^{\frac{1}{2}} + \frac{q(\mu+1)^2l^2}{2^n} \leq \frac{7q(\mu+1)^2l^2}{2^n}.\end{aligned}$$

□

By (9) and Lemma 12, we have

$$\mathsf{Adv}^{\mathsf{prg}}_{\mathsf{SCM.PRNG}^*}(q,\mu,\sigma,l) \leq \|\mathsf{T}_{\mathsf{re}} - \mathsf{T}_{\mathsf{id}}\| \leq \frac{8q(\mu+1)^2l^2}{2^n}.$$

4.4 Using Random IVs

One may want to instantiate nonces with random IVs for convenience of implementation. For the analysis of this instantiation, we need to introduce a new parameter r that denotes the highest multiplicity in IV collisions. Then we make the following observations.

1. The expected number of IV collisions is $\frac{q(q-1)}{2^{n-1}}$. By defining $\mu > q^{\frac{2}{3}}$ as a bad event, one can upper bound μ by $q^{\frac{2}{3}}$, while the probability of this bad event is upper bounded by $\frac{2q^{\frac{4}{3}}}{2^n}$ by Markov's inequality. Following the proof of Lemma 6 with this bad event, we have

$$\mathsf{Adv}^{\mathsf{mac}}_{\mathsf{SCM.MAC}^*[H]}(q,v) \leq \frac{16q^{\frac{8}{3}}}{2^{2n}} + \frac{3q^{\frac{4}{3}}}{2^n} + 4q^{\frac{4}{3}}\delta + \frac{4v}{2^n} + (2L+1)v\delta + 2^n\left(\frac{eq^{\frac{4}{3}}}{L2^n}\right)^L.$$

2. By closely looking at the proof of Lemma 7, one see that

$$\mathsf{Adv}^{\mathsf{prg}}_{\mathsf{SCM.PRNG}\#}(\mu,q,\sigma,l) \leq \frac{2\sigma^2 S}{2^{2n}} + \frac{4S}{2^n}$$

   where $S = \max_{\tau\in\Gamma}\left\{\sum_{N\in\mathcal{N}_m} s_N^2\right\}$. Since $\sum_{N\in\mathcal{N}_m} s_N^2 \leq \sigma rl$ and $\Pr[r \geq 4] \leq 3q^4/2^{3n}$, we have

$$\mathsf{Adv}^{\mathsf{prg}}_{\mathsf{SCM.PRNG}\#}(q,\sigma,l) \leq \frac{6\sigma^3 l}{2^{2n}} + \frac{12\sigma l}{2^n} + \frac{3q^4}{2^{3n}}.$$

3. In the proof of Lemma 8, it is assumed that exactly $\mu+1$ queries are made for each nonce. When nonces are instantiated with random IVs, $\mu+1$ can be replaced by r, obtaining the following bound.

$$\mathsf{Adv}^{\mathsf{prg}}_{\mathsf{SCM.PRNG\#}}(q,\sigma,l) \leq \frac{72ql^2}{2^n} + \frac{3q^4}{2^{3n}}.$$

All in all, we conclude that the security bound is dominated by

$$\min\left\{\frac{72ql^2}{2^n}, \frac{6\sigma^3 l}{2^{2n}} + \frac{12\sigma l}{2^n}\right\},$$

when $q \ll O(2^{\frac{3n}{4}})$ and $v \ll O(2^n)$.

References

1. Andreeva, E., et al.: COLM v1. Submission to the CAESAR competition (2016). https://competitions.cr.yp.to/round3/colmv1.pdf
2. Bellare, M., Rogaway, P., Wagner, D.: The EAX mode of operation. In: Roy, B., Meier, W. (eds.) FSE 2004. LNCS, vol. 3017, pp. 389–407. Springer, Heidelberg (2004). https://doi.org/10.1007/978-3-540-25937-4_25
3. Bhattacharya, S., Nandi, M.: Revisiting variable output length XOR pseudorandom function. IACR Trans. Symmetric Cryptol. **2018**(1), 314–335 (2018)
4. Bose, P., Hoang, V.T., Tessaro, S.: Revisiting AES-GCM-SIV: multi-user security, faster key derivation, and better bounds. In: Nielsen, J.B., Rijmen, V. (eds.) EUROCRYPT 2018. LNCS, vol. 10820, pp. 468–499. Springer, Cham (2018). https://doi.org/10.1007/978-3-319-78381-9_18
5. Choi, W., Lee, B., Lee, J., Lee, Y.: Toward a fully secure authenticated encryption scheme from a pseudorandom permutation. IACR Cryptology ePrint Archive, Report 2021/1168 (2021). http://eprint.iacr.org/2021/1168
6. Choi, W., Lee, B., Lee, Y., Lee, J.: Improved security analysis for nonce-based enhanced hash-then-mask MACs. In: Moriai, S., Wang, H. (eds.) ASIACRYPT 2020. LNCS, vol. 12491, pp. 697–723. Springer, Cham (2020). https://doi.org/10.1007/978-3-030-64837-4_23
7. Datta, N., Dutta, A., Nandi, M., Yasuda, K.: Encrypt or decrypt? To make a single-key beyond birthday secure nonce-based MAC. In: Shacham, H., Boldyreva, A. (eds.) CRYPTO 2018, Part I. LNCS, vol. 10991, pp. 631–661. Springer, Cham (2018). https://doi.org/10.1007/978-3-319-96884-1_21
8. Dobraunig, C., Eichlseder, M., Mendel, F., Schläffer, M.: Ascon v1.2. submission to the CAESAR competition (2016). https://competitions.cr.yp.to/round3/asconv12.pdf
9. Dutta, A., Nandi, M., Talnikar, S.: Beyond birthday bound secure MAC in faulty nonce model. In: Ishai, Y., Rijmen, V. (eds.) EUROCRYPT 2019, Part I. LNCS, vol. 11476, pp. 437–466. Springer, Cham (2019). https://doi.org/10.1007/978-3-030-17653-2_15
10. Gueron, S., Langley, A., Lindell, Y.: AES-GCM-SIV: nonce misuse-resistant authenticated encryption. RFC 8452, April 2019
11. Gueron, S., Lindell, Y.: GCM-SIV: full nonce misuse-resistant authenticated encryption at under one cycle per byte. In: Ray, I. (ed.) ACM SIGSAC Conference on Computer and Communications Security - CCS 2015, pp. 109–119. Association for Computing Machinery (2015)

12. Hoang, V.T., Krovetz, T., Rogaway, P.: Robust authenticated-encryption AEZ and the problem that it solves. In: Oswald, E., Fischlin, M. (eds.) EUROCRYPT 2015, Part I. LNCS, vol. 9056, pp. 15–44. Springer, Heidelberg (2015). https://doi.org/10.1007/978-3-662-46800-5_2
13. Hoang, V.T., Tessaro, S.: Key-alternating ciphers and key-length extension: exact bounds and multi-user security. In: Robshaw, M., Katz, J. (eds.) CRYPTO 2016. LNCS, vol. 9814, pp. 3–32. Springer, Heidelberg (2016). https://doi.org/10.1007/978-3-662-53018-4_1
14. Iwata, T.: Authenticated encryption mode for beyond the birthday bound security. In: Vaudenay, S. (ed.) AFRICACRYPT 2008. LNCS, vol. 5023, pp. 125–142. Springer, Heidelberg (2008). https://doi.org/10.1007/978-3-540-68164-9_9
15. Iwata, T., Minematsu, K.: Stronger security variants of GCM-SIV. IACR Trans. Symmetric Cryptol. **2016**(1), 134–157 (2016)
16. Iwata, T., Minematsu, K., Peyrin, T., Seurin, Y.: ZMAC: a fast tweakable block cipher mode for highly secure message authentication. In: Katz, J., Shacham, H. (eds.) CRYPTO 2017, Part III. LNCS, vol. 10403, pp. 34–65. Springer, Cham (2017). https://doi.org/10.1007/978-3-319-63697-9_2
17. Iwata, T., Seurin, Y.: Reconsidering the security bound of AES-GCM-SIV. IACR Trans. Symmetric Cryptol. **2017**(4), 240–267 (2017)
18. Jean, J., Nikolić, I., Peyrin, T., Seurin, Y.: Deoxys v1.41. Submission to the CAESAR competition (2016). https://competitions.cr.yp.to/round3/deoxysv141.pdf
19. Krovetz, T., Rogaway, P.: The software performance of authenticated-encryption modes. In: Joux, A. (ed.) FSE 2011. LNCS, vol. 6733, pp. 306–327. Springer, Heidelberg (2011). https://doi.org/10.1007/978-3-642-21702-9_18
20. Krovetz, T., Rogaway, P.: OCB (v1.1). Submission to the CAESAR competition (2016). https://competitions.cr.yp.to/round3/ocbv11.pdf
21. McGrew, D.A., Viega, J.: The security and performance of the Galois/counter mode (GCM) of operation. In: Canteaut, A., Viswanathan, K. (eds.) INDOCRYPT 2004. LNCS, vol. 3348, pp. 343–355. Springer, Heidelberg (2004). https://doi.org/10.1007/978-3-540-30556-9_27
22. Nir, Y., Langley, A.: ChaCha20 and Poly1305 for IETF protocols. RFC 7539 (2015)
23. Patarin, J.: Introduction to mirror theory: analysis of systems of linear equalities and linear non equalities for cryptography. IACR Cryptology ePrint Archive, Report 2010/287 (2010). http://eprint.iacr.org/2010/287
24. Patarin, J.: Mirror theory and cryptography. IACR Cryptology ePrint Archive, Report 2016/702 (2016). http://eprint.iacr.org/2016/702
25. Peyrin, T., Seurin, Y.: Counter-in-tweak: authenticated encryption modes for tweakable block ciphers. In: Robshaw, M., Katz, J. (eds.) CRYPTO 2016, Part I. LNCS, vol. 9814, pp. 33–63. Springer, Heidelberg (2016). https://doi.org/10.1007/978-3-662-53018-4_2
26. Rogaway, P., Shrimpton, T.: A provable-security treatment of the key-wrap problem. In: Vaudenay, S. (ed.) EUROCRYPT 2006. LNCS, vol. 4004, pp. 373–390. Springer, Heidelberg (2006). https://doi.org/10.1007/11761679_23
27. Whiting, D., Housley, R., Ferguson, N.: Counter with CBC-MAC (CCM). Submission to NIST (2002). https://csrc.nist.gov/groups/ST/toolkit/BCM/documents/proposedmodes/ccm/ccm.pdf
28. Wu, H.: ACORN: a lightweight authenticated cipher (v3). Submission to the CAESAR competition (2016). https://competitions.cr.yp.to/round3/acornv3.pdf
29. Wu, H., Preneel, B.: AEGIS: a fast authenticated encryption algorithm (v1.1). Submission to the CAESAR competition (2016). https://competitions.cr.yp.to/round3/aegisv11.pdf

Tight Security for Key-Alternating Ciphers with Correlated Sub-keys

Stefano Tessaro and Xihu Zhang(✉)

University of Washington, Seattle, USA
{tessaro,xihu}@cs.washington.edu

Abstract. A substantial effort has been devoted to proving optimal bounds for the security of key-alternating ciphers with independent sub-keys in the random permutation model (e.g., Chen and Steinberger, EUROCRYPT '14; Hoang and Tessaro, CRYPTO '16). While common in the study of multi-round constructions, the assumption that sub-keys are truly independent is not realistic, as these are generally highly correlated and generated from shorter keys.

In this paper, we show the existence of non-trivial distributions of limited independence for which a t-round key-alternating cipher achieves optimal security. Our work is a natural continuation of the work of Chen et al. (CRYPTO '14) which considered the case of $t = 2$ when all-subkeys are identical. Here, we show that key-alternating ciphers remain secure for a large class of $(t-1)$-wise and $(t-2)$-wise independent distribution of sub-keys.

Our proofs proceed by generalizations of the so-called Sum-Capture Theorem, which we prove using Fourier-analytic techniques.

Keywords: Provable security · Key-alternating ciphers

1 Introduction

Key-alternating ciphers (KACs) alternate the application of fixed, invertible, and key-independent permutations $P_1, \ldots, P_t$ on the n-bit strings with xor-ing $t+1$ n-bit sub-keys $s_0, s_1, \ldots, s_t$, i.e., the output of the KAC on input x and sub-keys $\boldsymbol{s} = (s_0, s_1, \ldots, s_t)$ is

$$\mathrm{KAC}_{\boldsymbol{s}}(x) = s_t + P_t(s_{t-1} + P_{t-1}(\cdots P_2(s_1 + P_1(s_0 + x))\cdots)),$$

where + denotes the bit-wise xor. Several modern block cipher designs are KACs – these include in particular Substitution-Permutation Networks (SPNs), like AES [10], PRESENT [3] and LED [14].

Most theoretical analyses of KACs [4,6,9,13,16,18,21] have proved their security as a (strong) pseudorandom permutation in a model where the permutations $P_1, \ldots, P_t$ are randomly and independently chosen, and can be queried by the adversary. Moreover, the sub-keys $\boldsymbol{s} = (s_0, s_1, \ldots, s_t)$ are also chosen

M. Tibouchi and H. Wang (Eds.): ASIACRYPT 2021, LNCS 13092, pp. 435–464, 2021.
https://doi.org/10.1007/978-3-030-92078-4_15

independently.[1] These results show that the number of queries q (to the keyed construction, as well as to the permutations) needed to break the construction is roughly $q = N^{t/(t+1)}$ (where $N = 2^n$), which has been shown to be optimal.

THIS PAPER: SECURITY WITH CORRELATED SUB-KEYS. Real sub-keys are however *not* independent, and are generated from a shorter key using a specific *key schedule* algorithm. However, very little progress has been made in understanding when such key schedules are secure, and independence assumptions are common even in cryptanalysis. In this paper, we therefore ask the following question:

> *For which distributions of sub-keys can we still obtain optimal security against $q = N^{t/(t+1)}$ queries?*

We note that this question was partially addressed by Dunkelman *et al.* [11] for $t = 1$ and later by Chen *et al.* [5], who proved such bounds for the case where $t = 2$, and the subkeys satisfy the constraint $s_0 = s_1 = s_2$.[2] Here, we consider the extension of their work beyond three rounds.

We also stress that our goal is not that of finding practical key schedules which are comparable to those used in actual block cipher designs. Rather, we aim for a broader understanding of correlated key schedules, and when they preserve optimal security. We also point out that with respect to our current state of knowledge, even modest savings in randomness to generate the keys are not known for multi-round KACs.

REDUCING KEY DEPENDENCE FOR ARBITRARY ROUNDS. As our first contribution, we show that for *any* t-round KAC with $t + 1$ subkeys, there are key schedules that merely depend on $t-1$ independent and uniform keys that achieve $q = \Omega(N^{t/(t+1)})$ security. This generalizes the result for $t = 2$ proved by Chen et al. [5] to multi-round instantiations.

We give a general sufficient condition on key distributions for $\boldsymbol{s}$ that achieve optimal security – specifically our condition considers distributions where the $t + 1$ subkeys $\boldsymbol{s}$ for the t-round KAC are a linear function of a vector $\boldsymbol{k}$ of $t - 1$ "master" keys, denoted as $\boldsymbol{s} = A\boldsymbol{k}$, in which we view each master key and subkey as an element of the field $\mathbb{F}_{2^n}$. The sufficient conditions for the key schedules are, in particular, as follows:

1. Any $t - 2$ rows of A forms a matrix of rank $t - 2$.
2. For any t rows of A,
   - the t rows form a matrix of rank $t - 1$.
   - there exists a linear combination of the t rows such that it gives zero vector and there are two neighboring rows with non-zero coefficients.

[1] In fact, Chen and Steinberger [6] already noted that their result holds in the case where the underlying subkeys are t-wise independent. The tight concrete bound proved by Hoang and Tessaro [16] also extends to t-wise independent setting.

[2] Actually, Chen *et al.* [5] also addressed reducing the number of keys and permutations in parallel. They showed that a 2-round KAC is secure against $q = \Omega(N^{2/3})$ queries when instantiated by a single permutation and a single key with a key schedule built over a linear orthomorphism.

For example, a suitable and natural key schedule that satisfies our condition is the one where $\boldsymbol{s}$ is from the $(t-1)$-wise independent distribution obtained by evaluating a random polynomial of degree $t-2$ at $t+1$ distinct points over $\mathbb{F}_{2^n}$. In fact, while our condition on key schedules is more restrictive than $(t-2)$-wise independence, it still allows for simple key schedules for small rounds (e.g. $t=3$ and $t=4$) that do not require field multiplication, which may be considered an expensive operation, i.e., for $t=3$, we show that one can set $\boldsymbol{s}=(k_0,k_0,k_1,k_1)$ to have $q=\Omega(N^{3/4})$. For $t=4$, we set $\boldsymbol{s}=(k_0,k_1,k_2,k_0+k_1,k_1+k_2)$ to have $q=\Omega(N^{4/5})$.

LESS INDEPENDENCE FOR MORE ROUNDS. Of course, we would like to understand whether even more randomness can be saved. We make progress by saving n more bits for a sufficiently large number of rounds. Again, we give a general condition on distributions characterized by linear functions mapping $t-2$ n-bit keys $\boldsymbol{k}$ to $t+1$ keys $\boldsymbol{s}$, i.e., $\boldsymbol{s}=A\boldsymbol{k}$. For any linear mapping A satisfying the property that each $t-2$ rows of A have rank $t-2$, our security proof shows, for $t>5$, a bound that gives security strictly better than $q=\Omega(N^{(t-1)/t})$ and for $t\geqslant 8$, we achieve $q=\Omega(N^{t/(t+1)})$ security. Again, one particular instantiation is obtained by evaluating a random polynomial of degree $t-3$ at $t+1$ distinct points over $\mathbb{F}_{2^n}$.

HOW FAR CAN WE GO? The end question is of course whether we can push our results even further. Ideally, it would be possible to use a single-key schedule (as in Chen *et al.*) for an arbitrary number of rounds. However, as we explain below, the classical approach to prove security for limited independence is via so-called "sum-capture theorems" [2,22]. In the paper below, we show that the sum-capture theorem necessary to study the trivial key schedule beyond two rounds is not true. This, of course, does *not* mean that the resulting construction is insecure, but improving beyond the results of this paper would require substantially new counting techniques. (See Sect. 4.3).

OTHER RELATED WORKS. Another aspect of theoretical analyses over KACs is to reduce the number of random permutations used in the construction. Recently, Wu *et al.* [23] showed that for a three round KAC instantiated with four uniform and independent subkeys and a single random permutation is secure against $q=\Omega(N^{3/4})$ adversarial queries. Dutta [12] considered minimizing the tweakable KAC by reducing the number of random permutations and proves the security of $q=\Omega(N^{2/3})$ for the 2-round tweakable KAC by Cogliati *et al.* [7] and 4-round tweakable KAC by Cogliati and Seurin [8].

1.1 Technical Overview

Our paper follows the well-established paradigm of proving security of key-alternating ciphers based on the *expectation method* by Hoang and Tessaro [16], combined with generalizations of sum-capture theorems as proposed by Chen *et al.* [5].

CHAIN-BASED ANALYSES. The core of existing analyses proceeds by identifying a set of *bad* transcripts which contains so-called *chains* – these are transcripts where the adversary has made direct queries to $P_1, P_2, \ldots, P_t$, and/or to the construction, which are linked together by the chosen subkeys. In the ideal world, such bad transcript would likely become inconsistent with the real world. i.e., the probability of obtaining the bad transcript from the real world can be zero. Formally, we represent a transcript as $\tau = (\mathcal{Q}_E, \mathcal{Q}_1, \ldots, \mathcal{Q}_t, \boldsymbol{k})$, where $\mathcal{Q}_E$ contains queries to the construction, and $\mathcal{Q}_i$'s are the queries to the individual permutations. Further, $\boldsymbol{k}$ are the keys from which the actual sub-keys $\boldsymbol{s} = (s_0, s_1, \ldots, s_t)$ are generated. (As our statements are independent of whether such queries occurred in the forward or in the backward direction, and of their order, we think of the transcript as being made of sets of input-output pairs.) We say that such a τ is *bad* if the subkeys $(s_0, s_1, \ldots, s_t)$ are such that there exist queries $(u_{t+1}, v_0) \in \mathcal{Q}_E, (u_1, v_1) \in \mathcal{Q}_1, \ldots, (u_t, v_t) \in \mathcal{Q}_t$ which constitutes a chain, i.e., if there exists an index i, such that for all $j \in \{0, \ldots, t\}$ satisfying $j \neq i$, one has $v_j + u_{j+1} = s_j$, then we say they form the i-th type of chain. If the sub-keys $\boldsymbol{s}$ are independent and uniform, then the number of chains is at most $(t+1) \cdot q^{t+1}$ (by a simple union bound over all types of chain), and thus, the probability that the transcript is bad is at most $O((t+1)q^{t+1}/N^t)$. (Note that every chain definition only involved t subkeys.)

HANDLING LIMITED INDEPENDENCE. This argument however does not work if $\boldsymbol{s}$ is generated (say) from $(t-1)$-wise independent and uniform n-bit keys, as we can expect (at best) to prove $O((t+1)q^{t+1}/N^{t-1})$. We resolve this by considering a generalized version of the sum-capture quantity which allows us to give tighter bound over the number of chains, namely we define

$$\mu_{\boldsymbol{c}}(V_0, \mathcal{Q}_1, \ldots, \mathcal{Q}_{t-1}, U_t) := \left| \left\{ (v_0, (u_1, v_1), \ldots, (u_{t-1}, v_{t-1}), u_t) \in V_0 \times \mathcal{Q}_1 \times \ldots \times \mathcal{Q}_{t-1} \times U_t \ : \sum_{i=0}^{t-1} c_i(v_i + u_{i+1}) = 0 \right\} \right| \quad (1)$$

where $V_0, U_t \subseteq \{0,1\}^n$ and the coefficients $\boldsymbol{c} = (c_0, \ldots, c_{t-1})$ are field elements of $\mathbb{F}_{2^n}$. A bound on this quantity can be used to bound the number of chains in a non-trivial fashion, as long as the coefficients arising are compatible with the underlying method to generate the sub-keys and satisfy certain conditions (which in turn will give our characterization of which distributions actually give the desired optimal security).

Concretely, when the linear coefficients $\boldsymbol{c} = (c_0, \ldots, c_{t-1})$ satisfies the condition that there is an index $0 \leqslant \mathsf{idx} < t-1$ such that $c_{\mathsf{idx}} \neq 0$ and $c_{\mathsf{idx}+1} \neq 0$, we prove the tight bound $\mu_{\boldsymbol{c}} = \Theta(q^{t+1}/N)$ using Fourier Analysis techniques.

REDUCING KEY DEPENDENCIES FURTHER. To obtain our results for construction with subkeys generated from $t-2$ independent and uniform keys, we need to upper bound an even more restrictive version of the above sum-capture quantity where two linear constraints are imposed, i.e.,

$$\mu_{\boldsymbol{c},\boldsymbol{d}}(V_0, \mathcal{Q}_1, \ldots, \mathcal{Q}_{t-1}, U_t) := \left| \left\{ (v_0, (u_1, v_1), \ldots, (u_{t-1}, v_{t-1}), u_t) \in V_0 \times \mathcal{Q}_1 \times \ldots \times \mathcal{Q}_{t-1} \times U_t \ : \sum_{i=0}^{t-1} c_i(v_i + u_{i+1}) = 0, \sum_{i=0}^{t-1} d_i(v_i + u_{i+1}) = 0 \right\} \right| \quad (2)$$

For the 2-constraint case, we in particular look at the coefficients $\boldsymbol{c} = (c_0, \ldots, c_{t-1})$ and $\boldsymbol{d} = (d_0, \ldots, d_{t-1})$ that characterize the underlying subkeys generated via the linear key schedule being $(t-2)$-wise independent and uniform. We then show that, with the subkeys generated from $t-2$ uniform and independent n-bit keys via a linear key schedule:

- for $t > 5$, the t-round KAC is secure against $q = \omega(N^{\frac{t-1}{t}})$ queries.
- for $t \geqslant 8$, the t-round KAC has tight security bound (i.e., $q = \Omega(N^{\frac{t}{t+1}})$)

Given that (2) is a natural generalization of its one constraint counterpart, it is tempting to conclude that upper-bounding (2) is not harder than upper-bounding (1). However, as the number of constraints becomes two, we stress that the problem of upper-bounding (2) is much harder. Moreover, the tightness of upper-bounding (1) crucially relies on a particular step which was referred to as the "Cauchy-Schwartz trick" [2,5,22], which does not seem to apply here. We bypass this limitation by introducing a novel representation for the upper bound of (2) as the 2-norm of a matrix. In particular, one can interpret the Cauchy-Schwartz trick upper bound as essentially a special case of the matrix norm bound in which each row and each column of the matrix contains at most one non-zero entry. Then we use the matrix Frobenius norm which is easier to compute for bounding the matrix 2-norm. Though our current technique only proves tight security bound for $t \geqslant 8$, we believe that the matrix 2-norm is the right characterization and one can extend the tightness result to $t \geqslant 4$ via a better tool to derive the 2-norm bound, as the usage of Frobenius norm is, in most cases, not tight[3].

While (2) remains to be a promising candidate to consider for saving two keys, we show that for $t = 3$, i.e., for the 3-round KAC with identical subkey and independent permutations, the quantity of (2) is lower bounded by q^3/N with good probability. Hence, a sum capture quantity with highly non-trivial characterizations or an alternative proof strategy for the 3-round KAC is needed to obtain the desired $q = \Omega(N^{3/4})$ security bound.

Good transcript analysis. As we have bounded the probability of a transcript being bad, we move to understand the remaining transcripts which we consider as good. We rely on the expectation method proposed by Hoang and

[3] In fact, the Frobenius norm and 2-norm can have up to $\sqrt{N}$ multiplicative gap for $N \times N$ matrix (e.g. the identity matrix), and we believe that a large gap exists in our Frobenius norm bound. However, to get a better 2-norm bound, it requires a much better understanding to our defined matrix for analyzing (2) than we do.

Tessaro [16], which is a generalization of the H-coefficient method [6,20]. In the expectation method, the final security upper bound is

$$\mathsf{Security\ bound} \leqslant \mathbb{E}_{X_1}[g(X_1)] + \mathsf{Pr}[X_1 \text{ is bad}]$$

in which X_1 is the random variable representing the transcript generated from the adversary interacting with the ideal world, and $g : \mathcal{T} \to [0, +\infty)$ is a non-negative function such that $g(\tau)$ upper bounds the real-world-ideal-world probability ratio of any good transcript τ. The goal is find a function $g : \mathcal{T} \to [0, +\infty)$ so that the value of $\mathbb{E}_{X_1}[g(X_1)]$ is minimized.

It is tempting to believe that the subkeys are needed to be at least t-wise independent and uniform when applying the techniques in [16] to achieve the tight security bound for the good transcripts. However, surprisingly, we show (in Sect. 5) that as long as the underlying subkeys $\boldsymbol{s} = (s_0, \ldots, s_t)$ are $(t-2)$-wise independent and uniform, we can pick a non-negative function g so that

$$\mathbb{E}_{X_1}[g(X_1)] \leqslant O(q^{t+1}/N^t).$$

Therefore, as long as the t-round KAC has a key schedule that gives $(t-2)$-wise independent and uniform subkeys, our result on the good transcript analysis can be applied as black-box.

1.2 Paper Organization

In Sect. 2 we define some basic notations and indistinguishability framework. In Sect. 3 we give the main theorems and show tight security for classes of t-round KAC. In Sect. 4 we analyze the sum capture quantity for upper-bounding the number of bad transcripts. Then we provide analysis for good transcripts in Sect. 5 and wrap up proof of theorems in Sect. 6. Finally we provide conclusions and open problems in Sect. 7.

2 Preliminaries

Notations. For a finite set S, we write $x \xleftarrow{\$} S$ to denote that x receives a uniformly sampled value from S. For an algorithm A, we write $y \leftarrow A(x_1, \ldots; r)$ to denote that A takes $x_1, \ldots$ as inputs and runs with the randomness r and assigning the output to y. We let $y \xleftarrow{\$} A(x_1, \ldots,)$ be that A, given the inputs, is executed over a randomly chosen r and the resulting value is assigned to y.

We use $\mathbb{F}_p$ to denote a finite field of size p. For any two elements $u, v \in \{0,1\}^n$, we use $\langle u, v\rangle = \sum_{i=1}^n u_i v_i$ to denote the inner product of u and v, where u_i, v_i are the i-th bit of u, v respectively. For any number $1 \leqslant b \leqslant a$, we write $a^{(b)} = a(a-1)\cdots(a-b+1)$ and take $a^{(0)} = 1$ by convention. In all the following, for any two elements $u, v \in \{0,1\}^n$, we take $u + v$ and uv as the field addition and multiplication in $\mathbb{F}_{2^n}$ respectively, in which $u + v$ is implemented as the bit-wise xor over $\{0,1\}^n$. For a fixed n, we write $N = 2^n$. For any vector u and matrix A, we write $u^\top$ and $A^\top$ as their transpose.

PRP SECURITY OF BLOCK CIPHERS. We study the security of the Key Alternating Cipher in the random permutation model. Let $E : \mathcal{K} \times \mathcal{M} \to \mathcal{M}$ be a blockcipher, which is constructed over a set of independent, random permutations $\boldsymbol{P} = (P_1, P_2, \ldots, P_t)$. Let $\mathcal{A}$ be an adversary, the strong PRP advantage of $\mathcal{A}$ is defined as

$$\mathsf{Adv}^{\pm\mathsf{prp}}_{E[\boldsymbol{P}]}(\mathcal{A}) := \Pr[K \xleftarrow{\$} \mathcal{K} : \mathcal{A}^{E[\boldsymbol{P}],\boldsymbol{P}} = 1] - \Pr[\mathcal{A}^{P_0,\boldsymbol{P}} = 1]$$

in which P_0 is a random permutation independent of $\boldsymbol{P}$, and "$\pm$" denotes that the adversary $\mathcal{A}$ can query the oracles in both forward direction and backward direction.

INDISTINGUISHABILITY FRAMEWORK. We consider a computationally unbounded distinguisher $\mathcal{A}$ interacting with two systems $\mathbf{S}_0$ and $\mathbf{S}_1$. The interaction between $\mathcal{A}$ and $\mathbf{S}_b$ (where $b \in \{0,1\}$) defines a transcript $\tau = ((u_1, v_1), \ldots, (u_q, v_q))$ that records the q pairs of queries/replies $\mathcal{A}$ made to/received from the system $\mathbf{S}_b$. Let X_b be the random variable representing the transcript, then the goal is to upper bound the following statistical distance

$$\Delta(X_0, X_1) = \sum_{\tau} \max\{0, \Pr[X_1 = \tau] - \Pr[X_0 = \tau]\}.$$

FORMULATING SYSTEMS. We follow [19] to describe the system behavior of $\mathbf{S}$ by associating every possible transcript $\tau = ((u_1, v_1), \ldots, (u_q, v_q))$ with a value $\mathsf{p}_{\mathbf{S}}(\tau) \in [0,1]$. One can interpret $\mathsf{p}_{\mathbf{S}}(\tau)$ as the probability that, if the queries $u_1, \ldots, u_q$ in τ are asked sequentially, $\mathbf{S}$ answers with $v_1, \ldots, v_q$ respectively. Note that $\mathsf{p}_{\mathbf{S}}(\cdot)$ is defined only by the underlying system $\mathbf{S}$ and is hence independent of any distinguisher. We also note that $\mathsf{p}_{\mathbf{S}}(\cdot)$ is not a probability distribution over the transcripts, as the sum over all $\mathsf{p}_{\mathbf{S}}(\tau)$ does not necessarily give one.

Since the distinguisher is computationally unbounded, it is sufficient to consider deterministic distinguishers only. Fix any deterministic distinguisher $\mathcal{A}$, let X denote the transcript distribution of $\mathcal{A}$ interacting with $\mathbf{S}$, then it holds that $\Pr[X = \tau] \in \{0, \mathsf{p}_{\mathbf{S}}(\tau)\}$ for any τ because, either $\mathcal{A}$ issues the queries $u_1, \ldots, u_q$ when given the answers $v_1, \ldots, v_q$, leading to $\Pr[X = \tau] = \mathsf{p}_{\mathbf{S}}(\tau)$, or it does not, resulting in $\Pr[X = \tau] = 0$.

Let $\mathcal{T}$ be the set of transcripts τ that has $\Pr[X_1 = \tau] > 0$. Further noting that $\Pr[X_0 = \tau] = \mathsf{p}_{\mathbf{S}_0}(\tau)$ if $\tau \in \mathcal{T}$, we can rewrite the statistical distance as

$$\Delta(X_0, X_1) = \sum_{\mathcal{T}} \max\{0, \mathsf{p}_{\mathbf{S}_1}(\tau) - \mathsf{p}_{\mathbf{S}_0}(\tau)\} = \sum_{\mathcal{T}} \mathsf{p}_{S_1}(\tau) \cdot \max\left\{0, 1 - \frac{\mathsf{p}_{\mathbf{S}_0}(\tau)}{\mathsf{p}_{\mathbf{S}_1}(\tau)}\right\}.$$

THE EXPECTATION METHOD. In this part we review the expectation method proposed by [16], which is developed based on the H-coefficient method [6,20]. In the H-coefficient method, the set of transcript $\mathcal{T}$ is partitioned into $\mathcal{T}_{\mathsf{good}}$ and $\mathcal{T}_{\mathsf{bad}}$ so that for any $\tau \in \mathcal{T}_{\mathsf{good}}$, $\mathsf{p}_{\mathbf{S}_0}(\tau)/\mathsf{p}_{\mathbf{S}_1}(\tau) \geqslant 1 - \varepsilon$ for some carefully chosen parameter ε. Then, an upper bound of the advantage directly follows. i.e.,

$$\Delta(X_0, X_1) \leqslant \varepsilon + \Pr[X_1 \in \mathcal{T}_{\mathsf{bad}}].$$

However, instead of giving a uniform bound over all good transcripts, we can associate each τ with a non-negative value $g(\tau)$ so that $\mathsf{ps}_0(\tau)/\mathsf{ps}_1(\tau) \geqslant 1-g(\tau)$ for every $\tau \in \mathcal{T}_{\mathsf{good}}$. Hence we can instead, derive the upper bound as

$$\Delta(X_0, X_1) \leqslant \sum_{\tau\in\mathcal{T}_{\mathsf{good}}} \mathsf{ps}_1(\tau)\cdot g(\tau) + \sum_{\tau\in\mathcal{T}_{\mathsf{bad}}} \mathsf{ps}_1(\tau) \leqslant \mathbb{E}_{X_1}[g(X_1)] + \sum_{\tau\in\mathcal{T}_{\mathsf{bad}}} \mathsf{ps}_1(\tau),$$

where we can take the expectation over all $\tau \in \mathcal{T}$ by the fact that $g(\cdot)$ is non-negative. Therefore, we have the following lemma.

Lemma 1 (The expectation method). *If there exists a partition of* $\mathcal{T} = \mathcal{T}_{\mathsf{good}} \sqcup \mathcal{T}_{\mathsf{bad}}$, *and a function* $g : \mathcal{T} \to [0, +\infty)$ *such that for any* $\tau \in \mathcal{T}_{\mathsf{good}}$, $\mathsf{ps}_0(\tau)/\mathsf{ps}_1(\tau) \geqslant 1 - g(\tau)$, *then*

$$\Delta(X_0, X_1) \leqslant \mathbb{E}_{X_1}[g(X_1)] + \mathsf{Pr}[X_1 \in \mathcal{T}_{\mathsf{bad}}].$$

3 Main Results

We consider the PRP security of t-round Key Alternating Cipher (KAC) that is built on t random permutations $\boldsymbol{P} = (P_1, \ldots, P_t)$ over $\{0,1\}^n$ and $t+1$ subkeys $(s_0, \ldots, s_t)$ in which $s_i \in \{0,1\}^n$. The t-round KAC, when given input $M \in \{0,1\}^n$, outputs

$$s_t + P_t(s_{t-1} + P_{t-1}(\cdots P_1(s_0 + M)\cdots)).$$

The subkeys are generated from the master key denoted as $(k_0, \ldots, k_w)$ in which k_i are sampled from $\{0,1\}^n$ uniformly and independently. Therefore, the length of the master key is $(w+1)n$ bits. Here we consider only linear key schedule algorithms, which can be represented as a matrix A over $\mathbb{F}_{2^n}$. We define the column vectors $\boldsymbol{s} = (s_0, \ldots, s_t)^\top$ and $\boldsymbol{k} = (k_0, \ldots, k_w)^\top$ in which we naturally take each n-bit string as an element in $\mathbb{F}_{2^n}$ and use $\boldsymbol{s} \leftarrow A\boldsymbol{k}$ to denote the key-scheduling process.

The case of A being an identity matrix of size $(t+1)\times(t+1)$ has been well studied, i.e. it was proved in [6,16] that, when the subkeys $s_0, \ldots, s_t$ are independent and uniform and the permutations $P_1, \ldots, P_t$ are independent, any adversary needs at least $q = \Omega(N^{t/(t+1)})$ queries to achieve constant distinguishing advantage. Here we consider the case in which the permutations are independent but the subkeys are correlated and are generated via linear key schedules from $t-1$ independent n-bit keys (considered Theorem 1) or $t-2$ independent n-bit keys (Theorem 2).

We starts with providing security bound of t-round KAC for a class of key schedules that generate $t+1$ subkeys from $t-1$ independent keys.

Theorem 1. *For the t-round* KAC *constructed over t random permutations* $\boldsymbol{P} = (P_1, \ldots, P_t)$, *let the key of KAC be* $\boldsymbol{k} = (k_0, k_1, \ldots, k_{t-2})^\top$ *in which k_i's are independently uniformly sampled from* $\mathbb{F}_{2^n}$. *Let subkeys* $\boldsymbol{s} = (s_0, s_1, \ldots, s_t)^\top$ *be derived by* $\boldsymbol{s} \leftarrow A\boldsymbol{k}$ *in which A is a* $(t+1)\times(t-1)$ *matrix over* $\mathbb{F}_{2^n}$, *with the rows denoted as* $A_0, \ldots, A_t$, *such that*

1. *Any* $t-2$ *rows of* A *forms a matrix of rank* $t-2$.
2. *For any* $I \subseteq \{0, \dots, t\}$, $|I| = t$, *then the row vectors* $(A_\ell)_{\ell \in I}$ *satisfy that*
   - $(A_\ell)_{\ell \in I}$ *forms a matrix of rank* $t-1$.
   - *there exists values* $(c_\ell)_{\ell \in I}$ *such that* $\sum_{\ell \in I} c_\ell A_\ell = \mathbf{0}$ *and there are two indices* $\mathsf{idx}_1, \mathsf{idx}_2 \in I$ *satisfying* $\mathsf{idx}_1 - \mathsf{idx}_2 \in \{1, t\}$ *and* $c_{\mathsf{idx}_1}, c_{\mathsf{idx}_2}$ *are both non-zero.*

Then for any adversary $\mathcal{A}$ *that issues at most* q *queries to* $\mathsf{KAC}, P_1, \dots, P_t$, *where* $9(t+2)n \leqslant q \leqslant N/4$,

$$\mathsf{Adv}^{\pm\mathsf{prp}}_{\mathsf{KAC}[\boldsymbol{P}]}(\mathcal{A}) \leqslant (t^2+t+1) \cdot \frac{4q^{t+1}}{N^t} + 3(t+1)\sqrt{\frac{q^{2t-1}(t+2)n}{N^{2t-2}}}.$$

First, we give a key schedule that gives $(t-1)$-wise independent and uniform subkeys for arbitrary t-round KAC.

Corollary 1. *For* $t < 2^n$, *pick distinct elements* $\alpha_0, \dots, \alpha_t \in \mathbb{F}_{2^n}$, *and let subkey* $s_i = F(\alpha_i)$ *in which* $F(X) = \sum_{j=0}^{t-2} k_j \cdot X^j$, *then an adversary needs* $\Omega(N^{t/(t+1)})$ *queries to achieve constant distinguishing advantage.*

Corollary 1 directly follows from the fact that A is a Vandermonde matrix so that every $t-1$ rows of A forms a full-rank sub-matrix. Hence, any t rows of A are linear dependent with the coefficients $(c_\ell)_{\ell \in I}$ satisfying $c_\ell \neq 0$ for all ℓ.

Note that by letting $t = 2$ in Corollary 1, our result implies the optimal security bound of 2-round KAC with identical subkeys and independent permutations proven by Chen *et al.* [5].

Though it is implied in the theorem statement that we need the subkeys being $(t-2)$-wise independent and uniform, for small round t, we still can obtain some simple key schedules that achieve the optimal bound for q while do not require any field multiplication operations, which may be considered an expensive operation in key-scheduling.

Corollary 2. *Let the* 3*-round* KAC *be with key schedule*

$$\boldsymbol{s} = (k_0, k_0, k_1, k_1)$$

in which k_0, k_1 *are two independently uniform* n*-bit keys, then an adversary needs* $\Omega(N^{3/4})$ *queries to achieve constant distinguishing advantage.*

Corollary 3. *Let the* 4*-round* KAC *be with key schedule*

$$\boldsymbol{s} = (k_0, k_1, k_2, k_0 + k_1, k_1 + k_2)$$

in which k_0, k_1, k_2 *are three independently uniform* n*-bit keys, then an adversary needs* $\Omega(N^{4/5})$ *queries to achieve constant distinguishing advantage.*

One can check that the subkeys in Corollary 2 (respectively Corollary 3) are 1-wise (pairwise) independent and uniform, and any t rows forms a sub-matrix of

Table 1. $q = \Omega(N^{\lambda})$ for constant security bound in Theorem 2.

t	3	4	5	6	7	8	9	10	...
$\lambda = \log_N q$	0.571	0.720	0.800	0.842	0.870	0.889	0.9	0.909	...
$t/(t+1)$	0.750	0.800	0.833	0.857	0.875	0.889	0.9	0.909	...

rank $t-1$ with the coefficients $(c_\ell)_{\ell \in I}$ satisfying the given conditions via Gaussian elimination.

As Theorem 1 gives tight bound for all t, one may optimistically expect similar results can be proved with ease when saving one more key. However, for the t-round KAC with subkeys generated from $t-2$ keys, we are only able to make partial progress and prove the following theorem that only implies tight security for $t \geqslant 8$.

Theorem 2. *For the t-round* KAC *constructed over t random permutations $\boldsymbol{P} = (P_1, \ldots, P_t)$, let the key of KAC be $\boldsymbol{k} = (k_0, k_1, \ldots, k_{t-3})^\top$ in which k_i's are independently and uniformly sampled from $\mathbb{F}_{2^n}$. Let subkeys $\boldsymbol{s} = (s_0, s_1, \ldots, s_t)^\top$ be derived by $\boldsymbol{s} = A\boldsymbol{k}$ in which A is a $(t+1) \times (t-2)$ matrix over $\mathbb{F}_{2^n}$ such that any $t-2$ rows of A forms a matrix of rank $t-2$. Then for any adversary $\mathcal{A}$ that issues at most $(t+2)nN^{2/3} \leqslant q \leqslant N/4$ queries to* KAC, $P_1, \ldots, P_t$,

$$\mathsf{Adv}^{\pm\mathsf{prp}}_{\mathsf{KAC}[\boldsymbol{P}]}(\mathcal{A}) \leqslant (t^2 + 2t) \cdot \frac{(5q)^{t+1}}{N^t} + (t+1)^2 \cdot \frac{(3q)^{2t-2.5}}{N^{2t-4}}.$$

Table 1 summarizes the order of q that leads the security bound to $\Omega(1)$. We can observe that, initially Theorem 2 does not give good bound for $t \leqslant 7$. From $t \geqslant 5$, the bound starts getting better than $q = \Omega(N^{(t-1)/t})$ which can be obtained by instantiating a $(t-1)$-round KAC from the provided $t-2$ keys and applying Theorem 1. When $t \geqslant 8$, the bound achieves the optimal $q = \Omega(N^{t/(t+1)})$. The tightness results for $t \leqslant 7$ are left open.

A feasible instantiation of Theorem 2 is to let the subkeys be the evaluations at $t+1$ distinct points of a degree $t-3$ polynomial. Then the following corollary holds.

Corollary 4. *For $8 \leqslant t < 2^n$, pick distinct elements $\alpha_0, \ldots, \alpha_t \in \mathbb{F}_{2^n}$, and let subkey $s_i = F(\alpha_i)$ in which $F(X) = \sum_{j=0}^{t-3} k_j \cdot X^j$, then an adversary needs $\Omega(N^{t/(t+1)})$ queries to achieve constant distinguishing advantage.*

Proof framework. We will use the expectation method (i.e. Lemma 1) to show both theorems. Given the query record $\mathcal{Q} = (\mathcal{Q}_E, \mathcal{Q}_1, \ldots, \mathcal{Q}_t)$, we will be generous and allow the adversary $\mathcal{A}$ to see the key $\boldsymbol{k}$ after making all the queries. Therefore, we let the transcript $\tau = (\mathcal{Q}, \boldsymbol{k})$ by attaching $\boldsymbol{k}$ to the end of $\mathcal{Q}$. In the ideal world, we sample and attach a dummy key $\boldsymbol{k}$ to $\mathcal{Q}$. Here we define the set of bad transcript for the t-round KAC.

Definition 1 (Bad transcripts). *For a t-round* KAC, *we say a transcript* $\tau = (\mathcal{Q}, \boldsymbol{k})$ *is bad if*

$$\boldsymbol{k} \in \mathsf{Badkey}_{\mathcal{Q}} = \bigcup_{i=0}^{t} \mathsf{Badkey}_{\mathcal{Q},i}$$

in which for every i,

$$\begin{aligned}\mathsf{Badkey}_{\mathcal{Q},i} := \{\boldsymbol{k} :\ & \boldsymbol{s} \leftarrow \mathsf{KeySchedule}(\boldsymbol{k}), \text{there exists } (u_{t+1}, v_0) \in \mathcal{Q}_E,\\ & (u_1, v_1) \in \mathcal{Q}_1, \ldots, (u_t, v_t) \in \mathcal{Q}_t\\ & \text{s.t. for all } 0 \leqslant j \leqslant t,\ j \neq i,\ v_j + s_j = u_{j+1}\},\end{aligned}$$

otherwise we say τ *is good. We use* $\mathcal{T}_{\mathsf{good}}$ *to denote the set of all good transcripts and* $\mathcal{T}_{\mathsf{bad}}$ *to denote the set of all bad transcripts. Hence* $\mathcal{T} = \mathcal{T}_{\mathsf{good}} \sqcup \mathcal{T}_{\mathsf{bad}}$.

Then, we break the analysis into the bad transcript case and the good transcript case. We will use the generalized sum capture quantity in Sect. 4 as an upper bound for the bad transcripts. We analyze the good transcripts in Sect. 5. The final proof of theorems will be presented in Sect. 6.

MORE FINE-GRAINED SECURITY. In the above theorems, we use q to be the uniform upper bound over all kinds of queries. However, we note that our proof technique also provides bounds when the number of cipher queries q_e and the number of permutation queries q_p are separated. We provide the bounds in the full version for both theorems.

4 Generalized Sum Capture Quantity for KAC

In [5] Chen *et al.* considered minimizing the 2-round KAC, where they proved a variant of "sum-capture" results [1,2,15,17,22]. The results are often stated that, for a randomly chosen set A of size q, the quantity

$$\mu(A) := \max_{\substack{X,Y \subseteq \mathbb{Z}_2^n\\ |X|=|Y|=q}} |\{(a, x, y) \in A \times X \times Y : a = x + y\}| \quad (3)$$

is close to its expected value q^3/N (when A, X, Y are all chosen at random) with high probability. In the 2-round KAC with identical key schedule, the sum-capture quantity is defined as

$$\mu(\mathcal{Q}) := \max_{\substack{X,Y \subseteq \mathbb{Z}_2^n\\ |X|=|Y|=q}} |\{(x, (u, v), y) \in X \times \mathcal{Q} \times Y : x + u = v + y\}| \quad (4)$$

where one can view the query transcript $\mathcal{Q}$ that derived from the interaction of an adversary $\mathcal{A}$ with the permutation, equivalently as the set A in (3) defined by $A = \{u + v \mid (u, v) \in \mathcal{Q}\}$.

However, both (3) and (4) consider only a single random permutation with a single linear constraints. To generalize the sum capture quantity so that we can handle the KAC that saves more keys, we consider the sum capture quantity that involves $(t-1)$ independently random permutations and $r \in \{1,2\}$ linear constraints over $\mathbb{F}_{2^n}$ for the t-round KAC with a linear key schedule.

For the $r = 1$ case, we are able to prove the tight bounds of sum capture quantity for any choice of linear constraint, leading to a feasible set of key schedule that enables saving two keys for arbitrary t-round KAC with tight security. However, as we increase the number of constraints to $r = 2$, the problem becomes more complicated and we do not have sophisticated technique to give a tight bound or handle arbitrary linear constraints. We are only able prove a loose upper bound for the linear-constraints that characterizes the underlying subkeys being $(t-2)$-wise independent, leading to partial result for saving three keys of t-round KAC.

FOURIER ANALYSIS. To prove the bounds, we will rely on the tool of Fourier analysis. In this part we define some notations for the Fourier analysis over $\{0,1\}^m$. Given a function $f : \{0,1\}^m \to \mathbb{R}$, the Fourier coefficient of f with $\alpha \in \{0,1\}^m$ is defined as

$$\hat{f}(\alpha) := \frac{1}{2^m} \sum_{x \in \{0,1\}^m} f(x)(-1)^{\langle \alpha, x \rangle}.$$

Then we have

$$f(x) = \sum_{\alpha \in \{0,1\}^m} \hat{f}(\alpha)(-1)^{\langle \alpha, x \rangle}. \tag{5}$$

For any set $S \subseteq \{0,1\}^m$, we let $\mathbb{1}_S : \{0,1\}^m \to \{0,1\}$ be the 0/1 indicator function of S. Then the following properties hold for $\mathbb{1}_S$:

$$\widehat{\mathbb{1}_S}(0) = \frac{|S|}{2^m} = \sum_{\alpha \in \{0,1\}^m} \widehat{\mathbb{1}_S}(\alpha)^2, \tag{6}$$

$$\forall \alpha \in \{0,1\}^m : |\widehat{\mathbb{1}_S}(\alpha)| \leqslant \widehat{\mathbb{1}_S}(0) = \frac{|S|}{2^m}. \tag{7}$$

4.1 1-Constraint Sum Capture Quantity

We let 1-constraint sum capture quantity be associated with a vector of coefficients $\mathbf{c} = (c_0, c_1, \ldots, c_{t-1})$, as

$$\mu_{\mathbf{c}}(V_0, \mathcal{Q}_1, \ldots, \mathcal{Q}_{t-1}, U_t) := \left| \left\{ (v_0, (u_1, v_1), \ldots, (u_{t-1}, v_{t-1}), u_t) \in V_0 \times \mathcal{Q}_1 \times \cdots \times \mathcal{Q}_{t-1} \times U_t \ : \ \sum_{j=0}^{t-1} c_j (v_j + u_{j+1}) = 0 \right\} \right|.$$

Lemma 2. *Let $t \geqslant 2$. Let $P_1, \ldots, P_{t-1}$ be $t-1$ independent uniformly random permutations of $\{0,1\}^n$, and let $\mathcal{A}$ be a probabilistic algorithm that makes adaptive queries to $P_1, \ldots, P_{t-1}$. Let $\mathcal{Q}_1, \ldots, \mathcal{Q}_{t-1}$ be the query transcripts of $P_1, \ldots, P_{t-1}$ interacting with $\mathcal{A}$. Let $\mathbf{c} = (c_0, \ldots, c_{t-1})$ be any coefficients so that there exists an index $0 \leqslant \mathsf{idx} < t-1$ satisfying $c_{\mathsf{idx}} \neq 0$ and $c_{\mathsf{idx}+1} \neq 0$, then for any $\mathcal{A}$ that makes at most q queries to each permutations,*

$$\mathsf{Pr}_{P_1,\ldots,P_{t-1}} \Bigg[\exists V_0, U_t \subseteq \mathbb{F}_{2^n}, |V_0| = |U_t| = q, \\ \mu_{\mathbf{c}}(V_0, \mathcal{Q}_1, \ldots, \mathcal{Q}_{t-1}, U_t) \geqslant \frac{3q^{t+1}}{N} + 3q^{t-1/2}\sqrt{(t+2)n} \Bigg] \leqslant \frac{2t}{N^t}.$$

We let $\Phi(\mathcal{Q}_i) := \max_{\alpha \neq 0, \beta \neq 0} N^2 |\widehat{\mathbb{1}_{Q_i}}(\alpha, \beta)|$ for the query records $\mathcal{Q}_1, \ldots, \mathcal{Q}_{t-1}$.

To show Lemma 2, we will first rely on the following Lemma 3, which states the upper bound in terms of $\Phi(\mathcal{Q}_i)$ we just defined. Then we will apply the later stated Lemma 4 by Chen *et al.* [5] that provides an upper bound for the $\Phi(\mathcal{Q}_i)$ term to conclude the proof.

Lemma 3. *Fix any $\mathbf{c} = (c_0, \ldots, c_{t-1})$ such that $c_{\mathsf{idx}} \neq 0$ and $c_{\mathsf{idx}+1} \neq 0$ for some index $0 \leqslant \mathsf{idx} < t-1$, then for any subsets V_0, U_t with $|V_0| = |U_t| = q$,*

$$\mu_{\mathbf{c}}(V_0, \mathcal{Q}_1, \ldots, \mathcal{Q}_{t-1}, U_t) \leqslant \frac{q^{t+1}}{N} + q^{t-1}\Phi(\mathcal{Q}_{\mathsf{idx}+1}).$$

Proof. The very first step is to write $\mu_{\mathbf{c}}$ as a sum over indicator functions, then we will perform Fourier transform over each indicator functions. The key point is that, even though the summation will be over many terms and Fourier coefficients, we can eliminate most of the summation term and simplify the equality so that it only sums over a single Fourier coefficient terms.

Here we sum over the indicator functions.

$$\mu_{\mathbf{c}}(V_0, \mathcal{Q}_1, \ldots, \mathcal{Q}_{t-1}, U_t) = \sum_{v_0} \sum_{u_1, v_1} \cdots \sum_{u_{t-1}, v_{t-1}} \sum_{u_t} \mathbb{1}_{V_0}(v_0) \mathbb{1}_{\mathcal{Q}_1}(u_1, v_1) \cdots \\ \cdots \mathbb{1}_{\mathcal{Q}_{t-1}}(u_{t-1}, v_{t-1}) \cdot \mathbb{1}_{U_t}(u_t) \cdot \mathbb{1}_{\mathsf{Eq}} \left(0, \sum_{j=0}^{t-1} c_j(v_j + u_{j+1}) \right)$$

in which $\mathbb{1}_{\mathsf{Eq}}(x, y)$ is the equality indicator function so that $\mathbb{1}_{\mathsf{Eq}}(x, y) = 1$ if and only if $x = y$. Note that for the equality indicator function, we can perform Fourier transformation and get

$$\mathbb{1}_{\mathsf{Eq}}(x, y) = \sum_{\alpha, \beta} \widehat{\mathbb{1}_{\mathsf{Eq}}}(\alpha, \beta) \cdot (-1)^{\langle \alpha, x \rangle + \langle \beta, y \rangle} = \frac{1}{N} \cdot \sum_{\alpha} (-1)^{\langle \alpha, x+y \rangle},$$

in which we use the fact that

$$\widehat{\mathbb{1}_{\mathsf{Eq}}}(\alpha, \beta) = \begin{cases} 1/N & \text{if } \alpha = \beta \\ 0 & o.w. \end{cases}$$

We expand each indicator function using Fourier transform and continue the calculation.

$$\begin{aligned}
&\mu_c(V_0, \mathcal{Q}_1, \ldots, \mathcal{Q}_{t-1}, U_t) \\
&= \sum_{\substack{v_0,u_1,v_1,\cdots \\ u_{t-1},v_{t-1},u_t}} \left(\sum_{\beta_0} \widehat{\mathbb{1}_{V_0}}(\beta_0)(-1)^{\langle \beta_0, v_0\rangle}\right) \cdot \left(\sum_{\alpha_1,\beta_1} \widehat{\mathbb{1}_{\mathcal{Q}_1}}(\alpha_1,\beta_1)(-1)^{\langle \alpha_1,u_1\rangle+\langle \beta_1,v_1\rangle}\right) \cdot \\
&\quad \cdots \left(\sum_{\alpha_{t-1},\beta_{t-1}} \widehat{\mathbb{1}_{\mathcal{Q}_{t-1}}}(\alpha_{t-1},\beta_{t-1})(-1)^{\langle \alpha_{t-1},u_{t-1}\rangle+\langle \beta_{t-1},v_{t-1}\rangle}\right) \\
&\quad \cdot \left(\sum_{\alpha_t} \widehat{\mathbb{1}_{U_t}}(\alpha_t)(-1)^{\langle \alpha_t,u_t\rangle}\right) \cdot \frac{1}{N}\left(\sum_{\gamma}(-1)^{\langle \gamma, \sum_{j=0}^{t-1} c_j(v_j+u_{j+1})\rangle}\right).
\end{aligned}$$

Here, notice that all Fourier coefficients only depend on the variables αs, βs and γ, so we can expand the multiplication and change the order of summation, and we obtain the following

$$\begin{aligned}
&\mu_c(V_0, \mathcal{Q}_1, \ldots, \mathcal{Q}_{t-1}, U_t) \\
&= \frac{1}{N}\sum_{\beta_0}\sum_{\alpha_1,\beta_1}\cdots\sum_{\alpha_{t-1},\beta_{t-1}}\sum_{\alpha_t}\sum_{\gamma} \widehat{\mathbb{1}_{V_0}}(\beta_0)\widehat{\mathbb{1}_{Q_1}}(\alpha_1,\beta_1)\cdots\widehat{\mathbb{1}_{Q_{t-1}}}(\alpha_{t-1},\beta_{t-1})\widehat{\mathbb{1}_{U_t}}(\alpha_t) \\
&\quad \cdot \sum_{v_0}\sum_{u_1,v_1}\cdots\sum_{u_{t-1},v_{t-1}}\sum_{u_t}(-1)^{\langle \beta_0,v_0\rangle}(-1)^{\langle \alpha_1,u_1\rangle+\langle \beta_1,v_1\rangle}\cdots \\
&\quad \cdots(-1)^{\langle \alpha_{t-1},u_{t-1}\rangle+\langle \beta_{t-1},v_{t-1}\rangle}\cdot(-1)^{\langle \alpha_t,u_t\rangle}\cdot(-1)^{\langle \gamma,\sum_{j=0}^{t-1} c_j(v_j+u_{j+1})\rangle} \\
&= \frac{1}{N}\sum_{\beta_0}\sum_{\alpha_1,\beta_1}\cdots\sum_{\alpha_{t-1},\beta_{t-1}}\sum_{\alpha_t}\sum_{\gamma} \widehat{\mathbb{1}_{V_0}}(\beta_0)\widehat{\mathbb{1}_{Q_1}}(\alpha_1,\beta_1)\cdots\widehat{\mathbb{1}_{Q_{t-1}}}(\alpha_{t-1},\beta_{t-1}) \\
&\quad \cdot \widehat{\mathbb{1}_{U_t}}(\alpha_t)\cdot\left(\sum_{v_0}(-1)^{\langle \beta_0,v_0\rangle+\langle \gamma,c_0v_0\rangle}\right)\cdot\left(\sum_{u_1}(-1)^{\langle \alpha_1,u_1\rangle+\langle \gamma,c_0u_1\rangle}\right) \\
&\quad \left(\sum_{v_1}(-1)^{\langle \beta_1,v_1\rangle+\langle \gamma,c_1v_1\rangle}\right)\cdots\left(\sum_{u_t}(-1)^{\langle \alpha_t,u_t\rangle+\langle \gamma,c_{t-1}u_t\rangle}\right)
\end{aligned}$$

The last equality is simply grouping the inner products that share the same u, v terms together. Note that the field multiplication of $c \cdot x$ can be represented as a matrix A_c[4] that applies to an n-dimensional vector x over $\mathbb{F}_2$. If $c = 0$, then $A_c = O$ where we use O to denote an all zero matrix, otherwise A_c is a full-rank matrix. Taking the summation over the v_0 term as an example, we rewrite the $\langle \gamma, c_0v_0\rangle$ term as $\langle \gamma, c_0v_0\rangle = \gamma^\top A_{c_0}v_0 = (A_{c_0}^\top\gamma)^\top v_0 = \langle A_{c_0}^\top\gamma, v_0\rangle$ where $A_{c_0}^\top$ is the transpose of A_{c_0}. So we get

[4] Since we are taking the natural field interpretation over $\{0,1\}^n$, in which the field addition is the bit-wise xor operation, we have the i-th column of A_c defined as the n-dimension vector representation of field element $c \cdot \nu_i$, in which ν_i is the field element that has the corresponding representation to be a basis vector with the i-th position being one and the rest positions being zero.

$$
\begin{aligned}
&\mu_c(V_0, \mathcal{Q}_1, \ldots, \mathcal{Q}_{t-1}, U_t) \\
&= \frac{1}{N} \cdot \sum_{\beta_0} \sum_{\alpha_1,\beta_1} \cdots \sum_{\alpha_{t-1},\beta_{t-1}} \sum_{\alpha_t} \sum_{\gamma} \widehat{\mathbb{1}_{V_0}}(\beta_0) \cdots \widehat{\mathbb{1}_{U_t}}(\alpha_t) \cdot \left(\sum_{v_0} (-1)^{\langle \beta_0 + A_{c_0}^\top \gamma, v_0 \rangle} \right) \\
&\quad \cdot \left(\sum_{u_1} (-1)^{\langle \alpha_1 + A_{c_0}^\top \gamma, u_1 \rangle} \right) \left(\sum_{v_1} (-1)^{\langle \beta_1 + A_{c_1}^\top \gamma, v_1 \rangle} \right) \cdots \\
&\quad \left(\sum_{v_{t-1}} (-1)^{\langle \beta_{t-1} + A_{c_{t-1}}^\top \gamma, v_{t-1} \rangle} \right) \left(\sum_{u_t} (-1)^{\langle \alpha_t + A_{c_{t-1}}^\top \gamma, u_t \rangle} \right).
\end{aligned}
$$

It is known that $\sum_{x \in \{0,1\}^n} (-1)^{\langle \alpha, x \rangle} = N$ if and only if $\alpha = 0$, otherwise it equals zero. So we are only interested in the case in which the fourier coefficients gives non-zero summation. And we observe that the set of interesting coefficients can be expressed in terms of γ, i.e., for all $i \in \{0, \ldots, t-1\}$: $\alpha_{i+1} = \beta_i = A_{c_i}^\top \gamma$. Hence the equality calculation can be greatly simplified as

$$
\begin{aligned}
&\mu_c(V_0, \mathcal{Q}_1, \ldots, \mathcal{Q}_{t-1}, U_t) \\
&= N^{2t-1} \sum_{\gamma} \widehat{\mathbb{1}_{V_0}}(A_{c_0}^\top \gamma) \widehat{\mathbb{1}_{Q_1}}(A_{c_0}^\top \gamma, A_{c_1}^\top \gamma) \cdots \widehat{\mathbb{1}_{Q_{t-1}}}(A_{c_{t-2}}^\top \gamma, A_{c_{t-1}}^\top \gamma) \widehat{\mathbb{1}_{U_t}}(A_{c_{t-1}}^\top \gamma) \\
&= \frac{q^{t+1}}{N} + N^{2t-1} \sum_{\gamma \neq 0} \widehat{\mathbb{1}_{V_0}}(A_{c_0}^\top \gamma) \widehat{\mathbb{1}_{Q_1}}(A_{c_0}^\top \gamma, A_{c_1}^\top \gamma) \cdots \widehat{\mathbb{1}_{U_t}}(A_{c_{t-1}}^\top \gamma) \\
&\leqslant \frac{q^{t+1}}{N} + N^{2t-1} \sum_{\gamma \neq 0} |\widehat{\mathbb{1}_{V_0}}(A_{c_0}^\top \gamma)| \cdot |\widehat{\mathbb{1}_{Q_1}}(A_{c_0}^\top \gamma, A_{c_1}^\top \gamma)| \cdots |\widehat{\mathbb{1}_{U_t}}(A_{c_{t-1}}^\top \gamma)|.
\end{aligned}
$$

Next, we let

$$
\begin{aligned}
\mathsf{left} &:= \text{min of } i \text{ such that } c_i \neq 0 \\
\mathsf{right} &:= \text{max of } i \text{ such that } c_i \neq 0
\end{aligned}
$$

To proceed with the calculation, case discussion over $(\mathsf{left}, \mathsf{right})$ is needed, here we consider the case of $\mathsf{left} = 0$ and $\mathsf{right} = t-1$ (i.e., $c_0 \neq 0$ and $c_{t-1} \neq 0$). The other cases give the same upper bound and we left them to the full version Therefore, we obtain

$$
\begin{aligned}
&\mu_c(V_0, \mathcal{Q}_1, \ldots, \mathcal{Q}_{t-1}, U_t) - \frac{q^{t+1}}{N} \\
&\leqslant N^{2t-1} \sum_{\gamma \neq 0} |\widehat{\mathbb{1}_{V_0}}(A_{c_0}^\top \gamma)| \cdot |\widehat{\mathbb{1}_{Q_1}}(A_{c_0}^\top \gamma, A_{c_1}^\top \gamma)| \cdots |\widehat{\mathbb{1}_{U_t}}(A_{c_{t-1}}^\top \gamma)| \\
&\leqslant N^{2t-3} \sum_{\gamma \neq 0} |\widehat{\mathbb{1}_{V_0}}(A_{c_0}^\top \gamma)| \cdot \left(\frac{q}{N^2} \right)^{t-2} \cdot \Phi(\mathcal{Q}_{\mathsf{idx}+1}) \cdot |\widehat{\mathbb{1}_{U_t}}(A_{c_{t-1}}^\top \gamma)| \\
&= q^{t-2} N \Phi(\mathcal{Q}_{\mathsf{idx}+1}) \cdot \sum_{\gamma \neq 0} |\widehat{\mathbb{1}_{V_0}}(A_{c_0}^\top \gamma)| \cdot |\widehat{\mathbb{1}_{U_t}}(A_{c_{t-1}}^\top \gamma)| \leqslant q^{t-1} \Phi(\mathcal{Q}_{\mathsf{idx}+1}). \qquad (8)
\end{aligned}
$$

Note that we have $N^2|\widehat{\mathbb{1}_{\mathcal{Q}_{\mathsf{idx}+1}}}(A_{c_{\mathsf{idx}}}\gamma, A_{c_{\mathsf{idx}+1}}\gamma)| \leqslant \Phi(\mathcal{Q}_{\mathsf{idx}+1})$ for any $\gamma \neq 0$ given the condition that $c_{\mathsf{idx}} \neq 0$ and $c_{\mathsf{idx}+1} \neq 0$. We also used the fact of (7) that, for any α, β, $|\widehat{\mathbb{1}_{\mathcal{Q}_i}}(\alpha, \beta)| \leqslant q/N^2$. The last step of inequality holds because by (6) we have $\sum_\gamma \widehat{\mathbb{1}_{V_0}}(A_{c_0}^\top \gamma)^2 = \sum_\gamma \widehat{\mathbb{1}_{U_t}}(A_{c_{t-1}}^\top \gamma)^2 = q/N$, so we can apply Cauchy-Schwartz inequality to obtain the result. This exact inequality step ensures the tight bound and was dubbed the *Cauchy-Schwartz trick* used in [2,5,22].

So we proved Lemma 3. □

Now the remaining step is to upper bound $\Phi(\mathcal{Q}_{\mathsf{idx}+1})$. Here we apply the following lemma, which has essentially the same proof of Lemma 6 proved by Chen *et al.* in [5], with the only adjustment of changing their parameter δ into $\delta = \sqrt{(12 \ln N)/q}$.

Lemma 4. *Assuming that* $9(t+2)n \leqslant q \leqslant N/2$. *Fix an adversary making* q *queries to a random permutation* P. *Let* Q *denote the transcript of interaction of* $\mathcal{A}$ *with* P. *Then for any* $\alpha, \beta \in \mathbb{F}_{2^n}$,

$$\Pr_{P,\omega}\left[\Phi(Q) \geqslant \frac{2q^2}{N} + 3\sqrt{(t+2)nq}\right] \leqslant \frac{2}{N^t},$$

in which the probability is taken over the random permutation P *and the random coins* ω *used by* $\mathcal{A}$.

Plugging in the inequality we get

$$\mu_{\mathbf{c}}(V_0, \mathcal{Q}_1, \ldots, \mathcal{Q}_{t-1}, U_t) \leqslant \frac{q^{t+1}}{N} + q^{t-1}\Phi(\mathcal{Q}_{\mathsf{idx}+1}) \leqslant \frac{3q^{t+1}}{N} + 3q^{t-1/2}\sqrt{(t+2)n}$$

with probability at least $1 - \frac{2t}{N^t}$. Hence we proved Lemma 2.

Tightness of Lemma 2. We examine the tightness of 1-constraints sum capture quantity in two aspects. One is, given the $\mathbf{c} = (c_0, \ldots, c_{t-1})$ in which there exists two neighboring c_i, c_{i+1} so that $c_i \neq 0, c_{i+1} \neq 0$, whether the upper bound is tight or not.

We first give the following proposition showing that, if there exists neighboring coefficients $c_i \neq 0$ and $c_{i+1} \neq 0$, then for moderately large q (e.g. $q > N^{2/3}$), $\mu_{\mathbf{c}} \geqslant q^{t+1}/2N$ with high probability. We left the detailed proof to the full version.

Proposition 1. *Let* q *be any positive integer of power of two. Fix any* $\mathbf{c} = (c_0, \ldots, c_{t-1})$ *such that there exists an index* $0 \leqslant i < t-1$ *satisfying* $c_i \neq 0$ *and* $c_{i+1} \neq 0$, *then there is an explicit algorithm* $\mathcal{A}$ *that makes at most* q *queries to each of* $P_1, \ldots, P_{t-1}$, *and* $V_0, U_t \subseteq \mathbb{F}_{2^n}$ *that have* $|V_0| = |U_t| = q$, *so that*

$$\Pr\left[\mu_{\mathbf{c}}(V_0, \mathcal{Q}_1, \ldots, \mathcal{Q}_{t-1}, U_t) \geqslant \frac{q^{t+1}}{2N}\right] \geqslant 1 - \frac{N}{q} \cdot e^{-q^2/8N}.$$

The following proposition, which is complementary to Proposition 1, states that, if $\mathbf{c} = (c_0, \ldots, c_{t-1})$ satisfies that for any $0 \leqslant i < t-1$, either $c_i = 0$ or $c_{i+1} = 0$, then $\mu_{\mathbf{c}}(V_0, \mathcal{Q}_1, \ldots, \mathcal{Q}_{t-1}, U_t)$ can achieve up to q^t, which is larger than q^{t+1}/N. We left the proof to the full version.

Proposition 2. *Let q be any positive integer of power of two. Fix any $\boldsymbol{c} = (c_0, \ldots, c_{t-1})$ such that for any $0 \leqslant i < t-1$, either $c_i = 0$ or $c_{i+1} = 0$, there is an explicit algorithm $\mathcal{A}$ that makes at most q queries to each of $P_1, \ldots, P_{t-1}$, and $V_0, U_t \subseteq \mathbb{F}_{2^n}$ that have $|V_0| = |U_t| = q$, so that*

$$\mu_{\boldsymbol{c}}(V_0, \mathcal{Q}_1, \ldots, \mathcal{Q}_{t-1}, U_t) \geqslant q^t.$$

4.2 2-Constraints Sum Capture Quantity

Now we move to consider the sum capture quantity in which the number of constraints $r = 2$. We let the 2-constraint sum capture quantity be associated with two vector of coefficients $\boldsymbol{c} = (c_0, c_1, \ldots, c_{t-1})$ and $\boldsymbol{d} = (d_0, d_1, \ldots, d_{t-1})$, as

$$\begin{aligned}\mu_{\boldsymbol{c},\boldsymbol{d}}(V_0, \mathcal{Q}_1, \ldots, \mathcal{Q}_{t-1}, U_t) :=\\ |\{(v_0, (u_1, v_1), \ldots, (u_{t-1}, v_{t-1}), u_t) \in V_0 \times \mathcal{Q}_1 \times \cdots \times \mathcal{Q}_{t-1} \times U_t \ :\\ \sum_{j=0}^{t-1} c_j(v_j + u_{j+1}) = 0, \sum_{j=0}^{t-1} d_j(v_j + u_{j+1}) = 0\}|. \quad (9)\end{aligned}$$

Though the 2-constraint sum capture quantity is a natural generalization of the 1-constraint case, we note that adding only one more constraint makes proving the tightest upper bound of (9) much harder. Here we only focus on giving bounds over the sum capture quantity with a specific class of coefficients $\boldsymbol{c}, \boldsymbol{d}$ that can be derived from the $(t-2)$-wise independently uniform subkeys. We obtain a bound that gives the tightest KAC security for $t \geqslant 8$. However, for $t < 5$, our 2-constraint upper bound is even worse than a reduction-based bound. While it is interesting to investigate whether our bound can be improved, for $t = 3$, in particular, we show that the above sum capture quantity is lower-bounded by $\Omega(q^3/N)$ and hence cannot be used to prove $q = \Omega(N^{3/4})$ for the 3-round KAC with identical subkeys.

We prove upper bounds for the class of linear constraint coefficients $\boldsymbol{c} = (c_0, \ldots, c_{t-1}), \boldsymbol{d} = (d_0, \ldots, d_{t-1})$ with the property that $c_0 = d_{t-1} = 1$, $c_{t-1} = d_0 = 0$, and for all $i \in \{1, \ldots, t-2\}$, $c_i \neq 0, d_i \neq 0$, and for all $i, j \in \{1, \ldots, t-2\}$ such that $i \neq j$, $c_i d_i^{-1} \neq c_j d_j^{-1}$. We justify that $\boldsymbol{c}, \boldsymbol{d}$ corresponds to the linear key schedule from $t-2$ independent keys that gives $(t-2)$-wise independently uniform subkeys.

Justification. We use $s_0, \ldots, s_{t-1}$ to denote the subkeys. Given the subkeys are generated linearly from $t-2$ independent keys and are $(t-2)$-wise independently uniform, the middle $t-2$ subkeys $s_1, \ldots, s_{t-2}$ uniquely fix the original master keys and hence the first subkey s_0 and the last subkeys s_{t-1} can be uniquely determined as a linear combination of $s_1, \ldots, s_{t-2}$. i.e.,

$$s_0 = \sum_{i=1}^{t-2} c_i s_i, \quad s_{t-1} = \sum_{i=1}^{t-2} d_i s_i.$$

Note that all c_i, d_i should be non-zero because otherwise we can obtain a linear combination $t-2$ subkeys that sum to zero, breaking the $(t-2)$-wise independence. Further, we show by contradiction, if there exists i, j such that $i \neq j$ and $c_i d_i^{-1} = c_j d_j^{-1}$, then we pick the set of subkeys $\{s_0, s_{t-1}\} \cup \{s_k \mid 1 \leqslant k \leqslant t-2 \wedge k \notin \{i, j\}\}$ and we have

$$s_0 + c_i d_i^{-1} s_{t-1} = \sum_{k \notin \{0,i,j,t\}} (c_i d_i^{-1} d_k + c_k) s_k$$

which is a linear dependence among $t-2$ subkeys. Thus all $c_i d_i^{-1}$ must be distinct.

Then we have the following lemma for the 2-constraints sum capture quantity.

Lemma 5. *Let $t \geqslant 3$. Let $P_1, \ldots, P_{t-1}$ be $t-1$ independent uniformly random permutations of $\{0,1\}^n$, and let $\mathcal{A}$ be a probabilistic algorithm that makes adaptive queries to $P_1, \ldots, P_{t-1}$. Let $\mathcal{Q}_1, \ldots, \mathcal{Q}_{t-1}$ be the query transcripts of $P_1, \ldots, P_{t-1}$ interacting with $\mathcal{A}$. Let coefficients $\mathbf{c}, \mathbf{d}$ be defined as above, then for any $\mathcal{A}$ that makes at most $q \geqslant (t+2)nN^{2/3}$ queries to each permutations,*

$$\mathsf{Pr}_{P_1,\ldots,P_{t-1}} \Big[\exists V_0, U_t \subseteq \mathbb{F}_{2^n}, |V_0| = |U_t| = q, \\ \mu_{\mathbf{c},\mathbf{d}}(V_0, \mathcal{Q}_1, \ldots, \mathcal{Q}_{t-1}, U_t) \geqslant \frac{q^{t+1}}{N^2} + t \cdot \frac{(3q)^{2t-3}}{N^{t-2}} + \frac{(3q)^{2t-2.5}}{N^{t-2}} \Big] \leqslant \frac{2t}{N^t}.$$

Discussion. Note that when $t \geqslant 5$, the security bound starts getting better than the $t-1$ round KAC bound $q = \Omega(N^{\frac{t-1}{t}})$. For $t \geqslant 8$, the security bound achieves optimal security of $q = \Omega(N^{\frac{t}{t+1}})$.

As in the case of 1-constraint, we will prove an upper bound of $\mu_{\mathbf{c},\mathbf{d}}$ conditioning on $\Phi(\mathcal{Q}_i)$ being small for all i.

Lemma 6. *Fix $\mathbf{c}, \mathbf{d}$ defined as in Lemma 5, then conditioning on $\Phi(\mathcal{Q}_i) \leqslant 9q^2/N$ for all $1 \leqslant i \leqslant t-1$, it holds that for any subsets $V_0, U_t \subseteq \mathbb{F}_{2^n}$ with $|V_0| = |U_t| = q$,*

$$\mu_{\mathbf{c},\mathbf{d}}(V_0, \mathcal{Q}_1, \ldots, \mathcal{Q}_{t-1}, U_t) \leqslant \frac{q^{t+1}}{N^2} + t \cdot \frac{(3q)^{2t-3}}{N^{t-2}} + \frac{(3q)^{2t-2.5}}{N^{t-2}}.$$

Proof. The initial calculation steps are similar to the 1-constraint case. We directly give the calculation result and left the details in the full version.

$$\mu_{\mathbf{c},\mathbf{d}}(V_0, \mathcal{Q}_1, \ldots, \mathcal{Q}_{t-1}, U_t) = \\ N^{2t-2} \sum_{\alpha,\beta} \widehat{\mathbb{1}_{V_0}}(\theta_0) \widehat{\mathbb{1}_{\mathcal{Q}_1}}(\theta_0, \theta_1) \widehat{\mathbb{1}_{\mathcal{Q}_2}}(\theta_1, \theta_2) \cdots \widehat{\mathbb{1}_{\mathcal{Q}_{t-1}}}(\theta_{t-2}, \theta_{t-1}) \widehat{\mathbb{1}_{U_t}}(\theta_{t-1})$$

in which

$$\theta_0 = \alpha, \quad \theta_{t-1} = \beta, \\ \forall i \in \{1, \ldots, t-2\} : \theta_i = A_{c_i}^\top \alpha + A_{d_i}^\top \beta.$$

We write $\mathsf{Coeff} = \{\theta_0, \theta_1, \ldots, \theta_{t-1}\}$. Here we partition the summation into three cases and discuss the set of (α, β) assignments that falls into each cases.

1. At least two θs in Coeff are zero.
2. Exactly one θ in Coeff is zero.
3. None of the θs in Coeff is zero.

The following claim shows that, if case one happens, then all coefficients θ are zero.

Claim 1. *If two θs in* Coeff *are zero, then* $\alpha = \beta = 0$.

Proof. If $\theta_0 = \alpha = \beta = \theta_{t-1} = 0$, then the claim is trivial. If $\alpha = \theta_0 = \theta_i = 0$ for some i with $1 \leqslant i \leqslant t-2$, then given $\theta_i = A_{c_i}^\top \alpha + A_{d_i}^\top \beta = A_{d_i}^\top \beta$ and $A_{d_i}^\top$ is full-rank (because $d_i \neq 0$), we can infer that $\beta = 0$. Similarly we can infer $\alpha = 0$ if $\beta = \theta_{t-1} = \theta_i = 0$ for some i with $1 \leqslant i \leqslant t-2$. Now, if $\theta_i = \theta_j = 0$ for some i, j such that $1 \leqslant i, j \leqslant t-2$ and $i \neq j$. Then the choice of (α, β) must satisfy

$$\begin{cases} A_{c_i}^\top \alpha + A_{d_i}^\top \beta = 0 \\ A_{c_j}^\top \alpha + A_{d_j}^\top \beta = 0 \end{cases}$$

implying $A_{d_{i+1}^{-1} c_{i+1}}^\top \alpha = (A_{d_{i+1}}^\top)^{-1} A_{c_{i+1}}^\top \alpha = \beta = (A_{d_{j+1}}^\top)^{-1} A_{c_{j+1}}^\top \alpha = A_{d_{j+1}^{-1} c_{j+1}}^\top \alpha$. Hence

$$\left(A_{d_{i+1}^{-1} c_{i+1}}^\top + A_{d_{j+1}^{-1} c_{j+1}}^\top \right) \alpha = \left(A_{d_{i+1}^{-1} c_{i+1} + d_{j+1}^{-1} c_{j+1}}^\top \right) \alpha = 0.$$

Here α can be non-zero only if $d_{i+1}^{-1} c_{i+1} = d_{j+1}^{-1} c_{j+1}$. However, this is impossible as we have justified from the $(t-2)$-wise independently uniform property of subkeys. □

Let μ_1, μ_2, μ_3 corresponds to summation for (α, β) that corresponds to case one, two, three, respectively.

Proposition 3

$$\mu_1 = \frac{q^{t+1}}{N^2}$$

Proof. Since case one only happens when $\alpha = \beta = 0$, we have $\theta_i = 0$ for all i. Therefore, a direct calculation using the fact that $\widehat{\mathbb{1}_{V_0}}(0) = \widehat{\mathbb{1}_{U_t}}(0) = q/N$ and $\widehat{\mathbb{1}_{Q_i}}(0, 0) = q/N^2$ proves the bound. □

Proposition 4

$$\mu_2 \leqslant \frac{t \cdot (3q)^{2t-3}}{N^{t-2}}$$

We note that the proof of Proposition 4 can be derived via a moderate tweak from the proof of 1-constraint sum capture quantity upper bound (i.e., Lemma 2), we left the complete proof to the full version.

Proposition 5

$$\mu_3 \leqslant \frac{(3q)^{2t-2.5}}{N^{t-2}}$$

Proof (of Proposition 5). We define a $N \times N$ matrix M with each entry labeled by $(\alpha, \beta) \in \mathbb{F}_{2^n} \times \mathbb{F}_{2^n}$ so that

$$M_{\alpha,\beta} = \begin{cases} 0 & \text{if some } \theta \in \mathsf{Coeff} \text{ is } 0 \\ \widehat{\mathbb{1}_{\mathcal{Q}_1}}(\alpha, A_{c_1}^\top \alpha + A_{d_1}^\top \beta) \cdots \widehat{\mathbb{1}_{\mathcal{Q}_{t-1}}}(A_{c_{t-2}}^\top \alpha + A_{d_{t-2}}^\top \beta, \beta) & o.w. \end{cases}$$

Note that M is a $2^n \times 2^n$ matrix. We also define the column vectors $\boldsymbol{v}$, $\boldsymbol{u}$ with each entry labeled by $\alpha \in \mathbb{F}_{2^n}$ so that $\boldsymbol{v}_\alpha = \widehat{\mathbb{1}_{V_0}(\alpha)}$ and $\boldsymbol{u}_\alpha = \widehat{\mathbb{1}_{U_t}(\alpha)}$. Therefore, we can write μ_3 as

$$\mu_3 = N^{2t-2} \sum_{\alpha,\beta \mid M_{\alpha,\beta} \neq 0} \widehat{\mathbb{1}_{V_0}(\alpha)} \cdot M_{\alpha,\beta} \cdot \widehat{\mathbb{1}_{U_t}(\beta)} = N^{2t-2} \boldsymbol{v}^\top M \boldsymbol{u}.$$

Noting that the equivalent definition for the matrix 2-norm as

$$\|M\|_2 := \sup_{\|x\|_2=1} \|Mx\|_2 = \sup_{\|x\|_2=1, \|y\|_2=1} y^\top M x,$$

we can use the matrix norm as the upper bound of μ_3, that is

$$\mu_3 = N^{2t-2} \cdot \boldsymbol{v}^\top M \boldsymbol{u} \leqslant N^{2t-2} \|\boldsymbol{v}\|_2 \|M\|_2 \|\boldsymbol{u}\|_2 .$$

By (6), we can infer that $\|\boldsymbol{v}\|_2 = \sqrt{\sum_\alpha v_\alpha^2} = \sqrt{\sum_\alpha \widehat{\mathbb{1}_{V_0}}(\alpha)^2} = \sqrt{q/N}$ and $\|\boldsymbol{u}\|_2 = \sqrt{q/N}$. We also use the fact that $\|M\|_2 \leqslant \|M\|_F$ where $\|M\|_F = \sqrt{\sum_{i,j} M_{i,j}^2}$ is the Frobenius norm, then we have

$$\mu_3 \leqslant N^{2t-2} \cdot \sqrt{\frac{q}{N}} \|M\|_2 \sqrt{\frac{q}{N}} \leqslant q N^{2t-3} \|M\|_F = q N^{2t-3} \sqrt{\sum_{\alpha,\beta} M_{\alpha,\beta}^2}$$

where

$$\begin{aligned} \sum_{\alpha,\beta} M_{\alpha,\beta}^2 &= \sum_{\alpha,\beta \mid M_{\alpha,\beta} \neq 0} \widehat{\mathbb{1}_{\mathcal{Q}_1}}(\alpha, A_{c_1}^\top \alpha + A_{d_1}^\top \beta)^2 \cdots \widehat{\mathbb{1}_{\mathcal{Q}_{t-1}}}(A_{c_{t-2}}^\top \alpha + A_{d_{t-2}}^\top \beta, \beta)^2 \\ &\leqslant \sum_{\alpha,\beta \mid M_{\alpha,\beta} \neq 0} \widehat{\mathbb{1}_{\mathcal{Q}_1}}(\alpha, A_{c_1}^\top \alpha + A_{d_1}^\top \beta)^2 \cdot \frac{(3q)^{4(t-2)}}{N^{6(t-2)}} \\ &\leqslant \frac{(3q)^{4(t-2)}}{N^{6(t-2)}} \sum_{\alpha,\beta} \widehat{\mathbb{1}_{\mathcal{Q}_1}}(\alpha, A_{c_1}^\top \alpha + A_{d_1}^\top \beta)^2 = \frac{(3q)^{4(t-2)}}{N^{6(t-2)}} \cdot \frac{q}{N^2} \leqslant \frac{(3q)^{4t-7}}{N^{6t-10}}. \end{aligned}$$

So we get

$$\mu_3 \leqslant q N^{2t-3} \cdot \frac{(3q)^{2t-3.5}}{N^{3t-5}} \leqslant \frac{(3q)^{2t-2.5}}{N^{t-2}}.$$

□

Putting the propositions all together, we have

$$\mu_{c,d} = \mu_1 + \mu_2 + \mu_3 \leqslant \frac{q^{t+1}}{N^2} + t \cdot \frac{(3q)^{2t-3}}{N^{t-2}} + \frac{(3q)^{2t-2.5}}{N^{t-2}}.$$

□

4.3 Tightness of 2-Constraint Sum Capture Quantity for 3-Round KAC

A natural question is whether the upper bound of the 2-constraint sum capture quantity can be improved so that it gives tight security bound for t-round KAC when $t < 7$. In particular, the most interesting case is to prove tight security bound $q = \Omega(N^{3/4})$ for 3-round KAC with identical subkeys, which corresponds to the instantiation in Corollary 4 when $t = 3$. However, for the 3-round KAC with identical key schedule, we show that it is impossible to show the conjectured optimal security bound via upper-bounding the sum capture quantity, as the sum capture quantity for 3-round identical-subkey KAC is lower-bounded by $\Omega(q^3/N)$ with high probability, giving $\mu_c/N = \Omega(q^3/N^2)$ instead of the desired q^4/N^3. The sum capture quantity lower bound for 3-round identical-subkey KAC directly follows from the following proposition with $c_1 = d_1 = 1$. We left the proof of proposition to the full version.

Proposition 6. *Let q be any positive integer of power of two. Let $t = 2$ and fix $\boldsymbol{c} = (1, c_1, 0)$, $\boldsymbol{d} = (0, d_1, 1)$ where c_1, d_1 are non-zero, then there exists an explicit algorithm $\mathcal{A}$ that makes at most q queries to each of P_1, P_2 and $V_0, U_3 \subseteq \mathbb{F}_{2^n}$ that have $|V_0| = |U_3| = q$, so that*

$$\mathsf{Pr}[\mu_{c,d}(V_0, \mathcal{Q}_1, \mathcal{Q}_2, U_3) \geqslant q^3/2N] \geqslant 1 - \frac{N}{q} \cdot e^{-q^2/8N}.$$

Though Proposition 6 gives a lower bound of $\Omega(q^3/N)$ for the sum capture quantity $\mu_{c,d}$, it does not immediately imply a distinguishing attack against the 3-round KAC. This is because the number of bad keys generated by our constructed $\mathcal{A}$ is at most q, so we have $\mathsf{Pr}[\boldsymbol{k} \in \mathsf{Badkey}] \leqslant q/N$. The reason of $\mu_{c,d}$ being too large is that a bad key may be counted multiple times in the sum capture quantity. Therefore, we cannot proceed with the sum capture quantity to prove the optimal $q = \Omega(N^{3/4})$ bound for 3-round KAC with identical subkeys if the overcounting cannot be eliminated.

5 Good Transcript Analysis

Our next goal is to obtain upper bounds of $1 - \mathsf{ps}_0(\tau)/\mathsf{ps}_1(\tau)$ for each $\tau \in \mathcal{T}_{\mathsf{good}}$. In particular, we will show the following lemma.

Lemma 7. *If the t-round KAC is instantiated with a key schedule that gives $(t-2)$-wise independently uniform subkeys, then there exists a function $g : \mathcal{T} \to [0, +\infty)$ so that for any $\tau = (\mathcal{Q}, \boldsymbol{k}) \in \mathcal{T}_{\mathsf{good}}$,*

$$1 - \frac{\mathsf{ps}_0(\tau)}{\mathsf{ps}_1(\tau)} \leqslant g(\tau),$$

and for any query records $\mathcal{Q}$,

$$\mathbb{E}_{\boldsymbol{k}}\left[g(\mathcal{Q}, \boldsymbol{k})\right] \leqslant \frac{t^2(4q)^{t+1}}{N^t}.$$

To obtain the desired function $g(\cdot)$, we need to understand the ratio $\mathsf{ps}_0(\tau)/\mathsf{ps}_1(\tau)$ first. Given the transcript $\tau = (\mathcal{Q}, \boldsymbol{k})$ in which $\mathcal{Q} = (\mathcal{Q}_E, \mathcal{Q}_1, \ldots, \mathcal{Q}_t)$, we write $E \downarrow \mathcal{Q}_E$ to denote that the real-world cipher construction E is consistent with the recorded query $\mathcal{Q}_E$, that is, for each $(x, y) \in \mathcal{Q}_E$, it holds that $E(x) = y$. Similarly, we write $P_i \downarrow \mathcal{Q}_i$ to denote that the permutation P_i is consistent with the recorded query $\mathcal{Q}_i$. Then following [5,16] one can derive that

$$\frac{\mathsf{ps}_0(\mathcal{Q}, \boldsymbol{k})}{\mathsf{ps}_1(\mathcal{Q}, \boldsymbol{k})} = N^{(|\mathcal{Q}_E|)} \cdot \mathsf{Pr}[E_{\boldsymbol{k}} \downarrow \mathcal{Q}_E \mid P_1 \downarrow \mathcal{Q}_1, \ldots, P_t \downarrow \mathcal{Q}_t], \tag{10}$$

where $N^{(|\mathcal{Q}_E|)} = N(N-1)\cdots(N-|\mathcal{Q}_E|+1)$. We provide a proof of (10) in the full version.

To analyze the probability term on the RHS, we need to take the following graph view for KAC, which was originally introduced by Chen and Steinberger in [6].

5.1 Graph Definition and an Useful Lemma

Let G be a graph that consists of vertices which can be divided into $m+1$ layers $L_0, \ldots, L_m$ such that each layer contains exactly N vertices, and edges that can be partition into m sets $\boldsymbol{E} = (E_{(0,1)}, E_{(1,2)}, \ldots, E_{(m-1,m)})$ such that $E_{(i,i+1)}$ forms a partial (but possibly perfect) matching from L_i to L_{i+1}.

We say a vertex $u \in L_i$, where $i < m$, is right-free if no edge connects u to any vertex in L_{i+1}. Analogously, we say a vertex $v \in L_j$, where $j > 0$, is left-free if no edge connects v to any vertex in L_{j-1}.

For any vertex $u \in L_0$ we define the following probabilistic procedure that generates a path $(w_0, w_1, \ldots w_m)$ from u to a vertex in L_m.

- Let $w_0 = u$.
- For i from 1 to m, if w_{i-1} is not right-free and connects to some vertex $w' \in L_i$, then let $w_i = w'$, otherwise let w_i be uniformly sampled from all left-free vertices in L_i.

We write $\mathsf{Pr}[u \to v]$ to denote the probability that the path $(u, w_1, \ldots, w_m)$ satisfies $w_m = v$. In particular, we are interested in the pair of (u, v) such that u is right-free and v is left-free.

For the layered graph G, we let $\mathcal{U}_G(a,b)$, where $a \leqslant b$, be the set of paths that starts at a left-free vertex in L_a and reaches a vertex in L_b. We note that the path in $\mathcal{U}_G(a,b)$ does not necessarily ends in L_b. We write $U_G(a,b) = |\mathcal{U}_G(a,b)|$. Note that $U_G(a,a)$ denotes the total number of left-free vertices in L_a.

Given any $\sigma = ((i_0,i_1),(i_1,i_2),\ldots,(i_{|\sigma|-1},i_{|\sigma|}))$ in which $i_0 < i_1 < \cdots < i_{|\sigma|}$, we say σ is an interesting (a,b)-segment partition with regard to the index set $\mathcal{I} \subseteq \{0,\ldots,m\}$ if $i_0 = a, i_{|\sigma|} = b$ and for all $1 < j < |\sigma|$ we have $i_j \in \mathcal{I}$. We use $\mathcal{B}_{\mathcal{I}}(a,b)$ to denote the set that contains all interesting (a,b)-segment partition of the set $\mathcal{I}$. Given a layered graph G, we let the interesting indices of G as

$$\mathcal{I}(G) := \{i \in \{0,1,2,\ldots,m\} \mid U_G(i,i) > 0\}.$$

Then we are ready to state the following lemma, which is a slightly different variant of the lemma proved by Chen and Steinberger in [6] but with essentially the same proof. We include the proof in the full version.

Lemma 8. *For any graph G defined as above, and any $u \in L_0, v \in L_m$ such that u is right-free and v is left-free, it holds that*

$$\mathsf{Pr}[u \to v] = \frac{1}{N} - \frac{1}{N} \sum_{\sigma \in \mathcal{B}_{\mathcal{I}(G)}(0,m)} (-1)^{|\sigma|} \prod_{h=1}^{|\sigma|} \frac{U_G(i_{h-1},i_h)}{U_G(i_h,i_h)}.$$

5.2 Graph View of KAC

The KAC can also be interpreted in the graph view. Given a transcript $\tau = (\boldsymbol{\mathcal{Q}}, \boldsymbol{k})$ where $\boldsymbol{\mathcal{Q}} = (\mathcal{Q}_E, \mathcal{Q}_1, \ldots, \mathcal{Q}_t)$ and let subkeys $\boldsymbol{s} = (s_0,\ldots,s_t)$ be generated from the key $\boldsymbol{k}$, we define $E_{(2i,2i+1)} := \{(v, v+s_i) \mid v \in L_{2i}\}$ for $i \in \{0,\ldots,t\}$. That is, L_{2i} and L_{2i+1} are connected by the "subkey edges", which corresponds to the step of xoring the subkey s_i in the KAC execution. For $i \in \{1,\ldots,t\}$, we let $E_{(2i-1,2i)} := \{(u,v) \mid (u,v) \in \mathcal{Q}_i\}$. This corresponds to the queries made to the permutation P_i. Now, note that the interesting indices for KAC can only be a subset of $\{0,2,4,\ldots,2t\}$.

For a fixed query records $\boldsymbol{\mathcal{Q}}$, let $Z_{\boldsymbol{s}}(a,b)$, where $a \leqslant b$, be the total number of paths that connects a vertex in L_a and a vertex in L_b when the subkeys are fixed to $\boldsymbol{s}$. Note that the paths do not necessarily start at L_a or end at L_b. For the ℓ-th cipher query (x_ℓ, y_ℓ), let $\alpha_\ell[\boldsymbol{s}]$ denote the largest possible index of the layer that is reachable from x_ℓ when the subkeys are fixed to be $\boldsymbol{s}$. let $\beta_\ell[\boldsymbol{s}]$ denote the smallest index of the layer than is reachable from y_ℓ. Note that in the good key case, we always have $\alpha_\ell[\boldsymbol{s}] < \beta_\ell[\boldsymbol{s}]$.

Now, to bound the probability $\mathsf{Pr}[E \downarrow \mathcal{Q}_E \mid P_1 \downarrow \mathcal{Q}_1, \ldots, P_t \downarrow \mathcal{Q}_t]$, we analyze the following experiment that can be divided into $|\mathcal{Q}_E|$ stages.

1. Initially, G_0 is defined according to the given transcript $\tau = (\boldsymbol{\mathcal{Q}}, \boldsymbol{k})$.
2. For ℓ from 1 to $|\mathcal{Q}_E|$, given $G_{\ell-1}$ is defined, the probabilistic path generating process is run for the ℓ-th query $(x_\ell, y_\ell) \in \mathcal{Q}_E$ over the graph $G_{\ell-1}$, from vertex $x_\ell \in L_0$.

- If the generated path from x_ℓ does not arrive at y_ℓ, the experiment outputs 0 and aborts.
- otherwise we first set $G_\ell = G_{\ell-1}$, then we remove all vertices on the path of (x_ℓ, y_ℓ) from G_ℓ. The new graph G_ℓ will have $N - \ell$ vertices in each layer.

3. If $G_{|\mathcal{Q}_E|}$ is successfully defined, the experiment outputs 1.

So we have

$$\frac{\mathsf{ps}_0(\mathcal{Q}, \boldsymbol{k})}{\mathsf{ps}_1(\mathcal{Q}, \boldsymbol{k})} = N^{(|\mathcal{Q}_E|)}\mathsf{Pr}[\mathsf{Exp}(\tau) = 1] = N^{(|\mathcal{Q}_E|)} \prod_{\ell=1}^{|\mathcal{Q}_E|} \mathsf{Pr}[x_\ell \to y_\ell \mid G_{\ell-1}]$$

Now we are ready to state the core lemma that defines the function $g(\mathcal{Q}, \boldsymbol{k})$ and prove it using Lemma 8.

Lemma 9. *For any query records $\mathcal{Q}$ with $q \leqslant N/4$ and subkeys $\boldsymbol{k}$ such that the transcript $\tau = (\mathcal{Q}, \boldsymbol{k}) \in \mathcal{T}_{\mathsf{good}}$,*

$$\frac{\mathsf{ps}_0(\mathcal{Q}, \boldsymbol{k})}{\mathsf{ps}_1(\mathcal{Q}, \boldsymbol{k})} \geqslant 1 - \sum_{\ell=1}^{q} \sum_{1 \leqslant a \leqslant b \leqslant t} \mathsf{R}_{2a-1,2b,\ell}[\boldsymbol{s}] \sum_{\sigma \in \mathcal{B}_{\mathcal{I}}(2a-1,2b),\ |\sigma| \geqslant 2} \prod_{h=1}^{|\sigma|} \frac{Z_{\boldsymbol{s}}(i_{h-1}, i_h)}{N - 2q}$$

in which the set of interesting indices $\mathcal{I}$ of the segment partition set $\mathcal{B}_{\mathcal{I}}$ is defined as $\mathcal{I} = \{0, 2, \ldots, 2t\}$, and $\mathsf{R}_{a,b,\ell}[\boldsymbol{s}] := \mathbb{1}(\alpha_\ell[\boldsymbol{s}] \geqslant a, \beta_\ell[\boldsymbol{s}] \leqslant b)$.

Proof. For the ℓ-th cipher query (x_ℓ, y_ℓ) given the graph support $G_{\ell-1}$, we can define a graph G from $G_{\ell-1}$ that removes all layers L_i for $i < \alpha_\ell[\boldsymbol{s}]$ and L_j for $j > \beta_\ell[\boldsymbol{s}]$. Thus, in the graph G we starts at a right-free vertex $u \in L_0$ and targets a left-free vertex $v \in L_m$, allowing us to apply Lemma 8.

$$\begin{aligned}
&\mathsf{Pr}_G[(x_\ell \to y_\ell) \mid G_{\ell-1}] \\
&= \frac{1}{N - \ell + 1}\left(1 - \sum_{\sigma \in \mathcal{B}_{\mathcal{I}(G)}(0,m)} (-1)^{|\sigma|} \prod_{h=1}^{|\sigma|} \frac{U_G(i_{h-1}, i_h)}{U_G(i_h, i_h)}\right) \\
&= \frac{1}{N - \ell + 1}\left(1 + \frac{U_G(0,m)}{U_G(m,m)} - \sum_{\sigma \in \mathcal{B}_{\mathcal{I}(G)}(0,m),\ |\sigma| \geqslant 2} (-1)^{|\sigma|} \prod_{h=1}^{|\sigma|} \frac{U_G(i_{h-1}, i_h)}{U_G(i_h, i_h)}\right) \\
&\geqslant \frac{1}{N - \ell + 1}\left(1 - \sum_{\sigma \in \mathcal{B}_{\mathcal{I}(G)}(0,m),\ |\sigma| \geqslant 2} \prod_{h=1}^{|\sigma|} \frac{U_G(i_{h-1}, i_h)}{U_G(i_h, i_h)}\right) \\
&\geqslant \frac{1}{N - \ell + 1}\left(1 - \sum_{\sigma \in \mathcal{B}_{\mathcal{I}}(\alpha_\ell[\boldsymbol{s}], \beta_\ell[\boldsymbol{s}]),\ |\sigma| \geqslant 2} \prod_{h=1}^{|\sigma|} \frac{Z_{\boldsymbol{s}}(i_{h-1}, i_h)}{N - 2q}\right) \qquad (11)
\end{aligned}$$

Now we only consider the case where the lower bound (11) $\geqslant 0$ for all ℓ. Otherwise Lemma 9 becomes trivially true. Hence we have

$$\frac{\mathsf{ps}_0(\mathcal{Q},\boldsymbol{k})}{\mathsf{ps}_1(\mathcal{Q},\boldsymbol{k})} \geqslant \prod_{\ell=1}^{q}\left(1-\sum_{\sigma\in\mathcal{B}_{\mathcal{I}}(\alpha_\ell[s],\beta_\ell[s]),\ |\sigma|\geqslant 2}\ \prod_{h=1}^{|\sigma|}\frac{Z_s(i_{h-1},i_h)}{N-2q}\right)$$

$$\geqslant 1-\sum_{\ell=1}^{q}\ \sum_{\sigma\in\mathcal{B}_{\mathcal{I}}(\alpha_\ell[s],\beta_\ell[s]),\ |\sigma|\geqslant 2}\ \prod_{h=1}^{|\sigma|}\frac{Z_s(i_{h-1},i_h)}{N-2q} \tag{12}$$

$$\geqslant 1-\sum_{\ell=1}^{q}\ \sum_{1\leqslant a\leqslant b\leqslant t}\mathsf{R}_{2a-1,2b,\ell}[\boldsymbol{s}]\ \sum_{\sigma\in\mathcal{B}_{\mathcal{I}}(2a-1,2b),\ |\sigma|\geqslant 2}\ \prod_{h=1}^{|\sigma|}\frac{Z_s(i_{h-1},i_h)}{N-2q} \tag{13}$$

in which (12) is due to $(1-a)(1-b)\geqslant 1-a-b$ for any $a,b\geqslant 0$ and (13) is due to the indicator function R is non-negative and satisfies $\mathsf{R}_{\alpha[s],\beta[s],\ell}[\boldsymbol{s}]=1$. We note that (13) is the exact quantity we pick for $1-g(\mathcal{Q},\boldsymbol{k})$. □

Lemma 10. *If* $q\leqslant N/4$, *then,*

$$\mathbb{E}_{\boldsymbol{k}}\left(\sum_{\ell=1}^{q}\ \sum_{1\leqslant a\leqslant b\leqslant t}\mathsf{R}_{2a-1,2b,\ell}[\boldsymbol{s}]\ \sum_{\sigma\in\mathcal{B}_{\mathcal{I}}(2a-1,2b),|\sigma|\geqslant 2}\ \prod_{h=1}^{|\sigma|}\frac{Z_s(i_{h-1},i_h)}{N-2q}\right)\leqslant\frac{t^2(4q)^{t+1}}{N^t}.$$

Proof. By the sum of expectation and noting that none of $\sigma\in\mathcal{B}_{\mathcal{I}}(2a-1,2b)$ would have $|\sigma|\geqslant 2$ if $a=b$, we have

$$\mathbb{E}_{\boldsymbol{k}}\left(\sum_{\ell=1}^{q}\ \sum_{1\leqslant a\leqslant b\leqslant t}\mathsf{R}_{2a-1,2b,\ell}[\boldsymbol{s}]\ \sum_{\sigma\in\mathcal{B}_{\mathcal{I}}(2a-1,2b),\ |\sigma|\geqslant 2}\ \prod_{h=1}^{|\sigma|}\frac{Z_s(i_{h-1},i_h)}{N-2q}\right)$$
$$=\sum_{\ell=1}^{q}\ \sum_{1\leqslant a<b\leqslant t}\ \sum_{\sigma\in\mathcal{B}_{\mathcal{I}}(2a-1,2b),\ |\sigma|\geqslant 2}\mathbb{E}_{s}\left(\mathsf{R}_{2a-1,2b,\ell}[\boldsymbol{s}]\cdot\prod_{h=1}^{|\sigma|}\frac{Z_s(i_{h-1},i_h)}{N-2q}\right).$$

Hence it is sufficient to derive bounds for each (a,b,σ). Note that for each a,b, $R_{2a-1,2b,j}[\boldsymbol{s}]$ only depends on the subkeys $s_0,\ldots,s_{a-2},s_{b+1},\ldots,s_t$, which are $(a-2+1)+(t-(b+1)+1)=t-b+a-1$ subkeys in total.

Next, given a fixed $\sigma=((i_0,i_1),(i_1,i_2),\ldots,(i_{|\sigma|-1},i_{|\sigma|}))$, we analyze the key dependency for each $Z_s(i_{h-1},i_h)$.

1. For $Z_s(i_0,i_1)$, note that $i_0=2a-1$ which is odd, and i_1 is even. So $Z_s(i_0,i_1)$ $(i_1-i_0-1)/2$ subkeys between L_{i_0} and L_{i_1}.
2. For any (i_{h-1},i_h) where $h>1$, given i_{h-1} is an even number, implying that $L_{i_{h-1}}$ and $L_{i_{h-1}+1}$ are connected by "key-edges", always forming a perfect matching regardless of the subkey choice. Then the equality $Z_s(i_{h-1},i_h)=Z_s(i_{h-1}+1,i_h)$ always holds. And we can see that $Z_s(i_{h-1}+1,i_h)$ only depends on $(i_h-i_{h-1}-2)/2$ subkeys.

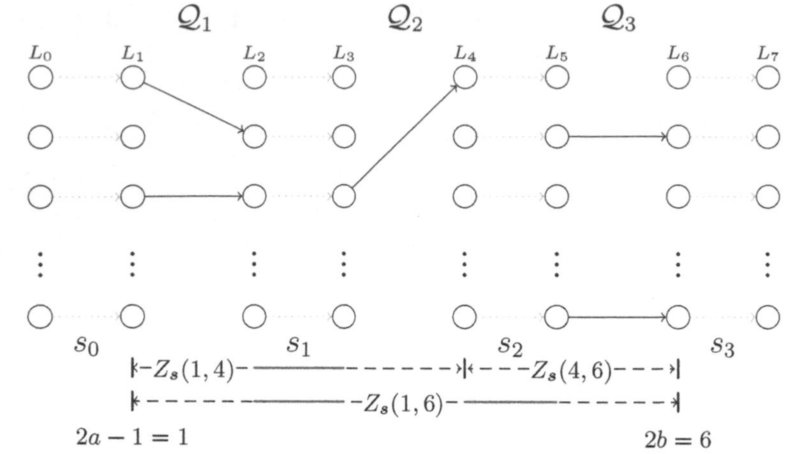

Fig. 1. A 3-round KAC with fixed query records $\mathcal{Q}_1, \mathcal{Q}_2, \mathcal{Q}_3$. The subkeys $\boldsymbol{s} = (s_0, \ldots, s_3)$ are random and to be sampled. The red solid line indicates that the $Z_{\boldsymbol{s}}(\mathsf{left}, \mathsf{right})$ that counts the number of paths from L_{left} to L_{right} depends on the corresponding subkeys. Consider $2a-1=1, 2b=6$, then $\mathsf{R}_{1,6,\ell}[\boldsymbol{s}] = 1$ and depends on $(a-1)+(3-b)=0$ subkeys, because any s_0 allows x_ℓ from L_0 to reach L_1, and y_ℓ from L_7 to L_6. For $\sigma = ((1,6))$, the value of $Z_{\boldsymbol{s}}(1,6)$ depends on two subkeys s_1, s_2. However, if the σ is further paritioned into $((1,4),(4,6))$, then $Z_{\boldsymbol{s}}(1,4)$ depends on s_1 but $Z_{\boldsymbol{s}}(4,6)$ does not depend on any subkeys, because $Z_{\boldsymbol{s}}(4,6) = Z_{\boldsymbol{s}}(5,6) = |\mathcal{Q}_3|$.

Also note that the sets of dependent subkeys for $Z_{\boldsymbol{s}}(i_{h-1}, i_h)$ and $\mathsf{R}_{2a-1,2b,j}[\boldsymbol{s}]$ are disjoint. Putting the results altogether, after fixing (a, b, σ), the total number of subkeys that each expectation term depends on are at most

$$\begin{aligned}
\#\text{dependent subkeys} &= (t-b+a-1) + \frac{i_1 - i_0 - 1}{2} + \sum_{h=2}^{|\sigma|}\left(\frac{i_h - i_{h-1}}{2} - 1\right) \\
&= (t-b+a-1) + \frac{\sum_{h=1}^{|\sigma|}(i_h - i_{h-1}) - 1}{2} - (|\sigma| - 1) \\
&= t - b + a - 1 + \frac{2b-2a}{2} - |\sigma| + 1 \\
&= t - |\sigma| \leqslant t - 2,
\end{aligned}$$

in which we observe that a summation term of (a, b, σ) depends on fewer subkeys if the size of σ is larger (See Fig. 1 for a specific case illustration). Because our construction ensures that any $t-2$ subkeys are independently and uniformly distributed, the random variables in each expectation terms are mutually independent and hence we can break the terms into

$$\mathbb{E}_k\left(\sum_{\ell=1}^{q}\sum_{1\leqslant a\leqslant b\leqslant t}\mathsf{R}_{2a-1,2b,\ell}[s]\sum_{\sigma\in\mathcal{B}_{\mathcal{I}}(2a-1,2b),\ |\sigma|\geqslant 2}\prod_{h=1}^{|\sigma|}\frac{Z_s(i_{h-1},i_h)}{N-2q}\right)$$

$$\leqslant\sum_{\ell=1}^{q}\sum_{1\leqslant a<b\leqslant t}\sum_{\sigma\in\mathcal{B}_{\mathcal{I}}(2a-1,2b),\ |\sigma|\geqslant 2}\mathbb{E}_s\left(\mathsf{R}_{2a-1,2b,\ell}[s]\cdot\prod_{h=1}^{|\sigma|}\frac{2Z_s(i_{h-1},i_h)}{N}\right)$$

$$=\sum_{\ell=1}^{q}\sum_{1\leqslant a<b\leqslant t}\sum_{\sigma\in\mathcal{B}_{\mathcal{I}}(2a-1,2b),\ |\sigma|\geqslant 2}\mathbb{E}_s\left(\mathsf{R}_{2a-1,2b,\ell}[s]\right)\cdot\prod_{h=1}^{|\sigma|}\mathbb{E}_s\left(\frac{2Z_s(i_{h-1},i_h)}{N}\right) \tag{14}$$

$$\leqslant\sum_{\ell=1}^{q}\sum_{1\leqslant a<b\leqslant t}\left(\frac{q}{N}\right)^{t-b+a-1}\sum_{\substack{\sigma\in\mathcal{B}_{\mathcal{I}}(2a-1,2b),\\ |\sigma|\geqslant 2}}\left(\frac{2q}{N}\right)^{(i_1-i_0+1)/2}\prod_{h=2}^{|\sigma|}\left(\frac{2q}{N}\right)^{(i_h-i_{h-1})/2} \tag{15}$$

$$\leqslant\sum_{\ell=1}^{q}\sum_{1\leqslant a<b\leqslant t}\left(\frac{q}{N}\right)^{t-b+a-1}\cdot\left(\frac{4q}{N}\right)^{b-a+1}\leqslant t^2\cdot\frac{(4q)^{t+1}}{N^t}. \tag{16}$$

In the above calculation, (14) is due to the subkeys are $(t-2)$-wise independent. The first "q/N" term of (15) comes from moving the $\mathbb{E}_s\left(\mathsf{R}_{2a-1,2b,\ell}[s]\right)$, and inside the summation the "$2q/N$" terms are the direct calculation upper bound of $\mathbb{E}_s\left(2Z_s(i_{h-1},i_h)/N\right)$ for each (i_{h-1},i_h). Finally we have the first inequality of (16) holds because the size of $\mathcal{B}_{\mathcal{I}}(2a-1,2b)$ is upper-bounded by 2^{b-a}, which is absorbed into "$2q/N$" term yielding a "$4q/N$" term. □

6 Concluding the Proof

Given the similarity of proofs for both theorems, we provide the proof of Theorem 1 here and left the proof of Theorem 2 to the full version.

6.1 Proof of Theorem 1

Proof. We partition the set of transcripts $\mathcal{T}=\mathcal{T}_{\mathsf{good}}\sqcup\mathcal{T}_{\mathsf{bad}}$ according to Definition 1. By applying Lemma 1, we have $\Delta(X_0,X_1)\leqslant\mathbb{E}_{X_1}[g(X_1)]+\mathsf{Pr}[X_1\in\mathcal{T}_{\mathsf{bad}}]$. We start with bounding $\mathsf{Pr}[X_1\in\mathcal{T}_{\mathsf{bad}}]$.

Claim

$$\mathsf{Pr}[X_1\in\mathcal{T}_{\mathsf{bad}}]\leqslant(t+1)\cdot\frac{3q^{t+1}}{N^t}+3(t+1)\sqrt{\frac{q^{2t-1}(t+2)n}{N^{2t-2}}}+\frac{t(t+1)}{N^t}.$$

Proof (of claim). We note that in the system $\mathbf{S}_1$, the set of bad keys $\mathsf{Badkey}_{\mathcal{Q}}$ is defined only by the query records $\mathcal{Q}=(\mathcal{Q}_E,\mathcal{Q}_1,\ldots,\mathcal{Q}_t)$. Therefore, we have

$$\mathsf{Pr}[X_1\in\mathcal{T}_{\mathsf{bad}}]\leqslant\mathsf{Pr}_{\mathcal{Q}}\left[|\mathsf{Badkey}_{\mathcal{Q}}|>C\right]+\frac{C}{N^{t-1}}.$$

To get the size bound for $\mathsf{Badkey}_{\mathcal{Q}}$, we compute the size of $\mathsf{Badkey}_{\mathcal{Q},i}$ for $0 \leqslant i \leqslant t$. Then, we have

$$\begin{aligned}|\mathsf{Badkey}_{\mathcal{Q},0}| &\leqslant \mu_{c_0}(V_1, \mathcal{Q}_2, \mathcal{Q}_3, \ldots, \mathcal{Q}_{t-1}, \mathcal{Q}_t, U_{t+1})\\ |\mathsf{Badkey}_{\mathcal{Q},1}| &\leqslant \mu_{c_1}(V_2, \mathcal{Q}_3, \mathcal{Q}_4, \ldots, \mathcal{Q}_t, \mathcal{Q}_E, U_1)\\ &\vdots\\ |\mathsf{Badkey}_{\mathcal{Q},t-1}| &\leqslant \mu_{c_{t-1}}(V_t, \mathcal{Q}_E, \mathcal{Q}_1, \ldots, \mathcal{Q}_{t-2}, U_{t-1})\\ |\mathsf{Badkey}_{\mathcal{Q},t}| &\leqslant \mu_{c_t}(V_0, \mathcal{Q}_1, \ldots, \mathcal{Q}_{t-1}, U_t).\end{aligned}$$

where the linear coefficient tuples $\boldsymbol{c}_i$ are given by the condition 2 of Theorem 1 so that there are two neighboring coefficients that are non-zero, and

$$\begin{aligned}\forall i \in \{1, \ldots, t\} : U_i &= \{u \mid \exists v : (u, v) \in \mathcal{Q}_i\}, & V_i &= \{v \mid \exists u : (u, v) \in \mathcal{Q}_i\}\\ U_{t+1} &= \{u \mid \exists v : (u, v) \in \mathcal{Q}_E\}, & V_0 &= \{v \mid \exists u : (u, v) \in \mathcal{Q}_E\}.\end{aligned}$$

The size of $\mathsf{Badkey}_{\mathcal{Q},i}$ is bounded by μ_{c_i} because any key $\boldsymbol{k} \in \mathsf{Badkey}_{\mathcal{Q},i}$ is uniquely mapped to the subkeys $(s_0, \ldots, s_{i-1}, s_{i+1}, s_t)$ as the linear mapping has rank $t-1$ (stated in condition 2 of Theorem 1).

Now we can apply Lemma 2 to upper bound $\mathsf{Badkey}_{\mathcal{Q},i}$ with high probability. For every i, by letting $C_i = \frac{3q^{t+1}}{N} + 3q^{t-1/2}\sqrt{(t+2)n}$, we obtain that $\mathsf{Pr}_{\mathcal{Q}}[|\mathsf{Badkey}_{\mathcal{Q},i}| > C_i] \leqslant \frac{2}{N^t}$. Therefore, setting $C = \sum_{i=0}^{t} C_i$, we have

$$\begin{aligned}\mathsf{Pr}[X_1 \in \mathcal{T}_{\mathsf{bad}}] &\leqslant \sum_{i=0}^{t} \mathsf{Pr}_{\mathcal{Q}}\left[|\mathsf{Badkey}_{\mathcal{Q}_i}| > C_i\right] + \frac{C}{N^{t-1}}\\ &\leqslant \frac{2t(t+1)}{N^t} + (t+1) \cdot \frac{3q^{t+1}}{N^t} + 3(t+1) \cdot \frac{q^{t-1/2}\sqrt{(t+2)n}}{N^{t-1}}\end{aligned}$$

Hence we proved the claim □

The next step is to pick a function g and upper bound $\mathbb{E}_{X_1}[g(X_1)]$. Note that by condition 1 of Theorem 1, any $t-2$ rows of key schedule matrix A has rank $t-2$, implying that any subset of $t-2$ subkeys are independent and uniform. Therefore we can apply Lemma 7 and obtain a function g. Noting that X_1 is in the ideal world so $\boldsymbol{k}$ is sampled independently of $\mathcal{Q}$, we have

$$\mathbb{E}_{X_1}[g(X_1)] = \mathbb{E}_{\mathcal{Q}}\mathbb{E}_{\boldsymbol{k}}[g(\mathcal{Q}, \boldsymbol{k})] \leqslant \mathbb{E}_{\mathcal{Q}}\left[\frac{t^2(4q)^{t+1}}{N^t}\right] = \frac{t^2(4q)^{t+1}}{N^t}.$$

Then by summing up the two quantities and numerical simplifications, the theorem follows. □

7 Conclusion and Open Problems

In this paper, we provided key schedules of limited independence for t-round key-alternating ciphers achieving tight security. We proved that the t-round key-alternating cipher remains tightly secure for a class of $(t-1)$-wise independent sub-key distributions and, when $t \geqslant 8$, for $(t-2)$-wise sub-key distributions.

While, for $3 \leqslant t \leqslant 7$, our result does not extends to $(t-2)$-wise independent sub-key distributions, we expect that a tighter analysis of the matrix 2-norm for the sum-capture quantity should give a proof for $4 \leqslant t \leqslant 7$. Also, it is interesting to investigate new methods for bounding the bad keys and proving tight security of 3-round key-alternating cipher with identical key schedule. Further, it would be also interesting to study whether the tightness result holds for $(t-3)$-wise distributions or beyond.

Acknowledgements. We thank the anonymous reviewers for sharing many helpful suggestions that improved the paper. Stefano Tessaro and Xihu Zhang were partially supported by NSF grants CNS-1930117 (CAREER), CNS1926324, CNS-2026774, a Sloan Research Fellowship, and a JP Morgan Faculty Award.

References

1. Alon, N., Kaufman, T., Krivelevich, M., Ron, D.: Testing triangle-freeness in general graphs. In: 17th SODA, pp. 279–288. ACM-SIAM, January 2006
2. Babai, L.: The Fourier transform and equations over finite abelian groups: an introduction to the method of trigonometric sums. Lecture Notes (1989). http://people.cs.uchicago.edu/~laci/reu02/fourier.pdf
3. Bogdanov, A., et al.: PRESENT: an ultra-lightweight block cipher. In: Paillier, P., Verbauwhede, I. (eds.) CHES 2007. LNCS, vol. 4727, pp. 450–466. Springer, Heidelberg (2007). https://doi.org/10.1007/978-3-540-74735-2_31
4. Bogdanov, A., Knudsen, L.R., Leander, G., Standaert, F.-X., Steinberger, J., Tischhauser, E.: Key-alternating ciphers in a provable setting: encryption using a small number of public permutations. In: Pointcheval, D., Johansson, T. (eds.) EUROCRYPT 2012. LNCS, vol. 7237, pp. 45–62. Springer, Heidelberg (2012). https://doi.org/10.1007/978-3-642-29011-4_5
5. Chen, S., Lampe, R., Lee, J., Seurin, Y., Steinberger, J.: Minimizing the two-round Even-Mansour cipher. In: Garay, J.A., Gennaro, R. (eds.) CRYPTO 2014. LNCS, vol. 8616, pp. 39–56. Springer, Heidelberg (2014). https://doi.org/10.1007/978-3-662-44371-2_3
6. Chen, S., Steinberger, J.: Tight security bounds for key-alternating ciphers. In: Nguyen, P.Q., Oswald, E. (eds.) EUROCRYPT 2014. LNCS, vol. 8441, pp. 327–350. Springer, Heidelberg (2014). https://doi.org/10.1007/978-3-642-55220-5_19
7. Cogliati, B., Lampe, R., Seurin, Y.: Tweaking Even-Mansour ciphers. In: Gennaro, R., Robshaw, M. (eds.) CRYPTO 2015. LNCS, vol. 9215, pp. 189–208. Springer, Heidelberg (2015). https://doi.org/10.1007/978-3-662-47989-6_9
8. Cogliati, B., Seurin, Y.: Beyond-birthday-bound security for tweakable Even-Mansour ciphers with linear tweak and key mixing. In: Iwata, T., Cheon, J.H. (eds.) ASIACRYPT 2015. LNCS, vol. 9453, pp. 134–158. Springer, Heidelberg (2015). https://doi.org/10.1007/978-3-662-48800-3_6
9. Cogliati, B., Seurin, Y.: On the provable security of the iterated Even-Mansour cipher against related-key and chosen-key attacks. In: Oswald, E., Fischlin, M. (eds.) EUROCRYPT 2015. LNCS, vol. 9056, pp. 584–613. Springer, Heidelberg (2015). https://doi.org/10.1007/978-3-662-46800-5_23
10. Daemen, J., Rijmen, V.: The Design of Rijndael, vol. 2. Springer, Heidelberg (2002). https://doi.org/10.1007/978-3-662-04722-4

11. Dunkelman, O., Keller, N., Shamir, A.: Minimalism in cryptography: the Even-Mansour scheme revisited. In: Pointcheval, D., Johansson, T. (eds.) EUROCRYPT 2012. LNCS, vol. 7237, pp. 336–354. Springer, Heidelberg (2012). https://doi.org/10.1007/978-3-642-29011-4_21
12. Dutta, A.: Minimizing the two-round tweakable Even-Mansour cipher. In: Moriai, S., Wang, H. (eds.) ASIACRYPT 2020. LNCS, vol. 12491, pp. 601–629. Springer, Cham (2020). https://doi.org/10.1007/978-3-030-64837-4_20
13. Even, S., Mansour, Y.: A construction of a cipher from a single pseudorandom permutation. J. Cryptol. **10**(3), 151–161 (1997). https://doi.org/10.1007/s001459900025
14. Guo, J., Peyrin, T., Poschmann, A., Robshaw, M.: The LED block cipher. In: Preneel, B., Takagi, T. (eds.) CHES 2011. LNCS, vol. 6917, pp. 326–341. Springer, Heidelberg (2011). https://doi.org/10.1007/978-3-642-23951-9_22
15. Hayes, T.P.: A large-deviation inequality for vector-valued martingales (2003). https://www.cs.unm.edu/~hayes/papers/VectorAzuma/VectorAzuma20050726.pdf
16. Hoang, V.T., Tessaro, S.: Key-alternating ciphers and key-length extension: exact bounds and multi-user security. In: Robshaw, M., Katz, J. (eds.) CRYPTO 2016. LNCS, vol. 9814, pp. 3–32. Springer, Heidelberg (2016). https://doi.org/10.1007/978-3-662-53018-4_1
17. Kiltz, E., Pietrzak, K., Szegedy, M.: Digital signatures with minimal overhead from indifferentiable random invertible functions. In: Canetti, R., Garay, J.A. (eds.) CRYPTO 2013. LNCS, vol. 8042, pp. 571–588. Springer, Heidelberg (2013). https://doi.org/10.1007/978-3-642-40041-4_31
18. Lampe, R., Patarin, J., Seurin, Y.: An asymptotically tight security analysis of the iterated Even-Mansour cipher. In: Wang, X., Sako, K. (eds.) ASIACRYPT 2012. LNCS, vol. 7658, pp. 278–295. Springer, Heidelberg (2012). https://doi.org/10.1007/978-3-642-34961-4_18
19. Maurer, U.: Indistinguishability of random systems. In: Knudsen, L.R. (ed.) EUROCRYPT 2002. LNCS, vol. 2332, pp. 110–132. Springer, Heidelberg (2002). https://doi.org/10.1007/3-540-46035-7_8
20. Patarin, J.: The "coefficients H" technique. In: Avanzi, R.M., Keliher, L., Sica, F. (eds.) SAC 2008. LNCS, vol. 5381, pp. 328–345. Springer, Heidelberg (2009). https://doi.org/10.1007/978-3-642-04159-4_21
21. Steinberger, J.: Improved security bounds for key-alternating ciphers via Hellinger distance. Cryptology ePrint Archive, Report 2012/481 (2012). http://eprint.iacr.org/2012/481
22. Steinberger, J.P.: Counting solutions to additive equations in random sets. CoRR, abs/1309.5582 (2013)
23. Wu, Y., Yu, L., Cao, Z., Dong, X.: Tight security analysis of 3-round key-alternating cipher with a single permutation. In: Moriai, S., Wang, H. (eds.) ASIACRYPT 2020. LNCS, vol. 12491, pp. 662–693. Springer, Cham (2020). https://doi.org/10.1007/978-3-030-64837-4_22

FAST: Secure and High Performance Format-Preserving Encryption and Tokenization

F. Betül Durak[1(✉)], Henning Horst[2], Michael Horst[2], and Serge Vaudenay[3]

[1] Microsoft Research, Redmond, USA
[2] Comforte AG, Wiesbaden, Germany
[3] EPFL, Lausanne, Switzerland

Abstract. We propose a new construction for format-preserving encryption. Our design provides the flexibility for use in format-preserving encryption (FPE) and for static table-driven tokenization. Our algorithm is a substitution-permutation network based on random Sboxes. Using pseudorandom generators and pseudorandom functions, we prove a strong adaptive security based on the super-pseudorandom permutation assumption of our core design. We obtain empirical parameters to reach this assumption. We suggest parameters for quantum security.

Our design accommodates very small domains, with a radix a from 4 to the Unicode alphabet size and a block length ℓ starting 2. The number of Sbox evaluations per encryption is asymptotically $\ell^{\frac{3}{2}}$, which is also the number of bytes we need to generate using AES in CTR mode for each tweak setup. For instance, we tokenize 10 decimal digits using 29 (parallel) AES computations to be done only once, when the tweak changes.

1 Introduction

Symmetric encryption offers an efficient way to keep data private. However, it is typically only length-preserving in the sense that a plaintext and a ciphertext occupy *exactly* the same space and structure in memory. However, length preservation falls short when we consider non-binary plaintext data such as bank account numbers, driver license numbers, tax ID's and so forth. This limitation can be overcome by format-preserving protection mechanisms. *Format-Preserving Encryption* (FPE) was proposed to encrypt data while retaining the original format and field size of the input data. It can, for instance, encrypt a 16-digit credit card number (or part of it), as a series of digits, and produce a ciphertext which is still 16-digits long. One difficulty with FPE is that the message space can be very small for common fields used in personal data processing scenarios, for example, age, a postal code, names, bank sort codes, subsets of larger fields, and so on. In particular, adversaries may be able to go through the message space exhaustively. Hence, FPE is strengthened with a *tweak*, following the tweakable encryption paradigm. Contrarily to a *nonce*, a tweak can be reused. Tweakable encryption was formalized by Liskov et al. [27].

M. Tibouchi and H. Wang (Eds.): ASIACRYPT 2021, LNCS 13092, pp. 465–489, 2021.
https://doi.org/10.1007/978-3-030-92078-4_16

Formally speaking, an FPE takes as input a key and a message, as well as parameters specifying the format and the tweak. In standard FPE, the format consists of a radix a and a length ℓ. The message domain has cardinality a^ℓ.

FPE first appeared as a *data-type preserving encryption* [13] and in the form of an *omnicipher* with the Hasty Pudding AES competitor [31]. The term FPE is due to Spies [33]. Rogaway presented a list of FPE schemes [29]. Some constructions are based on cycle walking [11]. The most popular FPEs are based on Feistel networks and have been standardized as FF1 and FF3 [1,3,7,8,12]. A weakness was found in FF1 and FF3 by Bellare et al. [6]. FF3 was broken and repaired by Durak and Vaudenay [18]. The attack was later improved by Hoang et al. [22,23]. There exist some dedicated constructions based on substitution-permutation network (SPN) such as TOY100 [20] and DEAN18 [5], but they are designed only for fixed blocks of decimal digits. Actually, one difficulty with SPN-based FPE is that the internal Sboxes must be adapted to the specific format of the input data. Another SPN-based construction allows more formats but suffers from lack of flexibility as well [15]. Another construction mixes the cycle walking techniques with SPN based on Sboxes working on a domain which is larger than the format [16]. However, this construction is not a pure SPN. It is rather based on one-time-pad with a keystream generated from an SPN. Hence, it needs a nonce and it has trivial chosen ciphertext decryption attacks.[1] We believe that substitution-permutation networks has been under-explored for FPE so far and will present a new FPE design based on an SPN.

Some cipher designs use pseudorandom Sboxes and use them in a pseudorandom sequence. Both random selections can be derived from the secret key. This approach was used in LUCIFER [19] (the preliminary version of DES), where Sboxes are invertible 4-bit to 4-bit functions selected from a pool of two using a binary key for each Sbox. It was used in KHUFU [28] as well, where Sboxes are pseudorandom 8-bit to 32-bit functions generated from the secret key. BLOWFISH [30] also used pseudorandom 8-bit to 32-bit functions. In our design, we use pseudorandom permutations over an alphabet set $\mathbf{Z}_a$, where a is the radix of the message to be encrypted. The key is used to select a sequence of Sboxes from a pool. The pool of Sboxes is generated by a secret too.

Tokenization is another concept for format-preserving data protection that introduces the notion of mapping cleartext values to substitute "token" values that retain format and structure of the original data, but no cleartext data, while logically isolating the process that performs the mapping. While encryption itself makes no assumption about key ownership, tokenization typically implies that tokenization secret(s) and mapping process are owned by a tokenization system, a strongly isolated single entity authenticating and auditing access to the token mapping process using the tokenization secret(s). ANSI X9.119-2 [2] defines three main approaches for tokenization: (1) On Demand Random Assignment (ODRA) which generates random tokens on demand and stores the

[1] Note that we want exact format preservation hence no stretch in theciphertext. Consequently, FPE cannot authenticate at the same time and authenticationcannot be used to defeat chosen ciphertext attacks.

association with the plaintext value in a dynamic mapping table which grows per new token generated. However, using the method, the large and constantly growing mapping table creates severe operational issues for environments requiring high performance and resilience. (2) Static table-driven tokenization (a.k.a. vault-less tokenization) generates tokens using a tokenization mapping process which operates using small pre-generated static random substitution tables used as the tokenization secret. (3) Encryption-based tokenization generates tokens using a suitable FPE or symmetric encryption algorithm where the key serves as tokenization secret. Our design can be used as base for static table-driven tokenization as well for encryption-based tokenization.

Our Contribution. In this paper, we design and analyze a new format-preserving protection construction method. We call our method FAST as for *Format-preserving Addition Substitution Transformation.*[2] FAST can be used in FPE or tokenization mode. Tokenization mode differs from FPE mode by having two specific inputs instead of one secret key: pre-generated random Sboxes as stateless table secret, which can be common to several domains, and a key, which is be used for domain separation. The stateless table secret is much more used than a given domain-specific key. Therefore, we consider a security model where the stateless table secret is revealed to the adversary and the rest works like in FPE security. In FPE mode, the pseudorandom Sboxes are generated from the key.

We formally define a strong security model for FPE which is essentially a multi-target chosen format and chosen tweak super-PRP (pseudorandom permutation) notion. Concretely, we consider adversaries who can choose all parameters, have many targets, choose the plaintexts and the ciphertexts. One challenge is that the encryption domain can be really small. Hence, the adversary could get the complete codebook for some tweaks and even look at their permutation parity. We model security by indistinguishability from an ideal FPE making only even permutations.[3]

We formally prove strong security based on a weak security assumption: that the core design is a super-PRP in a weak model where the adversary uses a single target, a single format, and a single tweak. More precisely, we reduce strong security to this weak security notion. We formally prove this reduction in a tight and quantifiable manner.

[2] There exists another FAST algorithm in the literature which is unrelated [14].

[3] A permutation π is called even if the number of (x, y) pairs such that $x < y$ and $\pi(x) > \pi(y)$ is even.

The single-instance security of the core design is heuristic. We find (what we believe to be) the best attacks on the core design. We optimize our parameters to reduce the number of Sbox applications down to $\ell^{\frac{3}{2}}$ (instead of ℓ^2). We set the number of rounds to twice the one we can break to have a good safety margin. We also consider quantum security.

We implement our algorithm and show good performance. Concretely, our design needs some AES applications to generate random bytes for each tweak. However, in contrast to the FF1 and FF3 algorithms which use AES as round functions in a Feistel network, our design allows for these generations to be parallelized and thus achieve much higher performance by design. Then, the core encryption needs no AES computation or expensive modular reductions. It is purely an SPN with Sboxes, additions, subtractions, and permutations.

Structure of this Paper. We first detail the specifications of FAST in Sect. 2. In Sect. 3, we give implementation results. We formally define a security model and we prove strong adaptive security of FAST based on the hypothesis that our core scheme is a super pseudorandom permutation in Sect. 4. Rationales are given in Sect. 5. The full version of this article [17] further include the formal proofs and the best known attacks which motivated our parameter choices.

2 Algorithm Specification

In what follows, we use the following integer parameters:

s: bit-security target
L: bitlength of key K
L_1: bitlength of key K_{SEQ}
L_2: bitlength of key K_S ($L_1 = L_2$)
a: the alphabet size a.k.a. radix ($a = 10$ for decimal digits) ($a \geq 4$)
ℓ: word length of input/output ($\ell \geq 2$)
m: number of Sboxes in the pool ($m = 256$)
n: total number of layers ($r = n/\ell$ rounds of ℓ layers)
w: a branch distance ($0 \leq w \leq \ell - 2$)
w': a second branch distance ($1 \leq w' \leq \ell - w - 1$)

Without loss of generality, the alphabet is $\mathbf{Z}_a = \{0, 1, \ldots, a-1\}$ to which we give the group structure defined by modulo a addition. The "input" is an element of $\mathbf{Z}_a^\ell$. An Sbox is a permutation of $\mathbf{Z}_a$. A pool of Sboxes is a tuple $S = (S_0, \ldots, S_{m-1})$ of m Sboxes.

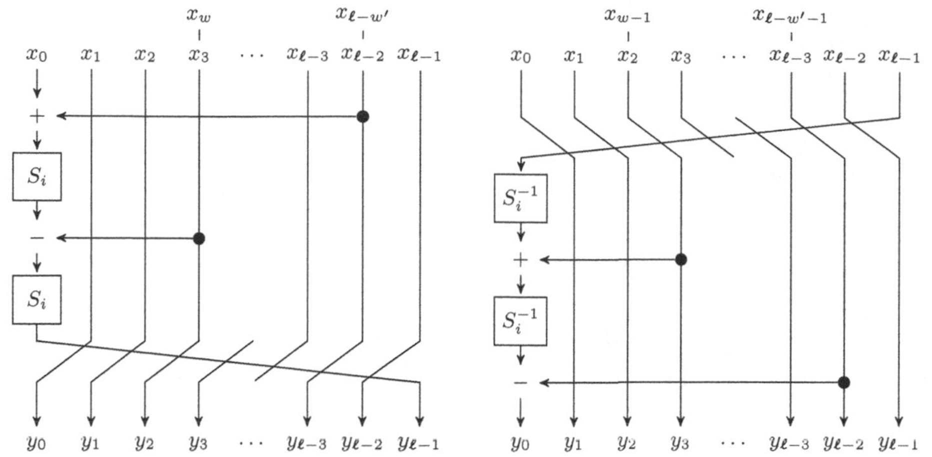

Fig. 1. One layer with circular shift of branches: forward (on the left) and backward (on the right) with $w = 3$, $w' = 2$

Layers of Encryption/Decryption. Given a pool S of m Sboxes and an index i in $\{0, \ldots, m-1\}$, we define the permutation $E_S[i]$ of $\mathbf{Z}_a^\ell$ as follows: for any $x = (x_0, \ldots, x_{\ell-1}) \in \mathbf{Z}_a^\ell$, we have

$$E_S[i](x) = \begin{cases} (x_1, \ldots, x_{\ell-1}, S_i(S_i(x_0 + x_{\ell-w'}))) & \text{if } w = 0 \\ (x_1, \ldots, x_{\ell-1}, S_i(S_i(x_0 + x_{\ell-w'}) - x_w)) & \text{if } w > 0 \end{cases}$$

as depicted in Fig. 1. We call it a *forward layer*. Similarly, we define a *backward layer*

$$D_S[i](x) = \begin{cases} (S_i^{-1}(S_i^{-1}(x_{\ell-1})) - x_{\ell-w'-1}, x_0, \ldots, x_{\ell-2}) & \text{if } w = 0 \\ (S_i^{-1}(S_i^{-1}(x_{\ell-1}) + x_{w-1}) - x_{\ell-w'-1}, x_0, \ldots, x_{\ell-2}) & \text{if } w > 0 \end{cases}$$

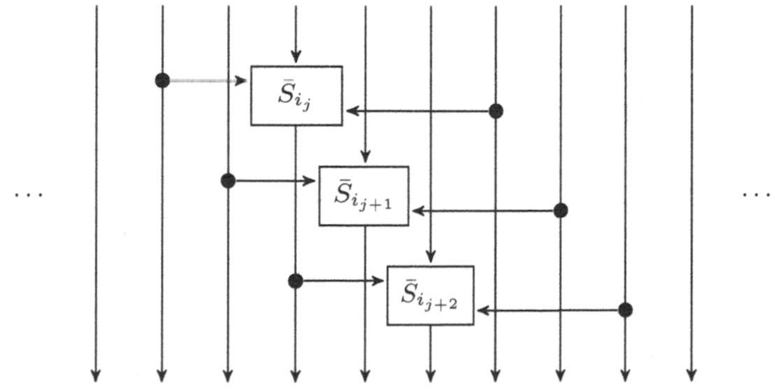

Fig. 2. Three consecutive layers with $w = 3$ and $w' = 2$ and without the circular shift of branches (Each $\bar{S}$ represents a double-Sbox)

If we represent layers without the circular shift of registers, the circuit of three consecutive layers looks like Fig. 2. Each layer involves one register which was modified w' layers before and one register which will be modified w layers later.

Given a sequence $i_0, \ldots, i_{n-1}$ of n indices, we define our m-layer core encryption/decryption functions

$$\mathsf{CEnc}_S[i_0, \ldots, i_{n-1}] = E_S[i_{n-1}] \circ \cdots \circ E_S[i_0]$$
$$\mathsf{CDec}_S[i_0, \ldots, i_{n-1}] = D_S[i_0] \circ \cdots \circ D_S[i_{n-1}]$$

so that $(\mathsf{CEnc}_S[i_0, \ldots, i_{n-1}])^{-1} = \mathsf{CDec}_S[i_0, \ldots, i_{n-1}]$. The n-layer encryption scheme is depicted in Fig. 3 with $\ell = 4$, $n = 16$, $w = 2$, and $w' = 1$. Since we require n to be multiple of ℓ, we consider n layers as being n/ℓ *rounds* of ℓ layers each.

Sbox Index Sequence Generation. Given an L_1-bit key K_{SEQ}, we generate a sequence $\mathsf{SEQ} = [i_0, i_1, i_2 \ldots, i_{n-1}]$ of n indices in $\{0, 1, \ldots, m-1\}$ using a pseudorandom generator:

$$\mathsf{SEQ} = \mathsf{PRNG}_{1,m,n}(K_{\mathsf{SEQ}})$$

The choice of this function $\mathsf{PRNG}_{1,m,n}$ is open. Our preferred option is the use of AES in CTR mode as later explained.

Sbox Generation. Given an L_2-bit key K_S,

$$S \leftarrow \mathsf{PRNG}_{2,a,m}(K_S)$$

The Sboxes can be any permutation of $\mathbf{Z}_a$. The choice of $\mathsf{PRNG}_{2,a,m}$ is open. We suggest one algorithm below.

Stateless Table-Driven Tokenization. The tokenization function uses a fixed pool S of Sboxes which plays the role of the stateless table secret. Given an L-bit key K (the key), a tweak tweak, a format specified by the parameters a and ℓ, the parameters (m, n, w, w'), the selected cipher suite $\mathsf{algo} = (\mathsf{PRNG}_1, \mathsf{PRF})$, and a plaintext $\mathsf{pt} \in \mathbf{Z}_a^\ell$, we define

$$\begin{aligned}
\mathsf{instance}_1 &= (a, m) \\
\mathsf{instance}_2 &= (\ell, n, w, w') \\
K_{\mathsf{SEQ}} &= \mathsf{PRF}^{L_1}(K, \mathsf{instance}_1, \mathsf{instance}_2, \mathsf{cste}_1, \mathsf{tweak}) \\
\mathsf{ct} &= \mathsf{CEnc}_S[\mathsf{PRNG}_{1,m,n}(K_{\mathsf{SEQ}})](\mathsf{pt}) \\
\mathsf{pt} &= \mathsf{CDec}_S[\mathsf{PRNG}_{1,m,n}(K_{\mathsf{SEQ}})](\mathsf{ct})
\end{aligned}$$

where K_{SEQ} is an L_1-bit key which is used to generate SEQ. The value of cste_1 is a constant which encodes the label "tokenization" and the size L_1. The function PRF^λ is a pseudorandom function with an L-bit key accepting an input of variable length and producing a λ-bit output.[4] With $\lambda = L_1$, we obtain a key K_{SEQ} for PRNG_1. The choice of PRF is open. Typically, we use AES-CMAC.

[4] We will only use $\lambda = L_1 = L_2$. So, the superscript λ is only an informative notation.

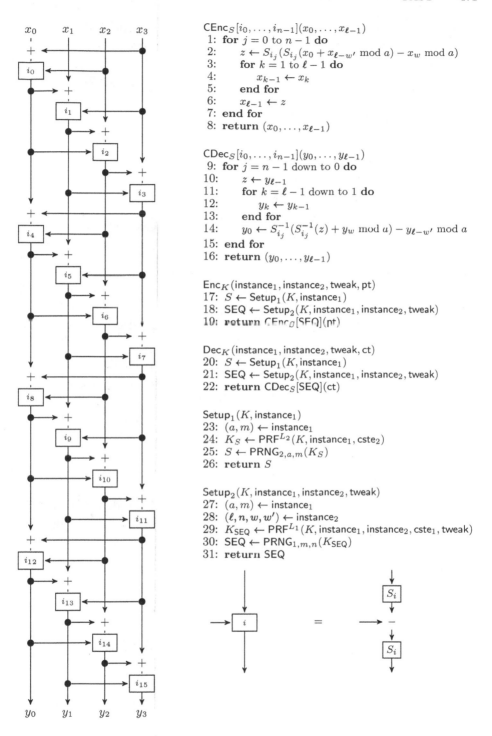

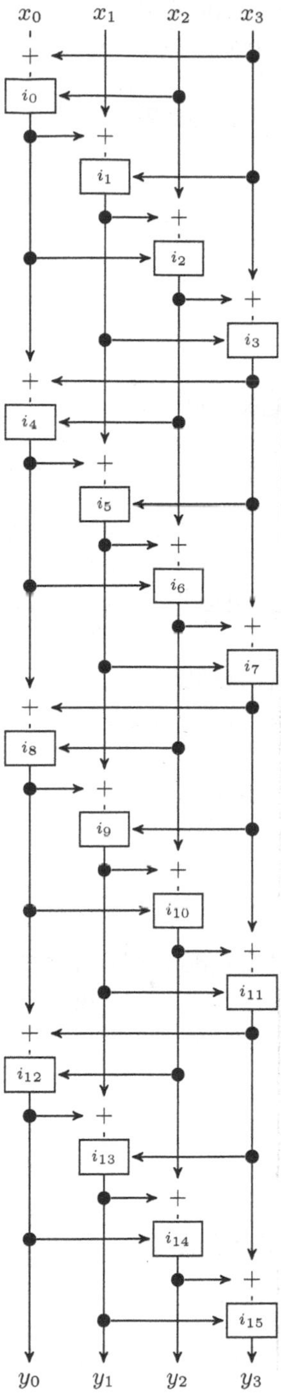

$\mathsf{CEnc}_S[i_0, \ldots, i_{n-1}](x_0, \ldots, x_{\ell-1})$
1: **for** $j = 0$ to $n - 1$ **do**
2:     $z \leftarrow S_{i_j}(S_{i_j}(x_0 + x_{\ell-w'} \bmod a) - x_w \bmod a)$
3:     **for** $k = 1$ to $\ell - 1$ **do**
4:         $x_{k-1} \leftarrow x_k$
5:     **end for**
6:     $x_{\ell-1} \leftarrow z$
7: **end for**
8: **return** $(x_0, \ldots, x_{\ell-1})$

$\mathsf{CDec}_S[i_0, \ldots, i_{n-1}](y_0, \ldots, y_{\ell-1})$
9: **for** $j = n - 1$ down to 0 **do**
10:     $z \leftarrow y_{\ell-1}$
11:     **for** $k = \ell - 1$ down to 1 **do**
12:         $y_k \leftarrow y_{k-1}$
13:     **end for**
14:     $y_0 \leftarrow S_{i_j}^{-1}(S_{i_j}^{-1}(z) + y_w \bmod a) - y_{\ell-w'} \bmod a$
15: **end for**
16: **return** $(y_0, \ldots, y_{\ell-1})$

$\mathsf{Enc}_K(\mathsf{instance}_1, \mathsf{instance}_2, \mathsf{tweak}, \mathsf{pt})$
17: $S \leftarrow \mathsf{Setup}_1(K, \mathsf{instance}_1)$
18: $\mathsf{SEQ} \leftarrow \mathsf{Setup}_2(K, \mathsf{instance}_1, \mathsf{instance}_2, \mathsf{tweak})$
19: **return** $\mathsf{CEnc}_S[\mathsf{SEQ}](\mathsf{pt})$

$\mathsf{Dec}_K(\mathsf{instance}_1, \mathsf{instance}_2, \mathsf{tweak}, \mathsf{ct})$
20: $S \leftarrow \mathsf{Setup}_1(K, \mathsf{instance}_1)$
21: $\mathsf{SEQ} \leftarrow \mathsf{Setup}_2(K, \mathsf{instance}_1, \mathsf{instance}_2, \mathsf{tweak})$
22: **return** $\mathsf{CDec}_S[\mathsf{SEQ}](\mathsf{ct})$

$\mathsf{Setup}_1(K, \mathsf{instance}_1)$
23: $(a, m) \leftarrow \mathsf{instance}_1$
24: $K_S \leftarrow \mathsf{PRF}^{L2}(K, \mathsf{instance}_1, \mathsf{cste}_2)$
25: $S \leftarrow \mathsf{PRNG}_{2,a,m}(K_S)$
26: **return** S

$\mathsf{Setup}_2(K, \mathsf{instance}_1, \mathsf{instance}_2, \mathsf{tweak})$
27: $(a, m) \leftarrow \mathsf{instance}_1$
28: $(\ell, n, w, w') \leftarrow \mathsf{instance}_2$
29: $K_{\mathsf{SEQ}} \leftarrow \mathsf{PRF}^{L1}(K, \mathsf{instance}_1, \mathsf{instance}_2, \mathsf{cste}_1, \mathsf{tweak})$
30: $\mathsf{SEQ} \leftarrow \mathsf{PRNG}_{1,m,n}(K_{\mathsf{SEQ}})$
31: **return** SEQ

Fig. 3. Core encryption $\mathsf{CEnc}[i_0, \ldots, i_{15}]$ with $\ell = 4$, $w = 2$, $w' = 1$, $n = 16$

Format-Preserving Encryption (FPE). The FPE uses a derived pool S of Sboxes. Given an L-bit key K, a tweak tweak, a format specified by the parameters a and ℓ, the parameters m and n, the selected cipher suite $\mathsf{algo} = (\mathsf{PRNG}_1, \mathsf{PRNG}_2, \mathsf{PRF})$, and an input $\mathsf{pt} \in \mathbf{Z}_a^\ell$, we define

$$\begin{aligned}
\mathsf{instance}_1 &= (a, m)\\
\mathsf{instance}_2 &= (\ell, n, w, w')\\
K_{\mathsf{SEQ}} &= \mathsf{PRF}^{L_1}(K, \mathsf{instance}_1, \mathsf{instance}_2, \mathsf{cste}_2, \mathsf{tweak})\\
K_S &= \mathsf{PRF}^{L_2}(K, \mathsf{instance}_1, \mathsf{cste}_3)\\
S &= \mathsf{PRNG}_{2,a,m}(K_S)\\
\mathsf{ct} &= \mathsf{CEnc}_S[\mathsf{PRNG}_{1,m,n}(K_{\mathsf{SEQ}})](\mathsf{pt})\\
\mathsf{pt} &= \mathsf{CDec}_S[\mathsf{PRNG}_{1,m,n}(K_{\mathsf{SEQ}})](\mathsf{ct})
\end{aligned}$$

where $\mathsf{instance}_1$, $\mathsf{instance}_2$, and PRF are like for tokenization, cste_2 is a constant which encodes the label "FPE SEQ" and the size L_1, and cste_3 is a constant which encodes the label "FPE Pool" and the size L_2. K_{SEQ} is an L_1-bit key which is used to generate SEQ. K_S is an L_2-bit key which is used to generate S. As m is the pool size and a is the Sbox size, changing m or a requires to recompute a new pool S, which is a tedious operation. However, changing ℓ should not require to recompute S. This is why we separate $\mathsf{instance}_1$ and $\mathsf{instance}_2$. In the pseudocode of Fig. 3, we separated the setup of S (in Setup_1 using $\mathsf{instance}_1$) and the setup of SEQ (in Setup_2 using $\mathsf{instance}_1$ and $\mathsf{instance}_2$).

Example. We consider $m = 256$ so that each Sbox index is a byte.

We define PRNG_1 from AES in CTR mode. We split $K_{\mathsf{SEQ}} = (K_1, \mathsf{IV}_1)$ with IV_1 of 128 bits with the last two bytes forced to 0.[5] Then,

$$\mathsf{PRNG}_{1,m,n}(K_{\mathsf{SEQ}}) =$$
$$\mathsf{trunc}_{8n}\left(\mathsf{AES}_{K_1}(\mathsf{IV}_1)\|\mathsf{AES}_{K_1}(\mathsf{IV}_1+1)\|\cdots\|\mathsf{AES}_{K_1}\left(\mathsf{IV}_1+\left\lceil\frac{n}{16}\right\rceil-1\right)\right)$$

where trunc_{8n} truncates to the first $8n$ bits and the addition is done modulo 2^{128}. The input of AES is an integer converted into a 128-bit string. We implicitly assume that the $8n$-bit result is converted into a sequence of bytes which define $(i_0, \ldots, i_{n-1})$.

The $\mathsf{PRNG}_{2,a,m}(K_S)$ generator first splits $K_S = (K_2, \mathsf{IV}_2)$ with IV_2 of 128 bits and generates a sequence

$$\mathsf{coins} = \mathsf{AES}_{K_2}(\mathsf{IV}_2)\|\mathsf{AES}_{K_2}(\mathsf{IV}_2+1)\|\cdots$$

of pseudorandom coins (this is AES in CTR mode) then applies a shuffling technique to generate each Sbox σ.[6] We can use the Fisher-Yates algorithm [24, p.145]:

---

[5] Forcing the last two bytes of IV to 0 avoids that some slide properties in coins such as $\mathsf{IV}' = \mathsf{IV} + 1$ and $K' = K$ may occur (although the complexity to obtain such properties could be very high).

[6] Interestingly, if the algorithm generating coins is secure, there is no need to care about constant-time implementation for the Sbox generations as discussed in Sect. 5.

initialize $\sigma(i) = i$ for $i = 0, \ldots, a-1$
for i from $a-1$ down to 1 **do**
    pick $j \in \{0, \ldots, i\}$ at random using the random coins
    exchange $\sigma[j]$ and $\sigma[i]$
end for

The way we generate j can follow many options [4,25,26]. To generate unbiased j from the random coins, we adapt a technique described by Lemire [25]. This approach uses L random input bits to generate a random value the range $[0, ..., i]$ (with $i < 2^L$) using only a multiplication with rejection probability $\frac{2^L \bmod (i+1)}{2^L}$. We choose L as a tradeoff between random bit consumption and rejection frequency: a value of $\lceil \log_2(i+1) \rceil + 4$ results in a maximum rejection probability of $1/2^4 = 0.0625$ and a much lower average rejection probability. We need on average a number of coins per Sbox equal to

$$\sum_{i=1}^{a-1} L \left(1 - \frac{2^L \bmod (i+1)}{2^L}\right)^{-1}$$

with $L = \lceil \log_2(i+1) \rceil + 4$. This generates unbiased Sboxes when the coins are random.

We define $\mathsf{PRF}^\lambda(K, \mathsf{list})$ as

$$\mathsf{trunc}_\lambda\left(\mathsf{AES\text{-}CMAC}_K(\mathsf{encode}(0, \mathsf{list})) \| \mathsf{AES\text{-}CMAC}_K(\mathsf{encode}(1, \mathsf{list})) \| \cdots\right)$$

which returns a λ-bit key. We only use $\lambda = L_1 = L_2$. In practice, we use $\lambda = 256$ or $\lambda = 384$ so that we only need 2 or 3 CMAC computations. Here, encode must be a non-ambiguous encoding of a list into a bitstring.

As an example, we can take $a = 10$ and $\ell = 10$ to encrypt a part of credit card numbers. For that, our recommended parameters below suggest to use $n = 390$ (i.e. 39 rounds of 10 layers), with $w = 3$ and $w' = 2$. We first need two AES computations to generate K_S (assuming encoding $(\mathsf{instance}_1, \mathsf{cste}_2)$ takes a single 128-bit block) and 129 (parallel) AES computations to generate the pool of Sboxes once for all. Thus, 131 AES for setting up the pool. Then, once for each tweak, we need 4 AES computations to generate K_{SEQ} then 25 AES computations to generate SEQ. Thus, 29 AES for each new tweak. This latter computation can be parallelized to have very fast processing. Finally, encryption/decryption requires no AES computation.

Security Goal. Our construction is supposed to offer a pretty high security (e.g. 128-bit security) even though the input domain could be of very small size a^ℓ. Security holds even when the adversary can choose the parameters, the tweak, the plaintexts, and the ciphertexts. We also have security when the pool of Sboxes is known, which may happen for instance when the stateless table secret leaks in tokenization. Towards this goal, we will need PRNG_1 and PRNG_2 to be secure pseudorandom generators, PRF to be a pseudorandom function, and we will reduce to the assumption that CEnc_S is a super-pseudorandom permutation (keyed by a random SEQ) when S is known but randomly set.

Recommended Parameters. An instance defines a (a, m, ℓ, n, w, w') tuple and a set of algorithms. Admissible $(\mathsf{instance}_1, \mathsf{instance}_2)$ instances are defined by a set $\mathcal{F}$. We define what admissible tuples are here, depending on the targeted security s. We recommend $L = s$, $L_1 = L_2 = 2s$, $m = 256$, $a \geq 4$, $\ell \geq 2$, n multiple of ℓ, and w, w', and n tuned as $w \sim \sqrt{\ell}$, $w' \sim \sqrt{\ell}$, and $n \sim \ell^{\frac{3}{2}}$. More precisely,

$$w = \min(\lfloor\sqrt{\ell}\rceil, \ell - 2)$$
$$w' = \max(1, w - 1)$$
$$n = \ell \times \left\lceil 2 \times \max\left(\frac{2s}{\ell \log_2 m}, \frac{s}{\sqrt{\ell}\ln(a-1)}, \frac{s}{\sqrt{\ell}\log_2(a-1)} + 2\sqrt{\ell}\right)\right\rceil$$

(Note that the $\ell - 2$ in the min defining w is reached only for $\ell \in \{2, 3\}$. Similarly, the 1 in the max defining w' is reached only for $\ell \in \{2, 3\}$. For, $\ell > 3$, we have $w = \lfloor\sqrt{\ell}\rceil$ and $w' = w - 1$.) These parameters were adjusted based on cryptanalysis and performance reasons. For $s = 128$, we write in Table 1 the number n/ℓ of "rounds" for a few sets of parameters.

Table 1. Number $r = n/\ell$ of rounds for 128-bit security

ℓ	2	3	4	5	6	7	8	9	10	12	16	32	50	64	100
$a = 4$	165	135	117	105	96	89	83	78	74	68	59	52	52	53	57
$a = 5$	131	107	93	83	76	70	66	62	59	54	48	46	47	48	53
$a = 6$	113	92	80	72	65	61	57	54	51	46	44	43	44	46	52
$a = 7$	102	83	72	64	59	55	51	48	46	43	41	41	43	45	50
$a = 8$	94	76	66	59	54	50	47	44	42	41	39	39	42	44	50
$a = 9$	88	72	62	56	51	47	44	42	40	39	38	38	41	43	49
$a = 10$	83	68	59	53	48	45	42	39	39	38	37	37	40	43	49
$a = 11$	79	65	56	50	46	43	40	38	38	37	36	37	40	42	48
$a = 12$	76	62	54	48	44	41	38	37	37	36	35	36	39	42	48
$a = 13$	73	60	52	47	43	39	37	36	36	35	34	36	39	41	48
$a = 14$	71	58	50	45	41	38	36	36	35	34	34	35	39	41	47
$a = 15$	69	57	49	44	40	37	36	35	34	34	33	35	38	41	47
$a = 16$	67	55	48	43	39	36	35	34	34	33	33	35	38	41	47
$a = 100$	40	33	28	27	26	26	25	25	25	26	26	30	34	37	44
$a = 128$	38	31	27	26	25	25	25	25	25	25	26	30	34	37	44
$a = 256$	33	27	25	24	23	23	23	23	23	24	25	29	33	37	44
$a = 1000$	32	22	21	21	21	21	21	21	21	22	23	28	32	36	43
$a = 1024$	32	22	21	21	21	21	21	21	21	22	23	28	32	36	43
$a = 10\,000$	32	22	18	18	18	18	19	19	19	20	21	27	32	35	42
$a = 65\,536$	32	22	17	17	17	17	17	18	18	19	21	26	31	35	42

For *quantum security*, we consider adversaries who can run quantum algorithms such as Grover [21] or Simon [32]. However, we do not assume quantum access to encryption/decryption oracles. To face quantum adversaries, we use the same formulas by replacing s by $2s$, except for $L_1 = L_2 = 3s$. We obtain that the number of rounds is doubled for the low ℓ values but remains unchanged for the large ones. This is because our security analysis suggests $n = \Omega(s\ell^{\frac{1}{2}} + \ell^{\frac{3}{2}})$. More details about figures are provided in the full version [17]. For quantum 128-bit security, there are a few changes in the underlying algorithms which should move to quantum 128-bit security. Namely, PRNG_1 and PRNG_2 are still AES-CTR but with a 256-bit key. As AES-CMAC does not offer 256-bit security, we need another algorithm or to twist CMAC with a 256-bit key.

Our design does not accommodate radix $a = 2$ or $a = 3$. We did not see as a disadvantage as radix $a = 4$ or 8 and $a = 9$ or 27 are possible if needed.

Rationales for w and w'. Our first design was using $w' = 1$ and $w = 0$ but had a powerful chosen ciphertext attack for up to ℓ^2 layers. Using $w > 0$ mitigated this attack and an optimal $w \sim \sqrt{\ell}$ was found. Then, we observed that decryption was faster than encryption because optimized compiled codes could process the computation of consecutive branches in parallel, but not for encryption. This motivated us to adopt a larger w', which is quite counter-intuitive. Indeed, it looks like slowing down the diffusion. However, our analysis did not show any need to increase the number of rounds. Using $w' \sim \sqrt{\ell}$ was good but we had to care for corner cases such as $\mathsf{gcd}(w, w', \ell) > 1$. Having $w' = w - 1$ ensures that $\mathsf{gcd}(w, w') = 1$.

3 Implementation Results

We implemented the algorithm in C++ on Intel Xeon 1.80GHz, using OpenSSL with AESNI support enabled.[7] It was compiled using g++ with flags

```
-O3 -Wall -Wextra -Wno-unused-const-variable -fPIC -DG_PLUS_PLUS
-falign-functions=32 -DHOT_ASSERTS=0
```

We took an open source implementation of FF1 and FF3[8] and optimized it for using AESNI and 128-bit arithmetic for modulo reduction where the input size allowed.[9]

Setting up a key and an instance requires generating the Sboxes. We need some AES computations to generate pseudorandom coins then apply the Fisher-Yates shuffling algorithm. Using our Sbox generation algorithm for $a = 10$, we need 61.8 random coins per Sbox on average. Hence, 124 AES parallel computations for $m = 256$. Note that our model allows S to be public, so even though side channel attacks might be considered against rejection sampling, this should be of no harm.

[7] We tested other Intel CPUs and obtained comparable results.

[8] https://github.com/0NG/Format-Preserving-Encryption.

[9] Our code is available on https://github.com/comForte/Format-Preserving-Encryption.

Setting up a tweak implies generating SEQ by some parallel AES computations. This can nicely exploit the AESNI pipeline architecture which is 3–4 times faster than the CBC mode of AES which is needed in FF1 and FF3. The SEQ sequence occupies a space of n bytes (with $m = 256$) in addition to the ma words of S, thus a total of 2-3KB for $a = 10$. For our implementation, we used a tweak of 8 bytes.

Finally, the core encryption needs no further AES computation. Due to $w' > 1$, consecutive encryption branches can be done in parallel, which speeds up the computation by the compiler. Similarly, $w > 1$ allows to run consecutive decryption branches in parallel.

We report here some implementation results showing a big advantage for FAST over FF1 and FF3. We plot in Fig. 4 the time for an encryption/decryption cycle per $\mathbf{Z}_a$ symbol (so it is $\frac{1}{\ell}$ of the encryption time) for FAST, FF1, and FF3. For FAST, we plot both the time when we reset the tweak or we reuse it (hence with no AES computation). For FF1 or FF3, changing the tweak or reusing it has no visible difference on the curve so we did not plot it. Essentially, the figures for FAST are as follows for Setup_1, Setup_2, and Enc/Dec:

- AES key setup: 572 cycles. (With 128-bit key $K/K_S/K_{\mathsf{SEQ}}$ in either AES-CTR or AES-CMAC.)
- S generation (in PRNG_2 based on AES-CTR, after AES key setup): about 88 cycles for each Sbox to generate for $a = 10$. (for various a, this is: 10 : 88, 16 : 137, 32 : 282, 64 : 617, 128 : 1334, 256 : 2831). This includes the generation of the random coins and the shuffle.
- K_{SEQ} and K_S derivation (PRF based on two parallel AES-CMAC, after AES key setup): $\sim$ 300 cycles per input block. With 16-byte instance encoding and 8-byte tweak, we need 7 AES computations in total (encryption of the zero-block, two CBC encryption of two blocks for K_{SEQ}, and two AES encryption of a single block for K_S); some of them could be done in parallel.
- SEQ derivation (in PRNG_1 based on AES-CTR, after AES key setup): 1.2 to 0.8 cycles for each of the n bytes.
- Core encryption/decryption: 5.7 cycles for each of the n layers, for $a = 10$.

For a best case comparison of most typical use cases, we optimized the open source FF1 implementation (which used big number modular arithmetic for all input lengths) to use the built-in (unsigned) `_int128` type provided by GCC as "native 128 bit integers" for this platform for $\ell \leq 32$. We did not change the implementation for $\ell > 32$ and acknowledge that it does not leverage full optimization potential. Therefore, we should take the $\ell > 32$ figures with a grain of salt, but we do have good performances compared to FF1/FF3 using built-in 128-bit integer arithmetic for $\ell \leq 32$ and nearly sustain this performance for longer inputs. (Note that FF3 limits to $\ell \leq 56$ and we abusively let an entry for $\ell = 64$.) We can safely say that FF1 performance per symbol is impacted negatively by the need for using a big integer library where modulo operands

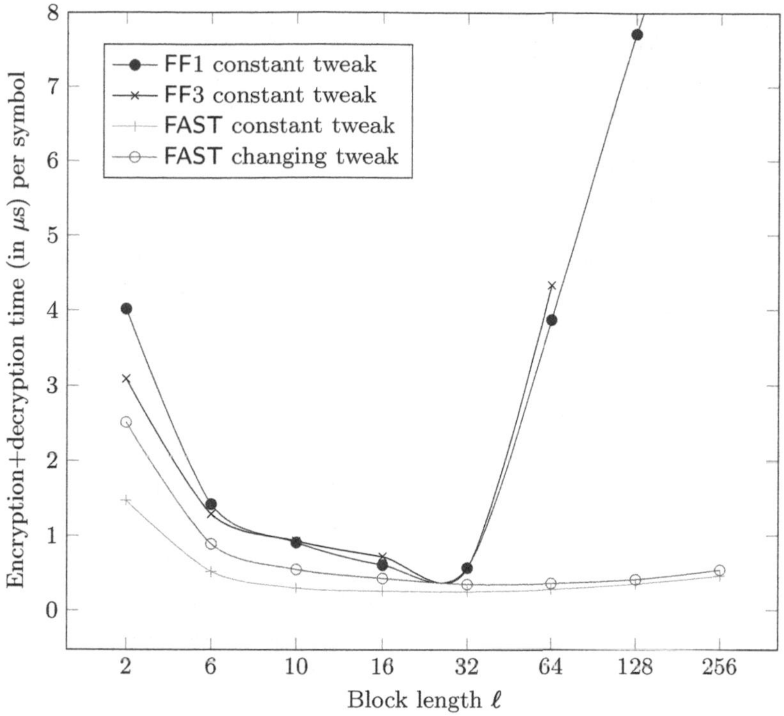

Fig. 4. Implementation results for $a = 10$ (FF3 limits $\ell \leq 56$)

do not fit into 128 bits. The performance breakdown of FF1 for larger strings is also acknowledged by other researchers.[10]

4 Security Proof

4.1 Security Definitions

We first define our strongest security notion by indistinguishability from an ideal FPE. It corresponds to the natural notion of tweakable super-pseudorandom permutation. I.e., the adversary can choose the tweak, a plaintext, a ciphertext. The adversary can further change the parameters (in the list $\mathcal{F}$ of allowed parameters). For instance, the adversary can change the format adaptively by keeping the same key.

First, we assume that the interface of the algorithm can be modeled by

$$F : K \mapsto \left(\mathsf{instance}_1, \mathsf{instance}_2, \mathsf{tweak} \mapsto \mathsf{even\ permutation\ of\ } \mathbf{Z}_a^\ell\right)$$

[10] See https://www.researchgate.net/publication/332088303_Evolution_of_Format_Preserving_Encryption_on_IoT_Devices_FF1 for instance.

with $\mathsf{instance}_1 = (a, m)$ and $\mathsf{instance}_2 = (\ell, n, w, w')$ (indeed, we will see in Sect. 5 that our permutations of $\mathbf{Z}_a^\ell$ are always even). We assume a set $\mathcal{F}$ of admissible instances. Given a secret k, F_k maps $\mathsf{instance}_1$, $\mathsf{instance}_2$, and tweak to an even permutation $F_k(\mathsf{instance}_1, \mathsf{instance}_2, \mathsf{tweak})$ of $\mathbf{Z}_a^\ell$. Hence,

$$\mathsf{ct} = F_k(\mathsf{instance}_1, \mathsf{instance}_2, \mathsf{tweak})(\mathsf{pt})$$
$$\mathsf{pt} = (F_k(\mathsf{instance}_1, \mathsf{instance}_2, \mathsf{tweak}))^{-1}(\mathsf{ct})$$

Based on this, we propose the security game in Fig. 5. In the Step 1 of the game, we implicitly mean that the game will define tables of $(\mathsf{pt}, \mathsf{ct})$ pairs for $(K, \mathsf{instance}_1, \mathsf{instance}_2, \mathsf{tweak})$ by lazy sampling, when needed in OTE and OTD. We obtain the following strong security notion.

The INDstrong security definition (as for "Strong INDistinguishability") gives oracle access (through OTE and OTD, as for "Oracle - Target Encryption/Decryption") to encryption/decryption with the ith target function with unknown key K_i. We limit the number of targets to a parameter τ as discussed below.

Definition 1. *We say that the algorithm is $(T, \tau, q, \varepsilon)$-INDstrong-secure if for any INDstrong-adversary $\mathcal{A}$ running the INDstrong game with τ targets, if the average complexity is limited by T, and if the average number of queries to the oracles is limited by q (we call this a (T, q)-limited adversary), the advantage is bounded by ε:*

$$\mathsf{Adv}_{\mathsf{INDstrong}}(\mathcal{A}) = \Pr[\mathsf{INDstrong}_1 \to 1] - \Pr[\mathsf{INDstrong}_0 \to 1] \leq \varepsilon$$

The average complexity is measured when running the game on average over all random coins (from the game and the adversary). We favor average number of queries instead of sharp upper bounds on the number of queries of each type.

Our security model is quite powerful as it allows the adversary to attack one of several target keys and also to mount attacks in which he can choose the tweak, as well as the instance. Namely, the adversary can adaptively choose the format (a, ℓ) and parameters (m, n, w, w') (as long as they are in an admissible set) and reuse the same keys with multiple instances. The adversary can further choose the input to the encryption or the decryption algorithm.

Regarding **passive related-key attacks**, since our key K is only used in a PRF, the security of PRF against passive related-key attacks and the security of our design in a multi-target model imply the security against passive related-key attacks. By *passive* related-key attack, we mean those in which the adversary launches many targets $K[1], \ldots, K[\tau]$ and expect some to be related by random selection. We could also address *active* related-key attacks in which the adversary can force the creation of a target in a related manner to another, e.g. the creation of $K[1]$ and $K[2]$ such that $K[2] = K[1] + 1$. We could prove that if PRF resists to related-key attacks, then the FPE as well. Unfortunately, the PRF which we use is based on AES which does not resist to this type of attacks for keys larger than 128 bits [10]. However, we are not aware of any related-key attack on our FPE.

Game $\mathsf{INDstrong}_b$:

pick F following the interface at random:
for each K, $\mathsf{instance}_1$ (including a), $\mathsf{instance}_2$ (including ℓ), tweak, $F_K(\mathsf{instance}_1, \mathsf{instance}_2, \mathsf{tweak})$ is an even permutation of $\mathbf{Z}_a^\ell$
pick $K[1], \ldots, K[\tau] \in \{0,1\}^L$ at random
run $\mathcal{A}^{\mathsf{OTE},\mathsf{OTD}} \to z$
return z

Oracle $\mathsf{OTE}(i, \mathsf{instance}_1, \mathsf{instance}_2, \mathsf{tweak}, \mathsf{pt})$
if $(\mathsf{instance}_1, \mathsf{instance}_2) \notin \mathcal{F}$ **then return** $\perp$
if $i \notin \{1, \ldots, \tau\}$ **then return** $\perp$
if $b = 0$ **then**
  return $F_{K_i}(\mathsf{instance}_1, \mathsf{instance}_2, \mathsf{tweak})(\mathsf{pt})$
else
  return $\mathsf{Enc}_{K_i}(\mathsf{instance}_1, \mathsf{instance}_2, \mathsf{tweak}, \mathsf{pt})$
end if

Oracle $\mathsf{OTD}(i, \mathsf{instance}_1, \mathsf{instance}_2, \mathsf{tweak}, \mathsf{ct})$
if $(\mathsf{instance}_1, \mathsf{instance}_2) \notin \mathcal{F}$ **then return** $\perp$
if $i \notin \{1, \ldots, \tau\}$ **then return** $\perp$
if $b = 0$ **then**
  return $\left(F_{K_i}(\mathsf{instance}_1, \mathsf{instance}_2, \mathsf{tweak})\right)^{-1}(\mathsf{ct})$
else
  return $\mathsf{Dec}_{K_i}(\mathsf{instance}_1, \mathsf{instance}_2, \mathsf{tweak}, \mathsf{ct})$
end if

Fig. 5. General indistinguishability game with access to ideal F

On Limiting the Number of Targets. An adversary can always prepare a dictionary of u keys with the encryption of a fixed plaintext, make a chosen plaintext attack on τ targets, and spot if any target belongs to the dictionary [9]. This gives an easy distinguisher with advantage $u\tau/2^L$. The value of τ could in principle reach a value close to q while the value of u would be proportional to the time complexity T. This type of attack applies well to AES too. With $L = 128$, we can take $u = \tau = 2^{64}$ and have a good distinguisher. In practice, it makes sense to assume that the number of targets is limited to a small number τ. Since we do not want to enlarge the key length due to this attack but still offer security with large q, we chose to introduce a low τ parameter.

Meaning of a 128-bit Security. We target a "128-bit security" (classical or quantum). However, the meaning of 128-bit security is often incorrectly understood as any attack would need at least $T = 2^{128}$ complexity to succeed. Attacks are however measured by several metrics such as T, q, ε, and τ. We could have attacks with a small T and a ridiculously low ε still 128-bit security.

It is hard to compare two attacks with different advantages. Sometimes, a (T, q, ε)-attack could be amplified into a $(kT, kq, k\varepsilon)$-attack (in which case we could say that the attack needs $k = \frac{1}{\varepsilon}$ to succeed, hence it has a normalized complexity of $\frac{T}{\varepsilon}$) but sometimes, the amplification works as a $(kT, kq, \sqrt{k}\varepsilon)$-attack (in which case we could say that the attack needs $k = \frac{1}{\varepsilon^2}$ to succeed, hence it has a normalized complexity of $\frac{T}{\varepsilon^2}$). It could also be the case that no amplification is possible. Hence, there is no general rule. We could try, as much as possible, to focus on adversaries achieving a constant advantage such as advantage $\frac{1}{2}$.

Another difficulty is the introduction of the multiple instances, target keys, and tweaks as mentioned above. Things become easier when the security notion implies a single key, a single target, and a single tweak.

Hence, by "128-bit security", we mean "like AES". We mean that in a same (q, ε, τ) configuration, we could have an attack against AES with a T which is lower or equal. If an adversary achieves a constant advantage with a single target, a single instance, and a single tweak, it must have a complexity comparable to an exhaustive search on a 128-bit key.

Indistinguishability to Even Permutations. Most of existing ciphers are even permutations. A random even permutation over a domain of size N is perfectly indistinguishable from a random permutation when the number of available input/output pairs does not reach $N - 1$. Block ciphers are defined over domains with large N so this is not a problem. In FPE, N can be very small and the parity may leak. Hence, we preferred to make sure that our FPE are even permutations and to adopt as a security model the indistinguishability to a random even permutation. In Sect. 5, we prove that our FPE with the selected parameters is even.

Known Pool Security. Our construction is based on a pool S of Sboxes. We can enrich the security notion to capture attacks in which the adversary learns S: a "known S attack".[11] There are several motivations for considering known S attacks:

- In tokenization mode, S is fixed once for all and the secret is only determining SEQ. We could imagine that by time, the pool S eventually leaks.
- Some (side-channel) attacks may uncover some Sboxes.
- Security in this model with single target and single instance offers some nice security reductions from strong security.

Hence, it is relevant to wonder if some attacks could exploit having the pool S as prior knowledge and with a random S and SEQ instead of a pseudorandom one. We enrich our security game as in Fig. 6. This is the INDKSsprp game (as for "Known-S Super-Pseudorandom Permutation"), working with the OE and OD oracles (as for "Oracle - Encryption/Decryption") and OT_1 and OT_2 oracles to set up the target parameters.

Definition 2. *We say that the algorithm is (T, q, ε)-INDKSsprp-secure if for any (T, q)-limited INDKSsprp-adversary $\mathcal{A}$ running the INDKSsprp game, the advantage is bounded by ε:*

$$\mathsf{Adv}_{\mathsf{INDKSsprp}}(\mathcal{A}) = \Pr[\mathsf{INDKSsprp}_1 \to 1] - \Pr[\mathsf{INDKSsprp}_0 \to 1] \leq \varepsilon$$

[11] A "chosen S attack" leads to trivial attacks. For instance, the adversary could pick all Sboxes equal, or all Sboxes linear (over $\mathbf{Z}_a$). Therefore, we do not consider chosen-S models.

Game $\mathsf{INDKSsprp}_b$:
run $\mathcal{A}^{\mathsf{OE},\mathsf{OD},\mathsf{OT}_1,\mathsf{OT}_2} \to z$
return z

Oracle $\mathsf{OT}_1(\mathsf{instance}_1)$
if S defined **then return** $\perp$
$(a, m) \leftarrow \mathsf{instance}_1$
pick $S_0, \ldots, S_{m-1}$ random permutations of $\mathbf{Z}_a$
$S \leftarrow (S_0, \ldots, S_{m-1})$
return S

Oracle $\mathsf{OT}_2(\mathsf{instance}_2)$
if SEQ defined **then return** $\perp$
if S undefined **then return** $\perp$
if $(\mathsf{instance}_1, \mathsf{instance}_2) \notin \mathcal{F}$ **then return** $\perp$
$(\boldsymbol{\ell}, \boldsymbol{n}, \boldsymbol{w}, \boldsymbol{w}') \leftarrow \mathsf{instance}_2$
pick a random even permutation F of $\mathbf{Z}_a^{\boldsymbol{\ell}}$
pick random $\mathsf{SEQ} \in \{0, \ldots, m-1\}^n$
return

Oracle $\mathsf{OE}(\mathsf{pt})$
if S or SEQ undefined **then return** $\perp$
if $b = 0$ **then**
  return $F(\mathsf{pt})$
else
  return $\mathsf{CEnc}_S[\mathsf{SEQ}](\mathsf{pt})$
end if

Oracle $\mathsf{OD}(\mathsf{ct})$
if S or SEQ undefined **then return** $\perp$
if $b = 0$ **then**
  return $F^{-1}(\mathsf{ct})$
else
  return $\mathsf{CDec}_S[\mathsf{SEQ}](\mathsf{ct})$
end if

Fig. 6. Single-Target/Instance/Tweak Known S indistinguishability game

We could also consider revealing K_S with the same arguments. We would then have to set S generated by PRNG_2 on a random K_S in the game. One advantage is that we would no longer need a specific security for PRNG_2 (it would be integrated in INDKSsprp with the above modification) and we could "compress" the storage of S by K_S if needed.

We finally define the one-time PRNG security and PRF security of our algorithms by the games in Fig. 7 and Fig. 8.

Definition 3. *We say that the algorithm is* (T, ε)-$\mathsf{INDPRNG}_1$*-secure if for any* T*-limited* $\mathsf{INDPRNG}_1$*-adversary* $\mathcal{A}$ *running the* $\mathsf{INDPRNG}_1$ *game, the advantage is bounded by* ε*:*

$$\mathsf{Adv}_{\mathsf{INDPRNG}_1}(\mathcal{A}) = \Pr[\mathsf{INDPRNG}_1^1 \to 1] - \Pr[\mathsf{INDPRNG}_1^0 \to 1] \leq \varepsilon$$

We similarly define $\mathsf{INDPRNG}_2$*-security. We similarly say that* PRF *is* (T, q, ε)-PRF*-secure if for any* (T, q)*-limited* PRF*-adversary* $\mathcal{A}$ *running the* PRF *game, the advantage is bounded by* ε*.*

We can now formally reduce the strong security INDstrong to the weak security INDKSsprp. The next step will be to heuristically assess the weak security of our construction.

Theorem 4. *There exists a (small) constant c such that for any s,* T*,* q*, and any* (T, τ, q)*-limited* INDstrong*-adversary* $\mathcal{A}$*, there exist* $q' \leq q$*, a* $(T + qc, q')$*-limited* INDKSsprp*-adversary* $\mathcal{A}'$*, a* $(T, q+1)$*-limited* PRF*-adversary* $\mathcal{B}$*, a* $(T+qc)$*-limited* $\mathsf{INDPRNG}_1$*-adversary* $\mathcal{C}$ *and a* $(T+qc)$*-limited* $\mathsf{INDPRNG}_2$*-adversary* $\mathcal{D}$ *such that*

```
Game INDPRNG_1^b:
  run A^OG → z
  return z

Oracle OG(m, n)
  if SEQ defined then return ⊥
  if b = 0 then
      pick random SEQ ∈ {0, ..., m − 1}^n
  else
      pick K_SEQ ∈ {0,1}^{L_1} at random
      SEQ ← PRNG_{1,m,n}(K_SEQ)
  end if
  return SEQ
```

```
Game INDPRNG_2^b:
  run A^OG → z
  return z

Oracle OG(a, m)
  if S defined then return ⊥
  if b = 0 then
      pick S_0, ..., S_{m−1}, random Z_a permutations
      S ← (S_0, ..., S_{m−1})
  else
      pick K_S ∈ {0,1}^{L_2} at random
      S ← PRNG_{2,a,m}(K_S)
  end if
  return S
```

Fig. 7. Indistinguishability game for PRNG

```
Game PRF^b:
  pick a random function F with same
    input/output domain as PRF
  pick K at random
  run A^OF → z
  return z

Oracle OF(x)
  if b = 0 then
      return F(x)
  else
      return PRF_K(x)
  end if
```

Fig. 8. Indistinguishability game for PRF

$$\mathsf{Adv}_{\mathsf{INDstrong}}(\mathcal{A}) \leq q \cdot \frac{\mathsf{Adv}_{\mathsf{INDKSsprp}}(\mathcal{A}')}{q'} + \tau \cdot \mathsf{Adv}_{\mathsf{PRF}}(\mathcal{B}) +$$
$$q \cdot (\mathsf{Adv}_{\mathsf{INDPRNG}_1}(\mathcal{C}) + \mathsf{Adv}_{\mathsf{INDPRNG}_2}(\mathcal{D})) + \frac{\tau^2}{2} \cdot 2^{-L}$$

In general, τ is limited by what is allowed in the implementation. The proof is provided in the full version [17].

Given that $\mathsf{Adv}_{\mathsf{INDKSsprp}}(\mathcal{A}')$, $\mathsf{Adv}_{\mathsf{INDPRNG}_1}(\mathcal{C})$, or $\mathsf{Adv}_{\mathsf{INDPRNG}_2}(\mathcal{D})$ can easily be as large as $T \cdot q' \cdot m^{-n}$, $T \cdot 2^{-L_1}$, or $T \cdot 2^{-L_2}$ respectively (by doing an exhaustive search on a list limited to T), it is crucial that $n \log_2 m$ and L_1 are both larger than $2s$. This will match the criteria (2) and (12) in Sect. 5. Similarly, $\mathsf{Adv}_{\mathsf{PRF}}(\mathcal{B})$ can be as large as $T \cdot 2^{-L} + q^2 \cdot 2^{-\lambda}$, with λ being the output length of the PRF^{λ}. By plugging all these values we obtain the upper bound $q \cdot T \cdot \left(m^{-n} + 2^{-L_1} + 2^{-L_2}\right) + \tau \cdot (T \cdot 2^{-L} + q^2 \cdot 2^{-\lambda}) + \frac{\tau^2}{2} \cdot 2^{-L}$ for $\mathsf{Adv}_{\mathsf{INDstrong}}(\mathcal{A})$. Given that $L = s$ and $n \log_2 m \approx \lambda = L_1 = L_2 = 2s$, this is $3q \cdot T \cdot 2^{-2s} + \tau \cdot (T \cdot 2^{-s} + q^2 \cdot 2^{-2s}) + \frac{\tau^2}{2} \cdot 2^{-s}$. The first term is fine. The other terms account for a normal degradation of the security by a factor τ in a multi-target setting. For instance, with the extreme case $q \approx T$, we need $T \approx \frac{1}{\tau} 2^s$ to reach a constant advantage.

The proof of Theorem 4 follows several reduction steps as follows.

- $\Gamma_b^0(\mathcal{A})$: We start with an $\mathsf{INDstrong}$ game.

- $\Gamma_j^1(\mathcal{A})$: Reduce to a game with independent F_i instead of $F_{K[i]}$. (Cost is $\frac{\tau^2}{2}2^{-L}$ due to possible collisions on $K[i]$.)
- $\Gamma_b^2(\mathcal{A}_j)$: Reduce to single target K. (Cost is a factor τ using an adversary for each target.)
- $\Gamma_b^3(\mathcal{A}_j)$: Replace PRF by a random function. (Cost is $\mathsf{Adv}_{\mathsf{PRF}}$.)
- $\Gamma_b^4(\mathcal{A}_j)$: Reduce to known S. (No cost.)
- $\Gamma_{j'}^5(\mathcal{A}_j)$—$\Gamma_b^6(\mathcal{A}_{j,j'})$: Reduce to single $\mathsf{instance}_1$ with hybrid games and single adversary, then several adversaries playing a unique single-instance game.
- $\Gamma_{j''}^7(\mathcal{A}_{j,j'})$—$\Gamma_b^8(\mathcal{A}_{j,j',j''})$: Reduce to single $(\mathsf{instance}_2, \mathsf{tweak})$ with the same method.
- $\Gamma_b^9(\mathcal{A}_{j,j',j''})$: Replace PRNG_1 by a truly random function. (Cost is $\mathsf{Adv}_{\mathsf{INDPRNG}_1}$.)
- $\mathsf{INDKSsprp}_b(\mathcal{A}_{j,j',j''})$: Replace PRNG_2 by a truly random function. (Cost is $\mathsf{Adv}_{\mathsf{INDPRNG}_2}$.)
- $\mathsf{INDKSsprp}_b(\mathcal{A}')$: We obtain an INDKSsprp game.

We use a trick to cumulate all hybrids which results in only a factor q. Namely, we take the hybrid with maximal $\frac{\mathsf{Adv}}{q'}$ and we upper bound the advantage of hybrids by their number of queries times this ratio. Summing them all results in $q \cdot \frac{\mathsf{Adv}}{q'}$

5 Rationales

On the choice of w'. The $\ell = 2$ is a special case where we shall use $w = 0$ and $w' = 1$. For $\ell > 2$, we use $w = \lfloor\sqrt{\ell}\rceil$ and we wonder how to select w'.

We clearly need $w' > 0$. Furthermore, it is required that $w < \ell - w'$ to avoid changes in branch orders. Without loss of generality, we assume $w' \leq w$ (with the exception of $\ell = 2$ for which $w = 0$). The previous design was using $w' = 1$. However, it may be nice for performances to have w' of same order of magnitude as w.

There is an easy attack when $d \geq 2$, with $d = \mathsf{gcd}(w, w', \ell)$: if two plaintexts pt and pt' have a difference of form $\mathsf{pt}' - \mathsf{pt} = (?0^{d-1})^{\ell/d}$, this property is preserved after d layers. Hence, we have a distinguisher with advantage close to 1 and any number of layers. To avoid this problem, we adopt $w' = \max(1, w - 1)$ which guaranties that $\mathsf{gcd}(w, w') = 1$ so $d = 1$ as well.

Parity of CEnc. We prove that the parity of encryption only depends on the parameters a, ℓ, and n. Hence, it does not leak.

Lemma 5. *For every y in a domain of size A, we consider a permutation P_y. The $(x, y) \mapsto (P_y(x), y)$ is a permutation with parity equal to the sum of the parities of every P_y.*

Proof. For y fixed, the permutation restricts to a permutation with same cycle structure as P_y. Hence, the permutation is a composition of permutations with same cycle structure as P_y, for every y. □

Lemma 6. *The $(x, y) \mapsto (x+y, y)$ permutation over $\mathbf{Z}_a^2$ is even when a is odd and has the parity of $\frac{a}{2}$ when a is even. The same holds for $(x, y) \mapsto (x-y, y)$.*

Proof. We let $P_y(x) = x+y \bmod a$ and we apply Lemma 5. P_y is the composition of $\frac{a}{k}$ cycles of length k, where k is the order of y in $\mathbf{Z}_a$. The parity of P_y is the parity of $\frac{a}{k}(k-1)$.

For $y = 0$, P_y is even.

For a odd, we notice that for $y \neq 0$, P_y and P_{-y} have the same parity hence cancel each other. Hence, the permutation is even when a is odd.

For a even, the same observation holds for $y \in \{1, \ldots, \frac{a}{2} - 1\}$. Hence, the parity is the same as the parity of $P_{a/2}$. We have $k = 2$ for $P_{a/2}$, thus its parity is the one of $\frac{a}{2}$. □

Lemma 7. *The parity of $\mathsf{CEnc}_S[i_0, \ldots, i_{n-1}]$ is as follows:*

- *for $a \bmod 4 \neq 3$, it is even;*
- *for $a \bmod 4 = 3$, it is the parity of $n(\ell - 1)$.*

(For this, we assume that $\ell = 2$ implies $w = 0$.)

Since n is a multiple of ℓ, $n(\ell - 1)$ is always even. Hence, the permutation $\mathsf{CEnc}_S[i_0, \ldots, i_{n-1}]$ is always even.

Proof. The encryption is the composition of permutations of n layers using $S_{i_0}, \ldots, S_{i_{n-1}}$. The layer using an Sbox σ is the composition of

P1 the permutation $(x_0, \ldots, x_{\ell-1}) \mapsto (x_0 + x_{\ell-1}, x_1, \ldots, x_{\ell-1})$,
P1′ the permutation $(x_0, \ldots, x_{\ell-1}) \mapsto (x_0 - x_w, x_1, \ldots, x_{\ell-1})$,
P2 the permutation $(x_0, \ldots, x_{\ell-1}) \mapsto (\sigma(x_0), x_1, \ldots, x_{\ell-1})$ (used twice),
P3 the permutation $(x_0, \ldots, x_{\ell-1}) \mapsto (x_1, \ldots, x_{\ell-1}, x_0)$.

By writing $P(x_0, x_{\ell-1}) = (x_0 + x_{\ell-1}, x_{\ell-1})$, for $\ell > 2$, P1 has the form of the permutation of Lemma 5 with y in a domain of size $A = a^{\ell-2}$ and all P_y set to P, so the parity of P1 is $a^{\ell-2}$ times the parity of P, which is the same as a times the parity of P. For $\ell = 2$, the permutation P1 is P so has the same parity. By using Lemma 6, we obtain the parity of P. Therefore, the parity of P1 is

- (a even and $\ell > 2$) even,
- (a even and $\ell = 2$) the parity of $\frac{a}{2}$,
- (a odd) even.

The same holds for P1′.

The second permutation P2 has the form of the permutation given in Lemma 5 with a fixed permutation $P = \sigma$ with y in a domain of size $A = a^{\ell-1}$. We obtain that the parity of P2 is the same as a times the parity of σ. Therefore, the parity of P2 is

- (a even and $\ell > 2$) even,
- (a even and $\ell = 2$) even,
- (a odd) the parity of σ.

However, P2 is used twice so its parity has no impact.

The third permutation P3 is the composition of $\ell - 1$ permutations of form $(x_0, \dots x_{\ell-1}) \mapsto (x_0, \dots, x_{i-1}, x_{i+1}, x_i, x_{i+2}, \dots, x_{\ell-1})$ exchanging the coordinates of index i and $i+1$. Those permutations can be written as in Lemma 5 for $\ell > 2$ with $P(x_i, x_{i+1}) = (x_{i+1}, x_i)$. This permutation has a fixed points and $\frac{a^2-a}{2}$ cycles of length two. Hence, it has the same parity as $\frac{a^2-a}{2}$. For $\ell > 2$, we deduce that the parity of P3 is the parity of $(\ell-1)a\frac{a^2-a}{2}$. For $\ell = 2$, the parity of P3 is the parity of $(\ell-1)\frac{a^2-a}{2}$. Therefore, the parity of P3 is

- (a even and $\ell > 2$) even,
- (a even and $\ell = 2$) the parity of $\frac{a^2-a}{2}$,
- (a odd) the parity of $(\ell-1)\frac{a^2-a}{2}$.

We sum the parities over the n layers and obtain the result. In the a even and $\ell > 2$ case, everything is even. In the a even and $\ell = 2$ case, we first observe that $w = 0$ so P1$'$ is unused. Then, we observe that the parity of $\frac{a}{2} + \frac{a^2-a}{2}$ is always even. In the a odd case, we observe that $\frac{a^2-a}{2}$ is even if and only if $a \bmod 4 = 1$. □

Slide Attack on Previous SEQ *Scheme.* A previous version of our construction was using SEQ with a sequence derived from a periodic repetition (or modified repetition) of an AES-generated sequence. This made the entire encryption process being a self-iteration on a simpler function, which is subject to a devastating slide attack. In our construction, SEQ is a random sequence of indices and the probability that it becomes periodic is negligible. So, the slide attack is defeated.

Best Known Attacks. We investigated several attack methods which we list here together with the requirement that security implies. They are detailed in the full version [17].

- Linear collapse. With too small parameters, there are chances that the encryption becomes linear over $\mathbf{Z}_a$.

$$\min(m,n) > \frac{s}{\log_2(a-1)! - \log_2 \varphi(a)} \tag{1}$$

- Known Sbox pool dictionary attack. With not enough layers, a partial dictionary attack can work.

$$n > \frac{2s}{\log_2 m} \tag{2}$$

- Chosen ciphertext distinguisher with $w = 0$ and $w' = 1$.

$$n > \ell(\ell-1) + \frac{s}{\log_2 \min(m, a\sqrt{a})} \qquad \text{if } w = 0 \text{ and } w' = 1 \tag{3}$$

- Chosen plaintext distinguisher with $w > 1$ and w and w' coprime.

$$n > (w'+1)(\ell - w') + \frac{s - 1 + 2\log_2 a}{\log_2 \min(m, a!)} \qquad \text{if } w > 1 \tag{4}$$

- Chosen ciphertext distinguisher with $w > 1$ and w and w' coprime.

$$n > (w+1)(\ell - w) + \frac{s - 1 + 2\log_2 a}{\log_2 \min(m, a!)} \qquad \text{if } w > 1 \tag{5}$$

- Chosen plaintext distinguisher with $w + w'$ factor of ℓ.

$$n > (w + w')\frac{s - 1 + \ell \log_2 a}{2\log_2(a-1)} \tag{6}$$

$$n > \frac{s - 1 + \ell \log_2 a}{\log_2 \min(m, a!)} \tag{7}$$

- Chosen plaintext distinguisher with w' factor of $\ell + 1$.

$$n > w'\frac{s - 1 + (\ell + 2)\log_2 a}{\log_2 a} \tag{8}$$

$$n > \frac{s - 1 + (\ell + 2)\log_2 a}{\log_2 \min(m, a!)} \tag{9}$$

- Differential and linear attacks. Given a framework which captures truncated differentials, impossible differentials, regular differentials, and linear hulls over the algebraic structure of $\mathbf{Z}_a$, we can derive a lower bound for n to achieve security.

$$n > \frac{s\sqrt{\ell}}{\ln(a-1)} \tag{10}$$

- Fixed point attacks. It may happen that all selected Sboxes have 0 as a fixed point, which would lead to a trivial attack.

$$n > \frac{s}{\log_2 a} \tag{11}$$

- Collision attacks. Trying many tweak until there is a collision on K_{SEQ} leads to a trivial distinguishing attack. Hence, the bitlength of K_{SEQ} must be at least $2s$.

$$L_1 \geq 2s \tag{12}$$

Choice of Parameters. The generic attacks have clearly shown that w should be around $\sqrt{\ell}$ but lower bounded by $\ell - 2$. As for the selection of n, we looked at all obtained requirements. For each a and ℓ, we computed the suggested w and the maximal requirement. Table 2 represents the minimal value for n with a subscript set to the equation number of the critical requirement. We set $s = 128$. For instance, $a = 10$ and $\ell = 6$ (encryption of 6 decimal digits) has entry 143_{10} which means that we need $n \geq 143$ layers (24 rounds) which is critical for Eq. (10), the differential and linear attacks. We suggest 48 rounds which gives a good security margin.

As we can see, low ℓ values have Eq. (10) (differential cryptanalysis) as critical while high ℓ have one of the generic attacks as critical. Large ℓ values have Eq. (6)

Table 2. Minimal number n of layers following criteria with reference to the critical one

ℓ	2	3	4	5	6	7	8	9	10	12	16	32	50	64	100
$a = 4$	165_{10}	202_{10}	234_{10}	261_{10}	286_{10}	309_{10}	330_{10}	350_{10}	369_{10}	404_{10}	467_{10}	663_6	931_6	1207_6	1960_6
$a = 5$	131_{10}	160_{10}	185_{10}	207_{10}	227_{10}	245_{10}	262_{10}	277_{10}	292_{10}	320_{10}	370_{10}	554_6	791_6	1034_6	1707_6
$a = 6$	113_{10}	138_{10}	160_{10}	178_{10}	195_{10}	211_{10}	225_{10}	239_{10}	252_{10}	276_{10}	319_{10}	497_6	718_6	945_6	1578_6
$a = 7$	102_{10}	124_{10}	143_{10}	160_{10}	175_{10}	190_{10}	203_{10}	215_{10}	226_{10}	248_{10}	286_{10}	462_6	673_6	890_6	1499_6
$a = 8$	94_{10}	114_{10}	132_{10}	148_{10}	162_{10}	175_{10}	187_{10}	198_{10}	209_{10}	228_{10}	264_{10}	437_6	642_6	853_6	1445_6
$a = 9$	88_{10}	107_{10}	124_{10}	138_{10}	151_{10}	163_{10}	175_{10}	185_{10}	195_{10}	214_{10}	247_{10}	419_6	619_6	825_6	1406_6
$a = 10$	83_{10}	101_{10}	117_{10}	131_{10}	143_{10}	155_{10}	165_{10}	175_{10}	185_{10}	202_{10}	234_{10}	405_6	602_6	804_6	1377_6
$a = 11$	79_{10}	97_{10}	112_{10}	125_{10}	137_{10}	148_{10}	158_{10}	167_{10}	176_{10}	193_{10}	223_{10}	394_6	587_6	787_6	1353_6
$a = 12$	76_{10}	93_{10}	107_{10}	120_{10}	131_{10}	142_{10}	151_{10}	161_{10}	169_{10}	185_{10}	214_{10}	385_6	576_6	773_6	1334_6
$a = 13$	73_{10}	90_{10}	104_{10}	116_{10}	127_{10}	137_{10}	146_{10}	155_{10}	163_{10}	179_{10}	207_{10}	377_6	566_6	762_6	1318_6
$a = 14$	71_{10}	87_{10}	100_{10}	112_{10}	123_{10}	133_{10}	142_{10}	150_{10}	158_{10}	173_{10}	200_{10}	370_6	558_6	752_6	1304_6
$a = 15$	69_{10}	85_{10}	98_{10}	109_{10}	119_{10}	129_{10}	138_{10}	146_{10}	154_{10}	169_{10}	195_{10}	365_6	551_6	743_6	1292_6
$a = 16$	67_{10}	82_{10}	95_{10}	106_{10}	116_{10}	126_{10}	134_{10}	142_{10}	150_{10}	164_{10}	190_{10}	359_6	545_6	736_6	1282_6
$a = 100$	40_{10}	49_{10}	56_{10}	63_{10}	69_{10}	74_{10}	79_{10}	84_{10}	89_{10}	97_{10}	124_6	282_6	451_6	625_6	1135_6
$a = 128$	38_{10}	46_{10}	53_{10}	60_{10}	65_{10}	70_{10}	75_{10}	80_{10}	84_{10}	92_{10}	120_6	277_6	444_6	618_6	1125_6
$a = 256$	33_{10}	41_{10}	47_{10}	52_{10}	57_{10}	62_{10}	66_{10}	70_{10}	74_{10}	81_{10}	112_6	264_6	429_6	600_6	1102_6
$a = 1000$	32_2	33_{10}	38_{10}	42_{10}	46_{10}	50_6	53_{10}	56_{10}	59_{10}	65_{10}	101_6	247_6	408_6	576_6	1072_6
$a = 1024$	32_2	32_2	37_{10}	42_{10}	46_{10}	50_6	53_{10}	56_{10}	59_{10}	64_{10}	101_6	246_6	408_6	576_6	1071_6
$a = 10\,000$	32_2	32_2	32_2	32_2	35_{10}	42_6	44_6	47_6	49_6	56_5	90_6	229_6	388_6	552_6	1041_6
$a = 65\,536$	32_2	32_2	32_2	32_2	32_2	38_6	40_5	44_5	48_5	56_5	84_6	220_6	377_6	540_6	1026_6

(differential chosen plaintext attack) as best attack. We can also see that Eq. (2) (Dictionary Attack) appears for low ℓ and large a. Actually, our lower bounds asymptotically give $n = \Omega(s\ell^{\frac{1}{2}} + \ell^{\frac{3}{2}})$ when s and ℓ grow to infinity. To select n, we doubled the requirement for a safety margin and we took the smallest acceptable multiple of ℓ by using Eq. (2), Eq. (10), and Eq. (6).

6 Conclusion

We constructed a flexible truly-SPN FPE. We proved that it is competitive in terms of both throughput and security, even when the encryption domain is very small. We encourage researchers to analyze the security.

References

1. Retail Financial Services - Requirements for Protection of Sensitive Payment Card Data - Part 1: Using Encryption Method. ANSI X9.119-1-2016. American National Standards Institute
2. Retail Financial Services - Requirements for Protection of Sensitive Payment Card Data - Part 2: Implementing Post Authorization Tokenization Systems. ANSI X9.119-2-2017. American National Standards Institute
3. Recommendation for Block Cipher Modes of Operation: Methods for Format Preserving Encryption. NIST Special Publication (SP) 800–38G. National Institute of Standards and Technology. http://dx.doi.org/10.6028/NIST.SP.800-38G

4. Baignères, T., Finiasz, M.: Dial C for cipher. In: Biham, E., Youssef, A.M. (eds.) SAC 2006. LNCS, vol. 4356, pp. 76–95. Springer, Heidelberg (2007). https://doi.org/10.1007/978-3-540-74462-7_7
5. Baignères, T., Stern, J., Vaudenay, S.: Linear cryptanalysis of non binary ciphers. In: Adams, C., Miri, A., Wiener, M. (eds.) SAC 2007. LNCS, vol. 4876, pp. 184–211. Springer, Heidelberg (2007). https://doi.org/10.1007/978-3-540-77360-3_13
6. Bellare, M., Hoang, V.T., Tessaro, S.: Message-recovery attacks on feistel-based format-preserving encryption. In: 23rd ACM Conference on Computer and Communications Security, Vienna, Austria, pp. 444–455. ACM Press (2016)
7. Bellare, M., Ristenpart, T., Rogaway, P., Stegers, T.: Format-preserving encryption. In: Jacobson, M.J., Rijmen, V., Safavi-Naini, R. (eds.) SAC 2009. LNCS, vol. 5867, pp. 295–312. Springer, Heidelberg (2009). https://doi.org/10.1007/978-3-642-05445-7_19
8. Bellare, M., Rogaway, P., Spies, T.: The FFX mode of operation for format-preserving encryption. http://csrc.nist.gov/groups/ST/toolkit/BCM/documents/proposedmodes/ffx/ffx-spec.pdf
9. Biham, E.: How to Decrypt or even Substitute DES-Encrypted Messages in 2^{28} steps. Inf. Process. Lett. **84**, 117–124 (2002)
10. Biryukov, A., Khovratovich, D.: Related-key cryptanalysis of the full AES-192 and AES-256. In: Matsui, M. (ed.) ASIACRYPT 2009. LNCS, vol. 5912, pp. 1–18. Springer, Heidelberg (2009). https://doi.org/10.1007/978-3-642-10366-7_1
11. Black, J., Rogaway, P.: Ciphers with arbitrary finite domains. In: Preneel, B. (ed.) CT-RSA 2002. LNCS, vol. 2271, pp. 114–130. Springer, Heidelberg (2002). https://doi.org/10.1007/3-540-45760-7_9
12. Brier, E., Peyrin, T., Stern, J.: BPS: a format-preserving encryption proposal. http://csrc.nist.gov/groups/ST/toolkit/BCM/documents/proposedmodes/bps/bps-spec.pdf
13. Brightwell, M., Smith, H.: Using datatype-preserving encryption to enhance data warehouse security. In: 20th NISSC Proceedings, pp. 141–149 (1997). http://csrc.nist.gov/nissc/1997/proceedings/141.pdf
14. Chakraborty, D., Ghosh, S., López, C.M., Sarkar, P.: FAST: Disk Encryption and Beyond. Eprint 2017/849 https://eprint.iacr.org/2017/849
15. Chang, D., et al.: SPF: a new family of efficient format-preserving encryption algorithms. In: Chen, K., Lin, D., Yung, M. (eds.) Inscrypt 2016. LNCS, vol. 10143, pp. 64–83. Springer, Cham (2017). https://doi.org/10.1007/978-3-319-54705-3_5
16. Chang, D., Ghosh, M., Jati, A., Kumar, A., Sanadhya, S.K.: eSPF: a family of format-preserving encryption algorithms using MDS matrices. In: Ali, S.S., Danger, J.-L., Eisenbarth, T. (eds.) SPACE 2017. LNCS, vol. 10662, pp. 133–150. Springer, Cham (2017). https://doi.org/10.1007/978-3-319-71501-8_8
17. Durak, F.B., Horst, H., Horst, M., Vaudenay, S.: FAST: Secure and High Performance Format-Preserving Encryption and Tokenization. Eprint 2021/1171 https://eprint.iacr.org/2021/1171
18. Durak, F.B., Vaudenay, S.: Breaking the FF3 format-preserving encryption standard over small domains. In: Katz, J., Shacham, H. (eds.) CRYPTO 2017. LNCS, vol. 10402, pp. 679–707. Springer, Cham (2017). https://doi.org/10.1007/978-3-319-63715-0_23. Eprint 2017/521 https://eprint.iacr.org/2017/521
19. Feistel, H.: Cryptography and computer privacy. Sci. Am. **228**(5), 15–23 (1973). https://www.jstor.org/stable/10.2307/24923044
20. Granboulan, L., Levieil, É., Piret, G.: Pseudorandom permutation families over abelian groups. In: Robshaw, M. (ed.) FSE 2006. LNCS, vol. 4047, pp. 57–77. Springer, Heidelberg (2006). https://doi.org/10.1007/11799313_5

21. Grover, L.K.: A fast quantum mechanical algorithm for database search. In: Proceedings of the 28th ACM Symposium on Theory of Computing, Philadelphia, Pennsylvania, U.S.A., pp. 212–219. ACM Press (1996)
22. Hoang, V.T., Miller, D., Trieu, N.: Attacks only get better: how to break FF3 on large domains. In: Ishai, Y., Rijmen, V. (eds.) EUROCRYPT 2019. LNCS, vol. 11477, pp. 85–116. Springer, Cham (2019). https://doi.org/10.1007/978-3-030-17656-3_4. Eprint 2019/244 https://eprint.iacr.org/2019/244
23. Hoang, V.T., Tessaro, S., Trieu, N.: The curse of small domains: new attacks on format-preserving encryption. In: Shacham, H., Boldyreva, A. (eds.) CRYPTO 2018. LNCS, vol. 10991, pp. 221–251. Springer, Cham (2018). https://doi.org/10.1007/978-3-319-96884-1_8. Eprint 2018/556 https://eprint.iacr.org/2018/556
24. Knuth, D.E.: Seminumerical Algorithms – The Art of Computer Programming (3rd ed.). Addison-Wesley, Boston (1998)
25. Lemire, D.: Fast Random Generation in an Interval. arXiv:1805.10941v4 (2018). https://arxiv.org/pdf/1805.10941.pdf
26. Lumbroso, J.: Optimal Discrete Uniform Generation from Coin Flips, and Applications. arXiv:1304.1916v1 (2013). https://arxiv.org/pdf/1304.1916.pdf
27. Liskov, M., Rivest, R.L., Wagner, D.: Tweakable block ciphers. J. Cryptol. **24**, 588–613 (2011)
28. Merkle, R.C.: Fast software encryption functions. In: Menezes, A.J., Vanstone, S.A. (eds.) CRYPTO 1990. LNCS, vol. 537, pp. 477–501. Springer, Heidelberg (1991). https://doi.org/10.1007/3-540-38424-3_34
29. Rogaway, P.: A synopsis of format preserving encryption (2010). http://web.cs.ucdavis.edu/~rogaway/papers/synopsis.pdf
30. Schneier, B.: Description of a new variable-length key, 64-bit block cipher (Blowfish). In: Anderson, R. (ed.) FSE 1993. LNCS, vol. 809, pp. 191–204. Springer, Heidelberg (1994). https://doi.org/10.1007/3-540-58108-1_24
31. Schroeppel, R.: The Hasty Pudding Cipher. AES submission (1998)
32. Simon, D.R.: On the power of quantum computation. SIAM J. Comput. **26**(5), 1474–1483 (1997)
33. Spies, T.: Format Preserving Encryption. White paper (2008). https://www.voltage.com/wp-content/uploads/Voltage-Security-WhitePaper-Format-Preserving-Encryption.pdf

Fine-Tuning the ISO/IEC Standard LightMAC

Soumya Chattopadhyay[1(✉)], Ashwin Jha[2], and Mridul Nandi[1]

[1] Indian Statistical Institute, Kolkata, India
[2] CISPA Helmholtz Center for Information Security, Saarbrücken, Germany
ashwin.jha@cispa.de

Abstract. LightMAC, by Luykx et al., is a block cipher based message authentication code (MAC). The simplicity of design and low overhead allows it to have very compact implementations. As a result, it has been recently chosen as an ISO/IEC standard MAC for lightweight applications. LightMAC has been shown to achieve query-length independent security bound of $O(q^2/2^n)$ when instantiated with two independently keyed n-bit block ciphers, where q denotes the number of MAC queries and the query-length is upper bounded by $(n - s)2^s$ bits for a fixed counter size s. In this paper, we aim to minimize the number of block cipher keys in LightMAC. First, we show that the original LightMAC instantiated with a single block cipher key, referred as 1k-LightMAC, achieves security bound of $O(q^2/2^n)$ while the query-length is at least $(n-s)$ bits and at most $(n-s)\min\{2^{n/4}, 2^s\}$ bits. Second, we show that a minor variant of 1k-LightMAC, dubbed as LightMAC-ds, achieves security bound of $O(q^2/2^n)$ while query-length is upper bounded by $(n - s)2^{s-1}$ bits. Of independent interest, our security proof of 1k-LightMAC employs a novel sampling approach, called the *reset-sampling*, as a subroutine within the H-coefficient proof setup.

Keywords: LightMAC · MAC · PRF · Single-key · Lightweight · ISO/IEC standard

1 Introduction

Lightweight cryptography endeavors to safeguard communications in resource-constrained environments. The advent of Internet of Things has given a great impetus to this field of research in the last decade or so. As a result, several standardization efforts have tried to systematize the field, most notably the CAESAR competition [1], NIST lightweight cryptography standardization project [2], and

Soumya Chattopadhyay and Mridul Nandi are supported by the project "Study and Analysis of IoT Security" under Government of India at R. C. Bose Centre for Cryptology and Security, Indian Statistical Institute, Kolkata. Ashwin Jha's work was carried out in the framework of the French-German-Center for Cybersecurity, a collaboration of CISPA and LORIA.

M. Tibouchi and H. Wang (Eds.): ASIACRYPT 2021, LNCS 13092, pp. 490–519, 2021.
https://doi.org/10.1007/978-3-030-92078-4_17

the ISO/IEC standardization [3]. Specifically, the ISO/IEC 29192-6:2019 standard [3] specifies three message authentication code (or MAC) algorithms for lightweight applications. MACs are symmetric-key primitives that achieve data authenticity and integrity. The ISO/IEC standard recommends LightMAC [4], Tsudik's keymode [5] and Chaskey-12 [6] as the three MAC algorithms. In this paper, we focus on LightMAC.

LightMAC, by Luykx et al. [4], is a parallelizable block cipher-based MAC. For an n-bit block cipher E instantiated with keys K_1 and K_2, and a global parameter $s < n$, a simplified[1] version of LightMAC can be defined as:

$$\mathsf{LightMAC}_{K_1,K_2}(m) := E_{K_2}(E_{K_1}(x[1]) \oplus \cdots \oplus E_{K_1}(x[\ell-1]) \oplus m[\ell] \| 10^{s-1}), \quad (1)$$

where $(m[1], \ldots, m[\ell])$ denotes the $(n-s)$-bit parsing of the input message m, and $x[i] = \langle i \rangle_s \| m[i]$ for $1 \leq i \leq \ell - 1$, where $\langle i \rangle_s$ denotes the s-bit binary representation of i. For obvious reasons s is also called the counter size. The counter-based encoding in LightMAC is inherited from some earlier MAC designs such as the XOR MACs by Bellare et al. [7] and Bernstein's protected counter sums [8]. The use of counter-based encoding limits the *rate*—ratio of the number of n-bit blocks in the message m to the number of block cipher calls required to process m. For example, LightMAC requires 4 calls to process a message of length $3n$ bits when the counter size $s = n/4$, whence the rate is $3/4$. Ideally, the rate should be as high as possible, with rate 1 or higher considered as holy grail. Dutta et al. [9] give optimal counter-based encoding strategies for some scenarios, resulting in significant speed-up. However, LightMAC still falls short on this account when compared to some other MAC schemes such as OMAC [10] and PMAC [11] etc.

However, LightMAC design is quite simple as it minimizes all auxiliary operations other than the block cipher call, which reduces the overhead to a minimum. For this reason, LightMAC is expected to have more compact implementations as compared to PMAC. Further, LightMAC is parallelizable like PMAC which enables it to exploit the parallel computing infrastructure, whenever available. As a result, LightMAC is a quite flexible algorithm, as it has qualities suitable for both memory-constrained environments as well as high performance computing.

Query-Length Independence: Yet another avenue where LightMAC gains over several other MAC schemes is its security guarantee. Many MAC algorithms, including PMAC and OMAC, have security bounds which degrade linearly with the query-length. Apparently, some sort of dependence on query-length is unavoidable in iterated MAC schemes. However, LightMAC is shown to have query-length independent security bounds.

It is well-known [12,13] that variable input length (VIL) pseudorandom functions (or PRFs) are good candidates for deterministic MACs. Indeed, almost all the security bounds on deterministic MAC schemes, in fact, quantify their PRF security. In the following discussion q and ℓ denote the number of queries and the bound on query-lengths, respectively.

[1] Assuming all messages have length $(n-s)r$ for some $1 \leq r \leq 2^s$.

Luykx et al. [4] showed that LightMAC achieves $O(q^2/2^n)$ bound on the success probability of any adversary (also referred as the PRF advantage). This bound is independent of the query-length ℓ, apart from the obvious bound of $\ell \leq (n-s)2^s$.

In comparison, arguably the most popular parallelizable MAC, PMAC, suffers from a linear degradation in security with increase in query-length. Some birthday-bound (PRF advantage is at least $q^2/2^n$) variants (or extensions) of PMAC, like PMAC with parity [14] and PMAC3 [15], do achieve query-length independence for a wide range of ℓ values. However, this costs significant increase in design complexity, such as more than two-fold increase in memory usage and relatively complex auxiliary operations like multiple masking operations or generating error correcting codes.

The situation does not improve much, when we consider birthday-bound sequential modes either. Schemes like CBC-MAC [16], XCBC [17] and OMAC exhibit similar degradation in security with increase in query-length as PMAC. EMAC [18,19] achieves query-length independence with slightly higher PRF advantage of $O(q/2^{n/2})$ while $\ell \leq 2^{n/4}$. However, EMAC only works for messages with "multiple-of-n" length. One can extend the construction to arbitrary domain by either using extra block cipher keys, as in ECBC and FCBC [17], or apply some injective padding rule on the input message before processing it through EMAC.

Beyond-the-birthday bound (BBB) secure constructions such as Sum-ECBC [20], PMAC+ [21], 3kf9 [22], PMACx [23], 1k-PMAC+ [24], and LightMAC+ [25], can also achieve query-length independent security bounds for a wide range of values of ℓ. However, these constructions require significantly more memory and additional operations (due to the BBB security requirement) as compared to LightMAC.

1.1 Motivation

ISO standards are widely used in communication protocols such as TLS, Bluetooth protocol, Zigbee etc. Being an ISO standard for lightweight cryptography, LightMAC is also widely recognized as a suitable MAC candidate for deployment in resource-constrained environments. Possibly, its simple and compact design and query-length independent security are the main reasons behind this perception. On a closer look, we see that the two independent keys greatly simplify the security argument of LightMAC. Due to the independence of keys, it can be viewed as an instance of the Hash-then-PRF paradigm [26,27], and hence the PRF security bound follows directly from LightMAC output collision probability.

However, maintaining two block cipher keys could be a burden in memory-constrained environments. Currently LightMAC with 2 keys requires 256 bits for key (128-bit block cipher key). Instead, one-key variants of LightMAC use 128 bits, which is a significant optimization in memory footprint both in hardware and software. The problem is further aggravated when implementations store precomputed round keys to reduce latency. For example, in case of AES128 [28], this precomputation would require 176 bytes of memory per key. This motivates us to look into the problem of minimizing the number of keys in LightMAC, while maintaining the query-length independence. Specifically, we ask the following question:

† : *Is there a single-key LightMAC variant which achieves similar query-length independent bounds as two-key LightMAC?*

As it turns out, the answer to this question is not straightforward. Recall the description of LightMAC from Eq. (1). Let $y_i := E_{K_1}(x_i)$ and $y^{\oplus} := y_1 \oplus \cdots \oplus y_{\ell-1} \oplus m_\ell \| 10^{s-1}$. We call x_i and y_i the i-th intermediate input and outputs, respectively and $y^{\oplus}$ and $t = E_{K_2}(y^{\oplus})$ the final input and output, respectively. There are two non-trivial bottlenecks (see Sect. 3.2) in answering the above questions:

1. Collisions between intermediate input and final input, and
2. Collisions between intermediate output and final output.

The naive way to handle these two cases is to bound the probability of these events to $O(q^2\ell/2^n)$ as there are at most $q\ell$ intermediate inputs/outputs and q final inputs/outputs. Clearly, this naive approach leads to a degradation in the security. So,

⋆ : *we need a more sophisticated strategy to prove the security of single-key LightMAC.*

Yet another approach is to explicitly separate the final inputs from intermediate inputs by fixing some input bit to 0 in intermediate inputs and 1 in final inputs. This will help in resolving the first bottleneck. However, the second bottleneck is still present. Hence, the resulting construction is not as straightforward as two-key LightMAC. Further, domain separation also introduces slight changes in the standardized design, which is not appreciated by end-users, in general. So,

⋆⋆ : *variants with very small modifications over the original LightMAC algorithm will be preferred.*

In this paper, we aim to answer † in affirmative using ⋆ and ⋆⋆ as general guidelines.

1.2 Our Contributions

Our contributions are twofold:

First, in Sect. 4, we show that *single-key* LightMAC, *denoted as* 1k-LightMAC, *is as secure as two-key* LightMAC, *while the query-lengths are lower bounded by $(n-s)$ bits and upper bounded by $(n-s)\min\{2^{n/4}, 2^s\}$ bits.* In other words, we show a security bound of $O(q^2/2^n)$ for 1k-LightMAC, while $(n-s) \le \ell \le (n-s)\min\{2^{n/4}, 2^s\}$.

In order to circumvent the two bottlenecks discussed in Sect. 1.1, we use a novel sampling approach, called the *reset-sampling* – a proof style much in the same vein as the reprogramming of random oracles [29]. At the highest

Table 1. A comparative summary of several birthday-bound block cipher based MAC algorithms. Here q denotes the number of queries, ℓ denotes the bound on query-length, and s denotes the counter size.

Mode	#BC keys	Aux. memory[a]	PRF bound	Restriction[b]
EMAC [18, 19]	2	0	$O\left(\frac{q}{2^{n/2}}\right)$ [33]	$\ell \leq n2^{n/4}$
ECBC,FCBC [17]	3	0	$O\left(\frac{q}{2^{n/2}}\right)$ [33]	$\ell \leq n2^{n/4}$
XCBC [17]	1	$2n$	$O\left(\frac{q^2\ell}{2^n}\right)$ [34]	$\ell \leq n2^{n/3}$
OMAC [10]	1	n	$O\left(\frac{q^2\ell}{2^n}\right)$ [35]	$\ell \leq n2^{n/4}$
PMAC [11]	1	n	$\Theta(\frac{q^2\ell}{2^n})$ [34, 36, 37]	-
PMAC3 [15]	2	$3n$	$O\left(\frac{q^2}{2^n}\right)$ [15, 38]	$\ell \leq n2^{n/2}$
LightMAC [3, 4]	2	s	$O\left(\frac{q^2}{2^n}\right)$ [4]	$\ell \leq (n-s)2^s$
1k-LightMAC	1	s	$O\left(\frac{q^2}{2^n}\right)$	$(n-s) \leq \ell \leq (n-s)\min\{2^{n/4}, 2^s\}$
LightMAC-ds	1	s	$O\left(\frac{q^2}{2^n}\right)$	$\ell \leq (n-s)2^{s-1}$

[a] The memory used to store masking keys or counter value.
[b] Upper bound on query-lengths for which the given security bound holds.

level, reset-sampling can be viewed as a subroutine in H-coefficient [30,31] or Expectation method [32] based proofs that can be employed in order to transform a possibly bad transcript into a good transcript given that certain conditions are fulfilled. In other words, it resets some bad transcript into a good transcript. For example, in our analysis we reset the intermediate outputs appropriately whenever the corresponding intermediate input collides with some final input.

Second, in Sect. 5, we propose a close variant of 1k-LightMAC, dubbed as LightMAC-ds, and show that *LightMAC-ds is asymptotically as secure as two-key LightMAC, i.e., it achieves security bound of $O(q^2/2^n)$ while $\ell \leq (n-s)2^{s-1}$*. The restriction on length is due to the loss of 1-bit from counter for domain separation.

Table 1 gives a comparison of LightMAC, 1k-LightMAC, and LightMAC-ds with several popular birthday-bound block cipher based MAC mode of operation. We deliberately refrain from enumerating beyond-the-birthday bound modes for a fair comparison, as they require relatively more memory and/or key material (due to the BBB security requirement). From the table, it is clear that the three LightMAC candidates are overall better than other modes considering security vs block cipher key size and security vs auxiliary memory. Further, *1k-LightMAC is almost as good as LightMAC and LightMAC-ds as long as $(n-s) \leq \ell \leq (n-s)\min\{2^{n/4}, 2^s\}$. Note that, the lower bound on ℓ is necessary to avoid some trivial collision events (see Sect. 3.2 for further details). Similarly, LightMAC-ds is as good as LightMAC as long as $\ell \leq (n-s)2^{s-1}$.*

Practical Significance: Our results are restricted in terms of the length of messages, especially, 1k-LightMAC which effectively bounds the message length to roughly $2^{35.5}$ bytes for 128-bit block size. However, we believe that this is a minor issue. Indeed, many real life communication protocols limit the message lengths to much less than 1 Gigabyte. For example, SRTP [39] limits the payload length to at most 1 Megabyte. So, the impact of length restriction could, in fact, be minimal in most applications. Furthermore, we emphasize that 1k-LightMAC can be used as a drop-in replacement, since the required changes are minimal. This is particularly a compelling feature for the intended application area of the ISO/IEC-29192-6:2019 standard, i.e. resource constrained environments, where additional deployment or maintenance cost is highly undesirable. In summary, our results have significant practical importance due to the ISO/IEC standardization of LightMAC and the inherent advantages of 1k-LightMAC and LightMAC-ds over LightMAC.

2 Preliminaries

NOTATIONAL SETUP: For $n \in \mathbb{N}$, $[n]$ denotes the set $\{1, 2, \ldots, n\}$. The set of all bit strings (including the empty string) is denoted $\{0,1\}^*$. The length of any bit string $X \in \{0,1\}^*$, denoted $|X|$, is the number of bits in X. For $n \in \mathbb{N}$, $\{0,1\}^n$ denotes the set of all bit strings of length n, and $\{0,1\}^{\leq n} := \bigcup_{i=0}^{n} \{0,1\}^i$. For any $A, B \in \{0,1\}^*$, we write $A \| B$ to denote the concatenation of A and B. For $n \in \mathbb{N}$ and $X \in \{0,1\}^*$, $(X_1, \ldots, X_l) \xleftarrow{n} X$ denotes the n-bit parsing of X where $|X_i| = n$ for all $1 \leq i \leq l-1$ and $0 \leq |X_l| \leq n-1$. For any $n \in \mathbb{N}$ and $M \in \{0,1\}^*$, we define $\mathsf{pad}_n(M) := M \| 10^d$ where d is the smallest integer such that $|\mathsf{pad}_n(M)|$ is a multiple of n. For $i, m \in \mathbb{N}$ such that $i < 2^m$, we define $\langle i \rangle_m$ as the m-bit binary encoding of the integer i. For $0 \leq k \leq n$, we define the falling factorial $(n)_k := n!/(n-k)! = n(n-1)\cdots(n-k+1)$. The set of all functions from $\mathcal{X}$ to $\mathcal{Y}$ is denoted $\mathcal{F}(\mathcal{X}, \mathcal{Y})$, and the set of all permutations of $\mathcal{X}$ is denoted $\mathcal{P}(\mathcal{X})$. We simply write $\mathcal{F}(a, b)$ and $\mathcal{P}(a)$, whenever $\mathcal{X} = \{0,1\}^a$ and $\mathcal{Y} = \{0,1\}^b$.

For a pair of q-tuples $\widetilde{X} = (X_1, \ldots, X_q)$ and $\widetilde{Y} = (Y_1, \ldots, Y_q)$, $(\widetilde{X}, \widetilde{Y})$ denotes the $2q$-tuple $(X_1, \ldots, X_q, Y_1, \ldots, Y_q)$. Similarly, one can extend notation for more than 2 tuples. Two q-tuples $\widetilde{X}$ and $\widetilde{Y}$ are said to be *permutation compatible*, denoted as $\widetilde{X} \leftrightsquigarrow \widetilde{Y}$, if $(X_i = X_j) \iff (Y_i = Y_j)$, for all $i \neq j$. By an abuse of notation, we also use $\widetilde{X}$ to denote the set $\{X_i : i \in [q]\}$.

For a finite set $\mathcal{X}$, $\mathsf{X} \leftarrow_{\$} \mathcal{X}$ denotes the uniform at random sampling of X from $\mathcal{X}$, and $\widetilde{\mathsf{X}} \leftarrow_{\#} \mathcal{X}$ denotes the without replacement sampling of a tuple $\widetilde{\mathsf{X}}$ from the set $\mathcal{X}$.

A USEFUL LEMMA: The following result from linear algebra will be very useful in later analysis.

Lemma 2.1. *Let* $(\mathsf{Y}_1, \ldots, \mathsf{Y}_l) \leftarrow_{\#} \mathcal{S} \subset \{0,1\}^n$ *with* $|\mathcal{S}| = N > l$. *Let* A *be a* $k \times l$ *binary matrix with rank* r. *We write the column vector* $(\mathsf{Y}_1, \ldots, \mathsf{Y}_l)^{tr}$ *as* $\widetilde{\mathsf{Y}}$. *Then, for any* $c \in (\{0,1\}^n)^k$, *we have*

$$\Pr\left[A \cdot \widetilde{\mathsf{Y}} = c\right] \leq \frac{1}{(N-l)^r}$$

Proof. Since the rank of the matrix A is r, we can identify $1 \leq i_1 < \cdots < i_r \leq l$ such that $\mathsf{Y}_{i_1}, \ldots \mathsf{Y}_{i_r}$ will be uniquely determined by fixing the value for the remaining $l-r$ variables. By conditioning on the values of these $l-r$ variables, the probability that $A \cdot \widetilde{\mathsf{Y}} = c$ is bounded by at most $\frac{1}{(N-l+r)_r}$ which is less than $\frac{1}{(N-l)^r}$. □

We will often employ this lemma for $k \geq 2$ cases.

2.1 Security Definitions

Distinguishers: A (q, T)-distinguisher $\mathscr{A}$ is an oracle Turing machine, that makes at most q oracle queries, runs in time at most T, and outputs a single bit. For any oracle $\mathcal{O}$, we write $\mathscr{A}^{\mathcal{O}}$ to denote the output of $\mathscr{A}$ after its interaction with $\mathcal{O}$. By convention, $T = \infty$ denotes computationally unbounded (information-theoretic) and deterministic distinguishers. In this paper, we assume that the distinguisher is non-trivial, i.e., it never makes a duplicate query. Let $\mathbb{A}(q, T)$ be the class of all non-trivial distinguishers limited to q queries and T computations.

Pseudorandom Function: A $(\mathcal{K}, \mathcal{X}, \mathcal{Y})$-*keyed function* F with key space $\mathcal{K}$, domain $\mathcal{X}$, and range $\mathcal{Y}$ is a function $F : \mathcal{K} \times \mathcal{X} \rightarrow \mathcal{Y}$. We write $F_K(X)$ for $F(K, X)$.

The *pseudorandom function* or PRF advantage of any distinguisher $\mathscr{A}$ against a $(\mathcal{K}, \mathcal{X}, \mathcal{Y})$-keyed function F is defined as

$$\mathbf{Adv}_F^{\mathsf{prf}}(\mathscr{A}) = \mathbf{Adv}_{F;\Gamma}(\mathscr{A}) := \left| \Pr_{\mathsf{K} \leftarrow\!\$\, \mathcal{K}} \left[\mathscr{A}^{F_{\mathsf{K}}} = 1\right] - \Pr_{\Gamma \leftarrow\!\$\, \mathcal{F}(\mathcal{X},\mathcal{Y})} \left[\mathscr{A}^{\Gamma} = 1\right] \right|. \quad (2)$$

The *PRF security* of F against $\mathbb{A}(q, T)$ is defined as

$$\mathbf{Adv}_F^{\mathsf{prf}}(q, T) := \max_{\mathscr{A} \in \mathbb{A}(q,T)} \mathbf{Adv}_F^{\mathsf{prf}}(\mathscr{A}).$$

Pseudorandom Permutation: A $(\mathcal{K}, \{0,1\}^n)$-*block cipher* E with key space $\mathcal{K}$ and block space $\{0,1\}^n$ is a $(\mathcal{K}, \{0,1\}^n, \{0,1\}^n)$-keyed function, such that $E(K, \cdot)$ is a permutation over $\{0,1\}^n$ for any key $K \in \mathcal{K}$. We write $E_K(X)$ for $E(K, X)$.

The *pseudorandom permutation* or PRP advantage of any distinguisher $\mathscr{A}$ against a $(\mathcal{K}, \{0,1\}^n)$-block cipher E is defined as

$$\mathbf{Adv}_E^{\mathsf{prp}}(\mathscr{A}) = \mathbf{Adv}_{E;\Pi}(\mathscr{A}) := \left| \Pr_{\mathsf{K} \leftarrow\!\$\, \mathcal{K}} \left[\mathscr{A}^{E_{\mathsf{K}}} = 1\right] - \Pr_{\Pi \leftarrow\!\$\, \mathcal{P}(n)} \left[\mathscr{A}^{\Pi} = 1\right] \right|. \quad (3)$$

The *PRP security* of E against $\mathbb{A}(q, T)$ is defined as

$$\mathbf{Adv}_E^{\mathsf{prp}}(q, T) := \max_{\mathscr{A} \in \mathbb{A}(q,T)} \mathbf{Adv}_E^{\mathsf{prp}}(\mathscr{A}).$$

2.2 H-Coefficient Technique

The H-coefficient technique by Patarin [30,31] is a tool to upper bound the distinguishing advantage of any deterministic and computationally unbounded distinguisher $\mathscr{A}$ in distinguishing the real oracle $\mathcal{R}$ from the ideal oracle $\mathcal{I}$. The collection of all queries and responses that $\mathscr{A}$ made and received to and from the oracle, is called the transcript of $\mathscr{A}$, denoted as τ.

Let $\mathbb{R}$ and $\mathbb{I}$ denote the transcript random variable induced by $\mathscr{A}$'s interaction with $\mathcal{R}$ and $\mathcal{I}$, respectively. Let $\mathcal{T}$ be the set of all transcripts. A transcript $\tau \in \mathcal{T}$ is said to be *attainable* if $\Pr[\mathbb{I} = \tau] > 0$, i.e., it can be realized by $\mathscr{A}$'s interaction with $\mathcal{I}$. Following these notations, we state the main result of H-coefficient technique in Theorem 2.1. A proof of this theorem is available in multiple papers, including [40,41].

Theorem 2.1 (H-coefficient). *For $\epsilon_1, \epsilon_2 \geq 0$, suppose there is a set $\mathcal{T}_{\mathsf{bad}} \subseteq \mathcal{T}$, that we call the set of all bad transcripts, such that the following conditions hold:*

- $\Pr[\mathbb{I} \in \mathcal{T}_{\mathsf{bad}}] \leq \epsilon_1$*; and*
- *For any $\tau \notin \mathcal{T}_{\mathsf{bad}}$, τ is attainable and* $\dfrac{\Pr[\mathbb{R} = \tau]}{\Pr[\mathbb{I} = \tau]} \geq 1 - \epsilon_2$.

Then, for any computationally unbounded and deterministic distinguisher $\mathscr{A}$, we have

$$\mathbf{Adv}_{\mathcal{R};\mathcal{I}}(\mathscr{A}) \leq \epsilon_1 + \epsilon_2.$$

3 Revisiting LightMAC

LightMAC is a block cipher-based parallelizable PRF construction by Luykx et al. [4]. It uses a counter-based encoding of input message blocks, much in the same vein as some of the previously proposed constructions like XMACC and XMACR [7] and protected counter sums [8]. Algorithm 3.1 gives the algorithmic description of LightMAC and Fig. 1 gives a pictorial illustration.

Throughout the rest of this paper, we refer to $x[i]$ and $y[i]$ as *intermediate input* and *output*, respectively, for all $i \in [\ell - 1]$ and $y^{\oplus}$ and t are referred as the *final input* and *output*, respectively.

Note that, the block size n and counter size s are application specific parameters that are fixed before any invocation. In order to argue the security of LightMAC, we must have $\langle i \rangle_s \neq \langle j \rangle_s$. When $i = 2^s + j$ for some $j \in [2^s - 1]$, then $\langle i \rangle_s = \langle j \rangle_s$. So, the maximum number of blocks in the padded message, denoted $\ell_{\max}$, must be less than 2^s. This will ensure that all the counters will be different.

3.1 Hash-Then-PRP and the Security of LightMAC

For some $\epsilon \geq 0$, a $(\mathcal{K}, \{0,1\}^{\leq (n-s)2^s}, \{0,1\}^n)$-keyed function H is called an ϵ-*universal hash function* if for all distinct $m, m' \in \{0,1\}^{\leq (n-s)2^s}$, we have

$$\Pr_{\mathsf{K} \leftarrow\$ \mathcal{K}}[H_{\mathsf{K}}(m) = H_{\mathsf{K}}(m')] \leq \epsilon.$$

Algorithm 3.1. LightMAC based on an n-bit block cipher E instantiated with two keys K_1, K_2. Here s denotes the counter size.

function $\mathsf{LightMAC}_{E_{K_1}, E_{K_2}}(m)$
  $y^{\oplus} \leftarrow 0^n$
  $(m[1], \ldots, m[\ell]) \xleftarrow{n-s} m$
  for $i = 1$ **to** $\ell - 1$ **do**
    $x[i] \leftarrow \langle i \rangle_s \| m[i]$ ▷ encoding $\langle i \rangle_s$ and $m[i]$ into $x[i]$
    $y[i] \leftarrow E_{K_1}(x[i])$ ▷ encrypting the encoded input
    $y^{\oplus} \leftarrow y^{\oplus} \oplus y[i]$ ▷ accumulating the intermediate output
  end for
  $y^{\oplus} \leftarrow y^{\oplus} \oplus \mathsf{pad}_n(m[\ell])$ ▷ accumulating final block of message
  $t \leftarrow E_{K_2}(y^{\oplus})$ ▷ tag generation
  return t
end function

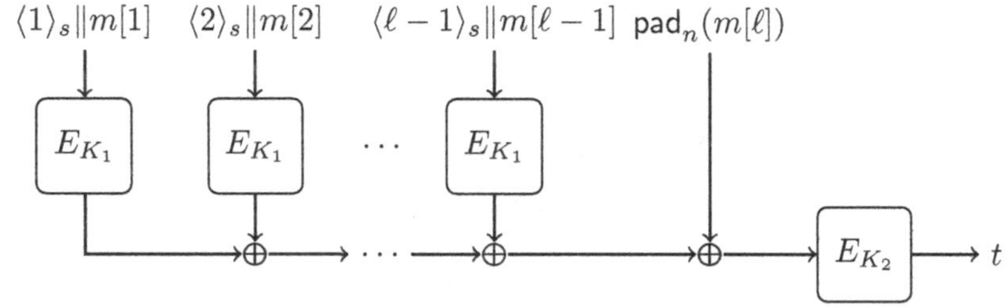

Fig. 1. LightMAC evaluated over an ℓ-block padded message m.

Universal hash functions are very useful in constructing PRFs via the Hash-then-PRP[2] paradigm [26,37]. In this paradigm, given independently keyed ϵ-universal hash function H_{K} and block cipher $E_{\mathsf{K}'}$, we define the Hash-then-PRP composition as $E_{K'} \circ H_K$. It is well-known that

$$\mathbf{Adv}^{\mathsf{prf}}_{E_{\mathsf{K}'} \circ H_{\mathsf{K}}}(q, T) \leq \mathbf{Adv}^{\mathsf{prp}}_{E}(q, T') + \binom{q}{2}\left(\frac{1}{2^n} + \epsilon\right), \tag{4}$$

where $T' = T + qO(T_E)$ and T_E denotes the runtime of E.

We skip the proof of this result as it is available in multiple papers including [37,42]. An informal justification for Eq. (4) is based on the observation that if the input to $E_{\mathsf{K}'}$ is distinct for all q queries then the outputs behave as "almost uniform at random". The probability that some inputs to $E_{\mathsf{K}'}$ collide is bounded by $\binom{q}{2}\epsilon$.

PRF Security of LightMAC: Consider a $(\mathcal{K}, \{0,1\}^{\leq (n-s)2^s}, \{0,1\}^n)$-keyed function LightHash, defined by the following mapping:

$$\forall m \in \{0,1\}^{\leq (n-s)2^s}, \quad \mathsf{LightHash}_{E_{K_1}}(m) := y^{\oplus},$$

[2] Here, we say PRP instead of PRF to highlight the use of block cipher based finalization.

where $y^{\oplus}$ is the final input corresponding to m in $\mathsf{LightMAC}_{E_{K_1},E_{K_2}}(m)$. Now, we can view LightMAC as an instantiation of Hash-then-PRP, by redefining LightMAC as

$$\mathsf{LightMAC}_{E_{K_1},E_{K_2}}(m) := E_{K_2}(\mathsf{LightHash}_{E_{K_1}}(m)).$$

Suppose, $\mathsf{LightHash}_{\Pi_1}$ is an ϵ_{LH}-universal hash for $\Pi_1 \leftarrow\!\!\$\, \mathcal{P}(n)$. Then, using Eq. (4), we have

$$\mathbf{Adv}^{\mathsf{prf}}_{\mathsf{LightMAC}}(q,T) \leq 2\mathbf{Adv}^{\mathsf{prp}}_{E}(\sigma,T') + \binom{q}{2}\left(\frac{1}{2^n} + \epsilon_{\mathsf{LH}}\right), \tag{5}$$

where σ denotes the total number of blocks in all q padded queries, and $T' = T + \sigma O(T_E)$ and T_E denotes the runtime of E.

In [4,9], it has been shown that $\epsilon_{\mathsf{LH}} \leq 1/(2^n - 2\ell_{\max})$, where $\ell_{\max}$ is the upper bound on the query-length in blocks. It is simply because for any $m \neq m'$ with lengths ℓ, ℓ' respectively, the event $\mathsf{LightHash}_{\Pi_1}(m) = \mathsf{LightHash}_{\Pi_1}(m')$ is identical with

$$\bigoplus_{i=1}^{\ell-1} \Pi_1(x[i]) \bigoplus_{j=1}^{\ell'-1} \Pi_1(x'[j]) = \mathsf{pad}_n(m[\ell]) \oplus \mathsf{pad}_n(m'[\ell']). \tag{6}$$

Now, since $m \neq m'$, either $(x[1],\ldots,x[\ell-1]) \neq (x'[1],\ldots,x'[\ell'-1])$, or

$$(x[1],\ldots,x[\ell-1]) = (x'[1],\ldots,x'[\ell'-1]) \wedge \mathsf{pad}_n(m[\ell]) \neq \mathsf{pad}_n(m'[\ell']).$$

The second case has zero probability. In the first case, assuming $\ell \geq \ell'$, we have at least one block say $x[i]$ which is distinct from all other blocks. Then, the probability of the event defined in Eq. (6) can be bounded above by probability that $\Pi_1(x[i])$ attains a certain value conditioned on the output of Π_1 on all other $x[j]$ and $x'[j']$ values for $j \in [\ell-1]\setminus\{i\}$ and $j' \in [\ell'-1]$. There are at most $2\ell_{\max}$ such values, i.e., Π_1 is already sampled on at most $2\ell_{\max}$ points. Therefore, the probability is bounded above by $1/(2^n - 2\ell_{\max})$.

By combining this bound with Eq. (5), we get the desired result for LightMAC in the following proposition.

Proposition 3.1. *For $\ell_{\max} < \min\{2^{n-2}, 2^s\}$, we have*

$$\mathbf{Adv}^{\mathsf{prf}}_{\mathsf{LightMAC}}(q,T) \leq 2\mathbf{Adv}^{\mathsf{prp}}_{E}(\sigma,T') + \frac{1.5q^2}{2^n},$$

where σ denotes the total number of blocks in all q padded queries, and $T' = T + \sigma O(T_E)$ and T_E denotes the runtime of E.

3.2 Bottlenecks for Single-Key LightMAC

We have just seen that the query-length independent security argument for LightMAC comes quite easily from the Hash-then-PRP paradigm. This is possible because K_1 and K_2 are independent of each other. A natural direction to explore

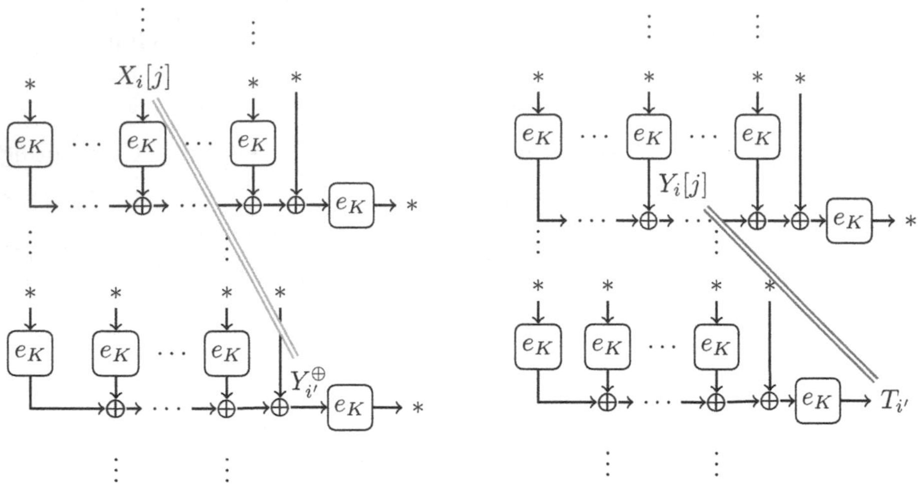

Fig. 2. `Icoll` (left) and `Ocoll` (right) events. In each case, labels with same color are equal, and double lines between two labels signify equality between the corresponding variables.

is the relaxation: $K_1 = K_2 = K$, i.e., LightMAC instantiated with a single key. Formally, we define the single-key LightMAC construction as follows:

$$\text{1k-LightMAC}_{E_K} := \text{LightMAC}_{E_K, E_K}.$$

We remark that *the additional nomenclature* 1k-LightMAC *is just for the sake of brevity. Indeed,* 1k-LightMAC *and* LightMAC *are algorithmically equivalent.* We have just instantiated $K_1 = K_2 = K$.

First thing to note is that Hash-then-PRP is no longer applicable as the hash function H_{K} and block cipher E_{K} are no longer independent. So, we have to look for a dedicated proof.

Suppose the adversary makes q queries $m_1, \ldots, m_q$ and the corresponding tuple of intermediate inputs and outputs are denoted $x_i = (x_i[1], \ldots, x_i[\ell_i - 1])$ and $y_i = (y_i[1], \ldots, y_i[\ell_i - 1])$, respectively. Similarly, the final input and output for the q queries is denoted $y_i^{\oplus}$ and t_i, respectively. Consider the events:

$$\begin{aligned} &\texttt{Icoll}: \ \exists (i, a) \in [q] \times [\ell_i - 1], j \in [q], \text{ such that } x_i[a] = y_j^{\oplus}; \\ &\texttt{Ocoll}: \ \exists (i, a) \in [q] \times [\ell_i - 1], j \in [q], \text{ such that } y_i[a] = t_j; \end{aligned}$$

`Icoll` denotes the event that a final input collides with some intermediate input and `Ocoll` denotes the analogous event for output collisions (see Fig. 2).

In a dedicated proof we must take care of these cases as they may lead to inconsistent transcripts. For example, it is possible that $x_i[a] = y_j^{\oplus}$ (`Icoll` holds) but $y_i[a] \neq t_j$ or vice-versa. The probability of realizing such a transcript is zero in the real world. In fact, one can easily create such inconsistencies by first making a query $m_1 = \langle 1 \rangle_s$, and then making another query $m_2 = 10^{n-s-1} \| x$, where x is any arbitrary bit string. Clearly, $x_2[1] = y_1^{\oplus}$, which implies that Icoll holds. This might help an adversary to mount an attack on 1k-LightMAC as it can access the internal variables using very short queries. Interestingly, if we swap the positions of counter and message block, then this trivial collision is no longer possible, and it might even be possible to show that the resulting variant is secure. Since our aim is to study the standardized algorithm, we simply assume that messages are at least $(n-s)$ bits long, thereby ensuring that at least one block cipher call is made in the hash layer. But, this only helps to avoid collisions in the corner case. We still have to consider the possibility of Icoll and Ocoll in the general case. We have to ensure that such inconsistencies do not occur with high probability. A straightforward bound on these events introduces a bound of the form $O(q^2 \ell_{\max}/2^n)$ since there are at most $q\ell_{\max}$ many (i,a) pairs and q choices for j. However, we aim to do better than this. In the next two sections, we show how we can handle these events in better way.

4 Security of 1k-LightMAC

This section is devoted to the PRF security of 1k-LightMAC. Throughout this section, we assume that messages are at least $(n-s)$-bit long. This assumption is used to avoid some trivial bad events, as discussed in Sect. 3.2.

Theorem 4.1. *Let $q, \ell_{\min}, \ell_{\max}, \sigma, t > 0$. For $\ell_{\min} \geq 2$, $q + 4\ell_{\max} \leq 2^{n-1}$, the PRF security of 1k-LightMAC against $\mathbb{A}(q,T)$ is given by*

$$\mathbf{Adv}^{\mathsf{prf}}_{\mathsf{1k\text{-}LightMAC}}(q,T) \leq \mathbf{Adv}^{\mathsf{prp}}_{E}(\sigma + q, T') + \frac{1.5q^2}{2^n} + \frac{7.5q^3\ell_{\max}^2}{2^{2n}} + \frac{4q^4\ell_{\max}^2}{2^{3n}} + \frac{2\sigma}{2^n},$$

where q denotes the number of queries, $\ell_{\max}$ (res. $\ell_{\min}$) denotes an upper (res. lower) bound on the number of blocks in any padded query, σ denotes the total number of blocks present in all q queries, $T' = T + \sigma O(T_E)$ and T_E denotes the runtime of E.

Further assuming $\ell_{\max} \leq \min\{2^{n/4}, 2^s\}$ and $q \leq \min\{2^{\frac{3n}{4}-2}, 2^{\frac{n}{2}-1.51}\}$, we have

$$\mathbf{Adv}^{\mathsf{prf}}_{\mathsf{1k\text{-}LightMAC}}(q,T) \leq \mathbf{Adv}^{\mathsf{prp}}_{E}(\sigma + q, T') + \frac{4q^2}{2^n} + \frac{2\sigma}{2^n}.$$

The proof of this theorem is described in the rest of this section. First of all, we switch to the information-theoretic setting, i.e., E_{K} is replaced with $\Pi \leftarrow\!\!\$\, \mathcal{P}(n)$ via a standard hybrid argument. Formally, we have

$$\mathbf{Adv}^{\mathsf{prf}}_{\mathsf{1k\text{-}LightMAC}}(q,T) \leq \mathbf{Adv}^{\mathsf{prp}}_{E}(\sigma + q, T') + \mathbf{Adv}^{\mathsf{prf}}_{\mathsf{1k\text{-}LightMAC}_{\Pi}}(q,\infty). \quad (7)$$

So it is enough to bound the PRF security of 1k-LightMAC$_{\Pi}$, henceforth also referred as the real oracle. We apply the H-coefficient technique to bound this term. Fix any $\mathscr{A} \in \mathbb{A}(q,\infty)$ such that

$$\mathbf{Adv}^{\mathsf{prf}}_{\mathsf{1k\text{-}LightMAC}_{\Pi}}(q,\infty) = \mathbf{Adv}^{\mathsf{prf}}_{\mathsf{1k\text{-}LightMAC}_{\Pi}}(\mathscr{A}).$$

Going forward, we will bound the advantage of $\mathscr{A}$.

4.1 Description of Oracles and Their Transcripts

Real Oracle: The real oracle corresponds to $\textsf{1k-LightMAC}_{\Pi}$. It responds faithfully to all the queries made by $\mathscr{A}$. Once the query-response phase is over, it releases all the intermediate inputs and outputs to $\mathscr{A}$.

In addition, the real oracle releases three binary variables, namely, $\textsf{FlagT}$, $\textsf{FlagZ}$, and $\textsf{FlagY}$, all of which are degenerately set to 0. The utility of these flags will become apparent from the description of ideal oracle. For now, it is sufficient to note that these flags are degenerate in the real world.
Formally, we have $\mathbb{R} := (\widetilde{\textsf{M}}, \widetilde{\textsf{T}}, \widetilde{\textsf{X}}, \widetilde{\textsf{Y}}, \textsf{FlagT}, \textsf{FlagZ}, \textsf{FlagY})$, where

- $\widetilde{\textsf{M}} = (\textsf{M}_1, \ldots, \textsf{M}_q)$ denotes the q-tuple of queries made by $\mathscr{A}$, where $\textsf{M}_i \in \{0,1\}^{\leq (n-s)2^s}$ for all $i \in [q]$. In addition, for all $i \in [q]$, let $\ell_i := \left\lfloor \frac{|\textsf{M}_i|}{n-s} \right\rfloor + 1$.
- $\widetilde{\textsf{T}} = (\textsf{T}_1, \ldots, \textsf{T}_q)$ denotes the q-tuple of final outputs received by $\mathscr{A}$, where $\textsf{T}_i \in \{0,1\}^n$.
- $\widetilde{\textsf{X}} = (\textsf{X}_1, \ldots, \textsf{X}_q)$, where $\textsf{X}_i$ denotes the intermediate input tuple for the i-th query, i.e., for all $a \in [\ell_i - 1]$, $\textsf{X}_i[a] = \langle a \rangle_s \| \textsf{M}_i[a]$.
- $\widetilde{\textsf{Y}} = (\textsf{Y}_1, \ldots, \textsf{Y}_q)$, where $\textsf{Y}_i$ denotes the intermediate output tuple for the i-th query, i.e., for all $a \in [\ell_i - 1]$, $\textsf{Y}_i[a] = \Pi(\textsf{X}_i[a])$. In addition, let $\widetilde{\textsf{Y}}^{\oplus} := (\textsf{Y}_1^{\oplus}, \ldots, \textsf{Y}_q^{\oplus})$, where $\textsf{Y}_i^{\oplus} := \bigoplus_{a \in [q]} \textsf{Y}_i[a] \oplus \textsf{pad}_n(\textsf{M}_i[\ell_i])$ for all $i \in [q]$.
- $\textsf{FlagI} = 0$ for all $\textsf{I} \in \{\textsf{T}, \textsf{Z}, \textsf{Y}\}$.

Note that, $\widetilde{\textsf{X}}$ is completely determined from $\widetilde{\textsf{M}}$. We have included it in the transcript just for the sake of simplicity. From the definition of $\textsf{1k-LightMAC}$, we know that $\Pi(\textsf{Y}_i^{\oplus}) = \textsf{T}_i$ for all $i \in [q]$. So, *in the real world we always have* $(\widetilde{\textsf{X}}, \widetilde{\textsf{Y}}^{\oplus}) \leftrightsquigarrow (\widetilde{\textsf{Y}}, \widetilde{\textsf{T}})$, *i.e.*, $(\widetilde{\textsf{X}}, \widetilde{\textsf{Y}}^{\oplus})$ *is permutation compatible with* $(\widetilde{\textsf{Y}}, \widetilde{\textsf{T}})$. We keep this observation in our mind when we simulate the ideal oracle.

Ideal Oracle: We reuse the variable notations from the real oracle description to represent the ideal oracle transcript $\mathbb{I}$, i.e., $\mathbb{I} := (\widetilde{\textsf{M}}, \widetilde{\textsf{T}}, \widetilde{\textsf{X}}, \widetilde{\textsf{Y}}, \textsf{FlagT}, \textsf{FlagZ}, \textsf{FlagY})$. This should not cause any confusion, as we never consider the random variables $\mathbb{R}$ and $\mathbb{I}$ jointly, whence the probability distributions of the constituent variables will always be clear from the context. The ideal oracle transcript is described in three phases, each contingent on some predicates defined over the previous stages. Specifically, the ideal oracle first initializes $\textsf{FlagT} = 0$, $\textsf{FlagZ} = 0$, $\textsf{FlagY} = 0$, and then follows the sampling mechanism given below:

<u>PHASE I (QUERY-RESPONSE PHASE)</u>: In the query-response phase, the ideal oracle faithfully simulates $\Gamma \leftarrow\!\!\$\ \mathcal{F}(\{0,1\}^{\leq (n-s)2^s}, \{0,1\}^n)$. Formally, for $i \in [q]$, at the i-th query $\textsf{M}_i \in \{0,1\}^{\leq (n-s)2^s}$, the ideal oracle outputs $\textsf{T}_i \leftarrow\!\!\$\ \{0,1\}^n$. The partial transcript generated at the end of the query-response phase is given by $(\widetilde{\textsf{M}}, \widetilde{\textsf{T}}, \widetilde{\textsf{X}})$, where

- $\widetilde{\textsf{M}} = (\textsf{M}_1, \ldots, \textsf{M}_q)$ and $\widetilde{\textsf{T}} = (\textsf{T}_1, \ldots, \textsf{T}_q)$.
- $\widetilde{\textsf{X}} = (\textsf{X}_1, \ldots, \textsf{X}_q)$, where $\textsf{X}_i = (\textsf{X}_i[1], \ldots, \textsf{X}_i[\ell_i - 1])$ and $\textsf{X}_i[a] := \langle a \rangle_s \| \textsf{M}_i[a]$ for all $(i, a) \in [q] \times [\ell_i - 1]$.

Now, we define a predicate on $\widetilde{\mathsf{T}}$:

$$\mathtt{BadT}: \ \exists i \neq j \in [q], \text{ such that } \mathsf{T}_i = \mathsf{T}_j.$$

If BadT is true, then FlagT is set to 1, and $\widetilde{\mathsf{Y}} = (\mathsf{Y}_1, \ldots, \mathsf{Y}_q)$ is defined degenerately: $\mathsf{Y}_i[a] = 0^n$ for all $(i, a) \in [q] \times [\ell_i - 1]$. Otherwise, the ideal oracle proceeds to the next phase.

PHASE II (OFFLINE INITIAL SAMPLING PHASE): Onward, we must have $\mathsf{T}_i \neq \mathsf{T}_j$ whenever $i \neq j$, and $\mathsf{FlagT} = 0$, since this phase is only executed when BadT is false. In the offline phase, the ideal oracle initially makes the following sampling:

$$(\mathsf{R}_{x_1}, \ldots, \mathsf{R}_{x_{\sigma'}}) \leftarrow_{\#} \{0,1\}^n \setminus \widetilde{\mathsf{T}},$$

where $(x_1, \ldots, x_{\sigma'})$ is an arbitrary ordering of the set

$$\mathbb{X}(\widetilde{\mathsf{X}}) := \{x : x = \mathsf{X}_i[a], (i, a) \in [q] \times [\ell_i - 1]\}.$$

Next, the ideal oracle sets

- $\mathsf{Z}_i[a] := \mathsf{R}_x$ if $x = \mathsf{X}_i[a]$, for all $(i, a) \in [q] \times [\ell_i - 1]$, and
- $\mathsf{Z}_i^{\oplus} := \bigoplus_{a=1}^{\ell_i - 1} \mathsf{Z}_i[a] \oplus \mathsf{pad}_n(\mathsf{M}_i[\ell_i])$.

At this stage we have $\mathsf{Z}_i[a] = \mathsf{Z}_j[b]$ if and only if $\mathsf{X}_i[a] = \mathsf{X}_j[b]$. In other words, $\widetilde{\mathsf{X}} \leftrightsquigarrow \widetilde{\mathsf{Z}}$. But *the same might not hold for* $\mathsf{Z}^{\oplus}$ and $\widetilde{\mathsf{T}}$. Now, we define four predicates on $(\widetilde{\mathsf{Z}}, \widetilde{\mathsf{X}})$:

$$\mathtt{BadZ1}: \ \exists i \neq j \in [q], \text{ such that } \mathsf{Z}_i^{\oplus} = \mathsf{Z}_j^{\oplus}.$$

$$\mathtt{BadZ2}: \ \exists (i, a) \in [q] \times [\ell_i - 1], \text{ such that } \mathsf{X}_i[a] = \mathsf{Z}_i^{\oplus}.$$

$$\mathtt{BadZ3}: \ \exists i \neq j \neq k \in [q], a \neq b \in [\ell_i - 1], \text{ such that}$$

$$(\mathsf{X}_i[a] = \mathsf{Z}_j^{\oplus}) \wedge (\mathsf{X}_i[b] = \mathsf{Z}_k^{\oplus}).$$

$$\mathtt{BadZ4}: \ \exists i \neq j \neq k \in [q], a \in [\ell_i - 1], b \in [\ell_j - 1], \text{ such that}$$

$$(\mathsf{X}_i[a] = \mathsf{Z}_j^{\oplus}) \wedge (\mathsf{X}_j[b] = \mathsf{Z}_k^{\oplus}).$$

We write $\mathtt{BadZ} := \mathtt{BadZ1} \vee \mathtt{BadZ2} \vee \mathtt{BadZ3} \vee \mathtt{BadZ4}$. Looking ahead momentarily, BadZ will represent bad scenarios that are difficult to fix in the third stage. For example, BadZ1 leads to permutation incompatibility between $\mathsf{Z}^{\oplus}$ and $\widetilde{\mathsf{T}}$ which is not desirable. We will discuss utility of the other three predicates in the description of next phase.

If BadZ is true, then FlagZ is set to 1, and $\widetilde{\mathsf{Y}} = (\mathsf{Y}_1, \ldots, \mathsf{Y}_q)$ is again defined degenerately, as in the case of BadT. Otherwise, the ideal oracle proceeds to the next phase.

PHASE III (OFFLINE RESETTING PHASE): At this point, we know that BadZ is false. In this phase, we will define the complete transcript generated in the ideal world, i.e., $\mathbb{I}$, by appropriately defining $\widetilde{\mathsf{Y}}$. Remember, our goal is to maintain $(\widetilde{\mathsf{X}}, \widetilde{\mathsf{Y}}^{\oplus}) \leftrightsquigarrow (\widetilde{\mathsf{Y}}, \widetilde{\mathsf{T}})$.

Definition 4.1 (full collision index). *Any query index $i \in [q]$ is called a full collision index if $\exists\ a \in [\ell_i - 1], j \in [q]$ such that $\mathsf{X}_i[a] = \mathsf{Z}_j^{\oplus}$. Additionally, let*

- $\mathcal{I} := \{i \in [q] : \mathsf{Z}_j^{\oplus} = \mathsf{X}_i[a],$ *for some* $a \in [\ell_i - 1], j \in [q]\}$.
- $\mathcal{J} := \{j \in [q] : \mathsf{Z}_j^{\oplus} = \mathsf{X}_i[a]$ *for some* $(i, a) \in [q] \times [\ell_i - 1]\}$.
- $\mathsf{FCT} := \{(i, a, j) : i, j \in [q], a \in [\ell_i - 1]$ *such that* $\mathsf{Z}_j^{\oplus} = \mathsf{X}_i[a]\}$. *Sometimes, we also use* $\widetilde{\mathsf{FCT}} := \{(i, a) \in [q] \times [\ell_i - 1] : \exists j \in [q]$ *such that* $\mathsf{Z}_j^{\oplus} = \mathsf{X}_i[a]\}$.

We refer to $i \in \mathcal{I}$ and $j \in \mathcal{J}$ as full-collision and resetting index, respectively.

Observe that we can simply set $\widetilde{\mathsf{Y}} = \widetilde{\mathsf{Z}}$, whenever $\mathcal{I} = \emptyset$, since $\neg(\mathtt{BadT} \vee \mathtt{BadZ})$ holds. However, we need a more involved method when $\mathcal{I} \neq \emptyset$. Next, we use a novel sampling approach, called *reset-sampling*, in context of the sampling for $\widetilde{\mathsf{Y}}$.

Reset-Sampling: The sampling of $\widetilde{\mathsf{Y}}$ is done in two stages:

STAGE 1: For all $(i, a) \in [q] \times [\ell_i - 1]$, set $\mathsf{Y}_i[a] = \mathsf{Z}_i[a]$.
STAGE 2: For all $(i, a, j) \in \mathsf{FCT}$, *reset* $\mathsf{Y}_i[a] = \mathsf{T}_j$.

Finally, define $\mathsf{Y}^{\oplus} := (\mathsf{Y}_1^{\oplus}, \ldots, \mathsf{Y}_q^{\oplus})$, where $\mathsf{Y}_i^{\oplus} = \bigoplus_{a \in [q]} \mathsf{Y}_i[q] \oplus \mathsf{pad}_n(\mathsf{M}_i[\ell_i])$.

In the second stage, we have reset $\mathsf{Y}_i[a]$ from $\mathsf{Z}_i[a]$ to T_j for all $(i, a, j) \in \mathsf{FCT}$. This fixes the previous inconsistency issue, i.e., $\mathsf{X}_i[a] = \mathsf{Z}_j^{\oplus}$ and $\mathsf{Y}_i[a] \neq \mathsf{T}_j$. Figure 3 gives a pictorial view of this step.

The following must hold due to the condition $\neg\mathtt{BadZ}$:

- For each $(i, a) \in \mathcal{I} \times [\ell_i - 1]$, there is a unique choice for j (if exists) such that $\mathsf{Y}_i[a]$ is reset to T_j. Otherwise, $\neg\mathtt{BadZ1}$ is violated.
- Continuing the previous point, we must have $j \neq i$. Otherwise, $\neg\mathtt{BadZ2}$ is violated. Indeed, $i = j$ incurs a trivial inconsistency: $(\mathsf{Y}_i[a] = \mathsf{T}_i) \wedge (\mathsf{X}_i[a] \neq \mathsf{Y}_i^{\oplus})$ due to the resetting mechanism.
- For each $i \in \mathcal{I}$, there exists at most one $a \in [\ell_i - 1]$, such that $\mathsf{Y}_i[a]$ is reset. Otherwise, $\neg\mathtt{BadZ3}$ is violated.
- For all $j \in \mathcal{J}$, none of the intermediate outputs are reset. Otherwise, $\neg\mathtt{BadZ4}$ is violated.

To summarize, the ideal oracle ensures that for each full collision index at most one intermediate output is reset, and the resetting index is uniquely determined. Further, a full collision index cannot be a resetting index. Thus, $\neg\mathtt{BadZ}$ helps in avoiding trivial inconsistencies as well as keeping the resetting to a minimum. Now, we define two predicates on $(\widetilde{\mathsf{X}}, \widetilde{\mathsf{Z}}, \widetilde{\mathsf{Y}})$:

$$\mathtt{BadY1}: \ \exists i \neq j, k \in [q], \exists a \in [\ell_i - 1], b \in [\ell_k - 1], \text{ such that } (\mathsf{X}_i[a] = \mathsf{Z}_j^{\oplus}) \wedge (\mathsf{Y}_i^{\oplus} = \mathsf{X}_k[b]).$$

$$\mathtt{BadY2}: \ \exists i \neq j \neq k \in [q], \exists a \in [\ell_i - 1], \text{ such that } (\mathsf{X}_i[a] = \mathsf{Z}_j^{\oplus}) \wedge (\mathsf{Y}_i^{\oplus} = \mathsf{Y}_k^{\oplus}).$$

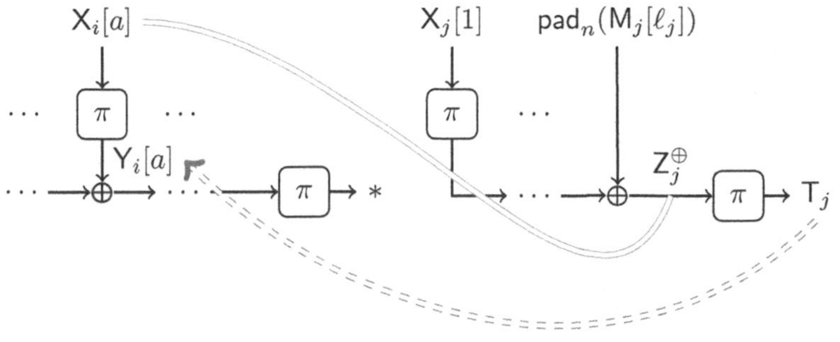

Fig. 3. Resetting of $Y_i[a]$ due to collision $X_i[a] = Z_j^{\oplus}$. The red double line represents a collision arising in phase II sampling. The blue dashed edge represents the corresponding resetting in phase III sampling. (Color figure online)

We write $\mathsf{BadY} := \mathsf{BadY1} \vee \mathsf{BadY2}$. It is easy to see that BadY simply handles the new inconsistencies that may arise due to the reset sampling. For example, BadY1 represents the scenario where resetting leads to collision between intermediate and final inputs. Similarly, BadY2 represents the scenario where resetting leads to collision between two final inputs.

If BadY is true, then FlagY is set to 1, and Y is redefined degenerately, as in the case of BadT and BadZ. At this point, the ideal oracle transcript is completely defined.

Intuitively, if the ideal oracle is not sampling $\widetilde{\mathsf{Y}}$ degenerately at any stage, then we must have $(\widetilde{\mathsf{X}}, \widetilde{\mathsf{Y}}^{\oplus}) \leftrightsquigarrow (\widetilde{\mathsf{Y}}, \widetilde{\mathsf{T}})$. We justify this intuition in the following proposition.

Proposition 4.1. *For* $\neg(\mathsf{BadT} \vee \mathsf{BadZ} \vee \mathsf{BadY})$, *we must have* $(\widetilde{\mathsf{X}}, \widetilde{\mathsf{Y}}^{\oplus}) \leftrightsquigarrow (\widetilde{\mathsf{Y}}, \widetilde{\mathsf{T}})$.

Proof. We have

- $\widetilde{\mathsf{X}} \leftrightsquigarrow \widetilde{\mathsf{Z}}$, by definition of $\widetilde{\mathsf{Z}}$. Moreover the resetting guarantees $\widetilde{\mathsf{Z}} \leftrightsquigarrow \widetilde{\mathsf{Y}}$. Thus, $\widetilde{\mathsf{X}} \leftrightsquigarrow \widetilde{\mathsf{Y}}$.
- We have $\mathsf{Y}_i[a] = \mathsf{T}_j$ if and only if $\mathsf{X}_i[a] = \mathsf{Z}_j^{\oplus}$. Now, $\neg\mathsf{BadZ4}$ implies that $j \notin \mathcal{I}$ thus, $\mathsf{Y}_j^{\oplus} = \mathsf{Z}_j^{\oplus}$. Therefore, $\mathsf{Y}_i[a] = \mathsf{T}_j \Rightarrow \mathsf{X}_i[a] = \mathsf{Y}_j^{\oplus}$. Also, $\mathsf{X}_i[a] = \mathsf{Y}_j^{\oplus}$ implies $j \notin \mathcal{I}$ (due to $\neg\mathsf{BadY1}$), thus, $\mathsf{Z}_j^{\oplus} = \mathsf{Y}_j^{\oplus}$. This gives us $\mathsf{X}_i[a] = \mathsf{Y}_j^{\oplus} \Rightarrow \mathsf{Y}_i[a] = \mathsf{T}_j$ from the second stage sampling of Y. Thus, $\mathsf{X}_i[a] = \mathsf{Y}_j^{\oplus} \Leftrightarrow \mathsf{Y}_i[a] = \mathsf{T}_j$.
- $\neg\mathsf{BadZ} \wedge \neg\mathsf{BadY}$ and definition of Y imply that $\mathsf{Y}_i^{\oplus}$'s are distinct. Also, $\neg\mathsf{BadT}$ implies that T_i's are distinct. Thus $\widetilde{\mathsf{Y}}^{\oplus} \leftrightsquigarrow \widetilde{\mathsf{T}}$.

These observations suffice to conclude that $(\widetilde{\mathsf{X}}, \widetilde{\mathsf{Y}}^{\oplus}) \leftrightsquigarrow (\widetilde{\mathsf{Y}}, \widetilde{\mathsf{T}})$. □

4.2 Transcript Analysis

Set of Transcripts: Given the description of transcript random variable corresponding to the ideal oracle, we can define the set of transcripts $\mathcal{T}$ as the set of all tuples $\tau = (\widetilde{m}, \widetilde{t}, \widetilde{x}, \widetilde{y}, \text{flagT}, \text{flagZ}, \text{flagY})$, where

- $\widetilde{m} = (m_1, \ldots, m_q)$, where $m_i \in \left(\{0,1\}^{\leq (n-s)2^s}\right)$ for $i \in [q]$. For $i \in [q]$, let $\ell_i = \left\lfloor \frac{|m_i|}{n-s} \right\rfloor + 1$.
- $\widetilde{t} = (t_1, \ldots, t_q)$, where $t_i \in \{0,1\}^n$ for $i \in [q]$;
- $\widetilde{x} = (x_1, \ldots, x_q)$, where $x_i = (x_i[1], \ldots, x_i[\ell_i - 1])$ for $i \in [q]$, and $x_i[a] = \langle a \rangle_s \| m_i[a]$ for all $a \in [\ell_i - 1]$;
- $\widetilde{y} = (y_1, \ldots, y_q)$, where $y_i = (y_i[1], \ldots, y_i[\ell_i - 1])$ for $i \in [q]$, and $y_i[a] \in \{0,1\}^n$ for all $a \in [\ell_i - 1]$.
- $\mathrm{flagT}, \mathrm{flagZ}, \mathrm{flagY} \in \{0,1\}$.

Furthermore, the following must always hold:

1. if $\mathrm{flagI} = 1$ for some $\mathrm{I} \in \{\mathrm{T}, \mathrm{Z}, \mathrm{Y}\}$, then $y_i[a] = 0^n$ for all $(i,a) \in [q] \times [\ell_i - 1]$.
2. if $\mathrm{flagT} = 0$, then t_i's are all distinct.
3. if $\mathrm{flagI} = 0$ for all $\mathrm{I} \in \{\mathrm{T}, \mathrm{Z}, \mathrm{Y}\}$, then $(\widetilde{x}, \widetilde{y}^{\oplus}) \leftrightsquigarrow (\widetilde{y}, \widetilde{t})$.

The first two conditions are obvious from the ideal oracle sampling mechanism. The last condition follows from Proposition 4.1 and the observation that in ideal oracle sampling for any $\mathsf{I} \in \{\mathsf{T}, \mathsf{Z}, \mathsf{Y}\}$, $\mathsf{FlagI} = 1$ if and only if BadI is true. Note that, condition 3 is vacuously true for real oracle transcripts.

Bad Transcript: A transcript $\tau \in \mathcal{T}$ is called *bad* if and only if the following predicate is true:

$$(\mathsf{FlagT} = 1) \vee (\mathsf{FlagZ} = 1) \vee (\mathsf{FlagY} = 1).$$

In other words, we term a transcript bad if the ideal oracle sets $\widetilde{\mathrm{Y}}$ degenerately. Let

$$\mathcal{T}_{\mathsf{bad}} := \{\tau \in \mathcal{T} : \tau \text{ is bad.}\}.$$

All other transcript $\tau' = (\widetilde{m}, \widetilde{t}, \widetilde{x}, \widetilde{y}, \mathrm{flagT}, \mathrm{flagZ}, \mathrm{flagY}) \in \mathcal{T} \setminus \mathcal{T}_{\mathsf{bad}}$ are called *good*. From the preceding characterization of the set of transcripts, we conclude that for any good transcript τ', we must have $(\widetilde{x}, \widetilde{y}^{\oplus}) \leftrightsquigarrow (\widetilde{y}, \widetilde{t})$. Henceforth, we drop flagT, flagZ, flagY notations for any good transcript with an implicit understanding that $\mathrm{flagT} = \mathrm{flagZ} = \mathrm{flagY} = 0$.

To apply the H-coefficient theorem we have to upper bound the probability $\Pr[\mathbb{I} \in \mathcal{T}_{\mathsf{bad}}]$ and lower bound the ratio $\Pr[\mathbb{R} = \tau]/\Pr[\mathbb{I} = \tau]$ for any $\tau \in \mathcal{T} \setminus \mathcal{T}_{\mathsf{bad}}$.

Lemma 4.1 (bad transcript analysis). *For $4\ell_{\max} + q \leq 2^{n-1}$, we have*

$$\Pr[\mathbb{I} \in \mathcal{T}_{\mathsf{bad}}] \leq \frac{3q^2}{2^{n+1}} + \frac{2.5q^3\ell_{\max}^2}{2^{2n}} + \frac{4q^3\ell_{\max}}{2^{2n}} + \frac{4q^4\ell_{\max}^2}{2^{3n}} + \frac{2\sigma}{2^n}.$$

The proof of this lemma is postponed to Sect. 4.3.

Good Transcript: Now, fix a good transcript $\tau = (\widetilde{m}, \widetilde{t}, \widetilde{x}, \widetilde{y})$. Let $\sigma' := |\widetilde{x}|$. Since, τ is good, we have $(\widetilde{x}, \widetilde{y}^{\oplus}) \leftrightsquigarrow (\widetilde{y}, \widetilde{t})$. Then, we must have $|\widetilde{y}^{\oplus}| = q$. Further, let $|\widetilde{x} \cap \widetilde{y}^{\oplus}| = r$. Thus, $|\widetilde{x} \cup \widetilde{y}^{\oplus}| = q + \sigma' - r$.

Real World: In the real world, the random permutation Π is sampled on exactly $q + \sigma' - r$ distinct points. Thus, we have

$$\Pr[\mathbb{R} = \tau] = \frac{1}{(2^n)_{q+\sigma'-r}}. \tag{8}$$

Ideal World: Here, the probability computation is slightly involved due to the two stage sampling employed in the ideal oracle. First of all, we have

$$\Pr\left[\widetilde{\mathsf{T}} = \widetilde{t}\right] = \frac{1}{2^{nq}}, \tag{9}$$

since each T_i is sampled uniformly from the set $\{0,1\}^n$ independent of others. Now, observe that all the full collision and resetting indices are fully determined from the transcript τ itself. In other words, we can enumerate the set $\widetilde{\mathsf{FCT}}$. Now, since the transcript is good, we must have $|\widetilde{\mathsf{FCT}}| = |\widetilde{x} \cap \widetilde{y}^{\oplus}| = r$, and for all indices $(i, a) \notin \widetilde{\mathsf{FCT}}$, we have $\mathsf{Y}_i[a] = \mathsf{Z}_i[a]$. Thus, we have

$$\begin{aligned} \Pr\left[\mathsf{Y}_i[a] = y_a^i \wedge (i,a) \notin \widetilde{\mathsf{FCT}} \mid \widetilde{\mathsf{T}} = \widetilde{t}\right] &= \Pr\left[\mathsf{Z}_i[a] = y_a^i \wedge (i,a) \notin \widetilde{\mathsf{FCT}} \mid \widetilde{\mathsf{T}} = \widetilde{t}\right] \\ &= \frac{1}{(2^n - q)_{\sigma'-r}}, \end{aligned} \tag{10}$$

where the second equality follows from the fact that truncation[3] of a without replacement sample from a set of size $(2^n - q)$ is still a without replacement sample from the same set. We have

$$\begin{aligned} \Pr[\mathbb{I} = \omega] &= \Pr\left[\widetilde{\mathsf{T}} = \widetilde{t}\right] \times \Pr\left[\widetilde{\mathsf{Y}} = \widetilde{y} \mid \widetilde{\mathsf{T}} = \widetilde{t}\right] \\ &\leq \frac{1}{2^{nq}} \times \Pr\left[\mathsf{Y}_i[a] - y_i[a] \wedge (i,a) \notin \widetilde{\mathsf{FCT}} \mid \widetilde{\mathsf{T}} = \widetilde{t}\right] \\ &= \frac{1}{2^{nq}} \times \frac{1}{(2^n - q)_{\sigma'-r}}. \end{aligned} \tag{11}$$

The above discussion on good transcripts can be summarized in shape of the following lemma.

Lemma 4.2. *For any $\tau \in \mathcal{T} \setminus \mathcal{T}_{\mathsf{bad}}$, we have*

$$\frac{\Pr[\mathbb{R} = \tau]}{\Pr[\mathbb{I} = \tau]} \geq 1.$$

Proof. The proof follows from dividing Eq. (8) by Eq. (11). □

From H-coefficient Theorem 2.1 and Lemma 4.1 and 4.2, we get

$$\mathbf{Adv}^{\mathsf{prf}}_{\mathsf{1k\text{-}LightMAC}_{\Pi}}(\mathscr{A}) \leq \frac{3q^2}{2^{n+1}} + \frac{2.5q^3\ell_{\max}^2}{2^{2n}} + \frac{4q^3\ell_{\max}}{2^{2n}} + \frac{4q^4\ell_{\max}^2}{2^{3n}} + \frac{2\sigma}{2^n}. \tag{12}$$

Theorem 4.1 follows from Eq. (7) and (12).

[3] Removing some elements from the tuple.

4.3 Proof of Lemma 4.1

We have

$$\begin{aligned}\Pr\left[\mathbb{I} \in \mathcal{T}_{\mathsf{bad}}\right] &= \Pr\left[(\mathsf{FlagT}=1) \vee (\mathsf{FlagZ}=1) \vee (\mathsf{FlagY}=1)\right] \\ &= \Pr\left[\mathtt{BadT} \vee \mathtt{BadZ} \vee \mathtt{BadY}\right] \\ &\leq \Pr\left[\mathtt{BadT}\right] \times \Pr\left[\mathtt{BadZ} \mid \neg\mathtt{BadT}\right] \times \Pr\left[\mathtt{BadY} \mid \neg(\mathtt{BadT} \vee \mathtt{BadZ})\right]\end{aligned}$$

We will handle the three terms on the right hand side separately. Before delving further, we introduce few more notations.

FEW MORE NOTATIONS: For simplicity, we denote the last padded block of any message m_i by $m_i[\ell_i]$ instead of $\mathsf{pad}_n(m_i[\ell_i])$. For any (i, a) with $i \in [q], a \in [\ell_i]$, $\mathsf{Z}_i^{\oplus\setminus a}$ (res. $\mathsf{Y}_i^{\oplus\setminus a}$) denotes $\bigoplus_{b \neq a} \mathsf{Z}_i[b] \oplus m_i[\ell_i]$ (res. $\bigoplus_{b \neq a} \mathsf{Y}_i[b] \oplus m_i[\ell_i]$).

While we bound the probability of bad events, we need to deal with system of equations in Z variables. Note that Z can be viewed as $\Pi(\mathsf{X})$ for the corresponding X variable. We will often employ Lemma 2.1 implicitly (without referring at each application) to bound the probability that these system of equations hold.

1. Bounding $\Pr[\mathtt{BadT}]$: Since, we have at most $\binom{q}{2}$ choice for i, j, and for each such pair, $\mathsf{T}_i = \mathsf{T}_j$ holds with exactly 2^{-n} probability. Thus, we have

$$\Pr\left[\mathtt{BadT}\right] \leq \frac{q^2}{2^{n+1}}. \tag{13}$$

2. Bounding $\Pr[\mathtt{BadZ} \mid \neg\mathtt{BadT}]$: Here, we have four cases.
   (a) $\mathtt{BadZ1}$: $\exists i \neq j \in [q]$, such that $\mathsf{Z}_i^{\oplus} = \mathsf{Z}_j^{\oplus}$. This is similar to $\mathtt{BadT}$ above. We have

$$\Pr\left[\mathtt{BadZ1} \mid \neg\mathtt{BadT}\right] \leq \frac{q^2}{2 \cdot (2^n - q - 2\ell_{\max})}.$$

   (b) $\mathtt{BadZ2}$: $\exists (i, a) \in [q] \times [\ell_i - 1]$, such that $\mathsf{X}_i[a] = \mathsf{Z}_i^{\oplus}$. It is easy to see that

$$\Pr\left[\mathtt{BadZ2} \mid \neg\mathtt{BadT}\right] \leq \sum_{i=1}^{q} \frac{\ell_i - 1}{2^n - q - \ell_{\max}} \leq \frac{\sigma}{2^n - q - \ell_{\max}}.$$

   (c) $\mathtt{BadZ3}$: $\exists i \neq j \neq k \in [q], a, b \in [\ell_i - 1]$, such that $(\mathsf{X}_i[a] = \mathsf{Z}_j^{\oplus}) \wedge (\mathsf{X}_i[b] = \mathsf{Z}_k^{\oplus})$. Here, $j \neq k$ implies that the system of equations has rank 2. Thus, using Lemma 2.1, we have

$$\Pr\left[\mathtt{BadZ3} \mid \neg\mathtt{BadT}\right] \leq \frac{q^3 \ell_{\max}^2}{12(2^n - q - 2\ell_{\max})^2}.$$

   (d) $\mathtt{BadZ4}$: $\exists i \neq j \neq k \in [q], a \in [\ell_i - 1], b \in [\ell_j - 1]$, such that $(\mathsf{X}_i[a] = \mathsf{Z}_j^{\oplus}) \wedge (\mathsf{X}_j[b] = \mathsf{Z}_k^{\oplus})$. Using similar argumentation as above, we have,

$$\Pr\left[\mathtt{BadZ4} \mid \neg\mathtt{BadT}\right] \leq \frac{q^3 \ell_{\max}^2}{12(2^n - q - 2\ell_{\max})^2}.$$

Combining all the four cases and assuming $q + 2\ell_{\max} \leq 2^{n-1}$, we have

$$\Pr[\mathtt{BadZ}|\neg\mathtt{BadT}] \leq \frac{q^2}{2^n} + \frac{0.34q^3\ell_{\max}^2}{2^{2n}} + \frac{2\sigma}{2^n} \tag{14}$$

3. Bounding $\Pr[\mathtt{BadY}|\neg(\mathtt{BadT} \vee \mathtt{BadZ})]$: Here, we have two cases:
   (a) $\mathtt{BadY1}$: $\exists i, j, k \in [q], \exists a \in [\ell_i - 1], b \in [\ell_k - 1]$ such that $(\mathsf{X}_i[a] = \mathsf{Z}_j^{\oplus}) \wedge (\mathsf{Y}_i^{\oplus} = \mathsf{X}_k[b])$. By virtue of resetting mechanism and $\neg\mathtt{BadZ}$, we arrive at an equivalent system of Z-equations

$$\begin{aligned} \mathsf{Z}_j^{\oplus} &= \mathsf{X}_i[a] \\ \mathsf{Z}_i^{\oplus\setminus a} &= \mathsf{X}_k[b] \oplus \mathsf{T}_j \end{aligned}$$

   We claim that the system always has rank 2. This can be argued as follows: Suppose the system has rank less than 2. Then, we must have $\mathsf{Z}_j^{\oplus} \oplus \mathsf{X}_i[a] \oplus \mathsf{Z}_i^{\oplus\setminus a} \oplus \mathsf{X}_k[b] \oplus \mathsf{T}_j = 0^n$. However, $\widetilde{\mathsf{Z}}$ are sampled from $\{0,1\}^n \setminus \widetilde{\mathsf{T}}$. Hence, T_j does not cancel out trivially. So, we must always have rank 2. Now if the rank is 2, then we can always rewrite the system of equations such that we have an equation in T_j and another equation involving some Z variables. Then, the first equation holds with at most $1/2^n$ probability (using the randomness of T_j) and conditioned on this the second equation holds with probability at most $1/(2^n - q - 2\ell_{\max})$. Thus, we have

$$\Pr[\mathtt{BadY1}|\neg(\mathtt{BadT} \vee \mathtt{BadZ})] \leq \frac{q^3\ell_{\max}^2}{2^n(2^n - q - 2\ell_{\max})}.$$

   (b) $\mathtt{BadY2}$: $\exists i, j, k \in [q], \exists a \in [\ell_i - 1]$, such that $(\mathsf{X}_i[a] = \mathsf{Z}_j^{\oplus}) \wedge (\mathsf{Y}_i^{\oplus} = \mathsf{Y}_k^{\oplus})$. Here we get $\mathsf{X}_i[a] = \mathsf{Z}_j^{\oplus} \wedge \mathsf{Z}_i^{\oplus\setminus a} = \mathsf{Y}_k^{\oplus} \oplus \mathsf{T}_j$ which changes according to the following subcases:
   Case A: when $k \notin \mathcal{I}$: Then the above system becomes

$$\begin{aligned} \mathsf{Z}_j^{\oplus} &= \mathsf{X}_i[a] \\ \mathsf{Z}_i^{\oplus\setminus a} &= \mathsf{Z}_k^{\oplus} \oplus \mathsf{T}_j \end{aligned}$$

   Using similar argumentation as before we can conclude that the system has rank 2. Therefore, we have

$$\Pr[\mathtt{BadY2} \wedge \text{Case A}|\neg(\mathtt{BadZ} \vee \mathtt{BadT})] \leq \frac{q^3\ell_{\max}}{(2^n - q - 3\ell_{\max})^2}.$$

   Case B: when $k \in \mathcal{I}$: In this case we have the following system of equations:

$$\begin{aligned} \mathsf{Z}_j^{\oplus} &= \mathsf{X}_i[a] \\ \mathsf{Z}_l^{\oplus} &= \mathsf{X}_k[b] \\ \mathsf{Z}_i^{\oplus\setminus a} \oplus \mathsf{Z}_k^{\oplus\setminus b} &= \mathsf{T}_j \oplus \mathsf{T}_l \end{aligned}$$

We must have $j \neq l$. Otherwise we will have $\mathsf{Z}_i^{\oplus} = \mathsf{Z}_k^{\oplus}$ which again violates $\neg$BadZ. Thus, $j \neq l$. Now, $j \neq l$ and $\neg$BadZ implies that $\mathsf{Z}_j^{\oplus} \neq \mathsf{Z}_l^{\oplus}$. Then, following a similar line of argument as before, we conclude that the system has rank 3. Therefore, we have

$$\Pr\left[\mathtt{BadY2} \wedge \text{Case B} | \neg(\mathtt{BadZ} \vee \mathtt{BadT})\right] \leq \frac{q^4 \ell_{\max}^2}{2^n (2^n - q - 4\ell_{\max})^2}.$$

Combining all the cases with the assumption that $q + 4\ell_{\max} \leq 2^{n-1}$, we have

$$\Pr\left[\mathtt{BadY} | \neg(\mathtt{BadT} \vee \mathtt{BadZ})\right] \leq \frac{2q^3 \ell_{\max}^2}{2^{2n}} + \frac{4q^3 \ell_{\max}}{2^{2n}} + \frac{4q^4 \ell_{\max}^2}{2^{3n}}. \quad (15)$$

The result follows from summing up Eq. (13)–(15). □

5 LightMAC-ds: A Minute Variant of Single-Key LightMAC

In the previous section we showed that single-key LightMAC achieves query-length independent security bounds while $\ell_{\min} \geq 2$ and $\ell_{\max} \leq 2^{n/4}$. Now, we propose a simple variant of LightMAC that achieves query-length independent security unconditionally.

5.1 Description of LightMAC-ds

For any $x \in \{0,1\}^n$ and $k < n$, let $\mathsf{chop}_k(x)$ denote the most significant $n - k$ bits of x. The complete algorithmic description of LightMAC-ds is given in Algorithm 5.1.

Algorithm 5.1. LightMAC-ds based on an n-bit block cipher E instantiated with a single key K. Here the counter size is $s - 1$. Highlighted lines point to the algorithmic differences with the LightMAC algorithm.

function $\mathsf{LightMAC\text{-}ds}_{E_K}(m)$
  $y^{\oplus} \leftarrow 0^n$
  $(m[1], \ldots, m[\ell]) \xleftarrow{n-s} m$
  for $i = 1$ **to** $\ell - 1$ **do**
    $x[i] \leftarrow 0 \| \langle i \rangle_{s-1} \| m[i]$ ▷ encoding $\langle i \rangle_{s-1}$ and $m[i]$ into $x[i]$
    $y[i] \leftarrow E_K(x[i])$ ▷ encrypting the encoded input
    $y^{\oplus} \leftarrow y^{\oplus} \oplus y[i]$ ▷ accumulating the intermediate output
  end for
  $y^{\oplus} \leftarrow y^{\oplus} \oplus \mathsf{pad}_n(m[\ell])$
  $t \leftarrow E_K(1 \| \mathsf{chop}_1(y^{\oplus}))$
  return t
end function

It is clear from the description that LightMAC-ds uses the familiar technique of domain separation to generate two "almost independent" instances of E. Specifically, we fix the most significant 1-bit of the block cipher input to

- 0 in the processing of encoded message blocks (see line no. 5 in Algorithm 5.1).
- 1 in the tag generation call (see line no. 10 in Algorithm 5.1).

Since 1-bit is reserved for domain separation, the effective counter size is reduced to $s-1$ for some global parameter $s < n$. Thus, the maximum message length can be at most $(n-s)2^{s-1}$, which is a slight drop from $(n-s)2^s$ in case of LightMAC, for large value of n and s.

5.2 Security of LightMAC-ds

Surprisingly (or not), the security argument for LightMAC-ds is quite similar to the one for single-key LightMAC. In fact, it is slightly easy to argue the security here, as we have already ensured $\neg$`Icoll` (see Sect. 3.2) by the virtue of domain separation. However, we still have to handle `Ocoll` (see Sect. 3.2) which would require a slight care while sampling the intermediate outputs in the ideal world. Note that, such complications do not arise in case of LightMAC for the obvious reason of independence between the primitives used to generate the intermediate and final outputs. The PRF security of LightMAC-ds is presented in Theorem 5.1.

Theorem 5.1. *Let $q, \ell_{\max}, T > 0$. For $q + 2\ell_{\max} \leq 2^{n-1}$, the PRF security of $\mathscr{A}$ against $\mathbb{A}(q,T)$ is given by*

$$\mathbf{Adv}^{\mathsf{prf}}_{\mathsf{LightMAC\text{-}ds}}(q,T) \leq \mathbf{Adv}^{\mathsf{prp}}_{E}(\sigma+q,T') + \frac{2.5q^2}{2^n},$$

where ℓ denotes an upper bound on the number of blocks in any padded query, $T' = T + O(T_E)$ and T_E denotes the runtime of E.

As expected, the proof is quite similar and a bit easier than the proof of Theorem 4.1. As the first step, we apply the hybrid argument to get

$$\mathbf{Adv}^{\mathsf{prf}}_{\mathsf{LightMAC\text{-}ds}}(q,T) \leq \mathbf{Adv}^{\mathsf{prp}}_{E}(\sigma+q,T') + \mathbf{Adv}^{\mathsf{prf}}_{\mathsf{LightMAC\text{-}ds}_\Pi}(q,\infty). \tag{16}$$

We are interested in a bound on the PRF security of LightMAC-ds$_\Pi$, henceforth also referred as the real oracle. Fix any $\mathscr{A} \in \mathbb{A}(q,\infty)$ such that

$$\mathbf{Adv}^{\mathsf{prf}}_{\mathsf{LightMAC\text{-}ds}_\Pi}(q,\infty) = \mathbf{Adv}^{\mathsf{prf}}_{\mathsf{LightMAC\text{-}ds}_\Pi}(\mathscr{A}).$$

Going forward, we will bound the advantage of $\mathscr{A}$ using H-coefficient technique.

5.3 Description of Oracles and Their Transcripts

Real Oracle: The real oracle is defined analogously as in the proof of Theorem 5.1. We describe it just for the sake of completeness. The real oracle faithfully responds to all the queries made by $\mathscr{A}$. Once the query-response phase is over, it releases all the intermediate inputs and outputs to $\mathscr{A}$. Additionally, the real oracle releases two binary flags, FlagT and FlagZ, that are degenerately set to 0. Formally, we have

$$\mathbb{R} := (\widetilde{\mathsf{M}}, \widetilde{\mathsf{T}}, \widetilde{\mathsf{X}}, \widetilde{\mathsf{Y}}, \mathsf{FlagT}, \mathsf{FlagZ}),$$

where

- $\widetilde{\mathsf{M}} = (\mathsf{M}_1, \ldots, \mathsf{M}_q)$ denotes the q-tuple of queries made by $\mathscr{A}$, where $\mathsf{M}_i \in \{0,1\}^{\leq (n-s)2^{s-1}}$ for all $i \in [q]$. In addition, for all $i \in [q]$, let $\ell_i := \lfloor \frac{|\mathsf{M}_i|}{n-s} \rfloor + 1$.
- $\widetilde{\mathsf{T}} = (\mathsf{T}_1, \ldots, \mathsf{T}_q)$ denotes the q-tuple of final outputs received by $\mathscr{A}$, where $\mathsf{T}_i \in \{0,1\}^n$.
- $\widetilde{\mathsf{X}} = (\mathsf{X}_1, \ldots, \mathsf{X}_q)$, where X_i denotes the intermediate input tuple for the i-th query, i.e., for all $a \in [\ell_i - 1]$, $\mathsf{X}_i[a] = 0\|\langle a \rangle_{s-1}\|\mathsf{M}_i[a]$.
- $\widetilde{\mathsf{Y}} = (\mathsf{Y}_1, \ldots, \mathsf{Y}_q)$, where Y_i denotes the intermediate output tuple for the i-th query, i.e., for all $a \in [\ell_i - 1]$, $\mathsf{Y}_i[a] = \Pi(\mathsf{X}_i[a])$. In addition, let $\widetilde{\mathsf{Y}}^{\oplus} := (\mathsf{Y}_1^{\oplus}, \ldots, \mathsf{Y}_q^{\oplus})$, where $\mathsf{Y}_i^{\oplus} := \bigoplus_{a \in [\ell_i - 1]} \mathsf{Y}_i[a] \oplus \mathsf{pad}_n(\mathsf{M}_i[\ell_i])$ for all $i \in [q]$.
- $\mathsf{FlagT} = \mathsf{FlagZ} = 0$.

Let $\mathsf{chop}_1(\widetilde{\mathsf{Y}}^{\oplus}) = (1\|\mathsf{chop}_1(\mathsf{Y}_i[1]), \ldots, 1\|\mathsf{chop}_1(\mathsf{Y}_i[\ell_i - 1]))$. It is straightforward to see that in the real world we always have $(\widetilde{\mathsf{X}}, \mathsf{chop}_1(\widetilde{\mathsf{Y}}^{\oplus})) \leftrightsquigarrow (\widetilde{\mathsf{Y}}, \widetilde{\mathsf{T}})$, i.e., $(\widetilde{\mathsf{X}}, \mathsf{chop}_1(\widetilde{\mathsf{Y}}^{\oplus}))$ is permutation compatible with $(\widetilde{\mathsf{Y}}, \widetilde{\mathsf{T}})$.

Ideal Oracle: We reuse the notations from real oracle description to represent the variables in the ideal oracle transcript $\mathbb{I}$, i.e.

$$\mathbb{I} := (\widetilde{\mathsf{M}}, \widetilde{\mathsf{T}}, \widetilde{\mathsf{X}}, \widetilde{\mathsf{Y}}, \mathsf{FlagT}, \mathsf{FlagZ}).$$

The ideal oracle transcript is described in two phases, with the second one contingent on some predicate defined over the first stage. Specifically, the ideal oracle initializes $\mathsf{FlagT} = \mathsf{FlagZ} = 0$, and then follows the sampling mechanism given below:

<u>Phase I (Query-Response Phase)</u>: In the query-response phase, the ideal oracle faithfully simulates $\Gamma \leftarrow\!\!\$\, \mathcal{F}(\{0,1\}^{\leq (n-s)2^{s-1}}, \{0,1\}^n)$. Formally, for $i \in [q]$, at the i-th query $\mathsf{M}_i \in \{0,1\}^{\leq (n-s)2^{s-1}}$, the ideal oracle outputs $\mathsf{T}_i \leftarrow\!\!\$\, \{0,1\}^n$. The partial transcript generated at the end of the query-response phase is given by $(\widetilde{\mathsf{M}}, \widetilde{\mathsf{T}}, \widetilde{\mathsf{X}})$, where

- $\widetilde{\mathsf{M}} = (\mathsf{M}_1, \ldots, \mathsf{M}_q)$ and $\widetilde{\mathsf{T}} = (\mathsf{T}_1, \ldots, \mathsf{T}_q)$.
- $\widetilde{\mathsf{X}} = (\mathsf{X}_1, \ldots, \mathsf{X}_q)$, where $\mathsf{X}_i = (\mathsf{X}_i[1], \ldots, \mathsf{X}_i[\ell_i - 1])$ and $\mathsf{X}_i[a] := 0\|\langle a \rangle_{s-1}\|\mathsf{M}_i[a]$ for all $(i, a) \in [q] \times [\ell_i - 1]$.

Now, we define a predicate on $\widetilde{\mathsf{T}}$:

$$\mathtt{BadT}: \ \exists i \neq j \in [q], \text{ such that } \mathsf{T}_i = \mathsf{T}_j.$$

If $\mathtt{BadT}$ is true, then $\mathsf{FlagT} = 1$, and $\widetilde{\mathsf{Y}} = (\mathsf{Y}_1, \ldots, \mathsf{Y}_q)$ is defined degenerately: $\mathsf{Y}_i[a] = 0^n$ for all $(i,a) \in [q] \times [\ell_i - 1]$. Otherwise, the ideal oracle proceeds to the next phase.

PHASE II (OFFLINE SAMPLING PHASE): In the offline phase, the ideal oracle initially makes the following sampling:

$$(\mathsf{R}_{x_1}, \ldots, \mathsf{R}_{x_t}) \leftarrow_{\#} \{0,1\}^n \setminus \widetilde{\mathsf{T}},$$

where $(x_1, \ldots, x_t)$ is an arbitrary ordering of the set

$$\mathbb{X}(\widetilde{\mathsf{X}}) := \{x : x = \mathsf{X}_i[a], (i,a) \in [q] \times [\ell_i - 1]\}.$$

Next, the ideal oracle sets

- $\mathsf{Z}_i[a] := \mathsf{R}_x$ if $x = \mathsf{X}_i[a]$, for all $(i,a) \in [q] \times [\ell_i - 1]$, and
- $\mathsf{Z}_i^{\oplus} := \bigoplus_{a=1}^{\ell_i - 1} \mathsf{Z}_i[a] \oplus \mathsf{pad}_n(\mathsf{M}_i[\ell_i])$.

At this stage we have $\mathsf{Z}_i[a] = \mathsf{Z}_j[b]$ if and only if $\mathsf{X}_i[a] = \mathsf{X}_j[b]$. In other words, $\widetilde{\mathsf{X}} \leftrightsquigarrow \widetilde{\mathsf{Z}}$. But *the same might not hold for* $\mathsf{chop}_1(\widetilde{\mathsf{Z}}^{\oplus})$ *and* $\widetilde{\mathsf{T}}$. Now, we define a predicate on $(\widetilde{\mathsf{Z}}, \widetilde{\mathsf{X}})$:

$$\mathtt{BadZ}: \ \exists i \neq j \in [q], \text{ such that } \mathsf{chop}_1(\mathsf{Z}_i^{\oplus}) = \mathsf{chop}_1(\mathsf{Z}_j^{\oplus}).$$

Note that, $\neg\mathtt{BadZ}$ ensures $\mathsf{chop}_1(\widetilde{\mathsf{Z}}^{\oplus}) \leftrightsquigarrow \widetilde{\mathsf{T}}$, that when coupled with the $\widetilde{\mathsf{X}} \leftrightsquigarrow \widetilde{\mathsf{Z}}$ due to the sampling mechanism ensures $(\widetilde{\mathsf{X}}, \mathsf{chop}_1(\widetilde{\mathsf{Z}}^{\oplus})) \leftrightsquigarrow (\widetilde{\mathsf{Z}}, \widetilde{\mathsf{T}})$. Intuitively, this makes the ideal world almost similar to the real world.

If $\mathtt{BadZ}$ is true, then $\mathsf{FlagZ} = 1$, and $\widetilde{\mathsf{Y}} := (\mathsf{Y}_1, \ldots, \mathsf{Y}_q)$ is again defined degenerately, as in the case of $\mathtt{BadT}$. Otherwise, $\widetilde{\mathsf{Y}} := \widetilde{\mathsf{Z}}$. At this point, the transcript random variable for the ideal world is completely determined.

5.4 Transcript Analysis

SET OF TRANSCRIPTS: Given the description of the transcript random variable corresponding to the ideal oracle, we can define the set of transcripts $\mathcal{T}$ as the set of all tuples $\tau = (\widetilde{m}, \widetilde{t}, \widetilde{x}, \widetilde{y}, \text{flagT}, \text{flagZ})$, where

- $\widetilde{m} = (m_1, \ldots, m_q)$, where $m_i \in \left(\{0,1\}^{\leq (n-s)2^{s-1}}\right)$ for $i \in [q]$. Let $\ell_i = \lfloor \frac{|m_i|}{n-s} \rfloor + 1$ for $i \in [q]$.
- $\widetilde{t} = (t_1, \ldots, t_q)$, where $t_i \in \{0,1\}^n$ for $i \in [q]$;
- $\widetilde{x} = (x_1, \ldots, x_q)$, where $x_i = (x_i[1], \ldots, x_i[\ell_i - 1])$ for $i \in [q]$, and $x_i[a] = 0\|\langle a \rangle_{s-1}\|m_i[a]$ for all $a \in [\ell_i - 1]$;

- $\widetilde{y} = (y_1, \ldots, y_q)$, where $y_i = (y_i[1], \ldots, y_i[\ell_i - 1])$ for $i \in [q]$, and $y_i[a] \in \{0,1\}^n$ for all $a \in [\ell_i - 1]$.
- flagT, flagZ $\in \{0,1\}$.

Furthermore, the following must always hold:

1. if flagI $= 1$ for some I $\in \{\mathrm{T}, \mathrm{Z}\}$, then $y_i[a] = 0^n$ for all $(i,a) \in [q] \times [\ell_i - 1]$.
2. if flagT $= 0$, then t_i's are all distinct.
3. if flagI $= 0$ for all I $\in \{\mathrm{T}, \mathrm{Z}\}$, then $(\widetilde{x}, \mathsf{chop}_1(\widetilde{\mathsf{Y}}^{\oplus})) \leftrightsquigarrow (\widetilde{y}, \widetilde{t})$.

Bad Transcript: A transcript $\tau \in \mathcal{T}$ is called *bad* if and only if the following predicate is true:

$$(\mathsf{FlagT} = 1) \vee (\mathsf{FlagZ} = 1).$$

In other words, we term a transcript bad if the ideal oracle sets $\widetilde{\mathsf{Y}}$ degenerately. Let

$$\mathcal{T}_{\mathsf{bad}} := \{\tau \in \mathcal{T} : \tau \text{ is bad.}\}.$$

All other transcript $\tau' = (\widetilde{m}, \widetilde{t}, \widetilde{x}, \widetilde{y}, \text{flagT}, \text{flagZ}) \in \mathcal{T} \setminus \mathcal{T}_{\mathsf{bad}}$ are called *good*. It is pretty straightforward to deduce that for any good transcript we must have $(\widetilde{x}, \mathsf{chop}_1(\widetilde{y}^{\oplus})) \leftrightsquigarrow (\widetilde{y}, \widetilde{t})$.

Lemma 5.1 (bad transcript analysis). *For $q + 2\ell_{\max} \leq 2^{n-1}$, we have*

$$\Pr[\mathbb{I} \in \mathcal{T}_{\mathsf{bad}}] \leq \frac{2.5q^2}{2^n}.$$

Proof. We have

$$\begin{aligned}\Pr[\mathbb{I} \in \mathcal{T}_{\mathsf{bad}}] &= \Pr[(\mathsf{FlagT} = 1) \vee (\mathsf{FlagZ} = 1)] \\ &= \Pr[\mathsf{BadT} \vee \mathsf{BadZ}] \\ &\leq \Pr[\mathsf{BadT}] \times \Pr[\mathsf{BadZ} | \mathsf{BadT}].\end{aligned}$$

We will handle the two terms on the right hand side separately:

1. Bounding $\Pr[\mathsf{BadT}]$: Since, we have at most $\binom{q}{2}$ choice for i, j, and for each such pair, $\mathsf{T}_i = \mathsf{T}_j$ holds with exactly 2^{-n} probability. Thus, we have

$$\Pr[\mathsf{BadT}] \leq \frac{q^2}{2^{n+1}}. \tag{17}$$

2. Bounding $\Pr[\mathsf{BadZ} | \neg\mathsf{BadT}]$: Fix two indices $i \neq j$. Now, we can have two cases:
   (a) $\ell_i = \ell_j$: Since $\mathsf{M}_i \neq \mathsf{M}_j$, we must have at least one index a, such that $\mathsf{M}_i[a] \neq \mathsf{M}_j[a]$, which implies that $\mathsf{X}_i[a] \neq \mathsf{X}_j[a]$. Further, note that $\mathsf{X}_i[a] \neq \mathsf{X}_k[b]$ for all $(k,b) \in \{i,j\} \times [\ell_k - 1]$. Then, by conditioning on the value of $\mathsf{Z}_k[b]$ for all $(k,b) \in \{i,j\} \times [\ell_k - 1] \setminus \{(i,a)\}$, we bound the probability that $\mathsf{chop}_1(\mathsf{Z}_i^{\oplus}) = \mathsf{chop}_1(\mathsf{Z}_i^{\oplus})$ to at most $2/(2^n - q - 2\ell_{\max})$, where the factor of 2 in the numerator is due to 1-bit chopping. There are at most $\binom{q}{2}$ choices for i, j, so in this case the probability is at most $q^2/(2^n - q - 2\ell_{\max})$.

(b) $\ell_i \neq \ell_j$: Without loss of generality we assume that $\ell_i > \ell_j$. Then, applying exactly the same argumentation as used in the preceding case with $(i, a) = (i, \ell_i - 1)$, we can bound the probability in this case to at most $q^2/(2^n - q - 2\ell_{\max})$.

Since the two cases are mutually exclusive, we have

$$\Pr[\mathsf{BadZ}|\neg\mathsf{BadT}] \leq \frac{q^2}{(2^n - q - 2\ell_{\max})}. \tag{18}$$

The result follows by summing up Eq. (17) and (18) and using $q + 2\ell_{\max} \leq 2^{n-1}$. □

Good Transcript: Fix a good transcript $\tau = (\widetilde{m}, \widetilde{t}, \widetilde{x}, \widetilde{y}, 0, 0)$. Let $\sigma' := |\widetilde{x}|$. Since, τ is good, we have $(\widetilde{x}, \mathsf{chop}_1(\widetilde{y}^{\oplus})) \leftrightsquigarrow (\widetilde{y}, \widetilde{t})$. Then, we must have $|\mathsf{chop}_1(\widetilde{y}^{\oplus})| = q$. Further, $\widetilde{x} \cap \mathsf{chop}_1(\widetilde{y}^{\oplus}) = \emptyset$ due to domain separation. Thus, $|\widetilde{x} \cup \mathsf{chop}_1(\widetilde{y}^{\oplus})| = q + \sigma'$.

Real World: In the real world, the random permutation Π is sampled on exactly $q + \sigma'$ distinct points. Thus, we have

$$\Pr[\mathbb{R} = \tau] = \frac{1}{(2^n)_{q+\sigma'}}. \tag{19}$$

Ideal World: In the ideal world, first $\widetilde{\mathsf{T}}$ is sampled in with replacement fashion from a set of size 2^n. Then, exactly σ' values are sampled corresponding to $\widetilde{\mathsf{Y}}$ in without replacement fashion from a set of size $2^n - q$. Thus, we have

$$\Pr[\mathbb{I} = \tau] = \frac{1}{2^{nq}} \times \frac{1}{(2^n - q)_{\sigma'}}. \tag{20}$$

On dividing Eq. (19) by (20), we get

$$\frac{\Pr[\mathbb{R} = \tau]}{\Pr[\mathbb{I} = \tau]} \geq 1.$$

From H-coefficient Theorem 2.1 and Lemma 5.1, we get

$$\mathbf{Adv}^{\mathsf{prf}}_{\mathsf{LightMAC\text{-}ds}_{\Pi}}(\mathscr{A}) \leq \frac{2.5q^2}{2^n}. \tag{21}$$

Theorem 5.1 follows from Eq. (16) and (21).

6 Conclusion

In this paper we studied the single-key instance of LightMAC, an ISO/IEC standard for lightweight message authentication codes. Our main contribution is a query-length independent security bound for 1k-LightMAC. Specifically, we showed that 1k-LightMAC achieves PRF security bound of $O(q^2/2^n)$ while $(n-s) \leq \ell \leq (n-s)\min\{2^{n/4}, 2^s\}$. Further, we proposed a slight variant of LightMAC, called LightMAC-ds that achieves security bound of $O(q^2/2^n)$ while $\ell \leq (n-s)2^{s-1}$.

6.1 Future Directions in Reset-Sampling

To prove the security of 1k-LightMAC, we used a novel sampling approach, called reset-sampling, that works as a subroutine within the H-coefficient proof setup. Although this approach is at a very nascent stage, we believe that reset-sampling could potentially be useful in deriving better security bounds for other single-key constructions. Indeed, OMAC [10] – another popular and standardized MAC algorithm – has a similar bottleneck as 1k-LightMAC, and might benefit from this sampling approach. In the following, we briefly discuss a possible reset-sampling approach for query-length independent security bounds for OMAC.

A simplified variant of OMAC for any message $m \in (\{0,1\}^n)^\ell$ can be defined as follows: $y[0] := 0^n$; for $1 \leq i \leq \ell - 1$, $x[i] = m[i] \oplus y[i-1]$ and $y[i] = E_K(x[i])$; $x[\ell] = m[\ell] \oplus y[\ell - 1] \oplus 2E_K(0^n)$; and $\mathsf{OMAC}_{E_K}(m) := y[\ell] = E_K(x[\ell])$.

For all $i \in [\ell - 1]$, $x[i]$ and $y[i]$ are referred as intermediate input and output, respectively, and $x[\ell]$ and $y[\ell]$ are referred as the final input and output respectively.

Suppose the adversary makes q queries. Given our analysis of 1k-LightMAC, it is easy to observe that the most contentious issue is the event when some intermediate input (res. output) collides with some final input (res. output). Intuitively, this leads to a leakage of internal values to the adversary. However, notice that this does not necessarily mean that the adversary can actually detect and exploit this to mount an attack. This is precisely the point where reset-sampling can help. As an example, consider the following sampling approach in the ideal world:

- The ideal oracle faithfully answers the q queries in the online phase.
- Once the query-response phase is over:
  - The ideal oracle samples the intermediate inputs/outputs by following the OMAC definition, except for one small change: the intermediate outputs are sampled outside the set of all final outputs. This helps in avoiding collisions between some intermediate output and some final output.
  - Now, we may have a situation where some intermediate input $x_i[a]$ collides with some final input $x_j[\ell_j]$, which is an inconsistency.
  - However, if $x_i[a+1]$ is fresh, i.e., it does not collide with any other intermediate/final input, then we can possibly reset $y_i[a]$ to $y_j[\ell_j]$ and redefine $x_i[a+1] := x'_i[a+1] = m_i[a+1] \oplus y_j[\ell_j]$.
  - This might result in a collision of the form $x'_i[a+1] = x_k[b]$, but as we have seen in case of 1k-LightMAC, the probability of such collisions are easily bounded to $O(q^3\ell^2/2^{2n})$ by considering the compound event $x_i[a] = x_j[\ell_j] \cap x'_i[a+1] = x_k[b]$. There will be some more inconsistencies arising due to the resetting. But we ignore them for the sake of brevity.
  - Finally, the ideal oracle releases the intermediate inputs and outputs.

A more formal and rigorous analysis of OMAC using reset-sampling will most probably require handling of several other bad events, and could be an interesting future research topic. Although the above description is very succinct and rough, it is expressive enough to demonstrate the idea of resetting. The technique is particularly useful for deriving improved bounds for single-key constructions, as demonstrated for 1k-LightMAC and outlined for OMAC. Interestingly, the dominating term in the bound of 1k-LightMAC is the collision probability. Indeed, the bad events introduced due to reset sampling only contribute beyond-the-birthday bound terms. In fact, this seems to be a general characteristic of reset sampling based proof, as the additional bad events are generally joint events involving two or more sources of randomness. Consequently, we believe that reset sampling may, in future, find wide applications in the analysis of single-key variant of BBB secure constructions, such as LightMAC+ [25], PMAC+ [21] etc.

References

1. CAESAR: Competition for authenticated encryption: security, applicability and robustness. Online Webpage (2014)
2. NIST: Lightweight cryptography standardization project. Online Webpage (2018)
3. 27, I.J.S.: Information technology – lightweight cryptography – part 6: Message authentication codes (MACs). ISO/IEC 29192-6, International Organization for Standardization (2019)
4. Luykx, A., Preneel, B., Tischhauser, E., Yasuda, K.: A MAC mode for lightweight block ciphers. In: Peyrin, T. (ed.) FSE 2016. LNCS, vol. 9783, pp. 43–59. Springer, Heidelberg (2016). https://doi.org/10.1007/978-3-662-52993-5_3
5. Tsudik, G.: Message authentication with one-way hash functions. In: Proceedings of the IEEE - INFOCOM 1992, pp. 2055–2059 (1992)
6. Mouha, N.: Chaskey: a MAC algorithm for microcontrollers - status update and proposal of Chaskey-12. IACR Cryptol. ePrint Arch. **2015**, 1182 (2015)
7. Bellare, M., Guérin, R., Rogaway, P.: XOR MACs: new methods for message authentication using finite pseudorandom functions. In: Coppersmith, D. (ed.) CRYPTO 1995. LNCS, vol. 963, pp. 15–28. Springer, Heidelberg (1995). https://doi.org/10.1007/3-540-44750-4_2
8. Bernstein, D.J.: How to stretch random functions: the security of protected counter sums. J. Cryptol. **12**(3), 185–192 (1999)
9. Dutta, A., Jha, A., Nandi, M.: A new look at counters: don't run like marathon in a hundred meter race. IEEE Trans. Comput. **66**(11), 1851–1864 (2017)
10. Iwata, T., Kurosawa, K.: OMAC: one-key CBC MAC. In: Johansson, T. (ed.) FSE 2003. LNCS, vol. 2887, pp. 129–153. Springer, Heidelberg (2003). https://doi.org/10.1007/978-3-540-39887-5_11
11. Black, J., Rogaway, P.: A block-cipher mode of operation for parallelizable message authentication. In: Knudsen, L.R. (ed.) EUROCRYPT 2002. LNCS, vol. 2332, pp. 384–397. Springer, Heidelberg (2002). https://doi.org/10.1007/3-540-46035-7_25
12. Goldreich, O., Goldwasser, S., Micali, S.: How to construct random functions (extended abstract). In: Proceedings of the Symposium on Foundations of Computer Science - FOCS 1984, pp. 464–479 (1984)
13. Bellare, M., Goldreich, O., Mityagin, A.: The power of verification queries in message authentication and authenticated encryption. IACR Cryptol. ePrint Arch. **2004**, 309 (2004)
14. Yasuda, K.: PMAC with parity: minimizing the query-length influence. In: Dunkelman, O. (ed.) CT-RSA 2012. LNCS, vol. 7178, pp. 203–214. Springer, Heidelberg (2012). https://doi.org/10.1007/978-3-642-27954-6_13

15. Naito, Y.: The exact security of PMAC with two powering-up masks. IACR Trans. Symmetric Cryptol. **2019**(2), 125–145 (2019)
16. Ehrsam, W.F., Meyer, C.H.W., Smith, J.L., Tuchman, W.L.: Message verification and transmission error detection by block chaining. Patent 4074066, USPTO (1976)
17. Black, J., Rogaway, P.: CBC MACs for arbitrary-length messages: the three-key constructions. In: Bellare, M. (ed.) CRYPTO 2000. LNCS, vol. 1880, pp. 197–215. Springer, Heidelberg (2000). https://doi.org/10.1007/3-540-44598-6_12
18. Bellare, M., Kilian, J., Rogaway, P.: The security of cipher block chaining. In: Desmedt, Y.G. (ed.) CRYPTO 1994. LNCS, vol. 839, pp. 341–358. Springer, Heidelberg (1994). https://doi.org/10.1007/3-540-48658-5_32
19. Berendschot, A., et al.: Final Report of RACE Integrity Primitives. Lecture Notes in Computer Science, vol. 1007. Springer, Heidelberg (1995)
20. Yasuda, K.: The sum of CBC MACs is a secure PRF. In: Pieprzyk, J. (ed.) CT-RSA 2010. LNCS, vol. 5985, pp. 366–381. Springer, Heidelberg (2010). https://doi.org/10.1007/978-3-642-11925-5_25
21. Yasuda, K.: A new variant of PMAC: beyond the birthday bound. In: Rogaway, P. (ed.) CRYPTO 2011. LNCS, vol. 6841, pp. 596–609. Springer, Heidelberg (2011). https://doi.org/10.1007/978-3-642-22792-9_34
22. Zhang, L., Wu, W., Sui, H., Wang, P.: 3kf9: enhancing 3GPP-MAC beyond the birthday bound. In: Wang, X., Sako, K. (eds.) ASIACRYPT 2012. LNCS, vol. 7658, pp. 296–312. Springer, Heidelberg (2012). https://doi.org/10.1007/978-3-642-34961-4_19
23. Zhang, Y.: Using an error-correction code for fast, beyond-birthday-bound authentication. In: Nyberg, K. (ed.) CT-RSA 2015. LNCS, vol. 9048, pp. 291–307. Springer, Cham (2015). https://doi.org/10.1007/978-3-319-16715-2_16
24. Datta, N., Dutta, A., Nandi, M., Paul, G., Zhang, L.: Single key variant of PMAC_Plus. IACR Trans. Symmetric Cryptol. **2017**(4), 268–305 (2017)
25. Naito, Y.: Blockcipher-based MACs: beyond the birthday bound without message length. In: Takagi, T., Peyrin, T. (eds.) ASIACRYPT 2017. LNCS, vol. 10626, pp. 446–470. Springer, Cham (2017). https://doi.org/10.1007/978-3-319-70700-6_16
26. Wegman, M.N., Carter, L.: New classes and applications of hash functions. In: Proceedings of the Symposium on Foundations of Computer Science - FOCS 1979, pp. 175–182 (1979)
27. Bellare, M., Pietrzak, K., Rogaway, P.: Improved security analyses for CBC MACs. In: Shoup, V. (ed.) CRYPTO 2005. LNCS, vol. 3621, pp. 527–545. Springer, Heidelberg (2005). https://doi.org/10.1007/11535218_32
28. NIST: Announcing the Advanced Encryption Standard (AES). FIPS 197, National Institute of Standards and Technology, U.S. Department of Commerce (2001)
29. Fischlin, M., Lehmann, A., Ristenpart, T., Shrimpton, T., Stam, M., Tessaro, S.: Random oracles with(out) programmability. In: Abe, M. (ed.) ASIACRYPT 2010. LNCS, vol. 6477, pp. 303–320. Springer, Heidelberg (2010). https://doi.org/10.1007/978-3-642-17373-8_18
30. Patarin, J.: Etude des Générateurs de Permutations Pseudo-aléatoires Basés sur le Schéma du DES. Ph.D. thesis, Université de Paris (1991)
31. Patarin, J.: The "coefficients H" technique. In: Avanzi, R.M., Keliher, L., Sica, F. (eds.) SAC 2008. LNCS, vol. 5381, pp. 328–345. Springer, Heidelberg (2009). https://doi.org/10.1007/978-3-642-04159-4_21
32. Hoang, V.T., Tessaro, S.: Key-alternating ciphers and key-length extension: exact bounds and multi-user security. In: Robshaw, M., Katz, J. (eds.) CRYPTO 2016. LNCS, vol. 9814, pp. 3–32. Springer, Heidelberg (2016). https://doi.org/10.1007/978-3-662-53018-4_1

33. Jha, A., Nandi, M.: Revisiting structure graphs: applications to CBC-MAC and EMAC. J. Math. Cryptol. **10**(3–4), 157–180 (2016)
34. Minematsu, K., Matsushima, T.: New bounds for PMAC, TMAC, and XCBC. In: Biryukov, A. (ed.) FSE 2007. LNCS, vol. 4593, pp. 434–451. Springer, Heidelberg (2007). https://doi.org/10.1007/978-3-540-74619-5_27
35. Nandi, M.: Improved security analysis for OMAC as a pseudorandom function. J. Math. Cryptol. **3**(2), 133–148 (2009)
36. Nandi, M., Mandal, A.: Improved security analysis of PMAC. J. Math. Cryptol. **2**(2), 149–162 (2008)
37. Gazi, P., Pietrzak, K., Rybár, M.: The exact security of PMAC. IACR Trans. Symmetric Cryptol. **2016**(2), 145–161 (2016)
38. Chakraborty, B., Chattopadhyay, S., Jha, A., Nandi, M.: On length independent security bounds for the PMAC family. IACR Cryptol. ePrint Arch. **2020**, 656 (2020)
39. Baugher, M., McGrew, D., Naslund, M., Carrara, E., Norrman, K.: The secure real-time transport protocol (SRTP). RFC 3711, IETF (2004)
40. Chen, S., Steinberger, J.: Tight security bounds for key-alternating ciphers. In: Nguyen, P.Q., Oswald, E. (eds.) EUROCRYPT 2014. LNCS, vol. 8441, pp. 327–350. Springer, Heidelberg (2014). https://doi.org/10.1007/978-3-642-55220-5_19
41. Mennink, B., Neves, S.: Encrypted Davies-Meyer and its dual: towards optimal security using mirror theory. In: Katz, J., Shacham, H. (eds.) CRYPTO 2017. LNCS, vol. 10403, pp. 556–583. Springer, Cham (2017). https://doi.org/10.1007/978-3-319-63697-9_19
42. Jha, A., Nandi, M.: A survey on applications of h-technique: Revisiting security analysis of PRP and PRF. IACR Cryptol. ePrint Arch. **2018**, 1130 (2018)

Categorization of Faulty Nonce Misuse Resistant Message Authentication

Yu Long Chen[1(✉)], Bart Mennink[2], and Bart Preneel[1]

[1] imec-COSIC, KU Leuven, Leuven, Belgium
{yulong.chen,bart.preneel}@kuleuven.be
[2] Digital Security Group, Radboud University, Nijmegen, The Netherlands
b.mennink@cs.ru.nl

Abstract. A growing number of lightweight block ciphers are proposed for environments such as the Internet of Things. An important contribution to the reduced implementation cost is a block length n of 64 or 96 bits rather than 128 bits. As a consequence, encryption modes and message authentication code (MAC) algorithms require security beyond the $2^{n/2}$ birthday bound. This paper provides an extensive treatment of MAC algorithms that offer beyond birthday bound PRF security for both nonce-respecting and nonce-misusing adversaries. We study constructions that use two block cipher calls, one universal hash function call and an arbitrary number of XOR operations. We start with the separate problem of generically identifying all possible secure n-to-n-bit pseudorandom functions (PRFs) based on two block cipher calls. The analysis shows that the existing constructions EDM, SoP, and EDMD are the only constructions of this kind that achieve beyond birthday bound security. Subsequently we deliver an exhaustive treatment of MAC algorithms, where the outcome of a universal hash function evaluation on the message may be entered at any point in the computation of the PRF. We conclude that there are a total amount of nine schemes that achieve beyond birthday bound security, and a tenth construction that cannot be proven using currently known proof techniques. For these former nine MAC algorithms, three constructions achieve optimal n-bit security in the nonce-respecting setting, but are completely insecure if the nonce is reused. The remaining six constructions have $3n/4$-bit security in the nonce-respecting setting, and only four out of these six constructions still achieve beyond the birthday bound security in the case of nonce misuse.

Keywords: PRF · Beyond birthday bound security · Faulty nonce model · EDM · SoP · EDMD

1 Introduction

Message authentication code (MAC) algorithms are one of the fundamental building blocks in cryptography. Given a message M, it allows a sender in possession of a secret key K to compute an authentication tag T, which can then be

M. Tibouchi and H. Wang (Eds.): ASIACRYPT 2021, LNCS 13092, pp. 520–550, 2021.
https://doi.org/10.1007/978-3-030-92078-4_18

verified by the receiver provided that it is also in possession of the key. The tag should be hard to forge, i.e., without knowledge of the key, it should be computationally infeasible to compute the tag corresponding to any new message. In this work, we will focus on nonce-based MAC algorithms. These functions take as additional input a nonce N that is used to randomize the scheme.

1.1 Wegman-Carter

Undoubtedly one of the most influential nonce-based MAC algorithms to date is due to Wegman and Carter [44], which was built on earlier work by Gilbert, MacWilliams, and Sloane [19]. Their construction first processes the message with a universal hash function H using a secret hash key, and subsequently masks the output with a pseudorandom function (PRF) F evaluated on the nonce:

$$\mathrm{WC}_{K,K_h}(N,M) = F_K(N) \oplus H_{K_h}(M).$$

The Wegman-Carter construction is proven to achieve n-bit security if H is an ϵ-almost XOR universal hash function with small ϵ ($\epsilon \approx 2^{-n}$), F is a PRF, and the nonce is never repeated [44].

One concern with WC is that dedicated PRFs are difficult to construct. The only exceptions are SURF [5], AES-PRF [31], and SipHash [1], which might ultimately considered to be permutation-based as well. Pseudorandom permutations (PRPs), on the other hand, are in abundance, but instantiating Wegman-Carter with a PRP instead of a PRF – the resulting function is known as Wegman-Carter-Shoup – only achieves close to birthday bound security [6,28,34,43]. This bound may be on the edge of what is desired if the construction is instantiated with a lightweight block cipher [2,3,8,10,16,20,42] with small block size n. For example, it only takes approximately $2^{32} \cdot 64$ bits of data (35 GB) to break Wegman-Carter-Shoup with a 64-bit block cipher.

1.2 Nonce-Misuse Resistance

A second concern about the Wegman-Carter construction is its strict dependency on the nonce. Any repetition of a single nonce will break the Wegman-Carter(-Shoup) MAC [21,24]: it would result in two tags $T = E_K(N) \oplus H_{K_h}(M)$ and $T' = E_K(N) \oplus H_{K_h}(M')$ for two different messages M, M' which might allow an attacker to deduce information about K_h.

In order to solve this nonce-misuse problem, Cogliati and Seurin introduced Encrypted Wegman-Carter with Davies-Meyer (EWCDM) [13]. EWCDM can be seen as a Wegman-Carter construction, with a Davies-Meyer construction as PRF, then followed by an encryption of the output. The security improvement in EWCDM lies in the "protection" of the outcome of this construction by an extra evaluation of a block cipher:

$$\mathrm{EWCDM}_{K_1,K_2,K_h}(N,M) = E_{K_2}(E_{K_1}(N) \oplus N \oplus H_{K_h}(M)).$$

Cogliati and Seurin [13] proved that this construction achieves $2n/3$-bit MAC security in the nonce-respecting scenario and $n/2$-bit MAC security in the nonce-misuse scenario. Mennink and Neves [30] proved almost n-bit PRF security of the mode in the nonce-respecting scenario. Later, a dual variant of EWCDM, called the Decrypted Wegman-Carter with Davies-Meyer (DWCDM), was introduced by Datta et al. [15]. Instead of making the second block cipher call using another independent key, DWCDM evaluates the block cipher in the inverse direction using the same key.

While these MAC algorithms provide security beyond the birthday barrier, most of them are only birthday bound secure if a nonce is reused. This might occur, for example, if a stateless device chooses nonces uniformly at random from a small set, if there is a faulty implementation of the cipher involved, or otherwise. For example, Böck et al. performed an internet-wide scan [7] and found 184 HTTPS servers that used a duplicate nonce for AES-GCM [29].

Dutta et al. [18] formalized the "faulty nonce model" for MAC algorithms. In the faulty nonce model, one considers a nonce-based MAC as usual, but labels a MAC query as "faulty" if it is performed for a repeated nonce. The authors furthermore introduced the nonce-based Enhanced Hash-then-Mask (nEHtM). At its base, nEHtM is a nonce-based variant of EHtM [32] where the random salt is replaced by a nonce and the PRF by a block cipher:

$$\mathrm{nEHtM}_{K,K_h}(N,M) = E_K(0 \parallel N) \oplus E_K(1 \parallel (N \oplus H_{K_h}(M))).$$

Dutta et al. proved that nEHtM achieves $2n/3$-bit security when the number of faulty nonces is below $2^{n/3}$, and proved graceful security degradation of at least $n/2$-bit security in the faulty model. Choi et al. [12] improved the security bound to $3n/4$-bit when the number of faulty nonces is below $2^{3n/8}$, and also proved graceful security degradation. Graceful degradation here means that the actual security level is between $3n/4$ (resp., $2n/3$) and $n/2$, depending on the total number of faulty queries that an adversary makes.

1.3 Our Contribution

In this work, we perform a general treatment of the design of block cipher based MAC algorithms that achieve beyond birthday bound PRF security in the nonce-respecting model. We subsequently consider how these schemes behave in the faulty nonce model. We restrict our focus to MAC algorithms based on a single universal hash function call on the input, two block cipher calls, and an arbitrary amount of XOR operations to combine the inputs and outcomes of the cryptographic building blocks.

Before diving into MAC design, however, we make one step backwards. Hidden in EWCDM is an n-bit PRF construction called the Encrypted Davies-Meyer construction EDM:

$$\mathrm{EDM}_{K_1,K_2}(N) = E_{K_2}(E_{K_1}(N) \oplus N). \tag{1}$$

Although one cannot reduce security of EWCDM to that of EDM [13], the proofs share similarities [13,30]. Likewise, nEHtM can be seen to hide the Sum of Permutation construction SoP [4]:

$$\mathrm{SoP}_{K_1,K_2}(N) = E_{K_1}(N) \oplus E_{K_2}(N). \tag{2}$$

We can conclude that one might have little hope in designing a MAC algorithm with beyond the birthday bound PRF security if that particular construction with the universal hash function evaluation omitted is not a good PRF in the first place. Therefore, in Sect. 3, we start with performing a general analysis of n-to-n-bit PRF designs from two block cipher calls. We prove that, although there are 2^6 constructions of that type to consider, for *all but six of them*, an attack in the birthday bound or faster can be mounted. The six remaining schemes are, perhaps unsurprisingly, EDM of (1), SoP of (2), the Encrypted Davies-Meyer Dual construction EDMD [30]:

$$\mathrm{EDMD}_{K_1,K_2}(N) = E_{K_2}(E_{K_1}(N)) \oplus E_{K_1}(N), \tag{3}$$

and the natural siblings of these three schemes that consist of XORing the input to the output.

Supported by these results, we go on to perform an exhaustive analysis of all MAC algorithms that can be constructed from two block cipher calls with a universal hash evaluation on the message. We prove that although there are 2^9 constructions of that type to consider, the quest leads to ten interesting MAC algorithms: five are based on EDM, three on SoP, and two on EDMD. The schemes are formalized in Sect. 4.

Out of these ten schemes, three of them are simply Wegman-Carter based on the PRFs EDM, SoP, and EDMD, respectively. These achieve n-bit security, but are completely insecure if the nonce is reused. The four remaining EDM-based schemes and two remaining SoP-based schemes achieve $3n/4$-bit security in the nonce-respecting scenario, and four out these six schemes still achieve beyond the birthday bound security in the case of nonce misuse. Note that there is always a safety margin that must be taken into account. This means that when we talk about $3n/4$-bit security, only $2^{3n/4-\delta}$ queries can be made, where δ is chosen such that the resulting advantage of the distinguisher remains negligible. Currently known proof techniques did not allow us to prove security of the final EDMD-based scheme, which was already mentioned (without proof) by Nandi [35]. We conjecture that this scheme has beyond birthday bound security against nonce-respecting adversaries. Our results are performed in the faulty nonce model of Dutta et al. [18] and are given in Sect. 4. These ten MAC algorithms are compared in terms of their security and efficiency in Table 1.

In Fig. 1, we show the four constructions that still achieve beyond the birthday bound security in the case of nonce misuse: two are serial, while the other two are parallel. The two serial constructions are new, and the two parallel constructions based on SoP are variants of the nEHtM construction of Dutta et al. [18] that uses two independent keys. The parallel constructions still achieve

Table 1. Comparison of the ten MAC algorithms, where μ is the number of faulty nonces. Here, n is the block size and E_{K_1} refers to the first block cipher evaluation in the construction. EWCDM was shown to achieve n-bits security using an unverified version of the mirror theory.

MAC	Nonce-resp. security ($\log_2$)	Nonce-misuse security ($\log_2$)	Computing E_{K_1} without M	Sequential/ parallel	Security tightness	Note
$F_{B_1}^{\mathrm{EDM}}$	n	0	✓	S	Tight	WC-with-EDM [44]
$F_{B_1}^{\mathrm{SoP}}$	n	0	✓	P	Tight	WC-with-SoP [44]
$F_{B_1}^{\mathrm{EDMD}}$	n	0	✓	S	Tight	WC-with-EDMD [44]
$F_{B_2}^{\mathrm{EDM}}$	$3n/4$ (n)	$n/2$	✓	S	Not (tight)	EWCDM [13], Thm. 2 ([30])
$F_{B_3}^{\mathrm{EDM}}$	$3n/4$	$n/2$	✓	S	Not	Thm. 2
$F_{B_4}^{\mathrm{EDM}}$	$3n/4$	$3n/4$ ($\mu < 2^{n/2}$)	—	S	?	Thm. 3
$F_{B_5}^{\mathrm{EDM}}$	$3n/4$	$3n/4$ ($\mu < 2^{n/2}$)	—	S	?	Thm. 3
$F_{B_2}^{\mathrm{SoP}}$	$3n/4$	$3n/4$ ($\mu \leq 2^{n/4}$)	✓	P	?	Thm. 4
$F_{B_3}^{\mathrm{SoP}}$	$3n/4$	$3n/4$ ($\mu \leq 2^{n/4}$)	✓	P	?	Thm. 4
$F_{B_2}^{\mathrm{EDMD}}$	?	?	✓	S	—	—

$3n/4$ security with $\mu \leq 2^{n/4}$ faulty nonces. Surprisingly, for the two serial constructions, the security does not decrease as long as the number of faulty nonces is below $2^{n/2}$. While parallel modes inherently profit most from modern parallel architectures, the Comb scheduling technique introduced in [9] can solve this problem even for serial modes on the server side. Besides, the serial structure can be particularly suited for the design of efficient dedicated primitives [17,31], while this is not the case for parallel modes. Therefore, an interesting consequence of our results is the introduction of two new constructions $F_{B_4}^{\mathrm{EDM}}$ and $F_{B_5}^{\mathrm{EDM}}$, where the security of these constructions remains the same as long as the number of faulty nonces is below $2^{n/2}$.

The security proofs in this work are performed using Patarin's H-coefficient technique [11,36,38], and using the mirror theory by Kim et al. [26]. We believe that the security bounds of the two SoP-based MAC algorithms can be improved by improving the mirror theory. The main security analysis is given in Sect. 5.3, where we show the PRF security of these MAC algorithms, the analysis straightforwardly generalizes to MAC security.

2 Preliminaries

For $n \in \mathbb{N}$, we denote by $\{0,1\}^n$ the set of bit strings of length n. For two bit strings $X, Y \in \{0,1\}^n$, we denote their bitwise addition as $X \oplus Y$. We denote by $\{0,1\}^*$ the set of bit strings of arbitrary length. For a value Z, we denote by $z \leftarrow Z$ the assignment of Z to the variable z. For a finite set S, we denote by $s \xleftarrow{\$} S$ the uniformly random selection of s from S. For an algorithm $\mathcal{D}$ and two oracles $\mathcal{O}, \mathcal{P}$, we denote by $\mathcal{D}^{\mathcal{O}}$ the evaluation of $\mathcal{D}$ with oracle interaction to $\mathcal{O}$,

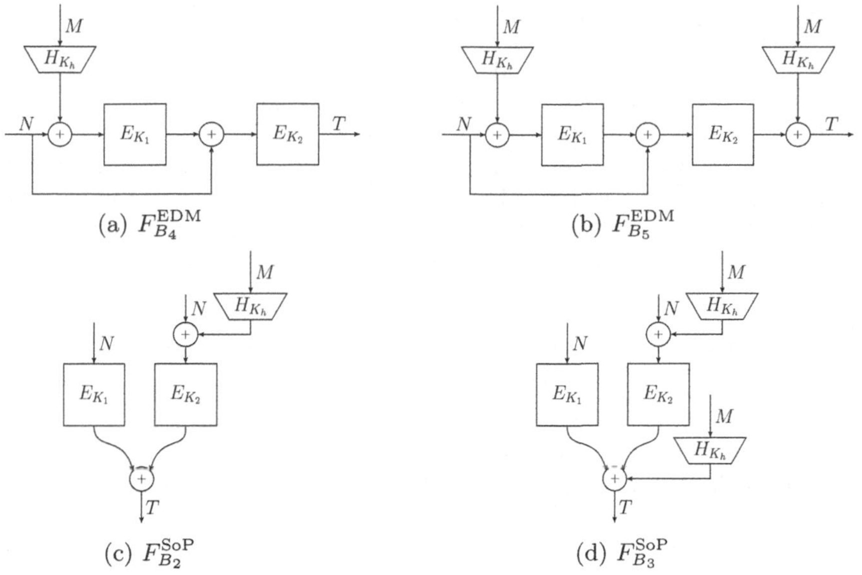

Fig. 1. Depiction of four MAC algorithms, where E is a block cipher and H a universal hash function.

and by $\Delta_{\mathcal{D}}\left(\mathcal{O}\,;\mathcal{P}\right)$ the advantage of $\mathcal{D}$ in distinguishing $\mathcal{O}$ from an oracle $\mathcal{P}$. For a primitive P, we denote by $\mathcal{O}[P]$ the oracle $\mathcal{O}$ built on the primitive P. We denote by $[q]$ the shorthand notation for $\{1,\ldots,q\}$. For two disjoint sets P and Q, we denote their (disjoint) union as $P \sqcup Q$.

2.1 Block Ciphers

For $k, n \in \mathbb{N}$, a block cipher is a function $E\colon \{0,1\}^k \times \{0,1\}^n \to \{0,1\}^n$ such that for fixed key $K \in \{0,1\}^k$, $E_K(\cdot) = E(K,\cdot)$ is a permutation on $\{0,1\}^n$.

Denote by $\mathrm{Perm}(n)$ the set of all permutations on $\{0,1\}^n$. The prp-security of a block cipher E is measured by considering a distinguisher $\mathcal{D}$ that is given forward access to either E_K for secret key $K \xleftarrow{\$} \{0,1\}^k$, or a random permutation $\pi \xleftarrow{\$} \mathrm{Perm}(n)$, and its goal is to determine which oracle it is given access to:

$$\mathbf{Adv}_E^{\mathrm{prp}}(\mathcal{D}) = \left|\Pr\left[K \xleftarrow{\$} \{0,1\}^k\colon \mathcal{D}^{E_K} = 1\right] - \Pr\left[\pi \xleftarrow{\$} \mathrm{Perm}(n)\colon \mathcal{D}^{\pi} = 1\right]\right|.$$

Note that we only consider the prp-security of block ciphers instead of the sprp-security, where $\mathcal{D}$ would have access to the inverse of E_K as well. The reason for this is that the constructions that we analyze only evaluate the underlying block ciphers in forward direction.

2.2 Nonce-Based Pseudorandom Functions

For $k, n \in \mathbb{N}$, a nonce-based pseudorandom function is a function $F: \{0,1\}^k \times \{0,1\}^n \times \{0,1\}^* \to \{0,1\}^n$, that takes as input a key $K \in \{0,1\}^k$, a nonce $N \in \{0,1\}^n$, a message $M \in \{0,1\}^*$, and outputs a tag $T \in \{0,1\}^n$.

We define a perfectly random oracle $\mathsf{Rand}: \{0,1\}^n \times \{0,1\}^* \to \{0,1\}^n$ as a function that for each new input in $\{0,1\}^n \times \{0,1\}^*$ generates a random string of length n bits. The prf-security of a function F is measured by considering a distinguisher $\mathcal{D}$ that is given access to either F_K for secret key $K \xleftarrow{\$} \{0,1\}^k$, or the random oracle Rand:

$$\mathbf{Adv}_F^{\mathrm{prf}}(\mathcal{D}) = \left|\Pr\left[K \xleftarrow{\$} \{0,1\}^k : \mathcal{D}^{F_K} = 1\right] - \Pr\left[\mathcal{D}^{\mathsf{Rand}} = 1\right]\right|.$$

We call a query a faulty query if the distinguisher $\mathcal{D}$ has already queried its oracle with the same nonce. The distinguisher $\mathcal{D}$ is allowed to make at most μ faulty queries. We call $\mathcal{D}$ a nonce-respecting adversary if $\mu = 0$, and nonce-misusing if $\mu \geq 1$.

2.3 Universal Hash Functions

For $n \in \mathbb{N}$, an universal hash function is a function $H: \mathcal{K}_h \times \{0,1\}^* \to \{0,1\}^n$, such that for fixed key $K_h \in \mathcal{K}_h$, we have $H_{K_h}(\cdot) = H(K_h, \cdot)$. We call H an ϵ-almost XOR universal (ϵ-AXU) hash function [27] if for all distinct $M, M' \in \{0,1\}^*$ and all $C \in \{0,1\}^n$, we have

$$\Pr\left[K_h \xleftarrow{\$} \mathcal{K}_h : H_{K_h}(M) \oplus H_{K_h}(M') = C\right] \leq \epsilon.$$

Unfortunately, we cannot immediately use this probability bound to bound the occurrence of the following event:

$$H_{K_{h_1}}(M_i) = H_{K_{h_1}}(M_j) \wedge H_{K_{h_2}}(M_j) = H_{K_{h_2}}(M_k) \wedge H_{K_{h_1}}(M_k) = H_{K_{h_1}}(M_l),$$

for $K_{h_1}, K_{h_2} \xleftarrow{\$} \mathcal{K}_h$. We cannot claim that the probability of this event is ϵ^3 for any fixed distinct M_i, M_j, M_k, and M_l, since the first and the last event are not independent. We will use the following lemma in our security proofs.

Lemma 1 (alternating events lemma [12,23]**).** *Let $q_i, q_j, q_k, q_l, q \in \mathbb{N}$ such that $q_i, q_j, q_k, q_l \leq q$. Let $X^q = (X_1, \ldots, X_q)$ be a q-tuple of random variables, and let $X^{q_i}, X^{q_j}, X^{q_k}, X^{q_l} \subseteq X^q$. For distinct $i \in [q_i], j \in [q_j]$, let $E_{i,j}$ be events associated with $X_i \in X^{q_i}$ and $X_j \in X^{q_j}$, possibly dependent, which all hold with probability at most ϵ. For distinct $i \in [q_i], j \in [q_j], k \in [q_k], l \in [q_l]$, let $F_{i,j,k,l}$ be events associated with $X_i \in X^{q_i}$, $X_j \in X^{q_j}$, $X_k \in X^{q_k}$, and $X_l \in X^{q_l}$ which all hold with probability at most ϵ'. Moreover, the collection of events $(F_{i,j,k,l})_{i,j,k,l}$ is independent with the collection of event $(E_{i,j})_{i,j}$. Then,*

$$\Pr[\exists i \in [q_i], j \in [q_j], k \in [q_k], l \in [q_l], E_{i,j} \wedge E_{k,l} \wedge F_{i,j,k,l}] \leq \sqrt{q_i q_j q_k q_l} \cdot \epsilon \cdot \sqrt{\epsilon'}.$$

Jha and Nandi [23] proved the alternating events lemma for $q_i, q_j, q_k, q_l = q$, the lemma can straightforwardly be generalized to different q_i, q_j, q_k, q_l, a similar proof for this is given in the bad transcripts analysis of the work by Choi et al. [12]. Note that Lemma 1 can be used to solve the above-mentioned example using the independent randomness of the hash keys K_{h_1} and K_{h_2}. For our constructions, we only have one hash key, hence we will use the randomly generated output tags as our second source of randomness.

2.4 Double Collision Attack

We will rely on the double collision attack by Nandi [35]. We recall the result of this attack in the following lemma.

Lemma 2 (double collision attack [35]**).** *For $k, n \in \mathbb{N}$, let $F1\colon \{0,1\}^k \times \{0,1\}^* \to \{0,1\}^n$ and $F2\colon \{0,1\}^k \times \{0,1\}^n \to \{0,1\}^n$ be non-injective functions. Consider $F3_{K_1,K_2} := F2_{K_2} \circ F1_{K_1}$. There is a non-negligible constant c such that for a distinguisher $\mathcal{D}$ making $(1/\sqrt{2}) \cdot 2^{n/2}$ queries, we have*

$$\mathbf{Adv}^{\mathrm{prf}}_{F3}(\mathcal{D}) \geq c.$$

3 Generalized Fixed-Input-Length PRF Construction

We present a synthetic categorization of all beyond birthday bound secure fixed-input-length PRFs from two block cipher calls and plain XOR operations.

Let $k, n \in \mathbb{N}$. Let $E\colon \{0,1\}^k \times \{0,1\}^n \to \{0,1\}^n$ be a block cipher. For a binary 3×3 matrix A of the form

$$A = \begin{pmatrix} a_{11} & 0 & 0 \\ a_{21} & a_{22} & 0 \\ a_{31} & a_{32} & a_{33} \end{pmatrix}, \tag{4}$$

our target PRF $F_A\colon \{0,1\}^{2k} \times \{0,1\}^n \to \{0,1\}^n$ defined by A is described in Algorithm 1 and given in Fig. 2. Note that any fixed-input-length PRF $F\colon \{0,1\}^n \to \{0,1\}^n$ based on two block cipher calls can be represented by this generic construction, omitting all possible constructions that can be obtained by applying linear transformations to the variables. In total, we thus analyze 2^6 fixed-input-length PRFs. However for some A, the resulting PRF is clearly not secure beyond the birthday bound. In Sect. 3.1, we first eliminate trivially insecure matrices. Then, in Sect. 3.2 we reason about the remaining ones.

3.1 Trivial Matrices

We call a matrix "trivial" if it does not make proper use of one or both block cipher calls. More formally, matrix A is called "non-trivial" if it satisfies the following properties:

Algorithm 1. PRF F_A with A of (4)

Input: $(K_1, K_2) \in \{0,1\}^{2k}$, $N \in \{0,1\}^n$
Output: $T \in \{0,1\}^n$

$u \leftarrow a_{11} \cdot N$
$v \leftarrow E_{K_1}(u)$
$x \leftarrow a_{21} \cdot N \oplus a_{22} \cdot v$
$y \leftarrow E_{K_2}(x)$
$T \leftarrow a_{31} \cdot N \oplus a_{32} \cdot v \oplus a_{33} \cdot y$
return T

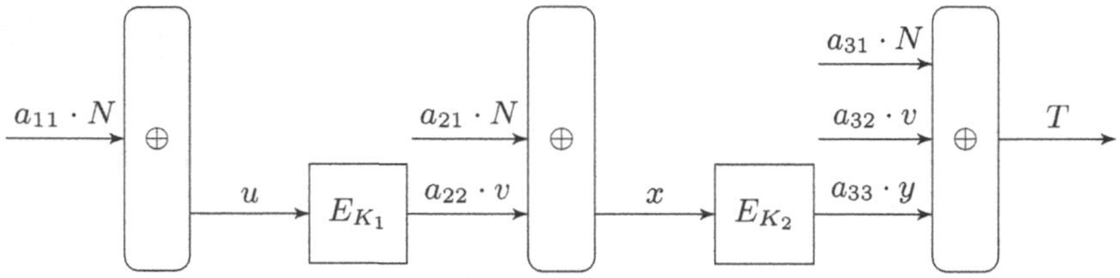

Fig. 2. PRF F_A based on two block ciphers E_{K_1} and E_{K_2}, and with A of (4).

(1) Each row of the matrix must contain at least one non-zero element. This requirement ensures that at least one input is XORed to each of the three XOR-operators. Note that the first two XOR-operations correspond respectively to the inputs of the two block ciphers. If no inputs are XORed to these XOR-operators, then the corresponding block cipher is independent of the inputs to the PRF. In this case, the resulting PRF can be broken in at most $2^{n/2}$ queries. The last XOR-operation corresponds to the output T, if no inputs are XORed to this XOR-operator, then the resulting PRF outputs a constant T for every query.
(2) Each column of the matrix must contain at least one non-zero element. This requirement ensures that each of the three inputs N, v, and y is used at least once.

We can derive the following four requirements from above properties:

$$a_{11} = 1, \qquad a_{33} = 1, \qquad a_{22} + a_{32} \geq 1, \qquad a_{21} + a_{22} \geq 1.$$

Notice that if $a_{11} = 0$, the block cipher E_{K_1} is not used in the computation; if $a_{33} = 0$, the block cipher E_{K_2} is not used in the output; if $a_{22} + a_{32} = 0$, the output of the block cipher E_{K_1} is not used in the output; and if $a_{21} + a_{22} = 0$, the block cipher E_{K_2} is not used in the computation. If one of the four requirements is not satisfied, then the resulting PRF can be broken in at most $2^{n/2}$ queries.

Thus, in the remainder, we focus on matrices A of the following form:

$$A = \begin{pmatrix} 1 & 0 & 0 \\ a_{21} & a_{22} & 0 \\ a_{31} & a_{32} & 1 \end{pmatrix}, \tag{5}$$

where $a_{21} + a_{22} \geq 1$ and $a_{22} + a_{32} \geq 1$ (ten schemes in total).

3.2 Generic Results for PRFs

Before we start with our generic analysis, we provide the following observation to simplify our analysis: XORing the input N to the output T does not influence the security of the PRF.

Proposition 1. *Let A be any non-trivial matrix of the form* (5). *Let*

$$A' := A \oplus \begin{pmatrix} 0\,0\,0 \\ 0\,0\,0 \\ 1\,0\,0 \end{pmatrix}.$$

For any distinguisher $\mathcal{D}$, there exists a distinguisher $\mathcal{D}'$ such that $\mathbf{Adv}^{\mathrm{prf}}_{F_A}(\mathcal{D}') \geq \mathbf{Adv}^{\mathrm{prf}}_{F_{A'}}(\mathcal{D})$ *and* $\mathbf{Adv}^{\mathrm{prf}}_{F_{A'}}(\mathcal{D}') \geq \mathbf{Adv}^{\mathrm{prf}}_{F_A}(\mathcal{D})$.

Proof. We only prove the part $\mathbf{Adv}^{\mathrm{prf}}_{F_{A'}}(\mathcal{D}') \geq \mathbf{Adv}^{\mathrm{prf}}_{F_A}(\mathcal{D})$, the part $\mathbf{Adv}^{\mathrm{prf}}_{F_A}(\mathcal{D}') \geq \mathbf{Adv}^{\mathrm{prf}}_{F_{A'}}(\mathcal{D})$ is proven in a similar way. Let $K_e = (K_1, K_2) \xleftarrow{\$} \{0,1\}^{2k}$, and note that $F_{A'}[E_{K_1}, E_{K_2}](N) = F_A[E_{K_1}, E_{K_2}](N) \oplus N$. For any distinguisher $\mathcal{D}$ whose goal is to distinguish the real world oracle $F_A[E_{K_1}, E_{K_2}]$ from the ideal world oracle $\varphi \xleftarrow{\$} \mathrm{Func}(n)$, we can build a distinguisher $\mathcal{D}'$ that has access to either $F_{A'}[E_{K_1}, E_{K_2}]$ or φ, and that simulates $\mathcal{D}$'s oracles. More precisely, for each query N made by $\mathcal{D}$, $\mathcal{D}'$ queries its oracle for N to retrieve a value T, and it returns $T \oplus N$ to $\mathcal{D}$. At the end, $\mathcal{D}'$ relays the decision bit output by $\mathcal{D}$. Distinguisher $\mathcal{D}'$ has at least the same success probability as $\mathcal{D}$, and this completes the proof. □

We are left with matrices A of the form

$$A = \begin{pmatrix} 1 & 0 & 0 \\ a_{21} & a_{22} & 0 \\ 0 & a_{32} & 1 \end{pmatrix}, \tag{6}$$

where $a_{21} + a_{22} \geq 1$ and $a_{22} + a_{32} \geq 1$. There are five options in total:

$$A_1 = \begin{pmatrix} 1\,0\,0 \\ 0\,1\,0 \\ 0\,0\,1 \end{pmatrix}, A_2 = \begin{pmatrix} 1\,0\,0 \\ 1\,1\,0 \\ 0\,0\,1 \end{pmatrix}, A_3 = \begin{pmatrix} 1\,0\,0 \\ 1\,0\,0 \\ 0\,1\,1 \end{pmatrix}, A_4 = \begin{pmatrix} 1\,0\,0 \\ 0\,1\,0 \\ 0\,1\,1 \end{pmatrix}, A_5 = \begin{pmatrix} 1\,0\,0 \\ 1\,1\,0 \\ 0\,1\,1 \end{pmatrix}. \tag{7}$$

Clearly, F_{A_1} is a cascade of two PRPs. This means that it does not have collisions and can be distinguished from a random function φ in around $2^{n/2}$ queries. Likewise, F_{A_5} is a composition of two PRFs. More specifically, F_{A_5} is equivalent to a cascade of two Davies-Meyer constructions (taking into account that $x = N \oplus v$ in the second Davies-Meyer construction), which is at most birthday bound secure due to Lemma 2. The remaining three functions for binary matrices A_2, A_3, A_4 are Encrypted Davies-Meyer [13], Sum of Permutation [4], and Encrypted Davies-Meyer Dual [30], respectively. All three constructions have been proven to achieve optimal n-bit security using Patarin's mirror theory [33,37,39,40], and the Sum of Permutation and the Encrypted Davies-Meyer Dual constructions have also been proven to achieve optimal n-bit security using the chi-squared method [14]. We thus arrive at the following results.

Proposition 2. *Let $k, n \in \mathbb{N}$. Let $E : \{0,1\}^k \times \{0,1\}^n \to \{0,1\}^n$ be a block cipher. For $x = 1, 5$, consider F_{A_x} of Algorithm 1 that is defined by binary matrix A_x of (7).*

(i) There is a distinguisher $\mathcal{D}$ making $2^{n/2}$ queries such that

$$\mathbf{Adv}^{\mathrm{prf}}_{F_{A_1}}(\mathcal{D}) \geq 1 - \frac{1}{e}.$$

(ii) There is a non-negligible constant c such that for a distinguisher $\mathcal{D}$ making $(1/\sqrt{2}) \cdot 2^{n/2}$ queries, we have

$$\mathbf{Adv}^{\mathrm{prf}}_{F_{A_5}}(\mathcal{D}) \geq c.$$

Proof. For case (i), consider a distinguisher $\mathcal{D}$ that makes $2^{n/2}$ queries and operates as follows. For $i = 1, \ldots, 2^{n/2}$, it selects arbitrary $N^{(i)}$'s to obtain $T^{(i)}$'s. If all $T^{(i)}$'s are distinct, output 1. Otherwise, output 0. In the real world, F_{A_1} behaves as a PRP, and thus $\Pr\left[\mathcal{D}^{F_{A_1}} = 1\right] = 1$. For the ideal world, we have

$$\Pr\left[\mathcal{D}^{\varphi} = 1\right] = \Pr\left[\cap_{i,i'} T^{(i)} \neq T^{(i')}\right] \leq 1 - \left(1 - e^{-\binom{q}{2}\frac{1}{2^n}}\right) = e^{-\binom{q}{2}\frac{1}{2^n}},$$

where $q = 2^{n/2}$.

The proof of case (ii) follows from Lemma 2. □

Theorem 1. *Let $k, n \in \mathbb{N}$. Let $E : \{0,1\}^k \times \{0,1\}^n \to \{0,1\}^n$ be a block cipher. For $x = 2, 3, 4$, consider F_{A_x} of Algorithm 1 that is defined by binary matrix A_x of (7).*

(i) Let ξ be any threshold, and for any distinguisher $\mathcal{D}$ making at most $q \leq 2^n/(67\xi^2)$ queries, we have

$$\mathbf{Adv}^{\mathrm{prf}}_{F_{A_2}}(\mathcal{D}) \leq \frac{q}{2^n} + \frac{\binom{q}{\xi+1}}{2^{n\xi}}.$$

(ii) For any distinguisher $\mathcal{D}$ making at most q queries, we have

$$\mathbf{Adv}^{\mathrm{prf}}_{F_{A_3}}(\mathcal{D}),\ \mathbf{Adv}^{\mathrm{prf}}_{F_{A_4}}(\mathcal{D}) \leq \frac{q}{2^n}.$$

Proof. We refer to Mennink and Neves [30] for the proofs of security of F_{A_2} and F_{A_4}, and to Dai et al. [14] for the proof of security of F_{A_3}. □

We conclude that EDM, SoP, and EDMD are the only three n-bit secure fixed-input-length PRFs that can be build using two block cipher calls and XOR operations (modulo the reduction of Proposition 1 that consists of feed-forwarding the input), and one should start from these fixed-input-length PRFs while building beyond birthday bound secure variable-input-length PRF algorithms.

Algorithm 2. Nonce-based PRF F_{A^*} with A^* of (8)

Input: $(K_1, K_2) \in \{0,1\}^{2k}$, $K_h \in \mathcal{K}_h$, $N \in \{0,1\}^n$, $M \in \{0,1\}^*$
Output: $T \in \{0,1\}^n$
1: $u \leftarrow a_{11} \cdot N \oplus b_1 \cdot H_{K_h}(M)$
2: $v \leftarrow E_{K_1}(u)$
3: $x \leftarrow a_{21} \cdot N \oplus a_{22} \cdot v \oplus b_2 \cdot H_{K_h}(M)$
4: $y \leftarrow E_{K_2}(x)$
5: $T \leftarrow a_{31} \cdot N \oplus a_{32} \cdot v \oplus a_{33} \cdot y \oplus b_3 \cdot H_{K_h}(M)$
6: **return** T

4 Generalized Nonce-Based PRF Construction

We consider how to generically construct a nonce-based PRF algorithm from two block cipher calls and one universal hash function call.

Let $k, n \in \mathbb{N}$. Let $E\colon \{0,1\}^k \times \{0,1\}^n \to \{0,1\}^n$ be a block cipher. For a binary 3×4 matrix A^* of the form

$$A^* = \begin{pmatrix} a_{11} & 0 & 0 & b_1 \\ a_{21} & a_{22} & 0 & b_2 \\ a_{31} & a_{32} & a_{33} & b_3 \end{pmatrix}, \tag{8}$$

our target nonce-based PRF $F_{A^*}\colon \{0,1\}^{2k} \times \mathcal{K}_h \times \{0,1\}^n \times \{0,1\}^* \to \{0,1\}^n$ defined by A^* is described in Algorithm 2 and given in Fig. 3. Note that any nonce-based PRF $F\colon \{0,1\}^n \times \{0,1\}^* \to \{0,1\}^n$ based on two block cipher calls and one universal hash function call can be represented by this generic construction, omitting all possible constructions that can be obtained by applying linear transformations to the variables. In total, we thus analyze 2^9 nonce-based PRFs. However for some A^*, the resulting construction is clearly not secure beyond the birthday bound. In Sect. 4.1, we first eliminate trivially insecure matrices. Then, we reason about the remaining ones.

4.1 Generic Results for Nonce-Based PRF Algorithms

Note that the reasoning of Sect. 3.1 also applies here: the distinguisher can eliminate the effect of the universal hash function by keeping the message M constant. Therefore, intuitively, a nonce-based PRF can only be secure if its underlying fixed-input-length PRF is built on a non-trivial matrix. We therefore focus on nonce-based PRF algorithm built on fixed-input-length PRFs from Eq. (6).

Thus, in the remainder, we focus on matrices A^* of the following form:

$$A^* = \begin{pmatrix} 1 & 0 & 0 & b_1 \\ a_{21} & a_{22} & 0 & b_2 \\ 0 & a_{32} & 1 & b_3 \end{pmatrix}, \tag{9}$$

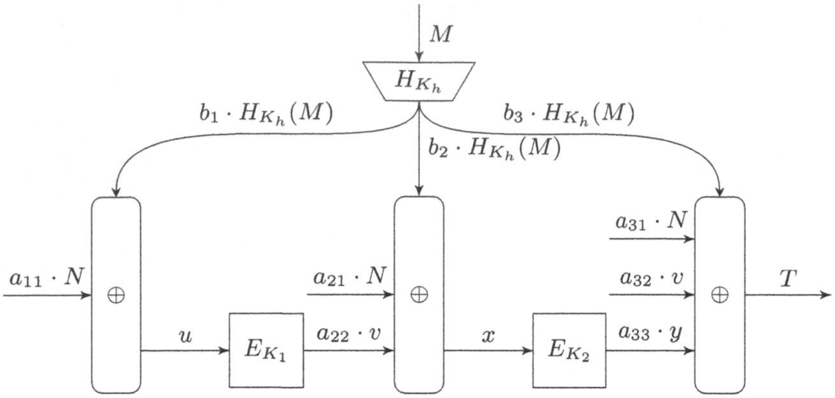

Fig. 3. Nonce-based PRF F_{A^*} based on two block ciphers E_{K_1}, E_{K_2}, and an universal hash function H_{K_h}, and with A^* of (8).

where $a_{21} + a_{22} \geq 1$, $a_{22} + a_{32} \geq 1$ and $b_1 + b_2 + b_3 \geq 1$. These options are:

$$A_1^* = \begin{pmatrix} 1\,0\,0\,b_1 \\ 0\,1\,0\,b_2 \\ 0\,0\,1\,b_3 \end{pmatrix}, A_2^* = \begin{pmatrix} 1\,0\,0\,b_1 \\ 1\,1\,0\,b_2 \\ 0\,0\,1\,b_3 \end{pmatrix}, A_3^* = \begin{pmatrix} 1\,0\,0\,b_1 \\ 1\,0\,0\,b_2 \\ 0\,1\,1\,b_3 \end{pmatrix}, \qquad A_4^* = \begin{pmatrix} 1\,0\,0\,b_1 \\ 0\,1\,0\,b_2 \\ 0\,1\,1\,b_3 \end{pmatrix}, A_5^* = \begin{pmatrix} 1\,0\,0\,b_1 \\ 1\,1\,0\,b_2 \\ 0\,1\,1\,b_3 \end{pmatrix}. \tag{10}$$

As in Sect. 3.2, nonce-based PRFs based on A_1^* cannot achieve beyond birthday bound security, as the distinguisher can make $2^{n/2}$ queries by keeping the message M constant and observe no collision in the tag. Nonce-based PRFs based on A_5^* also cannot achieve beyond birthday bound security, as these constructions can be seen as a cascade of two PRFs, and hence can be broken in the birthday bound using Lemma 2.

In the following, we denote $F_{B_x}^{\mathrm{EDM}}$, $F_{B_x}^{\mathrm{SoP}}$, and $F_{B_x}^{\mathrm{EDMD}}$ as the nonce-based PRFs based on matrices A_2^*, A_3^*, and A_4^*, respectively. For $x = 0, \ldots, 7$, we will consider all variants of B_x depending on the values of b_1, b_2, and b_3.

$$\begin{aligned} B_0 &= (0\,0\,0)\,, & B_4 &= (1\,0\,0)\,, \\ B_1 &= (0\,0\,1)\,, & B_5 &= (1\,0\,1)\,, \\ B_2 &= (0\,1\,0)\,, & B_6 &= (1\,1\,0)\,, \\ B_3 &= (0\,1\,1)\,, & B_7 &= (1\,1\,1)\,. \end{aligned} \tag{11}$$

4.2 Nonce-Based PRFs Based on A_2^* (Encrypted Davies-Meyer)

In this section, we consider nonce-based PRFs based on the Encrypted Davies-Meyer construction F^{EDM}. Let $k, n \in \mathbb{N}$, let $E\colon \{0,1\}^k \times \{0,1\}^n \to \{0,1\}^n$

be a block cipher, and $H\colon \mathcal{K}_h \times \{0,1\}^* \to \{0,1\}^n$ be an ϵ-AXU hash function. Consider generic construction $F^{\mathrm{EDM}}_{B_x}\colon \{0,1\}^{2k} \times \mathcal{K}_h \times \{0,1\}^n \times \{0,1\}^* \to \{0,1\}^n$:

$$\begin{aligned} &F^{\mathrm{EDM}}_{B_x}[E_{K_1}, E_{K_2}, H_{K_h}](N, M) = \\ &\qquad E_{K_2}(E_{K_1}(N \oplus b_1 \cdot H_{K_h}(M)) \oplus N \oplus b_2 \cdot H_{K_h}(M)) \oplus b_3 \cdot H_{K_h}(M), \end{aligned} \tag{12}$$

with $B_x \in \{B_0, B_1, \ldots, B_7\}$ of (11).

Here, $F^{\mathrm{EDM}}_{B_2}$ is the EWCDM construction of Cogliati and Seurin [13], which is shown to achieve $2n/3$-bit security against nonce-respecting adversaries. Using Patarin's mirror theory, Mennink and Neves [30] have shown that $F^{\mathrm{EDM}}_{B_2}$ also achieves n-bit security against nonce-respecting adversaries. The function $F^{\mathrm{EDM}}_{B_0}$ is trivially insecure and henceforth excluded. The function $F^{\mathrm{EDM}}_{B_1}$ is a Wegman-Carter construction with EDM as its underlying PRF, hence it is optimally n-bit secure against nonce-respecting adversaries, and totally broken when the nonce is reused. For the remaining six schemes, we show that four of these achieve beyond birthday bound security against nonce-respecting distinguisher. Moreover, two of these four constructions still provide the same amount of security in the faulty nonce model when the number of faulty nonces is below $2^{n/2}$, and the security drops to the birthday bound when $2^{n/2}$ faulty nonces are made. The security of the other two constructions drops to birthday bound once a single nonce is repeated.

Proposition 3. *Let $k, n \in \mathbb{N}$. Let $E : \{0,1\}^k \times \{0,1\}^n \to \{0,1\}^n$ be a block cipher, and $H\colon \mathcal{K}_h \times \{0,1\}^* \to \{0,1\}^n$ be an ϵ-AXU hash function. Consider $F^{\mathrm{EDM}}_{B_x}$ of Eq.* (12) *for binary matrix $B_x \in \{B_6, B_7\}$ of* (11)*. There is a nonce-respecting distinguisher $\mathcal{D}$ making $4 \cdot 2^{n/2}$ queries such that*

$$\mathbf{Adv}^{\mathrm{prf}}_{F^{\mathrm{EDM}}_{B_x}}(\mathcal{D}) \geq 1 - \frac{1}{2^n}.$$

Proof. The proof is given in the full version of the paper. □

Proposition 4. *Let $k, n \in \mathbb{N}$. Let $E : \{0,1\}^k \times \{0,1\}^n \to \{0,1\}^n$ be a block cipher, and $H\colon \mathcal{K}_h \times \{0,1\}^* \to \{0,1\}^n$ be an ϵ-AXU hash function. Consider $F^{\mathrm{EDM}}_{B_x}$ of Eq.* (12) *for binary matrix $B_x \in \{B_2, B_3\}$ of* (11)*. There is a distinguisher $\mathcal{D}$ making $2^{n/2} + 2$ queries with 2 faulty nonces such that*

$$\mathbf{Adv}^{\mathrm{prf}}_{F^{\mathrm{EDM}}_{B_x}}(\mathcal{D}) \geq 1 - \frac{1}{\sqrt{e}} - \frac{1}{2^n}.$$

Proof. The proof is given in the full version of the paper. □

Proposition 5. *Let $k, n \in \mathbb{N}$. Let $E : \{0,1\}^k \times \{0,1\}^n \to \{0,1\}^n$ be a block cipher, and $H\colon \mathcal{K}_h \times \{0,1\}^* \to \{0,1\}^n$ be an ϵ-AXU hash function. Consider $F^{\mathrm{EDM}}_{B_x}$ of Eq.* (12) *for binary matrix $B_x \in \{B_4, B_5\}$ of* (11)*. There is a distinguisher $\mathcal{D}$ making $2 \cdot 2^{n/2} + 4$ queries with $2^{n/2}$ faulty nonces such that*

$$\mathbf{Adv}^{\mathrm{prf}}_{F^{\mathrm{EDM}}_{B_x}}(\mathcal{D}) \geq 1 - \frac{1}{\sqrt{e}} - \frac{1}{2^n}.$$

Proof. The proof is given in the full version of the paper. □

Theorem 2. *Let $k, n \in \mathbb{N}$. Let $E : \{0,1\}^k \times \{0,1\}^n \to \{0,1\}^n$ be a block cipher, and $H : \mathcal{K}_h \times \{0,1\}^* \to \{0,1\}^n$ be an ϵ-AXU hash function. Consider $F^{\mathrm{EDM}}_{B_x}$ of Eq.* (12) *for binary matrix $B_x \in \{B_2, B_3\}$ of* (11)*. For any nonce-respecting distinguisher $\mathcal{D}$ making at most $q \leq 2^{3n/4}$ queries, there exist distinguishers $\mathcal{D}'_1$ and $\mathcal{D}'_2$ with the same query complexity such that*

$$\mathbf{Adv}^{\mathrm{prf}}_{F^{\mathrm{EDM}}_{B_2}}(\mathcal{D}) \leq \mathbf{Adv}^{\mathrm{prp}}_{E}(\mathcal{D}'_1) + \mathbf{Adv}^{\mathrm{prp}}_{E}(\mathcal{D}'_2) + \frac{q^2\epsilon}{2^n} + \frac{19q^{\frac{4}{3}}}{2^n} + \frac{6q^{\frac{8}{3}}}{2^{2n}} + \frac{18q^{\frac{7}{3}}}{2^{2n}} + \frac{q^2}{2^{2n}} + \frac{8q^4}{3 \cdot 2^{3n}},$$

$$\mathbf{Adv}^{\mathrm{prf}}_{F^{\mathrm{EDM}}_{B_3}}(\mathcal{D}) \leq \mathbf{Adv}^{\mathrm{prp}}_{E}(\mathcal{D}'_1) + \mathbf{Adv}^{\mathrm{prp}}_{E}(\mathcal{D}'_2) + \frac{q^2\epsilon}{2^n} + q^{\frac{4}{3}}\epsilon + \frac{18q^{\frac{4}{3}}}{2^n} + \frac{6q^{\frac{8}{3}}}{2^{2n}} + \frac{18q^{\frac{7}{3}}}{2^{2n}} + \frac{q^2}{2^{2n}} + \frac{8q^4}{3 \cdot 2^{3n}}.$$

Proof. The proof is given in Sect. 5.3. □

Theorem 3. *Let $k, n \in \mathbb{N}$. Let $E : \{0,1\}^k \times \{0,1\}^n \to \{0,1\}^n$ be a block cipher, and $H : \mathcal{K}_h \times \{0,1\}^* \to \{0,1\}^n$ be an ϵ-AXU hash function. Consider $F^{\mathrm{EDM}}_{B_x}$ of Eq.* (12) *for binary matrix $B_x \in \{B_4, B_5\}$ of* (11)*. Let μ be a fixed parameter. For any distinguisher $\mathcal{D}$ making at most $q \leq 2^{3n/4}$ queries, and at most μ faulty nonces, there exist distinguishers $\mathcal{D}'_1$ and $\mathcal{D}'_2$ with the same query complexity such that*

$$\mathbf{Adv}^{\mathrm{prf}}_{F^{\mathrm{EDM}}_{B_4}}(\mathcal{D}) \leq \mathbf{Adv}^{\mathrm{prp}}_{E}(\mathcal{D}'_1) + \mathbf{Adv}^{\mathrm{prp}}_{E}(\mathcal{D}'_2) + \frac{\mu^2}{2^n} + \mu^2\epsilon + \frac{q^2\epsilon}{2^n} + \frac{q^2\epsilon}{2^{n/2}} + \frac{q^2\sqrt{\epsilon}}{2^n} + q^{\frac{4}{3}}\epsilon + \frac{19q^{\frac{4}{3}}}{2^n} + \frac{6q^{\frac{8}{3}}}{2^{2n}} + \frac{18q^{\frac{7}{3}}}{2^{2n}} + \frac{q^2}{2^{2n}} + \frac{8q^4}{3 \cdot 2^{3n}},$$

$$\mathbf{Adv}^{\mathrm{prf}}_{F^{\mathrm{EDM}}_{B_5}}(\mathcal{D}) \leq \mathbf{Adv}^{\mathrm{prp}}_{E}(\mathcal{D}'_1) + \mathbf{Adv}^{\mathrm{prp}}_{E}(\mathcal{D}'_2) + 2\mu^2\epsilon + \frac{q^2\epsilon}{2^n} + \frac{q^2\epsilon}{2^{n/2}} + \frac{q^2\sqrt{\epsilon}}{2^n} + 2q^{\frac{4}{3}}\epsilon + \frac{18q^{\frac{4}{3}}}{2^n} + \frac{6q^{\frac{8}{3}}}{2^{2n}} + \frac{18q^{\frac{7}{3}}}{2^{2n}} + \frac{q^2}{2^{2n}} + \frac{8q^4}{3 \cdot 2^{3n}}.$$

Proof. The proof is given in Sect. 5.3. □

For Theorem 3, when μ is sufficiently smaller than $2^{n/2}$, $F^{\mathrm{EDM}}_{B_4}$ and $F^{\mathrm{EDM}}_{B_5}$ achieve $3n/4$-bit security. Note that this optimal bound holds under the assumption that ϵ is sufficiently small ($\epsilon \approx 2^{-n}$) and the block cipher E is sufficiently PRP secure, such that the other terms in the bound are dominating.

4.3 Nonce-Based PRFs Based on A_3^* (Sum of Permutations)

In this section, we consider nonce-based PRFs based on the Sum of Permutations construction F^{SoP}. Let $k, n \in \mathbb{N}$, let $E : \{0,1\}^k \times \{0,1\}^n \to \{0,1\}^n$ be a block cipher, and $H: \mathcal{K}_h \times \{0,1\}^* \to \{0,1\}^n$ be an ϵ-AXU hash function. Consider generic construction $F^{\mathrm{SoP}}_{B_x}: \{0,1\}^{2k} \times \mathcal{K}_h \times \{0,1\}^n \times \{0,1\}^* \to \{0,1\}^n$:

$$\begin{aligned} &F^{\mathrm{SoP}}_{B_x}[E_{K_1}, E_{K_2}, H_{K_h}](N, M) = \\ &\qquad E_{K_1}(N \oplus b_1 \cdot H_{K_h}(M)) \oplus E_{K_2}(N \oplus b_2 \cdot H_{K_h}(M)) \oplus b_3 \cdot H_{K_h}(M), \end{aligned} \tag{13}$$

with $B_x \in \{B_0, B_1, \ldots, B_7\}$ of (11).

The function $F^{\mathrm{SoP}}_{B_4}$ is symmetric to $F^{\mathrm{SoP}}_{B_2}$, and $F^{\mathrm{SoP}}_{B_5}$ is symmetric to $F^{\mathrm{SoP}}_{B_3}$, and hence $F^{\mathrm{SoP}}_{B_4}$ and $F^{\mathrm{SoP}}_{B_5}$ can be omitted. The function $F^{\mathrm{SoP}}_{B_2}$ is the two keyed variant of the nEHtM construction of Dutta et al. [18]. Dutta et al. have shown that nEHtM based on a single key with domain separation achieves $2n/3$-bit security when $2^{n/3}$ faulty nonces are made, and its security degrades in a graceful manner when the number of faulty nonces go beyond $2^{n/3}$. Later, Choi et al. [12] have shown that single keyed nEHtM actually achieves $3n/4$-bit security when up to $2^{3n/8}$ faulty nonces are made, and its security also degrades in a graceful manner. Here, $F^{\mathrm{SoP}}_{B_2}$ is the nEHtM construction based on two keys without domain separation. The function $F^{\mathrm{SoP}}_{B_0}$ is trivially insecure and henceforth excluded. The function $F^{\mathrm{SoP}}_{B_1}$ is a Wegman-Carter construction with SoP as its underlying PRF, hence it is optimally n-bit secure against nonce-respecting adversaries, and totally broken when the nonce is reused. For the remaining four schemes, we show that two of these schemes achieve beyond birthday bound security, even in the case of nonce reuse.

Proposition 6. *Let $k, n \in \mathbb{N}$. Let $E: \{0,1\}^k \times \{0,1\}^n \to \{0,1\}^n$ be a block cipher, and $H: \mathcal{K}_h \times \{0,1\}^* \to \{0,1\}^n$ be an ϵ-AXU hash function. Consider $F^{\mathrm{SoP}}_{B_x}$ of Eq. (13) for binary matrix $B_x \in \{B_6, B_7\}$ of (11). There is a nonce-respecting distinguisher $\mathcal{D}$ that making $4 \cdot 2^{n/2}$ queries such that*

$$\mathbf{Adv}^{\mathrm{prf}}_{F^{\mathrm{SoP}}_{B_x}}(\mathcal{D}) \geq 1 - \frac{1}{2^n}.$$

Proof. The proof is given in the full version of the paper. □

Theorem 4. *Let $k, n \in \mathbb{N}$. Let $E: \{0,1\}^k \times \{0,1\}^n \to \{0,1\}^n$ be a block cipher, and $H: \mathcal{K}_h \times \{0,1\}^* \to \{0,1\}^n$ be an ϵ-AXU hash function. Consider $F^{\mathrm{SoP}}_{B_x}$ of Eq. (13) for binary matrix $B_x \in \{B_2, B_3\}$ of (11). Let $\mu \leq q^{1/3}$. For any distinguisher $\mathcal{D}$ making at most $q \leq 2^{3n/4}$ queries, and at most μ faulty nonces, there exist distinguishers $\mathcal{D}_1'$ and $\mathcal{D}_2'$ with the same query complexity such that*

$$\begin{aligned} \mathbf{Adv}^{\mathrm{prf}}_{F^{\mathrm{SoP}}_{B_2}}(\mathcal{D}) \leq{}& \mathbf{Adv}^{\mathrm{prp}}_{E}(\mathcal{D}_1') + \mathbf{Adv}^{\mathrm{prp}}_{E}(\mathcal{D}_2') + \frac{\mu^2}{2^n} + \mu^2\epsilon + \frac{q^2\epsilon}{2^n} + 4\mu^2\epsilon + \frac{3\mu q^{3n/2}\epsilon}{2^{n/2}} \\ &+ q^{\frac{4}{3}}\epsilon + \frac{18q^{\frac{4}{3}}}{2^n} + \frac{6q^{\frac{8}{3}}}{2^{2n}} + \frac{18q^{\frac{7}{3}}}{2^{2n}} + \frac{q^2}{2^{2n}} + \frac{8q^4}{3 \cdot 2^{3n}}, \\ \mathbf{Adv}^{\mathrm{prf}}_{F^{\mathrm{SoP}}_{B_3}}(\mathcal{D}) \leq{}& \mathbf{Adv}^{\mathrm{prp}}_{E}(\mathcal{D}_1') + \mathbf{Adv}^{\mathrm{prp}}_{E}(\mathcal{D}_2') + 2\mu^2\epsilon + \frac{q^2\epsilon}{2^n} + 4\mu^2\epsilon + \frac{3\mu q^{3n/2}\epsilon}{2^{n/2}} + q^{\frac{4}{3}}\epsilon \\ &+ \frac{18q^{\frac{4}{3}}}{2^n} + \frac{6q^{\frac{8}{3}}}{2^{2n}} + \frac{18q^{\frac{7}{3}}}{2^{2n}} + \frac{q^2}{2^{2n}} + \frac{8q^4}{3 \cdot 2^{3n}}. \end{aligned}$$

Proof. The proof is given in Sect. 5.3. □

In that case $F^{\text{SoP}}_{B_2}$ and $F^{\text{SoP}}_{B_3}$ achieve $3n/4$-bit security with $\mu \le 2^{n/4}$. Although both nEHtM based on a single key and based on two independent keys achieve $3n/4$-bit security, the number of faulty nonces μ that can be made for our nEHtM based on two keys is $2^{n/4}$ when $q = 2^{3n/4}$, which is less than $2^{3n/8}$ for the case of single keyed nEHtM. This follows from the comparison with the results in [12], which is due to the version of mirror theory we are using here, since the versions of mirror theory used by Dutta et al. [18] and Choi et al. [12] are for single permutation, and cannot be applied for our nEHtM based on two keys. Our result can be improved by improving the mirror theory for two permutations. These optimal bounds again hold under the assumption that ϵ is sufficiently small ($\epsilon \approx 2^{-n}$) and the block cipher E is sufficiently PRP secure, such that the other terms in the bound are dominating.

4.4 Nonce-Based PRFs Based on A_4^* (Encrypted Davies-Meyer Dual)

In this section, we consider nonce-based PRFs based on the Encrypted Davies-Meyer Dual construction F^{EDMD}. Let $k, n \in \mathbb{N}$, let $E\colon \{0,1\}^k \times \{0,1\}^n \to \{0,1\}^n$ be a block cipher, and $H\colon \mathcal{K}_h \times \{0,1\}^* \to \{0,1\}^n$ be an ϵ-AXU hash function. Consider generic construction $F^{\text{EDMD}}_{B_x}\colon \{0,1\}^{2k} \times \mathcal{K}_h \times \{0,1\}^n \times \{0,1\}^* \to \{0,1\}^n$:

$$\begin{aligned} &F^{\text{EDMD}}_{B_x}[E_{K_1}, E_{K_2}, H_{K_h}](N, M) = \\ &E_{K_2}(E_{K_1}(N \oplus b_1 \cdot H_{K_h}(M)) \oplus b_2 \cdot H_{K_h}(M)) \oplus E_{K_1}(N \oplus b_1 \cdot H_{K_h}(M)) \oplus b_3 \cdot H_{K_h}(M), \end{aligned} \tag{14}$$

with $B_x \in \{B_0, B_1, \ldots, B_7\}$ of (11).

Again, the function $F^{\text{EDMD}}_{B_0}$ is trivially insecure and henceforth excluded. The function $F^{\text{EDMD}}_{B_1}$ is a Wegman-Carter construction with EDMD as its underlying PRF, hence it is optimally n-bit secure against nonce-respecting adversaries, and totally broken when the nonce is reused. For the remaining six schemes, we provide birthday bound attacks for five out these six schemes.

Proposition 7. *Let $k, n \in \mathbb{N}$. Let $E : \{0,1\}^k \times \{0,1\}^n \to \{0,1\}^n$ be a block cipher, and $H\colon \mathcal{K}_h \times \{0,1\}^* \to \{0,1\}^n$ be an ϵ-AXU hash function. Consider $F^{\text{EDMD}}_{B_x}$ of Eq.* (14) *for binary matrix $B_x \in \{B_3, B_4, B_5, B_6, B_7\}$ of* (11)*. There is a non-negligible constant c such that for a distinguisher $\mathcal{D}$ making $(1/\sqrt{2}) \cdot 2^{n/2}$ queries, we have*

$$\mathbf{Adv}^{\text{prf}}_{F^{\text{EDMD}}_{B_x}}(\mathcal{D}) \ge c.$$

Proof. These constructions can be seen as the composition of two random functions. The proposition follows straightforwardly from Lemma 2. □

We conclude that only $F^{\text{EDMD}}_{B_2}$ may achieve beyond birthday bound security. However, for all four constructions, the output of their second permutation E_{K_2} is XORed with its input, this makes it a non-trivial exercise to derive security beyond the birthday bound for these constructions.

5 Security Analysis

Our analysis is performed using the H-coefficients technique, recapped in Sect. 5.1, and Patarin's mirror theory, recapped in Sect. 5.2. The proof of Theorem 2 and 3 on EDM-based algorithms, and the proof of Theorem 4 on SoP-based algorithms, are given in Sect. 5.3.

5.1 H-coefficients Technique

We will use Patarin's H-coefficient technique [11,36,38] for our security proofs.

Consider two oracles $\mathcal{O}$ and $\mathcal{P}$, and a deterministic distinguisher $\mathcal{D}$ that has query access to either of these oracles. The distinguisher's goal is to distinguish both worlds, and we denote by

$$\mathbf{Adv}(\mathcal{D}) = \left|\Pr\left[\mathcal{D}^{\mathcal{O}} = 1\right] - \Pr\left[\mathcal{D}^{\mathcal{P}} = 1\right]\right|$$

its advantage. We define a transcript τ which summarizes all query-response tuples learned by $\mathcal{D}$ during its interaction with its oracle $\mathcal{O}$ or $\mathcal{P}$. We denote by $X_{\mathcal{O}}$ and $X_{\mathcal{P}}$ the probability distribution of transcripts when interacting with $\mathcal{O}$ and $\mathcal{P}$, respectively. We call a transcript $\tau \in \mathcal{T}$ attainable if $Pr[X_{\mathcal{P}} = \tau] > 0$, or in other words if the transcript τ can be obtained from an interaction with $\mathcal{P}$.

Lemma 3 (H-coefficients technique [22]**).** *Consider a deterministic distinguisher $\mathcal{D}$. Define a partition $\mathcal{T} = \mathcal{T}_{\text{good}} \sqcup \mathcal{T}_{\text{bad}}$, where $\mathcal{T}_{\text{good}}$ is the subset of $\mathcal{T}$ which contains all the "good" transcripts and $\mathcal{T}_{\text{bad}}$ is the subset with all the "bad" transcripts. Assume that there exists ε_1 such that for all attainable $\tau \in \mathcal{T}_{\text{good}}$:*

$$\frac{\Pr[X_{\mathcal{O}} = \tau]}{\Pr[X_{\mathcal{P}} = \tau]} \geq 1 - \varepsilon_1,$$

and that there exists ε_2 such that $\Pr[X_{\mathcal{P}} \in \mathcal{T}_{\text{bad}}] \leq \varepsilon_2$. *Then, we have*

$$\mathbf{Adv}(\mathcal{D}) \leq \varepsilon_1 + \varepsilon_2.$$

5.2 Mirror Theory

Patarin's mirror theory [33,37,39,40] was popularized by Mennink and Neves [30] and used to prove the optimal n-bit security of EDM and EWCDM. However, in Patarin's original work, the proof is highly complex and too difficult to verify, and it contains several gaps. In recent years, many different versions of mirror theory were presented [12,15,18,23,26]. We follow the description of the mirror theory by Kim et al. [26].

Let $G = (\mathcal{V}, \mathcal{S})$ be a graph and let $\overline{PQ} \in \mathcal{S}$ be an edge for $P, Q \in \mathcal{V}$. If this edge is labeled with $\lambda \in \{0,1\}^n$, then it means an equation $P \oplus Q = \lambda$, while if it is labeled with the symbol $\neq$, then it means that P and Q are distinct (since P and Q are from two independent sets). We write $P \overset{\star}{-} Q$ when an edge $\overline{PQ}$ is labeled with $\star \in \{0,1\}^n \cup \{\neq\}$.

Let $G^=$ denote the graph obtained by deleting all $\neq$-labeled edges from G. For $\ell > 0$ and a trail

$$\mathcal{L} : P_0 \overset{\lambda_1}{-} P_1 \overset{\lambda_2}{-} \dots \overset{\lambda_\ell}{-} P_\ell$$

in $G^=$, its label is defined as

$$\lambda(\mathcal{L}) = \lambda_1 \oplus \lambda_2 \oplus \dots \oplus \lambda_\ell.$$

We decompose $G^=$ into its connected components:

$$G^= = \mathcal{C}_1 \sqcup \mathcal{C}_2 \sqcup \dots \sqcup \mathcal{C}_\alpha \sqcup \mathcal{D}_1 \sqcup \mathcal{D}_2 \sqcup \dots \sqcup \mathcal{D}_\beta$$

for some $\alpha, \beta \geq 0$, where $\mathcal{C}_i$ denotes a component of size greater than 2, and $\mathcal{D}_i$ denotes a component of size 2. We will also write $\mathcal{C} = \mathcal{C}_1 \sqcup \mathcal{C}_2 \sqcup \dots \sqcup \mathcal{C}_\alpha$ and $\mathcal{D} = \mathcal{D}_1 \sqcup \mathcal{D}_2 \sqcup \dots \sqcup \mathcal{D}_\beta$. We call the graph G a *nice graph* if G satisfies the following two restrictions.

Definition 1 (acyclic). *$G^=$ contains no cycle.*

Definition 2 (non-zero path label (NPL)). *$\lambda(\mathcal{L}) \neq 0$ for any trail $\mathcal{L}$ of even length ℓ in $G^=$.*

Acyclic means that there is no linear combination of the equations that is independent of the unknowns, and NPL means that there is no linear combination of the equations that implies equality of two distinct unknowns. Given a nice graph $G = (\mathcal{V}, \mathcal{S})$, where the vertex set $\mathcal{V}$ is partitioned into two disjoint parts $\mathcal{P}$ and $\mathcal{Q}$, a solution to G should satisfy all the λ-labeled equations in $G^=$, while all the variables in $\mathcal{P}$ (resp., $\mathcal{Q}$) should take different values.

Lemma 4 (mirror theorem [26]). *Let G be a nice graph, and let q and q_c denote the number of edges of $G^=$ and $\mathcal{C}$, respectively. If $q < \frac{2^n}{8}$, then the number of solutions to G, denoted $h(G)$, satisfies*

$$\frac{h(G)2^{nq}}{(2^n)_{|\mathcal{P}|}(2^n)_{|\mathcal{Q}|}} \geq 1 - \frac{9q_c^2}{8 \cdot 2^n} - \frac{3q_c q^2}{2 \cdot 2^{2n}} - \frac{q^2}{2^{2n}} - \frac{9q_c^2 q}{8 \cdot 2^{2n}} - \frac{8q^4}{3 \cdot 2^{3n}}.$$

5.3 Proof of Theorem 2, 3, and 4

Recall that we consider the constructions $F_{B_2}^{\mathrm{EDM}}, F_{B_3}^{\mathrm{EDM}}$ in Theorem 2 for any nonce-respecting distinguisher, the constructions $F_{B_4}^{\mathrm{EDM}}, F_{B_5}^{\mathrm{EDM}}$ in Theorem 3 for any distinguisher making at most μ faulty nonces, and $F_{B_2}^{\mathrm{SoP}}, F_{B_3}^{\mathrm{SoP}}$ in Theorem 4 for any distinguisher making at most μ faulty nonces. The first part of the analyses of the three theorems is very similar. Only in Sect. 5.3.5 we consider the three theorems (and thus six schemes) independently.

Let $K_e = (K_1, K_2) \xleftarrow{\$} \{0,1\}^{2k}$, and $K_h \xleftarrow{\$} \mathcal{K}_h$. For $\mathcal{F} \in \{\mathrm{EDM}, \mathrm{SoP}\}$, consider any distinguisher $\mathcal{D}$ that has access to either the real world oracle $F_{B_x}^{\mathcal{F}}[E_{K_1}, E_{K_2}, H_{K_h}]$, with $x = 2, \dots, 5$ (resp., $x = 2, 3$) if $\mathcal{F} = \mathrm{EDM}$ (resp.,

$\mathcal{F} = \mathrm{SoP}$), or the ideal world oracle Rand. We first consider the case $\mathcal{F} = \mathrm{EDM}$. Instead of replacing the block ciphers E_{K_1}, E_{K_2} by π_1, π_2, we replace them by π_1, π_2^{-1}. As π_1, π_2 are drawn independently, these two constructions are provably equally secure. However it is more convenient to reason about the latter one, as an evaluation of the latter case can be viewed as the XOR of two permutations in the middle of the function. Let $\pi_1, \pi_2^{-1} \xleftarrow{\$} \mathrm{Perm}(n)$. We have

$$\begin{aligned}
&\mathbf{Adv}^{\mathrm{prf}}_{F^{\mathrm{EDM}}_{B_x}}(\mathcal{D}) \\
&\leq \Delta_{\mathcal{D}}\Big(F^{\mathrm{EDM}}_{B_x}[E_{K_1}, E_{K_2}, H_{K_h}]\ ;\ \mathsf{Rand}\Big) \\
&\leq \Delta_{\mathcal{D}}\Big(F^{\mathrm{EDM}}_{B_x}[\pi_1, \pi_2^{-1}, H_{K_h}]\ ;\ \mathsf{Rand}\Big) + \Delta_{\mathcal{D}'_1}\Big(E_{K_1}\ ;\ \pi_1\Big) + \Delta_{\mathcal{D}'_2}\Big(E_{K_2}\ ;\ \pi_2^{-1}\Big) \\
&= \Delta_{\mathcal{D}}\Big(F^{\mathrm{EDM}}_{B_x}[\pi_1, \pi_2^{-1}, H_{K_h}]\ ;\ \mathsf{Rand}\Big) + \mathbf{Adv}^{\mathrm{prp}}_{E}(\mathcal{D}'_1) + \mathbf{Adv}^{\mathrm{prp}}_{E}(\mathcal{D}'_2),
\end{aligned} \tag{15}$$

for some distinguishers $\mathcal{D}'_1$ and $\mathcal{D}'_2$ with the same complexity as $\mathcal{D}$. We focus on the remaining distance in (15). As of now, we drop $[\pi_1, \pi_2^{-1}, H_{K_h}]$ for readability, and assume $\mathcal{D}$ is computationally unbounded and deterministic. The case of $\mathcal{F} = \mathrm{SoP}$ is similar, but we replace the block ciphers E_{K_1}, E_{K_2} by π_1, π_2.

5.3.1 Transcripts

$\mathcal{D}$ makes q queries to $\mathcal{O} \in \{F^{\mathcal{F}}_{B_x}, \mathsf{Rand}\}$, and these are summarized in a transcript

$$\tau_m = \{(N^{(1)}, M^{(1)}, T^{(1)}), \ldots, (N^{(q)}, M^{(q)}, T^{(q)})\}.$$

After $\mathcal{D}$'s interaction with the oracles, but before it outputs its decision, we disclose the hash key K_h to the distinguisher. In the real world, this is the key used in the hash function. In the ideal world, K_h is a dummy key that is drawn uniformly at random. The complete view is denoted $\tau = (\tau_m, K_h)$.

5.3.2 Attainable Index Mappings

In the real world, each query $(N^{(i)}, M^{(i)}, T^{(i)}) \in \tau$ corresponds to an evaluation of the oracle $F^{\mathcal{F}}_{B_x}$. Note that each scheme consists of an evaluation of π_1 and an evaluation of π_2, these are of the form $X^{(i)} \mapsto \pi_1(X^{(i)})$ and $Y^{(i)} \mapsto \pi_2(Y^{(i)})$ such that $\pi_1(X^{(i)}) \oplus \pi_2(Y^{(i)}) = Z^{(i)}$. The values of $X^{(i)}, Y^{(i)}, Z^{(i)}$ are specific for the particular construction under analysis (recall that currently we consider six different constructions $F^{\mathrm{EDM}}_{B_2}, F^{\mathrm{EDM}}_{B_3}, F^{\mathrm{EDM}}_{B_4}, F^{\mathrm{EDM}}_{B_5}$ and $F^{\mathrm{SoP}}_{B_2}, F^{\mathrm{SoP}}_{B_3}$ at once), and can be deduced from τ. This will also become clear in Sect. 5.3.5, where the separate schemes are treated individually. The transcript τ defines q equations on the unknowns, and these q equations are the following:

$$\mathcal{E} = \begin{cases} \pi_1(X^{(1)}) \oplus \pi_2(Y^{(1)}) = Z^{(1)}, \\ \pi_1(X^{(2)}) \oplus \pi_2(Y^{(2)}) = Z^{(2)}, \\ \vdots \\ \pi_1(X^{(q)}) \oplus \pi_2(Y^{(q)}) = Z^{(q)}. \end{cases}$$

In the above q equations, some of the unknowns may be equal to each other. We have that $\pi_1(X^{(i)}) \neq \pi_1(X^{(j)})$ if and only if $X^{(i)} \neq X^{(j)}$, and $\pi_2(Y^{(i)}) \neq \pi_2(Y^{(j)})$ if and only if $Y^{(i)} \neq Y^{(j)}$. No condition holds for $\pi_1(X^{(i)})$ versus $\pi_2(Y^{(i)})$, as these are defined by independent permutations. Thus, $\{\pi_1(X^{(i)})\}_{1\leq i\leq q}$ and $\{\pi_2(Y^{(i)})\}_{1\leq i\leq q}$ are identified with two sets of unknowns

$$\mathcal{P} = \{P_1, \ldots, P_{q_1}\},$$
$$\mathcal{Q} = \{Q_1, \ldots, Q_{q_2}\}.$$

with $q_1, q_2 \leq q$. Since $\mathcal{P}$ and $\mathcal{Q}$ are defined by independent permutations, we know that $\mathcal{P}$ and $\mathcal{Q}$ are independent. We connect P_j and $Q_{j'}$ with a $Z^{(i)}$-labeled edge if $\pi_1(X^{(i)}) = P_j$ and $\pi_2(Y^{(i)}) = Q_{j'}$ for some i. Any pair of vertices in the same set (either $\mathcal{P}$ or $\mathcal{Q}$) are connected by a $\neq$-labeled edge. In this way, we obtain the transcript graph of τ on $\mathcal{P} \sqcup \mathcal{Q}$, and we denote it by G_τ.

5.3.3 Bad Transcripts

Informally, bad events are the properties which would make the mirror theory inapplicable. One can only apply the mirror theory if the transcript graph G_τ is (1) acyclic, (2) satisfies the NPL condition, and (3) the number of edges in $\mathcal{C}$ (i.e., edges in the components of size greater than two) is not greater than $\overline{q}_c$, for some parameter $\overline{q}_c$ that will be defined later on. The first two conditions come from Definitions 1 and 2, the last one is the condition on the number of edges in $\mathcal{C}$ in Lemma 4. Stated differently, we need to say that τ is a bad transcript if the corresponding transcript graph G_τ either includes a circle or a path of even length with $\lambda(\mathcal{L}) = 0$, or the number of edges in $\mathcal{C}$ exceeds $\overline{q}_c$.

The first two are implied if either of the following two events is set.

(i) G_τ contains an alternating circle of length 2 or an alternating path of length 2 such that $\lambda(\mathcal{L}) = 0$,
(ii) G_τ contains an alternating path of length 4 starting at the X-shore, or it contains an alternating path of length 4 starting at the Y-shore such that $\lambda(\mathcal{L}) = 0$.

We remark that it appears a bit odd to require the side-condition for the second part of event (ii) only. However, it turns out that by releasing that condition for this second part, we would not be able to derive a strong security bound for constructions based on SoP (see Sect. 5.3.5 for more details). Fortunately, it turns out that we *can* add this side-condition without problems, as negation of above two conditions (i)–(ii) indeed imply (1) and (2). Together with the third condition,

(iii) the number of edges in $\mathcal{C}$ is greater than $\overline{q}_c$,

these form the three conditions which a good transcript graph should satisfy. In other words, we say that $\tau \in \mathcal{T}_{\text{bad}}$ if and only if one of the above conditions holds.

Below, we will describe these three sets of bad events in more detail, the bad events for all six schemes are defined separately in the full version of the paper.

Recalling that we denote by $X^{(i)}$ the i-th input to π_1, $Y^{(i)}$ the i-th input to π_2, and $Z^{(i)} = \pi_1(X^{(i)}) \oplus \pi_2(Y^{(i)})$.

(i) This event is covered by AP2 = AP2a ∨ AP2b ∨ AP2c, defined as follows:

$$\begin{aligned}\text{AP2}a&: \exists\,\text{distinct}\,(i,j)\,\text{such that}\,X^{(i)} = X^{(j)} \wedge Y^{(i)} = Y^{(j)},\\ \text{AP2}b&: \exists\,\text{distinct}\,(i,j)\,\text{such that}\,X^{(i)} = X^{(j)} \wedge Z^{(i)} = Z^{(j)},\\ \text{AP2}c&: \exists\,\text{distinct}\,(i,j)\,\text{such that}\,Z^{(i)} = Z^{(j)} \wedge Y^{(i)} = Y^{(j)}.\end{aligned}$$

(ii) This event is covered by AP4 = AP4a ∨ AP4b, defined as follows:

$$\begin{aligned}\text{AP4}a&: \exists\,\text{distinct}\,(i,j,k,l)\,\text{such that}\,X^{(i)} = X^{(j)} \wedge Y^{(j)} = Y^{(k)} \wedge X^{(k)} = X^{(l)},\\ \text{AP4}b&: \exists\,\text{distinct}\,(i,j,k,l)\,\text{such that}\,Y^{(i)} = Y^{(j)} \wedge X^{(j)} = X^{(k)} \wedge Y^{(k)} = Y^{(l)}\\ &\qquad (\wedge\, Z^{(i)} \oplus Z^{(j)} \oplus Z^{(k)} \oplus Z^{(l)} = 0),\end{aligned}$$

where $Z^{(i)} \oplus Z^{(j)} \oplus Z^{(k)} \oplus Z^{(l)} = 0$ is the side condition of the event AP4b.

(iii) This event is covered by NC = NCa ∨ NCb, defined as follows:

$$\begin{aligned}\text{NC}a&: |\{(i,j)\,\text{such that}\,i \neq j \wedge X^{(i)} = X^{(j)}\}| \geq \overline{q}_c/4,\\ \text{NC}b&: |\{(i,j)\,\text{such that}\,i \neq j \wedge Y^{(i)} = Y^{(j)}\}| \geq \overline{q}_c/4.\end{aligned}$$

A distinct pair of "half-colliding" queries such that either $X^{(i)} = X^{(j)}$ or $Y^{(i)} = Y^{(j)}$ will add an edge to any component containing it, and make the size of the component greater than two; hence the number of edges in $\mathcal{C}$ cannot be twice as many as the number of half-collisions.

The probability that $\tau \in \mathcal{T}_{\text{bad}}$ happens, is given by

$$\Pr[\tau \in \mathcal{T}_{\text{bad}}] \leq \Pr[\text{AP2}] + \Pr[\text{AP4}] + \Pr[\text{NC}], \tag{16}$$

where AP2 = AP2a∨AP2b∨AP2c, AP4 = AP4a∨AP4b, and NC = NCa∨NCb.

5.3.4 Ratio for Good Transcripts for $F_{B_2}^{\text{EDM}}, F_{B_3}^{\text{EDM}}, F_{B_4}^{\text{EDM}}, F_{B_5}^{\text{EDM}}$, and $F_{B_2}^{\text{SoP}}, F_{B_3}^{\text{SoP}}$

Consider an attainable transcript $\tau \in \mathcal{T}_{\text{good}}$. We now lower bound $\Pr[X_{\mathcal{O}} = \tau]$ and compute $\Pr[X_{\mathcal{P}} = \tau]$ in order to obtain a lower bound for the ratio of these probabilities. We denote by $comp_{\mathcal{O}}(\tau)$ (resp., $comp_{\mathcal{P}}(\tau)$) the set of oracles in the real world (resp., the ideal world) that are compatible with τ. We first consider the ideal world $\mathcal{P}$, and obtain

$$\Pr[X_{\mathcal{P}} = \tau] = \Pr[\mathsf{Rand} \in comp_{\mathcal{P}}(\tau)] = \frac{1}{|\mathcal{K}_h|} \cdot \frac{1}{2^{nq}}.$$

For the real world oracle $\mathcal{O}$, the probability of obtaining τ is computed over the randomness of π_1 and π_2. Now, fix a parameter $\overline{q}_c$ (to be optimized later). For a transcript graph G_τ, let $G_\tau^{=}$ denote the graph obtained by deleting all

$\neq$-labeled edges from G_τ. Then $G_\tau^=$ is a bipartite graph with q edges. By the fact that the considered transcript τ is good, the induced graph G_τ (i) is acyclic, (ii) satisfies the NPL condition, and (iii) the number of edges in $\mathcal{C}$ (i.e., edges in the components of size greater than two) is not greater than $\overline{q}_c$. By Theorem 4 and since $q_c \leq \overline{q}_c$, the number of possible ways of fixing $\pi_1(X^{(i)})$ and $\pi_2(Y^{(i)})$ is lower bounded by $\frac{(2^n)_{|\mathcal{P}|}(2^n)_{|\mathcal{Q}|}}{2^{nq}}(1-\varepsilon_1)$ where

$$\varepsilon_1 = \frac{9\overline{q}_c^2}{8 \cdot 2^n} + \frac{3\overline{q}_c q^2}{2 \cdot 2^{2n}} + \frac{q^2}{2^{2n}} + \frac{9\overline{q}_c^2 q}{8 \cdot 2^{2n}} + \frac{8q^4}{3 \cdot 2^{3n}}. \tag{17}$$

The probability that π_1 and π_2 realize each assignment is exactly $1/(2^n)_{|\mathcal{P}|}(2^n)_{|\mathcal{Q}|}$. We thus obtain

$$\frac{\Pr[X_{\mathcal{O}} = \tau]}{\Pr[X_{\mathcal{P}} = \tau]} \geq 1 - \varepsilon_1.$$

5.3.5 Probability of Bad Transcripts for $F_{B_2}^{\mathrm{EDM}}, F_{B_3}^{\mathrm{EDM}}, F_{B_4}^{\mathrm{EDM}}, F_{B_5}^{\mathrm{EDM}}$, and $F_{B_2}^{\mathrm{SoP}}, F_{B_3}^{\mathrm{SoP}}$

The exact values of X, Y, and Z are, respectively,

MAC	X	Y	Z
$F_{B_2}^{\mathrm{EDM}}$	N	T	$N \oplus H_{K_h}(M)$
$F_{B_3}^{\mathrm{EDM}}$	N	$T \oplus H_{K_h}(M)$	$N \oplus H_{K_h}(M)$
$F_{B_4}^{\mathrm{EDM}}$	$N \oplus H_{K_h}(M)$	T	N
$F_{B_5}^{\mathrm{EDM}}$	$N \oplus H_{K_h}(M)$	$T \oplus H_{K_h}(M)$	N
$F_{B_2}^{\mathrm{SoP}}$	N	$N \oplus H_{K_h}(M)$	T
$F_{B_3}^{\mathrm{SoP}}$	N	$N \oplus H_{K_h}(M)$	$T \oplus H_{K_h}(M)$

Let $\overline{q}_c \in \mathbb{N}$. We denote by $\mathcal{I}$ the set of all query indices i such that $N^{(i)} = N^{(j)}$ for some $j \neq i$. One can see that $|\mathcal{I}| \leq 2\mu$. Note that $|\mathcal{I}| = 0$ for $F_{B_2}^{\mathrm{EDM}}$ and $F_{B_3}^{\mathrm{EDM}}$. We define by $\mathrm{AP2}^{\mathcal{F}}[B_x]$ (resp., $\mathrm{AP4}^{\mathcal{F}}[B_x]$ and $\mathrm{NC}^{\mathcal{F}}[B_x]$) the bad event AP2 (resp., AP4 and NC) for $F_{B_x}^{\mathrm{EDM}}$ with $x = 2, \ldots, 5$, or $F_{B_x}^{\mathrm{SoP}}$ with $x = 2, 3$. Note that we treat $F_{B_2}^{\mathrm{EDM}}$ and $F_{B_3}^{\mathrm{EDM}}$ for nonce-respecting distinguisher only, hence the bad events AP2a, AP2b, AP4a, AP4b, and NCa do not appear for these two constructions. We consider the bad events for each of the six construction separately.

(i) An alternating circle of length 2 or an alternating path of length such that $\lambda(\mathcal{L}) = 0$.

- $F_{B_4}^{\mathrm{EDM}}$. We first consider the bad event AP2a. The probability that $N^{(i)} \oplus H_{K_h}(M^{(i)}) = N^{(j)} \oplus H_{K_h}(M^{(j)})$ happens for fixed i, j is ϵ, and the probability that $T^{(i)} = T^{(j)}$ happens for fixed i, j is $1/2^n$. Summed over all q possible i's, and all q possible j's, we have

$$\Pr\left[\text{AP2}a^{\text{EDM}}[B_4]\right] \leq \frac{q^2\epsilon}{2^n}. \tag{18}$$

We then consider the bad event AP2b. The probability that $N^{(i)} \oplus H_{K_h}(M^{(i)}) = N^{(j)} \oplus H_{K_h}(M^{(j)})$ happens for fixed i, j is ϵ. Assume that $i < j$, which means that $N^{(j)}$ is a faulty nonce. Then the number of pairs (i, j) such that $N^{(i)} = N^{(j)}$ is at most μ^2, and we have

$$\Pr\left[\text{AP2}b^{\text{EDM}}[B_4]\right] \leq \mu^2\epsilon. \tag{19}$$

Bad event AP2c is similar to AP2b. However, the second event is $T^{(i)} = T^{(j)}$, which holds with probability $1/2^n$. Then the number of pairs (i, j) such that $N^{(i)} = N^{(j)}$ is at most μ^2, and we have

$$\Pr\left[\text{AP2}c^{\text{EDM}}[B_4]\right] \leq \frac{\mu^2}{2^n}. \tag{20}$$

- $F_{B_5}^{\text{EDM}}$. We first consider the bad event AP2a. The probability that $N^{(i)} \oplus H_{K_h}(M^{(i)}) = N^{(j)} \oplus H_{K_h}(M^{(j)})$ and $T^{(i)} \oplus H_{K_h}(M^{(i)}) = T^{(j)} \oplus H_{K_h}(M^{(j)})$ happens for fixed i, j is $\epsilon/2^n$. Summed over all q possible i's, and all q possible j's, we have

$$\Pr\left[\text{AP2}a^{\text{EDM}}[B_5]\right] \leq \frac{q^2\epsilon}{2^n}. \tag{21}$$

The bad event AP2b is already analyzed in (19). We then consider the bad event AP2c. The probability that $T^{(i)} \oplus H_{K_h}(M^{(i)}) = T^{(j)} \oplus H_{K_h}(M^{(j)})$ happens for fixed i, j is ϵ. Assume that $i < j$, which means that $N^{(j)}$ is a faulty nonce. Then the number of pairs (i, j) such that $N^{(i)} = N^{(j)}$ is at most μ^2, and we have

$$\Pr\left[\text{AP2}c^{\text{EDM}}[B_5]\right] \leq \mu^2\epsilon. \tag{22}$$

- $F_{B_2}^{\text{EDM}}$. Note that the X and Z values of $F_{B_2}^{\text{EDM}}$ are the reverse of those of $F_{B_4}^{\text{EDM}}$, and the Y value of the both constructions is the same. Hence the analysis is the same as that for $F_{B_4}^{\text{EDM}}$ with $\mu = 0$ because we consider nonce-respecting dinstinguishers for $F_{B_2}^{\text{EDM}}$.
- $F_{B_3}^{\text{EDM}}$. Note that the X and Z values of $F_{B_3}^{\text{EDM}}$ are the reverse of those of $F_{B_5}^{\text{EDM}}$, and the Y value of the both constructions is the same. Hence the analysis is the same as that for $F_{B_5}^{\text{EDM}}$ with $\mu = 0$ because we consider nonce-respecting dinstinguishers for $F_{B_3}^{\text{EDM}}$.
- $F_{B_2}^{\text{SoP}}$. Note that the X, Y, and Z values of $F_{B_2}^{\text{SoP}}$ are a reshuffling of the X, Y, and Z values of $F_{B_4}^{\text{EDM}}$. Hence we have that $\Pr\left[\text{AP2}^{\text{SoP}}[B_2]\right] = \Pr\left[\text{AP2}^{\text{EDM}}[B_4]\right]$.

- $F^{\text{SoP}}_{B_3}$. Note that the X, Y, and Z values of $F^{\text{SoP}}_{B_3}$ are a reshuffling of the X, Y, and Z values of $F^{\text{EDM}}_{B_5}$. Hence we have that $\Pr\left[\text{AP2}^{\text{SoP}}[B_3]\right] = \Pr\left[\text{AP2}^{\text{EDM}}[B_5]\right]$.

We have obtained

$$\Pr\left[\text{AP2}^{\text{EDM}}[B_2]\right] \leq \frac{q^2\epsilon}{2^n}, \tag{23}$$

$$\Pr\left[\text{AP2}^{\text{EDM}}[B_3]\right] \leq \frac{q^2\epsilon}{2^n}. \tag{24}$$

$$\Pr\left[\text{AP2}^{\text{EDM}}[B_4]\right], \Pr\left[\text{AP2}^{\text{SoP}}[B_2]\right] \leq \frac{\mu^2}{2^n} + \frac{q^2\epsilon}{2^n} + \mu^2\epsilon, \tag{25}$$

$$\Pr\left[\text{AP2}^{\text{EDM}}[B_5]\right], \Pr\left[\text{AP2}^{\text{SoP}}[B_3]\right] \leq 2\mu^2\epsilon + \frac{q^2\epsilon}{2^n}. \tag{26}$$

(ii) An Alternating Path of Length 4. We want to recall that since we treat $F^{\text{EDM}}_{B_2}$ and $F^{\text{EDM}}_{B_3}$ for nonce-respecting distinguisher only, alternating paths do not appear for these two constructions. Thus, we only have to consider $F^{\text{EDM}}_{B_4}$, $F^{\text{EDM}}_{B_5}$, $F^{\text{SoP}}_{B_2}$, and $F^{\text{SoP}}_{B_3}$.

- $F^{\text{EDM}}_{B_4}$. We will use Lemma 1 to bound the event, with $q_i = q_j = q_k = q_l = q$. We first consider the bad event AP4a. We denote $E_{i,j} : N^{(i)} \oplus H_{K_h}(M^{(i)}) = N^{(j)} \oplus H_{K_h}(M^{(j)})$ (same for $E_{k,\ell}$), and $F_{i,j,k,\ell} : T^{(j)} = T^{(k)}$. The probability that $E_{i,j}$ happens for fixed i, j is ϵ (same for $E_{k,\ell}$), and the probability that $F_{i,j,k,\ell}$ happens for fixed j, k is $1/2^n$. Summed over all possible i, j, k, ℓ's, we have

$$\Pr\left[\text{AP4}a^{\text{EDM}}[B_4]\right] \leq \frac{q^2\epsilon}{2^{n/2}}. \tag{27}$$

  Next, we consider the bad event AP4b, again with $q_i = q_j = q_k = q_l = q$. We drop the side-condition $Z^{(i)} \oplus Z^{(j)} \oplus Z^{(k)} \oplus Z^{(l)} = 0$ for simplicity. We denote $E_{i,j} : T^{(i)} = T^{(j)}$ (same for $E_{k,\ell}$), and $F_{i,j,k,\ell} : N^{(j)} \oplus H_{K_h}(M^{(j)}) = N^{(k)} \oplus H_{K_h}(M^{(k)})$. The probability that $E_{i,j}$ happens for fixed i, j is $1/2^n$ (same for $E_{k,\ell}$), and the probability that $F_{i,j,k,\ell}$ happens for fixed j, k is ϵ. Summed over all possible i, j, k, ℓ's, we have

$$\Pr\left[\text{AP4}b^{\text{EDM}}[B_4]\right] \leq \frac{q^2\sqrt{\epsilon}}{2^n}. \tag{28}$$

- $F^{\text{EDM}}_{B_5}$. The analysis is identical to the one of $F^{\text{EDM}}_{B_4}$. The only difference is that we have $Y = T \oplus H_{K_h}(M)$ instead of $Y = T$. However, we can still rely on the randomness of T.
- $F^{\text{SoP}}_{B_2}$ and $F^{\text{SoP}}_{B_3}$. Since the X and Y values are the same for these two constructions, we will consider these together. We first consider the bad event AP4a. The number of queries using any repeated nonce is at most 2μ. This means that the number of pairs (j, k) such that $N^{(j)} = N^{(i)}$ for some $i \neq j$

and $N^{(k)} = N^{(l)}$ for some $k \neq l$ is at most $4\mu^2$. The probability that $N^{(j)} \oplus H_{K_h}(M^{(j)}) = N^{(k)} \oplus H_{K_h}(M^{(k)})$ happens for fixed j, k is ϵ. Summed over all possible j, k's, we have

$$\Pr[\mathrm{AP4}a^{\mathrm{SoP}}[B_2]] \leq 4\mu^2\epsilon. \tag{29}$$

Next, we consider the bad event AP4b. Note that since the only randomness we have is the universal hash key K_h, we will explicitly rely on the side event $Z^{(i)} \oplus Z^{(j)} \oplus Z^{(k)} \oplus Z^{(l)} = 0$. We will use Lemma 1 to bound this event. We first consider the case that $k > \max\{i, j, l\}$ and the k-th query sets AP4b. We denote $E_{i,j} : N^{(i)} \oplus H_{K_h}(M^{(i)}) = N^{(j)} \oplus H_{K_h}(M^{(j)})$ (same for $E_{k,l}$), and $F_{i,j,k,l} : T^{(i)} \oplus T^{(j)} \oplus T^{(k)} \oplus T^{(l)} = 0$. The probability that $E_{i,j}$ happens for fixed i, j is ϵ (same for $E_{k,l}$), and the probability that $F_{i,j,k,l}$ happens for fixed i, j, k, l is $1/2^n$. For each fixed k, and summed over q possible i's, q possible j's, and q possible l's, and since the k-th query makes an inner edge of the trail, it should be a faulty query (there are μ possible k's in total). Therefore this case happens with probability at most

$$\mu\sqrt{\frac{q^3}{2^n}}\epsilon.$$

Next, consider the case that $l > \max\{i, j, k\}$ and the l-th query makes AP4b. We denote $E_{i,j} : N^{(i)} \oplus H_{K_h}(M^{(i)}) = N^{(j)} \oplus H_{K_h}(M^{(j)})$ (same for $E_{k,\ell}$), and $F_{i,j,k,\ell} : T^{(i)} \oplus T^{(j)} \oplus T^{(k)} \oplus T^{(l)} = 0$. The probability that $E_{i,j}$ happens for fixed i, j is ϵ (same for $E_{k,\ell}$), and the probability that $F_{i,j,k,\ell}$ happens for fixed i, j, k, l is $1/2^n$. For each fixed l (there are q possible l's in total), and summed over q possible i's, 2μ possible j's, and 2μ possible k's, this case happens with probability

$$2q\sqrt{\frac{\mu^2 q}{2^n}}\epsilon.$$

By symmetry, all other cases (i.e., $i > \max\{j, k, l\}$ and $j > \max\{i, k, l\}$) are also covered, we have

$$\Pr[\mathrm{AP4}b^{\mathrm{SoP}}[B_2]] \leq \mu\sqrt{\frac{q^3}{2^n}}\epsilon + 2q\sqrt{\frac{\mu^2 q}{2^n}}\epsilon = \frac{3\mu q^{3n/2}\epsilon}{2^{n/2}}. \tag{30}$$

We have obtained

$$\Pr\left[\mathrm{AP4}^{\mathrm{EDM}}[B_4]\right], \Pr\left[\mathrm{AP4}^{\mathrm{EDM}}[B_5]\right] \leq \frac{q^2\epsilon}{2^{n/2}} + \frac{q^2\sqrt{\epsilon}}{2^n}, \tag{31}$$

$$\Pr\left[\mathrm{AP4}^{\mathrm{SoP}}[B_2]\right], \Pr\left[\mathrm{AP4}^{\mathrm{SoP}}[B_3]\right] \leq 4\mu^2\epsilon + \frac{3\mu q^{3n/2}\epsilon}{2^{n/2}}. \tag{32}$$

(iii) The number of edges in $\mathcal{C}$ is greater than $\overline{q}_c$.

– $F^{\mathrm{EDM}}_{B_4}$. For NCa, $X = N \oplus H_{K_h}(M)$. Using Markov inequality, we have:

$$\Pr\left[\mathrm{NC}a^{\mathrm{EDM}}[B_4]\right] \leq \frac{4q^2\epsilon}{\overline{q}_c}. \tag{33}$$

For NCb, $Y = T$. Using Markov inequality, we have:

$$\Pr\left[\mathrm{NC}b^{\mathrm{EDM}}[B_4]\right] \leq \frac{4q^2}{\overline{q}_c \cdot 2^n}. \tag{34}$$

- $F^{\mathrm{EDM}}_{B_5}$. The bad event NCa is already analyzed in (33). For NCb, $Y = T \oplus H_{K_h}(M)$. Using Markov inequality, we have:

$$\Pr\left[\mathrm{NC}b^{\mathrm{EDM}}[B_5]\right] \leq \frac{4q^2\epsilon}{\overline{q}_c}. \tag{35}$$

- $F^{\mathrm{EDM}}_{B_2}$. The analysis is the same as that for $F^{\mathrm{EDM}}_{B_4}$, except that NCa would not happen due to $X = N$ and $\mu = 0$.
- $F^{\mathrm{EDM}}_{B_3}$. The analysis is the same as that for $F^{\mathrm{EDM}}_{B_5}$, except that NCa would not happen due to $X = N$ and $\mu = 0$.
- $F^{\mathrm{SoP}}_{B_2}$. Assuming that $\overline{q}_c/4 \geq \mu^2$ ($\overline{q}_c$ will be chosen later on to satisfy this condition), NCa would not happen. The bad event NCb is already analyzed in (33).
- $F^{\mathrm{SoP}}_{B_3}$. Assuming that $\overline{q}_c/4 \geq \mu^2$ ($\overline{q}_c$ will be chosen later on to satisfy this condition), NCa would not happen. The bad event NCb is already analyzed in (33).

We have obtained

$$\Pr\left[\mathrm{NC}^{\mathrm{EDM}}[B_2]\right] \leq \frac{4q^2}{\overline{q}_c \cdot 2^n}, \tag{36}$$

$$\Pr\left[\mathrm{NC}^{\mathrm{EDM}}[B_3]\right], \Pr\left[\mathrm{NC}^{\mathrm{SoP}}[B_2]\right], \Pr\left[\mathrm{NC}^{\mathrm{SoP}}[B_3]\right] \leq \frac{4q^2\epsilon}{\overline{q}_c}, \tag{37}$$

$$\Pr\left[\mathrm{NC}^{\mathrm{EDM}}[B_4]\right] \leq \frac{4q^2\epsilon}{\overline{q}_c} + \frac{4q^2}{\overline{q}_c \cdot 2^n}, \tag{38}$$

$$\Pr\left[\mathrm{NC}^{\mathrm{EDM}}[B_5]\right] \leq \frac{8q^2\epsilon}{\overline{q}_c}, \tag{39}$$

Conclusion for Bad Events. Combining (23)–(26), (31)–(32), and (36)–(39) with (16), we obtain

$$\Pr\left[\tau^{\mathrm{EDM}}[B_2] \in \mathcal{T}_{\mathrm{bad}}\right] \leq \frac{q^2\epsilon}{2^n} + \frac{4q^2}{\overline{q}_c \cdot 2^n},$$

$$\Pr\left[\tau^{\mathrm{EDM}}[B_3] \in \mathcal{T}_{\mathrm{bad}}\right] \leq \frac{q^2\epsilon}{2^n} + \frac{4q^2\epsilon}{\overline{q}_c},$$

$$\Pr\left[\tau^{\mathrm{EDM}}[B_4] \in \mathcal{T}_{\mathrm{bad}}\right] \leq \frac{\mu^2}{2^n} + \mu^2\epsilon + \frac{q^2\epsilon}{2^n} + \frac{q^2\epsilon}{2^{n/2}} + \frac{q^2\sqrt{\epsilon}}{2^n} + \frac{4q^2\epsilon}{\overline{q}_c} + \frac{4q^2}{\overline{q}_c \cdot 2^n},$$

$$\Pr\left[\tau^{\mathrm{EDM}}[B_5] \in \mathcal{T}_{\mathrm{bad}}\right] \leq 2\mu^2\epsilon + \frac{q^2\epsilon}{2^n} + \frac{q^2\epsilon}{2^{n/2}} + \frac{q^2\sqrt{\epsilon}}{2^n} + \frac{8q^2\epsilon}{\overline{q}_c},$$

$$\Pr\left[\tau^{\mathrm{SoP}}[B_2] \in \mathcal{T}_{\mathrm{bad}}\right] \le \frac{\mu^2}{2^n} + \mu^2\epsilon + \frac{q^2\epsilon}{2^n} + 4\mu^2\epsilon + \frac{3\mu q^{3n/2}\epsilon}{2^{n/2}} + \frac{4q^2\epsilon}{\overline{q}_c},$$
$$\Pr\left[\tau^{\mathrm{SoP}}[B_3] \in \mathcal{T}_{\mathrm{bad}}\right] \le 2\mu^2\epsilon + \frac{q^2\epsilon}{2^n} + 4\mu^2\epsilon + \frac{3\mu q^{3n/2}\epsilon}{2^{n/2}} + \frac{4q^2\epsilon}{\overline{q}_c}.$$

5.3.6 Conclusion

We will discuss the restrictions on the number of faulty queries for $F_{B_4}^{\mathrm{EDM}}, F_{B_5}^{\mathrm{EDM}}$, and $F_{B_2}^{\mathrm{SoP}}, F_{B_3}^{\mathrm{SoP}}$. We have assumed that $\overline{q}_c/4 \ge \mu^2$ for $F_{B_2}^{\mathrm{SoP}}$ and $F_{B_3}^{\mathrm{SoP}}$. In order to obtain $3n/4$-bit security, we choose $\overline{q}_c = 4q^{\frac{2}{3}}$. Above terms that include $\overline{q}_c$ get simplified as follows:

$$\frac{4q^2\epsilon}{\overline{q}_c} = q^{\frac{4}{3}}\epsilon,$$
$$\frac{4q^2}{\overline{q}_c \cdot 2^n} = \frac{q^{\frac{4}{3}}}{2^n}.$$

Based on this condition, we have $\mu \le q^{\frac{1}{3}}$ for $F_{B_2}^{\mathrm{SoP}}$ and $F_{B_3}^{\mathrm{SoP}}$, and there is no restriction on μ for $F_{B_4}^{\mathrm{EDM}}$ and $F_{B_5}^{\mathrm{EDM}}$. Using the H-coefficients Technique (Lemma 3) with

$$\varepsilon_1 = \frac{18q^{\frac{4}{3}}}{2^n} + \frac{6q^{\frac{8}{3}}}{2^{2n}} + \frac{18q^{\frac{7}{3}}}{2^{2n}} + \frac{q^2}{2^{2n}} + \frac{8q^4}{3 \cdot 2^{3n}},$$

we obtain the results stated in Theorem 2, Theorem 3, and Theorem 4.

Acknowledgments. This work was supported in part by the Research Council KU Leuven: GOA TENSE (C16/15/058). Yu Long Chen is supported by a Ph.D. Fellowship from the Research Foundation - Flanders (FWO). The authors would like to thank the anonymous reviewers for their comments and suggestions.

References

1. Aumasson, J.-P., Bernstein, D.J.: SipHash: a fast short-input PRF. In: Galbraith, S., Nandi, M. (eds.) INDOCRYPT 2012. LNCS, vol. 7668, pp. 489–508. Springer, Heidelberg (2012). https://doi.org/10.1007/978-3-642-34931-7_28
2. Beaulieu, R., Shors, D., Smith, J., Treatman-Clark, S., Weeks, B., Wingers, L.: The SIMON and SPECK families of lightweight block ciphers. Cryptology ePrint Archive, Report 2013/404 (2013)
3. Beierle, C., et al.: The SKINNY family of block ciphers and its low-latency variant MANTIS. In: Robshaw, M., Katz, J. (eds.) CRYPTO 2016. LNCS, vol. 9815, pp. 123–153. Springer, Heidelberg (2016). https://doi.org/10.1007/978-3-662-53008-5_5
4. Bellare, M., Krovetz, T., Rogaway, P.: Luby-Rackoff backwards: increasing security by making block ciphers non-invertible. In: Nyberg, K. (ed.) EUROCRYPT 1998. LNCS, vol. 1403, pp. 266–280. Springer, Heidelberg (1998). https://doi.org/10.1007/BFb0054132

5. Bernstein, D.J.: SURF: simple unpredictable random function, April 1997
6. Bernstein, D.J.: Stronger security bounds for Wegman-Carter-Shoup authenticators. In: Cramer, R. (ed.) EUROCRYPT 2005. LNCS, vol. 3494, pp. 164–180. Springer, Heidelberg (2005). https://doi.org/10.1007/11426639_10
7. Böck, H., Zauner, A., Devlin, S., Somorovsky, J., Jovanovic, P.: Nonce-disrespecting adversaries: practical forgery attacks on GCM in TLS. In: Silvanovich, N., Traynor, P. (eds.) USENIX WOOT 2016. USENIX Association (2016)
8. Bogdanov, A., et al.: PRESENT: an ultra-lightweight block cipher. In: Paillier, P., Verbauwhede, I. (eds.) CHES 2007. LNCS, vol. 4727, pp. 450–466. Springer, Heidelberg (2007). https://doi.org/10.1007/978-3-540-74735-2_31
9. Bogdanov, A., Lauridsen, M.M., Tischhauser, E.: Comb to pipeline: fast software encryption revisited. In: Leander, G. (ed.) FSE 2015. LNCS, vol. 9054, pp. 150–171. Springer, Heidelberg (2015). https://doi.org/10.1007/978-3-662-48116-5_8
10. Borghoff, J., et al.: PRINCE – a low-latency block cipher for pervasive computing applications. In: Wang, X., Sako, K. (eds.) ASIACRYPT 2012. LNCS, vol. 7658, pp. 208–225. Springer, Heidelberg (2012). https://doi.org/10.1007/978-3-642-34961-4_14
11. Chen, S., Steinberger, J.: Tight security bounds for key-alternating ciphers. In: Nguyen, P.Q., Oswald, E. (eds.) EUROCRYPT 2014. LNCS, vol. 8441, pp. 327–350. Springer, Heidelberg (2014). https://doi.org/10.1007/978-3-642-55220-5_19
12. Choi, W., Lee, B., Lee, Y., Lee, J.: Improved security analysis for nonce-based enhanced hash-then-mask MACs. In: Moriai, S., Wang, H. (eds.) ASIACRYPT 2020. LNCS, vol. 12491, pp. 697–723. Springer, Cham (2020). https://doi.org/10.1007/978-3-030-64837-4_23
13. Cogliati, B., Seurin, Y.: EWCDM: an efficient, beyond-birthday secure, nonce-misuse resistant MAC. In: Robshaw and Katz [41], pp. 121–149
14. Dai, W., Hoang, V.T., Tessaro, S.: Information-theoretic indistinguishability via the chi-squared method. In: Katz and Shacham [25], pp. 497–523
15. Datta, N., Dutta, A., Nandi, M., Yasuda, K.: Encrypt or decrypt? To make a single-key beyond birthday secure nonce-based MAC. In: Shacham, H., Boldyreva, A. (eds.) CRYPTO 2018. LNCS, vol. 10991, pp. 631–661. Springer, Cham (2018). https://doi.org/10.1007/978-3-319-96884-1_21
16. De Cannière, C., Dunkelman, O., Knežević, M.: KATAN and KTANTAN—a family of small and efficient hardware-oriented block ciphers. In: Clavier, C., Gaj, K. (eds.) CHES 2009. LNCS, vol. 5747, pp. 272–288. Springer, Heidelberg (2009). https://doi.org/10.1007/978-3-642-04138-9_20
17. Derbez, P., et al.: Cryptanalysis of AES-PRF and its dual. IACR Trans. Symmetric Cryptol. **2018**(2), 161–191 (2018)
18. Dutta, A., Nandi, M., Talnikar, S.: Beyond birthday bound secure MAC in faulty nonce model. In: Ishai, Y., Rijmen, V. (eds.) EUROCRYPT 2019. LNCS, vol. 11476, pp. 437–466. Springer, Cham (2019). https://doi.org/10.1007/978-3-030-17653-2_15
19. Gilbert, E.N., MacWilliams, F.J., Sloan, N.J.A.: Codes which detect deception. Bell Syst. Tech. J. **53**, 405–424 (1974)
20. Gong, Z., Nikova, S., Law, Y.W.: KLEIN: a new family of lightweight block ciphers. In: Juels, A., Paar, C. (eds.) RFIDSec 2011. LNCS, vol. 7055, pp. 1–18. Springer, Heidelberg (2012). https://doi.org/10.1007/978-3-642-25286-0_1
21. Handschuh, H., Preneel, B.: Key-recovery attacks on universal hash function based MAC algorithms. In: Wagner, D. (ed.) CRYPTO 2008. LNCS, vol. 5157, pp. 144–161. Springer, Heidelberg (2008). https://doi.org/10.1007/978-3-540-85174-5_9

22. Hoang, V.T., Tessaro, S.: Key-alternating ciphers and key-length extension: exact bounds and multi-user security. In: Robshaw and Katz [41], pp. 3–32
23. Jha, A., Nandi, M.: Tight security of cascaded LRW2. J. Cryptol. **33**(3), 1272–1317 (2020)
24. Joux, A.: Authentication failures in NIST version of GCM. Comments submitted to NIST Modes of Operation Process (2006)
25. Katz, J., Shacham, H. (eds.): CRYPTO 2017. LNCS, vol. 10403. Springer, Cham (2017). https://doi.org/10.1007/978-3-319-63697-9
26. Kim, S., Lee, B., Lee, J.: Tight security bounds for double-block hash-then-sum MACs. In: Canteaut, A., Ishai, Y. (eds.) EUROCRYPT 2020. LNCS, vol. 12105, pp. 435–465. Springer, Cham (2020). https://doi.org/10.1007/978-3-030-45721-1_16
27. Krawczyk, H.: LFSR-based hashing and authentication. In: Desmedt, Y.G. (ed.) CRYPTO 1994. LNCS, vol. 839, pp. 129–139. Springer, Heidelberg (1994). https://doi.org/10.1007/3-540-48658-5_15
28. Luykx, A., Preneel, B.: Optimal forgeries against polynomial-based MACs and GCM. In: Nielsen, J.B., Rijmen, V. (eds.) EUROCRYPT 2018. LNCS, vol. 10820, pp. 445–467. Springer, Cham (2018). https://doi.org/10.1007/978-3-319-78381-9_17
29. McGrew, D.A., Viega, J.: The security and performance of the Galois/Counter Mode (GCM) of operation. In: Canteaut, A., Viswanathan, K. (eds.) INDOCRYPT 2004. LNCS, vol. 3348, pp. 343–355. Springer, Heidelberg (2004). https://doi.org/10.1007/978-3-540-30556-9_27
30. Mennink, B., Neves, S.: Encrypted Davies-Meyer and its dual: towards optimal security using mirror theory. In: Katz and Shacham [25], pp. 556–583
31. Mennink, B., Neves, S.: Optimal PRFs from blockcipher designs. IACR Trans. Symmetric Cryptol. **2017**(3), 228–252 (2017)
32. Minematsu, K.: How to thwart birthday attacks against MACs via small randomness. In: Hong, S., Iwata, T. (eds.) FSE 2010. LNCS, vol. 6147, pp. 230–249. Springer, Heidelberg (2010). https://doi.org/10.1007/978-3-642-13858-4_13
33. Nachef, V., Patarin, J., Volte, E.: Feistel Ciphers - Security Proofs and Cryptanalysis. Springer, Cham (2017). https://doi.org/10.1007/978-3-319-49530-9
34. Nandi, M.: Bernstein bound on WCS is tight. In: Shacham, H., Boldyreva, A. (eds.) CRYPTO 2018. LNCS, vol. 10992, pp. 213–238. Springer, Cham (2018). https://doi.org/10.1007/978-3-319-96881-0_8
35. Nandi, M.: Mind the composition: birthday bound attacks on EWCDMD and SoKAC21. In: Canteaut, A., Ishai, Y. (eds.) EUROCRYPT 2020. LNCS, vol. 12105, pp. 203–220. Springer, Cham (2020). https://doi.org/10.1007/978-3-030-45721-1_8
36. Patarin, J.: Étude des Générateurs de Permutations Basés sur le Schéma du D.E.S. Ph.D. thesis, Université Paris 6, Paris, France, November 1991
37. Patarin, J.: On linear systems of equations with distinct variables and small block size. In: Won, D.H., Kim, S. (eds.) ICISC 2005. LNCS, vol. 3935, pp. 299–321. Springer, Heidelberg (2006). https://doi.org/10.1007/11734727_25
38. Patarin, J.: The "Coefficients H" technique. In: Avanzi, R.M., Keliher, L., Sica, F. (eds.) SAC 2008. LNCS, vol. 5381, pp. 328–345. Springer, Heidelberg (2009). https://doi.org/10.1007/978-3-642-04159-4_21
39. Patarin, J.: Introduction to mirror theory: analysis of systems of linear equalities and linear non equalities for cryptography. Cryptology ePrint Archive, Report 2010/287 (2010)
40. Patarin, J.: Mirror theory and cryptography. Cryptology ePrint Archive, Report 2016/702 (2016)

41. Robshaw, M., Katz, J. (eds.): CRYPTO 2016. LNCS, vol. 9814. Springer, Heidelberg (2016). https://doi.org/10.1007/978-3-662-53018-4
42. Shibutani, K., Isobe, T., Hiwatari, H., Mitsuda, A., Akishita, T., Shirai, T.: *Piccolo*: an ultra-lightweight blockcipher. In: Preneel, B., Takagi, T. (eds.) CHES 2011. LNCS, vol. 6917, pp. 342–357. Springer, Heidelberg (2011). https://doi.org/10.1007/978-3-642-23951-9_23
43. Shoup, V.: On fast and provably secure message authentication based on universal hashing. In: Koblitz, N. (ed.) CRYPTO 1996. LNCS, vol. 1109, pp. 313–328. Springer, Heidelberg (1996). https://doi.org/10.1007/3-540-68697-5_24
44. Wegman, M.N., Carter, L.: New hash functions and their use in authentication and set equality. J. Comput. Syst. Sci. **22**(3), 265–279 (1981)

Homomorphic Encryption and Encrypted Search

Balanced Non-adjacent Forms

Marc Joye(✉)

Zama, Paris, France
marc@zama.ai

Abstract. Integers can be decomposed in multiple ways. The choice of a recoding technique is generally dictated by performance considerations. The usual metric for optimizing the decomposition is the Hamming weight. In this work, we consider a different metric and propose new modified forms (i.e., integer representations using signed digits) that satisfy minimality requirements under the new metric. Specifically, we introduce what we call *balanced non-adjacent forms* and prove that they feature a minimal Euclidean weight. We also present efficient algorithms to produce these new minimal forms. We analyze their asymptotic and exact distributions. We extend the definition to modular integers and show similar optimality results. The balanced non-adjacent forms find natural applications in fully homomorphic encryption as they optimally reduce the noise variance in LWE-type ciphertexts.

Keywords: Integer recoding · Lattice cryptography · Fully homomorphic encryption · Gadget decomposition · Noise control · Implementation

1 Introduction

Let B be an integer ≥ 2. Every positive integer $k < B^n$ can be expressed uniquely as $k = \sum_{i=0}^{n-1} k_i\, B^i$ with $0 \leq k_i < B$. Integer B is referred to as the radix and integers k_i are called the digits. If the digit set is extended to $\{-(B-1), \dots, B-1\}$, integer k can also be written under the form

$$k = \sum_{i \geq 0} k'_i\, B^i \quad \text{with } -(B-1) \leq k'_i \leq B-1 \ .$$

The corresponding representation $(\dots, k'_2, k'_1, k'_0)_B$ is called a *modified radix-B form* for k. Modified radix-B forms are not unique. For example, $(2,2)_4$ and $(1,-2,2)_4$ are two modified radix-4 forms for 10.

Signed-Digit Representations. Minimal representations using signed digits find applications in the theory of arithmetic codes [24] and in fast arithmetic techniques [22]. In these applications, the minimality requirement relates to the Hamming weight of the representation (i.e., the number of nonzero digits). For radix 2, Reitwiesner [35] proved that the so-called non-adjacent form (NAF) is optimal in the sense that it has minimal Hamming weight among the modified radix-2 forms. The general case was later addressed by Clark and Liang [10].

M. Tibouchi and H. Wang (Eds.): ASIACRYPT 2021, LNCS 13092, pp. 553–576, 2021.
https://doi.org/10.1007/978-3-030-92078-4_19

They present a minimal representation for any signed-radix B. In that case, Arno and Wheeler [2] precisely estimated that the average proportion of nonzero digits is equal to $(B-1)/(B+1)$.

The main application of non-adjacent forms in cryptography resides in fast exponentiation [16]; in particular, in settings wherein the computation of an inverse is inexpensive like in elliptic curve groups [30]. Non-adjacent forms were further adapted to certain classes of elliptic curves by decomposing integers as power sums of the Frobenius endomorphism [21,26,37]. Another extension of the basic NAF representation is to consider a succession of w digits, at most one of them being nonzero [32,37,39]. Yet another extension of the basic NAF is to rely on certain digit sets of the form $\{0, 1, x\}$ with representations featuring the non-adjacency property [31]. Binary representations with respect to more general digit sets of the form $\{0, 1, x, y, \dots, z\}$ are investigated in [18]. Alternative minimal modified radix-B forms for fast exponentiation, but enabling to scan the exponent digits from the left to the right, are presented in [19,20,33].

Fully Homomorphic Encryption and Noise Propagation. A salient feature of known constructions for fully homomorphic encryption [14,36] is the presence of noise in the ciphertexts for security reasons. We refer the reader to [17] for an excellent survey on homomorphic encryption.

Here is a simple illustration. Multiplying a noisy ciphertext by a scalar may result in a ciphertext whose noise error exceeds tolerated bounds. A standard trick to control the noise growth is to decompose the scalar with respect to a (small) radix [3,4]. This technique has been applied in a number of fully homomorphic encryption schemes—at the heart of the encryption process or as an auxiliary tool for accompanying gadgets or procedures; see e.g. [1,4,6,7,9,13,15,28].

Let Enc denote a homomorphic encryption scheme. Imagine we need to evaluate $c \leftarrow k \cdot \mathrm{Enc}(x)$ for some scalar k and ciphertext $\mathrm{Enc}(x)$. Instead of directly computing $c \leftarrow k \cdot \mathrm{Enc}(x)$, letting $k = \sum_{i=0}^{n} k'_i\, B^i$ for a given radix B, we can alternatively obtain c as

$$c \leftarrow \sum_{i=0}^{n} k'_i\, \mathrm{Enc}(B^i\, x)$$

from the precomputed ciphertexts $\mathrm{Enc}(B^i\, x)$, for $0 \le i \le n$.

Let us look at the noise propagation in this second approach. For a random variable X, we respectively denote by $\mathbb{E}[X]$ and $\mathrm{Var}(X)$ its expectation and its variance. Suppose that scalar k with $|k| < B^n$ is drawn at random. Assuming that the noise is centered and that its variance is bounded by the same threshold σ^2 in $\mathrm{Enc}(x)$ and $\mathrm{Enc}(B^i\, x)$, the noise present in $c \leftarrow k \cdot \mathrm{Enc}(x)$ has its variance bounded by $(\mathrm{Var}(k) + \mathbb{E}[k]^2)\,\sigma^2 = \mathbb{E}[k^2]\,\sigma^2$ while the noise present in $c \leftarrow \sum_{i=0}^{n} k'_i\, \mathrm{Enc}(B^i\, x)$ has its variance bounded by $\big(\sum_{i=0}^{n}(\mathrm{Var}(k'_i) + \mathbb{E}[k'_i]^2)\big)\,\sigma^2 = \big(\sum_{i=0}^{n} \mathbb{E}[k'^2_i]\big)\,\sigma^2$. Observe that $\mathbb{E}[k^2] = \frac{1}{3}(B^n - 1)B^n$ if k is uniform over $\{-B^n+1, \dots, B^n-1\}$ and that $k'_i \in \{-B+1, \dots, B-1\}$ if $(k'_n, \dots, k'_0)$ is a modified radix-B for k. Hence, $\sum_{i=0}^{n} \mathbb{E}[k'^2_i]$ is expected to be much smaller than $\mathbb{E}[k^2]$; this is all the more true that $\sum_{i=0}^{n} \mathbb{E}[k'^2_i]$ is small. It is therefore of interest to produce modified radix-B forms that minimize this latter bound in order to contain the noise propagation in ciphertexts.

Contributions. Not all signed-digit representations equally perform. We saw for example that $(2, 2)_4$ and $(1, -2, 2)_4$ are two valid radix-4 representations for 10. Another representation for 10 is $(1, -1, -2)_4$, This paper seeks for modified radix-B forms $(k'_n, \ldots, k'_0)$ that minimize the quantity $\sum_{i=0}^{n} k_i'^2$. Back to our example, the form $(1, -1, -2)_4$ is actually what we call a "balanced non-adjacent form" and, as will be shown, constitutes an optimal choice for decomposing 10 in radix 4.

Our main results are:

- We define a new modified radix-B form that we call *balanced non-adjacent form* (or BNAF in short). These forms get one's name from the usual NAF because for $B = 2$ they exhibit the non-adjacency property. We prove that every integer has a BNAF and that the BNAF is unique.
- We propose a simple criterion to check whether or not a modified radix-B form is a BNAF. Based on it, we present algorithms for producing BNAFs on various input formats.
- We introduce the metric of Euclidean weight for modified radix-B forms and prove that it is optimally met by BNAFs. Specifically, we show that among all possible modified radix-B forms $(k'_n, \ldots, k'_0)$ for a given integer k, the BNAF always minimizes the quantity $\sum_{i=0}^{n} k_i'^2$.
- We study statistical properties of BNAFs:
  1. We use Markov chains to model the asymptotic behavior of the BNAF recoding process and provide estimates for the occurrence probability for the digits in a random BNAF.
  2. We determine the exact distribution of BNAFs for n-digit random integers.

Outline of the Paper. The rest of the paper is organized as follows. In the next section, we review some signed-digit representations. Section 3 is the core of the paper. We define the BNAF and prove important and useful properties the BNAF satisfies. In Sect. 4, we present a generic recoding algorithm. This algorithm is used to analyze the probability distribution of the BNAF representation under different settings. In Sect. 5, we extend the previous results to modular representations. Finally, we demonstrate a number of cryptographic applications in Sect. 6.

2 Balanced Signed-Digit Representations

Integers can always be recoded with digits in the set $\{-B_0, \ldots, B - 1 - B_0\}$ for any integer $0 \leq B_0 < B$. When $B_0 = \lfloor B/2 \rfloor$, the corresponding representation is known as *balanced* modified radix-B form [12, Chapter 9]. Remarkably, such a decomposition is at most one digit longer than the standard unsigned decomposition. In particular, any nonnegative integer $k < B^n$ can be recoded as a balanced radix-B form having at most $n + 1$ digits.

2.1 Odd Radices

If B is odd and $B_0 = \lfloor B/2 \rfloor$ then $-B_0 = -\frac{B-1}{2}$ and $B - 1 - B_0 = \frac{B-1}{2}$. In this case, the corresponding form with digits in the balanced set $\{-\frac{B-1}{2}, \dots, \frac{B-1}{2}\}$ for a nonnegative integer k is easily obtained. Analogously to obtaining the regular radix-B representation, the idea is to repeatedly divide by B, obtain the corresponding remainder, and repeat the process with the resulting quotient. The difference is that the remainders are chosen in the set $\{-\frac{B-1}{2}, \dots, \frac{B-1}{2}\}$ (instead of $\{0, \dots, B-1\}$).

Example 1. Take $B = 5$ and consider the integer $k = 93$. Starting with 93, we successively obtain $93 = 19 \cdot 5 - 2$, $19 = 4 \cdot 5 - 1$, $4 = 1 \cdot 5 - 1$, and $1 = 0 \cdot 5 + 1$. The balanced modified radix-5 for $k = 93$ is therefore $(1, -1, -1, -2)_5$.

2.2 Even Radices

The previous methodology similarly applies to an *even* value for $B \geq 4$ [11, § 3]. It produces a valid modified radix-B representation, which is however not [fully] balanced. The so-obtained digits k'_i belong to the set $\{-\frac{B}{2}, \dots, \frac{B}{2} - 1\}$. This is the recoding typically used with the gadget decomposition; see e.g. [9, Algorithm 1] for B a power of two.

Example 2. With radix $B = 4$, an application to $k = 93$ yields the representation $(1, -2, -2, -1, 1)_4$. Note that the digits are in the set $\{-2, \dots, 1\}$.

When the radix B is even, one has $-\frac{B}{2} \equiv \frac{B}{2} \pmod{B}$. Digits $-\frac{B}{2}$ and $\frac{B}{2}$ can then be used interchangeably. By allowing remainders of $\frac{B}{2}$, one can obtain different representations using the digit set $\{-\frac{B}{2}, \dots, \frac{B}{2}\}$.

Example 3. Continuing with Example 2, one can check that $(1, 2, -1, 1)_4$ is another valid modified radix-4 representation for $k = 93$—but now with digits in the set $\{-2, \dots, 2\}$.

3 Balanced Non-adjacent Forms

Here we introduce the balanced non-adjacent form and characterize its properties. This section mainly deals with integers; extensions to modular representations are covered in Sect. 5.

3.1 Definition

We start with the general definition.

Definition 1. *Let $B \geq 2$ be a radix. A modified radix-B representation*

$$(\dots, k'_2, k'_1, k'_0)$$

for an integer $k = \sum_i k'_i B^i$ is called a balanced non-adjacent form (BNAF) *if and only if, for all i,*

(C1) $|k'_i| \le \lfloor \frac{B}{2} \rfloor$;
(C2) $0 \le k'_i \cdot k'_{i+1} \le \lfloor \frac{B}{2} \rfloor (\lfloor \frac{B}{2} \rfloor - 1)$ *when* $|k'_i| = \lceil \frac{B}{2} \rceil$.

Remark 1. Conditions (C1) and (C2) are exclusive when the radix is odd. For an odd radix B, the definition of a BNAF simplifies to $|k'_i| \le \frac{B-1}{2}$ for all i.

For an even radix B, a pair of digits (k'_{i+1}, k'_i) with $|k'_{i+1}|, |k'_i| \le \lfloor \frac{B}{2} \rfloor$ that satisfies Condition (C2) is said *admissible*. Interestingly, the definition of a BNAF for $B = 2$ coincides with the definition of the non-adjacent form (NAF): $k'_i \in \{-1, 0, 1\}$ and $k'_i \cdot k'_{i+1} = 0$.

We present below a generic algorithm that converts any modified-radix form $(k'_n, \dots, k'_0)$ where $k'_i \in \{-(B-1), \dots, B-1\}$ for an integer k with $|k| < B^n$ into a BNAF. The algorithm is valid for both even and odd radices.

Algorithm 1: Conversion algorithm

```
Input: Modified radix-B form (k'_n, ..., k'_0) of an integer k = Σ_{i=0}^{n} k'_i B^i with
       |k| < B^n
Output: BNAF(k) ← (k'_n, ..., k'_0)
for i = 0 to n − 1 do
    σ_i ← sign(k'_i);
    if (|k'_i| > ⌊B/2⌋) ∨ ((|k'_i| = ⌈B/2⌉) ∧ ((−⌊B/2⌋ ≤ σ_i · k'_{i+1} ≤ −1) ∨ (⌊B/2⌋ ≤
      σ_i · k'_{i+1} ≤ B − 1))) then
        k'_i ← k'_i − σ_i · B;
        k'_{i+1} ← k'_{i+1} + σ_i;
    end if
end for
return (k'_n, ..., k'_0)
```

Lemma 1. *Algorithm 1 is correct.*

Proof. We have to prove that, on input a modified radix-B of an integer k with $|k| < B^n$, Algorithm 1 actually outputs a BNAF.

Iteration i of the for-loop at most modifies the values of digits k'_i and k'_{i+1}. As will become apparent, all along the algorithm, it holds that:

- $k'_i \in \{-B, \dots, B\}$ and $k'_{i+1} \in \{-B+1, \dots, B-1\}$ before entering iteration i;
- $|k'_i| \le \lfloor \frac{B}{2} \rfloor$ after exiting iteration i and the corresponding value for k'_i is unchanged by the next iterations.

We introduce some notation for more clarity. Let $({k'_n}^{(0)}, \dots, {k'_0}^{(0)})$ denote the input in Algorithm 1 of a modified radix-B form of an integer $k = \sum_{j=0}^{n} {k'_j}^{(0)} B^j$, $|k| < B^n$. More generally, let $({k'_n}^{(i)}, \dots, {k'_0}^{(i)})$ denote the representation entering iteration i in Algorithm 1—remark that $({k'_n}^{(i+1)}, \dots, {k'_0}^{(i+1)})$ also denotes the representation exiting iteration i. Moreover, we note that the algorithm is such that $\sum_{j=0}^{n} k'_j\, B^j$ always keeps equal to k; i.e., $\sum_{j=0}^{n} {k'_j}^{(i+1)}\, B^j = k$ for all $0 \le i \le n-1$. We also have $\sigma_i = \mathrm{sign}({k'_i}^{(i)})$. The output of Algorithm 1 is $\sum_{j=0}^{n} {k'_j}^{(n)}\, B^j$.

With the new notation, the two above observations can be rewritten as:

- ${k'_i}^{(i)} \in \{-B, \ldots, B\}$ and ${k'_{i+1}}^{(i)} \in \{-B+1, \ldots, B-1\}$;
- $|{k'_i}^{(i+1)}| \le \lfloor \frac{B}{2} \rfloor$ and ${k'_i}^{(j)} = {k'_i}^{(i+1)}$ for $i+1 < j \le n-1$.

The first observation and the relation ${k'_i}^{(j)} = {k'_i}^{(i+1)}$ for $i+1 < j \le n-1$ are easily verified by inspection of the algorithm. We now show that the relation $|{k'_i}^{(i+1)}| \le \lfloor \frac{B}{2} \rfloor$ is verified. If $|{k'_i}^{(i)}| > \lfloor \frac{B}{2} \rfloor$ (i.e., ${k'_i}^{(i)} \in \{-B, \ldots, -\lfloor \frac{B}{2} \rfloor - 1\} \cup \{\lfloor \frac{B}{2} \rfloor + 1, \ldots, B\}$), it is updated as ${k'_i}^{(i+1)} = {k'_i}^{(i)} - \sigma_i \cdot B \in \{-B + \lfloor \frac{B}{2} \rfloor + 1, \ldots, B - \lfloor \frac{B}{2} \rfloor - 1\} \subseteq \{-\lfloor \frac{B}{2} \rfloor, \ldots, \lfloor \frac{B}{2} \rfloor\}$. Observe also that when B is even and $|{k'_i}^{(i)}| = \lceil \frac{B}{2} \rceil = \lfloor \frac{B}{2} \rfloor$ and is updated then it becomes ${k'_i}^{(i+1)} = {k'_i}^{(i)} - \sigma_i \cdot B \in \{\pm \lfloor \frac{B}{2} \rfloor\}$. In all cases, the relation $|{k'_i}^{(i+1)}| \le \lfloor \frac{B}{2} \rfloor$ is therefore satisfied.

Since the for-loop iterates for i from 0 to $n-1$ and since ${k'_i}^{(j)} = {k'_i}^{(i+1)}$ for $j > i+1$, from the relation $|{k'_i}^{(i+1)}| \le \lfloor \frac{B}{2} \rfloor$, it follows that Condition (C1) holds true for all $0 \le i \le n-1$; i.e., $|{k'_i}^{(n)}| \le \lfloor \frac{B}{2} \rfloor$ for $0 \le i \le n-1$. It also holds true for the output k'_n because the algorithm keeps invariant $\sum_{j=0}^{n} {k'_j}^{(i+1)}\, B^j = k$; hence, the condition $|k| < B^n$ implies that the final output ${k'_n}^{(n)}$ lies in $\{0, 1, -1\}$ and thus $|{k'_n}^{(n)}| \le \lfloor \frac{B}{2} \rfloor$ because $B \ge 2$.

For even radices B, we need in addition to check that Condition (C2) is fulfilled. We so assume that B is even and so $\lfloor \frac{B}{2} \rfloor = \lceil \frac{B}{2} \rceil = \frac{B}{2}$. If the value of ${k'_i}^{(i)}$ entering iteration i satisfies $|{k'_i}^{(i)}| < \frac{B}{2}$ then this value remains unchanged until the end of the algorithm; as a consequence, the output ${k'_i}^{(n)}$ belongs to $\{-\frac{B}{2}+1, \ldots, \frac{B}{2}-1\}$. If the value of ${k'_i}^{(i)}$ entering iteration i satisfies $|{k'_i}^{(i)}| > \frac{B}{2}$ then it is updated as ${k'_i}^{(i+1)} = {k'_i}^{(i)} - \sigma_i \cdot B \in \{-\frac{B}{2}+1, \ldots, \frac{B}{2}-1\}$ and will no longer be modified by the subsequent iterations; as a consequence, the output ${k'_i}^{(n)}$ belongs to $\{-\frac{B}{2}+1, \ldots, \frac{B}{2}-1\}$. For output values ${k'_i}^{(n)} \in \{-\frac{B}{2}+1, \ldots, \frac{B}{2}-1\}$, Condition (C2) is always valid. Hence, the only case that needs to be analyzed is when the value of ${k'_i}^{(i)}$ entering iteration i is $\pm\frac{B}{2}$. There are four sub-cases according to the value of $\sigma_i \cdot {k'_{i+1}}^{(i)}$ entering iteration i.

- Sub-case 1: ${k'_i}^{(i)} \in \{\pm\frac{B}{2}\}$ and $\sigma_i \cdot {k'_{i+1}}^{(i)} \in \{-B+1, \ldots, -\frac{B}{2}-1\}$. In this case, as seen from Algorithm 1, k'_i and k'_{i+1} are not modified at iteration i. Hence, the final output value for k'_i is ${k'_i}^{(n)} = \frac{B}{2}$ if $\sigma_i = 1$ and ${k'_i}^{(n)} = -\frac{B}{2}$ if $\sigma_i = -1$. Furthermore, since ${k'_{i+1}}^{(i+1)} = {k'_{i+1}}^{(i)}$, if $\sigma_i = 1$ then ${k'_{i+1}}^{(i+1)} \in \{-B+1, \ldots, -\frac{B}{2}-1\}$ and so will be changed at iteration $i+1$ to eventually become the final output value ${k'_{i+1}}^{(n)} = {k'_{i+1}}^{(i+1)} - \sigma_{i+1} \cdot B \in \{1, \ldots, \frac{B}{2}-1\}$, which satisfies Condition (C2). Likewise, if $\sigma_i = -1$ then ${k'_{i+1}}^{(i+1)} \in \{\frac{B}{2}+1, \ldots, B-1\}$ and so will be changed at iteration $i+1$ to eventually become

${k'_{i+1}}^{(n)} = {k'_{i+1}}^{(i+1)} - \sigma_{i+1} \cdot B \in \{-\frac{B}{2}+1, \ldots, -1\}$, which again satisfies Condition (C2).

- Sub-case 2: ${k'_i}^{(i)} \in \{\pm\frac{B}{2}\}$ and $\sigma_i \cdot {k'_{i+1}}^{(i)} \in \{-\frac{B}{2}, \ldots, -1\}$. In this case, both k'_i and k'_{i+1} are updated at iteration i as ${k'_i}^{(i+1)} \leftarrow {k'_i}^{(i)} - \sigma_i \cdot B = -{k'_i}^{(i)} \in \{\mp\frac{B}{2}\}$ and ${k'_{i+1}}^{(i+1)} \leftarrow {k'_{i+1}}^{(i)} + \sigma_i$. Hence, at the end of iteration i, the resulting ${k'_{i+1}}^{(i+1)}$ belongs to $\{-\frac{B}{2}+1, \ldots, 0\}$ if $\sigma_i = 1$ and to $\{0, \ldots, \frac{B}{2}-1\}$ if $\sigma_i = -1$. In both cases, this value for ${k'_{i+1}}^{(i+1)}$ being such that $|{k'_{i+1}}^{(i+1)}| < \frac{B}{2}$, it won't be changed at iteration $i+1$. Moreover, as the resulting ${k'_i}^{(n)} = {k'_i}^{(i+1)}$ and ${k'_{i+1}}^{(n)} = {k'_{i+1}}^{(i+1)}$ have the same sign, the final output pair $({k'_{i+1}}^{(n)}, {k'_i}^{(n)})$ satisfies Condition (C2).
- Sub-case 3: ${k'_i}^{(i)} \in \{\pm\frac{B}{2}\}$ and $\sigma_i \cdot {k'_{i+1}}^{(i)} \in \{0, \ldots, \frac{B}{2}-1\}$. In this case, the values of k'_i and k'_{i+1} won't be changed at iteration i nor at iteration $i+1$. The final output values are therefore ${k'_i}^{(n)} = \frac{B}{2}$ and ${k'_{i+1}}^{(n)} \subset \{0, \ldots, \frac{B}{2}-1\}$ if $\sigma_i = 1$, and ${k'_i}^{(n)} = -\frac{B}{2}$ and ${k'_{i+1}}^{(n)} \in \{-\frac{B}{2}+1, \ldots, 0\}$ if $\sigma_i = -1$. Both cases satisfy Condition (C2).
- Sub-case 4: ${k'_i}^{(i)} \in \{\pm\frac{B}{2}\}$ and $\sigma_i \cdot {k'_{i+1}}^{(i)} \in \{\frac{B}{2}, \ldots, B-1\}$. In this case, the values of k'_i and k'_{i+1} are changed at iteration i as ${k'_i}^{(i+1)} = -{k'_i}^{(i)}$ and ${k'_{i+1}}^{(i+1)} = {k'_{i+1}}^{(i)} + \sigma_i \in \{\frac{B}{2}+1, \ldots, B\}$ if $\sigma_i = 1$ and $\in \{-B, \ldots, -\frac{B}{2}-1\}$ if $\sigma_i = -1$. In turn, ${k'_{i+1}}^{(i+1)}$ will be changed at iteration $i+1$ to eventually become ${k'_{i+1}}^{(n)} = {k'_{i+1}}^{(i+1)} - \sigma_{i+1} \cdot B = {k'_{i+1}}^{(i+1)} - \sigma_i \cdot B$. The final output values are therefore such that ${k'_i}^{(n)} = -\frac{B}{2}$ and ${k'_{i+1}}^{(n)} \in \{-\frac{B}{2}+1, \ldots, 0\}$ if $\sigma_i = 1$, and ${k'_i}^{(n)} = \frac{B}{2}$ and ${k'_{i+1}}^{(n)} \in \{0, \ldots, \frac{B}{2}-1\}$ if $\sigma_i = -1$. Again Condition (C2) is satisfied.

This shows that Algorithm 1 is correct and produces a BNAF. □

3.2 Properties

Although an integer can have several modified radix-B representations, the next theorem states that it has exactly one BNAF.

Theorem 1. *Every integer has a unique BNAF.*

Proof. Lemma 1 shows that there exists a BNAF for every integer. Suppose that an integer k possesses two different BNAF representations: $k = \sum_i k'_i B^i$ and $k = \sum_i k''_i B^i$. Let i^* denote the smallest index such that $k'_{i^*} \neq k''_{i^*}$. From $k = \sum_i k'_i B^i = \sum_i k''_i B^i$, we deduce that $(k'_{i^*} - k''_{i^*}) B^{i^*} \equiv 0 \pmod{B^{i^*+1}}$ and thus $k'_{i^*} - k''_{i^*} \equiv 0 \pmod{B}$.

The cases of odd radix and even radix are treated separately.

1. Consider the case of an odd radix B. Since $k'_{i^*} \neq k''_{i^*}$, the relation $k'_{i^*} - k''_{i^*} \equiv 0 \pmod{B}$ implies $k'_{i^*} - k''_{i^*} = \alpha B$ for some nonzero integer α. Since $|k'_{i^*}| \leq \lfloor\frac{B}{2}\rfloor = \frac{B-1}{2}$ and $|k''_{i^*}| \leq \lfloor\frac{B}{2}\rfloor = \frac{B-1}{2}$, it follows that $|k'_{i^*} - k''_{i^*}| \leq B-1$. The equation $k'_{i^*} - k''_{i^*} = \alpha B$ has therefore no nonzero solution α. A contradiction.

2. Consider now the case of an even radix B. Again, since by definition $|k'_{i^*}| \leq \lfloor \frac{B}{2} \rfloor = \frac{B}{2}$ and $|k''_{i^*}| \leq \lfloor \frac{B}{2} \rfloor = \frac{B}{2}$, and $k'_{i^*} \neq k''_{i^*}$, it thus follows from $k'_{i^*} - k''_{i^*} \equiv 0 \pmod{B}$ that $k'_{i^*} = -k''_{i^*} = \pm\frac{B}{2}$. Without loss of generality, we assume that $k'_{i^*} = \frac{B}{2}$ and $k''_{i^*} = -\frac{B}{2}$. From $\sum_i k'_i B^i \equiv \sum_i k''_i B^i \pmod{B^{i^*+2}}$, we deduce that $(k'_{i^*+1} - k''_{i^*+1})\, B + (k'_{i^*} - k''_{i^*}) \equiv 0 \pmod{B^2}$. In turn, this yields $(k'_{i^*+1} - k''_{i^*+1})\, B + B \equiv 0 \pmod{B^2}$ and therefore $k'_{i^*+1} - k''_{i^*+1} + 1 \equiv 0 \pmod{B} \iff k''_{i^*+1} \equiv k'_{i^*+1} + 1 \pmod{B}$. Furthermore, as $k'_{i^*} = \frac{B}{2}$ and $k''_{i^*} = -\frac{B}{2}$, we must have $0 \leq k'_{i^*+1} \leq \frac{B}{2} - 1$ and $-\frac{B}{2} + 1 \leq k''_{i^*+1} \leq 0$ to fulfill Condition (C2). From $k''_{i^*+1} \equiv k'_{i^*+1} + 1 \pmod{B}$, the requirement $0 \leq k'_{i^*+1} \leq \frac{B}{2} - 1$ leads to $k''_{i^*+1} \in \{1, \ldots, \frac{B}{2}\} \cup \{-\frac{B}{2}\}$, which contradicts the condition $-\frac{B}{2} + 1 \leq k''_{i^*+1} \leq 0$.

Consequently, the BNAF is unique. □

Integers can have multiple modified radix-B forms. The notion of weight relates an integer to its representation and enables to qualitatively distinguish among different representations.

Definition 2. *Given a base $B \geq 2$, the* Euclidean weight *of an integer k is the smallest value W such that there is a modified radix-B form*

$$(k'_n, \ldots, k'_0) \quad \text{such that} \sum_{i=0}^{n} k'_i B^i = k \text{ and } \sum_{i=0}^{n} {k'_i}^2 = W$$

for digits k'_i with $|k'_i| < B$.

The next theorem exhibits the main feature of the BNAF representation. It states that the BNAF of an integer k, $\mathrm{BNAF}(k) = (k'_n, \ldots, k'_0)$, minimizes the quantity $\sum_{i=0}^{n} {k'_i}^2$. The BNAF representation is in that sense optimal.

Theorem 2. *If $(k'_n, \ldots, k'_0)$ denotes the BNAF of an integer k then the Euclidean weight of k is equal to $\sum_{i=0}^{n} {k'_i}^2$.*

Proof. The proof relies on Algorithm 1.

We use the notation used in the proof of Lemma 1. We let $({k'_n}^{(i)}, \ldots, {k'_0}^{(i)})$ denote the representation entering iteration i in Algorithm 1; we also let $\sigma_i = \mathrm{sign}({k'_i}^{(i)})$. By abuse of language, for the representation $({k'_n}^{(i)}, \ldots, {k'_0}^{(i)})$, we call the quantity

$$W^{(i)} = \sum_{j=0}^{n} \left({k'_j}^{(i)}\right)^2$$

the Euclidean weight of $({k'_n}^{(i)}, \ldots, {k'_0}^{(i)})$ in Algorithm 1. The weight of the output of Algorithm 1 is given by $W^{(n)}$.

We now show that $W^{(n)} \leq W^{(0)}$, namely that the Euclidean weight of the output is smaller than or equal to the Euclidean weight of the input. Specifically, we show that if the if-branching is executed at iteration i then there exists an index j with $i < j \leq n$ such that $W^{(j)} \leq W^{(i)}$; if it is not executed then obviously $W^{(i+1)} = W^{(i)}$.

If the if-branching is executed at iteration i, it follows that $k_i'^{(i+1)} = k_i'^{(i)} - \sigma_i B$ and $k_{i+1}'^{(i+1)} = k_{i+1}'^{(i)} + \sigma_i$. The other values are unchanged. This yields

$$\begin{aligned} W^{(i+1)} - W^{(i)} &= \sum_{j=0}^{n} (k_j'^{(i+1)})^2 - \sum_{j=0}^{n} (k_j'^{(i)})^2 \qquad (*) \\ &= (k_i'^{(i+1)})^2 + (k_{i+1}'^{(i+1)})^2 - (k_i'^{(i)})^2 - (k_{i+1}'^{(i)})^2 \\ &= -\sigma_i B(2k_i'^{(i)} - \sigma_i B) + \sigma_i(2k_{i+1}'^{(i)} + \sigma_i) \\ &= -2B\,|k_i'^{(i)}| + B^2 + 2\sigma_i\, k_{i+1}'^{(i)} + 1 \ . \end{aligned}$$

The if-branching is executed at iteration i when (at least) one of the following conditions is met:

1. $|k_i'^{(i)}| > \lfloor \frac{B}{2} \rfloor$. There are several sub-cases.
   (a) B is even. Then, since $|k_i'^{(i)}| \geq \lfloor \frac{B}{2} \rfloor + 1 = \frac{B}{2} + 1$ and $\sigma_i\, k_{i+1}'^{(i)} \leq B - 1$, we get using (*)

   $$W^{(i+1)} - W^{(i)} \leq -2B(\tfrac{B}{2} + 1) + B^2 + 2(B-1) + 1 = -1 < 0\,,$$

   that is, $W^{(i+1)} < W^{(i)}$. We have $j = i + 1$.
   (b) B is odd and $\sigma_i\, k_{i+1}'^{(i)} \leq \lfloor \frac{B}{2} \rfloor$. When B is odd, we have $\lfloor \frac{B}{2} \rfloor = \frac{B-1}{2}$. This case is similar to the previous one. We obtain from (*)

   $$W^{(i+1)} - W^{(i)} \leq -2B(\tfrac{B-1}{2} + 1) + B^2 + 2(\tfrac{B-1}{2}) + 1 = 0\ .$$

   We get $W^{(i+1)} \leq W^{(i)}$ and have $j = i + 1$.
   (c) B is odd and $\sigma_i\, k_{i+1}'^{(i)} > \lfloor \frac{B}{2} \rfloor$. First, we note that $\sigma_i\, k_{i+1}'^{(i)} > \lfloor \frac{B}{2} \rfloor$ supposes $i \leq n - 2$ because for $i = n - 1$ we have $k_{i+1}'^{(i)} \in \{0, 1, -1\}$ ($|k| < B^n$). If the condition $\sigma_i\, k_{i+1}'^{(i)} > \lfloor \frac{B}{2} \rfloor$ holds, this can only occur if $\sigma_i = 1$ and $k_{i+1}'^{(i)} > \lfloor \frac{B}{2} \rfloor$ or if $\sigma_i = -1$ and $k_{i+1}'^{(i)} < -\lfloor \frac{B}{2} \rfloor$. Moreover, since we have $k_{i+1}'^{(i+1)} = k_{i+1}'^{(i)} + \sigma_i$, we infer that $\sigma_{i+1} = \sigma_i$. The if-branching is executed at both iterations i and $i+1$. A double application of (*) yields

   $$\begin{aligned} &W^{(i+2)} - W^{(i)} \\ &= (-2B\,|k_{i+1}'^{(i+1)}| + B^2 + 2\sigma_{i+1}\, k_{i+2}'^{(i+1)} + 1) \\ &\qquad + (-2B\,|k_i'^{(i)}| + B^2 + 2\sigma_i\, k_{i+1}'^{(i)} + 1) \\ &\leq -2(B-1)\,|k_{i+1}'^{(i)}| - 2B + 2B^2 + 2 + 2(B-1) - 2B(\tfrac{B-1}{2} + 1) \\ &\leq -2(B-1)\,|k_{i+1}'^{(i)}| + B(B-1) \\ &\leq -2(B-1)(\tfrac{B-1}{2} + 1) + B(B-1) = 1 - B \\ &< 0\ . \end{aligned}$$

Hence, we have $W^{(i+2)} < W^{(i)}$ and so $j = i + 2$.

2. $(|k_i'^{(i)}| = \lceil \frac{B}{2} \rceil) \wedge (-\lfloor \frac{B}{2} \rfloor \le \sigma_i \cdot {k_{i+1}'}^{(i)} \le -1)$. We assume w.lo.g. that B is even because when, it is odd, the condition $|k_i'^{(i)}| = \lceil \frac{B}{2} \rceil$ implies $|k_i'^{(i)}| > \lfloor \frac{B}{2} \rfloor$, which is covered in the previous case. We so get from (*)
$$W^{(i+1)} - W^{(i)} \le -2B\,\tfrac{B}{2} + B^2 + 2(-1) + 1 = -1 < 0$$
and thus $W^{(i+1)} < W^{(i)}$. We have $j = i + 1$.

3. $(|k_i'^{(i)}| = \lceil \frac{B}{2} \rceil) \wedge (\lfloor \frac{B}{2} \rfloor \le \sigma_i \cdot {k_{i+1}'}^{(i)} \le B - 1)$. Here too, we assume w.l.o.g. that B is even. We distinguish two sub-cases.
   (a) $\sigma_i \cdot {k_{i+1}'}^{(i)} > \lfloor \frac{B}{2} \rfloor = \frac{B}{2}$. This case is analogous to Case 1c. We have $\sigma_{i+1} = \sigma_i$. A double application of (*) yields
$$\begin{aligned} W^{(i+2)} - W^{(i)} &= (-2B\,|{k_{i+1}'}^{(i+1)}| + B^2 + 2\sigma_{i+1}\,{k_{i+2}'}^{(i+1)} + 1) \\ &\qquad + (-2B\,|k_i'^{(i)}| + B^2 + 2\sigma_i\,{k_{i+1}'}^{(i)} + 1) \\ &\le -2(B-1)\,|{k_{i+1}'}^{(i)}| \\ &\qquad - 2B + 2B^2 + 2 + 2(B-1) - 2B(\tfrac{B}{2}) \\ &\le -2(B-1)(\tfrac{B}{2} + 1) + B^2 = 2 - B < 0 \ . \end{aligned}$$
   We have $W^{(i+2)} < W^{(i)}$ and $j = i + 2$.
   (b) $\sigma_i \cdot {k_{i+1}'}^{(i)} = \lfloor \frac{B}{2} \rfloor = \frac{B}{2}$. Again, this requires $\sigma_{i+1} = \sigma_i$. We thus have ${k_{i+1}'}^{(i)} = k_i'^{(i)} \in \{\pm \frac{B}{2}\}$ or, equivalently, ${k_{i+1}'}^{(i)} = k_i'^{(i)} = \sigma_i \frac{B}{2}$. We let i^* denote the smallest index such that $i^* > i + 1$ and ${k_{i^*}'}^{(i)} \ne \sigma_i \frac{B}{2}$. Note that, for $B \ne 2$, $i^* \le n$ because ${k_n'}^{(l)} \in \{0, 1, -1\}$ for all $0 \le l \le n$ since $|k| < B^n$, and consequently, ${k_n'}^{(l)} \notin \{\pm \frac{B}{2}\}$. The same is true for $B = 2$ because if ${k_{n-1}'}^{(l)} \in \{\pm \frac{B}{2}\}$ for some $0 \le l \le n$ then ${k_n'}^{(l)} \ne {k_{n-1}'}^{(l)}$ since $|k| < B^n$. Moreover, note that $i^* \le n - 1$ when $\sigma_i\,{k_{i^*}'}^{(i)} > \frac{B}{2}$ because $({k_n'}^{(l)}, {k_{n-1}'}^{(l)}, {k_{n-2}'}^{(l)}) = (d, \sigma_i \frac{B}{2}, \sigma_i \frac{B}{2})$ for some digit $d > \sigma_i \frac{B}{2}$ contradicts $|k| < B^n$.
   We have $k_i'^{(i)} = {k_{i+1}'}^{(i)} = \cdots = {k_{i^*-1}'}^{(i)} = \sigma_i \frac{B}{2}$ and ${k_{i^*}'}^{(i)} \ne \sigma_i \frac{B}{2}$. At every subsequent iteration up to iteration $i^* - 1$, it turns out that the if-branching is executed, which results in
$$\begin{aligned} &({k_{i^*}'}^{(i^*)}, {k_{i^*-1}'}^{(i^*)}, \ldots, {k_{i+1}'}^{(i^*)}, k_i'^{(i^*)}) = \\ &\qquad ({k_{i^*}'}^{(i)} + \sigma_i, -\sigma_i(\tfrac{B}{2} - 1), \ldots, -\sigma_i(\tfrac{B}{2} - 1), -\sigma_i \tfrac{B}{2}) \ . \end{aligned}$$
   The cases of $\sigma_i\,{k_{i^*}'}^{(i)} < \frac{B}{2}$ and $\sigma_i\,{k_{i^*}'}^{(i)} > \frac{B}{2}$ are treated separately.

i. $\sigma_i\, k'_{i^*}{}^{(i)} < \frac{B}{2}$. In this case, we get

$$\begin{aligned} W^{(i^*)} - W^{(i)} &= (k'_{i^*}{}^{(i)} + \sigma_i)^2 + \sum_{l=i+1}^{i^*-1} (-\sigma_i(\tfrac{B}{2} - 1))^2 \\ &\quad + (-\sigma_i \tfrac{B}{2})^2 - (k'_{i^*}{}^{(i)})^2 - \sum_{l=i}^{i^*-1} (\sigma_i \tfrac{B}{2})^2 \\ &= 2\sigma_i\, k'_{i^*}{}^{(i)} + 1 - (i^* - i - 1)(B - 1) \\ &\leq 2(\tfrac{B}{2} - 1) + 1 - (B - 1) = 0 \end{aligned}$$

since $i^* \geq i + 2$. Hence, $W^{(i^*)} \leq W^{(i)}$ and we have $j = i^*$.

ii. $\sigma_i\, k'_{i^*}{}^{(i)} > \frac{B}{2}$. In this case, the if-branching is also executed at iteration i^*. We get

$$\begin{aligned} W^{(i^*+1)} - W^{(i)} &= (k'_{i^*+1}{}^{(i)} + \sigma_i)^2 + (k'_{i^*}{}^{(i)} - \sigma_i(B - 1))^2 \\ &\quad + \sum_{l=i+1}^{i^*-1} (-\sigma_i(\tfrac{B}{2} - 1))^2 + (-\sigma_i \tfrac{B}{2})^2 \\ &\quad - (k'_{i^*+1}{}^{(i)})^2 - (k'_{i^*}{}^{(i)})^2 - \sum_{l=i}^{i^*-1} (\sigma_i \tfrac{B}{2})^2 \\ &= 2\sigma_i\, k'_{i^*+1}{}^{(i)} + 1 - 2\sigma_i(B - 1)\, k'_{i^*}{}^{(i)} \\ &\quad + (B - 1)^2 - (i^* - i - 1)(B - 1) \\ &\leq 2(B - 1) + 1 - 2(B - 1)(\tfrac{B}{2} + 1) \\ &\quad + (B - 1)^2 - (B - 1) \\ &= 3 - 2B < 0\ . \end{aligned}$$

We so have $W^{(i^*+1)} < W^{(i)}$ and $j = i^* + 1$.

Theorem 1 teaches that the BNAF is unique. This means that, given an integer k and any modified radix-B representation of that integer, Definition 1 always returns the same modified radix-B form for k, namely the BNAF of k. Moreover, we just saw that the BNAF has an Euclidean weight that is smaller than or equal to the Euclidean weight of the input modified radix-B form. This implies that the BNAF representation has minimal Euclidean weight. In other words, if $(k'_n, \ldots, k'_0)$ is the BNAF of k, $|k| < B^n$, then the Euclidean weight of k is $W = \sum_{i=0}^{n} k_i'^2$. □

4 Recoding Algorithm

4.1 Description

The BNAF of an integer k can be obtained directly from the definition by repeatedly dividing k by B (integer division); if Conditions (C1) or (C2) (cf. Definition 1) are invalidated then a correction is applied to the resulting digit (and as well as to k). The "mod" operator in $K \bmod B$ indicates the unique value in $\{0, \ldots, B - 1\}$ that is congruent to K modulo B.

Algorithm 2: BNAF recoding

Input: Integer $k \neq 0$
Output: $\text{BNAF}(k) \leftarrow (k'_n, \ldots, k'_0)$ with $k'_i \in \{-\lfloor \frac{B}{2} \rfloor, \ldots, \lfloor \frac{B}{2} \rfloor\}$ s.t. $\sum_{i=0}^{n} k'_i B^i = k$

$K \leftarrow k$; $i \leftarrow 0$;
while $(K \neq 0)$ **do**
  $k'_i \leftarrow K \bmod B$; $K \leftarrow (K - k'_i)/B$;
  if $(k'_i > \lfloor \frac{B}{2} \rfloor) \vee \big((k'_i = \lceil \frac{B}{2} \rceil) \wedge ((K \bmod B) \geq \lfloor \frac{B}{2} \rfloor)\big)$ **then**
    $k'_i \leftarrow k'_i - B$; $K \leftarrow K + 1$;
  end if
  $i \leftarrow i + 1$;
end while
return $(k'_{i-1}, \ldots, k'_0)$

Remark 2. As indicated in Remark 1, Conditions (C1) and (C2) are exclusive when radix B is odd. In this case, the if-branching in Algorithm 2 simply reads as **if** $(k'_i > \lfloor \frac{B}{2} \rfloor)$ **then**.

4.2 Stochastic Analysis

This section studies the asymptotic behavior of the digits resulting from the BNAF recoding.

If $k'_i = K \bmod B$ then $(K - k'_i)/B = \lfloor K/B \rfloor$. Hence, we see that the output value of k'_i is at each iteration completely determined by the current values of $K \bmod B$ and of $\lfloor K/B \rfloor \bmod B$. A pair of digits (e, d) is therefore sufficient to describe each possible case.

It is useful to introduce some notation. We define the quantities K_i that keep track of the successive values of K entering the for-loop at iteration i, and represent $K_i \bmod B^2$ as the pair (e_i, d_i) with $0 \leq d_i, e_i < B$ such that $K_i \bmod B^2 = e_i\, B + d_i$. By construction, we have

$$\begin{cases} K_0 = k \\ K_{i+1} = \frac{K_i - k'_i}{B} \quad \text{for } 0 \leq i \leq n-1 \end{cases} .$$

Depending on the values of $K_i \bmod B^2 = (e_i, d_i)$, there are different cases to consider. This is detailed in Table 1.

From the last column in Tables 1(a) and 1(b), we remark that the knowledge of (e_i, d_i) only enables to obtain d_{i+1}. We have

$$d_{i+1} = K_{i+1} \bmod B = \frac{(K_i - k'_i) \bmod B^2}{B} = \frac{e_i B + d_i - k'_i}{B} \pmod B$$
$$= \begin{cases} e_i & \text{if } k'_i = d_i \\ e_i + 1 \pmod B & \text{if } k'_i = d_i - B \end{cases} .$$

Table 1. Output digit k'_i according to the pair (e_i, d_i).

(a) Odd radix B

State	(e_i, d_i)	k'_i	(e_{i+1}, d_{i+1})
a-1.	$\begin{cases} 0 \le d_i \le \frac{B-1}{2} \\ 0 \le e_i < B \end{cases}$	d_i	$(*, e_i)$
a-2.	$\begin{cases} \frac{B-1}{2} < d_i < B \\ 0 \le e_i < B \end{cases}$	$d_i - B$	$(*, (e_i + 1) \bmod B)$

(b) Even radix B

State	(e_i, d_i)	k'_i	(e_{i+1}, d_{i+1})
b-1.	$\begin{cases} 0 \le d_i < \frac{B}{2} \\ 0 \le e_i < B \end{cases}$	d_i	$(*, e_i)$
b-2.	$\begin{cases} d_i = \frac{B}{2} \\ 0 \le e_i < \frac{B}{2} \end{cases}$	$\frac{B}{2}$	$(*, e_i)$
b-3.	$\begin{cases} d_i = \frac{B}{2} \\ \frac{B}{2} \le e_i < B \end{cases}$	$-\frac{B}{2}$	$(*, (e_i + 1) \bmod B)$
b-4.	$\begin{cases} \frac{B}{2} < d_i < B \\ 0 \le e_i < B \end{cases}$	$d_i - B$	$(*, (e_i + 1) \bmod B)$

We also remark that if the radix-B digits forming k are uniformly random over $\{0, \ldots, B-1\}$ then so is e_{i+1}; in other words, e_{i+1} can take any value in $\{0, \ldots, B-1\}$ with a probability of $\frac{1}{B}$.

When B is odd (and thus $\lfloor \frac{B}{2} \rfloor = \frac{B-1}{2}$), from Table 1(a), we have $k'_i \leftarrow d_i \in \{0, \ldots, \frac{B-1}{2}\}$ or $k'_i \leftarrow d_i - B \in \{-\frac{B-1}{2}, \ldots, -1\}$. We therefrom infer that each digit is equiprobable in the recoding and so has an occurrence probability of $\Pr[k'_i = d] = \frac{1}{B}$ for any $d \in \{0, \ldots, \lfloor \frac{B}{2} \rfloor\}$.

When B is even, we obtain from Table 1(b) the following transition probabilities. For State b-1, since $d_{i+1} = e_i$ and $0 \le e_i < B$, there is a probability of $\frac{B/2}{B} = \frac{1}{2}$ to stay in State b-1 and a probability of $\frac{1/2}{B} = \frac{1}{2B}$ to transition to State b-2, and similarly of $\frac{1}{2B}$ to State b-3. The probability to transition to State b-4 from State b-1 is thus of $1 - \frac{1}{2} - \frac{1}{2B} - \frac{1}{2B} = \frac{B-2}{2B}$. For State b-2, since $d_{i+1} = e_i$ and $0 \le e_i < \frac{B}{2}$, the transition is necessarily to State b-1. For State b-3, since $d_{i+1} = e_i + 1 \bmod B$ and $\frac{B}{2} \le e_i < B$, there is a probability of $\frac{B/2-1}{B/2} = \frac{B-2}{B}$ to transition to State b-4 and a probability of $\frac{1}{B/2} = \frac{2}{B}$ to transition to State b-1 (i.e., when $e_i = B - 1$). Finally, for State b-4, since $d_{i+1} = e_i + 1 \bmod B$ and $0 \le e_i < B$, there is a probability of $\frac{B/2-1}{B} = \frac{B-2}{2B}$ to stay in State b-4 (i.e., when $e_i \in \{\frac{B}{2}, \ldots, B-2\}$), there is a probability of $\frac{1/2}{B}$ to transition either to

State b-2 or b-3 (i.e., when $e_i = \frac{B}{2} - 1$), and there is a probability of $\frac{B/2}{B} = \frac{1}{2}$ to transition to State b-1 (i.e., when $e_i \in \{0, \ldots, \frac{B}{2} - 2\} \cup \{B-1\}$).

Schematically, we have the automaton depicted in the next figure.

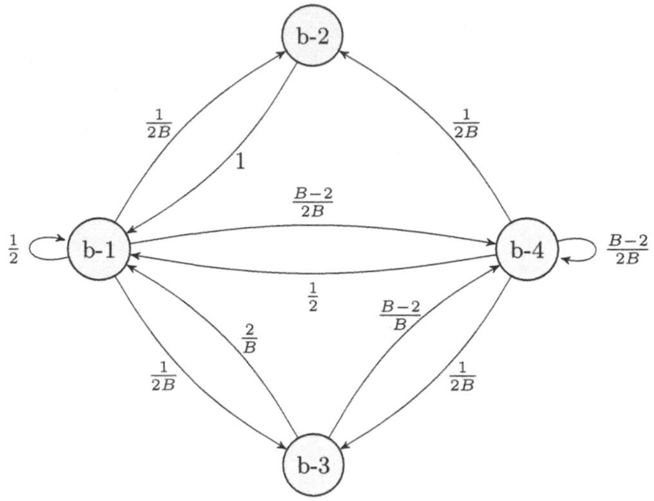

Fig. 1. Transition probabilities among the different states for an even radix B.

The corresponding Markov matrix $\mathbf{P}$ where element (i, j) denotes the probability for transitioning from State b-i to State b-j $(1 \le i, j \le 4)$ is given by

$$\mathbf{P} = \begin{pmatrix} \frac{1}{2} & \frac{1}{2B} & \frac{1}{2B} & \frac{B-2}{2B} \\ 1 & 0 & 0 & 0 \\ \frac{2}{B} & 0 & 0 & \frac{B-2}{B} \\ \frac{1}{2} & \frac{1}{2B} & \frac{1}{2B} & \frac{B-2}{2B} \end{pmatrix} .$$

The companion stationary probability vector $\boldsymbol{\pi} = (\pi_1, \pi_2, \pi_3, \pi_4)$ satisfies $\boldsymbol{\pi}\,\mathbf{P} = \boldsymbol{\pi}$ subject to $\sum_{1 \le j \le 4} \pi_j = 1$. We find

$$\boldsymbol{\pi} = \left(\frac{B^2 + B + 2}{2B(B+1)}, \frac{1}{2(B+1)}, \frac{1}{2(B+1)}, \frac{B-2}{2B}\right) .$$

We can now estimate the occurrence probability of each digit. This is made explicit in the next proposition.

Proposition 1. *Let $B \ge 2$ be a radix. Then a digit $k'_i \in \{-\lfloor \frac{B}{2} \rfloor, \ldots, \lfloor \frac{B}{2} \rfloor\}$ from a uniformly random radix-B BNAF features the following distribution*

$$\Pr[k'_i = d] = \begin{cases} \frac{B+2}{B+1}\frac{1}{B} & \text{if } d = 0 \text{ and } B \text{ is even} \\ \frac{1}{2(B+1)} & \text{if } d \in \{-\lfloor \frac{B}{2} \rfloor, \lfloor \frac{B}{2} \rfloor\} \text{ and } B \text{ is even} \\ \frac{1}{B} & \text{otherwise} \end{cases}$$

where $d \in \{-\lfloor \frac{B}{2} \rfloor, \ldots, \lfloor \frac{B}{2} \rfloor\}$.

Proof. We already showed that $\Pr[k_i' = d] = \frac{1}{B}$ when B is odd. We henceforth assume that B is even. Excluding the digit $d_i = 0$, States b-1 and b-4 in Table 1(b) are symmetric. We so deduce $\pi_1 = \Pr[k_i' = 0] + \pi_4$ and thus $\Pr[k_i' = 0] = \frac{B^2+B+2}{2B(B+1)} - \frac{B-2}{2B} = \frac{B+2}{B(B+1)}$. From Table 1(b), we also get $\Pr[k_i' = \frac{B}{2}] = \pi_2 = \frac{1}{2(B+1)}$ and $\Pr[k_i' = -\frac{B}{2}] = \pi_3 = \frac{1}{2(B+1)}$. For the remaining case (i.e., $d \notin \{-\frac{B}{2}, 0, \frac{B}{2}\}$), we infer from States b-1 and b-4 in Table 1(b) (excluding 0) that every digit is equiprobable and thus $(\pi_1 - \Pr[k_i' = 0]) + \pi_4 = (B-2)\Pr[k_i' = d \mid d \notin \{-\frac{B}{2}, 0, \frac{B}{2}\}] \iff \Pr[k_i' = d \mid d \notin \{-\frac{B}{2}, 0, \frac{B}{2}\}] = \frac{2\pi_4}{B-2} = \frac{1}{B}$. □

As a corollary, we can easily deduce the corresponding variance.

Corollary 1. *Let $B \geq 2$ be a radix. Then a digit k_i' in a uniformly random radix-B BNAF satisfies*

$$\mathbb{E}[k_i'] = 0 \quad \textit{and} \quad \mathrm{Var}(k_i') = \begin{cases} \frac{1}{12}(B^2-1) & \textit{if } B \textit{ is odd} \\ \frac{1}{12}\frac{(B+2)(B^2-B+1)}{B+1} & \textit{if } B \textit{ is even} \end{cases} .$$

Proof. This is immediate. We use the identity $\sum_{t=1}^{T} t^2 = \frac{1}{6}T(T+1)(2T+1)$. From its definition, since $\mathbb{E}[k_i'] = \sum_{-\lfloor\frac{B}{2}\rfloor \le d \le \lfloor\frac{B}{2}\rfloor} \Pr[k_i' = d]\, d = 0$ by symmetry, the variance is given by $\mathrm{Var}(k_i') = \sum_{\lfloor\frac{B}{2}\rfloor \le d \le \lfloor\frac{B}{2}\rfloor} \Pr[k_i' = d]\, d^2 = 2\sum_{d=1}^{\lfloor\frac{B}{2}\rfloor} \Pr[k_i' = d]\, d^2$. If B is odd, we get $\mathrm{Var}(k_i') = 2\frac{1}{B}\sum_{d=1}^{\frac{B-1}{2}} d^2 = \frac{B^2-1}{12}$. If B is even then we get $\mathrm{Var}(k_i') = 2\frac{1}{B}\sum_{d=1}^{\frac{B}{2}-1} d^2 + 2\frac{1}{2(B+1)}(\frac{B}{2})^2 = \frac{1}{12}(B-1)(B-2) + \frac{1}{4}\frac{B^2}{B+1} = \frac{(B+2)(B^2-B+1)}{12(B+1)}$. □

4.3 Exact Distribution

In this section, we consider the set of nonnegative integers whose standard radix-B representation consists of at most n digits; that is, the set $\{0, \ldots, B^n - 1\}$. The previous analysis shows that endowing this set with the uniform probability measure results in a digit distribution for the BNAF satisfying

$$\Pr[k_i'] \sim \begin{cases} \frac{1}{B} & \text{when } B \text{ is odd} \\ \frac{B+2}{B+1}\frac{1}{B} & \text{when } B \text{ is even} \end{cases} \quad \text{as } n \to \infty .$$

For a finite value of n, when B is even, the exact digit distribution for 0 and $\pm B/2$ oscillates around the asymptotic value according to the digit index. Indeed, if $({S_1}^{(i)}, {S_2}^{(i)}, {S_3}^{(i)}, {S_4}^{(i)})$ denotes the probability vector wherein component ${S_j}^{(i)}$ represents the probability of being in State b-j at iteration i in Algorithm 2 then

$$({S_1}^{(i+1)}, {S_2}^{(i+1)}, {S_3}^{(i+1)}, {S_4}^{(i+1)}) = ({S_1}^{(i-1)}, {S_2}^{(i-1)}, {S_3}^{(i-1)}, {S_4}^{(i-1)})\,\mathbf{P}$$

where $\mathbf{P}$ is the Markov matrix; see Sect. 4.2. For a uniformly random integer $k \in \{0, \ldots, B^n - 1\}$, letting $\mathrm{BNAF}(k) = (k_n', \ldots, k_0')$, the least significant digit

k'_0 is equiprobable amongst the possible values except for $\pm\frac{B}{2}$. Namely, we have $\Pr[k'_0 = d] = \frac{1}{B}$ if $d \in \{-\frac{B}{2}+1, \dots, \frac{B}{2}-1\}$ and $\Pr[k'_0 = d] = \frac{1}{2B}$ if $d \in \{\pm\frac{B}{2}\}$. We so deduce that $({S_1}^{(0)}, {S_2}^{(0)}, {S_3}^{(0)}, {S_4}^{(0)}) = (\frac{1}{2}, \frac{1}{2B}, \frac{1}{2B}, \frac{B-2}{2B})$. By induction, we find

$$\begin{aligned}({S_1}^{(i)}, {S_2}^{(i)}, {S_3}^{(i)}, {S_4}^{(i)}) &= ({S_1}^{(0)}, {S_2}^{(0)}, {S_3}^{(0)}, {S_4}^{(0)})\,\mathbf{P}^i \\ &= \Big(\frac{1}{2} + \frac{B^i + (-1)^{i+1}}{B^{i+1}(B+1)}, \\ &\qquad \frac{B^{i+1} - (-1)^{i+1}}{2B^{i+1}(B+1)}, \frac{B^{i+1} - (-1)^{i+1}}{2B^{i+1}(B+1)}, \frac{B-2}{2B}\Big) .\end{aligned}$$

Hence, since $\Pr\big[k'_i = \frac{B}{2}\big] = {S_2}^{(i)}$ and $\Pr\big[k'_i = -\frac{B}{2}\big] = {S_3}^{(i)}$, we obtain

$$\Pr\big[k'_i = \tfrac{B}{2}\big] = \Pr\big[k'_i = -\tfrac{B}{2}\big] = \frac{1}{2(B+1)} - (-1)^{i+1}\frac{1}{2B^{i+1}(B+1)} .$$

In the same way, from the symmetry between State b-1 without 0 and State b-4, we have ${S_1}^{(i)} + \Pr\big[k'_i = 0\big] = {S_4}^{(i)}$ and thus

$$\Pr[k'_i = 0] = \frac{1}{B} + \frac{B^i + (-1)^{i+1}}{B^{i+1}(B+1)} = \frac{B+2}{B(B+1)} + (-1)^{i+1}\frac{1}{B^{i+1}(B+1)} .$$

Furthermore, as the BNAF distribution is computed over the finite set of integers in $\{0, \dots, B^n - 1\}$, the exact digit distribution for the leading digits also differs from the asymptotic distribution. Owing to the BNAF definition, when B is even, the largest integer $k^* \in \{0, \dots, B^n - 1\}$ having the most significant of its BNAF equal to 0 has for BNAF $(k'_n, k'_{n-1}, k'_{n-2}, k'_{n-3}, \dots) = (0, \frac{B}{2}, \frac{B}{2}-1, \frac{B}{2}, \frac{B}{2}-1, \dots)$; that is, the BNAF starts with a leading 0 followed by a succession of the digits $(\frac{B}{2}, \frac{B}{2}-1)$. We need to distinguish the cases of n even or n odd. If n is even then $\mathrm{BNAF}(k^*) = (0, \frac{B}{2}, \frac{B}{2}-1, \frac{B}{2}, \frac{B}{2}-1, \dots, \frac{B}{2}, \frac{B}{2}-1)$, which corresponds to $k^* = \sum_{i=0}^{(n-2)/2}(\frac{B}{2}B + \frac{B}{2} - 1)\,B^{2i} = \frac{1}{2}(B^n - 1) + \frac{1}{2}\frac{B^n-1}{B+1} = \frac{1}{2}B^n\frac{B+2}{B+1} - \frac{B+2}{2(B+1)}$. If n is odd then $\mathrm{BNAF}(k^*) = (0, \frac{B}{2}, \frac{B}{2}-1, \frac{B}{2}, \frac{B}{2}-1, \dots, \frac{B}{2})$ and thus $k^* = \frac{B}{2}B^{n-1} + \sum_{i=0}^{(n-3)/2}((\frac{B}{2}-1)B + \frac{B}{2})\,B^{2i} = \frac{1}{2}(B^n - 1) + \frac{1}{2}\frac{B^n+1}{B+1} = \frac{1}{2}B^n\frac{B+2}{B+1} - \frac{B}{2(B+1)}$. As a consequence, it follows that

$$\Pr[k'_n = 0] = \frac{\frac{1}{2}B^n\frac{B+2}{B+1} - \frac{B+2}{2(B+1)} + 1}{B^n} = \frac{1}{2}\frac{B+2}{B+1} + \frac{1}{2B^n} - \frac{1}{2B^n(B+1)}$$

when n is even, and

$$\Pr[k'_n = 0] = \frac{\frac{1}{2}B^n\frac{B+2}{B+1} - \frac{B}{2(B+1)} + 1}{B^n} = \frac{1}{2}\frac{B+2}{B+1} + \frac{1}{2B^n} + \frac{1}{2B^n(B+1)}$$

when n is odd. Because $k \in \{0, \dots, B^n - 1\}$, k'_n must be 0 or 1. In turn, we have $\Pr[k'_n = 1] = 1 - \Pr[k'_n = 0] = \frac{1}{2}\frac{B}{B+1} - \frac{1}{2B^n} + \frac{1}{2B^n(B+1)}$ when n is even, and

$\Pr[k'_n = 1] = \frac{1}{2}\frac{B}{B+1} - \frac{1}{2B^n} - \frac{1}{2B^n(B+1)}$ when n is odd. The BNAF definition also prohibits k'_{n-1} to be equal to $-\frac{B}{2}$ when B is even—otherwise we would have $k'_n \le 0$, which contradicts the range definition $0 \le k \le B^n - 1$. As a result, since $-\frac{B}{2} \equiv \frac{B}{2} \pmod{B}$, the proportion of $\frac{B}{2}$ for k'_{n-1} grows accordingly. We so have $\Pr\left[k'_{n-1} = -\frac{B}{2}\right] = 0$ and $\Pr\left[k'_{n-1} = \frac{B}{2}\right] = \left(\frac{1}{2(B+1)} - (-1)^n \frac{1}{2B^n(B+1)}\right) + \left(\frac{1}{2(B+1)} - (-1)^n \frac{1}{2B^n(B+1)}\right) = \frac{1}{B+1} - (-1)^n \frac{1}{B^n(B+1)}$.

The case of an odd radix B is easier to deal with. We immediately have $\Pr[k'_i = d] = \frac{1}{B}$ for any $d \in \{-\lfloor\frac{B}{2}\rfloor, \ldots, \lfloor\frac{B}{2}\rfloor\}$, $0 \le i \le n-1$. This clearly appears from Algorithm 2; see Remark 2. For the most significant digit k'_n, it can only take values in $\{0,1\}$ due to range restrictions—recall that input integer $k \in \{0, \ldots, B^n - 1\}$. Specifically, we have $k'_n = 0$ if $k \in \{0, \ldots, \frac{B^n-1}{2}\}$ and $k'_n = 1$ if $k \in \{\frac{B^n+1}{2}, \ldots, B^n - 1\}$. We so get $\Pr[k'_n = 0] = \frac{(B^n+1)/2}{B^n}$ and $\Pr[k'_n = 1] = \frac{(B^n-1)/2}{B^n}$.

Putting it all together, we proved the following result.

Theorem 3. *Given a radix $B \ge 2$, let $(k'_n, \ldots, k'_0)$ represent the BNAF of an n-digit integer uniformly drawn at random in $\{0, \ldots, B-1\}^n$. Then*

- *for an even radix B:*

$$\Pr[k'_i = d \mid 0 \le i \le n-1] = \begin{cases} \frac{1}{B}\frac{B+2}{B+1} + (-1)^{i+1}\frac{1}{B^{i+1}(B+1)} & \text{if } d = 0 \\ \frac{1}{2(B+1)} - (-1)^{i+1}\frac{1}{2B^{i+1}(B+1)} & \text{if } d \in \{\pm\frac{B}{2}\} \text{ and } i \ne n-1 \\ \frac{1}{(B+1)} - (-1)^n\frac{1}{B^n(B+1)} & \text{if } d = \frac{B}{2} \text{ and } i = n-1 \\ 0 & \text{if } d = -\frac{B}{2} \text{ and } i = n-1 \\ \frac{1}{B} & \text{otherwise} \end{cases}$$

and

$$\Pr[k'_n = d] = \begin{cases} \frac{1}{2}\frac{B+2}{B+1} + \frac{1}{2B^n} + (-1)^{n+1}\frac{1}{2B^n(B+1)} & \text{if } d = 0 \\ \frac{1}{2}\frac{B}{B+1} - \frac{1}{2B^n} - (-1)^{n+1}\frac{1}{2B^n(B+1)} & \text{if } d = 1 \\ 0 & \text{otherwise} \end{cases};$$

- *for an odd radix B:*

$$\Pr[k'_i = d \mid 0 \le i \le n-1] = \frac{1}{B} \quad \text{and} \quad \Pr[k'_n = d] = \begin{cases} \frac{1}{2} + \frac{1}{2B^n} & \text{if } d = 0 \\ \frac{1}{2} - \frac{1}{2B^n} & \text{if } d = 1 \\ 0 & \text{otherwise} \end{cases}$$

where $d \in \{-\lfloor\frac{B}{2}\rfloor, \ldots, \lfloor\frac{B}{2}\rfloor\}$. □

5 Extensions

The balanced non-adjacent forms can be extended to modular representations.

Definition 3. *Let $B \geq 2$ be a radix. If there exists a BNAF $(k'_{n-1}, \dots, k'_0)$ such that*

$$k \equiv \sum_{i=0}^{n-1} k'_i B^i \pmod{B^n}$$

then $(k'_{n-1}, \dots, k'_0)$ is called a BNAF modulo B^n *for k.*

BNAF representations modulo B^n apply to integers in $\mathbb{Z}/B^n\mathbb{Z}$. They equally apply to discretized torus elements in $B^{-n}\mathbb{Z}/\mathbb{Z}$ by noting that $B^{-n}\mathbb{Z}/\mathbb{Z} \cong \frac{\mathbb{Z}/B^n\mathbb{Z}}{B^n}$. Indeed, a torus element $\tau \in B^{-n}\mathbb{Z}/\mathbb{Z}$ can always be rewritten as $\tau = k \cdot B^{-n}$ where $k \equiv \sum_{i=0}^{n-1} k'_i B^i \pmod{B^n}$. It is interesting to note that modular BNAFs do not need one more digit in their encoding.

The next two theorems are straightforward generalizations of Theorem 1 and Theorem 2.

Theorem 4. *Every integer k has a BNAF modulo B^n. This BNAF, say $(k'_{n-1}, k'_{n-2}, \dots, k'_0)$, is unique—unless B is even and $k'_{n-1} \in \{\pm\frac{B}{2}\}$, in which case $(-k'_{n-1}, k'_{n-2}, \dots, k'_0)$ is also a BNAF modulo B^n for k.* □

Theorem 5. *If $(k'_{n-1}, \dots, k'_0)$ is a BNAF modulo B^n of an integer k then the Euclidean weight of $k \pmod{B^n}$ is equal to $\sum_{i=0}^{n-1} k_i'^2$.* □

If k is an integer in $\{0, \dots, B^n - 1\}$ and if $(k'_n, \dots, k'_0) \leftarrow \mathrm{BNAF}(k)$, Theorem 3 tells that $k'_n \in \{0, 1\}$. More precisely, a close inspection of the proof shows that $k'_n = 0$ whenever

- $0 \leq k \leq \frac{B^n - 1}{2}$ if B is odd, or
- $0 \leq k \leq \frac{B^n(B+2) - B - 1 - (-1)^n}{2(B+1)}$ if B is even.

In all cases, we therefore have $k'_n = 0$ if $0 \leq k \leq \lfloor \frac{B^n}{2} \rfloor$. We define $\bar{k} = B^n - k$ and let $(\bar{k}'_n, \dots, \bar{k}'_0) \leftarrow \mathrm{BNAF}(\bar{k})$. If $\lfloor \frac{B}{2} \rfloor + 1 \leq k \leq B^n - 1$, we have by symmetry $\bar{k}'_n = 0$ since $0 \leq B^n - k \leq \lfloor \frac{B^n}{2} \rfloor$ for $\lfloor \frac{B}{2} \rfloor + 1 \leq k \leq B^n - 1$. Note also that $\mathrm{BNAF}(-\bar{k}) = -\mathrm{BNAF}(\bar{k})$. The BNAF modulo B^n of an integer k can therefore be defined as

$$\begin{cases} \mathrm{BNAF}(k \bmod B^n) & \text{if } k \bmod B^n \leq \lfloor \frac{B^n}{2} \rfloor \\ \mathrm{BNAF}\big((k \bmod B^n) - B^n\big) & \text{otherwise} \end{cases} \qquad (**)$$

where the BNAF is obtained as per Algorithm 2. This alternative definition makes the modular BNAF unique, except when B is even and $k \equiv \frac{B^n}{2} \bmod B^n$. In this latter case, there are two BNAFs modulo B^n: $\big(\frac{B}{2}, 0, \dots, 0\big)$ and $\big(-\frac{B}{2}, 0, \dots, 0\big)$.

Another benefit of the formulation (**) is that the distribution of the resulting BNAF digits is centered, provided that when B is even and $k \equiv \frac{B^n}{2} \pmod{B^n}$ one of the two forms $\big(\frac{B}{2}, 0, \dots, 0\big)$ or $\big(-\frac{B}{2}, 0, \dots, 0\big)$ is returned at

---

Algorithm 3: Modular BNAF recoding

Input: Integer $k \neq 0$ and $n \geq 1$
Output: $(k'_{n-1}, \ldots, k'_0)$ with $k'_i \in \{-\lfloor \frac{B}{2} \rfloor, \ldots, \lfloor \frac{B}{2} \rfloor\}$ s.t. $\sum_{i=0}^{n-1} k'_i B^i \equiv k \pmod{B^n}$

$K \leftarrow k \bmod B^n$; $i \leftarrow 0$;
if $(K > \lfloor \frac{B^n}{2} \rfloor) \vee ((K = \lceil \frac{B^n}{2} \rceil) \wedge (\texttt{random}() = 1))$ **then**
  $K \leftarrow K - B^n$;
end if
while $(K \neq 0)$ **do**
  $k'_i \leftarrow K \bmod B$; $K \leftarrow (K - k'_i)/B$;
  if $(k'_i > \lfloor \frac{B}{2} \rfloor) \vee ((k'_i = \lceil \frac{B}{2} \rceil) \wedge ((K \bmod B) \geq \lfloor \frac{B}{2} \rfloor))$ **then**
    $k'_i \leftarrow k'_i - B$; $K \leftarrow K + 1$;
  end if
  $i \leftarrow i + 1$;
end while
return $(k'_{i-1}, \ldots, k'_0)$

---

random; see Theorem 6. The corresponding algorithm is detailed in Algorithm 3. Given an integer k and a power n, it outputs the BNAF modulo B^n of k. The algorithm makes use of an internal routine random() that returns a uniformly random bit.

We state exactly the occurrence probability of each digit in the modular BNAF produced by Algorithm 3. We also state their expectation and variance.

Theorem 6. *Given a radix $B \geq 2$ and a power n, let $(k'_{n-1}, \ldots, k'_0)$ represent the BNAF modulo B^n of an integer uniformly drawn at random in $\{0, \ldots, B^n - 1\}$ as per Algorithm 3. Then*

- *for an even radix B:*

$$\Pr[k'_i = d \mid 0 \leq i \leq n-1] = \begin{cases} \frac{1}{B}\frac{B+2}{B+1} + (-1)^{i+1}\frac{1}{B^{i+1}(B+1)} & \text{if } d = 0 \\ \frac{1}{2(B+1)} - (-1)^{i+1}\frac{1}{2B^{i+1}(B+1)} & \text{if } d \in \{\pm\frac{B}{2}\} \\ \frac{1}{B} & \text{otherwise} \end{cases};$$

- *for an odd radix B:*

$$\Pr[k'_i = d \mid 0 \leq i \leq n-1] = \frac{1}{B}$$

where $d \in \{-\lfloor \frac{B}{2} \rfloor, \ldots, \lfloor \frac{B}{2} \rfloor\}$.

Proof. The theorem is a direct consequence of Theorem 3 using (**) and noting that $k'_n = 0$. When B is even, the digits $\frac{B}{2}$ and $-\frac{B}{2}$ are equiprobable for k'_{n-1} because of the random choice for $k \equiv \frac{B^n}{2} \pmod{B^n}$. We so infer from Theorem 3 that $\Pr[k'_{n-1} = \frac{B}{2}] = \Pr[k'_{n-1} = -\frac{B}{2}] = \frac{1}{2(B+1)} - (-1)^n \frac{1}{2B^n(B+1)}$ when B is even. The other cases are immediate. □

Corollary 2. *Given a radix $B \geq 2$ and a power n, let $(k'_{n-1}, \ldots, k'_0)$ represent the BNAF modulo B^n of an integer uniformly drawn at random in $\{0, \ldots, B^n - 1\}$ as per Algorithm 3. Then any digit k'_i in the representation $(k'_{n-1}, \ldots, k'_0)$ satisfies*

$$\mathbb{E}[k'_i] = 0 \quad \textit{and} \quad \operatorname{Var}(k'_i) = \begin{cases} \frac{1}{12}\,(B^2-1) & \textit{if } B \textit{ is odd} \\ \frac{1}{12}\,\frac{(B+2)(B^2-B+1)}{B+1} - \frac{(-1)^{i+1}}{4B^{i-1}(B+1)} & \textit{if } B \textit{ is even} \end{cases} .$$

Proof. The proof is analogous to that of Corollary 1. We have $\mathbb{E}[k'_i] = 0$ because the distribution is centered. For the variance, it then follows that $\operatorname{Var}(k'_i) = 2\sum_{d=1}^{\lfloor \frac{B}{2} \rfloor} \Pr[k'_i = d]\, d^2$. If B is odd, we get $\operatorname{Var}(k'_i) = 2\frac{1}{B}\sum_{d=1}^{\frac{B-1}{2}} d^2 = \frac{B^2-1}{12}$ and if B is even, $\operatorname{Var}(k'_i) = 2\frac{1}{B}\sum_{d=1}^{\frac{B}{2}-1} d^2 + 2\big(\frac{1}{2(B+1)} - (-1)^{i+1}\frac{1}{2B^{i+1}(B+1)}\big)(\frac{B}{2})^2 = \frac{1}{12}\,\frac{(B+2)(B^2-B+1)}{B+1} - \frac{(-1)^{i+1}}{4B^{i-1}(B+1)}$. □

6 Applications

As already mentioned in the introduction, a salient feature of lattice cryptosystems, notably those based on LWE [34] and its variants [5,8,23,25,38], is the presence of noise in the ciphertexts.

The noise can have different natures. It can be a parameter that is defined at setup time to guarantee a certain security level. It can be a quantity that evolves over time due to ciphertext evaluations as in fully homomorphic encryption. Finally, it can be algorithmic as the result of approximate computations or numerical errors.

Gadget Decomposition. Informally, an LWE ciphertext $\boldsymbol{c}$ can be seen as a $(d+1)$-dimensional vector such that its dot product with the key $\boldsymbol{t} = (-\boldsymbol{s}, 1)$ (also seen as a $(d+1)$-dimensional vector) equals the input plaintext μ plus some small noise error e. The noise term is typically removed by rounding. We write $\boldsymbol{c} \leftarrow \mathsf{LWE}_{\boldsymbol{s}}(\mu) \in (\mathbb{Z}/q\mathbb{Z})^{d+1}$. Ciphertext $\boldsymbol{c}$ can be multiplied by a small scalar k to give an encryption of $k\mu$. In order to support multiplication by an arbitrary scalar k, the multiplier needs first to be decomposed.

We follow the presentation of [29]; see also [17, Section 3]. Given a radix B and a level ℓ, the so-called gadget vector is given by $\boldsymbol{g} = (1, B, \ldots, B^{\ell-1}) \in (\mathbb{Z}/q\mathbb{Z})^{\ell}$ so that for any vector $\boldsymbol{v} \in (\mathbb{Z}/q\mathbb{Z})^{\ell}$ the product $\boldsymbol{v} \cdot \boldsymbol{g}^{\intercal}$ yields a scalar k in $\mathbb{Z}/q\mathbb{Z}$. We also consider the associated inverse transformation $g^{-1}\colon \mathbb{Z}/q\mathbb{Z} \to (\mathbb{Z}/q\mathbb{Z})^{\ell}$ such that for any scalar $k \in \mathbb{Z}/q\mathbb{Z}$, we have $g^{-1}(k) \cdot \boldsymbol{g}^{\intercal} = k$ and $g^{-1}(k)$ is "small". Explicitly, this inverse transformation replaces the input scalar by a (signed) radix-B expansion:

$$g^{-1}(k) = (k_0, \ldots, k_{\ell-1}) \quad \text{such that } k \equiv \textstyle\sum_{i=0}^{\ell-1} k_i\, B^i \pmod{q} .$$

From the basic LWE encryption scheme, an "extended" encryption scheme $\widehat{\mathsf{LWE}}$ is built by LWE-encrypting individually each component of plaintext vector $\mu\,\boldsymbol{g}$:

$\widehat{\mathsf{LWE}}_{\boldsymbol{s}}(\mu) \leftarrow (\mathsf{LWE}_{\boldsymbol{s}}(\mu), \mathsf{LWE}_{\boldsymbol{s}}(B\mu), \ldots, \mathsf{LWE}_{\boldsymbol{s}}(B^{\ell-1}\mu))$. The LWE encryption of $k\,\mu$ can then be obtained from $\widehat{\mathsf{LWE}}_{\boldsymbol{s}}(\mu)$ as $\mathsf{LWE}_{\boldsymbol{s}}(k\mu) \leftarrow g^{-1}(k) \cdot \widehat{\mathsf{LWE}}_{\boldsymbol{s}}(\mu)^{\intercal}$.

For an LWE ciphertext $\boldsymbol{c} \leftarrow \mathsf{LWE}_{\boldsymbol{s}}(\mu)$, we let $\mathrm{Err}(\boldsymbol{c})$ denote the noise error present in $\boldsymbol{c}$. We can then write $\langle \boldsymbol{c}, \boldsymbol{t} \rangle = \mu + \mathrm{Err}(\boldsymbol{c})$, where $\boldsymbol{t} = (-\boldsymbol{s}, 1)$. We define $\boldsymbol{C}_i := \mathsf{LWE}_{\boldsymbol{s}}(B^i\mu)$ and $\boldsymbol{C}' := g^{-1}(k) \cdot \widehat{\mathsf{LWE}}_{\boldsymbol{s}}(\mu)^{\intercal}$. We so obtain

$$\begin{aligned}\langle \boldsymbol{C}', \boldsymbol{t} \rangle &= \langle \textstyle\sum_{i=0}^{\ell-1} k_i \,\mathsf{LWE}_{\boldsymbol{s}}(B^i\mu), \boldsymbol{t} \rangle = \textstyle\sum_{i=0}^{\ell-1} k_i \,\langle \mathsf{LWE}_{\boldsymbol{s}}(B^i\mu), \boldsymbol{t} \rangle \\ &= \textstyle\sum_{i=0}^{\ell-1} k_i (B^i\,\mu + \mathrm{Err}(\boldsymbol{C}_i)) = (\textstyle\sum_{i=0}^{\ell-1} k_i B^i)\mu + \textstyle\sum_{i=0}^{\ell-1} \mathrm{Err}(\boldsymbol{C}_i)) \\ &= k\,\mu + \textstyle\sum_{i=0}^{\ell-1} k_i \mathrm{Err}(\boldsymbol{C}_i)\ .\end{aligned}$$

The noise present in $\boldsymbol{C}'$ only amounts to $\mathrm{Err}(\boldsymbol{C}') = \sum_{i=0}^{\ell-1} k_i\mathrm{Err}(\boldsymbol{C}_i)$—this has to be compared with the noise $k\mathrm{Err}(\boldsymbol{c})$ present in $\boldsymbol{c}' \leftarrow k\,\mathsf{LWE}_{\boldsymbol{s}}(\mu)$. Hence, using the gadget decomposition, the error only grows logarithmically in q instead of linearly. Furthermore, the gadget decomposition can accommodate any digit expansion. As a consequence, selecting the BNAF for $g^{-1}(k)$ further improves the situation since the variance $\mathrm{Var}(\mathrm{Err}(\boldsymbol{C}'))$ is then minimal.

We note that the gadget decomposition applies to all LWE-type encryption schemes. It also extends naturally to vectors and matrices as done for example in the GSW encryption scheme [15] for the multiplication of ciphertexts.

Key Switching. LWE-type ciphertexts under a given key can be converted into ciphertexts under another key in different parameter sets thanks to a key switching procedure [6, § 1.2]. Its implementation requires key-switching keys: they essentially consist of an encryption of the key components of the original $\boldsymbol{s} = (s_1, \ldots, s_d)$ with respect to the new key $\boldsymbol{s}'$. More precisely, using the previous notation, the d key switching keys are given $\mathsf{ksk}[j] \leftarrow \widehat{\mathsf{LWE}}_{\boldsymbol{s}'}(s_j)$, $1 \le j \le d$. An input LWE ciphertext $\boldsymbol{c} \leftarrow \mathsf{LWE}_{\boldsymbol{s}}(\mu) := (a_1, \ldots, a_d, b)$ is then turned into the ciphertext

$$\boldsymbol{c}' \leftarrow (0, \ldots, 0, b) - \sum_{j=1}^{d} g^{-1}(a_j)\,\mathsf{ksk}[j]\ .$$

We are back to a setting similar to the previous one. Letting $g^{-1}(a_j) = (a_{j,0}, \ldots, a_{j,\ell-1})$, $\mathsf{ksk}[j] = (\mathsf{ksk}[j]_0, \ldots, \mathsf{ksk}[j]_{\ell-1})$ and $\boldsymbol{t}' = (-\boldsymbol{s}', 1)$, we can check that

$$\begin{aligned}\langle \boldsymbol{c}', \boldsymbol{t}' \rangle &= \langle (0, \ldots, 0, b), \boldsymbol{t}' \rangle - \textstyle\sum_{j=1}^{d} \langle g^{-1}(a_j)\,\mathsf{ksk}[j], \boldsymbol{t}' \rangle \\ &= b - \sum_{j=1}^{d} \Big(a_j s_j + \textstyle\sum_{i=0}^{\ell-1} a_{j,i}\mathrm{Err}(\mathsf{ksk}[j]_i)\Big) \\ &= \langle \boldsymbol{c}, \boldsymbol{t} \rangle - \sum_{j=1}^{d}\sum_{i=0}^{\ell-1} a_{j,i}\mathrm{Err}(\mathsf{ksk}[j]_i)\,,\end{aligned}$$

that is, an LWE encryption of μ under key $\boldsymbol{s}'$—provided that the noise keeps small.

Here too, it is crucial to adopt the BNAF representation for the gadget decomposition. The gain quickly becomes significant as the error not only is amplified by the number ℓ of levels but also by the dimension d of the input ciphertext (typically of the order of $10^3 \approx 2^{10}$ at a 128-bit security level).

Fast Fourier Transform. Crandall and Fagin [11, § 3] empirically observe that when floating-point FFTs are employed, it is advantageous to make use of balanced representations. Indeed, they tend to reduce the convolution errors attendant to floating-point arithmetic, including those resulting from round-off errors. Algorithm 3 produces decompositions that are perfectly balanced: they on average have a zero mean; see Corollary 2. FFT techniques are well suited to module lattices as a way to reduce the computation time in lattice cryptography [27]. They for example play a central role in the fast bootstrapping procedure of FHEW [13] or of TFHE [9].

References

1. Alperin-Sheriff, J., Peikert, C.: Faster bootstrapping with polynomial error. In: Garay, J.A., Gennaro, R. (eds.) CRYPTO 2014. LNCS, vol. 8616, pp. 297–314. Springer, Heidelberg (2014). https://doi.org/10.1007/978-3-662-44371-2_17
2. Arno, S., Wheeler, F.S.: Signed digit representations of minimal Hamming weight. IEEE Trans. Comput. **42**(8), 1007–1110 (1993). https://doi.org/10.1109/12.238495
3. Brakerski, Z.: Fully homomorphic encryption without modulus switching from classical GapSVP. In: Safavi-Naini, R., Canetti, R. (eds.) CRYPTO 2012. LNCS, vol. 7417, pp. 868–886. Springer, Heidelberg (2012). https://doi.org/10.1007/978-3-642-32009-5_50
4. Brakerski, Z., Gentry, C., Vaikuntanathan, V.: (Leveled) fully homomorphic encryption without bootstrapping. ACM Trans. Computa. Theory **6**(3), 13:1–13:36 (2014). https://doi.org/10.1145/2633600. Earlier version in ITCS 2012
5. Brakerski, Z., Langlois, A., Peikert, C., Regev, O., Stehlé, D.: Classical hardness of learning with errors. In: Boneh, D., Roughgarden, T., Feigenbaum, J. (eds.) 45th Annual ACM Symposium on Theory of Computing, pp. 575–584. ACM Press (2013). https://doi.org/10.1145/2488608.2488680
6. Brakerski, Z., Vaikuntanathan, V.: Efficient fully homomorphic encryption from (standard) LWE. SIAM J. Comput. **43**(2), 831–871 (2014). https://doi.org/10.1137/120868669
7. Cheon, J.H., Kim, A., Kim, M., Song, Y.: Homomorphic encryption for arithmetic of approximate numbers. In: Takagi, T., Peyrin, T. (eds.) ASIACRYPT 2017. LNCS, vol. 10624, pp. 409–437. Springer, Cham (2017). https://doi.org/10.1007/978-3-319-70694-8_15
8. Cheon, J.H., Stehlé, D.: Fully homomophic encryption over the integers revisited. In: Oswald, E., Fischlin, M. (eds.) EUROCRYPT 2015. LNCS, vol. 9056, pp. 513–536. Springer, Heidelberg (2015). https://doi.org/10.1007/978-3-662-46800-5_20
9. Chillotti, I., Gama, N., Georgieva, M., Izabachène, M.: TFHE: fast fully homomorphic encryption over the torus. J. Cryptol. **33**(1), 34–91 (2019). https://doi.org/10.1007/s00145-019-09319-x
10. Clark, W.E., Liang, J.J.: On arithmetic weight for a general radix representation of integers. IEEE Trans. Inf. Theory **19**(6), 823–826 (1973). https://doi.org/10.1109/TIT.1973.1055100

11. Crandall, R., Fagin, B.: Discrete weighted transforms and large-integer arithmetic. Math. Comput. **62**(205), 305–324 (1994). https://doi.org/10.1090/S0025-5718-1994-1185244-1
12. Crandall, R., Pomerance, C.: Prime Numbers: A Computational Perspective. Springer, New York (2001). https://doi.org/10.1007/978-1-4684-9316-0
13. Ducas, L., Micciancio, D.: FHEW: bootstrapping homomorphic encryption in less than a second. In: Oswald, E., Fischlin, M. (eds.) EUROCRYPT 2015. LNCS, vol. 9056, pp. 617–640. Springer, Heidelberg (2015). https://doi.org/10.1007/978-3-662-46800-5_24
14. Gentry, C.: Computing arbitrary functions of encrypted data. Commun. ACM **53**(3), 97–105 (2010). https://doi.org/10.1145/1666420.1666444
15. Gentry, C., Sahai, A., Waters, B.: Homomorphic encryption from learning with errors: conceptually-simpler, asymptotically-faster, attribute-based. In: Canetti, R., Garay, J.A. (eds.) CRYPTO 2013. LNCS, vol. 8042, pp. 75–92. Springer, Heidelberg (2013). https://doi.org/10.1007/978-3-642-40041-4_5
16. Gordon, D.M.: A survey of fast exponentiation methods. J. Algorithms **27**(1), 129–146 (1998). https://doi.org/10.1006/jagm.1997.0913
17. Halevi, S.: Homomorphic encryption. In: Lindell, Y. (ed.) Tutorials on the Foundations of Cryptography. ISC, pp. 219–276. Springer, Cham (2017). https://doi.org/10.1007/978-3-319-57048-8_5
18. Jao, D., Raju, S.R., Venkatesan, R.: Digit set randomization in elliptic curve cryptography. In: Hromkovič, J., Královič, R., Nunkesser, M., Widmayer, P. (eds.) SAGA 2007. LNCS, vol. 4665, pp. 105–117. Springer, Heidelberg (2007). https://doi.org/10.1007/978-3-540-74871-7_10
19. Joye, M., Yen, S.M.: Optimal left-to-right binary signed-digit exponent recoding. IEEE Trans. Comput. **49**(7), 740–748 (2000). https://doi.org/10.1109/12.863044
20. Joye, M., Yen, S.-M.: New minimal modified radix-r representation with applications to smart cards. In: Naccache, D., Paillier, P. (eds.) PKC 2002. LNCS, vol. 2274, pp. 375–383. Springer, Heidelberg (2002). https://doi.org/10.1007/3-540-45664-3_27
21. Koblitz, N.: CM-curves with good cryptographic properties. In: Feigenbaum, J. (ed.) CRYPTO 1991. LNCS, vol. 576, pp. 279–287. Springer, Heidelberg (1992). https://doi.org/10.1007/3-540-46766-1_22
22. Koren, I.: Computer Arithmetic Algorithms, 2nd edn. A K Peters/CRC Press (2002). https://doi.org/10.1201/9781315275567
23. Langlois, A., Stehlé, D.: Worst-case to average-case reductions for module lattices. Des. Codes Crypt. **75**(3), 565–599 (2014). https://doi.org/10.1007/s10623-014-9938-4
24. van Lint, J.H.: Introduction to Coding Theory. Graduate Texts in Mathematics, vol. 86, 3rd edn. Springer, Heidelberg. (1999). https://doi.org/10.1007/978-3-642-58575-3
25. Lyubashevsky, V., Peikert, C., Regev, O.: On ideal lattices and learning with errors over rings. J. ACM **60**(6), 43:1–43:35 (2013). https://doi.org/10.1145/2535925
26. Meier, W., Staffelbach, O.: Efficient multiplication on certain nonsupersingular elliptic curves. In: Brickell, E.F. (ed.) CRYPTO 1992. LNCS, vol. 740, pp. 333–344. Springer, Heidelberg (1993). https://doi.org/10.1007/3-540-48071-4_24
27. Micciancio, D.: Generalized compact knapsacks, cyclic lattices, and efficient one-way functions. Comput. Complex. **16**(4), 365–411 (2007). https://doi.org/10.1007/s00037-007-0234-9

28. Micciancio, D., Peikert, C.: Trapdoors for lattices: simpler, tighter, faster, smaller. In: Pointcheval, D., Johansson, T. (eds.) EUROCRYPT 2012. LNCS, vol. 7237, pp. 700–718. Springer, Heidelberg (2012). https://doi.org/10.1007/978-3-642-29011-4_41
29. Micciancio, D., Polyakov, Y.: Bootstrapping in FHEW-like cryptosystems. Cryptology ePrint Archive, Report 2020/086 (2020). https://ia.cr/2020/086
30. Morain, F., Olivos, J.: Speeding up the computations on an elliptic curve using addition-subtraction chains. RAIRO Theoret. Inform. Appl. **24**(6), 531–543 (1990). https://doi.org/10.1051/ita/1990240605311
31. Muir, J.A., Stinson, D.R.: Alternative digit sets for nonadjacent representations. In: Matsui, M., Zuccherato, R.J. (eds.) SAC 2003. LNCS, vol. 3006, pp. 306–319. Springer, Heidelberg (2004). https://doi.org/10.1007/978-3-540-24654-1_22
32. Muir, J.A., Stinson, D.R.: Minimality and other properties of the width-w nonadjacent form. Math. Comput. **75**(253), 369–384 (2005). https://doi.org/10.1090/S0025-5718-05-01769-2
33. Qin, B., Li, M., Kong, F., Li, D.: New left-to-right minimal weight signed-digit radix-r representation. Comput. Electr. Eng. **35**(1), 150–158 (2008). https://doi.org/10.1016/j.compeleceng.2008.09.007
34. Regev, O.: On lattices, learning with errors, random linear codes, and cryptography. J. ACM **56**(6), 34:1–34:40 (2009). https://doi.org/10.1145/1568318.1568324
35. Reitwiesner, G.W.: Binary arithmetic. Adv. Comput. **1**, 231–308 (1960). https://doi.org/10.1016/S0065-2458(08)60610-5
36. Rivest, R.L., Adleman, L., Detouzos, M.L.: On data banks and privacy homomorphisms. In: DeMillo, R.A., Dobkin, D.P., Jones, A.K., Lipton, R.J. (eds.) Foundations of Secure Computation. pp. 165–179. Academic Press (1978). https://people.csail.mit.edu/rivest/pubs.html#RAD78
37. Solinas, J.A.: Efficient arithmetic on Koblitz curves. Des. Codes Crypt. **19**(2/3), 195–249 (2000). https://doi.org/10.1023/A:1008306223194
38. Stehlé, D., Steinfeld, R., Tanaka, K., Xagawa, K.: Efficient public key encryption based on ideal lattices. In: Matsui, M. (ed.) ASIACRYPT 2009. LNCS, vol. 5912, pp. 617–635. Springer, Heidelberg (2009). https://doi.org/10.1007/978-3-642-10366-7_36
39. Takagi, T., Yen, S.-M., Wu, B.-C.: Radix-r non-adjacent form. In: Zhang, K., Zheng, Y. (eds.) ISC 2004. LNCS, vol. 3225, pp. 99–110. Springer, Heidelberg (2004). https://doi.org/10.1007/978-3-540-30144-8_9

Efficient Boolean Search over Encrypted Data with Reduced Leakage

Sarvar Patel[1(✉)], Giuseppe Persiano[1,2], Joon Young Seo[1], and Kevin Yeo[1]

[1] Google LLC, Mountain View, USA
{sarvar,jyseo,kwlyeo}@google.com
[2] Università di Salerno, Fisciano, Italy

Abstract. Encrypted multi-maps enable outsourcing the storage of a multi-map to an untrusted server while maintaining the ability to query privately. We focus on encrypted Boolean multi-maps that support arbitrary Boolean queries over the multi-map. Kamara and Moataz [Eurocrypt'17] presented the first encrypted multi-map, BIEX, that supports CNF queries with optimal communication, worst-case sublinear search time and non-trivial leakage.

We improve on previous work by presenting a new construction CNFFilter for CNF queries with significantly less leakage than BIEX, while maintaining both optimal communication and worst-case sublinear search time. As a direct consequence our construction shows additional resistance to leakage-abuse attacks in comparison to prior works. For most CNF queries, CNFFilter avoids leaking the result sets for any singleton queries for labels appearing in the CNF query. As an example, for the CNF query of the form $(\ell_1 \vee \ell_2) \wedge \ell_3$, our scheme does not leak the result sizes of queries to ℓ_1, ℓ_2 or ℓ_3 individually. On the other hand, BIEX does leak some of this information. This is just an example of the reduced leakage obtained by CNFFilter. The core of CNFFilter is a new *filtering* algorithm that performs set intersections with significantly less leakage compared to prior works.

We implement CNFFilter and show that CNFFilter achieves faster search times and similar communication overhead compared to BIEX at the cost of a small increase in server storage.

1 Introduction

In this work, we study the notion of *structured encryption* that was introduced by Chase and Kamara [17]. Structured encryption (STE) is a general cryptographic primitive that considers the scenario where a data owner (commonly referred to as the client) wishes to store a data structure on a potentially untrusted server such as a cloud storage provider. STE schemes should ensure that clients are able to perform all necessary data structure operations correctly over the server-stored encrypted data while ensuring that the adversarial server learns as little information as possible.

For the full version of this paper, please see [38].

M. Tibouchi and H. Wang (Eds.): ASIACRYPT 2021, LNCS 13092, pp. 577–607, 2021.
https://doi.org/10.1007/978-3-030-92078-4_20

The privacy goal of a STE scheme is to reveal little information about the contents of the outsourced data structure as well as the operations that are performed on the data structure. In an ideal world, these schemes would leak no information about either the underlying data or the executed algorithms. However, the only known ways to achieve this desired privacy is through the use of extremely expensive cryptographic primitives such as oblivious RAM [24] and/or fully homomorphic encryption [23]. In contrast, structured encryption considers a more relaxed privacy requirement with the hope of achieving the small overhead necessary for practical applications. In more detail, structured encryption are defined by a leakage function that is an upper bound on the information that may be learned by the adversarial server. As a result, some schemes have larger than ideal leakage, but avoid using heavy cryptographic primitives. However, we note that caution is necessary when picking leakage functions as there have been many works (see [8,13,25–27,33,35,44] as some examples) showing that various leakage profiles may be utilized by intelligent adversaries to compromise privacy in certain settings.

In our work, we will focus on an important type of STE scheme called *encrypted multi-maps*. An encrypted multi-map EMM structurally encrypts a multi-map MM consisting of pairs $(\ell, \vec{v})$ of labels ℓ and tuples $\vec{v}$ of values. We use the writing $\mathsf{MM}[\ell]$ to denote the tuple associated to label ℓ by MM. We focus on encrypted multi-maps due to its significance in a wide range of important real-world applications. Encrypted multi-maps have been the basis of many *searchable encryption* (or *encrypted search*) constructions. Searchable encryption was introduced by Song *et al.* [42] and enables a client to perform keyword searches over a corpus of documents outsourced to a server. There has been a long line of work (see [7,9,18] and references therein as examples) that considers single keyword search to determine a list of documents containing a single queried keyword. There have been many subsequent works for improving efficiency [14,21], dynamicity [32,36,43], forward and/or backward privacy [10,12], suppressing leakage [30,31,40] and improving locality [5,16,19,20] to list some examples. Faber *et al.* [22] build on [15] to obtain more complex queries such as range, substring, and wildcard queries. There also has been work for efficiency lower bounds for searchable encryption/structured encryption [11,39]. We note that many of the above searchable encryption schemes are also encrypted multi-map schemes. Chase and Kamara [17] introduced structured encryption, which is an extension of encryption for general data structures beyond search indices. Encrypted multi-maps are also used in encrypted relational databases where clients wish to perform SQL queries over encrypted databases [29].

Many previous works consider the simplest setting of encrypted multi-map schemes that enable clients to perform *exact* queries for a label ℓ and return the associated value tuple $\mathsf{MM}[\ell]$ if it exists. More recently, there has been work on improving the utility of encrypted multi-map schemes by supporting more complex and expressive queries. In our work, we focus on *encrypted Boolean multi-maps* where the client queries a Boolean formula Φ over labels and the result should be the set of values satisfying the formula Φ. For example, a query for formula $\Phi = \ell_1 \wedge \ell_2$ asks for all values v such that $(v \in \mathsf{MM}[\ell_1]) \wedge (v \in \mathsf{MM}[\ell_2])$.

This problem has been studied in several works such as [15,37]. Kamara and Moataz [28] presented BIEX[1], the first non-interactive, encrypted Boolean multi-map scheme with non-trivial leakage, optimal communication and worst-case sublinear search time. In our work, we will present new constructions with strictly smaller leakage and similar or better efficiency than all prior works.

1.1 Background and Goals

In this section, we present naive solutions and identify their shortcomings that we address in our work. Before we begin, we denote the notion of *volume* as the number of results that are associated with a specific query. We will also denote this as the *query volume.* We will also utilize the notions of response-revealing and response-hiding. Response-revealing encrypted multi-maps mean that the responses to queries are revealed to the server in plaintext. Response-hiding schemes ensure that the servers see responses in encrypted form and may only infer the size of the response.

Naive Solutions. A simple construction to enable Boolean queries is to utilize any response-hiding encrypted multi-map that can handle exact queries. For any Boolean formula Φ over labels $\ell_1, \ldots, \ell_q$, the client issues q queries, one for each of $\ell_1, \ldots, \ell_q$. The client receives all q result sets $\mathsf{MM}[\ell_1], \ldots, \mathsf{MM}[\ell_q]$ and evaluates Φ locally. The scheme is sub-optimal in terms of communication. For example, if Φ is a conjunction, the size of the result set $|\mathsf{MM}[\ell_1] \cap \ldots \cap \mathsf{MM}[\ell_q]|$ will be much smaller than the size of all q result sets, $|\mathsf{MM}[\ell_1]| + \ldots + |\mathsf{MM}[\ell_q]|$. Therefore, the server's response is larger than necessary.

To obtain optimal communication, we consider another simple encrypted Boolean multi-map that utilizes a response-revealing encrypted multi-map supporting exact queries. The client once again issues q queries, one for each of the q labels $\ell_1, \ldots, \ell_q$. The server learns the responses of all q queries and applies Φ before returning the result set to the client. The above construction obtains optimal communication as the server response consists of exactly the result set. Unfortunately, the leakage is horrible as the server learns all sets $\mathsf{MM}[\ell_1], \ldots, \mathsf{MM}[\ell_q]$ in plaintext.

The above solution can be extended to hide the plaintext values in a standard manner. Each value appearing in the multi-map will be stored as a tag (a PRF evaluation) as well as an encryption under private keys held by the client. All tags are computed under the same private key. The client issues q queries for $\ell_1, \ldots, \ell_q$ and the server learns the tags and encryptions of all values in $\mathsf{MM}[\ell_1], \ldots, \mathsf{MM}[\ell_q]$. The tags suffice to perform arbitrary set operations to apply the Boolean formula Φ since they are computed under the same key. Communication remains optimal since the server will only return encryptions of values that satisfy Φ. While the server does not learn the plaintext values in each

[1] While BIEX considers Boolean searchable encryption, the basic construction is an encrypted Boolean multi-map.

of $\mathsf{MM}[\ell_1], \ldots, \mathsf{MM}[\ell_q]$, the server learns the volumes of the singleton queries for each of the labels $\ell_1, \ldots, \ell_q$. Using the tags, the server can perform arbitrary set intersections and unions over the q results $\mathsf{MM}[\ell_1], \ldots, \mathsf{MM}[\ell_q]$ and not just the ones needed for Φ. As a consequence, the server may also learn the volumes (i.e., result sizes) for any arbitrary Boolean queries over the q labels, $\ell_1, \ldots, \ell_q$. Going forward, we will refer to this last solution as the *canonical naive solution.*

Leakage. Given the above naive solutions, an important privacy goal of encrypted Boolean multi-maps is to reduce the volume leakage for arbitrary Boolean queries. Note that optimal communication schemes must leak the volume of the query $\Phi(\ell_1, \ldots, \ell_q)$, and the goal is to limit the leakage of any additional volumes for queries that are related to the original query. Mapping this back to the canonical naive solution, we note that, since the volumes of all singleton queries for labels $\ell_1, \ldots, \ell_q$ are revealed, an adversary can compute the volume for queries $\Psi(\ell_1, \ldots, \ell_q)$ for any Boolean formula Ψ. For convenience, we define the *base query set of leakage* for the canonical naive construction as $\mathsf{B} = \{\ell_1, \ldots, \ell_q\}$ and call the span $\mathsf{Span}(\mathsf{B})$, the set of all queries for which an adversary can construct the volume from the volumes of the queries in the set B. We will formally define the notion of the base query set of leakage later. In our work, we improve the state-of-the-art by presenting non-interactive and efficient schemes with the smallest volume leakage to our knowledge.

Beyond volume leakage, we note that many encrypted multi-map schemes have non-trivial leakage about queries themselves. This leakage could include whether two Boolean queries are identical, whether a label appears in two different Boolean queries, the structure of the Boolean query, etc. For simplicity, we split off our analysis into the leakage of query volumes and all other leakage unrelated to query volumes. In our work, we ensure that our constructions have the same query leakage as prior works [15,28].

Efficiency Goals. Finally, we discuss our efficiency goals. We will aim for our constructions to be non-interactive with optimal communication and worst-case sublinear search times, while only incurring small additional storage overhead compared to prior works. To obtain optimal communication, the response of the server should be exactly the size of the query's result and the client's request size should be independent of the server-stored multi-map. Worst-case sublinear search time implies that the scheme should not unnecessarily process the entire encrypted multi-map when answering queries. Finally, the storage overhead should be small enough for practical usage.

1.2 Related Works

We survey existing constructions of encrypted Boolean multi-maps with smaller leakage compared to the canonical naive solution discussed in Sect. 1.1.

OXT. Cash *et al.* [15] present the oblivious cross-tag (OXT) protocol that is a non-interactive encrypted Boolean multi-map. OXT is able to handle all conjunctive queries and Boolean queries in *Searchable Normal Form* (that is, of the form

$\ell_1 \wedge \Phi(\ell_2, \ldots, \ell_q)$) with worst-case sublinear search times. Unfortunately, queries for many Boolean formulae may end up having linear search times. We note that Faber *et al.* [22] extend OXT for more (but not all) Boolean queries including range, substring and wildcard queries. The core cryptographic operation in OXT are expensive public-key operations (exponentiation in a Diffie-Hellman group). As a result, queries may end up being computationally expensive even for formulae for which the algorithm operates on a sublinear portion of the database.

BlindSeer. Pappas *et al.* [37] present BlindSeer that handles all arbitrary Boolean queries with worst-case sublinear search time unlike OXT. BlindSeer encodes the underlying multi-map using a search tree combined with Bloom filters. To traverse the tree during query time, BlindSeer utilizes secure computation to determine the next node in the search tree to visit. By using secure computation, the majority of the core cryptographic operations in BlindSeer end up being symmetric key operations. However, the search algorithm in BlindSeer still ends up being slower than OXT as the secure computation techniques require multiple rounds of client-server interactions (even if the majority of operations are symmetric-key). Given this knowledge, it is clear that reducing interaction is necessary for constructing efficient query algorithms.

BIEX. Kamara and Moataz [28] present BIEX that combines several good properties of both OXT and BlindSeer. In particular, BIEX is the first non-interactive encrypted Boolean multi-map that is able to handle arbitrary Boolean queries with worst-case sublinear search times and non-trivial leakage smaller than the canonical naive solution. Furthermore, the search algorithms of BIEX utilize only symmetric-key primitives. As a result, the search algorithm of BIEX is more efficient than both OXT and BlindSeer.

For the leakage of BIEX, consider a CNF query $\Phi = D_1 \wedge \ldots \wedge D_m$ where each clause D_i is a disjunction $(\ell_{i,1} \vee \ldots \vee \ell_{i,q_i})$. The *base query set of leakage* (see discussion in Sect. 1.3) consists of all singleton labels appearing in the first clause and all 2-conjunctions of labels with the first appearing in the first clause and the second label appearing in the second clause onward:

$$\{\ell_{1,i} \mid i \in [q_1]\} \cup \{(\ell_{1,i} \wedge \ell_{j,k}) \mid i \in [q_1], 2 \leq j \leq m, k \in [q_j]\}.$$

While this is significantly smaller leakage than the canonical naive solution, it includes all q_1 singleton labels appearing in the first clause. In other words, the leakage from querying Φ is at least as large as performing q_1 exact queries for all labels in the first clause, which is not ideal.

In our work, we present the first constructions with *no singleton labels in the base query set of leakage* for all Boolean queries except for disjunctions (i.e., single-term CNF). Our constructions enjoy all the good properties of BIEX including non-interaction, optimal response size, sublinear search time, and exclusive use of symmetric-key primitives.

Relation to Leakage-Abuse Attacks. Finally, we discuss prior works on leakage-abuse attacks on encrypted multi-maps (or encrypted search). The SPAR final report [4] describes data sets and query distributions that arise from real life applications. Most prior works mainly consider either exact [8,13,27] or range [25,26,33,35] queries. Given the lack of attacks, it may seem that reducing leakage for Boolean queries is not important at first. However, it turns out that the attacks for exact or range queries may also be applied in the Boolean query setting.

Consider the leakage of BIEX as an example. For a CNF query, the adversary learns the volumes of each of q_1 labels in the first clause. In other words, the adversary could simulate and obtain leakage of q_1 exact queries using a single Boolean query to BIEX. This means that exact query attacks may be applied to encrypted Boolean multi-maps using fewer Boolean queries if we do not reduce leakage. The same idea may be applied for range query attacks. Suppose that labels come from an ordered set (such as the integers). i A single Boolean query to BIEX with q_1 labels means leakage for q_1 ranges of length 1. In the worst case when all q_1 labels are consecutive in the ordered set (such as $\{1, \ldots, q_1\}$), a single Boolean query to BIEX would end up leaking the volumes of $O(q_1^2)$ ranges ($[i, j]$ where $1 \leq i \leq j \leq q_1$).

With the above in mind, an important goal is to design encrypted Boolean multi-maps that reduce leakage. By reducing leakage, we improve the chance of our constructions resisting leakage-abuse attacks (both ones that are currently known and ones that will be developed in the future). In this work, we present constructions that avoid leaking volumes corresponding to either exact or range queries for most Boolean queries. Therefore, our construction shows additional resistance to leakage-abuse attacks in comparison to prior works.

1.3 Our Contributions

In our work, we present new encrypted Boolean multi-maps with reduced leakage and similar or better efficiency compared to prior works. As our main technical tool, we present a new *filtering* algorithm that uses only private-key primitives and performs set intersections with small leakage. By utilizing this filtering algorithm, we obtain new constructions for handling conjunctions and CNF queries with reduced leakage and optimal communication complexity as the response to a query contains exactly one ciphertext per each item in the response set. In addition, our constructions are non-interactive and require sub-linear work.

To compare leakage, we will utilize the notion of a *base query set of leakage*. Let B be the base query set of leakage for any construction. Then, the adversary may recover volumes for any Boolean query Ψ in the *span* $\mathsf{Span}(\mathsf{B})$ of the base query set of leakage B; that is, $\mathsf{Span}(\mathsf{B})$ consists of all formulae $\Psi(x_1, \ldots, x_t)$ with $x_i \in \mathsf{B}$, for $i = 1, \ldots, t$.

The worst leakage is obtained when B contains all singleton labels $\mathsf{B} = \{\ell_1, \ldots, \ell_q\}$ in which case $\mathsf{Span}(\mathsf{B})$ includes all Boolean formulae over the labels $\ell_1, \ldots, \ell_q$. This is the leakage obtained by the canonical naive solution.

Throughout our work, we will only consider constructions that satisfy all the good properties of BIEX. Our constructions will be non-interactive, handle arbitrary Boolean queries with worst-case sublinear computation and only utilize symmetric key primitives.

Our first construction ConjFilter supports conjunctive queries $\ell_1 \wedge \ldots \wedge \ell_q$. We will use ConjFilter as a building block when constructing an encrypted multi-map for CNF queries. Even though it is only a building block, ConjFilter has smaller leakage compared to all previous efficient solutions that support conjunctions. Specifically, the base query set of leakage for ConjFilter is

$$\{(\ell_1 \wedge \ell_2), (\ell_1 \wedge \ell_2 \wedge \ell_3), (\ell_1 \wedge \ell_2 \wedge \ell_4), \ldots, (\ell_1 \wedge \ell_2 \wedge \ell_q)\}.$$

Theorem 1 (Informal). ConjFilter *is a non-interactive scheme supporting conjunctive queries that is adaptively-secure with optimal communication and worst-case sub-linear search time. For a conjunctive query* $\Phi = \ell_1 \wedge \ldots \wedge \ell_q$, *the adversary may recover the volumes of all queries of the form* $\Psi(x_1, \ldots, x_t)$ *where each* $x_i \in \{(\ell_1 \wedge \ell_2), (\ell_1 \wedge \ell_2 \wedge \ell_3), \ldots, (\ell_1 \wedge \ell_2 \wedge \ell_q)\}$ *and* Ψ *is any Boolean query.*

In particular, the queries whose volumes are leaked by ConjFilter is a subset of those leaked by prior works. As an example of the reduced leakage of ConjFilter, note that the adversary cannot recover the volume for any 2-conjunctive queries beyond $(\ell_1 \wedge \ell_2)$. In contrast, the base query set of leakage for prior non-interactive constructions OXT [15] and BIEX [28] consists of $\{(\ell_1 \wedge \ell_2), \ldots, (\ell_1 \wedge \ell_q)\}$ that enables recovering volumes for many 2-conjunctions. By playing with the base sets, one can find many queries whose volumes are leaked by prior works, but not by ConjFilter.

Next, we present an encrypted Boolean multi-map CNFFilter that supports CNF queries using ConjFilter as a building block. CNF queries are of the form $D_1 \wedge \ldots \wedge D_m$ where each clause D_i is a disjunction $(\ell_{i,1} \vee \ldots \vee \ell_{i,q_i})$ with q_i unique labels. The base query set of leakage for CNFFilter may be broken down into two parts. The first part consists of all 2-conjunctions of labels from the first and second clause:

$$\mathsf{B}' = \{(\ell_{1,i} \wedge \ell_{2,j}) \mid i \in [q_1], j \in [q_2]\}.$$

The second part consists of all 3-conjunctions of labels from the first clause, second clause and the last label appearing in the third clause onward:

$$\mathsf{B}'' = \{(b' \wedge \ell_{k,l}) \mid b' \in \mathsf{B}', 3 \leq k \leq m, l \in [q_k]\}.$$

The base query set of leakage B of CNFFilter is equal to $\mathsf{B} = \mathsf{B}' \cup \mathsf{B}''$.

Theorem 2 (Informal). CNFFilter *is a non-interactive scheme supporting CNF queries that is adaptively-secure with optimal communication and worst-case sub-linear search time. For a CNF query* $\Phi = D_1 \wedge \ldots \wedge D_m$ *where each clause* D_i *is a disjunction* $(\ell_{i,1} \vee \ldots \vee \ell_{i,q_i})$, *the adversary may recover the volumes of all queries of the form* $\Psi(x_1, \ldots, x_t)$ *where each* $x_i \in \mathsf{B}' \cup \mathsf{B}''$ *and* Ψ *is a Boolean query.*

For comparison, note that the base query set of leakage for BIEX consists of all singleton labels appearing in the first clause and all 2-conjunctions of labels with the first appearing in the first clause and the second label appearing in the second clause onward:

$$\{\ell_{1,i} \mid i \in [q_1]\} \cup \{(\ell_{1,i} \wedge \ell_{j,k}) \mid i \in [q_1], 2 \leq j \leq m, k \in [q_j]\}.$$

Note that for any CNF query Φ, the span of the base query set of leakage of CNFFilter is a subset of the one of BIEX. As a simple example of reduced leakage, unless the query is a disjunction, CNFFilter does not leak volumes for any singleton queries unlike BIEX. Many more examples of queries whose volumes are leaked by BIEX and not by CNFFilter may be found.

The above comparison only considered leakage resulting from one conjunctive/CNF query. In practice, these constructions will answer and leak information about multiple conjunctive/CNF queries. Consider the example of two queries resulting in the base query sets of leakage B_1 and B_2. In the worst case, the adversary may recover volumes of any queries of the form $\Phi(x_1, \ldots, x_t)$, where $x_i \in \mathsf{B}_1 \cup \mathsf{B}_2$. In other words, leakage may explode as more queries are performed. Therefore, it is integral to minimize the base query set leakage for individual queries.

Referring back to leakage-abuse attacks, CNFFilter does not leak volumes about exact queries except when querying disjunctions. Furthermore, the base query set of leakage for CNFFilter consists of only intersections ignoring disjunction queries. So, there is no leakage about range queries either as ranges correspond to unions of one or more consecutive labels. As a result, CNFFilter seems to be more resistant to known leakage-abuse attacks compared to BIEX.

Finally, we present a comparison of efficiency with our solution and BIEX. We obtain all the same properties including non-interaction, sublinear search times and only using symmetric-key primitives. From our implementation, we show that CNFFilter obtains faster search times than BIEX. For storage, CNFFilter only incurs 20% additional storage overhead compared to BIEX in exchange for reduced leakage and faster search times.

Both ConjFilter and CNFFilter are proved adaptively secure in the ROM. Note that the assumption of random oracles as well as their programmability are required for adaptive security by previous works [15,28] as well. Non-adaptive security for both constructions can instead be proved in the standard model.

1.4 Our Techniques

We present our new techniques used to construct ConjFilter and CNFFilter. The core of our new technique is an improved filtering algorithm for conjunctions.

Conjunctions. We start by presenting the approach to handling conjunctive queries used in previous works [15,28][2]. Consider the conjunctive query $\ell_1 \wedge \ldots \wedge \ell_q$. The main idea of prior works is to decompose the query into $(q-1)$ 2-conjunctions: $(\ell_1 \wedge \ell_2) \wedge (\ell_1 \wedge \ell_3) \wedge \ldots \wedge (\ell_1 \wedge \ell_q)$. Each of the $(q-1)$ 2-conjunction queries are computed independently such that the resulting response

[2] In [28], the authors only present a construction for CNF queries. To derive a conjunction scheme, we consider the case where each disjunction clause is a single label.

sets are all PRF evaluations under the key solely depending on label ℓ_1. Then, the server returns the intersection of all $q-1$ sets. In this way, the size of the server's response is proportional to the result of the query and thus optimal.

There are several drawbacks to using this approach. The scheme leaks the volumes of the $(q-1)$ 2-conjunctions. As all response sets are PRF evaluations under the same key, the adversary may learn volumes of more complex queries. For example, the intersections of any two response sets yields the volume of a 3-conjunction. In general, the adversary can compute any Boolean function over the response sets. That is, the base query set of leakage is $\{(\ell_1 \wedge \ell_2), (\ell_1 \wedge \ell_3), \ldots, (\ell_1 \wedge \ell_q)\}$. In terms of computation cost, the server must perform computation on the order of $|\mathsf{MM}[\ell_1 \wedge \ell_2]| + \ldots + |\mathsf{MM}[\ell_1 \wedge \ell_q]|$. This is quite wasteful as the response set $\mathsf{MM}[\ell_1 \wedge \ell_2]$ is already a superset of the final response. Ideally, the server's computation should not need to be much larger than $|\mathsf{MM}[\ell_1 \wedge \ell_2]|$.

To address these drawbacks, while keeping the size of the server's response optimal, we present a new *filtering* algorithm that will be utilized by ConjFilter. First, we compute the response set $S_2 := \mathsf{MM}[\ell_1 \wedge \ell_2]$ such that each value in S_2 is a PRF evaluation under a key depending solely on label ℓ_1. Next, we compute the intersection $S_3 := S_2 \cap \mathsf{MM}[\ell_1 \wedge \ell_3]$ by directly filtering S_2 and removing elements of S_2 that do not appear in $\mathsf{MM}[\ell_1 \wedge \ell_3]$. To do this, we maintain an additional data structure $\mathcal{X}$ that allows the server to check whether a value $v \in S_2$ belongs to $\mathsf{MM}[\ell_1 \wedge \ell_3]$ without retrieving the entire $\mathsf{MM}[\ell_1 \wedge \ell_3]$, thereby avoiding volume leakage for the query $\ell_1 \wedge \ell_3$. We repeat this filtering to compute each $S_i = S_{i-1} \cap \mathsf{MM}[\ell_1 \wedge \ell_i]$ until we compute the set S_q that is the result for the original query.

At a high level, the data structure $\mathcal{X}$ is constructed as follows. For each label pair (ℓ_a, ℓ_b) and for each value $v \in \mathsf{MM}[\ell_a \wedge \ell_b]$, $\mathcal{X}$ stores a *double tag* of v. A *double tag* of v is computed by applying two successive PRF evaluations, where the first evaluation is under the key solely depending on ℓ_a, say $K^{\mathsf{t}}_{\ell_a}$, and the second evaluation is under the key depending on ℓ_a and ℓ_b, say $K^{\times}_{\ell_a,\ell_b}$. Thus, given a tag of $v \in \mathsf{MM}[\ell_a \wedge \ell_b]$ under the key $K^{\mathsf{t}}_{\ell_a}$, the server can determine whether v belongs to $\mathsf{MM}[\ell_a \wedge \ell_c]$ by simply applying PRF under the key $K^{\times}_{\ell_a,\ell_c}$ and checking whether the resulting evaluation belongs to $\mathcal{X}$. In particular, note that the volume of $\mathsf{MM}[\ell_a \wedge \ell_c]$ is never revealed.

We note that the above filtering algorithm leaks volumes for only a subset of queries whose volumes are leaked by prior works. In particular, the base query set of leakage is $\{(\ell_1 \wedge \ell_2), (\ell_1 \wedge \ell_2 \wedge \ell_3), \ldots, (\ell_1 \wedge \ell_2 \wedge \ell_q)\}$. As an example of reduced leakage, note that the only 2-conjunction whose volume may be recovered in ConjFilter is $\ell_1 \wedge \ell_2$ whereas the volume of $(q-1)$ 2-conjunctions of the form $(\ell_1 \wedge \ell_2), \ldots, (\ell_1 \wedge \ell_q)$ are leaked by prior works.

We note our filtering algorithm is reminiscent but starkly different from the cross-tag protocols presented by Cash *et al.* [15]. In particular, our new filtering algorithm only use symmetric key primitives (PRFs) while the cross-tag protocols in [15] require public-key operations (i.e., exponentiation in a Diffie-Hellman group).

CNFs. Next, we show how to support CNF queries using the filtering algorithm of $\mathsf{ConjFilter}$ as a building block. We start by reviewing the BIEX construction [28] for CNF queries. Consider a CNF query of the form $D_1 \wedge \ldots \wedge D_\ell$ where $D_i = (\ell_{i,1} \vee \ldots \vee \ell_{i,q_i})$. In the first step, BIEX computes $\mathsf{MM}[D_1]$. The scheme for computing disjunction D_1 ends up leaking the volumes for q_1 singleton queries for labels $\ell_{1,1}, \ldots, \ell_{1,q_1}$. The main problem is that there is no known scheme supporting disjunctions that do not reveal singleton query volumes.

To avoid this leakage, $\mathsf{CNFFilter}$ combines the first two clauses $D_1 \wedge D_2$ that may be rewritten as:

$$D_1 \wedge D_2 = (\ell_{1,1} \vee \ldots \vee \ell_{1,q_1}) \wedge (\ell_{2,1} \vee \ldots \vee \ell_{2,q_2}) = \bigvee_{i \in [q_1], j \in [q_2]} (\ell_{1,i} \wedge \ell_{2,j}).$$

In other words, $D_1 \wedge D_2$ becomes a disjunction over $q_1 q_2$ 2-conjunction queries. Next, we can apply the algorithm for computing disjunctions over the $q_1 q_2$ 2-conjunction result sets to obtain $S_2 := \mathsf{MM}[D_1 \wedge D_2]$. While the volumes of all 2-conjunction sets are revealed, no volumes for singleton queries are leaked.

We apply the filtering algorithm again to incorporate the remaining clauses $D_3, \ldots, D_m$, while keeping the server's response, and thus communication, optimal in size. If $D_3 = \ell_{3,1} \vee \ldots \vee \ell_{3,q_3}$, then $S_2 \cap \mathsf{MM}[D_3] = (S_2 \cap \mathsf{MM}[\ell_{3,1}]) \cup \ldots \cup (S_2 \cap \mathsf{MM}[\ell_{3,q_3}])$. At a high level, the filtering algorithm may be applied on S_2 for each of the labels $\ell_{3,1}, \ldots, \ell_{3,q_3}$. By repeating this for each of the clauses $D_3, \ldots, D_m$, the server successfully computes the set $\mathsf{MM}[D_1 \wedge \ldots \wedge D_m]$. The filtering scheme allows $\mathsf{CNFFilter}$ to avoid volume leakage for many queries.

$\mathsf{CNFFilter}$ also improves search times compared to BIEX. Recall that BIEX initially computes the set $\mathsf{MM}[D_1]$. Instead, $\mathsf{CNFFilter}$ first computes the set $\mathsf{MM}[D_1 \wedge D_2]$ that will later be filtered. As $\mathsf{MM}[D_1 \wedge D_2]$ is a subset of $\mathsf{MM}[D_1]$ and typically smaller, searching in $\mathsf{CNFFilter}$ ends up being faster than BIEX.

2 Preliminaries

2.1 Boolean Encrypted Multi-Maps

A multi-map data structure maintains a set of m label to value tuple pairs $\mathsf{MM} = \{(\ell_t, \vec{v}_t)\}_{t \in [m]}$, where each ℓ_i comes from the *label universe* $\mathcal{U}$ and $\vec{v}_i$ is a tuple of values where each value comes from the *value universe* $\mathcal{V}$. Different labels may be associated with tuples of different length. We assume that all m labels are unique. If any two labels are equal, then the two associated value tuples may be combined into a single value tuple.

The multi-map data structure supports the *query operation* that receives a multi-map $\mathsf{MM} = \{(\ell_t, \vec{v}_t)\}_{t \in [m]}$ and a label $\ell \in \mathcal{U}$ as arguments. If there exists $t \in [m]$ such that $\ell_t = \ell$, then the query returns $\vec{v}_t$. Otherwise, the query returns $\perp$. For convenience, if $(\ell, \vec{v}) \in \mathsf{MM}$ then we denote $\mathsf{MM}[\ell] = \vec{v}$. If ℓ does not appear in MM, then $\mathsf{MM}[\ell] = \perp$.

We consider the extended *Boolean multi-map* that enables more complex query operations beyond simply retrieving the value tuple associated with a label. More formally, a Boolean multi-map is associated with a supported class of

Boolean formulae queries $\mathbb{B}$ over labels. We consider query classes: conjunctions and CNFs. For the set of conjunctions of the form $\Phi = \ell_1 \wedge \ldots \ell_q$, the query for Φ returns the intersection $\mathsf{MM}[\ell_1] \cap \ldots \cap \mathsf{MM}[\ell_q]$. For the set of CNF queries of the form $\Phi = (\ell_{1,1} \vee \ldots \vee \ell_{1,q_1}) \wedge \ldots \wedge (\ell_{m,1} \vee \ldots \vee \ell_{m,q_m})$, the query for Φ returns the set of values $(\mathsf{MM}[\ell_{1,1}] \cup \ldots \cup \mathsf{MM}[\ell_{1,q_1}]) \cap \ldots \cap (\mathsf{MM}[\ell_{m,1}] \cup \ldots \cup \mathsf{MM}[\ell_{m,q_m}])$. For convenience, we denote the result set for any query Φ by $\mathsf{MM}[\Phi]$.

Next, we define the notion of an *encrypted Boolean multi-map*, which is the structured encryption (STE) for Boolean multi-maps. Our STE definition of encrypted Boolean multi-map will be *non-interactive*. That is, the query consists of a single client request followed by the server's reply.

Definition 1. *Let $\mathbb{B}$ be a class of Boolean formulae. A* non-interactive encrypted Boolean multi-map $\Sigma = (\mathsf{Setup}, \mathsf{Token}, \mathsf{Search}, \mathsf{Resolve})$ *for the class $\mathbb{B}$ consists of the following four algorithms:*

1. $(\mathtt{msk}, \mathsf{eBMM}) \leftarrow \Sigma.\mathsf{Setup}(1^\lambda, \mathsf{MM})$*: The setup algorithm is executed by the client and takes as input the security parameter 1^λ and a multi-map* MM. *It outputs the* master secret key $\mathtt{msk}$ *and the* encrypted multi-map eBMM. *The client keeps the master secret key $\mathtt{msk}$ while the encrypted multi-map* eBMM *is sent to the server.*
2. $\mathtt{tok}_\Phi \leftarrow \Sigma.\mathsf{Token}(\mathtt{msk}, \Phi)$*: The token generation algorithm is executed by the client and receives the master secret key $\mathtt{msk}$ and a Boolean formula $\Phi \in \mathbb{B}$ as input. It returns the* token $\mathtt{tok}_\Phi$ *that is sent to the server.*
3. $\mathtt{ans} \leftarrow \Sigma.\mathsf{Search}(\mathsf{eBMM}, \mathtt{tok})$*: The search algorithm is executed by the server and takes as input the token $\mathtt{tok}$ sent by the client and the encrypted multi-map* eBMM. *It returns the* encrypted answer $\mathtt{ans}$ *that is sent to the client.*
4. $\mathsf{MM}[\Phi] \leftarrow \Sigma.\mathsf{Resolve}(\mathtt{msk}, \mathtt{ans})$*: The resolve algorithm is executed by the client and takes the encrypted answer $\mathtt{ans}$ sent by the server and the master secret key $\mathtt{msk}$. It computes the answer* $\mathsf{MM}[\Phi]$.

We impose the following natural correctness condition. For every MM *and for every $\Phi \in \mathbb{B}$, it holds that* $\Sigma.\mathsf{Resolve}(\mathtt{msk}, \mathsf{Search}(\mathsf{eBMM}, \mathtt{tok})) = \mathsf{MM}[\Phi]$, *provided that* $(\mathtt{msk}, \mathsf{eBMM}) \leftarrow \Sigma.\mathsf{Setup}(1^\lambda, \mathsf{MM})$ *and* $\mathtt{tok} = \Sigma.\mathsf{Token}(\mathtt{msk}, \Phi)$.

2.2 Security Notions

For encrypted Boolean multi-maps, we utilize the same security notions as typically done in structured encryption using leakage functions. The adversary's leakage is upper bounded by a pair $\mathcal{L} = (\mathcal{L}_{\mathsf{Setup}}, \mathcal{L}_{\mathsf{Query}})$ of leakage functions. The leakage function $\mathcal{L}_{\mathsf{Setup}}$ provides an upper bound on the knowledge gained by the adversarial server when given eBMM. $\mathcal{L}_{\mathsf{Query}}$ is an upper bound on the knowledge gained by the adversary when receiving a token from the client generated using the Token algorithm and when applying the token on the encrypted multi-map in the Search algorithm.

To formalize the security notion, we use the simulation-based approach. We present definitions for adaptive adversaries. We define the following real and ideal experiments with a stateful, honest-but-curious adaptive PPT adversary $\mathcal{A}$ and a stateful, PPT simulator $\mathcal{S}$ for an encrypted Boolean multi-map $\Sigma = (\Sigma.\mathsf{Setup}, \Sigma.\mathsf{Token}, \Sigma.\mathsf{Search}, \Sigma.\mathsf{Resolve})$ for a class $\mathbb{B}$ of Boolean formulae and for leakage function $\mathcal{L} = (\mathcal{L}_{\mathsf{Setup}}, \mathcal{L}_{\mathsf{Query}})$.

$\mathbf{Real}^{\mathsf{a}}_{\Sigma,\mathcal{A}}(1^\lambda)$:

1. The adversary $\mathcal{A}$ generates multi-map MM and passes it to the challenger $\mathcal{C}$.
2. The challenger $\mathcal{C}$ executes $(\mathtt{msk}, \mathsf{eBMM}) \leftarrow \Sigma.\mathsf{Setup}(1^\lambda, \mathsf{MM})$ and passes eBMM to the adversary $\mathcal{A}$.
3. For $i = 1, \ldots, \mathsf{poly}(\lambda)$, the adversary $\mathcal{A}$ adaptively picks Boolean formula query $\Phi_i \in \mathbb{B}$ and sends it to the challenger $\mathcal{C}$. Using Φ_i, the challenger $\mathcal{C}$ executes $\mathtt{tok}_i \leftarrow \Sigma.\mathsf{Token}(\mathtt{msk}, \Phi_i)$ and sends $\mathtt{tok}_i$ to the adversary $\mathcal{A}$.
4. The adversary $\mathcal{A}$ outputs a bit $b \in \{0, 1\}$.

$\mathbf{Ideal}^{\mathsf{a}}_{\Sigma,\mathcal{A},\mathcal{L},\mathcal{S}}(1^\lambda)$:

1. The adversary $\mathcal{A}$ generates multi-map MM and passes it to the challenger $\mathcal{C}$.
2. The simulator $\mathcal{S}$ receives $\mathcal{L}_{\mathsf{Setup}}(\mathsf{MM})$ and returns an encrypted multi-map eBMM to the adversary $\mathcal{A}$.
3. For $i = 1, \ldots, \mathsf{poly}(\lambda)$, the adversary $\mathcal{A}$ adaptively picks Boolean formula query $\Phi_i \in \mathbb{B}$ and sends it to the challenger $\mathcal{C}$. The simulator receives $\mathcal{L}_{\mathsf{Query}}(\mathsf{MM}, \Phi_1, \ldots, \Phi_{i-1})$ from $\mathcal{C}$ and computes $\mathtt{tok}_i$ which is returned to the adversary $\mathcal{A}$.
4. The adversary $\mathcal{A}$ outputs a bit $b \in \{0, 1\}$.

Definition 2. *The non-interactive encrypted Boolean multi-map Σ is* adaptively *$\mathcal{L}$-secure if there exists a stateful, PPT simulator $\mathcal{S}$ such that for all adaptive, PPT adversaries $\mathcal{A}$:*

$$\left|\Pr[\mathbf{Real}^{\mathsf{a}}_{\Sigma,\mathcal{A}}(1^\lambda) = 1] - \Pr[\mathbf{Ideal}^{\mathsf{a}}_{\Sigma,\mathcal{A},\mathcal{L},\mathcal{S}}(1^\lambda) = 1]\right| \leq \mathsf{negl}(\lambda).$$

For presentation, we split up query leakage $\mathcal{L}_{\mathsf{Query}}$ into token leakage $\mathcal{L}_{\mathsf{Token}}$ and search leakage $\mathcal{L}_{\mathsf{Search}}$. $\mathcal{L}_{\mathsf{Token}}$ encompasses all leakage derived by the adversary viewing only the search token. $\mathcal{L}_{\mathsf{Search}}$ contains all leakage from the adversary applying the search token onto the encrypted multi-map. At a high level, $\mathcal{L}_{\mathsf{Token}}$ reveals information about the query on its own such as the number of unique labels, number of CNF clauses, etc. On the other hand, $\mathcal{L}_{\mathsf{Search}}$ reveals information about the underlying multi-map. In particular, the majority of $\mathcal{L}_{\mathsf{Search}}$ consists of volume leakage for a set of queries. Suppose Q is the set of all queries whose volumes are leaked in $\mathcal{L}_{\mathsf{Search}}$. We denote the base query set of leakage S such that all queries $q \in Q$ may be written as a Boolean function $f(x_1, \ldots, x_t)$ where each $x_i \in S$. In other words, using the volumes of queries in S, one can recover the volumes for all queries in Q.

2.3 Encrypted Multi-maps

In our work, we will utilize response-revealing encrypted multi-maps sEMM in a blackbox manner. As the name implies, response-revealing means that the values in the response are revealed to the server in plaintext. In contrast, response-hiding encrypted multi-maps ensure that the server sees each value in an encrypted manner. At a high level, response-hiding schemes will reveal only the number of values in a response as opposed to the response itself.

There are several non-interactive, adaptively-secure encrypted multi-maps with minimal leakage such as $\mathsf{2Lev}$ [15] or ZMF [28] that are response-revealing. We now describe the efficiency and leakage properties of these schemes. For an MM of size n, the sEMM output by the Setup algorithm uses storage of $\Theta(n)$ ciphertexts. The Token algorithm results in a single ciphertext while the resulting answer for a keyword ℓ computed by the server using Search consists of exactly the set $\mathsf{MM}[\ell]$ in plaintext. In terms of leakage, the setup leakage of sEMM consists of the multi-set of all values that appear in the underlying multi-map; we denote this leakage $\mathcal{L}_{\mathsf{Setup}} = \mathsf{vals}(\mathsf{MM})$. As all values will be encryptions in our constructions, the setup leakage of sEMM would only consists of the number of values. The leakage during querying consists of the *query repetition pattern*, qeq, describing which two queries are performed on the same label. For a query sequence $Q = (q_1, q_2, \ldots)$, $\mathsf{qeq}(Q)$ is a $|Q| \times |Q|$ matrix M such that $M[i][j] = 1$ if and only if i-th and j-th query in Q are equal. As the scheme is response-revealing, the plaintext response, $\mathsf{resp}(\mathsf{MM}, Q) = (\mathsf{MM}[q_1], \mathsf{MM}[q_2], \ldots)$. So, $\mathcal{L}_{\mathsf{Query}} = (\mathsf{qeq}, \mathsf{resp})$.

Theorem 3. *If one-way functions exist, there exists a non-interactive, response-revealing* sEMM *that is adaptively* $(\mathcal{L}_{\mathsf{Setup}}, \mathcal{L}_{\mathsf{Query}})$*-secure, uses* $\Theta(n)$ *storage and* $O(|\mathsf{MM}[\ell]|)$ *ciphertexts of communication for a query to label* ℓ*.*

3 Conjunctive Queries

In this section, we present our new construction $\mathsf{ConjFilter}$ of an encrypted Boolean multi-map supporting the class of conjunctive queries. $\mathsf{ConjFilter}$ is non-interactive with optimal communication and sublinear search time. A formal description of $\mathsf{ConjFilter}$ is found in Fig. 1.

3.1 Construction ConjFilter

$\mathsf{ConjFilter}$ follows BIEX [28] by pre-computing answers to all possible 2-conjunction queries, but diverges from BIEX in the method used to compute conjunctions. We start by describing the setup algorithm of $\mathsf{ConjFilter}$.

Given an input multi-map $\mathsf{MM} = \{(\ell_i, \vec{v}_i)\}_{i \in [m]}$, the setup of $\mathsf{ConjFilter}$ constructs a multi-map MM^{p} in the following way. The multi-map MM^{p} will store a tuple of values for each pair of labels (a, b) that appear in MM. The

- $(\mathtt{msk}, \mathsf{eBMM}) \leftarrow \mathsf{ConjFilter.Setup}(1^\lambda, \mathsf{MM} = \{(\ell_i, \vec{v}_i)\}_{i\in[m]})$:
  1. Randomly select PRF seeds $K^{\mathsf{p}}, K^{\mathsf{t}}, K^{\times} \leftarrow \{0,1\}^\lambda$.
  2. Randomly select encryption key $K^{\mathsf{enc}} \leftarrow \{0,1\}^\lambda$.
  3. Set $\mathsf{MM}^{\mathsf{p}} \leftarrow \{\ \}$.
  4. For all pairs $(\mathtt{a}, \mathtt{b})$ of labels appearing in MM:
     (a) Compute *tag seed* $K^{\mathsf{t}}_{\mathsf{a}} \leftarrow F(K^{\mathsf{t}}, \mathtt{a})$.
     (b) Compute *encryption key* $K^{\mathsf{enc}}_{\mathsf{a,b}} \leftarrow F(K^{\mathsf{p}}, \mathtt{a} \mid\mid \mathtt{b})$.
     (c) Set $\mathsf{MM}^{\mathsf{p}}[(\mathtt{a}, \mathtt{b})] \leftarrow \emptyset$.
     (d) For all $v \in \mathsf{MM}[\mathtt{a}] \cap \mathsf{MM}[\mathtt{b}]$:
        i. Compute *tag* $\mathsf{tag}_{\mathsf{a},v} \leftarrow F(K^{\mathsf{t}}_{\mathsf{a}}, v)$ and *encrypted tag* $\mathsf{etag}_{\mathsf{a,b},v} = \mathsf{Enc}(K^{\mathsf{enc}}_{\mathsf{a,b}}, \mathsf{tag}_{\mathsf{a},v})$.
        ii. Compute *encrypted value* $\mathsf{ev}_v = \mathsf{Enc}(K^{\mathsf{enc}}, v)$.
        iii. Add $(\mathsf{etag}_{\mathsf{a},v}, \mathsf{ev}_v)$ to $\mathsf{MM}^{\mathsf{p}}[(\mathtt{a}, \mathtt{b})]$.
  5. Execute $(\mathtt{msk}^{\mathsf{p}}, \mathsf{EMM}^{\mathsf{p}}) \leftarrow \mathsf{sEMM.Setup}(1^\lambda, \mathsf{MM}^{\mathsf{p}})$.
  6. Initialize $\mathcal{X} = \emptyset$.
  7. For all pairs $(\mathtt{a}, \mathtt{b})$ of labels appearing in MM:
     (a) Compute double-tag seed $K^{\times}_{\mathsf{a,b}} = F(K^{\times}, \mathtt{a} \mid\mid \mathtt{b})$.
     (b) For all $v \in \mathsf{MM}[\mathtt{a}] \cap \mathsf{MM}[\mathtt{b}]$:
        i. Compute double tag $F(K^{\times}_{\mathsf{a,b}}, \mathsf{tag}_{\mathsf{a},v})$ and add it to $\mathcal{X}$.
  8. Randomly permute $\mathcal{X}$.
  9. Return $(\mathtt{msk} = (K^{\mathsf{p}}, K^{\times}, K^{\mathsf{enc}}, \mathtt{msk}^{\mathsf{p}}), \mathsf{EMM} = (\mathsf{EMM}^{\mathsf{p}}, \mathcal{X}))$.
- $\mathtt{tok}_\Phi \leftarrow \mathsf{ConjFilter.Token}(\mathtt{msk} = (K^{\mathsf{p}}, K^{\times}, K^{\mathsf{enc}}, \mathtt{msk}^{\mathsf{p}}), \Phi = (\ell_1 \wedge \ell_2 \wedge \ldots \wedge \ell_q))$:
  1. Compute $\mathtt{tok}^{\mathsf{p}} \leftarrow \mathsf{sEMM.Token}(\mathtt{msk}^{\mathsf{p}}, (\ell_1, \ell_2))$.
  2. Compute *encryption key* $K^{\mathsf{enc}}_{\ell_1,\ell_2} \leftarrow F(K^{\mathsf{p}}, \ell_1 \mid\mid \ell_2)$.
  3. For $d = 3, \ldots, q$:
     (a) Compute *double-tag seed* $K^{\times}_d = F(K^{\times}, \ell_1 \mid\mid \ell_d)$.
  4. Return $\mathtt{tok}_\Phi = (\mathtt{tok}^{\mathsf{p}}, K^{\mathsf{enc}}_{\ell_1,\ell_2}, K^{\times}_3, \ldots, K^{\times}_q)$.
- $\mathtt{ans} \leftarrow \mathsf{ConjFilter.Search}(\mathtt{tok}_\Phi = (\mathtt{tok}^{\mathsf{p}}, K^{\mathsf{enc}}_{\ell_1,\ell_2}, K^{\times}_3, \ldots, K^{\times}_q), \mathsf{EMM} = (\mathsf{EMM}^{\mathsf{p}}, \mathcal{X}))$:
  1. Retrieve $\{(\mathsf{etag}_l, \mathsf{ev}_l)\}_{l\in[L]} \leftarrow \mathsf{sEMM.Search}(\mathtt{tok}^{\mathsf{p}}, \mathsf{EMM}^{\mathsf{p}})$.
  2. For $l = 1, \ldots, L$:
     (a) Compute $\mathsf{tag}_l \leftarrow \mathsf{Dec}(K^{\mathsf{enc}}_{\ell_1,\ell_2}, \mathsf{etag}_l)$.
  3. Set $\mathtt{ans} \leftarrow \emptyset$.
  4. For $l = 1, \ldots, L$:
     (a) For $d = 3, \ldots, q$:
        i. Compute *double tag* $\mathsf{dtag}_{l,d} \leftarrow F(K^{\times}_l, \mathsf{tag}_d)$.
     (b) If all $\mathsf{dtag}_{l,3}, \ldots, \mathsf{dtag}_{l,q} \in \mathcal{X}$, then add ev_l to $\mathtt{ans}$.
  5. Return $\mathtt{ans}$.
- $\mathtt{ans} \leftarrow \mathsf{ConjFilter.Resolve}((\mathsf{ev}_1, \ldots, \mathsf{ev}_r), \mathtt{msk} = (K^{\mathsf{p}}, K^{\times}, K^{\mathsf{enc}}, \mathtt{msk}^{\mathsf{p}}))$:
  1. Return $\{\mathsf{Dec}(K^{\mathsf{enc}}, \mathsf{ev}_1), \ldots, \mathsf{Dec}(K^{\mathsf{enc}}, \mathsf{ev}_r)\}$.

Fig. 1. Pseudocode for construction ConjFilter.

values in MM^{p} will consists of pairs of an *encrypted tag* and an *encrypted value*. For each $v \in \mathsf{MM}[\mathtt{a}] \cap \mathsf{MM}[\mathtt{b}]$, the tuple $\mathsf{MM}^{\mathsf{p}}[(\mathtt{a}, \mathtt{b})]$ will store a pair of encrypted tags and encrypted value for v. The tag for v stored in $\mathsf{MM}^{\mathsf{p}}[(\mathtt{a}, \mathtt{b})]$

is computed as $\mathsf{tag}_{\mathsf{a},v} = F(K^{\mathsf{t}}_{\mathsf{a}}, v)$ where F is a PRF. Both the tag and value are encrypted using an IND-CPA encryption scheme Enc to obtain the pair $(\mathsf{etag}_{\mathsf{a,b},v}, \mathsf{ev}_v) := (\mathsf{Enc}(K^{\mathsf{enc}}_{\mathsf{a,b}}, \mathsf{tag}_{\mathsf{a},v}), \mathsf{Enc}(K^{\mathsf{enc}}, v))$ that will be added to tuple $\mathsf{MM}^{\mathsf{p}}[(\mathsf{a}, \mathsf{b})]$. Note that the seed $K^{\mathsf{t}}_{\mathsf{a}}$ used to compute the tag depends solely on the first label of the pair a, whereas the encryption key $K^{\mathsf{enc}}_{\mathsf{a,b}}$ depends on both labels. K^{enc} is a system-wide encryption key. Both $K^{\mathsf{t}}_{\mathsf{a}}$ and $K^{\mathsf{enc}}_{\mathsf{a,b}}$ are pseudorandomly generated to ensure that the client storage remains small. The multi-map MM^{p} is then encrypted using a response-revealing encrypted multi-map (see Sect. 2.3) to construct $\mathsf{EMM}^{\mathsf{p}}$ that is sent to the server. In addition to $\mathsf{EMM}^{\mathsf{p}}$, ConjFilter will also construct a set $\mathcal{X}$ of *double tags* that will also be stored by the server. For each pair of labels (a, b) and for each value $v \in \mathsf{MM}[\mathsf{a}] \cap \mathsf{MM}[\mathsf{b}]$, $\mathcal{X}$ will store the double tag $\mathsf{dtag}_{\mathsf{a,b},v} = F(K^{\times}_{\mathsf{a,b}}, \mathsf{tag}_{\mathsf{a},v})$, which is essentially a PRF evaluation of the tag $\mathsf{tag}_{\mathsf{a},v}$ that was stored in the encrypted multi-map $\mathsf{EMM}^{\mathsf{p}}$. The PRF seed $K^{\times}_{\mathsf{a,b}}$ will be pseudorandomly generated from a secret master key and the labels a and b. $\mathcal{X}$ is the new structure of ConjFilter that enables filtering in a way that reduces volume leakage.

To answer a query for conjunction $\ell_1 \wedge \ldots \wedge \ell_q$, the client issues a query token to $\mathsf{EMM}^{\mathsf{p}}$ for (ℓ_1, ℓ_2). As $\mathsf{EMM}^{\mathsf{p}}$ is response-revealing, the server will learn the entry $\mathsf{MM}^{\mathsf{p}}[(\ell_1, \ell_2)]$ in plaintext. In addition, the client also sends the encryption key $K^{\mathsf{enc}}_{\ell_1,\ell_2}$ that enables the server to decrypt all encrypted tags that appear in $\mathsf{MM}^{\mathsf{p}}[(\ell_1, \ell_2)]$. As a result, the server may decrypt the encrypted tags in $\mathsf{MM}[\ell_1 \wedge \ell_2]$ to obtain set $S_2 = \{(\mathsf{tag}_1, \mathsf{ev}_1), (\mathsf{tag}_2, \mathsf{ev}_2), \ldots\}$ of pairs of tags and encrypted values. Note, the server may only decrypt encrypted tags but may not decrypt the encrypted values. Next, we want to filter S_2 to only keep pairs of tags and encrypted values that correspond to values that appear in $\mathsf{MM}[\ell_3]$. To do this, we utilize the set of double tags $\mathcal{X}$. In the request, the client issues the PRF seed $K^{\times}_{\ell_1,\ell_3}$ for filtering S_2 with $\mathsf{MM}[\ell_3]$. For each tag_i in S_2, the server computes $F(K^{\times}_{\ell_1,\ell_3}, \mathsf{tag}_i)$ and checks whether the PRF evaluation appears in $\mathcal{X}$. The server computes the set $S_3 \subseteq S_2$ such that S_3 contains the pair $(\mathsf{tag}_i, \mathsf{ev}_i)$ from S_2 if and only if $F(K^{\times}_{\ell_1,\ell_3}, \mathsf{tag}_i) \in \mathcal{X}$. We note that S_3 consists only of the tag and encrypted value pairs corresponding to values that appear in $\mathsf{MM}[\ell_1 \wedge \ell_2 \wedge \ell_3]$. As a result, the server successfully filters S_2 to keep elements that also appear in $\mathsf{MM}[\ell_3]$. By repeating the filtering algorithm for each $\ell_3, \ldots, \ell_q$, the server will exactly compute an encrypted version of $\mathsf{MM}[\ell_1 \wedge \ldots \wedge \ell_q]$.

We note that handling singleton queries (1-conjunctions) of the form ℓ is a special case where only a single query to $\mathsf{EMM}^{\mathsf{p}}$ for entry ℓ is issued by the client. The server returns the response set that may be decrypted by the client to obtain $\mathsf{MM}[\ell]$. For convenience, we do not add this special case of Fig. 1 to focus the pseudocode on the new techniques.

3.2 Efficiency

The encrypted multi-map of ConjFilter consists of two structures: $\mathsf{EMM}^{\mathsf{p}}$ and $\mathcal{X}$. Altogether, both structures store three objects for each value appearing in $\mathsf{MM}[\mathsf{a}] \cap \mathsf{MM}[\mathsf{b}]$ for each pair of labels (a, b). Therefore, the encrypted multi-map

$\mathsf{ConjFilter}$ requires server storage $O(\sum_{\mathsf{a},\mathsf{b}\in\mathcal{U}} |\mathsf{MM}[\mathsf{a}] \cap \mathsf{MM}[\mathsf{b}]|)$. The client only stores $O(1)$ PRF seeds and encryption keys.

For communication, consider a conjunctive query Φ over q labels. The token $\mathtt{tok}$ for Φ contains a token for $\mathsf{EMM}^{\mathsf{p}}$, a decryption key and $q-2$ double-tag seeds. As the token size of $\mathsf{EMM}^{\mathsf{p}}$ is $O(1)$, we get that the total size of tokens for $\mathsf{ConjFilter}$ is $O(q)$. In particular, the token size is independent on the size of the underlying multi-map. The server response size is optimal as there is exactly one ciphertext returned for each value that appears in the response $\mathsf{MM}[\Phi]$.

Finally, we consider the computational cost of the server performing the query. Note, the server first computes a response set for the query $\mathsf{MM}[\ell_1 \wedge \ell_2]$. Afterwards, the server filters the set for each of the other labels $\ell_3, \ldots, \ell_q$. As a result, the server computation becomes $O(q \cdot |\mathsf{MM}[\ell_1 \wedge \ell_2]|)$. In the natural setting that $|\mathsf{MM}[\ell_1] \cap \mathsf{MM}[\ell_2]|$ is sublinear in the size of the input multi-map, $\mathsf{ConjFilter}$ performs sublinear work in the input multi-map.

3.3 Formal Description of Leakage for ConjFilter

In this section, we give a formal description of the leakage function for $\mathsf{ConjFilter}$. For our leakage descriptions, we consider an input multi-map MM and a sequence $Q = (\Phi^1, \Phi^2, \ldots)$ of conjunctive queries, where the i-th query is the conjunction $\Phi^i = (\ell_1^i \wedge \ldots \wedge \ell_{q_i}^i)$. We split the information leaked by $\mathsf{ConjFilter}$ for an input multi-map MM and a query sequence Q into three leakages:

1. The *setup leakage*, $\mathcal{L}_{\mathsf{Setup}}$, learned by the adversary from viewing the encrypted Boolean multi-map $(\mathsf{EMM}^{\mathsf{p}}, \mathcal{X})$;
2. The *token leakage*, $\mathcal{L}_{\mathsf{Token}}$, learned by the adversary from viewing the tokens;
3. The *search leakage*, $\mathcal{L}_{\mathsf{Search}}$, learned by the adversary when applying the tokens to the encrypted Boolean multi-map $(\mathsf{EMM}^{\mathsf{p}}, \mathcal{X})$.

Query leakage, $\mathcal{L}_{\mathsf{Query}} = (\mathcal{L}_{\mathsf{Token}}, \mathcal{L}_{\mathsf{Search}})$, is the union of token and search leakage.

Before presenting our leakage, we define the notion of *repetition patterns*. Note that $\mathsf{ConjFilter}$ makes extensive use of PRFs to compute various cryptographic objects. As PRF functions are deterministic, this means that these objects might repeatedly appear several times in query tokens or during server processing. In the description of the leakage of our constructions we will make use of repetition patterns to encode information about the appearances of an object. In general, suppose we have T occurrences of an object. For a fixed ordering of the T occurrences, the repetition pattern will consist of a sequence of T integers, one for each occurrence of the object. Each integer will correspond to the first index of this object was encountered. Two entries of the sequence are equal if and only if they correspond to the same instance of the object. An example of the repetition pattern is the query equality pattern appearing in many encrypted multi-map schemes (such as [31,40]) that reveals whether two queries are the same as well as the first time this query was previously seen. We will utilize repetition patterns for tags, double tags, decryption keys and PRF seeds used to compute double tags.

Setup Leakage. The setup leakage $\mathcal{L}_{\mathsf{Setup}}$ is the information learned by the adversary from the encrypted multi-map $\mathsf{EMM}^{\mathsf{p}}$ and set $\mathcal{X}$ of double tags computed by ConjFilter.Setup. We utilize a response-revealing encrypted multi-map from Sect. 2.3. Recall that the setup leakage of $\mathsf{EMM}^{\mathsf{p}}$ is the set of values appearing in the underlying input multi-map MM^{p}. As all values are pairs of encryptions, the leakage is simply the size of MM^{p}. Each element of $\mathcal{X}$ is a PRF evaluation. Therefore, the adversary learns no information beyond the size of $\mathcal{X}$, that is identical to the size of MM^{p}. To complete the description, the setup leakage is $\mathcal{L}^{\mathsf{st}}_{\mathsf{ConjFilter}}(\mathsf{MM}) = N = \sum_{\ell,\ell' \in \mathcal{U}} |\mathsf{MM}[\ell] \cap \mathsf{MM}[\ell']|$, which is the size of MM^{p} and $\mathcal{X}$.

Token Leakage. The token leakage consists of the information learned by the adversary from tokens. First of all, note that the number of double tags in the i-th token leaks the number of labels appearing in i-th query. We denote this leakage function by $\#\mathsf{labels}(Q) = (q_1, \ldots, q_{|Q|})$.

Next, we note that the encryption key in the token of the i-th query is pseudorandomly generated using the first two labels, ℓ^i_1 and ℓ^i_2, of the query. Therefore if two queries share the first two labels, the corresponding tokens contain the same encryption key. Thus $\mathsf{EMM}^{\mathsf{p}}$ leaks the *encryption key repetition pattern* denoted by encryptionKeyRP. Formally, encryptionKeyRP is an array whose length is the number of queries and encryptionKeyRP$[i]$ is the smallest $j \leq i$ such that the i-th and the j-th tokens contain the same encryption key.

Similarly, the leakage also consists of *double tag PRF seed repetition patterns* denoted by doubleTagSeedRP. Similarly, doubleTagSeedRP is an array whose length is the number of double-tag PRF seeds seen and each entry is an index of when the corresponding double-tag PRF seed was first encountered.

A similar leakage is obtained from double tags. Consider two queries Φ^i and Φ^j with the same first label such that the s-th label of Φ^i is equal to the t-th label of Φ^j. That is,

$$\ell^i_1 = \ell^j_1 \text{ and } \ell^i_s = \ell^j_t.$$

Then double-tag PRF seed $K^{\times}_{i,s}$ in the query token for Φ^i is equal to double-tag PRF seed $K^{\times}_{j,t}$ in the query token for Φ^j. We encode these repetitions in array doubleTagSeedRP where, for each (i, s), doubleTagSeedRP$[i, s] = (j, t)$ where $j \leq i$ is the smallest index such that the j-th query has the same t-th label as the s-th label of the i-th query. The token leakage is thus set to $\mathcal{L}^{\mathsf{t}}_{\mathsf{ConjFilter}} = (\#\mathsf{labels}, \mathsf{encryptionKeyRP}, \mathsf{doubleTagSeedRP})$.

Search Leakage. For search leakage, we note that the server sees in the plaintext both tags and double tags. As a result, the search leakage consists of the tag and double tag repetition patterns tagRP and doubleTagRP. The leakage tagRP is an array whose length is equal to the number of tags seen. Each entry corresponds to the index that the tag was first seen. The function doubleTagRP is defined similarly for double tags.

When the tokens are applied to the Boolean encrypted multi-map, the adversary sees tags (obtained by decrypting the encrypted tags from MM^{p}) and the double tags and which of them belongs to $\mathcal{X}$. Thus the execution of search leaks the number and the repetition pattern tagRP of tags, and the number, the repetition pattern $\mathsf{doubleTagRP}$ and the membership in $\mathcal{X}$ of the double tags.

Let us discuss what this tells us about MM and Q, starting from the tags.

The number L_i of tags obtained from EMM^p in the i-th search invocation corresponds to the size of $\mathsf{MM}[\ell_1^i \wedge \ell_2^i]$. To understand the tag repetition pattern, note that the tag is a function of the first label of a query and of the actual value v. Thus if the l_1-th tag of query i_1 is the same as the l_2-th tag of query i_2, the two queries have the same first label, that is $\ell_1^{i_1} = \ell_1^{i_2}$, and there exists $v \in \mathsf{MM}[\ell_1^{i_1} \wedge \ell_1^{i_2}]$. Therefore, by counting the number of common tags between query i_1 and query i_2, it is possible to compute the size of

$$\mathsf{MM}[\ell_1^{i_1} \wedge \ell_2^{i_1} \wedge \ell_1^{i_2} \wedge \ell_2^{i_2}] = \mathsf{MM}[\ell_1^{i_1} \wedge \ell_2^{i_1} \wedge \ell_2^{i_2}].$$

This can be extended to compute the size of conjunction of four or more labels that come from queries with the same first label.

For the double tags, observe that a double tag is obtained from a tag and a double-tag seed and thus associated repetition pattern $\mathsf{doubleTagRP}$ can be obtained from the tag repetition pattern tagRP and the double-tag seed repetition pattern $\mathsf{doubleTagSeedRP}$. We include it in the leakage for convenience. Membership in $\mathcal{X}$ of double tags can be encoded by q matrices $\mathsf{MX}_1, \ldots, \mathsf{MX}_q$, one for each query, defined as follows:

$$\mathsf{MX}_i[l][d] = \begin{cases} 1, & \text{if } \mathsf{dtag}_{l,d} \in \mathcal{X} \text{ for the } i\text{-th query;} \\ 0, & \text{otherwise.} \end{cases}$$

By counting the number of 1's in column d of MX_i, one obtains the size of $\mathsf{MM}[\ell_1^i \wedge \ell_2^i \wedge \ell_d^i]$. This can be extended to the computation of the size of conjunctions of four or more labels, by counting the number of common rows that contain 1 in two or more columns.

Finally, we note that the server learns whether a double tag appears in the set $\mathcal{X}$ or not. For each query Φ^i, we denote the leakage MX_i as an array of length $|\mathsf{MM}^\mathsf{p}[(\ell_1^i, \ell_i^2)]| \cdot (q-2)$ with one entry for each double tag seen when processing Φ^i. An entry of MX_i is 1 if and only if the corresponding double tag appears in $\mathcal{X}$ or not. Recall that a double tag is pseudorandomly generated based on two labels (a, b) and a value v. If the corresponding MX_i entry is 1, it means that the value appears in the intersection of $\mathsf{MM}[\mathsf{a}] \cap \mathsf{MM}[\mathsf{b}]$. Therefore, we have that $\mathcal{L}_{\mathsf{Search}} = (\mathsf{tagRP}, \mathsf{doubleTagRP}, \{\mathsf{MX}_i\}_{i \in [|Q|]})$.

We can re-interpret the volume leakage of $\mathcal{L}_{\mathsf{Search}}$ to determine the base query set of leakage with respect to a single conjunctive query $\ell_1 \wedge \ldots \wedge \ell_q$. Note the query to $\mathsf{MM}[\ell_1 \wedge \ell_2]$ reveals the volume of $(\ell_1 \wedge \ell_2)$. The double tags reveal the volumes of $(\ell_1 \wedge \ell_2 \wedge \ell_i)$ for all $i \geq 3$. As all the sets of PRF evaluations are under the same key, the adversary may perform arbitrary set intersections and unions over the responses. Therefore, the adversary learns the volume of any query of the form $\Psi(x_1, \ldots, x_t)$ where $x_i \in \mathsf{B} = \{(\ell_1 \wedge \ell_2), (\ell_1 \wedge \ell_2 \wedge \ell_3), \ldots, (\ell_1 \wedge \ell_2 \wedge \ell_q)\}$ where B is the base query set of leakage. The above analysis works when the query is a conjunction of two or more labels. For singleton label queries, the volume of the single queried label is leaked, which is unavoidable when insisting on optimal download sizes.

The query leakage consists of both the token and search leakage, $\mathcal{L}_{\mathsf{Query}} = (\mathcal{L}_{\mathsf{Token}}, \mathcal{L}_{\mathsf{Search}})$. We prove the following theorem in the full version.

Theorem 4. ConjFilter *is an adaptively* $(\mathcal{L}_{\mathsf{Setup}}, \mathcal{L}_{\mathsf{Query}})$*-secure encrypted Boolean multi-map scheme that supports conjunctive queries in the random oracle model.*

3.4 Comparison with BIEX [28]

For completeness, we present a comprehensive overview of the techniques used in BIEX in our full version. These similar ideas were also used in prior works such as [15]. In terms of setup and token leakage, it turns out that both ConjFilter and BIEX have identical leakage. The main difference in leakage occurs during search time. To exhibit the differences, we start by comparing the set of plaintext tags that are revealed to the server. For a query $\Phi = \ell_1 \wedge \ldots \ell_q$, ConjFilter only reveals the tags appearing in the multi-map entry $\mathsf{MM}^{\mathsf{P}}[\ell_1 \wedge \ell_2]$. On the other hand, BIEX reveals all plaintext tags appearing in $q-1$ multi-map entries $\mathsf{MM}^{\mathsf{P}}[\ell_1 \wedge \ell_2], \ldots, \mathsf{MM}^{\mathsf{P}}[\ell_1 \wedge \ell_q]$. As an immediate consequence, ConjFilter only leaks volumes for a single 2-conjunction $(\ell_1 \wedge \ell_2)$ while BIEX leaks volumes for $q-1$ 2-conjunctions $(\ell_1 \wedge \ell_2), \ldots, (\ell_1 \wedge \ell_q)$.

Note that ConjFilter reveals double tags that do not exist in BIEX. The leakage reveals whether the double tag corresponding to labels (ℓ_1, ℓ_i) and a value $v \in \mathsf{MM}[\ell_1 \wedge \ell_2]$ appears in $\mathcal{X}$. Note this is true if and only if $v \in \mathsf{MM}[\ell_1 \wedge \ell_2 \wedge \ell_i]$. Therefore, ConjFilter ends up leaking the volumes of 3-conjunctions of the form $\ell_1 \wedge \ell_2 \wedge \ell_i$ where $i \in \{3, \ldots, q\}$. These are the only sets of PRF evaluations that are leaked by ConjFilter on top of the 2-conjunction result $\ell_1 \wedge \ell_2$. As these sets are evaluated under the same PRF key, the adversary may perform arbitrary set operations over them to derive volumes of other queries. Therefore, the base query set of leakage is $\{(\ell_1 \wedge \ell_2), (\ell_1 \wedge \ell_2 \wedge \ell_3), \ldots, (\ell_1 \wedge \ell_2 \wedge \ell_q)\}$.

Going back to BIEX, the only sets of PRF evaluations leaked consist of 2-conjunctions from the set $\{(\ell_1 \wedge \ell_2), \ldots, (\ell_1 \wedge \ell_q)\}$. This ends up being the base set of query leakage as all PRF evaluations are under the same key. It is easy to see that the span of the base query set of leakage of ConjFilter is a subset of the span of the base query set of leakage of BIEX. This means that BIEX ends up leaking volumes of more queries. To see some concrete reduced leakage, BIEX already leaks volumes of more 2-conjunctions than ConjFilter. Looking at 3-conjunctions, ConjFilter leaks only 3-conjunctions of the form $(\ell_1 \wedge \ell_2 \wedge \ell_3), \ldots, (\ell_1 \wedge \ell_2 \wedge \ell_q)$. On the other hand, BIEX leaks volumes for 3-conjunctions of the form $\ell_1 \wedge \ell_i \wedge \ell_j$ where $i < j \in \{2, \ldots, q\}$. Therefore, it is clear ConjFilter leaks volumes for less 3-conjunctions than BIEX. One can find many more queries for which volumes are leaked by BIEX and not ConjFilter using the base sets. As leakage explodes as more conjunctive queries are handled by BIEX and ConjFilter, the leakage reduction on ConjFilter only gets better when considering leakage of multiple conjunctive queries.

As a caveat, we note that ConjFilter and BIEX leak volumes for identical query sets in only two cases. The first case is singleton label queries where it is necessary to leak the response size due to optimal communication requirements. The other case is 2-conjunctions where both schemes leak only the volume of the 2-conjunctive query. For conjunctions with 3 or more labels, the set of queries for which volumes are leaked for ConjFilter is always a strict subset of BIEX.

4 CNF Queries

In this section, we present CNFFilter, a construction supporting general CNF queries that extends the filtering techniques of ConjFilter. The formal description of CNFFilter may be found in Fig. 2.

4.1 Construction CNFFilter

The CNFFilter.Setup algorithm is identical to ConjFilter.Setup that computes the encrypted multi-map $\mathsf{EMM}^{\mathsf{p}}$ and set $\mathcal{X}$.

Next, we show how CNFFilter handles CNF queries using $\mathsf{EMM}^{\mathsf{p}}$ and $\mathcal{X}$. We start with the simple case of a CNF formulae $\Phi = D_1 \wedge D_2$ with only two clauses where each clause $D_d = \ell_{d,1} \vee \ldots \vee \ell_{d,q_d}$, for $d = 1, 2$. For all $i \in \{1, \ldots, q_1\}$, we define the set S_i as

$$S_i := (\mathsf{MM}[\ell_{1,i}] \cap \mathsf{MM}[D_2]) \setminus \left(\mathsf{MM}[\ell_{1,i}] \cap \mathsf{MM}[D_2] \cap \left(\bigcup_{r=i+1}^{q_1} \mathsf{MM}[\ell_{1,r}]\right)\right).$$

Note that any two sets, S_i and S_j, are disjoint as long as $i \neq j$. Furthermore, the union of all q_1 sets is exactly $\mathsf{MM}[D_1 \wedge D_2]$. In other words, $S_1, \ldots, S_{q_1}$ is a partition of $\mathsf{MM}[D_1 \wedge D_2]$ and this is crucial to obtain optimal communication. Let us show how the search algorithm will compute the sets $S_1, \ldots, S_{q_1}$. Its output will consists of the union of the q_1 sets.

The client will issue tokens $\mathtt{tok}_1, \ldots, \mathtt{tok}_{q_1}$ to compute each of the sets $S_1, \ldots, S_{q_1}$. The first part of $\mathtt{tok}_i$ corresponding to S_i will be the q_2 tokens to query entries $(\ell_{1,i}, \ell_{2,j})$, for all $j \in \{1, \ldots, q_2\}$, in $\mathsf{EMM}^{\mathsf{p}}$. Additionally, $\mathtt{tok}_i$ will contain the encryption keys to decrypt all tags that appear in the tuples $\mathsf{MM}^{\mathsf{p}}[(\ell_{1,i}, \ell_{2,j})]$, for all $j \in \{1, \ldots, q_2\}$. As a result, the server will be able to obtain the tags in the tuples $\mathsf{MM}[\ell_{1,i} \wedge \ell_{2,1}], \ldots, \mathsf{MM}[\ell_{1,i} \wedge \ell_{2,q_2}]$. Using the tags, the server may also compute the union of all q_2 sets, which we denote as S_i, that is a superset of the final answer. Note, that S_i is currently equal to the set $\mathsf{MM}[\ell_{1,i}] \cap \mathsf{MM}[D_2]$. Two different parts S_i and S_j might not be disjoint at the moment. For example, there might be a value $v \in \mathsf{MM}[\ell_{1,i}] \cap \mathsf{MM}[\ell_{1,j}] \cap \mathsf{MM}[D_2]$ that appears in both S_i and S_j. To ensure all parts are disjoint, and thus guarantee optimal communication, we filter each S_i and remove all values that will appear in sets $S_{i+1}, S_{i+2}, \ldots, S_{q_1}$. If any value v appears in $S_i \cap S_j$, it must appear in $\mathsf{MM}[\ell_{1,i} \wedge \ell_{1,j}]$. Therefore, we can use $\mathcal{X}$ to filter any values in S_i that also will also appear in S_j. To do this for any $i < j$, the client sends the PRF seed $K^{\times}_{\ell_{1,i},\ell_{1,j}}$. The server computes the PRF evaluation of every tag in S_i using $K^{\times}_{\ell_{1,i},\ell_{1,j}}$ (i.e. the double tag). Every pair whose double tag appears in $\mathcal{X}$ may be safely removed from S_i as it will appear in S_j. After filtering all sets $S_1, \ldots, S_{q_1}$, the server obtains a partitioning of $\mathsf{MM}[D_1 \wedge D_2]$.

Next, we explain the extension to CNF queries with any number of clauses. As described above, we have successfully retrieved the q_1 sets $S_1, \ldots, S_{q_1}$ whose union is the answer to the query $D_1 \wedge D_2$. Given a new clause $D_3 = (\ell_{3,1} \vee \ldots \vee \ell_{3,q_3})$, we show how to compute the filtered sets $S_1 \cap \mathsf{MM}[D_3], \ldots, S_{q_1} \cap \mathsf{MM}[D_3]$ whose union corresponds to the response to the query $D_1 \wedge D_2 \wedge D_3$. Recall that all tags in each set S_i are computed using a PRF seed depending solely on label $\ell_{1,i}$. It suffices to remove all items in S_i that do not appear in any of the sets $\mathsf{MM}[\ell_{1,i} \wedge \ell_{3,1}], \ldots, \mathsf{MM}[\ell_{1,i} \wedge \ell_{3,q_3}]$. To do this, we once again use filtering via the set $\mathcal{X}$. The client will send the PRF seeds $K^{\times}_{\ell_{1,i},\ell_{3,1}}, \ldots, K^{\times}_{\ell_{1,i},\ell 3,q_3}$ and applies each of them to each tag in S_i and checks whether the resulting double tag appears in $\mathcal{X}$ or not. If any value in S_i whose corresponding q_3 double tags do not appear in $\mathcal{X}$, the value will be removed from S_i as it does not appear in $\mathsf{MM}[D_1 \wedge D_2 \wedge D_3]$. By removing all these tags, the server successfully computes $S_i \wedge D_3$ for all q_1 sets. For a CNF query of the form $D_1 \wedge D_2 \wedge \ldots \wedge D_\ell$, we can repeat the above filtering for all $D_3, \ldots, D_\ell$ to compute the final response.

We note the above description considers CNF queries with at least two clauses. For the special case of a CNF query with a single clause, the query will be a disjunction. In this case, we revert to the same algorithms for BIEX [28]. No additional storage is necessary as BIEX only requires $\mathsf{EMM}^{\mathsf{p}}$. To our knowledge, there is no way to serve disjunctions without leaking volumes of singleton labels. We leave it as an important open question to answer whether it is possible to compute disjunctions without leaking volumes of singleton labels. We omit the special case from the pseudocode in Fig. 2 to focus on our new techniques.

4.2 Efficiency

The storage of $\mathsf{CNFFilter}$ is identical to $\mathsf{ConjFilter}$ as they store the same structures $\mathsf{EMM}^{\mathsf{p}}$ and $\mathcal{X}$. So, $\mathsf{CNFFilter}$ stores $O(\sum_{\mathsf{a},\mathsf{b} \in \mathcal{U}} |\mathsf{MM}[\mathsf{a}] \cap \mathsf{MM}[\mathsf{b}]|)$ ciphertexts.

Moving on, we consider the costs of computing CNF queries of the form $\Phi = D_1 \wedge \ldots \wedge D_\ell$ where each D_i is a disjunction over q_i keys. For convenience, we denote $q = q_1 + \ldots + q_\ell$. The token for Φ contains a $\mathsf{EMM}^{\mathsf{p}}$ token and an encryption key for each pair of keys (a, b) where a appears in the first clause D_1 and b appears in the second clause D_2. As a result, there are $O(q_1 q_2)$ such keys and tokens. Additionally, for each key appearing in any of the clauses $D_3, \ldots, D_\ell$ and each key appearing in the first D_1, the token for Φ contains a PRF key. This results in an additional $O(q_1 \cdot (q - q_1 - q_2))$ PRF keys. So, the token size of $\mathsf{CNFFilter}$ is $O(q_1 \cdot q) = O(q^2)$, which is independent of the stored multi-map. The server response size is optimal as there is exactly one ciphertext returned for each value in the response $\mathsf{MM}[\Phi]$.

In terms of server computation, the server computes response sets for all queries of the form $\mathsf{MM}[\mathsf{a} \wedge \mathsf{b}]$ where a is a label from the clause D_1 and b is a label from the clause D_2. We may upper bound the size of all these $q_1 \cdot q_2$

- $(\mathtt{msk}, \mathsf{EMM}) \leftarrow \mathsf{CNFFilter.Setup}(1^\lambda, \mathsf{MM} = \{(\ell_t, \vec{v}_t)\}_{t\in[m]})$:
  1. Compute $(\mathtt{msk}, \mathsf{EMM}) \leftarrow \mathsf{ConjFilter.Setup}(1^\lambda, \mathsf{MM})$.
  2. Return $(\mathtt{msk}, \mathsf{EMM})$.
- $\mathtt{tok}_\Phi \leftarrow \mathsf{CNFFilter.Token}(\mathtt{msk} = (K^{\mathsf{p}}, K^{\mathsf{x}}, K^{\mathsf{enc}}, \mathtt{msk}^{\mathsf{p}}), \Phi = D_1 \wedge \ldots \wedge D_\ell)$:
  1. For $d = 1, \ldots, \ell$, parse D_d as $(\ell_{d,1} \vee \ldots \vee \ell_{d,q_d})$.
  2. For $i = 1, \ldots, q_1$:
     (a) For $j = 1, \ldots, q_2$:
        i. Compute $K^{\mathsf{enc}}_{i,j} \leftarrow F(K, \ell_{1,i} \,||\, \ell_{2,j})$.
        ii. Compute $\mathtt{tok}^{\mathsf{p}}_{i,j} \leftarrow \mathsf{sEMM.Token}(\mathtt{msk}^{\mathsf{p}}, (\ell_{1,i}, \ell_{2,j}))$.
  3. For $i = 1, \ldots, q_1$:
     (a) For $r = i+1 \ldots, q_1$:
        i. Compute $K^{\mathsf{x}}_{\ell_{1,i},\ell_{1,r}} = F(K^{\mathsf{x}}, \ell_{1,i} \,||\, \ell_{1,r})$.
  4. For $d = 3, \ldots, \ell$:
     (a) For $i = 1, \ldots, q_1$:
        i. For $r = 1, \ldots, q_d$:
           A. Compute $K^{\mathsf{x}}_{\ell_{1,i},\ell_{d,r}} = F(K^{\mathsf{x}}, \ell_{1,i} \,||\, \ell_{d,r})$.
  5. Return $(\{(K^{\mathsf{enc}}_{i,j}, \mathtt{tok}^{\mathsf{p}}_{i,j})\}_{(i,j)\in[q_1]\times[q_2]}, \{K^{\mathsf{x}}_{\ell_{1,i},\ell_{1,r}}\}_{i<r\in[q_1]\times[q_1]},$
     $\{K^{\mathsf{x}}_{\ell_{1,i},\ell_{3,j}}\}_{(i,j)\in[q_1]\times[q_3]}, \ldots, \{K^{\mathsf{x}}_{\ell_{1,i},\ell_{\ell,j}}\}_{(i,j)\in[q_1]\times[q_\ell]})$.
- $\mathsf{ans} \leftarrow \mathsf{CNFFilter.Search}(\mathtt{tok}_\Phi, \mathsf{EMM} = (\mathsf{EMM}^{\mathsf{p}}, \mathcal{X}))$.
  1. Parse $\mathtt{tok}_\Phi = (\{(K^{\mathsf{enc}}_{i,j}, \mathtt{tok}^{\mathsf{p}}_{i,j})\}_{(i,j)\in[q_1]\times[q_2]}, \{K^{\mathsf{x}}_{\ell_{1,i},\ell_{1,r}}\}_{i<r\in[q_1]\times[q_1]},$
     $\{K^{\mathsf{x}}_{\ell_{1,i},\ell_{3,j}}\}_{(i,j)\in[q_1]\times[q_3]}, \ldots, \{K^{\mathsf{x}}_{\ell_{1,i},\ell_{\ell,j}}\}_{(i,j)\in[q_1]\times[q_\ell]})$.
  2. For $i = 1, \ldots, q_1$: `# Compute partition of` $\mathtt{D_1 \wedge D_2}$
     (a) Set $S_i \leftarrow \emptyset$.
     (b) For $j = 1, \ldots, q_2$:
        i. Set $S_i \leftarrow S_i \cup \mathsf{sEMM.Search}(\mathtt{tok}^{\mathsf{p}}_{i,j}, \mathsf{EMM}^{\mathsf{p}})$.
     (c) Use decryption key $K^{\mathsf{enc}}_{i,j}$ to decrypt the first component of every pair of S_i and remove pairs from S_i until all pairs have distinct first component.
     (d) Parse S_i as $\{(\mathsf{tag}_1, \mathsf{ev}_1), \ldots, (\mathsf{tag}_{|S_i|}, \mathsf{ev}_{|S_i|})\}$.
     (e) For each $(\mathsf{tag}, \mathsf{ev}) \in S_i$:
        i. Compute double tag $\mathsf{dtag}_r \leftarrow F(K^{\mathsf{x}}_{\ell_{1,i},\ell_{1,r}}, \mathsf{tag})$, for $r = i+1, \ldots, q_1$.
        ii. If one of the double tags belongs to $\mathcal{X}$, then remove the pairs containing tag from S_i.
  3. For $d = 3, \ldots, \ell$: `# Filtering using clause` $\mathtt{D_d}$
     (a) For $i = 1, \ldots, q_1$:
        i. For each $(\mathsf{tag}, \mathsf{ev}) \in S_i$:
           A. Compute $\mathsf{dtag}_j \leftarrow F(K^{\mathsf{x}}_{\ell_{1,i},\ell_{d,j}}, \mathsf{tag})$, for $j = 1, \ldots, q_d$.
           B. If one of $\mathsf{dtag}_1, \ldots \mathsf{dtag}_{q_d}$ belongs to $\mathcal{X}$ then, set $S \leftarrow S \setminus \{(\mathsf{tag}, \mathsf{ev})\}$.
  4. Return all second components appearing in $S = S_1 \cup S_2 \cup \ldots \cup S_{q_1}$. That is, parse S as $S = \{(\mathsf{tag}_1, \mathsf{ev}_1), \ldots, (\mathsf{tag}_{|S|}, \mathsf{ev}_{|S|})\}$ and return $\mathsf{ans} = \{\mathsf{ev}_1, \ldots, \mathsf{ev}_{|S|}\}$.
- $\mathsf{ans} \leftarrow \mathsf{CNFFilter.Resolve}(\mathsf{ans} = \{\mathsf{ev}_1, \ldots, \mathsf{ev}_{|\mathsf{ans}|}\}, \mathtt{msk} = (K^{\mathsf{p}}, K^{\mathsf{x}}, K^{\mathsf{enc}}, \mathtt{msk}^{\mathsf{p}}))$
  1. Return $\mathsf{Dec}(K^{\mathsf{enc}}, \mathsf{ev}_1), \ldots, \mathsf{Dec}(K^{\mathsf{enc}}, \mathsf{ev}_{|\mathsf{ans}|})$.

Fig. 2. Pseudocode for construction CNFFilter

responses by $O(q_1 \cdot q_2 \cdot |\mathsf{MM}[D_1 \wedge D_2]|)$. Each tag that appears in the response set is hashed using an additional PRF key depending on another label that appears in any of the clauses $D_3, \ldots, D_\ell$. This incurs an additional $O((q - q_1 - q_2) \cdot |\mathsf{MM}[D_1 \wedge D_2]|)$ server computation. Altogether, the total server computation is $O(q \cdot q_1 \cdot |\mathsf{MM}[D_1 \wedge D_2]|) = O(q^2 \cdot |\mathsf{MM}[D_1 \wedge D_2])$. This is sublinear in the input multi-map size as long as $\mathsf{MM}[D_1 \wedge D_2]$ is sublinear in the input multi-map size. On average, our scheme has smaller server computation as it depends only on $|\mathsf{MM}[D_1 \wedge D_2]$ compared to BIEX whose server computation depends on the size $|\mathsf{MM}[D_1]|$ that is most likely larger. We show that our scheme has better concrete server computation in our experiments in Sect. 5.

4.3 Formal Description of Leakage of CNFFilter

In this section, we give a formal description of the leakage for CNFFilter. We will utilize the partitioning of leakage into setup $\mathcal{L}_{\mathsf{Setup}}$, token $\mathcal{L}_{\mathsf{Token}}$ and search $\mathcal{L}_{\mathsf{Search}}$ leakage as done in ConjFilter.

Consider a multi-map $\mathsf{MM} = \{(\ell_t, \vec{v}_t)\}_{t\in[m]}$ and a CNF query sequence $Q = (\Phi^1, \ldots, \Phi^{|Q|})$, where $\Phi^p = (D_1^p \wedge \ldots \wedge D_{m^p}^p)$ consists of m^p clauses. The d-th clause D_d^p of Φ^p consists of q_d^p labels, $D_d^p = (\ell_{d,1}^p \vee \ldots \vee \ell_{d,q_d^p}^p)$.

Setup Leakage. As ConjFilter and CNFFilter have identical setup algorithms, the setup leakages are also identical. Thus, $\mathcal{L}_{\mathsf{Setup}}(\mathsf{MM}, Q) = N = \sum_{\ell,\ell' \in \mathcal{U}} |\mathsf{MM}[\ell] \cap \mathsf{MM}[\ell']|$.

Token Leakage. The token leakage consists of repetition patterns for both the decryption keys and PRF seeds for double tags. denoted by encryptionKeyRP and doubleTagSeedRP defined as follows. Each entry of encryptionKeyRP and doubleTagSeedRP will correspond to the decryption key or PRF seeds unique identifier. The token for the p-th query Φ^p contains one decryption key for each pair consisting of a label from the first clause and a label from the second clause. Therefore, for query Φ^p, $\mathsf{encryptionKeyRP}_p$ contains an entry $\mathsf{encryptionKeyRP}_p[i, j]$ for each $1 \le i \le q_1^p$ and $1 \le j \le q_2^p$. A repetition $\mathsf{encryptionKeyRP}_p[i, j] = \mathsf{encryptionKeyRP}_{p'}[i', j']$ occurs if and only if

$$\ell_{1,i}^p = \ell_{1,i'}^{p'} \text{ and } \ell_{2,j}^p = \ell_{2,j'}^{p'}.$$

In other words, the encryptionKeyRP tells us whether the first two clauses of two queries share two labels.

The token for the p-th query Φ^p contains one double-tag seed for each pair consisting of a label from the first clause and a label from a clause following the second clause. Therefore, for query Φ^p, $\mathsf{doubleTagSeedRP}_p$ contains an entry $\mathsf{doubleTagSeedRP}_p[i, d, j]$ for each $1 \le i \le q_1^p$, $1 \le d \le l^p$, and $1 \le j \le q_d^p$. A repetition $\mathsf{doubleTagSeedRP}_p[i, d, j] = \mathsf{doubleTagSeedRP}_{p'}[i', d', j']$ occurs if and only if

$$\ell_{1,i}^p = \ell_{1,i'}^{p'} \text{ and } \ell_{d,j}^p = \ell_{d,j'}^{p'}.$$

In other words, the doubleTagSeedRP tells us whether the first clauses and the d-th and d'-th clause of two queries share two labels.

Search Leakage. The execution of the Search algorithm reveals both tags and double tags. The tags are revealed after decrypting the response to the queries MM^p. The double tags are computed during filtering with the set $\mathcal{X}$. As both tags and double tags are pseudorandomly generated, they also leak repetition patterns.

In addition, double tags leak membership in $\mathcal{X}$ which is encoded in the matrices MX. Therefore, we have that

$$\mathcal{L}^{\mathsf{sr}}_{\mathsf{CNFFilter}}(\mathsf{MM}, Q) = (\mathsf{tagRP}, \mathsf{doubleTagRP}, \mathsf{MX}).$$

Let us now see what $\mathcal{L}^{\mathsf{sr}}_{\mathsf{CNFFilter}}$ tells us about MM. In computing the response to Φ^p, the number of tags obtained from each query to the underlying MM^p gives the volume of the 2-conjunction $\ell^p_{1,i} \wedge \ell^p_{2,j}$. In addition, observe that if the responses to 2-conjunction $(\ell^p_{1,i} \wedge \ell^p_{2,j})$ and to 2-conjunction $(\ell^{p'}_{1,i'} \wedge \ell^p_{2,j'})$ share a tag then it must be the case that $\ell^p_{1,i} = \ell^{p'}_{1,i'}$ and that there exists $v \in \mathsf{MM}[\ell^p_{1,i} \wedge \ell^p_{2,j} \wedge \ell^p_{2,j'}]$. Therefore, by counting the number of common tags between the responses to the two 2-conjunction one can obtain the volume of the 3-conjunction

$$(\ell^p_{1,i} \wedge \ell^p_{2,j}) \wedge \left(\ell^{p'}_{1,i'} \wedge \ell^p_{2,j'}\right) = \left(\ell^p_{1,i} \wedge \ell^p_{2,j} \wedge \ell^p_{2,j'}\right).$$

Clearly, tags appearing in the results of three or more 2-conjunctions give the volume of conjunctions with four or more labels.

In sums, we can say that the tag repetition pattern leaks the volume of 2-conjunctions, one for each query to MM^p, that can be combined to compute the volume of larger conjunctions.

The double-tag repetition pattern doubleTagRP can be computed from tagRP and doubleTagSeedRP. Indeed, two double tags are equal iff they are obtained by applying the same double-tag seed to the same tag (except with negligible in λ probability). Therefore no further information is leaked by doubleTagRP.

Finally, let us look at the double-tag membership in $\mathcal{X}$ pattern. For each query, the membership information MX^p for query Φ^p has a matrix $\mathsf{MX}^p_{i,j}$ for each pair of label $\ell^p_{1,i}$ of the first clause and label $\ell^p_{2,j}$ of the second clause. Matrix $\mathsf{MX}^p_{i,j}$ has a row for each tag tag that is obtained by decrypting the response to the query for $\mathsf{MM}^\mathsf{p}[\ell^p_{1,i} \wedge \ell^p_{2,j}]$ and a column for each double-tag seed dstag and $\mathsf{MX}^p_{i,j}[\mathsf{tag}, \mathsf{dstag}] = 1$ iff the corresponding double tag is found in $\mathcal{X}$. It is easy to see that the number of 1 in the column of double-tag seed for $\ell^p_{1,i}$ and $\ell^p_{1,r}$ gives the volume of 3-conjunction $(\ell^p_{1,i} \wedge \ell^p_{2,j} \wedge \ell^p_{1,r})$. Similarly the columns of the double-tag seed for $\ell^p_{1,i}$ and $\ell^p_{d,r}$ gives the volume of 3-conjunction $(\ell^p_{1,i} \wedge \ell^p_{2,j} \wedge \ell^p_{d,r})$. And, as before, the volume of 3-conjunctions can be combined together to obtain the volume of conjunction of size 4 or larger. In sums the membership in $\mathcal{X}$ gives the volume of conjunctions of size 3 or larger.

We denote the query leakage as the combination of token and search leakage $\mathcal{L}_{\mathsf{Query}} = (\mathcal{L}_{\mathsf{Token}}, \mathcal{L}_{\mathsf{Search}})$. We prove the following theorem in the full version.

Theorem 5. CNFFilter *is an adaptively* $(\mathcal{L}_{\mathsf{Setup}}, \mathcal{L}_{\mathsf{Query}})$*-secure encrypted Boolean multi-map scheme that supports CNF queries in the random oracle model.*

4.4 Comparing the Leakage

We now compare the leakage of our construction with the one of BIEX (a description of BIEX may be found in the full version).

We start by considering the tags that are revealed by $\mathsf{CNFFilter}$. Consider a CNF query with m clauses of the form $(\ell_{1,1} \vee \ldots \vee \ell_{1,q_1}) \wedge \ldots \wedge (\ell_{m,1} \vee \ldots \vee \ell_{m,q_m})$. $\mathsf{CNFFilter}$ reveals the tags for all values in $\mathsf{MM}[\ell_{1,i} \wedge \ell_{2,j}]$ for all label pairs of the form $(\ell_{1,i}, \ell_{2,j})$. On the other hand, BIEX reveals all plaintext tags appearing in $\mathsf{MM}[\ell_{1,i}]$ for all labels $\ell_{1,i}$. Additionally, it reveals all plaintext tags appearing in $\mathsf{MM}[\ell_{1,i} \wedge \ell_{j,k}]$ for all label pairs of the form $(\ell_{1,i}, \ell_{j,k})$ where $j \geq 2$.

Note that $\mathsf{CNFFilter}$ reveals double tags that do not exist in BIEX. The leakage reveals whether the double tag corresponding to label pair $(\ell_{1,i}, \ell_{k,l})$ and a value $v \in \mathsf{MM}[\ell_{1,i} \wedge \ell_{2,j}]$ appears in $\mathcal{X}$. Note that this is true if and only if $v \in \mathsf{MM}[\ell_{1,i} \wedge \ell_{2,j} \wedge \ell_{k,l}]$. Therefore, $\mathsf{CNFFilter}$ ends up leaking the volumes of 3-conjunctions of the form $\ell_{1,i} \wedge \ell_{2,j} \wedge \ell_{k,l}$ where $k \geq 3$. These are the only sets of PRF evaluations that are leaked by $\mathsf{CNFFilter}$ on top of the 2-conjunction results $\ell_{1,i} \wedge \ell_{2,j}$. Therefore, the base query set of leakage is $\mathsf{B}' \cup \{(b' \wedge \ell_{k,l}) \mid b' \in \mathsf{B}', 3 \leq k \leq m, l \in [q_k]\}$ where $\mathsf{B}' = \{(\ell_{1,i} \wedge \ell_{2,j}) \mid i \in [q_1], j \in [q_2]\}$.

On the other hand, the sets of PRF evaluations leaked by BIEX consist of queries from the set $\{\ell_{1,i} \mid i \in [q_1]\} \cup \{(\ell_{1,i} \wedge \ell_{j,k}) \mid i \in [q_1], 2 \leq j \leq m, k \in [q_j]\}$. This also turns out to be the base set of query leakage for BIEX.

It is easy to verify that the span of the base set of query leakage of $\mathsf{CNFFilter}$ is a subset of the span of the base set of query leakage of BIEX. First, BIEX leaks volumes for all singleton labels $\ell_{1,i}$ which $\mathsf{CNFFilter}$ doesn't leak, unless the query is a disjunction (recall that $\mathsf{CNFFilter}$ falls back to using BIEX in this case). Additionally, while $\mathsf{CNFFilter}$ only leaks 2-conjunctions of the form $\ell_{1,i} \wedge \ell_{2,j}$, BIEX leaks 2-conjunctions of the form $\ell_{1,i} \wedge \ell_{j,k}$ for all $j \geq 2$. Note that the 3-conjunctions $\ell_{1,i} \wedge \ell_{2,j} \wedge \ell_{k,l}$ leaked by $\mathsf{CNFFilter}$ are also leaked by BIEX since the server can compute this from the response sets of 2-conjunctions $\ell_{1,i} \wedge \ell_{2,j}$ and $\ell_{1,i} \wedge \ell_{k,l}$. Thus, it follows that $\mathsf{CNFFilter}$ does not leak more than BIEX.

As a caveat, we note that $\mathsf{CNFFilter}$ and BIEX leak volumes for the same set of queries in only two cases. The first case happens when the query is a disjunction of the form $\ell_1 \vee \ldots \vee \ell_q$, in which case $\mathsf{CNFFilter}$ falls back to the default implementation of BIEX. The other case happens when the query is a 2-conjunction of the form $\ell_1 \wedge \ell_2$. In every other case, $\mathsf{CNFFilter}$ leaks strictly less than BIEX.

5 Experiments

In this section, we present our experimental evaluation for our main construction, $\mathsf{CNFFilter}$, that supports CNF queries with reduced volume leakage. We start by describing our experimental setup as well as the choice of parameters and primitives for our construction. Afterwards, we compare with the construction of BIEX described in [28].

Using the results of these experiments, we will try to answer the following question: *how do the concrete efficiency costs of our construction* CNFFilter *compare to the previous, state-of-the-art BIEX* [28]*?*

Note that we will use multipliers to describe efficiency improvements. If construction A is a 2x improvement over construction in B in computation, we mean that construction A uses half the computation compared to construction B.

5.1 Setup of Experiments

Our experiments are conducted using the identical machines for both the client and the server. The machines are Ubuntu PCs with 12 cores, 3.65 GHz Intel Xeon E5-1650 and 32 GB of RAM. All experimental results that are reported have standard deviations less than 10% of their average over 50 executions. All network costs are measured at the application layer. Both our client and server are implemented in C++ using the gRPC library [2].

Input Dataset. For our experiments, we utilize the Enron email dataset [34]. We parse the Enron email dataset using the Natural Language Toolkit (NLTK) in Python [3]. Before indexing the dataset, we perform canonicalization and stemming [41] using NLTK. Afterwards, we create a multi-map over the Enron email dataset mapping keywords to email identifiers. In our experiments, we will consider executing schemes over an input multi-map with a target number of values n. To obtain an input multi-map of size n from the Enron email dataset, we perform sampling in the following way. Pick emails uniformly at random and add them to the multi-map until there are at least n total keyword-identifier pairs in the multi-map.

Primitives. In all our experiments, we will utilize HMAC-SHA256 as our PRF with 16 byte keys. For our symmetric encryption scheme, we utilize AES in CTR mode with 16 byte keys. For the case of when encrypting pseudorandom values that will never repeat, we will utilize AES in CTR mode with a fixed IV. Our implementations utilize OpenSSL for both HMAC-SHA256 and AES. For the underlying standard encrypted multi-map of Sect. 2.3, we utilize the response-revealing 2Lev construction from [14] with parameters big block size $B = 100$ and small block size $b = 8$.

Selectivity of Clauses. In our experiments, we vary the selectivity of the first and second clauses in the CNF queries while fixing the selectivities of the remaining clauses. This is a reasonable setup as the search times of BIEX and CNFFilter depend mainly on the selectivity of the first and second clauses.

5.2 Implementation of BIEX [28]

The BIEX construction was presented in [28] along with an implementation in Java [1]. To provide a fair comparison with our C++ implementation of CNFFilter, we re-implement BIEX in C++ with the same underlying primitives

Table 1. Microbenchmarks for the search time of CNFFilter and BIEX [28] on randomly chosen queries of the form $D_1 \wedge D_2 \wedge D_3$ where each D_i is a four label disjunction. The leftmost column and the topmost row denote the number of values associated with each label in the first and the second clause, respectively. The number of values associated with labels in D_3 are fixed to 10000. All search times are measured in milliseconds.

	100		500		1,000		5,000		10,000	
	CNFFilter	BIEX	CNFFilter	BIEX	CNFFilter	BIEX	CNFFilter	BIEX	CNFFilter	BIEX
100	**<0.01**	<0.01	**<0.01**	<0.01	**<0.01**	<0.01	**<0.01**	<0.01	**<0.01**	<0.01
500	**<0.01**	0.24	**<0.01**	0.16	**<0.01**	0.08	**<0.01**	0.16	**0.04**	0.18
1000	**<0.01**	1.28	**<0.01**	1.22	**<0.01**	1.24	**0.32**	1.30	**0.82**	1.36
5000	**<0.01**	9.80	**<0.01**	9.98	**0.64**	10.18	**3.01**	10.72	**5.01**	11.30
10000	**<0.01**	21.84	**0.46**	20.34	**1.16**	21.98	**5.44**	22.36	**9.46**	22.76

as CNFFilter. All our reported results for BIEX will be using our C++ implementation. We note that the tags stored in the encrypted multi-map of BIEX will be the first 8 bytes of the HMAC-SHA256 output. As tags are pseudorandom and won't collide (except with small probability), we encrypt tags using AES-CTR mode with a fixed IV. All encryption and PRF keys used are 16 bytes long. We did not implement their new underlying encrypted multi-map ZMF, filtering optimization or online cipher HBC1 [6], as they mainly improve the underlying encrypted multi-map which are used by both schemes in similar ways.

Compared to the Java implementation of BIEX [1], our C++ implementation of BIEX runs 20x faster than results reported in [28]. Recall that the server computation time depends on the selectivity of the first clause in the CNF query. For a query of the form $D_1 \wedge \ldots \wedge D_\ell$ over q distinct labels and each D_i is a disjunction, then BIEX search algorithm runs in time $O(q^2 \cdot |\mathsf{MM}[D_1]|)$. As the size of $\mathsf{MM}[D_1]$ grows, the server running time also grows as seen in Table 1.

5.3 Cost of CNFFilter

We also implement our construction CNFFilter in C++. The tags stored in the encrypted multi-map and the double tags stored in $\mathcal{X}$ will be the first 8 bytes of the HMAC-SHA256 output. As tags are pseudorandom and do not repeat (except with small probability), we encrypt tags using AES-CTR mode with a fixed IV. All encryption and PRF keys used in CNFFilter are 16 bytes long.

Recall that search computation time of CNFFilter depends on the selectivity of the conjunction of the first two clauses of a CNF query. For a CNF query of the form $D_1 \wedge \ldots \wedge D_\ell$ over q distinct labels, the running time of the search algorithm of CNFFilter grows in the size of $\mathsf{MM}[D_1 \wedge D_2]$. As $\mathsf{MM}[D_1 \wedge D_2]$ is a subset of $\mathsf{MM}[D_1]$, the running time of CNFFilter is expected to be faster than BIEX. Our experimental results in Table 1 confirm these expectations by showing that the search time of CNFFilter is at least 2x faster and may be more than 40x faster compared to BIEX for the same queries and the same input multi-map.

For communication, both CNFFilter and BIEX obtain optimal download communication complexity. In terms of upload communication costs (i.e. token size),

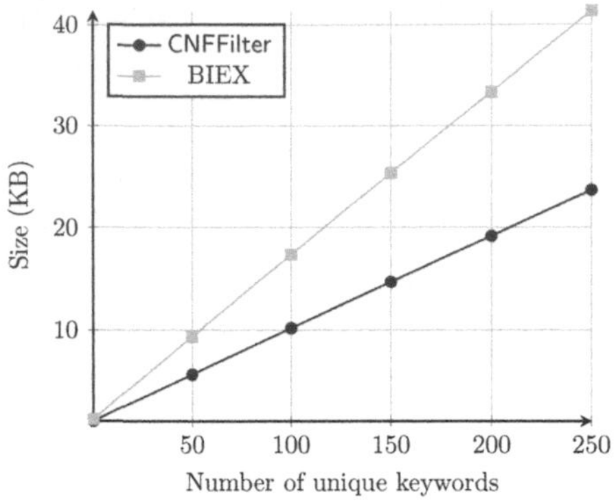

Fig. 3. Search token sizes of CNFFilter and BIEX [28] for 3-clause CNFs $D_1 \wedge D_2 \wedge D_3$ where the D_1 and D_2 contain 5 labels and the x-axis indicates the number of labels in D_3.

Table 2. Storage and setup time of CNFFilter and BIEX [28].

	Input multi-map size in number of key-value pairs (n)									
	10,000		50,000		100,000		500,000		1,000,000	
	CNFFilter	BIEX	CNFFilter	BIEX	CNFFilter	BIEX	CNFFilter	BIEX	CNFFilter	BIEX
Storage size (MB)	115	95	480	401	941	773	4,661	3,702	16,408	13,173
Setup time (seconds)	3	2	13	8	24	13	137	72	662	308

CNFFilter requires smaller tokens compared to BIEX as shown in Fig. 3. Recall that if the CNF query has q_1 labels in the first clause and q total labels overall, then BIEX executes $q_1 \cdot (q - q_1)$ queries to 2Lev. On the other hand, CNFFilter performs only $q_1 \cdot q_2$ 2Lev queries where q_2 is the number of labels in the second clause. The remaining operations in CNFFilter involve hashing and checking membership in $\mathcal{X}$. These operations only require the client to send a PRF key of 16 byte size. This is around 60% of the token size of performing a query to 2Lev. Therefore, CNFFilter obtains smaller token sizes.

Finally, we consider the storage costs of CNFFilter and BIEX. Both schemes store an identical encrypted multi-map for all 2-conjunctions. In addition, CNFFilter must also store the set of hashes $\mathcal{X}$ that does not exist in BIEX. As a result, CNFFilter will have larger storage costs. However, the set $\mathcal{X}$ only consists of double tags of 8 byte length. As a result, $\mathcal{X}$ occupies much smaller space compared to the storage of the encrypted multi-map. This is observed in Table 2 that shows CNFFilter only incurs a 20–25% increase in storage over BIEX, which seems reasonable given the leakage, communication and server computation improvements.

6 Conclusions

In this work, we continue work on designing encrypted Boolean multi-maps. Our new construction CNFFilter mitigates volume leakage better than all previous works while simultaneously achieving optimal communication and worst-case sublinear search times. In terms of volume leakage reduction, CNFFilter substantially improves upon the previous constructions.

References

1. Clusion. https://github.com/orochi89/Clusion
2. gRPC - an RPC library and framework. https://github.com/grpc/grpc
3. Natural language toolkit. http://nltk.org
4. SPAR Pilot Evaluation. MIT Lincoln Laboratory (2015)
5. Asharov, G., Segev, G., Shahaf, I.: Tight tradeoffs in searchable symmetric encryption. In: Shacham, H., Boldyreva, A. (eds.) CRYPTO 2018. LNCS, vol. 10991, pp. 407–436. Springer, Cham (2018). https://doi.org/10.1007/978-3-319-96884-1_14
6. Bellare, M., Boldyreva, A., Knudsen, L., Namprempre, C.: On-line ciphers and the hash-CBC constructions. J. Cryptol. **25**, 640–679 (2012)
7. Bellare, M., Boldyreva, A., O'Neill, A.: Deterministic and efficiently searchable encryption. In: Menezes, A. (ed.) CRYPTO 2007. LNCS, vol. 4622, pp. 535–552. Springer, Heidelberg (2007). https://doi.org/10.1007/978-3-540-74143-5_30
8. Blackstone, L., Kamara, S., Moataz, T.: Revisiting leakage abuse attacks. In: NDSS 2020 (2020)
9. Boneh, D., Di Crescenzo, G., Ostrovsky, R., Persiano, G.: Public key encryption with keyword search. In: Cachin, C., Camenisch, J.L. (eds.) EUROCRYPT 2004. LNCS, vol. 3027, pp. 506–522. Springer, Heidelberg (2004). https://doi.org/10.1007/978-3-540-24676-3_30
10. Bost, R.: Sophos: forward secure searchable encryption. In: CCS 2016 (2016)
11. Bost, R., Fouque, P.-A.: Security-efficiency tradeoffs in searchable encryption - lower bounds and optimal constructions. In: PoPETS 2019 (2019)
12. Bost, R., Minaud, B., Ohrimenko, O.: Forward and backward private searchable encryption from constrained cryptographic primitives. In: CCS 2017 (2017)
13. Cash, D., Grubbs, P., Perry, J., Ristenpart, T.: Leakage-abuse attacks against searchable encryption. In: CCS 2015 (2015)
14. Cash, D., et al.: Dynamic searchable encryption in very-large databases: data structures and implementation. In: NDSS 2014 (2014)
15. Cash, D., Jarecki, S., Jutla, C., Krawczyk, H., Roşu, M.-C., Steiner, M.: Highly-scalable searchable symmetric encryption with support for boolean queries. In: Canetti, R., Garay, J.A. (eds.) CRYPTO 2013. LNCS, vol. 8042, pp. 353–373. Springer, Heidelberg (2013). https://doi.org/10.1007/978-3-642-40041-4_20
16. Cash, D., Tessaro, S.: The locality of searchable symmetric encryption. In: Nguyen, P.Q., Oswald, E. (eds.) EUROCRYPT 2014. LNCS, vol. 8441, pp. 351–368. Springer, Heidelberg (2014). https://doi.org/10.1007/978-3-642-55220-5_20
17. Chase, M., Kamara, S.: Structured encryption and controlled disclosure. In: Abe, M. (ed.) ASIACRYPT 2010. LNCS, vol. 6477, pp. 577–594. Springer, Heidelberg (2010). https://doi.org/10.1007/978-3-642-17373-8_33
18. Curtmola, R., Garay, J., Kamara, S., Ostrovsky, R.: Searchable symmetric encryption: improved definitions and efficient constructions. J. Comput. Secur. **19**, 895–934 (2011)
19. Demertzis, I., Papadopoulos, D., Papamanthou, C.: Searchable encryption with optimal locality: achieving sublogarithmic read efficiency. In: Shacham, H., Boldyreva, A. (eds.) CRYPTO 2018. LNCS, vol. 10991, pp. 371–406. Springer, Cham (2018). https://doi.org/10.1007/978-3-319-96884-1_13

20. Demertzis, I., Papamanthou, C.: Fast searchable encryption with tunable locality. In: SIGMOD 2017 (2017)
21. Demertzis, I., Talapatra, R., Papamanthou, C.: Efficient searchable encryption through compression. In: PVLDB 2018 (2018)
22. Faber, S., Jarecki, S., Krawczyk, H., Nguyen, Q., Rosu, M., Steiner, M.: Rich queries on encrypted data: beyond exact matches. In: Pernul, G., Ryan, P.Y.A., Weippl, E. (eds.) ESORICS 2015. LNCS, vol. 9327, pp. 123–145. Springer, Cham (2015). https://doi.org/10.1007/978-3-319-24177-7_7
23. Gentry, C.: Fully homomorphic encryption using ideal lattices. In: STOC 2009 (2009)
24. Goldreich, O., Ostrovsky, R.: Software protection and simulation on oblivious RAMs. J. ACM **43**(3), 431–473 (1996)
25. Grubbs, P., Lacharité, M., Minaud, B., Paterson, K.G.: Learning to reconstruct: statistical learning theory and encrypted database attacks. In: IEEE S&P 2019 (2019)
26. Grubbs, P., Lacharité, M., Minaud, B., Paterson, K.G.: Pump up the volume: practical database reconstruction from volume leakage on range queries. In: CCS 2018 (2018)
27. Islam, M.S., Kuzu, M., Kantarcioglu, M.: Access pattern disclosure on searchable encryption: ramification, attack and mitigation. In: NDSS 2012 (2012)
28. Kamara, S., Moataz, T.: Boolean searchable symmetric encryption with worst-case sub-linear complexity. In: Coron, J.-S., Nielsen, J.B. (eds.) EUROCRYPT 2017. LNCS, vol. 10212, pp. 94–124. Springer, Cham (2017). https://doi.org/10.1007/978-3-319-56617-7_4
29. Kamara, S., Moataz, T.: SQL on structurally-encrypted databases. In: Peyrin, T., Galbraith, S. (eds.) ASIACRYPT 2018. LNCS, vol. 11272, pp. 149–180. Springer, Cham (2018). https://doi.org/10.1007/978-3-030-03326-2_6
30. Kamara, S., Moataz, T.: Computationally volume-hiding structured encryption. In: Ishai, Y., Rijmen, V. (eds.) EUROCRYPT 2019. LNCS, vol. 11477, pp. 183–213. Springer, Cham (2019). https://doi.org/10.1007/978-3-030-17656-3_7
31. Kamara, S., Moataz, T., Ohrimenko, O.: Structured encryption and leakage suppression. In: Shacham, H., Boldyreva, A. (eds.) CRYPTO 2018. LNCS, vol. 10991, pp. 339–370. Springer, Cham (2018). https://doi.org/10.1007/978-3-319-96884-1_12
32. Kamara, S., Papamanthou, C., Roeder, T.: Dynamic searchable symmetric encryption. In: CCS 2012 (2012)
33. Kellaris, G., Kollios, G., Nissim, K., O'Neill, A.: Generic attacks on secure outsourced databases. In: CCS 2016 (2016)
34. Klimt, B., Yang, Y.: The enron corpus: a new dataset for email classification research. In: Boulicaut, J.-F., Esposito, F., Giannotti, F., Pedreschi, D. (eds.) ECML 2004. LNCS (LNAI), vol. 3201, pp. 217–226. Springer, Heidelberg (2004). https://doi.org/10.1007/978-3-540-30115-8_22
35. Lacharité, M., Minaud, B., Paterson, K.G.: Improved reconstruction attacks on encrypted data using range query leakage. In: IEEE S&P 2018 (2018)
36. Miers, I., Mohassel, P.: IO-DSSE: scaling dynamic searchable encryption to millions of indexes by improving locality. In: NDSS 2017 (2017)
37. Pappas, V., et al.: Blind seer: a scalable private DBMS. In: IEEE S&P 2014 (2014)
38. Patel, S., Persiano, G., Seo, J.Y., Yeo, K.: Efficient boolean search over encrypted data with reduced leakage. Cryptology ePrint Archive, Report 2021/1227 (2021)
39. Patel, S., Persiano, G., Yeo, K.: Leakage cell probe model: lower bounds for key-equality mitigation in encrypted multi-maps. In: Crypto 2020 (2020)

40. Patel, S., Persiano, G., Yeo, K., Yung, M.: Mitigating leakage in secure cloud-hosted data structures: volume-hiding for multi-maps via hashing. In: CCS 2019 (2019)
41. Porter, M.: The Porter stemming algorithm. https://tartarus.org/martin/PorterStemmer/
42. Song, D., Wagner, D., Perrig, A.: Practical techniques for searches on encrypted data. In: IEEE S&P 2000 (2000)
43. Stefanov, E., Papamanthou, C., Shi, E.: Practical dynamic searchable encryption with small leakage. In: NDSS 2014 (2014)
44. Zhang, Y., Katz, J., Papamanthou, C.: All your queries are belong to us: the power of file-injection attacks on searchable encryption. In: USENIX Security Symposium, pp. 707–720 (2016)

Revisiting Homomorphic Encryption Schemes for Finite Fields

Andrey Kim[1,2], Yuriy Polyakov[1,3](✉), and Vincent Zucca[4,5,6]

[1] New Jersey Institute of Technology, Newark, USA
[2] Samsung Advanced Institute of Technology, Suwon, Republic of Korea
andrey.kim@samsung.com
[3] Duality Technologies, Newark, USA
ypolyakov@dualitytech.com
[4] DALI, Université de Perpignan Via Domitia, Perpignan, France
vincent.zucca@univ-perp.fr
[5] LIRMM, Univ Montpellier, Montpellier, France
[6] imec-COSIC, KU Leuven, Leuven, Belgium

Abstract. The Brakerski-Gentry-Vaikuntanathan (BGV) and Brakerski/ Fan-Vercauteren (BFV) schemes are the two main homomorphic encryption (HE) schemes to perform exact computations over finite fields and integers. Although the schemes work with the same plaintext space, there are significant differences in their noise management, algorithms for the core homomorphic multiplication operation, message encoding, and practical usability. The main goal of our work is to revisit both schemes, focusing on closing the gap between the schemes by improving their noise growth, computational complexity of the core algorithms, and usability. The other goal of our work is to provide both theoretical and experimental performance comparison of BGV and BFV.

More precisely, we propose an improved variant of BFV where the encryption operation is modified to significantly reduce the noise growth, which makes the BFV noise growth somewhat better than for BGV (in contrast to prior results showing that BGV has smaller noise growth for larger plaintext moduli). We also modify the homomorphic multiplication procedure, which is the main bottleneck in BFV, to reduce its algorithmic complexity. Our work introduces several other novel optimizations, including lazy scaling in BFV homomorphic multiplication and an improved BFV decryption procedure in the Residue Number System (RNS) representation. We also develop a usable variant of BGV as a more efficient alternative to BFV for common practical scenarios.

We implement our improved variants of BFV and BGV in PALISADE and evaluate their experimental performance for several benchmark computations. The experimental results suggest that our BGV implementation is faster for intermediate and large plaintext moduli, which are often used in practical scenarios with ciphertext packing, while our BFV implementation is faster for small plaintext moduli.

The full version of the paper is available at https://eprint.iacr.org/2021/204.

M. Tibouchi and H. Wang (Eds.): ASIACRYPT 2021, LNCS 13092, pp. 608–639, 2021.
https://doi.org/10.1007/978-3-030-92078-4_21

1 Introduction

Homomorphic encryption (HE) is a powerful cryptographic primitive that enables performing computations over encrypted data without having access to the secret key. The HE research area has seen a lot of progress since the formulation of the first fully homomorphic encryption construction by Gentry in 2009 [17], and the schemes implemented in modern HE libraries are multiple orders of magnitude faster than the initial implementation of Gentry's scheme [18]. The most common HE schemes are typically grouped into three classes based on the data types they support computations on. The first class primarily works with Boolean circuits and decision diagrams, similar to the original Gentry scheme, and includes the FHEW and TFHE schemes [12,15]. The second class supports modular arithmetic over finite fields, which typically correspond to vectors of integers mod t, where t is a prime power commonly called as the plaintext modulus. The second class is also sometimes used for small-integer arithmetic. This class includes Brakerski-Gentry-Vaikuntantan (BGV) and Brakerski/Fan-Vercauteren (BFV) schemes [8,9,16]. The third, and most recent, class supports approximate computations over vectors of real and complex numbers, and is represented by the Cheon-Kim-Kim-Song (CKKS) scheme [11]. All these schemes are based on the hardness of the Ring Learning With Errors (RLWE) problem, where noise is added during encryption and key generation to achieve the hardness properties. The noise grows as encrypted computations are performed, and the main functional parameter in all these schemes, the ciphertext modulus Q, needs to be large enough to accommodate the noise growth, or a special bootstrapping procedure may be used to reset the noise and keep the value of Q relatively small.

Our work focuses on the HE schemes of the second class. Although the BGV and BFV schemes work with the same plaintext algebra, they use different strategies for encoding the message composed of integers in $\mathbb{Z}_t$ and controlling the noise. The BGV scheme encodes the message in the least significant digit (LSD) of integers in $\mathbb{Z}_Q$ and applies the modulus switching technique to keep the noise magnitude constant, i.e., it scales down Q by a factor that corresponds to the noise added after the previous modulus switching call. The BFV scheme encodes the message in the most significant digit (MSD) of integers in $\mathbb{Z}_Q$ and uses a special form of homomorphic multiplication, where ciphertext polynomials are multiplied without modular reduction and then scaled down by Q/t. In BFV, the value of Q is typically constant and the noise magnitude increases at a rate similar to how Q decreases in BGV. The difference in noise management strategies between BGV and BFV affects the noise growth and efficiency of the schemes. Costache and Smart performed a noise growth comparison, which suggested that BGV has better noise growth for larger t than BFV [13]. However, the authors did not examine the computational complexity difference, and it has not been clear up to this moment how the schemes compare in terms of practical performance, both from the perspective of computational complexity and actual experimental measurements.

The main goal of this paper is to present improved variants of BFV and BGV schemes, which also close the gap between the schemes. The other goal is to compare the theoretical complexity of their primitive operations, and experimental performance of BGV and BFV for several different scenarios using our software implementation in the PALISADE library [2].

Modified BFV Scheme. We propose two modifications for the BFV scheme. The first modification deals with encryption, and the second modification revises the homomorphic multiplication operation. The net effects of these modifications are smaller noise growth and faster homomorphic multiplication in BFV.

The encryption in BFV can be represented as $\boldsymbol{a} \cdot \boldsymbol{s} + \boldsymbol{e} + \Delta \boldsymbol{m}$ (for simplicity, we focus here on the secret-key formulation), where $\boldsymbol{a}$ is a uniformly random ring element in cyclotomic ring $\mathcal{R}_Q$, $\boldsymbol{s}$ and $\boldsymbol{e}$ are the secret key and Gaussian noise ring elements in $\mathcal{R}$, $\boldsymbol{m}$ is a message in $\mathcal{R}_t$, and $\Delta = \lfloor Q/t \rfloor$ is the scaling factor. Our analysis shows that the difference between Δ and Q/t, which is often described in terms of $r_t(Q) := Q - t\Delta$, brings about a significant error (proportional to $r_t(Q)$) that affects the first homomorphic multiplication and increases the noise growth in BFV as compared to BGV for larger t. If this error is removed, i.e., $r_t(Q) \approx 0$, the noise growth in BFV becomes the same, or actually somewhat better, as in BGV. In view of this, our first modification suggested for BFV is to replace the encryption operation in BFV with $\boldsymbol{a} \cdot \boldsymbol{s} + \boldsymbol{e} + \left\lceil \frac{Q}{t} \boldsymbol{m} \right\rfloor$, which is a more natural choice as compared to the one in the original BFV. This encryption function also significantly simplifies the noise analysis and estimates for BFV homomorphic multiplication. Note that this modification can be likewise applied to the original Brakerski LWE scheme [8].

The most expensive operation in BFV is homomorphic multiplication as it requires a multiplication of two ciphertexts $\mathbf{c}_1$ and $\mathbf{c}_2$ without modular reduction, followed by scaling the results of the tensor product by t/Q. Algorithmically, this requires extending both ciphertexts to modulus QP, where P is sufficiently larger than Q, performing a tensor product which involves expensive Number Theoretic Transforms (NTTs), scaling down the result by Q/t, and finally switching the scaling result from P to Q. We propose a more efficient procedure for homomorphic multiplication where the values of $P \approx Q$, which saves some expensive modulus extension operations and NTTs. The main idea is to apply modulus switching to one of the ciphertexts, e.g., $\mathbf{c}_2$, to change it from Q to P (denote it as $\mathbf{c}_2'$), and then do scaling by t/P after the tensor product. This removes the requirement for extending the scaling result from P to Q (it will already be in Q) at the expense of doing a smaller number of modulus extensions during the modulus switching of $\mathbf{c}_2$. The other benefit is that the tensor product of $\mathbf{c}_1$ and $\mathbf{c}_2'$ can be scaled by t/P directly in PQ, i.e., we have a tensor product mod PQ instead of a tensor product without modular reduction.

We also introduce a leveled version of BFV homomorphic multiplication, where ciphertexts modulo a larger modulus Q are internally scaled down to a smaller modulus Q_ℓ (or P_ℓ), the standard homomorphic multiplication operations are performed, and then the results are scaled back up to Q. The benefit of this approach is that the ciphertexts still look the same (modulo Q) outside the homomorphic multiplication operations, but we get BGV-like benefits of working with smaller moduli in multiplication. The combined effect of our improvements in homomorphic multiplication is the speed-up of up to 4x, as compared to a prior state-of-the-art BFV implementation, when dealing with multiplications at deeper levels of computation.

BFV Scheme Optimizations. We also introduce several algorithmic optimizations that equally apply to the classical BFV and our modified variant. The first optimization is for the scenarios where we need to add multiple BFV ciphertexts that were just obtained by BFV multiplication. The standard way is to perform many expensive BFV multiplications and then add up the result. However, we can delay the scaling by t/Q (or by t/P in our BFV variant) in each homomorphic multiplication until the sum is computed, and then just do one scaling at the end. This saves many expensive NTTs and modulus extension operations. We denote this optimization as *lazy scaling*. The lazy scaling can be combined with previously known lazy relinearization to push most of the expensive computations in a homomorphic multiplication, i.e., scaling and relinearization, to the end, after the aggregation is done.

Some of the other optimizations apply to Residue Number Systems (RNS) variants of BFV, where multi-precision integers in $\mathbb{Z}_Q$ are split into vectors of smaller integers using the Chinese Remainder Theorem (CRT) to perform operations efficiently using native (64-bit) integer types. The RNS variants are now predominately used in practice, and are implemented in the SEAL [29], PALISADE [2], and Lattigo [1] software libraries. There are two main RNS variants of BFV: the Bajard-Eynard-Hasan-Zucca (BEHZ) variant based on modular integer arithmetic and Montgomery reductions and the Halevi-Polyakov-Shoup (HPS) variant based on a combination of modular integer arithmetic and floating-point approximations [5,21].

A significant limitation of the HPS approach is that high-precision ("long double" or even quad-precision) floating-point arithmetic is required to support larger CRT moduli: long doubles are needed for CRT moduli from 47 to 58 bits, and quad-precision floats are needed for higher CRT moduli [21]. We introduce a general-purpose digit decomposition technique (inspired by digit decomposition in key switching) and apply it to the HPS decryption procedure to add support for arbitrary CRT moduli using only regular double-precision floating-point arithmetic, thus overcoming this limitation of the HPS variant. This digit decomposition technique can be applied to other mixed integer/floating-point RNS operations to reduce precision requirements for floating-point arithmetic.

We also apply the full RNS variant of hybrid key switching [24] recently proposed for the CKKS scheme to both BFV RNS variants, and demonstrate how some auxiliary CRT moduli needed for homomorphic multiplication can be reused for hybrid key switching. This key switching method has some benefits (smaller noise growth, better efficiency for deeper computations) over the residue decomposition key switching method previously used in both RNS variants of BFV.

BGV Scheme Optimizations and Usability Improvements. We use the Gentry-Halevi-Smart (GHS) variant of BGV as the basis for our BGV instantiation [20,23]. Although the original GHS variant performs some operations in RNS, it still uses multiprecision integer arithmetic for key switching and some scenarios of modulus switching. For instance, although the GHS paper originally introduced the hybrid key switching technique, the authors used multiprecision arithmetic for the digit decomposition step. We apply the full RNS version of hybrid key switching to our BGV instantiation and eliminate any multiprecision arithmetic from our BGV implementation, thus significantly improving its efficiency.

One of the challenges in the GHS variant is the need to perform dynamic noise estimation, which makes the BGV implementation less robust and usable as compared to the BFV variants where noise estimation is typically needed only at the parameter generation phase. We develop a more usable and robust variant of BGV that is essentially as simple to use as the current BFV implementations. This variant only needs to know the multiplicative depth and maximum number of additions per level for many common scenarios. The main advantage of this BGV variant is that it is significantly faster than our BFV implementations for certain practical scenarios, yet its usability matches that of BFV.

Implementation and Performance Comparison. We implement the improved variants of BFV and BGV in PALISADE, and provide their comparison for specific benchmark computations. To the best of our knowledge, this is the first publicly available implementation of both schemes in the same software library. We also perform theoretical comparison of the computational complexity for the operations that differ between BFV and BGV.

The comparison results can be summarized as follows:

- Our improved variant of BFV has somewhat better noise growth than BGV, in contrast to prior results for the original BFV scheme that showed better noise growth for BGV at larger plaintext moduli [13].
- Our best variant of BFV is faster than BGV for small plaintext moduli, while BGV is faster for intermediate and large plaintext moduli used in many practical scenarios.
- The speed-up in homomorphic multiplication of our best BFV variant compared to a prior state-of-the-art RNS implementation of BFV goes up to 4x for deeper computations.

Related work. Costache et al. further examine the difference between the noise growth in BFV and BGV [14] to improve the analysis presented in [13]. They explore an alternative heuristic noise analysis approach to obtain tighter noise bounds. We point out that this new analysis has some inacurracies, e.g., the effect of extra noise due to $r_t(Q)$ in BFV homomorphic multiplication is not accounted for. We show that this extra noise determines the higher noise growth in BFV for large plaintext moduli, and demonstrate how this noise is removed in our BFV variant. Moreover, we show that this analysis can be carried out independently of the chosen heuristic for noise analysis. The authors also do not consider the difference in the complexity of homomorphic encryption operations between BGV and BFV, which affects their conclusions. In view of the above, we primarily compare our results with the prior work [13].

The encoding of a message in the MSD of a ciphertext as $\lceil \frac{Q}{t}\boldsymbol{m}\rfloor$ was already used in the Key Encapsulation Mechanism (KEM) Kyber [7]. But in the case of Kyber, the plaintext modulus $t = 2$, i.e., the coefficients of the messages are either 0 or 1. Therefore, the messages can be recovered directly during decryption by checking whether the coefficients are closer to $\lceil Q/2\rfloor$ or 0, and the noise is not affected.

SEAL also independently added to v3.4.0 a modification of BFV encryption similar to what we describe in our work [29]. However, no underlying noise analysis was presented, and the prior paper related to SEAL [14] included noise analysis inaccuracies involving the rounding term $r_t(Q)$, suggesting that the full effect of this change was not well-understood.

Note that the FHEW and TFHE schemes can also support arithmetic over finite fields for small plaintext moduli (typically up to 4 bits) [28], and can be considered as an alternative to BGV and BFV for these scenarios. These schemes support fast bootstrapping (the latency is much lower than for BGV and BFV bootstrapping [22]), but their main limitation is the lack of support for CRT packing, which makes the BGV/BFV approach much more appealing when large arrays of numbers need to be computed on/bootstrapped because one ciphertext operation can perform thousands of integer operations at once.

Organization. The rest of the paper is organized as follows. In Sect. 2 we provide the necessary background on BGV and BFV. In Sects. 3 and 4, we present our improved variants of BFV and BGV, respectively. Section 5 includes the theoretical comparison of the schemes, and discussion of the experimental results. Section 6 provides the conclusions and outlines the ideas for future work.

2 Background

All logarithms are expressed in base 2 if not indicated otherwise. Let N be a power of two. We denote the $2N$-th cyclotomic ring $\mathcal{R} = \mathbb{Z}[X]/(X^N + 1)$ and $\mathcal{R}_Q := \mathcal{R}/Q\mathcal{R}$.[1] Ring elements are indicated in bold, e.g. $\boldsymbol{a}$. For an integer $Q > 1$, we identify the ring $\mathbb{Z}_Q$ with $(-Q/2, Q/2] \cap \mathbb{Z}$ as a representative interval and for $z \in \mathbb{Z}$, $[z]_Q \in \mathbb{Z}_Q$ denotes the centered remainder of z modulo Q, while $r_Q(z)$ denotes the classical Euclidean remainder in $[0, Q) \cap \mathbb{Z}$. For $x \in \mathbb{Q}$, $\lfloor x \rfloor$, $\lfloor x \rceil$ and $\lceil x \rceil$ denote the rounding to the lower, closest and higher integer, respectively. We extend these notations to elements of $\mathcal{R}$ by applying them coordinate-wise. For $\boldsymbol{a} = a_0 + a_1 \cdot X + \cdots + a_{N-1} \cdot X^{N-1} \in \mathcal{R}$, we denote the ℓ_∞ norm of $\boldsymbol{a}$ as $\|\boldsymbol{a}\|_\infty = \max_{0 \le i < N}\{|a_i|\}$. There exists a constant $\delta_{\mathcal{R}}$ such that $\|\boldsymbol{a} \cdot \boldsymbol{b}\|_\infty \le \delta_{\mathcal{R}} \|\boldsymbol{a}\|_\infty \|\boldsymbol{b}\|_\infty$ for any $(a, b) \in \mathcal{R}^2$. It is well-known that for $\mathcal{R} = \mathbb{Z}[X]/(X^N + 1)$, $\delta_{\mathcal{R}} = N$. However in practice this bound is only reached with exponentially low probability. As shown in [21], the bound $\delta_{\mathcal{R}} = 2\sqrt{N}$ is much closer to what we observe experimentally, and can be used to achieve

[1] More general cyclotomic rings are also supported, and all results of our work equally apply to these non-power-of-two rings; please see [23] for more details on general cyclotomic rings.

tighter noise bounds. Another approach consists in estimating the noise size using the canonical embedding norm [20], as currently done in HElib [23]. Nonetheless, in this work we estimate the noise size using the expansion factor $\delta_{\mathcal{R}}$ with the method of [21] as it is simpler and precise enough for our purpose.

We use $\boldsymbol{a} \leftarrow \chi$ to denote the sampling of $\boldsymbol{a} \in \mathcal{R}$ according to a distribution χ. $\chi_{\mathtt{key}}$ denotes the *uniform ternary* distribution, i.e., all the coefficients of $\boldsymbol{a} \leftarrow \chi_{\mathtt{key}}$ are selected uniformly and independently from $\{-1, 0, 1\}$. This distribution is commonly used for secret key generation as it is the most efficient option conforming to the HE standard [4]. $\chi_{\mathtt{err}}$ denotes a *discrete Gaussian* distribution with standard deviation $\sigma_{\mathtt{err}}$, i.e. all the coefficients of $\boldsymbol{a} \leftarrow \chi_{\mathtt{err}}$ are selected independently from a truncated discrete Gaussian distribution with standard deviation $\sigma_{\mathtt{err}}$. Truncated discrete Gaussian distributions are commonly used to generate error polynomials to meet the desired hardness requirement [4]. We assume that the polynomials sampled from $\chi_{\mathtt{key}}$ and $\chi_{\mathtt{err}}$ have their coefficients bounded by $B_{\mathtt{key}} = 1$ and $B_{\mathtt{err}} = 6\sigma_{\mathtt{err}}$, respectively. Although a Gaussian distribution is not bounded by nature, the probability for a Gaussian coefficient to be larger than $B_{\mathtt{err}} = 6\sigma_{\mathtt{err}}$, is less than 2^{-30}, therefore the two distributions are very close in practice. $\mathcal{U}_Q$ denotes the *uniform distribution* over $\mathcal{R}_Q$, where every coefficient of $\boldsymbol{a}$ is sampled uniformly and independently from $\mathbb{Z}_Q$.

2.1 Plaintext Space

We are interested in the BGV and BFV homomorphic encryption schemes which both share the same plaintext space $\mathcal{R}_t$ for some integer $t > 1$. Hence, the most natural way to represent plaintext messages of these schemes is to think of them as vectors of size N with their coefficients taken modulo t. However, $\mathcal{R}_t$ has many algebraic properties, in particular when $t = p^r$ is a prime power with p coprime to $2N$. In this case $\mathcal{R}_t$ is actually a $\mathbb{Z}_t$-algebra, which means that it contains a subring isomorphic to $\mathbb{Z}_t$. In this paper we focus on the case $r = 1$, where $t = p$ is a prime. The interested reader can nonetheless refer to [23] for further details regarding the general case. $\mathbb{Z}_t$-algebra supports efficent Single-Instruction Multiple-Data (SIMD) packing/batching. For more details on the packing, the reader is referred to [30].

2.2 Homomorphic Encryption Schemes for Finite Field Arithmetic

The two schemes studied in this work: BGV and BFV are actually two instantiations of the same idea, and share, therefore, many common features. First, according to the desired security level λ and the targeted application, one starts by selecting public parameters for the considered scheme: ring dimension $N = 2^d$, the plaintext modulus t, a ciphertext modulus Q and two probability distributions χ_{key} and χ_{err} on the ring $\mathcal{R}$. In both cases, the secret key will be an element $\boldsymbol{s} \leftarrow \chi_{\mathtt{key}}$. Note that BGV and BFV may be viewed as different modes of a unified scheme, where the ciphertexts may be switched from one mode/scheme to the other (see the full version for details).

Original BGV Scheme. In 2011, Brakerski et al. designed a leveled homomorphic scheme, namely capable of evaluating circuits of arbitrary size, but known beforehand [9]. The key tool of their construction is the *modulus switching* procedure which allows to switch a ciphertext $\mathtt{ct}$ encrypted under a modulus Q to a smaller modulus Q' in order to maintain the noise level "constant". As a consequence, one must select a chain of $L+1$ moduli $Q_0 \mid Q_1 \mid \ldots \mid Q_L = Q$ such that t and Q_L are coprime. The public key is formed as:

$$\mathsf{pk} = \left([\boldsymbol{a} \cdot \boldsymbol{s} + t\boldsymbol{e}]_{Q_L}, -\boldsymbol{a}\right) \in \mathcal{R}^2_{Q_L},$$

which is equivalent to the Ring-LWE sample $([\boldsymbol{a}/t \cdot \boldsymbol{s} + \boldsymbol{e}]_{Q_L}, [-\boldsymbol{a}/t]_{Q_L})$ (since t and Q_L are coprime) associated to $\boldsymbol{s}$ and Q_L with $\boldsymbol{a} \leftarrow \mathcal{U}_{Q_L}$ and $\boldsymbol{e} \leftarrow \chi_{\mathtt{err}}$.

A ciphertext $\mathtt{ct} = (\boldsymbol{c}_0, \boldsymbol{c}_1) \in \mathcal{R}^2_Q$ corresponds to a degree 1 polynomial whose coefficients lie in $\mathcal{R}_Q$. The message $\boldsymbol{m} \in \mathcal{R}_t$ is hidden in the LSD of the first coefficient $\boldsymbol{c}_0$ of the ciphertext as follows:

$$\mathtt{ct} = \left([[\boldsymbol{m}]_t + \boldsymbol{u} \cdot \mathbf{pk}_0 + t\boldsymbol{e}_0]_{Q_L}, [\boldsymbol{u} \cdot \mathbf{pk}_1 + t\boldsymbol{e}_1]_{Q_L}\right)$$

with $\boldsymbol{u} \leftarrow \chi_{\mathtt{key}}$ and $\boldsymbol{e}_0, \boldsymbol{e}_1 \leftarrow \chi_{\mathtt{err}}$. The noise contained in a ciphertext $\mathtt{ct} = (\boldsymbol{c}_0, \boldsymbol{c}_1)$ appears explicitly once the ciphertext is evaluated on the secret key $\boldsymbol{s}$.

$$\boldsymbol{c}_0 + \boldsymbol{c}_1 \cdot \boldsymbol{s} = [\boldsymbol{m}]_t + t(\boldsymbol{u} \cdot \boldsymbol{e} + \boldsymbol{e}_1 \cdot \boldsymbol{s} + \boldsymbol{e}_0) = [\boldsymbol{m}]_t + t\boldsymbol{v}_{\mathtt{fresh}} \bmod Q_L, \quad (1)$$

where the term $\boldsymbol{v}_{\mathtt{fresh}} = \boldsymbol{u} \cdot \boldsymbol{e} + \boldsymbol{e}_1 \cdot \boldsymbol{s} + \boldsymbol{e}_0$ is the noise inherent to a "freshly" encrypted ciphertext. Since $Q_0 \mid Q_1 \mid \ldots \mid Q_L$, encryptions can be performed equivalently at any level i, i.e., modulo Q_i.

To decrypt a ciphertext $\mathtt{ct} = (\boldsymbol{c}_0, \boldsymbol{c}_1) \in \mathcal{R}^2_{Q_i}$ with $i \in [0, L]$, one computes $\boldsymbol{m}' = [\boldsymbol{c}_0 + \boldsymbol{c}_1 \cdot \boldsymbol{s}]_{Q_i}$ and then outputs $[\boldsymbol{m}']_t$. To ensure correctness of the decryption, the noise $\boldsymbol{v}$ must be "small enough" such that $\boldsymbol{m}' = [\boldsymbol{m}]_t + t\boldsymbol{v}$ does not wrap-around modulo Q_i. As a consequence, decryption remains correct as long as:

$$\|\boldsymbol{v}\|_\infty < \frac{Q_0}{2t} - \frac{1}{2}.$$

One can add two ciphertexts $\mathtt{ct}$ and $\mathtt{ct}'$ encrypting $\boldsymbol{m}$ and $\boldsymbol{m}'$, respectively, at the same level i to yield:

$$\boldsymbol{c}_0 + \boldsymbol{c}_0' + (\boldsymbol{c}_1 + \boldsymbol{c}_1') \cdot \boldsymbol{s} = [\boldsymbol{m} + \boldsymbol{m}']_t + t(\boldsymbol{v} + \boldsymbol{v}' + \boldsymbol{u}) \bmod Q_i,$$

with $\|\boldsymbol{u}\|_\infty \leq 1$. This means that

$$\mathtt{ct}_{\mathsf{add}} = ([\boldsymbol{c}_0 + \boldsymbol{c}_0']_{Q_i}, [\boldsymbol{c}_1 + \boldsymbol{c}_1']_{Q_i})$$

is a level-i encryption of $[\boldsymbol{m} + \boldsymbol{m}']_t$ and its noise is almost the sum of the noises of $\mathtt{ct}$ and $\mathtt{ct}'$:

$$\|\boldsymbol{v}_{\mathsf{add}}\|_\infty = \|\boldsymbol{v} + \boldsymbol{v}' + \boldsymbol{u}\|_\infty \leq \|\boldsymbol{v}\|_\infty + \|\boldsymbol{v}'\|_\infty + 1.$$

Similarly to addition, we can multiply two level-i ciphertexts $\mathtt{ct}$ and $\mathtt{ct}'$ to obtain the following congruence modulo Q_i:

$$(\boldsymbol{c}_0 + \boldsymbol{c}_1 \cdot \boldsymbol{s}) \cdot (\boldsymbol{c}_0' + \boldsymbol{c}_1' \cdot \boldsymbol{s}) = [\boldsymbol{m} \cdot \boldsymbol{m}']_t + t([\boldsymbol{m}]_t \cdot \boldsymbol{v}' + \boldsymbol{v} \cdot [\boldsymbol{m}']_t + t\boldsymbol{v} \cdot \boldsymbol{v}' + \boldsymbol{r}_m)$$

with $[\boldsymbol{m}]_t \cdot [\boldsymbol{m}']_t = [\boldsymbol{m} \cdot \boldsymbol{m}']_t + t\boldsymbol{r}_m$ and $\|\boldsymbol{r}_m\|_\infty \leq \delta_{\mathcal{R}} t/2$. This means that

$$\mathtt{ct}_{\mathtt{mult}} = ([\boldsymbol{c}_0 \cdot \boldsymbol{c}_0']_{Q_i}, [\boldsymbol{c}_0 \cdot \boldsymbol{c}_1' + \boldsymbol{c}_1 \cdot \boldsymbol{c}_0']_{Q_i}, [\boldsymbol{c}_1 \cdot \boldsymbol{c}_1']_{Q_i}) \in \mathcal{R}_{Q_i}^3$$

is a degree-2 ciphertext encrypting $[\boldsymbol{m} \cdot \boldsymbol{m}']_t$ and its noise is bounded by

$$\begin{aligned} \|\boldsymbol{v}_{\mathtt{mult}}\|_\infty &= \|[\boldsymbol{m}]_t \cdot \boldsymbol{v}' + \boldsymbol{v} \cdot [\boldsymbol{m}']_t + t\boldsymbol{v} \cdot \boldsymbol{v}' + \boldsymbol{r}_m\|_\infty \\ &\leq \frac{\delta_{\mathcal{R}} t}{2} \left(2 \|\boldsymbol{v}\|_\infty \|\boldsymbol{v}'\|_\infty + \|\boldsymbol{v}\|_\infty + \|\boldsymbol{v}'\|_\infty + 1\right). \end{aligned}$$

Remark 1. The reader can notice that the degree, and thus the size, of a ciphertext increases after each multiplication, increasing therefore the future communication and computational costs. Since this is something one wants to avoid in practice, the degree-2 ciphertexts are "relinearized" after a homomorphic multiplication to degree-1 ciphertexts using a key-switching procedure (see the full version).

The main issue with homomorphic multiplication is its quadratic noise growth, which implies that by choosing $Q_L \approx \|\boldsymbol{v}_{\mathtt{fresh}}\|_\infty^L$ one could only perform $\log_2 L$ consecutive multiplications. The idea of modulus switching is to reduce the size of the noise after each multiplication to keep it constant and prevent the quadratic blow-up. This is achieved by scaling the ciphertext $\mathtt{ct}$ by Q_i/Q_j for $i < j$, which scales down the noise by roughly the same factor. More precisely, let $\mathtt{ct} = (\boldsymbol{c}_0, \boldsymbol{c}_1)$ be a level $j \in (0, L] \cap \mathbb{Z}$ encryption of a message $\boldsymbol{m}$ with noise $\boldsymbol{v}$ and let i be an integer smaller than j, then set:

$$\boldsymbol{\delta} = \left(t[-\boldsymbol{c}_0/t]_{Q_j/Q_i}, t[-\boldsymbol{c}_1/t]_{Q_j/Q_i}\right) \in \mathcal{R}^2.$$

Then one can compute

$$\mathtt{ct}' = \frac{Q_i}{Q_j} \cdot (\boldsymbol{c}_0 + \boldsymbol{\delta}_0, \boldsymbol{c}_1 + \boldsymbol{\delta}_1) \bmod Q_i.$$

Brakerski et al. showed that if $\mathtt{ct} = (\boldsymbol{c}_0, \boldsymbol{c}_1)$ is such that

$$\left\|[\boldsymbol{c}_0 + \boldsymbol{c}_1 \cdot \boldsymbol{s}]_{Q_j}\right\|_\infty < \frac{Q_j}{2} - \frac{tQ_j}{2Q_i}(1 + \delta_{\mathcal{R}} B_{\mathtt{key}}),$$

then $\mathtt{ct}'$ is an encryption of $[Q_i/Q_j \boldsymbol{m}]_t$ whose noise $\boldsymbol{v}'$ is bounded by

$$\|\boldsymbol{v}'\|_\infty \leq \frac{Q_i}{Q_j} \|\boldsymbol{v}\|_\infty + \|\boldsymbol{v}_{\mathtt{ms}}\|_\infty$$

with $\|\boldsymbol{v}_{\mathtt{ms}}\|_\infty \leq (1 + \delta_{\mathcal{R}} B_{\mathtt{key}})/2$. Therefore by choosing the encryption parameters such that performing modulus switching after a homomorphic multiplication (plus a key-switching) brings the noise back to its initial level, one can perform L consecutive multiplications instead of approximately $\log_2 L$ initially.

Gentry-Halevi-Smart (GHS) Variant of BGV. Since the modulus-switching procedure outputs an encryption of the message scaled by a factor $[Q_i/Q_j]_t$, Brakerski et al. proposed to choose the moduli $Q_i = 1 \bmod t$. This approach, although very convenient in theory, becomes challenging in practice when using a large t since it reduces significantly the range of possible moduli for the Q_i. As a consequence, Gentry, Halevi, and Smart proposed to keep track of the scaling factor for each ciphertext instead [20]. In particular, they suggested to encrypt $[Q_L \boldsymbol{m}]_t$ instead of $[\boldsymbol{m}]_t$ in Eq. (1), which provides natural downscaling to $[Q_i \boldsymbol{m}]_t$ as modulus switching operations are applied. However in this case, one has to pay attention when adding two ciphertexts with different scaling factors. Nonetheless this can be achieved without impacting significantly the noise by following the methodology of [25].

Gentry et al. also proposed several optimizations related to noise management. The first one is to perform modulus switching after encryption and before first multiplication, in order to reduce the noise from $\|\boldsymbol{v}_{\texttt{fresh}}\|_\infty$ to $\|\boldsymbol{v}_{\texttt{ms}}\|_\infty$. The second one is to perform modulus switching just before the next multiplication instead of just after a multiplication. This permits to reduce the noise accumulated due to other operations, such as additions or key switching, that are performed between two subsequent multiplications.

Original BFV Scheme. In [8], Brakerski proposed a *scale-invariant* construction that achieves asymptotically the same noise growth as BGV, but does not *explicitly* call the modulus-switching procedure, embedding it internally in the homomorphic multiplication. Fan and Vercauteren then ported Brakerski's construction to the Ring-LWE setting [16], and the scheme is now commonly referred to as BFV. The BFV scheme uses a public key

$$\mathsf{pk} = \left([\boldsymbol{a} \cdot \boldsymbol{s} + \boldsymbol{e}]_Q, -\boldsymbol{a}\right) \in \mathcal{R}_Q^2,$$

which corresponds exactly to a Ring-LWE sample associated to $\boldsymbol{s}$ and Q with $\boldsymbol{a} \leftarrow \mathcal{U}_Q$ and $\boldsymbol{e} \leftarrow \chi_{\texttt{err}}$. The main difference between BGV and BFV is that BFV ciphertexts encode messages in their MSD instead of LSD:

$$\texttt{ct} = \left([\Delta[\boldsymbol{m}]_t + \boldsymbol{u} \cdot \mathbf{pk}_0 + \boldsymbol{e}_0]_Q, [\boldsymbol{u} \cdot \mathbf{pk}_1 + \boldsymbol{e}_1]_Q\right)$$

with $\Delta = \lfloor Q/t \rfloor$, $\boldsymbol{u} \leftarrow \chi_{\texttt{key}}$ and $\boldsymbol{e}_0, \boldsymbol{e}_1 \leftarrow \chi_{\texttt{err}}$. Similarly to BGV, the noise contained in a ciphertext $\texttt{ct} = (\boldsymbol{c}_0, \boldsymbol{c}_1)$ appears explicitly once the ciphertext is evaluated on the secret key $\boldsymbol{s}$:

$$\boldsymbol{c}_0 + \boldsymbol{c}_1 \cdot \boldsymbol{s} = \Delta[\boldsymbol{m}]_t + \boldsymbol{u} \cdot \boldsymbol{e} + \boldsymbol{e}_1 \cdot \boldsymbol{s} + \boldsymbol{e}_0 = \Delta[\boldsymbol{m}]_t + \boldsymbol{v}_{\texttt{fresh}} \bmod Q,$$

where the "fresh" noise $\boldsymbol{v}_{\texttt{fresh}} = \boldsymbol{u} \cdot \boldsymbol{e} + \boldsymbol{e}_1 \cdot \boldsymbol{s} + \boldsymbol{e}_0$ is the same as for BGV.

To decrypt the ciphertext ct, one needs to scale and round $\texttt{ct}(\boldsymbol{s})$ by t/Q to remove the factor Δ. Hence the decryption procedure requires computing

$$\boldsymbol{m}' = \left\lfloor \frac{t}{Q} [\boldsymbol{c}_0 + \boldsymbol{c}_1 \cdot \boldsymbol{s}]_Q \right\rceil,$$

and the decryption will be correct as long as:

$$\|\boldsymbol{v}\|_\infty < \frac{Q}{2t} - \frac{r_t(Q)}{2}. \tag{2}$$

Note that the term $r_t(Q)/2$ is the error inherited from the difference between Δ^{-1} and t/Q: $\Delta t/Q = 1 - r_t(Q)/Q$. Addition of two ciphertexts $\mathtt{ct}$ and $\mathtt{ct}'$ is done like in BGV, but the noise growth is slightly different since the carry of the addition of the two messages is scaled by Δ:

$$\boldsymbol{c}_0 + \boldsymbol{c}_0' + (\boldsymbol{c}_1 + \boldsymbol{c}_1') \cdot \boldsymbol{s} = \Delta[\boldsymbol{m} + \boldsymbol{m}']_t + \boldsymbol{v} + \boldsymbol{v}' - r_t(Q)\boldsymbol{u} \bmod Q,$$

with $\|\boldsymbol{u}\|_\infty \leq 1$. This implies that

$$\mathtt{ct}_{\mathtt{add}} = ([\boldsymbol{c}_0 + \boldsymbol{c}_0']_Q, [\boldsymbol{c}_1 + \boldsymbol{c}_1']_Q)$$

is an encryption of $[\boldsymbol{m} + \boldsymbol{m}']_t$, and its noise is bounded by

$$\|\boldsymbol{v}_{\mathtt{add}}\|_\infty = \|\boldsymbol{v} + \boldsymbol{v}' + r_t(Q)\boldsymbol{u}\|_\infty \leq \|\boldsymbol{v}\|_\infty + \|\boldsymbol{v}'\|_\infty + r_t(Q). \tag{3}$$

The BFV multiplication of two ciphertexts $\mathtt{ct}$ and $\mathtt{ct}'$ is done differently, as compared to BGV, since once the product is computed, it gets scaled by Δ^2, which has two important consequences. First, the product of $\mathtt{ct}$ and $\mathtt{ct}'$ cannot be reduced modulo Q, therefore it must be done in $\mathcal{R}$, i.e., without any modular reduction. Second, the product must be scaled down by $t/Q \approx \Delta^{-1}$ to remove the extra Δ factor and reduce the noise similarly to modulus switching in BGV. We describe the two steps of the homomorphic multiplication separately. The first part, called the *tensoring*, consists in computing the product of two ciphertexts in $\mathcal{R}$:

$$\mathtt{ct}_{\mathtt{tensor}} = (\boldsymbol{c}_0 \cdot \boldsymbol{c}_0', \boldsymbol{c}_0 \cdot \boldsymbol{c}_1' + \boldsymbol{c}_1 \cdot \boldsymbol{c}_0', \boldsymbol{c}_1 \cdot \boldsymbol{c}_1') \in \mathcal{R}^3.$$

When evaluating $\mathtt{ct}_{\mathtt{tensor}}$ on the secret key, one obtains:

$$\begin{aligned}(\boldsymbol{c}_0 + \boldsymbol{c}_1 \cdot \boldsymbol{s}) \cdot (\boldsymbol{c}_0' + \boldsymbol{c}_1' \cdot \boldsymbol{s}) &= (\Delta[\boldsymbol{m}]_t + \boldsymbol{v} + Q\boldsymbol{k}) \cdot (\Delta[\boldsymbol{m}']_t + \boldsymbol{v}' + Q\boldsymbol{k}') \\ &= \frac{Q}{t}\Delta\left[\boldsymbol{m} \cdot \boldsymbol{m}'\right]_t + \frac{Q}{t}\boldsymbol{v}_{\mathtt{tensor}} + \frac{Q^2}{t}\boldsymbol{k}_{\mathtt{tensor}},\end{aligned}$$

where

$$\begin{aligned}\boldsymbol{v}_{\mathtt{tensor}} = &\ \frac{t\boldsymbol{v} \cdot \boldsymbol{v}'}{Q} + \frac{t\Delta}{Q}\left([\boldsymbol{m}]_t \cdot \boldsymbol{v}' + [\boldsymbol{m}']_t \cdot \boldsymbol{v}\right) + t(\boldsymbol{v} \cdot \boldsymbol{k}' + \boldsymbol{v}' \cdot \boldsymbol{k}) \\ &- r_t(Q)\left([\boldsymbol{m}]_t \cdot \boldsymbol{k}' + [\boldsymbol{m}']_t \cdot \boldsymbol{k} + \boldsymbol{r}_m + \frac{\Delta}{Q}[\boldsymbol{m}]_t \cdot [\boldsymbol{m}']_t\right),\end{aligned}$$

$$\boldsymbol{k}_{\mathtt{tensor}} = [\boldsymbol{m}]_t \cdot \boldsymbol{k}' + [\boldsymbol{m}']_t \cdot \boldsymbol{k} + t\boldsymbol{k} \cdot \boldsymbol{k}' + \boldsymbol{r}_m$$

with $\|\boldsymbol{r}_m\|_\infty \leq \delta_{\mathcal{R}} t/2$ like for BGV. Also note that $\boldsymbol{k} = (\boldsymbol{c}_0 + \boldsymbol{c}_1 \cdot \boldsymbol{s} - \Delta[\boldsymbol{m}]_t - \boldsymbol{v})/Q$ and $\boldsymbol{k}' = (\boldsymbol{c}_0' + \boldsymbol{c}_1' \cdot \boldsymbol{s} - \Delta[\boldsymbol{m}']_t - \boldsymbol{v}')/Q$ have their norm bounded by $(\delta_{\mathcal{R}} B_{\mathtt{key}} + 3)/2$.

The scaling operation is done in $\mathcal{R}_Q$ and outputs a result modulo Q:

$$\mathtt{ct}_{\mathtt{scale}} = \left[\left\lceil \frac{t}{Q}\mathtt{ct}_{\mathtt{tensor}} \right\rfloor\right]_Q \in \mathcal{R}_Q^3.$$

The scaling leads to

$$\frac{t}{Q}\left(\boldsymbol{c}_{\mathtt{tensor}_0} + \boldsymbol{c}_{\mathtt{tensor}_1} \cdot \boldsymbol{s} + \boldsymbol{c}_{\mathtt{tensor}_2} \cdot \boldsymbol{s}^2\right) = \Delta\left[\boldsymbol{m} \cdot \boldsymbol{m}'\right] + \boldsymbol{v}_{\mathtt{tensor}} + Q\boldsymbol{k}_{\mathtt{tensor}}.$$

The rounding of scaled terms introduces an additional error $\boldsymbol{v}_r$ such that

$$\mathtt{ct}_{\mathtt{scale}_0} + \mathtt{ct}_{\mathtt{scale}_1} \cdot \boldsymbol{s} + \mathtt{ct}_{\mathtt{scale}_2} \cdot \boldsymbol{s}^2 = \Delta\left[\boldsymbol{m} \cdot \boldsymbol{m}'\right] + \boldsymbol{v}_{\mathtt{tensor}} + \boldsymbol{v}_{\mathtt{r}} \bmod Q,$$

with $\|\boldsymbol{v}_r\|_\infty \leq \ (1 + \delta_{\mathcal{R}} B_{\mathtt{key}} + \delta_{\mathcal{R}}^2 B_{\mathtt{key}}^2)/2$. Hence the total multiplication noise $\boldsymbol{v}_{\mathtt{mult}} = \boldsymbol{v}_{\mathtt{tensor}} + \boldsymbol{v}_{\mathtt{r}}$ is bounded by

$$\begin{aligned}\|\boldsymbol{v}_{\mathtt{mult}}\|_\infty \leq \frac{\delta_{\mathcal{R}} t}{2}\Bigg(&\frac{2\|\boldsymbol{v}\|_\infty \|\boldsymbol{v}'\|_\infty}{Q} + (4 + \delta_{\mathcal{R}} B_{\mathtt{key}})\left(\|\boldsymbol{v}\|_\infty + \|\boldsymbol{v}'\|_\infty\right) \\ &+ r_t(Q)\left(\delta_{\mathcal{R}} B_{\mathtt{key}} + 5\right)\Bigg) + \frac{1 + \delta_{\mathcal{R}} B_{\mathtt{key}} + \delta_{\mathcal{R}}^2 B_{\mathtt{key}}^2}{2},\end{aligned} \tag{4}$$

For the same reasons as for BGV, one needs to perform a key-switching operation to relinearize the resulting degree-2 ciphertext. The key-switching procedure is the same for both schemes, and we refer to the full version for further details.

2.3 RNS Representation

The Chinese Remainder Theorem (CRT) permits decomposing multi-precision integers in $\mathbb{Z}_Q$ into vectors of smaller integers to perform operations efficiently using native (64-bit) integer data types. The integer CRT representation is also often referred to as the Residue-Number-System (RNS) representation. As a consequence, the ciphertext modulus is usually chosen as a product of "small", i.e., fitting in a machine word, co-prime moduli so that elements of $\mathcal{R}_Q$ are represented with their residues modulo the different q_i's. For BGV, we choose $Q = q_0 \cdots q_L$ and we denote $Q_i = q_0 \cdots q_i$ for $0 \leq i \leq L$, where each $q_i = 1 \bmod 2N$, to use the efficient NTT algorithm for the multiplication of elements in $\mathcal{R}_Q$. For BFV, we choose $Q = q_1 \cdots q_k$, with $q_i = 1 \bmod 2N$ for $1 \leq i \leq k$ and similarly to BGV we denote $Q_i = q_1 \cdots q_i$ for $1 \leq i \leq k$. Note that we have chosen different notations on purpose since in the original BGV the size of the moduli is directly related to the noise reduction we want to achieve by modulus switching, and is therefore dependent on the circuit one wants to evaluate. However, this constraint can be removed by considering a granular approach with dynamic noise estimation, as implemented in HElib [23] (see the discussion in Sect. 4 for more details on dynamic vs static noise estimation in BGV). On the other hand, in BFV the size of the moduli is independent of the circuit and, hence, the moduli are usually chosen as large as possible within the limit of a machine word.

When performing computations in RNS, and more particularly when implementing BGV and BFV, it is sometimes needed to switch the RNS basis, i.e., convert $\boldsymbol{a} \in \mathcal{R}_Q$ from its residues modulo $Q = q_1 \cdots q_k$ to $[\boldsymbol{a}]_Q$ modulo P for some $P = p_1 \cdots p_{k'}$. This can be achieved using a *basis extension* formulated as

$$\texttt{FastBaseExtension}(\boldsymbol{a}, Q, P) = \sum_{i=1}^{k} \left[\boldsymbol{a} \left(\frac{Q}{q_i} \right)^{-1} \right]_{q_i} \frac{Q}{q_i} \bmod p_j. \tag{5}$$

Note that the basis extension does not yield $[\boldsymbol{a}]_Q \bmod P$ but rather $[\boldsymbol{a}]_Q + \boldsymbol{u}Q \bmod P$ with $\|\boldsymbol{u}\|_\infty < k/2$. When the result of this extension is divided by Q, as in many procedures of BGV and BFV, the error caused by this Q-overflow $\boldsymbol{u}$ can be neglected most of the times. However in certain cases, as in the BFV decryption procedure, this overflow cannot be tolerated and needs to be removed/corrected. This can be achieved either using integer instructions with the so-called γ*-correction* technique of [5], or using floating-point instructions to retrieve $\boldsymbol{u}$ as in [21] since

$$\boldsymbol{u} = \left\lfloor \sum_{i=1}^{k} \left[\boldsymbol{a} \left(\frac{Q}{q_i} \right)^{-1} \right]_{q_i} \frac{1}{q_i} \right\rceil. \tag{6}$$

The same problem occurs during BFV homomorphic multiplication, and if it is not handled using either of the techniques of [5] or [21], the impact of $\boldsymbol{u}$ on the noise growth will be significant [6].

2.4 Hybrid Key Switching in RNS

Key switching transforms a ciphertext $\texttt{ct} = (\boldsymbol{c}_0, \boldsymbol{c}_1) \in \mathcal{R}_Q^2$, which can be decrypted with $\boldsymbol{s}_A$, into a ciphertext $\texttt{ct}' = (\boldsymbol{c}_0', \boldsymbol{c}_1') \in \mathcal{R}_Q^2$ encrypting the same message as ct, but decryptable with another secret key $\boldsymbol{s}_B$. This procedure is needed to compute automorphisms (rotations) of the ciphertexts [19], or to relinearize ciphertexts after a homomorphic multiplication. Note that this procedure adds a noise $\boldsymbol{v}_{\texttt{ks}}$ to the ciphertexts.

Several ways of performing the key-switching procedure have been found over the years. The first one was formulated by Brakerski and Vaikuntanathan (BV) in [10] and extended to RNS in [5]. This technique is based on digit decomposition of one ring element in the ciphertext. Unfortunately the BV key switching requires a quadratic number of NTTs to be computed, and hence becomes the main bottleneck of the scheme (asymptotically, and often in practice), and causes a relatively large noise growth. In [20], Gentry, Halevi, and Smart proposed another alternative for key switching. Their method, which we refer to as the GHS key switching, has a smaller noise growth than BV, and is also more efficient (asymptotically, and in many practical cases) since it only requires a linear number of NTTs. The drawback of this method is that one either needs to double the dimension N or reduce the size of Q by a factor of 2 for security reasons. Gentry, Halevi, and Smart also presented a hybrid key switching technique, which combines BV digit decomposition and larger modulus from GHS to provide the best tradeoff between the two techniques. The RNS versions of hybrid key switching were later derived for the CKKS scheme in [26] (for one small special prime) and in [24] for the more general case. The hybrid key switching technique [24] is the most efficient one in practice, both in terms of performance and noise growth, as our detailed comparison of the BV, GHS, and Hybrid key switching in the full version shows. Hence we use the hybrid key switching in our implementation.

3 Improved BFV Scheme

One can notice from Eqs. (2), (3) and (4) that the noise of BFV is impacted by the $r_t(Q)$ factor which does not appear in BGV. This factor causes faster noise growth for BFV when using larger plaintext moduli, as compared to BGV. In this section we show that this problem is not inherent to the MSD encoding of BFV, but rather comes from the choice for its instantiation in [16] and prior LWE-based Brakerski scheme [8]. We show that by instantiating the scheme in a more natural way, we can get rid of this $r_t(Q)$ term. We also present a modified homomorphic multiplication procedure that significantly improves the complexity of BFV homomorphic multiplication, as compared to all prior variants of BFV.

In this section, $\mathtt{ct} = (\boldsymbol{c}_0, \boldsymbol{c}_1)$ and $\mathtt{ct}' = (\boldsymbol{c}_0', \boldsymbol{c}_1')$ denote two BFV ciphertexts encrypting, respectively, the messages $[\boldsymbol{m}]_t$ and $[\boldsymbol{m}']_t$ with noise $\boldsymbol{v}$ and $\boldsymbol{v}'$.

3.1 Noise Reduction

To fully understand the problem with faster noise growth in BFV for larger plaintext moduli, let us examine more carefully the noise bound after a multiplication in BFV (Eq. (4)). This bound can be simplified by analyzing only the dominant terms, which determine the noise magnitude. More precisely, if we assume that the two ciphertexts have their noise bounded by V, and $B_{\mathtt{key}} = 1$, the size of the noise of their multiplication can be reasonably approximated by

$$\delta_{\mathcal{R}} t\left((5+\delta_{\mathcal{R}})V + \frac{r_t(Q)}{2}(\delta_{\mathcal{R}}+5)\right) + \frac{\delta_{\mathcal{R}}^2}{2} \approx \delta_{\mathcal{R}}^2 t\left(V + \frac{r_t(Q)}{2}\right). \quad (7)$$

Since the noise grows significantly with homomorphic multiplications, V becomes larger than $r_t(Q)/2 < t$ after we perform the first multiplication. However, this is not necessarily true for the first multiplication itself since, like in BGV, the noise of fresh ciphertexts in BFV is bounded by $B_{\mathtt{err}}(2\delta_{\mathcal{R}} B_{\mathtt{key}} + 1) \approx 2\delta_{\mathcal{R}} B_{\mathtt{err}}$. The homomorphic encryption standard [4] recommends using an error distribution with $\sigma_{\mathtt{err}} = 3.2$. Therefore, the noise of a fresh ciphertext can be estimated as $V_{\mathtt{init}} = 2 \times 6 \times 3.2 \times 2\sqrt{N} < 77\sqrt{N}$. Since in practice the dimension N typically does not exceed 2^{16}, a fresh ciphertext always has its noise size not higher than 14 bits, while $r_t(Q)$ can be as large as t. As a consequence, when $r_t(Q)$ is larger than 2^{15}, it becomes responsible for the larger noise growth after the first multiplication in BFV. For instance, if $t = 2^{32}$ and $r_t(Q) \approx t/2 \approx 2^{31}$, the noise after the first multiplication will be at least 16 bits larger than in the case when $r_t(Q) < V_{\texttt{init}}$. Note that this difference will not lead to a larger noise growth on the next multiplications since, as shown in Eq. (7), the noise growth after a multiplication is linear in V. However, this difference of 16+ bits will be carried through until the end of the computation. In the case of $t = 2^{60}$, this difference would become at least 44 bits.

The easiest way to circumvent this problem would be to choose the moduli q_i, as in the original BGV, i.e., such that $q_i = 1 \bmod t$, which would lead to $r_t(Q) = 1$. However, for the same reasons as in BGV, this restriction would make the finding of the moduli challenging for large t. Although it is possible to relax this condition by choosing, for instance, $r_t(Q) < \sqrt{N}$, i.e., finding $r_t(Q)$ through trial and error, we believe this would be a patch rather than a real solution. We show next that there is a more natural way to fix this problem.

Indeed, the $r_t(Q)$ term comes from the difference between Δ^{-1} and t/Q since when computing $\Delta t/Q$ (during decryption and homomorphic multiplication), one obtains $1 - r_t(Q)/Q$. Therefore, to solve this issue we propose to modify the original BFV encryption algorithm by encoding $[\boldsymbol{m}]_t$ in the ciphertext in a more natural way as $\lfloor Q[\boldsymbol{m}]_t/t \rceil$ instead of $\Delta[\boldsymbol{m}]_t$. The first benefit is seen in the decryption bound since now

$$\left\lfloor \frac{t}{Q}[\boldsymbol{c}_0 + \boldsymbol{c}_1 \cdot \boldsymbol{s}]_Q \right\rceil = \left\lfloor \frac{t}{Q}\left(\frac{Q}{t}[\boldsymbol{m}]_t + \boldsymbol{v} + \boldsymbol{\varepsilon} + \boldsymbol{k}Q\right) \right\rceil = [\boldsymbol{m}]_t + \left\lfloor \frac{t}{Q}(\boldsymbol{v} + \boldsymbol{\varepsilon}) \right\rceil + t\boldsymbol{k}$$
$$= [\boldsymbol{m}]_t + \left\lfloor \frac{t}{Q}(\boldsymbol{v} + \boldsymbol{\varepsilon}) \right\rceil \bmod t,$$

where $\boldsymbol{k} \in \mathcal{R}$ and $\boldsymbol{\varepsilon}$ is the rounding error coming from $\lfloor Q[\boldsymbol{m}]_t/t \rceil = Q[\boldsymbol{m}]_t/t + \boldsymbol{\varepsilon}$, such that $\|\boldsymbol{\varepsilon}\|_\infty \leq 1/2$. Therefore the decryption will be correct as long as:

$$\frac{t}{Q}\|\boldsymbol{v} + \boldsymbol{\varepsilon}\|_\infty < \frac{1}{2},$$

which is satisfied if

$$\|\boldsymbol{v}\|_\infty < \frac{Q}{2t} - \frac{1}{2}. \tag{8}$$

Remark 2. Note that one can compute $\lfloor Q[\boldsymbol{m}]_t/t \rceil \bmod Q$ directly in RNS as long as t and Q are coprime since

$$\left\lfloor \frac{Q[\boldsymbol{m}]_t}{t} \right\rceil = \frac{Q[\boldsymbol{m}]_t - [Q\boldsymbol{m}]_t}{t} = -\frac{[Q\boldsymbol{m}]_t}{t} \bmod Q.$$

The second benefit is observed in the addition since now we have

$$\begin{aligned}\boldsymbol{c}_0 + \boldsymbol{c}_1 \cdot \boldsymbol{s} + \boldsymbol{c}'_0 + \boldsymbol{c}'_1 \cdot \boldsymbol{s} &= \frac{Q}{t}([\boldsymbol{m}]_t + [\boldsymbol{m}']_t) + \boldsymbol{v} + \boldsymbol{v}' + \boldsymbol{\varepsilon} + \boldsymbol{\varepsilon}' \\ &= \frac{Q}{t}([\boldsymbol{m} + \boldsymbol{m}']_t + t\boldsymbol{u}) + \boldsymbol{v} + \boldsymbol{v}' + \boldsymbol{\varepsilon} + \boldsymbol{\varepsilon}' \\ &= \frac{Q}{t}[\boldsymbol{m} + \boldsymbol{m}']_t + \boldsymbol{v} + \boldsymbol{v}' + \boldsymbol{\varepsilon} + \boldsymbol{\varepsilon}' \bmod Q.\end{aligned}$$

Hence the noise after a homomorphic addition is bounded by

$$\|\boldsymbol{v}_{\texttt{new-add}}\|_\infty \le \|\boldsymbol{v}\|_\infty + \|\boldsymbol{v}'\|_\infty + 1. \tag{9}$$

Note that the decryption bound (8) and the addition bound (9) are now exactly the same as for BGV.

The equations for homomorphic multiplication can be simplified the same way. Denoting $\tilde{\boldsymbol{v}} = \boldsymbol{v} + \boldsymbol{\varepsilon}$, $\mathtt{ct}_{\mathtt{tensor}}$ is computed as

$$\begin{aligned}(\boldsymbol{c}_0 + \boldsymbol{c}_1 \cdot \boldsymbol{s}) \cdot (\boldsymbol{c}_0' + \boldsymbol{c}_1' \cdot \boldsymbol{s}) &= \left(\frac{Q}{t}[\boldsymbol{m}]_t + \tilde{\boldsymbol{v}} + \boldsymbol{k}Q\right) \cdot \left(\frac{Q}{t}[\boldsymbol{m}']_t + \tilde{\boldsymbol{v}}' + \boldsymbol{k}'Q\right) \\ &= \frac{Q^2}{t^2}[\boldsymbol{m} \cdot \boldsymbol{m}']_t + \frac{Q}{t}\boldsymbol{v}_{\texttt{new-tensor}} + \frac{Q^2}{t}\boldsymbol{k}_{\texttt{new-tensor}},\end{aligned}$$

where

$$\begin{aligned}\boldsymbol{v}_{\texttt{new-tensor}} &= [\boldsymbol{m}]_t \cdot \tilde{\boldsymbol{v}}' + [\boldsymbol{m}']_t \cdot \tilde{\boldsymbol{v}} + \frac{t}{Q}\tilde{\boldsymbol{v}} \cdot \tilde{\boldsymbol{v}}' + t(\tilde{\boldsymbol{v}} \cdot \boldsymbol{k}' + \tilde{\boldsymbol{v}}' \cdot \boldsymbol{k}), \\ \boldsymbol{k}_{\texttt{new-tensor}} &= [\boldsymbol{m}]_t \cdot \boldsymbol{k}' + [\boldsymbol{m}']_t \cdot \boldsymbol{k} + t\boldsymbol{k} \cdot \boldsymbol{k}' + \boldsymbol{r}_m.\end{aligned}$$

Then after the scaling by t/Q and rounding, similarly to the original BFV scheme, the noise of the multiplication is given by: $\boldsymbol{v}_{\texttt{new-mult}} = \boldsymbol{v}_{\texttt{new-tensor}} + \boldsymbol{v}_r$, and is bounded by:

$$\begin{aligned}\|\boldsymbol{v}_{\texttt{new-mult}}\|_\infty \le& \frac{\delta_{\mathcal{R}} t}{2}\left(\frac{2\|\tilde{\boldsymbol{v}}\|_\infty \|\tilde{\boldsymbol{v}}'\|_\infty}{Q} + (4 + \delta_{\mathcal{R}} B_{\texttt{key}})(\|\tilde{\boldsymbol{v}}\|_\infty + \|\tilde{\boldsymbol{v}}'\|_\infty)\right) \\ &+ \frac{1 + \delta_{\mathcal{R}} B_{\texttt{key}} + \delta_{\mathcal{R}}^2 B_{\texttt{key}}^2}{2}.\end{aligned} \tag{10}$$

We will see in Sect. 5 that this bound is similar to the bound for BGV.

Similarly to [27], we can derive a bound on the noise after having evaluated a binary tree of depth L from (10). By assuming that the size of the noise of ciphertexts is bounded by V before the first multiplication, the noise of the resulting ciphertext will be bounded by

$$C_1^L V + C_2 \sum_{i=0}^{L-1} C_1^i \le C_1^L V + L C_2 C_1^{L-1}$$

with $C_1 = \delta_{\mathcal{R}} t(5 + \delta_{\mathcal{R}} B_{\texttt{key}})$ and $C_2 = (1 + \delta_{\mathcal{R}} B_{\texttt{key}} + \delta_{\mathcal{R}}^2 B_{\texttt{key}}^2)/2 + V_{\texttt{ks}}$ where $V_{\texttt{ks}}$ represents the noise added by the key-switching (see the full version).

Last we want to highlight further the similarity between BGV and BFV. Just like in the GHS variant of BGV, one can encrypt a ciphertext ct in BFV using a slightly larger modulus Qp and then rescale the ciphertext by $1/p$, which will have the same effect as modulus switching in BGV:

$$\mathtt{ct}_{\mathtt{scale}} = \left\lfloor \frac{1}{p}\mathtt{ct} \right\rceil \bmod Q,$$

so that its noise after scaling is bounded by

$$\|\boldsymbol{v}_{\texttt{scale}}\|_\infty \leq \frac{\|\boldsymbol{v}\|_\infty}{p} + \frac{1}{2p} + \frac{1+\delta_{\mathcal{R}}B_{\texttt{key}}}{2}.$$

Therefore, like in BGV, this allows to reduce the noise of a freshly encrypted to $(1+\delta_{\mathcal{R}}B_{\texttt{key}})/2 \approx \delta_{\mathcal{R}}/2$. Note that the noise benefit of the BFV encryption proposed in our work will become more significant as the fresh noise is several bits larger than the modulus switching noise. Moreover, when using GHS or Hybrid key switching, p can be chosen as one of the moduli of the key-switching basis, and therefore this technique will not impact the selection of Ring-LWE security parameters.

3.2 Modified Homomorphic Multiplication

In the previous subsection, we showed how to instantiate BFV in such a way that it is not worse than BGV in terms of noise growth. Now the main difference left between the two schemes is in the complexity of their homomorphic multiplication procedure. In a nutshell, in BGV the tensoring can be done directly modulo Q while in BFV it must be done without any modular reduction. In practice, this requires using a second RNS basis $P = p_1 \cdots p_{k'}$ such that $\texttt{ct}(\boldsymbol{s}) \cdot \texttt{ct}'(\boldsymbol{s}')$ does not wrap around modulo PQ. More precisely, the critical part in practice is to avoid the wraparound of the dominant term $Qt\boldsymbol{k} \cdot \boldsymbol{k}'$ modulo P during the scaling (see Sect. 2.2). This requires to choose $P > t\delta_{\mathcal{R}}^3 Q/4$, which in practice is satisfied by setting $k' = k+1$ for the RNS instantiation. Algorithm 1 recalls the original homomorphic multiplication procedure of BFV.

Algorithm 1 . Original BFV Multiplication Algorithm

procedure OriginalMult($\texttt{ct} = (\boldsymbol{c}_0, \boldsymbol{c}_1) \in \mathcal{R}_Q^2, \texttt{ct}' = (\boldsymbol{c}_0', \boldsymbol{c}_1') \in \mathcal{R}_Q^2$)
  Expand: $\texttt{ct} \in \mathcal{R}_Q^2$ and $\texttt{ct}' \in \mathcal{R}_Q^2 \to \texttt{ct} \in \mathcal{R}_{QP}^2$ and $\texttt{ct}' \in \mathcal{R}_{QP}^2$:
   ▷ $\texttt{ct}(\boldsymbol{s}) = \Delta[\boldsymbol{m}]_t + \boldsymbol{v} + Q\boldsymbol{k} \pmod{\mathcal{R}_{QP}}$
   ▷ $\texttt{ct}'(\boldsymbol{s}) = \Delta[\boldsymbol{m}']_t + \boldsymbol{v}' + Q\boldsymbol{k}' \pmod{\mathcal{R}_{QP}}$
  Tensor: $\texttt{ct}_{\texttt{tensor}} = (\boldsymbol{c}_0 \cdot \boldsymbol{c}_0', \boldsymbol{c}_0 \cdot \boldsymbol{c}_1' + \boldsymbol{c}_1 \cdot \boldsymbol{c}_0', \boldsymbol{c}_1 \cdot \boldsymbol{c}_1') \in \mathcal{R}_{QP}^3$:
   ▷ $\texttt{ct}_{\texttt{tensor}}(\boldsymbol{s}) = \frac{Q}{t}\Delta\left[\boldsymbol{m} \cdot \boldsymbol{m}'\right]_t + \frac{Q}{t}\boldsymbol{v}_{\texttt{tensor}} + \frac{Q^2}{t}\boldsymbol{k}_{\texttt{tensor}} \pmod{\mathcal{R}_{QP}}$
  ScaleDown: $\texttt{ct}_{\texttt{scale}} = \lfloor \frac{t}{Q}\texttt{ct}_{\texttt{tensor}} \rceil \in \mathcal{R}_P^3$
   ▷ $\texttt{ct}_{\texttt{scale}}(\boldsymbol{s}) = \Delta\left[\boldsymbol{m} \cdot \boldsymbol{m}'\right]_t + \boldsymbol{v}_{\texttt{tensor}} + Q\boldsymbol{k}_{\texttt{tensor}} + \boldsymbol{v}_r \pmod{\mathcal{R}_P}$
  SwitchBasis: $\texttt{ct}_{\texttt{scale}} \in \mathcal{R}_P^3 \to \texttt{ct}_{\texttt{scale}} \in \mathcal{R}_Q^3$:
   ▷ $\texttt{ct}_{\texttt{scale}}(\boldsymbol{s}) = \Delta\left[\boldsymbol{m} \cdot \boldsymbol{m}'\right]_t + \boldsymbol{v}_{\texttt{tensor}} + \boldsymbol{v}_r \pmod{\mathcal{R}_Q}$

We propose a new homomorphic multiplication algorithm, with a reduced computational complexity. Instead of multiplying two ciphertexts modulo Q and dealing with a multiple of Q^2 modulo QP, the idea is to switch one of the two ciphertexts to modulus P so that after the tensoring we obtain a multiple of PQ that vanishes modulo PQ. As explained in the above paragraph, this would allow us to reduce the size of P since the original dominant term would now disappear. More precisely, the procedure starts as usual with two ciphertexts encrypted modulo Q:

$$\mathtt{ct}(\boldsymbol{s}) = \frac{Q}{t}[\boldsymbol{m}]_t + \tilde{\boldsymbol{v}} + \boldsymbol{k}Q \text{ and } \mathtt{ct}'(\boldsymbol{s}) = \frac{Q}{t}[\boldsymbol{m}']_t + \tilde{\boldsymbol{v}}' + \boldsymbol{k}'Q.$$

with $\tilde{\boldsymbol{v}} = \boldsymbol{v} + \boldsymbol{\varepsilon}$ and $\tilde{\boldsymbol{v}}' = \boldsymbol{v}' + \boldsymbol{\varepsilon}'$, like in Sect. 3.1.

Then one can perform the modulus switching of one of the two ciphertexts, say $\mathtt{ct}$, to convert it to modulus P by computing

$$\hat{\mathtt{ct}} = \left\lfloor \frac{P}{Q}\mathtt{ct} \right\rceil \bmod P,$$

which satisfies:

$$\hat{\mathtt{ct}}(\boldsymbol{s}) = \frac{P}{t}[\boldsymbol{m}]_t + \frac{P\tilde{\boldsymbol{v}}}{Q} + \boldsymbol{k}P + \boldsymbol{\varepsilon}_{\mathtt{round}} \bmod P,$$

where the rounding error $\boldsymbol{\varepsilon}_{\mathtt{round}} = \hat{\mathtt{ct}}(\boldsymbol{s}) - P\mathtt{ct}(\boldsymbol{s})/Q$ has its norm bounded by $(1 + \delta_{\mathcal{R}}B_{\mathtt{key}})/2$ as usual. From there, $\hat{\mathtt{ct}}$ is expanded from P to QP, $\mathtt{ct}'$ is expanded from Q to QP, and one can perform the tensoring as usual to obtain

$$\begin{aligned}\hat{\mathtt{ct}}_{\mathtt{tensor}}(\boldsymbol{s}) = \; & \frac{PQ}{t^2}[\boldsymbol{m}\cdot\boldsymbol{m}']_t + \frac{P}{t}\hat{\boldsymbol{v}}_{\mathtt{tensor}} + \frac{QP}{t}\hat{\boldsymbol{k}}_{\mathtt{tensor}} \\ & + \boldsymbol{\varepsilon}_{\mathtt{round}} \cdot \left(\frac{Q}{t}[\boldsymbol{m}']_t + \tilde{\boldsymbol{v}}' + \boldsymbol{k}'Q\right) \bmod PQ,\end{aligned}$$

with $\hat{\boldsymbol{v}}_{\mathtt{tensor}} = \boldsymbol{v}_{\mathtt{new\text{-}tensor}}$ from Sect. 3.1 and

$$\hat{\boldsymbol{k}}_{\mathtt{tensor}} = [\boldsymbol{m}]_t \cdot \boldsymbol{k}' + [\boldsymbol{m}']_t \cdot \boldsymbol{k} + \boldsymbol{r}_m \in \mathcal{R}.$$

Note that this time $\hat{\boldsymbol{k}}_{\mathtt{tensor}}$ does not contain a multiple of $\boldsymbol{k}\cdot\boldsymbol{k}'$. Then to get back a valid ciphertext modulo Q, one must scale down the result by t/P, instead of t/Q in the original case, which leads to

$$\frac{t}{P}\hat{\mathtt{ct}}_{\mathtt{tensor}}(\boldsymbol{s}) = \frac{Q}{t}[\boldsymbol{m}\cdot\boldsymbol{m}']_t + \hat{\boldsymbol{v}}_{\mathtt{tensor}} + Q\hat{\boldsymbol{k}}_{\mathtt{tensor}} + \frac{t\boldsymbol{\varepsilon}_{\mathtt{round}}}{P} \cdot \left(\frac{Q}{t}[\boldsymbol{m}']_t + \tilde{\boldsymbol{v}}' + \boldsymbol{k}'Q\right).$$

After the rounding, the multiple of Q will vanish modulo Q and one will have to take into account the rounding error term $\boldsymbol{v}_r$ of norm bounded by $(1 + \delta_{\mathcal{R}}B_{\mathtt{key}} + \delta_{\mathcal{R}}^2B_{\mathtt{key}}^2)/2$, which adds to the noise, like in the original BFV scheme. Therefore, the noise of this variant of homomorphic multiplication is bounded by

$$\|\hat{\boldsymbol{v}}_{\mathtt{new\text{-}mult}}\|_\infty \leq \|\boldsymbol{v}_{\mathtt{new\text{-}mult}}\|_\infty + \frac{t\delta_{\mathcal{R}}(\delta_{\mathcal{R}}B_{\mathtt{key}} + 1)}{2P}\left(\|\tilde{\boldsymbol{v}}\|_\infty' + \frac{Q(\delta_{\mathcal{R}}B_{\mathtt{key}} + 4)}{2}\right). \tag{11}$$

Notice that the only difference in the noise growth between Eq. (10) and Eq. (11) is due to rounding error $\boldsymbol{\varepsilon}_{\mathtt{round}}$ occuring during the first modulus switching.

However, we can control the size of this noise with P. As explained in Sect. 3.1, the norm of $\boldsymbol{v}_{\texttt{new-mult}}$ is dominated by $\delta_{\mathcal{R}}^2 tV$, where V is the bound on the size of the noise of $\tilde{\boldsymbol{v}}$ and $\tilde{\boldsymbol{v}}'$. If we look carefully at the other term and choose $P \approx Q$, it will be dominated by $\delta_{\mathcal{R}}^3 t/4$. Since the noise of a fresh ciphertext, even scaled-down after encryption, has always a size larger than $\delta_{\mathcal{R}}/2$, this error term will add at most half a bit to the noise of the first multiplication in the worst case, which can be considered as neglible in practice as a larger cushion is typically added to the heuristic expression for δ_R, or, more precisely, δ_R^3 in this case. This means that one can choose $P \approx Q$ and hence $k' = k$, instead of $k' = k+1$ in the original case, which reduces the size of P and still achieves the same noise growth as in Sect. 3.1. We summarize our new multiplication algorithm in Algorithm 2.

Algorithm 2 . New BFV Multiplication Algorithm

procedure NewMult($\texttt{ct} = (\boldsymbol{c}_0, \boldsymbol{c}_1) \in \mathcal{R}_Q^2, \texttt{ct}' = (\boldsymbol{c}_0', \boldsymbol{c}_1') \in \mathcal{R}_Q^2$)
  ModSwitch: $\texttt{ct} \in \mathcal{R}_Q^2 \to \hat{\texttt{ct}} \in \mathcal{R}_P^2$
  Expand: $\hat{\texttt{ct}} \in \mathcal{R}_P^2 \to \hat{\texttt{ct}} \in \mathcal{R}_{QP}^2$ and $\texttt{ct}' \in \mathcal{R}_Q^2 \to \texttt{ct}' \in \mathcal{R}_{QP}^2$
   ▷ $\hat{\texttt{ct}}(\boldsymbol{s}) = \frac{P}{t}[\boldsymbol{m}]_t + \frac{P}{Q}\tilde{\boldsymbol{v}} + P\boldsymbol{k} + \boldsymbol{\varepsilon}_{\text{round}} \pmod{\mathcal{R}_{QP}}$
   ▷ $\texttt{ct}'(\boldsymbol{s}) = \frac{Q}{t}[\boldsymbol{m}']_t + \tilde{\boldsymbol{v}}' + Q\boldsymbol{k}' \pmod{\mathcal{R}_{QP}}$
  Tensor: $\hat{\texttt{ct}}_{\texttt{tensor}} = (\hat{\boldsymbol{c}}_0 \cdot \boldsymbol{c}_0', \hat{\boldsymbol{c}}_0 \cdot \boldsymbol{c}_1' + \hat{\boldsymbol{c}}_1 \cdot \boldsymbol{c}_0', \hat{\boldsymbol{c}}_1 \cdot \boldsymbol{c}_1') \in \mathcal{R}_{QP}^3$:
   ▷ $\hat{\texttt{ct}}_{\texttt{tensor}}(\boldsymbol{s}) = \frac{QP}{t^2}\left[\boldsymbol{m} \cdot \boldsymbol{m}'\right]_t + \frac{P}{t}\hat{\boldsymbol{v}}_{\texttt{tensor}} + \frac{QP}{t}\hat{\boldsymbol{k}}_{\texttt{tensor}} \pmod{\mathcal{R}_{QP}}$
  ScaleDown: $\texttt{ct}_{\texttt{scale}} = \left\lfloor \frac{t}{P}\hat{\texttt{ct}}_{\texttt{tensor}} \right\rceil \in \mathcal{R}_Q^3$
   ▷ $\texttt{ct}_{\texttt{scale}}(\boldsymbol{s}) = \frac{Q}{t}\left[\boldsymbol{m} \cdot \boldsymbol{m}'\right]_t + \hat{\boldsymbol{v}}_{\texttt{tensor}} + \boldsymbol{v}_r \pmod{\mathcal{R}_Q}$

Remark 3. Notice that since one must scale the tensored ciphertext by t/P instead of t/Q, it can be done directly in the basis Q. Therefore the homomorphic multiplication procedure requires 2 basis extensions from Q to P for $\texttt{ct} = (\boldsymbol{c}_0, \boldsymbol{c}_1)$ in the beginning, 4 more basis extensions to expand the two ciphertexts $\hat{\texttt{ct}} = (\hat{\boldsymbol{c}}_0, \hat{\boldsymbol{c}}_1)$ and $\texttt{ct}' = (\boldsymbol{c}_0', \boldsymbol{c}_1')$ from P and Q, respectively, to PQ. Finally one needs 3 additional basis extensions from PQ to Q for $\hat{\texttt{ct}}_{\texttt{tensor}} \in \mathcal{R}_{PQ}^3$ to perform the downscaling modulo Q. Thus it requires a total of 9 basis extensions instead of $4+3+3=10$ in the original BFV algorithm. Moreover, since P is slightly smaller, each basis extension will be cheaper to compute.

Leveled BFV Multiplication. If one wants to make BFV even closer to BGV in terms of performance, one could consider a "leveled" approach to BFV by working with ciphertexts modulo $Q_\ell = q_1 \cdots q_\ell$ and performing modulus switching as the computation progresses. However, as in BGV, one would have to manage ciphertexts at different levels and deal with more challenging noise estimation.

To keep the usability of BFV, we propose instead a "leveled" multiplication that pre-scales both ciphertexts by $\frac{Q_\ell}{Q}$ (using internal modulus switching to Q_ℓ), and then multiplies the result by $\frac{Q}{Q_\ell}$ after the multiplication procedure. In this case, the ciphertexts will always stay modulo Q outside the multiplication procedure, but the multiplication will be done internally modulo $Q_\ell < Q$ and hence will be more efficient.

In this case, the noise of input ciphertexts after internal modulus switching from Q to Q_ℓ will be equal to

$$\hat{\boldsymbol{v}} = \frac{Q_\ell}{Q}\boldsymbol{v} + \boldsymbol{\varepsilon}_{\texttt{round}} \text{ and } \hat{\boldsymbol{v}}' = \frac{Q_\ell}{Q}\boldsymbol{v}' + \boldsymbol{\varepsilon}'_{\texttt{round}},$$

where $\boldsymbol{\varepsilon}_{\texttt{round}}$ and $\boldsymbol{\varepsilon}'_{\texttt{round}}$ have their norm bounded by $(1 + \delta_{\mathcal{R}} B_{\texttt{key}})/2 \approx \delta_{\mathcal{R}}/2$. On the one hand, the main consideration here is to choose ℓ such that $\frac{Q_\ell}{Q}\|\boldsymbol{v}\|_\infty$ remains significantly larger than $\|\boldsymbol{\varepsilon}_{\texttt{round}}\|_\infty \approx \frac{\delta_{\mathcal{R}}}{2}$, so that the noise brought about by the modulus switching procedure will not significantly impact the overall noise growth. This is equivalent to

$$\|\boldsymbol{v}\|_\infty \gg \frac{Q\delta_{\mathcal{R}}}{2Q_\ell} \text{ and } \|\boldsymbol{v}\|'_\infty \gg \frac{Q\delta_{\mathcal{R}}}{2Q_\ell},$$

or in practice

$$\|\boldsymbol{v}\|_\infty > 8\frac{Q\delta_{\mathcal{R}}}{Q_\ell} \text{ and } \|\boldsymbol{v}\|'_\infty > 8\frac{Q\delta_{\mathcal{R}}}{Q_\ell}. \tag{12}$$

On the other hand, in order to gain as much as possible in efficiency, Q_ℓ must be chosen as the smallest modulus satisfying inequalities (12). Theoretically this requires to have a precise estimate of the average (or lower bound within a certain confidence interval) noise size. But in practice it is enough to add a heuristic "cushion" to our worst-case bound. See the full version for details.

Algorithm 3 . New Leveled BFV Multiplication Algorithm

procedure LEVELEDNEWMULT($\texttt{ct} = (\boldsymbol{c}_0, \boldsymbol{c}_1) \in \mathcal{R}_Q^2, \texttt{ct}' = (\boldsymbol{c}'_0, \boldsymbol{c}'_1) \in \mathcal{R}_Q^2$)
- ModSwitchDown: $\hat{\texttt{ct}} = \lfloor \frac{Q_\ell}{Q}\texttt{ct} \rceil \in \mathcal{R}_{Q_\ell}^2$ and $\hat{\texttt{ct}}' = \lfloor \frac{Q_\ell}{Q}\texttt{ct}' \rceil \in \mathcal{R}_{Q_\ell}^2$
  - $\triangleright\ \hat{\boldsymbol{v}} = \frac{Q_\ell}{Q}\boldsymbol{v} + \boldsymbol{\varepsilon}_{\texttt{round}}$ and $\triangleright\ \hat{\boldsymbol{v}}' = \frac{Q_\ell}{Q}\boldsymbol{v}' + \boldsymbol{\varepsilon}'_{\texttt{round}}$
- $\hat{\texttt{ct}}_{\texttt{m}} = \texttt{NewMult}(\hat{\texttt{ct}}, \hat{\texttt{ct}}') \in \mathcal{R}_{Q_\ell}^3$
  - $\triangleright\ \hat{\texttt{ct}}_{\texttt{m}}(\boldsymbol{s}) = \frac{Q_\ell}{t}[\boldsymbol{m}_1\boldsymbol{m}_2]_t + \hat{\boldsymbol{v}}_{\texttt{m}} \pmod{\mathcal{R}_{Q_\ell}}$
- ModSwitchUp: $\texttt{ct}_{\texttt{m}} = \lfloor \frac{Q}{Q_\ell}\hat{\texttt{ct}}_{\texttt{m}} \rceil \in \mathcal{R}_Q^3$
  - $\triangleright\ \texttt{ct}_{\texttt{m}}(\boldsymbol{s}) = \frac{Q}{t}[\boldsymbol{m}_1\boldsymbol{m}_2]_t + \boldsymbol{v}_{\texttt{m}} \pmod{\mathcal{R}_Q}$
  - $\triangleright\ \boldsymbol{v}_{\texttt{m}} = \frac{Q}{Q_\ell}\hat{\boldsymbol{v}}_{\texttt{m}} + \boldsymbol{v}_r$

Remark 4. Note that this "leveled" optimization can be equally applied to key switching. The only difference in this case would be to ensure that the noise of the scaled ciphertext remains larger than the noise brought about by the key-switching procedure itself.

Table 1. Complexities of different multiplication methods.

	# NTTs	# integer-mult	# floating-point-oper
MultOld	$14k+7$	$(10k^2+26k+9)n$	$(10k+3)n$
MultNew	$14k$	$(9k^2+15k)n$	$7kn$
MultNewLeveled	14ℓ	$(4k\ell+5\ell^2+2k+18\ell)n$	$(2k+5\ell)n$

Remark 5. Modulus switching from Q to Q_ℓ and then from Q_ℓ to P_ℓ in Algorithm 3 can be combined into a single modulus switching from Q directly to P_ℓ. This reduces the number of integer multiplications from $(k\ell+\ell^2+2\ell)n$ to $(k\ell+\ell)n$. Note that an approximate modulus switching (instead of an exact one with a floating-point correction technique from [21]) can be employed by adding extra $\log k$ bits to the noise estimate used for reducing the number of levels inside homomorphic multiplication. Both exact and approximate procedures for switching the moduli of ciphertexts between arbitrary RNS bases are described in the full version.

Table 1 summarizes the computational complexities of different multiplication algorithms by assuming that the extension from Q to QP is performed using the technique from [21] with floating-point operations.

Lazy Scaling in BFV Multiplication. An additional optimization can be implemented by noticing that tensoring and scaling can be separated to optimize some evaluation circuits. For example, consider the inner product circuit of two vectors of ciphertexts. We evaluate it by multiplying (tensoring and scaling) the pairs of ciphertexts and then adding the results $\pmod{\mathcal{R}_Q}$. It is more efficient to do this in a different way: first we apply the tensoring subroutine to the pairs of ciphertexts, then add the results $\pmod{\mathcal{R}_{QP}}$, and finally perform the expensive scaling subroutine only once. Indeed, after tensoring we already have the information about the multiplicative noise $v_{\texttt{tensor}}$, thus changing the order of scaling and additions does not affect the $v_{\texttt{tensor}}$ noise. Moreover, as we perform the scaling down only once instead of doing it for each pair of ciphertexts, the total noise from the inner product is actually reduced. We call this technique *lazy scaling* and describe the pseudocode in the full version. The experimental results in the full version suggest that this optimization can speed up inner products by more than 2x in practice.

3.3 Improved Decryption in the HPS RNS Variant

A significant practical limitation of the HPS approach is that high-precision ("long double" or even quad-precision) floating-point arithmetic is required to support larger CRT moduli [21]. We introduce a general-purpose digit decomposition technique (inspired by digit decomposition in key switching) and apply it to the HPS decryption procedure to add support for arbitrary CRT moduli using only regular double-precision floating-point arithmetic, hence overcoming this limitation of the HPS variant.

The idea of HPS scaling [21] for decryption can be briefly explained as follows: for $x \in \mathbb{Z}_Q$ with CRT representation $(x_1, \ldots, x_k)$ we want to compute an integer $y = \lceil t/Qx \rfloor \in \mathbb{Z}_t$, and use a CRT composition formula to derive the following expression:

$$y := \left\lceil \frac{t}{Q} x \right\rfloor = \left\lceil \left(\sum_{i=1}^{k} x_i \cdot \left[\left(\frac{Q}{q_i} \right)^{-1} \right]_{q_i} \cdot \frac{Q}{q_i} \cdot \frac{t}{Q} \right) - u \cdot Q \cdot \frac{t}{Q} \right\rfloor$$

$$= \left[\left\lceil \left(\sum_{i=1}^{k} x_i \cdot \left(\left[\left(\frac{Q}{q_i} \right)^{-1} \right]_{q_i} \cdot \frac{t}{q_i} \right) \right) \right\rfloor \right]_t = \left[\left(\sum_{i=1}^{k} x_i \cdot \omega_i \right) + \left\lceil \sum_{i=1}^{k} x_i \cdot \theta_i \right\rfloor \right]_t,$$

$$\text{where } \left[\left(\frac{Q}{q_i} \right)^{-1} \right]_{q_i} \cdot \frac{t}{q_i} = \omega_i + \theta_i \text{ with } \omega_i \in \mathbb{Z}_t \text{ and } \theta_i \in \left[-\frac{1}{2}, \frac{1}{2} \right).$$

As we can only store approximate values $\tilde{\theta}_i = \theta_i + \epsilon_i$, the magnitude of the error term $|\epsilon'| = |\sum_i x_i \epsilon_i|$ in the fractional part is limited by $k q_m \epsilon_m$, where $q_m = \max_i(q_i)$ and $\epsilon_m = \max_i(\epsilon_i)$. If we restrict the floating-point precision to "doubles", which are natively supported by modern CPUs, we have to introduce a constraint $k q_m < 2^{51}$. To support larger CRT moduli, we need "long doubles" or even quad-precision arithmetic: long doubles are needed for CRT moduli from 47 to 58 bits, and quad-precision floats are needed for higher CRT moduli [21].

Our main idea is to perform digit decomposition, somewhat similar to how digit decomposition is done in BV key-switching, to replace the factor q_m with a smaller digit of it. For base $B_s \in \mathbb{Z}$, $B_s \geq 2$, let $d_s = \lceil \log(q_m)/\log(B_s) \rceil$. Let $x_i = \sum_{j=0}^{d_s-1} x_{i,j} \cdot B_s^j$ be the B_s base decomposition of x_i. Then the expression for y can be rewritten as

$$y = \left[\left\lceil \left(\sum_{i=1}^{k} \sum_{j=0}^{d_s-1} x_{i,j} \cdot \left(\frac{t}{q_i} \cdot \left[\left[\left(\frac{Q}{q_i} \right)^{-1} \right]_{q_i} \cdot B_s^j \right]_{q_i} \right) \right) \right\rfloor \right]_t$$

$$= \left[\left(\sum_{i=1}^{k} \sum_{j=0}^{d_s-1} [x_{i,j} \cdot \omega_{i,j}]_t \right) + \left\lceil \sum_{i=1}^{k} \sum_{j=0}^{d_s-1} x_{i,j} \cdot \theta_{i,j} \right\rfloor \right]_t,$$

$$\text{where } \frac{t}{q_i} \cdot \left[\left[\left(\frac{Q}{q_i} \right)^{-1} \right]_{q_i} \cdot B_s^j \right]_{q_i} = \omega_{i,j} + \theta_{i,j}, \text{ with } \omega_{i,j} \in \mathbb{Z}_t \text{ and } \theta_{i,j} \in \left[-\frac{1}{2}, \frac{1}{2} \right).$$

Note that $\omega_{i,j}$ and $\theta_{i,j}$ are the new precomputation factors instead of ω_i and θ_i.

Error Analysis. The magnitude of the error term $|\epsilon'| = |\sum_{i,j} x_{i_j} \epsilon_{i,j}|$ is now limited by $\left|\sum_{i,j} x_{i,j} \epsilon_{i,j}\right| < k d_s B_s \epsilon_m$. In practice, our moduli q_i are normally bounded by 64 (or often by 60) bits. We have already considered the case of $kq_m < 2^{51}$. If $kq_m > 2^{51}$, we can take $d_s = 2$, $B_s = 2^{\lceil \log_2 q_m/2 \rceil}$. Then $|\epsilon'| < 2^{-19}k < 1/4$ for $k < 2^{17}$. Hence the floating-point error will have no effect on the result for any practically reasonable value of k.

Complexity Analysis. The procedure takes kd_s floating-point multiplications, kd_s modular integer multiplications, some modular additions, and one rounding to compute $\lceil u \rfloor$. However, if $tkd_sB_s < 2^{64}$, then we can replace modular multiplications and modular additions by plain integer multiplications and additions respectively, and do one modular reduction at the end.

Remark 6. Note that this digit decomposition technique can be applied to other mixed integer/floating-point RNS operations to reduce precision requirements for floating-point arithmetic or avoid extra noise due to floating-point rounding. For instance, it can be used in the scaling for homomorphic multiplication.

4 More Usable BGV Scheme

The practical use of the BGV scheme requires accurate dynamic noise estimation to decide when the modulus operation should be executed, and what scaling factor should be chosen for modulus switching [20]. Each modulus switching decision may significantly impact the noise not only for the current operation, but also for all subsequent operations. An error in a noise estimate may eventually lead even to a decryption failure. Therefore, fine-tuned noise estimation techniques are used to estimate the noise for various operations (see [23] for a more detailed discussion). In contrast, the BFV scheme is much more robust to inaccuracies in noise estimation and typically only requires an upper bound on the error for the desired multiplicative depth. This robustness of BFV is related to the use of the MSD encoding and scaling down by a large factor Q/t during BFV homomorphic multiplication, and the "fragility" of BGV is caused by the LSD encoding and scaling down by a small factor, comparable in magnitude to the noise incurred in operations after the previous modulus switching. For this reason, many modern homomorphic encryption libraries implement BFV as the scheme for finite fields, while only HELib and PALISADE (since quite recently) provide efficient implementations of BGV.

We present an alternative approach for instantiating BGV, which does not require dynamic noise estimation. For this instantiation, one only needs to specify the multiplicative depth of the computation, maximum number of additions per multiplicative level, and the number of additions and automorphisms before first multiplication. Then all moduli $Q_L, Q_{L-1}, \ldots, Q_1, Q_0$ are chosen so that a small, constant level of noise can be maintained throughout the computation. All modulus switching operations are automatically performed right before a homomorphic multiplication. Conceptually, this BGV instantiation is similar in usability to BFV, where only the multiplicative depth needs to be specified upfront and all "modulus switching" operations are performed automatically.

The logic for choosing the moduli is as follows. We start with a fresh encryption that has a noise $\|\boldsymbol{v}_{\texttt{fresh}}\|_\infty = B_{\texttt{err}}(2\delta_{\mathcal{R}}B_{\texttt{key}}+1)$. Then we perform automorphism operations and additions, and apply modulus switching right before the first multiplication. This additional modulus switching before first multiplication allows us to reset the noise to a value comparable to the modulus switching noise, which will be the constant noise level $\|\boldsymbol{v}_{\mathsf{c}}\|_\infty$ we will maintain throughout the computation. This can be expressed as

$$\frac{Q_L}{Q_{L+1}}\left((n_{\text{add}}+1)\|\boldsymbol{v}_{\texttt{fresh}}\|_\infty + n_{\text{ks}}\|\boldsymbol{v}_{\texttt{ks}}\|_\infty\right) + \frac{1+\delta_{\mathcal{R}}B_{\texttt{key}}}{2} \le \|\boldsymbol{v}_{\mathsf{c}}\|_\infty ,$$

where n_{add} and n_{ks} are the numbers of additions and automorphism operations, respectively, that are performed before first multiplication, and $\|\boldsymbol{v}_{\texttt{ks}}\|_\infty$ is the bound on key switching noise. Note that here we introduced a new level and corresponding new modulus Q_{L+1} to account for an extra level we added before first multiplication. It is best to choose Q_{L+1}/Q_L such that $\|\boldsymbol{v}_{\mathsf{c}}\|_\infty \approx 1+\delta_{\mathcal{R}}B_{\texttt{key}}$ to achieve the smallest constant error because this error will allow us to minimize the subsequent values of Q_{i+1}/Q_i for most practical scenarios, hence resulting in the minimum value of ciphertext modulus Q_{L+1} (see the full version for more details, and more general expression for optimal $\|\boldsymbol{v}_{\mathsf{c}}\|_\infty$).

Then for multiplication levels (from L to 1), we have to satisfy

$$\frac{Q_i}{Q_{i+1}}\left((n'_{\text{add}}+1)\frac{\delta_{\mathcal{R}}t}{2}(2\|\boldsymbol{v}_{\mathsf{c}}\|_\infty^2 + 2\|\boldsymbol{v}_{\mathsf{c}}\|_\infty + 1) + (n'_{\text{ks}}+1)\|\boldsymbol{v}_{\texttt{ks}}\|_\infty\right) + \frac{1+\delta_{\mathcal{R}}B_{\texttt{key}}}{2} \le \|\boldsymbol{v}_{\mathsf{c}}\|_\infty ,$$

where n'_{add} and n'_{ks} are the maximum numbers of additions and key switching operations, respectively, allowed per any multiplication level (going from L down to 1). For simplicity we use these maximum values across all levels so that Q_{i+1}/Q_i could have roughly same value for all $i \in \{1,\ldots,L-1\}$. Note that for `Hybrid` key switching and relatively large plaintext moduli, such as $t = 2^{16}+1$, which is often used for CRT packing, the multiplication noise is always much higher than $\|\boldsymbol{v}_{\texttt{ks}}\|_\infty$ (see derivations in the full version). Hence for this case we can rewrite the expression as

$$\frac{Q_i}{Q_{i+1}}\left((n'_{\text{add}}+1)\frac{\delta_{\mathcal{R}}t}{2}(2\|\boldsymbol{v}_{\mathsf{c}}\|_\infty^2 + 2\|\boldsymbol{v}_{\mathsf{c}}\|_\infty + 1)\right) + \frac{1+\delta_{\mathcal{R}}B_{\texttt{key}}}{2} \le \|\boldsymbol{v}_{\mathsf{c}}\|_\infty .$$

The last modulus Q_0 is chosen such that decryption is correct for a ciphertext with noise bounded by $\|\boldsymbol{v}_{\mathsf{c}}\|_\infty$. This implies that $Q_0 > 2t\|\boldsymbol{v}_{\mathsf{c}}\|_\infty - t$.

It is easy to show that once $L, n_{\text{add}}, n_{\text{ks}}, n'_{\text{add}}$, and n'_{ks} (only needed for small t) are given, all moduli Q_i can be derived. First we compute Q_0, then all values $Q_1,\ldots,Q_L$, and finally we can find Q_{L+1}.

This logic is simple to implement and avoids any dynamic noise estimation during the computation. It is also robust to inaccurate estimates as long as the upper bound for δ_R is chosen appropriately, which is very similar to what is done for BFV. There is a cost for this simplicity and robustness. The moduli Q_{L+1} may be larger than the values obtained using the more granular approach with dynamic noise estimation [23] because we use the maximum values of n'_{add} and n'_{ks} over all intermediate levels. However, our experimental results show that this instantiation of BGV can be significantly faster than the improved BFV implementation described in Sect. 3.

Remarks on the RNS Instantiation. Recall that for original BGV, we choose $Q = q_0 \cdots q_L$ and denote $Q_i = q_0 \cdots q_i$ for $0 \leq i \leq L$, where all $q_i = 1 \bmod 2N$ and co-prime to each other. In the case of our BGV variant, an extra q_{L+1} is introduced to reset the "fresh" noise to modulus switching noise. It is easy to show that for this setup, $Q_0 = q_0$, $Q_{i+1}/Q_i = q_{i+1}$, and $Q_{L+1}/Q_L = q_{L+1}$.

The expressions for finding q_0, q_i, q_{L+1}, where $i \in \{1, \ldots, L\}$, can be written as follows:

$$q_0 > 2t \left\| \boldsymbol{v}_{\mathsf{c}} \right\|_\infty - t, \tag{13}$$

$$q_i > 2 \left((n'_{\text{add}} + 1) \frac{\delta_{\mathcal{R}} t}{2} (2 \left\| \boldsymbol{v}_{\mathsf{c}} \right\|_\infty + 2 + \frac{1}{\left\| \boldsymbol{v}_{\mathsf{c}} \right\|_\infty}) + (n'_{\text{ks}} + 1) \frac{\left\| \boldsymbol{v}_{\mathtt{ks}} \right\|_\infty}{\left\| \boldsymbol{v}_{\mathsf{c}} \right\|_\infty} \right), \tag{14}$$

$$q_{L+1} > 2 \left((n_{\text{add}} + 1) \frac{\left\| \boldsymbol{v}_{\mathtt{fresh}} \right\|_\infty}{\left\| \boldsymbol{v}_{\mathsf{c}} \right\|_\infty} + n_{\text{ks}} \frac{\left\| \boldsymbol{v}_{\mathtt{ks}} \right\|_\infty}{\left\| \boldsymbol{v}_{\mathsf{c}} \right\|_\infty} \right),$$

where we take $\left\| \boldsymbol{v}_{\mathsf{c}} \right\|_\infty = 1 + \delta_{\mathcal{R}} B_{\mathtt{key}}$.

Handling Crosslevel Operations and Scaling Factors. The GHS variant implemented in HELib uses ciphertext-specific scaling factors, which introduces some complications that may affect the usability and may require additional scalar multiplications to bring two ciphertexts to the same scaling factor. In our BGV variant, we chose a simpler approach where the same scaling factor is used for all ciphertexts at a specific level, which reduces the number of scalar multiplications. This approach was originally introduced for the CKKS scheme in [25], and in our work we adapt it to BGV.

5 Comparison of BFV and BGV

5.1 Noise Growth

When comparing BGV and BFV, it is convenient to use the leveled approach of BGV, first comparing Q_0, then Q_i, and finally Q_{L+1}.

For Q_0, our modified variant of BFV has identical noise as BGV, i.e., Eq. (8) is exactly the same as Eq. (13).

For Q_{i+1}/Q_i, which corresponds to each multiplicative level, the dominant term in the BFV expression given by Eq. (11) is $\delta_R^2 t B_{\mathtt{key}} V$, where V is the largest of the errors in two multiplied ciphertexts. For BGV, Eq. (14) suggests that the dominant term is $2\delta_R^2 t B_{\mathtt{key}} V$. In other words, the expressions for BFV and BGV are identical except for the extra multiplicative factor of 2. This factor appears in BGV because we ensure that at each level the downscaled noise matches the added modulus switching noise, keeping the noise level constant at twice the modulus switching noise (see the full version for details). In the case of BFV, the quadratic noise (product of prior noises for each ciphertext) is negligible as we downscale the ciphertext by a large factor Q/t, and we only observe the pure modulus switching noise. In other words, BFV has a small benefit of using one bit less per multiplication level.

There is also an extra advantage of BFV for small plaintext moduli, e.g., $t = 2$. As the analysis in the full version shows, the key switching noise in this case becomes comparable to multiplication noise for BGV, which implies higher values of Q_{i+1}/Q_i. In contrast, the key switching noise may only affect the initial level in BFV, as afterwards the accumulated noise from prior multiplications will be much higher than additive key switching noise, which is independent of current ciphertext noise. When we switch to larger plaintext moduli, this BFV advantage disappears as the key-switching noise in BGV becomes negligible compared to multiplication noise (as shown in the full version).

Using the $(L+1)$-th level (q_{L+1} in the RNS version) is preferred in BGV to achieve the smallest constant noise (twice the modulus switching noise). If $(L+1)$-th level is not used, then the fresh noise will make each Q_{i+1}/Q_i larger by a factor $\|\boldsymbol{v}_{\mathtt{fresh}}\|_\infty / \|\boldsymbol{v}_{\mathtt{c}}\|_\infty \approx 2B_{\mathtt{err}} \approx 37$. Although one could use an auxiliary modulus in hybrid key switching during encryption instead (see the end of Sect. 3.1), extra noise can be accumulated from additions and/or key switching operations performed before first multiplication, which would increase all subsequent Q_{i+1}/Q_i. So the least level of constant noise in BGV, and hence smallest Q_{i+1}/Q_i, can be guaranteed only by introducing a relatively small extra "noise budget" for pseudo-level $L+1$. Note that in BFV it is best to use an auxiliary modulus to reset the fresh noise to smaller modulus switching noise, without increasing the ciphertext modulus (see Sect. 3.1). Hence no pseudo-level $L+1$ is needed in BFV, which is another small advantage of BFV over BGV.

In summary, the improved variants of BFV and BGV presented in this work have very similar noise growth, but BFV has some minor advantages over BGV, resulting in somewhat reduced ciphertext moduli needed to support the same computations.

5.2 Computational Complexity

The main difference between BFV and BGV in terms of computational complexity is due to the scaling method used in the multiplication operation. As was previously mentioned, BFV uses the MSD encoding and scales down the tensor product by a large Q/t factor, while BGV uses the LSD encoding technique to scale the tensor product only by a relatively small factor, comparable to the noise of previous multiplication. Considering that the noise growth is very similar in both schemes, one can expect that the computational complexity of BFV multiplication will be significantly higher. The purpose of this section is to quantify this difference, and examine the effect of plaintext moduli on this difference. Note that all other operations, such as addition and automorphism, use the same approach in both schemes, and do not have any significant difference in terms of theoretical complexity. Hence we focus on the operation of multiplication.

The analysis in Sect. 3.2 shows that our leveled BFV multiplication takes 14ℓ NTTs and $(4k\ell + 5\ell^2 + 2k + 18\ell)n$ integer multiplications (we ignore for simplicity a much smaller contribution of floating-point operations). We also add the computational cost of hybrid key switching used for relinearization as there is a difference in its cost between BFV and BGV. For key-switching we assume that the ciphertext element is decomposed into $d_{\text{num}} = \ell/\alpha$ digits, i.e. each digit is considered modulo α moduli. The cost of relinearization for BFV is $4\ell + 2\alpha$ NTTs and $n(3\alpha\ell + 2d_{\text{num}}\ell + 2\alpha + 5\ell)$ integer multiplications (see the full version for details). Here, for simplicity of analysis we assume that ℓ is the same for leveled BFV multiplication and subsequent relinearization. The total cost of multiplication and relinearization in BFV is $17\ell + 2\alpha$ NTTs and $n(4k\ell + 5\ell^2 + 2k + 23\ell + 3\alpha\ell + 2d_{\text{num}}\ell + 2\alpha)$ integer multiplications.

In the case of our BGV variant, the total cost of multiplication includes two modulus switching operations for input ciphertexts, the tensor product, and, finally, the relinearization. The cost of modulus switching is $4(\ell' + 1)$ NTTs and $4n(\ell' + 2)$ integer multiplications, where ℓ' is the number of CRT moduli after modulus switching. The cost of tensor product is $4n\ell'$ integer multiplications. The cost of relinearization in the case of BGV is: $4\ell' + 2\alpha'$ NTTs and $n(3\alpha'\ell' + 2d_{\text{num}}\ell' + 4\alpha' + 7\ell')$ integer multiplications. Hence the total cost of multiplication and relinearization is $8\ell' + 4 + 2\alpha'$ NTTs and $n(3\alpha'\ell' + 2d_{\text{num}}\ell' + 4\alpha' + 15\ell' + 8)$ integer multiplications.

One can observe that the number of NTTs needed for BFV multiplication appears to be 2x or even higher than for BGV. But we should keep in mind that typically $\ell' > \ell$. For example, when $t = 2$, we can even have $\ell' > 3\ell$ since in BFV we work with large (60-bit) moduli vs the moduli of size $\delta_R^2 t$ (less than 20 bits) in BGV. On the other hand, the cost of integer multiplications in BFV appears to be significantly higher due to multiple basis extension operations. The above may suggest that the complexity of BFV could be lower than for BGV at small t, while more significant benefits of BGV are expected as t is increased, when the ratio of ℓ'/ℓ becomes smaller than 2, which corresponds to the typical value of $t = 2^{16} + 1$ used for CRT packing. One could argue that this is essentially due to the assumption that the computations modulo each CRT moduli are implemented on different machine words, which is typically true for practical implementations of homomorphic encryption. As a consequence, while BGV might be practically slower than BFV at small t for classical implementations, we stress that this is only due to the way the CRT representation is usually implemented and that BGV still has a lower theoretical complexity than BFV even for small plaintext moduli.

Remark 7. To reduce even further the computational cost of BGV, one could trunk some CRT moduli together in the same 64-bit machine word. This would allow one to divide the number of moduli ℓ', and thus of NTTs, by a factor of 2 when the moduli are smaller than 30 bits ($t \approx 2^{11}$) and by a factor of 3 when they are smaller than 20 bits ($t \approx 2$).

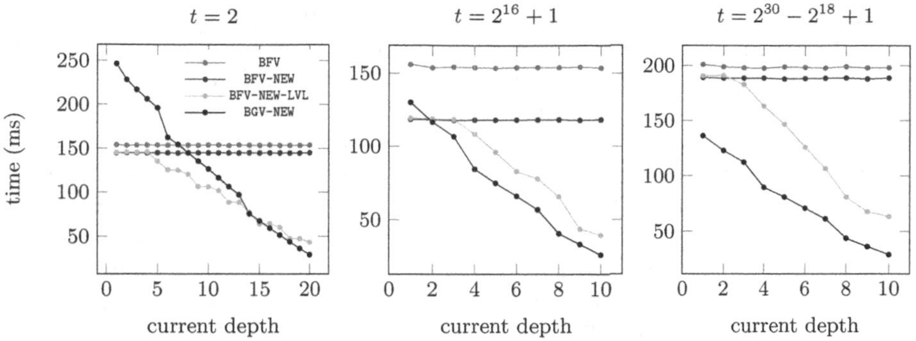

Fig. 1. Comparison of homomorphic multiplication runtimes for BFV and BGV variants at various depths as a function of plaintext modulus t. Hybrid key switching with 3 digits, i.e., $d_{\mathrm{num}} = 3$, was used, and N was set to 2^{15}.

5.3 Software Implementation and Experimentation Setup

We implemented all variants of BFV and BGV in PALISADE v1.10.4. The evaluation environment was a commodity desktop computer system with an Intel(R) Core(TM) i7-9700 CPU @ 3.00 GHz and 64 GB of RAM, running Ubuntu 18.04 LTS. The compiler was g++ 9.3.0. All experiments were executed in the single-threaded mode.

PALISADE includes the implementation of both BEHZ and HPS variants of BFV. The runtime results and noise growth for both variants are roughly the same (as shown in Sect. 5.4). We chose the HPS variant as the main RNS variant for our BFV modifications due to its relative simplicity. We denote our modified BFV variant as BFV-NEW, our modified BFV variant with leveled multiplication as BFV-NEW-LVL, and our BGV variant as BGV-NEW. Note that our implementation does not trunk small CRT moduli in BGV for small values of t, i.e., it does not include the optimization suggested in Remark 7.

5.4 Performance Comparison

Figure 1 illustrates the comparison of homomorphic multiplication runtimes for the BFV and BGV variants developed in this work to the baseline for the prior state-of-the-art BFV implementation of the HPS variant [21]. The first major observation is that BFV-NEW-LVL outperforms BGV-NEW for small plaintext moduli (at least up to depth 20), while BGV-NEW runs significantly faster than BFV-NEW-LVL for intermediate and large plaintext moduli, i.e., $t = 2^{16}+1$ and $t = 2^{30}-2^{18}+1$. This observation is in agreement with our theoretical complexity analysis in Sect. 5.2 since our implementation does not include the optimization suggested in Remark 7, i.e., small moduli are not trunked together. The second significant observation is that our best BFV variant, labeled as BFV-NEW-LVL, speeds up the runtime of deeper multiplications (depth-20 for $t = 2$ and depth-10 for higher t) by 3x-4x, as compared to the BFV baseline.

Table 2 shows the comparison of noise growth and runtimes for a binary tree computation ranging in multiplicative depth from 1 to 7. First, we want to point out that the noise growth and runtimes for the BEHZ and HPS variants are very close, with HPS having somewhat better runtime efficiency, which agrees well with the noise analysis in [6] and runtime comparison in [3]. In view of this, we chose HPS as the main variant for our `BFV` improvements (but similar gains can be expected for the BEHZ variant). Our next observation is that `BGV` has a slightly faster noise growth, as compared to all `BFV` variants, with the difference in noise increasing with depth (as predicted in Sect. 5.1). Note that the original `BFV` variants have somewhat higher noise (by almost constant number of bits) as compared to our `BFV` variants because they do not use the technique of encrypting with a slightly larger modulus Qp, followed with scaling by p. Our final observation is that `BGV-NEW` has a minor speed-up over the best `BFV` variant for the chosen plaintext modulus $t = 2^{16} + 1$. Note that the speed-up is observed only for this or higher plaintext moduli, with `BFV-NEW-LVL` becoming faster for $t = 2$ (see the full version for details). Tables in the appendix of the full version also show the more significant effect of $r_t(Q)$ on noise magnitude at larger plaintext moduli for the original `BFV`, as theoretically predicted in Sect. 3.

Table 2. Comparison of noise growth and runtimes of `BFV` and `BGV` variants for a benchmark computation $\prod_{i=1}^{2^k} x_i$. Hybrid key switching with 3 digits, i.e., $d_{\text{num}} = 3$, was used, t was set to $2^{16}+1$, and $\lambda \geq 128$. Here, e denotes the current noise magnitude, $\log Q$, the size of the `BFV` ciphertext modulus, and $\log Q_L$, the equivalent ciphertext modulus in `BGV` without the last CRT modulus q_{L+1}.

k	Original BFV							Our BFV							Our BGV				
	params			BEHZ		HPS		params			BFV-NEW		BFV-NEW-LVL		params			BGV-NEW	
	$\log N$	$\log q_i$	$\log Q$	$\log e$	Time (s)	$\log e$	Time (s)	$\log N$	$\log q_i$	$\log Q$	$\log e$	Time (s)	$\log e$	Time (s)	$\log N$	$\log q_i$	$\log Q_L$	$\log e$	Time (s)
1	13	31	62	45	0.011	44	0.01	13	59	59	36	0.004	35	0.004	13	33	58	34	0.005
2	13	47	94	66	0.034	66	0.03	13	45	90	63	0.025	63	0.025	13	33	91	67	0.02
3	14	43	129	102	0.24	103	0.21	14	41	123	95	0.19	96	0.18	13	33	124	100	0.063
4	14	53	159	131	0.52	132	0.45	14	52	156	125	0.4	125	0.39	13	33	157	133	0.17
5	14	48	192	158	1.41	161	1.2	14	47	188	155	1.07	155	1.04	14	34	196	171	0.8
6	14	56	224	189	2.85	189	2.44	14	55	220	184	2.18	184	2.13	14	34	230	205	2.03
7	14	51	255	221	7.61	220	6.51	14	50	250	214	5.98	214	5.73	14	34	264	239	4.86

Table 3 illustrates the comparison of noise growth and runtimes for a polynomial evaluation benchmark. Our first observation is that `BGV-NEW` has a significantly higher noise than all `BFV` variants because the moduli q_i in this case require extra room for the additions at each level (the deepest level has the most significant effect on all q_i's). `BGV-NEW` again has a minor advantage in terms of runtime as compared to our best `BFV` variant for $t = 2^{16} + 1$, but `BFV-NEW-LVL` becomes faster when we decrease t to smaller values (see the full version for details). Note that for $k = 8$, `BGV-NEW` has a smaller ring dimension than all `BFV` variants, which is an effect of the automated logic for hybrid key switching used in the implementation, rather than a result of better noise growth in `BGV` (since $\log Q$ in `BFV` is significantly smaller than $\log Q_L$ in `BGV`).

Table 3. Comparison of noise growth and runtimes of BFV and BGV variants for a benchmark computation $\prod_{i=0}^{k} a_i x^i$: $|a_i| < 16$. Hybrid key switching with 3 digits, i.e., $d_{\text{num}} = 3$, was used, t was set to $2^{16}+1$, and $\lambda \geq 128$. Here, e denotes the current noise magnitude, $\log Q$, the BFV ciphertext modulus, and $\log Q_L$, the equivalent ciphertext modulus in BGV without the last CRT modulus q_{L+1}.

k	Original BFV							Our BFV							Our BGV				
	params			BEHZ		HPS		params			BFV-NEW		BFV-NEW-LVL		params			BGV-NEW	
	$\log N$	$\log q_i$	$\log Q$	$\log e$	Time (s)	$\log e$	Time (s)	$\log N$	$\log q_i$	$\log Q$	$\log e$	Time (s)	$\log e$	Time (s)	$\log N$	$\log q_i$	$\log Q_L$	$\log e$	Time (s)
2	13	34	68	41	0.012	40	0.01	13	32	64	35	0.009	36	0.009 s	13	38	68	38	0.007
4	13	50	100	76	0.034	76	0.03	13	48	96	67	0.026	67	0.025 s	13	38	107	74	0.024
8	14	45	135	106	0.25	107	0.22	14	43	129	100	0.19	100	0.18 s	13	39	148	116	0.061
16	14	56	168	138	0.53	138	0.46	14	54	162	130	0.4	130	0.33 s	14	41	197	163	0.28
32	14	50	200	166	1.43	167	1.22	14	49	196	161	1.1	161	0.78 s	14	42	244	208	0.61
48	14	58	232	197	2.16	198	1.85	14	57	228	191	1.66	190	1.22 s	14	42	286	251	1.07
64	14	58	232	199	2.89	199	2.48	14	57	228	191	2.22	191	1.54 s	14	43	293	256	1.27

6 Concluding Remarks

Our theoretical analysis and experimental results show that the modified BFV variant has somewhat better noise growth than BGV for all plaintext moduli, though previous results suggested that BGV has a better noise growth than BFV for larger plaintext moduli [13,14]. This result is mainly due to our modification of the BFV encryption procedure. The other major conclusion is that, when the moduli of BGV are not trunked together, BFV is significantly faster for small plaintext moduli, e.g., $t = 2$, with BGV becoming faster as the plaintext modulus is increased.

The variant of BGV presented in this paper was mainly motivated by improving the usability of the scheme, which is known to be more challenging for use than BFV. From this perspective, this BGV variant is as easy to use as the implementation of BFV in PALISADE. However, the usability also has some performance cost, e.g., we have to choose the size of CRT moduli more conservatively. It would be interesting to examine how the performance of our BGV variant compares to the BGV design with dynamic noise estimation, which is implemented in HElib. It would not be fair to compare the PALISADE implementation directly with the HElib implementation as one would mostly observe the effect of differences in the efficiency of primitive ring operations, such as NTTs, rather than the differences between the BGV variants. For a fair comparison, a PALISADE implementation of the dynamic-noise BGV variant would be needed. Another potential improvement for BGV is to consider the idea of trunking multiple small CRT moduli mentioned in Remark 7. We plan to examine both ideas in our future work.

Acknowledgments. Andrey Kim and Yuriy Polyakov's NJIT work was supported in part by the Defense Advanced Research Projects Agency (DARPA) and the US Navy SPAWAR Systems Center Pacific (SSCPAC) under Contract Number N66001-17-1-4043 and the Office of the Director of National Intelligence (ODNI), Intelligence Advanced Research Projects Activity (IARPA), via Contract No. 2019-1902070006. The views and conclusions contained herein are those of the authors and should not be interpreted as necessarily representing the official policies, either expressed or implied, of the Department of Defense, ODNI, IARPA, or the U.S. Government. Vincent Zucca's KU Leuven work was supported in part by the Research Council KU Leuven grant C14/18/067, CyberSecurity Research Flanders with reference number VR20192203, and the IARPA HECTOR project under the solicitation number IARPA-BAA-17-05. We also thank Charlotte Bonte for a careful review of the first version of the paper, her feedback, and fruitful discussions that helped us to improve the paper.

References

1. Lattigo v2.1.1, December 2020. http://github.com/ldsec/lattigo. ePFL-LDS
2. PALISADE Lattice Cryptography Library (release 1.10.6), December 2020. https://palisade-crypto.org/
3. Al Badawi, A., Polyakov, Y., Aung, K.M.M., Veeravalli, B., Rohloff, K.: Implementation and performance evaluation of RNS variants of the BFV homomorphic encryption scheme. IEEE Trans. Emerg. Top. Comput. **9**(2), 941–956 (2021). https://doi.org/10.1109/TETC.2019.2902799
4. Albrecht, M., Chase, M., Chen, H., et al.: Homomorphic encryption security standard. Technical report, HomomorphicEncryption.org, Toronto, Canada, November 2018
5. Bajard, J.-C., Eynard, J., Hasan, M.A., Zucca, V.: A full RNS variant of FV like somewhat homomorphic encryption schemes. In: Avanzi, R., Heys, H. (eds.) SAC 2016. LNCS, vol. 10532, pp. 423–442. Springer, Cham (2017). https://doi.org/10.1007/978-3-319-69453-5_23
6. Bajard, J.C., Eynard, J., Martins, P., Sousa, L., Zucca, V.: Note on the noise growth of the RNS variants of the BFV scheme. Cryptology ePrint Archive, Report 2019/1266 (2019). https://eprint.iacr.org/2019/1266
7. Bos, J., et al.: CRYSTALS - kyber: a CCA-secure module-lattice-based KEM. In: 2018 IEEE European Symposium on Security and Privacy (EuroS P), pp. 353–367 (2018). https://doi.org/10.1109/EuroSP.2018.00032
8. Brakerski, Z.: Fully homomorphic encryption without modulus switching from classical GapSVP. In: Safavi-Naini, R., Canetti, R. (eds.) CRYPTO 2012. LNCS, vol. 7417, pp. 868–886. Springer, Heidelberg (2012). https://doi.org/10.1007/978-3-642-32009-5_50
9. Brakerski, Z., Gentry, C., Vaikuntanathan, V.: (leveled) fully homomorphic encryption without bootstrapping. ACM Trans. Comput. Theory (TOCT) **6**(3), 1–36 (2014)
10. Brakerski, Z., Vaikuntanathan, V.: Fully homomorphic encryption from ring-LWE and security for key dependent messages. In: Rogaway, P. (ed.) CRYPTO 2011. LNCS, vol. 6841, pp. 505–524. Springer, Heidelberg (2011). https://doi.org/10.1007/978-3-642-22792-9_29
11. Cheon, J.H., Kim, A., Kim, M., Song, Y.: Homomorphic encryption for arithmetic of approximate numbers. In: Takagi, T., Peyrin, T. (eds.) ASIACRYPT 2017. LNCS, vol. 10624, pp. 409–437. Springer, Cham (2017). https://doi.org/10.1007/978-3-319-70694-8_15
12. Chillotti, I., Gama, N., Georgieva, M., Izabachène, M.: Faster fully homomorphic encryption: bootstrapping in less than 0.1 seconds. In: Cheon, J.H., Takagi, T. (eds.) ASIACRYPT 2016. LNCS, vol. 10031, pp. 3–33. Springer, Heidelberg (2016). https://doi.org/10.1007/978-3-662-53887-6_1

13. Costache, A., Smart, N.P.: Which ring based somewhat homomorphic encryption scheme is best? In: Sako, K. (ed.) CT-RSA 2016. LNCS, vol. 9610, pp. 325–340. Springer, Cham (2016). https://doi.org/10.1007/978-3-319-29485-8_19
14. Costache, A., Laine, K., Player, R.: Evaluating the effectiveness of heuristic worst-case noise analysis in FHE. In: Chen, L., Li, N., Liang, K., Schneider, S. (eds.) ESORICS 2020. LNCS, vol. 12309, pp. 546–565. Springer, Cham (2020). https://doi.org/10.1007/978-3-030-59013-0_27
15. Ducas, L., Micciancio, D.: FHEW: bootstrapping homomorphic encryption in less than a second. In: Oswald, E., Fischlin, M. (eds.) EUROCRYPT 2015. LNCS, vol. 9056, pp. 617–640. Springer, Heidelberg (2015). https://doi.org/10.1007/978-3-662-46800-5_24
16. Fan, J., Vercauteren, F.: Somewhat practical fully homomorphic encryption. IACR Cryptol. ePrint Arch. **2012**, 144 (2012)
17. Gentry, C.: Fully homomorphic encryption using ideal lattices. In: Proceedings of the Forty-First Annual ACM Symposium on Theory of Computing, pp. 169–178 (2009)
18. Gentry, C., Halevi, S.: Implementing gentry's fully-homomorphic encryption scheme. In: Paterson, K.G. (ed.) EUROCRYPT 2011. LNCS, vol. 6632, pp. 129–148. Springer, Heidelberg (2011). https://doi.org/10.1007/978-3-642-20465-4_9
19. Gentry, C., Halevi, S., Smart, N.P.: Fully homomorphic encryption with polylog overhead. In: Pointcheval, D., Johansson, T. (eds.) EUROCRYPT 2012. LNCS, vol. 7237, pp. 465–482. Springer, Heidelberg (2012). https://doi.org/10.1007/978-3-642-29011-4_28
20. Gentry, C., Halevi, S., Smart, N.P.: Homomorphic evaluation of the AES circuit. In: Safavi-Naini, R., Canetti, R. (eds.) CRYPTO 2012. LNCS, vol. 7417, pp. 850–867. Springer, Heidelberg (2012). https://doi.org/10.1007/978-3-642-32009-5_49
21. Halevi, S., Polyakov, Y., Shoup, V.: An improved RNS variant of the BFV homomorphic encryption scheme. In: Matsui, M. (ed.) CT-RSA 2019. LNCS, vol. 11405, pp. 83–105. Springer, Cham (2019). https://doi.org/10.1007/978-3-030-12612-4_5
22. Halevi, S., Shoup, V.: Bootstrapping for HElib. Cryptology ePrint Archive, Report 2014/873 (2014). https://eprint.iacr.org/2014/873
23. Halevi, S., Shoup, V.: Design and implementation of HElib: a homomorphic encryption library. Cryptology ePrint Archive, Report 2020/1481 (2020)
24. Han, K., Ki, D.: Better bootstrapping for approximate homomorphic encryption. In: Jarecki, S. (ed.) CT-RSA 2020. LNCS, vol. 12006, pp. 364–390. Springer, Cham (2020). https://doi.org/10.1007/978-3-030-40186-3_16
25. Kim, A., Papadimitriou, A., Polyakov, Y.: Approximate homomorphic encryption with reduced approximation error. Cryptology ePrint Archive, Report 2020/1118 (2020). https://eprint.iacr.org/2020/1118
26. Kim, M., Song, Y., Li, B., Micciancio, D.: Semi-parallel logistic regression for GWAS on encrypted data. BMC Med. Genomics **13**(7), 1–13 (2020)
27. Lepoint, T., Naehrig, M.: A comparison of the homomorphic encryption schemes FV and YASHE. In: Pointcheval, D., Vergnaud, D. (eds.) AFRICACRYPT 2014. LNCS, vol. 8469, pp. 318–335. Springer, Cham (2014). https://doi.org/10.1007/978-3-319-06734-6_20
28. Micciancio, D., Polyakov, Y.: Bootstrapping in FHEW-like cryptosystems. Cryptology ePrint Archive, Report 2020/086 (2020). https://eprint.iacr.org/2020/086
29. Microsoft SEAL (2020). https://github.com/Microsoft/SEAL
30. Smart, N.P., Vercauteren, F.: Fully homomorphic SIMD operations. Des. Codes Crypt. **71**(1), 57–81 (2012). https://doi.org/10.1007/s10623-012-9720-4

Transciphering Framework for Approximate Homomorphic Encryption

Jihoon Cho[1(✉)], Jincheol Ha[2], Seongkwang Kim[2(✉)], Byeonghak Lee[2], Joohee Lee[1], Jooyoung Lee[2(✉)], Dukjae Moon[1], and Hyojin Yoon[1]

[1] Samsung SDS, Seoul, Korea
{jihoon1.cho,joohee1.lee,dukjae.moon,hj1230.yoon}@samsung.com
[2] KAIST, Daejeon, Korea
{smilecjf,ksg0923,lbh0307,hicalf}@kaist.ac.kr

Abstract. Homomorphic encryption (HE) is a promising cryptographic primitive that enables computation over encrypted data, with a variety of applications including medical, genomic, and financial tasks. In Asiacrypt 2017, Cheon et al. proposed the CKKS scheme to efficiently support approximate computation over encrypted data of real numbers. HE schemes including CKKS, nevertheless, still suffer from slow encryption speed and large ciphertext expansion compared to symmetric cryptography.

In this paper, we propose a novel hybrid framework, dubbed RtF (Real-to-Finite-field) framework, that supports CKKS. The main idea behind this construction is to combine the CKKS and the FV homomorphic encryption schemes, and use a stream cipher using modular arithmetic in between. As a result, real numbers can be encrypted without significant ciphertext expansion or computational overload on the client side.

As an instantiation of the stream cipher in our framework, we propose a new HE-friendly cipher, dubbed HERA, and extensively analyze its security and efficiency. The main feature of HERA is that it uses a simple randomized key schedule. Compared to recent HE-friendly ciphers such as FLIP and Rasta using randomized linear layers, HERA requires a smaller number of random bits. For this reason, HERA significantly outperforms existing HE-friendly ciphers on both the client and the server sides.

With the RtF transciphering framework combined with HERA at the 128-bit security level, we achieve small ciphertext expansion ratio with a range of 1.23 to 1.54, which is at least 23 times smaller than using (symmetric) CKKS-only, assuming the same precision bits and the same level of ciphertexts at the end of the framework. We also achieve 1.6 μs and 21.7 MB/s for latency and throughput on the client side, which are 9085 times and 17.8 times faster than the CKKS-only environment, respectively.

Keywords: Homomorphic encryption · Transciphering framework · Stream cipher · HE-friendly cipher

Jooyoung Lee—This work was supported by the National Research Foundation of Korea (NRF) grant funded by the Korea government (MSIT) (No. 2021R1F1A 1047146).

M. Tibouchi and H. Wang (Eds.): ASIACRYPT 2021, LNCS 13092, pp. 640–669, 2021.
https://doi.org/10.1007/978-3-030-92078-4_22

1 Introduction

Cryptography has been extensively used to protect data when it is stored (data-at-rest) or when it is being transmitted (data-in-transit). We also see increasing needs that data should be protected while it is being used, since it is often processed within untrusted environments. For example, organizations might want to migrate their computing environment from on-premise to public cloud, and to collaborate with their data without necessarily trusting each other. If data is protected by an encryption scheme which is *homomorphic*, then the cloud would be able to perform meaningful computations on the encrypted data, supporting a wide range of applications such as machine learning over a large amount of data preserving its privacy.

HOMOMORPHIC ENCRYPTION (FOR APPROXIMATE COMPUTATION). An encryption scheme that enables addition and multiplication over encrypted data without decryption key is called a *homomorphic encryption* (HE) scheme. Since the emergence of Gentry's blueprint [27], there has been a large amount of research in this area [10,18,25,29]. Various applications of HE to medical, genomic, and financial tasks have also been proposed [15,17,37,45].

However, real-world data typically contain some errors from their true values since they are represented by real numbers rather than bits or integers. Even in the case that input data are represented by exact numbers without approximation, one might have to approximate intermediate values during data processing for efficiency. Therefore, it would be practically relevant to support approximate computation over encrypted data. To the best of our knowledge, the CKKS encryption scheme [16] is the only one that provides the desirable feature using an efficient encoder for real numbers. Due to this feature, CKKS achieves good performance in various applications, for example, to securely evaluate machine learning algorithms on a real dataset [9,46].

Unfortunately, HE schemes including CKKS commonly have two technical problems: slow encryption speed and large ciphertext expansion; the encryption/decryption time and the evaluation time of HE schemes are relatively slow compared to conventional encryption schemes. In particular, ciphertext expansion seems to be an intrinsic problem of homomorphic encryption due to the noise used in the encryption algorithm. Although the ciphertext expansion has been significantly reduced down to the order of hundreds in terms of the ratio of a ciphertext size to its plaintext size since the invention of the batching technique [28], it does not seem to be acceptable from a practical view point. Furthermore, this ratio becomes even worse when it comes to encryption of a short message; encryption of a single bit might result in a ciphertext of a few megabytes.

TRANSCIPHERING FRAMEWORK FOR EXACT COMPUTATION. To address the issue of the ciphertext expansion and the client-side computational overload, a hybrid framework, also called a *transciphering framework*, has been proposed [45] (see Fig. 1). In the client-sever model, a client encrypts a message $\mathbf{m}$ using a symmetric cipher E with a secret key $\mathbf{k}$; this secret key is also encrypted

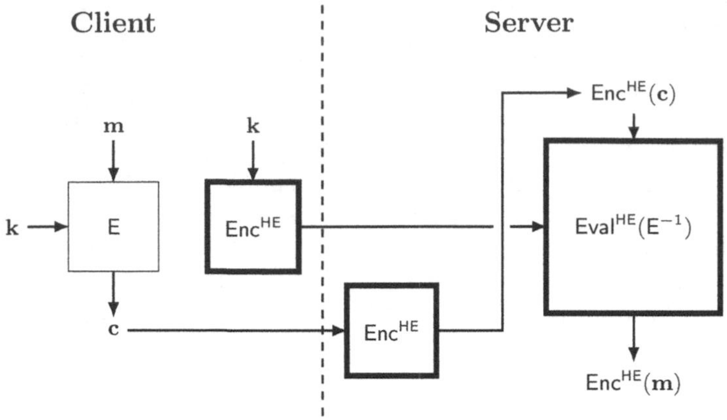

Fig. 1. The (basic) transciphering framework. Homomorphic operations are performed in the boxes with thick lines.

using an HE algorithm $\mathsf{Enc}^{\mathsf{HE}}$. The resulting ciphertexts $\mathbf{c} = \mathsf{E}_{\mathbf{k}}(\mathbf{m})$ and $\mathsf{Enc}^{\mathsf{HE}}(\mathbf{k})$ are stored in the server.

When the server wants to compute $\mathsf{Enc}^{\mathsf{HE}}(\mathbf{m})$ (for computation over encrypted data), it first computes $\mathsf{Enc}^{\mathsf{HE}}(\mathbf{c})$ for the corresponding ciphertext $\mathbf{c}$. Then the server homomorphically evaluates E^{-1} over $\mathsf{Enc}^{\mathsf{HE}}(\mathbf{c})$ and $\mathsf{Enc}^{\mathsf{HE}}(\mathbf{k})$, securely obtaining $\mathsf{Enc}^{\mathsf{HE}}(\mathbf{m})$.

Given a symmetric cipher with low multiplicative depth and complexity, this framework has the following advantages on the client side.

- A client does not need to encrypt all its data using an HE algorithm (except the symmetric key). All the data can be encrypted using only a symmetric cipher, significantly saving computational resources in terms of time and memory.
- Symmetric encryption does not result in ciphertext expansion, so the communication overload between the client and the server will be significantly low compared to using any homomorphic encryption scheme alone.

All these merits come at the cost of computational overload on the server side. That said, this trade-off would be worth considering in practice since servers are typically more powerful than clients.

HE-FRIENDLY CIPHERS. Symmetric ciphers are built on top of linear and nonlinear layers, and in a conventional environment, there has been no need to take different design principles for the two types of layers with respect to their implementation cost. However, when a symmetric cipher is combined with BGV/FV-style HE schemes in a transciphering framework, homomorphic addition becomes way cheaper than homomorphic multiplication in terms of computation time and noise growth. With this observation, efficiency of an HE-friendly cipher is evaluated by its multiplicative complexity and depth. In an arithmetic circuit, its multiplicative complexity is represented by the number of multiplications (ANDs in the binary case). Multiplicative depth is the depth of the tree that represents the arithmetic circuit, closely related to the noise growth in the HE-ciphertexts. These two metrics have brought a new direction in the design of symmetric ciphers: to use simple nonlinear layers at the cost of highly randomized linear layers as adopted in the design of FLIP [44] and Rasta [21].

1.1 Our Contribution

The main contribution of this paper is two-fold. First, we propose a new transciphering framework for the CKKS scheme that supports approximate computation over encrypted data. Second, we propose a new stream cipher, dubbed HERA (HE-friendly cipher with a RAndomized key schedule), to be built in our framework. Using our new transciphering framework combined with HERA, real numbers can be encrypted without significant ciphertext expansion or computational overload on the client side.

RtF TRANSCIPHERING FRAMEWORK. The transciphering framework in Fig. 1 does not directly apply to the CKKS scheme. The main reason is that it is infeasible to design an HE-friendly (deterministic) symmetric cipher E operating on real (or complex) numbers; if an HE-friendly symmetric cipher E over the real field exists, then E is given as a real polynomial map, and any ciphertext will be represented by a polynomial in the corresponding plaintext and the secret key over $\mathbb{R}$. Then, for given plaintext-ciphertext pairs $(\mathbf{m}_i, \mathbf{c}_i)$, an adversary will be able to establish a system of polynomial equations in the unknown key $\mathbf{k}$. The sum of $\|\mathsf{E}_{\mathbf{k}}(\mathbf{m}_i) - \mathbf{c}_i\|_2^2$ over the plaintext-ciphertext pairs also becomes a real polynomial, where the actual key is the zero of this function. Since this polynomial is differentiable, its (approximate) zeros will be efficiently found by using iterative algorithms such as the gradient descent algorithm. By taking multiple plaintext-ciphertext pairs, the probability of finding any false key will be negligible.

In order to overcome this problem, we combine CKKS with FV which is a homomorphic encryption scheme using modular arithmetic [25], obtaining a novel hybrid framework, dubbed the RtF (Real-to-Finite-field) transciphering framework. This framework inherits a wide range of usability from the previous transciphering framework, such as efficient short message encryption or flexible repacking of data on the server side. Additionally, our framework does not require to use the complex domain for message spaces (as in the CKKS scheme), or any expertise of the CKKS parameter setting on the client side.

In brief, the RtF framework works as follows. First, the client scales up and rounds off real messages into $\mathbb{Z}_t$. Then it encrypts the messages using a stream cipher E over $\mathbb{Z}_t$. This "E-ciphertext" will be sent to the server with an FV-encrypted secret key of E, and stored there.

Whenever a "CKKS-ciphertext" is needed for any message $\mathbf{m}$, the server encrypts the E-ciphertext of $\mathbf{m}$ in coefficients, using the FV scheme. With the resulting FV-ciphertext, say $\mathcal{C}$, and the FV-encrypted key, the server homomorphically evaluates the stream cipher E and moves the resulting keystreams from slots to coefficients using $\mathsf{SlotToCoeff}^{\mathsf{FV}}$. By subtracting this ciphertext from $\mathcal{C}$, the server obtains the FV-ciphertext of $\mathbf{m}$ in coefficients, not in slots. Finally, in order to translate this FV-ciphertext into the corresponding CKKS-ciphertext of $\mathbf{m}$ in slots, the server CKKS-bootstraps it. Since the message $\mathbf{m}$ should be moved from the coefficients to the slots, the last step of the bootstrapping, $\mathsf{SlotToCoeff}^{\mathsf{CKKS}}$, can be omitted. As a result, the server will be able to approximately evaluate any circuit on the CKKS-ciphertexts. Details of the framework are given in Sect. 3.

LOW-DEPTH STREAM CIPHERS USING MODULAR ARITHMETIC. In the RtF transciphering framework, a stream cipher using modular arithmetic is required as a building block. There are only a few ciphers using modular arithmetic [2,4,5,30], and even such algorithms are not suitable for our transciphering framework due to their high multiplicative depths. In order to make our transciphering framework efficiently work, we propose a new HE-friendly cipher HERA, operating on a modular space with low multiplicative depth.

Recent constructions for HE-friendly ciphers such as FLIP and Rasta use randomized linear layers in order to reduce the multiplicative depth without security degradation. However, this type of ciphers spend too many random bits to generate random matrices, slowing down the overall speed on both the client and the server sides. Instead of generating random matrices, we propose to randomize the key schedule algorithm by combining the secret key with a (public) random value for every round.

IMPLEMENTATION. We implement the RtF transciphering framework with the stream cipher HERA in public repository[1]. In Sect. 5.2, we present the benchmark of the client-side encryption in C++ and the server-side transciphering using the `Lattigo` library. We also compare our framework to PEGASUS [40] and CKKS only. In the full version of this paper [19], we compare HERA to existing HE-friendly ciphers using the `HElib` library.

In summary, we achieve small ciphertext expansion ratio with a range of 1.23 to 1.54 on the client side, which is 23 times smaller than the (symmetric) CKKS-only environment assuming similar precision and the same level of ciphertexts at the end of the framework. When it comes to latency and throughput, we achieve 1.6 μs and 21.7 MB/s on the client side, which is 9085 times and 17.8 times faster than the CKKS-only environment respectively. We refer to Sect. 5.2 for more details.

1.2 Related Work

HOMOMORPHIC EVALUATION OF SYMMETRIC CIPHERS. Since the transciphering framework has been introduced [45], early works have been focused on homomorphic evaluation of popular symmetric ciphers (e.g., AES [28], SIMON [39], and PRINCE [23]). Such ciphers have been designed without any consideration on their arithmetic complexity, so the performance of their homomorphic evaluation

[1] https://github.com/KAIST-CryptLab/RtF-Transciphering.

was not satisfactory. In this line of research, LowMC [3] is the first construction that aims to minimize the depth and the number of AND gates. However, it turned out that LowMC is vulnerable to algebraic attacks [20,22,47], so it has been revised later.[2]

Canteaut et al. [11] claimed that stream ciphers would be advantageous in terms of online complexity compared to block ciphers, and proposed a new stream cipher Kreyvium. However, its practical relevance is limited since the multiplicative depth (with respect to the secret key) keeps growing as keystreams are generated. The FLIP stream cipher [44] is based on a novel design strategy that its permutation layer is randomly generated for every encryption without increasing the algebraic degree in its secret key. Furthermore, it has been reported that FiLIP [43], a generalized instantiation of FLIP, can be efficiently evaluated with the TFHE scheme [34]. Rasta [21] is a stream cipher aiming at higher throughput at the cost of high latency using random linear layers, which are generated by an extendable output function. Dasta [33], a variant of Rasta using affine layers with lower entropy, boosts up the client-side computation. As another variant of Rasta, Masta [31] operates on a modular domain, improving upon Rasta in terms of the throughput of homomorphic evaluation.

Compression of HE Ciphertexts. In order to reduce the memory overhead when encrypting short messages, Chen et al. [12] also proposed an efficient LWEs-to-RLWE conversion method which enables transciphering to the CKKS ciphertexts: small messages can be encrypted by LWE-based symmetric encryption with a smaller ciphertext size (compared to RLWE-based encryption), and a collection of LWE ciphertexts can be repacked to an RLWE ciphertext to perform a homomorphic evaluation. Lu et al. [40] proposed a faster LWEs-to-RLWE conversion algorithm in a hybrid construction of FHEW and CKKS, dubbed PEGASUS, where the conversion is not limited to a small number of slots.

Chen et al. [13] proposed a hybrid HE scheme using the CKKS encoding algorithm and a variant of FV. This hybrid scheme makes the ciphertext size a few times smaller compared to using CKKS only, in particular, when the number of slots is small. However, the ciphertexts from this hybrid scheme are of size larger than tens of kilobytes, which limits its practical relevance.

2 Preliminaries

Notations. Throughout the paper, bold lowercase letters (resp. bold uppercase letters) denote vectors (resp. matrices). For a real number r, $\lfloor r \rceil$ denotes the nearest integer to r, rounding upwards in case of a tie. For an integer q, we identify $\mathbb{Z}_q$ with $\mathbb{Z} \cap (-q/2, q/2]$, and for any real number z, $[z]_q$ denotes the mod q reduction of z into $(-q/2, q/2]$. The notation $\lfloor \cdot \rceil$ and $[\cdot]_q$ are extended to vectors (resp. polynomials) to denote their component-wise (resp. coefficient-wise) reduction. For a complex vector $\mathbf{x}$, its ℓ_p-norm is denoted by $\|\mathbf{x}\|_p$. When

[2] https://github.com/LowMC/lowmc/blob/master/determine_rounds.py.

we say ℓ_p-norm of a polynomial, it means that the ℓ_p-norm of the coefficient vector of the polynomial.

Usual dot products of vectors are denoted by $\langle \cdot, \cdot \rangle$. Throughout the paper, ζ and ξ denote a $2N$-th primitive root of unity over the complex field $\mathbb{C}$, and the finite field $\mathbb{Z}_t$, respectively, for fixed parameters N and t. We denote the multiplicative group of $\mathbb{Z}_t$ by $\mathbb{Z}_t^\times$. The set of strings of arbitrary length over a set S is denoted by S^*. For two vectors (strings) $\mathbf{a}$ and $\mathbf{b}$, their concatenation is denoted by $\mathbf{a}\|\mathbf{b}$. For a set S, we will write $a \leftarrow S$ to denote that a is chosen from S uniformly at random. For a probability distribution $\mathcal{D}$, $a \leftarrow \mathcal{D}$ will denote that a is sampled according to the distribution $\mathcal{D}$. Unless stated otherwise, all logarithms are to the base 2.

2.1 Homomorphic Encryption

As the building blocks of our transciphering framework, we will briefly review the FV and CKKS homomorphic encryption schemes of which security is based on the hardness of Ring Learning With Errors (RLWE) problem [41,48]. For more details, we refer to [16,25].

It is remarkable that FV and CKKS use the same ciphertext space; for a positive integer q, an integer M which is a power of two, and $N = M/2$, both schemes use

$$\mathcal{R}_q = \mathbb{Z}_q[X]/(\Phi_M(X))$$

as their ciphertext spaces, where $\Phi_M(X) = X^N + 1$. They also use similar algorithms for key generation, encryption, decryption, and homomorphic addition and multiplication. However, the FV scheme supports *exact* computation modulo t (which satisfies $t \equiv 1 \pmod M$ throughout this paper), while the CKKS scheme supports *approximate* computation over the real numbers by taking different strategies to efficiently encode messages.

Encoders and Decoders. The main difference between FV and CKKS comes from their methods to encode messages lying in distinct spaces. The encoder $\mathsf{Ecd}_\ell^{\mathsf{FV}} : \mathbb{Z}_t^\ell \to \mathcal{R}_t$ of the FV scheme is the inverse of the decoder $\mathsf{Dcd}_\ell^{\mathsf{FV}}$ defined by, for $p(X) = \sum_{k=0}^{\ell-1} a_k X^{kN/\ell} \in \mathcal{R}_t$,

$$\mathsf{Dcd}_\ell^{\mathsf{FV}}(p(X)) = (p(\alpha_0), \cdots, p(\alpha_{\ell-1})) \in \mathbb{Z}_t^\ell,$$

where $\alpha_i = \xi^{5^i \cdot N/\ell} \pmod t$ for $0 \le i \le \ell/2 - 1$ and $\alpha_i = \xi^{-5^{i-\ell/2} \cdot N/\ell} \pmod t$ for $\ell/2 \le i \le \ell - 1$.[3]

Let Δ_{CKKS} be a positive real number (called a scaling factor in [16]). The CKKS encoder $\mathsf{Ecd}_{\ell/2}^{\mathsf{CKKS}} : \mathbb{C}^{\ell/2} \to \mathcal{R}$ is the (approximate) inverse of the decoder $\mathsf{Dcd}_{\ell/2}^{\mathsf{CKKS}} : \mathcal{R} \to \mathbb{C}^{\ell/2}$, where for $p(X) = \sum_{k=0}^{\ell-1} a_k X^{kN/\ell} \in \mathcal{R}$,

$$\mathsf{Dcd}_{\ell/2}^{\mathsf{CKKS}}(p(X)) = \Delta_{\mathsf{CKKS}}^{-1} \cdot (p(\beta_0), p(\beta_1), \cdots, p(\beta_{\ell/2-1})) \in \mathbb{C}^{\ell/2},$$

where $\beta_j = \zeta^{5^j \cdot N/\ell} \in \mathbb{C}$ for $0 \le j \le \ell/2 - 1$.

[3] A primitive root of unity ξ exists if the characteristic t of the message space is an odd prime such that $t \equiv 1 \pmod M$.

ALGORITHMS. FV and CKKS share a common key generation algorithm. The descriptions of those two schemes have also been merged, so that one can easily compare the differences between FV and CKKS.

- Key generation: given a security parameter $\lambda > 0$, fix integers N, P, and $q_0, \ldots, q_L$ such that q_i divides q_{i+1} for $0 \le i \le L-1$, and distributions $\mathcal{D}_{key}$, $\mathcal{D}_{err}$ and $\mathcal{D}_{enc}$ over $\mathcal{R}$ in a way that the resulting scheme is secure against any adversary with computational resource of $O(2^\lambda)$.
  1. Sample $a \leftarrow \mathcal{R}_{q_L}$, $s \leftarrow \mathcal{D}_{key}$, and $e \leftarrow \mathcal{D}_{err}$.
  2. The secret key is defined as $sk = (1, s) \in \mathcal{R}^2$, and the corresponding public key is defined as $pk = (b, a) \in \mathcal{R}^2_{q_L}$, where $b = [-a \cdot s + e]_{q_L}$.
  3. Sample $a' \leftarrow \mathcal{R}_{P \cdot q_L}$ and $e' \leftarrow \mathcal{D}_{err}$.
  4. The evaluation key is defined as $evk = (b', a') \in \mathcal{R}^2_{P \cdot q_L}$, where $b' = [-a' \cdot s + e' + Ps']_{P \cdot q_L}$ for $s' = [s^2]_{q_L}$.
- Encryption: given a public key $pk \in \mathcal{R}^2_{q_L}$ and a plaintext $m \in \mathcal{R}$,
  1. Sample $r \leftarrow \mathcal{D}_{enc}$ and $e_0, e_1 \leftarrow \mathcal{D}_{err}$.
  2. Compute $\mathsf{Enc}(pk, 0) = [r \cdot pk + (e_0, e_1)]_{q_L}$.
  - For FV, $\mathsf{Enc}^{\mathsf{FV}}(pk, m) = [\mathsf{Enc}(pk, 0) + (\Delta_{\mathsf{FV}} \cdot [m]_t, 0)]_{q_L}$, where $\Delta_{\mathsf{FV}} = \lfloor q_L / t \rceil$.
  - For CKKS, $\mathsf{Enc}^{\mathsf{CKKS}}(pk, m) = [\mathsf{Enc}(pk, 0) + (m, 0)]_{q_L}$.
- Decryption: given a secret key $sk \in \mathcal{R}^2$ and a ciphertext $ct \in \mathcal{R}^2_{q_l}$,

$$\mathsf{Dec}^{\mathsf{FV}}(sk, ct) = \left\lfloor \frac{t}{q_l} [\langle sk, ct \rangle]_{q_l} \right\rceil;$$

$$\mathsf{Dec}^{\mathsf{CKKS}}(sk, ct) = [\langle sk, ct \rangle]_{q_l}.$$

- Addition: given ciphertexts ct_1 and ct_2 in $\mathcal{R}^2_{q_l}$, their sum is defined as

$$ct_{add} = [ct_1 + ct_2]_{q_l}.$$

- Multiplication: given ciphertexts $ct_1 = (b_1, a_1)$ and $ct_2 = (b_2, a_2)$ in $\mathcal{R}^2_{q_l}$ and an evaluation key evk, their product is defined as

$$ct_{mult} = \left[(d_0, d_1) + \left\lfloor P^{-1} \cdot d_2 \cdot evk \right\rceil\right]_{q_l},$$

  where (d_0, d_1, d_2) is defined by $[(b_1 b_2, a_1 b_2 + a_2 b_1, a_1 a_2)]_{q_l}$ when using CKKS and $\left[\left\lfloor \frac{t}{q_l}(b_1 b_2, a_1 b_2 + a_2 b_1, a_1 a_2) \right\rceil\right]_{q_l}$ when using FV.
- Rescaling (Modulus switching): given a ciphertext $ct \in \mathcal{R}^2_{q_l}$ and $l' < l$, its rescaled ciphertext is defined as

$$\mathsf{Rescale}_{l \to l'}(ct) = \left[\left\lfloor \frac{q_{l'}}{q_l} \cdot ct \right\rceil\right]_{q_{l'}}.$$

2.2 Some Notable Homomorphic Operations

Bootstrapping for CKKS. The bootstrapping procedure for CKKS has been actively studied recently [8,14,32,38]. Let ct be a CKKS-ciphertext of $m(Y) \in \mathbb{Z}[Y]/(Y^\ell + 1)$ with respect to the secret key sk and the ciphertext modulus q, where $Y = X^{N/\ell}$, namely, $m(Y) = [\langle ct, sk \rangle]_q$. In this case, $m(Y)$ has $\ell/2$ slots. The CKKS bootstrapping aims to find a larger modulus $Q > q$ and a ciphertext ct' such that $m(Y) = [\langle ct', sk \rangle]_Q$. It consists of five steps: ModRaise, SubSum, $\mathsf{CoeffToSlot}^{\mathsf{CKKS}}$, EvalMod, and $\mathsf{SlotToCoeff}^{\mathsf{CKKS}}$.

- ModRaise: If we set $t(X) = \langle ct, sk \rangle \in \mathcal{R}$, then $t(X) = q \cdot I(X) + m(Y)$ for some $I(X) \in \mathcal{R}$. ModRaise raises the ciphertext modulus to $Q \gg q$ so that ct is regarded as an encryption of $t(X)$ with respect to modulus Q.
- SubSum: If $N \neq \ell$, then SubSum maps $I(X)$ to a polynomial in Y, that is, $q \cdot I(X) + m(Y)$ to $(N/\ell) \cdot (q \cdot \tilde{I}(Y) + m(Y))$.
- $\mathsf{CoeffToSlot}^{\mathsf{CKKS}}$: Since the message $q \cdot I(X) + m(Y)$ is in the coefficient domain, it requires homomorphic evaluation of the encoding algorithm to enable slot-wise modulo q operation. $\mathsf{CoeffToSlot}^{\mathsf{CKKS}}$ performs homomorphic evaluation of the inverse Discrete Fourier Transform (DFT) to obtain the ciphertext(s) of $\mathsf{Ecd}^{\mathsf{CKKS}}(q \cdot I(X) + m(Y))$.
- EvalMod: To approximate the modulo q operation, EvalMod homomorphically evaluates a polynomial approximation of $f(t) = \frac{q}{2\pi} \sin\left(\frac{2\pi t}{q}\right)$. In recent works [8,32], Chebyshev polynomial approximations are used.
- $\mathsf{SlotToCoeff}^{\mathsf{CKKS}}$: It performs homomorphic evaluation of DFT to output a ciphertext of $m(Y)$ back in its coefficient domain.

Operations in FV. In the FV scheme, there are two operations between slots and coefficients.

- $\mathsf{CoeffToSlot}^{\mathsf{FV}}$: It is a homomorphic evaluation of FV-encoding function. It semantically puts the coefficients of a plaintext polynomial into the vector of slots. It is done by multiplying the inverse Number Theoretic Transform (NTT) matrix.
- $\mathsf{SlotToCoeff}^{\mathsf{FV}}$: It is a homomorphic evaluation of FV-decoding function. It semantically puts the slot vector of a message into the coefficients of the plaintext polynomial. It is also done by multiplying the NTT matrix.

3 RtF Transciphering Framework

In this section, we describe how the RtF transciphering framework works, and analyze the message precision of the framework.

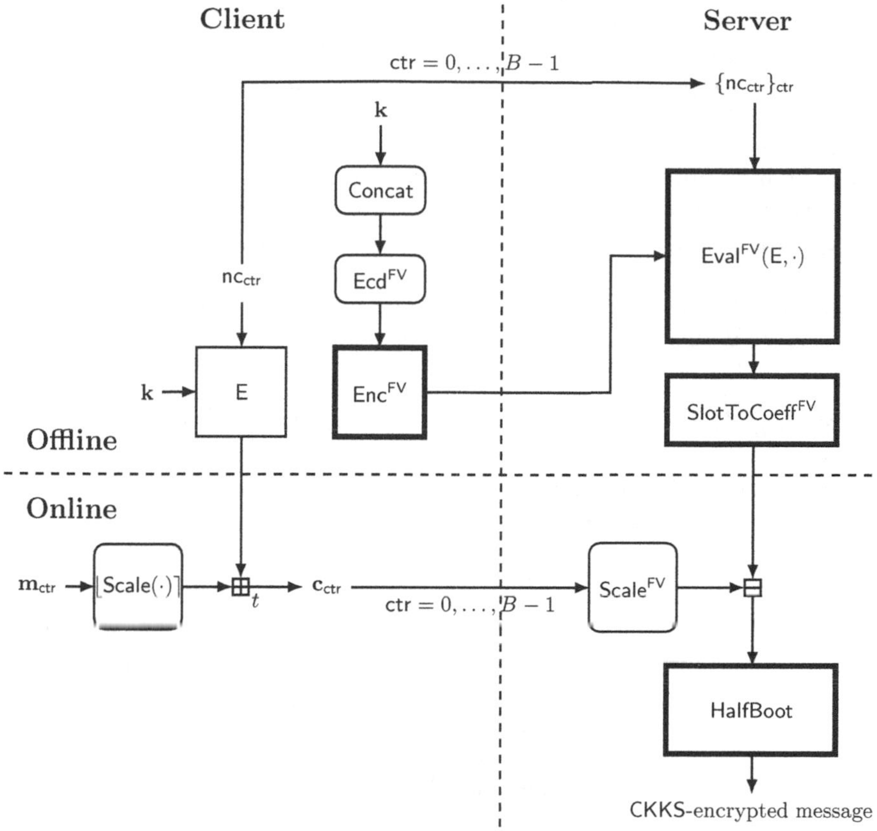

Fig. 2. The RtF transciphering framework. Homomorphic encryption and evaluation is performed in the boxes with thick lines. Operations in the boxes with rounded corners do not use any secret information. The vertical dashed line distinguishes the client-side and the server-side computation, while the horizontal dashed line distinguishes the offline and the online computation. The client sends ciphertexts block by block, while the server gathers B ciphertext blocks and recovers the CKKS-encrypted message of the ciphertexts.

3.1 Overview of the Framework

Our RtF transciphering framework aims to replace the (basic) transciphering framework in Fig. 1 to support CKKS, when equipped with any suitable stream cipher. The overall design is depicted in Fig. 2. At a high level, we propose to use a stream cipher operating on $\mathbb{Z}_t^n$ to encrypt real number messages on the client side and to convert the ciphertexts into the corresponding CKKS ciphertexts on the server side. In this regard, it is required to employ an additional HE scheme which provides homomorphic evaluation of keystreams of the stream cipher over the modulo t spaces efficiently, and we use FV for this purpose.

The main idea of the RtF framework is to inject real messages into the coefficients of plaintext polynomials of FV and to delegate encoding/decoding to the server via SlotToCoeff and CoeffToSlot for FV and CKKS which is described more precisely as follows.

First, a message of real numbers $\mathbf{m}_{\mathsf{ctr}} \in \mathbb{R}^n$ is scaled into $\mathbb{Z}_t^n$ by multiplying by a constant and rounding, and encrypted to $\mathbf{c}_{\mathsf{ctr}}$ on the client side. After gathering symmetric ciphertexts $\mathbf{c}_{\mathsf{ctr}}$'s from the client, the server generates a polynomial $C \in \mathcal{R}_t$ whose coefficients are components of $\mathbf{c}_{\mathsf{ctr}}$'s. Then the polynomial is scaled up into the FV ciphertext space by multiplying Δ_{FV}, say $\mathcal{C} = (\Delta_{\mathsf{FV}} \cdot C, 0)$.[4] On the other hand, when the server evaluates the symmetric cipher, a bunch of the keystream is FV-encrypted in slots. In order to match the domain of computation, the server evaluates

$$\mathsf{SlotToCoeff}^{\mathsf{FV}} : \mathsf{Enc}^{\mathsf{FV}}(\mathsf{Ecd}^{\mathsf{FV}}(z_0, \ldots, z_{N-1})) \mapsto \mathsf{Enc}^{\mathsf{FV}}(z_0 + \cdots + z_{N-1}X^{N-1})$$

after evaluation of the cipher, where $(z_0, \ldots, z_{N-1})$ is the concatenated keystream. Then, homomorphically computing

$$(\Delta_{\mathsf{FV}} \cdot C, 0) - \mathsf{Enc}^{\mathsf{FV}}(z_0 + \cdots + z_{N-1}X^{N-1}),$$

we have $\mathsf{Enc}^{\mathsf{FV}}(m_0 + \cdots + m_{N-1}X^{N-1})$, where $(m_0, \ldots, m_{N-1})$ is the concatenated message. The next step is to convert the type of encryption to CKKS and then to put the messages into slots, which can be done by HalfBoot.

In the bootstrapping procedure, there are five steps as follows:

$$\mathsf{ModRaise} \rightarrow \mathsf{SubSum} \rightarrow \mathsf{CoeffToSlot}^{\mathsf{CKKS}} \rightarrow \mathsf{EvalMod} \rightarrow \mathsf{SlotToCoeff}^{\mathsf{CKKS}}.$$

HalfBoot basically follows the procedure of CKKS bootstrapping, except the final $\mathsf{SlotToCoeff}^{\mathsf{CKKS}}$ step. Since the input ciphertext of HalfBoot contains the original message $(m_0, \ldots, m_{N-1})$ in coefficients rather than slots, it does not require to move data in slots back to coefficients after EvalMod. Furthermore, with an appropriate rescaling, HalfBoot gives an effect of full bootstrapping to enable further approximate computations on the output CKKS ciphertexts.

3.2 Specification

For a fixed security parameter λ, all the other parameters for the FV and the CKKS schemes will be set accordingly, including the degree of the polynomial modulus N, the ciphertext moduli $\{q_i\}_{i=0}^{L}$ (used for both FV and CKKS), and the FV plaintext modulus t. With these parameters fixed, we will describe how the framework works, distinguishing four parts; initialization, client-side computation, and offline/online server-side computation (see Fig. 2). The client-side and server-side computations are described in Algorithm 1 and Algorithm 2, respectively.

---

[4] We note that $\mathbf{c}_{\mathsf{ctr}}$'s are in coefficients, not in slots.

Algorithm 1: Client-side symmetric key encryption of the RtF transciphering framework

Input:
- Nonce $\mathsf{nc}_{\mathsf{ctr}} \in \{0,1\}^\lambda$
- Symmetric key $\mathbf{k} \in \mathbb{Z}_t^n$
- Tuple of messages $\mathbf{m}_{\mathsf{ctr}} \in \mathbb{R}^n$
- Scaling factor δ

Output:
- Symmetric ciphertext $\mathbf{c}_{\mathsf{ctr}} \in \mathbb{Z}_t^n$

$\mathbf{z}_{\mathsf{ctr}} \leftarrow \mathsf{E}(\mathbf{k}_{\mathsf{ctr}}, \mathsf{nc}_{\mathsf{ctr}})$
$\widetilde{\mathbf{m}}_{\mathsf{ctr}} \leftarrow \lfloor \delta \cdot \mathbf{m}_{\mathsf{ctr}} \rceil$
$\mathbf{c}_{\mathsf{ctr}} \leftarrow [\widetilde{\mathbf{m}}_{\mathsf{ctr}} + \mathbf{z}_{\mathsf{ctr}}]_t$
return $\mathbf{c}_{\mathsf{ctr}}$

INITIALIZATION. We use FV and CKKS with the same cyclotomic polynomial of degree N, and the same public-private key pair (pk, sk). The public key pk is shared by the server and the client. Let ℓ be the number of used slots per FV-ciphertext to encrypt $\mathbf{k} \in \mathbb{Z}_t^n$ which satisfies $n \mid \ell$ and $\ell \mid N$. To enable SIMD evaluation for keystreams, we consider the following matrix of B duplications of $\mathbf{k}$.

$$\mathsf{Concat}(\mathbf{k}) := \underbrace{(\mathbf{k}\|\mathbf{k}\| \cdots \|\mathbf{k})}_{B\text{-times}} \in \mathbb{Z}_t^{n \times B}.$$

The client can pack the coefficients of matrix $\mathsf{Concat}(\mathbf{k})$ column-wisely into one glued column vector in $\mathbb{Z}_t^{nB}$ or row-by-row manner, which are called column-wise and row-wise packing, respectively. The number of keystreams calculated in a single ciphertext (resp. n ciphertexts) is $B = \ell/n$ for column-wise packing (resp. $B = \ell$ for row-wise packing). We refer to the full version [19] for more details.

To summarize, the client computes

$$\mathcal{K} := \mathsf{Enc}^{\mathsf{FV}}(pk, \mathsf{Ecd}^{\mathsf{FV}}(\mathsf{Concat}(\mathbf{k}))),$$

and sends $\mathcal{K}$ to the server. We note that this initialization phase can be done only once at the beginning of the RtF framework. The client also generates a random value $\mathsf{nc} \in \{0,1\}^\lambda$ and sends it to the server.

CLIENT-SIDE COMPUTATION. Given a nonce $\mathsf{nc} \in \{0,1\}^\lambda$, a secret key $\mathbf{k} \in \mathbb{Z}_t^n$ of E, an n-tuple of real messages $\mathbf{m} = (m_0, \ldots, m_{n-1}) \in \mathbb{R}^n$, and a scaling factor $\delta > 0$, the client executes the following encryption algorithm as described in Algorithm 1.

The client computes keystream $\mathbf{z} = \mathsf{E}_{\mathbf{k}}(\mathsf{nc}) \in \mathbb{Z}_t^n$. Then, the client scales the message $\mathbf{m}$ by multiplying δ to every component of $\mathbf{m}$. Rounding it off gives a

Algorithm 2: Server-side homomorphic evaluation of decryption of the RtF transciphering framework

Input:
- Set of nonces $\mathsf{nc}_0, \ldots, \mathsf{nc}_{B-1} \in \{0,1\}^\lambda$
- Homomorphically encrypted keys $\mathcal{K} = \mathsf{Enc}^{\mathsf{FV}}\left(\mathsf{Ecd}^{\mathsf{FV}}(\mathsf{Concat}(\mathbf{k}))\right)$
- Tuple of symmetric ciphertexts $\mathbf{c} = (\mathbf{c}_0, \ldots, \mathbf{c}_{B-1}) \in (\mathbb{Z}_t^n)^B$

Output:
- CKKS-encrypted message $\mathcal{M}$

$\mathcal{V} \leftarrow \mathsf{Eval}^{\mathsf{FV}}(\mathsf{E}, \mathcal{K}, \{\mathsf{nc}_{\mathsf{ctr}}\}_{\mathsf{ctr}})$
$\mathcal{Z} \leftarrow \mathsf{SlotToCoeff}^{\mathsf{FV}}(\mathcal{V})$
$C \leftarrow \mathsf{VecToPoly}(\mathbf{c})$
$\mathcal{C} \leftarrow (\Delta_{\mathsf{FV}} \cdot C, 0)$
$\mathcal{X} \leftarrow [\mathcal{C} - \mathcal{Z}]_q$
$\mathcal{X} \leftarrow \mathsf{Rescale}_{\rightarrow 0}(\mathcal{X})$ `// Rescale to the lowest level`
$\mathcal{M} \leftarrow \mathsf{HalfBoot}(\mathcal{X})$
return $\mathcal{M}$

vector $\widetilde{\mathbf{m}} \in \mathbb{Z}^n$. If t and δ are appropriately chosen, the norm $\|\widetilde{\mathbf{m}}\|_\infty$ can be upper bounded by $t/2$. Finally, the client computes

$$\mathbf{c} := [\widetilde{\mathbf{m}} + \mathbf{z}]_t ,$$

and sends it to the server.

Offline Server-side Computation. Given a tuple of nonces $(\mathsf{nc}_0, \ldots, \mathsf{nc}_{B-1})$ and the FV-encrypted key $\mathcal{K}$, the server is able to construct a circuit for the homomorphic evaluation of E, denoted by $\mathsf{Eval}^{\mathsf{FV}}(\mathsf{E}, \{\mathsf{nc}_{\mathsf{ctr}}\}_{\mathsf{ctr}}, \cdot)$. The circuit constructed for column-wise (resp. row-wise) packing method returns 1 ciphertext (resp. n ciphertexts) which packs ℓ/n keystreams (resp. ℓ keystreams). With the FV-encrypted key $\mathcal{K}$, the server homomorphically computes $\mathcal{V} := \mathsf{Eval}^{\mathsf{FV}}(\mathsf{E}, \{\mathsf{nc}_{\mathsf{ctr}}\}_{\mathsf{ctr}}, \mathcal{K})$. For ease of notation, we explain the remaining parts with column-wise packing method. Denoting the concatenation of ℓ/n keystreams by $(z_0, \ldots, z_{\ell-1}) \in \mathbb{Z}_t^\ell$, the resulting FV-ciphertext $\mathcal{V}$ can be represented as

$$\mathsf{Enc}^{\mathsf{FV}}\left(\mathsf{Ecd}_\ell^{\mathsf{FV}}(z_0, \ldots, z_{\ell-1})\right).$$

Finally, the server computes

$$\mathcal{Z} := \mathsf{SlotToCoeff}^{\mathsf{FV}}(\mathcal{V}) = \mathsf{Enc}^{\mathsf{FV}}\left(\sum_{k=0}^{\ell-1} z_k X^{k \cdot N/\ell}\right).$$

ONLINE SERVER-SIDE COMPUTATION. Given a tuple of symmetric ciphertexts $\mathbf{c} = (\mathbf{c}_0, \ldots, \mathbf{c}_{\ell/n-1}) \in (\mathbb{Z}_t^n)^{\ell/n}$, the server scales up $\mathbf{c}$ into FV-ciphertext space to enable FV evaluation, namely

$$C := \mathsf{VecToPoly}(\mathbf{c}),$$
$$\mathcal{C} := (\Delta_{\mathsf{FV}} \cdot C, 0),$$

where VecToPoly is defined by

$$\mathsf{VecToPoly}: \quad \mathbb{R}^\ell \longrightarrow \mathbb{R}[X]/(\Phi_{2N}(X))$$
$$(m_0, \ldots, m_{\ell-1}) \mapsto \sum_{k=0}^{\ell-1} m_k X^{k \cdot N/\ell}.$$

Then, server computes $\mathcal{X} := [\mathcal{C} - \mathcal{Z}]_q$, where q is the ciphertext modulus of $\mathcal{Z}$, and rescales it to the lowest level of CKKS.

Now, the only remaining procedure is HalfBoot, which combines ModRaise, SubSum, $\mathsf{CoeffToSlot}^{\mathsf{CKKS}}$, and EvalMod sequentially. Denoting the scaled message by $(\widetilde{\mathbf{m}}_0, \ldots, \widetilde{\mathbf{m}}_{\ell/n-1}) := (\widetilde{m}_0, \ldots, \widetilde{m}_{\ell-1}) \in \mathbb{Z}^\ell$, the resulting ciphertext can be represented as

$$\mathcal{X} := \mathsf{Enc}^{\mathsf{CKKS}}\left(\sum_{k=0}^{\ell-1} \widetilde{m}_k X^{k \cdot N/\ell}\right).$$

Then, after ModRaise, we have

$$\mathcal{X}' := \mathsf{Enc}^{\mathsf{CKKS}}\left(\sum_{k=0}^{\ell-1} \widetilde{m}_k X^{k \cdot N/\ell} + q_0 \cdot I(X)\right)$$

for some polynomial $I(X) = r_0 + \cdots + r_{N-1}X^{N-1} \in \mathcal{R}$. By evaluating SubSum, the polynomial $I(X)$ becomes sparsely packed

$$\widetilde{I}(X) = \frac{N}{\ell} \sum_{k=0}^{\ell-1} r_{k \cdot N/\ell} X^{k \cdot N/\ell}$$

and the message is scaled by N/ℓ, say $\widetilde{m}_k \leftarrow (N/\ell) \cdot \widetilde{m}_k$. Evaluating $\mathsf{CoeffToSlot}^{\mathsf{CKKS}}$ gives two ciphertexts as follows.

$$\mathcal{Y}_0 = \mathsf{Enc}^{\mathsf{CKKS}}\left(\mathsf{Ecd}_{\ell/2}^{\mathsf{CKKS}}(\widetilde{m}_0 + q_0\widetilde{r}_0, \ldots, \widetilde{m}_{\ell/2-1} + q_0\widetilde{r}_{\ell/2-1})\right)$$
$$\mathcal{Y}_1 = \mathsf{Enc}^{\mathsf{CKKS}}\left(\mathsf{Ecd}_{\ell/2}^{\mathsf{CKKS}}(\widetilde{m}_{\ell/2} + q_0\widetilde{r}_{\ell/2}, \ldots, \widetilde{m}_{\ell-1} + q_0\widetilde{r}_{\ell-1})\right)$$

where $\widetilde{r}_k = (N/\ell) \cdot r_{k \cdot N/\ell}$ for $k = 0, 1, \ldots, \ell - 1$. If $\ell \neq N$, then those two ciphertexts can be packed in a ciphertext. As EvalMod evaluates the modulo-q_0 operation approximately, EvalMod operation results in what we want.

3.3 Message Precision

As the CKKS scheme adds some noise for every arithmetic operation, it is important to analyze how close the output $\mathcal{M}$ of Algorithm 2 is to the original message. In this section, we bound the error occurred in the RtF framework. First, we bound the error in the middle state $\mathcal{X}$ in Algorithm 2.

Let $\mathbf{m} \in \mathbb{R}^\ell$ be an (ℓ/n)-concatenation of the client's message as an input to Algorithm 1 such that $\widetilde{\mathbf{m}} = \lfloor \delta \cdot \mathbf{m} \rceil$ and $\|\widetilde{\mathbf{m}}\|_\infty \leq \lfloor t/2 \rfloor$, and let $\mathcal{X}$ be the state in line 5 of Algorithm 2 before rescaling to zero level and HalfBoot in Algorithm 2. If $e_{\mathsf{eval}} \in \mathcal{R}$ is an error from homomorphic evaluation of E with FV such that $\|e_{\mathsf{eval}}\|_\infty < \Delta_{\mathsf{FV}}/2$ (i.e., the ciphertext is correctly FV-decryptable), then we have

$$\left\| \mathsf{VecToPoly}(\mathbf{m}) - \frac{\mathsf{Dec}^{\mathsf{CKKS}}(\mathcal{X})}{\delta \Delta_{\mathsf{FV}}} \right\|_\infty \leq \frac{1}{2\delta} + \frac{\|e_{\mathsf{eval}}\|_\infty}{\Delta_{\mathsf{FV}}\delta}$$
$$\leq \frac{1}{2\delta} + \frac{1}{2\delta} = \frac{1}{\delta}$$

since $\|\mathbf{m} - \widetilde{\mathbf{m}}/\delta\|_\infty \leq \frac{1}{2\delta}$ and $[\widetilde{\mathbf{m}}]_t = \widetilde{\mathbf{m}}$. We remark that e_{eval} depends on the construction of E, which will be bounded appropriately for our new stream cipher and proposed parameters for HE.

The change of the message precision in HalfBoot varies according to which specific algorithm is used. We basically follow the work of Bossuat et al. [8] of CKKS bootstrapping, and we describe the message precision using those results.

In the bootstrapping procedure, the most significant step is to approximate modular reduction, which corresponds to EvalMod. As modular reduction itself is not well-matched with polynomial approximation, the sine function is commonly used as a stepping-stone to evaluate modular reduction in bootstrapping algorithms. As a result, there are two kinds of error to be considered in EvalMod: one from distance between modular reduction and sine function, and the other from polynomial approximation of the sine function.

The first one, from distance between modular reduction and the sine function, is mainly determined by the ratio of the bootstrapping scaling factor Δ' to the modulus q_0. Bootstrapping algorithms use scaling factor Δ' larger than default scaling factor Δ_{CKKS} used for basic arithmetic, since approximating modular reduction induces much larger error. In this case, the distance between the modular reduction and the sine function is bounded by Taylor's theorem as follows.

$$\left| \frac{q_0}{\Delta'} \left[\frac{\Delta'}{q_0} x \right]_1 - \frac{q_0}{2\pi\Delta'} \sin\left(\frac{2\pi\Delta' x}{q_0} \right) \right| \leq \frac{q_0}{2\pi\Delta'} \cdot \frac{1}{3!} \left(\frac{2\pi\Delta'}{q_0} \right)^3 = \frac{2\pi^2}{3} \left(\frac{\Delta'}{q_0} \right)^2 \quad (1)$$

provided that $|x| \leq 1$.

The other error from polynomial approximation of the sine function is determined by the polynomial interpolation algorithms. In this step, Bossuat et al. [8] adopt a specialized Chebyshev interpolation proposed by Han and Ki [32] for sparse keys, and combine it with their optimization method, which is called errorless polynomial evaluation. The error bound is calculated based on the distribution of Chebyshev nodes which is empirically achieved, and we recommend to see [32] for further discussion. Similarly to (1), this error bound also decreases when Δ'/q_0 gets smaller. Thus, we present an experimental result of correlation between Δ'/q_0 and the message precision in Table 1.

Table 1. This table presents experimental error of HalfBoot for various Δ'/q_0. The value ε is the mean error occurred by HalfBoot. The experiment is done by using parameter `Par-128` in Table 4 except Δ'/q_0.

Δ'/q_0	2^{-6}	2^{-7}	2^{-8}	2^{-9}	2^{-10}	2^{-11}	2^{-12}
$-\log\varepsilon$	11.29	13.29	15.30	17.29	19.28	21.24	22.73

In our transciphering framework, the value Δ'/q_0 is approximately δ/t. The plaintext modulus t should be larger than the number of precision bits, which is the reason for ciphertext expansion in our framework. This expansion can be reduced when arcsin is evaluated after the sine function.

After HalfBoot, we obtain a refreshed CKKS ciphertext of pre-determined scale Δ_{CKKS} as a result of RtF framework. Although we can freely choose the final scale Δ_{CKKS}, the message precision of the RtF framework cannot exceed $\log\delta$ bits. Hence it is enough to choose $\Delta_{\mathsf{CKKS}} \gg \delta N$ to ensure maximum precision $\log\delta$ against scaling error.

4 A New Stream Cipher over $\mathbb{Z}_t$

The RtF transciphering framework requires a stream cipher with a variable plaintext modulus. In this section, we propose a new stream cipher HERA using modular arithmetic, and analyze its security.

4.1 Specification

A stream cipher HERA for λ-bit security takes as input a symmetric key $\mathbf{k} \in \mathbb{Z}_t^{16}$, a nonce $\mathsf{nc} \in \{0,1\}^\lambda$, and returns a keystream $\mathbf{k}_{\mathsf{nc}} \in \mathbb{Z}_t^{16}$, where the nonce is fed to the underlying extendable output function (XOF) that outputs an element in $(\mathbb{Z}_t^{16})^*$. In a nutshell, HERA is defined as follows.

$$\mathsf{HERA}[\mathbf{k},\mathsf{nc}] = \mathsf{Fin}[\mathbf{k},\mathsf{nc},r] \circ \mathsf{RF}[\mathbf{k},\mathsf{nc},r-1] \circ \cdots \circ \mathsf{RF}[\mathbf{k},\mathsf{nc},1] \circ \mathsf{ARK}[\mathbf{k},\mathsf{nc},0]$$

where the i-th round function $\mathsf{RF}[\mathbf{k},\mathsf{nc},i]$ is defined as

$$\mathsf{RF}[\mathbf{k},\mathsf{nc},i] = \mathsf{ARK}[\mathbf{k},\mathsf{nc},i] \circ \mathsf{Cube} \circ \mathsf{MixRows} \circ \mathsf{MixColumns}$$

and the final round function Fin is defined as

$$\mathsf{Fin}[\mathbf{k}, \mathsf{nc}, r] = \\ \mathsf{ARK}[\mathbf{k}, \mathsf{nc}, r] \circ \mathsf{MixRows} \circ \mathsf{MixColumns} \circ \mathsf{Cube} \circ \mathsf{MixRows} \circ \mathsf{MixColumns}$$

for $i = 1, 2, \ldots, r-1$ (see Fig. 3).

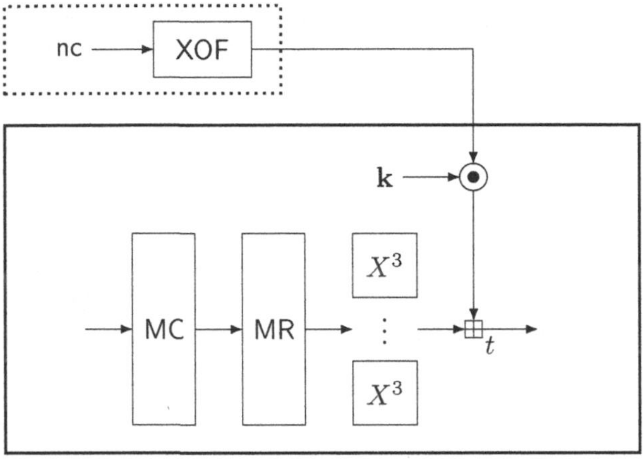

Fig. 3. The round function of HERA. Operations in the box with dotted (resp. thick) lines are public (resp. secret). "MC" and "MR" represent MixColumns and MixRows, respectively.

KEY SCHEDULE. The round key schedule can be simply seen as component-wise product between a random value and the master key $\mathbf{k}$, where the uniformly random value in $\mathbb{Z}_t^\times$ is obtained from a certain extendable output function XOF with an input nc. Given a sequence of the outputs from XOF, say $\mathbf{rc} = (\mathbf{rc}_0, \ldots, \mathbf{rc}_r) \in (\mathbb{Z}_t^{16})^{r+1}$, ARK is defined as follows.

$$\mathsf{ARK}[\mathbf{k}, \mathsf{nc}, i](\mathbf{x}) = \mathbf{x} + \mathbf{k} \bullet \mathbf{rc}_i$$

for $i = 0, \ldots, r$, and $\mathbf{x} \in \mathbb{Z}_t^{16}$, where $\bullet$ (resp. $+$) denotes component-wise multiplication (resp. addition) modulo t. The extendable output function XOF might be instantiated with a sponge-type hash function SHAKE256 [24].

LINEAR LAYERS. Each linear layer is the composition of MixColumns and MixRows. Similarly to AES, MixColumns multiplies a certain 4×4-matrix to each column of the state, where the state of HERA is also viewed as a 4×4-matrix over $\mathbb{Z}_t$ (see Fig. 4). MixColumns and MixRows are defined as in Fig. 5a and Fig. 5b, respectively. The only difference of our construction from AES is that each entry of the matrix is an element of $\mathbb{Z}_t$.

x_{00}	x_{01}	x_{02}	x_{03}
x_{10}	x_{11}	x_{12}	x_{13}
x_{20}	x_{21}	x_{22}	x_{23}
x_{30}	x_{31}	x_{32}	x_{33}

Fig. 4. State of HERA. Each square stands for the component in $\mathbb{Z}_t$.

$$\begin{bmatrix} y_{0c} \\ y_{1c} \\ y_{2c} \\ y_{3c} \end{bmatrix} = \begin{bmatrix} 2 & 3 & 1 & 1 \\ 1 & 2 & 3 & 1 \\ 1 & 1 & 2 & 3 \\ 3 & 1 & 1 & 2 \end{bmatrix} \cdot \begin{bmatrix} x_{0c} \\ x_{1c} \\ x_{2c} \\ x_{3c} \end{bmatrix}$$

(a) MixColumns

$$\begin{bmatrix} y_{c0} \\ y_{c1} \\ y_{c2} \\ y_{c3} \end{bmatrix} = \begin{bmatrix} 2 & 3 & 1 & 1 \\ 1 & 2 & 3 & 1 \\ 1 & 1 & 2 & 3 \\ 3 & 1 & 1 & 2 \end{bmatrix} \cdot \begin{bmatrix} x_{c0} \\ x_{c1} \\ x_{c2} \\ x_{c3} \end{bmatrix}$$

(b) MixRows

Fig. 5. Definition of MixColumns and MixRows. For $c \in \{0, 1, 2, 3\}$, x_{ij} and y_{ij} are defined as in Fig. 4.

NONLINEAR LAYERS. The nonlinear map Cube is the concatenation of 16 copies of the same S-box, where the S-box is defined by $x \mapsto x^3$ over $\mathbb{Z}_t$. So, for $\mathbf{x} = (x_0, \ldots, x_{15}) \in \mathbb{Z}_t^{16}$, we have

$$\mathsf{Cube}(\mathbf{x}) = (x_0^3, \ldots, x_{15}^3).$$

For the bijectivity of S-boxes, it is required that $\gcd(3, t-1) = 1$.

ENCRYPTION MODE. When a keystream of k blocks (in $(\mathbb{Z}_t^{16})^k$) is needed for some $k > 0$, the "inner-counter mode" can be used; for $\mathsf{ctr} = 0, 1, \ldots, k-1$, one computes

$$\mathbf{z}[\mathsf{ctr}] = \mathsf{HERA}\,[\mathbf{k}, \mathsf{nc} \| \mathsf{ctr}]\,(\mathbf{ic}),$$

where $\mathbf{ic}$ denotes a constant $(1, 2, \ldots, 16) \in \mathbb{Z}_t^{16}$.

4.2 Design Rationale

Symmetric cipher designs for advanced protocols so far have been targeted at homomorphic encryption as well as various privacy preserving protocols such as multiparty computation (MPC) and zero knowledge proof (ZKP). In such protocols, multiplication is significantly more expensive than addition, so a new design principle has begun to attract attention in the literature: to use simple nonlinear layers at the cost of highly randomized linear layers (e.g., FLIP [44] and Rasta [21]). However, to the best of our knowledge, most symmetric ciphers following this new design principle operate only on binary spaces, rendering it difficult to apply them to our hybrid framework.

One might consider literally extending FLIP [44] or Rasta [21] to modular spaces. This straightforward approach will degrade the overall efficiency of the cipher. Furthermore, unlike MPC and ZKP, linear maps over homomorphically encrypted data may not be simply "free". In order to use the batching techniques for homomorphic evaluation, the random linear layers should be encoded into HE-plaintexts, and then applied to HE-ciphertexts. Since multiplication between (encoded) plaintexts and ciphertexts require $O(N \log N)$ time (besides many HE rotations), randomized linear layers might not be that practical except that a small number of rounds are sufficient to mitigate algebraic attacks. For this reason, we opted for fixed linear layers.

In Table 2, we compare different types of linear maps to the (nonlinear) Cube map in terms of evaluation time and noise budget consumption. This experiment is conducted with the HE-parameters $(N, \lceil \log q \rceil) = (32768, 275)$ using row-wise packing, where the noise budget after the initialization is set to 239 bits. In this table, "Fixed matrix" and "Freshly-generated matrix" represent a non-sparse fixed matrix, and a set of distinct matrices freshly generated over different slots, respectively, where all the matrices are 16×16 square matrices and randomly generated. We see that a freshly-generated linear layer takes more time than Cube. A fixed linear layer is better than a freshly-generated one, but its time complexity is not negligible yet compared to Cube. On the other hand, our linear layer is even faster than (uniformly sampled) fixed linear layer due to its sparsity.

Table 2. Comparisons of different types of maps in terms of evaluation time and noise budget consumption.

	Time (ms)	Consumed Budget (bits)
MixRows ∘ MixColumns	23.55	4
Fixed matrix	461.68	27
Freshly-generated matrix	4006.03	34.9
Cube	3479.07	86.4

The HERA cipher uses a sparse linear layer, whose design is motivated by the MixColumns layer in AES, enjoying a number of nice features; it is easy to analyze since its construction is based on an MDS (Maximum Distance Separable) matrix and needs a small number of multiplications due to the sparsity of the matrix. We design a $\mathbb{Z}_t$-variant of the matrix and use it in the linear layers; it turns out to be an MDS matrix over $\mathbb{Z}_t$ when t is a prime number such that $t > 17$. Instead of using ShiftRows of AES, HERA uses an additional layer MixRows which is a "row version" of MixColumns to enhance the security against algebraic attacks; the composition of two linear functions generates all possible monomials, which makes algebraic attacks infeasible. Also, using MixRows mitigates linear cryptanalysis; the branch number of the linear layer is 8 (see the full version [19]) so that HERA does not have a high-probability linear trail.

In the nonlinear layer, Cube takes the component-wise cube of the input. The cube map is studied from earlier multivariate cryptography [42], recently attracting renewed interest for the use in MPC/ZKP-friendly ciphers [2,4]. The cube map has good linear/differential characteristics, whose inverse is of high degree, mitigating meet-in-the-middle algebraic attacks.

As multiplicative depth heavily impacts on noise growth of HE-ciphertexts, it is desirable to design HE-friendly ciphers using a small number of rounds. One of the most threatening attacks on ciphers with low algebraic degrees is the higher order differential attack. For a λ-bit secure (possibly non-binary) cipher, the algebraic degree of the cipher should be at least $\lambda - 1$. However, the attack is not available on randomized ciphers such as FLIP and Rasta.

To balance between efficiency and security, we propose a new direction: randomizing the key schedule. A randomized key schedule (RKS) is motivated by the tweakey framework [36]. In the tweakey framework, a key schedule takes as input a public value (called a tweak) and a key, where an adversary is allowed to take control of tweaks. On the other hand, RKS is a key schedule which takes as input a randomized public value and a key together, where the random value comes from a certain pseudorandom function. So, in our design, an adversary is not able to freely choose the random value.

The design principle behind our RKS is simple: to use as small number of multiplications as possible. One might consider simply adding a fresh random value to the master key for every round. This type of key schedule might provide security against differential cryptanalysis, but it still might be vulnerable to algebraic attacks and linear cryptanalysis. It is important to enlarge the number of monomials in the first linear layer, while this candidate cannot obtain this effect since an adversary is able to use the linear change of variables (see the full version [19]). Based on this observation, we opt for component-wise multiplication. It offers better security on algebraic attacks and linear cryptanalysis. For a traditional block cipher using fixed keys, outer affine layers do not affect its overall security; when it comes to HERA, the first and the last affine layers, combined with the randomized key schedule, increases the number of monomials.

The input constant $\mathbf{ic} = (1, 2, \ldots, 16)$ consists of distinct numbers in $\mathbb{Z}_t^{16}$; it will make a larger number of monomials in the polynomial representation of the cipher (compared to using a too simple constant, say the all-zero vector), enhancing security against algebraic attacks.

4.3 Security Analysis of HERA

In this section, we provide a summary of the security analysis of HERA (due to the page limit). All the details are given in the full version [19]. Table 3 shows the number of rounds to prevent each of the attacks considered in this section according to the security level λ, where we assume that $t > 2^{16}$.

Assumptions and the Scope of Analysis. We limit the number of encryptions under the same key up to the birthday bound with respect to λ, i.e., $2^{\lambda/2}$, since otherwise one would not be able to avoid a nonce collision (when nonces are chosen uniformly at random).

Table 3. Recommended number of rounds with respect to each attack.

Attack	λ			
	80	128	192	256
Trivial Linearization	4	5	6	7
GCD Attack	1	1	1	7
Gröbner Basis Attack	4	5	6	7
Interpolation Attack	4	5	6	7
Linear Cryptanalysis	2	4	4	6

In this work, we will consider the standard "secret-key model", where an adversary arbitrarily chooses a nonce, and obtains the corresponding keystream without any information on the secret key. The related-key and the known-key models are beyond the scope of this paper.

Since HERA takes as input counters, an adversary is not able to control the differences of the inputs. Nonces can be adversarially chosen, while they are also fed to the extendable output function, which is modeled as a random oracle. So one cannot control the difference of the internal variables. For this reason, we believe that our construction is secure against any type of chosen-plaintext attack including (higher-order) differential, truncated differential, invariant subspace trail and cube attacks. A recent generalization of an integral attack [7] requires only a small number of chosen plaintexts, while it is not applicable to HERA within the birthday bound.

The HERA cipher can be represented by a set of polynomials over $\mathbb{Z}_t$ in unknowns $k_0, \dots, k_{15}$, where $k_i \in \mathbb{Z}_t$ denotes the i-th component of the secret key $\mathbf{k} \in \mathbb{Z}_t^{16}$. Since multiplication is more expensive than addition in HE schemes, most HE-friendly ciphers have been designed to have a low multiplicative depth. This property might possibly make such ciphers vulnerable to algebraic attacks. With this observation, our analysis will be focused on algebraic attacks.

TRIVIAL LINEARIZATION. Trivial linearization is to solve a system of linear equations by replacing all monomials by new variables. When applied to the r-round HERA cipher, the number of monomials appearing in this system is upper bounded by

$$S = \sum_{i=0}^{3^r} \binom{16 + i - 1}{i}.$$

Therefore, at most S equations will be enough to solve this system of equations. All the monomials of degree at most 3^r are expected to appear after r rounds of HERA (as explained in detail in the full version [19]). Therefore, we can conclude that this attack requires $O(S)$ data and $O(S^\omega)$ time, where $2 \leq \omega \leq 3$. An adversary might take the *guess and determine* strategy before trivial linearization. However, this strategy will not be useful when $t > 2^{16}$.

GCD ATTACK. The GCD attack seeks to compute the greatest common divisor (GCD) of univariate polynomials, and it can be useful for a cipher operating on a large field with its representation being a polynomial in a single variable. This attack can be extended to a system of multivariate polynomial equations by guessing all the key variables except one. For r-round HERA, the complexity of GCD attack is estimated as $O(t^{15}r^2 3^r)$. For a security parameter $\lambda \leq 240$, HERA will be secure against the GCD attack even with a single round as long as $t > 2^{16}$. If $\lambda = 256$, then the number of round should be at least 7.

GRÖBNER BASIS ATTACK. The Gröbner basis attack is to solve a system of equations by computing a Gröbner basis of the system. We analyze the security of HERA against the Gröbner basis attack under the semi-regular assumption, which is reasonable as conjectured in [26].

The degree of regularity of the system can be computed as the degree of the first non-positive coefficient in the Hilbert series

$$HS(z) = \left(1 - z^{3^r}\right)^{m-16} \left(\sum_{i=0}^{3^r-1} z^i\right)^{16}$$

where r is the number of rounds and m is the number of equations. Since the summation does not have any negative term, one easily see that the degree d_{reg} of regularity cannot be smaller than 3^r. Therefore, the time complexity of the Gröbner basis attack is lower bounded by

$$O\left(\binom{16 + 3^r}{3^r}^2\right).$$

Any variant based on the guess-and-determine strategy requires even higher complexity when $r \leq 6$. Even for $r = 7$, there is no significant impact on the security.

Instead of a system of equations of degree 3^r, one can establish a system of $16rk$ cubic equations in $16(r-1)k + 16$ variables, where k is the block length of each query. In this case, the complexity is estimated as

$$O\left(\binom{16(r-1)k + 16 + d_{reg}(r,k)}{d_{reg}(r,k)}^{\omega}\right).$$

In the full version [19], we compute the degree $d_{reg}(r,k)$ of regularity and estimate the time complexity of the attack.

INTERPOLATION ATTACK. The interpolation attack is to establish an encryption polynomial in plaintext variables without any information on the secret key and to distinguish it from a random permutation [35]. It is known that the data complexity of this attack depends on the number of monomials in the polynomial representation of the cipher.

For the r-round HERA cipher, let $\mathbf{rc} = (\mathbf{rc}_0, \ldots, \mathbf{rc}_r) \in (\mathbb{Z}_t^{16})^{r+1}$ be a sequence of the outputs from XOF. For $i = 0, \ldots, r$, $\mathbf{rc}_i$ is evaluated by a polynomial of degree 3^{r-i}. As we expect that the r-round HERA cipher has almost all monomials of degree $\leq 3^r$ in its polynomial representation, the number of monomials is lower bounded by

$$\sum_{j=0}^{r}\sum_{i=0}^{3^j}\binom{16+i-1}{i}.$$

One might try to recover the secret key using the interpolation attack on $r-1$ rounds. However, HERA uses the full key material for every round. It implies that the key recovery attack needs brute-force search for the full key space.

The inverse of the cube map is of degree $(2t-1)/3$, so the degree of the equation in the middle state will be too high to recover all its coefficients. So we conclude that the meet-in-the-middle approach is not applicable to HERA.

Linear Cryptanalysis. Linear cryptanalysis typically applies to block ciphers operating on binary spaces. However, linear cryptanalysis can be extended to non-binary spaces [6]; for a prime t, the linear probability of a cipher $\mathsf{E} : \mathbb{Z}_t^n \to \mathbb{Z}_t^n$ with respect to input and output masks $\mathbf{a}, \mathbf{b} \in \mathbb{Z}_t^n$ can be defined as

$$\mathrm{LP}^{\mathsf{E}}(\mathbf{a},\mathbf{b}) = \left|\mathbb{E}_{\mathbf{m}}\left[\exp\left\{\frac{2\pi i}{t}\Big(-\langle \mathbf{a},\mathbf{m}\rangle + \langle \mathbf{b}, \mathsf{E}(\mathbf{m})\rangle\Big)\right\}\right]\right|^2,$$

where $\mathbf{m}$ follows the uniform distribution over $\mathbb{Z}_t^n$. When E is a random permutation, the expected linear probability is denoted by

$$\mathrm{ELP}^{\mathsf{E}}(\mathbf{a},\mathbf{b}) = \mathbb{E}_{\mathsf{E}}[\mathrm{LP}^{\mathsf{E}}(\mathbf{a},\mathbf{b})].$$

One might consider two different approaches in the application of linear cryptanalysis on HERA according to how to take the input variables: the XOF output variables or the key variables. In the first case, unlike traditional linear cryptanalysis, the probability of any linear trail of HERA depends on the key since it is multiplied to the input. It seems infeasible to make a plausible linear trail without any information on the key material.

In the second case, the attack is reduced to solving an LWE-like problem as follows; given pairs $(\mathsf{nc}_i, \mathbf{y}_i)$ such that $\mathsf{HERA}(\mathbf{k}, \mathsf{nc}_i) = \mathbf{y}_i$, one can establish

$$\langle \mathbf{b}, \mathbf{y}_i\rangle = \langle \mathbf{a}, \mathbf{k}\rangle + e_i$$

for some vectors $\mathbf{a} \neq \mathbf{0}, \mathbf{b} \in \mathbb{Z}_t^n$ and error e_i sampled according to a certain distribution χ. It requires $1/\mathrm{ELP}^{\mathsf{E}}(\mathbf{a},\mathbf{b})$ samples to distinguish χ from the uniform distribution [6]. The linear probability of r-round HERA is upper bounded by $(\mathrm{LP}^S)^{B_\ell \cdot \lfloor \frac{r}{2} \rfloor}$, where LP^S and B_ℓ denote the linear probability of the S-box and the (linear) branch number of the linear layer, respectively. Therefore, the data complexity for linear cryptanalysis is lower bounded approximately by $1/(\mathrm{LP}^S)^{B_\ell \cdot \lfloor \frac{r}{2} \rfloor}$. Again, we have $\mathrm{LP}^S \leq 4/t$ as seen in the full version [19]. As the branch number of the linear layer of HERA is 8 (as shown in the full version [19]), we can conclude that r-round HERA provides λ-bit security against linear cryptanalysis when

$$\left(\frac{t}{4}\right)^{8\cdot\lfloor \frac{r}{2} \rfloor} > 2^{\lambda}.$$

5 Implementation

In this section, we evaluate the performance of the RtF framework combined with the HERA cipher in terms of encryption speed and ciphertext expansion. The source codes of server-side computation are developed in Golang version 1.16.4 with `Lattigo` library [1] which implements RNS variants of the FV and CKKS schemes. The source codes of client-side computation are developed in C++17, using GNU C++ 7.5.0 compiler with AVX2 instruction set. XOF is instantiated with SHAKE256 in `XKCP` library [49]. Our experiments are done in AMD Ryzen 7 2700X @ 3.70 GHz single-threaded with 64 GB memory.

Additionally, we evaluate the performance of HERA combined with BGV only in order to make a fair comparison with previous works. One can find the result in the full version [19].

5.1 Parameter

The sets of parameters used in our implementation are given in Table 4, where

- λ is the security parameter;
- p is the number of precision bits of the RtF framework;
- L' is the ciphertext level at the end of the framework;
- t is the plaintext modulus;
- r is the number of rounds of the symmetric ciphers;
- N is the degree of the polynomial modulus in the HE schemes;
- ℓ is the number of slots in the FV scheme in the RtF framework;
- QP is the largest ciphertext modulus of the HE schemes including special primes.

For the CKKS scheme, the message space is $\mathbb{C}^{\ell/2}$.

In Table 4, we recommend secure parameters of HERA when combined with the RtF framework. For the parameters related to bootstrapping, we follow the choice of bootstrapping parameters in [8]. Specifically,

- the hamming weight h of the secret key is 192;
- the range K of the sine evaluation is 25;
- the number R of the double angle formula is 2;
- the degree $d_{\sin}$ of the sine evaluation is 63;
- the degree $d_{\arcsin}$ of the inverse sine evaluation is 7, if necessary.

We also experiment the effect of the inverse sine evaluation [38]. The parameter names ending with a stands for the evaluation of the inverse sine function. The parameter sets ending with s stands for a small number of slots. It uses 16 slots in order to evaluate HERA. Parameter q_0/Δ' is the ratio of the first ciphertext modulus q_0 to the bootstrapping scaling factor Δ' which is introduced in Sect. 3.3. We use 128-bit secure HE parameters for all parameter sets. If an application requires more depth with 80-bit security, then a few dozens of level can be appended without raising N and degradation of security.

Table 4. Selected sets of parameters used in our implementation. The rest of the bootstrapping parameters is set to be $(h, K, R, d_{\sin}, d_{\text{arcsin}}) = (192, 25, 2, 63, 0/7)$.

Set	λ	SKE		HE					
		$\lceil \log t \rceil$	r	$\log N$	$\log \ell$	$\lceil \log QP \rceil$	Δ_{CKKS}	q_0/Δ'	arcsin
Par-80	80	28	4	16	16	1533	2^{40}	512	✗
Par-80a	80	25	4	16	16	1533	2^{45}	16	✓
Par-80s	80	28	4	16	4	1533	2^{40}	512	✗
Par-80as	80	25	4	16	4	1533	2^{45}	16	✓
Par-128	128	28	5	16	16	1533	2^{40}	512	✗
Par-128a	128	25	5	16	16	1533	2^{45}	16	✓
Par-128s	128	28	5	16	4	1533	2^{40}	512	✗
Par-128as	128	25	5	16	4	1533	2^{45}	16	✓

Table 5. Performance of the RtF transciphering framework with HERA.

Set	CER	Client-side		Server-side			p	$\log q_{L'}$
		Lat	Thrp	Lat.		Thrp		
		(μs)	(MB/s)	Off (s)	On (s)	(KB/s)		
Par-80	1.54	1.520	22.86	98.56	16.84	5.066	17.22	500
Par-80a	1.24	1.443	26.62	91.09	20.68	5.412	19.13	375
Par-80s	1.53	1.520	22.95	71.89	13.23	0.0019	17.29	500
Par-80as	1.23	1.443	26.77	68.31	14.14	0.0020	19.25	375
Par-128	1.54	1.599	21.73	128.7	19.00	4.738	17.22	500
Par-128a	1.24	1.520	25.26	120.7	20.88	5.077	19.13	375
Par-128s	1.54	1.599	21.72	89.62	13.34	0.0018	17.21	500
Par-128as	1.23	1.520	25.26	84.02	14.31	0.0019	19.35	375

5.2 Benchmarks

We measure the performance of the RtF framework, distinguishing two different parts: the client-side and the server-side as separated in Fig. 2. On the client-side, the latency includes time for generating pseudorandom numbers (needed to generate a single keystream in $\mathbb{Z}_t^{16}$), keystream generation from HERA, message scaling, rounding and vector addition over $\mathbb{Z}_t$. The extendable output function is instantiated with SHAKE256 in XKCP.

The server-side offline latency includes time for the randomized key schedule, homomorphic evaluation of the keystreams from HERA, and $\mathsf{SlotToCoeff}^{\mathsf{FV}}$. HERA is homomorphically evaluated by using row-wise packing. The online latency includes scaling up to FV-ciphertext space, the homomorphic subtraction, rescaling to the lowest level, and HalfBoot. We measure the latency until the first HE-ciphertext comes out, while the throughput is measured until all the 16 HE-ciphertexts come out. We note that our evaluation does not take into account key encryption since the encrypted key will be used over multiple sessions once it is computed. For the same reason, the initialization process of the HE schemes is not considered.

We summarize our implementation results in Table 5. This table includes ciphertext expansion ratio (CER), time-relevant measurements, precision, and homomorphic capacity. One can see that the parameters with arcsin (`Par-a`) offer smaller CER while the remaining levels are less than other parameters. On the other hand, the parameters with small slots (`Par-s`) take less time for evaluation since the complexity of evaluating $\mathsf{SlotToCoeff}^{\mathsf{FV}}$ and $\mathsf{CoeffToSlot}^{\mathsf{CKKS}}$ is affected by the number of slots.

Comparison. We compare the result to the recent implementation of LWEs-to-RLWE conversions [40] and CKKS itself. The comparison is summarized in Table 6. We run all those schemes by ourselves except the †-marked one. The source codes of LWEs-to-RLWE conversion is taken from the `OpenPegasus` library[5]. As `OpenPegasus` library does not include symmetric LWE encryption, we implement (seeded) symmetric LWE encryption with AVX2-optimized SHAKE256. We use `Lattigo` library for CKKS encryption.

In this table, the security parameter λ is set to 128. For the fairness of comparison, we try to make L' equal. Regardless of ℓ, the number of real number messages encrypted on the client side using RtF and LWE is 16 and 1 respectively. We evaluate the LWE encryption in LWEs-to-RLWE and the CKKS encryption in CKKS-only environment as (seeded) symmetric encryptions since they offer smaller ciphertext expansion ratio. For all experiments, we sample the domain of each component of the message vector from uniform distribution over $(-1, 1)$. When computing the ciphertext expansion ratio, we use the formula $\log t/(p+1)$, which excludes the effect of sending a public nonce. Multiple use of different nonces can be dealt with a counter so that the effect of nonce to the ratio is asymptotically zero.

Since the `OpenPegasus` library supports only selected sets of parameters in terms of the number of slots and the ciphertext modulus (at the point of submission), we implemented LWEs-to-RLWE for $N = 2^{16}$ and $\ell = 2^{10}$ which does not provide exactly the same functionality as ours with full available slots; we additionally implemented the RtF framework with HERA using the parameter $\ell = 2^9$ which processes the same number of data in order to make a fair comparison.

One can see that our RtF framework outperforms the LWEs-to-RLWE conversion and the CKKS-only environment with respect to CER and client-side performance, achieving the main purpose of the transciphering framework. On the server-side, the RtF framework enjoys larger throughput at the cost of larger latency due to the highly nonlinear structure of the HERA compared to LWE encryption. We note that the CKKS-only environment requires no additional computation since it uses CKKS-ciphertexts with nonzero level.

[5] https://github.com/Alibaba-Gemini-Lab/OpenPEGASUS.

Table 6. Comparison of the RtF transciphering framework with HERA to LWEs-to-RLWE conversion (denoted by LWE) and the CKKS-only environment. All the experiments are done with 128-bit security. Parameter N in parentheses implies the dimension of LWE. The parameter p stands for the bits of precision. "–" indicates that the previous work did not report the value.

Scheme	N	ℓ	Ctxt. Exp.		Client		Server		p	L'
			Ctxt. (KB)	Ratio	Lat. (μs)	Thrp. (MB/s)	Lat. (s)	Thrp. (KB/s)		
RtF	2^{16}	2^{16}	0.055	1.54	1.599	21.73	147.68	4.738	17.2	11
RtF	2^{16}	2^{9}	0.055	1.53	1.599	21.78	117.71	0.051	17.2	11
LWE [40]	$2^{16}(2^{10})$	2^{10}	0.007	4.84	21.60	0.051	89.61	0.006	9.2	11
LWE [40]†	$2^{16}(2^{10})$	2^{13}	0.007	–	–	–	51.71	–	–	6
CKKS	2^{14}	2^{14}	640	35.31	14527	1.218	none		17.1	11

†: data is directly from the paper.

References

1. Lattigo v2.1.1.: ePFL-LDS (December 2020). http://github.com/ldsec/lattigo
2. Albrecht, M., Grassi, L., Rechberger, C., Roy, A., Tiessen, T.: MiMC: efficient encryption and cryptographic hashing with minimal multiplicative complexity. In: Cheon, J.H., Takagi, T. (eds.) ASIACRYPT 2016. LNCS, vol. 10031, pp. 191–219. Springer, Heidelberg (2016). https://doi.org/10.1007/978-3-662-53887-6_7
3. Albrecht, M.R., Rechberger, C., Schneider, T., Tiessen, T., Zohner, M.: Ciphers for MPC and FHE. In: Oswald, E., Fischlin, M. (eds.) EUROCRYPT 2015. LNCS, vol. 9056, pp. 430–454. Springer, Heidelberg (2015). https://doi.org/10.1007/978-3-662-46800-5_17
4. Aly, A., Ashur, T., Ben-Sasson, E., Dhooghe, S., Szepieniec, A.: Design of symmetric-key primitives for advanced cryptographic protocols. IACR Trans. Symmetric Cryptol. **2020**(3), 1–45 (2020)
5. Ashur, T., Dhooghe, S.: MARVELlous: a STARK-Friendly Family of Cryptographic Primitives. IACR Cryptology ePrint Archive, Report 2018/1098 (2018). https://eprint.iacr.org/2018/1098
6. Baignères, T., Stern, J., Vaudenay, S.: Linear cryptanalysis of non binary ciphers. In: Adams, C., Miri, A., Wiener, M. (eds.) SAC 2007. LNCS, vol. 4876, pp. 184–211. Springer, Heidelberg (2007). https://doi.org/10.1007/978-3-540-77360-3_13
7. Beyne, T., et al.: Out of oddity – new cryptanalytic techniques against symmetric primitives optimized for integrity proof systems. In: Micciancio, D., Ristenpart, T. (eds.) CRYPTO 2020. LNCS, vol. 12172, pp. 299–328. Springer, Cham (2020). https://doi.org/10.1007/978-3-030-56877-1_11
8. Bossuat, J.-P., Mouchet, C., Troncoso-Pastoriza, J., Hubaux, J.-P.: Efficient bootstrapping for approximate homomorphic encryption with non-sparse keys. In: Canteaut, A., Standaert, F.-X. (eds.) EUROCRYPT 2021. LNCS, vol. 12696, pp. 587–617. Springer, Cham (2021). https://doi.org/10.1007/978-3-030-77870-5_21
9. Boura, C., Gama, N., Georgieva, M., Jetchev, D.: Simulating homomorphic evaluation of deep learning predictions. In: Dolev, S., Hendler, D., Lodha, S., Yung, M. (eds.) CSCML 2019. LNCS, vol. 11527, pp. 212–230. Springer, Cham (2019). https://doi.org/10.1007/978-3-030-20951-3_20

10. Brakerski, Z., Gentry, C., Vaikuntanathan, V.: (Leveled) fully homomorphic encryption without bootstrapping. In: Proceedings of the 3rd Innovations in Theoretical Computer Science Conference, pp. 309–325. ACM (2012)
11. Canteaut, A., et al.: Stream ciphers: a practical solution for efficient homomorphic-ciphertext compression. J. Cryptol. **31**(3), 885–916 (2018)
12. Chen, H., Dai, W., Kim, M., Song, Y.: Efficient homomorphic conversion between (Ring) LWE ciphertexts. In: Sako, K., Tippenhauer, N.O. (eds.) ACNS 2021. LNCS, vol. 12726, pp. 460–479. Springer, Cham (2021). https://doi.org/10.1007/978-3-030-78372-3_18
13. Chen, H., Iliashenko, I., Laine, K.: When HEAAN Meets FV: a New Somewhat Homomorphic Encryption with Reduced Memory Overhead. IACR Cryptology ePrint Archive, Report 2020/121 (2020), https://eprint.iacr.org/2020/121
14. Cheon, J.H., Han, K., Kim, A., Kim, M., Song, Y.: Bootstrapping for approximate homomorphic encryption. In: Nielsen, J.B., Rijmen, V. (eds.) EUROCRYPT 2018. LNCS, vol. 10820, pp. 360–384. Springer, Cham (2018). https://doi.org/10.1007/978-3-319-78381-9_14
15. Cheon, J.H., Jeong, J., Lee, J., Lee, K.: Privacy-preserving computations of predictive medical models with minimax approximation and non-adjacent form. In: Brenner, M., et al. (eds.) FC 2017. LNCS, vol. 10323, pp. 53–74. Springer, Cham (2017). https://doi.org/10.1007/978-3-319-70278-0_4
16. Cheon, J.H., Kim, A., Kim, M., Song, Y.: Homomorphic encryption for arithmetic of approximate numbers. In: Takagi, T., Peyrin, T. (eds.) ASIACRYPT 2017. LNCS, vol. 10624, pp. 409–437. Springer, Cham (2017). https://doi.org/10.1007/978-3-319-70694-8_15
17. Cheon, J.H., Kim, M., Lauter, K.: Homomorphic computation of edit distance. In: Brenner, M., Christin, N., Johnson, B., Rohloff, K. (eds.) FC 2015. LNCS, vol. 8976, pp. 194–212. Springer, Heidelberg (2015). https://doi.org/10.1007/978-3-662-48051-9_15
18. Chillotti, I., Gama, N., Georgieva, M., Izabachène, M.: TFHE: fast fully homomorphic encryption over the torus. J. Cryptol. **33**(1), 34–91 (2020)
19. Cho, J., et al.: Transciphering Framework for Approximate Homomorphic Encryption (Full Version). Cryptology ePrint Archive, Report 2020/1335 (2020). https://eprint.iacr.org/2020/1335
20. Dinur, I., Liu, Y., Meier, W., Wang, Q.: Optimized interpolation attacks on LowMC. In: Iwata, T., Cheon, J.H. (eds.) ASIACRYPT 2015. LNCS, vol. 9453, pp. 535–560. Springer, Heidelberg (2015). https://doi.org/10.1007/978-3-662-48800-3_22
21. Dobraunig, C., et al.: Rasta: a cipher with low ANDdepth and few ANDs per bit. In: Shacham, H., Boldyreva, A. (eds.) CRYPTO 2018. LNCS, vol. 10991, pp. 662–692. Springer, Cham (2018). https://doi.org/10.1007/978-3-319-96884-1_22
22. Dobraunig, C., Eichlseder, M., Mendel, F.: Higher-order cryptanalysis of LowMC. In: Kwon, S., Yun, A. (eds.) ICISC 2015. LNCS, vol. 9558, pp. 87–101. Springer, Cham (2016). https://doi.org/10.1007/978-3-319-30840-1_6
23. Doröz, Y., Shahverdi, A., Eisenbarth, T., Sunar, B.: Toward practical homomorphic evaluation of block ciphers using prince. In: Böhme, R., Brenner, M., Moore, T., Smith, M. (eds.) FC 2014. LNCS, vol. 8438, pp. 208–220. Springer, Heidelberg (2014). https://doi.org/10.1007/978-3-662-44774-1_17
24. Dworkin, M.J.: SHA-3 Standard: Permutation-Based Hash and Extendable-Output Functions. Technical report, National Institute of Standards and Technology (2015)

25. Fan, J., Vercauteren, F.: Somewhat Practical Fully Homomorphic Encryption. IACR Cryptology ePrint Archive, Report 2012/144 (2012). https://eprint.iacr.org/2012/144
26. Fröberg, R.: An inequality for Hilbert series of graded algebras. Math. Scand. **56**, 117–144 (1985)
27. Gentry, C.: Fully homomorphic encryption using ideal lattices. In: Proceedings of the Forty-First Annual ACM Symposium on Theory of Computing, pp. 169–178. ACM (2009)
28. Gentry, C., Halevi, S., Smart, N.P.: Homomorphic evaluation of the AES circuit. In: Safavi-Naini, R., Canetti, R. (eds.) CRYPTO 2012. LNCS, vol. 7417, pp. 850–867. Springer, Heidelberg (2012). https://doi.org/10.1007/978-3-642-32009-5_49
29. Gentry, C., Sahai, A., Waters, B.: Homomorphic encryption from learning with errors: conceptually-simpler, asymptotically-faster, attribute-based. In: Canetti, R., Garay, J.A. (eds.) CRYPTO 2013. LNCS, vol. 8042, pp. 75–92. Springer, Heidelberg (2013). https://doi.org/10.1007/978-3-642-40041-4_5
30. Grassi, L., Rechberger, C., Rotaru, D., Scholl, P., Smart, N.P.: MPC-friendly symmetric key primitives. In: Proceedings of the 2016 ACM SIGSAC Conference on Computer and Communications Security, pp. 430–443. ACM (2016)
31. Ha, J., et al.: Masta: an HE-friendly cipher using modular arithmetic. IEEE Access **8**, 194741–194751 (2020)
32. Han, K., Ki, D.: Better bootstrapping for approximate homomorphic encryption. In: Jarecki, S. (ed.) CT-RSA 2020. LNCS, vol. 12006, pp. 364–390. Springer, Cham (2020). https://doi.org/10.1007/978-3-030-40186-3_16
33. Hebborn, P., Leander, G.: Dasta - alternative linear layer for rasta. IACR Trans. Symmetric Cryptol. **2020**(3), 46–86 (2020)
34. Hoffmann, C., Méaux, P., Ricosset, T.: Transciphering, using FiLIP and TFHE for an efficient delegation of computation. In: Bhargavan, K., Oswald, E., Prabhakaran, M. (eds.) INDOCRYPT 2020. LNCS, vol. 12578, pp. 39–61. Springer, Cham (2020). https://doi.org/10.1007/978-3-030-65277-7_3
35. Jakobsen, T., Knudsen, L.R.: The interpolation attack on block ciphers. In: Biham, E. (ed.) FSE 1997. LNCS, vol. 1267, pp. 28–40. Springer, Heidelberg (1997). https://doi.org/10.1007/BFb0052332
36. Jean, J., Nikolić, I., Peyrin, T.: Tweaks and keys for block ciphers: the TWEAKEY framework. In: Sarkar, P., Iwata, T. (eds.) ASIACRYPT 2014. LNCS, vol. 8874, pp. 274–288. Springer, Heidelberg (2014). https://doi.org/10.1007/978-3-662-45608-8_15
37. Juvekar, C., Vaikuntanathan, V., Chandrakasan, A.: GAZELLE: a low latency framework for secure neural network inference. In: Proceedings of the 27th USENIX Conference on Security Symposium, pp. 1651–1668. USENIX Association (2018)
38. Lee, J.-W., Lee, E., Lee, Y., Kim, Y.-S., No, J.-S.: High-precision bootstrapping of RNS-CKKS homomorphic encryption using optimal minimax polynomial approximation and inverse sine function. In: Canteaut, A., Standaert, F.-X. (eds.) EUROCRYPT 2021. LNCS, vol. 12696, pp. 618–647. Springer, Cham (2021). https://doi.org/10.1007/978-3-030-77870-5_22
39. Lepoint, T., Naehrig, M.: A comparison of the homomorphic encryption schemes FV and YASHE. In: Pointcheval, D., Vergnaud, D. (eds.) AFRICACRYPT 2014. LNCS, vol. 8469, pp. 318–335. Springer, Cham (2014). https://doi.org/10.1007/978-3-319-06734-6_20

40. Lu, W., Huang, Z., Hong, C., Ma, Y., Qu, H.: PEGASUS: bridging polynomial and non-polynomial evaluations in homomorphic encryption. In: 2021 2021 IEEE Symposium on Security and Privacy (SP), pp. 1057–1073. IEEE Computer Society (May 2021)
41. Lyubashevsky, V., Peikert, C., Regev, O.: On ideal lattices and learning with errors over rings. In: Gilbert, H. (ed.) EUROCRYPT 2010. LNCS, vol. 6110, pp. 1–23. Springer, Heidelberg (2010). https://doi.org/10.1007/978-3-642-13190-5_1
42. Matsumoto, T., Imai, H.: Public quadratic polynomial-tuples for efficient signature-verification and message-encryption. In: Barstow, D., et al. (eds.) EUROCRYPT 1988. LNCS, vol. 330, pp. 419–453. Springer, Heidelberg (1988). https://doi.org/10.1007/3-540-45961-8_39
43. Méaux, P., Carlet, C., Journault, A., Standaert, F.-X.: Improved filter permutators for efficient FHE: better instances and implementations. In: Hao, F., Ruj, S., Sen Gupta, S. (eds.) INDOCRYPT 2019. LNCS, vol. 11898, pp. 68–91. Springer, Cham (2019). https://doi.org/10.1007/978-3-030-35423-7_4
44. Méaux, P., Journault, A., Standaert, F.-X., Carlet, C.: Towards stream ciphers for efficient FHE with low-noise ciphertexts. In: Fischlin, M., Coron, J.-S. (eds.) EUROCRYPT 2016. LNCS, vol. 9665, pp. 311–343. Springer, Heidelberg (2016). https://doi.org/10.1007/978-3-662-49890-3_13
45. Naehrig, M., Lauter, K., Vaikuntanathan, V.: Can homomorphic encryption be practical? In: Proceedings of the 3rd ACM Workshop on Cloud Computing Security Workshop, pp. 113–124. ACM (2011)
46. Park, S., Byun, J., Lee, J., Cheon, J.H., Lee, J.: HE-friendly algorithm for privacy-preserving SVM training. IEEE Access **8**, 57414–57425 (2020)
47. Rechberger, C., Soleimany, H., Tiessen, T.: Cryptanalysis of low-data instances of full LowMCv2. IACR Trans. Symmetric Cryptol. **2018**(3), 163–181 (2018)
48. Regev, O.: On lattices, learning with errors, random linear codes, and cryptography. J. ACM **56**(6), 1–40 (2009)
49. XKCP: eXtended Keccak Code Package (August 2020). https://github.com/XKCP/XKCP

Improved Programmable Bootstrapping with Larger Precision and Efficient Arithmetic Circuits for TFHE

Ilaria Chillotti(✉), Damien Ligier(✉), Jean-Baptiste Orfila(✉), and Samuel Tap(✉)

Zama, Paris, France
{ilaria.chillotti,damien.ligier,jb.orfila,samuel.tap}@zama.ai
https://zama.ai/

Abstract. *Fully Homomorphic Encryption* (FHE) schemes enable to compute over encrypted data. Among them, TFHE [8] has the great advantage of offering an efficient method for *bootstrapping noisy ciphertexts*, i.e., reduce the noise. Indeed, homomorphic computation increases the noise in ciphertexts and might compromise the encrypted message. TFHE bootstrapping, in addition to reducing the noise, also evaluates (for free) *univariate functions* expressed as look-up tables. It however requires to have the most significant bit of the plaintext to be known *a priori*, resulting in the loss of one bit of space to store messages. Furthermore it represents a non negligible overhead in terms of computation in many use cases.

In this paper, we propose a solution to overcome this limitation, that we call Programmable Bootstrapping Without Padding (**WoP-PBS**). This approach relies on two building blocks. The first one is the multiplication *à la* BFV [13] that we incorporate into TFHE. This is possible thanks to a thorough noise analysis showing that correct multiplications can be computed using practical TFHE parameters. The second building block is the generalization of TFHE bootstrapping introduced in this paper. It offers the flexibility to select any chunk of bits in an encrypted plaintext during a bootstrap. It also enables to evaluate many LUTs at the same time when working with small enough precision. All these improvements are particularly helpful in some applications such as the evaluation of Boolean circuits (where a bootstrap is no longer required in each evaluated gate) and, more generally, in the efficient evaluation of arithmetic circuits even with large integers. Those results improve TFHE circuit bootstrapping as well. Moreover, we show that bootstrapping large precision integers is now possible using much smaller parameters than those obtained by scaling TFHE ones.

Keywords: FHE · TFHE · Bootstrapping

1 Introduction

Fully Homomorphic Encryption (FHE) is a family of encryption schemes allowing to perform computation over encrypted data. FHE schemes use noisy cipher-

M. Tibouchi and H. Wang (Eds.): ASIACRYPT 2021, LNCS 13092, pp. 670–699, 2021.
https://doi.org/10.1007/978-3-030-92078-4_23

texts for security reasons, i.e., ciphertexts containing some randomness. This noise grows after every performed homomorphic operation, and, if not controlled, can compromise the message and prevent the user from decrypting correctly. A technique called *bootstrapping* and introduced by Gentry [14] allows to reduce the noise, by mean of a public key called *bootstrapping key*. By using bootstrapping frequently, thus reducing the noise when needed, one can perform as many homomorphic operations as she wants, but it remains an expensive technique, both in terms of execution time and memory usage.

Nowadays, the most practical FHE schemes are based on the hardness assumption called *Learning With Errors* (LWE), introduced by Regev in 2005 [20], and on its *ring* variant (RLWE) [19,22]. Even if bootstrapping is possible for all these schemes, some of them (such as BGV [3], BFV [2,13] and CKKS [6]) actually avoid it because the technique remains a bottleneck. These schemes make use of RLWE ciphertexts exclusively and adopt a *leveled approach*, which consists in choosing parameters that are large enough to tolerate all the noise produced during the computation. These schemes take advantage of *SIMD encoding* [21] to pack many messages in a single ciphertext and perform the homomorphic evaluations in parallel on all of these messages at the same time, and they naturally perform homomorphic multiplications between RLWE ciphertexts by doing a *(tensor) product* followed by a *relinearization/key switching*.

TFHE [7–9] is also an (R)LWE-based FHE scheme which differentiates from the other (R)LWE-based cryptosystems because it supports a *very efficient bootstrapping* technique. TFHE was originally proposed as an improvement of *FHEW* [12], a GSW [15] based scheme with a fast bootstrapping for the evaluation of homomorphic Boolean gates. Apart from improving FHEW bootstrapping, TFHE also introduces new techniques in order to support more functionalities than the ones proposed by FHEW and to improve homomorphic evaluation of complex circuits. TFHE efficiency comes in part from the choice of a small ciphertext modulus which allows to use CPU native types to represent a ciphertext both in the standard domain and in Fourier domain. This is what we call the *TFHE context*.

TFHE encrypts messages in the most significant bits, meaning a message $m \in \mathbb{Z}$ is rescaled by a factor $\Delta \in \mathbb{Z}$ before being reduced modulo q. The small noise $e \in \mathbb{Z}$ is added in the least significant bit, so a noisy plaintext looks like $\Delta \cdot m + e \mod q$. In this paper, when we refer to *bits of precision*, we mean the quantity $p = \log_2(\frac{q}{\Delta})$. We illustrate this in Fig. 1. Note that if $m > 2^p$ some of the information in m will be lost because of the modulo q.

TFHE *bootstrapping* is very efficient, but also *programmable*, meaning that a univariate function can be evaluated at the same time as the noise is being reduced. It is often called *programmable bootstrapping* [10,11] and noted PBS. The function to be evaluated is represented as a *look-up table* (LUT) and the bootstrapping rotates this table (stored in an encrypted polynomial) in order to output the correct element in the table. The LUT has to have redundancy (each coefficient is repeated a certain amount of time consecutively) in order to remove the input ciphertext noise during the PBS.

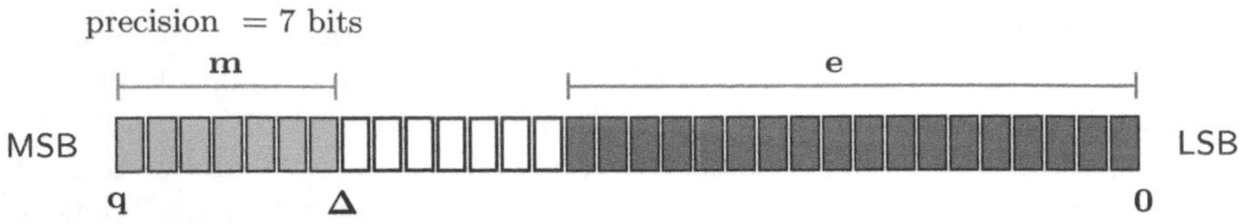

Fig. 1. In TFHE, messages are encoded in the most significant bits (MSB), and so it is rescaled by a scaling factor Δ, while the error appears in the least significant bits (LSB). The precision is $\log_2(\frac{q}{\Delta})$, i.e 7 bits in the figure.

A multi-output version of the PBS is described in [4] allowing the evaluation of multiple (negacyclic) functions $\{f_i\}_i$ over one encrypted input. Each function f_i is encoded as a LUT in a polynomial P_i. One can find a shared polynomial Q such that we can decompose each P_i as $Q \cdot P_i'$ and compute $\mathsf{CT}_{\mathsf{out}} \leftarrow \mathbf{PBS}(\mathsf{ct}_{\mathsf{in}}, \mathsf{BSK}, Q)$. Then, one needs to multiply $\mathsf{CT}_{\mathsf{out}}$ by each of P_i' and sample extract the resulting ciphertexts. One would have obtained the evaluation of each function. One drawback of this method is that the noise inside the i-th output ciphertexts depends on P_i'.

A recent paper revisits the TFHE bootstrapping [16]. It gives two algorithms and a few optimizations to compute programmable bootstrapping on large precision ciphertexts encrypting one message decomposed in a certain base. Those algorithms could be used to homomorphically compute multivariate functions if we call them with the right lookup tables.

The BGV/BFV/CKKS leveled approach is very convenient when the circuit that has to be homomorphically evaluated is small in terms of multiplicative depth, but also known in advance. When multiple inputs have to be evaluated with the same circuit at once, this approach is also very good in terms of amortized computation time. However, when the circuit is deep and unknown *a priori*, the TFHE approach is more convenient.

A recent work by Boura et al., called Chimera [1], tries to take advantage of both approaches, by building bridges between FHE schemes (TFHE, BFV and CKKS), in order to switch between them depending on which functionality is needed.

TFHE and its fast PBS are very powerful, but have some *limitations*:

A In general, to correctly bootstrap a ciphertext, its encrypted plaintext needs to have its *first Most Significant Bit (MSB) set to zero* (or at least known). The only exception is when the univariate function evaluated is negacyclic.

B One cannot bootstrap efficiently a message with a *large precision* (e.g., more than 6 bits). The number of bits of the message we bootstrap is strictly related to the dimension N of the ring chosen for the PBS. This means that the more we increase the precision, the more we have to increase the parameter N, and the *slower* the computation is.

C The PBS algorithm is *not multi-thread friendly*. Indeed, it is a loop working on an accumulator.

D There exists *no native multiplication* between two LWE ciphertexts. There are two approaches to multiply LWE ciphertexts: (*i*) use two programmable bootstrappings to evaluate the function $x \mapsto \frac{x^2}{4}$ so we can build the multiplication $x \cdot y = \frac{(x+y)^2}{4} - \frac{(x-y)^2}{4}$; (*ii*) use 1 or more TFHE circuit bootstrappings [8, Alg. 6] in order to convert one of the inputs into a GGSW (if not given as input) and then performing an external product. Since both techniques use PBS, they both suffer from limitations A and B.

E Because of limitations A and B it is not possible, in an efficient manner, to homomorphically *split a message* contained in a single ciphertext into several ciphertexts containing smaller chunks of the original message.

F The PBS can evaluate only a *single function per call*. Using the [4] trick, we can evaluate multiple Look-Up Tables at the same time, but the output will have an additional amount of noise which depends on the function evaluated.

G TFHE gate bootstrapping represents a very easy solution for evaluating *homomorphic Boolean circuits*. However, this technique requires a PBS for each binary gate, which results in a *costly execution*. Furthermore, when we want to apply a similar approach to the arithmetic circuit with bigger integers (more than 1 bit), TFHE does not provide a solution.

H TFHE circuit bootstrapping requires ℓ PBS followed by many key switchings which is quite time consuming.

Contributions. In this paper we overcome the above-mentioned TFHE limitations. First, we *generalize TFHE PBS* so it can evaluate *several functions at once* without additional computation or noise. This approach is possible when the message to bootstrap is small enough. It overcomes limitation F and enables to compute a single generalized PBS when computing a circuit bootstrapping instead of ℓ PBS, overcoming limitation H. Circuit bootstrapping is particularly interesting in the leveled evaluation of Look-Up Tables, as shown in [8].

Furthermore, we thoroughly study the noise growth when computing a tensor product followed by a relinearization (i.e., the BFV-like multiplication) and found *parameters compatible with the TFHE context* representing a new way of computing LWE multiplications in TFHE. This multiplication is efficient and does not require a PBS which overcomes limitation D. We also propose a packed use of this algorithm to compute several LWE products at once or a sum of several LWE products at once. Our noise analysis is also valid for BFV-like schemes and can help estimate the noise growth there.

From this multiplication, we define a *new PBS procedure* that does not require the MSB to be set to zero, overcoming limitation A. This new procedure is composed of few generalized PBS that can be computed in parallel which makes it more multi-thread compatible (limitation C). Observe that, differently from Chimera, which builds bridges to move between different schemes, we add the support for a BFV-like multiplication into TFHE, in order to remove some of the TFHE limitations. In this way, we don't need to switch between schemes, and we can remain all the time in the TFHE context.

From this new PBS we are able to *homomorphically decompose* a plaintext from a single ciphertext into several ciphertexts encrypting blocks of the input plaintext, overcoming limitation E, and also relax the need for PBS at every gate in the gate bootstrapping and its generalization, overcoming limitation G.

From this new decomposition algorithm and the Tree-PBS algorithm [16], we are able to create a *fast PBS for larger input messages*, overcoming limitation B. We can also in an even faster manner refresh the noise (bootstrap, not PBS) in a ciphertext from this new decomposition algorithm.

2 Background and Notations

The parameter q is a positive integer and represents the modulo for the integers we are working with. We note $\mathbb{Z}_q$ the ring $\mathbb{Z}/q\mathbb{Z}$. The parameter N is a power of 2 and represents the *size of polynomials* we are working with. We note $\mathfrak{R}_q$ the ring $\mathbb{Z}_q[X]/(X^N+1)$. A *Gaussian distribution* with a mean set to zero and a standard deviation set to σ is written χ_σ. We use the symbol $||$ for concatenation. When ι is an integer, we note by $[\cdot]_\iota$ the reduction modulo ι and by $\lfloor \cdot \rceil_\iota$ the rounding then the reduction modulo ι. We refer to the *most* (resp. *least*) *significant bits* of an integer as MSB (resp. LSB). We alse refer to *look-up tables* as LUT. The (computational) complexity of an algorithm Alg, potentially dependent on some parameters $p_1, \cdots, p_n$, is denoted $\mathbb{C}_{\mathsf{Alg}}^{p_1,\cdots,p_n}$.

Remark 1. Observe that in this paper we use different notations compared to TFHE [7–9]. In TFHE, the message and ciphertext spaces are expressed by using the real torus $\mathbb{T} = \mathbb{R}/\mathbb{Z}$. On a computer, they implemented $\mathbb{T}$ by using native arithmetic modulo 2^{32} or 2^{64}, which means that they work on $\mathbb{Z}_q$ (with $q = 2^{32}$ or $q = 2^{64}$). This is why we prefer to use $\mathbb{Z}_q$ instead of $\mathbb{T}$, as already adopted in [10]. It is made possible because there is an isomorphism between $\mathbb{Z}_q$ and $\frac{1}{q}\mathbb{Z}/\mathbb{Z}$ as explained in [1, Sect. 1].

LWE, RLWE and GLWE Ciphertexts. A GLWE ciphertext of a message $M \in \mathfrak{R}_q$ with the scaling factor $\Delta \in \mathbb{Z}_q$ under the secret key $\mathbf{S} \in \mathfrak{R}_q^k$ is defined as follows:

$$\mathsf{CT} = (A_1, \cdots, A_k, B = \sum_{i=1}^{k} A_i \cdot S_i + \lfloor M \cdot \Delta \rceil_q + E) = \mathsf{GLWE}_{\mathbf{S}}(M \cdot \Delta) \in \mathfrak{R}_q^{k+1}$$

such that $\mathbf{S} = (S_1, \cdots, S_k) \in \mathfrak{R}_q^k$ is the secret key with coefficients either sampled from a uniform binary, uniform ternary or Gaussian distribution, $\{A_i\}_{i=1}^k$ are polynomials in $\mathfrak{R}_q$ with coefficients sampled from the uniform distribution in $\mathbb{Z}_q$, E is an noise (error) polynomial in $\mathfrak{R}_q$ such that its coefficients are sampled from a Gaussian distributions χ_σ. The parameter k is a positive integer and represents the number of polynomials in the GLWE secret key. To simplify notations, we sometimes define S_{k+1} as -1.

A GLWE ciphertext with $N = 1$ is an *LWE ciphertext* and in this case we consider the parameter $n = k$ for the size of the LWE secret key and we note both the ciphertext and the secret with a lower case e.g. ct and $\mathbf{s}$. A GLWE ciphertext with $k = 1$ and $N > 1$ is an *RLWE ciphertext*.

Lev, RLev and GLev Ciphertexts. A GLev ciphertext with the base $\mathfrak{B} \in \mathbb{N}^*$ and $\ell \in \mathbb{N}^*$ levels, of a message $M \in \mathfrak{R}_q$ under the GLWE secret key $\mathbf{S} \in \mathfrak{R}_q^k$ is defined as the following vector of GLWE ciphertexts:

$$\overline{\mathsf{CT}} = (\mathsf{CT}_1, \cdots, \mathsf{CT}_\ell) = \mathsf{GLev}_{\mathbf{S}}^{\mathfrak{B},\ell}(M) \in \mathfrak{R}_q^{\ell \times (k+1)}$$

where $\mathsf{CT}_i = \mathsf{GLWE}_{\mathbf{S}}(M \cdot \frac{q}{\mathfrak{B}^i})$ is a GLWE ciphertext.

A GLev ciphertext with $N = 1$ is a *Lev ciphertext* and in this case we consider the parameter $n = k$ for the size of the LWE secret key. A GLev ciphertext with $k = 1$ and $N > 1$ is a *RLev ciphertext.*

Decomposition Algorithms. The decomposition algorithm in the integer base $\mathfrak{B} \in \mathbb{N}^*$ with $\ell \in \mathbb{N}^*$ levels is written $\mathsf{dec}^{(\mathfrak{B},\ell)}$ and takes as input an integer $x \in \mathbb{Z}_q$ and output a decomposition vector of integers $(x_1, \cdots, x_\ell) \in \mathbb{Z}_q^\ell$ such that:

$$\left\langle \mathsf{dec}^{(\mathfrak{B},\ell)}(x), \left(\frac{q}{\mathfrak{B}^1}, \cdots, \frac{q}{\mathfrak{B}^\ell}\right)\right\rangle = \left\lfloor x \cdot \frac{\mathfrak{B}^\ell}{q} \right\rceil \cdot \frac{q}{\mathfrak{B}^\ell} \in \mathbb{Z}_q$$

Note that this decomposition starts from the MSB. When we apply this decomposition on a vector of integers, we end up with a vector of decomposition vector of integers.

We can also decompose an integer polynomials $X \in \mathfrak{R}_q$ into a decomposition vector of polynomials $(X_1, \cdots, X_\ell) \in \mathfrak{R}_q^\ell$ such that:

$$\left\langle \mathsf{dec}^{(\mathfrak{B},\ell)}(X), \left(\frac{q}{\mathfrak{B}^1}, \cdots, \frac{q}{\mathfrak{B}^\ell}\right)\right\rangle = \left\lfloor X \cdot \frac{\mathfrak{B}^\ell}{q} \right\rceil \cdot \frac{q}{\mathfrak{B}^\ell} \in \mathfrak{R}_q$$

When we apply this decomposition on a vector of polynomials, we end up with a vector of decomposition vectors of polynomials.

Key Switching. A technique that is often used in FHE, called *key switching*, allows to change parameters and keys in the ciphertext. The key switching makes the noise grow and is performed using a so-called *key-switching key* which is a public key composed of encryptions of secret key elements.

There are different types of key switchings: we will quickly list and describe the ones that are interesting for the understanding of the paper. The LWE-to-GLWE key-switching key is noted KSK and is equal to $\mathsf{KSK} = \left\{\overline{\mathsf{CT}}_i = \mathsf{GLev}_{\mathbf{S}'}^{\mathfrak{B},\ell}(s_i)\right\}_{1 \le i \le n}$, where $\mathbf{s} = (s_1, \ldots, s_n) \in \mathbb{Z}_q^n$ is the input LWE secret key and $\mathbf{S}' = (S'_1, \ldots, S'_k) \in \mathfrak{R}_q^k$ is the output GLWE secret key.

- $\boxed{\mathsf{CT}_{\mathsf{out}} \leftarrow \mathbf{PrivateKS}(\{\mathsf{ct}_i\}_{i \in \{1,\ldots,p\}}, \mathsf{KSK})}$: allows to apply a private linear function $f : (\mathbb{Z}/q\mathbb{Z})^p \longrightarrow \mathbb{Z}/q\mathbb{Z}[X]$ over p LWE ciphertexts $\{\mathsf{ct}_i = \mathsf{LWE}_{\mathbf{s}}(m_1)\}_{i \in \{1,\ldots,p\}}$ and creates a GLWE ciphertext $\mathsf{CT}_{\mathsf{out}} = \mathsf{GLWE}_{\mathbf{S}'}(f(m_1, \cdots, m_p))$. For more details check [8, Algorithm 2].

- $\boxed{\mathsf{CT}_{\mathsf{out}} \leftarrow \textbf{PublicKS}(\{\mathsf{ct}_i\}_{i\in\{1,\ldots,p\}}, \mathsf{KSK}, f)}$: is a public version of the previous key switching, i.e., a key switching with a public linear function f. For more details check [8, Algorithm 1]. The *key switching used in TFHE PBS* is a public key switching, where the function f is the identity function and the output GLWE is instantiated with $k = n'$ and $N = 1$ (i.e., as an LWE instance).
- $\boxed{\mathsf{CT}_{\mathsf{out}} \leftarrow \textbf{PackingKS}(\{\mathsf{ct}_j\}_{j=1}^{p}, \{i_j\}_{j=1}^{p}, \mathsf{KSK})}$: is a (public) key switching procedure enabling to pack several LWE ciphertexts into one GLWE. It takes as input a set of p LWE ciphertexts as well as a set of p indexes. Given the set of indexes $\{i_j\}_{j=1}^{p}$, the function f has the following shape: $f(\{m_j\}_{j=1}^{p}) \longrightarrow \sum_{j=1}^{p} m_j \cdot X^{i_j}$.

GSW, RGSW and GGSW Ciphertexts. A GGSW ciphertext with the base $\mathfrak{B} \in \mathbb{N}^*$ and $\ell \in \mathbb{N}^*$ levels, of a message $M \in \mathfrak{R}_q$ under the GLWE secret key $\mathbf{s} = (S_1, \cdots, S_k) \in \mathfrak{R}_q^k$ is defined as the following vector of GLev ciphertexts:

$$\overline{\overline{\mathsf{CT}}} = \left(\overline{\mathsf{CT}}_1, \cdots, \overline{\mathsf{CT}}_{k+1}\right) = \mathsf{GGSW}_{\mathbf{S}}^{(\mathfrak{B},\ell)}(M) \in \mathfrak{R}_q^{(k+1)\times\ell\times(k+1)}$$

where $\overline{\mathsf{CT}}_i = \mathsf{GLev}_{\mathbf{S}}^{(\mathfrak{B},\ell)}(-S_i \cdot M)$ is a GLev ciphertext. Remember that we note $S_{k+1} = -1$.

A GGSW ciphertext with $N = 1$ is a *GSW ciphertext*, and a GGSW ciphertext with $k = 1$ and $N > 1$ is a *RGSW ciphertext.*

TFHE PBS. The bootstrapping of TFHE has a double functionality: it reduces the noise in the ciphertexts and at the same time evaluates a univariate function. We call it PBS for *programmable bootstrapping.* In order to be performed, the PBS uses a so called *bootstrapping key*, i.e., a list of GGSW encryptions of the elements of the secret key used to encrypt the input LWE (noisy) ciphertext of the PBS. The procedure is composed of three major steps:

- *Modulus Switching*: the input LWE ciphertext in $\mathbb{Z}_q^{n+1}$ is converted into a ciphertext in $\mathbb{Z}_{2N}^{n+1}$;
- *Blind Rotation*: a GLWE encryption of a *redundant LUT*[1] is rotated (by using a loop of CMux operations [9]) according to the LWE ciphertext produced in the previous step and the public bootstrapping key;
- *Sample Extraction*: the constant coefficient of the GLWE output of the previous step is extracted as a LWE ciphertext.

TFHE Circuit Bootstrapping. In 2017, TFHE authors propose a technique called *citcuit bootstrapping* [8, Algorithm 6], to convert an LWE ciphertext into a

[1] A *redundant LUT* is a LUT corresponding to a function f, whose entries are redundantly represented inside the coefficients of a polynomial in $\mathfrak{R}_q$. In practice, the redundancy consists in a r times (with r a system parameter) repetition of the entries $f(i)$ of the LUT with a certain shift: $P_f = X^{-r/2} \cdot \sum_{i=0}^{N/r-1} X^{i\cdot r} \cdot \left(\sum_{j=0}^{r-1} f(i) \cdot X^j\right)$. The redundancy is used to perform the rounding operation during bootstrapping.

GGSW ciphertext, and to reduce its noise at the same time. The circuit bootstrapping is composed by a series of ℓ TFHE PBS, followed by a list of $(k+1)\ell$ private key switching procedures. The goal is to build one by one all the GLWE ciphertexts composing the output GGSW.

3 Building Blocks

In this section we describe two building blocks: the LWE multiplication, that uses an existing GLWE multiplication together with some key switchings and sample extraction, and a generalized version of TFHE PBS. Both techniques are necessaries in order to build our constructions in the rest of the paper.

3.1 LWE Multiplication

We first recall the multiplication algorithm for GLWE ciphertexts in Algorithm 1. It is composed of a *tensor product* followed by a *relinearization* and is widely used in the literature [13] (we recall the GLWE [3] algorithm, instead of the more limited RLWE version). Since this algorithm is largely used in the rest of the paper, we thoroughly study its noise growth and provide a formal noise analysis where $\mathsf{Var}(S)$ is the variance of a GLWE secret key polynomial $S \in \mathfrak{R}_q$, $\mathsf{Var}(S'_{\mathsf{even}})$ (resp. $\mathsf{Var}(S'_{\mathsf{odd}})$) is the variance of even (resp. odd) coefficients in S^2 and $\mathsf{Var}(S'')$ is the variance of coefficients in $S_i \cdot S_j$ which is the product between two independent secret key polynomials $S_i, S_j \in \mathfrak{R}_q$. We provide concrete cryptographic parameters depending on the precision and the multiplicative depth in the Table 1.

Table 1. Parameters depending on the GLWE multiplicative depth and the precision.

Precision	1	2	3	4	5	6	7	8	9	10	11	12	13	14	15	16	17	18	19	20	21	22	23	24
Max. depth	32	16	16	8	8	8	8	4	4	4	4	4	4	2	2	2	2	2	2	2	2	2	2	2
$\log_2(N)$	12	11	12	11	11	12	12	11	11	11	12	12	12	11	11	11	11	11	11	11	12	12	12	12
$\log_2(\mathfrak{B})$	8	5	8	12	10	8	8	20	17	15	17	17	8	30	30	20	20	20	20	20	20	20	20	20
ℓ	8	10	8	4	5	8	8	2	3	3	3	3	8	1	1	2	2	2	2	2	2	2	2	2

Theorem 1 (GLWE multiplication). *Let* $\mathsf{CT}_1 = \mathsf{GLWE}_{\mathbf{S}}(\mathsf{PT}_1) \in \mathfrak{R}_q^{k+1}$ *and* $\mathsf{CT}_2 = \mathsf{GLWE}_{\mathbf{S}}(\mathsf{PT}_2) \in \mathfrak{R}_q^{k+1}$ *be two GLWE ciphertexts, encrypting respectively* $\mathsf{PT}_1 = M_1\Delta_1 \in \mathfrak{R}_q$ *and* $\mathsf{PT}_2 = M_2\Delta_2 \in \mathfrak{R}_q$, *under the same secret key* $\mathbf{S}=(S_1,\ldots,S_k)\in\mathfrak{R}_q^k$, *with noise sampled respectively from* χ_{σ_1} *and* χ_{σ_2}. *Let* $\mathsf{RLK} = \left\{\overline{\mathsf{CT}}_{i,j} = \mathsf{GLev}_{\mathbf{S}}^{(\mathfrak{B},\ell)}(S_i \cdot S_j) \in \mathfrak{R}_q^{\ell \times (k+1)}\right\}_{1\le i\le k}^{1\le j\le i}$ *be a relinearization key for the GLWE secret key* $\mathbf{S}$, *with noise sampled from* $\chi_{\sigma_{\mathsf{RLK}}}$.

Algorithm 1 computes a new GLWE ciphertext CT *encrypting the product* $\mathsf{PT}_1 \cdot \mathsf{PT}_2 / \Delta \in \mathfrak{R}_q$ *where* $\Delta = min(\Delta_1, \Delta_2)$ *(a scaling factor), under the secret key* $\mathbf{S}$, *with a noise variance* $\mathsf{Var}_{\mathsf{GLWEMult}}$ *estimated by the following formula:*

$$
\begin{aligned}
\mathsf{Var}_{\mathbf{GLWEMult}} = & \tfrac{N}{\Delta^2}\left(\Delta_1^2 ||M_1||_\infty^2 \sigma_2^2 + \Delta_2^2 ||M_2||_\infty^2 \sigma_1^2 + \sigma_1^2\sigma_2^2\right) \\
& + \tfrac{N}{\Delta^2}\left(\tfrac{q^2-1}{12}\left(1+kN\mathsf{Var}(S)+kN\mathbb{E}^2(S)\right)+\tfrac{kN}{4}\mathsf{Var}(S)+\tfrac{1}{4}(1+kN\mathbb{E}(S))^2\right)(\sigma_1^2+\sigma_2^2) \\
& + \tfrac{1}{12}+\tfrac{kN}{12\Delta^2}\cdot\left((\Delta^2-1)\cdot\left(\mathsf{Var}(S)+\mathbb{E}^2(S)\right)+3\cdot\mathsf{Var}(S)\right)+\tfrac{k(k-1)N}{24\Delta^2}\cdot\left((\Delta^2-1)\cdot\left(\mathsf{Var}(S'')+\mathbb{E}^2(S'')\right)+3\cdot\mathsf{Var}(S'')\right) \\
& + \tfrac{kN}{24\Delta^2}\cdot\left((\Delta^2-1)\cdot\left(\mathsf{Var}(S'_{\mathsf{odd}})+\mathsf{Var}(S'_{\mathsf{even}})+2\cdot\mathbb{E}^2(S'_{\mathsf{mean}})\right)+3\cdot\left(\mathsf{Var}(S'_{\mathsf{odd}})+\mathsf{Var}(S'_{\mathsf{even}})\right)\right)+k\ell N\sigma_{\mathsf{RLK}}^2\cdot\tfrac{(k+1)}{2}\cdot\tfrac{\mathfrak{B}^2+2}{12} \\
& + \tfrac{kN}{2}\left(\tfrac{q^2}{12\mathfrak{B}^{2\ell}}-\tfrac{1}{12}\right)\left((k-1)\cdot(\mathsf{Var}(S'')+\mathbb{E}^2(S''_{\mathsf{mean}}))+\mathsf{Var}(S'_{\mathsf{odd}})+\mathsf{Var}(S'_{\mathsf{even}})+2\mathbb{E}^2(S'_{\mathsf{mean}})\right) \\
& + \tfrac{kN}{8}\cdot\left((k-1)\cdot\mathsf{Var}(S'')+\mathsf{Var}(S'_{\mathsf{odd}})+\mathsf{Var}(S'_{\mathsf{even}})\right).
\end{aligned}
\tag{1}
$$

Let $k^* = \frac{k(k+1)}{2}$ *and* $k^+ = \frac{(k+1)(k+2)}{2}$. *The complexity of the algorithm is:*

$$
\begin{aligned}
\mathbb{C}_{\mathsf{GLWEMult}}^{(k,\ell,n,N)} &= \mathbb{C}_{\mathsf{TensorProduct}}^{(k,N)} + \mathbb{C}_{\mathsf{Relin}}^{(k,\ell,N)}, \textit{with} \\
\mathbb{C}_{\mathsf{TensorProduct}}^{(k,N)} &= 2(k+1)\mathbb{C}_{\mathsf{FFT}} + k^+\mathbb{C}_{\mathsf{iFFT}} + (k+1)^2 N\mathbb{C}_{\mathsf{multFFT}} + k^* N\mathbb{C}_{\mathsf{addFFT}}, \textit{and} \\
\mathbb{C}_{\mathsf{Relin}}^{(k,\ell,N)} &= N\ell k^*\mathbb{C}_{\mathsf{dec}} + k^*\ell\mathbb{C}_{\mathsf{FFT}} + k^*\ell(k+1)N\mathbb{C}_{\mathsf{multFFT}} + (k^*\ell-1)(k+1)N\mathbb{C}_{\mathsf{addFFT}} + (k+1)\mathbb{C}_{\mathsf{iFFT}}
\end{aligned}
\tag{2}
$$

Proof (sketch). In the proof, we compute the decryption of the resulting ciphertext, obtaining the message plus the noise so we can estimate its variance. The detailed computation leading us to the aforementioned noise formula is provided in the full version of the paper. □

The same Algorithm 1 can be adapted in order to perform a GLWE square: the square is more efficient since $R'_{i,j}$ and A'_i are computed with a single multiplication instead of two. For more details, we refer to the full version of the paper.

3.1.1 Single LWE Multiplication

We now define Algorithm 2 for homomorphically *multiply two LWE ciphertexts*. It requires the *sample extraction* procedure, which is an algorithm adding no noise to the ciphertext and consisting in simply rearranging some of the coefficients of the GLWE input ciphertext to build the output LWE ciphertext encrypting one of the coefficients of the input polynomial plaintext. The sample extraction is described in [9, Sect. 4.2] for RLWE inputs, and can be easily extended to GLWE ones. Due to page constraint, this algorithm is described in the full version of the paper.

Theorem 2 (LWE-to-GLWE Packing Key Switch). *We start with the simplest case were we pack a single LWE ciphertext. Let* $\mathsf{ct}_{\mathsf{in}} = \mathsf{LWE}_{\mathbf{s}}(m\cdot\Delta) \in \mathbb{Z}_q^{n+1}$ *be an LWE ciphertext encrypting* $m\cdot\Delta \in \mathbb{Z}_q$*, under the LWE secret key* $\mathbf{s} = (s_1, \ldots, s_n) \in \mathbb{Z}_q^n$*, with noise sampled respectively from* χ_σ*. Let* $\mathbf{S}'$ *be a GLWE secret key such that* $\mathbf{S}' = (S'_1, \ldots, S'_k)\, in\, \mathfrak{R}_q^{k+1}$*. Let* $\mathsf{KSK} = \{\overline{\mathsf{CT}}_i = \mathsf{GLev}_{\mathbf{S}'}^{\mathfrak{B},\ell}(s_i) \in \mathfrak{R}_q^{\ell\times(k+1)}\}_{1\le i\le n}$ *be a key switching key from* $\mathbf{s}$ *to* $\mathbf{S}'$ *with noise sampled from* $\chi_{\sigma_{\mathsf{KSK}}}$*.*

There are two different variances after a packing key switch: one for the coefficient we just filled written $\mathsf{Var}_{\mathsf{fill}}$ *and another for the empty coefficients* $\mathsf{Var}_{\mathsf{emp}}$*. Those variances are estimated by:*

$$
\begin{aligned}
\mathsf{Var}_{\mathsf{fill}}^{(1)} &= \sigma^2 + n\cdot\left(\frac{q^2}{12\mathfrak{B}^{2\ell}}-\frac{1}{12}\right)\cdot\left(\mathsf{Var}(s_i)+\mathbb{E}^2(s_i)\right)+\frac{n}{4}\cdot\mathsf{Var}(s_i)+n\cdot\ell\cdot\sigma_{\mathsf{KSK}}^2\cdot\frac{\mathfrak{B}^2+2}{12} \\
\mathsf{Var}_{\mathsf{emp}}^{(1)} &= n\cdot\ell\cdot\sigma_{\mathsf{KSK}}^2\cdot\frac{\mathfrak{B}^2+2}{12}
\end{aligned}
\tag{3}
$$

Algorithm 1: $\mathsf{CT} \leftarrow$ **GLWEMult** $(\mathsf{CT}_1, \mathsf{CT}_2, \mathsf{RLK})$

Context: $\begin{cases} \mathbf{S} = (S_1, \dots, S_k) \in \mathfrak{R}_q^k : \text{ a GLWE secret key} \\ \Delta = \min(\Delta_1, \Delta_2) \in \mathbb{Z}_q \\ \mathsf{PT}_1 = M_1\Delta_1 \in \mathfrak{R}_q \\ \mathsf{PT}_2 = M_2\Delta_2 \in \mathfrak{R}_q \end{cases}$

Input: $\begin{cases} \mathsf{CT}_1 = \mathsf{GLWE}_{\mathbf{S}}(\mathsf{PT}_1) = (A_{1,1}, \cdots, A_{1,k}, B_1) \in \mathfrak{R}_q^{k+1} \\ \mathsf{CT}_2 = \mathsf{GLWE}_{\mathbf{S}}(\mathsf{PT}_2) = (A_{2,1}, \cdots, A_{2,k}, B_2) \in \mathfrak{R}_q^{k+1} \\ \mathsf{RLK} = \left\{\overline{\mathsf{CT}}_{i,j} = \mathsf{GLev}_{\mathbf{S}}^{(\mathfrak{B},\ell)}(S_i \cdot S_j)\right\}_{1\le i\le k}^{1\le j\le i} : \text{ a relinearization key for } \mathbf{S} \end{cases}$

Output: $\mathsf{CT} = \mathsf{GLWE}_{\mathbf{S}}\left(\frac{\mathsf{PT}_1 \cdot \mathsf{PT}_2}{\Delta}\right) \in \mathfrak{R}_q^{k+1}$

```
begin
    /* Tensor product                                              */
    for 1 ≤ i ≤ k do
        T'_i ← [⌊[A_{1,i}·A_{2,i}]_Q / Δ⌉]_q
    end
    for 1 ≤ i ≤ k, 1 ≤ j < i do
        R'_{i,j} ← [⌊[A_{1,i}·A_{2,j} + A_{1,j}·A_{2,i}]_Q / Δ⌉]_q
    end
    for 1 ≤ i ≤ k do
        A'_i ← [⌊[A_{1,i}·B_2 + B_1·A_{2,i}]_Q / Δ⌉]_q
    end
    B' ← [⌊[B_1·B_2]_Q / Δ⌉]_q
    /* Relinearization                                             */
    CT ←
    (A'_1, ···, A'_k, B') + Σ_{i=1}^{k} ⟨CT̄_{i,i}, dec^{(𝔅,ℓ)}(T'_i)⟩ + Σ_{1≤i≤k}^{1≤j<i} ⟨CT̄_{i,j} · dec^{(𝔅,ℓ)}(R'_{i,j})⟩
end
```

When we pack $1 \le \alpha \le N$ LWE ciphertexts, we have $\mathsf{Var}_{\mathsf{fill}}^{(\alpha)} = \mathsf{Var}_{\mathsf{fill}}^{(1)} + (\alpha-1)\cdot\mathsf{Var}_{\mathsf{emp}}^{(1)}$ *and* $\mathsf{Var}_{\mathsf{emp}}^{(\alpha)} = \alpha\cdot\mathsf{Var}_{\mathsf{emp}}^{(1)}$ *The complexity of the algorithm is:*

$$\mathbb{C}_{\mathsf{PackingKS}}^{(\alpha,\ell,n,k,N)} = \alpha\ell n\mathbb{C}_{\mathsf{dec}} + \alpha\ell n(k+1)N\mathbb{C}_{\mathsf{mul}} + ((\alpha\ell n - 1)(k+1)N + \alpha)\mathbb{C}_{\mathsf{add}}$$

Proof (sketch). In the proof, we compute the decryption of the resulting ciphertext, obtaining the message plus the noise so we can estimate the two variances. The detailed computation leading us to the aforementioned noise formulas are provided in the full version of the paper. □

Theorem 3 (LWE Multiplication). *Let* $\mathsf{ct}^{(1)} = \mathsf{LWE}_{\mathbf{s}}(m_1\cdot\Delta_1)$ *and* $\mathsf{ct}^{(2)} = \mathsf{LWE}_{\mathbf{s}}(m_2\cdot\Delta_2)$ *be two LWE ciphertexts, encrypting respectively* $m_1\cdot\Delta_1$ *and* $m_2\cdot\Delta_2$, *both encrypted under the LWE secret key* $\mathbf{s} = (s_1, \dots, s_n)$, *with noise sampled respectively from* χ_{σ_1} *and* χ_{σ_2}. *Let* $\mathsf{KSK} = \left\{\overline{\mathsf{CT}}_i = \mathsf{GLev}_{\mathbf{S}'}^{\mathfrak{B},\ell}(s_i)\right\}_{1\le i\le n}$ *a key switching key from* $\mathbf{s}$ *to* $\mathbf{S}'$ *where* $\mathbf{S}' = (S'_1, \dots, S'_k)$, *with noise sampled from* $\chi_{\sigma_{\mathsf{KSK}}}$. *Let* RLK *be a relinearization key for* $\mathbf{S}'$, *defined as in Theorem 1.*

Algorithm 2 computes a new LWE ciphertext $\mathsf{ct}_{\mathsf{out}}$, *encrypting the product* $m_1\cdot m_2\cdot\Delta_{\mathsf{out}}$, *where* $\Delta_{\mathsf{out}} = max(\Delta_1, \Delta_2)$, *under the secret key* $\mathbf{s}'$. *The variance of the noise in* $\mathsf{ct}_{\mathsf{out}}$ *can be estimated by replacing the variances* σ_1 *and* σ_2 *in the RLWE*

Algorithm 2: $\mathsf{ct}_{\mathsf{out}} \leftarrow$ **LWEMult** $(\mathsf{ct}_1, \mathsf{ct}_2, \mathsf{RLK}, \mathsf{KSK})$

Context: $\begin{cases} \mathbf{s} = (s_1, \cdots, s_n) \in \mathbb{Z}_q^n : \text{ the LWE input secret key} \\ \mathbf{s}' = (s'_1, \cdots, s'_{kN}) \in \mathbb{Z}_q^{kN} : \text{ the LWE output secret key} \\ \mathbf{S}' = (S'_1, \dots, S'_k) \in \mathfrak{R}_q^k : \text{ a GLWE secret key} \\ \forall 1 \le i \le k,\ S'_i = \sum_{j=0}^{N-1} s'_{(i-1)\cdot N+j+1} X^j \in \mathfrak{R}_q \\ \Delta_{\mathsf{out}} = \max(\Delta_1, \Delta_2) \in \mathbb{Z}_q \end{cases}$

Input: $\begin{cases} \mathsf{ct}_1 = \mathsf{LWE}_{\mathbf{s}}(m_1 \cdot \Delta_1) \in \mathbb{Z}_q^{n+1} \\ \mathsf{ct}_2 = \mathsf{LWE}_{\mathbf{s}}(m_2 \cdot \Delta_2) \in \mathbb{Z}_q^{n+1} \\ \mathsf{RLK} : \text{ a relinearization key for } \mathbf{S}' \text{ as defined in Algorithm 1} \\ \mathsf{KSK} = \left\{ \overline{\mathsf{CT}}_i = \mathsf{GLev}_{\mathbf{S}'}^{\mathfrak{B},\ell}(s_i) \right\}_{1 \le i \le n} : \text{ a key switching key from } \mathbf{s} \text{ to } \mathbf{S}' \end{cases}$

Output: $\mathsf{ct}_{\mathsf{out}} = \mathsf{LWE}_{\mathbf{s}'}(m_1 \cdot m_2 \cdot \Delta_{\mathsf{out}}) \in \mathbb{Z}_q^{kN+1}$

begin

  /* KS from LWE to GLWE */

  $\mathsf{CT}_1 = \mathsf{GLWE}_{\mathbf{S}'}(m_1 \cdot \Delta_1) \leftarrow$ **PackingKS**$(\{\mathsf{ct}_1\}, \{0\}, \mathsf{KSK})$;

  $\mathsf{CT}_2 = \mathsf{GLWE}_{\mathbf{S}'}(m_2 \cdot \Delta_2) \leftarrow$ **PackingKS**$(\{\mathsf{ct}_2\}, \{0\}, \mathsf{KSK})$;

  /* GLWE multiplication: Tensor product + Relinearization */

  $\mathsf{CT} = \mathsf{GLWE}_{\mathbf{S}'}(m_1 \cdot m_2 \cdot \Delta_{\mathsf{out}}) \leftarrow$ **GLWEMult**$(\mathsf{CT}_1, \mathsf{CT}_2, \mathsf{RLK})$

  /* Sample extract the constant term */

  $\mathsf{ct}_{\mathsf{out}} = \mathsf{LWE}_{\mathbf{s}'}(m_1 \cdot m_2 \cdot \Delta_{\mathsf{out}}) \leftarrow$ **SampleExtract** $(\mathsf{CT}, 0)$

end

multiplication (Formula 1, Theorem 1) with the variance estimated after a packing key switch (Formula 3, Theorem 2). The complexity is:

$$\mathbb{C}_{\mathsf{LWEMult}}^{(\ell_{\mathbf{KS}}, \ell_{\mathbf{RL}}, n, k, N)} = 2 \cdot \mathbb{C}_{\mathsf{PackingKS}}^{(1, \ell_{\mathbf{KS}}, n, k, N)} + \mathbb{C}_{\mathsf{GLWEMult}}^{(k, \ell_{\mathbf{RL}}, n, N)} + \mathbb{C}_{\mathsf{SampleExtract}}^{(N)}$$

3.1.2 Packed Products and Packed Sum of Products

It is possible to use algorithm 2 to compute with a single multiplication several products, or several squares, or a sum of several products, or even a sum of several squares.

These four functionalities can be easily achieved by slightly modifying Algorithm 2. In the case of **PackedMult** and **PackedSumProducts**, the algorithm take in input two sets of LWE ciphertexts $\left\{\mathsf{ct}_i^{(1)}\right\} = \left\{\mathsf{LWE}_{\mathbf{s}}(m_i^{(1)} \cdot \Delta_1)\right\}_{0 \le i < \alpha}$ and $\left\{\mathsf{ct}_i^{(2)}\right\} = \left\{\mathsf{LWE}_{\mathbf{s}}(m_i^{(2)} \cdot \Delta_2)\right\}_{0 \le i < \alpha}$:

1. **PackedMult:** the goal is to compute LWE encryptions of the products $m_i^{(1)} \cdot m_i^{(2)} \cdot \Delta_{\mathsf{out}}$, where $\Delta_{\mathsf{out}} = max(\Delta_1, \Delta_2)$. The two input sets are packed with a packing key switch into two GLWE ciphertexts with indexes $\mathscr{L}_1 = \{0, 1, 2, \cdots, \alpha - 1\}$ and $\mathscr{L}_2 = \{0, \alpha, 2\alpha, \cdots, (\alpha - 1)\alpha\}$ respectively. The resulting GLWE ciphertexts are multiplied with the GLWE multiplication (Algorithm 1) and finally all the coefficients at indexes $i \cdot (\alpha + 1)$ (for $0 \le i < \alpha$) are extracted.
2. **PackedSumProducts:** the goal is to compute a LWE encryption of the sum of products $\sum_{i=0}^{\alpha-1} m_i^{(1)} \cdot m_i^{(2)} \cdot \Delta_{\mathsf{out}}$, where $\Delta_{\mathsf{out}} = max(\Delta_1, \Delta_2)$. The two input sets are packed with a packing key switch into two GLWE ciphertexts with indexes $\mathscr{L}_1 = \{0, 1, 2, \cdots, \alpha - 1\}$ and $\mathscr{L}_2 = \{\alpha - 1, \alpha - 2, \alpha - 3, \cdots, 0\}$ respectively. The resulting GLWE ciphertexts are multiplied with the GLWE multiplication (Algorithm 1) and finally the coefficient at index $\alpha - 1$ is extracted.

Note that it is possible to compute packed squares and a packed sum of squares if the two LWE input sets are equal. It is also possible to compute squares and a sum of squares by computing a RLWE multiplication between an RLWE ciphertext and itself. In that case, a single set of LWE input in provided $\{\mathsf{ct}_i\} = \{\mathsf{LWE}_{\mathbf{s}}(m_i \cdot \Delta)\}_{0 \leq i < \alpha}$:

1. **PackedSquares:** the goal is to compute LWE encryptions of the squares $m_i^2 \cdot \Delta$. The input set is packed with a packing key switch into a GLWE ciphertext with indexes $\mathscr{L} = \{2^0 - 1, 2^1 - 1, 2^2 - 1, \cdots, 2^{\alpha-1} - 1\}$. The resulting GLWE ciphertext is squared by using the GLWE square algorithm and finally all the coefficients at indexes $2^{i+1} - 2$ (for $0 \leq i < \alpha$) are extracted.
2. **PackedSumSquares:** the goal is to compute a LWE encryption of the sum of squares $\sum_{i=0}^{\alpha-1} m_i^2 \cdot 2\Delta$. To achieve this goal, the input set is packed with a packing key switch into a GLWE ciphertext with redundancy, using two indexes sets $\mathscr{L}_1 = \{0, 1, 2, \cdots, \alpha - 1\}$ and $\mathscr{L}_2 = \{2\alpha - 1, 2\alpha - 2, 2\alpha - 3, \cdots, \alpha\}$. The resulting GLWE ciphertext is squared by using the GLWE square algorithm and finally the coefficient at index $2\alpha - 1$ is extracted.

Note that we could also compute packed products and a packed sum of products with a GLWE square algorithm by changing $\mathscr{L}$, $\mathscr{L}_1$ and $\mathscr{L}_2$ and also extracting different coefficients. Also note that for these four algorithms, there are restrictions regarding the maximum value that α can take each time. We provide more details in the the full version of the paper.

3.2 Generalized PBS

We propose a *more versatile* algorithm for the PBS where we are able to bootstrap a precise chunk of bits, instead of only the MSB as described in TFHE, and to also apply several function evaluations at once. We describe this generalization in Algorithm 3. We introduce two *new parameters*, $\varkappa$ and ϑ, which redefine the *modulus switching* step of TFHE PBS. In particular, $\varkappa$ defines the number of MSB that are not considered in the PBS, while 2^ϑ defines the number of functions that can be evaluated at the same time in a single generalized PBS.

The two parameters $\varkappa$ and ϑ are illustrated in Fig. 2, where "input" represents the plaintext (with noise) that is encrypted the input ciphertext of the modulus switching, and "output" illustrates the plaintext (with noise) that is encrypted inside the output ciphertext (after modulus switching). The first $\varkappa$ MSB will not impact the following steps of the generalized PBS and ϑ bits will be set to 0 in order to encode 2^ϑ functions in the LUT stored in P_f (see Sect. 4.3 for more details). Observe that the case $(\varkappa, \vartheta) = (0, 0)$ corresponds to the original TFHE PBS.

We also define the *"plaintext modulus switching"* function written **PTModSwitch** to recover the plaintext of the encrypted output of a modulus switching algorithm. Let $m \in \mathbb{Z}_q$ be a message, $\Delta \in \mathbb{Z}_q$ its scaling factor, $\varkappa \in \mathbb{Z}$ and $\vartheta \in \mathbb{N}$ the parameters of a modulus switching. We define $q' = \frac{q}{\Delta 2^\varkappa}$. The case where $\varkappa \geq 0$ is illustrated in Fig. 3. We defined $(\beta, m') \leftarrow \mathbf{PTModSwitch}_q(m, \Delta, \varkappa, \vartheta) \in \{0,1\} \times \mathbb{N}$ as follow:

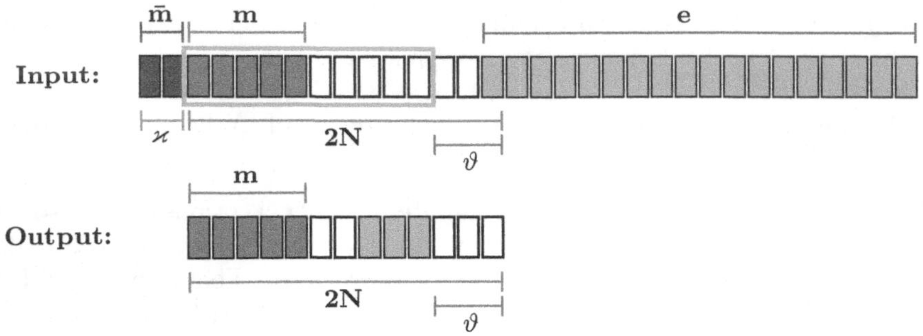

Fig. 2. Modulus switching operation in the generalized PBS (Algorithm 3): on top of the figures we illustrate the data $(\bar{m}, m, e)$, on the bottom the dimensions $(\varkappa,\, 2N,\, \vartheta)$.

$$\text{If } \varkappa \geq 0: \begin{cases} m' = m \mod \frac{q'}{2} \\ \text{if } m \mod q' < \frac{q'}{2},\ \beta = 0,\ \text{else } \beta = 1 \end{cases} \qquad \text{Else}: \begin{cases} m' = m \\ \beta \text{ is a random bit} \end{cases}$$

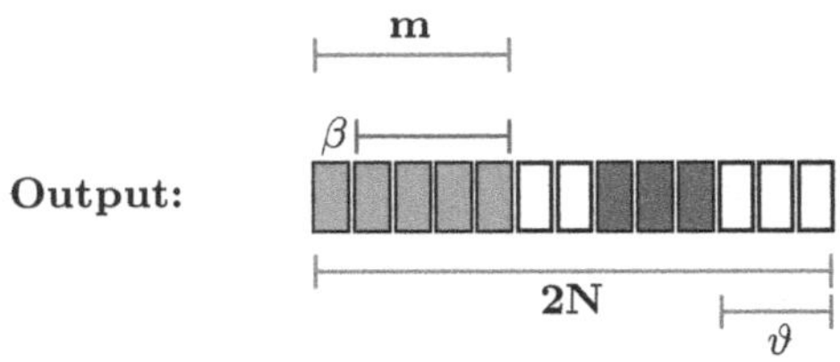

Fig. 3. Plaintext after the modulus switching from the generalized PBS (Algorithm 3) where $\varkappa \geq 0$: on top of the figure we illustrate the data$(m,\, \beta,\, m')$, on the bottom the dimensions $(2N,\, \vartheta)$.

Note that for simplicity purpose, we provide the generalized PBS noise formula *only for binary secret keys.* However, in the full version of the paper we provide formulas as well as proofs for more key distributions (binary, ternary and Gaussian).

Theorem 4 (Generalized PBS). *Let* $\mathbf{s} = (s_1, \cdots, s_n) \in \mathbb{Z}_q^n$ *be a binary LWE secret key. Let* $\mathbf{S}' = (S'_1, \ldots, S'_k) \in \mathfrak{R}_q^k$ *be a GLWE binary secret key such that* $S'_i = \sum_{j=0}^{N-1} s'_{(i-1)\cdot N+j+1} \cdot X^j$*, and* $\mathbf{s}' = (s'_1, \cdots, s'_{kN})$ *be the corresponding binary LWE secret key. Let* P_f *be a r-redundant LUT for a function* $f: \mathbb{Z} \to \mathbb{Z}$ *and* Δ_{out} *be the output scaling factor. Let* $(\varkappa, \vartheta)$ *be the two integer variables defining (along with N) the window size to be modulus switched, such that* $\frac{q 2^{\vartheta}}{\Delta_{\mathsf{in}} 2^{\varkappa}} < 2N$*, and let* $(\beta, m') = \mathbf{PTModSwitch}_q(m, \Delta_{\mathsf{in}}, \varkappa, \vartheta) \in \{0,1\} \times \mathbb{N}$.

Then Algorithm 3 takes as input a LWE ciphertext $\mathsf{ct}_{\mathsf{in}} = \mathsf{LWE}_{\mathbf{s}}(m \cdot \Delta_{\mathsf{in}}) \in \mathbb{Z}_q^{n+1}$ *with noise distribution from* $\chi_{\sigma_{\mathsf{in}}}$, *a bootstrapping key* $\mathsf{BSK} = \left\{ \overline{\overline{\mathsf{CT}}}_i = \mathsf{GGSW}_{\mathbf{S}'}^{\mathfrak{B},\ell}(s_i) \right\}_{i=1}^{n}$ *from* $\mathbf{s}$ *to* $\mathbf{S}'$ *and a (possibly trivial) GLWE encryption of* $P_f \cdot \Delta_{\mathsf{out}}$, *and returns an LWE ciphertext* $\mathsf{ct}_{\mathsf{out}}$ *under the secret key* $\mathbf{s}'$, *encrypting the message* $(-1)^{\beta} \cdot f(m') \cdot \Delta_{\mathsf{out}}$ *if and only if the input noise has variance* $\sigma_{\mathsf{in}}^2 < \frac{\Delta_{\mathsf{in}}^2}{4\Gamma^2} - \frac{q'^2}{12w^2} + \frac{1}{12} - \frac{nq'^2}{24w^2} - \frac{n}{48}$, *where* Γ *is a variable depending on the probability of correctness defined as* $P = \mathsf{erf}\left(\frac{\Gamma}{\sqrt{2}}\right)$, $w = 2N \cdot 2^{-\vartheta}$ *and* $q' = q \cdot 2^{-\varkappa}$.

The output noise after the generalized PBS is estimated by the formula:

$$\mathsf{Var}(\mathsf{PBS}) = n\ell(k+1)N\frac{\mathfrak{B}^2+2}{12}\mathsf{Var}(\mathsf{BSK}) + n\frac{q^2-\mathfrak{B}^{2\ell}}{24\mathfrak{B}^{2\ell}}\left(1+\frac{kN}{2}\right) + \frac{nkN}{32} + \frac{n}{16}\left(1-\frac{kN}{2}\right)^2.$$

The complexity of Algorithm 3 is the same as the complexity of TFHE bootstrapping [9], *i.e.,*

$$\mathbb{C}_{\mathsf{GenPBS}}^{(n,\ell,k,N)} = \mathbb{C}_{\mathsf{ModulusSwitching}}^{(n)} + n\mathbb{C}_{\mathsf{CMUX}}^{(n,\ell,k,N)}\mathbb{C}_{\mathsf{SampleExtract}}^{(N)} \quad \textit{with}$$

$$\begin{cases} \mathbb{C}_{\mathsf{ModulusSwitching}}^{(n)} & = (n+1)\mathbb{C}_{\mathsf{Scale\&Round}} \\ \mathbb{C}_{\mathsf{CMUX}}^{(n,\ell,k,N)} & = (k+1)(n+1)\mathbb{C}_{\mathsf{Rotation}}^{(N)} + 2n(k+1)N\mathbb{C}_{\mathsf{Add}} + \mathbb{C}_{\mathsf{ExternalProduct}}^{(n,\ell,k,N)} \\ \mathbb{C}_{\mathsf{ExternalProduct}}^{(n,\ell,k,N)} & = n\ell(k+1)N\mathbb{C}_{\mathsf{dec}} + n\ell(k+1)\mathbb{C}_{\mathsf{FFT}} + n(k+1)\ell(k+1)N\mathbb{C}_{\mathsf{multFFT}} + \\ & \quad + n(k+1)(\ell(k+1)-1)N\mathbb{C}_{\mathsf{addFFT}} + n(k+1)\mathbb{C}_{\mathsf{iFFT}} \end{cases}$$

Proof (sketch). In the proof, we compute the decryption of the resulting ciphertext, obtaining the message plus the noise so we can estimate its variance. The detailed proof of this theorem is provided in the full version of the paper. □

4 Upgraded Bootstrapping

This section describes our main contributions, i.e., the **WoP-PBS** (PBS without a bit of padding) and the PBS evaluating multiple look-up tables at the same time (we call this algorithm **PBSmanyLUT**).

4.1 WoP-PBS First Version

A big constraint with TFHE PBS is the *negacyclicity of the rotation of the LUT*. It implies a need of a *padding bit* (as mentioned in Limitation A). We propose a solution to remove that requirement, by using the aforementioned LWE multiplication (Algorithm 1) and the generalized PBS (Algorithm 3). This new bootstrapping is called the *programmable bootstrapping without padding* (**WoP-PBS**) and a first version is described in Algorithm 4.

Theorem 5 (PBS Without Padding (V1)). *Let* $\mathbf{s} = (s_1, \cdots, s_n) \in \mathbb{Z}_q^n$ *be a binary LWE secret key. Let* $\mathbf{S}' = (S'_1, \ldots, S'_k) \in \mathfrak{R}_q^k$ *be a GLWE secret key such that* $S'_i = \sum_{j=0}^{N-1} s'_{(i-1)\cdot N+j+1} X^j \in \mathfrak{R}_q$, *and* $\mathbf{s}' = (s'_1, \cdots, s'_{kN}) \in \mathbb{Z}_q^{kN}$ *be the corresponding binary LWE key. Let* $P_f \in \mathfrak{R}_q$ *(resp.* $P_{\mathbb{1}} \in \mathfrak{R}_q$*) be a* r*-redundant LUT for the function* $f : \mathbb{Z} \mapsto \mathbb{Z}$, *(resp. the constant function* $x \mapsto 1$*) and* $\Delta_{\mathsf{out}} \in \mathbb{Z}_q$ *be the output scaling factor.*

Algorithm 3: $\mathsf{ct}_{\mathsf{out}} \leftarrow \mathbf{GenPBS}\left(\mathsf{ct}_{\mathsf{in}}, \mathsf{BSK}, \mathsf{CT}_f, \varkappa, \vartheta\right)$

Context:
$$\begin{cases} \mathbf{s} = (s_1, \cdots, s_n) \in \mathbb{Z}_q^n : \text{ the LWE input secret key} \\ \mathbf{s}' = (s'_1, \cdots, s'_{kN}) \in \mathbb{Z}_q^{kN} : \text{ the LWE output secret key} \\ \mathbf{S}' = (S'_1, \ldots, S'_k) \in \mathfrak{R}_q^k : \text{ a GLWE secret key} \\ \forall 1 \leq i \leq k,\ S'_i = \sum_{j=0}^{N-1} s'_{(i-1)\cdot N+j+1} X^j \in \mathfrak{R}_q \\ P_f \in \mathfrak{R}_q : \text{a } r\text{-redundant LUT for } x \mapsto f(x) \\ \Delta_{\mathsf{out}} \in \mathbb{Z}_q : \text{ the output scaling factor} \\ f : \mathbb{Z} \to \mathbb{Z} : \text{a function} \\ (\beta, m') = \mathbf{PTModSwitch}_q(m, \Delta_{\mathsf{in}}, \varkappa, \vartheta) \in \{0,1\} \times \mathbb{N} \end{cases}$$

Input:
$$\begin{cases} \mathsf{ct}_{\mathsf{in}} = \mathsf{LWE}_{\mathbf{s}}(m \cdot \Delta_{\mathsf{in}}) = (a_1, \cdots, a_n, a_{n+1} = b) \in \mathbb{Z}_q^{n+1} \\ \mathsf{BSK} = \left\{\overline{\overline{\mathsf{CT}}}_i = \mathsf{GGSW}_{\mathbf{S}'}^{\mathfrak{B},\ell}(s_i)\right\}_{i=1}^{n} : \text{ a bootstrapping key from } \mathbf{s} \text{ to } \mathbf{S}' \\ \mathsf{CT}_f = \mathsf{GLWE}_{\mathbf{S}'}(P_f \cdot \Delta_{\mathsf{out}}) \in \mathfrak{R}_q^{k+1} \\ (\varkappa, \vartheta) \in \mathbb{Z} \times \mathbb{N} : \text{define along with } N \text{ the chunk of the plaintext to bootstrap} \end{cases}$$

Output: $\mathsf{ct}_{\mathsf{out}} = \mathsf{LWE}_{\mathbf{s}'}\left((-1)^{\beta} \cdot f(m') \cdot \Delta_{\mathsf{out}}\right)$ if we respect requirements in Theorem 4

begin
- /* modulus switching */
- **for** $1 \leq i \leq n+1$ **do**
  - $a'_i \leftarrow \left\lceil \left\lfloor \frac{a_i \cdot 2N \cdot 2^{\varkappa - \vartheta}}{q} \right\rceil \cdot 2^{\vartheta} \right\rfloor_{2N}$
- **end**
- /* blind rotate of the LUT */
- $\mathsf{CT} \leftarrow \mathbf{BlindRotate}\left(\mathsf{CT}_f, \{a'_i\}_{i=1}^{n+1}, \mathsf{BSK}\right)$;
- /* sample extract the constant term */
- $\mathsf{ct}_{\mathsf{out}} \leftarrow \mathbf{SampleExtract}(\mathsf{CT}, 0)$

end

Let CT_f *be a (possibly trivial) GLWE encryption of* $P_f \cdot \Delta_{\mathsf{out}}$ *and* $\mathsf{CT}_{\mathbb{1}}$ *be a trivial GLWE encryption of* $P_{\mathbb{1}} \cdot \Delta_{\mathsf{out}}$. *Let* $(\varkappa, \vartheta) \in \mathbb{Z} \times \mathbb{N}$ *be the two integer variables defining (along with* N*) the chunk of the plaintext that is going to be bootstrapped, such that* $\frac{q 2^{\vartheta}}{\Delta_{\mathsf{in}} 2^{\varkappa}} < 2N$, *and let* $(\beta, m') = \mathbf{PTModSwitch}_q(m, \Delta_{\mathsf{in}}, \varkappa, \vartheta) \in \{0,1\} \times \mathbb{N}$.

Let $\mathsf{KSK} = \left\{\overline{\mathsf{CT}}_i = \mathsf{GLev}_{\mathbf{S}'}^{(\mathfrak{B},\ell)}(s'_i)\right\}_{1 \leq i \leq n}$ *be a key switching key from* $\mathbf{s}'$ *to* $\mathbf{S}'$, *with noise sampled respectively from* $\chi_{\sigma^{(1)}}$ *and* $\chi_{\sigma^{(2)}}$. *Let* $\mathsf{RLK} = \left\{\overline{\mathsf{CT}}_{i,j} = \mathsf{GLev}_{\mathbf{S}'}^{(\mathfrak{B},\ell)}(S'_i \cdot S'_j)\right\}_{1 \leq i \leq k}^{1 \leq j \leq i}$ *be a relinearization key for* $\mathbf{S}'$, *defined as in Theorem 1. Let* $\mathsf{BSK} = \left\{\overline{\overline{\mathsf{CT}}}_i = \mathsf{GGSW}_{\mathbf{S}'}^{\mathfrak{B},\ell}(s_i)\right\}_{i=1}^{n}$ *be a bootstrapping key from* $\mathbf{s}$ *to* $\mathbf{S}'$.

Then the Algorithm 4 takes in input a LWE ciphertext $\mathsf{ct}_{\mathsf{in}} = \mathsf{LWE}_{\mathbf{s}}(m \cdot \Delta_{\mathsf{in}}) \in \mathbb{Z}_q^{n+1}$ *where* $\mathsf{ct}_{\mathsf{in}} = (a_1, \cdots, a_n, a_{n+1} = b)$, *with noise sampled from* $\chi_{\sigma_{\mathsf{in}}}$, *and returns an LWE ciphertext* $\mathsf{ct}_{\mathsf{out}} \in \mathbb{Z}_q^{kN+1}$ *under the secret key* $\mathbf{s}'$ *encrypting the messages* $f(m') \cdot \Delta_{\mathsf{out}}$ *if and only if the input noise has variance verifying Theorem 3.*

The output ciphertext noise variance verifies $\mathsf{Var}(\mathbf{WoP\text{-}PBS}_1) = \mathsf{Var}(\mathbf{LWEMult})$ *with input variances for the LWE multiplication (Algorithm 2) defined as* $\sigma_i = \mathsf{Var}(\mathbf{GenPBS})$, *for* $i \in \{1, 2\}$.

The complexity of Algorithm 4 is:

$$\mathbb{C}_{\mathbf{WoP\text{-}PBS}_1}^{(n, \ell_{\mathbf{PBS}}, k_1, N_1, \ell_{\mathbf{KS}}, \ell_{\mathbf{RL}}, k_2, N_2)} = 2\mathbb{C}_{\mathsf{GenPBS}}^{(n, \ell_{\mathbf{PBS}}, k_1, N_1)} + \mathbb{C}_{\mathsf{LWEMult}}^{(\ell_{\mathbf{KS}}, \ell_{\mathbf{RL}}, N_1, k_2, N_2)}$$

Proof (Sketch). We only provide a proof of correctness of the algorithm, considering that the noise and the complexity are directly deduced from the **GenPBS** and **LWEMult** algorithms. Both of the **GenPBS** are applied with the same parameters except for the evaluated function (P_f or $P_{\mathbb{1}}$). Thus, in both cipher-

Algorithm 4: $\mathsf{ct}_{\mathsf{out}} \leftarrow \mathbf{WoP\text{-}PBS}_1(\mathsf{ct}_{\mathsf{in}}, \mathsf{BSK}, \mathsf{RLK}, \mathsf{KSK}, P_f, \Delta_{\mathsf{out}}, \varkappa, \vartheta)$

Context:
$$\begin{cases} \mathbf{s} = (s_1, \cdots, s_n) \in \mathbb{Z}_q^n \\ \mathbf{s}' = (s'_1, \cdots, s'_{kN}) \in \mathbb{Z}_q^{kN} \\ \mathbf{S}' = \left(S'^{(1)}, \ldots, S'^{(k)}\right) \in \mathfrak{R}_q^k \\ \forall 1 \le i \le k,\ S'^{(i)} = \sum_{j=0}^{N-1} s'_{(i-1)\cdot N+j+1} X^j \in \mathfrak{R}_q \\ f : \mathbb{Z} \to \mathbb{Z} : \text{a function} \\ P_{\mathbb{1}} \in \mathfrak{R}_q : \text{ a redundant LUT for } x \mapsto 1 \\ (\beta, m') = \mathbf{PTModSwitch}_q(m, \Delta, \varkappa, \vartheta) \in \{0,1\} \times \mathbb{N} \\ \mathsf{CT}_f = \mathsf{GLWE}_{\mathbf{S}'}(P_f \cdot \Delta_{\mathsf{out}}) \in \mathfrak{R}_q^{k+1} \text{ (might be a trivial encryption)} \\ \mathsf{CT}_{\mathbb{1}} \in \mathfrak{R}_q^{k+1} : \text{ a trivial encryption of } P_{\mathbb{1}} \cdot \Delta_{\mathsf{out}} \end{cases}$$

Input:
$$\begin{cases} \mathsf{ct}_{\mathsf{in}} = \mathsf{LWE}_{\mathbf{s}}(m \cdot \Delta_{\mathsf{in}}) = (a_1, \cdots, a_n, a_{n+1} = b) \in \mathbb{Z}_q^{n+1} \\ \mathsf{BSK} = \left\{\mathsf{BSK}_i = \mathsf{GGSW}_{\mathbf{S}'}^{(\mathfrak{B},\ell)}(s_i)\right\}_{1 \le i \le n} : \text{ a bootstrapping key from } \mathbf{s} \text{ to } \mathbf{S}' \\ \mathsf{RLK} = \left\{\overline{\mathsf{CT}}_{i,j} = \mathsf{GLev}_{\mathbf{S}'}^{(\mathfrak{B},\ell)}\left(S'_i \cdot S'_j\right)\right\}_{1 \le i \le k}^{1 \le j \le i} : \text{ a relinearization key for } \mathbf{S}' \\ \mathsf{KSK} = \left\{\overline{\mathsf{CT}}_i = \mathsf{GLev}_{\mathbf{S}'}^{(\mathfrak{B},\ell)}(s'_i)\right\}_{1 \le i \le kN} : \text{ a key switching key from } \mathbf{s}' \text{ to } \mathbf{S}' \\ P_f \in \mathfrak{R} : \text{a redundant LUT for } x \mapsto f(x) \\ \Delta_{\mathsf{out}} \in \mathbb{Z}_q : \text{the output scaling factor} \\ (\varkappa, \vartheta) \in \mathbb{Z} \times \mathbb{N} : \text{define along with } N \text{ the window size} \end{cases}$$

Output: $\mathsf{ct}_{\mathsf{out}} = \mathsf{LWE}_{\mathbf{s}'}(f(m') \cdot \Delta_{\mathsf{out}})$ if we respect requirements in Theorem 5

1 **begin**

/* Compute two PBS in parallel: */

2 $\mathsf{ct}_f = \mathsf{LWE}_{\mathbf{s}'}((-1)^{\beta} \cdot f(m') \cdot \Delta_{\mathsf{out}}) \leftarrow$ **GenPBS** $(\mathsf{ct}_{\mathsf{in}}, \mathsf{BSK}, \mathsf{CT}_f, \varkappa - 1, \vartheta)$;

3 $\mathsf{ct}_{\mathsf{Sign}} = \mathsf{LWE}_{\mathbf{s}'}((-1)^{\beta} \cdot \Delta_{\mathsf{out}}) \leftarrow$ **GenPBS** $(\mathsf{ct}_{\mathsf{in}}, \mathsf{BSK}, \mathsf{CT}_{\mathbb{1}}, \varkappa - 1, \vartheta)$;

/* Compute the multiplication */

4 $\mathsf{ct}_{\mathsf{out}} \leftarrow$ **LWEMult**$(\mathsf{ct}_f, \mathsf{ct}_{\mathsf{Sign}}, \mathsf{RLK}, \mathsf{KSK})$;

5 **end**

texts ct_f and $\mathsf{ct}_{\mathsf{Sign}}$ the value of β is the same. Then, $\mathsf{ct}_{\mathsf{out}} = \mathsf{LWE}_{\mathbf{s}}((-1)^{2\beta} \cdot f(m') \cdot \Delta_{\mathsf{out}}) = \mathsf{LWE}_{\mathbf{s}}(f(m') \cdot \Delta_{\mathsf{out}})$. □

Remark 2. Observe that, in Algorithm 4 we set KSK as a key switching key for $\mathbf{s}'$ to $\mathbf{S}'$ where $\mathbf{s}'$ is the LWE secret key composed of the coefficients in $\mathbf{S}'$. In practice, the key switching can be done to a key $\mathbf{S}''$, that has nothing to do with $\mathbf{s}'$. In this case, the RLK should be adapted as well to the key $\mathbf{S}''$.

It shall be noticed that in Algorithm 4:

- The two **GenPBS** have the same input ciphertext. To make the evaluation more efficient (evaluating a single bootstrapping instead of two), it is possible to use either the multi-value bootstrap described in [4], which will be faster but at the cost of a higher output noise. Another option would be to take advantage of the **PBSmanyLUT**, that we describe in detail in Algorithm 6 if the input message is small enough (*cf.* Remark 3).
- There could be only one key switching done in **LWEMult** (instead of two) if one of the two inputs is provided as a GLWE ciphertext (one **GenPBS** does not perform the final sample extraction).
- The **LWEMult** on line 4 can be replaced be a **MultSquareLWE** which is faster.

These improvements could impact both increase the noise but improve the complexity of the algorithm.

4.2 WoP-PBS Second Version

Another big constraint with TFHE PBS is that *the polynomial size is directly linked to the size of the message we want to bootstrap* (as mentioned in Limitation B). The smallest growth of the polynomial size slows down the computation by more than a factor 2 as TFHE PBS complexity is proportional to the FFT complexity: $N \log_2(N)$ with N the polynomial size. Keeping that in mind, we offer a different way to perform a bootstrap without padding in Algorithm 5 which can be more efficient in a multi-threaded machine. The main idea behind this Algorithm is to write a message m as $\beta || m'$ with β the most significant bit and m' the rest of the message. The function f to be computed is broken into two functions: f_0 and f_1. We want f_0 if β is equal to 0 and f_1 if $\beta = 1$. We use β as an encrypted decision bit, so we can choose between $f_0(m')$ or $f_1(m')$ thanks to the **LWEMult** algorithm.

We give the complete set of cryptographic parameters for different precisions in the full version of the paper. In a nutshell, for precisions from 1 to 5 bits, we use $\log_2(N) = 11$ and for 6 and 7 bits of precisions, we use $\log_2(N) = 12$.

Algorithm 5: $\mathsf{ct}_{\mathsf{out}} \leftarrow \textbf{WoP-PBS}_2(\mathsf{ct}_{\mathsf{in}}, \mathsf{BSK}, \mathsf{RLK}, \mathsf{KSK}, P_f, \Delta_{\mathsf{out}}, \varkappa, \vartheta)$

Context:
$$\begin{cases} \mathbf{s} = (s_1, \cdots, s_n) \in \mathbb{Z}_q^n \\ \mathbf{s}' = (s'_1, \cdots, s'_{kN}) \in \mathbb{Z}_q^{kN} \\ \mathbf{S}' = \left(S'^{(1)}, \ldots, S'^{(k)}\right) \in \mathfrak{R}_q^k \\ \forall 1 \le i \le k,\ S'^{(i)} = \sum_{j=0}^{N-1} s'_{(i-1)\cdot N+j+1} X^j \in \mathfrak{R}_q \\ f_0(x) = f(x) = f_1(x-p) \text{ for a certain } p \\ (\beta, m') = \textbf{PTModSwitch}_q(m, \Delta, \varkappa, \vartheta) \in \{0,1\} \times \mathbb{N} \\ P_{\mathbb{1}} \in \mathfrak{R}_q : \text{ as defined in Algorithm 4} \\ \mathsf{CT}_{f_i} = \mathsf{GLWE}_{\mathbf{S}'}\left(P_{f_i} \cdot \Delta_{\mathsf{out}}\right) \in \mathfrak{R}_q^{k+1} \text{ (might be a trivial encryption)} \\ \mathsf{CT}_{\mathbb{1}} \in \mathfrak{R}_q^{k+1} : \text{ a trivial encryption of } P_{\mathbb{1}} \cdot \frac{\Delta_{\mathsf{out}}}{2} \\ P_{f_0}, P_{f_1} \in \mathfrak{R}_q : \text{ redundant LUTs of the two halves of } P_f \end{cases}$$

Input:
$$\begin{cases} \mathsf{ct}_{\mathsf{in}} = \mathsf{LWE}_{\mathbf{s}}(m \cdot \Delta_{\mathsf{in}}) = (a_1, \cdots, a_n, a_{n+1} = b) \in \mathbb{Z}_q^{n+1} \\ \mathsf{BSK}, \mathsf{KSK}, \mathsf{RLK} : \text{ as defined in Algorithm 4} \\ P_f \in \mathfrak{R}_q : \text{ a redundant LUT for } x \mapsto f(x) \\ \Delta_{\mathsf{out}} \in \mathbb{Z}_q : \text{ the output scaling factor} \\ (\varkappa, \vartheta) \in \mathbb{Z} \times \mathbb{N} : \text{ define along with } N \text{ the window size} \end{cases}$$

Output: $\mathsf{ct}_{\mathsf{out}} = \mathsf{LWE}_{\mathbf{s}'}(f(m') \cdot \Delta_{\mathsf{out}})$ if we respect requirements in Theorem 6

begin

/* Compute in parallel 3 PBS: */

$\mathsf{ct}_{\mathsf{f}_0} = \mathsf{LWE}_{\mathbf{s}'}((-1)^\beta \cdot \Delta_{\mathsf{out}} \cdot f_0(m')) \leftarrow \textbf{GenPBS}(\mathsf{ct}_{\mathsf{in}}, \mathsf{BSK}, \mathsf{CT}_{f_0}, \varkappa, \vartheta)$;

$\mathsf{ct}_{\mathsf{f}_1} = \mathsf{LWE}_{\mathbf{s}'}((-1)^\beta \cdot \Delta_{\mathsf{out}} \cdot f_1(m')) \leftarrow \textbf{GenPBS}(\mathsf{ct}_{\mathsf{in}}, \mathsf{BSK}, \mathsf{CT}_{f_1}, \varkappa, \vartheta)$;

$\mathsf{ct}_{\mathsf{Sign}} = \mathsf{LWE}_{\mathbf{s}'}((-1)^\beta \cdot \frac{\Delta_{\mathsf{out}}}{2}) \leftarrow \textbf{GenPBS}(\mathsf{ct}_{\mathsf{in}}, \mathsf{BSK}, \mathsf{CT}_{\mathbb{1}}, \varkappa, \vartheta)$;

/* Compute two sums in parallel: */

$\mathsf{ct}_{\beta_0} = \mathsf{LWE}_{\mathbf{s}'}((1-\beta) \cdot \Delta_{\mathsf{out}}) \leftarrow \mathsf{ct}_{\mathsf{Sign}} + (\mathbf{0}, \frac{\Delta_{\mathsf{out}}}{2})$;

$\mathsf{ct}_{\beta_1} = \mathsf{LWE}_{\mathbf{s}'}(-\beta \cdot \Delta_{\mathsf{out}}) \leftarrow \mathsf{ct}_{\mathsf{Sign}} - (\mathbf{0}, \frac{\Delta_{\mathsf{out}}}{2})$;

/* Compute two multiplications in parallel: */

$\mathsf{ct}_{\beta \cdot \mathsf{f}_0} \leftarrow \textbf{LWEMult}(\mathsf{ct}_{\mathsf{f}_0}, \mathsf{ct}_{\beta_0}, \mathsf{RLK}, \mathsf{KSK})$;

$\mathsf{ct}_{\beta \cdot \mathsf{f}_1} \leftarrow \textbf{LWEMult}(\mathsf{ct}_{\mathsf{f}_1}, \mathsf{ct}_{\beta_1}, \mathsf{RLK}, \mathsf{KSK})$;

/* Add the previous results: */

$\mathsf{ct}_{\mathsf{out}} \leftarrow \mathsf{ct}_{\beta \cdot \mathsf{f}_0} + \mathsf{ct}_{\beta \cdot \mathsf{f}_1}$;

end

Theorem 6 (PBS Without Padding (V2)). *Let f_0 and f_1 be the two functions representing f such that $f_0(x) = f(x) = f_1(x-p)$ for a certain $p \in \mathbb{N}$. Then, under the same hypothesis of Theorem 5, the Algorithm 5 takes in input a LWE ciphertext $\mathsf{ct}_{\mathsf{in}} = \mathsf{LWE}_{\mathbf{s}}(m \cdot \Delta_{\mathsf{in}}) = (a_1, \cdots, a_n, a_{n+1}=b)$, with noise from $\chi_{\sigma_{\mathsf{in}}}$, and returns in output a LWE ciphertext $\mathsf{ct}_{\mathsf{out}}$ under the secret key $\mathbf{s}'$ encrypting the messages $f(m') \cdot \Delta_{\mathsf{out}}$ if and only if the input noise has variance verifying the Theorem 3.*

The output ciphertext noise variance verifies $\mathsf{Var}(\mathbf{WoP\text{-}PBS}_2) = 2 \cdot \mathsf{Var}(\mathbf{LWEMult})$ with input variances for the **LWEMult** *defined as $\sigma_i = \mathsf{Var}(\mathbf{GenPBS})$, for $i \in \{1, 2\}$.*

The complexity of Algorithm 4 is:

$$\mathbb{C}_{\mathbf{WoP\text{-}PBS}_2}^{(n, \ell_{\mathbf{PBS}}, k_1, N_1, \ell_{\mathbf{KS}}, \ell_{\mathbf{RL}}, k_2, N_2)} = 3\mathbb{C}_{\mathsf{GenPBS}}^{(n, \ell_{\mathbf{PBS}}, k_1, N_1)} + 2\mathbb{C}_{\mathsf{LWEMult}}^{(\ell_{\mathbf{KS}}, \ell_{\mathbf{RL}}, N_1, k_2, N_2)} + (N_2 + 3)\mathbb{C}_{\mathsf{add}}$$

Proof (Sketch). We have $\mathsf{ct}_{\beta_0} = \mathsf{LWE}_{\mathbf{s}'}(\frac{\Delta_{\mathsf{out}}}{2}((-1)^\beta + 1))$. If $\beta = 0$, then $\mathsf{ct}_{\beta_0} = \mathsf{LWE}_{\mathbf{s}'}(\Delta_{\mathsf{out}})$ else $\mathsf{ct}_{\beta_0} = \mathsf{LWE}_{\mathbf{s}'}(0)$. Then, $\mathsf{ct}_{\beta_0} = \mathsf{LWE}_{\mathbf{s}'}((1-\beta)\Delta_{\mathsf{out}})$. Similarly, we obtain $\mathsf{ct}_{\beta_1} = \mathsf{LWE}_{\mathbf{s}'}((-\beta)\Delta_{\mathsf{out}})$. The output ciphertext $\mathsf{ct}_{\mathsf{out}}$ is then equal to $\mathsf{LWE}_{\mathbf{s}'}(((-1)^\beta(1-\beta)\Delta_{\mathsf{out}} f_0(m') + (-1)^\beta(-\beta)\Delta_{\mathsf{out}} f_1(m'))$. Thus, if $\beta = 0$, $\mathsf{ct}_{\mathsf{out}} = f_0(m')$ else $\mathsf{ct}_{\mathsf{out}} = f_1(m')$, as expected. □

It shall be noticed that in Algorithm 5:

- The three **GenPBS** have the same input ciphertext. As we observed for Algorithm 4, to make the evaluation more efficient by evaluating a single bootstrapping instead of three, it is possible to use either the multi-value bootstrap described in [4] or to take advantage of the **PBSmanyLUT** (Algorithm 6 and *cf.* Remark 3).
- We could remove two key switches (among four) as explained for the $\mathbf{WoP\text{-}PBS}_1$.
- To improve both performance and noise, in practice, we can do a lazy relinearization as described in [18], i.e., the step of relinearization of the two **LWEMult** will be done after the final addition.
- The two **LWEMult** followed by the final addition can be replaced by a **PackedSumProducts** (described in the full version of the paper).

These improvements could increase the noise but also improve the complexity of the algorithm.

4.3 A Multi-output PBS

We are able to extract any chunk of the encrypted plaintext with ϑ, $\varkappa$ and N. When possible, one can define a smaller chunk for the plaintext by trimming the bound in the LSB using a $\vartheta > 0$. It means that after the modulus switching there are ϑ LSB set to 0. More formally, after the modulus switching, a plaintext m^* will be of the form $m^* = m \cdot \Delta + e \cdot 2^\vartheta \in \mathbb{Z}_q$.

Thank to the ϑ LSB set to 0 in the plaintext, one can evaluate 2^ϑ functions at the cost of only one **GenPBS** without increasing the noise compared to a regular TFHE PBS. The procedure is described in Algorithm 6.

The form of the LUT polynomial is set accordingly to the ϑ parameter so that it contains up to 2^ϑ functions. As for TFHE bootstrapping, one needs to have

Algorithm 6: $\mathsf{ct}_1, \dots, \mathsf{ct}_{2^\vartheta} \leftarrow \mathbf{PBSmanyLUT}(\mathsf{ct}_{\mathsf{in}}, \mathsf{BSK}, P_{(f_1, \dots f_{2^\vartheta})}, \Delta_{\mathsf{out}}, \varkappa, \vartheta)$

Context:
$$\begin{cases} \mathbf{s} = (s_1, \dots, s_n) \in \mathbb{Z}_q^n \\ \mathbf{s}' = (s'_1, \dots, s'_{kN}) \in \mathbb{Z}_q^{kN} \\ \mathbf{S}' = \left(S'^{(1)}, \dots, S'^{(k)}\right) \in \mathfrak{R}_q^k \\ \forall 1 \le i \le k,\ S'^{(i)} = \sum_{j=0}^{N-1} s'_{(i-1)\cdot N+j+1} X^j \in \mathfrak{R}_q \\ f_1, \dots, f_{2^\vartheta} : \mathbb{Z} \to \mathbb{Z} \\ (\beta, m') = \mathbf{PTModSwitch}_q(m, \Delta, \varkappa, \vartheta) \in \{0,1\} \times \mathbb{N} \\ \mathsf{CT}_{(f_1, \dots, f_{2^\vartheta})} = \mathsf{GLWE}_{\mathbf{S}'}\left(P_{(f_1, \dots, f_{2^\vartheta})} \cdot \Delta_{\mathsf{out}}\right) \text{ (might be a trivial encryption)} \end{cases}$$

Input:
$$\begin{cases} \mathsf{ct}_{\mathsf{in}} = \mathsf{LWE}_{\mathbf{s}}(m \cdot \Delta_{\mathsf{in}}) = (a_1, \cdots, a_n, a_{n+1} = b) \in \mathbb{Z}_q^{n+1} \\ \mathsf{BSK} = \left\{\mathsf{BSK}_i = \mathsf{GGSW}_{\mathbf{S}'}^{(\mathfrak{B}, \ell)}(s_i)\right\}_{1 \le i \le n} \\ P_{(f_1, \dots, f_{2^\vartheta})} : \text{a redundant LUT for} : x \mapsto f_1(x) || \dots || f_{2^\vartheta}(x) \\ (\varkappa, \vartheta) \in \mathbb{Z} \times \mathbb{N} : \text{define along with N the window size} \end{cases}$$

Output: $\mathsf{ct}_1, \dots, \mathsf{ct}_{2^\vartheta}$ such that $\mathsf{ct}_j = \mathsf{LWE}_{\mathbf{s}'}\left((-1)^\beta \cdot f_j(m') \cdot \Delta_{\mathsf{out}}\right)$

begin
- /* modulus switching */
- **for** $1 \le i \le n+1$ **do**
  - $a'_i \leftarrow \left[\left\lfloor \frac{a_i \cdot 2N \cdot 2^{\varkappa - \vartheta}}{q} \right\rceil \cdot 2^\vartheta\right]_{2N}$
- **end**
- /* blind rotate of the LUT */
- $\mathsf{CT} \leftarrow \mathbf{BlindRotate}\left(\mathsf{CT}_{(f_1, \cdots, f_{2^\vartheta})}, \{a'_i\}_{1 \le i \le n+1}, \mathsf{BSK}\right)$;
- /* sample extract the first 2^ϑ terms (coeffs. from 0 to $2^\vartheta - 1$) */
- **for** $1 \le j \le 2^\vartheta$ **do**
  - $\mathsf{ct}_j \leftarrow \mathbf{SampleExtract}_{j-1}(\mathsf{CT})$
- **end**

end

redundancy in the LUT to remove the input noise. Each block of functions (i.e., the sequence of $f_i, i \in [1, 2^\vartheta]$ coefficients) is repeated all along the polynomial. The LUT can be build as follow:

$$P_{(f_1, \dots, f_{2^\vartheta})} = X^{\frac{N}{2p}} \sum_{j=0}^{p-1} X^{j \frac{N}{p}} \sum_{k=0}^{\frac{N}{p 2^\vartheta} - 1} X^{k \cdot 2^\vartheta} \sum_{i=0}^{2^\vartheta - 1} f_{i+1}(j) X^i, \text{ with } p = \frac{q}{\Delta_{\mathsf{in}} \cdot 2^{\varkappa + 1}}$$

By doing so, one can sample extract at the end 2^ϑ coefficients which leads to 2^ϑ output ciphertexts, one for each evaluated functions. By neglecting the computational cost of the ϑ sample extractions, the complexity is the same than for a PBS evaluating only one function. The noise is also not impacted.

This method is particularly efficient when the polynomial size is constrained by the desired output noise. If the polynomial size is chosen large enough, there will be bits set to zero between the modulus switching noise and the message. This new method allows to exploit these bits to compute different functions on the same input ciphertext.

Theorem 7 (Multi-output PBS). *Let* $\mathbf{s} = (s_1, \cdots, s_n) \in \mathbb{Z}_q^n$ *be a binary LWE secret key. Let* $\mathbf{S}' = (S'_1, \dots, S'_k) \in \mathfrak{R}_q^k$ *be a GLWE secret key such that* $S'_i = \sum_{j=0}^{N-1} s'_{(i-1)\cdot N+j+1} X^j \in \mathfrak{R}_q$, *and* $\mathbf{s}' = (s'_1, \cdots, s'_{kN}) \in \mathbb{Z}_q^{kN}$ *be the corresponding LWE key.*

Let $P_{(f_1,\cdots f_{2^\vartheta})} \in \mathfrak{R}_q$ *be a r-redundant LUT for the functions* $x \mapsto f_1(x) || \ldots || f_{2^\vartheta}(x)$ *and* $\Delta_{\mathsf{out}} \in \mathbb{Z}_q$ *be the output scaling factor. Let* $(\varkappa, \vartheta) \in \mathbb{Z} \times \mathbb{N}$ *be the two integer variables defining (along with N) the window size to be modulus switched, such that* $\frac{q 2^\vartheta}{\Delta_{\mathsf{in}} 2^\varkappa} < 2N$, *and let* $(\beta, m') = \mathbf{PTModSwitch}_q(m, \Delta_{\mathsf{in}}, \varkappa, \vartheta)$.

Then, the Algorithm 6 takes in input a LWE ciphertext $\mathsf{ct_{in}} = \mathsf{LWE_s}(m \cdot \Delta_{\mathsf{in}}) = (a_1, \cdots, a_n, a_{n+1} = b)$, *with noise distribution from* $\chi_{\sigma_{\mathsf{in}}}$, *a bootstrapping key* $\mathsf{BSK} = \left\{ \overline{\overline{\mathsf{CT}}}_i = \mathsf{GGSW}^{\mathfrak{B}, \ell}_{\mathbf{S}'}(s_i) \right\}_{i=1}^{n}$ *from* $\mathbf{s}$ *to* $\mathbf{S}'$ *and a (trivial) GLWE encryption of* $P_f \cdot \Delta_{\mathsf{out}}$, *and returns in output* 2^ϑ *LWE ciphertexts* $\{\mathsf{ct}_j\}_{j \in [0, 2^\vartheta]}$ *under the secret key* $\mathbf{s}'$ *encrypting the messages* $(-1)^\beta \cdot f_j(m') \cdot \Delta_{\mathsf{out}}$ *if and only if the input noise has variance verifying the Theorem 3.*

The complexity of the algorithm is:

$$\mathbb{C}^{(n,\ell,k,N,\vartheta)}_{\mathbf{PBSmanyLUT}} = \mathbb{C}^{(n,\ell,k,N)}_{\mathsf{GenPBS}} + 2^\vartheta \mathbb{C}^{(N)}_{\mathsf{SampleExtract}}$$

Proof. The proof is the mainly the same as the one from the **GenPBS** (provided in the full version of the paper). Let $p = \frac{q}{\Delta_{\mathsf{in}} \cdot 2^{\varkappa+1}}$ be the number of possible values for each $f_i, i \in [0, 2^\vartheta]$. Let $m \in [0, p-1]$ be a plaintext value. The polynomial $P_{(f_0, \cdots, f_{2^\vartheta})}$ encodes the following LUT:

$$\underbrace{\left(\ldots, \underbrace{f_1(m), \ldots, f_{2^\vartheta}(m), \ldots, f_1(m), \ldots, f_{2^\vartheta}(m)}_{N/p \text{ elements}}, \underbrace{f_1(m+1), \ldots, f_{2^\vartheta}(m+1), \ldots, f_1(m+1), \ldots, f_{2^\vartheta}(m+1)}_{N/p \text{ elements}}, \ldots \right)}_{p \text{ blocks}}$$

From the **GenPBS**, ϑ bits are set to 0. Then, by construction of the LUT, $\mathsf{LUT}_{(f_0, \cdots, f_{2^\vartheta})}[m^* + i] = f_{i+1}(m')$ for $i \in [0, 2^\vartheta - 1]$, so that sample extracting gives the expected result. □

Remark 3. Observe that **PBSmanyLUT** and **WoP-PBS** algorithms can be combined in two different ways:

1. Using **PBSmanyLUT** to improve **WoP-PBS**: In **WoP-PBS**$_1$, the ct_{Sign} and each ct_{f_i} resulting from distinct **GenPBS** can be evaluated at once by using a single **PBSmanyLUT**. Similarly, in **WoP-PBS**$_2$, ct_{Sign} and each $\mathsf{ct}_{f_{0,i}}$ and $\mathsf{ct}_{f_{1,i}}$ could be evaluated at once. In both cases, this variant can be applied only if the polynomial size chosen for the **WoP-PBS** is large enough to allow multiple LUT evaluations (i.e, if precision is not yet a bottleneck condition): this variant of the **WoP-PBS** will improve the complexity of the algorithm, without impacting the noise growth.
2. Using **WoP-PBS** to improve **PBSmanyLUT**: The **PBSmanyLUT** algorithm implicitly performs a **GenPBS** with a special modulus switching. This **GenPBS** can actually be replaced by a **WoP-PBS** (with the same special modulus switching) as a **WoP-PBS** performs the same operation as **GenPBS**, without the bit of padding constraint. This technique is what we call **WoPBSmanyLUT**.

Remark 4. A technique to evaluate many LUTs at the same time by performing a single TFHE bootstrapping (plus a bunch of polynomial multiplications per

LUT) has been already proposed in [4] and used in [16]. Their technique does not impose a strong constraint on the polynomial size used for the bootstrapping, however it results in a larger output noise, that strictly depends on the function that is evaluated. If the noise constraints at the output of the bootstrapping are a problem, the technique of [4] will require to increase the polynomial size.

Our new **PBSmanyLUT** is a better alternative to this technique in some situations as the output noise will be independent of the function evaluated. But this comes at the cost of having enough space for the evaluation of the different LUTs (i.e., ϑ bits on the modulus switching to evaluate 2^{ϑ} functions so a large enough polynomial size N must be chosen). If we already are working with large enough polynomials, there is no computation overhead nor noise growth when replacing a **GenPBS** by a **PBSmanyLUT**.

5 Applications

In this section we present some of the applications that take advantage from our new techniques. In particular, we show that:

- Using a combination of **LWEMult** and **GenPBS** improves the gate bootstrapping technique of TFHE [9], because it allows to perform leveled binary operations between bootstrappings (instead of bootstrapping every single gate).
- The improved gate bootstrapping technique can be extended in order to evaluate arithmetic circuits with larger precision, by using a combination of **LWEMult** and **WoP-PBS** (or its variants).
- Using the **PBSmanyLUT** technique allows to improve the Circuit Bootstrapping of TFHE by a factor ℓ, without affecting the noise growth.
- The **WoP-PBS** technique (and its variants) can be used to bootstrap on larger precision inputs.

5.1 Fast Arithmetic

We start by describing an improvement of FHE Boolean circuit evaluation. Then, we extend it to arithmetic circuits dealing with integers encoded in more than a single bit. Finally, we describe how to use the later to build exact computation on bigger encrypted integers.

5.1.1 Fast Boolean Arithmetic

In TFHE [7], authors improve techniques proposed in FHEW [12] to perform fast homomorphic evaluation of Boolean circuits and called this feature *gate bootstrapping*. It is very easy to use, because it performs one bootstrapping for each bivariate Boolean gate evaluated: there is no need to be careful with the noise management anymore because each gate reset the noise systematically. This also makes the conversion between the cleartext Boolean circuits and the encrypted circuits quite straightforward in practice.

However, performing a bootstrapping at each bivariate Boolean gate is very expensive when we want to evaluate large circuits and seem unnecessary. One idea to make the evaluation more efficient would be to mix the bootstrapping with some leveled operations, at the cost of loosing the ease of not caring about noise growth. But this idea cannot be immediately applied when it comes to gate bootstrapping: in fact, the bootstrapping also takes care of ensuring a fixed encoding in the ciphertexts, that may not be ensured if we introduce leveled operations. Furthermore, TFHE can only evaluate linear combinations between LWE ciphertexts; non linear operations would require the use of bootstrapping or of a non native product between LWE ciphertexts (e.g., an external product which is not composable because it makes use of different input ciphertext types). This is especially problematic when we want to evaluate an **AND** gate, for instance.

To be more clear, in gate bootstrapping, messages are encoded with what we call one *"bit of padding"*: meaning that we know that the MSB of the plaintext (without noise) is set to zero. This bit is used to perform a linear combination while preserving the (plaintext) MSB of this combination so we can bootstrap it (the function is negacyclic, so do not need an additional bit of padding) and get a correct result. Roughly speaking, the initial linear combination evaluates the linear part of the gate and consumes the bit of padding, while the bootstrapping takes care of the evaluation of the non-linear part of the gate, reduces the noise and brings the bit of padding back to be able to perform a future operation.

We propose a novel approach based on the **GenPBS** and **LWEMult** which removes both the constraint of padding bits and the difficulties with the non-linear leveled evaluations. Thus, this offers the possibility of computing series of Boolean gates without the need of computing a bootstrap for every gate. A **GenPBS** should only be computed to reduce the noise when needed. In Lemma 1, we only describe some of the most common Boolean gates (i.e., **XOR**, **NOT** and **AND**), whose combination offers functional completeness. The other gates can be obtained by combining these operations.

Lemma 1. *Let* $b_i \in \{0,1\}$ *such that* $\mathsf{ct}_i = \mathsf{LWE}_{\mathbf{s}}(b_i \cdot \frac{q}{2}) \in \mathbb{Z}_q^{n+1}$, *for* $i \in \{1,2\}$. *Let* $\left(\mathbf{0}, \frac{q}{2}\right) \in \mathbb{Z}_q^{n+1}$ *be a trivial LWE ciphertext. Then, the following equalities between Boolean gates and homormorphic operators hold:*

$$\begin{aligned} \mathsf{ct}_1 \,\mathbf{XOR}\, \mathsf{ct}_2 &= \mathsf{ct}_1 + \mathsf{ct}_2 \\ \mathsf{ct}_1 \,\mathbf{AND}\, \mathsf{ct}_2 &= \mathbf{LWEMult}(\mathsf{ct}_1, \mathsf{ct}_2, \mathsf{RLK}, \mathsf{KSK}) \\ \mathbf{NOT}\, \mathsf{ct}_1 &= \mathsf{ct}_1 + \left(\mathbf{0}, \frac{q}{2}\right) \end{aligned}$$

Proof (Sketch). A bit is naturally encoded as a 0 (resp. $\frac{q}{2}$) if its value is 0 (resp. 1). Then the Boolean gates **XOR** and **NOT** stem from that encoding. The **AND** is a direct application of the **LWEMult**. □

The noise increases after each computed gate since no bootstrap is performed. Then, after chaining many of them, a noise reduction might be required. We propose two simple processes exploiting the **GenPBS** with the (negacyclic) sign function.

Lemma 2. *Let* $\mathsf{ct_{in}}$ *be a LWE ciphertext resulting from a Boolean circuit with gates defined as in Lemma 1. Then, each of the following operators allows to bootstrap the ciphertext during the Boolean circuit evaluation:*

$$\mathsf{ct_{out}} \leftarrow \mathbf{GenPBS}(\mathsf{ct_{in}}, \mathsf{BSK}, P_{\mathbb{1}} \cdot X^{N/2}, \Delta_{\mathsf{out}} = \frac{q}{4}, \varkappa = 0, \vartheta = 0) + \left(\mathbf{0}, \frac{q}{4}\right) \quad (4)$$

$$\mathsf{ct_{out}} \leftarrow \mathbf{GenPBS}(\mathsf{ct_{in}}, \mathsf{BSK}, P_f = \sum_{i=\frac{N}{4}}^{\frac{3N}{4}-1} X^i, \Delta_{\mathsf{out}} = \frac{q}{2}, \varkappa = -1, \vartheta = 0) \quad (5)$$

Proof. The first method 4 uses **GenPBS** with the parameters $\Delta_{\mathsf{out}} = \frac{q}{4}, \varkappa = 0, \vartheta = 0$ and $P_f = P_{\mathbb{1}} * X^{N/2}$. The output of the **GenPBS** gives $\mathsf{ct_{tmp}} = \mathsf{LWE_s}(\pm\frac{q}{4})$. Then, depending on the sign, the term $\mathsf{ct_{tmp}} + (\mathbf{0}, \frac{q}{4})$ is equal to $\mathsf{LWE_s}(0)$ or $\mathsf{ct_{tmp}} = \mathsf{LWE_s}(\frac{q}{2})$.

The second approach 5 uses other parameters for the modulus switching which can be seen as shifted of one bit, i.e., $\varkappa = -1$, $\vartheta = 0$ and $\Delta_{\mathsf{out}} = \frac{q}{2}$. In this case, the sign does not impact the value of the encoded bit, since $\pm 0 = 0$ and $\pm\frac{q}{2} = \frac{q}{2}$. Then, evaluating **GenPBS** with the function $P_f = \sum_{i=\frac{N}{4}}^{\frac{3N}{4}-1} X^i$ and $\Delta_{\mathsf{out}} = \frac{q}{2}$, we obtain $\mathsf{ct_{out}} = \mathsf{LWE_s}(\pm 0)$ or $\mathsf{LWE_s}(\pm\frac{q}{2})$. □

5.1.2 Modular Power of 2 Arithmetic

We generalize the faster Boolean circuit method (described in Lemma 1) to any power of two modular integer circuits. This enables a more efficient exact arithmetic modulo 2^p for some integer p. For $i \in \{1, 2\}$, let $\mathsf{ct}_i = \mathsf{LWE_s}(m_i \cdot \frac{q}{2^p})$ be a LWE ciphertext encrypting the message $m_i \in [\![0, 2^p[\![$ (i.e., m_i has a precision of p bits). As in the case of faster Boolean arithmetic, we define three natural homomorphic operators to mimic modular 2^p arithmetic: the addition ($\mathbf{Add}_{2^p}$) that is evaluated as an homomorphic LWE addition, the multiplication ($\mathbf{Mul}_{2^p}$) that is evaluated as a **LWEMult**, and the unary opposite ($\mathbf{Opp}_{2^p}$) that is obtained by simply negating the LWE input.

When we deal with integers encoded with more than one bit, functions we have to apply during a PBS are no longer negacyclic. It means that without a **WoP-PBS** we would have to have at least 2 bits of padding (one for a linear combination and another one for the PBS with non-negacyclic function evaluation). This results in a big N when we want to work with larger powers of two. With a **WoP-PBS**, we do not need to have bits of padding. Then, we can simply compute leveled additions and multiplications, and only use a **WoP-PBS** when we have to reset the noise to a lower level.

5.1.3 From Power of 2 Modular Arithmetic to Exact Integer Arithmetic

We now present some operators allowing to extend homomorphic computation modulo a power of two modular to bigger integer arithmetic. To do so, we will use a few LWE ciphertexts to represent a single big integer. These required operations offer the possibility to compute an exact integer multiplication between two LWE ciphertexts as in Sect. 5.1.2 and keeping the LSB of the computation.

However, we also need to be able to recover the MSB of additions and multiplications for carry propgation when we deal with big integers encrypted with several ciphertexts. The operators keeping the MSB of the computation between two messages $m_1, m_2 \in [\![0, 2^p[\![$ are defined as: $\mathbf{Add}_{2\mathrm{P}}^{\mathrm{MSB}} : (m_1, m_2) \mapsto \left\lfloor \frac{m_1 + m_2}{2^p} \right\rfloor \bmod 2^p$ and $\mathbf{Mul}_{2\mathrm{P}}^{\mathrm{MSB}} : (m_1, m_2) \mapsto \left\lfloor \frac{m_1 \cdot m_2}{2^p} \right\rfloor \bmod 2^p$ and their implementation is described in Algorithm 7.

In Algorithm 7, to improve efficiency, we can remove both **PublicKS** and include them in the relinearization steps of the previous **WoP-PBS**. If parameters allow it, one might also replace Lines 6 and 7 of Algorithm 7 by a single **WoP-PBS** to extract the MSB directly.

Algorithm 7: $\mathsf{ct}_{\mathsf{out}} \leftarrow$ [$\mathbf{Add}_{2\mathrm{P}}^{\mathrm{MSB}}$] | [$\mathbf{Mul}_{2\mathrm{P}}^{\mathrm{MSB}}$] $(\mathsf{ct}_1, \mathsf{ct}_2, \mathsf{BSK}, \mathsf{KSK}_1, \mathsf{KSK}_2, \mathsf{RLK})$

Context:
$$\begin{cases} \mathbf{s} = (s_1, \cdots, s_n) \in \mathbb{Z}_q^n \\ \mathbf{s}' = (s'_1, \cdots, s'_{kN}) \in \mathbb{Z}_q^{kN} \\ \mathbf{S}' = \left(S'^{(1)}, \ldots, S'^{(k)}\right) \in \mathfrak{R}_q^k \\ \forall 1 \leq i \leq k,\ S'^{(i)} = \sum_{j=0}^{N-1} s'_{(i-1)\cdot N+j+1} X^j \in \mathfrak{R}_q \\ \Delta = \frac{q}{2^p} \in \mathbb{Z}_q \\ 0 \leq m_1, m_2 < 2^p \\ P_{\mathsf{Id}} : \text{a redundant LUT for } x \mapsto x \text{ (identity function)} \end{cases}$$

Input:
$$\begin{cases} \mathsf{ct}_1 = \mathsf{LWE}_{\mathbf{s}}(m_1 \cdot \Delta) \in \mathbb{Z}_q^{n+1} \\ \mathsf{ct}_2 = \mathsf{LWE}_{\mathbf{s}}(m_2 \cdot \Delta) \in \mathbb{Z}_q^{n+1} \\ \mathsf{BSK} = \left\{\mathsf{BSK}_i = \mathsf{GGSW}_{\mathbf{S}'}^{(\mathfrak{B},\ell)}(s_i)\right\}_{1 \leq i \leq n} : \text{a bootstrapping key from } \mathbf{s} \text{ to } \mathbf{S}' \\ \mathsf{KSK}_1 = \left\{\overline{\mathsf{CT}}_i = \mathsf{GLev}_{\mathbf{S}'}^{(\mathfrak{B},\ell)}(s'_i)\right\}_{1 \leq i \leq kN} : \text{a key switching key from } \mathbf{s}' \text{ to } \mathbf{S}' \\ \mathsf{KSK}_2 = \left\{\overline{\mathsf{ct}}_i = \mathsf{Lev}_{\mathbf{s}}^{(\mathfrak{B},\ell)}(s'_i)\right\}_{1 \leq i \leq kN} : \text{a key switching key from } \mathbf{s}' \text{ to } \mathbf{s} \\ \mathsf{RLK} = \left\{\overline{\mathsf{CT}}_{i,j} = \mathsf{GLev}_{\mathbf{S}'}^{(\mathfrak{B},\ell)}\left(S'_i \cdot S'_j\right)\right\}_{1 \leq i \leq k}^{1 \leq j \leq i} : \text{a relinearization key for } \mathbf{S}' \end{cases}$$

Output: [$\mathsf{ct}_{\mathsf{out}} = \mathsf{LWE}_{\mathbf{s}}\left(\left[\left\lfloor \frac{m_1+m_2}{2^p} \right\rfloor\right]_{2^p} \cdot \Delta\right)$] | [$\mathsf{ct}_{\mathsf{out}} = \mathsf{LWE}_{\mathbf{s}}\left(\left[\left\lfloor \frac{m_1 \cdot m_2}{2^p} \right\rfloor\right]_{2^p} \cdot \Delta\right)$]

1 **begin**

/* add p bits of padding */

2 $\mathsf{ct}'_1 \leftarrow$ **WoP-PBS**$(\mathsf{ct}_1, \mathsf{BSK}, \mathsf{RLK}, \mathsf{KSK}_1, P_{\mathsf{Id}}, \Delta/2^p, 0, 0)$;

3 $\mathsf{ct}'_2 \leftarrow$ **WoP-PBS**$(\mathsf{ct}_2, \mathsf{BSK}, \mathsf{RLK}, \mathsf{KSK}_1, P_{\mathsf{Id}}, \Delta/2^p, 0, 0)$;

/* compute the operation */

4 [$\mathsf{ct}' \leftarrow \mathsf{ct}'_1 + \mathsf{ct}'_2$] | [$\mathsf{ct}' \leftarrow$ **LWEMult**$(\mathsf{ct}'_1, \mathsf{ct}'_2, \mathsf{RLK}, \mathsf{KSK}_1)$] ;

/* key switch */

5 $\mathsf{ct}'' \leftarrow$ **PublicKS**$(\mathsf{ct}', \mathsf{KSK}_2, \mathsf{Id})$;

/* extract the LSB */

6 $\mathsf{ct}'_{\mathsf{LSB}} \leftarrow$ **WoP-PBS**$(\mathsf{ct}'', \mathsf{BSK}, \mathsf{RLK}, \mathsf{KSK}_1, P_{\mathsf{Id}}, \Delta/2^p, p, 0)$;

/* subtract the LSB to only keep the MSB */

7 $\mathsf{ct} \leftarrow \mathsf{ct}' - \mathsf{ct}'_{\mathsf{LSB}}$;

/* key switch */

8 $\mathsf{ct}_{\mathsf{out}} \leftarrow$ **PublicKS**$(\mathsf{ct}, \mathsf{KSK}_2, \mathsf{Id})$;

9 **end**

Lemma 3 (MSB operations). *For $i \in \{1, 2\}$, let $\mathsf{ct}_i = \mathsf{LWE}_{\mathbf{s}}(m_i \cdot \Delta)$ be two LWE ciphertexts, encrypting $m_i \cdot \Delta$ with $0 \leq m_i < 2^p$ and $\Delta = \frac{q}{2^p}$, both encrypted under the same secret key $\mathbf{s} = (s_1, \ldots, s_n) \in \mathbb{Z}_q^n$, with noise sampled in χ_{σ_i}. Let* $\mathsf{BSK}, \mathsf{KSK}, \mathsf{RLK}$ *be defined as in Theorem 5.*

Then, Algorithm 7 is able to compute a new LWE ciphertext $\mathsf{ct}_{\mathsf{out}}$*, encrypting the MSB of the sum, i.e., the carry,* $\left[\left\lfloor \frac{m_1+m_2}{2^p} \right\rceil\right]_{2^p} \cdot \Delta$ *(resp. a new LWE ciphertext* $\mathsf{ct}_{\mathsf{out}}$*, encrypting the MSB of the product* $\left[\left\lfloor \frac{m_1 \cdot m_2}{2^p} \right\rceil\right]_{2^p} \cdot \Delta$*), under the secret key* $\mathbf{s}'$*. The variance of the noise of* $\mathsf{ct}_{\mathsf{out}}$ *can be estimated by composing the noise formulas of the different operations composing the algorithm.*

The complexity of Algorithm 7 is:

$$\begin{aligned}
\mathbb{C}_{\mathbf{Add}_{2^p}^{\mathrm{MSB}}}^{(n,\ell_{\mathbf{PBS}},k_1,N_1,\ell_{\mathbf{KS}},\ell_{\mathbf{RL}},k_2,N_2)} &= 3\mathbb{C}_{\mathbf{WoP\text{-}PBS}}^{(n,\ell_{\mathbf{PBS}},k_1,N_1,\ell_{\mathbf{KS}},\ell_{\mathbf{RL}},k_2,N_2)} + 2\mathbb{C}_{\mathsf{PublicKS}}^{(1,\ell_{\mathbf{KS}},k_2N_2,1,n)} \\
&\quad + 2(N_2+1)\mathbb{C}_{\mathsf{add}} \\
\mathbb{C}_{\mathbf{Mul}_{2^p}^{\mathrm{MSB}}}^{(n,\ell_{\mathbf{PBS}},k_1,N_1,\ell_{\mathbf{KS}},\ell_{\mathbf{RL}},k_2,N_2)} &= 3\mathbb{C}_{\mathbf{WoP\text{-}PBS}}^{(n,\ell_{\mathbf{PBS}},k_1,N_1,\ell_{\mathbf{KS}},\ell_{\mathbf{RL}},k_2,N_2)} + 2\mathbb{C}_{\mathsf{PublicKS}}^{(1,\ell_{\mathbf{KS}},k_2N_2,1,n)} \\
&\quad + (N_2+1)\mathbb{C}_{\mathsf{add}} + \mathbb{C}_{\mathsf{LWEMult}}^{(\ell_{\mathbf{KS}},\ell_{\mathbf{RL}},k_2N_2,1,k_2N_2)}
\end{aligned} \tag{6}$$

Proof (sketch). The first two **WoP-PBS** of the algorithm send the two messages m_1 and m_2 to a lower scaling factor $\frac{q}{2^{2p}}$. This way, when the leveled addition (resp. the **LWEMult**) operation is performed, the new precision $2p$ will be able to store the entire (both MSB and LSB) exact result. The third **WoP-PBS** is used to extract only the LSB of the result, that will be subtracted from the result of the previous computation to obtain an encryption of the MSB at scaling factor $\frac{q}{2^p}$, i.e, ready to be used in the following computation. Observe that the **PublicKS** are used in order to switch the secret key in order to be compatible with the following operation. □

5.2 Faster Circuit Bootstrapping

In TFHE [8], authors present a technique called *circuit bootstrapping*, that allows to convert an LWE ciphertext into an GGSW ciphertext. The circuit bootstrapping is necessary for leveled evaluations using the external product: the latter's inputs are both GLWE and GGSW ciphertexts, while its output is a GLWE ciphertext. To sum up, circuit bootstrapping allows to build a new GGSW ciphertext from an LWE ciphertext so one can use it as input to an external product for instance.

The authors of [8] observe that a GGSW ciphertext, encrypting a message $\mu \in \mathbb{Z}$ (μ is binary in their application) under the secret key $\mathbf{S} = (S_1, \ldots, S_k, S_{k+1} = -1)$, is composed by $(k+1)\ell$ GLWE ciphertexts encrypting $\mu \cdot S_i \cdot \frac{q}{\mathfrak{B}^j}$, for $1 \le i \le k+1$ and $1 \le j \le \ell$. As already mentioned in Sect. 2, the goal of circuit bootstrapping is to build one by one all the GLWE ciphertexts composing the output GGSW. In order to do that, it performs the following two steps:

- The first step performs ℓ *independent TFHE PBS* to transform the input LWE encryption of μ into independent LWE encryptions of $\mu \cdot \frac{q}{\mathfrak{B}^j}$.
- The second step performs a list of $(k+1)\ell$ private key switchings from LWE to GLWE to multiply the messages $\mu \cdot \frac{q}{\mathfrak{B}^j}$ obtained in the first step by the elements of the secret key S_i, and so to obtain the different lines of the output GGSW.

Table 2. Generalization of TFHE gate bootstrapping.

	Gate bootstrap TFHE	Binary arithmetic ($p = 1$) as in Sect. 5.1.1	Integer arithmetic ($p > 1$) generalization in Sect. 5.1.3
$\mathbf{Opp}_{2^p}$	Negation	Addition with a constant	Negation
$\mathbf{Add}_{2^p}$	Bootstrapped XOR	Homomorphic Add	Homomorphic Add
$\mathbf{Add}_{2^p}^{\mathrm{MSB}}$	Bootstrapped AND	MultLWE	3 WoPBS + 2 Homomorphic Add + 2 public key switch
$\mathbf{Mul}_{2^p}$	Bootstrapped AND	MultLWE	MultLWE
$\mathbf{Mul}_{2^p}^{\mathrm{MSB}}$	$x \mapsto 0$	$x \mapsto 0$	3 WoPBS + MultLWE + Homomorphic Add + 2 public key switch
Noise reduction frequency	PBS at each gate	PBS when necessary	WoPBS when necessary

Here, we propose a faster method based on the **PBSmanyLUT** algorithm (Algorithm 6). In a nutshell, the idea is to replace the ℓ PBS of the first step by only one **PBSmanyLUT** (that costs exactly the same as a one of the ℓ original PBS and do not increase the noise). Since the most costly part of the circuit boostrapping is due to the PBS part, the overall complexity is then roughly reduced by a factor ℓ. In [8], $\ell = 2$, so we have an improvement of a factor 2 on the PBS part, without any impact on the noise.

Lemma 4. *Let consider the circuit boostrapping algorithm as described in [8, Alg. 11]. The ℓ independent bootstrappings (line 2) could be replaced by:*

$$\begin{cases} \{\mathsf{ct}_i\}_{i\in[1,\ell]} \leftarrow \mathbf{PBSmanyLUT}(\mathsf{ct}_{\mathsf{in}}, \mathsf{BSK}, P\cdot X^{N/2^{\rho+1}}, 1, \varkappa = 0, \rho = \lceil \log_2(\ell) \rceil) \\ \forall i \in [1,\ell], \mathsf{ct}_i + \left(\mathbf{0}, \frac{q}{2\mathfrak{B}^i}\right) \end{cases}$$

$$\textit{with } P(X) = \sum_{i=0}^{\frac{N}{2^\rho}-1} \sum_{j=0}^{2^\rho - 1} \frac{q}{2\mathfrak{B}^j} X^{2^\rho \cdot i + j}.$$

Proof. By calling **PBSmanyLUT** with $\rho = \lceil \log_2(\ell) \rceil$, we are able to compute ℓ **PBS** in parallel. The polynomial P represents the LUT:

$$\underbrace{\left(\underbrace{\frac{q}{2\mathfrak{B}^1}, \ldots, \frac{q}{2\mathfrak{B}^\ell}, 0, \ldots, 0}_{2^\rho \text{ elements}}, \underbrace{\frac{q}{2\mathfrak{B}^1}, \ldots, \frac{q}{2\mathfrak{B}^\ell}, 0, \ldots, 0}_{2^\rho \text{ elements}}, \ldots, \underbrace{\frac{q}{2\mathfrak{B}^1}, \ldots, \frac{q}{2\mathfrak{B}^\ell}, 0, \ldots, 0}_{2^\rho \text{ elements}}\right)}_{N' = N/2^\rho \text{ elements}}$$

In the end, for $i \in [1, \ell]$, $\mathsf{ct}_i = \mathsf{LWE}_{\mathbf{s}}(\pm \frac{q}{2\mathfrak{B}^i})$, with the sign depending on the plaintext value. By adding the trivial ciphertext $(\mathbf{0}, \frac{q}{2\mathfrak{B}^i})$ to the ct_i, we either get $\mathsf{ct}_i = \mathsf{LWE}_{\mathbf{s}}(\frac{q}{\mathfrak{B}^i})$ or $\mathsf{LWE}_{\mathbf{s}}(0)$, as expected. □

5.3 Large Precision Without Padding (Programmable) Bootstrapping

We first describe a way to efficiently bootstrap an LWE ciphertext with larger precision and then show how to also compute a PBS on such ciphertexts. These algorithms do not require the input LWE ciphertext to have a bit of padding.

5.3.1 Larger Precision Without Padding Bootstrapping

We introduce a new procedure in Algorithm 8 to homomorphically decompose a message encrypted inside a ciphertext in α ciphertexts each encrypting a small chunk of the original message. The key of the efficiency of this algorithm is to begin by extracting the least significant bits instead of the most significant bits. To do so, we use the previously introduced parameter $\varkappa$ to remove some of the most significant bits of the input message m and apply the bootstrapping algorithm on the remaining bits as described in Subsect. 3.2. The bootstrapping algorithm must be a **WoP-PBS** (Algorithm 4 or 5) as the value of most significant bit is not guaranteed to be set to zero. This procedure allows us to obtain an encryption of the least significant bits of the message. Next, by subtracting this result to the input ciphertext, we remove the least significant bits of the input message. This gives a new ciphertext encrypting only the most significant bits of the input message. From now on, this procedure is then repeated on the resulting ciphertext until we obtain α ciphertexts, each encrypting $m_i \Delta_i$ such that $m_{\mathsf{in}} \Delta_{\mathsf{in}} = \sum_{i=0}^{\alpha-1} m_i \Delta_i$. This process is somehow similar to the approach called *Digit Extraction* applied on the BGV/BFV schemes, presented in [5,17].

This entails a significantly better complexity than the solution explained in the Limitation E as each bootstrap only needs a ring dimension big enough to bootstrap correctly the number of bits of each chunk instead of having to be big enough to bootstrap correctly the total number of bits of the input ciphertext.

Efficiency might be improved within the multiplication inside each **WoP-PBS** by adding a keyswitching during the relinearization step to reduce the size of the LWE dimension. As the complexity of the **WoP-PBS** depends on this LWE dimension, this will result in a faster version of Algorithm 8.

Lemma 5. *Let* $\mathsf{ct}_{\mathsf{in}} = \mathsf{LWE}_{\mathbf{s}}(m_{\mathsf{in}} \cdot \Delta_{\mathsf{in}}) \in \mathbb{Z}_q^{n+1}$ *be a LWE ciphertext, encrypting* $m_{\mathsf{in}} \cdot \Delta_{\mathsf{in}} \in \mathbb{Z}_q$. *under the LWE secret key* $\mathbf{s} = (s_1, \ldots, s_n) \in \mathbb{Z}_q^n$, *with noise sampled from* χ_σ. *Let* $\mathsf{BSK}, \mathsf{KSK}$ *and* RLK *as defined in Theorem 5. Let* $\mathscr{L} = \{d_i\}_{i \in [0, \alpha-1]}$ *with* $d_i \in \mathbb{N}^*$ *s.t.* $\Delta_{\mathsf{in}} 2^{\sum_{i=0}^{\alpha-1} d_i} \leq q$ *be the list defining the bit size of each output chunk. Algorithm 8 computes* $\alpha \in \mathbb{N}^*$ *new LWE ciphertexts* $\{\mathsf{ct}_{\mathsf{out},i}\}_{i \in [0, \alpha-1]}$, *where each one of them encrypts* $m_i \cdot \Delta_i$, *where* $\Delta_i = \Delta_{\mathsf{in}} \cdot 2^{\sum_{j=1}^{i-1} d_j}$, *under the secret key* $\mathbf{s}'$. *The variances of the noise is* $\mathsf{Var}(\mathsf{ct}_{\mathsf{out},i}) = \mathsf{Var}(\mathbf{WoP\text{-}PBS})$. *The complexity is:* $\mathbb{C}_{\mathsf{Decomp}}^{(n, \ell_{\mathbf{PBS}}, k_1, N_1, \ell_{\mathbf{KS}}, \ell_{\mathbf{RL}}, \alpha)} = \alpha \mathbb{C}_{\mathbf{WoP\text{-}PBS}_1}^{(n, \ell_{\mathbf{PBS}}, k_1, N_1, \ell_{\mathbf{KS}}, \ell_{\mathbf{RL}}, 1, n)} + \alpha(n+1)\mathbb{C}_{\mathsf{add}} + (\frac{\alpha(\alpha+1)}{2})\mathbb{C}_{\mathsf{add}}$.

Algorithm 8: $\mathsf{ct}_{\mathsf{out}} \leftarrow \mathbf{Decomp}(\mathsf{ct}_{\mathsf{in}}, \mathsf{BSK}, \mathsf{RLK}, \mathsf{KSK}, \mathscr{L})$

Context:
$$\begin{cases} \mathbf{s} = (s_1, \cdots, s_n) \in \mathbb{Z}_q^n \\ \mathbf{s}' = (s'_1, \cdots, s'_N) \in \mathbb{Z}_q^{kN} \\ \mathbf{S}' = \left(S'^{(1)}, \ldots, S'^{(k)}\right) \in \mathfrak{R}_q^k \\ \forall 1 \leq i \leq k,\ S'^{(i)} = \sum_{j=0}^{N-1} s'_{(i-1)\cdot N+j+1} X^j \in \mathfrak{R}_q \\ \{P_{f_i}\}_{i\in[0,\alpha-1]} : \text{LUTs for the functions } f_i \\ \forall i \in [1, \alpha-1], \Delta_i = \Delta_{\mathsf{in}} \cdot 2^{\sum_{j=1}^{i-1} d_j} \leq q \\ \Delta_0 = \Delta_{\mathsf{in}}, m_{\mathsf{in}}\Delta_{\mathsf{in}} = \sum_{i=0}^{\alpha-1} m_i \Delta_i \end{cases}$$

Input:
$$\begin{cases} \mathsf{ct}_{\mathsf{in}} = \mathsf{LWE}_{\mathbf{s}}(m_{\mathsf{in}} \cdot \Delta_{\mathsf{in}}) \in \mathbb{Z}_q^{n+1} \\ \mathsf{BSK}, \mathsf{KSK}, \mathsf{RLK} : \text{as defined in Algorithm 4} \\ \mathscr{L} = \{d_i\}_{i\in[0,\alpha-1]} \text{ with } d_i \in \mathbb{N}^* \end{cases}$$

Output: $\{\mathsf{ct}_{\mathsf{out},i} = \mathsf{LWE}_{\mathbf{s}'}(m_i \cdot \Delta_i)\}_{i\in[0,\alpha-1]}$

```
begin
    ct ← ct_in
    for i ∈ [0, α − 1] do
        ϰ_i ← Σ_{j=i+1}^{α−1} d_j
        ct_out,i ← WoP-PBS(ct, BSK, RLK, KSK, P_{f_i}, Δ_i, ϰ_i, 0)
        ct ← ct − ct_out,i
    end
end
```

An immediate application of Algorithm 8 is a high precision bootstrap algorithm. By using the decomposition and then adding each $\mathsf{ct}_{\mathsf{out},i}$, one can get - with the right parameters- a noise smaller than the one of the input ciphertext.

5.3.2 Larger Precision WoP-PBS

The **Tree-PBS** and the **ChainPBS** algorithms introduced in [16] allow to compute large precision programmable bootstrappings assuming that the input ciphertexts are already decomposed in chunks. In a nutshell, the idea behind the **Tree-PBS** is to encode a high-precision function in several LUTs. The first input ciphertext is used to select a subset among all the LUTs. This subset is then rearranged thanks to a key switching to build new encrypted LUTs. The previous steps can be repeated on the second input ciphertext, and so on. The **Tree-PBS** relies on the multi-output bootstrap from [4].

Thanks to the Algorithm 8, we are able to efficiently decompose a ciphertext. This allows to quickly switch from one representation (one ciphertext for one message) to another (e.g., several ciphertexts for one message) before calling the **Tree-PBS** or the **ChainPBS** algorithms. Moreover, we can replace the calls to PBS in both of the algorithms by a **WoP-PBS**. This relaxes the need to call **Tree-PBS** or **ChainPBS** with ciphertexts having a bit of padding. We call these two algorithms respectively the **Tree-WoP-PBS** and the **Chained-WoP-PBS**. Note that these algorithms can also be used to implement the $\mathbf{Add}_{2\mathrm{P}}^{\mathrm{MSB}}$ and $\mathbf{Mul}_{2\mathrm{P}}^{\mathrm{MSB}}$ operators.

6 Conclusion

This paper extends TFHE by exceeding some of its limitations. In particular, we present a new technique that allows to bootstrap messages without requiring a bit of padding, taking advantage of the GLWE multiplication (tensor product plus relinearization) and of our generalized version of TFHE's PBS. The latter additionally allows to evaluate multiple LUTs in a single PBS for free when possible. These two techniques are particularly interesting when used to improve both the gate bootstrapping and the circuit bootstrapping techniques of TFHE. Thank to this new programmable bootstrapping, there is no need to compute a systematic PBS in every homomorphic Boolean gates as leveled additions and multiplications can be evaluated between when noise allows it. Additionally, the evaluation of Boolean circuits can be extended in order to support the evaluation of larger powers of 2 modular arithmetic and exact integer arithmetic. The circuit bootstrapping can be drastically improved, by replacing the evaluation of multiple PBS in the algorithm by a single **PBSmanyLUT** (that costs exactly as a PBS), without affecting the noise growth. Finally, we introduce two new efficient methods to bootstrap ciphertexts with large precision: a bootstrapping method to bring the noise down as well as a programmable bootstrapping evaluating univariate functions.

Open Problems. All the new techniques proposed improve the state of the art by adding new features to TFHE and getting rid of some of its constraints. However, many enhancements could be added. In particular, one of the major bottleneck concerns the computation of the negacyclic convolutions of polynomials. The most efficient method based on the FFT inherently adds noise to ciphertext due to the use of floating points over 64 bits. When applied with larger floating point representation, the performances collapse. Thus, the study of alternative methods compatible with the TFHE parameters might improve the practical performances.

References

1. Boura, C., Gama, N., Georgieva, M., Jetchev, D.: CHIMERA: combining ring-LWE-based fully homomorphic encryption schemes. J. Math. Cryptol. **14**(1), 316–338 (2020)
2. Brakerski, Z.: Fully homomorphic encryption without modulus switching from classical GapSVP. IACR Cryptology ePrint Archive 2012 (2012). http://eprint.iacr.org/2012/078
3. Brakerski, Z., Gentry, C., Vaikuntanathan, V.: (Leveled) fully homomorphic encryption without bootstrapping. In: Innovations in Theoretical Computer Science 2012, Cambridge, MA, USA, 8–10 January 2012 (2012)
4. Carpov, S., Izabachène, M., Mollimard, V.: New techniques for multi-value input homomorphic evaluation and applications. In: Matsui, M. (ed.) CT-RSA 2019. LNCS, vol. 11405, pp. 106–126. Springer, Cham (2019). https://doi.org/10.1007/978-3-030-12612-4_6
5. Chen, H., Han, K.: Homomorphic lower digits removal and improved FHE bootstrapping. In: Nielsen, J.B., Rijmen, V. (eds.) EUROCRYPT 2018. LNCS, vol. 10820, pp. 315–337. Springer, Cham (2018). https://doi.org/10.1007/978-3-319-78381-9_12
6. Cheon, J.H., Kim, A., Kim, M., Song, Y.: Homomorphic encryption for arithmetic of approximate numbers. In: Takagi, T., Peyrin, T. (eds.) ASIACRYPT

2017. LNCS, vol. 10624, pp. 409–437. Springer, Cham (2017). https://doi.org/10.1007/978-3-319-70694-8_15
7. Chillotti, I., Gama, N., Georgieva, M., Izabachène, M.: Faster fully homomorphic encryption: bootstrapping in less than 0.1 seconds. In: Cheon, J.H., Takagi, T. (eds.) ASIACRYPT 2016. LNCS, vol. 10031, pp. 3–33. Springer, Heidelberg (2016). https://doi.org/10.1007/978-3-662-53887-6_1
8. Chillotti, I., Gama, N., Georgieva, M., Izabachène, M.: Faster packed homomorphic operations and efficient circuit bootstrapping for TFHE. In: Takagi, T., Peyrin, T. (eds.) ASIACRYPT 2017. LNCS, vol. 10624, pp. 377–408. Springer, Cham (2017). https://doi.org/10.1007/978-3-319-70694-8_14
9. Chillotti, I., Gama, N., Georgieva, M., Izabachène, M.: TFHE: fast fully homomorphic encryption over the torus. J. Cryptol. **33**(1), 34–91 (2020)
10. Chillotti, I., Joye, M., Ligier, D., Orfila, J.B., Tap, S.: CONCRETE: concrete operates on ciphertexts rapidly by extending TFHE. In: WAHC 2020–8th Workshop on Encrypted Computing & Applied Homomorphic Cryptography, vol. 15 (2020)
11. Chillotti, I., Joye, M., Paillier, P.: Programmable bootstrapping enables efficient homomorphic inference of deep neural networks. In: Dolev, S., Margalit, O., Pinkas, B., Schwarzmann, A. (eds.) CSCML 2021. LNCS, vol. 12716, pp. 1–19. Springer, Cham (2021). https://doi.org/10.1007/978-3-030-78086-9_1
12. Ducas, L., Micciancio, D.: FHEW: bootstrapping homomorphic encryption in less than a second. In: Oswald, E., Fischlin, M. (eds.) EUROCRYPT 2015. LNCS, vol. 9056, pp. 617–640. Springer, Heidelberg (2015). https://doi.org/10.1007/978-3-662-46800-5_24
13. Fan, J., Vercauteren, F.: Somewhat practical fully homomorphic encryption. IACR Cryptology ePrint Archive 2012 (2012). http://eprint.iacr.org/2012/144
14. Gentry, C.: Fully homomorphic encryption using ideal lattices. In: Proceedings of the 41st Annual ACM Symposium on Theory of Computing, STOC 2009, Bethesda, MD, USA, 31 May–2 June 2009 (2009)
15. Gentry, C., Sahai, A., Waters, B.: Homomorphic encryption from learning with errors: Conceptually-simpler, asymptotically-faster, attribute-based. IACR Cryptology ePrint Archive 2013 (2013). http://eprint.iacr.org/2013/340
16. Guimarães, A., Borin, E., Aranha, D.F.: Revisiting the functional bootstrap in TFHE. IACR Trans. Cryptogr. Hardw. Embed. Syst. **2021**(2) (2021)
17. Halevi, S., Shoup, V.: Bootstrapping for HElib. In: Oswald, E., Fischlin, M. (eds.) EUROCRYPT 2015. LNCS, vol. 9056, pp. 641–670. Springer, Heidelberg (2015). https://doi.org/10.1007/978-3-662-46800-5_25
18. Lee, Y., Lee, J., Kim, Y.S., Kang, H., No, J.S.: High-precision and low-complexity approximate homomorphic encryption by error variance minimization. Cryptology ePrint Archive, Report 2020/1549 (2020). https://eprint.iacr.org/2020/1549
19. Lyubashevsky, V., Peikert, C., Regev, O.: On ideal lattices and learning with errors over rings. In: Gilbert, H. (ed.) EUROCRYPT 2010. LNCS, vol. 6110, pp. 1–23. Springer, Heidelberg (2010). https://doi.org/10.1007/978-3-642-13190-5_1
20. Regev, O.: On lattices, learning with errors, random linear codes, and cryptography. In: Gabow, H.N., Fagin, R. (eds.) Proceedings of the 37th Annual ACM Symposium on Theory of Computing, 2005. ACM (2005)
21. Smart, N.P., Vercauteren, F.: Fully homomorphic SIMD operations. Des. Codes Cryptogr. **71**(1), 57–81 (2014)
22. Stehlé, D., Steinfeld, R., Tanaka, K., Xagawa, K.: Efficient public key encryption based on ideal lattices. In: Matsui, M. (ed.) ASIACRYPT 2009. LNCS, vol. 5912, pp. 617–635. Springer, Heidelberg (2009). https://doi.org/10.1007/978-3-642-10366-7_36

Author Index

Printed in the United States
by Baker & Taylor Publisher Services